THE ENGLISH
LEGAL SYSTEM

WALKER & WALKER

THE ENGLISH LEGAL SYSTEM

SIXTH EDITION

by

R. J. WALKER, LL.B.(Lond.)

of Gray's Inn and the Inner Temple,
One of Her Majesty's Counsel,
and of the South-Eastern Circuit

LONDON
BUTTERWORTHS
1985

United Kingdom	Butterworth & Co (Publishers) Ltd 88 Kingsway, London WC2B 6AB, and 61A North Castle Street, Edinburgh EH2 3LJ
Australia	Butterworths Pty Ltd Sydney, Melbourne, Brisbane, Adelaide, Perth, Canberra and Hobart
Canada	Butterworth & Co (Canada) Ltd Toronto and Vancouver
New Zealand	Butterworths of New Zealand Ltd Wellington and Auckland
Singapore	Butterworth & Co (Asia) Pte Ltd Singapore
South Africa	Butterworth & Co (South Africa) (Pty) Ltd Durban and Pretoria
U.S.A.	Butterworth Legal Publishers St Paul, Minnesota; Seattle, Washington, Boston, Massachusetts, Austin, Texas and D & S Publishers, Clearwater, Florida

ISBN Hardcover 0 406 67760 3
Softcover 0 406 67761 1

Printed and bound in Great Britain by Mackays of Chatham Ltd

Preface

Considerable changes in the areas of law and practice covered by this work have necessitated this new edition. I have taken the opportunity of rewriting many chapters not only in order to reflect these changes but also to present a fuller account of topics such as judicial review, *Anton Piller* orders, *Mareva* injunctions and legal aid, which seem to me to require more detailed attention in view of their practical importance in the modern administration of justice. I have sought to incorporate all of the relevant new statutory provisions, notably the Magistrates' Courts Act 1980, Supreme Court Act 1981, Contempt of Court Act 1981, Legal Aid Act 1982, Criminal Justice Act 1982 and County Courts Act 1984, and to illustrate the text by reference to the most recent authorities.

I have endeavoured to state the law as at May 1, 1985 although I have indicated, where appropriate, changes which will be effected when the relevant provisions of the Police and Criminal Evidence Act 1984 are brought into operation.

May 1985   Ronald Walker

Table of Contents

PART III—THE ADMINISTRATION OF JUSTICE

PART IV—CIVIL PROCEDURE

Table of Statutes

References in this Table to "*Statutes*" are to Halsbury's
Statutes of England (Third Edition) showing the volume and
page at which the annotated text of the Act will be found.

Table of European Communities Legislation

List of Cases

A

PART I

The Historical Sources
of English Law

SUMMARY

CHAPTER 1

Common Law

A ORIGINS OF THE COMMON LAW

It is normal to regard common law as the primary historical source of English law, with equity and legislation, the two other principal historical sources, each evolving later as a "gloss" on the common law. This view is only tenable if English law is regarded as originating in 1066 with the Norman Conquest. In fact, although modern lawyers hardly ever look beyond the common law to ascertain the existence of a legal rule, the common law has in itself a number of historical sources which were, prior to the Conquest, embodied in local custom. The unique contribution of the Norman Conquest was to unify these local customs into one system of law common to all men, for this reason termed the "common law".

It would be a mistake to suppose that William I by one legislative act created a central system of courts to which was transferred all the jurisdiction of the various local courts and in which was administered a code of law created by the King. This would have been impossible, not only because of the administrative difficulty involved, but because the local courts constituted an important source of revenue to the barons and landowners who consequently resisted attempts to diminish their jurisdiction. What did in fact happen was that the King, over a period of time, assumed control of the administration of justice throughout the land through his judges and justices and created a central system of courts. The jurisdiction of the local courts was never formally abolished but, for various reasons, declined as the jurisdiction of the King's courts grew. This was, however, a slow process and between 1066 and about 1154 the jurisdiction of the King's courts was confined to Pleas of the Crown, disputes between tenants-in-chief over title to land and supervision of the inferior courts.

The ascendancy of the King's courts over the local courts[1] was achieved only over a period of three centuries and may be accounted for by the following factors:-

---

[1] The principal courts existing prior to the creation of royal courts were the communal courts of the shire and hundred and the feudal courts held by landowners. See Potter, *Outlines of English Legal History*, Chap. 3.

1   The decline in the authority of the sheriff

The sheriff exercised both a civil jurisdiction, in the shire or county court, and a criminal jurisdiction on his "tourn". He was, at the time of the Conquest, an immensely powerful figure and challenged the authority of the King himself. Consequently the growth and consolidation of the King's authority was marked by a corresponding reduction in the status of the sheriff. His civil jurisdiction declined after the Conquest since pleas relating to land were transferred to the feudal courts and later the royal courts, and pleas not relating to land were generally tried either by the King's justices or by the sheriff himself, sitting by royal commission, or by borough courts, or other local courts, established under royal franchise. In addition the interpretation put on the Statute of Gloucester 1278 limited the sheriff's jurisdiction to 40s. The sheriff's criminal jurisdiction was assumed by the King's judges in assizes and the itinerant justices in quarter sessions and, in relation to lesser offences, by the franchise courts known as "courts leet" and, subsequently, by the justices in petty sessions. Clause 24 of Magna Carta prohibited the sheriff from hearing Pleas of the Crown and by the end of the twelfth century the King's justices exercised an exclusive jurisdiction over all serious crime. In 1461 the remaining jurisdiction of the sheriff's tourn was substantially transferred to justices.[2] As one textbook writer has put it:[3]

> "Parliament repeatedly ignored the existence of the old county assembly as it heaped new duties of all kinds upon the magistrates. What had happened in reality was that the Crown had taken the county from the sheriff and put it into commission."

However, the sheriff continued to supervise the system of "frank-pledge".[4]

2   The evolution of the writ system[5]

The King, as fountain of justice, would grant a writ to a suitor to enable him to petition the King for a remedy where there was a denial of justice in the local courts. These writs became formalised and a Register of Writs kept with the result that an increasing number of rights arose which were enforceable in the King's courts. This increase resulted in a gradual decline of the civil jurisdiction of the feudal courts, particularly since the early writs were concerned with protecting title to land, disputes concerning which were the principal business transacted in the feudal courts. Those local courts whose jurisdiction survived longest, and indeed thrived, were the borough and city courts exercising jurisdiction by virtue of royal franchise. They exercised a

---

2   By 1 Edw. IV, c. 2.
3   Baker, *An Introduction to English Legal History*, (2nd Edn.), p. 24.
4   This system was introduced by William I as a result of the large numbers of Normans slain who had no relatives to bring the criminal to justice. It imposed communal responsibility by making every person without substantial property a member of a group of ten called a "tithing". If one committed a crime the other nine would be responsible for bringing him to trial, failing which they would be liable to pay a fine. A special fine was payable by a hundred in which a murderer was located unless it could be shown that his victim was not a Norman but an Anglo-Saxon ("presentment of Englishry").
5   See p. 20, *post*.

local jurisdiction over small civil claims. Basically they applied the common law (but not subject to the procedural complexities which dogged the common law courts) although, being patronised by merchants, some of them gave effect to the law merchant.[6]

3   The introduction by Henry II of the system of Grand and Petty Assizes[7]

The Grand Assize enabled the defendant to a suit concerning land held by freehold tenure (writ of right) to claim trial by jury in the royal courts as an alternative to battle. Petty (or possessory) Assizes enabled a person who had been disseised of land[8] to regain possession summarily without having to undergo the cumbersome procedure attendant upon a writ of right.

4   The ownership of land becoming centralised in the King

Thus originated the modern concept that landowners own not the land itself but an estate in the land, for example, a freehold estate. Consequently all disputes concerning estates in land affected the King's interest. By the reign of Henry II it was established that any suit concerning free tenure had to be commenced by a writ of right issuing from the Chancery. Although the issue raised by the writ was at first tried in the feudal courts, later, proceedings were removable to the royal courts[9] by writ of Pone which alleged a defect in proceedings in the feudal court on which ground the action was removed from its jurisdiction. This allegation was fictitious but the parties were not able to deny its truth. This constitutes an early example of the use of legal fictions to acquire jurisdiction.[10]

5   The increase in the scope of Pleas of the Crown

Such a Plea was based upon a breach of the King's peace[11] and redressible by punishment which usually involved fine or forfeiture. Consequently these pleas were a source of royal revenue and their scope increased with the power of the monarchy. The pleas were principally criminal in modern terms although from them probably developed the great writ of trespass, the basis of the modern law of torts.[12]

6   The Statute of Gloucester 1278

This Statute was passed as an attempt to curb the jurisdiction of the common law courts over personal actions which was growing principally through the

---

[6] See p. 67, *post*.

[7] The word "Assizes" is not here used in its primary sense of a sitting of a court, but as a procedure established by an ordinance passed at such a sitting (bearing in mind that "court" included, at this time, legislative assemblies).

[8] See p. 22, *post*.

[9] To the Court of Common Pleas.

[10] See p. 42, *post*.

[11] As opposed to a Common Plea which was a pure dispute between subjects.

[12] See p. 24, *post*.

recently created writ of trespass. It expressly provided that no action involving less than 40s. could be commenced in the royal courts. In fact the measure backfired because the common law judges interpreted this to mean that no personal actions involving more than 40s. could be tried in the local courts. With the decline in the value of money in the Middle Ages the jurisdiction of the local courts over personal actions correspondingly diminished. To this Statute may be attributed the gradual disappearance of the feudal courts which eventually necessitated the statutory creation of the modern county courts in 1846.

Thus the common law courts grew and gradually superseded the local courts. The latter have virtually ceased to function. Most have been abolished by statute. As part of the reform of the system of courts effected by the Courts Act 1971 most of the local courts which did function actively were abolished. These were the Bristol Tolzey and Pie Poudre Courts, the Liverpool Court of Passage, the Norwich Guildhall Court and the Salford Hundred Court.[13] The Courts, prior to their abolition, exercised a civil jurisdiction roughly equivalent to that of county courts. The only other inferior local court regularly functioning prior to the Courts Act 1971 was the Mayor's and City of London Court. This court was formally abolished also; however it has effectively been retained since the Courts Act makes the City of London a county court district and provides that the county court for that district shall be known as the Mayor's and City of London Court.[14]

The Local Government Act 1972 abolished, as from 1 April 1974, the remaining borough civil courts, the jurisdiction of which was, for the most part, derived from borough charters.[15] Finally, the Administration of Justice Act 1977, implementing recommendations of the Law Commission,[16] removed the jurisdiction of obsolete classes of courts and nominate courts.[17] However, to preserve tradition, these courts are permitted to sit and exercise their traditional, and largely formal, non-judicial functions.[18] The Lord Chancellor has power to make provision by order for enabling any jurisdiction abolished by the Act to be exercised instead by the High Court, the Crown Court, a county court or a magistrates' court.[19]

---

[13] Courts Act 1971, s. 43.
[14] *Ibid.*, s. 42.
[15] Local Government Act 1972, s. 221 and Sch. 28; see p. 68, fn. 14, *post.*
[16] Jurisdiction of Certain Ancient Courts (Law Com. no. 72).
[17] Administration of Justice Act 1977, s. 23 and Sch. 4; the courts concerned were Courts Baron, Courts Leet (other than the Court Leet for the Manor of Laxton), Customary Courts of the Manor, Courts of Pie Poudre, Courts of the Staple (see p. 69, *post*), Courts of the Clerks of the Markets, Hundred Courts, Law Days, Views of Frankpledge, Common Law (or Sheriff's) county courts as known before the passing of the County Courts Act 1846 (see p. 80, *post*) and a number of other specified courts. The Act did not, however, affect courts which were not found by the Law Commission to be obsolete, notably the Court of Chivalry (see p. 218, *post*), Coroners' Courts (see p. 210, *post*), the Ecclesiastical Courts (see p. 216, *post*) and Courts of Survey.
[18] See Sch. 4, Part III of the 1977 Act for a description of business customary for certain courts.
[19] *Ibid.*, s. 23(4).

B COURTS OF THE COMMON LAW

1 The Curia Regis

The fountain of justice at common law is the King himself. Consequently all common law courts derive their jurisdiction from the King. Modern society accepts the desirability of a separation of the powers of the executive, the legislature and the judiciary. However in medieval times all three functions were exercised by the King in Council. The King's Council is thus the predecessor not only of Parliament but of the courts.

The medieval pattern was for courts to separate from the Council and eventually acquire a jurisdiction independent of it. However the King at all times retained a residual power deriving from his prerogative powers. Thus the three main common law courts, the Court of Exchequer, the Court of Common Pleas and the Court of King's Bench, split off from the Council and their judges exercised jurisdiction to decide civil disputes and major criminal cases in London and on assize. The King's justices assumed jurisdiction over criminal offences. Nevertheless the undefined residual jurisdiction of the King led to other courts deriving their jurisdiction from the Curia Regis, notably the Court of Chancery and the Star Chamber. Indeed it was not until the seventeenth century that the Council itself discontinued its judicial function. The functions of these courts were to remedy the procedural defects and restrictions of the common law courts and to dispense justice where the common law courts were for some reason unable to do so. The obvious results of this *ad hoc* method of creating courts were clashes between them and the common law courts over the extent of their respective jurisdiction.

2 The Court of Exchequer

This was the first of the three central common law courts to split off from the Curia Regis. In the reign of Henry I the Exchequer became a separate department of the Council dealing with the collection and distribution of royal revenue. By the reign of Henry II it had become a court, the judges of which were Exchequer Barons presided over by the Chief Baron who was, after the fourteenth century, always a lawyer, frequently of great distinction.

Originally the jurisdiction of the court was confined to disputes between subjects and the Crown concerning revenue. Later the court acquired jurisdiction over disputes between subjects, such as writs of debt and covenant,[20] through the fiction of "Quominus". This depended upon a fictitious allegation of a debt owed by the plaintiff to the Crown which the plaintiff was the less able (*quominus*) to pay because of the debt owing to him by the defendant. This fictitious allegation enabled the court to determine the substantive issue between the parties.[1]

In addition the court appears, at least in its early days, to have exercised an equity jurisdiction, though its procedure was that of the common law courts rather than of the Court of Chancery.

---

[20] See p. 23, *post*.
[1] See Baker, *op. cit.*, pp. 44–45.

When the court was finally abolished in 1875 its jurisdiction was transferred to the newly-formed High Court, its common law jurisdiction being exercised by the Queen's Bench Division after 1880, and its revenue jurisdiction by the Chancery Division. Its equity jurisdiction had been transferred by statute to the Chancery in 1841.[2]

3   The Court of Common Pleas

While the King was determining civil disputes in Council suitors were obliged to follow the court wherever it travelled. Because of the inconvenience this caused it became the practice for judges to remain permanently in Westminster Hall to try Common Pleas[3] and Magna Carta, c. 17, provided that the common pleas should be held in a "certain place" which was fixed at Westminster.

The judges of the court were full time lawyers appointed from the ranks of the serjeants-at-law, the senior advocates who had an exclusive right of audience in the court. The serjeants were the leaders of the legal profession and consequently the most highly paid. This fact, coupled with the excessive formality of pleading attendant upon the real actions[4] (over which the court had a monopoly), made proceedings in the Common Pleas dilatory and expensive.

The jurisdiction of the court existed over disputes between subjects where the King's interest was not involved. Hence it tried all the real actions and the personal actions of debt, covenant and detinue. It also tried actions of trespass where the title to land was involved. It must be remembered that only wealthy landowners could afford to litigate in the royal courts so that most civil actions in the early Middle Ages in fact involved disputes over title to land. Thus the Common Pleas in the early period of the development of the common law exercised a far wider jurisdiction than the Exchequer or the King's Bench.

The court was abolished in 1875 and its jurisdiction transferred to the High Court, being exercised by the Queen's Bench Division after 1880.

4   The Court of King's Bench

This was the last of the three central courts to break away from the Council. Consequently it has always remained closer to the King than the Exchequer and the Common Pleas. This is not to say that the King's Bench was not separate from the Curia Regis. Although they were closely associated there is ample evidence that the judges of the King's Bench acted independently of the King[5] by the reign of Edward I and attempts by James I to sit in the court were defeated by Coke. However, because of its association with the King, it acquired jurisdiction to issue the prerogative writs (now "orders") of mandamus, prohibition and certiorari, restraining excesses and abuses of

---

2   5 Vict., c. 5.
3   As opposed to Pleas of the Crown; see p. 5, *ante*.
4   See p. 21, *post*.
5   See Plucknett, *A Concise History of the Common Law*, (5th Edn.), p. 151.

jurisdiction by inferior courts and public officials.[6] In addition the writ of habeas corpus, which it had power to issue, was later of great constitutional importance in curbing the personal exercise by the King of his prerogative powers. Its wide appellate jurisdiction may also be traced to the exercise of the royal duty to correct deficiencies in cases tried in other courts.

The judicial function was exercised by the judges of the court presided over by the Chief Justice of England, an office ranking above that of Chief Justice of the Common Pleas.[7] This function was both original and appellate and both civil and criminal.

The original jurisdiction of the King's Bench was exercised principally in civil matters, although the judges of the court exercised original criminal jurisdiction in courts of assize. The civil jurisdiction, which derived from the Pleas of the Crown and in particular from the writ of trespass, developed in about 1250.[8] This operated to confer upon the court jurisdiction over most actions in tort since nearly all torts are offshoots of trespass. It did not acquire jurisdiction over contract until the writ of assumpsit in the late sixteenth century evolved to replace the writ of debt.[9] However it filched jurisdiction from the Common Pleas over writs of debt by means of the fictitious Bill of Middlesex procedure. The King's Bench had jurisdiction over all cases[10] where the defendant was in the custody of the warden of the King's Bench prison. Consequently the Sheriff of Middlesex was directed by bill to arrest the defendant for a trespass *vi et armis* and take him into custody. Since the court had jurisdiction over trespass actions it was able to try the real cause of action ancillary to the fictitious trespass suit which was in fact dropped. If the defendant was in a county other than Middlesex the Sheriff would mark the bill *non est inventus* and a writ of *latitat* would then direct him to arrest the defendant wherever he "lurks and runs" (*latitat et discurrit*). By the sixteenth century the issue of the fictitious Bill of Middlesex was dispensed with and the action could be commenced with the *latitat*. This did not limit the plaintiff to any particular form of action and therefore afforded greater flexibility than did the highly formal system of pleading that by now existed in the Common Pleas. It resulted in a huge increase in the business of the King's Bench, so much so that the very existence of the Common Pleas was threatened. Parliament intervened in 1661[11] by removing the power to compel appearance by arrest where the true cause of action was not specified in the bill. The King's Bench countered this by issuing process requiring the defendant to answer in a plea of trespass and also (*ac etiam*) in a plea of debt. The only solution for the Common Pleas, and that which it ultimately adopted, was to sanction the *ac etiam* procedure itself, thereby relaxing some of the formalities of pleading attendant upon debt actions in the Common Pleas.[12]

---

[6] This jurisdiction is now exercised by the divisional court of the Queen's Bench Division by way of "judicial review" proceedings; see p. 174, *post*.

[7] Coke, for example, was promoted from the latter office to the former.

[8] See p. 24, *post*.

[9] See p. 26, *post*.

[10] Excluding the real actions which remained in the exclusive jurisdiction of the Court of Common Pleas.

[11] 13 Car. II (sess. ii), c. 2.

[12] For a fuller account of this struggle for jurisdiction between the King's Bench and the Common Pleas, see Baker, *op. cit.*, pp. 40–43.

The appellate jurisdiction of the King's Bench existed in both civil and criminal cases. However the right of appeal was based on an error in procedure in the court below.[13]

5   The Courts of Exchequer Chamber

There were, at different periods of history, no less than four courts bearing the title "Exchequer Chamber". The jurisdiction of all of them was appellate.

(1) The oldest was established by statute in 1357[14] as a result of the refusal of the Exchequer to submit to the appellate jurisdiction of the King's Bench. The court was created to sit in "any council room nigh the exchequer" (hence the name "Exchequer Chamber") and to consist of the Chancellor and the Treasurer with assistance from judges of the common law courts as assessors. Its jurisdiction was solely as a court of error from the Exchequer. Hence the business of the court was limited as it was also by the difficulty of getting the Chancellor and the Treasurer together, particularly when the latter office was vacant.

(2) There existed, even before 1357, a practice of judges reserving difficult points of law for consideration by a bench of judges drawn from all three common law courts and, later, the Chancery. These meetings were no doubt informal at first and the authority of the opinions delivered purely persuasive. They remained informal in the sense that no litigant had a right to require a judge to refer any point of law for consideration. However, the judgments were by the fifteenth century regarded as binding[15] and the informal meetings, by now usually held in the Exchequer Chamber, constituted the sitting of a court. Hence such a court was also termed a Court of Exchequer Chamber. Many of the leading cases of the common law were decided in this court before twelve judges[16] and the court sat until the seventeenth century to determine civil cases and until the nineteenth century in criminal cases.

(3) A third Court of Exchequer Chamber was set up during the existence of the two already described by statute in 1585.[17] It was set up as a court of error from the King's Bench in cases of debt, detinue, covenant, account, action upon the case, ejectment or trespass commenced[18] in the King's Bench. It consisted of any six judges drawn from the Exchequer Barons and the justices of the Common Pleas. Thus there were at this time three courts of error; *viz.* the Court of Exchequer Chamber (1357) from the Court of Exchequer, the King's Bench from the Common Pleas and the Court of Exchequer Chamber (1585) from the King's Bench. In addition error still lay direct from the King's Bench to the House of Lords. This somewhat complex hierarchy prevailed until the creation of the last Court of Exchequer Chamber in 1830.

---

[13] See p. 31, *post*.

[14] 31 Edw. 3, St. 1, c. 12.

[15] In 1483 the Chief Justice of the Common Pleas followed a decision of the Exchequer Chamber even though he thought it wrong (Y.B. 1 Ric. 3, Michs, no. 2).

[16] Examples are *Slade* v. *Morley* (1602), Yelv. 2; *Hampden's Case* (1637), 3 State Tr. 825; *Godden* v. *Hales* (1686), 11 State Tr. 1254.

[17] 31 Eliz. 1, c. 1.

[18] This had the effect of confining it to proceedings commenced by bill since actions by writ were "commenced" in the Chancery.

(4) The court created in 1830[19] was the court of error from all three common law courts and was composed of judges of the two courts other than the one in which the trial at first instance took place. Appeal lay from the court to the House of Lords. The court existed until 1875 when its jurisdiction was transferred to the Court of Appeal.

6 Assizes

It was, during the Middle Ages, and indeed always has been, impossible to administer the criminal law on the basis of all trials taking place in London. Consequently, Norman and Plantagenet monarchs adopted the system, which appears to have existed even before the Conquest, of sending out royal justices throughout the kingdom to hold "assizes" (or sittings) of the royal courts. The jurisdiction of these assize courts, at first purely criminal, was later extended to civil proceedings.

The assize judges were generally the judges of the common law courts, but could also be serjeants-at-law or even prominent laymen. Consequently they exercised no jurisdiction *virtute officii* but only by reason of commissions issued by the Sovereign. The commissions conferring criminal jurisdiction were the commission of *Oyer and Terminer* and the commission of *Gaol Delivery*. The first directed the persons named in the commission to hear and determine all offences in respect of which the accused had been "presented" by the grand jury of the county.[20] The second directed them to deliver from the gaols of the county, and to try, all persons there awaiting trial.[1]

So successful and popular was the assize system that Edward I organised the circuits on the modern basis with each circuit consisting of a group of counties visited regularly three or four times a year by royal judges. In addition the Statute of Nisi Prius 1285 extended the system to certain civil actions. The basic reason for this extension was the difficulty of transporting local juries to Westminster. Consequently in those personal actions, such as trespass, triable in the King's Bench and Common Pleas with a jury, the sheriff was directed to secure the attendance of a jury at Westminster "unless before" (*nisi prius*) that day the justices of assize should visit that county. The system was extended in the fourteenth and fifteenth centuries to all types of civil action. It would, however, be incorrect to suppose that a trial at *nisi prius* was at this time a trial of the whole action. In fact only the issues of fact were tried at *nisi prius*. The pleading took place *in banc* (in Westminster) and the jury verdict was added to the record of the case to be sent back to Westminster for judgment to be entered since the commissioner of assize had no power to enter judgment. Later, when the commissioners were always lawyers and advocates went on circuit, the whole trial took place at the assize so that the trial of actions might take place in London or at an assize.[2]

---

[19] 11 Geo. 4 & 1 Will. 4, c. 70.

[20] See p. 16, *post*.

[1] These commissions were created by the Assizes of Clarendon 1166, and Northampton 1176 and continued to issue until their effective abolition under the provisions of the Courts Act 1971.

[2] The assize system survived until the 1st January 1972—the date on which the Courts Act 1971 came into operation; section 1(2) provides that "All courts of assize are hereby abolished, and Commissions, whether ordinary or special, to hold any court of assize shall not be issued."

7   Justices of the Peace

Originally the office of justice of the peace was an administrative rather than a judicial office but a judicial function was given to it in the fourteenth century as a direct result of the declining criminal jurisdiction of the local courts and the inability of the assizes to deal with the growing number of offenders.

The origin of the justices of the peace is to be found in a royal proclamation of 1195 creating the knights of the peace to assist the sheriff in enforcing the law. This function was of an administrative and police character rather than of a judicial character. With the decline of the office of sheriff in the fourteenth century the "keepers of the peace" (*custodes pacis*) as they were by now known,[3] were given a judicial function in addition to their administrative tasks. The former function has increased as the latter has diminished. In 1330 the holders of this new office had become so powerful locally that they were given statutory power to punish the sheriff, if he abused his powers of granting bail to prisoners.

As a result of the effects of the Black Death on the labour market, Statutes of Labourers were passed from 1351 in an attempt to regulate prices and wages and to reorganise labour generally. The enforcement of these statutes was placed in the hands of "justices of labourers" who were, in 1361, included in the same commissions as the keepers of the peace. It is from this date that the office of J.P. in its modern sense originates. The new justices of the peace were laymen and not usually legally qualified, a tradition which exists at the present day.[4] Their criminal jurisdiction was at first exercised solely in the sessions which they were, by statute,[5] compelled to hold in each county four times a year. These were the "quarter sessions" and in 1590 the justices in quarter sessions were given jurisdiction over all criminal offences not excluding capital felonies. It was, indeed, not until the Quarter Sessions Act 1842 that the jurisdiction of quarter sessions was limited to exclude treason, murder and felonies punishable with life imprisonment.

Later, in Tudor times, a number of statutes conferred jurisdiction on justices to try offences out of sessions. From these statutes, the first of which was passed in 1496,[6] stems the summary jurisdiction of the justices of the peace in "petty sessions". This summary jurisdiction, which is entirely statutory, is exercised without a jury and justices exercising this jurisdiction are now termed a "magistrates' court".[7]

As indicated earlier, the administrative jurisdiction of justices of the peace declined through the years as the criminal jurisdiction grew. Most of the administrative jurisdiction formerly exercised by justices is now in the hands of local authorities. However certain important functions remain. The

---

3 The nomenclature "justice of the peace" appears to date from about 1327, and to be an official title after 1361; Plucknett, *A Concise History of the Common Law*, (5th Edn.), p. 168.
4 See p. 206, *post*.
5 36 Edw. 3, st. 1, c. 12.
6 11 Hen. 7, c. 3; see Plucknett, *op. cit.*, p. 169.
7 See p. 206, *post*.

common law power to issue warrants of arrest and summonses still exists. The important task of conducting preliminary investigations into indictable offences[8] was conferred on justices of the peace by statutes of 1554[9] and 1555.[10] This procedure eventually superseded the procedure of presentment by a grand jury.[11]

8 The General Eyre

In addition to the royal commissions issued to the justices of assize and to the justices of the peace, described above, there was a far wider commission which existed only until about 1340. This was the commission *ad omnia placita* and the justices to whom this commission was issued constituted the "general eyre". The eyre was in a sense the forerunner of the whole system of itinerant justices. The justices in eyre were concerned to safeguard royal interests of all kinds. For example they supervised the collection of royal revenue due from fines and forfeitures. Also the eyre, once in every seven years, held an inquisition in each county into the whole system of the local administration of justice including frankpledge, police duties and the conduct of the sheriff. The procedure involved a series of questions known as the "articles of the eyre" (*capitula itineris*) being put to a special session of the local county court. During the session of the eyre local sessions of the assizes were suspended and the cases heard by the eyre. Thus the general eyre undoubtedly exercised a judicial function superior to that of the assizes, though inferior to the Court of King's Bench.

It is hardly surprising that the visits of the eyre were extremely unpopular and there is on record an incident in which the men of Cornwall fled to the woods rather than face the eyre. The final extinction of the eyre in about 1340 may be attributed to the growth of Parliament. An unfortunate feature of its extinction was that a useful means of reform of the legal system was lost.

9 The Star Chamber

It is strictly erroneous to classify the Star Chamber as a common law court. It derived its jurisdiction from the King in the same way as the common law courts but it did not administer the common law and, more particularly, adopted a criminal and civil procedure repugnant to that obtaining in the common law courts. In addition, whereas the common law courts quite early in their existence became independent of the Council, the Star Chamber appears always to have retained the closest link with the Council. Hence it administered the royal prerogative rather than the common law although, by doing so, it added considerably to the scope of the criminal law. It has been described as a court of "criminal equity",[12] though the description "equity" is misleading.

---

8 See p. 476, *post*.
9 1 & 2 P. & M., c. 13.
10 2 & 3 P. & M., c. 10.
11 See p. 16, *post*.
12 Radcliffe and Cross, *The English Legal System* (5th Edn.), p. 134.

Opinions differ as to the origins of the court. It seems to have originated from sittings of the Council in a chamber in Westminster known as the Star Chamber, possibly on account simply of its interior décor. The ancient theory that the court was created by a statute of 1487 (*pro camera stellata*) is now discounted, although this Act did confer jurisdiction upon the court to try certain offences such as riot and rout. The court of Star Chamber consisted of members of the Council, the Chancellor. Treasurer and Privy Seal and common law judges.

The court had a miscellaneous civil jurisdiction over matters outside the common law such as mercantile and ecclesiastical disputes. It also assumed jurisdiction over matters within the scope of the common law courts and for this reason it fell into disfavour with common law judges. The growth of the Court of Chancery during the same period[13] effectively restricted the civil jurisdiction of the Star Chamber since both were at this time conciliar courts.

It is the criminal jurisdiction of the Star Chamber which is of far greater interest and importance since, while the court did not try felonies, it recognised and tried many new offences which were, in modern terms, "misdemeanours". Many of these were offences of a public nature such as riot, unlawful assembly, conspiracy, criminal libel, perjury, forgery and criminal attempts. All these crimes were created to fill gaps in the existing criminal law as administered in the assizes and quarter sessions.

Procedure in the Star Chamber differed radically from procedure in the common law courts. The civil procedure resembled more closely Chancery procedure than the dilatory formality of the common law. Criminal procedure was even more fundamentally different. Proceedings were commenced, not by presentment by the grand jury, but by information filed by the Attorney-General. An inquisitorial procedure followed whereby the defendant was examined on oath, sometimes under torture. Witnesses' evidence was frequently given by affidavit thus denying the accused any opportunity of cross-examination. Finally, there was no jury, guilt being determined by the members of the court. In a modern situation such a procedure would be unthinkable and condemned as a total denial of justice. Nevertheless, it was at that time justifiable in the light of the influence on juries which certain persons exercised, the bitterness of the state trials for treason (which took place before juries) and, following the Wars of the Roses, the anarchic situation throughout the realm which the existing criminal law and courts could not remedy. Even Coke, that most noted champion of the common law, described the court as "the most honourable Court (our Parliament excepted) that is in the Christian world".[14]

Nevertheless, in spite of its popularity in Tudor times, the accession of the Stuarts and, in particular, the Civil War resulted in the court becoming a symbol of prerogative power in the eyes of the Puritans and Parliamentarians and one of the first legislative acts of the Long Parliament was the abolition of the Star Chamber in 1641.

---

[13] See p. 44, *post.*
[14] 4 Inst., p. 65.

C CRIMINAL PROCEDURE IN THE COMMON LAW COURTS

There have, at different times, been three principal methods of prosecuting accused persons in the royal courts. These methods each involved a different method of trial. The two principal methods of trial, trial on indictment and summary trial, still exist. The third, appeal of felony, existed until the fifteenth century. Each of these procedures must be examined briefly.

1 Appeal of felony

The striking feature of ancient criminal procedure prior to the Norman Conquest was that the responsibility for bringing a person to justice lay not with the Crown but with the individual against whom the crime had been committed. Although most of the ancient procedure became obsolete under the Normans, the appeal of felony created by them perpetuated the ancient concept of private prosecution. The appellant was the victim or his representative and his appeal, originally brought in the local courts, could eventually be brought in the King's Bench. The distinguishing feature of procedure by appeal was that the defendant had a right to call for trial by battle, a method of trial introduced by the Normans.

With the rise of the jury, appeal of felony fell into disfavour with the common law judges who introduced excessive technicalities with which the appellor had to comply. Consequently the procedure became rare although appeals of murder were apparently common until the fifteenth century. An appeal of murder could not be brought for a year and a day after death whereas an indictment could, in the fifteenth century, be brought at once. Consequently the latter procedure had precedence although an acquittal on indictment was no bar to a subsequent appeal of felony. The procedure died out from the fifteenth century onwards but was not finally abolished until 1819[15] following a case which reminded the legislature that the right to claim battle still existed.[16]

2 Trial on indictment

This is the most important method of trial conceived by the common law. Its importance stems from the fact that it is the only one of the three methods which involved the use of the jury. The conduct of the prosecution of a person accused on indictment may be conveniently divided into four stages: arrest, presentation for trial, trial and sentence.

a Arrest

Prior to the Conquest there appears to have been very little public responsibility for the apprehension of criminals. The Normans' interest in their apprehension was at least partly financial since the new public crimes known as "felonies" involved the prisoner, if convicted, in forfeiture of his

---

[15] 59 Geo. 3, c. 46.
[16] *Ashford* v. *Thornton* (1818), 1 B. & Ald. 405.

property and escheat of his lands to the Crown. The earliest procedure which evolved to secure the apprehension of criminals was the system of "frank-pledge" described above.[17] Later, the Assize of Clarendon 1166 provided that juries of each hundred should present to the royal commissioners when they came on circuit all persons suspected of felony on any ground including information supplied by the sheriff.[18] The creation of these juries illustrates the lack of royal trust in the sheriffs.

After the frankpledge system died out in the fourteenth century the practice grew of every parish appointing a "constable" upon whom were conferred wider powers of arrest than those available to the general public. Also, as the control over the administration of justice passed from the sheriff to the justices of the peace, the latter acquired the right to issue warrants of arrest to the constables.

b   Presentation for trial

This stage of the proceedings has involved, at different periods of history, two bodies; the grand jury and justices of the peace.

The grand jury was the earliest type of jury used at assizes and quarter sessions. Consisting of between twelve and twenty-four freeholders of the country, it originated in the fourteenth century and was the successor of the jury of presentment of the hundred created by the Assize of Clarendon 1166. The early function of the grand jury was to present persons for trial before the royal justices, frequently on the basis of the jurors' personal knowledge. Hence the members of the grand jury would often be witnesses or at least persons with local knowledge. Later, with the growth of the constabulary, the grand jury exercised the function, which was subsequently assumed by justices of the peace, of inquiring into allegations of crime in order to decide whether to present a bill of indictment against the prisoner. This function of presenting the bill of indictment was taken over by justices of the peace with the creation of the modern preliminary investigation by statutes of 1554 and 1555. Thereafter the sole function of the grand jury was to certify a bill of indictment preferred at quarter sessions or assizes as a "true bill". Thus it had become redundant and was virtually abolished (save for a few exceptional cases) by the Administration of Justice (Miscellaneous Provisions) Act 1933 and finally abolished by the Criminal Justice Act 1948.

Finally, whatever jurisdiction the grand jury had to act as a trial jury was abolished by a statute of 1352[19] which allowed a member of the trial jury to be challenged on the ground of his having been a member of the jury of presentment. From this date the petty (or trial) jury is seen as completely distinct from the grand jury.

c   Trial

The earliest method of trial in the royal courts was trial by ordeal. This method of trial had, of course, existed long before the common law and indeed long before Christianity. Trial by ordeal was regarded as an appeal to

---

[17] See p. 4, *ante.*
[18] The sheriff still supervised the system of frankpledge.
[19] 25 Edw. 3, st. 5, c. 3.

God to decide the guilt or innocence of the accused and might take various forms. Ordeal by fire or boiling water was common.[20] This involved burning or scalding the prisoner's hands and bandaging them. The bandages were removed after three days, when guilt would be established if the hands had not healed. A more subtle appeal to the supernatural was "wager of law". This involved the prisoner finding a special number (generally twelve) of oath-swearers to swear to his innocence. If he could not do so, or his oath-swearers faltered in their oath, he was immediately presumed guilty. In an age when the oath would not be sworn lightly it was no doubt difficult to secure oath-swearers if the prisoner was patently guilty. Indeed the ecclesiastical courts retained compurgation until well after the Restoration. Compurgation also existed as a means whereby a defendant could evade liability in certain civil actions.[1]

All these forms of ordeal were attended with elaborate religious ceremony which accounts for the credence placed in their efficacy. Thus when Pope Innocent III in the Lateran Council in 1215 forbade members of the clergy from performing ceremonial at ordeals, the ordeal was effectively abolished as a means of trial.[2] This raised the need for a new method of trial to be found and led to the establishment of trial by jury.

The petty (or trial) jury was created not by statute, but by prerogative exercised through the King's judges. At first, no person could be compelled to submit to trial by jury without his consent. If he remained silent when asked to plead to treason or misdemeanour, this was treated as a plea of guilty. However this was not so in cases of felony. In such cases he had to submit to jury trial and was pressed by heavy weights of iron upon his chest until he did consent or died. This barbaric procedure (known as *peine forte et dure*) usually resulted in acquiescence but many died rather than submit to jury trial. The result was that they did not die convicted felons and so did not forfeit their property to the Crown. There is record of a prisoner being pressed to death as late as 1658. In 1772[3] this procedure was abolished and a provision introduced that silence be treated as a plea of guilty in all cases. In 1827 statute[4] altered the position by providing that standing mute be treated as a plea of not guilty.

Trial by jury in the fifteenth century bore a passing resemblance to a modern jury trial. The most notable differences were: that in cases of treason or felony the accused could only have counsel to speak for him on matters of law, not on issues of fact; that he had no right to call any witnesses of his own in cases of felony; that there were few if any rules of evidence; that he could not give evidence on his own behalf[5] and, perhaps most significant of all, that the jury which tried him could be fined or imprisoned if the judge considered their verdict perverse. This practice was held to be illegal by VAUGHAN, C.J. in *Bushell's Case*[6] in 1670 after which date no juror could be punished for his decision.

---

[20] See Plucknett, *op. cit.*, p. 114.
[1] See p. 23, *post*.
[2] Except for ordeal by battle which continued to exist to determine appeals of felony.
[3] 12 Geo. 3, c. 20.
[4] 7 & 8 Geo. 4, c. 28.
[5] This impediment was not removed until the Criminal Evidence Act 1898.
[6] (1670), Vaugh. 135.

d   Sentence

If found guilty, the prisoner's punishment depended upon whether he stood convicted of felony or misdemeanour. Conviction for felony was punishable by death or maiming and forfeiture of the felon's land and chattels to the Crown. Conviction for misdemeanour, on the other hand, was punishable by fine, whipping or imprisonment. Various means were adopted to mitigate the severity of the punishment on a conviction for felony. Indeed, by the end of the eighteenth century only about one condemned prisoner in eight was actually executed. In many cases the death sentence would be remitted through the exercise of the royal prerogative of mercy. This would often take the form of a pardon conditional upon transportation for life of the prisoner to the American or Australian colonies. In other cases juries fictitiously assessed the value of stolen property at less than one shilling since this reduced the offence from larceny to petty larceny, which was not a capital offence. This is another example of the use of fictions at common law. However a far more important fiction which was used to mitigate the severity of the criminal law was the fiction of "benefit of clergy".

Following the murder of Becket, Henry II was prompted by remorse to concede to the clergy[7] the privilege of exemption from trial in the King's courts. The "criminous clerk" would instead be tried in the ecclesiastical courts where the punishments were far less severe than in the common law courts. In addition there was no jury trial in the ecclesiastical courts but only trial by compurgation (wager of law)[8] which made convictions rare.

As a direct result of the excessive severity of punishment for felony in the common law courts, benefit of clergy was made available[9] to secular as well as religious clerks. The test to determine whether an accused person was a clerk was whether or not he could read. To show ability to read the accused had only to recite a verse of Latin commonly supposed to have been Psalm 51, v. 1 and known, for obvious reasons, as the "neck verse". The privilege could, by the fourteenth century, be claimed after conviction and before sentence. If a plea after conviction succeeded the accused could not be subjected to any corporal punishment although he was not exempt from forfeiture of property, the other incident of conviction for felony.

Originally, the plea could be made on any trial for treason or felony (but not for misdemeanour). However a series of statutes beginning in the fifteenth century effectively limited the availability of the privilege. A statute of 1490[10] ensured that the privilege could only claimed by a first offender by providing that he be branded upon successfully pleading his clergy. Subsequently benefit of clergy was withdrawn from murder committed *ex malitia praecogitata*.[11] In 1576 statute[12] provided that criminous clerks should not be handed over to the church but should be released completely, thus severing

---

7 See Plucknett, *op. cit.*, p. 439.
8 See p. 17, *ante*.
9 By the statute of 25 Edw. 3, st. 3, c. 4 (1352).
10 4 Hen. 7, c. 13.
11 By 23 Hen. 8, c. 1, 25 Hen. 8, c. 3, 1 Ed. 6, c. 12, 5 & 6 Ed. 6, c. 10. This was the origin of the distinction between murder and manslaughter in the English criminal law; cf. *Hyam* v. *Director of Public Prosecutions*, [1975] A.C. 55, at p. 66; [1974] 2 All E.R. 41, at p. 45, *per* LORD HAILSHAM.
12 18 Eliz. 1, c. 7.

the plea from any connection with the ecclesiastical courts. However the same Act conferred a discretionary power on the court to imprison the offender for up to one year. A series of post-Reformation statutes which codified the common law as to felonies such as rape, piracy, robbery and burglary expressly made these offences non-clergyable so that benefit of clergy became available only in the case of certain common law felonies. It was finally abolished by the Criminal Law Act 1827.

From the brief account above, it will be apparent that at the very root of early criminal law and procedure was the division of crimes into felonies and misdemeanours. The earliest, and basic, offences such as murder, manslaughter, rape, robbery, burglary and larceny were felonies while the offences created later, either by the Star Chamber or by statute, were misdemeanours and upon this distinction depended sentence and, to a lesser extent, procedure. The death penalty for felony as such was abolished early in the development of the common law by the combined operation of the fiction of benefit of clergy and statute. Forfeiture for felony was not abolished until the Forfeiture Act 1870. Thereafter the distinction between felony and misdemeanour was an anachronism; nevertheless a number of irritating consequences flowed from the distinction—to take but one example, the offences of misprision, compounding and being accessory after the fact existed in relation to felony but not in relation to misdemeanour.

The distinction was eventually abolished by the Criminal Law Act 1967, section 1(1) of which provides that "All distinctions between felony and misdemeanour are hereby abolished". Section 1(2) goes on to state that:[13]

> "on all matters on which a distinction has previously been made between felony and misdemeanour, including mode of trial, the law and practice in relation to all offences cognisable under the law of England and Wales (including piracy) shall be the law and practice applicable at the commencement of this Act in relation to misdemeanour."

3 Summary trial

The third, and latest, method of trial created by the common law was summary trial; trial without a jury. This method of trial in its modern sense was entirely created by statute and was only available where statute so provided. The trial was before justices of the peace holding "petty sessions".[14] Nevertheless, even before the statutory creation of petty sessions, minor offences were not, of course, dealt with by the assizes or quarter sessions. They were dealt with by the sheriff in his "tourn" in the hundred court or in a "court leet" which was a franchise court, the franchise being in the hands of the lord of the manor or a borough. In the sixteenth century these courts declined as their jurisdiction was, by successive statutes, vested in justices of the peace.

---

[13] References in the Act to felony do not include treason (s. 12(6)) so that offences of misprision, compounding and being accessory after the fact still exist in relation to treason. Since the Treason Act 1945 there has been no procedural distinction between treason and felony.

[14] Although certain local courts had, by royal charter, jurisdiction over summary offences which excluded that of the ordinary justices. All such jurisdiction may now be regarded as obsolete so that exclusive summary jurisdiction is vested in magistrates' courts: see *R. v. East Powder Magistrates' Court, Ex parte Lampshire*, [1979] Q.B. 616; [1979] 2 All E.R. 329.

A statute of 1848[15] (Sir John Jervis's Act) for the first time created a uniform procedure for summary trials. In modern times the vast bulk of criminal offences are tried in this way.[16]

D   CIVIL PROCEDURE AT COMMON LAW

It is not proposed to examine procedure in the local or feudal courts although there is no doubt that most common law actions were triable in these courts until the fourteenth century. These courts each had different methods of securing the defendant's presence, different rules of pleading and different modes of trial. The earliest forms of action tried in the common law courts concerned disputes over title to land. Between 1250 and 1400 the common law provided for the trial of personal actions in the royal courts and by 1400 very few of such actions were not triable at common law.

There is one basic principle underlying the growth of the common law. This is that a common law right only existed if there was a procedure for enforcing it (*ubi remedium ibi ius*). Consequently, substantive law is inextricably bound up with procedure. Maine expressed the situation thus:

> "So great is the ascendancy of the Law of Actions in the infancy of Courts of Justice, that substantive law has at first the look of being gradually secreted in the interstices of procedure".[17]

With this principle in mind it is possible to examine the history of civil procedure. The course of a civil action in the common law courts may be broadly divided into three stages: (a) the issue of the appropriate writ; (b) pleadings; and (c) trial.

1   Issue of the writ

An action at common law was commenced by the plaintiff purchasing from the Chancery a writ.[18] This writ, when issued, was not in the form of the modern writ of summons (which is directed to the defendant himself). The common law writ was directed to the sheriff of the county where the action was brought and directed the sheriff to command (*praecipe*) the defendant to do some act by way of giving effect to the plaintiff's right (e.g. to pay money or surrender up property to the plaintiff) or to attend court to explain why he would not. Such a writ was termed a *praecipe* writ. It will be appreciated that, unlike the modern writ, it was not in a standard form. There was a different form of writ for each form of action. Indeed a cause of action only existed if the facts fell within the scope of an existing writ on the register of writs. The modern student might legitimately enquire why the courts did not simply sanction the issue of new forms of writ to meet factual situations apparently calling for remedy as and when the same arose. The primary explanation is the inherent conservatism of the judges. English judges have

---

15 Summary Jurisdiction Act 1848.
16 Summary procedure is dealt with at length, at pp. 542, *et seq, post.*
17 Maine, *Early Law and Custom*, p. 389.
18 Other methods, such as proceedings by bill, were superseded by the writ system. However, as we have seen (pp. 7–9, *ante*) both the King's Bench and the Exchequer developed bill procedures so as to acquire jurisdiction over debt and other actions.

always regarded the creation of new causes of action with extreme reserve,[19] attaching a peculiar reverence to the achievement of legal certainty. Secondly, since litigation was an important source of local as well as royal revenue, feudal barons were extremely reluctant to agree to any development which would operate to deprive their courts of business and indeed the history of the early period of the common law is marked by the struggle between the local courts and the common law courts with the latter prevailing only gradually. Consequently the various forms of action developed over some six centuries. The precise content and nature of the individual forms of action is clearly a matter of substantive law but it is convenient at this point to outline the historical evolution of the forms of action.[20]

2　The forms of action

a　Real actions

The earliest civil matters over which the common law courts were anxious to assume jurisdiction were those concerning land. Therefore, not unnaturally, the earliest forms of action were actions for the recovery of land. These are termed real actions. Personal actions are actions for damages. Actions in which both land and damages are sought are described as mixed actions. The growth of the real actions is extremely complex. The earliest form of real action was the writ of right. This was not a means of commencing an action in the royal courts but a direction from the King commanding the feudal lord to try a dispute concerning title to freehold land between the "demandant" (plaintiff) and the "tenant" (defendant). The action would be tried in the feudal court by battle. Where the tenant in chief of the two claimants was the King himself the issue on the writ would be triable by the King. Thus the earliest jurisdiction of the King derives from his position as a feudal lord. Henry II attempted to extend this form of writ of right so as to by-pass the court of the feudal overlord and make any writ of right triable in the royal courts. His attempt was premature and clause 34 of Magna Carta provided that this writ (*praecipe quod reddat*) should not be issued in future so as to deprive any free man of his court. This did not, however, affect the form of writ of right appropriate where the King was tenant in chief (*praecipe in capite*). Thus there were after 1215 two forms of writ of right, only one of which was properly within the jurisdiction of the common law courts. Nevertheless, even where the issue on the writ was triable in the feudal rather than the royal court, the royal writ had first to be obtained.

　　The writ of right was effectively brought within the jurisdiction of the royal judges by the introduction, under Henry II, of the Grand Assize. This gave the tenant (defendant) the option of submitting to trial before twelve knights[1] as an alternative to battle. This concept of "jury" trial was further

---

[19] See, for example, *Best v. Samuel Fox & Co., Ltd.,* [1952] A.C. 716; [1952] 2 All E.R. 394; *Chapman v. Honig,* [1963] 2 Q.B. 502; [1963] 2 All E.R. 513. Maitland describes this force as the *vis inertiae.*

[20] For a simple and lucid guide to this complex historical development see Maitland, *The Forms of Action at Common Law.*

[1] This was not a jury in the modern sense since the knights were witnesses rather than judges of fact.

developed by Henry II with the creation of the Possessory (or Petty) Assizes, the method of trial of which was similar to that obtaining at the Grand Assize.[2] The two[3] principal possessory assizes were *Novel Disseisin* and *Mort d'Ancestor*. The first lay at the suit of a plaintiff who had been recently dispossessed (disseised) of his rightful freehold tenement. The latter was available to the heir of a person[4] who died seised as of fee against a person who had obtained seisin before the heir. The actions are often described as mixed actions since damages could be awarded as well as recovery of land. The feature of the Possessory Assizes was that they did not involve declarations as to absolute title but only as to comparative rights to possession (seisin) of freehold land. From these actions stems the modern concept of title to land as being comparative (rather than absolute) and being based upon possession (rather than ownership). Because the Possessory Assizes did not involve the complex ceremonial and procedure attendant upon writs of right, they largely replaced the latter. Nevertheless they were, by their terms, limited in scope and, even at this stage, the common law judges were reluctant to extend the scope of the existing forms of action. This led to the creation of a new type of action—the writ of entry.

Writs of entry were originally created as variations on the Possessory Assizes. However, due to the relative speed of procedure, they became popular and were extended by the Statute of Marlborough 1267, to any suit in which the demandant alleged a flaw in the tenant's title even though the demandant had not been disseised. The result was that writs of entry became available to determine almost any dispute over title and they were used widely until the fifteenth century when they were in turn superseded by the mixed action of ejectment.[5] The real actions were almost entirely abolished by the Real Property Limitation Act 1833. The few remaining after this date were abolished by the Common Law Procedure Acts 1852–1860.

b   Personal actions prior to 1285

The earliest forms of personal actions were virtually indistinguishable from the real actions. They were commenced by *praecipe quod reddat* commanding the defendant to return personal property (money or chattels) to the plaintiff and ordering the sheriff to bring the defendant before the royal court[6] if he failed to do so. In fact the actions were only distinguishable from the real actions by the relief sought. In Maitland's own words:

---

2   Although the recognitors need not be knights but only good and lawful men of the neighbourhood.

3   There were two other possessory assizes; *darrein presentment* and *utrum*.

4   Seisin did not pass automatically on the death of the tenant; it only arose when the heir physically entered into possession of the land. Hence the need to provide the heir with a right of action against a person who entered the land before the heir could do so. The degrees of ancestry within the assizes of mort d'ancestor were extended by the later actions of *Aiel* (grandfather), *Besaiel* (great-grandfather) and *Cosinage* (cousin). The original writ extended only to father, mother, brother, sister, uncle and aunt.

5   See p. 25, *post*.

6   Usually the Court of Common Pleas.

"We are tempted to say that Debt is a 'real' action, that the vast gulf which to our minds divides the 'Give me what I own' and 'Give me what I am owed' has not yet become apparent."[7]

The earliest personal actions at common law were *debt, detinue, covenant* and *account*.[8] *Debt* was an action for a fixed sum of money in return for an executed consideration. Although it was, in modern terms, contractual in nature, it was very far removed from the modern action in contract because of its inherent limitations. The action only lay for a liquidated sum[9] due in full. It was not an action for damages. Also the plaintiff had no right of action until he had fully performed his obligation.[10] Finally the writ became subject to an elaborate and artificial system of pleading and was subject to wager of law.[11]

The writ of *detinue* was similar to debt and certainly the two actions had a similar origin. The praecipe directed the defendant to return a specific chattel which he was wrongfully refusing to return. However, if unsuccessful the defendant always had the option of paying damages rather than returning the chattel. Thus the action was not an action for a specific *res* but an action for damages.[12] Detinue, like debt, was triable by wager of law.

The writ of *account* is one of the few writs which has contributed to modern procedure rather than to substantive law.[13] It was used, as it is today, to compel an "accounting party" such as a manorial bailiff or a business partner to account to the plaintiff for money received on the latter's behalf. The writ was later superseded by the equitable jurisdiction of the Chancellor to take accounts since accounts by bill in the Court of Chancery did not involve the elaborate and expensive procedure of the Court of Common Pleas.

The last of these important early forms of action was the writ of *covenant*. This form of action bears testimony to the peculiar sanctity with which the common law has always regarded the seal. The writ lay for breach of any obligation under the defendant's seal. It was wider than debt in that it lay for the recovery of unliquidated damages and lay for the failure to perform virtually any obligation. However it was restrictive in that there was no action unless the obligation were contained in writing under seal. It appears that the writ was widely used to enforce leases since the obligations between lessor and lessee were originally purely personal. It should be noted that covenant could not be brought for the recovery of a debt, even under seal. The action in such a case would have to be in debt.

By the thirteenth century the Register of Original Writs contained some fifty writs, though these were all factual variations upon the basic writs described above. The immediate result of this proliferation of actions,

---

[7] Maitland, *The Forms of Action at Common Law* (1936 Edn.), p. 38.

[8] *Replevin* was an additional form but of lesser importance being confined to wrongful distress and triable generally in the local courts rather than in the Court of Common Pleas.

[9] It is possible that the action was originally for the return of specific coin.

[10] Alternatively the acknowledgement of a debt by a deed under seal was sufficient to found an action of debt.

[11] See p. 17, *ante*.

[12] Detinue, as a nominate tort, existed until abolished by s. 2(1) of the Torts (Interference with Goods) Act 1977.

[13] For details of this procedure, see p. 328, *post*.

especially the advent of the great writ of trespass during this period, was a decline in the revenue of the local courts. The barons, ever anxious to halt the centralisation of litigation, consequently forced Henry III to agree that no new writs of course (*de cursu*) should be sealed by the Chancellor without the consent of the whole Council. This concession was contained in the Provisions of Oxford 1258. It is questionable how far these Provisions had the force of law but they were undoubtedly instrumental in stunting the growth of the common law and providing for the very narrow course which the subsequent development of the forms of action was to take.

c The Writ of Trespass

The great writ of trespass, "that fertile mother of actions",[14] may be seen as the link between the early forms of action already described and the later writs which are the historical source of most of the modern law of contract and torts. There are conflicting theories about the origins of trespass. A common theory, advanced notably by Maitland, is that the writ had its roots in the old appeal of felony. Though a criminal proceeding this had much in common with a civil action since it was instituted by an individual on his own behalf rather than by the Crown. A second theory regards trespass as an offshoot of the assize of novel disseisin.[15] This is supported by the fact that damages could be awarded in that action. Other scholars attribute the origins of the writ to local procedure and Roman law.

The nature of trespass was that it was a breach of the King's peace by a positive wrongful act. Unlike the *praecipe* writs, the writ of trespass directed the sheriff forthwith to summon the defendant to show why he had committed the alleged wrong. It did not give him the opportunity of first doing right by the plaintiff. All writs of trespass contained the words *vi et armis et contra pacem domini regis* (by force of arms and against the King's peace). This wrongful act might be directed at the plaintiff's person (*vi et armis*), goods (*de bonis asportatis*) or land (*quare clausum fregit*), but in all cases the act had to be direct. Trespass did not extend to damage indirectly caused. Further limits to the scope of the writ were that it did not protect intangible rights, such as reputation, and that it was a wrong against possession, providing no remedy where the interference was with rights to possession or title to goods or land rather than with actual possession. Trespasses were regarded so seriously that they were (and, of course, still are) actionable *per se* (without proof of damage) and were, for a long time, wrongs of strict liability. Trespass actions were never subject to wager of law, but were triable before a jury, usually in the Court of King's Bench.

d Actions on the case

Since a writ corresponded rather to a factual situation than to a legal right the limitation on the creation of new writs imposed by the Provisions of Oxford 1258 brought obvious injustice. The facts of the plaintiff's case might not be precisely covered by an existing writ, in which event he would have no

---

[14] Maitland, *op. cit.*, p. 48.
[15] See Woodbine, *Origins of the Action of Trespass*, 33 Yale Law Journal, pp. 799–816; 34 *ibid.*, pp. 343–370.

remedy. To remedy this injustice the Statute of Westminster II 1285, c. 24, provided:

> "And whensoever from henceforth it shall fortune in the Chancery, that in one case a writ is found, and in like case (*in consimili casu*) falling under like law, and requiring like remedy, is found none, the clerks of the Chancery shall agree in making the writ. . . ."[16]

The immediate result of this provision was a rapid growth in the number of original writs. By 1300 there were some 300 writs on the Register but it must be stressed that all the new writs were factual variations upon the existing writs and did not have the effect of recognising new rights. However, as more and more factual variations on the writ of trespass were allowed, the effect was eventually that new forms of action were created protecting hitherto unprotected rights and enforcing new types of duty. These actions were the actions on the case. The name "case" suggests that these actions have their origin firmly in the statute *in consimili casu*. This view was expressed by Coke[17] and was also favoured by the older legal historians such as Maitland. The more modern view is that the Statute of Westminster II is not the source of actions on the case but the position is not free from doubt.

The new actions on the case filled the obvious gaps in the writ of trespass. For example, trespass did not extend to damage indirectly caused. Trespass on the case remedied this by providing a remedy where the defendant caused physical damage to the plaintiff indirectly, for example by leaving a log in the road over which the plaintiff's horse stumbled.[18] In addition, there grew from trespass on the case three important new forms of action which were to go far towards shaping the growth of contract and tort. These were the actions of *ejectment, trover* and *assumpsit*.

The important action of *ejectment* filled the gap between the real actions and the writ of trespass. Originally a purely personal action (remediable only by damages) it became, by the end of the fifteenth century, a mixed action in that the plaintiff could claim both damages and the recovery of land. It will be recalled that the plaintiff had no remedy in trespass unless he was in possession of the land in question at the time of the alleged wrong. Hence trespass was not available to a landlord or reversioner. A person out of possession of land had two remedies for its recovery. He could exercise his common law privilege of self-help and re-enter the land. However this was not really satisfactory particularly after the Forcible Entry Act 1381, which made forcible re-entry a criminal offence. Alternatively the real actions were available to him. These, however, had by this time become unpopular with litigants because of the cumbersome and expensive procedure attendant upon them. It was in order to avoid the cumbersome real actions that the action of ejectment was developed.

Ejectment was originally an action by a lessee to recover leasehold land from which he had been wrongly ejected. It was only extended to freehold land by the use of an incredibly elaborate fiction. The freeholder would

---

[16] This translation is taken from Maitland, *op. cit.*, p. 51.
[17] 2 Inst., f. 407.
[18] These facts are those of one of the earliest recorded actions of trespass on the case.

allege a fictitious demise (lease) of his land to a fictitious character invariably named John Doe. John Doe would in turn allege that he had been ejected by a second fictitious character named Richard Roe.[19] The plaintiff would then write a letter to the substantive defendant asking him to defend the action and signing it "your loving friend Richard Roe". The action, in form an action by an ejected lessee, would then enable the substantial dispute as to title to freehold land to be tried. Such actions may be recognised in law reports by the title *Doe d.*[20] *A.* v. *B.*

This action almost entirely superseded the real actions and became the universal form of action for the recovery of land. The famous John Doe in fact existed until his own demise was finally effected by the Common Law Procedure Act 1852. The modern "possession" action, available to any person entitled to possession of land, was created in 1875.

Just as ejectment used a legal fiction to extend a narrow form of action to a very wide set of facts so *trover*, strictly an action depending upon loss and finding, was extended to fill the gap between detinue and trespass to goods. Trover (conversion) went beyond the scope of these two writs since it extended the plaintiff's protection to all acts which constituted an unjustifiable denial of his title to chattels. In the sixteenth century trover largely superseded detinue[1] because of the relatively streamlined procedure attaching to actions on the case. In addition detinue, like debt, was subject to the anachronistic wager of law.

Assumpsit is perhaps the most important of all the actions on the case since from this single writ derive the basic principles of the modern law of contract. Until this time the only "contractual" actions at common law were debt and covenant; thus parties could create a relationship enforceable in the common law courts only by fixing the amount of remuneration in advance (which could only create a cause of action for one of the parties) or by incorporating their agreement in a deed under seal. There was no action on an executory agreement not under seal. In such cases the parties would be compelled to pursue their remedies in the inferior courts with the result that much of the profitable litigation arising out of England's growing mercantile power was outside the scope of the King's courts. In addition the common lawyers were conscious that, unless they took action, the new courts of equity[2] would assume jurisdiction over contract litigation. It was against this background that the common lawyers developed the writ of assumpsit. Assumpsit grew to supersede debt but grew, not out of the writ of debt, but as an offshoot of trespass. Thus it might be said that the law of contract and the law of torts have the same origin—trespass. In fact assumpsit in its early history was tortious in nature. The basis of liability was that the defendant was in breach of an obligation which he had assumed (assumpsit). In the fourteenth and fifteenth centuries the defendant's failure could not be mere non-performance. He was at first only liable if he undertook a task, for

---

[19] Or William Styles.

[20] "d." means "on the demise of".

[1] Until 1854 when s. 78 of the Common Law Procedure Act gave the court power to order specific restitution of chattels in actions of detinue. The power is now generally available in any proceedings for "wrongful interference" with goods as defined in s. 1 of the Torts (Interference with Goods) Act 1977; *ibid.*, s. 3(2).

[2] See p. 44, *post*.

example, to cure a horse or look after goods as a bailee, and performed it badly (misfeasance).[3] He might also be liable for malfeasance if he gave an oral undertaking which proved to be false. Assumpsit for malfeasance is virtually equivalent to deceit. Finally, in the sixteenth century, assumpsit was extended to non-feasance and at this point of time contract and tort separated. At this time assumpsit could only replace the unpopular writ of debt if the defendant had assumed an obligation to pay the debt, for example by acknowledgement. However in *Slade's Case*[4] in 1602 all the common law judges decided that "every contract executory imports in itself an assumpsit" at which stage assumpsit superseded debt.

Subsequent actions on the case protected intangible rights; *libel, slander, deceit* and *nuisance* are examples.

The history of *libel* and *slander* is complex. Until the late fifteenth century defamation was regarded as a wrong of an essentially spiritual nature and was thus dealt with by the ecclesiastical courts.[5] With the invention of printing the dissemination of libel presented a threat to national security and was recognised as a crime by the Court of Star Chamber, though damages might also be awarded. Slander, however, was not punishable in the Star Chamber, which accounts for the fact that slander, unlike libel, is not a criminal offence at the present day; it may also account for the fact that libel is actionable *per se* whereas slander is not. In the sixteenth century the common law courts recognised a new action on the case for words, though this action was at first confined to allegations of crime. With the abolition of the Star Chamber, the action on the case for words was extended to include libel.

Although the tort of *deceit* was recognised, in its modern form, only in the late eighteenth century,[6] there was, as early as the fourteenth century, a right of action against one who by fraudulent representation induced another to enter into a contract. This form of action was closely associated with assumpsit[7] and was contractual rather than tortious in nature. As stated above, deceit outside the context of a contractual relationship, became actionable in the eighteenth century and the modern definition of fraud, as including recklessness, was laid down a century later.[8]

An assize of *nuisance* appears to have existed prior to the evolution of trespass. This was, however, a real rather than a personal action. The modern tort of nuisance, an action for damages for wrongful interference with another's use or enjoyment of land (or, in the case of public nuisance, with another's exercise of a public right) derives from an action on the case developed in the sixteenth century. This action on the case supplanted the old assize of nuisance and extended the action, which had formerly been

---

3 In *Waldon* v. *Marshall* (1370), Y.B. Mich, 43 Ed. 3, f. 33, pl. 38, one of the earliest actions of its type, the defendant was held liable when a horse which the defendant had undertaken to cure died through his negligence.
4 4 Rep. 926.
5 Although the common law courts had jurisdiction to hear actions in relation to the slander of magnates under the *Scandalum Magnatum* provision of the Statute of Westminster I 1275. Although falling into disuse this provision was not in fact repealed until the Statute Law Revision Act 1888.
6 *Pasley* v. *Freeman* (1789), 3 Term Rep. 51.
7 See p. 26, *ante*.
8 *Derry* v. *Peek* (1889), 14 App. Cas 337.

confined to instances of disseisin, to a wide variety of forms of interference.[9]

In addition to these named actions there existed the innominate action on the case. This special action on the case has been used, albeit cautiously, to provide a remedy where none of the known actions exactly covered the situation. As WILLES, C.J. explained (somewhat optimistically) in 1745:

> "A special action on the case was introduced for this reason, that the law will never suffer an injury and a damage without a remedy."[10]

In fact common law judges have usually been reluctant to recognise a new cause of action. The torts of malicious falsehood,[11] inducing a breach of contract,[12] intentionally causing physical harm[13] and even the modern tort of negligence have their origin in the special action on the case.

The nineteenth century is universally recognised as being the great era of law reform and among the first topics for reform was the existence of the constricting writ system outlined above. The reform was piecemeal. The Real Property Limitation Act 1833 almost entirely abolished the real actions. The Common Law Procedure Act 1852 removed the necessity for specifying a form of action in a writ of summons. This abolished the writ system insofar as the plaintiff no longer had to settle on a choice of writ. However the pleader would, even after this date, still have to follow the precedents of pleading applicable to one of the forms of action. The final abolition of the forms of action was not completed until the passing of the Judicature Acts 1873–1875.[14] These Acts introduced the modern system of pleading whereby the plaintiff merely has to plead facts leaving the court to determine their legal effect.

Nevertheless the common law forms of action are still of great significance. Maitland's famous dictum "The forms of action we have buried but they still rule us from their graves",[15] is an overstatement. However it is important to bear in mind that the forms of action were both procedural and substantive. All that the nineteenth century legislation did was to abolish the procedure. Thus the modern significance of the forms of action is purely substantive. If the plaintiff's case could not have been prosecuted under the terms of a writ prior to 1852, then, generally, he has no cause of action.[16] Similarly if he fails to plead facts essential to a cause of action he cannot succeed in that action.[17] However, if he pleads facts which give rise to a cause

---

9 Many of these are enumerated in *Aldred's Case* (1610), 9 Co. Rep. 57b; see also *Walter* v. *Selfe* (1851), 4 De G. & Sm. 315.

10 *Winsmore* v. *Greenbank* (1745), *Willes* 578.

11 *Shepherd* v. *Wakeman* (1662), Sid. 79.

12 *Lumley* v. *Gye* (1853), 2 E. & B. 216.

13 *Wilkinson* v. *Downton*, [1897] 2 Q.B. 57.

14 Not all countries administering common law systems have introduced similar reforms. In Australia, for example, a system of pleading similar to that existing in this country prior to 1875 still exists so that actions may still fail on purely technical points of pleading; this is well illustrated by the decision of the Judicial Committee of the Privy Council, on appeal from the High Court of Australia, in *Mutual Life and Citizens' Assurance Co., Ltd.* v. *Evatt*, [1971] A.C. 793; [1971] 1 All E.R. 150.

15 Maitland, *Equity* (1916 Edn.), p. 296.

16 See, for example, *Bradford Corporation* v. *Pickles*, [1895] A.C. 587; *Best* v. *Samuel Fox & Co., Ltd.*, [1952] A.C. 716; [1952] 2 All E.R. 394; *Chapman* v. *Honig*, [1963] 2 Q.B. 502; [1963] 2 All E.R. 513; see p. 34, *post*.

17 As to the importance of pleadings, see p. 339, *post*.

of action, then he will not fail simply because he has specified the wrong cause of action or been guilty of some other procedural irregularity, as he would have done prior to 1875.[18]

3 Pleadings at common law

Having been issued with a writ the plaintiff was very far from obtaining his remedy in the common law courts. He had first to satisfy the rigorous formality of pleading attendant upon each writ. An action could easily be won or lost in the pleading. This fact prompted Littleton to advise his son:[19]

> "It is one of the most honourable, laudable and profitable things in our law to have the science of well pleading in actions real and personal, and therefore I counsel thee especially to employ thy courage and care to learn this."

Originally pleadings were delivered orally in open court and entered on the court record by the clerk. This, no doubt, placed a heavy burden on the pleader to be precise. At this stage pleadings appear to have constituted evidence of the truth of the facts pleaded, so that oral pleadings were at once allegations of fact and evidence in support of those facts. These oral pleadings were in Norman French.[20] By the fifteenth century the pleadings had become separate from the trial and were in writing. Thus the parties were able to fix the issue between them and then argue in support of that issue at the trial. However there could only be one issue in each action. The plaintiff could not plead causes of action in the alternative.[1] The defendant could not raise alternative defences but had to rely upon one defence either of law or of fact.

A defence based on a point of law was termed a "demurrer" and necessarily involved the defendant admitting all the facts alleged by the plaintiff. A defence on the facts might take the form of a special plea, such as self-defence in assault, or limitation, or a plea of the "general issue".[2] This amounted to a straight denial of the facts alleged in the issue against the defendant. There was a special form of general issue in each form of action. In covenant the general issue was *non est factum*, in debt *nil debet*, in assumpsit *non assumpsit*. Each plea had to be set out according to the hallowed formula or the plea would founder. Choice of the wrong plea would lose the action as surely as choice of the wrong writ. It might appear that this system of pleading would ensure a speedy trial if nothing else. In fact the reverse was true because the defendant's plea of the general issue told the plaintiff nothing about the defence to be raised against him. Thus by pleading *non assumpsit* the defendant could raise at the trial matters relating, for example, to capacity, lack of consideration, discharge, release or the Statute of Frauds. Consequently, the pleadings were extremely general and the plaintiff would have to be prepared to meet any possible defence at

---

[18] *Fouldes* v. *Willoughby* (1841), 8 M. & W. 540; *cf. Letang* v. *Cooper*, [1965] 1 Q.B. 197; [1964] 2 All E.R. 929. See R.S.C. (Revision) 1965, O. 2, r. 1.

[19] Littleton, *Of Tenures*, s. 534.

[20] They were in English, in fact, after 1362. The plea rolls, however, were in Latin until 1731 after which date they too were in English.

[1] This inconvenient rule against duplicity was removed by 4 & 5 Anne, c. 3 in 1705.

[2] A plea of "not guilty" in a criminal case is equivalent to pleading the old "general issue".

the trial. The need for pleadings to be more specific was introduced eventually by statute. The Civil Procedure Act 1833 conferred power upon the judges to make rules of procedure; this led to the famous Hilary Rules of 1834 which required the defendant to plead his defences specifically. These Rules remedied the abuse of parties concealing their hands until the trial but they created more, rather than less, formality and complexity of pleading. The process of breaking this down began soon afterwards with the passing of the Common Law Procedure Acts 1852–1860, and was perfected by the Judicature Acts 1873–1875, which created the modern system of pleading.[3]

4   Trial

The mode of trial depended upon the form of action. Writs of right were triable by battle, debt and detinue by the archaic wager of law. However all other actions were triable by judge and jury, the method which has survived to the present day, though the jury is rapidly disappearing in favour of trial by a judge alone.

Where an issue of law was raised on a demurrer no jury was involved since juries never decided points of law. The parties would simply appear at one of the three superior common law courts at Westminster and argue the point before the judges of that court. Thus the whole trial would take place *in banc*.

Where, on the other hand, the issue raised was one of fact, for example by the defendant pleading the general issue, this issue had to be decided by a jury. It is noteworthy that the jury in civil cases has a different origin from the criminal jury. While the latter derives from the jury of presentment of the hundred, the civil jury has its origin in the Assizes of Clarendon 1166, and Northampton 1176, which created the Grand and Petty Assizes. Thus the only jury which ever existed in civil actions was the petty jury, twelve in number. However, just as in criminal cases, the civil jury was originally a body of local witnesses and only later came to act as judges of fact. Since all writs of trespass and actions on the case were triable by jury, the effect was that, at common law, virtually all actions in contract and tort were tried by a jury. As the jurors were, at least until the fifteenth century, witnesses, other witnesses were rarely required at the trial and the jurors *qua* witnesses could be punished for a perverse verdict. *Bushell's Case* in 1670[4] established that jurors could no longer be punished for their verdicts from which, one deduces, the concept of jurors as witnesses had completely disappeared.

Jury trials at assizes took place in two stages. The issue of fact was tried at *nisi prius* by the jury and their verdict sent back to the trial court at Westminster since judgment could not be entered at *nisi prius* but only *in banc*. The central court at Westminster then entered judgment on the record in accordance with the jury verdict. Later the whole action became triable on assize or in London although judgments at *nisi prius* were still entered at Westminster as a formality.

For the enforcement of judgments there was a further set of writs avail-

---

3   See p. 83, *post*.
4   (1670), Vaugh. 135.

able. These too were directed to the sheriff.[5] The most important of them were the writ of attachment (whereby the defendant had to provide security for his attendance), *distringas* (ordering seizure of the defendant's property) and *capias ad respondendum* (ordering the defendant's arrest).

There was no appeal by way of rehearing at common law. This was not introduced until 1875.[6] The first method of appeal from the decision of a common law court was by writ of error alleging an error on the record. This would not extend to any question of fact and could only extend to such points of law as would appear on the record; for example, defects in pleadings or failure to summon all parties to the proceedings. Proceedings in error were also apparently extended to appeals against the decision of a judge on the trial of a demurrer. Where a point of law was not contained in the court record the trial judge might be asked to seal a "Bill of Exceptions" which was annexed to the record and was deemed, by the Statute of Westminster II 1285, c. 31, to be part of the record for the purpose of proceedings in error. The Bill of Exceptions contained points of law not otherwise enrolled such as rulings on the admissibility of evidence or the burden of proof.[7]

Finally in the seventeenth century it became possible for a litigant to "move for a new trial", a procedure which is still an alternative to appeal by way of rehearing in civil actions.

E   CONTENT OF COMMON LAW

We have seen that the development of the common law (excluding crime) took place by means of the formulation and extension of forms of action so that a right existed if, and only if, there was a procedure for enforcing it. It is for this reason that the forms of action are so important in any consideration of the origins of English law and in the forms of action is to be found the content of the common law, that is to say the basic principles of the law of property and the law of contract and tort.

1   Law of property

a   Real and personal property

In most continental systems the word "property" is used to indicate subject matter in which rights exist—consequently the fundamental distinction in such systems is between movable and immovable property. In the English legal system, however, although that meaning of property is not unknown (and is often used in statutes, for example the Theft Act 1968) "property" is traditionally used to describe not the object itself but rather that interest in the object that the law recognises. Within this framework of definition the writ system gave rise to a distinction between "real" property (consisting of rights enforceable by one of the real actions) and "personal" property (consisting of rights enforceable by one of the personal actions). Although the

---

[5] As is the only surviving writ of execution, the writ of *fieri facias* (see p. 391, *post*).
[6] Judicature Acts 1873–1875.
[7] Bills of exceptions were apparently unpopular with common law judges and there is evidence that many of them flatly refused to seal bills. See, for example, *Bridgman* v. *Holt* (1693), Show. Parl. Cas. 111.

real actions were, as has been seen, superseded by the personal action of ejectment, the distinction between real property (realty) and personal property (personalty) has persisted throughout our legal history.

To the layman (and indeed to the continental lawyer) the distinction has little in the way of logic to commend it. In particular it produced the anomalous consequence that leaseholds were (and are) personal property rather than real property. Until 1926 (when the Law of Property Act 1925 came into operation) this distinction was of great significance, in particular because the rules of succession on intestacy differed radically according to whether the property of the deceased was real or personal. Real property passed to the heir at law, to the exclusion of other sons and daughters; personal property, with which the feudal system was little concerned, devolved upon the next of kin. Consequently there is, in the law reports, a considerable volume of litigation dealing with the distinction between real and personal property. The equitable doctrine of conversion, for example, arose entirely out of this type of dispute between the heir at law and the next of kin.

Virtually all distinctions between the old rules relating to real and personal property were abolished by the 1925 legislation, including the intestate succession rules. Nevertheless the distinction is still drawn. For example, a testator who makes a bequest of "all my realty" to a named beneficiary will not succeed in passing to him any leasehold interests he may have. Similarly, since personal property may be seized in execution of a judgment, a leasehold interest may theoretically be taken in execution whereas a freehold interest cannot be seized (although it can be reached by charging order).[8]

Since the personal actions protected intangible possessions, such as debts, it follows that personal property may exist in something having no physical existence, such as debts, rights under negotiable instruments, trade marks, copyrights and the like; such property is described in English law as "choses in action" and may be distinguished from "choses in possession" which term comprises rights in objects capable of physical possession, such as cars, furniture or domestic animals.

b   Tenures and estates

It is beyond the scope of a work of this nature to consider in detail the various interests in land created by the common law. Nevertheless it would be inappropriate to omit from the most cursory description of the historical origins of the law of property some mention of tenures and estates.[9]

The fundamental proposition, and one which holds good to the present day, is that land cannot be owned in the absolute sense in which there may be ownership of chattels. The Sovereign is the absolute owner of all the land in the realm. Individuals may only hold estates in the land by a form of tenure.

Tenures—According to English law all landowners are tenants of the Sovereign. The word "tenure" is used to describe the form of the holding or tenancy. In the Middle Ages there were several forms of tenure, the obligations which were imposed upon the tenant in return for his tenure being

---

8   See p. 393, *post.*
9   See, generally, Baker, *An Introduction to English Legal History*, (2nd Edn.), pp. 193–262.

termed the "incidents" of that form of tenure. Tenures differed according to whether the holder was a freeman or a villein.

The tenures held by freemen were known as "freehold" tenures. The two principal forms of freehold tenure in the Middle Ages were tenure by "knight service" and "socage" tenure.[10] Knight service involved the tenant providing a certain number of knights to fight in the lord's army. In time of peace this requirement was replaced by an obligation to pay a sum of money known as *scutagium* (shield-money). Military tenure was abolished in 1660[11] and converted into the second form of tenure-socage. The incidents of socage tenure varied considerably. They might involve the provision of weapons for the lord's army or of agricultural services. One standard incident of socage tenure was escheat, whereby the land was forfeited to the superior lord if the tenant died without heir.[12]

Villeins could also hold land. The incidents attaching to unfree tenure varied but generally involved the payment of money, the rendering of agricultural services, escheat and the payment of fines on alienation (transfer) of the land. Unfree tenure was evidenced by an entry on the roll of the manorial court. It thus became known as tenure by copy of the roll—"copyhold" tenure. Copyhold tenure might be converted into freehold tenure by enfranchisement. Those copyholds which were not so enfranchised were converted into socage tenure by the Law of Property Act 1922 (which came into force on January 1, 1926).[13] It may, therefore, appear that the history of tenure is of no more than academic interest. Nevertheless it does illustrate the basis of the modern system of land ownership and it is the basis of the doctrine of estates.

Before examining briefly the nature of estates in land it should be recalled that leasehold was not a feudal tenure, so that a leasehold estate in land does not arise from tenure in the same way as does a freehold estate.

Estates—While tenure concerns the relationship between the lord and his tenant, the interest which the latter has in the land is termed an "estate". At common law there were several different estates which a person might hold in land and several estates might exist simultaneously in a single parcel of land. It is sufficient to state that, since 1926, there have been only two legal estates in land: (1) an estate in fee simple absolute in possession (freehold), and (2) a term of years absolute (leasehold). The freehold estate is held by socage tenure, although this is of no practical significance. Leasehold was not, originally, an estate at all and leases in the Middle Ages were regarded as creating no more than purely personal obligations between the parties. It was only when the same form of action[14] became used for both the freeholder and the leaseholder to recover possession of the land, in the fifteenth century, that the leaseholder was recognised as having an estate in land.

---

[10] Other forms of freehold tenure were *frankalmoign* (whereby religious houses undertook to say prayers for the soul of the superior feudal lord) and *serjeanty* (whereby the tenant had to provide various honorary services), a useful chart of the various forms of tenure can be found in Baker, *op. cit.*, p. 221.

[11] By the Tenures Abolition Act.

[12] When the device of the trust was conceived in equity (see p. 149, *post*) one of its uses was to avoid some of the burdensome incidents of feudal tenure.

[13] Section 128 and Sch. 12.

[14] The action of ejectment; see p. 25, *ante*.

Apart from the estates which existed, and continue to exist, in land, there were other rights enforceable by one or more of the forms of action. These are described as "interests" in land, rather than estates. At the present day there is an important distinction (from the standpoint of conveyancing) between "legal interests", such as easements and charges by way of legal mortgage, and "equitable interests", such as interest under a trust. The former derive from the forms of action at common law while the latter, as their title would indicate, have their origins in equity.[15]

2   Contract and tort

a   Law of torts

A tort may be defined as the infringement of a legal right not arising exclusively out of a contract or trust and giving rise to a cause of action for unliquidated damages. This definition, like most other definitions of torts, is not of much assistance in identifying the nature of a tort. It is only possible to identify a tort by possessing a prior knowledge of the rights which the law of torts protects. The infringement of one of these rights is a tort. The general function of the law of torts is to provide compensation to a person in respect of damage caused by another. However, this is not the basis upon which the law of torts has grown. Thus there are many cases in which one person may cause loss or damage to another without committing a tort or indeed any actionable wrong. There is no action for infringement of privacy,[16] nor for loss caused by legitimate business competition. A wife has no action for the loss of her husband's consortium[17] nor has a tenant any remedy if given notice to quit by a landlord for giving evidence against the latter in judicial proceedings.[18] Every legal right involves a correlative legal duty imposed on another person or persons. A right protected by the law of torts involves a correlative duty owed by every member of the community, unlike a contractual right which only involves a duty on the part of the other contracting party. Nevertheless a tort is no easier to identify looked at from the standpoint of the defendant's duty. It has no general moral character. While certain torts involve conduct on the part of the defendant which would be regarded as immoral or anti-social (for example, battery, deceit, malicious prosecution, defamation), others have no moral content whatsoever (such as trespass to land, nuisance and the concept of vicarious liability). Also by

---

15 See p. 49, *post*.

16 See: *Lord Bernstein of Leigh* v. *Skyviews and General, Ltd.*, [1978] Q.B. 479; [1977] 2 All E.R. 902 in which the plaintiff, albeit unsuccessfully, sought to protect his privacy by framing his action as a trespass to the air space above his land; *Malone* v. *Metropolitan Police Commissioner (No. 2)*, [1979] Ch. 344; [1979] 2 All E.R. 620 in which the plaintiff sought to invoke the European Convention for the Protection of Human Rights and Fundamental Freedoms (1950) in an attempt to demonstrate a right not to have his telephone "tapped"; he failed since the Convention is not part of English law and there is no right of property (apart from copyright) in words transmitted by telephone lines (see p. 63, *post*).

17 *Best* v. *Samuel Fox & Co. Ltd.*, [1952] A.C. 716; [1952] 2 All E.R. 394. At common law the husband had a right of action against a person who deprived him of his wife's services or consortium and a parent had a right of action for deprivation of the services of a child; these causes of action were abolished by the Administration of Justice Act 1982, s. 2.

18 *Chapman* v. *Honig*, [1963] 2 Q.B. 502; [1963] 2 All E.R. 513.

no means all conduct which is immoral or intended to cause damage to another is tortious. Treason, obscenity, contempt of court[18] and perjury[19] are not torts even where their commission causes and is intended to cause damage to another.

Conversely certain conduct is tortious even though it causes the plaintiff no damage or loss whatsoever. "The least touching of another in anger is battery."[1] Any act of trespass, however trivial, is actionable *per se*. Similarly there are some torts which not only do not depend upon the fault of the defendant but do not even require him to have intended to commit the tortious act. The conclusion to be drawn is that there is nothing intrinsic in the nature of conduct which marks it as tortious.

The only way in which it is possible to identify tortious conduct is by reference to the historical development of tort. The plaintiff in an action in tort can succeed only if he can show a right historically protected by the law of torts, can persuade the court to vary an existing right to such an extent as, in fact, to create a new right or if he has a statutory right. This means that new rights of action in tort can be created either judicially or by legislation. In modern times the judiciary is so restricted by the operation of the doctrine of precedent[2] that it is extremely rare for a new right to be created judicially. Examples of new torts which have evolved through the willingness of judges to extend existing causes of action in comparatively recent times are the tort of inducing a breach of contract, which was created in the case of *Lumley* v. *Gye*[3] in 1853 as an extension of the existing tort of enticement of a servant, and liability under the rule in *Rylands* v. *Fletcher*[4] which evolved as an offshoot of nuisance in 1866.

Virtually the whole of the modern law of torts (excluding, of course, breach of statutory duty) derives from the writ of trespass and the actions on the case which evolved from the writ.[5] Until the fourteenth century trespass constituted the whole of the existing law of torts with the exception of detinue, an even older action deriving from the action of debt.[6] One commentator has stated that[7]

> "had there been a medieval *Salmond* or *Winfield* trespass would have been the title, not of a chapter but of the book".

In the nineteenth century the writ system was abolished by the Common Law Procedure Act 1852. This dispensed with the necessity for the plaintiff to select one form of action to fit his claim. Thereafter he merely had to plead facts leaving the court to decide whether he had a remedy. The effect of this was to give the law of torts a certain fluidity but not to increase the scope of the existing torts.

The only real development which the abolition of the forms of action has brought about is that the name given to a tort is purely descriptive. Certain

---

[19] *Hargreaves* v. *Bretherton*, [1959] 1 Q.B. 45; [1958] 3 All E.R. 122.
[1] *Cole* v. *Turner* (1704), 6 Mod. Rep. 149, *per* HOLT, C.J.
[2] See p. 133, *post*.
[3] (1853), 2 E. & B. 216.
[4] (1866), L.R. 1 Exch. 265; affirmed (1868), L.R. 3 H.L. 330.
[5] See p. 24, *ante*.
[6] See p. 23, *ante*.
[7] 74 L.Q.R. 407 (Milsom).

factual situations give rise to a cause of action; others do not. To identify these factual situations as deceit, nuisance or negligence is useful only for the purposes of classification. At the present day no practical consequence can follow from classifying one factual situation as trespass and another as negligence rather than vice versa. This point is particularly clearly illustrated by the case of *Letang* v. *Cooper*.[8] The plaintiff was run over by a car which was allegedly being driven negligently by the defendant. She contended that this gave rise to two causes of action; trespass and negligence. The action for negligence was clearly statute-barred but the plaintiff maintained that, on a true construction of the Limitation Acts, her action for trespass was not. This argument found favour with the judge at first instance, but his decision was reversed by the Court of Appeal. DIPLOCK, L.J. (as he then was) explained the situation thus:[9]

> "A cause of action is simply a factual situation the existence of which entitles one person to obtain from the court a remedy against another person. Historically the means by which the remedy was obtained varied with the nature of the factual situation and causes of action were divided into categories according to the 'form of action' by which the remedy was obtained in the particular kind of factual situation which constituted the cause of action; . . . But it is essential to realise that when, since 1873, the name of a form of action is used to identify a cause of action, it is used as a convenient and succinct description of a particular category of factual situation which entitles one person to obtain from the court a remedy against another person. To forget this will indeed encourage the old forms of action to rule us from their graves. . . . The description 'negligence' was in fact used by the plaintiff's pleader; but this cannot be decisive, for we are concerned not with the description applied by the pleader to the factual situation and the action founded on it, but with the description applied to it by Parliament in the enactment to be construed. It is true that the factual situation also falls within the description of the tort of 'trespass to the person'. But that, as I have endeavoured to show, does not mean that there are two causes of action. It merely means that there are two apt descriptions of the same cause of action. It does not cease to be the tort of 'negligence', because it can also be called by another name. An action founded on it is none the less an 'action for negligence' because it can also be called an 'action for trespass to the person'."

It might be supposed from the foregoing that the law of torts has fossilized. In fact nothing could be further from the truth. Within the last twenty years there has been an enormous expansion of the scope of potential rights and liabilities through judicial expansion of the tort of negligence. Negligence differs from other torts in that liability is approached from the point of view of the defendant's conduct rather than the plaintiff's right; hence it bears little or no affinity to the forms of action at common law. The principle, usually called the "neighbour" principle,[10] is that a person owes a duty of care to other persons whom he ought reasonably to foresee as likely to be affected by his acts or omissions and that if he is in breach of that duty (by failing to exercise reasonable care) he is liable to such of those other persons as suffer damage. Originally confined to physical damage, the tort has been

---

8 [1965] 1 Q.B. 232; [1964] 2 All E.R. 929.
9 [1965] 1 Q.B., at p. 242; [1964] 2 All E.R., at p. 934.
10 Derived from the famous speech of LORD ATKIN in *M'Alister* (*or Donoghue*) v. *Stevenson*, [1932] A.C. 562.

extended to purely financial loss[11] and, in recent years, to an ever-increasing range of factual situations.[12] LORD WILBERFORCE, in one of the leading recent cases, summarised the current state of the law:[13]

> "the position has now been reached that in order to establish that a duty of care arises in a particular situation, it is not necessary to bring the facts of that situation within those of previous situations in which a duty of care has been held to exist. Rather the question has to be approached in two stages. First one has to ask whether, as between the alleged wrongdoer and the person who has suffered damage there is a sufficient relationship of proximity or neighbourhood such that, in the reasonable contemplation of the former, carelessness on his part may be likely to cause damage to the latter, in which case a prima facie duty of care arises. Secondly, if the first question is answered affirmatively, it is necessary to consider whether there are any considerations which ought to negative, or to reduce or limit the scope of the duty or the class of person to whom it is owed or the damages to which a breach of it may give rise."

Most actions in tort these days are, in fact, based upon negligence or breach of statutory duty, so that very little of the modern law of torts is directly traceable to the forms of action at common law.

b   Law of contract

Whereas the law of torts developed (with the exception of the tort of detinue) from the writ of trespass, the modern law of contract has its orgins in the writ of assumpsit,[14] and, to a lesser extent, in the earlier writs of debt and covenant. It will be recalled that assumpsit replaced debt and provided a general means of enforcing bargains. It should, however, be noted that assumpsit did not supersede the writ of covenant, the result being that obligations under seal are, to this day, enforceable without proof of consideration whereas, in contracts not under seal, consideration is essential.

Although many of the rules applicable to contracts have changed, and although both equity[15] and legislation have contributed to the modern law of contract, the basic principles derive from the common law forms of action. A "contract", in English law, means an agreement which would have been enforceable in the common law courts prior to 1852 by use of one of the three writs of debts, covenant or assumpsit. This is more than a matter of mere historical interest, for two reasons. First, the rules relating to contract generally do not necessarily apply to other consensual transactions such as conveyances or marriages. Secondly, statutory provisions which are expressed to apply to contracts are clearly not intended to apply to every legal relationship created consensually.

It would be beyond the scope of this work to investigate the principles of

---

[11] *Hedley Byrne & Co., Ltd.* v. *Heller & Partners, Ltd.*, [1964] A.C. 465; [1963] 2 All E.R. 575.
[12] The landmarks since *Hedley Byrne* (*supra*) have been *Home Office* v. *Dorset Yacht Co., Ltd.*, [1970] A.C. 1004; [1970] 2 All E.R. 294; *Anns* v. *Merton London Borough Council*, [1978] A.C. 728; [1977] 2 All E.R. 492; *Junior Books, Ltd.* v. *Veitchi Co., Ltd.*, [1983] 1 A.C. 520; [1982] 3 All E.R. 201, all decisions of the House of Lords.
[13] *Anns* v. *Merton London Borough Council*, [1978] A.C. 728, at p. 751; [1977] 2 All E.R. 492, at 498.
[14] See p. 26, *ante*.
[15] See p. 48, *post*.

the law of contract. Suffice it to mention that the essential elements of a valid contract are as follows:

(1)   there must be an agreement consisting of an offer by one party and an acceptance by the other;
(2)   either the contract must be contained in a deed under seal or there must be valuable consideration given by each party;
(3)   the agreement must have been reached with the intention of creating a legal relationship and must, by its character, be capable of so doing;
(4)   the parties must have the legal capacity to contract; and
(5)   in some cases the transaction must comply with certain formalities prescribed by law.

Case law has created exceptions to these principles and, in some cases, has almost succeeded in distorting them.[16] Judicial inroads into the doctrine of consideration provide a graphic illustration of this. Nevertheless each element remains essential to the creation of a valid enforceable contract. *Quasi-contract*[17]—A particularly interesting result of the merger of the whole of the writ of debt into assumpsit was that assumpsit became available for the recovery of monies such as judgment debts, statutory fines and customary dues hitherto within the province of debt on a record. This was anomalous since these debts did not arise, in many cases, by agreement and are thus not properly describable as contractual. This branch of the law is known as "quasi-contract" and is a striking demonstration of the fact that the nature of a contractual obligation is ascertainable by reference to the history of contract rather than to the conduct of the parties or the inherent nature of the transaction.

Since debt had already assimilated the ancient writ of account there were many other forms of quasi-contract where the defendant had received money to the plaintiff's use and had failed to account to him for it. The common law courts provided remedies in such circumstances by the development of various actions on the case, extending *assumpsit* to either implied or fictitious undertakings to pay. One such was the action for a *quantum meruit* whereby in the absence of an express agreement as to price a person could (and still can) be ordered to pay for the value of goods or services that he had ordered. Similarly if one person expended money on behalf of another the courts would compel the latter to reimburse the former on the fictitious basis that he had assumed an indebtedness (*indebitatus assumpsit*). This was later used as the basis upon which contributions could be recovered between co-sureties or joint contractors.[18] The courts have since used the concept of quasi-contract to enforce restitution wherever one person is unjustly enriched at the expense of another. For example, money paid under a mistake of fact and money paid in pursuance of a void contract or an illegal contract is recoverable in quasi-contract.

---

16   For a recent illustration of the difficulty which is sometimes encountered in fitting a cause of action into the framework created by the forms of action at common law, see *Jackson* v. *Horizon Holidays, Ltd.*, [1975] 3 All E.R. 92; [1975] 1 W.L.R. 1468.
17   For a comprehensive summary of the development of the various forms of quasi-contractual liability, see Baker, *op. cit.*, pp. 300–314.
18   *Cowell* v. *Edwards* (1800), 2 Bos. & P. 268. This branch of the law is now codified in the Civil Liability (Contribution) Act 1978.

c   The relationship between contract and tort

Although both contract and tort have their foundation in the writ system, the nature and characteristics of each of these branches of the common law differ in that obligations in contract are primarily fixed by the parties themselves whereas rights and duties protected and enforced by actions in tort are primarily fixed by law.

In certain cases, due to the tortious nature of assumpsit for misfeasance and malfeasance, the same act may constitute both a tort and a breach of contract, generally where the defendant's conduct is alleged to be negligent or fraudulent. Thus, for example, a dentist who negligently extracts a private patient's tooth is liable for breach of his contractual obligation to exercise proper care in the plaintiff's treatment and is also liable in the tort of negligence.[19] Similarly a negligent act may constitute both a breach of contract to one person, an employer for instance, and a tort to another. This occurred in *Lister* v. *Romford Ice and Cold Storage Co., Ltd.*,[20] where the negligence of a driver towards his passengers was held to be a breach of contract towards his employer. VISCOUNT SIMONDS, in that case, observed that:[1]

> "It is trite law that a single act of negligence may give rise to a claim either in tort or for breach of a term express or implied in a contract. Of this the negligence of a servant in performance of his duty is a clear example."

Often the coincidence of contractual and tortious liability will be of no importance. The plaintiff's success will not depend upon whether he chooses to describe his action as an action in contract or an action in tort. However there are certain rules of English law which are expressed to apply only to "contract" or only to "tort". Consequently there are several cases where the course of an action will be affected according to whether it is termed an action in contract or an action in tort. Generally the plaintiff will plead both causes of action in the alternative. The question then arises as to the approach the court will adopt in classifying the nature of the action. It seems clear that if the plaintiff can derive any advantage from framing his action in contract rather than tort he will be allowed to do so. For instance in *Matthews* v. *Kuwait Bechtel Corporation*[2] the plaintiff suffered injury while working in Kuwait for the defendant corporation under a contract to be governed, according to its terms, by English law. He sought leave[3] to serve a writ out of the jurisdiction which he could in an action in contract but not in an action in tort. He was granted leave on the basis that he had a cause of action in contract irrespective of the fact that he also had an action in tort. The case of *Chesworth* v. *Farrar*[4] provides an illustration of the importance of characterisation. This case involved an action brought against the estate of a deceased person for the proceeds of sale of certain antiques owned by the plaintiff, the action being brought more than six months after the grant of

---

[19] *Edwards* v. *Mallan*, [1908] 1 K.B. 1002. There would, probably, be no contract with a National Health Service patient.

[20] [1957] A.C. 555; [1957] 1 All E.R. 125.

[1] [1957] A.C., at p. 573; [1957] 1 All E.R., at p. 131. See also *Donoghue* v. *Stevenson*, [1932] A.C. 562 which serves to illustrate this point.

[2] [1959] 2 Q.B. 57; [1959] 2 All E.R. 345.

[3] Under (what is now) R.S.C. (Revision) 1965, O. 11, r. 1; see p. 315, *post*.

[4] [1967] 1 Q.B. 407; [1966] 2 All E.R. 107.

representation to the estate. It followed (from the Law Reform (Miscellaneous Provisions) Act 1934, s. 1(3)) that, insofar as the action lay in tort, it was statute-barred.[5] However EDMUND DAVIES, J. (as he then was) held that the plaintiff's right to the proceeds of sale of his goods sounded in quasi-contract rather than in tort, so that the cause of action was not an "action in tort" within the 1934 Act and was, therefore, not statute-barred.[6]

However it more frequently happens that the plaintiff might derive an advantage from framing his action in tort rather than in contract. This is all the more likely now that an action in negligence may be maintained in respect of financial loss. For example, the measure of damages in tort is somewhat wider than in contract; aggravated damages are recoverable in tort but not usually in contract;[7] limitation periods differ since a cause of action in contract accrues upon breach whereas in most torts it accrues only when damage is suffered. The approach which the courts adopt in this sort of case may be described as unpredictable. In several actions against solicitors in respect of professional negligence, plaintiffs have failed to recover for certain heads of damage on the basis that they were too remote in an action in contract, notwithstanding that they might not have been too remote in tort.[8] Nor can these cases be explained solely by reference to the history of the solicitor-client relationship, which has always been entirely contractual. In *Bagot* v. *Stevens Scanlan & Co.*,[9] DIPLOCK, L.J. (sitting at first instance) stated a wider principle, namely that all professional relationships in contract give rise to a contractual duty alone and not to any duty independent of contract. The question in that case arose in a neat form. The defendant architects had supervised the construction and installation of a drainage system in pursuance of a contract with the plaintiff. This supervision ended in February, 1957. The drains were alleged to have been constructed negligently in that the pipes began to crack and cause flooding in or about the end of 1961. The writ was issued in April, 1963, by which time it was admitted that an action in contract would be statute-barred, the six year period of limitation having commenced in February, 1957, and thus expired before the issue of the writ. DIPLOCK, L.J. (as he then was) held, on the trial of a preliminary point of law, that no action would lie in tort even though such an action might not be statute-barred, expressly adopting the following statement of law set out in the judgment of GREER, L.J. in *Jarvis* v. *Moy, Davies, Smith, Vandervell & Co.*:[10]

> "The distinction in the modern view, for this purpose, between contract and tort may be put thus: where the breach of duty alleged arises out of a liability independently of the personal obligation undertaken by contract, it is tort, and it

---

[5] This would no longer be so, there being now no special period of limitation for proceedings in tort against the estates of deceased persons: Proceedings Against Estates Act 1970, s. 1.

[6] Though the action for breach of bailment, being based upon the infringement of a right of possession, was tortious in nature (although the bailment was contractual) and therefore barred.

[7] *Addis* v. *Gramophone Co., Ltd.*, [1909] A.C. 488. The rules of remoteness also differ; see *The Heron II*, [1969] 1 A.C. 350; [1967] 3 All E.R. 686; *Doyle* v. *Olby (Ironmongers), Ltd.*, [1969] 2 Q.B. 158; [1969] 2 All E.R. 119.

[8] *Groom* v. *Crocker*, [1939] 1 K.B. 194; [1938] 2 All E.R. 394; *Hall* v. *Meyrick*, [1957] 2 Q.B. 455; [1957] 2 All E.R. 722; *Clark* v. *Kirby-Smith*, [1964] Ch. 506; [1964] 2 All E.R. 835.

[9] [1966] 1 Q.B. 197; [1964] 3 All E.R. 577.

[10] [1936] 1 K.B. 399, at p. 405.

may be tort even though there may happen to be a contract between the parties, if the duty in fact arises independently of that contract. Breach of contract occurs where that which is complained of is a breach of duty arising out of the obligations undertaken by the contract.''

DIPLOCK, L.J., having stated this wide principle, went on to acknowledge that there were exceptional relationships where a duty was owed in tort as well as in contract:

> "I think that on examination all those will turn out to be cases where the law in the old days recognised either something in the nature of a status like a public calling (such as common carrier, common innkeeper, or a bailor and bailee) or the status of master and servant. There it can be properly said, as it was in such cases as *Lister* v. *Romford Ice and Cold Storage Co., Ltd.*[11] that, independently of contract, there existed from the mere status a relationship which gave rise to a duty of care not dependent on the existence of a contract between the parties.''[12]

However this case, together with *Groom* v. *Crocker* and *Clark* v. *Kirby-Smith (supra)* was not followed by OLIVER, J. (as he then was) in *Midland Bank Trust Co., Ltd.* v. *Hett, Stubbs and Kemp*[13] and had previously been considered, without apparent enthusiasm, by the Court of Appeal in *Esso Petroleum Co., Ltd.* v. *Mardon*[14] and *Batty* v. *Metropolitan Property Realizations, Ltd.*[15] and it now seems to be the law that, notwithstanding the existence of a contract, a plaintiff, if he has an independent cause of action in tort, may frame his action accordingly if to do so affords him any advantage. However, as a matter of public policy, a plaintiff can never enforce an unenforceable contract by framing his action in tort, and there are many authorities to support this proposition.[16]

The "pigeonhole" approach owes its existence in English law to the medieval writ system. It can, occasionally, cause injustice. This is well illustrated by the anomalous doctrine of privity of contract. *X* enters into a contract with *Y* for the benefit of *Z*. There is no logical reason why *Z* should not be able to sue upon that contract for to allow him to do so would impose upon *Y* no greater obligation than he had agreed to undertake. Nevertheless *Z* has no right of action.[17]

---

[11] [1957] A.C. 555; [1957] 1 All E.R. 125.

[12] [1964] 3 All E.R. 577, at p. 580. It seems that if, in this type of case, the action in tort is, for some reason, barred no action will lie in contract: *Turner* v. *Stallibrass*, [1898] 1 Q.B. 56; *Ballet* v. *Mingay*, [1943] K.B. 281; [1943] 1 All E.R. 143.

[13] [1979] Ch. 384; [1978] 3 All E.R. 571.

[14] [1976] Q.B. 801; [1976] 2 All E.R. 5.

[15] [1978] Q.B. 554; [1978] 2 All E.R. 445.

[16] Examples are *Jennings* v. *Rundall* (1799), 8 Term Rep. 335; *R. Leslie, Ltd.* v. *Sheill*, [1914] 3 K.B. 607; *cf. Burnard* v. *Haggis* (1863), 14 C.B.N.S. 45.

[17] *Tweddle* v. *Atkinson* (1861), 1 B. & S. 393; *cf. Beswick* v. *Beswick*, [1968] A.C. 58; [1967] 2 All E.R. 1197; see p. 53, *post*. But even this principle yields to the "neighbour" principle of the tort of negligence so that in a case falling within the principles stated by LORD WILBERFORCE in *Anns* (see p. 37, *ante*) the doctrine of privity may be avoided; see *Junior Books, Ltd.* v. *Veitchi Co. Ltd.*, [1983] 1 A.C. 520; [1982] 3 All E.R. 201, which is likely to prove to be a watershed in this branch of the law.

CHAPTER 2

Equity

A ORIGINS OF EQUITY

It may be apparent from the preceding chapter that substantive common law and procedure were hidebound by formality and restrictions. The common law partly avoided its own rigidity by the extensive use of fictions. Fictions were used for three basic purposes. First, they were employed to avoid the severity of the criminal law, benefit of clergy being the most notable example.[1] Secondly, fictions were used to extend the scope of the original writs in order to expand substantive law; trover, ejectment and assumpsit were all extended far beyond their literal scope to this end.[2] Finally, fictions were used to assume jurisdiction. Early fictions, such as the writ of pone, were used to acquire jurisdiction from the local courts in matters concerning title to land. Subsequently the common law courts used fictions to acquire jurisdiction from one another. Quominus and Bill of Middlesex[3] are notable examples of this trend which can be explained by the fact that the prosperity of courts and judges depended upon the volume of litigation conducted.

However fictions were not capable in themselves of remedying all the defects of common law. These included the strictness of the application of common law doctrines and the inadequacy of the remedies available at common law. The overriding defect was, of course, the way in which substantive law was entirely bound up with procedure. Legislation, the principal modern agency of law reform, was not widely used in the Middle Ages and did not become the major organ of law reform until the seventeenth century.

Consequently an alternative means of providing a gloss on the common law was required. This led to the evolution of the second major historical source of English law—equity.

Equity is not peculiar to the English legal system. Continental systems of law recognise the existence of equity. However, in continental systems equity is purely conceptual. It is almost a synonym for "natural justice". In England this is not so. Natural justice is not a concept which forms the basis

---

[1] See p. 18, *ante*.
[2] See p. 25, *ante*.
[3] See pp. 7, 9, *ante*.

of English decisions although it no doubt affects the interpretation which judges put on the law. Hence equity in the English legal system does not mean natural justice[4] although its rules are in part based on the concept of justice, particularly where these rules were created to remedy injustice in the common law. Equity, in English law, has been defined by Maitland as—

> "that body of rules administered by our English Courts which were it not for the operation of the Judicature Acts, would be administered by those Courts which would be known as Courts of Equity".

This definition may appear to beg the question but it serves to illustrate that the nature of modern equity can be understood only by reference to its historical origins and development.

Equity, in its original sense of natural justice, was administered in the common law courts until the fourteenth century. Common law judges, particularly the judges of the Court of Exchequer, could exercise some discretion in their application of the law particularly in the question of whether or not to recognise the validity of writs issued out of the Chancery. This discretion was, no doubt, exercised on the basis of doing justice in individual cases and thus amounted to what the continental lawyer would describe as equity. Unfortunately during the fourteenth century the common law became hidebound by formality and so became rigid and inflexible. Provided a litigant could find a writ to fit his case and could surmount the intricacies of pleading attendant upon the writ he had a right to a remedy. No discretion was involved. It has always been a feature of the common law that common law remedies are available as of right. The plaintiff who can show the infringement of his legal right must be granted a remedy irrespective of his conduct or personality.

During this period, also, common law judges ceased to be drawn from the ranks of clerics and were recruited from the ranks of a legal profession whose inclination was toward learning and mastering the intricacies of pleading rather than attempting to reform the law.

Furthermore the political climate of the Middle Ages resulted in measures such as the Provisions of Oxford 1258, the tendency of which was to restrict the expansion of the writ system and to force it to develop along very narrow lines.

Finally the General Eyre, probably the last organ through which equity could be applied in the common law courts, declined in the same period as a result of local unpopularity.

Consequently the common law became, quite early in its existence, incapable of providing a means of remedying its own inherent restrictions. This meant that injustices were bound to occur. For example a litigant who had suffered damage might not be able to find an existing form of action into which he could fit his case. Even if he found a form of action he might falter in pleading or might, in debt or detinue, be met by the defendant waging his

---

[4] But see *Earl* v. *Slater and Wheeler (Airlyne), Ltd.,* [1973] 1 All E.R. 145; [1973] 1 W.L.R. 51 in which the (now defunct) National Industrial Relations Court held that a statutory provision requiring the question of whether a dismissal of an employee was fair or unfair to be determined "in accordance with equity and the substantial merits of the case" was to be interpreted as requiring determination in accordance with common sense and common fairness rather than in accordance with the principles of equity (as opposed to common law).

law. Alternatively if he were a defendant it might be that a remedy would be granted against him contrary to the justice of the case.

A practice grew, in such cases, of dissatisfied litigants petitioning the King to exercise his prerogative in their favour. For a time the King in Council determined these petitions himself. Later they became so numerous that the King delegated this task to his principal minister, the Chancellor. The Chancellor was, it will be recalled, an officer of the common law since he had custody of the Great Seal and controlled the issue of original writs out of the Chancery to litigants at common law. In addition he sat, from time to time, as a judge in the Council and the Court of Exchequer Chamber. He was, until the fall of Wolsey (1515–1529), an ecclesiastic.

In 1474 there is the first recorded instance of the Chancellor issuing a decree in his own name rather than in the name of the King. At this point of time the Court of Chancery was created and became, as the common law courts had become, independent of the King and of the Council.

B   COURTS OF EQUITY

1   The Court of Chancery

This was the principal court of equity and, as stated above, modern equity is the system of law administered in this court. The earliest jurisdiction of the Chancellor, often termed the "Latin" jurisdiction because the proceedings were recorded in Latin,[5] consisted of hearing petitions by litigants to whom a remedy had been denied or against whom an order had been unjustly made at common law. If there had been injustice the Chancellor would remit the case to the King's Bench for investigation. If that court found that a party had been guilty of corruption he would be punished summarily in the name of the King. This is, historically, the less important aspect of the Chancellor's jurisdiction and was extinguished with the abolition of the Court of Star Chamber to which it was transferred when Conciliar jurisdiction was transferred from the Chancellor to that court.

By far the most important aspect of the Chancellor's jurisdiction consisted of the recognition and enforcement of a diverse set of principles now identifiable as the rules of equity.

It is debatable whether equity grew out of the jurisdiction of the Chancellor or whether the Chancellor's jurisdiction developed out of the principles of equity. In any event the growth of equity is inextricably tied up with the office of Chancellor. This was, at different times, both a good and a bad feature of the system. It was a good feature in that brilliant lawyers such as Sir Thomas More (1529–1532), Lord Ellesmere (1596–1617), Sir Francis Bacon (1618–1621), Lord Nottingham (1673–1682) and Lord Hardwicke (1737–1756) were each able to create and mould principles of equity without which it is difficult to imagine how English law could today continue to function. On the other hand, since the Court of Chancery habitually bore the characteristics of the Chancellor, any personal shortcomings which he might

---

[5] The equitable jurisdiction of the Chancellor is generally described as the "English" jurisdiction since proceedings were recorded in English.

possess would become ingrained in procedure in the court. Thus the court was brought into disrepute in the seventeenth century by the sale of offices in the court. All offices, including that of Master of the Rolls, were sold by the Chancellor.[6] Indeed so great was corruption in the court during this period that on the bursting of the South Sea Bubble in 1725 a deficiency of some £100,000 in court funds was discovered as a result of which Lord Macclesfield was impeached and fined £30,000.

A further defect in the Court of Chancery was the organisation of the court. There was an excess of court officials who attempted to extend the ambit of their duties so as to increase their revenue. Apart from the abuse which the sale of these clerkships created the proliferation of Chancery clerks naturally made litigation in the court extremely slow and expensive. The excess of court officers was equalled only by the paucity of judges. At first the Chancellor himself was the only judge. In practice he was unable to hear all cases himself and by the sixteenth century was accustomed to delegate his judicial function to the Masters in Chancery although judgment was delivered only by the Chancellor himself. The chief of these Masters was the Master of the Rolls who in 1729[7] effectively became a second judge of the court. However this did little to speed up the conduct of litigation since the parties had a right to apply to the Chancellor for a re-hearing. Arrears of work were handed down through successive Chancellors. Matters reached a head in the nineteenth century with the elevation of Lord Eldon to the office of Chancellor. Lord Eldon (1801–1827) was a distinguished lawyer but unfortunately suffered from an excess of caution. He would not deliver any judgment or make any order without considering every available authority. There are records of judgments being reserved for months and even years. While this stabilised the court it also brought it into discredit with suitors and the backlog of cases pending became enormous. In 1813 Lord Eldon approved the appointment of a Vice-Chancellor as an additional judge of the Court but this brought little improvement since an appeal lay from his decisions to the Chancellor. Apart from this measure Lord Eldon stood fast against any reform and used the power of his office to thwart any attempt at reform of the judicial system. This obdurate conservatism contributed greatly to the welter of reform which in fact began shortly after his resignation from office in 1827. The Court of Chancery was finally abolished by the Judicature Acts 1873–1875 and its jurisdiction substantially transferred to the Chancery Division of the High Court.

In addition to its equitable jurisdiction the Court, because of its close association with the Crown, acquired jurisdiction over other miscellaneous matters. For example the Crown, as *parens patriae*, had protective custody of all infants within the realm; this jurisdiction, which comprised such matters as the power to appoint guardians, was assigned to the Court of Chancery but is now exercised by the Family Division.[8]

A similar concept existed in relation to persons of unsound mind; since they too were in need of protection the Sovereign assumed responsibility for

---

[6] The office of Master of the Rolls was apparently worth £6,000 in the eighteenth century. See *Ex parte the Six Clerks* (1798), 3 Ves. 589.

[7] By 3 Geo. 2, c. 30.

[8] Wardship proceedings were transferred from the Chancery Division to the Family Division by the Administration of Justice Act 1970, s. 1; Sch. 1.

the care of lunatics and their property. This responsibility was, as with infants, delegated to the Chancellor and is today exercised, for the most part, by the Court of Protection, the judges of which are judges of the Chancery Division.[9]

Procedure in the Court of Chancery

Since proceedings in the Court of Chancery were not commenced by writ the court was never a slave of procedure in the same way as were the common law courts. Consequently, Chancellors were able to create rights and remedies *de novo* as justice required. There was never any pretence that equitable rules dated from time immemorial.[10] It was this that prompted John Selden's immortal aphorism that "Equity varies as the length of the Chancellor's foot".[11]

A Chancery suit was commenced by a petition or bill filed by the plaintiff in the court. This petition originally had not to comply with any particular formality so that its potential scope was unlimited. Later, through the intervention of lawyers, uniformity and complexity came to be required in the drafting of Chancery bills and petitions which became as tortuous as common law pleadings.

Provided that the petition disclosed some reason for the Chancellor's intervention a writ of subpoena would be issued and served on the defendant compelling him to attend in answer to the petition. The defendant was then required to draft an answer to the allegations in the petition. This answer had to be on oath and is the origin of the modern interrogatories. It was a far longer and more detailed document than a common law defence since it disclosed not only the defence but also other factors to influence the Chancellor to exercise his discretion in favour of the defendant. Issue was thereby joined and the action proceeded to trial.

At the trial the evidence of witnesses was often not required and where testimony was required it was given on affidavit so that proceedings before the Chancellor were confined to legal arguments on both sides.[12] Where the case involved the existence of a common law right the Chancellor would call for the assistance of two common law judges to act as assessors. Finally the Chancellor would issue a decree in his own name. However this was not the end of the matter. An account might remain to be taken or an estate administered. Also the unsuccessful party might always apply to the Chancellor for a rehearing which would be granted even if the first hearing had been before the Chancellor himself. Even then the matter was not closed because there might be a further appeal to the House of Lords.[13]

---

[9] See p. 219, *post*.
[10] See *Re Hallett* (1880), 13 Ch.D. 696, at p. 710, *per* JESSEL, M.R.
[11] Selden, *Table Talk*.
[12] In modern Chancery Division proceedings the evidence is usually given on affidavit in the first instance followed, in the event of a dispute on the facts, by cross-examination of the deponents.
[13] This appeal dates from *Shirley* v. *Fagg* (1675), 6 State Tr. 1146.

2 The Court of Appeal in Chancery

This court was established in 1851[14] to hear appeals from decisions of the Vice-Chancellors (of whom there were by this time three) and the Master of the Rolls. The Lord Chancellor had almost ceased to act as a first-instance judge. The court consisted of the Chancellor and two Lords Justices (the first time that this nomenclature had been adopted). In addition the Chancellor might require any Vice-Chancellor or the Master of the Rolls to sit as an additional judge. There was a further appeal from the Court of Appeal in Chancery to the House of Lords. The court was abolished by the Judicature Acts 1873–1875 and its jurisdiction effectively transferred to the Court of Appeal.

3 The Court of Requests[15]

This court emerged in the fifteenth century from a committee of the Council established to grant relief to poor litigants who were denied a remedy at common law. Hence its jurisdiction was similar to that of the Chancery although it tended only to try cases of minor importance. In these cases the court could dispense equity more quickly and cheaply than could the Court of Chancery. This made the court popular with litigants but unpopular with common lawyers since it frequently meddled in the conduct of actions proceeding in the common law courts. The court was in 1598[16] declared "illegal" and to have "not any power by commission by statute or by common law". In spite of this rebuke the court continued to hold sittings until these were suspended in 1642 on the outbreak of the civil war. The court was not formally abolished but after the Restoration, although the Court of Chancery continued to thrive, the Court of Requests did not and because of the very close association between the court and the Council Charles II did not dare to attempt to revive its jurisdiction.

C NATURE AND CONTENT OF EQUITY

1 Nature of equity

One of the best definitions of the nature of equity is that of LORD COWPER in *Dudley* v. *Dudley*.[17]

> "Now equity is no part of the law, but a moral virtue, which qualifies, moderates, and reforms the rigour, hardness, and edge of the law, and is an universal truth; it does also assist the law where it is defective and weak in the constitution (which is the life of the law) and defends the law from crafty evasions, delusions, and new subtilties, invented and contrived to evade and delude the common law,

---

[14] 14 & 15 Vict., c. 83.
[15] This court should not be confused with the Courts of Requests which were established in the eighteenth century to hear small claims (usually less than 40s.) and which were the forerunners of the modern county courts.
[16] *Stepney* v. *Flood* (1598), Cro. Eliz. 646.
[17] (1705), Prec. Ch. 241, at p. 244; cited by LORD HODSON in *National Provincial Bank, Ltd.* v. *Ainsworth*, [1965] A.C. 1175, at p. 1224; [1965] 2 All E.R. 472, at p. 480.

whereby such as have undoubted right are made remediless; and this is the office of equity, to support and protect the common law from shifts and crafty contrivances against the justice of the law. Equity therefore does not destroy the law, nor create it, but assist it."

The basic nature of equity is expressed in the renowned "maxims of equity". Thus equity provided new remedies where a remedy at common law was deficient on the basis that "equity does not suffer a wrong to be without a remedy". "Equity will not assist a volunteer" embodies the principle that a decree of specific performance will not be granted to a person who has given no consideration in return for the obligation which he seeks to have enforced. Similarly equity does not provide a remedy to a person who has behaved unconscionably (for example, a beneficiary who has acquiesced in a breach of trust) since "he who comes to equity must come with clean hands".[18]

Equity's effect upon English law has been felt mainly in relation to the law of property and the law of contract. It has both a positive and a negative aspect to its operation. Its positive operation is demonstrated by the principle that equity will give effect to parties' intentions notwithstanding the absence of some formality required by the common law ("equity looks on that as done which ought to be done"); thus, an agreement to create a formal lease is equivalent to the lease itself;[19] the doctrine of part performance enables a contract to be enforced even though, by reason of the Statute of Frauds, it could not be proved at common law.[20] The negative aspect of equity centres on the equitable doctrine of fraud[1] and operates to restrain persons from enforcing rights which they could otherwise enforce, where to do so would be a fraud (in the equitable sense) on other parties. Thus, to take a simple example, a trustee, notwithstanding his capacity to dispose of the legal estate, will be restrained from so doing in breach of trust;[2] the doctrine of equitable estoppel[3] is founded on a similar principle.

The negative aspect of equity is, usually, rendered effective by the remedy of injunction.

Finally, an important principle of equity is that equity acts *in personam* rather than *in rem*; thus the right of a beneficiary is essentially a personal right against the trustee rather than a right in the trust property itself. This fact is often obscured because the right is both assignable and enforceable against a transferee of the legal estate; however, the fact that it is not enforceable against a *bona fide* purchaser for value of the legal estate without notice

---

[18] *Snell's Principles of Equity* (27th Edn.), at pp. 27 *et seq.* lists and explains twelve maxims of equity.

[19] *Walsh* v. *Lonsdale* (1882), 21 Ch.D. 9.

[20] *Maddison* v. *Alderson* (1883), 8 App. Cas. 467; this, like other equitable doctrines, is capable of expansion and adaptation: see *Steadman* v. *Steadman* [1974] Q.B. 161; [1973] 3 All E.R. 977.

[1] See p. 54, *post.*

[2] For a modern illustration, see *Waller* v. *Waller*, [1967] 1 All E.R. 305; [1967] 1 W.L.R. 451; see also *Lloyds Bank, Ltd.* v. *Bundy*, [1975] Q.B. 326; [1974] 3 All E.R. 757, especially the judgment of Lord Denning, M.R. at pp. 336–339 and 763–765 of the respective reports. The principle of "inequality of bargaining power" referred to in that judgment is now much canvassed, particularly in actions by banks against their customers.

[3] *Central London Property Trust, Ltd.* v. *High Trees House, Ltd.*, [1947] K.B. 130; [1956] 1 All E.R. 256n.

of the trust demonstrates the personal nature of an equitable interest. An interesting illustration of the maxim that equity acts *in personam* is that specific performance may be ordered of an agreement relating to land abroad, notwithstanding that an English court would have no jurisdiction to make an order in relation to the land itself.[4]

2 Content of equity

Although equitable rules were created on the basis of conscience, they soon became uniform and certain in extent. This development was essential because most equitable rights were rights in land capable of devolution and transfer. For this reason the rules of equity affecting land law soon became quite as rigid and certain as the corresponding common law rules.

The rules of equity were nearly all created between the end of Wolsey's term of office in 1529 and the end of Lord Eldon's Chancellorship in 1827.[5] The most important of these rules are considered below. They resulted sometimes in the recognition of new rights wholly unrecognised in the common law courts (the "exclusive" jurisdiction) and sometimes in the granting of new remedies which the common law did not provide (the "concurrent" jurisdiction).

a New rights

The rights of a beneficiary under a use or trust—A use or trust may be defined as a relationship in which one person has property vested in him subject to an obligation to permit another person to have the beneficial enjoyment of the property. The first person is described as a trustee, the second as a beneficiary or *cestui que trust*.

The existence of the use, as it was first known, dates back to the thirteenth century. It had even at this date certain advantages. For example, it enabled the Franciscans to enjoy the use of vast estates even though they were pledged to poverty by their order.[6] It made it possible for crusaders to arrange for their land to be held for them while they were in the Holy Land. Until the passing of the Statute of Wills 1540, freehold land could not be devised by will, so that to achieve the devolution of his land in accordance with his wishes the freeholder created uses in his lifetime. None of these methods of employing the use was particularly objectionable to the Crown. However in the fourteenth and fifteenth centuries it was appreciated that the use could be a device for defrauding creditors and in particular for depriving

---

4 *Penn* v. *Lord Baltimore* (1750), 1 Ves. Sen. 444.

5 Equity after this date became rigidly defined and there have been very few equitable rights or doctrines formulated since then although the existing doctrines are constantly being revised. Notable exceptions are the enforcement of restrictive covenants (*Tulk* v. *Moxhay* (1848), 2 Ph. 774) and the doctrine of quasi-estoppel (*Central London Property Trust, Ltd.* v. *High Trees House, Ltd.,* [1947] K.B. 130; [1956] 1 All E.R. 256n.). In recent years this doctrine has been developed so as to create, in effect, new rights; see, notably, *E.R. Ives Investments, Ltd.* v. *High,* [1967] 2 Q.B. 379; [1967] 1 All E.R. 504; *Inwards* v. *Baker,* [1965] 2 Q.B. 29; [1965] 1 All E.R. 446; *Crabb* v. *Arun District Council,* [1976] Ch. 179; [1975] 3 All E.R. 865. For the difficulties involved in the recognition of a new equitable interest in land see *National Provincial Bank, Ltd.* v. *Ainsworth,* [1965] A.C. 1175; [1965] 2 All E.R. 472.

6 The papacy declared in 1279 that it was lawful for friars to be beneficiaries under uses.

the feudal overlord of the revenue from the incidents of feudal tenure. This loss of revenue eventually meant a loss to the Crown and it was this factor which prompted Henry VIII, never indifferent to a possible loss of revenue, to "force upon an extremely unwilling Parliament"[7] the Statute of Uses 1535. This statute attempted to abolish uses of land by providing that where a person was seised to the use, confidence or trust of another that other was to be treated as seised. Thus if land were granted "to X to the use of Y" the legal estate would vest immediately in Y and X would take no interest whatsoever. The intended effect of this statute was to abolish the use. It did not however extinguish uses altogether since there were many loopholes in the statute. For example the statute did not extend to uses of copyholds, leaseholds or pure personalty since seisin could never exist in these types of property. In addition the statute was held not to apply to "active uses", that is to say uses which imposed a positive duty on the trustee. Finally the common law judges held in 1558[8] that where there was a use upon a use (i.e. "to A to the use of B to the use of C") the Statute of Uses did not execute the second use but only the first (i.e. B, not C, took the legal estate). This was of small significance at common law since the common law judges would not recognise that the second *cestui que use* (C) had any interest. However the Court of Chancery would recognise and enforce the second use because it appeared unconscionable to defeat the donor's intention by giving the first *cestui que use* an unfettered interest. In *Sambach* v. *Dalston*[9] the Chancellor established that the second use was enforceable in equity. Thus the use or trust, as it was becoming known, had become an equitable interest. It may appear illogical that the common law courts would not recognise trusts which were a considerable source of revenue to the Court of Chancery. The reason is that the constricting writ system could not be adapted to encompass the growing law of trusts. Had it been possible to reorganise common law procedure at this stage rather than two centuries later it is probable that equity in the modern sense would never have existed.

Nevertheless trusts were enforceable only in the courts of equity. They were at no time enforceable at common law. It soon became established that the beneficiary could enforce his right not only against the trustee personally but against any transferee of the legal estate (except a bona fide purchaser without notice). Consequently the trust in equity created an interest in property as well as personal rights against the trustee.

The incidents of feudal tenure were abolished in 1660[10] but by this date the trust was being used to serve other purposes. For example the trust could be used to bequeath property for charitable purposes. In the seventeenth and eighteenth centuries the trust was used in the creation of strict settlements of large estates so as to keep family estates from being broken up and sold. Another way in which the trust was employed to meet social conditions was in the creation of marriage settlements by which a father could create a trust in favour of his daughter on marriage thus giving her a beneficial interest

---

[7] Maitland, *Equity*, (1916 Edn.) p. 35. For an enlightening account of the Parliamentary progress of the Statute of Uses see Plucknett, *A Concise History of the Common Law*, (5th Edn.) pp. 584–587.

[8] *Tyrrel's Case* (1558), Dyer 1.55.

[9] (1634), Toth. 188.

[10] 12 Car. 2, c. 24.

which did not pass to the husband on marriage with the rest of her property.

Indeed, to combat the social evil of fortune hunting husbands, wives could be restrained by the terms of the trust from disposing of future income from the trust. This was the "restraint upon anticipation" which was not abolished until 1935 when the legal position of a married woman as regards property was finally equated to that of her husband.[11] In more modern times the trust has proved an invaluable device in the avoidance of the incidence of estate duty and, latterly, capital transfer tax.

The equity of redemption—There is a maxim of equity to the effect that "equity looks to the intent and not to the form". This maxim embodies that aspect of the Chancellor's "conscience" which led equity to intervene in the common law relating to mortgages. In the sixteenth century the classical form of common law mortgage was a conveyance of the land to the mortgagee subject to a covenant to reconvey to the mortgagor on payment of the loan and interest on or before a specified date. This was construed strictly by the common law judges so that the right to a reconveyance was lost after the due date for redemption had passed. This strict view caused injustice and there are records of persons amassing vast fortunes by the simple expedient of advancing money on mortgage and absenting themselves until after the due date for redemption. This practice was the very type of occurrence calculated to prompt the intervention of the Chancellor and so it did. The Court of Chancery recognised a right to redeem after the due date for redemption has passed at law. This right was termed the "equity of redemption" and was an equitable interest in land which the mortgagor could deal with in the same way as a beneficiary under a trust could deal with his beneficial interest. Thus any person who took the legal estate in the land took it subject to the equity of redemption (unless he took it for value without notice). The only way in which the mortgagee could free himself of the fetter of the equity of redemption was to apply to the Court of Chancery to foreclose the mortgage.[12]

The effect of equity recognising these new rights in land was that the Court of Chancery acquired a vast quantity of litigation since by the nineteenth century most estates were the subject of settlements or mortgages.

b New remedies

Injunction—An injunction is an order of the court compelling or restraining the performance of some act. An injunction which orders the defendant to perform some act is termed "mandatory", as opposed to a "prohibitory" injunction which restrains the defendant from committing some wrong, usually a tort.

The injunction is an equitable remedy but it had its counterpart in the common law writ of prohibition. This writ could be directed at inferior courts to prevent them from exceeding their jurisdiction[13] or at the sheriff to

---

[11] Law Reform (Married Women and Tortfeasors) Act 1935.

[12] Mortgage by conveyance of the fee simple was abolished by the Law of Property Act 1925 which substituted mortgage by grant of a term of years and created also the charge by way of legal mortgage. Any attempt at mortgage by conveyance now takes effect as a lease for a term of 3,000 years.

[13] This is the scope of the present day order of prohibition.

prevent the defendant infringing the plaintiff's right. However the injunction went beyond this writ since it could be directed at the defendant personally ("equity acts *in personam*") and failure to comply resulted in the imprisonment of the defendant for contempt of court.

Injunctions could be issued by the Chancellor not only in respect of equitable interests but also as a remedy for the infringement of common law rights. Thus equity contributed to the growth of the law of torts by providing a remedy where damages were inadequate redress, for example to restrain the commission of a nuisance or the publication of a libel. Unfortunately, the Court of Chancery could not, until 1858, award damages so that the plaintiff who sought damages and an injunction would have to bring two separate actions. The Chancery Amendment Act 1858 (Lord Cairns' Act) eventually remedied this by enabling the Court of Chancery to award damages as well as an injunction.

One particular form of injunction was the bone of contention between the common law courts and the Court of Chancery. This was the "common injunction" by which the Chancellor could restrain a litigant from proceeding to enforce his common law right in the common law courts or from enforcing a judgment obtained at common law, where this would violate principles of equity.[14]

Injunctions, like all equitable remedies, are discretionary. Even where the plaintiff can show that he has an equitable right he will not be awarded an injunction unless he has acted with conscience. In addition an injunction will not be granted where damages would be an adequate remedy nor where the interests of the public at large outweigh those of the individual. Thus in a recent case,[15] the Court of Appeal, by majority, refused to grant an injunction against a cricket club to restrain the playing of cricket on a village ground, where it had been played since 1905, although the plaintiff, an adjoining householder whose property had been damaged in the past and was likely to be damaged in the future by cricket balls, had established that the playing of cricket there constituted a private nuisance and recovered substantial damages. However this discretion can only limit rather than extend the scope of injunction. Thus there is no discretion to grant an injunction to restrain an act which does not constitute an infringement of any right legal or equitable.[16] To this rule there are some minor exceptions in that the court can grant an injunction to restrain an act which would constitute an abuse of its own process for example by impeding the conduct of a pending action. It may restrain proceedings in a foreign court.[17] Finally it appears that the court has power to restrain a suspected criminal from disposing of the proceeds of his crime;[18] the basis of this jurisdiction is difficult to iden-

---

[14] The common injunction was abolished by the Judicature Act 1873 but there is still power to restrain litigants from proceeding in inferior or foreign courts: see *infra*.

[15] *Miller* v. *Jackson*, [1977] Q.B. 966; [1977] 3 All E.R. 338.

[16] *Day* v. *Brownrigg* (1878), 10 Ch.D. 294; *Paton* v. *Trustees of British Pregnancy Advisory Service*, [1979] Q.B. 276; [1978] 2 All E.R. 987 (husband refused injunction to restrain wife from having an abortion, he having no legal right to control the destiny of the foetus conceived by him).

[17] See *British Airways Board* v. *Laker Airways, Ltd.*, [1985] A.C. 58; [1984] 3 All E.R. 39.

[18] *Chief Constable of Kent* v. *V*, [1983] Q.B. 34; [1982] 3 All E.R. 36; the power only exists in relation to identifiable property so that in *Chief Constable of Hampshire* v. *A*, [1984] 2 All

tify, but it appears to be the public interest in ensuring that the proceeds of crime are not dissipated. The power of the High Court to grant injunctions is now expressly set out in section 37(1) of the Supreme Court Act 1981, which provides that:

"The High Court may by order (whether interlocutory or final) grant an injunction or appoint a receiver in all cases in which it appears to the court to be just and convenient to do so."

Despite the generality of that provision, it does not create a power to grant injunctions beyond the general equitable jurisdiction described above, that is to say as ancillary to a legal or equitable right.[19] Nevertheless the scope of injunctions is wider than the scope of common law remedies in that, while the latter could only be granted after the wrongful act had been performed, an injunction can issue to restrain an apprehended wrong, such an injunction being termed a *quia timet* injunction.[20] In addition, interlocutory injunctions are an invaluable means of preserving the *status quo* pending the trial of an action.[1]

Specific performance—A decree of specific performance is an order of the court compelling a person to perform an obligation existing under either a contract or a trust. The remedy is particularly appropriate to actions in contract. It shares the characteristics of injunction and other equitable remedies in that its grant is discretionary and it will not be awarded either where the plaintiff has not behaved equitably (for example has given inadequate consideration) or where damages would be an adequate remedy. For this reason specific performance is only available to redress breaches of certain contracts, for example where the subject matter of a contract of sale is a chattel of a rare or personal nature[2] or, more usually, land.[3]

E.R. 385; [1984] 2 W.L.R. 954, the Court of Appeal held that there was no power to restrain payments out from a bank account in which the proceeds of crime had been mingled with legitimately obtained monies.

[19] The contrary view, namely that the section confers an unlimited power in any case, was advanced by LORD DENNING, M.R. in *Chief Constable of Kent* v. *V* (*supra*) but has not been adopted by others and may safely be regarded as incorrect.

[20] The effect of Lord Cairns' Act in this respect is that a plaintiff may be awarded damages for proprietary loss even though no common law or proprietary right has been infringed: *Leeds Industrial Co-operative Society, Ltd.* v. *Slack*, [1924] A.C. 851. In *Seager* v. *Copydex, Ltd.*, [1967] 2 All E.R. 415; [1967] 1 W.L.R. 923 the plaintiff, an inventor, was awarded damages against a company that made use of confidential information supplied to them by the plaintiff, on the basis of the equitable doctrine of breach of confidence. Virtually the only distinction between the plaintiff's cause of action and an action in tort seems to be that the damages were not recoverable as a matter of right, but only as a matter of discretion.

[1] See p. 333, *post*. In recent years the courts have developed two new forms of interlocutory injunction which have achieved considerable practical importance; the first is the *Mareva* injunction by which a plaintiff may restrain an alleged debtor from disposing of or removing from the jurisdiction his assets (*Mareva Compania Naviera S.A. of Panama* v. *International Bulkcarriers S.A.*, [1980] 1 All E.R. 213; see p. 297, *post*); the second is the *Anton Piller* order which permits a plaintiff to enter a defendant's premises to inspect, remove or make copies of documents belonging to the plaintiff, usually in breach of copyright cases (*Anton Piller K.G.* v. *Manufacturing Processes, Ltd.*, [1976] Ch. 55; [1976] 1 All E.R. 779; see p. 296, *post*).

[2] *Pusey* v. *Pusey* (1684), 1 Vern. 273.

[3] Specific performance may be ordered of an obligation to pay money where the payee is not the plaintiff so that damages would not be an adequate remedy: *Beswick* v. *Beswick*, [1968] A.C. 58; [1967] 2 All E.R. 1197.

The Chancery Amendment Act 1858 enabled the Court of Chancery to award damages in lieu of, or in addition to, specific performance.[4]

Rectification—The common law has always attached a peculiar sanctity to obligations under seal. It would enforce an obligation merely because it was under seal even though there was no consideration. Equity would not. Unfortunately the common law provided very few defences to an action on the defendant's seal. It was no defence at common law that the instrument did not accurately reflect the true intention of the parties. However equity did provide a defence. Where the instrument did not reflect the true intention of the parties, through a mistake in transcribing, the Court of Chancery claimed jurisdiction to rectify the document. Rectification lay only for mistake and did not allow contracts to be rectified but only documents. Rectification was apparently first used in respect of marriage settlements but was later extended to voluntary settlements and to written contracts. It was originally confined to cases of mutual mistake but now extends, not only to cases of mutual mistake, but also to cases where there is a mistake on the part of one party of which the other party is aware (but does not draw to the former's alteration) so that it would be inequitable to allow the latter to take advantage of the mistake.[5]

Rescission—This remedy, like rectification, grew out of the inability of the common law to prevent a party from suing on a contract or covenant where it was obviously unjust for him to do so because of some collateral matter. In certain circumstances the Court of Chancery would rescind a contract where it was possible to restore the *status quo* between the parties. There were several grounds for applying for rescission, the most important being fraud and innocent misrepresentation.

Fraud in equity is a much wider concept than common law fraud. Fraud only gave rise to an action at common law in the action for deceit, in which case the fraud had to be a false representation of existing fact.[6] The equitable doctrine of fraud certainly encompassed this and went much further. It extended to virtually all circumstances which the layman would describe as instances of fraudulent conduct, such as taking unfair advantage of the weakness or ignorance of another, abusing a fiduciary relationship or disposing of property to defraud creditors.[7] In all such cases the offended party might do nothing and resist a suit for specific performance. However if he had already parted with property this would be inadequate. In such a case he could apply to the court to rescind the contract.

A second ground for ordering rescission was innocent misrepresentation.

---

4   These are assessed in the same manner as damages at common law. Furthermore the effect of an order for specific performance of a contract is simply to continue the contract under the court's control so that, if the order is not complied with, the party in whose favour it was made may then ask the court to discharge the order and terminate the contract, whereupon he may be awarded damages at common law for breach of contract: *Johnson* v. *Agnew*, [1980] A.C. 367; [1979] 1 All E.R. 883.

5   *Bates (Thomas) & Son, Ltd.* v. *Wyndham's (Lingerie), Ltd.*, [1981] 1 All E.R. 1077; [1981] 1 W.L.R. 505.

6   *Derry* v. *Peek* (1889), 14 App. Cas. 337.

7   For a classification of the various aspects of equitable fraud, see *Snell's Principles of Equity* (27th Edn.), pp. 543–560 and for recent illustrations of the extension of the doctrine and its adaptation to new circumstances, see *Lloyds Bank, Ltd.* v. *Bundy*, [1975] Q.B. 326; [1974] 3 All E.R. 757; *O'Sullivan* v. *Management Agency and Music, Ltd.*, [1984] 3 W.L.R. 448.

Innocent misrepresentation at common law was confined to terms of the contract and gave rise only to an action for damages. Misrepresentation in equity extended to representations which did not form part of the contract. Such a representation gave no right to damages but did give a right in equity to rescind, thus filling a gap in the common law.[8]

The remaining equitable remedies are account,[9] appointment of a receiver,[10] delivery up and cancellation of documents[11] and discovery.[12]

D RELATIONSHIP BETWEEN COMMON LAW AND EQUITY

1 Prior to 1875

By the very nature of the jurisdiction it exercised the Court of Chancery was bound to come into conflict with the courts of the common law. Equity both supplemented the common law and corrected its deficiencies. Where equity supplemented the common law, as by the recognition of uses and the grant of equitable remedies for the infringement of legal rights, it was not particularly repugnant to common lawyers because it did not countermand their authority. However this was not the case where equity corrected the common law. In these instances there was a direct conflict between the common law courts and the Chancellor. Thus the Chancellor would rescind a contract or rectify a deed where the common law courts would enforce it in accordance with its original terms. Equity would allow a mortgagor to redeem where the common law would recognise no fetter on the mortgagee's legal estate. In such a case equity would have to prevail or be of no effect. Consequently, in order to assert its prevalence, the Court of Chancery began to issue common injunctions which, although directed at the litigant personally rather than at the common law courts, had the effect of limiting common law jurisdiction. This practice became particularly prevalent during Wolsey's term of office, so much so that the practice was incorporated in the articles of his impeachment. To smooth over the conflict a common lawyer, Sir Thomas More, was appointed as Chancellor. This had no lasting effect and by the end of the sixteenth century the common injunction was once again a well established weapon in the Chancellor's armoury. In 1598 the common lawyers denounced the Court of Requests as an illegal court as a protest against the use of prerogative powers. The conflict with the Chancery itself came soon afterwards with the appointment of Coke as Chief Justice of the Common Pleas in 1606. Coke, a bitter opponent of prerogative power, attacked vigorously the jurisdiction of all the courts exercising this jurisdiction. In 1613 he was transferred to the King's Bench in which court he held in a case in 1615[13] that where a common law court had decided a case the Court of Chancery

---

[8] See now the Misrepresentation Act 1967.
[9] See p. 328, *post* for details of the procedure for obtaining this remedy.
[10] See p. 395, *post* for the use of this remedy as a method of enforcing judgments.
[11] See *Snell's Principles of Equity* (27th Edn.), p. 608.
[12] Cf. *Norwich Pharmacal Co.* v. *Customs and Excise Commissioners*, [1974] A.C. 133; [1973] 2 All E.R. 943; for a discussion of this case, see p. 358, *post*.
[13] *Courtney* v. *Glanvil* (1615), Cro. Jac. 343.

had no power to intervene between the parties, and that any parties who appealed from a common law decision to the Chancellor would be imprisoned under the Statute of Praemunire. Lord Ellesmere, the Lord Chancellor, brought the dispute to a head in the same year by declaring, in the *Earl of Oxford's Case*,[14] the power of the Chancery to set aside common law judgments "not for any error or defect in the judgment, but for the hard conscience of the party". The dispute was referred to the King, James I. James I, after consulting his Attorney-General, Sir Francis Bacon (Coke's bitterest opponent and destined to be Ellesmere's successor as Chancellor), decided in favour of the Court of Chancery and upheld the validity of the common injunction. Thus the supremacy of equity was established though in the next eighty years this supremacy was by no means unchallenged. As late as 1690 a bill was introduced into Parliament to give the common law courts power to issue writs of prohibition to prohibit the Chancery from encroaching upon their jurisdiction. The bill never became law and the efforts of the common lawyers to evade the consequences of the *Earl of Oxford's Case* thereafter petered out. Nonetheless, by this time most of the rules and principles of equity had become as firmly established as those of the common law and equity had virtually ceased to evolve as a corrective to the common law. The evolution of the doctrine of binding precedent must be blamed for this, though the conservatism of the judges doubtless played a part. LORD ELDON's attitude is epitomised in the following famous extract from one of his judgments:[15]

> "The doctrines of this court ought to be as well settled, and made as uniform almost, as those of the Common Law. . . . Nothing would inflict on me greater pain, in quitting this place, than the recollection that I had done anything to justify the reproach that the equity of this court varies like the Chancellor's foot."

By the time of the Judicature Acts even as imaginative a lawyer as SIR GEORGE JESSEL, M.R. could observe:[16]

> "This Court is not, as I have often said, a Court of Conscience, but a Court of Law."

2   Equity after the Judicature Acts 1873–1875

The major reforms effected by these Acts are considered in detail below.[17] The Acts abolished the conflict between the common law courts and the Court of Chancery by abolishing these courts themselves and transferring their jurisdiction to the new Supreme Court of Judicature. Consequently the common injunction was abolished and an injunction cannot now issue out of one Division of the High Court to restrain proceedings in any other Division.

However the Judicature Acts fused only the administration of common law and equity. They did not fuse the substantive rules. Thus an award of damages is still a legal remedy and available as of right for infringement of a

---

[14] (1615), 1 Rep. Ch. 1.
[15] *Gee* v. *Pritchard* (1818), 2 Swan. 402, at p. 414.
[16] *Re National Funds Assurance Co.* (1878), 10 Ch.D. 118, at p. 128.
[17] See p. 81, *post*.

legal right whereas equitable remedies are still discretionary. There is no longer any duality of jurisdiction since the Supreme Court must give effect to both legal and equitable rights and remedies. Where there is conflict between the rules of common law and equity with reference to the same matter, the rules of equity prevail.[18] The effect of this provision is that certain rules of common law have been extinguished. With respect to interests in land most possible sources of conflict were removed by the property legislation of 1925.

As has already been noted[19] there have been very few equitable rights or doctrines formulated since the early nineteenth century. The creation of rights by equitable estoppel is certainly the most significant development. Recent attempts to extend the equitable jurisdiction to grant relief against forfeiture and penalties, so as to relieve contracting parties from the stipulated consequences of failing to perform their contractual obligations in time, have been firmly resisted by the House of Lords.[20] On the other hand the rapid and important growth of *Mareva* injunctions and *Anton Piller* orders[1] may be seen as significant developments of equity although they are, of course, judicial extensions of the remedy of interlocutory injunction rather than wholly new remedies.

---

[18] Supreme Court Act 1981, s. 49(1); see p. 84, *post.*
[19] See p. 49, *ante.*
[20] *Scandinavian Trading Tanker Co. AB* v. *Flota Petrolera Ecuatoriana*, [1983] 2 A.C. 694; [1983] 2 All E.R. 763; *Sport International Bussum BV* v. *Inter-Footwear, Ltd.*, [1984] 2 All E.R. 321; [1984] 1 W.L.R. 776.
[1] See p. 53, fn. 1, *ante.*

CHAPTER 3

Other Historical Sources

A LEGISLATION

Legislation is, after common law and equity, the third major historical source of English law. At the present day legislation is the principal agency of law reform and, with the tendency toward codification, is becoming the most important source of English law. In addition practically all the rules relating to the composition and jurisdiction of the modern courts and procedure applicable therein are statutory. It perhaps presents an accurate picture to say that, while most principles of English law have their origins in common law and equity, most of the detail is now contained in statute.

Early legislation was scarcely distinguishable from common law. Norman and early Angevin monarchs promulgated charters,[1] ordinances[2] and assizes[3] but these are hardly legislation in the modern sense since the concept of a separate legislature had not yet evolved. It is uncertain how far these governmental acts were regarded as authoritative. No doubt many were accepted as having the force of statutes but it was not until the end of the Middle Ages that legislative acts of less authority than statutes ceased to appear. Even statutes did not enjoy the absolute authority accorded to them at the present day. There are many instances in the Year Books of judges refusing to apply statutes because they conflicted with the common law, which was still regarded as sovereign.

The fifteenth century saw the recognition of statutes as being of absolute, literal authority. This corresponded with the emergence of Parliament as the legislature and, in Tudor times, with the printing and publication of statutes which allayed earlier doubts as to authenticity. But the early seventeenth century Coke could state of Parliament's legislative power:

> "it is so transcendent and absolute as it cannot be confined either for causes or persons within any bounds".[4]

---

[1] E.g., Magna Carta 1215.
[2] E.g., Ordinance of Labourers 1349.
[3] E.g., Assize of Northampton 1176.
[4] 2 Inst., Proem.

The nineteenth century heralded the era of codification and statutory definition of the jurisdiction of the courts. In this era legislation passed from being a fairly minor source of law, used mainly to guide the development of the common law, to being a major source of law transcending common law and equity.

Legislation as a source of law differs from common law and equity in several respects. Common law and equity, because of the doctrine of precedent, are inherently limited and can only develop new principles by varying and extending the application of existing principles. Legislation, on the other hand, can embody wholly new principles of law formulated without reference to any existing principles and, more important, can categorically repeal existing law which common law and equity cannot do. These are the principal advantages of legislation as an agency of law reform.

Finally legislation differs from other historical sources of law in another important respect. In the case of common law, equity and other historical sources the rules can only be ascertained by reference to other legal sources, notably precedents. Legislation is its own legal source. For this reason interpretation of statutes is a most important technique since it is only by interpreting the words of a statute that the law which it contains can be deduced from it. This important topic is dealt with fully below.[5]

B LAW OF THE EUROPEAN COMMUNITIES

1 Applicability of European Community law

The United Kingdom has, since January 1, 1973 (the date specified in the Treaty of Accession), been a member state of the European Communities,[6] together with Belgium, France, the Federal Republic of Germany, Italy, Luxembourg, Netherlands, Denmark, the Republic of Ireland and Greece.[7]

The general implementation of the Community Treaties was effected, in the United Kingdom, by section 2(1) of the European Communities Act 1972, which provides that:

> "All such rights, powers, liabilities, obligations and restrictions from time to time created or arising by or under the Treaties, and all such remedies and procedures from time to time provided for by or under the Treaties, as in accordance with the Treaties are without further enactment to be given legal effect or used in the United Kingdom shall be recognised and available in law, and be enforced, allowed and followed accordingly; and the expression 'enforceable Community right' and similar expressions shall be read as referring to one to which this subsection applies."

The effect of this provision is to incorporate into English law present and future Community law which, under the Treaties, is to be given legal effect without further enactment. This law may take the form of the Treaties themselves or regulations, directives or decisions of the Council or the

---

[5] See p. 102, *post*.
[6] The most important of these is the European Economic Community (E.E.C.), the others being the European Coal and Steel Community (E.C.S.C.) and the European Atomic Energy Community (Euratom).
[7] Spain and Portugal are due to become member states in 1986.

Commission which have legislative powers under the Treaties.[8] Those provisions which have the effect of creating rights and duties in individuals within the member states are said to be "directly applicable". If a provision is not directly applicable then, although it may impose obligations upon the United Kingdom, it does not affect the rights and duties of individuals and, as such, has no impact within the domestic system. Whether or not a provision of community law is directly applicable depends upon interpretation of the provision itself. In the United Kingdom this is primarily a matter for the court which is called upon to consider the provision in question, although there is power (and in some circumstances a duty) to refer the matter to the European Court.[9] The constitution and jurisdiction of the European Court is considered in detail elsewhere in this work.[10]

Those provisions of Community law which take effect without further enactment are sometimes described as "self-executing". Not all Community law is within this category. Directives and decisions of the Council and Commission usually[11] require implementation by specific enactment within the member states. In the United Kingdom power to implement such provisions by statutory instrument is contained in section 2(2) of the European Communities Act 1972.

Finally, there is a third category of legislative provision which requires implementation within the United Kingdom either by Act of Parliament or statutory instrument made under an Act of Parliament (other than the European Communities Act 1972). This requirement arises out of section 2(2) and Schedule 2 of the 1972 Act, since it is expressly provided in that schedule that the power to implement subordinate Community legislation by statutory instrument does not include power—

(*a*) to make any provision imposing or increasing taxation; or
(*b*) to make any provision taking effect from a date earlier than that of the making of the instrument containing the provision; or
(*c*) to confer any power to legislate by means of orders, rules, regulations or other subordinate instrument, other than rules of procedure for any court or tribunal; or
(*d*) to create any new criminal offence punishable with imprisonment for more than two years or punishable on summary conviction with imprisonment for more than three months or with a fine of more than £400 (if not calculated on a daily basis) or with a fine of more than £100[12] a day.

To summarise the position, European Community law is created by the Treaties creating the Communities, by the legislative organs of the Communities (the Council and the Commission)[13] and by the European Court, in the

---

[8] See p. 127, *post* for details of the forms of Community legislation.
[9] E.E.C. Treaty, Art. 177; see p. 185, *post* for details of this procedure.
[10] See p. 184, *post*.
[11] But not invariably; see Case 41/74: *Van Duyn* v. *Home Office (No. 2)*, [1975] Ch. 358; [1975] 3 All E.R. 190; [1974] E.C.R. 1337 and p. 185, *post*.
[12] The figure was raised from £5 to £100 by the Criminal Law Act 1977, s. 32(3).
[13] The fourth Institution of the Community (after the Council, the Commission and the Court) is the Assembly; the functions of the Assembly may be categorised as advisory and supervisory (E.E.C. Treaty, Art. 137). It has the right to put oral or written questions to the

manner in which it interprets the Treaties and Community instruments. It becomes part of the law of the United Kingdom if:

(1) it is by its nature, in accordance with the Treaties, self-executing; or
(2) it is implemented by statutory instrument under section 2(2) of the 1972 Act; or
(3) it is the subject of a separate enactment by Act of Parliament.

Finally it must, as a matter of interpretation, be "directly applicable" in the sense of creating rights and obligations enforceable by and against individuals. If it is not then it creates only obligations on the part of the United Kingdom government and is not to be regarded as part of English law.

It is important to bear in mind that European Community law, as such, concerns only rights and duties arising out of matters with a European element. As LORD DENNING, M.R. put it in *H.P. Bulmer, Ltd.* v. *J. Bollinger S.A.*[14]

> "The first and fundamental point is that the treaty concerns only those matters which have a European element, that is to say matters which affect people or property in the nine [*sic*] countries of the Common Market besides ourselves. The treaty does not touch any of the matters which concern solely the mainland of England and the people in it. These are still governed by English law. They are not affected by the treaty. But when we come to matters with a European element, the treaty is like an incoming tide. It flows into the estuaries and up the rivers. It cannot be held back."

The above statement accurately reflects the application of European Community law as a direct source. However, European Community law may also be an indirect source of law in the sense that where Parliament passes an Act, or a statutory instrument is made under an Act, that Act or instrument is part of the domestic legislation of the United Kingdom, irrespective of the fact that it happens to have been passed to give effect to a Community directive, and it may well affect "matters which concern solely the mainland of England and the people in it". Thus section 9 of the European Communities Act 1972 effects important changes in English company law. Although it was passed to give effect to a directive of the Council of the E.E.C. on Harmonisation of Company Law,[15] it is by no means limited to matters with a European element and, indeed, has the same effect as any of the provisions of any other United Kingdom statute, such as the Companies Act 1948.

Commission, to censure the activities of the Commission and a duty to discuss in open session the annual report submitted to it by the Commission; it also has the right to be consulted on certain specific matters. The Assembly consists of delegates from the member countries, the United Kingdom delegates being directly elected: European Assembly Elections Act 1978, s. 1.
[14] [1974] Ch. 401, at p. 418; [1974] 2 All E.R. 1226, at p. 1231; for the points arising from this important case, see p. 380, *post*. The principle is illustrated by the decision of the European Court in Case 175/78: *R.* v. *Saunders*, [1980] Q.B. 72; [1979] 2 All E.R. 267 to the effect that Article 48 (which provides for the free movement of workers within the Community) had no effect in a wholly domestic situation and therefore did not invalidate a binding-over order made by the Crown Court whereby the defendant was required to proceed to Northern Ireland and not to return to England or Wales for a period of three years.
[15] E.E.C. Directive 68/151/C.E.E.; published in [1968] J.O.L. 65, pp. 8–9; the Companies Act 1980 (Parts I to III) was passed to implement the E.E.C. Second Directive 77/91/E.E.C., 1977 J.D. L.26/1.

It must be noted that where there is a conflict between Community law and national law the former must prevail. Thus a national court, in applying provisions of Community law, is under a duty to give full effect to those provisions, if necessary refusing of its own motion to apply any conflicting national measure, whether adopted prior to or after the relevant Community provision. It is not necessary for the conflicting national measure to be set aside, since, in accordance with the principle of precedence of Community law, the entry into force of a directly applicable provision of Community law automatically supersedes any existing conflicting national law and precludes the valid adoption of any new, incompatible national measure.[16] This happened, in relation to this country, in *Macarthys, Ltd.* v. *Smith*[17] in which the Court of Appeal was called upon to consider the interaction of section 1 of the Equal Pay Act 1970 and Article 119 of the E.E.C. Treaty. It referred to the European Court questions concerning the proper construction of that Article. The European Court decided that the applicant, a female employee, was entitled to be paid the equivalent amount to that paid by her employers to the male employee who had previously done the job. Under the Equal Pay Act 1970 she was not so entitled (because the provisions for equal pay in that Act only applied where the man and the woman were employed at the same time). The Court of Appeal, applying the decision of the European Court (as it was, of course, bound to) held that Article 119 had precedence over the 1970 Act, so that the application succeeded. This principle may be regarded as a substantial limitation upon the traditional sovereignty of Parliament.

2   Content of European Community law

Most of the provisions in the Treaties and in the secondary legislation of the Communities are not directly applicable and are concerned with creating and enforcing obligations of an economic character between the member states rather than between individuals within the states. Implementation of the common agricultural policy has, for example, been the aim of a great deal of Community legislation.

However a number of Articles of the E.E.C. Treaty have been held by the European Court to be directly applicable and these may, therefore, be taken to create rights and obligations within the English legal system. These include Article 12 (which prohibits the introduction of new customs duties),[18] Article 53 (which prohibits the introduction by member states of new restrictions on the establishment in their territories of nationals of other member states),[19] Article 95 (which prohibits the imposition by a member state of internal charges on the products of other member states in excess of those applied to similar domestic products),[20] Article 119 (which states that men and women should receive equal pay for equal work)[1] and Article 48 (which requires the abolition of discrimination based on nationality between

---

[16] Case 106/77: *Amministrazione Delle Finanze Dello Stato* v. *Simmenthal Sp A*, [1978] E.C.R. 629.
[17] [1981] Q.B. 180; [1981] 1 All E.R. 111.
[18] Case 26/62: *Van Gend en Loos* v. *Netherlands Fiscal Administration*, [1963] C.M.L.R. 105.
[19] Case 6/64: *Costa* v. *Enel*, [1964] C.M.L.R. 425.
[20] Case 57/65: *Firma Alfons Lutticke* v. *Hauptzollamt Sarrelouis*, [1971] C.M.L.R. 674.
[1] Case 43/75: *De Frenne* v. *Sabena*, [1981] 1 All E.R. 122; *Macarthys, Ltd.* v. *Smith* (*supra*).

workers of the member states and the taking of steps to ensure the free movement of workers within the Community).[2] In *Schorsch Meier G.m.b.H.* v. *Hennin*[3] the Court of Appeal treated the direct applicability of Article 106 (by which each member state undertakes to authorise in the currency of the member state in which the creditor or beneficiary resides any payments connected with the movement of goods, services or capital) as justifying departure from the fundamental rule that judgments in England must be expressed in sterling. Consequently the Court of Appeal, in that case, gave judgment expressed in deutschmarks. However the case was only argued on one side and in *Miliangos* v. *George Frank (Textiles), Ltd.*[4] a majority of the House of Lords doubted the direct applicability of Article 106.

A duty created by Community law is a statutory duty, breach of which enables an English court to award any remedy available to the court, such as damages.[5]

European Convention on Human Rights—The United Kingdom is a subscriber to the Convention for the Protection of Human Rights and Fundamental Freedoms (1950),[6] often referred to as the European Convention on Human Rights. This Convention established both the European Commission of Human Rights and the European Court of Human Rights, the jurisdiction of which extends to all cases concerning the interpretation or application of the Convention. The rights and freedoms recognised by the Convention include the right to life, the right not to be subjected to torture or to inhuman or degrading treatment or punishment, not to be held in slavery or servitude, not to be required to perform forced or compulsory labour, the right to liberty and security of person, to a fair hearing, to respect for private life and correspondence, to marry, to respect for family life and home, to peaceful enjoyment of possessions, to education, to freedom of thought, conscience and religion, to freedom of expression, freedom of assembly, freedom of association and free elections.

Nevertheless it must be stressed that the Convention is not a part of English law, in which essential respect it must be distinguished from Community law. A person who alleges violation of his rights or freedoms under the Convention may apply to the European Commission of Human Rights and any state which is a party to the Convention may refer to the Commission any alleged breach of the Convention by any state which is a party. The applicant must show that he has exhausted all effective remedies in his own country and the application must be lodged within six months of a final decision in his case by a national court or authority. The Commission may then refer these matters to the European Court of Human Rights for decision

---

2 Case 41/74: *Van Duyn* v. *Home Office (No. 2)*, [1975] Ch. 358; [1975] 3 All E.R. 190; [1974] E.C.R. 1337; see p. 129, *post*.
3 [1975] Q.B. 416; [1975] 1 All E.R. 152.
4 [1975] 3 All E.R. 801; [1976] A.C. 443; see p. 147, *post*.
5 *Garden Cottage Foods, Ltd.* v. *Milk Marketing Board*, [1984] A.C. 130; [1983] 2 All E.R. 770 in which the House of Lords held that the Milk Marketing Board would be liable in damages to a butter distributor if the latter suffered loss as a result of the board's "abuse of a dominant position within the Common Market" (which would amount to a breach of Article 86 of the E.E.C. Treaty).
6 Cmd. 8969 (T.S. 71(1953)).

and report. It will then be the duty of the member state concerned to enforce the decision and, if it does not, the final sanction is suspension of membership of the Council of Europe. Under Article 50 of the Convention the Court has power to afford to the injured party "just satisfaction" which may involve ordering the state concerned to pay a sum of money in respect of pecuniary or non-pecuniary damage suffered together with costs or expenses, including lawyers' fees.[7] The Court of Appeal has stated that it will "have regard" to the Convention when applying English law, even though it is not part of English law,[8] so that to this very limited extent the Convention may be regarded as a source of law. However no rights directly enforceable in the English courts are conferred upon any individual by any provision in the Convention.[9]

C CUSTOM

The word "custom" may be used in several different senses. In one sense custom is the principal source of the whole of English law since it is the original source of common law. The early common law was not an entirely new set of rules imported into England by the Normans but rather that body of rules resulting from the welding of the law and custom of England into one system of law. In 1350 counsel declared that "common usage is common law".[10] These customs, such as monogamy, parental rights, the right to use the seashore for navigation and fishing[11] and most of the early criminal law, are no longer regarded as a separate source of law since they have either become part of the common law or been incorporated in statute.

A second use of the word "custom" is to describe conventional trade or business usage. This is really a misuse of the word since trade usage is usually relevant only to imply terms into contracts, so that the court can ascertain what unexpressed terms the parties intended to apply. These are questions of fact rather than questions of law so that custom, in this context, is not a source of law at all. Trade customs need not be ancient[12] provided that they

---

[7] See J. L. Sharpe, *Awards of Costs and Expenses under Article 50 of the European Convention on Human Rights* (1984) The Law Society's Gazette, p. 905.

[8] *Ahmad* v. *Inner London Education Authority*, [1978] Q.B. 36; [1978] 1 All E.R. 574; *R.* v. *Chief Immigration Officer, Heathrow Airport, Ex parte Salamet Bibi*, [1976] 3 All E.R. 843; [1976] 1 W.L.R. 979.

[9] See *Malone* v. *Metropolitan Police Commissioner* (*No. 2*), [1979] Ch. 344; [1979] 2 All E.R. 620 in which SIR ROBERT MEGARRY, V.-C., in holding that telephone "tapping" did not give rise to any cause of action, expressly rejected arguments based on alleged infringement of Art. 8 of the Convention on the basis that the Convention, while it might indicate what English law ought to be, did not indicate what it was and was itself no part of English law. Mr. Malone did then apply to the Commission who referred the matter to the Court where his complaint was upheld, the Court deciding that there had been a violation of his right to respect for private life and correspondence: *Malone* v. *United Kingdom* (Application 869/79) (1984) Council of Europe Press Release, 2 August. This was the twelfth case in which the Court had considered complaints involving the United Kingdom; in only one of these was there found to have been no breach of the Convention. The explanation for this high success rate by applicants is, of course, that the numerous unmeritorious complaints are rejected by the Commission and thus never reach the Court.

[10] Y.B. 30 Edw. 3, ff. 25, 26.

[11] Though not for bathing or beachcombing; see *Alfred F. Beckett, Ltd.* v. *Lyons*, [1967] Ch. 449; [1967] 1 All E.R. 833.

[12] See *Noble* v. *Kennoway* (1780), 2 Doug. 510, at p. 513, *per* LORD MANSFIELD.

can be proved to be certain. However they must not be illegal or unreasonable and they may always be expressly excluded. Many trade customs were originally an elaborate method of granting discount to purchasers; hence the "baker's dozen" and the fact that 1,000 rabbits mean 1,200 rabbits to rabbit-dealers.[13] Ancient mercantile custom fulfilled a wider function than modern commercial usage since it was the basis of a set of rules of law collectively described as the law merchant. The law merchant, unlike trade usage, is a source of law and is considered below.[14]

The third common use of the word "custom" is to describe local custom: rules of law which apply only in a definite locality. Custom, in this sense of the word, is a separate source of law.

Local custom

Local custom as a source of law, distinct from common law, has two elementary and unvarying characteristics; first, it must be an exception to the common law and, second, it must be confined in its application to a particular locality such as a county, borough or parish. It may be further limited to a class of persons within that locality, for example fishermen, but it cannot apply to a class of persons generally throughout the kingdom, for if it did it would be part of the common law and not an exception to it.

The modern tendency is to standardise the law by statute and this has resulted in the statutory abolition of many local customs. Customary forms of land tenure and succession[15] were all abolished by the Law of Property Acts 1922 and 1925. The type of local customary right still existing is in the nature of a right of way, or right to indulge in sports and pastimes on a village green[16] or a right to dry fishing-nets[17] on land within the parish. However, a customary profit-à-prendre cannot exist in favour of an indefinite number of persons, such as the inhabitants of a locality, since this would be liable to destroy entirely the subject-matter of the profit.[18]

Customary rules of law, unlike rules of common law, are not judicially noticed until settled by judicial decision. Thus any person who alleges a customary right must plead it and prove its existence. This involves showing that the alleged custom satisfies certain tests. Blackstone's classification of these tests is the generally accepted arrangement and is as follows.

a Antiquity

Local custom must have existed from "time whereof the memory of man runneth not to the contrary" (time immemorial). This has been fixed by statute[19] at 1189, the first year of the reign of Richard I. In practice positive proof of existence in 1189 is rarely available so that the courts are willing to

---

[13] *Smith* v. *Wilson* (1832), 3 B. & Ad. 728.
[14] See p. 67, *post.*
[15] Examples were "Gavelkind" (a customary method of descent applicable in Kent) and "Borough English" (a customary method of descent applicable in Nottingham, Bristol and certain other boroughs whereby freeholds passed on intestacy to the youngest son or brother).
[16] *New Windsor Corporation* v. *Mellor*, [1975] Ch. 380; [1975] 3 All E.R. 44.
[17] *Mercer* v. *Denne*, [1905] 2 Ch. 538.
[18] *Alfred F. Beckett, Ltd.* v. *Lyons*, [1967] Ch. 449; [1967] 1 All E.R. 833.
[19] Statute of Westminster I 1275.

accept as proof evidence that the custom has existed for a long time. This is
often done by calling the oldest available local inhabitant as a witness. The
burden is then on the party denying the existence of the custom to prove
either that it did not exist in 1189 or that it could not have existed in 1189.
Thus in *Simpson* v. *Wells*[20] the appellant, who had been charged with
obstructing a public foot-way by setting up a refreshment stall, alleged that
he had a customary right to do so deriving from "statute sessions".[1] It was
shown that statute sessions were first authorised by the Statutes of Labourers
in the fourteenth century so that the right could not have existed in 1189.

b   Continuance

This is Blackstone's second test for proving custom. The right must have
existed uninterrupted. Any interruption of the custom since 1189 defeats its
existence. On the other hand mere non-use does not defeat the custom; a
customary right, once acquired, can only be abolished or extinguished by
Act of Parliament.[2]

c   Peaceable enjoyment

A custom can only exist by common consent. It must not have been exercised
by the use of force, nor secretly, nor under a revocable licence (since this
would make the custom dependent upon the will of one individual rather
than on public observance): *nec per vim nec clam nec precario*. Thus, where
the right to fish depended upon the grant of a licence by the owners of an
oyster fishery, it was held that there was no customary right to fish since
enjoyment had never been as of right, but only by licence.[3]

d   Obligatory force

Where the custom imposes a specific duty that duty must be obligatory. This
is true of all rules of law. Indeed it is this which distinguishes a rule of law
from a social convention or a moral obligation. Thus, notes Blackstone:

> "a custom that all the inhabitants shall be rated towards the maintenance of a
> bridge, will be good; but a custom that every man is to contribute thereto at his
> own pleasure, is idle and absurd, and indeed no custom at all".

e   Certainty

A custom must be certain for, as JESSEL, M.R. observed, "the notion of law
means a certain rule of some kind".[4] For this reason a usage was held bad
which provided that a man in Hereford had capacity to sell land when he
could measure an ell[5] and count up to twelve since "one person is twenty

---

[20] (1872), L.R. 7 Q.B. 214.
[1] These were ancient fairs held for the purpose of hiring servants.
[2] *Hammerton* v. *Honey* (1876), 24 W.R. 603; *New Windsor Corporation* v. *Mellor*, [1975] Ch.
380; [1975] 3 All E.R. 44.
[3] *Mills* v. *Colchester Corporation* (1867), L.R. 2 C.P. 476; see also *Alfred F. Beckett, Ltd.* v.
Lyons, [1967] Ch. 449; [1967] 1 All E.R. 833.
[4] *Hammerton* v. *Honey* (*supra*).
[5] 45 inches.

years old before he knows how to measure an ell, and another knows how when he is seven years old".[6] Similarly an alleged manorial custom enabling tenants to take away turf "in such quantity as occasion may require" has been held void for uncertainty.[7]

f Consistency

Customs must be consistent with one another. They are, by their nature, inconsistent with the common law but they cannot, in a defined locality, be inconsistent with one another, for as Blackstone observed:

> "if one man prescribes that by custom he has a right to have windows looking into another's garden, the other cannot claim a right by custom to stop up or obstruct those windows: for these contradictory customs cannot both be good, nor both stand together".[8]

The appropriate course of procedure is to deny the existence of a custom inconsistent with one's own customary right. This is not, however, possible if that custom has been settled by judicial decision for then it will be judicially noticed.

g Reasonableness

The last and most important test that custom must satisfy is that of reasonableness. It is for the party refuting the custom to show that it is unreasonable. A custom which is repugnant to a fundamental principle of common law cannot be reasonable. For this reason the House of Lords rejected a custom which enabled a manorial lord to undermine his tenant's land without paying compensation for damage to buildings thereby caused.[9] Equally a customary right to commit a crime could not be reasonable.

Furthermore, if a custom must obviously have been unreasonable in 1189 (though not necessarily unreasonable at the present day) this will tend to show that the custom could not have existed in 1189 and it will be rejected on this ground rather than on the basis of it being unreasonable. In *Bryant* v. *Foot*[10] the rector of a parish claimed thirteen shillings as a customary fee for the celebration of a marriage in the parish. It was held that, having regard to the value of money in 1189, the amount was totally unreasonable so that the custom could not have existed at that date.

D   LAW MERCHANT

The law of contract as administered in the common law courts in the thirteenth and fourteenth centuries was extremely rudimentary. Broadly speaking an action could only be brought within the narrow terms of the writ of debt or in respect of the breach of an obligation under seal (writ of

---

[6] Y.B. 12, f. 13 Edw. 3 (R.S.) 23.
[7] *Wilson* v. *Willes* (1806), 7 East 121.
[8] Bl. Comm. 78.
[9] *Wolstanton, Ltd. and Duchy of Lancaster* v. *Newcastle-under-Lyme Corporation*, [1940] A.C. 860; [1940] 3 All E.R. 101.
[10] (1868), L.R. 3 Q.B. 497.

covenant). In addition the local courts had only a limited jurisdiction in contract since the Statute of Gloucester 1278, had effectively reduced their jurisdiction to claims involving less than forty shillings.[11]

Thus the existing courts were ill-equipped to deal with the increasing volume of litigation arising from England's growth as a trading centre. The result was that a new set of courts sprang up to deal solely with disputes between merchants. Since these courts were not common law courts they were not rigidly tied to the common law, and a new set of rules originating partly in custom and partly in international law evolved in these courts as a gloss on the common law. Since their decisions were subject to review by the Court of King's Bench by way of writ of error their rules and doctrines of necessity followed the fundamental tenets of the common law.

1   Courts administering the law merchant

a   Courts of fairs and boroughs

Most mercantile transactions in the Middle Ages were conducted at fairs and markets which were held in fixed places on fixed days. The most important and permanent fairs were held in boroughs which were communities granted a franchise by the King in return for payment of royal dues known as "tolls". The charter granted by the King usually conferred the right to hold a court in the borough. Officers of the borough were also given power to hold courts at the fairs and markets so that the courts of the fairs were generally special sessions of the borough court. These courts were known as courts of "pie poudre",[12] and naturally attracted merchants because of the speed and simplicity of procedure and because the law administered in the courts gave effect to their own customs which formed the basis of their dealings.

The thirteenth and fourteenth centuries were the heyday of these courts. Thereafter various factors contributed to their obsolescence. In 1466[13] the Court of Common Pleas held that an appeal lay by writ of error to the common law courts. This intervention by the common lawyers was the very thing the merchants wished to avoid. The nature of commerce changed and merchants became less peripatetic. The courts themselves began to acquire a cumbersome and technical procedure while the common law courts, with the evolution of assumpsit, broadened their jurisdiction. By the eighteenth century almost all of the courts of pie poudre had ceased to function.[14]

---

[11] See p. 5, *ante.*

[12] Possibly deriving from the Latin *pes pulvericatus* (dusty foot) or from the old French *pied pulderaux* (pedlar).

[13] Y.B. 6 Edw. 4, M., pl. 9.

[14] The last of these courts, the Bristol Tolzey and Pie Poudre Courts, were abolished by s. 43 of the Courts Act 1971. Some of the borough courts were abolished by the Municipal Corporations Act 1883, s. 2 and the Justices of the Peace Act 1949, s. 10 while as part of the reorganisation of local government whereby boroughs were abolished, 141 borough civil courts were abolished by the Local Government Act 1972, s. 221 and Sch. 28. Finally, the jurisdiction of most of the remaining local courts, including all courts of pie poudre, was formally abolished by the Administration of Justice Act 1977, s. 23 and Sch. 4; see p. 6, *ante.*

b   Staple courts

In order to facilitate the collection of customs duties from foreign merchants, statutes were passed[15] confining dealing in certain basic commodities such as wool and tin to certain towns. In each of these "staple"[16] towns there was a court which had exclusive jurisdiction over merchants, save in matters involving title to land or felony. These courts of staple thus exercised both a civil and criminal jurisdiction and applied a pot-pourri of the common law and mercantile custom.

These courts later assumed jurisdiction over persons who were not merchants but they soon became obsolete with the decline of the staple system.[17]

c   High Court of Admiralty

It has at all times been difficult to separate mercantile and maritime law. Both had their origins in foreign legal systems and mercantile custom. The High Court of Admiralty, created in the fourteenth century, had both a civil and a criminal jurisdiction over matters arising on the high seas. The court also assumed jurisdiction over contracts made on land, in the fifteenth century, by the fictitious assumption that the contract was in fact made "on the high seas". The court was closely associated with the Council and the Tudors, particularly Henry VIII, extended its jurisdiction to a wide range of civil and criminal[18] matters having little or no connection with admiralty. The combined effect of this upsurge in the fortunes of the High Court of Admiralty and the corresponding decline of the courts of pie poudre and staple was that the former acquired most of the jurisdiction of the latter.

Unfortunately for the Admiralty this euphoric state of affairs was to be of limited duration. The same close association with the Council which had helped the rise in the court's fortunes later contributed to their decline. The court, in common with the other conciliar courts, the Court of Chancery, the Court of Star Chamber and the Court of Requests, met the full force of Coke's attack on prerogative powers on his accession to the bench in 1606. He denied that the court was a court of record and regarded it as an inferior court having no power to fine or imprison and being subject to the royal writ of prohibition. The effect of these attacks was not sufficiently strong to overthrow the court but it was sufficient to limit its jurisdiction, in civil cases, to matters actually arising on the high seas. It lost all its jurisdiction over such matters as contracts made abroad. Indeed the common law encroached further upon admiralty jurisdiction and assumed jurisdiction over contracts made either abroad or on the high seas by the fiction (yet another example of the use of fictions to acquire jurisdiction) that the contract was made "in the parish of St. Mary-le-Bow in the Ward of Cheap". Thus all that remained of admiralty jurisdiction were cases involving

---

[15] Notably 27 Edw. 3, st. 2 (1353).

[16] From the old French *estape* meaning a market (4 Co. Inst. 238).

[17] The jurisdiction of all staple courts was formally abolished by the Administration of Justice Act 1977, s. 23 and Sch. 4; see p. 6, *ante.*

[18] A statute of 1536, 28 Hen. 8, c. 15, confirmed the court's jurisdiction over crimes committed on the high seas and provided for trial by jury before commissioners. Later, when the court became unpopular with the common lawyers, these commissioners were invariably common lawyers so that the common law in fact controlled the criminal jurisdiction of the court.

collisions at sea, salvage and, in the eighteenth and nineteenth centuries, prize. All this jurisdiction was transferred to the new Probate, Divorce and Admiralty Division of the High Court in 1875.[19] The criminal jurisdiction of the Admiralty commissioners, which derived from the statute of 1536, was given to the Central Criminal Court in 1834 and to courts of assize in 1844.[20] Since this date no admiralty sessions have been held.

Appeal lay from the High Court of Admiralty to the Council originally, later to the High Court of Delegates and finally, after 1832, to the Privy Council.

Thus by the seventeenth century the law merchant had passed largely into the jurisdiction of the common law courts.

2   The content of the law merchant

Although the law merchant was, by the seventeenth century, administered in the common law courts, the common law judges did not regard it as part of the common law. They were ever aware that it was based on usage. In the leading case of *Goodwin* v. *Robarts*[1] COCKBURN, C.J. described the *lex mercatoria* in the following words:

> "It is neither more nor less than the usages of merchants and traders in the different departments of trade, ratified by the decisions of courts of law."

The effect of the law merchant being derived from custom was that since the common lawyers required proof of the existence of a custom they would not recognise a rule of the law merchant which was unreasonable or repugnant to the common law. On the other hand mercantile customs, unlike local customs, were not required to date from time immemorial so that recent customs could be accepted into the law. Thus, just as equity grew as a gloss on the common law, the law merchant was a gloss on the law of contract which was, even after the evolution of assumpsit, scarcely adequate to meet mercantile needs.

Perhaps the greatest contribution of the law merchant to the common law was the concept of negotiability. This was introduced in the seventeenth century by means of a special action on the case on the custom of merchants to fill the gap left by the refusal of the common law to recognise the assignability of choses in action. Eventually the necessity for pleading this special action on the case disappeared and, largely due to the pioneering of Holt, C.J., bills of exchange were accepted at common law. Holt, C.J. (Chief Justice of the King's Bench 1689–1710) formulated the principles of transfer by endorsement, presumption of consideration and the rule that a *bona fide* holder's title was not invalidated by defects in the title of the

---

[19] It is now administered in the "Admiralty Court" of the Queen's Bench Division; Supreme Court Act 1981, ss. 20–24; see p. 371, *post*. The Admiralty Court's practice was to award interest (which the common law courts did not do prior to the Civil Procedure Act 1833). Hence the High Court, when exercising its Admiralty jurisdiction (under section 20 of the Supreme Court Act 1981; see p. 196, *post*) has an extra-statutory jurisdiction to award interest, which it does not possess when exercising jurisdiction derived from common law: *President of India* v. *La Pintada Cia Navegacion SA*, [1984] 2 All E.R. 773; [1984] 3 W.L.R. 10.
[20] The criminal jurisdiction of the Admiralty is now exercised by the Crown Court.
[1] (1875), L.R. 10 Ex. 337.

transferor. Holt's work was perfected by the great Scots lawyer Lord Mansfield who was Chief Justice of the King's Bench between 1756 and 1788. The negotiable instrument is by no means the sole contribution of the law merchant to English law. Partnership, the law of agency and insurance are three major branches of the law which have the custom of merchants as their primary source. The nineteenth century, the age of codification, saw the incorporation of much of the law merchant into statute. The Bills of Exchange Act 1882, the Partnership Act 1890 and the Sale of Goods Act 1893 are examples of such statutes.

E CANON LAW

The canon law, the law of the Western or Catholic Church, has influenced the growth of English law in two ways. First it was the basis of many concepts which were formulated in the lay courts and as such is a primary source of other sources of law. Examples of common law concepts which originated in the canon law are: the nature of criminal law and its close association with moral fault, imprisonment as a punishment for crime (the purpose of which the canonists conceived to be the possibility of repentance through solitary contemplation), wager of law as a method of trial and, of course, the nature of Christian marriage and family rights. In addition the common law trial by ordeal relied for its efficacy on the participation of the clergy. Canon law also influenced the nature of equity, the strong moral content of which is attributable to the fact of the early Chancellors being clerics. Specific concepts of equity, such as the recognition of marriage as good consideration for a marriage settlement, are undoubtedly identifiable with a canon law origin.

The second, and more important, way in which canon law became a source of English law was by its application in the ecclesiastical courts. In this context canon law was a system of law wholly independent of the common law since the ecclesiastical courts were, during the Middle Ages, completely outside the control of the King.

1   Ecclesiastical courts

It would be impossible in a general outline of the historical sources of English law to deal fully with the myriad of ecclesiastical courts which have existed at different times in history. Only a broad outline is possible.

a   Hierarchy

The lowest ecclesiastical court was the court of the archdeacon. Above the archdeaconry courts were the diocesan courts of the bishops, the consistory courts. These were the courts of first instance in all matters not concerning members of the clergy. The consistory courts also exercised appellate jurisdiction over clergy discipline as administered in the archdeaconry courts. Appeal lay from the consistory courts to the provincial courts of the two archbishops (York Chancery and Court of Arches).[2]

---

2 For the present hierarchy and jurisdiction of the ecclesiastical courts, see p. 216, *post*.

Until the Reformation the Papal Curia was at the summit of the hierarchy. The Pope possessed both legislative and judicial power over the English clergy; his judicial function was both original and appellate but was, obviously, confined to cases of major importance. The result of the Reformation was the abolition of all Papal jurisdiction. The legislative power of the Pope passed to Parliament and Convocations of the clergy. The jurisdiction to hear appeals from the provincial courts was assumed by the Court of Delegates established by statute[3] in 1533. The commissioners, appointed by the Crown, might be bishops, common law judges or "civilian" lawyers. The unsatisfactory composition of the court prevented it from enjoying any great respect. In addition it followed no system of precedent and did not record its decisions. Its jurisdiction in both ecclesiastical and admiralty matters was transferred to the Privy Council in 1832.

b Procedure

Procedure in the ecclesiastical courts resembled procedure in the Court of Chancery rather than common law procedure. Proceedings were instituted by a document known as a "libel" which was similar in form to a Chancery petition. The parties were examined in court and could be represented by the proctors and advocates who composed that part of the legal profession which practised in the ecclesiastical courts and had been schooled in civil law at the universities of Oxford and Cambridge.[4] The judges of the consistory and provincial courts were styled Chancellors and they sat without a jury. Judgment was in the form of a decree.

c Conflict with the common law

All courts outside the common law system clashed with the common lawyers at one time or another. The ecclesiastical courts were no exception to this rule. The conflict between Church and State in the reign of Henry II precipitated the question of the scope of the jurisdiction of the Church courts. In 1164 the English bishops were induced to agree the concessions of jurisdiction contained in the Constitutions of Clarendon. The most important concessions of jurisdiction were over *advowsons* (the right[5] to nominate clergymen to an ecclesiastical benefice), disputes over which were conceded to be outside the jurisdiction of the ecclesiastical courts, disputes over whether land was held under common law or spiritual tenure (*frankalmoign*)[6] and, finally, the right of the common law courts to try clerics for criminal offences in respect of which they had been convicted in the church court. This last concession of jurisdiction was removed after the murder of

---

3 25 Hen. 8, c. 19. The Court of Delegates also heard appeals from the High Court of Admiralty.

4 Eventually the degree of Doctor of Civil Law, obtainable only at these Universities, became an essential qualification for practice in the ecclesiastical or admiralty courts. Those qualified had their chambers in buildings called "Doctors' Commons" in which the Court of Arches and the High Court of Admiralty sat.

5 The right, which generally belonged to the person who had endowed the church, was a valuable right in property and capable of conveyance.

6 This was decided by an "assize *utrum*". If land were found to be held in *frankalmoign* any dispute passed into the jurisdiction of the ecclesiastical courts.

Becket which was the origin of the long history of the privilege of "benefit of clergy"[7]

After this the jurisdiction of the ecclesiastical courts became fairly clearly defined and did not cause any serious clash with the common lawyers until the seventeenth century when the whole system of ecclesiastical courts was brought down by the Civil War. The system was reinstated by the Restoration but shortly afterwards lost its jurisdiction over the laity in matters of criminal law and moral offences.

The surviving jurisdiction of the ecclesiastical courts over the laity comprised probate and matrimonial jurisdiction. This in turn became resented by the common lawyers and was removed by the Matrimonial Causes Act 1857 and the Court of Probate Act 1857. Since this date the jurisdiction of the ecclesiastical courts has been confined to matters affecting members of the Church where this jurisdiction does not conflict with the jurisdiction of the ordinary courts.[8]

2 Content of the canon law as administered in the ecclesiastical courts

That part of the ecclesiastical courts' jurisdiction which concerned the enforcement of doctrine and morals and matters concerning only the clergy has not passed into English law and remains solely the province of the ecclesiastical courts. Thus offences such as incontinence, adultery, usury and slander have not become part of the general criminal law. On the other hand, blasphemy and blasphemous libel, offences originally justiciable in the ecclesiastical courts,[9] continue to be offences and, as the House of Lords has recently confirmed,[10] they are offences of strict liability in the sense that the only intent required is an intent to publish material which is in fact blasphemous, not a specific intent to blaspheme.

The part of canon law which is a source of the general English law is that part which concerns probate and matrimony. By no means the whole of the law of probate was within the control of the church courts. Their jurisdiction was in fact confined to wills of personalty (including leaseholds). This jurisdiction also extended to granting letters of administration on intestacy. However no probate or letters of administration were required in respect of realty. Disputes as to the validity of wills, so far as they disposed of realty, could only be determined in the common law courts.[11] Although matters concerning the validity of wills were within the jurisdiction of the ecclesiastical courts, matters concerning their construction and the administration of estates were not. These were dealt with by the Court of Chancery. This

---

[7] See p. 18, *ante.*

[8] See p. 216, *post.*

[9] See *Bowman* v. *Secular Society, Ltd.,* [1917] A.C. 406 for an account of the history of these offences.

[10] *R.* v. *Lemon,* [1979] A.C. 617; [1979] 1 All E.R. 898 (the "Gay News" case); a blasphemous publication is one which "contains any contemptuous, reviling, scurrilous or ludicrous matter relating to God, Jesus Christ or the Bible, or the formularies of the Church of England as by law established": Stephen's *Digest of the Criminal Law* (9th Edn.), art. 214, cited with approval in *R.* v. *Lemon (supra).*

[11] The procedure was by action of ejectment by the devisee against the heir-at-law.

unfortunate dichotomy of jurisdiction was perpetuated by the Judicature Acts and existed until the Administration of Justice Act 1970 re-named the Probate, Divorce and Admiralty Division the Family Division and transferred contentious probate business to the Chancery Division.[12] Probate jurisdiction was transferred to the newly-created Court of Probate by the Act of 1857. The Court was given power to hear and determine all questions relating to testamentary matters. This jurisdiction was finally assigned to the Probate, Divorce and Admiralty Division in 1875.

Perhaps the most important aspect of modern law which has its origin in the canon law as administered in the ecclesiastical courts is family law. Although a common law marriage was (and still is) possible in special circumstances most marriages were celebrated in church so that marriage was, and always has been, a relationship with strong religious implications. Although the ecclesiastical courts, accepting marriage as indissoluble, had no power to grant a divorce in the modern sense they did have power to pronounce decrees of nullity, restitution of conjugal rights[13] (calling on a deserting spouse to return to the other) and a "divorce" a *mensa et thoro* (judicial separation, which relieves one spouse of the duty of cohabiting with the other). Divorce *a vinculo* became possible by private Act of Parliament in the latter half of the seventeenth century, though this was exceedingly expensive. Divorce by judicial decree was made possible for the first time by the Matrimonial Causes Act 1857.[14] This Act, passed to give effect to the report of a royal commission set up in 1850 to consider this branch of the law, transferred the matrimonial jurisdiction of the ecclesiastical courts to the new Divorce Court. This jurisdiction was assigned by the Judicature Acts to the Probate, Divorce and Admiralty Division of the High Court.

The ecclesiastical courts conflicted in certain respects with the common law courts. Thus, although the ecclesiastical courts recognised legitimation by subsequent marriage of the parents, the common law did not and excluded such children from succession under a disposition to "children". The ecclesiastical concept of legitimation was not, in fact, recognised in English law until the passing of the Legitimacy Act 1926.

F ROMAN LAW

Roman law, the basis of most continental systems of law, is, surprisingly, of very minor importance as a source of English law. It is not a direct source at all in the sense that there was never a system of English courts applying solely Roman law. Any influence that Roman law has had on the growth of English law has been indirect. The source of law which owes most to Roman law is canon law. The reason is that the Chancellors and advocates in the ecclesias-

---

[12] Administration of Justice Act 1970, s. 1(4); see p. 194, *post*.

[13] The sanction for failure to comply with the decree could be excommunication until the Ecclesiastical Courts Act 1813 which replaced this with power to commit for contempt. This was in turn abolished by the Matrimonial Causes Act 1884. The decree was abolished by the Divorce Reform Act 1969.

[14] For an entertaining summary of the history of divorce law, see Baker, *An Introduction to English Legal History*, (2nd Edn.), pp. 401–410.

tical courts were indoctrinated with the civil law through their studies at Oxford and Cambridge. Thus the formal requirements of wills in many cases have their counterpart in Roman law as have many of the rules relating to parental authority.

Roman law also undoubtedly influenced maritime and mercantile law since the Venetian and Genoese mercantile customs which these branches of the law utilised had a civilian basis.

The common law itself has from time to time borrowed from Roman law. The principal link between Roman law and common law is Bracton's treatise *De Legibus et Consuetudinibus Angliae* written in Latin in about the year 1250. Bracton was well versed in Roman law and the civilian principles he incorporated into his treatise owed much to the writings of the Roman jurist Justinian. Thus common law judges, faced with a case of first impression with little or no assistance to be gleaned from English precedents, have looked to Bracton for assistance and in doing so have adopted Romanist principles. The leading example is the judgment of HOLT, C.J. in *Coggs* v. *Bernard*[15] which classifies bailments in accordance with Bracton's classification, itself based on Roman law. Similarly, in *Dalton* v. *Angus*[16] LORD BLACKBURN, one of the greatest of common law judges, considered the Roman doctrine of *usucapio* (prescription) when deciding a difficult question on the subject of easements. Also, in a modern case,[17] the question of whether the owner of a swarm of bees could follow them on to the land of another was answered by reference to Justinian's Institutes which, as every student of Roman law knows, deals with that precise question.

---

[15] (1703), 2 Ld. Raym. 969.
[16] (1881), 6 App. Cas. 740.
[17] *Kearry* v. *Pattinson*, [1939] 1 K.B. 471; [1939] 1 All E.R. 65.

CHAPTER 4

Administrative Reforms of the Nineteenth Century

A THE NEED FOR REFORM

English law has been compared to a river which is "first fed by the springs of the common law" and later by "the fountain of equity, and the wells of the law merchant and ecclesiastical law".[1] The chief cause for concern at the beginning of the nineteenth century was not the existence of separate sources of law, for these complemented and supplemented one another to produce one body of English law, but the fact that these sources were being administered in different courts. Thus the common law was administered principally by the three superior common law courts, equity by the Court of Chancery, canon law by the ecclesiastical courts and the law merchant and maritime by the High Court of Admiralty. In addition procedure in the individual courts was generally defective in one or more respects. The restrictive operation of the doctrine of precedent together with the inherent conservatism of judges made it impossible for judicial reform to correct the major deficiencies which existed. Only sweeping legislation could clear the dead wood and the nineteenth century was to be the great era of legislative reform. It must not be supposed that the need for reform was universally accepted. Those who profited by the general corruption of the officials of the Court of Chancery or by the complexity of pleading in the common law courts were by no means anxious to alter their situation. Others could not conceive that so majestic a system as the English Legal System could be in any way improved. Thus Blackstone in his *Commentaries on the Laws of England* published in 1765 painted a rosy picture of the system. Lord Eldon opposed virtually every reformative measure introduced during his Chancellorship (1801–1827). Fortunately there were others such as Jeremy Bentham, Sir Samuel Romilly and Lord Brougham who could detect the fundamental flaws which existed. The principal matters needing reform were as follows:

---

[1] Potter, *op. cit.* (5th Edn.), p. 1.

(1) the duality of jurisdiction between the common law courts and the Court of Chancery whereby a plaintiff might have to commence two separate actions in respect of one set of facts: an action in the common law courts to obtain damages and a separate action in the Chancery for an equitable remedy such as an injunction;

(2) the system whereby the Chancellor could restrain a litigant from enforcing his common law rights by means of a common injunction;

(3) the fact that the ecclesiastical courts exercised exclusive jurisdiction in matters of probate and matrimonial causes over persons who were not members of the Church of England;

(4) the conflict of jurisdiction between the common law courts and the High Court of Admiralty;

(5) the fact that the jurisdiction of the three superior common law courts had become co-extensive in many cases through the widespread use of fictions such as Bill of Middlesex and *Quominus*;

(6) the lack of a system of courts to try small civil claims. Those local courts and borough courts which had fulfilled the useful function of dispensing justice summarily and cheaply had, by the nineteenth century, been almost entirely swallowed up by the superior courts of the common law. The result was the creation of a vacuum since the considerable costs of proceedings in Westminster or at *nisi prius* made litigation impracticable where the sum involved was not large;

(7) the complex and inadequate system of appeals in both civil and criminal cases at common law (the right to appeal against a finding of fact in criminal cases, a long-felt need, was not in fact introduced until 1907);[2]

(8) the formal and artificial procedure existing in the common law courts.[3] The cornerstone of procedural difficulty at common law was, of course, the writ system with its many different forms of action, each subject to a different procedure and a different system of pleading. If the plaintiff was unfortunate enough to choose the wrong writ he would be non-suited and would have to start his action all over again. His error could not be cured by amendment, nor could he plead in the alternative;

(9) the scandalous condition of the Court of Chancery. The complete inadequacy of the judicial staff of the court led to an ever-increasing backlog of cases which became even greater under Lord Eldon due to that Chancellor's excessive caution and dilatory conduct. The inadequacy of the judicial staff was matched only by the welter of court officials whose bribery and corruption have already been noted.[4]

Almost all of these defects were corrected by legislation between 1825 and 1875, culminating in the Judicature Acts 1873–1875. The Judicature Acts were so comprehensive and sweeping as to merit separate consideration, but, before that, the principal steps leading to their passing must be traced.

---

[2] Criminal Appeal Act 1907.
[3] See p. 20, *ante.*
[4] See p. 45, *ante.*

B   REFORMS PRIOR TO 1873

1   Reforms of the common law courts and procedure

a   *Uniformity of Process Act 1832*

This Act was the first of the procedural reforms. It abolished the various different forms of commencing proceedings and substituted one form of writ of summons to be used for commencing personal actions in all three common law courts. It did not affect real actions. It must not be supposed that the Act abolished the necessity for selecting a particular form of action. It did not. The plaintiff still had to specify his cause of action by reference to one form of action and if he selected the wrong one he would be nonsuited just as before.

b   *Real Property Limitation Act 1833*

This statute formally abolished almost all the real actions. In fact the statute had but slight effect since it did not affect the action of ejectment which had long superseded the real actions nor did it affect the procedure for bringing those real actions which were not abolished.

c   *Civil Procedure Act 1833*

This Act extended the procedural reforms commenced by the Uniformity of Process Act 1832. Apart from finally abolishing wager of law and, for the first time, making it possible for the defendant to pay money into court in satisfaction of the plaintiff's claim and conferring power to award interest on debt or damages, the Act created a new system of pleading. Although this system swept away many of the anachronistic rules of pleading it scarcely simplified pleading and eventually had to be repealed because it created a system which proved to be far more complex than the system which it was intended to replace.

d   *Common Law Procedure Acts 1852–1860*

The three Common Law Procedure Acts of 1852, 1854 and 1860 constituted the first real attempts at comprehensive reform of the common law system. Each was passed following recommendations contained in the reports of the Civil Procedure Commissioners appointed in 1850.

The Common Law Procedure Act 1852 revised completely proceedings at first instance and on appeal and created many of the rules of procedure which were eventually incorporated in the Rules of the Supreme Court annexed to the Judicature Acts. The fundamental reform was the abolition of the forms of action. After 1852 the necessity for naming a specific form of action on the writ of summons was removed. Consequently joinder of causes of action, hitherto impossible, was recognised and one source of duplicity of proceedings removed. The action of ejectment and its two protagonists John Doe and Richard Roe were laid to rest and replaced by the modern action for the recovery of land. Amendment of pleadings became possible, judgment in default of appearance was introduced and service outside the jurisdiction allowed for the first time.

The 1852 Act was concerned principally with reforming the internal structure of common law procedure. The Common Law Procedure Act 1854 was the first major step in fusing the administration of law and equity. This important Act for the first time enabled a defendant in the common law courts to raise an equitable defence. Such a defence, for example fraud or undue influence, could be raised in any case in which the defendant would be entitled to equitable relief against the common law judgment, that is to say cases where the Chancellor would issue a common injunction. The same Act gave the common law courts power to grant injunctions and to compel discovery of documents and administer interrogatories. A final important innovation of the 1854 Act was the provision that a judge might, with the consent of the parties, try issues of fact without a jury. This was the first step in the rapid decline of the jury in civil cases.

2 Chancery reforms

Compared with the striking reforms of common law procedure in the nineteenth century, Chancery reforms in the corresponding period were somewhat minor. The creation of the Chancery Court of Appeal to relieve the Chancellor of most of his work as a judge at first instance,[5] the appointment of Vice-Chancellors in 1813 and 1841[6] and the authorisation of the Master of the Rolls to sit as a regular Court in 1833[7] were all reforms aimed at clearing the arrears of litigation which had accumulated through the insufficient number of judges in the Court of Chancery.

Procedural reforms along the lines of the Common Law Procedure Acts 1852–1860 tended during the same period to assimilate Chancery procedure and common law procedure. The Court of Chancery Procedure Act 1852 abolished the need for every fact in the plaintiff's bill to be contained in interrogatories appended to the bill, which was henceforth to contain simply numbered paragraphs setting out the material facts on which the plaintiff relied concluding with a prayer for relief. The same Act abolished the need for the Court of Chancery to state a case for the opinion of the common law courts and enabled the Court of Chancery itself to decide all questions of law and fact arising in any case before it.

Finally, the Chancery Amendment Act 1858 (Lord Cairns' Act) empowered the Court of Chancery to award damages either in addition to or in lieu of an injunction or a decree of specific performance in respect of infringement of a common law right. This removed the necessity for bringing separate actions in the common law courts and the Chancery in respect of one cause of action. Lord Cairns' Act also provided for issues of fact and assessment of damages to be determined by a jury, but this revolutionary power was never exercised.

3 Creation of the county courts

In the nineteenth century, due to the decline of the jurisdiction of the borough courts of record, there was an urgent need for the creation of a system of small claims courts.

---

[5] Court of Chancery Act 1851.
[6] Court of Chancery Act 1841.
[7] 3 & 4 W. 4, c. 94.

One attempt to satisfy this need took the form of the creation, by private Acts of Parliament, of Courts of Requests for actions concerning small debts. These courts were not a great success since the judges were often local people, unqualified in the law with no great respect for evidence or rules of procedure.

In 1749 an Act[8] attempted to revive the jurisdiction of the ancient Middlesex county court by allowing the county clerk (a barrister) and the . suitors of the court to sit in the various hundreds in turn to try cases involving not more than 40s. This experiment of a permanent judge touring the county to deal with small claims was successful and upon it was modelled the system of county courts established in 1846.

The County Courts Act 1846 ("An Act for the recovery of small debts and demands") created some 500 county courts divided into sixty circuits each with its own judge who was to be a barrister of at least seven years standing appointed by the Chancellor. The upper limit of the jurisdiction of these courts was fixed at £20 but so popular did they become that it was raised to £50 in 1850. The power to remit cases from the superior courts at Westminster to the county courts was created in 1856 in respect of actions of contract where the sum claimed did not exceed £50. Since their creation the financial limits of the county courts' jurisdiction have risen steadily and the courts can no longer properly be described as small claims courts. Nevertheless the advent of legal aid has brought most county court proceedings within the reach of all.

4   Creation of the Courts of Probate and Divorce

The Court of Probate Act 1857 and the Matrimonial Causes Act 1857 had the combined effect of terminating the jurisdiction of the ecclesiastical courts over persons who were not members of the Church. Henceforth the jurisdiction of the ecclesiastical courts was confined to internal matters. The new Court of Probate was presided over by a judge who was also a judge of the newly formed Divorce Court.[9] These courts, together with the High Court of Admiralty, moved to Westminster Hall so that Doctors' Commons were abolished. The existing doctors and proctors had a right of audience before these courts but, since this right was also shared by all barristers, their office became extinct.

The jurisdiction of the Courts of Probate and Divorce has already been considered.[10]

---

[8] 23 Geo. 2, c. 33.
[9] Sir Cresswell Cresswell was appointed the first judge of the Probate and Divorce Courts.
[10] See pp. 71–73, *ante.*

C THE JUDICATURE ACTS 1873–1875[11]

1 The Supreme Court of Judicature

The Judicature Acts of 1873 and 1875 came into operation together[12] on November 1, 1875. Their principal effect was to create a new Supreme Court of Judicature to which was transferred the jurisdiction of all the superior courts of law and equity except the Chancery Courts of the Counties Palatine of Lancaster and Durham[13] which were unaffected. The Supreme Court was divided into two parts, the High Court of Justice and the Court of Appeal.[14]

a High Court of Justice

The High Court was given the jurisdiction formerly exercised by the three common law courts,[15] the Court of Chancery, the Courts for Probate and Divorce and Matrimonial Causes, the High Court of Admiralty, the Courts of Common Pleas at Lancaster and Durham, and the courts created by the commissions of oyer and terminer, gaol delivery and assize.[16] The High Court was also given jurisdiction to hear appeals from the county courts, but this jurisdiction was transferred to the Court of Appeal in 1934.[17]

The High Court was formed in five divisions; Chancery Division, Probate, Divorce and Admiralty Division, Queen's Bench Division, Common Pleas Division and Exchequer Division. It was, however, provided that the number of divisions might be altered by Order in Council[18] and, after the deaths of the Chief Justice of the Queen's Bench and Chief Baron of the Exchequer in 1880, the Common Pleas and Exchequer Divisions were merged in the Queen's Bench Division and LORD COLERIDGE became the first Lord Chief Justice of England. Since that date, therefore, there have been three divisions of the High Court.[19]

The divisions of the High Court are not separate courts. Thus each division has equal competence and a judge of one division had jurisdiction to sit in any division and may, indeed, be required to do so by the Lord Chancellor.

The principle of equal competence is aptly illustrated by the decision of the Court of Appeal in *Re L*.[20] The case turned on the question of whether a judge of the Probate, Divorce and Admiralty Division had power to order a blood test on an infant for the purpose of determining paternity. It was

---

[11] These statutes, the full short titles of which are the Supreme Court of Judicature Acts 1873–1875, were replaced by the Supreme Court of Judicature (Consolidation) Act 1925 (commonly cited as the Judicature Act 1925) which in turn was consolidated with amendments in the Supreme Court Act 1981.

[12] The Judicature Act 1873 was intended to come into operation on November 2, 1874 but this was postponed when it was appreciated that further amendments were necessary.

[13] See p. 191, *post*.

[14] The Supreme Court now consists of the Court of Appeal, the High Court and the Crown Court; Supreme Court Act 1981, s. 1(1); as to the Crown Court, see p. 198, *post*.

[15] The Court of Exchequer, Court of Common Pleas and Court of King's Bench.

[16] The jurisdiction of the London Court of Bankruptcy was added by the Bankruptcy Act 1883.

[17] Administration of Justice (Appeals) Act 1934.

[18] Judicature Act 1873, ss. 32–36.

[19] See p. 191, *post*. The Probate, Divorce and Admiralty Division has, however, been renamed the Family Division (Administration of Justice Act 1970, s. 1(1)).

[20] [1968] P. 119; [1968] 1 All E.R. 20; applying *R. v. Gyngall*, [1893] 2 Q.B. 232.

argued that, if jurisdiction to order a blood test existed, it derived from the inherent custodial jurisdiction of the Court of Chancery[1] and could, therefore, be exercised only by a judge of the Chancery Division in wardship proceedings. LORD DENNING, M.R. disposed of this argument as follows.[2]

> "This wide jurisdiction of the old Court of Chancery is now vested in the High Court of Justice and can be exercised by any judge of the High Court. As a matter of convenience, the jurisdiction is exercised by making the child a ward of court and putting it under the care of a judge of the Chancery Division; but that is only machinery. If a question arises as to the welfare of a child before any judge of the High Court, he can make such order as may be appropriate in the circumstances. He need not send the case over to a Chancery judge."

Nevertheless business is distributed between the three divisions in approximately the same way as it was distributed between the courts whose jurisdiction the High Court assumed in 1875.[3] Common law matters are generally dealt with in the Queen's Bench Division, equity suits in the Chancery Division and matrimonial causes and matters affecting children in the Family Division.[4] In many cases there is a choice as to whether to proceed in one division or another and if an action is commenced in one division it may be transferred to another division. Such a transfer is made, however, for convenience rather than for want of jurisdiction.

b   Court of Appeal

The Court of Appeal was established by the Acts rather on the model of the Court of Appeal in Chancery than on the Exchequer Chamber, that is to say, with permanent judges rather than judges of first instance sitting in turn to hear appeals from one another's decisions. To the Court of Appeal was transferred the jurisdiction of the Court of Exchequer Chamber, the Court of Appeal in Chancery, the Court of Appeal from Lancaster, the Court of the Lord Warden of the Stannaries[5] and the admiralty jurisdiction (except in prize cases) of the Judicial Committee of the Privy Council.

The Court of Appeal is composed of a number of ex-officio judges, of whom only the Master of the Rolls and the Lord Chief Justice usually sit, and permanent Lords Justices of Appeal.[6]

The jurisdiction of the Court of Appeal was originally intended to be concerned mainly with appeals from the High Court. Since 1875, however, the appellate jurisdiction of the divisional court of the Queen's Bench Divi-

---

[1] See p. 45, *ante.*
[2] [1968] P., at pp. 156–157; [1968] 1 All E.R., at pp. 24–25. The substantive point of the case is now of purely historical interest since specific power to order blood tests is now contained in the Family Law Reform Act 1969, s. 20 and, furthermore, wardship jurisdiction is now assigned to the Family Division by the Supreme Court Act 1981, s. 61 and Sch. 1.
[3] Although a certain amount of redistribution, notably in relation to probate, admiralty and wardship business, was effected by the Administration of Justice Act 1970.
[4] For details of the present jurisdiction of the divisions of the High Court, see p. 191, *post.*
[5] A franchise court of the Stannaries in Cornwall. The Court of the Vice-Warden of the Stannaries was abolished by the Stannaries Court (Abolition) Act 1896 and its jurisdiction transferred to county courts in Cornwall; for the history of the stannaries courts and a recent unsuccessful attempt to revive their jurisdiction, see *R. v. East Powder Magistrates' Court, Ex parte Lampshire*, [1979] Q.B. 616; [1979] 2 All E.R. 329.
[6] See p. 189, *post.*

sion in civil matters has declined so that the appellate jurisdiction of the Court of Appeal has widened in scope. Thus the power to entertain applications for a new trial was transferred from the divisional court of the Queen's Bench Division to the Court of Appeal in 1890.[7] More important still were the transfer of county court appeals to the Court of Appeal in 1934 and of criminal appeals in 1966.[8]

c   Procedure

Before the nineteenth century each court regulated its own internal procedure with very little intervention by Parliament. The nineteenth century saw a change of attitude and the setting-up of commissions by Parliament to consider procedure in the courts. It was as a result of the reports of these commissions that the Common Law Procedure Acts 1852–1860 and the various Chancery Procedure and Chancery Amendment Acts, particularly the Acts of 1852 and 1858,[9] were passed. The purpose of these Acts was to assimilate common law and equity procedure. This process was completed by the Judicature Acts which created a single set of rules of procedure to apply throughout the Supreme Court. The first set of Rules of the Supreme Court was contained in a schedule to the Judicature Act 1875. Section 17 of the 1875 Act also provided power for judges of the Supreme Court to make rules of procedure, a function now carried out by the Rule Committee. These Rules are constantly varied to provide for new causes of action and new statutory provisions.[10] The original rules comprised those features of common law procedure introduced in 1852 which had proved workable together with the most useful rules of procedure hitherto applicable in the Court of Chancery. The result has been a happy one in that the formalism of the old system of pleading has almost entirely disappeared and substantive law and procedure have become completely separate, the former no longer the servant of the latter. The function of modern procedure is to facilitate the enforcement of rights not to create them. Although it is still possible for an action to be won or lost in the pleadings[11] this hardly ever occurs and procedural errors do not have the catastrophic effect they once had.

2   The House of Lords

The House of Lords in the nineteenth century was under constant fire from critics because the judicial strength of the House fell far short of that required of the highest court of appeal in the realm. Lay peers could and did sit and it was not uncommon for only one lawyer, the Lord Chancellor, to sit on the hearing of an important appeal. An attempt was made to strengthen the composition of the House by conferring a life peerage upon the leading Exchequer Baron, PARKE, B. However the Committee of Privileges held

---

[7] Judicature Act 1890, s. 1.
[8] Criminal Appeal Act 1966.
[9] See p. 79, *ante*.
[10] See p. 293, *post*.
[11] See, for example, *Esso Petroleum Co., Ltd.* v. *Southport Corporation*, [1956] A.C. 218; [1955] 3 All E.R. 864.

that, as a life peer, he had no right to sit and vote in the House.[12] The result was that the Judicature Act 1873 contained a provision abolishing the judicial function of the House of Lords. This section never took effect because it was repealed before the Judicature Act 1873 came into force. The eventual solution was to provide for the creation of salaried life peers who were legally qualified to exercise the House's judicial function. This was effected by the Appellate Jurisdiction Act 1876. Since this date lay peers have, by convention, taken no part in the judicial sessions of the House. Nevertheless the House of Lords was not made a part of the Supreme Court of Judicature and is still not a part of the Supreme Court. Consequently the House of Lords retains the right to regulate its own procedure in regard to the hearing of appeals.[13]

3   Fusion of the administration of law and equity

The primary effect of the Judicature Acts on the relationship between law and equity was to fuse their administration. This was done by transferring the jurisdiction of the existing superior courts of law and equity to one court—the Supreme Court of Judicature. The Supreme Court judges were directed by the Acts to give effect to both legal and equitable rights and remedies.[14] Thus the duality of jurisdiction which existed prior to 1875, whereby two actions might have to be brought to enforce one right, was abolished. Also abolished was the common injunction, the need for which stemmed from the pre-existing duality of jurisdiction.

It is an open question how far the Judicature Acts fused the rules of law and equity by fusing their administration. This question cannot be answered categorically because of the differing natures of certain rules of equity. Most rules of equity grew, not in conflict with common law rules, but as a gloss upon them. Thus the equitable rights and duties arising out of the creation of a trust are not inconsistent with the legal rights in the subject matter of the trust. The legal estate of the trustee is not denied by the equitable interest of the beneficiary; it is merely subject to the beneficial interest. Maitland himself perceived very little direct conflict between the rules of law and equity, seeing equity as a gloss on the common law.[15] Nevertheless, certain rules of equity undoubtedly grew in direct conflict with corresponding common law rules. In such cases the Chancellor would issue a common injunction restraining one party from exercising his common law right. For example the Chancellor would restrain a party from suing to enforce an obligation which had been induced by fraud, duress or undue influence. Since these defences could, after 1875, be pleaded in the Supreme Court of Judicature, it is possible to say that the common law rule has been merged into the corresponding rule of equity. In such a case the Judicature Acts did more than fuse the administration of law and equity; they fused the rules themselves. The framers of the Judicature Acts specified nine particular cases of conflict and provided that in these cases and in all other cases of conflict or variance

---

[12] *Wensleydale Peerage Case* (1865), 5 H.L. Cas. 958.
[13] For details of the jurisdiction of the House of Lords, see p. 186, *post*.
[14] Judicature Act 1873, ss. 24, 25.
[15] Maitland, *Equity*, pp. 16–20.

the equitable rule should prevail.[16] Section 49(1) of the Supreme Court Act 1981 now provides that:

> "Subject to the provisions of this or any other Act, every court exercising jurisdiction in England or Wales in any civil cause or matter shall continue to administer law and equity on the basis that, wherever there is any conflict or variance between the rules of equity and the rules of the common law with reference to the same matter, the rules of equity shall prevail."

There have, in fact, been few cases in which common law and equity have conflicted since 1875 but wherever there has been a conflict the equitable rule has prevailed.[17]

One such conflict, over the question of whether time limits prescribed by a rent review clause in a lease were of the essence, reached the House of Lords in 1977.[18] The rule of equity (namely that stipulations in contracts as to the time by which various steps should be taken are not of the essence unless in the circumstances it would be inequitable not to treat the failure of one party to comply with the stipulations as relieving the other party from the duty to perform his obligations) prevailed. LORD DIPLOCK availed himself of the opportunity to comment upon the fusion of law and equity in the following terms.[19]

> "to perpetuate a dichotomy between rules of equity and rules of common law which it was a major purpose of the Supreme Court of Judicature Act 1873 to do away with is, in my view, conducive to erroneous conclusions as to the ways in which the law of England has developed in the last 100 years.
>
> Your Lordships have been referred to the vivid phrase traceable to the first edition of Ashburner, *Principles of Equity*[20] where, speaking in 1902 of the effect of the Judicature Act, he says 'the two streams of jurisdiction [*sc.* law and equity], though they run in the same channel, run side by side and do not mingle their waters'. My Lords, by 1977 this metaphor has in my view become both mischievous and deceptive. The innate conservatism of English lawyers may have made them slow to recognise that by the Judicature Act 1873 the two systems of substantive and adjectival law formerly administered by courts of law and courts of chancery (as well as those administered by courts of admiralty, probate and matrimonial causes), were fused. As at the confluence of the Rhone and Saone, it may be possible for a short distance to discern the source from which each part of the combined stream came, but there comes a point at which this ceases to be possible. If Professor Ashburner's fluvial metaphor is to be retained at all, the waters of the confluent streams of law and equity have surely mingled now."

---

[16] Judicature Act 1873, s. 25.

[17] Examples are *Job* v. *Job* (1877), 6 Ch.D. 562 (liability of executors); *Walsh* v. *Lonsdale* (1882), 21 Ch.D. 9 (enforceability of an agreement for a lease); *Berry* v. *Berry*, [1929] 2 K.B. 316 (variation of a deed by parol evidence). In an amusing exchange between bench and bar at the conclusion of a modern case (*Hill* v. *C.A. Parsons & Co., Ltd.*, [1972] Ch. 305; [1971] 3 All E.R. 1345) LORD DENNING, M.R. remarked "It is the common lawyers who now do equity!", the point being that, in a case in which the Court of Appeal had by majority granted an interlocutory injunction, the dissenting member of the Court, STAMP, L.J., was the only judge who had come to the Court of Appeal from the Chancery Division.

[18] *United Scientific Holdings, Ltd.* v. *Burnley Borough Council*, [1978] A.C. 904; [1977] 2 All E.R. 62.

[19] [1978] A.C., at pp. 924–925; [1977] 2 All E.R., at p. 68.

[20] (1902), p. 23.

PART II

The Legal and Literary
Sources of English Law

The word "source" is used in various senses in relation to law. A *formal* source of law is that from which a system of law derives its validity, whether that be, for example, the general will or the will of a dictator; consideration of formal sources is a matter of jurisprudence rather than of the legal system and is thus outside the scope of the present work. The *historical* sources of English law have been examined. It remains to consider the *legal* and *literary* sources. The authority for any proposition of law is the legal source of that proposition; the legal sources have been defined as the gates through which new principles can find entrance into the law. Literary sources are simply the materials in which the legal sources are recorded; every legal source has its corresponding literary source. The principal legal sources of English law are legislation and judicial precedents (though custom, which is treated in the present work as a purely historical source, is regarded by some as a legal source). The corresponding literary sources are, with respect to legislation, the various publications of statutes, notably the Queen's Printer's Copy, and, in the case of the law of the European Communities, the texts of the Treaties themselves and the Official Journal of the European Communities, and, with respect to precedents, law reports. Text books are an indirect literary source of all legal sources, though the old "books of authority" are a legal source in themselves.

CHAPTER 5

Legislation

A THE FUNCTIONS OF LEGISLATION

The broad function of all legislation is to create, alter or revoke law to give effect to the intention of the legislative body. Subordinate legislation fulfils various specific functions, scarcely capable of classification. The functions of Acts of Parliament, by far the most important form of legislation, may be classified as follows.

1 Revision of substantive rules of law

Although all statutes are concerned with law revision in the broadest sense relatively few statutes are concerned with altering or revising substantive rules of law or "lawyers' law" as it is sometimes called. Such statutes are frequently passed when the law, through the restrictive operation of the doctrine of judicial precedent, has become stale and incapable of adaptation. The need for reform often manifests itself in a House of Lords decision. Where a decision of the House of Lords is unpopular the law is usually altered by statute. There are many examples on the statute book of Acts passed with the apparent intention of overruling the effect of a House of Lords decision.[1] When a more general reform of the law is required the initiative frequently comes from lawyers. Until 1965 the machinery for generating law reform was conspicuously erratic in its operation, consisting mainly of the Law Revision Committee and, subsequently, the Law Reform Committee which considered, on their own initiative or at the invitation of the Lord Chancellor, branches of the law requiring reform and then published reports containing recommendations. The Committees consisted of practising lawyers who met from time to time, when pressure of other work permitted. Their recommendations often, but by no means always, were subsequently taken up by Parliament. Where the question was of wider

---

[1] Examples are: Parliamentary Papers Act 1840; Limitation Act 1963; Trade Disputes Act 1965; War Damage Act 1965; Criminal Evidence Act 1979 (see p. 679, *post*). The apparent intention of these Acts is to reverse House of Lords decisions immediately preceding them though Acts of Parliament do not expressly name cases which they are obviously intended to overrule.

public importance, heads of government departments might refer the question to a special committee for report or the Crown might set up a Royal Commission. A modern example of law reform based on the recommendations of a Royal Commission is the Courts Act 1971 which follows basically the recommendations of the so-called "Beeching Commission".[2]

However a major addition to the machinery of law reform was made by the Law Commissions Act 1965 which established the Law Commissions. Section 3(1) of the Act defines the duty of the Commissions (there is a separate Commission for Scotland) thus:

> "It shall be the duty of each of the Commissions to take and keep under review all the law with which they are respectively concerned with a view to its systematic development and reform, including in particular the codification of such law, the elimination of anomalies, the repeal of obsolete and unnecessary enactments, the reduction of the number of separate enactments and generally the simplification and modernisation of the law."

The creation of the Law Commission has been universally acknowledged as an important step forward in law reform, for which the former Lord Chancellor, Lord Gardiner, must take most of the credit. The Commissions, by reason of the appointment of full-time Commissioners of the highest calibre and of full-time administrative staff, have been able to produce a steady flow of reports, recommendations and draft Bills, most of which have been implemented by Act of Parliament within a relatively short time. Thus, for example, out of 76 Public Acts which received the Royal Assent in 1971, no fewer than 11 were based wholly or in part on recommendations of the Law Commission.[3]

2   Consolidation of enactments

Where a branch of the law has evolved piecemeal, a consolidating statute may be passed, for the purpose of clarification, containing substantially the existing law in a consolidated form. There are three sorts of consolidating Acts: (1) "pure" consolidation (simple re-enactment); (2) consolidation under the Consolidation of Enactments (Procedure) Act 1949, which allows "corrections and minor improvements";[4] (3) consolidation with amendments recommended by the Law Commission, under a procedure adopted by Parliament since 1965. Consolidation Acts are not subject to parliamentary debate, but there are special procedures designed to ensure that the bill, when enacted, does not depart from the pre-existing statutory provisions which are

---

[2]   *Report of the Royal Commission on Assizes and Quarter Sessions*; Cmnd. 4153 (1969).
[3]   These were the Vehicles (Excise) Act, the Animals Act, the Coinage Act, the Administration of Estates Act, the National Savings Bank Act, the Law Reform (Miscellaneous Provisions) Act, the Nullity of Marriage Act, the Criminal Damage Act, the Statute Law (Repeals) Act, the Recognition of Divorces and Legal Separations Act and the Law Reform (Jurisdiction in Delict) (Scotland) Act.
[4]   These are defined by s. 2 of the 1949 Act as "amendments of which the effect is confined to resolving ambiguities, removing doubts, bringing obsolete provisions into conformity with modern practice or removing unnecessary provisions or anomalies which are not of substantial importance, and amendments designed to facilitate improvement in the form or manner in which the law is stated, and includes any transitional provisions which may be necessary in consequence of such amendments".

to be consolidated.[5] The type of consolidation effected appears from the long title of the Act in question which will, in the case of pure consolidation, be in the form "An Act to consolidate . . . " while, in the case of consolidation with amendments under the 1949 procedure or with "Law Commission" amendments the long title will refer to the 1949 Act or to the Law Commission as the case may be.[6]

There are many who believe that the process of consolidation should be taken to the point of producing a consolidated statute book, similar to that which exists in many other countries, in which the whole of our statute law would be arranged under titles and kept up to date by textual amendment. However desirable this might be it is clear that it is not a reform which is likely to be implemented in the foreseeable future. In May 1973 the government set up a departmental committee under the chairmanship of Sir David Renton to review the form in which public Bills are drafted "with a view to achieving greater simplicity and clarity in statute law". The Renton Committee reported in 1975[7] and concluded that "it would not be practicable to consolidate the whole statute book within a limited number of years, nor to do so on the principle of 'one Act, one subject'." Although the Committee made some 87 separate recommendations, notably that the preparation of a comprehensive new Interpretation Act should be put in hand, little if any radical change in the law was recommended and, although there was an Interpretation Act passed in 1978, this was only a consolidating Act, with Law Commission amendments, and it is difficult to envisage any sweeping reforms in the foreseeable future.

3 Codification

Codification differs from consolidation in that an Act may only be said to consolidate statute law, whereas it may codify both case law and statute law. Nevertheless codification is similar in function to consolidation in that in both cases the object of the statute is to simplify and clarify the existing law rather than to effect substantial alterations to it. Notable examples of codifying statutes are the Offences against the Person Act 1861 and the Sale of Goods Act 1893.

There is, in many areas of the law, a pressing need for codification. This is due to the manner in which Parliament approaches the task of amendment of statutes. Rather than produce a comprehensive re-enactment which would enable the relevant law on a topic to be clearly set out in a single statute, it is the practice simply to amend piecemeal by sections tucked away in a statute which may deal with a large number of different topics and amend an equally large number of earlier statutes. Subsequently the amending provision may itself be repealed or re-amended with the result that, in order to discover

---

5 For an explanation of this, and of the significance of the consolidating procedures in the context of construction of statutes, see the speech of Lord Simon in *Farrell* v. *Alexander*, [1977] A.C. 59, at pp. 82–85; [1976] 2 All E.R. 721, at pp. 733–736.

6 See, for examples, Employment Protection (Consolidation) Act 1978 (pure consolidation); Rent Act 1977 (Law Commission amendments); Juries Act 1974 (1949 Act "corrections and improvements").

7 *The Preparation of Legislation*: Cmnd. 6053 (1975).

what the law is, it is necessary to pick one's way through a maze of separate statutory provisions.

This situation, in the field of industrial relations legislation, led to the following trenchant remarks by SIR JOHN DONALDSON, M.R. in a recent case:[8]

> "My plea is that Parliament, when legislating in respect of circumstances which directly affect the 'man or woman in the street' or the 'man or woman on the shop floor', should give as high a priority to clarity and simplicity of expression as to refinements of policy. Where possible statutes, or complete parts of statutes, should not be amended but re-enacted in an amended form so that those concerned can read the rules in a single document. When formulating policy, ministers, of whatever political persuasion, should at all times be asking themselves and asking parliamentary counsel: 'Is this concept too refined to be capable of expression in basic English? If so, is there some way in which we can modify the policy so that it can be so expressed?' Having to ask such questions would no doubt be frustrating for ministers and the legislature generally, but in my judgment this is part of the price which has to be paid if the rule of law is to be maintained."

These remarks were expressly adopted by LORD DIPLOCK when the case reached the House of Lords.[9] What (if any) fruit they bear remains to be seen.

4   Collection of revenue

The annual Finance Act implementing the Budget proposals is concerned primarily with the collection of revenue by the Crown. Other Acts, notably the Income and Corporation Taxes Act 1970, fulfil the same function. Possibly on account of the considerable energies expended on the task of tax avoidance these statutes tend to promote rather more litigation than the average statute, including numerous "test cases" in which the Inland Revenue is concerned to discover whether the drafting of a measure has achieved the desired effect.

5   Implementation of treaties

The United Kingdom, by entering into treaties, undertakes to implement the laws which form the subject matter of the treaty. We have already noted that directives and decisions of the Council and Commission of the E.E.C. usually require implementation either by statute or statutory instrument[10] and that, arising out of its subscription to the European Convention on Human Rights, the United Kingdom has a duty to legislate so as to enforce decisions of the European Court of Human Rights.[11] With a view to standardising or harmonising branches of the law with an international element, the United Kingdom subscribes to specific treaties or conventions, following

---

[8] *Merkur Island Shipping Corporation.* v. *Laughton*, [1983] 2 A.C. 570, at pp. 594–595; [1983] 1 All E.R. 334, at p. 351.
[9] [1983] 2 A.C., at p. 612; [1983] 2 All E.R. 189, at pp. 198–9.
[10] See p. 60, *ante*.
[11] See p. 64, *ante*.

which they are implemented by domestic legislation. Recent examples of such legislation are the Civil Jurisdiction and Judgments Act 1982, the Taking of Hostages Act 1982, the International Transport Conventions Act 1983 and the Data Protection Act 1984.

6 Social legislation

The law student, faced with a list of the Acts of Parliament passed in any single year, will probably feel that most of them do not concern him at all and will regard them as of secondary importance. These Acts are varied in their scope and functions but may be classified together as social legislation. Such Acts are concerned with regulating the day to day running of the social system rather than with creating criminal offences or rights and duties between individuals. There is an increasing tendency for Parliament to delegate to subordinate bodies the power to make regulations of this nature. It is, of course, wrong to suppose that social legislation is of no interest to the lawyer. When legislation attempts to strike a balance between competing social priorities there is an inevitable tendency towards dispute and, as a result, litigation. An obvious modern example is legislation concerning landlord and tenant. Population increases, immigration and the centralisation of industry have resulted in housing becoming a major social problem. Acts passed as a result, such as the Landlord and Tenant Acts and the Rent Acts, have become the subject of a huge volume of litigation over their interpretation.

B FORMS OF LEGISLATION

Early legislation in England took several different forms, such as charters, provisions, ordinances and statutes. At the present day, however, there are only three different forms which United Kingdom legislation may take: Acts of Parliament, delegated legislation and autonomic legislation. There are, in addition, the various forms of European legislation and these are considered at the end of this chapter.

1 Acts of Parliament

Subject to compliance with the overriding legislation of the European Communities, discussed below, Parliament is recognised as sovereign and as possessing unlimited legislative power. This has not always been so[12] but in modern times it had not, until recently, been seriously contended that the courts have any power to override the intention of the legislature. However in *British Railways Board* v. *Pickin*[13] an attempt was made to impugn the validity of a private Act of Parliament, the British Railways Act 1968, on the ground that, in obtaining the enactment of part of the Act, the British Railways Board had fraudulently concealed certain matters from Parliament

---

[12] See, for example, dicta of COKE, C.J. in *Bonham's Case* (1609), 8 Co. Rep. 113b and of HOLT, C.J. in *City of London* v. *Wood* (1701), 12 Mod. Rep. 669.
[13] [1974] A.C. 765; [1974] 1 All E.R. 609.

and thereby misled Parliament into an enactment which operated to deprive the plaintiff of his land or proprietary rights. If it was surprising that such a point should be pleaded it was, perhaps, more surprising that the Court of Appeal should have held that it raised a triable issue.[14] The House of Lords, however, allowed the Board's appeal and restored the judge's order that the pleading be struck out as being frivolous, vexatious and an abuse of the process of the court.[15] Accordingly, it is now clear that no court is entitled to go behind that which Parliament has enacted and that this rule is equally applicable to public and private Acts. The procedure[16] is, briefly, that a Bill is drafted by Parliamentary draftsmen under supervision, generally, of a minister of the Crown. The Bill is then introduced in either the House of Commons or the House of Lords by a member of Parliament. If it passes through all its stages within the Parliamentary session it receives the Royal Assent and becomes an Act of Parliament. The contents of the Act are set out in various publications, though references to present day Acts are to the Queen's Printer's Copy published by Her Majesty's Stationery Office and on sale there to the general public. The Stationery Office publishes these copies in annual volumes and also publishes annually an Index to the Statutes in Force, for reference purposes. In addition the Incorporated Council of Law Reporting publishes annually the texts of Acts taken from the Queen's Printer's Copies.

The mode of citation of statutes has undergone change. Early statutes were cited by the name of the place where Parliament met.[17] Subsequently statutes were cited by reference to their regnal year and chapter. Thus, for example, the Criminal Justice Act 1948 would be cited as 11 & 12 *Geo.* 6, *c.* 58 indicating that the Act was the fifty-eighth passed in the Parliamentary session extending over the eleventh and twelfth years of the reign of George VI. This exceedingly cumbersome method of citation was not abolished until 1962.[18] Although Acts still have chapter numbers (a legacy of the fiction that only one Act was passed in a Parliamentary session), reference is now to the calendar year rather than to the regnal year. In practice Acts are commonly cited by reference to their short title, and this is permissible by section 2 of the Short Titles Act 1896. Many Acts passed prior to 1896 have been endowed with short titles retrospectively and Acts passed since that date contain a section conferring upon themselves a short title.

2   Delegated legislation

"Delegated legislation" is the description given to the vast body of rules, orders, regulations and bye-laws created by subordinate bodies under specific powers delegated to those bodies by Parliament. The advantage of delegated legislation is that it enables regulations to be made and altered

---

14 The decision of the Court of Appeal is reported at [1973] Q.B. 219; [1972] 3 All E.R. 923. For a further unsuccessful attempt to have an Act of Parliament declared *ultra vires* (in this case the Canada Act 1982 at the suit of 124 Canadian Indian Chiefs) see *Manuel* v. *A.-G.,* [1983] Ch. 77; [1982] 3 All E.R. 822.

15 Under R.S.C., O. 18, r. 19; see p. 344, *post* for details of this procedure.

16 Details of Parliamentary procedure will be found in works on constitutional law.

17 E.g., Statute of Gloucester 1278; Provisions of Oxford 1258.

18 Acts of Parliament Numbering and Citation Act 1962 (10 & 11 Eliz. 2, c. 34).

quickly without the need, usually, for placing them before Parliament. The vital feature which distinguishes Parliament from any other person or body having legislative power is that the latter is not sovereign. Delegated legislation is valid only if it is within the legislative powers conferred by Parliament (*intra vires*). If it is not it is said to be *ultra vires* and is, in that event, inoperative. Thus, for example, the Rules of the Supreme Court are delegated legislation, being passed by a Rule Committee under powers conferred by the Supreme Court Act 1981.[19] The power conferred upon the Committee is limited to creating rules of procedure. Consequently, if any Rule of the Supreme Court has the characteristic of a rule of substantive law rather than a rule of procedure it is ineffective.[20] However, unless and until declared *ultra vires* by a final judgment in an action in the courts, a statutory instrument must be treated as part of the law and enforced accordingly.[1] Delegated legislation which is concerned solely with implementing the detail of a general policy contained in an Act of Parliament is useful and unexceptionable. However, the powers delegated are frequently defined in the widest terms with the effect of conferring a legislative function on some body almost equivalent to that of Parliament itself.[2] This power is always, of course, subject to control by Parliament but, where the legislative power is conferred upon a Minister of the Crown, this may not be an effective control.[3]

The highest form of delegated legislation is Order in Council which is nominally an order of the Privy Council consisting of the Sovereign and Privy Councillors. Many Acts are brought into operation by Order in Council, the power to make the Order being contained in the Act itself.[4] In fact, though not in theory, an Order in Council is generally made by the Government and merely sanctioned by the Privy Council. The effect, therefore, is to confer wide legislative power upon Government departments.[5]

---

[19] S. 84; the current Rules were made under powers conferred by the now repealed Judicature Act 1925, s. 99.

[20] See *Re Grosvenor Hotel, London (No. 2)*, [1965] Ch. 1210; [1964] 3 All E.R. 354; *Ward* v. *James*, [1966] 1 Q.B. 273; [1965] 1 All E.R. 563.

[1] Cf. *Hoffman-La Roche (F.) & Co. A.G.* v. *Secretary of State for Trade and Industry*, [1975] A.C. 295 at p. 329; [1974] 2 All E.R. 1128.

[2] The powers tend to be very widely defined in time of war. See, for example, the extraordinarily wide powers to make Defence Regulations conferred by the Supplies and Services (Transitional Powers) Act 1945 and the Supplies and Services (Extended Purposes) Act 1947, cited in *Law in the Making*, by C.K. Allen (7th Edn.), pp. 540 *et seq.*

[3] *Liversidge* v. *Anderson*, [1942] A.C. 206; [1941] 3 All E.R. 338; see also *Kruse* v. *Johnson*, [1898] 2 Q.B. 91; *Buck* v. *A.-G.*, [1965] Ch. 745; [1964] 2 All E.R. 663.

[4] An Act may be brought into force by Order in Council even though the power to make the Order derives from the Act itself: Interpretation Act 1978, s. 13.

[5] In this context attention may be drawn to section 2(2) of the European Communities Act 1972 which provides that:

"Subject to Schedule 2 to this Act, at any time after its passing Her Majesty may by Order in Council, and any designated Minister or department may by regulations, make provision—

(*a*) for the purpose of implementing any community obligation of the United Kingdom, or enabling any such obligation to be implemented, or of enabling any rights enjoyed or to be enjoyed by the United Kingdom under or by virtue of the Treaties to be exercised; or

(*b*) for the purpose of dealing with matters arising out of or related to any such obligation or rights or the coming into force, or the operation from time to time, of subsection (1) above;

and in the exercise of any statutory power of duty, including any power to give directions or to legislate by means of orders, rules, regulations or other subordinate instrument, the person

Orders in Council and certain other Regulations are published in Statutory Instruments[6] (formerly Statutory Rules and Orders) by the Queen's Printer and available at Her Majesty's Stationery Office. They are cited by calendar year and number (for example: *S.I.* 1959, *No.* 64) and, often, by a short title.

3   Autonomic legislation

This differs from delegated legislation in that an autonomous body has an independent power to legislate for its own members and, in some cases, for members of the general public. Though this power is usually conferred by Parliament this is not always so. The power is in all cases, however, sanctioned by Parliament. Examples of autonomous legislative bodies are public undertakings such as transport and gas authorities whose bye-laws affect the public at large. The Church of England, the General Medical Council, The Law Society, trade unions and even limited companies are autonomous in the sense that they have power to control their own internal structure and to legislate for their members. It is arguable that such legislation does not affect the public but it does in a negative sense in that any individual who causes a breach of the regulations created by an autonomous body may commit a civil wrong.

In almost all cases autonomic legislation is confined in its extent by an Act of Parliament in which event it is subject to the doctrine of *ultra vires*. An important exception, however, is constituted by the prerogative jurisdiction of the Privy Council. This jurisdiction is principally concerned with legislating by Order in Council for Crown Colonies. The power is subject to the ordinary rules of English law though not to the doctrine of *ultra vires*.[7] It will thus be apparent that Orders in Council may be passed either under powers conferred by individual Acts or under a general prerogative power independent of statute. Both of these are subject to the law, although only the first is subject to the doctrine of *ultra vires*.[8]

Codes of Practice—Before leaving the topic of forms of legislation, it is necessary to refer to Codes of Practice, which are of increasing significance in certain legislative contexts. The most important of these, in practice, are the codes issued by the Advisory, Conciliation and Arbitration Service

---

entrusted with the power or duty may have regard to the objects of the Communities and to any such obligation or rights as aforesaid.''

The above provision has been widely criticised on the ground that it confers legislative power which is so extensive that it ought properly to be exercised only by Parliament directly. Schedule 2 of the Act does, in fact, limit the powers somewhat in that it excludes power to make any provision imposing or increasing taxation, to make any retrospective provision or to create any new criminal offence punishable with imprisonment for more than two years or punishable on summary conviction with imprisonment for more than three months or with a fine of more than £400 (or £5 a day if calculated on a daily basis).

6   Statutory Instruments Act 1946. Statutes conferring subordinate legislative powers frequently, though not always, provide that the Statutory Instrument made thereunder shall be laid before Parliament. In this event a copy of the Instrument must be so laid before it comes into operation: Statutory Instruments Act 1946, s. 4. The effect of laying the Instrument before Parliament varies. In some cases the Instrument does not take effect until expressly approved by resolution while in others it takes effect immediately subject to cancellation by negative resolution within forty ''sitting'' days.

7   *The Zamora*, [1916] 2 A.C. 77 (P.C.).

8   See *Buck* v. *A.-G.*, [1965] Ch. 745; [1964] 2 All E.R. 663.

("ACAS") under section 6 of the Employment Protection Act 1975. ACAS may issue Codes of Practice containing "such practical guidance as the Service thinks fit for the purpose of promoting the improvement of industrial relations".[9] Provision for codes of this type was first made by the Industrial Relations Act 1971 and the first such code, the Code of Practice on Disciplinary Practice and Procedures in Employment, has been of immense importance, particularly in unfair dismissal cases, where the tribunals and courts have developed principles of "procedural unfairness", whereby a dismissal, although not substantially unfair, may be held unfair because of failure on the part of the employer to adopt a fair procedure, in accordance with the Code of Practice, prior to dismissal, for example by failure to carry out a proper investigation of allegations against an employee or failure to give an employee an opportunity to state his case. As VISCOUNT DILHORNE observed in a recent unfair dismissal case.[10]

> "It does not follow that non-compliance with the Code necessarily renders a dismissal unfair, but I agree with the view expressed by Sir JOHN DONALDSON, P. in *Earl* v. *Slater and Wheeler (Airlyne), Ltd.*[11] that a failure to follow a procedure prescribed in the Code may lead to the conclusion that a dismissal was unfair, which, if that procedure had been followed, would have been held to have been fair."

Whether Codes of Practice promulgated pursuant to Acts of Parliament are classifiable as "legislation" is a moot point. In one sense they have the characteristic of delegated legislation in that the power to issue the code is conferred by statute upon a specified body and, presumably, a Code of Practice could be declared *ultra vires*. On the other hand a Code of Practice does not, by its very nature, have the force of law. That is not to say that it does not have legal effect. Codes issued under the 1975 Act are admissible in any proceedings before an industrial tribunal or the Central Arbitration Committee.[12] Codes of Practice approved or issued by the Health and Safety Commission under section 16 of the Health and Safety at Work etc. Act 1974 have even greater force in that, in criminal proceedings under the Act, not only is the relevant Code admissible in evidence, but failure to comply with the Code amounts to *prima facie* proof of contravention of the provisions of the Act to which the Code relates.[13] Reference may also be made to the Highway Code, first issued pursuant to the Road Traffic Act 1930, failure to comply with the provisions of which is not, in itself, an offence but may be relied upon by any party in either civil or criminal proceedings.[14]

C THE OPERATION OF STATUTES

In defining the scope of a statute it is necessary to advert both to its geographical area of operation and to the time during which it is operative.

---

[9] Employment Protection Act 1975, s. 6(1).
[10] *W. Devis & Sons, Ltd.* v. *Atkins*, [1977] A.C. 931, at p. 955; [1977] 3 All E.R. 40, at p. 49.
[11] [1973] 1 All E.R. 145; [1973] 1 W.L.R. 51.
[12] Employment Protection Act 1975, s. 6(11); see p. 221, *post*.
[13] Health and Safety at Work etc. Act 1974, s. 17(2).
[14] Road Traffic Act 1972, s. 37(5).

1   Geographical operation

There is a presumption that an Act of Parliament is operative throughout the United Kingdom[15] but not elsewhere unless in either case a contrary intention appears in the Act itself. The contrary intention may either limit or extend the geographical operation of the Act. Thus Acts frequently contain a section restricting their operation to exclude Scotland or Northern Ireland. The Limitation Act 1963, for example, was in three parts: Part I applying to England and Wales, Part II to Scotland and Part III to Northern Ireland. A similar reduction in the geographical operation of legislation occurs in the case of Acts which are expressed to apply only to a limited locality; such Acts are described as "local Acts". An Act may be partly local and partly general. For example, sections 83 and 86 of the Fires Prevention (Metropolis) Act 1774 were held to be applicable throughout the United Kingdom although the operation of the Act as a whole was confined to the London area.

Conversely an Act may expressly or by necessary implication extend outside the United Kingdom, though there is a presumption against this.[16] For example, section 57 of the Offences against the Person Act 1861 provides that the crime of bigamy is committed "whether the second marriage shall have taken place in England or Ireland, *or elsewhere.*" An Act which does have extraterritorial operation is, however, generally limited to apply only to British subjects or persons owing allegiance to the Crown.[17]

2   Temporal operation

a   When a statute begins to be operative

Until 1793[18] a statute came into force on the first day of the Parliamentary session in which it was passed. Consequently virtually all legislation was retrospective. The present law is that a statute comes into force on the day on

---

[15] Since it lies within the prerogative power of the Crown to extend its sovereignty and jurisdiction to areas of land or sea over which it has not previously asserted sovereignty or jurisdiction, the words "United Kingdom" incorporate such area of land or sea as may from time to time be formally declared by the Crown to be subject to its sovereignty and jurisdiction as part of the United Kingdom: see *Post Office* v. *Estuary Radio, Ltd.*, [1968] 2 Q.B. 740, at p. 748; [1967] 3 All E.R. 663, at p. 680, *per* DIPLOCK, L.J. (as he then was).

[16] The presumption is particularly strong in criminal cases; see *Cox* v. *Army Council*, [1963] A.C. 48; [1962] 1 All E.R. 880; *Air-India* v. *Wiggins*, [1980] 2 All E.R. 593; [1980] 1 W.L.R. 815.

[17] *Joyce* v. *Director of Public Prosecutions*, [1946] A.C. 347; [1946] 1 All E.R. 186; but cf. Internationally Protected Persons Act 1978, under which attacks upon the person or property of "protected persons" (such as heads of state and their families) are offences justiciable in the United Kingdom, even though committed outside the United Kingdom by a person "whether a citizen of the United Kingdom and Colonies or not" (s. 1); there are similar provisions in the Suppression of Terrorism Act 1978, s. 4 in relation to certain offences specified in Sch. 1 to that Act (e.g. murder, manslaughter, kidnapping and various offences under the Offences Against the Person Act 1861) when committed in countries who subscribed to the European Convention on the Suppression of Terrorism 1977, and in the Taking of Hostages Act 1982. See also the Protection of Trading Interests Act 1980 under which the Secretary of State for Trade is given powers to make orders prohibiting compliance with the laws of overseas countries where they may be damaging to the trading interests of the United Kingdom.

[18] Acts of Parliament (Commencement) Act.

which it receives the Royal Assent, unless some other date is specified in the Act itself. Frequently some future date will be specified to enable persons affected by the Act to prepare for its operation. Thus the Highways (Miscellaneous Provisions) Act 1961 came into operation on August 3, 1964, the delay being for the purpose of enabling highway authorities, upon whom a new duty to maintain highways was imposed, to effect such repairs as were necessary to comply with the stringent provisions of the Act. Alternatively an Act may provide that it is to come into force on a "day to be appointed". The day is appointed by Order in Council unless the Act provides for appointment by a Minister. In either case the appointed day is published in a Statutory Instrument. The disadvantage of this practice is that it is slightly more difficult to determine when the Act is coming into force and it is necessary to consult the calender of appointed days. Different parts of an Act or sections in an Act may be brought into force at different times and it appears that there are portions of Acts in existence which have never been brought into force.[19]

The effect of a statute coming into operation is that, if it is a Public Act, and every Act passed since 1850 is presumed to be a Public Act in the absence of a contrary provision, it immediately becomes effective and the courts take judicial notice of it.[20]

Delegated legislation generally comes into force when it is passed but section 3(2) of the Statutory Instruments Act 1946 provides that where a person is charged with contravening the provisions of a Statutory Instrument it shall be a defence to prove that the Instrument had not been issued by Her Majesty's Stationery Office at the date of the alleged contravention, unless it is proved that at that date reasonable steps had been taken for the purpose of bringing the purport of the Instrument to the notice of the public, or of persons likely to be affected by it, or of the person charged.[1]

Retrospective operation. As a general rule a statute only affects factual situations which arise during the period of its operation. There is a presumption against the statute being retroactive. This presumption is particularly strong where the statute in question creates criminal penalties or tax obligations or would operate to deprive a person of a vested right in property.[2] However, Parliament is sovereign and statutes may be, and occasionally are, expressed to be retroactive even where this operates to deprive a person of a vested right in property. A modern illustration was the controversial War Damage Act 1965 which operated to remove vested rights to compensation from the Crown and which was exceptional in that it was also expressed to

---

[19] A notable example of this is the Children and Young Persons Act 1969, parts of which, notably ss. 4 and 5, have yet to be brought into operation (see p. 208, *post*); cf. *R.* v. *Kynaston* (1927), 19 Cr. App. Rep. 180.

[20] Interpretation Act 1978, s. 3.

[1] See *R.* v. *Sheer Metalcraft, Ltd.*, [1954] 1 Q.B. 586; [1954] 1 All E.R. 542.

[2] *Yew Bon Tew* v. *Kenderaan Bas Mara*, [1983] 1 A.C. 553; [1982] 3 All E.R. 833. In *R.* v. *Fisher* [1969] 1 All E.R. 100; [1969] 1 W.L.R. 8 the rule against retrospective operation operated, for once, against the accused in that he was convicted of an offence which had, at the time of his trial, been abolished by statute since the conduct in question had been, at the time of commission, an offence; see also *R.* v. *West London Stipendiary Magistrate, Ex parte Simeon*, [1983] 1 A.C. 234; *sub. nom. Metropolitan Police Commissioner* v. *Simeon*, [1982] 2 All E.R. 813. But a retrospective statute may affect a pending action: *Zainal bin Hashim* v. *Government of Malaysia*, [1980] A.C. 734; [1979] 3 All E.R. 241.

apply to proceedings commenced before the Act came into force.[3] Also, statutes aimed at preventing tax avoidance are sometimes expressed to be retroactive and there seems to be no presumption against retroactivity in the case of statutes of this type.[4] An Act of indemnity, the purpose of which is to validate or legalise *ex post facto* that which was initially invalid or illegal, must by its nature be retroactive.[5] It seems that Parliament's intention to make a statute retroactive need not, in exceptional cases, be expressed provided the intention can be clearly implied from the statute read as a whole. Thus in *Williams* v. *Williams*[6] the new financial provisions of the Matrimonial Proceedings and Property Act 1970 were held to apply to a case in which the decree of divorce was granted before the 1970 Act came into force, notwithstanding that the changes in the law effected by the Act were clearly substantive rather than procedural and notwithstanding also the absence of any express provision making the 1970 Act provisions retroactive. A statute which alters rules of evidence or procedure rather than rules of substantive law is always retroactive, in the absence of a contrary intention, since the rules of evidence and procedure which a court is bound to observe are those in existence at the time of the hearing.[7]

Where a statute applies to a situation arising from a continuing state of affairs it is a moot point whether the statute may properly be said to be retrospective. Thus the provision in the Road Traffic Act 1962 which required a court to impose disqualification upon a driver who had two previous endorsements on his driving licence, was held to apply where the first of the accused's previous convictions occurred before the Act came into force.[8] This was not regarded by the court as a retrospective application of the statute in question.

b   When a statute ceases to be operative

No statute becomes obsolete by the passing of time. Nevertheless there are many ancient statutes more honoured in the breach than in the observance. In the past the approach of the legislature has generally been to do nothing until the need for repeal manifested itself. Thus the plaintiff in a nineteenth century case was no doubt disturbed to discover that his opponent had a right to claim trial by battle;[9] two cases in recent years have involved statutes of

---

3   Section 1(2). The action affected was *Burmah Oil Co., Ltd.* v. *Lord Advocate*, [1965] A.C. 75; [1964] 2 All E.R. 348.
4   See, for example, Finance Act 1936, s. 18; *Lord Howard de Walden* v. *Inland Revenue Commissioners*, [1942] 1 K.B. 389; [1942] 1 All E.R. 287.
5   Examples of Acts of indemnity are: Indemnity Act 1920; Indian Divorces (Validity) Act 1921; Charitable Trusts (Validation) Act 1954.
6   [1971] P. 271; [1971] 2 All E.R. 764.
7   See *Blyth* v. *Blyth*, [1966] A.C. 643; [1966] 1 All E.R. 524 (evidence); cf. *Yew Bon Tew* v. *Kenderaan Bas Mara*, [1983] 1 A.C. 553; [1982] 3 All E.R. 833 (limitation statute in Malaysia held not to revive statute-barred cause of action).
8   *Carter-Fea* v. *Graham* (1964), 62 L.G.R. 279. The "totting-up" procedure is now based on accumulation of penalty points rather than endorsements (Transport Act 1981, s. 19). A similar approach is adopted where the statute imposes increased penalties for offences committed before it came into force: *Director of Public Prosecutions* v. *Lamb*, [1941] 2 K.B. 89; [1941] 2 All E.R. 499.
9   *Ashford* v. *Thornton* (1818), 1 B. & Ald. 405.

1351 and 1381 respectively[10] while recent cases concerning the rights of "squatters" on other person's premises have involved consideration of the 1429 Statute of Forcible Entry.[11] As a final example of ancient legislation which is still utilitarian may be cited the Justices of the Peace Act 1361 under the provisions of which prosecutions are sometimes brought and persons bound over to keep the peace.[12]

There are indications at last, however, that the pragmatic approach to statute revision is gradually yielding to a systematic reform of legislation. The Law Commissions are expressly required to review "obsolete and unnecessary enactments" with a view to repeal.[13] Steps in this direction were taken by the passing of the Criminal Law Act 1967, Part II of which was devoted to the repeal of unnecessary and obsolete enactments, listed in Schedules 3 and 4 of the Act, the Statute Law (Repeals) Act 1969 which repealed numerous obsolete enactments, including the Sunday Observance Acts, the Law Reform (Miscellaneous Provisions) Act 1970 which abolished the anachronistic actions for breach of promise of marriage, damages for adultery, enticement and harbouring of a spouse and enticement, harbouring and seduction of a child, and further Statute Law (Repeals) Acts in 1971 and in most years since 1973 which have repealed many hundreds of obsolete statutory provisions in whole or in part. All of these recent Acts were passed following recommendations by the Law Commissions.

To the above rule that statutes do not become obsolete with the passing of time there is an exception. Certain statutes are expressed to be operative only for a limited period, usually because they are experimental or transitional though the best known statutes of this type, the Army Act and the Air Force Act are re-enacted periodically so as to avoid the prohibition on keeping a standing army in time of peace.[14] There have been notable recent examples of statutes containing the seeds of their own desuetude. Thus the Murder (Abolition of Death Penalty) Act 1965 was expressed to expire on the 31st July 1970 unless Parliament by affirmative resolution of both Houses otherwise determined (which it did in 1969). The Prevention of Terrorism (Temporary Provisions) Act 1984 requires annual renewal by order of the Home Secretary and ceases to have effect in 1989 in any event.[15] These temporary statutes may acquire a new lease of life by the passing of an Expiring Laws Continuance Act which is effected solely for the purpose of renewing statutes which would otherwise expire. Thus Part I of the Commonwealth Immigrants Act 1962, an experimental measure expressed

---

[10] *Hemmings* v. *Stoke Poges Golf Club, Ltd.*, [1920] 1 K.B. 720; *Joyce* v. *Director of Public Prosecutions*, [1946] A.C. 347; [1946] 1 All E.R. 186.
[11] *R.* v. *Robinson*, [1971] 1 Q.B. 156; [1970] 3 All E.R. 369; *R.* v. *Mountford*, [1972] 1 Q.B. 28; [1971] 2 All E.R. 81. This Act, in common with other ancient Statutes of Forcible Entry, was abolished by the Criminal Law Act 1977, s. 65 and Sch. 13.
[12] See *R.* v. *Aubrey-Fletcher, Ex parte Thompson*, [1969] 2 All E.R. 846; [1969] 1 W.L.R. 872.
[13] Law Commissions Act 1965, s. 3(1).
[14] Prior to 1955 this was done by means of annual Acts. However a new procedure was established by the Army Act 1955, s. 226 and the Air Force Act 1955, s. 224. Under this procedure the Acts are renewable annually by Order in Council, a new Act of Parliament being required only every five years.
[15] When a further Act will be passed should the situation in Northern Ireland not be resolved. The 1984 Act was passed to replace the Prevention of Terrorism (Temporary Provisions) Act 1976 which was renewable (and in fact renewed) annually.

to last for only one year, was renewed annually until 1971 when the Immigration Act 1971 was passed to supersede it.

Unless it is one of those which are expressed to be operative for a limited period a statute ceases to have effect only when repealed by another statute, since only Parliament is competent to repeal its own enactments.[16] Repeal may be express or implied. In modern times almost all repeal is express and it is common for a statute to include a schedule of repeals, expressly incorporated into the body of the Act, where there are several provisions repealed. Implied repeal is possible and occurs where two statutory provisions are inconsistent with one another. In this situation the later provision impliedly repeals the earlier to the extent of the inconsistency.[17] The courts, however, lean against implied repeal and will attempt to reconcile seemingly conflicting provisions wherever possible. In addition there is a rule that a public Act does not impliedly repeal a private or local Act (*generalia specialibus non derogant*).[18] Unless the contrary intention appears repeal does not have the effect of revivifying any earlier repealed rule of law, statutory[19] or otherwise.[20]

D   THE INTERPRETATION AND CONSTRUCTION OF STATUTES

1   The need for interpretation and construction

Where the words of a statute are clear and unambiguous persons affected by its provisions will regulate their conduct according to the terms of the statute and the need for judicial interpretation will not arise. However, if the meaning or extent of a statute is uncertain or ambiguous litigation is inevitable and the statute will fall to be interpreted. There is a technical distinction between interpretation and construction. "Interpretation" is simply the process whereby a meaning is assigned to the words in a statute. "Construction", on the other hand, is the process whereby uncertainties or ambiguities in a statute are resolved. It follows that every statute which comes before a court is interpreted whereas only uncertain or ambiguous provisions require construction. The processes are not usually distinguished by judges since, by the nature of things, litigation only arises around the wording of a statute where it is ambiguous or, at least, uncertain. However, LAWSON, J. clearly did distinguish the process of interpretation and construction in one case:[1]

---

[16] Unless the enactment is impliedly repealed by legislation of the European Communities: *Amministrazione Delle Finanze Dello Stato* v. *Simmenthal Sp A*, [1978] E.C.R. 629; see p. 62, *ante*.

[17] See, for example, *Smith* v. *Benabo*, [1937] 1 K.B. 518; [1937] 1 All E.R. 523; *Ellen Street Estates* v. *Minister of Health*, [1934] 1 K.B. 590; *Dryden* v. *Dryden*, [1973] Fam. 217; [1973] 3 All E.R. 526.

[18] Thus it was held in *Bishop of Gloucester* v. *Cunnington*, [1943] K.B. 101; [1943] 1 All E.R. 61, that the restrictions on the recovery of leasehold property imposed by the Rent and Mortgage Interest Restriction Acts 1920–1939 did not affect the right of a bishop to recover possession of a parsonage under the Pluralities Act 1838.

[19] Interpretation Act 1978, s. 15.

[20] *Ibid.*, s. 16(1).

[1] *Franklin* v. *A.-G.*, [1974] Q.B. 185, at p. 199; [1973] 1 All E.R. 879, at p. 886 (one of the cases arising out of the attempt by the plaintiff to proceed against the Crown by way of the ancient remedy of "petition of right"; see p. 303, *post*).

"I approach the answer to the question in two stages. Stage one is this: whether the meaning of the Cyprus Act 1960 in this respect is clear and unambiguous, and if so, what does it mean? At this stage I look at the words of the enactment as a whole, including the Schedule, and I use no further aids, no further extrinsic aids in order to reach a conclusion as to the clear and unambiguous meaning of the words . . . If I find that the answer on the first stage in my inquiry is that the meaning of the Act in this respect is ambiguous, then I have to go on to the second stage and consider two possible different meanings . . .

Now if I get to this second stage, then in my judgment, and then only, am I entitled to look at extrinsic aids,[2] such as the long title, the heading, the side notes, other legislation; then only am I entitled to resort to maxims of construction . . ."

a Ambiguity

Ambiguity arises through an error in drafting whereby words used in a statute are found to be capable of bearing two or more literal meanings. Language is an imprecise tool and even Parliamentary draftsmen, in using words intended to convey one meaning, occasionally contrive to give rise to an alternative meaning which neither they nor the legislature ever envisaged. Thus the Restriction of Offensive Weapons Act 1959 made it an offence to "offer for sale" certain offensive weapons including "flick knives". A shopkeeper who displayed weapons of this type in his window was held, by a divisional court, to be not guilty of an offence under the Act because, as every student of the law of contract knows, the exhibition of goods in a shop window does not constitute an offer.[3] Where the subject matter of a statute is a branch of the law which is intrinsically complex, such as landlord and tenant or income tax, it seems to be virtually impossible to choose language which is entirely free from ambiguity. Nevertheless the judiciary has on occasion been less than sympathetic to the draftsman's plight. Thus in *R. v. Royle*,[4] section 16 of the Theft Act 1968 was described as being so obscure as to have "created a judicial nightmare" while in *Central Asbestos Co., Ltd. v. Dodd*[5] LORD REID said of the Limitation Act 1963 that it had "a strong claim to the distinction of being the worst drafted Act on the statute book".[6]

---

2 The aids then referred to by LAWSON, J. are generally referred to as intrinsic (rather than extrinsic) aids since they appear in the text of the Queen's Printer's copy of the Act; see p. 116, *post*.

3 *Fisher* v. *Bell*, [1961] 1 Q.B. 394; [1960] 3 All E.R. 731; see also *Partridge* v. *Crittenden*, [1968] 2 All E.R. 421; [1968] 1 W.L.R. 1204.

4 [1971] 3 All E.R. 1359, at p. 1363; [1971] 1 W.L.R. 1764, at p. 1767, *per* EDMUND DAVIES, L.J. (as he then was); cf. *Director of Public Prosecutions* v. *Turner*, [1974] A.C. 357; [1973] 3 All E.R. 124 in which the House of Lords expressed its own dim view of the same section. The offending part of the section (s. 16(2)(a)) was eventually repealed and replaced by the Theft Act 1978.

5 [1973] A.C. 518, at p. 529; [1972] 2 All E.R. 1135, at p. 1138; the Limitation Act 1975 (replacing that part of the 1963 Act) seemed to aim at similar distinction. The Acts concerned are now consolidated in the Limitation Act 1980.

6 See also, *Great Western Rail. Co.* v. *Bater*, [1922] 2 A.C. 1, at p. 11; *Barentz* v. *Whiting*, [1965] 1 All E.R. 685; [1965] 1 W.L.R. 433; *London County Council* v. *Lees*, [1939] 1 All E.R. 191; *Davies* v. *Warwick*, [1943] K.B. 329; [1943] 1 All E.R. 309. For an enlightening insight into the draftsman's problems, and techniques for resolving them, see F. Bennion, "Legislative Technique", 129 New Law Journal, p. 748.

b   Uncertainty

Uncertainty is far more common than ambiguity. Uncertainty occurs where the words of a statute are intended to apply to various factual situations and the courts are called upon to decide whether or not the set of facts before them amounts to a factual situation envisaged by the Act. For example the words "an accident arising out of and in the course of his employment" in the Workmen's Compensation Acts were the source of innumerable cases, not because they were in any way ambiguous but because their scope was uncertain, being adaptable to endless permutations of facts.[7] The use of general, and ostensibly clearly defined, words such as "road",[8] "park",[9] "premises",[10] and "loudspeaker"[11] has created problems of construction which the legislature could not have envisaged, while, more recently, the courts have been called upon to resolve such conundrums as whether the cremation of humans is "the subjection of goods or materials to any process"[12] and whether an orange squeezed by hand is a "manufactured beverage".[13] LORD DENNING has expressed the difficulty as follows:[14]

> "It must be remembered that it is not within human powers to foresee the manifold sets of facts which may arise, and, even if it were, it is not possible to provide for them in terms free from all ambiguity."

The primary difficulty in such cases is that the words themselves are almost the only guide which may be used to the meaning which Parliament intended. The view is often expressed, even by members of the judiciary themselves,[15] that the legislature should publish a statement of its aims in relation to any particular Act.[16] In fact such statements often are published but, in interpreting and construing the Act in question, the judiciary for some reason diligently eschews them.[17]

2   Judicial approaches to interpretation

The basic task of the judge is to ascertain the intention of Parliament. Nevertheless there are alternative approaches to this task. These approaches,

---

[7] The words now appear in the Social Security Act 1975, s. 50 where they continue to cause trouble: see *R.* v. *National Insurance Commissioner, Ex parte Michael*, [1977] 2 All E.R. 420; [1977] 1 W.L.R. 109.

[8] *Griffin* v. *Squires*, [1958] 3 All E.R. 468; [1958] 1 W.L.R. 1106.

[9] *Re Ripon (Highfield) Housing Order, 1938*, [1939] 2 K.B. 838; [1939] 3 All E.R. 548.

[10] *Whitley* v. *Stumbles*, [1930] A.C. 544; *Maunsell* v. *Olins*, [1975] A.C. 373; [1975] 1 All E.R. 16.

[11] *Reynolds* v. *John*, [1956] 1 Q.B. 650; [1956] 1 All E.R. 306.

[12] *Bourne (Inspector of Taxes)* v. *Norwich Crematorium, Ltd.*, [1967] 2 All E.R. 567; [1967] 1 W.L.R. 691.

[13] *Customs and Excise Commissioners* v. *Savoy Hotel, Ltd.*, [1966] 2 All E.R. 299; [1966] 1 W.L.R. 948. For a delightfully sardonic exposition of the difficulty of ascertaining the "right" meaning of words, see the judgment of DIPLOCK, L.J. (as he then was) in *Slim* v. *Daily Telegraph, Ltd.*, [1968] 2 Q.B. 157, at pp. 171–172; [1968] 1 All E.R. 497, at p. 504.

[14] *Seaford Court Estates, Ltd.* v. *Asher*, [1949] 2 K.B. 481, at p. 499; [1949] 2 All E.R. 155, at p. 164 (affirmed [1951] A.C. 508; [1950] 1 All E.R. 1018).

[15] See, for example, observations of LORD DU PARCQ in *Cutler* v. *Wandsworth Stadium, Ltd. (in Liquidation)*, [1949] A.C. 398, at p. 410; [1949] 1 All E.R. 544, at p. 549.

[16] The long title frequently does this, but generally too briefly to be of real assistance: see p. 117, *post*.

[17] See *London County Council* v. *Central Land Board*, [1959] Ch. 386; [1958] 3 All E.R. 676.

which differ radically, are commonly known as the "literal" approach and the "purposive" approach. It is never possible to know in advance which approach any particular court will favour. Certain decisions have been based on one of these approaches, others on the application of another.

Each of these approaches to interpretation must be considered individually.[18]

a The literal approach

The basic approach to statutory interpretation, as already stated, is to ascertain the intention of the legislature. The literal rule of interpretation is that this intention must be found in the ordinary and natural meaning of the words used. If these words, interpreted literally, are capable of alternative meanings the literal rule clearly cannot be applied. Hence the approach breaks down in the face of an ambiguity. However, if the words are capable of only one literal meaning the literal rule is that this meaning must be applied even if it appears unlikely or absurd. The rule may be expressed as an irrebuttable presumption that Parliament intends the ordinary and natural meaning of the words it employs. The rule will, in most cases, produce a reasonable interpretation of the statute. However, in extreme cases where the statute has been carelessly drafted, the rule may produce a manifest absurdity. Thus in *Inland Revenue Commissioners* v. *Hinchy*[19] the House of Lords was called upon to construe section 25(3) of the Income Tax Act 1952 which provided that any person delivering an incorrect tax return should forfeit ". . . treble the tax which he ought to be charged under this Act". Although Parliament presumably intended[20] a penalty of treble the unpaid tax the House of Lords held that the literal meaning of the words of the subsection was that the respondent was liable to pay treble the whole amount of tax payable by him for the year. *Fisher* v. *Bell*, quoted earlier,[1] is a further example of the application of the literal rule producing a result which appeared contrary to the intention of the legislature.

Although there are numerous cases in which the literal rule has been applied strictly[2] there appears to be a modern judicial tendency to apply the purposive approach in cases where the literal rule would produce a perverse decision. This tendency is exemplified, characteristically, in the following words of LORD DENNING, M.R.:[3]

---

[18] As to the approach to the interpretation of legislation of the European Communities, see p. 128, *post*.

[19] [1960] A.C. 748; [1960] 1 All E.R. 505.

[20] The law was in fact changed shortly after this decision by the Finance Act 1960, s. 44.

[1] [1961] 1 Q.B. 394; [1960] 3 All E.R. 731; see p. 103, *ante*.

[2] See, for example: *Magor and St. Mellons Rural District Council* v. *Newport Corporation*, [1952] A.C. 189; [1951] 2 All E.R. 839; *Prince Ernest of Hanover* v. *A.-G.*, [1957] A.C. 88; [1957] 1 All E.R. 49; *Barclays Bank, Ltd.* v. *Cole*, [1967] 2 Q.B. 738; [1966] 3 All E.R. 948; *R.* v. *West Yorkshire Coroner, Ex parte Smith*, [1983] Q.B. 335; [1982] 3 All E.R. 1098; The Law Commission report, *The Interpretation of Statutes* (1969 Law Com. No. 21) recommended a statutory provision to the effect that "a construction which would promote the general legislative purpose underlying the provision in question is to be preferred to a construction which would not".

[3] *Corocraft* v. *Pan American Airways, Inc.*, [1969] 1 Q.B. 616, at p. 655; [1969] 1 All E.R. 82, at p. 88.

". . . the literal meaning of the words is never allowed to prevail where it would produce manifest absurdity or consequences which can never have been intended by the legislature."

The diversity of judicial approach is well illustrated by the speeches of the House of Lords in *Kammins Ballrooms Co., Ltd.* v. *Zenith Investments (Torquay), Ltd.*[4] The case turned on the interpretation of section 29(3) of the Landlord and Tenant Act 1954 which provides that "No application [for the grant of a new tenancy] shall be entertained unless it is made not less than two nor more than four months" after (*inter alia*) the tenant's request for a new tenancy. On the question of whether the court had power to consider an application made less than two months after the tenant's request, the House of Lords (VISCOUNT DILHORNE dissenting) held that the court did have such power, thereby appearing to disregard the clear words of the section for as VISCOUNT DILHORNE observed.[5]

"The appellants' contention here is that the words 'no application . . . shall be entertained' must be interpreted as meaning that an application shall in certain circumstances be entertained notwithstanding that it is made too early or too late. That seems to me to involve implying something wholly inconsistent with the words expressly used. True it is that English is a flexible language but that does not mean that one can disregard the natural and ordinary meaning of the words used unless it is apparent that some other meaning was intended.

If language is clear and explicit, the court must give effect to it 'for in that case the words of the statute speak the intention of the legislature' (*Warburton* v. *Loveland* (1832), 2 Dow. & Cl. 480, *per* TINDAL, C.J. at p. 489). 'And in so doing it must bear in mind that its function is *jus dicere*, not *jus dare*: the words of a statute must not be overruled by the judges, but reform of the law must be left in the hands of Parliament' (*Maxwell on Interpretation of Statutes*, 12th edn. (1969), p. 1)."

VISCOUNT DILHORNE was, however, a lone voice in support of this traditional approach. LORD REID acknowledged that.[6]

"If the words of an Act are so inflexible that they are incapable in any context of having but one meaning, then the court must apply that meaning, no matter how unreasonable the result—it cannot insert other words. But such cases are rare because the English language is a flexible tool."

LORD REID then went on to find, somewhat ingeniously, that the words were not, in fact, unambiguous, thus enabling him to reject the apparent literal meaning. LORD DIPLOCK, on the other hand, made no pretence of applying the literal rule and his speech typifies the trend away from rigid adherence to literal interpretation.[7]

"Upon the literal approach, semantics and the rules of syntax alone could never justify the conclusion that the words '*No application . . . shall* be entertained

---

4 [1971] A.C. 850; [1970] 2 All E.R. 871.
5 [1971] A.C. 850, at p. 869; [1970] 2 All E.R. 871, at p. 883.
6 [1971] A.C. 850, at p. 859; [1970] 2 All E.R. 871, at p. 874.
7 [1971] A.C. 850, at p. 880; [1970] 2 All E.R. 871, at p. 892. This approach was enthusiastically adopted by LORD DENNING, M.R. in *Nothman* v. *London Borough of Barnet*, [1978] 1 All E.R. 1243; [1978] 1 W.L.R. 220 but, although the House of Lords upheld the decision in that case, LORD RUSSELL expressly disclaimed what he called the "sweeping comments" of the Master of the Rolls ([1979] 1 All E.R. 142, at p. 151; [1979] 1 W.L.R. 67, at p. 77).

unless' meant that some applications should be entertained notwithstanding that neither of the conditions which follow the word 'unless' was fulfilled . . . It can be justified only upon the assumption that the draftsman of the Act omitted to state in any words he used in the subsection an exception to the absolute prohibition to which Parliament must have intended it to be subject.

A conclusion that an exception was intended by Parliament, and what that exception was can only be reached by using the purposive approach.''

However, it must not be supposed that the literal approach has fallen into desuetude. The House of Lords, differently constituted save for VISCOUNT DILHORNE, returned to the theme in *Stock* v. *Frank Jones (Tipton), Ltd.*[8] VISCOUNT DILHORNE, in defence of the literal approach, repeated substantially what he had said in the *Kammins Ballrooms Case.*[9] LORD SCARMAN also favoured the literal approach, save where "the consequences are so absurd that, without going outside the statute, one can see that Parliament must have made a drafting mistake".[10] LORD SIMON dealt with the rationale of the literal rule in considerably greater depth and, while favouring the literal approach, acknowledged that where this produced an anomaly a court would be justified in departing from the plain words, but only were it satisfied that:

"(1) there is clear and gross balance of anomaly; (2) Parliament, the legislative promoters and the draftsman could not have envisaged such anomaly and could not have been prepared to accept it in the interest of a supervening legislative objective; (3) the anomaly can be obviated without detriment to such legislative objective; (4) the language of the statute is susceptible of the modification required to obviate the anomaly.''[11]

b The purposive approach

The purposive approach to statutory interpretation, sometimes known as the "golden rule", is that words in a statute must be interpreted according to their natural, ordinary and grammatical meaning, so far as possible, but only to the extent that such an interpretation does not produce a manifestly absurd result. Perhaps the best known statement of the rule is to be found in the judgment of PARKE, B. in *Becke* v. *Smith:*[12]

"It is a very useful rule in the construction of a statute to adhere to the ordinary meaning of the words used, and to the grammatical construction, unless that is at variance with the intention of the legislature to be collected from the statute itself, or leads to any manifest absurdity or repugnance, in which case the

---

[8] [1978] 1 All E.R. 948; [1978] 1 W.L.R. 231.

[9] [1978] 1 All E.R., at pp. 951–952; [1978] 1 W.L.R., at pp. 234–235; LORD FRASER expressly agreed with VISCOUNT DILHORNE's speech.

[10] [1978] 1 All E.R., at p. 955; [1978] 1 W.L.R., at p. 239.

[11] [1978] 1 All E.R., at pp. 952–954; [1978] 1 W.L.R., at pp. 235–237; the whole of this speech repays study. Of the remaining law lords, LORD FRASER expressly agreed with VISCOUNT DILHORNE's speech, while LORD EDMUND-DAVIES, finding the statutory language clear, simply applied it.

[12] (1836), 2 M. & W., at p. 195. The statement of LORD WENSLEYDALE in *Grey* v. *Pearson* (1857), 6 H.L. Cas. 61, at p. 106, expressed in very similar terms, is also frequently cited as stating the rule; see, for example, *Lord Advocate* v. *de Rosa*, [1974] 2 All E.R. 849; [1974] 1 W.L.R. 946. See, also, *Vacher* v. *The London Society of Compositors*, [1913] A.C. 107.

language may be varied or modified so as to avoid such inconvenience, but no further.''

Where the statute permits of two or more literal interpretations the court must adopt that interpretation which produces the least absurd or repugnant result. This application of the golden rule is not, of course, inconsistent with the literal rule since the latter cannot be applied in a case of ambiguity. This is the narrow aspect of the golden rule and has been adopted in several well-known cases. Thus, for example, section 57 of the Offences against the Person Act 1861 provides that "Whosoever, being married, shall *marry* any other person during the life of the former husband or wife" shall be guilty of bigamy. The word *marry* permits of alternative meanings. It may be construed to mean *contracts a valid marriage* or *goes through a ceremony of marriage*. Since the former meaning would produce an absurd result, the latter must be applied.[13]

However, where the statute is capable of only one literal meaning and the court rejects that meaning in favour of a construction which is obviously more rational the golden rule is, in effect, being applied in preference to the literal rule. There have been relatively few cases in which this wide application of the golden rule has been adopted. Of the few cases in which this has been done perhaps the best known is *Re Sigsworth*[14] in which the golden rule was applied to prevent a murderer from taking on the intestacy of his victim although he was, as her son, the sole "issue" on a literal interpretation of the Administration of Estates Act 1925. More recently, in interpreting section 47 of the same Act, HARMAN, J. (as he then was) rejected a literal interpretation which he considered absurd in these words:[15]

"I take this course because I am convinced that Parliament, in laying down rules for ascertaining next-of-kin, cannot have intended to promote those more remote over those nearer in blood."

Similarly in the recent case of *Federal Steam Navigation Co., Ltd.* v. *Department of Trade and Industry*[16] the House of Lords, in interpreting a somewhat carelessly drafted provision in the Oil in Navigable Waters Act 1955, to the effect that "the owner *or* master of the ship" should be punishable in the case of discharge of oil, held (by a bare majority) that *both* the owner and master were liable to be prosecuted, on the basis that "or", in effect, meant "and"—an interpretation which (as the dissenting minority pointed out) involved flat rejection of the normal and grammatical exclusionary sense of the word used.[17]

A major criticism of the wide application of the golden rule in preference to the literal rule is that it is inherently subjective. The judge who decides that a literal interpretation is contrary to the intention of the legislature is, *ipso*

---

13 *R.* v. *Allen* (1872), L.R. 1 C.C.R. 367; see also *Young* v. *Clarey*, [1948] Ch. 191; [1948] 1 All E.R. 197; *Mills* v. *Cooper*, [1967] 2 Q.B. 459; [1967] 2 All E.R. 100.

14 [1935] Ch. 89.

15 *Re Lockwood*, [1958] Ch. 231, at p. 238; [1957] 3 All E.R. 520, at p. 524.

16 [1974] 2 All E.R. 97; [1974] 1 W.L.R. 505.

17 This would appear to be an example of a "drafting mistake", such as LORD SCARMAN envisaged, in *Stock* v. *Frank Jones (Tipton), Ltd.*, [1978] 1 All E.R. 948; [1978] 1 W.L.R. 231 (*supra*), would justify departure from the literal rule, and certainly a "clear and gross balance of anomaly" as envisaged by LORD SIMON in that case.

facto, ascertaining the intention of the legislature from some source or sources other than the statute itself, and this is, strictly, beyond his judicial function. Moreover he may expose himself to the criticism that he is giving effect to his own views as to what the policy of Parliament ought to be.[18]

Rejection of a literal interpretation on the ground of absurdity is, however, only possible where there is available a more rational interpretation of the provision under consideration. Thus if there is no other possible interpretation or only an alternative which is equally, or even more, absurd than the literal interpretation, the court has to adopt the latter.[19]

Supplying omissions.—An interesting problem of construction arises when the court is faced with a factual situation for which the statute has not provided. Such a situation is termed a *casus omissus*. It can only be remedied by attributing to Parliament an intention which Parliament never had. This amounts to a legislative act on the part of the judiciary and is a function which the more conservative judges are slow to adopt. Thus DENNING, L.J. (as he then was) explained, in the Court of Appeal, the judicial function in respect of omissions as follows:[20]

> "We sit here to find out the intention of Parliament and of Ministers and carry it out, and we do this better by filling in the gaps and making sense of the enactment than by opening it up to destructive analysis."

On appeal LORD SIMONDS roundly condemned this approach and, in a now famous dictum, described it as a "naked usurpation of the legislative function under the thin disguise of interpretation".[1] "If a gap is disclosed," LORD SIMONDS explained, "the remedy lies in an amending Act." Nonetheless it is a truism that hard cases make bad law and the courts have, from time to time, been prepared to assume the authority to supply omissions left by the legislature. An illustration of this is to be found in the majority decision of the House of Lords in *Edwards* v. *Porter*[2] where it was held that, although a husband "need not be joined" in an action against his wife, he could be joined if the plaintiff so wished. The Married Women's Property Act 1882, the Act in question, was silent on this point.[3]

---

[18] See *Duport Steels, Ltd.* v. *Sirs*, [1980] 1 All E.R. 529; [1980] 1 W.L.R. 142; *R.* v. *Barnet London Borough Council, Ex parte Shah*, [1983] 2 A.C. 309; (*sub nom. Shah* v. *Barnet London Borough Council*, [1983] 1 All E.R. 226) in both of which cases the House of Lords warned the judiciary against this pitfall; see p. 233, *post*.

[19] The House of Lords found itself in this unenviable position in *Metropolitan Police Commissioner* v. *Curran*, [1976] 1 All E.R. 162; [1976] 1 W.L.R. 87 and had to content itself with a unanimous and scathing attack on the draftsmanship of the provisions in question (s. 9(3) and Sch. 4 of the Road Traffic Act 1972).

[20] *Magor and St. Mellons Rural District Council* v. *Newport Corporation*, [1950] 2 All E.R. 1226 at p. 1236.

[1] [1952] A.C. 189, at p. 191; [1951] 2 All E.R. 839, at p. 841. In *James Buchanan & Co., Ltd.* v. *Babco Forwarding and Shipping (U.K.), Ltd.*, [1977] Q.B. 208; [1977] 1 All E.R. 518, LORD DENNING reiterated what he had said in *Magor and St. Mellons* in relation to a statute enacting an international convention (as to which, see p. 122, *post*) on the basis of the more liberal approach to statutory interpretation adopted by the European Court (see p. 128, *post*); but the House of Lords, once again, did not support his view ([1978] A.C. 141; [1977] 3 All E.R. 1048).

[2] [1925] A.C. 1.

[3] See also: *Astor* v. *Perry*, [1935] A.C. 398; *Re Radio Communications in Canada* (*Regulation and Control*), [1932] A.C. 304; *Chandris* v. *Isbrandtsen Moller Co., Inc.*, [1951] 1 K.B. 240; [1950] 1 All E.R. 768; *Wagg* v. *The Law Society*, [1957] Ch. 405; [1957] 2 All E.R. 274; *Williams* v. *Williams*, [1971] P. 271; [1971] 2 All E.R. 764 (see p. 100, *ante*).

Whichever approach to interpretation is adopted, the court is still bound to interpret the words of the Act before it. If interpretation discloses an uncertainty or ambiguity the court will then be bound to construe the statute. The judges themselves have formulated a large body of rules for the interpretation and construction of statutes. These rules, which equate approximately to the rules for the construction of documents generally, are exceedingly complex and only those most commonly encountered are discussed below, by way of example.

3 Rules of interpretation and construction

a The statute must be read as a whole

Words in isolation may import meanings different from that which they bear in conjunction.[4] A statute must be read as a whole. Every section must be read in the light of every other section, especially in the light of an interpretation section,[5] and schedules, if incorporated into the body of the Act, must be read with the Act.

An interesting illustration of this, and other rules of interpretation, is afforded by the decision of the House of Lords in the leading case of *Beswick* v. *Beswick*.[6] The case raised the question of whether Parliament had by section 56 of the Law of Property Act 1925 inadvertently abrogated the common law rule that a person cannot sue on a contract to which he is not a party. Section 56(1) provides that "A person may take an . . . interest in land or other property, or the benefit of any condition, right of entry, covenant or agreement over or respecting land or other property, although he may not be named as a party to the conveyance or other instrument. . . ." Section 205(1) of the 1925 Act, the interpretation section, provides that "In this Act *unless the context otherwise requires* . . . (xx) 'Property' includes any thing in action. . . ." It was argued that the combined effect of these provisions was to enable a stranger to a contract to enforce the contract. This argument prevailed in the Court of Appeal[7] but was rejected by the House of Lords. Their lordships pointed out that section 56 is one of 25 sections in the Act grouped under the heading "Conveyances and other instruments" and in those circumstances held that the context did require the word property to be limited in its effect to real property.

The long title and the short title, being part of the enactment, must, strictly, be consulted in interpreting any part of the Act though, in practice, the courts will only refer to the long title to resolve an ambiguity and do not regard the short title as an aid to interpretation at all.[8] Headings, marginal

---

4 See observations on the words "unfair competition" in *Lee* v. *Showmen's Guild of Great Britain*, [1952] 2 Q.B. 329, at p. 338; [1952] 1 All E.R. 1175, at p. 1178.

5 See p. 120, *post.*

6 [1968] A.C. 58; [1967] 2 All E.R. 1197; see also *Crook* v. *Edmondson*, [1966] 2 Q.B. 81; [1966] 1 All E.R. 833.

7 [1966] Ch. 538; [1966] 3 All E.R. 1. The Court of Appeal appear to have overlooked the vital words "unless the context otherwise requires" in s. 205(1). In the event the House of Lords was able to uphold the decision of the Court of Appeal by an ingenious use of the remedy of specific performance; see p. 53, *ante.*

8 See p. 118, *post.*

notes, punctuation and schedules which are not expressly incorporated into the text are not part of the enactment and are, accordingly, not aids to interpretation.

b The mischief rule

The "mischief rule", or rule in *Heydon's Case*, is that where a statute was passed to remedy a mischief the court will, if possible, adopt the interpretation of the statute which will have the effect of correcting the mischief in question. In *Heydon's Case*,[9] itself, the rule was defined thus:

> ". . . four things are to be discussed and considered: (1) what was the common law before the making of the Act; (2) what was the mischief and defect for which the common law did not provide; (3) what remedy the Parliament hath resolved and appointed to cure the disease of the commonwealth; and (4) the true reason of the remedy."

A more modern formulation is that of LORD DIPLOCK in *Jones* v. *Wrotham Park Settled Estates*, where he specified three conditions which must be satisfied before the rule can be applied:[10]

> (1) it must be possible to determine from consideration of the Act as a whole[11] precisely the mischief that it was the purpose of the Act to remedy;
> (2) it must be apparent that the draftsman and Parliament had inadvertently overlooked, and so omitted to deal with, the mischief;
> (3) it must be possible to state "with certainty"[12] what were the additional words that would have been inserted by the draftsman and approved by Parliament had the omission been drawn to their attention.

The rule is often used to resolve ambiguities in cases in which the literal rule cannot be applied. For example, a "single woman" for the purposes of affiliation proceedings is a woman with no husband to support her, not necessarily an unmarried woman, since the mischief which the Acts were passed to remedy is the possibility of a woman having an illegitimate child with no means of supporting it.[13]

In order to ascertain the mischief which the statute was passed to correct the judge may legitimately have regard to the preamble of the statute, the long title,[14] headings[15] and to extrinsic sources such as reports of Royal Commissions or Law Reform Committees which may indicate the state of the law before the passing of the Act.[16]

---

9 (1584), 3 Co. Rep. 7a.

10 [1980] A.C. 74, at 105; [1979] 1 All E.R. 286, at 289.

11 In fact, in a case of ambiguity the court may look to extrinsic aids (*infra*).

12 This cannot mean that the precise words that would have been used can be ascertained with total confidence, as the Court of Appeal pointed out in *Inland Revenue Commissioners* v. *Trustees of Sir John Aird's Settlement*, [1982] 2 All E.R. 929; [1982] 1 W.L.R. 270.

13 *Kruhlak* v. *Kruhlak*, [1958] 2 Q.B. 32; [1958] 1 All E.R. 154.

14 *Suffolk County Council* v. *Mason*, [1979] 2 All E.R. 369; [1979] 2 W.L.R. 571; see p. 119, *post*.

15 *Qualter, Hall & Co., Ltd.* v. *Board of Trade*, [1962] Ch. 273; [1961] 3 All E.R. 389.

16 See, generally, the full discussion of this topic by the House of Lords in *Black-Clawson International, Ltd.* v. *Papierwerke Waldhof-Aschaffenburgh A.G.*, [1975] A.C. 591; [1975] 1 All E.R. 810.

c   *The* eiusdem generis *rule*

This rule is but a particular aspect of the wider rule that the statute must be read as a whole. The rule is that general words which follow two or more particular words in an Act must be confined to a meaning of the same kind (*eiusdem generis*) as the particular words. It is common drafting practice, when the intention is to cover a wide range of similar circumstances, to use two or three particular examples to create a *genus* followed by a general expression, such as "or other place", which has the effect of extending the operation of the enactment to all particular circumstances which are within the *genus* created. The operation of the rule can best be illustrated by two examples.

Section 1 of the Betting Act 1853 prohibited the keeping of a "house, office, room or other place" for betting with persons resorting thereto. In *Powell* v. *Kempton Park Racecourse Co.*[17] the point at issue was whether Tattersalls' ring at a racecourse was an "other place" within the meaning of the Act. The House of Lords held that it was not since the words "house, office, room" created a *genus* of indoor places within which a racecourse, being outdoor, did not fall.

Similarly in *Brownsea Haven Properties, Ltd.* v. *Poole Corporation*[18] it was held that regulations enabling a local authority to make orders for the direction of traffic "in all times of public processions, rejoicings, or illuminations, and in any case when the streets are thronged or liable to be obstructed" did not confer power to create a one-way traffic system for the six months of the summer holiday season.

It should be noted that there must be at least two specific words to create a *genus*. Thus where an Act referred to "theatres and other places of amusement" it was held that a funfair was within the Act even though not *eiusdem generis* with the word "theatres".[19]

d   *Penal provisions are construed narrowly*

Where a statute imposes criminal liability or tax obligations (which are treated as penal) and the statute is ambiguous or uncertain, it should be construed in favour of the individual.[20] Thus it has been held that the offence of "knowingly possessing an explosive" requires knowledge on the part of the accused that the substance possessed is explosive, not merely that he possesses the substance.[1] One aspect of this general rule is the presumption against the imposition of liability without fault.[2]

---

[17] [1899] A.C. 143; cf., *Culley* v. *Harrison*, [1956] 2 Q.B. 71; [1956] 2 All E.R. 254.

[18] [1958] Ch. 574; [1958] 1 All E.R. 205; see also *R.* v. *Jordan*, [1977] A.C. 699; [1976] 3 All E.R. 775 (obscene publication justified "as being for the public good on the ground that it is in the interests of science, literature, art or learning, or of other objects of general concern" (Obscene Publications Act 1959, s. 4(1)); the House of Lords held that "other objects of general concern", having regard to the preceding generic words, did not include the psychotherapeutic value of pornography to sexual deviants; see p. 655, *post*).

[19] *Allen* v. *Emmerson*, [1944] K.B. 362; [1944] 1 All E.R. 344. For a striking illustration of the operation of the rule see *Customs and Excise Commissioners* v. *Savoy Hotel, Ltd.*, [1966] 2 All E.R. 299; [1966] 1 W.L.R. 948.

[20] *Dock Co. at Kingston-upon-Hull* v. *Browne* (1831), 2 B. & Ad. 43; *D'Avigdor-Goldsmid* v. *Inland Revenue Commissioners*, [1953] A.C. 347; [1953] 1 All E.R. 403.

[1] *R.* v. *Hallam*, [1957] 1 Q.B. 569; [1957] 1 All E.R. 665.

[2] See p. 114, *post*.

However, this rule of interpretation is not strong enough to displace the literal rule. Consequently, where a statute unambiguously creates a criminal penalty or a tax the court is bound to give effect to it even though it appears unjust.[3]

e   Interpretation Act 1978

This Act, which consolidates with amendments the Interpretation Act 1889, prescribes definitions of certain words and phrases which are commonly encountered in Acts of Parliament. Thus:

> ". . . unless the contrary intention appears (*a*) words importing the masculine gender include the feminine; (*b*) words importing the feminine gender include the masculine; (*c*) words in the singular include the plural and words in the plural include the singular."[4]
>
> ". . . 'month' means calendar month".[5]

However these, and other, definitions are only presumptive and yield to a contrary intention, express or implied, in the Act being interpreted. Thus, although the word "person" is defined in Schedule 1 of the Interpretation Act to include a body corporate, it was held in one case that a corporation which undertook legal work was not guilty of the offence of acting as an unqualified "person" since the enactment in question could only apply to persons who could qualify as solicitors.[6]

4   Presumptions in construction

It is possible to express almost any rule of statutory interpretation in the form of a presumption. The rules against retrospective operation and against extra-territorial operation are often expressed as presumptions. The reasons for rules of statutory interpretation being described as presumptions is that their operation is rebutted by an express provision to the contrary in the Act itself. They thus have the quality of evidentiary presumptions. Nevertheless, although it is probably a mere matter of terminology, the following are always described as presumptions rather than as rules.

a   Presumption against alteration of the law

Parliament, like the judiciary, is presumed to know the law. Consequently if an Act does not expressly alter the law it will be presumed that Parliament did not intend it to have that effect. In the words of DEVLIN, J. (as he then was).[7]

---

[3]   E.g., *R.* v. *Hare*, [1934] 1 K.B. 354; *Inland Revenue Commissioners* v. *Hinchy*, [1960] A.C. 748; [1960] 1 All E.R. 505, see p. 105, *ante*.

[4]   Section 6. For a recent illustration of the application of this rule, see *Floor* v. *Davis*, [1980] A.C. 695; [1979] 2 All E.R. 677.

[5]   Section 5 and Sch. 1.

[6]   *Law Society* v. *United Service Bureau, Ltd.*, [1934] 1 K.B. 343. This *lacuna* was filled by s. 22 of the Solicitors Act 1957; see also *Penn-Texas Corporation* v. *Murat-Anstalt*, [1964] 2 Q.B. 647; [1964] 2 All E.R. 594.

[7]   *National Assistance Board* v. *Wilkinson*, [1952] 2 Q.B. 648, at p. 661; [1952] 2 All E.R. 255, at p. 260.

"A statute is not to be taken as effecting a fundamental alteration in the general law unless it uses words which point unmistakably to that conclusion."

Thus, prior to the Criminal Evidence Act 1898 a wife was incompetent to give evidence against her husband. That Act made her competent to do so but, in the absence of an express provision, the House of Lords in *Leach* v. *R.*[8] held that it did not make her compellable.

Nevertheless it is important to remember that Parliament can expressly make fundamental alterations to the common law and, if such a change appears from a literal interpretation of the words used, the use of any presumption to the contrary is out of place. The presumption against fundamental change also applies in relation to statute law, one aspect being the presumption that a consolidating statute does not, simply by verbal alteration in the provision re-enacted, thereby introduce a fundamental change of meaning.[9] Conversely the mere fact that a statutory provision is re-enacted (whether by way of consolidation or otherwise) does not necessarily mean that Parliament is intending to give statutory force to judicial interpretations of the earlier enactment. The court must interpret the enactment as it stands though, if the scales were equally balanced, the fact that Parliament had re-enacted a provision which had been the subject of judicial interpretation might tip the balance in favour of that interpretation.[10]

b   Presumption against the imposition of liability without fault

This may be regarded as an aspect of the general presumption against fundamental change in the common law by mere implication. At common law *mens rea* is an element in all crimes,[11] though not in all torts. Although the legislature can, and frequently does, create offences of strict or absolute liability the intention so to do must be clear and unambiguous. LORD REID, in the leading case of *Sweet* v. *Parsley*, explained the judicial approach as follows:[12]

"Our first duty is to consider the words of the Act; if they show a clear intention to create an absolute offence, that is an end of the matter. But such cases are very rare.[13] Sometimes the words of the section which creates a particular offence make it clear that *mens rea* is required in one form or another. Such cases are quite frequent.[14] But in a very large number of cases there is no clear indication either way. In such cases there has for centuries been a presumption that Parliament did not intend to make criminals of persons who were in no way blameworthy in what they did. That means that, whenever a section is silent as to *mens*

---

8 [1912] A.C. 305; see p. 631, *post; Beswick* v. *Beswick*, [1968] A.C. 58; [1967] 2 All E.R. 1197 (p. 110, *ante*) is a paradigm of this presumption; see also *Black-Clawson International, Ltd.* v. *Papierwerke Waldhof-Aschaffenburg A.G.*, [1975] A.C. 591; [1975] 1 All E.R. 810.

9 See *Beswick* v. *Beswick* (*supra*); *Woolley* v. *Woolley*, [1968] P. 29; [1966] 3 All E.R. 855.

10 See p. 125, *post*.

11 See *R.* v. *Tolson* (1889), 23 Q.B.D. 168, at p. 181; *Younghusband* v. *Luftig*, [1949] 2 K.B. 354; [1949] 2 All E.R. 72.

12 [1970] A.C. 132, at p. 148; [1969] 1 All E.R. 347, at p. 349. See also *R.* v. *Gould*, [1968] 2 Q.B. 65; [1968] 1 All E.R. 849.

13 See, for examples, *R.* v. *Prince* (1875), L.R. 2 C.C.R. 154; *Cundy* v. *Le Coq* (1884), 13 Q.B.D. 207.

14 See, for examples, *R.* v. *Hallam*, [1957] 1 Q.B. 569; [1957] 1 All E.R. 665; *Vane* v. *Yiannopoullos*, [1965] A.C. 486; [1964] 3 All E.R. 820.

rea, there is a presumption that, in order to give effect to the will of Parliament, we must read in words appropriate to require *mens rea*."

c Presumption against depriving a person of a vested right

In the absence of express provision the courts will not construe a statute as having the effect of depriving a person of a right vested in him before the statute came into operation. This is linked with the presumption against retrospective operation though it is more than an illustration of the latter presumption. For example, every person has a right to the use and enjoyment of his own land. The remedy for infringement of this right is an action in trespass or nuisance, depending on the character of the interference. Consequently where a statute authorises the performance of an act, which constitutes a nuisance to the plaintiff, the statute will not be construed as having the effect of removing the plaintiff's right unless it is clearly intended to have that effect.[15] Even stronger is the presumption against removing a right to compensation.[16] Nevertheless, this can be done expressly as evidenced by the War Damage Act 1965 which removed a right to compensation from the Crown in respect of damage to or destruction of property caused by the Crown in time of war, or in contemplation of the outbreak of war.[17]

d Presumption against ousting the jurisdiction of the courts

Individuals cannot, by contract, exclude the jurisdiction of the courts. Although Parliament may exclude an individual's recourse to the courts, the provision purporting so to do must be absolutely clear and unambiguous since the courts are extremely wary about permitting legislative or executive interference with their jurisdiction. The principle was stated by VISCOUNT SIMONDS as follows in *Pyx Granite, Ltd.* v. *Ministry of Housing and Local Government.*[18]

> ". . . it is a principle not by any means to be whittled down that the subject's recourse to Her Majesty's courts for the determination of his rights is not to be excluded except by clear words. That is, as McNAIR, J. called it in *Francis* v. *Yiewsley and West Drayton Urban District Council*[19] a 'fundamental rule' from which I would not for my part sanction any departure."

---

[15] *Metropolitan Asylum District* v. *Hill* (1881), 6 App. Cas. 193.

[16] *Minister of Health* v. *Stafford Corporation*, [1952] Ch. 730; [1952] 2 All E.R. 386. It was on this basis that the Court of Appeal held in *Allen* v. *Thorn Electrical Industries, Ltd.*, [1967] 1 Q.B. 487; [1967] 2 All E.R. 1137 that the prohibition on pay increases introduced by the Prices and Incomes Act 1966 did not deprive the plaintiff of his right to an increase which had been agreed upon before the prohibition came into effect.

[17] The right had been held to exist in *Burmah Oil Co., Ltd.* v. *Lord Advocate*, [1965] A.C. 75; [1964] 2 All E.R. 348.

[18] [1960] A.C. 260, at p. 286; [1959] 3 All E.R. 1, at p. 6, cited with approval by LORD DONOVAN in *Ealing London Borough* v. *Race Relations Board*, [1972] A.C. 342, at p. 353; [1972] 1 All E.R. 105, at p. 108; the decision illustrates the application of the presumption in that the House of Lords held that the machinery established under the Race Relations Act 1968 for referring disputes to certain nominated county courts did not exclude the inherent jurisdiction of the High Court to make a declaration as to rights under the Act; see p. 344, *post*.

[19] [1957] 2 Q.B. 136, at p. 148; the passage referred to does not appear in the report of the case in [1957] 1 All E.R. 825.

One application of this rule is the principle that a provision which expressly states that the decision of an inferior court, tribunal or administrative body shall be "final" does not exclude the prerogative jurisdiction of the High Court to review the decision.

> "... if a tribunal goes wrong in law and the error appears on the face of the record, the High Court will interfere by certiorari to quash the decision. It is not to be deterred by the enactment that the decision is 'final'. The decision may be final on the facts but it is not final on the law."[20]

e   Presumption that a statute does not bind the Crown

One of the few relics of the prerogative of the Crown is the rule that the Crown is not bound by a statute unless expressly named in it. The rule extends to the Crown and to its servants and agents though not to nationalised industries.[1] The Crown Proceedings Act 1947 placed the Crown, with certain exceptions, in the same position as a private person in the law of torts. Consequently, statutes which affect common law rights and duties are usually expressed to bind the Crown. Examples are the Limitation Act 1980 and the Occupiers' Liability Act 1957. The Crown is no longer a preferred creditor in bankruptcy[2] and the general trend of modern legislation is towards the removal of the Crown's privileges and immunities.[3]

5   Material aids to construction

The distinction between interpretation and construction has already been noted. All statutes require interpretation but only statutes whose provisions are ambiguous or uncertain in extent require construction, though the processes of interpretation and construction are inextricably interrelated. Judges frequently make no attempt to distinguish the processes of interpretation and construction. The distinction is, however, material since not all aids to construction are legitimate aids to interpretation. Thus the aids to construction which do not form part of the enactment may only be consulted where the process of interpretation has disclosed an uncertainty or an ambiguity.

There are two classes of aids to construction; internal aids and external aids.

a   Internal aids

An internal (or intrinsic) aid is an aid which is to be found within the Queen's Printer's copy of the statute itself. Those parts of the statute which form part of the enactment must, of course, be consulted as part of the general process

---

20 *Tehrani* v. *Rostron*, [1972] 1 Q.B. 182, at p. 187; [1971] 3 All E.R. 790, at p. 793, *per* LORD DENNING, M.R.; see also *R.* v. *Medical Appeal Tribunal, Ex Parte Gilmore*, [1957] 1 Q.B. 574; [1957] 1 All E.R. 796, where the earlier authorities are reviewed; *Sagnata Investments, Ltd.* v. *Norwich Corporation*, [1971] 2 Q.B. 614; [1971] 2 All E.R. 1441.
1 *Tamlin* v. *Hannaford*, [1950] 1 K.B. 18; [1949] 2 All E.R. 327.
2 Bankruptcy Act 1914, s. 151.
3 See *Madras Electric Supply Corporation* (*in liquidation*) v. *Boarland* (*Inspector of Taxes*), [1955] A.C. 667; [1955] 1 All E.R. 753.

of interpretation in applying the general rule that the statute must be read as a whole. Other parts of the Queen's Printer's copy are not aids to interpretation though some, but not all, are aids to construction. There has not, however, been a universal judicial adherence to these basic principles and the modern tendency is to regard those parts of the statute which are not strictly part of the enactment, that is to say punctuation, headings and marginal notes, as aids to construction in cases of ambiguity. Thus in *Director of Public Prosecutions* v. *Schildkamp* LORD REID stated.[4]

> ". . . it may be more realistic to accept the Act as printed as being the product of the whole legislative process, and to give due weight to everything found in the printed Act. I say more realistic because in very many cases the provision before the court was never even mentioned in debate in either House, and it may be that its wording was never closely scrutinised by any member of either House. In such a case it is not very meaningful to say that the words of the Act represent the intention of Parliament but that punctuation, cross-headings and sidenotes do not.
>
> So if the authorities are equivocal and one is free to deal with the whole matter I would not object to taking all these matters into account provided that we realise that they cannot have equal weight with the words of the Act. Punctuation can be of some assistance in construction. A cross-heading ought to indicate the scope of the sections which follow it.[5] But a sidenote is a poor guide to the scope of the section for it can do no more than indicate the main subject with which the section deals."

It is necessary to identify and distinguish the constituent parts of a statute.
Long title— The long title of an Act begins with the words "An Act" and goes on to describe the general effect of the Act. Thus the Act whose short title is the "Law of Property Act 1925" has the long title: "An Act to consolidate the enactments relating to Conveyancing and the Law of Property in England and Wales." It might be supposed that the insertion of a long title would afford Parliament the opportunity of stating its general intention in passing the Act, but in fact long titles tend to be succinct rather than explanatory and generally do little more than identify the subject matter of the Act. Their insertion would appear to rest rather on tradition than on utility.

Until the nineteenth century the long title was not part of the Act itself and was therefore not regarded as a legitimate aid to interpretation. The modern long title, however, is part of the enactment and may be the subject of debate

---

4 [1971] A.C. 1, at p. 10; [1969] 3 All E.R. 1640, at p. 1641; see also *Limb & Co. (Stevedores)* v. *British Transport Docks Board*, [1971] 1 All E.R. 828; [1971] 1 W.L.R. 311.
5 LINDLEY, M.R. in *Fielding* v. *Morley Corporation*, [1899] 1 Ch. 1. at p. 3; see also *Vacher* v. *London Society of Compositors*, [1913] A.C. 107, at p. 128; *R.* v. *Delmayne*, [1970] 2 Q.B. 170, at p. 175; [1969] 2 All E.R. 980, at p. 983; *Black-Clawson International, Ltd.* v. *Papierwerke Waldhof-Aschaffenburg A.G.*, [1975] A.C. 591; [1975] 1 All E.R. 810 in which LORD REID, VISCOUNT DILHORNE and LORD SIMON all referred to the long title of the Foreign Judgments (Reciprocal Enforcement) Act 1933, as an aid to the construction of section 8 of that Act, although LORD REID only did do because he regarded the section itself as ambiguous; on the authorities this was too narrow a view and, as LORD SIMON stated, the long title, being part of the enactment, can be consulted before getting to the stage of finding the text of the section ambiguous. See also *Suffolk County Council* v. *Mason*, [1979] A.C. 705; [1979] 2 All E.R. 369.

and amendment in Parliament. Consequently, it may be regarded as a legitimate aid both to interpretation and construction. A Master of the Rolls observed in 1899:

> "I read the title advisedly because now and for some years past the title of an Act of Parliament has been part of the Act. In the old days it used not to be so, and in the old books we are told not to regard it, but now the title is an important part of the Act and is so treated by both Houses of Parliament".

Although the long title is part of the Act, it is a minor aid to construction. There have been conspicuously few cases in which it has been consulted and it certainly cannot prevail over an express provision in the body of the Act. Thus "An Act to amend the law with respect to wills of personal estate made by British subjects" (Wills Act 1861) has been held to apply to the will of an alien.[6] The long title should not be confused with the preamble though, now that preambles are rarely encountered, judges do occasionally describe the long title as the preamble.[7]

Short title—This is the title by which Acts are commonly, and properly, cited. In theory the short title is a valid aid both to interpretation and to construction, but there appears to be no reported case in which the short title has been used to determine a point of construction, though reference has sometimes been made to it. The short title could certainly not be used to introduce ambiguity into the body of the Act and, indeed, the short titles of certain Acts do not reflect the content of the Act accurately. The Criminal Procedure Act 1865, for example, applies to both civil and criminal proceedings.

Preamble—The preamble is that part of the statute which precedes the enacting words and sets out the reason for the statute being passed, for example the mischief which the statute is passed to remedy. In old cases great weight was attached to the preamble as an aid to construction.[8] Important Acts such as the Statute of Uses 1535, the Statute of Frauds 1677 and the Parliament Act 1911 have long and instructive preambles. Probably the best known preamble is that of the Charitable Uses Act 1601 which is still regarded as containing the criteria to be adopted when considering whether a particular object is a "charitable" one.[9] Where a statute has a preamble, it traditionally begins with the word "Whereas". Modern statutes, however, rarely contain a preamble and where one is included it is generally too brief to be of assistance.[10] Consequently the preamble is of declining importance as an aid to construction. Although the preamble is part of the enactment, like the long title, it cannot be introduced to create an ambiguity in the body of the Act. In the words of LORD HALSBURY:[11]

---

6   *Re Groos*, [1904] P. 269; see also *R.* v. *Bates*, [1952] 2 All E.R. 842; [1953] 1 W.L.R. 77; *Re Wykes*, [1961] Ch. 229, at p. 242; [1961] 1 All E.R. 470, at p. 475.

7   E.g. WINN, L.J. in *Crook* v. *Edmondson*, [1966] 2 Q.B. 81, at p. 89; [1966] 1 All E.R. 833, at p. 835; BAKER, J. (as he then was) in *Limb & Co.* (*Stevedores*) v. *British Transport Docks Board* (*supra*).

8   *Belasco* v. *Hannant* (1862), 3 B. & S. 13; *Sussex Peerage Claim* (1844), 11 Cl. & F. 85.

9   See, for example, the consideration of this preamble in *Incorporated Council of Law Reporting for England and Wales* v. *A.-G.*, [1971] Ch. 626; [1971] 3 All E.R. 1029.

10   Compare secondary legislation of the European Communities which invariably has a long preamble; for the reasons for this, see p. 129, *post*.

11   *Powell* v. *Kempton Park Racecourse Co.*, [1899] A.C. 143, at p. 157.

". . . If an enactment is itself clear and unambiguous, no preamble can qualify or cut down the enactment".

It might be argued that, since the preamble and the long title form part of the enactment, the enactment cannot be "clear and unambiguous" if the long title or the preamble is inconsistent with the body of the Act. The courts have not generally acceded to this line of argument.[12]

Headings—A section or group of sections in an Act may be preceded by a heading. Such headings are not part of the enactment and for that reason logic would suggest their exclusion. Notwithstanding, headings are often consulted as an aid to construction where the enactment is uncertain or ambiguous.[13] The modern judicial tendency appears to be to treat a heading as if it were a preamble.[14] In *Director of Public Prosecutions* v. *Schildkamp*[15] LORD UPJOHN was in favour of according greater weight to headings than were the other law lords, and accordingly observed:[16]

"In my opinion, it is wrong to confine their role to the resolution of ambiguities in the body of the Act. When the court construing the Act is reading it through to understand it, it must read the cross-headings as well as the body of the Act and that will always be a useful pointer as to the intention of Parliament in enacting the immediately following sections. Whether the cross-heading is no more than a pointer or label or is helpful in assisting to construe or even in some cases to control the meaning or ambit of those sections must necessarily depend on the circumstances of each case."

Marginal notes—Marginal notes are not part of an Act and are inserted by the draftsman purely for facility of reference. It has happened that a marginal note has borne no relation to the content of a section which had been considerably altered during the passage of the Bill.[17] For this reason the old rule was that marginal notes were not regarded as a legitimate aid to construction, even in the event of ambiguity.[18] Nevertheless there have been cases in which the court has clearly adverted to the marginal note in construing a section.[19] Thus UPJOHN, L.J. (as he then was) observed in one case.[20]

---

[12] *A.-G.* v. *Prince Ernest Augustus of Hanover*, [1957] A.C. 436; [1957] 1 All E.R. 49; *Ward* v. *Holman*, [1964] 2 Q.B. 580; [1964] 2 All E.R. 729; *Powell* v. *Kempton Park Racecourse Co.* (*supra*).
[13] For an instructive recent case see *Crook* v. *Edmondson*, [1966] 2 Q.B. 81; [1966] 1 All E.R. 833 in which the words "immoral purposes" were construed in the light of the group of sections of the Sexual Offences Act 1956 in which those words occurred; see also *Beswick* v. *Beswick*, [1968] A.C. 58; [1967] 2 All E.R. 1197 (p. 110, *ante*).
[14] *Martins* v. *Fowler*, [1926] A.C. 746; *Re Carlton*, [1945] 1 Ch. 280; [1945] 2 All E.R. 370; *Qualter, Hall & Co., Ltd.* v. *Board of Trade*, [1962] Ch. 273; [1961] 3 All E.R. 389.
[15] [1971] A.C. 1; [1969] 3 All E.R. 1640.
[16] [1971] A.C., at p. 28; [1969] 3 All E.R., at p. 1656.
[17] Married Women (Maintenance in Case of Desertion) Act 1886, s. 1(2).
[18] See *R.* v. *Bates*, [1952] 2 All E.R. 842; [1953] 1 W.L.R. 77; *Chandler* v. *Director of Public Prosecutions*, [1964] A.C. 763; [1962] 3 All E.R. 142.
[19] E.g., *Pride of Derby and Derbyshire Angling Association, Ltd.* v. *British Celanese, Ltd.*, [1953] Ch. 149; [1952] 1 All E.R. 179; *R.* v. *Vickers*, [1957] 2 Q.B. 664; [1957] 2 All E.R. 741.
[20] *Stephens* v. *Cuckfield Rural District Council*, [1960] 2 Q.B. 373, at p. 383; *Limb & Co. (Stevedores)* v. *British Transport Docks Board*, [1971] 1 All E.R. 828; [1971] 1 W.L.R. 311 (*supra*).

"While the marginal note to a section cannot control the language used in the section, it is at least permissible to approach a consideration of its general purpose and the mischief at which it is aimed with the note in mind."

In the light of the speeches of the House of Lords in *Director of Public Prosecutions* v. *Schildkamp* (*supra*), it now appears that the court is entitled to look at marginal notes in cases of ambiguity, though they clearly carry little weight and certainly cannot displace a meaning which appears from the enactment proper.[1]

Punctuation— Before 1850 Acts of Parliament were not punctuated; even after that punctuation was left to the draftsman and not scrutinised by Parliament. Accordingly there was some old authority for the proposition that punctuation could not be taken into account as an aid to construction. However the courts now adopt a far more realistic attitude and, following the observations of LORD REID in *Director of Public Prosecutions* v. *Schildkamp* (*supra*), the House of Lords has now held[2] that punctuation can and should be taken into account by judges in interpreting statutes.

Interpretation sections—It is a relatively modern drafting technique to include an interpretation section in an Act. The Law of Property Act 1925, for example, has a long section containing definitions of, and guides to the interpretation of, numerous words and phrases employed in that Act.[3] Although an interpretation section is as much a part of the Act as any other section, the interpretation of a word depends rather on its context than on the interpretation section, and, in any event, if there is an inconsistency between an interpretation section and the body of an Act the latter prevails. This is especially so when the interpretation section uses the word "includes". In this case the interpretation section will be regarded as extending rather than restricting the normal meaning of the words in question. Thus where an interpretation section[4] defined "street" by stating that it "should apply to and include any highway, not being a turnpike road", the Court of Appeal held that the word "street" could include a turnpike road since the interpretation section extended rather than restricted the ordinary and natural meaning of the word.[5]

Schedules—Schedules are part of the enactment if expressly incorporated by a section in the Act itself. They are used (*inter alia*) for prescribing forms, furnishing illustrations, listing repeals effected by the Act and setting out transitional provisions. They cannot be regarded as altering or enlarging the ordinary meaning of words used in the Act. Thus in *Ellerman Lines, Ltd.* v. *Murray*[6] the House of Lords, in interpreting an Act passed to give effect to an International Convention, steadfastly refused to look at a schedule to the Act in which was set out the text of the Convention because the words of the Act were unambiguous. It is to be presumed that the House would ·have considered the schedule, had the Act been uncertain or ambiguous, in order to apply the mischief rule.[7] If the situation which arose in *Ellerman Lines,*

---

1   See *R.* v. *Kelt*, [1977] 3 All E.R. 1099; [1977] 1 ·W.L.R. 1365.
2   *Hanlon* v. *The Law Society*, [1981] A.C. 124; [1980] 2 All E.R. 199.
3   Section 205; see *Beswick* v. *Beswick* (*supra*).
4   Public Health Act 1848, s. 2.
5   *Nutter* v. *Accrington Local Board* (1879), 4 Q.B.D. 375.
6   [1931] A.C. 126.
7   See *Salomon* v. *Customs and Excise Commissioners*, [1967] 2 Q.B. 116; [1966] 3 All E.R.

Ltd. v. *Murray* were to arise at the present day the contrary approach would be adopted, and, indeed, the case itself was disapproved by the House of Lords in *James Buchanan & Co.* v. *Babco Forwarding and Shipping (U.K.), Ltd.*[8] With the increasing number of statutes which are passed to implement international conventions a new difficulty has arisen; that is that the convention (which is part of the enactment) is sometimes in a foreign language and, indeed, is sometimes set out in more than one language. The House of Lords grappled with this difficulty, in construing the French and English texts of the Warsaw Convention contained in Schedule 1 of the Carriage by Air Act 1961, in *Fothergill* v. *Monarch Airlines, Ltd.*[9] Reversing the decision of the Court of Appeal, it held that a loss of articles from a suitcase constituted "damage" to baggage. This conclusion was reached by not applying a literal interpretation of the word "damage" but rather a purposive one and by looking at extrinsic sources so as to ascertain that the word "avarie" (used in the French text) is capable of meaning "loss" as well as "damage".

The Consumer Credit Act 1974 utilises what appears to be a novel concept in Parliamentary drafting—the use of examples. Section 188(1) provides that "Schedule 2 shall have effect for illustrating the use of terminology employed in this Act" and that Schedule contains 24 examples, each expressed in the form of a set of facts and an analysis of the application of the new terminology to those facts. The examples are expressed not to be exhaustive and section 188(3) provides that in the case of conflict between Schedule 2 and any other provision of the Act, the latter shall prevail. First impressions suggest that this innovation may be of considerable value in the interpretation of complicated legislation (particularly where new terminology is used). The examples are in the nature of an extended interpretation section so that there would seem to be no reason to suppose that they will lead to any greater difficulties than those which arise in acts having conventional interpretation sections.

b External aids

An external (or extrinsic) aid to construction is an aid which is not to be found in the Queen's Printer's copy of the Act. Since the function of the courts is to ascertain the intention of the legislature, it might be thought that they would readily refer to statements made in Parliament as to the intention of the member or party introducing the Bill. In fact the reverse is the case. The reports of debates on the Bill in its passage through Parliament are rigidly excluded[10] as are explanatory memoranda upon the effects of the Act,

---

871. In *Corocraft, Ltd.* v. *Pan American Airways, Inc.*, [1969] 1 Q.B. 616; [1969] 1 All E.R. 82 there was no ambiguity or uncertainty in the English Act but the Court of Appeal nevertheless adopted the text of the Convention (the meaning of which differed from that of the Act, the Carriage by Air Act 1932), distinguishing *Ellerman Lines, Ltd.* v. *Murray* on the basis that in that case the intention of Parliament had been to give effect to the English text of the Convention whereas in the present case the intention was to give effect to the original Convention. There is a presumption that Parliament intended to fulfil, rather than break, its international obligations; cf. *The Andrea Ursula*, [1973] Q.B. 265; [1971] 1 All E.R. 821.

8 [1978] A.C. 141; [1977] 3 All E.R. 1048.

9 [1981] A.C. 251; [1980] 2 All E.R. 696. The 1961 Act, s. 1(2) expressly provides that in the event of inconsistency between the English and French texts, the latter is to prevail.

10 *Assam Railways and Trading Co., Ltd.* v. *Inland Revenue Commissioners*, [1935] A.C. 445; *R.* v. *Hertford College* (1878), 3 Q.B.D. 693. In *Beswick* v. *Beswick*, [1968] A.C. 58, at p. 74;

where these are issued.[11] In a case this century[12] LORD HALSBURY, L.C. refused to deliver a speech on the interpretation of a statute which he had helped to draft. This rigid and widely criticised rule appears to have entered English law in the eighteenth century.[13] Perhaps the most striking illustration of the rule excluding extrinsic aids to interpretation is the case of *Ellerman Lines, Ltd.* v. *Murray*, noted above, in which the House of Lords refused to look at the text of an International Convention when interpreting a statute passed to give effect to that Convention. However, in the event of ambiguity, it is now clearly established that, when construing a statute passed to enact matters agreed at an International Convention, the court is entitled to look at the Convention to ascertain what Parliament must have intended.[14] Thus it probably makes no difference whether the text of the Convention is scheduled to the Act or not. Where the Convention is printed in more than one language (as will usually be the case) it is permissible to look at foreign texts as well as the English text, although the majority of the House of Lords in *James Buchanan & Co., Ltd.* v. *Babco Forwarding and Shipping (U.K.), Ltd.*[15] expressed the view that this was only permissible if the English text was ambiguous. This principle and the presumption that Parliament intends to fulfil its international obligations will doubtless be of considerable practical importance in the coming years when the courts are called upon to construe

---

[1967] 2 All E.R. 1197, at p. 1202 reasons advanced for the rule were that it would add to the time and expense of preparing cases if counsel had to read all the debates in *Hansard* and that reports of debates in select committees are not available to the public. In *Davis* v. *Johnson*, [1979] A.C. 264; [1978] 1 All E.R. 1132, the House of Lords unanimously reaffirmed the rule that Hansard can never be relied upon by counsel in any court and can never be relied upon by the court in construing a statute or for any other purpose.

[11] *London County Council* v. *Central Land Board*, [1959] Ch. 386; [1958] 3 All E.R. 676. However, in *Sagnata Investments, Ltd.* v. *Norwich Corporation*, [1971] 2 Q.B. 614; [1971] 2 All E.R. 1441, LORD DENNING, M.R. did refer to *Hansard, Parliamentary Debates* when considering the mischief intended to be remedied by the Betting, Gaming and Lotteries Act 1963, Sch. 6 and did so again in *R.* v. *Greater London Council, Ex parte Blackburn*, [1976] 3 All E.R. 184; [1976] 1 W.L.R. 50 (albeit having first said "I know that we are not supposed to do this"). The Renton Committee Report, *The Preparation of Legislation* (Cmnd. 6053 of 1975) (see p. 91, *ante*) recommended against the use of such external aids to interpretation.

[12] *Hilder* v. *Dexter*, [1902] A.C. 474.

[13] *Millar* v. *Taylor* (1769), 4 Burr. 2303. In *Race Relations Board* v. *Docker's Labour Club and Institute, Ltd.*, [1976] A.C. 285; [1974] 3 All E.R. 592 the House of Lords (for the fourth time in less than three years) had to interpret the controversial Race Relations Act 1968 (now the Race Relations Act 1976) and, in particular, the words "section of the public" in section 2(1), so as to determine whether discrimination in the instant case was in the public domain (and therefore prohibited by the Act). This led to LORD SIMON suggesting the creation of a constitutional convention to the effect that where the promoter of a Bill, or a Minister supporting it, is asked whether it will apply in a given circumstance, and expresses an opinion, that circumstance should be made the subject of a specific provision in the enactment, so as to give effect to the intention of Parliament. To date no such practice appears to have been adopted.

[14] *The Banco*, [1971] P. 137; [1971] 1 All E.R. 524; cf. the cases cited in fn. 7, p. 120, *ante*.

[15] [1978] A.C. 141; [1977] 3 All E.R. 1048; LORD WILBERFORCE was in favour of consulting the foreign text for assistance, "if assistance is needed" without first discovering ambiguity in the English text, but if there were no ambiguity (or, at least, uncertainty) in the English text, it is difficult to see why assistance would be needed; cf. *Fothergill* v. *Monarch Airlines, Ltd.*, [1981] A.C. 251; [1980] 2 All E.R. 696 (see p. 121, *ante*) where some members of the House appear to have regarded the word "damage" as ambiguous in its context; but since the French text was the primary text, it could clearly have been relied upon by the parties whether the English text was ambiguous or not and the court would be bound to give effect to the French text. This is an important distinction between the two cases.

the legislation which will be passed to implement the instruments of the European Community Institutions. It may be observed that most continental countries adopt the opposite approach and encourage consultation of the Parliamentary and political history of the statute. These materials are known as *travaux préparatoires* and are an invaluable aid to the task of discovering the intention of continental legislatures. In *Fothergill* v. *Monarch Airlines, Ltd.*[16] the House of Lords accepted that in construing the text of an international convention, embodied in a domestic statute, the English courts could in certain circumstances consider *travaux préparatoires* relating to the convention, although there was not general agreement as to what those circumstances would be, and a certain lack of enthusiasm for their use is discernible in all of the speeches. However, although the general rule in relation to external aids is one of exclusion,[17] there are certain legitimate external aids to construction and these are set out below.

Dictionaries—Words in statutes are presumed to bear their ordinary and natural meaning and it is legitimate to consult a dictionary to ascertain the meaning of words which have no particular legal meaning. Thus in *Re Rippon (Highfield) Housing Confirmation Order* 1938[18] the court adopted the Oxford English Dictionary definition of the word "park". Nevertheless dictionaries bear only slight weight and, in context, the dictionary meaning may not be the one which Parliament presumably intended. Thus in *Mills* v. *Cooper*[19] a divisional court rejected the Shorter Oxford English Dictionary definition of a "gypsy" while in *Thornton* v. *Fisher and Ludlow, Ltd.*[20] the same dictionary's definition of a "passage" was not adopted. Words and phrases which have a particular legal meaning are described as "terms of art" and do not necessarily bear the meaning which laymen would attribute to them.[1] In interpreting a foreign text of a convention, the court is entitled to consult foreign dictionaries, textbooks and articles and, indeed, to receive expert evidence.[2]

Reports of Committees—Although the Parliamentary history of an Act is rejected as an aid to construction, reports of the Law Commissions, Law

---

[16] *Supra.* Note also s. 3(3) of the Civil Jurisdiction and Judgments Act 1982 which expressly provides that in interpreting the conventions implemented by that Act, the court may consider certain reports by named individuals (which are reproduced in the Official Journal of the Communities).

[17] The Law Commission report, *The Interpretation of Statutes* (1969, Law Com. No. 21) recommended the admission of extrinsic material, other than reports of Parliamentary proceedings. LORD SIMON has more than once advocated reference to Parliamentary proceedings and other preparatory material as an aid to judicial interpretation of statutes (cf. *McMillan* v. *Crouch*, [1972] 3 All E.R. 61, at p. 76; [1972] 1 W.L.R. 1102, at p. 1119; *Race Relations Board* v. *Charter*, [1973] A.C. 868, at p. 900; [1973] 1 All E.R. 512, at p. 527) but his views on this topic have attracted little support.

[18] [1939] 2 K.B. 838; [1939] 3 All E.R. 548.

[19] [1967] 2 Q.B. 459; [1967] 2 All E.R. 100.

[20] [1968] 2 All E.R. 241; [1968] 1 W.L.R. 655.

[1] See *Sydall* v. *Castings, Ltd.*, [1967] 1 Q.B. 302; [1966] 3 All E.R. 770, on the construction of the word "descendants" as a term of art; see also *Barclays Bank, Ltd.* v. *Cole*, [1967] 2 Q.B. 738; [1966] 3 All E.R. 948, on the meaning of the word "fraud" and compare *Lloyds Bank, Ltd.* v. *Marcan*, [1973] 2 All E.R. 359 [1973] 1 W.L.R. 339 where PENNYCUICK, V.-C. gave a much wider meaning to the word "defraud" in s. 172(1) of the Law of Property Act 1925 on the basis that the section was replacing a provision in an Act of 1571 in which the words "hinder, delay or defraud" were used.

[2] *Fothergill* v. *Monarch Airlines, Ltd.* (*supra*).

Reform Committees and similar bodies are legitimate aids to discovering the
state of the pre-existing law and the mischief which the statute was passed to
remedy.[3] It is not, however, legitimate to interpret the words of an Act in
accordance with the recommendations of a Committee which preceded its
passing.[4] Thus in *Letang* v. *Cooper*[5] the Court of Appeal held that the words
"negligence, nuisance or breach of duty" in the Law Reform (Limitation of
Actions, etc.) Act 1954 were wide enough to embrace the tort of trespass to
the person even though the Tucker Committee report,[6] which preceded the
1954 Act, expressed an intention to exclude this form of action from the
shorter limitation period recommended in that report.

Other statutes—Where the words of one statute are ambiguous or uncertain,
assistance as to their meaning may sometimes be gained from consideration
of the way in which similar words have been used in other statutes, provided
that they are *in pari materia* with the provision under consideration. Thus in
R. v. *Wheatley*[7] the question before the Court of Appeal, Criminal Division,
was whether a metal pipe bomb filled with fire-dampened sodium chlorate
mixed with sugar was an "explosive" substance within the meaning of
section 4 of the Explosive Substances Act 1883. The defendant's expert
evidence was to the effect that the materials would produce only a pyrotechnic effect, and not an explosive one. The trial judge directed the jury that
this was no defence, having regard to the definition of "explosive" in section
3(1) of the Explosives Act 1875, which included a substance used with a view
to producing a "pyrotechnic effect". It was held that this direction was
correct since, having regard to the long title of the 1883 Act ("An Act to
amend the Law relating to Explosive Substances"), that Act was intended to
amend, *inter alia*, the 1875 Act and both Acts were *in pari materia*. It followed that what was an explosive substance within section 4 of the 1883 Act
was to be determined by applying the definition of "explosive" in
section 3(1) of the 1875 Act.

c   Judicial precedents

The application of the doctrine of judicial precedent to the interpretation of
statutes was explained as follows by the late LORD UPJOHN:[8]

> "It is quite clear that judicial statements as to the construction and intention of
> an Act must never be allowed to supplant or supersede its proper construction
> and courts must beware of falling into the error of treating the law to be that laid
> down by the judge in construing the Act rather than found in the Act itself. No

---

[3]   See, for example, *Rookes* v. *Barnard*, [1964] A.C. 1129; [1964] 1 All E.R. 367; *National
Provincial Bank, Ltd.* v. *Ainsworth*, [1965] A.C. 1175; [1965] 2 All E.R. 472; *Black-Clawson
International, Ltd.* v. *Papierwerke Waldhof-Aschaffenburg A.-G.*, [1975] A.C. 591; [1975] 1
All E.R. 810.

[4]   *Black-Clawson International, Ltd.* v. *Papierwerke Waldhof-Aschaffenburg A.G.* (*supra*).

[5]   [1965] 1 Q.B. 232; [1964] 2 All E.R. 929.

[6]   Cmd. 7740. In *Sagnata Investments, Ltd.* v. *Norwich Corporation* (*supra*) LORD DENNING,
M.R., in considering the legislative history of the Betting, Gaming and Lotteries Act 1963
took into account the recommendations of the Royal Commission on Betting, Lotteries and
Gaming (Cmd. 8190 of 1951).

[7]   [1979] 1 All E.R. 954; [1979] 1 W.L.R. 144.

[8]   *Ogden Industries, Pty., Ltd.* v. *Lucas*, [1970] A.C. 113, at p. 127; [1969] 1 All E.R. 121, at p.
126.

doubt a decision on particular words binds inferior courts on the construction of those words on similar facts, but beyond that the observations of judges on the construction of statutes may be of the greatest help and guidance but are entitled to no more than respect and cannot absolve the court from its duty in exercising an independent judgment.''

Thus where a superior court has interpreted the words of an Act, an inferior court in the hierarchy is bound to adopt that interpretation if faced with the same words in the same Act. Similarly the Court of Appeal is bound to follow its own previous decision upon the interpretation of a statute to the same extent as it is bound to follow any other of its previous decisions. The position is less clear if the later court is called upon to interpret the same or similar words in another part of the same Act or in another Act. In this event the earlier decision may be referred to if the two provisions in the Acts in question are *in pari materia* (deal with the same subject matter). This occurs most commonly when the later Act is a consolidating statute and the earlier Act is one of those repealed and consolidated. However, even in the case of consolidation Acts, the court is not bound by a precedent based upon an earlier Act consolidated by the Act under construction. The correct approach is for the court to interpret the Act in accordance with the usual principles of statutory interpretation. Only where there is a real or substantial difficulty or ambiguity should the court refer to the legislation which has been repealed or precedents based upon that legislation.[9]

Similarly, if the later Act employs words or phrases which have been the subject of judicial interpretation in an earlier Act dealing with the same subject matter it may be inferred that they are intended to bear the same meaning, on the basis that Parliament is presumed to know the law.[10] For example, the House of Lords, in assigning a meaning to the word ''wreck'' in the Merchant Shipping Act 1925, adopted the interpretation of that word which had been given in a case decided on the wording of the Merchant Shipping Act 1894.[11] It is, however, no more than a possible inference and it must not be supposed that by re-enacting a statutory provision which has been the subject of judicial interpretation Parliament is thereby, in effect, giving statutory force to that interpretation. If it is a wrong interpretation then (provided it is not binding on the court in accordance with the doctrine of precedent) a court is perfectly free to disregard it.[12] This is of particular importance now that the House of Lords is free to depart from its own previous decisions.[13] Moreover, where the earlier decision is upon similar

---

[9] *Farrell* v. *Alexander*, [1977] A.C. 59; [1976] 2 All E.R. 721; *R.* v. *Heron*, [1982] 1 All E.R. 993; [1982] 1 W.L.R. 451.

[10] Cf. *Maxwell on Interpretation of Statutes* (11th edn. 1962) p. 303, cited with approval in *R.* v. *Freeman*, [1970] 2 All E.R. 413; [1970] 1 W.L.R. 788 in which the Court of Appeal held that, since there was no relevant distinction between the definition of ''firearm'' in s. 57(1) of the Firearms Act 1968 and the definitions in earlier Firearms Acts, Parliament must be taken to have adopted in the 1968 Act the interpretation which had been placed on the definition in the Firearms Act 1920.

[11] *The Olympic*, [1913] P. 92; *Barras* v. *Aberdeen Steam Trawling and Fishing Co., Ltd.*, [1933] A.C. 402.

[12] See *Dun* v. *Dun*, [1959] A.C. 272; [1959] 2 All E.R. 134; *Farrell* v. *Alexander (supra)*; *R.* v. *Chard*, [1984] A.C. 279; [1983] 3 All E.R. 637 (in which the House of Lords expressly disapproved *dicta* to the contrary in *Barras* v. *Aberdeen Steam Trawling and Fishing Co., Ltd. (supra)*).

[13] See p. 146, *post*.

words in a statute which is not *in pari materia* with the statute requiring interpretation, or where the words are used in a different context, that decision is of little, if any, value.[14]

E LEGISLATION OF THE EUROPEAN COMMUNITIES

1 Forms of Community legislation

The primary legislation of the European Communities consists of the Treaties themselves.[15]

Under the Treaties the Council and Commission of the Communities have the duty, in accordance with the provisions of the Treaties, to make *regulations*, issue *directives*, make *decisions*, make *recommendations* and deliver *opinions*.[16] These are the instruments by which the policy of the Treaties is implemented. It is usually effected by the Commission submitting a proposal to the Council for the latter's consideration following which the instrument is duly promulgated, although in certain cases the Commission may itself make regulations or issue directives.

Not all of the Community instruments have binding legislative force. Thus *recommendations* and *opinions* have no binding force on the member states or other persons or institutions to whom they are addressed. They are not, however, without significance within our legal system since they are "Community instruments" and as such may be implemented in the United Kingdom by subordinate legislation.[17] Those Community instruments which may be classified as legislation are *regulations, directives* and *decisions*.

a Regulations

These have general application, are binding in their entirety and directly applicable[18] to all member states. Thus they confer individual rights and duties which the national courts of the member states must protect. It follows that, in the United Kingdom, there is no need for further legislation to implement Community regulations any more than there is any need to implement the Treaties. Furthermore, it is expressly provided[19] that any enactment has effect subject to existing "enforceable Community rights" so that the sovereignty of Parliament is limited to passing legislation which does not conflict with the overriding legislation of the European Communities.

---

14 *London Corporation* v. *Cusack-Smith*, [1955] A.C. 337; [1955] 1 All E.R. 302; *Goodrich* v. *Paisner*, [1957] A.C. 65; [1956] 2 All E.R. 176.
15 The original, and main, treaties comprise the Treaty of Paris which established the European Coal and Steel Community (the "E.C.S.C. Treaty"), the Treaty of Rome, which established the European Economic Community (the "E.E.C. Treaty"), a second Treaty of Rome, which established the European Atomic Energy Community (the "Euratom Treaty") and further Treaties of Brussels and Luxembourg which merged the main institutions of the Communities. Futhermore, there are numerous ancillarly treaties in the form of international agreements, protocols and annexes, declared to be treaties by Order in Council under s. 1(3) of the 1972 Act.
16 E.E.C. Treaty, Art. 189.
17 European Communities Act 1972, s. 2(2); see p. 60, *ante*.
18 *Ibid.*, s. 2(1).
19 *Ibid.*, s. 2(4).

b   Directives

Unlike regulations, directives do not necessarily have immediate binding force. They are addressed to member states but it is left to the individual national authorities to implement them. In the United Kingdom this may be done by Order in Council or by regulations made by a designated Minister or department by way of statutory instrument.[20]

Nevertheless, although Article 189 of the E.E.C. Treaty distinguishes between regulations, which are not only binding but also directly applicable in the member states, and directives, which, while binding on the member states have, in principle, no direct effect, it seems that the European Court is prepared to look beyond this legal categorisation so that directives have sometimes been given direct effect as conferring rights upon individuals even where member states have done nothing to implement the directive in question. A notable example of this is afforded by the decision of the European Court in case 41/74: *Van Duyn* v. *Home Office (No. 2)*[1] in which a directive was held to be of immediate binding effect so as to confer rights upon the plaintiff even though the United Kingdom had not implemented that directive.

Accordingly, when faced with a directive, it is necessary to examine in each case whether the wording, nature and scheme of the provisions in question are capable of producing direct effects between the member states to which the directive is addressed and their subjects.[2]

c   Decisions

These may be made by the Council and Commission as a formal method of enunciating policies or initiating actions. They are binding on those to whom they are addressed. Although not expressed to be "directly applicable" they can, in the same way as directives, have this effect and, indeed, the European Court has indicated that they may operate to create for individuals rights which national courts must safeguard.[3]

The literary source of the Treaties is, of course, the text of the Treaties themselves. All regulations and, in practice, directives and the principal decisions are published in the Official Journal of the European Communities, which is published in Luxembourg. In the United Kingdom judicial notice is taken of the Treaties and of the Official Journal and the latter is admissible as evidence of any instrument or other act therein contained.[4] The Official Journal is a huge work, and in 1973 and 1974 no less than 8,164 regulations, directives and decisions were published in it. Accordingly, those

---

[20] *Ibid.*, s. 2(2).

[1] [1975] Ch. 358; [1975] 3 All E.R. 190; [1974] E.C.R. 1337. See also *Shields* v. *E. Coomes (Holdings), Ltd.*, [1979] 1 All E.R. 456; [1978] 1 W.L.R. 1408; *R.* v. *Secretary of State for the Home Department, Ex parte Santillo*, [1981] Q.B. 778; [1981] 2 All E.R. 897; *R.* v. *Bouchereau*, [1978] Q.B. 732; [1981] 2 All E.R. 924; [1977] E.C.R. 1999.

[2] See D. Wyatt, *Directly Applicable Provisions of EEC Law*, 125 New Law Journal pp. 458, 575, 669, 793.

[3] Case 9/70: *Franz Grad* v. *Finanzamt Traustein*, [1971] C.M.L.R. 1.

[4] European Communities Act 1972, s. 3(2). Otherwise a Community instrument is proved by production of a copy certified by an official of the institution which has promulgated that instrument (*ibid.*, s. 3(3)) or by production of a copy purporting to be printed by the Queen's Printer (*ibid.*, s. 3(4)).

researching into Community legislation will, in practice, find that the most expeditious course is to consult *Halsbury's Statutes of England* (Volume 42A) in which both primary and secondary legislation are grouped under the appropriate subject titles used in *Halsbury's Statutes*, the primary legislation being printed in full while the secondary legislation is summarised in a convenient form.

2   Operation of Community legislation

The Treaties themselves, being both primary legislation of the Communities and the source of the power to make the secondary legislation thereof, are not subject to review in either the European Court or the courts of the member states, although they are, of course, subject to interpretation.

As with subordinate legislation in the United Kingdom, the secondary legislation (regulations, directives and decisions) are subject to review by both the European Court and the courts of the member states. Moreover they are subject to review on wider grounds than are statutory instruments within the United Kingdom. As has been explained, the latter may only be impugned if they are *ultra vires*[5] or conflict with European Community legislation[6] and they are valid and effective until otherwise declared by the final decision of a court. Secondary legislation of the European Community institutions, on the other hand, may be impugned on the grounds of lack of competence, infringement of any essential procedural requirement, infringement of the Treaties or of any rule of law relating to their application or misuse of powers.[7] A review by the European Court may be obtained either by action taken for this purpose by a member state, by the Council or by the Commission or by way of appeal by an individual against a decision which is either addressed to him or is of direct and specific concern to him.[6] On such a review the European Court has power to declare the instrument void. The question of the validity of secondary legislation may also be determined by the national courts so that it would be open to a court in the United Kingdom to treat a secondary enactment as invalid (although it is to be expected that the court would be more likely to refer the question of validity under Article 177). This power is implicit in the terms of Article 177.[8]

Regulations come into force on the date specified in them or, in the absence of a specified date, on the twentieth day following their publication.[9] Directives and decisions take effect on the date on which they are notified to those to whom they are addressed.[9]

3   Interpretation of Community legislation.

The rules, refinements, technicalities and artifices which English courts have developed over the centuries in their approach to the interpretation of statutes have been demonstrated earlier in this chapter. They have led to, and

---

5 See p. 95, *ante.*
6 European Communities Act 1972, s. 2(4).
7 E.E.C. Treaty, Art. 173.
8 See p. 185, *post.*
9 E.E.C. Treaty, Art. 191.

sprung from, the meticulous care which is exercised in the drafting of our legislation. Community legislation is not drafted in the same mould. It is expressed (as the domestic legislation of the other Common Market countries tends to be drafted) in terms of broad principle, leaving the courts to supply the detail by giving effect, in particular cases, to the general intention of the institution that has enacted the instrument in question. Thus regulations, directives and decisions of the Council and of the Commission have to state the reasons on which they have been based and have to refer to any proposals or opinions which were required to be obtained pursuant to the Treaties.[10] These reasons are normally set out in the preamble to the instrument in question.

Accordingly, in terms of the traditional approaches to interpretation which have been adopted in this country,[11] the "literal rule" plays little or no part in the Community legislation, the purposive approach being the appropriate one.

Thus, for example, a fundamental question of interpretation which arises in relation to provisions in the Treaties, or directives or decisions, is whether the provision in question is "directly applicable", that is to say whether it operates to confer directly upon individuals rights enforceable by them in the courts of a member state, or whether it simply gives rise to reciprocal rights and obligations in international law.[12] The first two questions referred by PENNYCUICK, V.-C. in *Van Duyn* v. *Home Office*[13] were whether Article 48 of the E.E.C. Treaty and Directive 64/221 (adopted on February 25, 1964) were directly applicable. In deciding these questions affirmatively, the European Court stated that:[14]

> "It is necessary to examine, in every case, whether the nature, general scheme and wording of the provision in question are capable of having direct effects on the relations between member states and individuals."

It would seem to be incumbent upon English judges, when interpreting a provision, whether in the Treaties or in a Community instrument, to adopt a similar approach based upon adherence to principle rather than the letter of the law. This was recognised by LORD DENNING, M.R. in the course of his seminal judgment in *H.P. Bulmer, Ltd.* v. *J. Bollinger S.A.*[15]

> "What then are the principles of interpretation to be applied? Beyond doubt the English courts must follow the same principles as the European Court. Otherwise there would be differences between the countries of the nine. That would never do. All the courts of all nine countries should interpret the Treaty in the

---

10 *Ibid.*, Art. 190.
11 See p. 105, *ante.*
12 See p. 61, *ante.*
13 [1974] 3 All E.R. 178; [1974] 1 W.L.R. 1107; see p. 185, *post.*
14 Case 41/74; *Van Duyn* v. *Home Office (No. 2)*, [1975] Ch. 358, at p. 357; [1975] 3 All E.R. 190, at p. 205.
15 [1974] Ch. 401, at pp. 425–426; [1974] 2 All E.R. 1226, at pp. 1237–1238; for further points arising from the judgment of LORD DENNING, M.R. in this case (on the principles applicable in deciding whether or not to refer a case to the European Court under Article 177) see p. 380, *post.* See, also, *Application des Gaz S.A.* v. *Falks Veritas, Ltd.*, [1974] Ch. 381, at pp. 393–394; [1974] 3 All E.R. 51, at pp. 56–57 for further observations of LORD DENNING upon the style of Community legislation and the proper approach to be adopted in the interpretation thereof.

130 Part II—The Legal and Literary Sources of English Law

same way. They should all apply the same principles. It is enjoined on the English courts by section 3 of the European Communities Act 1972 which I have read.

What a task is thus set before us! The Treaty is quite unlike any of the enactments to which we have become accustomed. The draftsmen of our statutes have striven to express themselves with the utmost exactness. They have tried to foresee all possible circumstances that may arise and to provide for them. They have sacrificed style and simplicity. They have foregone brevity. They have become long and involved. In consequence, the judges have followed suit. They interpret a statute as applying only to the circumstances covered by the very words. They give them a literal interpretation. If the words of the statute do not cover a new situation—which was not foreseen—the judges hold that they have no power to fill the gap. To do so would be a 'naked usurpation of the legislative function': see *Magor and St. Mellons Rural District Council* v. *Newport Corporation*.[16] The gap must remain open until Parliament finds time to fill it.

How different is the Treaty! It lays down general principles. It expresses its aims and purposes. All in sentences of moderate length and commendable style. But it lacks precision. It uses words and phrases without defining what they mean. An English lawyer would look for an interpretation clause, but he would look in vain. There is none. All the way through the Treaty there are gaps and lacunae. These have to be filled in by the judges, or by regulations or directives. It is the European way. That appears from the decision or the Hamburg Court in *Re Tax on Imported Lemons*."[17]

Having dealt with the Treaty, LORD DENNING then turned to deal with the secondary legislation.

"Likewise the regulations and directives. They are enacted by the Council sitting in Brussels for everyone to obey. They are quite unlike our statutory instruments. They have to give the reasons on which they are based: article 190. So they start off with pages of preambles, 'whereas' and 'whereas' and 'whereas'. These show the purpose and intent of the regulations and directives. They follow the provisions which are to be obeyed. Here again words and phrases are used without defining their import. Such as 'personal conduct' in the Directive 64/221, article 3 (E.E.C.) which was considered by Pennycuick V.-C. in *Van Duyn* v. *Home Office*.[18] In case of difficulty, recourse is had to the preambles. These are useful to show the purpose and intent behind it all. But much is left to the judges. The enactments give only an outline plan. The details are to be filled in by the judges.

Seeing these differences, what are the English courts to do when they are faced with a problem of interpretation? They must follow the European pattern. No longer must they examine the words in meticulous detail. No longer must they argue about the precise grammatical sense. They must look to the purpose or intent. To quote the words of the European Court in the *Da Costa*[19] case, they must deduce 'from the wording and the spirit of the Treaty the meaning of the Community rules'. They must not confine themselves to the English text. They must consider, if need be, all the authentic texts, of which there are now six: see *Sociale Verzekeringsbank* v. *Van der Vecht*.[20] They must divine the spirit of the

16 [1952] A.C. 189, at p. 191; [1951] 2 All E.R. 839, at p. 841; the quoted words are from the speech of LORD SIMONDS, rebuking LORD DENNING himself in relation to his judgment in the Court of Appeal in that case; see p. 109, *ante*.
17 [1968] C.M.L.R. 1.
18 [1974] 3 All E.R. 178; [1974] 1 W.L.R. 1107.
19 Case 28–30/62: *Da Costa en Schaake NV* v. *Nederlandse Belastingadministratie*, [1963] C.M.L.R. 224, at p. 237.
20 [1968] C.M.L.R. 151.

Treaty and gain inspiration from it. If they find a gap, they must fill it as best they can. They must do what the framers of the instrument would have done if they had thought about it. So we must do the same. Those are the principles, as I understand it, on which the European Court acts.''

Where a Community directive or decision is implemented in the United Kingdom by means of subordinate legislation under section 2(2) of the 1972 Act,[1] the task of the English court will, *prima facie*, be to interpret the English statutory instrument rather than the Community instrument itself: in so doing the traditional rules of statutory interpretation would apply. It will be appreciated that inconsistency would arise if the English statutory instrument did not, on its true construction, bear the same meaning as that indicated by the Community instrument. The answer to this situation is provided by section 2(4) of the 1972 Act[2]—the English instrument would be of no effect to the extent of the inconsistency so that the directive or decision would remain, to that extent, unimplemented in the United Kingdom.

[1] See p. 60, *ante.*
[2] See p. 128, *ante.*

CHAPTER 6

Law Reports and Precedents

A THE RELATIONSHIP BETWEEN LAW REPORTS AND THE DOCTRINE OF PRECEDENT

The operation of the doctrine of precedent is inextricably bound up with law reporting. The rule is that any decision may be cited to a court provided that it is vouched for by a member of the Bar who was present when judgment was delivered. In addition, since judges take judicial notice of the whole of English law, an individual judge may rely upon a precedent of which he is aware even though the decision is unreported.[1] There is, thus, no rule that a case may only be cited or relied upon as a precedent if it is reported. Nevertheless personal recollection by judges or counsel is so impermanent and haphazard that it could not possibly form the basis of a workable system. Hence precedents are almost always contained in law reports. The close nexus between law reporting and the doctrine of judicial precedent is evidenced by the fact that the modern doctrine of binding precedent was formulated only when an integrated system of law reporting evolved in the nineteenth century.

In the face of the undoubted principle that reported and unreported cases are of equal authority some recent remarks of LORD DIPLOCK (with which all the other members of the House concurred) in *Roberts Petroleum, Ltd.* v. *Bernard Kenny, Ltd.*[2] caused considerable consternation among some sections of the profession.[3] After referring to a growing practice of citing unreported decisions of the Court of Appeal, LORD DIPLOCK went on:

> "My Lords, in my opinion, the time has come when your Lordships should adopt the practice of declining to allow transcripts of unreported judgments of the Civil Division of the Court of Appeal to be cited on the hearing of appeals to this House unless leave is given to do so, and that such leave should only be

---

[1] In addition, transcripts of judgments of the House of Lords and Court of Appeal are filed in the Supreme Court Library in London. Until 1951 no record was maintained anywhere of judgments of the Court of Appeal: see *Gibson* v. *South American Stores (Gath and Chaves) Ltd.*, [1950] Ch. 177, at p. 195; [1949] 2 All E.R. 985, at p. 995.

[2] [1983] 2 A.C. 192, at pp. 200–202; [1983] 1 All E.R. 564, at pp. 566–568.

[3] See, for example, Harrison, 'Unreported Cases: Myth and Reality', (1984) The Law Society's Gazette, p. 257.

granted on counsel's giving an assurance that the transcript contains a statement of some principle of law, relevant to an issue in the appeal to this House, that is binding on the Court of Appeal and of which the substance, as distinct from the mere choice, of phraseology, is not to be found in one of the generalised or specialised series of reports.''

A few days earlier, SIR JOHN DONALDSON, M.R., in the Court of Appeal, had contented himself with expressing the hope that counsel would display suitable restraint in the citation of precedent.[4]

It is important to distinguish a law report from a court record. The court record contains, basically, the names of the parties, the form of action (until these were abolished), the pleadings and the decision or order of the court. A law report contains most of these and, in addition, the judgment of the court containing the reasoning upon which the decision has been based. It is this reasoning which is the important element in the decision for the purposes of the doctrine of precedent. For this reason court records, such as the Plea Rolls, copies of which dating from the twelfth century are preserved in the Public Record Office, are of little value as precedents.

One might suppose that, because law reports are fundamental to the doctrine of precedent which is the cornerstone of the English legal system, the courts would have created a methodical system of producing law reports. It is an extraordinary anomaly that this has never been done. Law reporting has been left entirely to private enterprise so that, even at the present day, there is an element of chance and individual preference in the matter of whether or not a case is reported.

The historical evolution of the modern system of law reporting is considered below, but first the operation of the precedent system requires detailed examination.

B THE OPERATION OF THE DOCTRINE OF PRECEDENT

1 The doctrine of binding precedent

The traditional view of the function of an English judge is that it is not to make law but to decide cases in accordance with existing legal rules. This gives rise to the doctrine of binding precedent whereby the judge is not merely referred to earlier decisions for guidance; he is bound to apply the rules of law contained in those decisions. The operation of the doctrine depends upon the hierarchy of the courts. All courts stand in a definite relationship to one another. A court is bound by decisions of a court above itself in the hierarchy and, usually, by a court of equivalent standing. Given that the doctrine of precedent has binding force within this framework, the question naturally arises of how the law may develop if cases are always to be determined according to ageless principles. In practice there are several ways in which the doctrine retains its flexibility. These are dealt with in detail below[5] but it is sufficient to note at this juncture two basic principles: first,

---

[4] *Stanley* v. *International Harvester Co. of Great Britain, Ltd.*, (1983) *The Times*, 7 February.
[5] See p. 140, *post.*

that superior courts have power to overrule decisions of inferior courts and, in certain cases, to overrule their own earlier decisions, and, secondly, that any rule of law may be changed by statute. Consequently every rule of law is subject to change, either by the judges themselves or by Parliament. However, the disadvantage of legislation as a source of law is that statutes require interpretation by judges, and these interpretations are in themselves judicial precedents. Therefore it is an oversimplification to regard legislation as superior to precedent as a source of law.

The advantages of the precedent system are said to be certainty, precision and flexibility.[6] Legal certainty is achieved, in theory at least, in that, if the legal problem raised has been solved before, the judge is bound to adopt that solution. Precision is achieved by the sheer volume of reported cases containing solutions to innumerable factual situations arising in any particular branch of the law. No code or statute, no matter how carefully drafted, could anticipate the legal problems which these variations of fact may promote. Consequently, the judge in a continental legal system must generally decide cases on the basis of broad principles. Finally, flexibility is achieved by the possibility of decisions being overruled and by the possibility of distinguishing and confining the operation of decisions which appear unsound, the latter process being of particular importance.

The obvious disadvantages of the system are its inherent rigidity, which may occasionally cause hardship, and the vast and ever-increasing bulk of reported cases to which the court must advert to determine what is the law, since an excess of case law tends to obscure basic principles.[7]

Finally, it is self-evident that there cannot be an infinite regression. Every rule of law must have its origin. If it was not created by statute, then it must have been created by a court. Thus where there is no precedent the doctrine breaks down and the judge is bound to reach a decision in accordance with general principles. Even in modern times cases arise for which there is no precedent. These cases are described as cases of first impression and require the judge to make law rather than to apply it.[8] This he will do by reference to analogous principles but even legal principles must have their origin so that the declaratory theory of the common law is not of universal application.[9]

---

6. See observations of RUSSELL, L.J. (as he then was) in *Gallie* v. *Lee*, [1969] 2 Ch. 17, at p. 41; [1969] 1 All E.R. 1062, at p. 1076 (affirmed *sub. nom. Saunders* v. *Anglia Building Society*, [1971] A.C. 1004; [1970] 3 All E.R. 961) and of LORD HAILSHAM in *Cassell & Co., Ltd.* v. *Broome*, [1972] A.C. 1027, at p. 1054; [1972] 1 All E.R. 801, at p. 809 ("in legal matters, some degree of certainty is at least as valuable a part of justice as perfection").

7. Thus, for example, in *Qureshi* v. *Qureshi*, [1972] Fam. 173; [1971] 1 All E.R. 325 some 94 authorities (and 8 textbooks) appear to have been cited to the court. The current attitude of appellate courts, faced with ever-increasing demands upon court time, is to discourage extensive citation of authorities, particularly where they are merely illustrative of general principles which are adequately set out in a leading case; see observations of LORD DIPLOCK in *Lambert* v. *Lewis*, [1982] A.C. 225; [1981] 1 All E.R. 1185.

8. E.g., *Philips* v. *Brooks*, [1919] 2 K.B. 243; *Noble* v. *Harrison*, [1926] 2 K.B. 332; *Lancashire Loans, Ltd.* v. *Black*, [1934] 1 K.B. 380; *British Transport Commission* v. *Gourley*, [1956] A.C. 185; [1955] 3 All E.R. 796; *Malone* v. *Metropolitan Police Commissioner (No. 2)*, [1979] Ch. 344; [1979] 2 All E.R. 620; *Midland Bank Trust Co., Ltd.* v. *Green (No. 3)*, [1982] Ch. 529; [1981] 3 All E.R. 744; *Parker* v. *British Airways Board*, [1982] Q.B. 1004; [1982] 1 All E.R. 834.

9. See LORD SIMON's observations upon the declaratory theory of the common law in *Jones* v. *Secretary of State for Social Services*, [1972] A.C. 944, at p. 1026; [1972] 1 All E.R. 145, at p. 198, quoted at p. 234, *post*.

Before considering in detail the doctrine of binding precedent (or *stare decisis*) it is necessary to express a possible reservation as to its universal applicability in the English courts, which arises from the judgments of the majority of the Court of Appeal in *Trendtex Trading Corporation, Ltd.* v. *Central Bank of Nigeria*.[10] The question at issue was whether the defendant bank could claim sovereign immunity from action,[11] on the basis that it was a department or organ of the state of Nigeria. The Court of Appeal held that it could not; first, because it had not established that it was a department of the state (a ground upon which the court was unanimous) and secondly (STEPHENSON, L.J. dissenting) on the ground that there was a rule of international law that the doctrine of sovereign immunity was not applicable to the ordinary commercial transactions, as distinct from the governmental acts, of a sovereign state, which rule was part of English law. The difficulty in the path of the second ground was that there was authority of the Court of Appeal against it which, according to the ordinary rules,[12] would bind the court in the instant case. However, LORD DENNING, M.R., with whom SHAW, L.J. agreed, overcame this difficulty by stating, as a principle, that the rule of *stare decisis* had no application to the rules of international law and, therefore, no application to that part of English law which embodies current international law. If this reasoning is upheld in subsequent cases, it will constitute an important, albeit limited, exception to the doctrine of binding precedent, and being a decision of the Court of Appeal it must, for the time being, be taken as an accurate statement of what the law is.

2 The binding element in precedents

a The ratio decidendi

It is a misstatement to speak of a "decision" as being binding, just as it is not technically correct to regard a "decision" as overruled. It is not the decision which binds, any more than it is the decision which is overruled; it is the rule of law contained in the decision. This element in a decision is termed the *ratio decidendi* of the case. Not every statement of law made by a judge in the course of his judgment is part of the *ratio*. For this reason it is important to be able to analyse a decision and isolate from it the *ratio decidendi*.

Every decision contains the following basic ingredients:

(1) findings of material facts, direct and inferential. An inferential finding of fact is the inference which the judge (or jury if there is one) draws from the direct, or perceptible, facts. For example, from the direct facts of the speed of a vehicle, the length of skid marks and the state of the road the judge or jury may infer negligence. Negligence is an inferential finding of fact. Similarly, unreasonable behaviour, in matrimonial proceedings, is an inference of fact which may or may not be drawn from the direct facts of the respondent spouse's treatment of the other spouse during the marriage;

---

[10] [1977] Q.B. 529; [1977] 1 All E.R. 881. The question at issue in the case has now been resolved by the State Immunity Act 1978, s. 3(1); see p. 304, *post*.

[11] See p. 304, *post*.

[12] As to which, see p. 148, *post*.

(2) statements of the principles of law applicable to the legal problems disclosed by the facts; and

(3) judgment based on the combined effect of (1) and (2).

For the purposes of the parties themselves and their privies, (3) is the material element in the decision for it determines finally their rights and liabilities in relation to the subject matter of the action. It is the judgment that estops the parties from reopening the dispute.[13]

However, for the purpose of the doctrine of precedent, (2) is the vital element in the decision. This is, indeed, the *ratio decidendi*. Thus the *ratio decidendi* may be defined as the statement of law applied to the legal problems raised by the facts as found upon which the decision is based. The two other elements in the decision are not precedents. The judgment is not binding (except directly on the parties themselves); nor are the findings of fact. This means that, even where the direct facts of an earlier case appear to be identical to those of the case before the court, the judge or jury is not bound to draw the same inference as that drawn in the earlier case. This point is well illustrated by the leading case of *Qualcast (Wolverhampton) Ltd.* v. *Haynes*.[14] In that case an employee sued his employers for damages for negligence in failing to provide a safe system of work. The county court judge, at first instance, held himself bound to find the defendant liable by earlier cases in which employers, having taken similar precautions to those taken by the defendants in the present case, had been held liable. This was wrong for, as the House of Lords explained, these cases, even though decided by a judge sitting alone rather than with a jury, were decisions based upon inferences of fact which were not to be regarded as binding. Otherwise, as LORD SOMERVELL observed:[15] "the precedent system will die from a surfeit of authorities".

Moreover, not every statement of law in a judgment is binding. Only those statements which are based upon the facts as found and upon which the decision is based are binding. Any other statement of law is, strictly, superfluous and is described as an *obiter dictum* (something said "by the way").

b   Obiter dicta

There are two types of *obiter dicta*. First, a statement of law is regarded as *obiter* if it is based upon facts which either were not found to exist or, if found, were not found to be material. For example, the famous statement of equitable estoppel contained in the judgment of DENNING, J. (as he then was) in *Central London Property Trust, Ltd.* v. *High Trees House, Ltd.*[16] is clearly *obiter* since it applied to a set of facts which were not found to be present in the case. Similarly, in *Rondel* v. *Worsley*[17] the House of Lords expressed opinions to the effect that a barrister might be held liable in tort

---

13 See p. 589, *post*.
14 [1959] A.C. 743; [1959] 2 All E.R. 38.
15 [1959] A.C., at p. 758; [1959] 2 All E.R., at p. 43. It should be remembered that, in the tort of negligence, only the existence of a duty of care is a question of law; whether or not the defendant has broken his duty is a question of fact.
16 [1947] K.B. 30; [1956] 1 All E.R. 256n.
17 [1969] 1 A.C. 191; [1967] 3 All E.R. 993; see p. 270, *post*.

when acting outside the province of litigation and that a solicitor, when acting as advocate, might enjoy immunity from action. Since the case concerned only the liability of a barrister when acting as advocate, the opinions in question were necessarily *obiter*.

A second type of *obiter dictum* is a statement of law which, although based on the facts as found, does not form the basis of the decision. An obvious example is a statement of law in support of a dissenting judgment. Similarly, where a court makes statements of law leading to one conclusion and then adopts a contrary decision on the facts for a different reason, those statements are necessarily *obiter* since they do not support the decision. This is illustrated by the decision of the House of Lords in *Hedley Byrne & Co., Ltd. v. Heller & Partners, Ltd.*[18] The proposition of law in that case, that the maker of a statement owes a duty of care, in certain circumstances, to persons whom he may expect to rely upon that statement, is, strictly, *obiter* since the bank which gave the advice was protected by its disclaimer of responsibility. That being so, the further statement as to what rule of law would have been applied but for the disclaimer cannot be regarded as essential to the decision. This was recognized by DANCKWERTS, L.J. in *Rondel v. Worsley*[19] where that Lord Justice expressed the view that the wide statement of the law made by the House of Lords in *Hedley Byrne* was no more than a *dictum*. Nevertheless, *Hedley Byrne* does illustrate that the strict rules for isolating the *ratio decidendi* of a case are sometimes of little value since, the reasoning of the House of Lords, having been expressly applied in the Court of Appeal and approved in the House of Lords,[20] undoubtedly represents the present English law. It seems that where the House of Lords states a rule of law and expressly overrules earlier contrary decisions, that statement will be treated as binding even though not strictly essential to the decision.[1]

In some cases the court decides a case and goes on to state a principle of law which is of much wider application than the decision requires. In such a case only that part of the statement of law which applies to the actual facts of the case before the court is *ratio*, the wider principle embodied in the statement being *obiter*. A good illustration of this may be found in the line of cases concerning the liability of hospitals for the negligence of surgeons and other hospital staff. In *Hillyer v. St. Bartholomew's Hospital*[2] the Court of Appeal, in considering the liability of a hospital for the negligence of a consultant surgeon, stated a broad principle that a hospital was not vicariously liable for the negligence of any doctor, because the hospital could not control the manner in which he performed his work. This statement was clearly wider than was necessary for the decision and the Court of Appeal, in

---

[18] [1964] A.C. 465; [1963] 2 All E.R. 575.
[19] [1967] 1 Q.B. 443; [1966] 3 All E.R. 657; (affirmed [1969] 1 A.C. 191; [1967] 3 All E.R. 993).
[20] *Arenson v. Casson, Beckman, Rutley & Co.*, [1977] A.C. 405; [1975] 3 All E.R. 901.
[1] A similar example is afforded by the case of *Fairman v. Perpetual Investment Building Society*, [1923] A.C. 74, where the statement of law as to whether the plaintiff was an invitee or a licensee was not essential to the decision and, therefore, strictly *obiter*. Nevertheless the House of Lords subsequently regarded this statement as a second *ratio* of the case in *Jacobs v. London County Council*, [1950] A.C. 361; [1950] 1 All E.R. 737; the cases are now of purely academic interest since s. 1 of the Occupiers' Liability Act 1957 has abolished the common law distinction between invitees and licensees.
[2] [1909] 2 K.B. 820.

a later case,[3] limited the principle to liability for consultant surgeons and held it not to apply to a resident surgeon, since the basis of vicarious liability is the existence of a contract of service rather than the ability of the employer to control the manner in which the employee performs his work.[4]

It is difficult to isolate the *ratio decidendi* of a case which is argued on more than one ground. If the court is willing to decide the case on one ground it will usually refrain from expressing an opinion on any other point of law raised. Such a point is then said to be "left open". There are numerous important points of law which have been left open and which remain, as yet, undecided.[5] However the court sometimes feels constrained to deal with every point of law raised and then to give its decision. Which of these statements of law is the *ratio decidendi* of the case? The problem often arises when considering the decisions of appellate courts where different members of the court have arrived at the same conclusion, but for different reasons. A reason adopted by a majority of the court is, *prima facie, ratio* whereas a reason adopted only by a minority is usually regarded as inessential to the decision and, therefore, not binding. The position is even more complicated where no one reason is favoured by a majority. Clearly every case must have a *ratio decidendi* and the answer seems to be that it depends upon which of the alternative reasons subsequent courts are prepared to accept as *rationes*. It is certainly possible for a case to have two or more *rationes decidendi*. The case of *Fairman* v. *Perpetual Investment Building Society*[6] is an example. The House of Lords in that case gave two reasons for its decision, both of which were accepted as binding by the House itself in *Jacobs* v. *London County Council*.[7] On the other hand, in *Read* v. *J. Lyons & Co., Ltd.*[8] the House of Lords advanced two reasons for its decision that the defendants were not liable under the rule in *Rylands* v. *Fletcher*:[9] (1) that the rule did not apply in the absence of an escape of the dangerous substance from the defendant's occupation or control; and (2) that the rule did not apply unless the plaintiff had an interest in land affected by the escape. The second reason, which is principally contained in the speech of LORD MACMILLAN, was, in a later case,[10] treated by the Court of Appeal as *obiter*, on the basis that it was not essential to the decision. The position is complicated in that

---

[3] *Cassidy* v. *Ministry of Health*, [1951] 2 K.B. 343; [1951] 1 All E.R. 574; see also *Gold* v. *Essex County Council*, [1942] 2 K.B. 293; [1942] 2 All E.R. 237.

[4] For an illustration of a wide principle being subsequently narrowed see *Re Grosvenor Hotel, London* (*No. 2*), [1965] Ch. 1210; [1964] 3 All E.R. 354, in which the Court of Appeal treated as *obiter* (and wrong) the wide statement of the law relating to Crown privilege made by the then Lord Chancellor in *Duncan* v. *Cammell, Laird & Co., Ltd.*, [1942] A.C. 624; [1942] 1 All E.R. 587, notwithstanding that the statement in question had been applied by appellate courts on several occasions; see now *Conway* v. *Rimmer*, [1968] A.C. 910; [1968] 1 All E.R. 874.

[5] See *Minter* v. *Priest*, [1930] A.C. 558; *Dunne* v. *North-Western Gas Board*, [1964] 2 Q.B. 806; [1963] 3 All E.R. 916.

[6] [1923] A.C. 74.

[7] [1950] A.C. 361; [1950] 1 All E.R. 737. The case is particularly notable in that one of the two reasons given in *Fairman*'s case was clearly not essential to the decision. See fn. 1, p. 137, *ante*.

[8] [1947] A.C. 146; [1946] 2 All E.R. 471.

[9] (1868), L.R. 3 H.L. 330.

[10] *Perry* v. *Kendricks Transport, Ltd.*, [1956] 1 All E.R. 154; [1956] 1 W.L.R. 85.

the statement to this effect in the Court of Appeal case was, itself, *obiter* because the plaintiff's action failed for another reason. Consequently it remains undecided whether the second reason in *Read* v. *J. Lyons & Co., Ltd.* is *ratio* or *obiter*.[11]

A variation of the difficulty described above arises where the majority of a court favour a reason which does not support the decision which the court in the event gives. That reason cannot, by definition, be a *ratio decidendi* because it does not support the decision; on the other hand to treat the contrary reasoning of the minority as *ratio*, although theoretically defensible, is logically odd. The occasions on which such a dilemma will arise are likely to be very rare, but the hearing by the House of Lords of the appeal in *Central Asbestos Co., Ltd.* v. *Dodd*[12] was such an occasion. The question before the House turned on the construction of the ill-drafted provisions of section 7(3) of the Limitation Act 1963. LORDS REID and MORRIS took one view of the law, LORDS SIMON and SALMON a different view. The fifth member of the court, LORD PEARSON, was in favour of deciding the appeal in the same way as LORDS REID and MORRIS, but for a different reason, his view on the point of law substantially supporting that of LORDS SIMON and SALMON.

It was not long before the Court of Appeal was called upon to decide the point of law which had arisen in *Dodd*'s case (which was, put simply, whether time ran against a plaintiff who knew the facts upon which his action was based but did not know that these facts gave him a cause of action). The Court of Appeal held[13] that, since *Dodd*'s case had no discernible *ratio decidendi*, the Court of Appeal would go back to the law as contained in the earlier cases.

It would be erroneous to suppose that *obiter dicta* are of no authority. Strictly, they are not of binding authority but have only persuasive authority. Nevertheless, where the statement in question has fallen from a court of high authority and is a deliberate statement of law as opposed to a casual expression of opinion it will usually be followed in the absence of binding authority to the contrary. By way of example may be cited the case of *Adams* v. *Naylor*[14] in which the House of Lords disapproved the practice of Government departments setting up a nominal defendant to avoid the Crown's immunity from actions in tort. Although this disapproval was *obiter*, the Court of Appeal in *Royster* v. *Cavey*[15] adopted it and refused to sanction this

---

[11] The Court of Appeal in *Dunne* v. *North-Western Gas Board*, [1964] 2 Q.B. 806; [1963] 3 All E.R. 916, expressly left the point open.

[12] [1973] A.C. 518; [1972] 2 All E.R. 1135.

[13] *Harper* v. *National Coal Board*, [1974] Q.B. 614; [1974] 2 All E.R. 441. The cases are of no more than academic interest, so far as the limitation point is concerned, since Parliament intervened by passing the Limitation Act 1975 (now the Limitation Act 1980), which supports the view that the interpretation of the law intended by Parliament was that favoured by the minority in *Dodd*'s case. In *Miliangos* v. *George Frank (Textiles), Ltd.*, [1976] A.C. 443, at p. 479; [1975] 3 All E.R. 801, at p. 822 LORD SIMON was critical of the Court of Appeal in *Harper* for not following the minority reasoning in *Dodd* but, since that reasoning did not support the decision, it is difficult to support LORD SIMON's criticism and, indeed, difficult to see what other course was open to the Court of Appeal.

[14] [1946] A.C. 443; [1946] 2 All E.R. 241.

[15] [1947] K.B. 204; [1946] 2 All E.R. 642. This decision precipitated the passing of the Crown Proceedings Act 1947 which enabled the Crown to be sued in tort.

long-standing practice. Similarly, the statement of the principle of equitable estoppel made by DENNING, J. (as he then was) in *Central London Property Trust, Ltd.* v. *High Trees House, Ltd.*,[16] although clearly *obiter*, has been adopted by superior courts and is now an accepted rule of equity.[17] There could be no more striking example, finally, than the "neighbour principle" propounded by LORD ATKIN in *M'Alister (or Donoghue)* v. *Stevenson*.[18] This statement of law, though far wider than the decision required, has become the basis of the modern tort of negligence and has been cited and applied on occasions too numerous to mention.

3   Precedents which are not binding

a   Persuasive authorities

Only the *ratio decidendi* of a decision is binding. *Obiter dicta* are of persuasive authority. It has already been noted that the *dicta* of an appellate court may carry great weight. However, *dicta*, of whatever weight, may be rejected if a later court wishes to adopt a contrary solution.

Other persuasive precedents are decisions of courts inferior in the hierarchy to the court which is invited to follow their decisions. Thus, for example, Court of Appeal decisions are of persuasive authority in the House of Lords.

A third class of persuasive authorities consists of the decisions of Scottish, Irish, Commonwealth and foreign courts. There is an increasing tendency on the part of English judges to draw analogies from other legal systems but these authorities are accepted as being of persuasive authority only. Special mention must be made of "decisions" of the Judicial Committee of the Privy Council. The advice of the Privy Council to Her Majesty is not strictly binding on any English judge. Thus, even a first instance judge may legitimately decline to follow a decision of the Privy Council.[19] However, Privy Council decisions are of very great persuasive authority for the obvious reason that the Council is in practice composed, for judicial sittings, of those persons who usually sit in the House of Lords. Nevertheless, despite the similarity in composition between the Privy Council and the House of Lords, there had not, until recently, been any suggestion that Privy Council authorities were of equivalent weight to House of Lords cases. However, the Court of Appeal in the case of *Doughty* v. *Turner Manufacturing Co., Ltd.*[20] expressed the view (albeit *obiter*) that the Court of Appeal's own decision in *Re Polemis*[1] was no longer good law in the light of the subsequent Privy Council decision in *The Wagon Mound*.[2] More recently, in *Worcester Works Finance, Ltd.* v. *Cooden Engineering Co., Ltd.*,[3] the Court of Appeal, faced

---

16 [1947] K.B. 130; [1956] 1 All E.R. 256n.
17 See *Tool Metal Manufacturing Co., Ltd.* v. *Tungsten Electric Co., Ltd.*, [1955] 2 All E.R. 657; *D. and C. Builders, Ltd.* v. *Rees*, [1966] 2 Q.B. 617; [1965] 3 All E.R. 837.
18 [1932] A.C. 562.
19 DIPLOCK, J. (as he then was) did so in *Port Line, Ltd.* v. *Ben Line Steamers, Ltd.*, [1958] 2 Q.B. 146; [1958] 1 All E.R. 787. See also *Dulieu* v. *White*, [1901] 2 K.B. 669.
20 [1964] 1 Q.B. 518; [1964] 1 All E.R. 98.
1 [1921] 3 K.B. 560.
2 *Overseas Tankship (U.K.), Ltd.* v. *Morts Dock and Engineering Co., Ltd.*, [1961] A.C. 388; [1961] 1 All E.R. 404.
3 [1972] 1 Q.B. 210; [1971] 3 All E.R. 708.

with a conflict of authority between previous decisions of the Court of Appeal and a later decision of the Privy Council, had no hesitation in preferring the latter, LORD DENNING, M.R., laying down the principle that when the Privy Council disapproves of a previous decision of the Court of Appeal, the latter is at liberty to depart from its previous decision. In the light of these decisions it now seems that decisions of the Privy Council enjoy a standing as precedents superior to that of precedents of the Court of Appeal.

b Precedents which have been overruled

A precedent does not lose its authority with the passing of time. Indeed the strength of a precedent increases with age in that courts tend to be reluctant to overrule long-standing authorities, unless they are clearly wrong. Apart from the desirability of attaining certainty, the main reason for the reluctance of judges to overrule old decisions is the fact that, since overruling operates retrospectively, it might have the effect of disturbing financial arrangements, depriving persons of vested proprietary rights and even imposing criminal liability. Thus in *Re Compton*[4] the Court of Appeal would not overrule a long line of old authorities concerning charitable trusts although it considered these cases anomalous. Similarly the rule in *Pinnel's Case*,[5] though plainly anomalous, has never been overruled. In *Foakes* v. *Beer*[6] the House of Lords would not overrule *Pinnel's Case*; LORD FITZGERALD, though doubting that the rule was a good one, did not feel that the House would be justified in overruling it having regard simply to its longevity.[7] On the other hand there is little hesitation felt in overruling decisions which the court considers to be clearly wrong. Thus in *Bourne* v. *Keane*[8] the House, considering an aspect of the law of trusts, overruled by a majority a series of long-standing decisions even though this had the effect of disturbing many existing trusts and settlements. More recently in *Button* v. *Director of Public Prosecutions*[9] the House of Lords, in holding that the common law offence of affray could be committed in a private place, overruled a line of authority to the effect that an affray could take place only in a public place, while in the leading case of *Miliangos* v. *George Frank (Textiles), Ltd*.[10] the House of Lords overruled[11] its own decision in *Re United Railways of the Havana and Regla Warehouses, Ltd*.[12] which embodied one of the clearest and most firmly entrenched rules of English law, namely that judgment must be given in sterling.

The process of overruling must be carefully distinguished from the process of reversing a decision. A decision altered on appeal is said to be "reversed". Reversing differs from overruling in that the former affects the decision in

---

[4] [1945] Ch. 123; [1945] 1 All E.R. 198.
[5] (1602), 5 Rep. 117a.
[6] (1884), 9 App. Cas. 605.
[7] *Ibid.*, at p. 630. The rule has, of course, been undermined by the doctrine of equitable estoppel: see *D. and C. Builders, Ltd.* v. *Rees*, [1966] 2 Q.B. 617; [1965] 3 All E.R. 837.
[8] [1919] A.C. 815.
[9] [1966] A.C. 591; [1965] 3 All E.R. 587.
[10] [1976] A.C. 443; [1975] 3 All E.R. 801.
[11] Although the majority of the House stated that it was "departing from" the decision in the *Havana* case, it amounts in effect to overruling that case.
[12] [1961] A.C. 1007; [1960] 2 All E.R. 332.

the case whereas the latter only affects the rule of law upon which the decision is based.[13] Strictly, it is not correct to speak of a decision as "overruled" since it is only the rule of law contained in the decision which is affected, not the decision itself.

A decision may be overruled either by statute or by a higher court. If it is overruled by a higher court the earlier decision is deemed to have been based on a misunderstanding of the law. The earlier rule of law is deemed never to have existed. This is the declaratory theory of the common law. The common law is never changed; it is merely restated correctly. Consequently all judicial overruling operates retrospectively. It is this which distinguishes judicial overruling from overruling by statute, since the latter (in the absence of an express provision to the contrary) operates only when the statute becomes operative. Another difference between judicial overruling and overruling by statute is that statutes, unlike judges, do not expressly name the decisions which they overrule. Nevertheless it is not usually difficult to identify the cases which are overruled by a statute, particularly where the statute follows closely upon an unpopular decision of a superior court, often the House of Lords.

It appears that in the Supreme Court of the United States there is power to overrule decisions prospectively, that is to apply the earlier decision to the facts of the instant case but to overrule it in so far as it may affect future cases.[14] In the United States Supreme Court the power is held to be based on the common law, though it has never been recognised in this country. However, in *Jones* v. *Secretary of State for Social Services*[15] a case in which the House of Lords declined to overrule a previous decision of the House although a majority were of the opinion that the *ratio* of the earlier decision was wrong, LORD SIMON advanced the opinion that the most satisfactory method of dealing with the appeal would have been to allow it on the basis that, it was covered by the earlier decision but to have overruled the earlier decision prospectively. In the event, however, he simply concurred in allowing the appeal and went on to say that, although an extension of judicial power to include prospective overruling should be considered (a suggestion with which LORD DIPLOCK agreed), it would preferably be the subject of Parliamentary enactment, adding:[16]

> "In the first place, informed professional opinion is probably to the effect that your Lordships have no power to overrule decisions with prospective effect only; such opinion is itself a source of law; and your Lordships, sitting judicially, are bound by any rule of law arising extra-judicially. Secondly, to proceed by Act of Parliament would obviate any suspicion of endeavouring to upset one-sidedly the constitutional balance between executive, legislature and judiciary. Thirdly, concomitant problems could receive consideration—for example whether other courts supreme within their own jurisdictions should have similar

---

[13] See *Metropolitan Police District Receiver* v. *Croydon Corporation*, [1957] 2 Q.B. 154; [1957] 1 All E.R. 478.

[14] *Linkletter* v. *Walker* (1965), 381 U.S. 618, cited in *Jones* v. *Secretary of State for Social Services* (*infra*).

[15] [1972] A.C. 944; [1972] 1 All E.R. 145; see p. 146, *post*.

[16] [1972] A.C., at pp. 1026–1027; [1972] 1 All E.R., at p. 198; LORD SIMON advanced substantially similar suggestions in *Miliangos* v. *George Frank (Textiles), Ltd.*, [1976] A.C. 443, at p. 490; [1975] 3 All E.R. 801, at p. 832.

powers as regards the rule of precedent; whether machinery could and should be devised to apprise the courts of the potential repercussions of any particular decision; and whether any court (including the appellate committee of your Lordships' House) should sit in banc when invited to review a previous decision.''

The passage above illustrates clearly the reasons why it is preferable for major changes in the law to be made by Parliament, rather than by the judiciary.

c Precedents which can be distinguished

The process of "distinguishing" is probably the major factor in enabling the doctrine of precedent to remain flexible and adaptable. Cases are distinguished on their facts. The *ratio decidendi* of a case is, by definition, based upon the material facts of that case. Consequently if the court is willing to regard as material any fact not common to the case before it and the precedent cited, the two cases can be distinguished. The law reports are full of strained distinctions where the court was evidently anxious not to follow an apparently binding precedent. In theory it is possible to distinguish virtually any precedent since factual situations will almost never precisely duplicate themselves. Nevertheless there are practical limits beyond which the court will be unlikely to go. Cases which are indistinguishable are described as being "on all fours" with one another. To illustrate how fine a distinction may be drawn between ostensibly parallel factual situations reference may be made to two well known cases concerning the tort of conversion. In *England* v. *Cowley*[17] the defendant refused to allow the plaintiff to remove goods from his, the defendant's, premises. This was held not to be conversion since there was no absolute denial of title. This case was distinguished by the Court of Appeal in *Oakley* v. *Lyster*[18] in which the defendant refused to allow the plaintiff to remove material from his, the defendant's, land and, in addition, asserted his own title to the material. This was held to be an act of conversion, the assertion of title apparently making the denial of title absolute.

d Statements of law made per incuriam

The Court of Appeal in the leading case of *Young* v. *Bristol Aeroplane Co., Ltd.*[19] established the principle that the Court of Appeal was not bound to follow its own earlier decision if satisfied that the decision in question was reached *per incuriam* (through lack of care). This means that some relevant statutory provision or precedent, which would have affected the decision, was not brought to the attention of the court. Although the principle in *Young's* case was expressed to apply only to the Court of Appeal, it has been applied in other courts. Thus in *R.* v. *Northumberland Compensation Appeal Tribunal, Ex parte Shaw*[20] a divisional court of the King's Bench Division declined to follow a Court of Appeal decision on the ground that

---

[17] (1873), L.R. 8 Exch. 126.
[18] [1931] 1 K.B. 148.
[19] [1944] L.B. 718; [1944] 2 All E.R. 293 (affirmed [1946] A.C. 163; [1946] 1 All E.R. 98); see p. 148, *post*.
[20] [1951] 1 K.B. 711; [1951] 1 All E.R. 268.

the latter had been reached *per incuriam*, a relevant House of Lords decision not having been cited to the Court of Appeal. In *Cassell & Co., Ltd.* v. *Broome*[1] the House of Lords rejected in condemnatory terms the Court of Appeal's decision to the effect that the decision of the House of Lords in *Rookes* v. *Barnard*[2] on the issue of exemplary damages had been reached *per incuriam* because of two previous decisions of the House. LORD HAILSHAM, L.C., in the course of the leading speech for the majority, asserted that[3]

> "it is not open to the Court of Appeal to give gratuitous advice to judges of first instance to ignore decisions of the House of Lords in this way . . . The course taken would have put judges of first instance in an embarrassing position, as driving them to take sides in an unedifying dispute between the Court of Appeal . . . and the House of Lords."

while LORD REID[4] took the view that it was "obvious that the Court of Appeal failed to understand LORD DEVLIN's speech". The words of LORD HAILSHAM proved to be prophetic because in *Miliangos* v. *George Frank (Textiles), Ltd.*[5] BRISTOW, J. (as he expressly acknowledged) found himself in the position of embarrassment foreseen by LORD HAILSHAM. That the learned judge found himself in such a position was due to the fact that in *Schorsch Meier G.m.b.H.* v. *Hennin*[6] the Court of Appeal had held that the rule of law whereby money judgments could only be expressed in sterling had ceased to exist, notwithstanding clear House of Lords authority for the existence of the rule. BRISTOW, J. preferred to follow the House of Lords authority; the Court of Appeal (perhaps not surprisingly) stated that he was wrong in so doing because *Schorsch Meier* was binding upon him. On appeal[7] the House of Lords decision in question[8] was overruled, although not on any of the grounds on which the Court of Appeal had cited either in the instant case or in *Schorsch Meier*.

The *per incuriam* principle is of limited application. Very few decisions have subsequently been regarded as having been reached *per incuriam* and in *Morelle, Ltd.* v. *Wakeling*[9] SIR RAYMOND EVERSHED, M.R. reaffirmed that:

> "As a general rule the only cases in which decisions should be held to have been given *per incuriam* are those of decisions given in ignorance or forgetfulness of

[1] [1972] A.C. 1027; [1972] 1 All E.R. 801.
[2] [1964] A.C. 1129; [1964] 1 All E.R. 367. This decision had already been subjected to devastating criticism in the courts of the Commonwealth and had been repudiated by the Privy Council; see *Australian Consolidated Press, Ltd.* v. *Uren*, [1969] 1 A.C. 590; [1967] 3 All E.R. 523. No less devastating was the criticism of LORD DENNING, M.R., culminating in the description of the doctrine laid down by LORD DEVLIN in *Rookes* v. *Barnard* as "hopelessly illogical and inconsistent"; *Broome* v. *Cassell & Co., Ltd.*, [1971] 2 Q.B. 354, at p. 381; [1971] 2 All E.R. 187, at p. 199, an approach which attracted vehement criticism from the majority of the House of Lords.
[3] [1972] A.C. 1027, at p. 1054; [1972] 1 All E.R. 801, at p. 809.
[4] [1972] A.C., at p. 1084; [1972] 1 All E.R., at p. 835.
[5] [1975] Q.B. 487; [1975] 1 All E.R. 1076.
[6] [1975] Q.B. 416; [1975] 1 All E.R. 152; [1975] 1 C.M.L.R. 20.
[7] [1976] A.C. 443; [1975] 3 All E.R. 801.
[8] *Re United Railways of the Havana and Ragla Warehouses, Ltd.*, [1961] A.C. 1007; [1960] 2 All E.R. 332 (a decision to which LORD DENNING himself had been a party).
[9] [1955] 2 Q.B. 379, at p. 406; [1955] 1 All E.R. 708, at p. 718; see also *Miliangos* v. *George Frank (Textiles), Ltd.*, [1976] A.C. 443, at p. 477; [1975] 3 All E.R. 801, at p. 821, *per* LORD SIMON.

some inconsistent statutory provision or of some authority binding on the court concerned: so that in such cases some part of the decision or some step in the reasoning on which it is based is found, on that account, to be demonstrably wrong. This definition is not necessarily exhaustive, but cases not strictly within it which can properly be held to have been decided *per incuriam* must, in our judgment, consistently with the *stare decisis* rule which is an essential feature of our law, be, in the language of LORD GREENE, M.R. of the rarest occurrence.''

Thus the doctrine will not be extended to cases which were merely not fully or expertly argued,[10] or were argued on one side only (as *Schorsch Meier* was), or were cases in which the court appeared to misunderstand the law or was not aware of considerations of policy underlying a statute[11] or adopted a statutory interpretation which appears to be wrong. However, if it appeared to a court that a previous court's interpretation of a statute was an impossible interpretation (as opposed merely to an incorrect one) then it would seem that the duty of the later court is to apply a correct interpretation;[11] whether this would be an example of the *per incuriam* doctrine or simply an illustration of the general rules relating to the interpretation of statutes, and the obligations of judges in relation thereto, is problematical.

4 The hierarchy of the courts

It has already been noted that the doctrine of binding precedent depends for its operation upon the underlying principle that the courts form a hierarchy with each court standing in a definite position in relation to every other court. The structure of this hierarchy must now be considered for the purposes of the doctrine of precedent.

a European Court

In matters concerning: (1) the interpretation of the Treaties; (2) the validity and interpretation of acts of the Community institutions; and (3) the interpretation of the statutes of bodies established by an act of the Council, the Court of Justice of the European Communities[12] is now the supreme tribunal. Accordingly its decisions, in these areas of jurisdiction, will be binding on all English courts. Indeed section 3(1) of the European Communities Act 1972 expressly provides that:

"For the purpose of all legal proceedings any question as to the meaning or effect of any of the Treaties, or as to the validity, meaning or effect of any Community instrument, shall be treated as a question of law (and, if not referred

---

[10] *Joscelyne* v. *Nissen*, [1970] 2 Q.B. 86; [1970] 1 All E.R. 1213; *Morelle, Ltd.* v. *Wakeling* (*supra*).

[11] *Farrell* v. *Alexander*, [1976] Q.B. 345; [1976] 1 All E.R. 129 (decision reversed [1977] A.C. 59; [1976] 2 All E.R. 721); but see *Industrial Properties (Barton Hill), Ltd.* v. *Associated Electrical Industries, Ltd.*, [1977] Q.B. 580; [1977] 2 All E.R. 293 in which the Court of Appeal declared one of its previous decisions *per incuriam* where the court had misunderstood an earlier case because of deficiencies in the law report of that case to which it had been referred, and *Dixon* v. *British Broadcasting Corporation*, [1979] Q.B. 546; [1979] 2 All E.R. 112 in which one *ratio* of an earlier case was treated as *per incuriam* on the ground that the statutory provision under construction had apparently been considered in isolation rather than in context; see also *Williams* v. *Fawcett*, [1985] 1 All E.R. 787; [1985] 1 W.L.R. 501.

[12] See p. 183, *post*.

to the European Court, be for determination as such in accordance with the principles laid down by and any relevant decision of the European Court)."

The European Court appears not to observe a doctrine of binding precedent and does not regard itself as bound by its previous decisions.[13]

b   House of Lords

The House of Lords stands at the summit of the English hierarchy of courts. Decisions of the House of Lords are binding upon all other courts trying civil or criminal cases, whether or not appeal lies to the House from those courts.

Until recently the House of Lords regarded itself as strictly bound by its own earlier decisions, which were thus immutable except by legislation. This principle was finally established in the case of *London Street Tramways Co.* v. *L.C.C.*[14] at the end of the last century, although in ensuing years the principle had, on occasion, been doubted.

In 1966 the rule in the *London Street Tramways* case was finally discredited. LORD GARDINER, L.C., on behalf of himself and the Lords of Appeal in Ordinary, made a statement to the effect that their Lordships proposed in future to depart from their own earlier decisions "when it appears right to do so".[15] They would, however, bear in mind the danger of disturbing retrospectively financial arrangements and rights in property and the special need for preserving certainty in the criminal law. The Lord Chancellor made it clear, moreover, that this statement was not intended to apply elsewhere than in the House of Lords.

Although this statement was not made in the context of an actual decision it has been regarded as having the force of law, so that the House does depart from its own earlier decision when the occasion arises to do so.

The practical consequences of this change in the law were, at first, slight. In the five years following LORD GARDINER's statement the House of Lords did not overrule any of its previous decisions. Their reticence is aptly demonstrated by *Jones* v. *Secretary of State for Social Services.*[16] In this important case, involving the construction of the National Insurance (Industrial Injuries) Act 1946, a majority of the House (consisting of seven members) declined to overrule a previous decision of the House[17] although a majority of their lordships were of opinion that the *ratio* of the earlier decision was wrong. Since there was no suggestion that the earlier authority could be distinguished it might appear that, a majority of the House being of the opinion that the decision was wrong, there would be no alternative but to overrule it. Three of the majority of four who believed the earlier authority to be wrong were in favour of overruling it and had the fourth, LORD SIMON, agreed, the House would undoubtedly have overruled its own earlier decision. However LORD SIMON gave several reasons why, in his opinion, it

---

13 Case 28-30/62: *Da Costa en Schaake N.V.* v. *Nederlandse Belastingadministratie*, [1963] C.M.L.R. 224, cited in *H.P. Bulmer, Ltd.* v. *J. Bollinger S.A.*, [1974] Ch. 401; [1974] 2 All E.R. 1226.
14 [1898] A.C. 375.
15 Reported at [1966] 3 All E.R. 77; [1966] 1 W.L.R. 1234.
16 [1972] A.C. 944; [1972] 1 All E.R. 145.
17 *R.* v. *Deputy Industrial Injuries Commissioner, Ex parte Amalgamated Engineering Union, Re Dowling*, [1967] 1 A.C. 725; [1967] 1 All E.R. 210.

would be wrong to depart from *Dowling*'s case, notably that the power to depart from a previous decision "is one to be most sparingly exercised", and that a variation of view on a matter of statutory construction would rarely provide a suitable occasion.

However, the wait for a suitable occasion was not a long one and in *British Railways Board* v. *Herrington*[18] the House, on the question of the extent of the duty of care owed by an occupier of land to trespassers, restated the law and refused to follow the statement of the law, which had stood for over 40 years, laid down in *R. Addie & Sons (Collieries), Ltd. v. Dumbreck*.[19]

As indicated above, the power is exercised sparingly. As LORD REID observed in one case:[20]

". . . our change of practice in no longer regarding previous decisions of this House as absolutely binding does not mean that whenever we think a previous decision was wrong we should reverse it. In the general interest of certainty in the law we must be sure that there is some very good reason before we so act."

Nevertheless in 1975 the enormous potential impact of the 1966 declaration upon English law was demonstrated by the decision of the House in *Miliangos* v. *George Frank (Textiles), Ltd.*[1] In this case the House of Lords, departing from its earlier decision in *Re United Railways of the Havana and Regla Warehouses, Ltd.*,[2] overruled what had been one of the most firmly established rules of English law, namely that money judgments could only be expressed in sterling and not in a foreign currency. The basis upon which the House felt it right to alter this rule was the change in foreign exchange conditions generally and the position of sterling in particular.

Apart from the possibility of the House of Lords being prepared to depart from its own earlier decisions there are three basic means by which a House of Lords decision may lose its authority. First, and most obviously, it may be overruled by statute or a decision of the European Court. Secondly, it may be distinguished. The process of distinguishing applies in the House of Lords as in other courts. Indeed, in the past it has been applied with more force in the House of Lords than elsewhere because there was no other judicial means of avoiding an undesirable precedent. Thus in *Scruttons, Ltd. v. Midland Silicones, Ltd.*[3] the House of Lords distinguished its own earlier decision in *Elder, Dempster & Co., Ltd. v. Paterson, Zochonis & Co., Ltd.*[4] on the facts even though the legal problem raised in each case, namely whether a stranger to a contract can take advantage of a contractual exemption clause, appeared very similar. Indeed LORD DENNING, though describing himself as

---

18 [1972] A.C. 877; [1972] 1 All E.R. 749.
19 [1929] A.C. 358; see also *The Johanna Oldendorff*, [1974] A.C. 749; [1973] 3 All E.R. 148; *Vestey* v. *Inland Revenue Commissioners*, [1980] A.C. 1148; [1979] 3 All E.R. 976.
20 *Knuller (Publishing, Printing and Promotions), Ltd.* v. *Director of Public Prosecutions*, [1973] A.C. 435, at p. 455; [1972] 2 All E.R. 898, at p. 903; see also, to similar effect, *Fitzleet Estates, Ltd.* v. *Cherry*, [1977] 3 All E.R. 996; [1977] 1 W.L.R. 1345.
1 [1976] A.C. 443; [1975] 3 All E.R. 801. It is, perhaps, interesting to note that only one of their lordships who had sat in *Knuller* (*supra*) sat in this case and he (LORD SIMON) dissented while of the two members who had sat in *Jones* v. *Secretary of State for Social Services* (*supra*) one was LORD SIMON and the other (LORD WILBERFORCE) had dissented in that case.
2 [1961] A.C. 1007; [1960] 2 All E.R. 332; see p. 144, *ante*.
3 [1962] A.C. 446; [1962] 1 All E.R. 1.
4 [1924] A.C. 522; see also *Adler* v. *Dickson*, [1955] 1 Q.B. 158; [1954] 3 All E.R. 397.

"not unduly attached to the strict doctrine of precedent" doubted whether the cases were distinguishable. Since the 1966 declaration, the need for such strained distinctions has, of course, disappeared.

Finally, it is possible for a House of Lords decision to be rejected if given *per incuriam*. This possibility was expressly mentioned by LORD HALSBURY, L.C. in the *London Street Tramways* case. In modern conditions it would be most unlikely for a case to pass through the House of Lords with an important authority not cited. As stated above, the Court of Appeal in *Broome* v. *Cassell & Co., Ltd.*⁵ regarded a House of Lords decision as being given *per incuriam* on the basis that two House of Lords authorities were not cited to the House. Reference has already been made to the manner in which the House of Lords disapproved the Court of Appeal's application of the *per incuriam* doctrine. LORD DIPLOCK was alone, however, in going so far as to state that the Court of Appeal had no power to treat a decision of the House of Lords in this way:⁶

> "The Court of Appeal found themselves able to disregard the decision of this House in *Rookes* v. *Barnard* by applying to it the label *per incuriam*. That label is relevant only to the right of an appellate court to decline to follow one of its own previous decisions, not to its right to disregard a decision of a higher appellate court or to the right of a judge of the High Court to disregard a decision of the Court of Appeal."

In view of the support which this *dictum* has received⁷ it may fairly be said to represent the law as it now stands.

c   Court of Appeal

Civil division—Decisions of the Court of Appeal are binding on all inferior courts trying civil or criminal cases, including divisional courts.⁸ There seems to be no reason to suppose that inferior criminal courts will not be bound by decisions of the civil division of the Court of Appeal. The Court of Appeal is bound by decisions of the European Court, the House of Lords, and by its own earlier decisions.⁹ The latter principle was affirmatively established in the leading case of *Young* v. *Bristol Aeroplane Co., Ltd.*¹⁰ LORD GREENE, M.R., who delivered the judgment of the court, cited three exceptional circumstances in which an earlier decision of the Court of Appeal would not be regarded as binding.

(1) Where there are two conflicting decisions, the Court may choose which it will follow, the decision not followed being deemed to be overruled. Thus, in *Fisher* v. *Ruislip-Northwood Urban District Council*¹¹ the Court, of

---

⁵ [1971] 2 Q.B. 354; [1971] 2 All E.R. 187; see p. 144, *ante*.

⁶ *Broome* v. *Cassell & Co., Ltd.*, [1972] A.C. 1027, at p. 1131; [1972] 1 All E.R. 801, at p. 874.

⁷ See *Baker* v. *R.*, [1975] A.C. 774; [1975] 3 All E.R. 55; *Miliangos* v. *George Frank (Textiles)*, *Ltd.*, [1976] A.C., at p. 479; [1975] 3 All E.R., at pp. 822–823, *per* LORD SIMON.

⁸ *Brownsea Haven Properties, Ltd.* v. *Poole Corporation*, [1958] Ch. 574; [1958] 1 All E.R. 205.

⁹ *Sed quaere*: is it bound by a decision of the Judicial Committee of the Privy Council? See p. 140, *ante*. The Court of Appeal is also bound by decisions of courts which exercised equivalent jurisdiction prior to 1875: the Court of Exchequer Chamber and the Chancery Court of Appeal; see *Ex parte M'George* (1882), 20 Ch.D. 697.

¹⁰ [1944] K.B. 718; [1944] 2 All E.R. 293 (affirmed [1946] A.C. 163; [1946] 1 All E.R. 98).

¹¹ [1945] K.B. 584; [1945] 2 All E.R. 458.

which LORD GREENE was again a member, was required to choose between conflicting lines of authorities concerning the liability of local authorities to motorists who collided with unlit air-raid shelters while in *Tiverton Estates, Ltd.* v. *Wearwell, Ltd.*[12] the Court of Appeal was able to avoid following its own recent decision in the controversial case of *Law* v. *Jones*[13] (to the effect that it was unnecessary for a memorandum under section 40 of the Law of Property Act 1925 to acknowledge the existence of a contract) because it was in conflict with earlier decisions of the Court.

(2) The Court is bound to refuse to follow a decision of its own which, though not expressly overruled, cannot stand with a later House of Lords decision.[14]

(3) The Court is not bound to follow a decision of its own if that decision was given *per incuriam*. This principle, explained earlier, is not confined to the Court of Appeal.

During his tenure of the office of Master of the Rolls, LORD DENNING engaged in a tireless, but ultimately unsuccessful, campaign to gain for the Court of Appeal the freedom that the House of Lords has to depart from its own previous decisions at will. In *Gallie* v. *Lee*[15] LORD DENNING evinced a desire to depart from the rule in *Young*'s case in the following words:[16]

> "We are, of course, bound by the decisions of the House [of Lords], but I do not think we are bound by prior decisions of our own, or at any rate, not absolutely bound. We are not fettered as it was once thought. It was a self-imposed limitation; and we who imposed it can also remove it. The House of Lords have done it. So why should not we do likewise?"

This was, however, a minority opinion, RUSSELL, L.J. (as he then was) saw the position of the House of Lords in quite a different light, saying of the Master of the Rolls:[17]

---

[12] [1975] Ch. 146; [1974] 1 All E.R. 209.

[13] [1974] Ch. 112; [1973] 2 All E.R. 437; see also *Starr* v. *National Coal Board*, [1977] 1 All E.R. 243; [1977] 1 W.L.R. 63; *Sherratt (W.A.), Ltd.* v. *John Bromley (Church Stretton), Ltd.*, [1985] 1 All E.R. 216.

[14] This exception, it will be observed, does not apply to cases in which a decision of the Court of Appeal is inconsistent with an earlier House of Lords decision. It may be that LORD GREENE did not entertain this as a possibility and indeed it is clearly a situation which should not arise since the Court of Appeal, unless it was not referred to the earlier House of Lords decision (in which event its own decision would be *per incuriam*) should not reach decisions which are inconsistent with existing authority of the House of Lords. If however the situation does arise, probably the better view is that the Court of Appeal should follow its own decision and give leave to appeal to the House of Lords; cf. *Miliangos* v. *George Frank (Textiles), Ltd.*, [1976] A.C., at p. 479; [1975] 3 All E.R., at p. 823, *per* LORD SIMON. But see *Verrall* v. *Great Yarmouth Borough Council*, [1981] Q.B. 202; [1980] 1 All E.R. 839, where the Court of Appeal simply declined to follow its own decision in *Thompson* v. *Park*, [1944] K.B. 408; [1944] 2 All E.R. 477 on the ground that it was inconsistent with the decision of the House of Lords in *Winter Garden Theatre (London), Ltd.* v. *Millenium Productions, Ltd.*, [1948] A.C. 173; [1947] 2 All E.R. 331.

[15] [1969] 2 Ch. 17; [1969] 1 All E.R. 1062 (affirmed *sub nom. Saunders* v. *Anglia Building Society*, [1971] A.C. 1004; [1970] 3 All E.R. 961).

[16] [1969] 2 Ch., at p. 37; [1969] 1 All E.R., at p. 1072.

[17] [1969] 2 Ch., at p. 41; [1969] 1 All E.R., at p. 1082; the third member of the court, SALMON, L.J. (as he then was), took a middle view and stated that a change in policy, though possibly desirable, would require a pronouncement of the whole Court of Appeal. Nevertheless, in *Davis* v. *Johnson*, [1979] A.C. 264; [1978] 1 All E.R. 1132 LORD SALMON. in common with the other members of the House of Lords, expressly reaffirmed *Young*'s case.

"I think that in one respect he has sought to wield a broom labelled 'For the use of the House of Lords only' . . . I do not support the suggestion that this court is free to override its own decisions . . . the availability of the House of Lords to correct error in the Court of Appeal makes it in my view unnecessary for this court to depart from its existing discipline."

Again in *Barrington* v. *Lee*,[18] a case concerned with liability as between vendor and purchaser in respect of an estate agent's default over a deposit, LORD DENNING, dealing with the effect of the Court of Appeal's decision in *Burt* v. *Claude Cousins & Co., Ltd.*[19] on similar facts, boldly asserted:[20]

"We are not absolutely bound by *Burt*'s case. We no longer look to see if the case can be brought within the exceptions stated in *Young* v. *Bristol Aeroplane Co., Ltd.*

Once again, however, LORD DENNING was expressing a minority view for EDMUND DAVIES, L.J. (as he then was) and STEPHENSON, L.J., though concurring in the result of the appeal by distinguishing *Burt*'s case, both re-affirmed the principles of *Young*'s case and disagreed with the view of LORD DENNING quoted above. STEPHENSON, L.J.'s judgment epitomises the traditional approach:[1]

"what may be thought timorous subservience to judicial precedent is, in my judgment, preferable to the uncertainty which will be introduced into the law in fields not easy to delimit by the bolder work of demolition and restoration proposed by LORD DENNING, M.R., in this case . . . We must take care lest in struggling to straighten out the law we bend it until it breaks."

Faced with such opposition to his views LORD DENNING was constrained to resile from the statements he had made in *Gallie* v. *Lee* and *Barrington* v. *Lee*; indeed in *Miliangos* v. *George Frank (Textiles), Ltd.*[2] the Master of the Rolls expressly applied the principles in *Young* v. *Bristol Aeroplane Co., Ltd.* Nevertheless in *Davis* v. *Johnson*,[3] a controversial case dealing with the power of the courts to protect "battered wives", LORD DENNING led the full Court of Appeal in yet another attack on *Young*'s case, which attack was, again, repulsed when the case reached the House of Lords,[4] where the rule in *Young* was, in LORD DIPLOCK's words, "expressly, unequivocally and unanimously" reaffirmed. It is not now to be anticipated that any further attempt will be made by the Court of Appeal to suggest that it is not bound by its own previous decisions (subject to the recognised exceptional cases referred to in *Young*).

The civil division of the Court of Appeal is certainly not bound by decisions of the now defunct Court of Criminal Appeal. It is uncertain whether the civil division will regard itself as bound by decisions of the criminal

---

[18] [1972] 1 Q.B. 326; [1971] 3 All E.R. 1231.
[19] [1971] 2 Q.B. 426; [1971] 2 All E.R. 611.
[20] [1972] 1 Q.B., at p. 338; [1971] 3 All E.R., at p. 1238; see also *Hanning* v. *Maitland (No. 2)*, [1970] 1 Q.B. 580, at p. 587; [1970] 1 All E.R. 812, at p. 815.
[1] [1972] 1 Q.B., at p. 345; [1971] 3 All E.R., at p. 1245. The law was, eventually, clarified by the House of Lords in *Sorrell* v. *Finch*, [1977] A.C. 728; [1976] 2 All E.R. 371. See also *Tiverton Estates, Ltd.* v. *Wearwell, Ltd*; [1975] Ch. 146; [1974] 1 All E.R. 209.
[2] [1975] Q.B. 487; [1975] 1 All E.R. 1076 *(supra)*.
[3] [1979] A.C. 264; [1978] 1 All E.R. 841.
[4] [1979] A.C. 264; [1978] 1 All E.R. 1132.

division of the Court of Appeal, which now exercises that jurisdiction formerly exercised by the Court of Criminal Appeal. The better view appears to be that the civil division will regard itself as bound by decisions of the criminal division so that the inelegant conflict which has, in the past, existed between the civil and criminal appeal courts[5] is now unlikely to recur.

It may be noted finally that a "full court" of five or more judges of the civil division is sometimes convened to hear cases involving particularly important or difficult points of law. The full court of the civil division has, however, no greater authority than the normal court and its decisions carry no more weight as precedents.[6]

Criminal division—Decisions of the criminal division of the Court of Appeal bind inferior courts trying criminal cases, including the divisional court of the Queen's Bench Division, and will probably be regarded as binding upon inferior courts trying civil cases. The division regards itself as bound by decisions of its predecessor, the Court of Criminal Appeal, and by decisions of the civil division of the Court of Appeal subject to the exceptions contained in *Young* v. *Bristol Aeroplane Co., Ltd.*[7] Thus in *R.* v. *Merriman*[8] the criminal division allowed an appeal, totally lacking in merit, "with the utmost reluctance" because of the existence of a direct authority of the Court of Criminal Appeal[9] in favour of the appellant. However, the court certified a point of law of general public importance and granted leave to appeal to the House of Lords where the appeal was allowed and the earlier authority overruled.[10]

The Court of Criminal Appeal formulated the principle that it would not be bound by its own previous decision where this would cause injustice to an appellant, the rationale of this principle being that the desire for attaining justice transcends the desirability of certainty. The rule was stated by LORD GODDARD, C.J. in *R.* v. *Taylor*[11] in the following terms:

> "This court, however, has to deal with questions involving the liberty of the subject, and if it finds, on reconsideration, that, in the opinion of a full court assembled for that purpose, the law has been either misapplied or misunderstood in a decision which it has previously given, and that, on the strength of that decision, an accused person has been sentenced and imprisoned, it is the

---

5 The historic conflict occurred in the cases of *R.* v. *Denyer*, [1926] 2 K.B. 258 (C.C.A.) and *Hardie and Lane* v. *Chiltern*, [1928] 1 K.B. 306 (C.A.) in which the Court of Appeal, on the subject of the legality of trade stop-lists, declined to follow the earlier decision of the Court of Criminal Appeal and expressly disapproved it. The conflict on this point could thus be solved only by the House of Lords and this was done in *Thorne* v. *Motor Trade Association*, [1937] A.C. 797; 3 All E.R. 157.

6 This was established in *Young* v. *Bristol Aeroplane Co., Ltd.*, [1944] K.B. 718; [1944] 2 All E.R. 293.

7 For an example of the criminal division treating an earlier decision of the Court as *per incuriam*, see *R.* v. *Ewing*, [1983] Q.B. 1039; [1983] 2 All E.R. 645.

8 [1971] 2 Q.B. 310; [1971] 2 All E.R. 1424.

9 *R.* v. *Scaramanga*, [1963] 2 Q.B. 807; [1963] 2 All E.R. 852.

10 [1973] A.C. 584; [1972] 3 All E.R. 42; for the point in the case, see p. 492, *post*. A similar course was followed in *Director of Public Prosecutions* v. *Kilbourne*, [1973] A.C. 729; [1973] 1 All E.R. 440; see p. 623, *post* for a discussion of this case.

11 [1950] 2 K.B. 368; [1950] 2 All E.R. 170; overruling *R.* v. *Treanor* (or *McAvoy*), [1939] 1 All E.R. 330; see also observations of LORD DIPLOCK in *Director of Public Prosecutions* v. *Merriman*, [1973] A.C. 584, at 605; [1972] 3 All E.R. 42, at 58, but cf. *R.* v. *Charles*, [1976] 1 All E.R. 659; [1976] 1 W.L.R. 248 (affirmed [1977] A.C. 177; [1976] 3 All E.R. 112).

bounden duty of the court to reconsider the earlier decision with a view to seeing whether that person had been properly convicted. The exceptions which apply in civil cases ought not to be the only ones applied in such a case as the present.''

This rule was adopted by the criminal division of the Court of Appeal in *R. v. Gould*[12]

In the past, decisions of the Court of Criminal Appeal have been somewhat less reliable as precedents than the decisions of other appellate courts. This is accounted for by the fact that the court rarely reserved judgment, that only one judgment was usually given and that dissents were not recorded. Although the Supreme Court Act 1981, s. 59 expressly provides that separate judgments may be pronounced on a question of law, precedents of the criminal division of the Court of Appeal are still regarded with more circumspection than decisions of the civil division.

d   High Court

Divisional courts—In civil matters divisional courts are bound by decisions of the House of Lords and Court of Appeal (including, probably, the criminal division), subject to the exceptions set out in *Young* v. *Bristol Aeroplane Co., Ltd.*,[13] and also by their own earlier decisions. The latter principle was clearly established in *Police Authority for Huddersfield* v. *Watson.*[14] Divisional court decisions in civil cases are binding on judges of the same division of the High Court sitting alone, and, possibly,[15] on judges of other divisions.[16]

In criminal cases the position of the divisional court of the Queen's Bench Division is closely analogous to that of the criminal division of the Court of Appeal. Thus it is free to depart from its own decisions in the same circumstances as is that court.[17] When exercising its supervisory jurisdiction, a divisional court is in the same position as a High Court judge sitting alone; thus it may depart from its own previous decision when convinced that such decision is wrong. The above principles appear from the decision of the

---

[12] [1968] 2 Q.B. 65; [1968] 1 All E.R. 849; the necessity for a "full court" of five or more judges seems to have been tacitly abolished; cf. *R.* v. *Newsome*, [1970] 2 Q.B. 711; [1970] 3 All E.R. 455 which appears to assert greater power for a court of five to depart from the earlier decision of a court of three than a court of three would possess. In *R.* v. *Jackson*, [1974] Q.B. 802; [1974] 1 All E.R. 640, a case in which the court had to choose between conflicting decisions on an important question of sentencing principle, a full court was convened, and it seems likely that on occasions where the need to choose between conflicting decisions is likely to arise, this practice will be adopted: see, generally, G. Zellick, *Precedent in the Court of Appeal, Criminal Division*, [1974] Crim. L.R. 222.

[13] See p. 148, *ante*: *R.* v. *Northumberland Compensation Tribunal, Ex parte Shaw*, [1952] 1 K.B. 338; [1952] 1 All E.R. 122.

[14] [1947] K.B. 842; [1947] 2 All E.R. 193.

[15] *Bretherton* v. *United Kingdom Totalisator Co., Ltd.*, [1945] K.B. 555; [1945] 2 All E.R. 202.

[16] See *Re Seaford, Seaford* v. *Seifert*, [1967] P. 325; [1967] 2 All E.R. 458 (reversed [1968] P. 53; [1968] 1 All E.R. 482) in which a judge of the Probate, Divorce and Admiralty Division regarded himself as bound by a decision of the divisional court of the Queen's Bench Division; cf. *Elderton* v. *United Kingdom Totalisator Co., Ltd.* (1945), 61 T.L.R. 529; (affirmed [1945] 2 All E.R. 624).

[17] See p. 151, *ante*.

Queen's Bench divisional court, delivered by GOFF, L.J., in *R.* v. *Greater Manchester Coroner, Ex parte Tal.*[18]
Judges at first instance—Decisions of High Court judges sitting alone at first instance are binding on inferior courts but are not binding on other High Court judges. For this reason it is a dangerous practice to rely upon principles of law which are contained only in first instance decisions, since they are not binding in any High Court action. Naturally, they are of persuasive authority and a High Court judge will hesitate before "not following" the decision of one of his brethren, if only for reasons of comity. Nevertheless, where a first instance judge is clearly convinced that an earlier decision at first instance is wrong, he will be free to refuse to follow that decision. There have been several direct clashes between decisions of first instance judges, a notable recent example occurring in relation to the question of whether failure on the part of a driver or passenger in a motor vehicle to wear a seat belt amounted to contributory negligence in the event that injury suffered in an accident was aggravated by such failure. This question virtually divided the judges of the Queen's Bench Division in some fourteen reported cases on the topic between 1970 and 1975 until the Court of Appeal resolved the conflict in *Froom* v. *Butcher*[19] where it was held that failure to wear a seat belt did, in the ordinary way, amount to contributory negligence.[20]

It is sometimes said that judges of the Chancery Division are less willing to depart from decisions of their brethren than are judges of other divisions. This is only true insofar as to depart from any earlier authority might have the effect of disturbing financial arrangements or depriving a person of a vested proprietary right.

High Court judges are bound by decisions of the Court of Appeal and House of Lords. Where there appears to be a conflict between previous decisions of the Court of Appeal and House of Lords, the High Court judge should give effect to the decision of the immediately higher court, viz. the Court of Appeal. The reasoning behind this is that the conflict could only arise if the Court of Appeal had been able to distinguish or otherwise avoid following a House of Lords decision; in those circumstances the High Court judge should assume that the Court of Appeal had correctly distinguished or otherwise avoided such decision.[1]

---

18 [1984] 3 All E.R. 240; [1984] 3 W.L.R. 643. A "full" divisional court of five or more judges has no greater authority than the normal court of two or three (*Younghusband* v. *Luftig*, [1949] 2 K.B. 354; [1949] 2 All E.R. 72).
19 [1976] Q.B. 286; [1975] 3 All E.R. 520; all of the reported cases on the subject are reviewed in the judgment of LORD DENNING, M.R. in this case.
20 For other illustrations of clashes between judges at first instance, see *Esso Petroleum Co., Ltd.* v. *Harper's Garage (Stourport), Ltd.*, [1966] 2 Q.B. 514; [1965] 2 All E.R. 933 and *Petrofina, Ltd.* v. *Martin*, [1965] Ch. 1073; [1965] 2 All E.R. 176; *Metropolitan Police District Receiver* v. *Croydon Corporation*, [1956] 2 All E.R. 785; [1956] 1 W.L.R. 1113 and *Monmouthshire C.C.* v. *Smith*, [1957] 1 All E.R. 78; [1956] 1 W.L.R. 1132; *Wood* v. *Luscombe*, [1966] 1 Q.B. 169; [1964] 3 All E.R. 972 and *Randolph* v. *Tuck*, [1962] 1 Q.B. 175; [1961] 1 All E.R. 814: see p. 592, *post.*
1 This was the analysis of LORD SIMON in *Miliangos* v. *George Frank (Textiles), Ltd.*, [1976] A.C. 443; [1975] 3 All E.R. 801; see p. 144, *ante.*

e   Inferior and other courts

Magistrates' courts, county courts and other inferior tribunals are bound by the decisions of all superior courts, not excluding first instance decisions of the High Court. The position of the Crown Court in the hierarchy, in relation to the doctrine of precedent, has not been authoritatively determined. When a High Court judge presides the court is, presumably, equivalent to a judge of the High Court sitting at first instance. However, when a Circuit judge or Recorder presides it would seem reasonable to regard the court as inferior in status to a judge of the High Court and, therefore, bound by decisions of the High Court.[2] The decisions of one inferior court are not binding upon any other inferior court, chiefly because the decisions of inferior courts are not reported. The Employment Appeal Tribunal[3] is bound by decisions of the Court of Appeal and House of Lords but does not regard itself as bound by decisions of the High Court (nor, presumably by its own decisions) or of the Tribunal's predecessor, the National Industrial Relations Court.[4]

In conclusion it would probably be optimistic to state categorically that the doctrine of binding precedent as applied in English courts achieves certainty while retaining flexibility. Its operation depends, as with the interpretation of statutes, on the conception of the particular judge or court trying a case of the judicial function. The rules for determining the *ratio decidendi* of a case and the hierarchy of the courts are sufficiently well defined to achieve legal certainty. On the other hand, the *per incuriam* doctrine, the process of distinguishing, the capacity of superior courts to overrule decisions and the absolute power of Parliament to change the law all serve to keep the doctrine flexible. In the last analysis the doctrine of precedent is usually seen to operate fairly, though how far this is attributable to the inherent qualities of the doctrine and how far to the rationalism of English judges is a matter of debate.

C   THE HISTORICAL DEVELOPMENT OF LAW REPORTING

As stated at the beginning of this chapter, the doctrine of binding precedent became a part of English law only when the system of law reporting had become comprehensive. The doctrine of precedent, as such, is of far greater antiquity but it was only in the nineteenth century that precedents became binding rather than merely persuasive. As late as 1762 LORD MANSFIELD, a bitter opponent of mulish adherence to precedent, could state:[5]

---

2   In *R. v. Colyer*, [1974] Crim. L.R. 243 a Circuit judge presiding over the Crown Court at Ipswich took the bold course of refusing to follow a decision of the divisional court of the Queen's Bench Division on the ground that it was not binding on him. This must surely have been incorrect. Since the divisional court is bound by its own previous decisions (*supra*) it would be bizarre if a Circuit judge were not bound by them.

3   As to which, see p. 204, *post*.

4   *Portec (U.K.), Ltd.* v. *Mogenson*, [1976] 3 All E.R. 565.

5   *Fisher* v. *Prince* (1762), 3 Burr. 1363. This theme runs through many of LORD MANSFIELD's judgments. See, for example: *Jones* v. *Randall* (1774), Cowp. 37; *R. v. Bembridge* (1783), 3 Doug. 327.

"the reason and spirit of cases make law, not the letter of particular precedents".

Nevertheless the growth of a comprehensive system of law reporting brought with it the modern doctrine of binding precedent. If it were possible to mark the turning point, the decision of PARKE, B. in *Mirehouse* v. *Rennell* in 1833[6] would appear to herald the evolution of the modern system.

It is, therefore, instructive to trace the evolution of law reporting and, incidentally, to note the methods of citation and reference.

The history of law reporting can be roughly divided into three periods: first, the period of the Year Books extending approximately from 1272 to 1535; secondly, the period of the private named[7] reporters extending from 1535 to 1865 and, thirdly, the modern semi-official system of reporting which began in 1865.

1 The Year Books

The Year Books are the first available law reports. They were first compiled during the reign of Edward I. Exactly what function they were intended to and did fulfil at that time is uncertain. They were certainly not intended for use by the judges as precedents, and were probably simply notes compiled by students and junior advocates for use, by advocates, as guides to pleading and procedure. While they contain legal argument of counsel and notes of exchanges between bench and bar they are very far from being law reports in the modern sense. Since most litigation in the thirteenth and fourteenth centuries took the form of disputes over title to land it is natural to find that most Year Book cases are land law cases, generally being decisions of the Court of Common Pleas.

Although Year Book reports were in no sense official and were not, apparently, intended for use by the judges, there are indications that they may have been used by some judges as a direct source of precedent. Thus in 1310 STANTON, J. referred to a case decided at least ten years earlier[8] while BEREFORD, C.J. in 1312 cited a decision some twenty-five years old.[9] Even allowing for the longevity of judicial recollection of case law, it seems likely that these judges were basing their knowledge upon some written record of the cases in question. By the fifteenth century there are many examples of Year Book cases in which the judge is reported as having relied upon a number of very old authorities. This is the origin of the doctrine of precedent in English law and there is ample evidence[10] that the judges were conscious that their decisions were being recorded for use as precedents.

With the introduction of printing in the fifteenth century many Year Book manuscripts were printed in the so-called "Black Letter" editions. The most widely used modern printed editions of the Year Books are the Rolls Series (R.S.) and the Selden Society Series (S.S.). Both series date from early

---

6 (1833), 1 Cl. & F. 527.
7 Private reports are still published, though not, as formerly, under the name of the individual reporter.
8 *Kembeare* v. *K.*, Y.B. 4 Ed. 2 (S.S. iv), 153. Note the method of citation by regnal year.
9 *Anon.*, Y.B. 6 Ed. 2 (S.S. xiii), 43.
10 For examples see Allen, *Law in the Making* (7th Edn.), pp. 190 *et seq.*

in the present century and contain the original text of the Year Book manuscripts, which are in "law French", a peculiar combination of Norman French, English and Latin, together with an English translation. The Selden Society continue to edit and produce collections of Year Book reports. Citation of Year Book cases is usually by reference to one of these two editions.

Abridgements

The excellence of the printed editions of the original Year Books which are available has rather lessened the value of the Abridgements. These are merely collections of Year Book cases according to their subject matter in chronological order compiled by judges and lawyers, generally for their own use. Some of these Abridgements were published and may be compared to modern case books. The best known Abridgements are those of Fitzherbert and Brooke, published in 1516 and 1568 respectively.

2   The private reports

Compilation of printed Year Books ceased in about 1535.[11] Almost immediately private sets of reports began to be produced, printed and published under the name of the law reporter. At first the private reports were scarcely fuller than the Year Book reports had been. Very soon, however, many sets of private reports became far more detailed, reproducing much of counsel's argument and virtually the whole of the judgment. The private reporters generally attached themselves to one court, probably the court in which they intended to practise, and took notes of the proceedings. These notes would later be revised and published as reports. The citation of precedents became progressively more common as the private reports became more comprehensive.

The private reporters proliferated in the period 1535 to 1865. The standard of reporting varied greatly. At one end of the scale were the reporters whose reports contain what are still regarded today as classic expositions of the common law. These reporters did not, until the end of the eighteenth century, produce their reports contemporaneously with the decisions they were reporting. Consequently the reporter's invention and personality played no little part in the compilation of the reports. This is particularly true of Coke, possibly the greatest of all law reporters. Coke's Reports (Co. Rep.) are so well known as to be citable merely as "Reports" (Rep.). They contain comprehensive expositions of virtually every aspect of the common law supported by a wealth of authority assiduously gleaned from the Year Books and even the ancient Plea Rolls, which Coke had copied for his own use. Coke's great industry and scholarship have made his Reports and text-books a primary literary source of the common law. Nowadays there is rarely any need to look beyond Coke to trace the origin of any common law rule. His Reports, published between 1600 and 1658, contain many of the great consti-

---

[11] Although manuscript Year Books continued to be produced into the seventeenth century.

tutional cases of the seventeenth century, such as *Prohibitions del Roy*,[12] *Proclamations*,[13] and *Magdalen College*.[14]

It will be observed that Coke was a judge as well as a law reporter. This is true of many of the great reporters, notably Dyer, who was Chief Justice of the Common Pleas, and Saunders, Chief Justice of the King's Bench. To the great names of Coke, Dyer and Saunders may be added those of Plowden and, later, Burrow. Burrow's Reports are of cases in the Court of King's Bench between 1751 and 1772 and thus include many of Lord Mansfield's famous judgments. They are widely regarded as the first set of law reports produced in the modern pattern. They contain headnotes and the argument of counsel is carefully separated from the judgment. Nevertheless they were not contemporaneous reports. The first reports which attempted to be contemporaneous were the Term Reports which are of cases in the King's Bench in the period 1785–1800.

It must not be thought that every one of the private law reporters was a Plowden or a Coke. At the other end of the scale were reporters such as Barnardiston, Atkyns and Espinasse whose reports became virtually uncitable, so low were they held in judicial esteem.[15] Lord Mansfield, in particular, would not permit certain series of reports to be cited to him, while HOLT, C.J. observed feelingly that "these scambling reports . . . will make us appear to posterity for a parcel of blockheads".[16]

Citation of private reports

The private reports are cited by the name of the reporter (usually abbreviated) and a volume and page number. The date of the report is not part of the reference but is usually inserted in ordinary round (not square) brackets. Thus the reference to the case of *Ashford* v. *Thornton* is

> (1818), 1 B. & Ald. 405

which indicates that the case is reported in volume 1 of Barnewall and Alderson's Reports at page 405. The reference to *Pillans* v. *Van Mierop*

> (1765), 3 Burr. 1663

indicates that the case can be found in the third volume of Burrow's Reports at page 1663.

In practice most law libraries have the reports of the private reporters in the reprinted edition known as "The English Reports" (E.R. or Eng. Rep.). The English Reports are published in 176 volumes and contain all the available reports of the private reporters. With the English Reports is published a reference chart showing in which volume the reports of any individual reporter are contained.

---

[12] (1607), 12 Rep. 63.

[13] (1610), 12 Rep. 74.

[14] (1615), 11 Rep. 666.

[15] For an assessment of the relative merits of the private reporters see Allen, *Law in the Making* (7th Edn.), pp. 221 *et seq.*

[16] *Slater* v. *May* (1704), 2 Ld. Raym. 1072.

3   The present system of law reporting

a   The Law Reports

In 1865 the system of private reporting gave way to the system which still exists at the present day. A Council was established to publish, as cheaply as possible, reports of decisions of superior courts. The Council was, from its inception, under professional control and contained representatives of the Inns of Court and The Law Society. The Council was incorporated in 1870 as the Incorporated Council of Law Reporting for England and Wales.[17] The reports which the Council produces are described simply as the "Law Reports" and have superseded most of the private series of reports. The Law Reports are not an official publication but, by convention, they are the series of reports to which counsel should refer when citing a case which is reported in the Law Reports.[18] In addition the judges are given the opportunity of revising reports of their own judgments. The reporters for the Law Reports are, of course, barristers and they must be present in court when judgment is delivered. This demonstrates that, even at the present day, a precedent is not citable merely because it is reported but only if it is vouched for by a barrister who was present when judgment was delivered.

b   The Weekly Law Reports

Up to and including 1952 the Incorporated Council of Law Reporting published "Weekly Notes" (W.N.). These reports were in the form of a current précis and did not enjoy the authority of the Law Reports. They were, indeed, not strictly citable as reports.[19]

Weekly Notes were replaced in 1953 by the Weekly Law Reports. The Weekly Law Reports include a report of every decision which will ultimately appear in the Law Reports proper. The cases are reported in full, except that legal argument is omitted because of the restriction on space. In addition many cases are published in the Weekly Law Reports which it is not intended to include subsequently in the Law Reports. These cases are published in Volume 1 of the Weekly Law Reports whereas cases which are destined to reach the Law Reports are published in Volumes 2 and 3.

c   Citation of the Law Reports and the Weekly Law Reports

The citation of the Law Reports prior to 1891 was somewhat complex. Before 1875 a case was cited by reference to the court in which it was decided and a serial number dating from 1865, prefixed by the letters L.R. The date, not being part of the reference, was inserted in ordinary round brackets.

---

[17] The Council is a charity; *Incorporated Council of Law Reporting for England and Wales* v. *A.-G.*, [1972] Ch. 73; [1971] 3 All E.R. 1029.

[18] An advantage of the Law Reports over other series is that legal argument, as well as the judgments, is published. Where the court has adjourned to take time to consider its decision judgment is said to be "reserved". This fact is indicated in reports by the insertion of the words *curia advisari vult* (*cur. ad. vult* or *c.a.v.*) before the judgment. Reserved judgments are generally accorded greater weight than *ex tempore* judgments.

[19] See *Re Loveridge*, [1902] 2 Ch. 859, at p. 865, *per* BUCKLEY, J.

Thus

> *Irving* v. *Askew* (1870), L.R. 5 Q.B. 208

was reported in the fifth volume of Reports of cases in the Court of Queen's Bench at page 208.

Between 1875 and 1890 citation was by an abbreviation of the appropriate division of the High Court (Ch. D.; Q.B.D.; P.D.; C.P.D.; Ex. D.[20]) or App. Cas. for an appeal case. The date was still not part of the reference and the serial number dated from 1875. The prefix L.R. was dropped. An example of citation during this period is

> *Symons* v. *Rees* (1876), 1 Ex. D. 416.

In 1891 the date was, for the first time, made part of the reference in place of a serial number and the letter D. (for Division) was dropped. The fact that the date is part of the reference is signified by its inclusion in square brackets. There is a separate volume of Reports for each division of the High Court (Q.B.; Ch.; Fam.[1]) and a separate volume for House of Lords and Privy Council cases (A.C.).[2] Court of Appeal decisions are reported in the volume for the division of the High Court from which the appeal came. County court appeals and appeals to the criminal division of the Court of Appeal are usually reported in the volume for the Queen's Bench Division. There is thus nothing in the reference to distinguish a Court of Appeal decision from a decision at first instance. This is the modern method of citation.

In the case of the Weekly Law Reports the year is, as with the Law Reports, part of the reference and appears in square brackets. There is, however, no attempt to classify cases by the court in which they were decided. All cases appear in 1 W.L.R., 2 W.L.R. or 3 W.L.R. irrespective of whether they are House of Lords or first instance decisions.

d Other series of reports

A case which is reported in the Law Reports should be cited by its Law Report reference in preference to any other reference, though only as a matter of practice. Although the Law Reports superseded most of the series of private reports, certain series of private reports are still published. The most highly regarded of these private reports are the All England Law

---

[20] The last two were abolished in 1880 with the fusion of the Common Pleas Division and the Exchequer Division into the Queen's Bench Division; see p. 81, *ante*.

[1] When the Family Division was named the Probate, Divorce and Admiralty Division, this volume of Reports was cited by the letter P.

[2] It may be noted that, prior to 1974, when a case reached the House of Lords (or Privy Council or divisional court on appeal) the appellant's name used to be cited first. Thus, for example, the case known in the Court of Appeal as *Lever Brothers, Ltd.* v. *Bell*, [1931] 1 K.B. 557 became *Bell* v. *Lever Brothers, Ltd.*, [1932] A.C. 161 in the House of Lords because the defendant, Bell, was the appellant in the House of Lords. However this practice was altered, in relation to House of Lords cases, by a *Procedure Direction* issued on February 5, 1974 (reported at [1974] 1 All E.R. 752; [1974] 1 W.L.R. 305) whereby petitions for leave to appeal and appeals to the House of Lords will carry the same title as that which obtained in the court of first instance. In criminal cases this has the effect of terminating the practice (which appears to have dated from *Director of Public Prosecutions* v. *Beard*, [1920] A.C. 479) whereby the *Director of Public Prosecutions* was substituted for *Rex* (or *Regina*). The All England Law Reports appear now (since 1979) to have adopted the new method of citation.

Reports. These are published weekly and their virtue lies principally in the speed with which they follow the decision. In addition many cases are reported in the All England Law Reports which do not find their way into the Law Reports. The All England Law Reports are cited by the year in square brackets followed by the abbreviation All E.R. and a page number. There are usually three volumes of All England Law Reports published each year though, unlike the Weekly Law Reports, there is no significance in the volume number.

The Law Journal Reports (L.J.) and Law Times Reports (L.T.) have been incorporated in the All England Law Reports. The Times Law Reports (T.L.R.) have also ceased to function independently. However, the Criminal Appeal Reports (C.A.R. or Cr. App. Rep.), first published shortly after the creation of the Court of Criminal Appeal, are still produced and report a number of criminal cases not reported elsewhere. Similarly Lloyd's List Law Reports (Lloyd's Rep.) contain a number of commercial cases not reported elsewhere while the Road Traffic Reports (R.T.R.) contain, as the title would suggest, reports of road traffic cases. Other specialist series in general use are Local Government Reports (L.G.R.), Reports of Patent Cases (R.P.C.), Reports of Tax Cases (T.C.), Simon's Tax Cases (S.T.C.), Ryde's Rating Cases (R.R.C.) and Fleet Street Patent Law Reports (F.S.R.) while in the growing area of industrial law there are Knight's Industrial Law Reports (K.I.L.R. (formerly K.I.R.)) and the Industrial Cases Reports (I.C.R.) and Industrial Relations Law Reports (I.R.L.R.) which report decisions of the Employment Appeal Tribunal and of industrial tribunals, which are usually not reported elsewhere. European Community law decisions are to be found principally in the Common Market Law Reports (C.M.L.R.) and European Court Reports (E.C.R.). Periodicals such as the *Solicitors' Journal, Justice of the Peace, Estate Gazette, Criminal Law Review, New Law Journal* and *Current Law* include notes of cases to which reference may be made in the absence of a full report in a recognised series.[3] Among newspapers only the reports of *The Times* are commonly cited (not to be confused with the Times Law Reports).

The chief criticism which may be advanced of the present system of law reporting in England is its informality. Although there cannot be many cases of importance which escape the elaborate net of the law reporters there are undoubtedly some. The citation of unreported cases in court is still by no means unknown while the citation of cases reported only in series of reports other than the Law Reports is quite common.[4] With the advent of computerised data bases, such as LEXIS, unreported decisions, together with decisions of overseas courts, have become much more accessible to practitioners. It was this phenomenon, and the spectre of protraction of legal

---

3 See *Worthy* v. *Lloyd*, [1939] 2 K.B. 612; [1939] 1 All E.R. 474.
4 For examples see Allen, *Law in the Making* (7th Edn.) pp. 367 *et seq*; see also *Barrington* v. *Lee*, [1972] 1 Q.B. 326; [1971] 3 All E.R. 1231 from which it appears that the Court of Appeal in *Ryan* v. *Pilkington*, [1959] 1 All E.R. 689; [1959] 1 W.L.R. 403 may have gone wrong because two important unreported authorities were not before the Court. These cases, decided in 1948 and 1958 have since been reported (in [1971] 2 Q.B. 439, 443; [1971] 2 All E.R. 628, 631).

argument that it spawned, which led LORD DIPLOCK to make the contro-
versial statement which he did in *Roberts Petroleum, Ltd.* v. *Bernard Kenny,
Ltd.*,[5] restricting counsel's right to cite unreported transcripts of the Court of
Appeal in either the Court of Appeal or the House of Lords.

A second criticism of the system is the unnecessary duplication of effort.
Many cases are reported more or less fully in three or four different series of
reports and noted in many periodicals.

On the initiative of the then Lord Chancellor a Committee was set up to
report on the state of law reporting. Its report, published in 1940, was
somewhat negative in character. It rejected the proposal to grant a monopoly
to the Incorporated Council of Law Reporting, being content to state that
the Law Reports should be cited in preference to any other series. The
Committee also rejected, in the interest of publicity of judicial proceedings,
a proposal to grant licences to reporters without which they would be incompetent to report. Most of the positive recommendations in the 1940 Report
were contained in the minority report of Professor Goodhart. Professor
Goodhart's main suggestion was that each court, through an official shorthand writer and the judge, should produce an authenticated transcript which
would be filed with the court records. Copies of these transcripts would be
available for sale to law reporters and other interested persons. This would
amount to making law reports official. The majority of the Committee
rejected Professor Goodhart's proposal as expensive and inconvenient. At
the present day the main objection to Professor Goodhart's proposal would
be the additional strain it would impose upon an already overworked
judiciary.

---

[5] [1983] 2 A.C. 192, at 200–202; [1983] 1 All E.R. 564, at 566–568 (see p. 132, *ante*).

CHAPTER 7

Text Books

A text book differs from a statute or a law report in that it is not an original literary source of law. Text books, even if of the highest authority, contain only opinions as to the state of the law. In short they are descriptive rather than creative. Nevertheless it would be unrealistic in any consideration of the literary sources of English law to ignore text books for they are, in some cases, the earliest authority for the existence of a common law rule. The importance of text books as a source of law is, historically, in inverse proportion to the availability of law reports. Thus, in modern times text books are of comparatively little value since direct authority can almost always be found in a law report. Conversely, in the infancy of law reporting when such reports as existed were of a highly personalised nature the text books were, and are, the main source of authority. Indeed the line between a law report and a text book opinion is often a narrow one, particularly in the case of Coke whose *Institutes* (*Inst.*) are cited quite as often as his Reports and are generally accorded equivalent authority.

It will thus be apparent that there are two types of legal text book. The first is the ancient text book which is commonly used as an original source of common law. This type of book is a book of authority. The second type of text book is the modern text book which, however well respected and frequently cited, is not a book of authority. That is to say it is not a source of law and is only of use in that it indicates where a direct source, such as a statute or a law report, may be found. The dividing line between books of authority and modern text books is purely historical and depends, as stated above, on the availability of direct literary sources. Blackstone's *Commentaries on the Laws of England*, published in 1765, is probably the watershed in that, although it is often cited as a book of authority, it was also the forerunner of the modern text book.

A SOME BOOKS OF AUTHORITY

Text books of English law have not become books of authority merely by reason of their antiquity. Of the many works produced as legal text books, only about a dozen are universally accepted by the legal profession and the judiciary alike as books of authority. It is no accident that almost all the authors of these works were judges. The academic lawyer in the modern sense did not appear until Blackstone, in the eighteenth century, and Blackstone himself was also a judge. The following are some of the major text book writers whose works may be said to be sources of English law.

1   Glanvill and Bracton

Glanvill's treatise *De Legibus et Consuetudinibus Angliae* (concerning the laws and customs of England), written in about 1187, is the first major commentary on the common law in existence. Written in Latin, the manuscripts merely indicate that the treatise was written in the time of Glanvill who was Henry II's chief justiciar,[1] so that it is doubtful whether Glanvill was personally responsible for its composition. The subject matter of the treatise principally concerns land law, the basis of the common law. The form of the treatise set the pattern for legal writing for centuries to come in that it approached the common law from the standpoint of procedure, setting out the existing forms of action with a commentary on the scope of each. Glanvill is still cited as a book of authority[2] though not as frequently as the larger and more comprehensive treatise of Bracton.

Bracton's treatise, written in about 1250, was, like Glanvill's treatise, written in Latin and intituled *De Legibus et Consuetudinibus Angliae*. Although uncompleted it is a far more ambitious and comprehensive survey of English law than Glanvill's work. It adopted Glanvill's pattern of a summary of the forms of action glossed with a commentary but went further in that it illustrated the commentaries with case law. The cases in Bracton's treatise are set out very fully, generally including as much detail as the Year Books. In addition the treatise contains a long exposition of English law by way of introduction. Bracton appears to have been thoroughly grounded in Roman law and his treatise draws many Roman law analogies. Virtually all the principles of Roman law which have found their way into English law have done so *via* Bracton.[3] Perhaps the best known case in which Bracton's civilian analogies have been adopted into English law is *Coggs* v. *Bernard*[4] in which HOLT, C.J. developed the law of bailments in accordance with Roman law concepts gleaned from Bracton. The development of the law of easements also owes much to Bracton's exposition of Roman law.[5] Nevertheless, Bracton is first and foremost a chronicler of the common law and his treatise stands as the major academic work on the common law prior to Coke's *Institutes*.

2   Littleton

After Bracton there is no book of authority until the late fifteenth century when Littleton's treatise *Of Tenures* was published. This important work

---

1   The justiciar was the forerunner of the Chancellor.
2   See, for example: *Ashford* v. *Thornton* (1818), 1 B. & Ald. 405; *Warner* v. *Sampson*, [1959] 1 Q.B. 297; [1959] 1 All E.R. 120.
3   See p. 74, *ante*.
4   (1703), 2 Ld. Raym. 909.
5   *Dalton* v. *Angus* (1881), 6 App. Cas. 740.

was the first comprehensive study of English land law which was, at the time, exceedingly complex. The work differs from that of Bracton in that it approaches the subject from the standpoint of substantive law rather than of procedure. Also it appears that the work was intended for use as a text book and it was, in fact, used for this purpose for centuries after its composition. Coke's praise of Littleton was fulsome and he described the work as being of absolute perfection, "the ornament of the common law, and the most perfect and absolute work that ever was written in any human science". Indeed, the first of Coke's *Institutes* is a commentary on Littleton's *Of Tenures*.

The work is also notable as being the first major legal work to be printed, rather than written.

3   Coke

Probably the greatest of text book writers was Coke himself. This may be added to his other accomplishments as a judge, Parliamentarian and law reporter. Coke's great contribution to academic literature, apart from the Reports, which undoubtedly contain much subjective exposition, are his *Institutes of the Laws of England*. Coke's *Institutes* were composed chiefly towards the end of his life after he had ceased to hold judicial office. They are so well known as to be citable merely as *Inst.* without reference to the author.

There are four *Institutes*. The first, published in 1628, is a treatise on Littleton's *Of Tenures* and is commonly cited as *Co. Litt.* The second, and perhaps least valuable, Institute is a summary of the principal medieval statutes. The third is concerned with criminal law, defining and describing all the Pleas of the Crown, and the fourth Institute deals with the jurisdiction of the courts. The reason for the exalted position of the *Institutes* as a direct source of the common law is Coke's acquaintance with the Year Books. Coke's mastery of the Year Books has probably never been equalled and his recollection in the *Institutes* is so accurate that, even shortly after his death, virtually no one would look beyond Coke as a direct source. For this reason the Year Books are cited comparatively infrequently while the *Institutes* have been cited to English courts probably more frequently than any other book of authority.

A recent instance of reliance upon Coke as a work of authority is to be found in the decision of the Court of Appeal in *Reid* v. *Metropolitan Police Commissioner*.[6] The case was concerned with the meaning of the words "market overt" in section 22(1) of the Sale of Goods Act 1893 and, in particular, whether the operation of that section was confined to sales between sunrise and sunset.

> "To solve this question we have to go back to the works of Sir Edward Coke. In 1596 there was an important case about market overt;[7] Coke reported it. He afterwards expounded the law of market overt in his Institutes[8]. . . I think we should follow the words of Sir Edward Coke rather than those of Sir William Blackstone."[9]

---

6   [1973] Q.B. 551; [1973] 2 All E.R. 97.
7   *Market-Overt Case* (1596), 5 Co. Rep. 83b.
8   (1642), vol. 2, pp. 713, 714.
9   [1973] Q.B. 551, at p. 559; [1973] 2 All E.R. 97, at p. 99, *per* LORD DENNING, M.R.

The words that the Court of Appeal followed began

> "The sale must not be in the night, but between the rising of the sun, and the going downe of the same"[10]

so that a purchaser who bought the plaintiff's goods some one hour before sunrise at the New Caledonian Market in Southwark was held not to have acquired a good title to them under the Sale of Goods Act.

The only weakness in Coke's work is his total devotion to the common law to the exclusion of every other branch of English law. His total abhorrence of equity and admiralty undoubtedly did much to maintain the separate administration of these branches of the law for so long.

4 Blackstone

After Coke a large number of legal text books were produced. A few of these, such as the works of Hale, Hawkins and Foster are citable as books of authority particularly in relation to the criminal law.[11] Due to the poverty of early reports of criminal cases judges, when faced with a question of basic principles of criminal law, usually look no further than the early text books, particularly those of Coke, Hale, Hawkins, Foster and Blackstone. In the leading case of *Joyce* v. *Director of Public Prosecutions*[12] the House of Lords, in deciding that a foreigner who enjoyed the protection of the Crown could be guilty of treason under the Treason Act 1351, relied almost entirely on Foster's *Crown Cases*, Hale's *Pleas of the Crown*, Hawkins' *Pleas of the Crown*, East's *Pleas of the Crown* and Coke's *Institutes*. More recently, in defining the common law offence of affray in the House of Lords, LORD GARDINER, L.C. referred (*inter alia*) to Fitzherbert, Coke, Hale, Hawkins and Blackstone.[13]

Blackstone's *Commentaries on the Laws of England*, published in 1765, is probably the last book of authority to be written. It differs from works such as those of Hale and Hawkins in that it covers a far wider field. The four books comprising the *Commentaries* deal with constitutional law, family law, the law of real and personal property, succession, contract and tort, criminal law and civil and criminal procedure. It is, however, in the fields of tort and criminal law that Blackstone's authority is greatest. The authority of the *Commentaries* is rather less weighty than the authority of the earlier works cited in this section.[14] There are two reasons for this. First, the scope of the work is so wide that it cannot do more than state principles where works of narrower range can probe detail. Secondly, the *Commentaries* are later in point of time than Coke, Hale, Foster and the others so that in the event of an inconsistency between them the earlier work is almost bound to prevail. This is well illustrated by the case of *Button* v. *Director of Public Prosecutions*[15] in which a statement of Blackstone[16] to the effect that a

---

10 *Market-Overt Case* (1596), 5 Co. Rep. 83b.
11 See *Ashford* v. *Thornton* (1818), 1 B. & Ald. 405; *R*. v. *Casement* [1917] 1 K.B. 98; *Joyce* v. *Director of Public Prosecutions*, [1946] A.C. 347; [1946] 1 All E.R. 186.
12 [1946] A.C. 347; [1946] 1 All E.R. 186.
13 *Button* v. *Director of Public Prosecutions*, [1966] A.C. 591; [1965] 3 All E.R. 587.
14 Cf. *Reid* v. *Metropolitan Police Commissioner* (*supra*) in which Blackstone's definition of market overt was rejected in favour of that of Coke.
15 *Supra*.
16 4 Comm. 145.

common law affray could take place only in a public place was rejected by the House of Lords as inconsistent with earlier statements in the works of Hale and Hawkins.

B   MODERN TEXT BOOKS

The growth of law reporting after Blackstone's era and the fact that the basic principles of the common law were well established and chronicled by that time have made it unnecessary to look at any more recent text book as a direct source of a common law rule. Nineteenth-century works such as Stephen's *Commentaries on the Laws of England* are sometimes consulted but only as guides, not as sources. They are not books of authority. There are, in addition, many standard text books widely used by the legal profession, and even by judges, which are of the highest persuasive authority. Virtually every branch of the law has its standard work and the judge will think twice before gainsaying a statement of law appearing in such a work. Nevertheless judges never lose sight of the fact that these works are not books of authority and, in the event of a statement in a standard text book being inconsistent with a principle contained in a precedent or a statute, the latter will always prevail. For example, in *Watson v. Thomas S. Whitney & Co., Ltd.*[17] the Court of Appeal, in deciding that an appeal from the registrar of the (now defunct) Liverpool Court of Passage lay to the Court of Appeal, declined to adopt clear statements in *Halsbury's Laws of England* and the *Annual Practice 1966*, to the effect that the appeal lay to the divisional court of the Queen's Bench Division. Similarly, in *Button v. Director of Public Prosecutions*[18] the House of Lords drew attention to errors in Archbold's *Pleading, Evidence & Practice in Criminal Cases* and Russell on *Crimes and Misdemeanours*, both standard works on the criminal law. In *Shenton v. Tyler*[19] the then Master of the Rolls, in considering the scope of marital privilege, referred to some dozen text books on evidence, including those of Best, Cockle, Phipson and Stephen, before deciding that all were wrong.

The above, however, are exceptional occurrences. On the whole the persuasive authority of a standard text book is of considerable weight. There have been several cases in which a court has been willing to accept almost *verbatim* the view of a distinguished academician upon the law. Thus the description of easements contained in Cheshire's *Modern Real Property* was adopted by the Court of Appeal in *Re Ellenborough Park*,[20] while the House of Lords in *A.-G. v. De Keyser's Royal Hotel, Ltd.*[1] expressly accepted Dicey's definition of the royal prerogative. To go one step further, counsel for the respondents in *Rookes v. Barnard*[2] postulated the rather startling proposition that the tort of intimidation had been created by Sir John Salmond in his leading work on the law of torts.

---

[17] [1966] 1 All E.R. 122; [1966] 1 W.L.R. 57.
[18] [1966] A.C. 591; [1965] 3 All E.R. 587 (*supra*).
[19] [1939] Ch. 620; [1939] 1 All E.R. 827.
[20] [1956] Ch. 131; [1955] 3 All E.R. 667.
[1] [1920] A.C. 508.
[2] [1964] A.C. 1129; [1964] All E.R. 367.

There was formerly a rule of practice that a text book could not be cited in court during the lifetime of its author. The rule, which appears to have rested on no very logical foundation, has now been discounted and several text book writers, and even the authors of articles in legal periodicals, have had the satisfaction of seeing their opinions judicially endorsed during their own lifetimes.[3]

---

[3] See, for example, *Performing Right Society, Ltd.* v. *Mitchell and Booker* (*Palais de Dance*), *Ltd.*, [1924] 1 K.B. 762; *Read* v. *J. Lyons & Co., Ltd.*, [1945] K.B. 216; [1945] 1 All E.R. 106 (affirmed [1947] A.C. 156; [1946] 2 All E.R. 471); *R.* v. *Humphrys* [1977] A.C. 1; [1976] 2 All E.R. 497.

PART III

The Administration of Justice

SUMMARY

CHAPTER 8

The Royal Prerogative and Judicial Review

A THE ROYAL PREROGATIVE

Historically the Sovereign is the fountain of justice in England. For this reason the administration of justice is, strictly speaking, a prerogative of the Crown. This prerogative has, however, been substantially whittled away. Thus it was decided by COKE, C.J. in the case of *Prohibitions del Roy*,[1] that the King (James I) could not, in his own person, judge any case. The general immunity from civil proceedings which the Crown enjoyed at common law has been drastically curtailed by the Crown Proceedings Act 1947, although the personal immunity which the Sovereign enjoys from both civil and criminal proceedings remains. It is customarily accepted that the Crown no longer has a general power to create new courts by prerogative although it can, apparently, create courts to administer only the common law. This was established by the Privy Council in *Re Lord Bishop of Natal*.[2] Nevertheless this power is worthless since any court so created would be powerless to apply any rules of law other than common law rules and would, presumably, have difficulty in obtaining Parliamentary authority for the finance required to maintain such a court.[3] The best-known definition of the prerogative, in the present century, is that of Dicey,[4] which is as follows:

> "The prerogative is the name for the remaining portion of the Crown's original authority, and is therefore, as already pointed out, the name for the residue of discretionary power left at any moment in the hands of the Crown, whether such power be in fact exercised by the King himself or by his Ministers."

Most of the remaining vestiges of prerogative control over the administration of justice are now found in formality rather than in

---

[1] (1607), 12 Co. Rep. 63.
[2] (1865), 3 Moo. P.C. N.S. 115.
[3] The creation of the Criminal Injuries Compensation Board, is, however, a recent example of a tribunal created by prerogative act; see p. 222, *post*.
[4] *Introduction to the Study of the Law of the Constitution* (8th Edn., 1915), p. 421, cited with approval in *A.-G.* v. *De Keyser's Royal Hotel Ltd.*, [1920] A.C. 508.

substance. The superior courts are termed the "Queen's Courts" and the judges of those courts styled "Her Majesty's Judges". Criminal proceedings, on indictment, are pursued in the name of the Queen and all criminal proceedings are conducted on behalf of the Crown. These so-called prerogatives are, however, illusory. Judges are appointed "on the advice of" the Lord Chancellor or, in some cases, the Prime Minister. There is no power in the Crown to intervene in civil proceedings and criminal proceedings may usually be commenced by any private individual. The substantial remnants of the royal prerogative over the administration of justice are few. Among them may be included the power of the Attorney-General to stop a prosecution on indictment by entering a *nolle prosequi*, the power to pardon a convicted person and the prerogative of mercy under which the Crown may, through the Home Secretary, suspend, commute or remit any sentence.[5] Furthermore it has recently been affirmed that in certain peculiar circumstances arising outside the jurisdiction, the exercise of the prerogative may be invoked by petition of right.[6]

One aspect of the exercise of the royal prerogative which does merit mention is the prerogative of Her Majesty, acting on the advice of her Ministers, to enter into treaties. This prerogative cannot be questioned by the courts.[7] Thus the United Kingdom, on the 22nd January 1972, was a party to the Treaty of Accession by which it joined the European Economic Community, thereby, in effect, relinquishing some of the sovereignty of Parliament.[8]

Judicial review of prerogative action—The scope of the courts' powers, by judicial review, to control administrative action is considered in detail below but reference must at this stage be made to the specific question: is the exercise of the royal prerogative subject to review by the courts? Traditionally the view has been that the court's power is limited to ascertaining whether or not a prerogative power exists;[9] having ascertained that such a power did exist the courts would not assume jurisdiction to adjudicate upon or seek to control the manner of its exercise. This principle went hand in hand with the view that in matters affecting the interests of the state, it was the state and not the courts that had the last word. This view was upheld by the House of Lords, in the context of discovery of documents, in *Duncan* v. *Cammell, Laird & Co., Ltd.*[10]

However, within the last thirty years or so the attitude of the courts has radically altered. It is no longer the law that the Crown's claim for privilege from disclosure of documents cannot be scrutinised and, if necessary, over-

---

5 Of more doubtful validity is the practice of the Inland Revenue Commissioners in granting extra-statutory concessions against tax liabilities, for example, a concession to miners whereby income tax is not charged on a miner's free coal and allowances in lieu thereof; cf. *Vestey* v. *Inland Revenue Commissioners (No. 2)*, [1980] A.C. 1148; [1979] 3 All E.R. 976.

6 *Franklin* v. *R.*, [1974] Q.B. 202; [1973] 3 All E.R. 861; see p. 303, *post*.

7 Cf. *Blackburn* v. *A.-G.*, [1971] 2 All E.R. 1380; [1971] 1 W.L.R. 1037.

8 In Case 6/64: *Costa* v. *ENEL*, [1964] C.M.L.R. 425 the European Court of Justice stated (at p. 455) that ". . . the member States, albeit within limited spheres, have restricted their sovereign rights and created a body of law applicable both to their nationals and to themselves".

9 *A.-G.* v. *De Keyser's Royal Hotel*, [1920] A.C. 508.

10 [1942] A.C. 624; [1942] 1 All E.R. 587; see p. 598, *post* for a discussion of this case and the authorities which ensued on this topic.

ridden by the courts.[11] In a prosecution under the Official Secrets Act based on conduct said to be "prejudicial to the safety or interest of the state", it is for the Crown to prove this and it cannot do so simply by asserting its opinion as to the existence of such prejudice.[12]

There is now direct authority for the proposition that the exercise of prerogative power is subject to judicial review. This is the decision of a divisional court of the Queen's Bench Division in *R. v. Criminal Injuries Compensation Board, Ex parte Lain*,[13] holding that decisions of the Board, a body established by prerogative to administer a scheme for the provision of compensation to victims of crimes of violence, were subject to judicial review. The principle is also illustrated by the decision of the Court of Appeal in *Laker Airways, Ltd. v. Department of Trade*[14] in which it was held that the court could intervene to prevent the exercise, by the Secretary of State for Trade, of a prerogative power to cancel the plaintiff's designation as a scheduled service operator and recommend the withdrawal of its air transport licence granted under the Civil Aviation Act 1971.

Thus there seems to be no doubt but that the courts will seek to interfere, by way of judicial review, with decisions of administrative bodies acting in the exercise of powers conferred upon them by royal prerogative. What remains uncertain is the extent to which the courts will similarly intervene in relation to the direct exercise of the royal prerogative. This question, of fundamental constitutional importance, was raised and discussed in the speeches of the House of Lords in *Council of Civil Service Unions v. Minister for the Civil Service*.[15] The litigation arose out of an instruction by the minister to the effect that the conditions of employment of staff at Government Communications Headquarters (GCHQ) would be revised so as to prohibit membership of any trade union (other than an approved departmental staff association). This instruction was issued pursuant to power conferred upon the minister by an Order in Council made under the royal prerogative. The appellants applied for judicial review of the minister's instruction. It was contended (*inter alia*) on behalf of the minister that the instruction was not open to review by the courts because it was an emanation of the prerogative. In the event adjudication on this contention became unnecessary because the House of Lords held that the evidence disclosed that the minister's instruction to have been justified on the ground of national security. This being so, any observations by their Lordships upon the contention raised were necessarily *obiter*. Nevertheless the *dicta* of LORDS SCARMAN, DIPLOCK and ROSKILL are illuminating.[16] From them may be deduced the following principles.

---

[11] Cf. *Conway* v. *Rimmer*, [1968] A.C. 910; [1968] 1 All E.R. 874.

[12] *Chandler* v. *Director of Public Prosecutions*, [1964] A.C. 763; [1962] 3 All E.R. 142; see also *R. v. Secretary of State for the Home Dept., Ex parte Hosenball*, [1977] 3 All E.R. 452; [1977] 1 W.L.R. 766.

[13] [1967] 2 Q.B. 864; [1967] 2 All E.R. 770, described as a "landmark" case by LORD SCARMAN and LORD ROSKILL in *Council of Civil Service Unions* v. *Minister for the Civil Service (infra)*; see p. 222, *post*.

[14] [1977] Q.B. 643; [1977] 2 All E.R. 182.

[15] [1984] 3 All E.R. 935; [1984] 3 W.L.R. 1174.

[16] The remaining law lords sitting on the appeal, LORDS FRASER and BRIGHTMAN, preferred not to express their concluded view on the topic.

(1) The exercise by an administrative body of delegated powers emanating from a prerogative power is subject to judicial review.[17]

(2) The exercise of certain prerogative powers is not subject to judicial review because their nature and subject matter is such as not to be amenable to the judicial process; these include the making of treaties, the defence of the realm, the prerogative of mercy, the grant of honours, the dissolution of Parliament and the appointment of ministers.

(3) The direct exercise of prerogative powers, not being within the category envisaged in (2) above, is subject to judicial review on grounds of "illegality", "procedural impropriety" or (probably) "irrationality".

LORD SCARMAN summarised the modern approach as follow:[18]

"My Lords, I would wish to add a few, very few, words on the reviewability of the exercise of the royal prerogative. Like my noble and learned friend Lord Diplock, I believe that the law relating to judicial review has now reached the stage where it can be said with confidence that, if the subject matter in respect of which prerogative power is exercised is justiciable, that is to say if it is a matter on which the court can adjudicate, the exercise of the power is subject to review in accordance with the principles developed in respect of the review of the exercise of statutory power. Without usurping the role of legal historian, for which I claim no special qualification, I would observe that the royal prerogative has always been regarded as part of the common law, and that Coke CJ had no doubt that it was subject to the common law: see *Prohibitions Del Roy* (1607) 12 Co. Rep. 63, 77 E.R. 1342 and *Case of Proclamations* (1611) 12 Co. Rep. 74, 77 E.R. 1352. In the latter case he declared that 'the King hath no prerogative, but that which the law of the land allows him' (see 12 Co. Rep. 74 at 76, 77 E.R. 1352 at 1354). It is, of course, beyond doubt that in Coke's time and thereafter judicial review of the exercise of prerogative power was limited to inquiring into whether a particular power existed and, if it did, into its extent: see *A.-G.* v. *De Keyser's Royal Hotel Ltd.* [1920] A.C. 508, [1920] All E.R. Rep. 80. But this limitation has now gone, overwhelmed by the developing modern law of judicial review: see *R.* v. *Criminal Injuries Compensation Board, ex. p. Lain* [1967] 2 All E.R. 770, [1967] 2 Q.B. 864 (a landmark case comparable in its generation with the *Case of Proclamations*) and *R.* v. *Secretary of State for the Home Dept, ex. p. Hosenball* [1977] 3 All E.R. 452, [1977] 1 W.L.R. 766. Just as ancient restrictions in the law relating to the prerogative writs and orders have not prevented the courts from extending the requirement of natural justice, namely the duty to act fairly, so that it is required of a purely administrative act, so also has the modern law, a vivid sketch of which my noble and learned friend Lord Diplock has included in his speech, extended the range of judicial review in respect of the exercise of prerogative power. Today, therefore, the controlling factor in determining whether the exercise of prerogative power is subject to judicial review is not its source but its subject matter."

B   JUDICIAL REVIEW

1   Historical origins of the powers of the High Court

We have seen[19] that the earliest method of appealing at common law was by writ of error, and that this was eventually superseded by a proper appeals

---

17 LORD FRASER and, tacitly, LORD BRIGHTMAN agreed with this principle.
18 [1984] 3 All E.R. 935, at p. 948; [1984] 3 W.L.R. 1174, at p. 1193.
19 See p. 31, *ante.*

procedure. However this procedure only applied within the superior common law courts. The common law courts also wished to control the conduct of inferior courts of record, so as to provide a remedy where they acted in excess of jurisdiction or otherwise contrary to law. This was regarded as a prerogative power and was exercised by means of use of a number of prerogative writs. These writs were also used to enforce the "rule of law", whereby all exercise of authority is subject to the control of the law, exercised by the courts. After about 1600 this jurisdiction was in fact exercised by the Court of King's Bench.[20]

The prerogative writs within the category described above were:

(1) *prohibition* whereby inferior courts or administrative bodies could be prohibited from acting in excess of jurisdiction or unlawfully;

(2) *mandamus* whereby an inferior court could be ordered to exercise jurisdiction where it was declining to do so or an official ordered to perform a function which the law required of him;

(3) *certiorari* whereby the record of an inferior court could be examined by the King's Bench and the proceedings quashed on the ground of error of law, excess of jurisdiction or abuse of process;

(4) *habeas corpus* requiring a person holding another in custody to justify the confinement to the court; and

(5) *quo warranto* enabling a party to challenge the jurisdiction of a court or person in public office purporting to exercise jurisdiction over him by means of a writ ordering the sheriff to summon the claimant to show by what authority (*quo warranto*) he asserted jurisdiction.

Of the above, *quo warranto* fell into disuse long before its abolition in 1938[1] while the various forms of the writ of *habeas corpus*[2] still exist and the writ of *habeas corpus ad subjiciendum* is still frequently used, often as a means of testing the validity of detention effected for the purpose of extradition.

The remaining three writs were abolished in 1938 but replaced by *orders* of *prohibition, mandamus* and *certiorari*.[3] They constitute the supervisory jurisdiction of the High Court and the procedure whereby this jurisdiction is invoked and exercised is now termed "judicial review". An application for any of the orders named above[4] must be made by way of application for judicial review.

2 Procedure

The procedure on applications for judicial review is governed by R.S.C. Order 53.

---

20 See Baker, *An Introduction to English Legal History* (2nd Edn.), pp. 123–132; Jaffe and Henderson, *Judicial Review and the Rule of Law: Historical Origins* (1956) 72 Law Quarterly Review 345.

1 By Administration of Justice (Miscellaneous Provisions) Act 1938, s. 9, which provided that the remedy would, in effect, be replaced by injunction; see now Supreme Court Act 1981, s. 30.

2 There are five forms still in use; see notes to R.S.C. Order 54, r. 1 in the Supreme Court Practice 1985.

3 Administration of Justice (Miscellaneous Provisions) Act 1938, s. 7.

4 Or for an injunction under s. 30 of the Supreme Court Act 1981 (*supra*) (ibid., s. 31(1)).

The application must be made promptly and in any event within three months from the date when the grounds for the application first arose unless the court considers that there is good reason for extending this period.[5] The application is by originating motion, to a divisional court of the Queen's Bench Division in criminal matters or to a judge sitting in open court in other cases.[6]

The applicant requires leave to apply for judicial review and this is sought by *ex parte* application to a judge. The application is in a prescribed form and must contain the relief sought and the grounds relied upon and must be accompanied by an affidavit verifying the facts relied on. The judge may determine the application without a hearing (unless a hearing is requested in the notice of application). If the application for leave is refused the applicant may renew it by applying, in criminal cases to the divisional court or, in any other case, to a single judge sitting in open court or, if the court so directs, to the divisional court.[7]

Applications for interlocutory orders, such as discovery, interrogatories, cross-examination of witnesses, may be made to a judge or master.[8]

On the hearing of the application for judicial review the court will hear any party served with the motion or summons and any other person who appears to be a proper person to be heard. The court has power to make orders of *prohibition, mandamus* or *certiorari*, to grant an injunction or declaration and to award damages if the applicant could have recovered damages had he proceeded by action, rather than application for judicial review.[9]

The court has power to grant interim relief,[10] such as an interlocutory injunction. Where the relief sought is a declaration, an injunction or damages the court may, in certain circumstances, order the proceedings to continue as if they had been commenced by writ.[11]

The essential feature of judicial review is that it applies to public law rather than private law matters. Thus it is not appropriate where the applicant's complaint is of a purely private nature, for example that he has been wrongfully dismissed by his employer, even where that employer is a public authority.[12] Conversely, if the applicant wishes to challenge a public law decision he must proceed by way of application for judicial review and he cannot avoid the procedural requirements of Order 53 (notably the need for leave to move and the prescribed time limit) by bringing an ordinary action seeking a declaration or an injunction.[13]

---

[5] O. 53, r. 4.

[6] O. 53, r. 5(2) although the court may (except in criminal cases) direct that the application shall be made by originating summons to a judge in chambers or by originating motion to the divisional court (*ibid.*).

[7] O. 53, r. 3; see this rule for full details of the procedural requirements.

[8] O. 53, r. 8.

[9] Supreme Court Act 1981, s. 31(4); any claim for damages must be included in the statement filed in support of the application (*ibid.*).

[10] O. 53, r. 3(10).

[11] O. 53, r. 9(5).

[12] *R.* v. *B.B.C., Ex parte Lavelle*, [1983] 1 All E.R. 241; [1983] 1 W.L.R. 23.

[13] *O'Reilly* v. *Mackman*, [1983] 2 A.C. 237; [1982] 3 All E.R. 1124; *Cocks* v. *Thanet District Council*, [1983] 2 A.C. 286; [1982] 3 All E.R. 1135.

3 Bodies amenable to judicial review

In *R.* v. *Electricity Commissioners, Ex parte London Electricity Joint Committee Co.* (*1920*) *Ltd.*[14] ATKIN, L.J. (as he then was) laid down certain requirements as conditions precedent to the exercise of the supervisory jurisdiction of the High Court. One of these was that a body was not amenable to such jurisdiction unless it had a duty to act "judicially". This led to a large number of decisions on the issue of whether the decision it was sought to attack was "quasi-judicial" or only "administrative". Fortunately this requirement was swept away by the decision of the House of Lords in *Ridge* v. *Baldwin*[15] and the law now is that judicial review lies against any inferior court or tribunal and against any body exercising functions conferred by law which may affect the rights or legitimate expectations of subjects.[16] It lies therefore against, for example, a local authority watch committee,[17] a coroner,[18] the Criminal Injuries Compensation Board,[19] a board of prison visitors,[20] immigration officers,[1] ministers of the Crown.[2] But it does not lie against bodies exercising a non-public function (such as an employer). Nor does it lie against superior courts. However, the Crown Court is amenable to judicial review when acting as an appellate court (for which purpose it is an inferior court) and, indeed, in any other case "other than its jurisdiction in matters relating to trial on indictment".[3]

4 Grounds for judicial review

The most important factor to bear in mind is that judicial review is not a form of appeal. The High Court will not substitute its own decision for that of the court, tribunal or body below on the ground that it appears to be wrong. The circumstances in which the court will interfere are want or excess of jurisdiction,[4] error on the face of the record,[5] failure to comply with the rules of natural justice (these vary from case to case but generally include the

---

[14] [1924] 1 K.B. 171.
[15] [1964] A.C. 40; [1963] 2 All E.R. 66.
[16] As to the interpretation of "legitimate expectations" (a new concept), see *Findlay* v. *Secretary of State for the Home Dept.*, [1984] 3 All E.R. 801; [1984] 3 W.L.R. 1159; *Council of Civil Service Unions* v. *Minister for the Civil Service*, [1984] 3 All E.R. 935; [1984] 3 W.L.R. 1174.
[17] *Ridge* v. *Baldwin* (*supra*).
[18] *R.* v. *West Yorkshire Coroner, Ex parte Smith*, [1983] Q.B. 335; [1982] 3 All E.R. 1098; see p. 211, *post*.
[19] *R.* v. *Criminal Injuries Compensation Board, Ex parte Lain*, [1967] 2 Q.B. 864; [1967] 2 All E.R. 770; see p. 222, *post*.
[20] *O'Reilly* v. *Mackman* (*supra*).
[1] *R.* v. *Secretary of State for the Home Dept., Ex parte Khawaja*, [1984] A.C. 74; [1983] 1 All E.R. 765.
[2] *R.* v. *Secretary of State for the Home Dept., Ex parte Hosenball*, [1977] 3 All E.R. 452; [1977] 1 W.L.R. 766.
[3] Supreme Court Act 1981, s. 29(3); see p. 198, *post*.
[4] *Anisminic* v. *Foreign Compensation Commission*, [1969] 2 A.C. 147; [1969] 1 All E.R. 208.
[5] This used to be confined to the record itself and excluded jurisdiction to correct errors in the reasons leading to the record but it is now held to extend to errors in reasons given in support of the recorded decision: *R.* v. *Crown Court at Knightsbrige, Ex parte International Sporting Club* (*London*), *Ltd.*, [1982] Q.B. 304; [1981] 3 All E.R. 417.

right of each party to state his case, the prohibition on a person being judge in his own cause, the right to be informed of the reasons for a decision and, in some cases, the right to legal representation before a tribunal). In addition the court will intervene when it considers that the decision is one which no reasonable body could have reached on the facts if it had correctly construed its duty — this is called the *"Wednesbury* principle"[6] and *"Wednesbury* unreasonableness" is a concept much canvassed by applicants for judicial review.

In *Council of Civil Service Unions* v. *Minister for the Civil Service*[7] LORD DIPLOCK suggested classifying the grounds on which administrative action is subject to judicial review as (1) "illegality"; (2) "irrationality" (viz. *Wednesbury* unreasonableness); and (3) "procedural impropriety".

---

6   *Associated Provincial Picture Houses, Ltd.* v. *Wednesbury Corpn.*, [1948] 1 K.B. 223; [1947] 2 All E.R. 680.
7   *Supra.*

CHAPTER 9

The Courts

A INTRODUCTION

All English courts derive their jurisdiction directly or indirectly from the Crown, the jurisdiction of judges being, in theory, an extension of the royal prerogative. There are, within the English legal system, a large number of courts of varying degrees of standing and jurisdiction. There are various ways of classifying courts. The two fundamental divisions of English courts are; (1) courts of record and courts not of record; and (2) superior and inferior courts. Before explaining further the significance of this classification it may be noted that there are other classifications, though these are not of universal application. Thus it is possible to classify courts according to their functions. The obvious classification in this repect would be into courts of civil and courts of criminal jurisdiction. This classification is not, however, a valid one since, although certain courts do exercise a purely civil or criminal jurisdiction, most English courts hear both civil and criminal cases. Thus the House of Lords, Court of Appeal, High Court, Crown Court and magistrates' courts exercise jurisdiction in both civil and criminal matters. A second classification would be into courts of original and courts of appellate jurisdiction. Nor is this division of general application. Although certain courts, such as the Court of Appeal and the House of Lords, exercise a purely appellate jurisdiction, while other courts, such as magistrates' courts, have no appellate jurisdiction, many courts, notably the High Court and the Crown Court, exercise both original and appellate jurisdiction.

The Court of Justice of the European Communities (the European Court) is, of course, *sui generis* since, although not an English court, it exercises jurisdiction within the English legal system and the position of this Court within the system must be considered.

It may sometimes be a matter of dispute whether a particular tribunal is properly described as a "court" or not. This is not central to the question of whether the supervisory jurisdiction of the High Court extends to the body in question, since that jurisdiction is not limited to courts properly so called.[1] It is, however, important in the context of contempt of court[2] since the offence

---

[1] See p. 177, *ante*.
[2] See p. 237, *post*.

of contempt of court is, by definition, capable of commission only in relation to a "court". In *A.-G.* v. *British Broadcasting Corporation*[3] the House of Lords (reversing the decision of the Court of Appeal) held that a valuation court constituted under section 88 of the General Rate Act 1967 was not "an inferior court", for the purposes of R.S.C. Ord. 52, r. 1(2) since, although it was termed a court, its functions were essentially administrative and it was not a court of law established to exercise the judicial power of the state. The House was, however, divided on the question of whether it was a court at all (*viz.* for any purpose other than contempt proceedings). This is no doubt of academic interest but it appears to be of no other practical significance whether a tribunal is properly describable as a "court" or not.

1   Superior and inferior courts

A traditional classification of English courts is their division into superior and inferior courts. The nature of superior courts is that their jurisdiction is limited neither by the value of the subject matter of an action nor geographically. The jurisdiction of inferior courts is limited both geographically and according to the value of the subject matter of the dispute.[4] The superior courts are the House of Lords, Court of Appeal, High Court, Crown Court, Judicial Committee of the Privy Council, Restrictive Practices Court and the Employment Appeal Tribunal. One of the distinctive features of inferior courts is that they are amenable to the supervisory jurisdiction of the High Court exercised by prerogative order,[5] though this applies also to the Crown Court in the exercise of its appellate jurisdiction even though the Crown Court is, as stated above, a superior court.[6] The most important of the inferior courts are county courts and magistrates' courts although all courts not listed above as superior are inferior courts. The distinction is also of importance in relation to contempt of court, since the penalties which may be imposed by inferior courts are far less than superior courts have power to inflict.[7]

2   Courts of record

An ancient division of courts is into courts of record and courts which are not courts of record. The basic historical distinction depended upon whether or not the court in question maintained a record of its proceedings. The records of courts of record are preserved in the Public Record Office. Courts of record may be inferior or superior. The essential characteristic of a court of record is no longer that it maintains a record; it is that it has power to punish

---

3   [1981] A.C. 303; [1980] 3 All E.R. 161.
4   Whether a court is an inferior or a superior court can usually be ascertained by reference to the historical origins of the court or, if it was created by statute, by the terms of the statute creating it. However where the statute is silent it is necessary to look at the nature and powers of the court so as to decide whether they are analogous to those of a superior or an inferior court; see *R.* v. *Cripps, Ex parte Muldoon*, [1984] Q.B. 68; [1983] 3 All E.R. 72 in which the Queen's Bench divisional court held an election court (under the Representation of the People Act) to be an inferior court.
5   See p. 177, *ante.*
6   See p. 198, *post.*
7   See p. 237, *post.*

for contempt. Consequently any court which has jurisdiction to punish contempt is a court of record. The powers of superior and inferior courts of record, and of magistrates' courts, to commit for contempt are now set out in the Contempt of Court Act 1981.[8] In addition the High Court has a common law jurisdiction to punish contempts committed before courts which are not courts of record.[9]

3 The principle of open justice

Before considering individually the constitution and jurisdiction of English courts attention may be drawn to the general principle of "open justice". The first aspect of this is that courts should sit in public. Ever since the abolition of the Court of Star Chamber English judges have rebelled against the notion of private sittings of courts. In the famous words of LORD HEWART, C.J. in *R.* v. *Sussex Justices, Ex parte McCarthy*:[10]

> "A long line of cases shows that it is not merely of some importance but is of fundamental importance that justice should not only be done, but should manifestly and undoubtedly be seen to be done."

The principle, and the circumstances which would justify departure from it were explained by SIR JOHN DONALDSON, M.R. in *R.* v. *Chief Registrar of Friendly Societies, Ex parte New Cross Building Society*,[11] as follows:

> "It is fundamental to British justice as we know it, and as our forbears have known it, that the Queen's courts are open to all. And when I say that they are open to all I do not limit this to those who have business in the courts. The judges administer justice in the Queen's name on behalf of the whole community. No one is more entitled than a member of the general public to see for himself that justice is done. Nevertheless it is well settled that occasions can arise when it becomes the duty of the court to close its doors.
>   This problem was considered in depth by the House of Lords in *Scott* v. *Scott* [1913] A.C. 417, [1911–13] All E.R. Rep. 1. The guidance which I get from their lordships' speeches can be summarised as follows. The general rule that the courts shall conduct their proceedings in public is but an aid, albeit a very important aid, to the achievement of the paramount object of the courts, which is to do justice in accordance with the law. It is only if, in wholly exceptional circumstances, the presence of the public or public knowledge of the proceedings is likely to defeat that paramount object that the courts are justified in proceeding in camera. These circumstances are incapable of definition. Each application for privacy must be considered on its merits, but the applicant must satisfy the court that nothing short of total privacy will enable justice to be done. It is not sufficient that a public hearing will create embarrassment for some or all of those concerned. It must be shown that a public hearing is likely to lead, directly or indirectly, to a denial of justice."

---

[8] See p. 238, *post*.
[9] *R.* v. *Davies*, [1906] 1 K.B. 32; see p. 240, *post*.
[10] [1924] 1 K.B. 256, at p. 259; see also *Scott* v. *Scott*, [1913] A.C. 417; *R.* v. *Denbigh Justices, Ex parte Williams*, [1974] Q.B. 759; [1974] 2 All E.R. 1052; Supreme Court Act 1981, s. 67.
[11] [1984] 2 All E.R. 27, at p. 31; [1984] 2 W.L.R. 370, at p. 377. In this case "wholly exceptional circumstances" to justify sitting *in camera* were found to exist, namely that the financial standing of a building society was in issue and publicity of the proceedings might have led to the loss of public confidence in the society with the result that it would be forced to close, thereby rendering nugatory the relief sought in the proceedings.

There are several specific situations in which courts are justified in sitting *in camera*. These are, principally, in wardship proceedings, proceedings involving a secret process, cases involving evidence of sexual capacity in suits for nullity of marriage, proceedings relating to declarations of legitimacy, certain proceedings for injunctions[12] or financial relief in matrimonial causes, juvenile court proceedings,[13] proceedings under the Official Secrets Act[14] and other proceedings where the presence of the public would make the administration of justice impracticable. In addition where an appeal or an application for leave to appeal is brought against the decision of a court which had power to sit in private, the appellate court has similar power.[15]

The general rule that proceedings should be conducted publicly is zealously enforced since it is regarded as being at the heart of our system of procedure. Thus where justices, considering an adoption application, took a social worker in the case into their room with them when they retired, the President of the Family Division described this as "a most extraordinary and unfortunate procedure" and a "grave irregularity" and on this (among other) grounds a re-hearing was ordered.[16]

In exercising its discretion whether to conduct proceedings *in camera*, the court must take into account the effect of publicity on the parties, particularly in relation to their health and occupations and on third parties who, for example, might be distressed by the disclosure of family secrets and weigh against that the value of publicity in eliciting further evidence and the traditional rule of public policy that justice should be administered publicly.[17] Where the public is wrongly excluded from proceedings, those proceedings may be set aside.[18]

The second aspect of the principle of open justice is that all the evidence should be communicated publicly and the third is that nothing should be done to discourage or prevent publication of fair and accurate reports of judicial proceedings. However, just as there are limitations on the principle that proceedings should be conducted in public, so are there circumstances which may justify a court restricting publicity of evidence, either within or outside the courtroom. To quote a common example, victims of blackmail are usually permitted to communicate their names and addresses in court by writing them down and to be referred to throughout the proceedings as "Mr. X" or some such title. There are provisions in the Sexual Offences (Amendment) Act 1976 for preserving the anonymity of complainants and defendants in rape and similar offences.[19]

---

12 See *Practice Direction* (*Matrimonial Causes: Injunction*), [1974] 2 All E.R. 1119; [1974] 1 W.L.R. 936; see also p. 296, *post* as to hearing applications for *Anton Piller* orders.
13 Though *bona fide* representatives of the press may not be excluded: Children and Young Persons Act 1933, s. 37.
14 Official Secrets Act 1920, s. 8.
15 Domestic and Appellate Proceedings (Restriction of Publicity) Act 1968, s. 1.
16 *Re B* (*a minor*), [1975] Fam. 127; [1975] 2 All E.R. 449.
17 *Barritt* v. *A.-G.*, [1971] 3 All E.R. 1183; [1971] 1 W.L.R. 1713.
18 *McPherson* v. *McPherson*, [1936] A.C. 177.
19 Sexual Offences (Amendment) Act 1976, ss. 4–6; after a person has been "accused" (as to which, see s. 4(6)) of a rape offence it is an offence to publish in a written publication or broadcast any matter likely to lead members of the public to identify a woman as the complainant (s. 4) or the defendant as the person accused (except after his conviction) (s. 6); in each case a judge of the Crown Court has power, on application, to remove these restrictions in certain circumstances; see p. 579, *post*.

This area of the law was recently considered by the House of Lords in *A.-G.* v. *Leveller Magazine, Ltd.*[20] The House accepted that, in exercising its control over the proceedings before it, a court was entitled to derogate from the principle of open justice by sitting in private or permitting a witness not to disclose his name when giving evidence if it was necessary to do so in the interests of the due administration of justice. However VISCOUNT DILHORNE and LORD EDMUND-DAVIES both stated that a court has no power to make an order directed to and binding on the public *ipso jure* prohibiting the publication of information which might, for example, enable a witness to be identified (although, of course, such publication might, in certain circumstances, amount to contempt if it threatened the administration of justice either in the particular case or in relation to cases which might be brought in the future). In the event in that case the absence of a clear direction or order restricting publication and the fact that the identity of the witness in question was readily ascertainable from other evidence which was freely reportable combined to lead to the convictions for contempt being quashed.

Where a court has power to order a name or other matter to be withheld from the public in proceedings before the court, section 11 of the Contempt of Court Act 1981 empowers the court to give "such directions . . . as appear to the court to be necessary" for giving effect to any order which it makes. It should be noted, however, that this section does not create a power to order a name or other matter to be withheld; it simply regulates the exercise of such power as the court may inherently possess.

B THE EUROPEAN COURT

1 The place of the European Court in the English legal system

Prior to January 1, 1973, the date upon which the United Kingdom became a member of the European Communities, the House of Lords was the court of final appeal. The position has now altered for, above the House of Lords, stands the Court of Justice of the European Communities (the European Court). It is important to appreciate at the outset that the European Court's jurisdiction does not extend to purely internal disputes between subjects so that in the vast majority of cases arising within the United Kingdom there is no question of the dispute going further than the House of Lords. LORD DENNING, M.R. explained the position in *H.P. Bulmer, Ltd* v. *J. Bollinger S.A.*[1]

> "The first and fundamental point is that the Treaty concerns only those matters which have a European element, that is to say, matters which affect people or property in the nine countries of the Common Market besides ourselves. The Treaty does not touch any of the matters which concern solely England and the people in it. These are still governed by English law. They are not affected by the Treaty. But when we come to matters with a European element the Treaty is like an incoming tide. It flows into the estuaries and up the rivers. It cannot be held back . . . It is important to distinguish between the task of interpreting the Treaty—to see what it means—and the task of *applying* it—to

---

[20] [1979] A.C. 440; [1979] 1 All E.R. 745—the so-called "Colonel B" case.
[1] [1974] Ch. 401, at pp. 418–419; [1974] 2 All E.R. 1226, at pp. 1231–1232.

apply its provisions to the case in hand. Let me put on one side the task of applying the Treaty. On this matter in our courts, the English judges have the final word. They are the only judges who are empowered to decide the case itself. They have to find the facts, to state the issues, to give judgment for one side or the other, and to see that the judgment is enforced.

Before the English judges can apply the Treaty, they have to see what it means and what is its effect. In the task of *interpreting* the Treaty, the English judges are no longer the final authority. They no longer carry the law in their breasts. They are no longer in a position to give rulings which are of binding force. The supreme tribunal for *interpreting* the Treaty is the European Court of Justice, at Luxembourg.''

In United Kingdom courts, judicial notice must be taken of any decision of, or expression of opinion by, the European Court on any question as to the validity, meaning or effect of any of the Treaties, or as to the validity, meaning or effect of any Community instrument.[2]

2   Constitution and procedure of the European Court

The Court of Justice consists of ten judges[3] and is assisted by four Advocates-General[4] whose duties are to present publicly, with complete impartiality and independence, reasoned conclusions on cases submitted to the Court with a view to assisting the latter in the performance of its duties.[3]

Judges and Advocates-General are chosen "from among persons of indisputable independence who fulfil the conditions required for the holding of the highest judicial office in their respective countries or who are jurists of recognised competence".[5] They are appointed for a term of six years by the governments of member states acting in common agreement.[6] They retire in rota and are eligible for re-appointment; the President of the Court is appointed, for a term of three years by the judges from among their number.[7] The Court appoints its own registrar and lays down rules governing his service.[8]

The Court has power to adopt its own rules of procedure, which must be submitted to the Council of the European Communities for unanimous approval.[9] The Court must sit in plenary session save that it may set up chambers, composed of three or five judges, to deal with certain categories of cases[10] although it must always sit in plenary session to hear cases submitted to it by a member state or by one of the institutions of the Community[11] or to deal with preliminary questions submitted to it pursuant to Article 177.[5]

---

[2] European Communities Act 1972, s. 3(2).
[3] Act of Accession, Art. 17 (as amended).
[4] *Ibid.*, Art. 18 (as amended).
[5] E.E.C. Treaty, Art. 165; for references under Art. 177, see *infra.*
[6] Act of Accession, Art. 18 (as amended).
[7] E.E.C. Treaty, Art. 167.
[8] *Ibid.*, Art. 168.
[9] *Ibid.*, Art. 188.
[10] *Ibid.*, Art. 165.
[11] There are four Institutions of the Community: the Assembly, the Council, the Commission and the Court of Justice.

3 Jurisdiction of the Court

There are, basically, two aspects of the jurisdiction of the European Court. The first of these is quite outside our own legal system and comprises such matters as the hearing of complaints brought by member states or the Commission (or, indeed, on the Court's own initiative) that a member state has failed to fulfil its obligations under the Treaties,[12] the review of the legality of acts of the Council and of the Commission and the hearing of disputes between member states which relate to the subject matter of the Treaties.

The aspect of the Court's jurisdiction which is of direct concern to the English lawyer is that which arises under Article 177 of the E.E.C. Treaty.[13] This Article provides as follows:

"(1) The Court of Justice shall have jurisdiction to give preliminary rulings concerning:
(a) the interpretation of this Treaty;
(b) the validity and interpretation of acts of the institutions of the Community;
(c) the interpretation of the statutes of bodies established by an act of the Council, where those statutes so provide.
(2) Where such a question is raised before any court or tribunal of a Member State, that court or tribunal may, if it considers that a decision on the question is necessary to enable it to give judgment, request the Court of Justice to give a ruling thereon.
(3) Where any such question is raised in a case pending before a court or tribunal of a Member State, against whose decisions there is no judicial remedy under national law, that court or tribunal shall bring the matter before the Court of Justice".

Accordingly, save in cases to which (3) above applies the court or tribunal has a discretion as to whether or not to refer a case to the European Court. The factors which ought to be taken into account in exercising that discretion and the principles applicable were considered by LORD DENNING, M.R. in *H.P. Bulmer, Ltd.* v. *Bollinger S.A.*[14] Where (3) above applies, no such discretion exists and there must be a reference. This clearly applies to the House of Lords but it is doubtful whether it would apply to courts below the House of Lords even where the decision of the court was not one from which an appeal would lie in the particular case in question. This doubt is based upon what appears to be a proper construction of Article 177(3) which makes the supremacy of the court rather than the finality of a particular decision the governing factor.

The first reference from a United Kingdom court was made by PENNY-CUICK, V.-C. in *Van Duyn* v. *Home Office*,[15] the questions raised being

[12] Thus a complaint against the United Kingdom was upheld for failure to implement a Regulation providing for compulsory installation of tachographs in vehicles used for the carriage of dangerous goods: Case 128/78: *Re Tachographs, E.C. Commission* v. *United Kingdom*, [1979] 2 C.M.L.R. 45. However, the Court does not have jurisdiction to entertain a direct action brought by an individual against a member state: *D.* v. *Grand Duchy of Luxembourg*, [1982] E.C.R. 3709.
[13] Similar jurisdiction is conferred by Art. 150 of the Euratom Treaty and by Art. 41 of the E.C.S.C. Treaty.
[14] [1974] Ch. 401; [1974] 2 All E.R. 1126; for a summary of these principles, see p. 380, *post*.
[15] [1974] 3 All E.R. 178; [1974] 1 W.L.R. 1107; see p. 127, *ante*.

questions of the direct applicability and interpretation of Article 48 of the E.E.C. Treaty and Directive 64/221, arising out of the decision of the Home Secretary to refuse entry into the United Kingdom to a Dutch national on the ground of her association with the Church of Scientology. The Court of Justice decided[16] that a member State is permitted to prohibit, on the grounds of public policy, an individual from entering its territory where the individual is associated with an organisation which the member state considers to be socially harmful and is proposing to enter the territory of the member state in order to take up employment with the organisation.

Although it is through Article 177 that the jurisdiction of the Court has by far the greatest impact upon litigants, or prospective litigants, in this country it may be noted that the Court does have specific jurisdiction to deal with certain cases concerning disputes to which ordinary individuals (as opposed to member states or Community Institutions) may be parties. Thus, it has jurisdiction in disputes relating to compensation for damage caused by the Institutions of the Communities or by their servants in the performance of their duties[17] and in disputes between the Communities and their servants within the limits and under the conditions laid down in the staff regulations or the conditions of employment.[18]

C THE HOUSE OF LORDS

1 Constitution and procedure

Parliament is the oldest court of the common law although it is not usual nowadays to refer to it as a court. Nevertheless reference is still made to the High Court of Parliament as a judicial body. Leaving aside the jurisdiction of each House to regulate its own procedure, the judicial function of Parliament is now exercised by the House of Lords.

In theory, though not in fact, an appeal to the House of Lords is an appeal to the whole House, not merely to those members who are in fact sitting to hear the appeal. Until the nineteenth century this was literally true in that any member of the House could and did vote in judicial sessions. Not unnaturally decisions of the House of Lords at that time enjoyed no very great authority, particularly since those peers who were lawyers and took the most prominent part in the exercise of the House's jurisdiction were by no means the senior and most respected judges of their day, a remark which also applies to certain Lord Chancellors of the nineteenth century. As a matter of practice puisne judges were frequently invited to advise their Lordships on the law. Indeed this is still possible though it does not appear to have been done since 1898.[19] However it was not until the Appellate Jurisdiction Act 1876 provided for the creation of salaried life peers to hear appeals that the

---

[16] [1975] Ch. 358; [1975] 3 All E.R. 190; the report of the decision affords an illuminating insight into the procedure of the European Court and the manner in which references are dealt with.

[17] E.E.C. Treaty, Art. 178.

[18] *Ibid.*, Art. 179; cf. *Berti* v. *E.C. Commission*, [1982] E.C.R. 3493.

[19] *Allen* v. *Flood*, [1898] A.C. 1.

convention against lay peers participating in judicial sittings of the House was firmly established.[20]

This Act provided that at the hearing of an appeal there should be present at least three of the following—the Lord Chancellor, the Lords of Appeal in Ordinary ("law lords") and such peers who hold or have held "high judicial office" as defined in the Act. In practice most appeals are heard solely by the Lords of Appeal in Ordinary. These are the senior members of the judiciary and are generally appointed from the ranks of the Court of Appeal, though exceptionally a first instance judge may be elevated directly to the "chill and distant heights". They must either have held high judicial office for two years or be practising barristers of not less than fifteen years' standing.[1] They have the same rights as other peers but in practice they sit on the cross benches and take no part in political sittings of the House unless the matter concerns the administration of justice. By custom, one or two of the law lords are Scots and the Scottish members generally sit when the House is hearing appeals from the Court of Session, which is the Scottish equivalent of the Court of Appeal. The number of law lords, originally fixed at two, is now not less than seven nor more than eleven.[2]

Argument in appeals no longer takes place, as it used to do, in the chamber of the House. The appeal is argued in one of the committee rooms, their lordships sitting unrobed. The opinions of their lordships are not usually read in the chamber[3] although they retire to the chamber to state whether they would allow or dismiss the appeal. These opinions are not strictly "judgments" but speeches in support of the members' votes on the motion made by the Lord Chancellor or senior Lord. Where the House is equally divided the appeal is dismissed. Equal division does not in practice occur because an uneven number of members invariably sits. Nevertheless the situation has arisen on a few occasions and arose in the case of *Kennedy* v. *Spratt*.[4] In that case the appeal would have been dismissed by a majority of three to two but for the fact that one of the majority, LORD UPJOHN, died between the hearing of the appeal and the delivery of judgment having, however, recorded his opinion before his death. In the result, the votes being equal, the appeal was dismissed in any event.[5] The House of Lords has no power to pass judgment. It may only remit the case to the Court of Appeal or the trial judge with its recommendations which must then be translated by that court into a judgment.

---

[20] An earlier attempt to create life peers by prerogative had been rejected by the House— *Wensleydale Peerage Case* (1856), 5 H.L. Cas. 958.

[1] Appellate Jurisdiction Act 1876, s. 6.

[2] Appellate Jurisdiction Act 1947; Administration of Justice Act 1968, s. 1(1) (*a*); this number may be increased by Order in Council (*ibid.*, s. 1(2)).

[3] See *Practice Direction*, [1963] 1 W.L.R. 1382.

[4] [1972] A.C. 83; [1971] All E.R. 805.

[5] See *Kennedy* v. *Spratt* (*Background Note*), [1972] A.C. 99. Had LORD UPJOHN's written opinion indicated that he was in favour of allowing the appeal an anomalous situation would have arisen whereby his death would, in effect, have deprived the appellant of success. In such an event the members of the House would surely have changed their votes so that the appeal would be allowed or, possibly, taken no vote and had the appeal reheard by a differently constituted committee.

2   Jurisdiction

a   Original jurisdiction

The House of Lords has very little original jurisdiction. The right of a peer to be "tried by his peers", which was thought to have been created by Magna Carta, was finally abolished by the Criminal Justice Act 1948 and now all persons, whether peer or commoner, are subject to the ordinary jurisdiction of the English criminal courts.

Impeachment is a procedure whereby persons may be prosecuted by the House of Commons before the House of Lords. It has always been confined to the prosecution of political offenders. Although impeachment has not been abolished it is in practice obsolete and the jurisdiction has not been exercised since the impeachments of Warren Hastings and Viscount Melville in 1795 and 1805 respectively.

The Committee of Privileges, which is by convention composed of lawyers in the House, makes recommendations to the whole House arising out of the Committee trying, at the instance of the Sovereign, a disputed claim to a peerage.[6]

Finally both the House of Lords and the House of Commons have jurisdiction over breaches of privilege, which include contempt of the House in question and wrongs committed within the precincts of each House. Either House may imprison the offender who has no right of appeal and may not move for habeas corpus.

b   Appellate jurisdiction

The jurisdiction of the House of Lords is almost entirely appellate.

In civil cases it hears appeals from the Court of Appeal but only with leave of either the Court of Appeal or the Appeals Committee of the House itself.[7] The ground of appeal does not have to be a point of law as it does in criminal cases but most cases which reach the House of Lords do in fact involve a point of law of public importance, in nine out of ten cases being concerned with the correct construction of Acts of Parliament.[8] The Administration of Justice Act 1969 introduced a "leap-frog" procedure whereby there can be an appeal direct from the trial court to the House of Lords without the need for a prior appeal to the Court of Appeal. Such an appeal lies subject to two conditions; first the trial judge must grant a certificate,[9] which he may do only if all parties consent and the case involves a point of law of general public importance which either relates wholly or mainly to the construction of an enactment or is one in respect of which the judge was bound by a previous decision of the Court of Appeal or House of Lords;

---

6   The Committee sat, in 1976, to hear the celebrated *Ampthill Peerage Case*, [1977] A.C. 547; [1976] 2 All E.R. 411; it consisted of nine peers, four of whom were law lords and delivered speeches.

7   Administration of Justice (Appeals) Act 1934. The House also hears appeals from the equivalent civil courts of Scotland (Court of Session) and Northern Ireland (Court of Appeal).

8   See observations of LORD HAILSHAM to this effect in *Johnson* v. *Moreton*, [1980] A.C. 37, at p. 53; [1978] 3 All E.R. 37, at p. 44.

9   Act of 1969, s. 12(1); there is no appeal against the grant or refusal of a certificate (s. 12(5)).

secondly the House of Lords must grant leave.[10]

The appeal to the House of Lords in criminal cases is of modern origin. Although a writ of error was available before this century, there was no general right of appeal until the Criminal Appeal Act 1907, which provided for an appeal from the Court of Criminal Appeal[11] established by the Act. The right of appeal from the divisional court of the Queen's Bench Division was created by the Administration of Justice Act 1960 and the conditions for appealing to the House of Lords in a criminal matter are now contained in that Act. These conditions are discussed fully in Part V of this book.[12]

Appeal lies, subject to similar condition, from the High Court and Court of Appeal of Northern Ireland and from the Courts-Martial Appeal Court.

D THE COURT OF APPEAL

The Supreme Court of Judicature was the product of the complete reorganisation of the English superior courts effected by the Supreme Court of Judicature Acts 1873–1875. These Acts are now consolidated in the Supreme Court Act 1981. The Acts created the Supreme Court of Judicature to which was transferred the original and appellate jurisdiction of the existing superior courts of first instance and appeal.[13] The Supreme Court now consists of the Court of Appeal, the High Court and the Crown Court. The appellate jurisdiction of the superior courts of law and equity was transferred to the Court of Appeal, while the original jurisdiction was, broadly speaking, transferred to the High Court, the Crown Court having been added by the Courts Act 1971.[14]

1 Constitution

The Court of Appeal is composed of the Lord Chancellor, the Lord Chief Justice, the Master of the Rolls, the President of the Family Division of the High Court, the Vice-Chancellor,[15] former Lord Chancellors, the Lords of Appeal in Ordinary[16] (all the above being *ex officio* judges) and the Lords Justices of Appeal. Ordinarily, of the *ex officio* judges only the Master of the Rolls (in civil cases) and the Lord Chief Justice (in criminal cases) sit in the court. They are, in fact, the presidents of the civil and criminal divisions respectively. The Master of the Rolls was a first instance judge in the Court

---

[10] *Ibid.*, s. 13. The grant of leave precludes appeal to the Court of Appeal. The "leapfrog" procedure was adopted in *Ealing London Borough* v. *Race Relations Board*, [1972] A.C. 342; [1972] 1 All E.R. 105; see p. 115, *ante*.

[11] The jurisdiction of this Court was transferred to the criminal division of the Court of Appeal by the Criminal Appeal Act 1966.

[12] See pp. 540, 555, *post*.

[13] See p. 81, *ante*.

[14] See p. 198, *post*.

[15] The Vice-Chancellor became a judge of the Court of Appeal upon the implementation of the Supreme Court Act 1981.

[16] In recent years the Court has sometimes been composed of three law lords: see, for examples, *Mallett* v. *Restormel Borough Council*, [1978] 2 All E.R. 1057; *Re Amirteymour*, [1978] 3 All E.R. 637; [1979] 1 W.L.R. 63. Furthermore, in November 1979, the criminal division of the Court sat at the law courts in Cardiff, the first time the Court had sat outside London.

of Chancery, and, indeed, in the Chancery Division of the High Court until 1881. In modern times some of the greatest lawyers of their day have held the office of Master of the Rolls. The Lords Justices of Appeal are appointed by Her Majesty by letters patent. They must have been judges of the High Court or barristers of at least fifteen years' standing.[17] There must be not more than 23 Lords Justices.[18]

In addition to the regular judges of the court the Lord Chancellor may require any High Court judge, and may request any former judge of the High Court or of the Court of Appeal, to sit in the civil division and the Lord Chief Justice may require (or request as the case may be) any such judge or former judge to sit in the criminal division;[19] indeed, the criminal division more often than not contains a Queen's Bench Division judge and, in practice, the first court of the criminal division usually consists of the Lord Chief Justice, a Lord Justice of Appeal and one puisne judge while a second court comprises one Lord Justice of Appeal and two puisnes.

By section 3(5) of the Supreme Court Act 1981 any number of courts of either division of the Court of Appeal may sit at the same time. In the civil division the court is duly constituted if it consists of either two or an uneven number of judges not less than three.[20] The criminal division is duly constituted with either two or an uneven number of justices not less than three, save that only a court of three or more can (*a*) determine an appeal against conviction or a verdict of not guilty by reason of insanity or a finding of unfitness to plead, an application for leave to appeal to the House of Lords; or (*b*) refuse an application for leave to appeal against conviction (or any such verdict or finding referred to above) other than an application which has been refused by a single judge.[1] In addition a single judge of the criminal division (who may be, and usually is, a High Court judge) has certain jurisdiction under the Criminal Appeal Act 1968, s. 31 (as amended), notably to hear applications for leave to appeal. Occasionally a "full court" of five or more members is convened to hear appeals involving novel or difficult points of law in both the civil and criminal divisions, although such a court has no wider powers than the normal court.

2   Jurisdiction

Since October 1, 1966, the date upon which the Criminal Appeal Act 1966 came into operation, the Court of Appeal has consisted of a civil and a criminal division.

a   Civil division

The civil division exercises (*a*) all jurisdiction conferred on it by the Supreme Court Act 1981 or any other Act; and (*b*) all jurisdiction exercisable by it

---

[17] Supreme Court Act 1981, s. 10(3).

[18] *Ibid.*, s. 2; this number may be increased by Order in Council (s. 2(4)) and was so increased (from 18 to 23) in 1983.

[19] *Ibid.*, s. 9.

[20] *Ibid.*, s. 54; Court of Appeal (Civil Division) Order 1982; see p. 427, *post* for details of procedure on appeals.

[1] *Ibid.*, s. 55; for details of procedure on appeal to the criminal division, see p. 527, *post*.

prior to the commencement of the 1981 Act.[2] This is set out more fully in Chapter 22 of this book.[3] It is sufficient to note at this stage that the civil division has no criminal jurisdiction and hardly any original jurisdiction. Its jurisdiction is entirely civil and almost entirely appellate. It hears appeals from the High Court, county courts, the Restrictive Practices Court, the Employment Appeal Tribunal and various tribunals, notably the Lands Tribunal. Appeal is by way of rehearing, except in the case of certain appeals from tribunals where it is by case stated.[4]

b   Criminal division

The criminal division of the Court of Appeal is the successor of the Court of Criminal Appeal, the jurisdiction of the latter being transferred to the former by section 1(1) of the Criminal Appeal Act 1966.

The Court of Criminal Appeal emerged as a result of the deficient system of criminal appeals which existed prior to 1907. The court was created by the Criminal Appeal Act 1907 and superseded the Court for Crown Cases Reserved and the right of appeal by writ of error to the Queen's Bench Division.

The jurisdiction of the criminal division is set out fully in Part V of this book.[5] Briefly, it hears appeals by persons convicted and, in certain cases, considers points of law referred to the Court by the Attorney-General following acquittal,[6] following trial in the Crown Court. It also hears appeals against sentence from this court. In addition the Home Secretary may refer a case to the division, under section 17 of the Criminal Appeal Act 1968, for assistance on any point or for determination as an appeal. The criminal division of the Court of Appeal has no civil jurisdiction and no original jurisdiction, its jurisdiction being solely appellate.

E   THE HIGH COURT OF JUSTICE

The High Court was established by the Judicature Acts and to it was transferred the jurisdiction of the three superior common law courts of first instance, the Court of Chancery, the Courts of Admiralty, Probate, Divorce and Matrimonial Causes and other superior courts of civil and criminal jurisdiction (except the Chancery Courts of the Counties Palatine of Lancaster and Durham[7]). Its constitution and jurisdiction are now contained in the Supreme Court Act 1981. Prior to 1971 the High Court sat in the Royal Courts of Justice in the Strand, London, though High Court judges constituted a court of the High Court for all purposes when they tried cases on assize. Nevertheless their jurisdiction on assize derived not from their office

---

2   *Ibid.*, s. 15(2).
3   See p. 423, *post*.
4   Rules of the Supreme Court (Revision) 1965, O. 61.
5   See p. 527, *post*.
6   See Chapter 25, *post*.
7   These courts, which were superior courts, continued to exercise a Chancery jurisdiction equivalent to that of the High Court in the County Palatine of Lancaster and the County Borough of Teesside until their abolition by the Courts Act 1971, s. 41 which merged them with the High Court.

but from the Commissions under which they sat. The Courts Act 1971 abolished all courts of assize but section 71 of the Supreme Court Act now provides that sittings of the High Court may be conducted at any place in England or Wales;[8] the centres at which sittings of the High Court are, in fact, held are determined in accordance with directions of the Lord Chancellor. Although there are standing directions, it is always open to the Lord Chancellor to give an *ad hoc* direction to enable a particular sitting to take place at a particular place if there is sufficient reason for it. Thus in *St. Edmundsbury and Ipswich Diocesan Board of Finance* v. *Clark*,[9] a case concerning a claim to a right of way over a disputed strip of land at Iken, a small village in Suffolk, a direction was given on behalf of the Lord Chancellor, at the request of the trial judge, MEGARRY, J., authorising the court to sit at Iken.[10] The jurisdiction of the High Court is both civil and criminal and both original and appellate. It has virtually unlimited jurisdiction in civil actions, though this is not generally an exclusive jurisdiction and where the action concerns a small sum it is usually brought in the county courts.

The High Court, when created, consisted of five divisions, but these were reduced in 1880 to the three which now exist[11] (save that the Probate, Divorce and Admiralty Division has been re-named the Family Division[12]). Although all three divisions have equal competence each division, in fact, exercises a separate jurisdiction. This is not dictated by convenience but by the Rules of the Supreme Court which govern procedure and practice throughout the Supreme Court (except in the Crown Court where there are separate rules, the Crown Court Rules).[13] These Rules specify the manner in which an action or matter may be commenced and prosecuted in the High Court. Consequently certain types of action are confined to a particular division. Thus matrimonial causes in the High Court may only be heard in the Family Division and not in either of the two other divisions. In certain cases the jurisdiction of the divisions overlaps and it is possible to start certain proceedings in one or other of them. For example, two modern cases concerning similar conditions in similar contracts were tried within a short space of time.

---

8 Although evidence, including a view by the judge, may be taken outside the jurisdiction; cf. *Tito* v. *Waddell*, [1975] 3 All E.R. 997; [1975] 1 W.L.R. 1303; see p. 194, *post*.

9 [1973] Ch. 323; [1973] 2 All E.R. 1155.

10 MEGARRY, J. had requested such a direction out of an abundance of caution since he had already decided that he had power to adjourn the hearing of the action to Iken under R.S.C., O. 35, r. 3.

11 Under s. 7 of the Supreme Court Act, Her Majesty may by Order in Council, on a recommendation of the Lord Chancellor, the Lord Chief Justice, the Master of the Rolls, the President of the Family Division and the Vice-Chancellor, increase or reduce the number of divisions.

12 Administration of Justice Act 1970, s. 1. The same section also effected redistribution of business between the divisions as a consequence of the main purpose of the change which was to create a division which deals solely with family and domestic matters. Thus the Admiralty jurisdiction of the High Court was assigned to the Queen's Bench Division to be exercised by the new "Admiralty Court" created by s. 2 of the Act, while contentious probate business was assigned to the Chancery Division, thereby eradicating the unsatisfactory duality of jurisdiction which had hitherto existed, whereby disputes concerning the validity of wills were heard in the Probate, Divorce and Admiralty Division, while questions of the construction of wills were determined in the Chancery Division.

13 See p. 203, *post*; though the inherent jurisdiction of the High Court is exercisable by a judge of any Division; see *Re L*, [1968] P. 119; [1968] 1 All E.R. 20; p. 81, *ante*.

The first[14] was tried in the Chancery Division, the second[15] in the Queen's Bench Division. It is important to bear in mind that the divisions of the High Court are not different courts, so that the jurisdiction of any one High Court judge is exercisable by any other High Court judge, irrespective of the division to which he is assigned.[16] Furthermore the Lord Chancellor, with the concurrence of the Lord Chief Justice and the President of the Family Division, has directed that:

> "any Division of the High Court to which a cause or matter is assigned shall have jurisdiction to grant in that cause or matter any remedy or relief arising out of or related to or connected with any claim made in the cause or matter notwithstanding that proceedings for such remedy or relief are assigned by or under any Act to another Division of the court."[17]

Nevertheless, as a matter of practice, the effect of statutes and rules of procedure is usually to confer upon each division jurisdiction which is independent of that exercised by the other two divisions.[18]

As the volume of litigation has increased so has the number of High Court judges. The maximum number is now 80 and this number may be increased by Order in Council.[19] High Court judges, sometimes styled "puisne" judges, must be barristers of not less than ten years' standing. In practice High Court judges are appointed from the ranks of Queen's Counsel (or treasury juniors) and, albeit not very often, also from the ranks of Circuit judges. High Court judges are appointed to a particular division by the Lord Chancellor, depending usually on the practice which the appointee had at the bar prior to appointment. This is particularly true of the Chancery Division where the very specialised nature of the cases heard requires that new judges be appointed from the Chancery Bar, whose members are usually to be found in chambers in Lincoln's Inn. Appointments are made by the Crown on the advice of the Lord Chancellor.[20]

a Chancery Division

The Chancery Division consists of the Lord Chancellor, who, although nominal head of the Division, never sits at first instance, a Vice-Chancellor and such of the puisne judges as the Lord Chancellor may nominate.[1] Before 1972, sittings of the Chancery Division were held only in the Royal Courts of Justice and Chancery judges did not go on assize (though a concurrent Chancery jurisdiction was exercised by the now defunct Chancery Courts of the Counties Palatine of Lancaster and Durham). Although the Supreme Court Act authorises sittings of the High Court to be held at any place in England and Wales, in practice most Chancery business continues to be

14 *Petrofina (Great Britain), Ltd.* v. *Martin*, [1965] Ch. 1073; [1965] 2 All E.R. 176.
15 *Esso Petroleum Co., Ltd.* v. *Harpers Garage (Stourport), Ltd.*, [1966] 2 Q.B. 514; [1965] 2 All E.R. 933.
16 See *Re Hastings (No. 3)*, [1959] Ch. 368; [1959] 1 All E.R. 698; *Re Kray*, [1965] Ch. 736; [1965] 1 All E.R. 710; *Re L*, [1968] P. 144; [1968] 1 All E.R. 20.
17 *Practice Direction (High Court: Divisions)*, [1973] 2 All E.R. 233; [1973] 1 W.L.R. 627.
18 For the distribution of business between the divisions, see Supreme Court Act 1981, s. 61 and Sched. 1.
19 *Ibid.*, s. 4(4).
20 For details of the position of Her Majesty's judges, see p. 229, *post.*
1 Supreme Court Act 1981, s. 5; there are at present 13.

taken in London, members of the Chancery bench and bar not being notice-ably peripatetic.[2] However the Vice-Chancellor of the County Palatine of Lancaster (who is now a Circuit judge[3]) sits as a judge of the High Court[4] at Liverpool, Manchester and Preston and, time permitting, at Leeds and Newcastle-upon-Tyne for the hearing of proceedings assigned to the Chancery Division.

Original jurisdiction—Section 34 of the Judicature Act 1873 assigned to the Chancery Division jurisdiction over matters which were heard in the Court of Chancery prior to the abolition of that court in 1875. The distribution of High Court business between the divisions is now governed by section 61 and Schedule 1 of the Supreme Court Act. Under that Schedule are assigned to the Chancery Division all causes and matters relating to:

"(*a*) the sale, exchange or partition of land, or the raising of charges on land;

(*b*) the redemption or foreclosure of mortgages;

(*c*) the execution of trusts;

(*d*) the administration of estates of deceased persons;

(*e*) bankruptcy;

(*f*) the dissolution of partnerships or the taking of partnership or other accounts;

(*g*) the rectification, setting aside or cancellation of deeds or other instruments in writing;

(*h*) probate business, other than non-contentious or common form business;

(*i*) patents, trade marks, registered designs or copyright;

(*j*) the appointment of a guardian of a minor's estate,

and all causes and matters involving the exercise of the High Court's jurisdiction under the enactments relating to companies."

This jurisdiction is augmented by statutes and rules of procedure. Thus the Chancery Division, in addition to the matters set out above, exercises juris-diction over revenue matters, town and country planning and landlord and tenant disputes. Judges of the Division when sitting as the Court of Protection[5] hear applications under the Mental Health Act 1983 concerning the management of the property and affairs of mental patients.

Patents Court—There are three "specialist courts" within the High Court, *viz.* the Patents Court, the Admiralty Court and the Commercial Court.[6] Of these the first is part of the Chancery Division (the other two being part of the Queen's Bench Division). It was established by the Patents Act 1977 and consists of nominated judges of the division. It hears patent actions at first

---

2   Although MEGARRY, J. (as he then was) cast doubt upon this belief, not only by conducting a sitting of his court at a village in Suffolk (*St. Edmundsbury and Ipswich Diocesan Board of Finance* v. *Clark* (*supra*)) but by visiting two islands in the western Pacific for the purpose of conducting a view (*Tito* v. *Waddell* (*supra*), p. 192).

3   By virtue of Courts Act 1971, s. 16; Sch. 2.

4   Pursuant to the request of the Lord Chancellor made under s. 9 of the Supreme Court Act under which section Circuit judges or Recorders may sit as judges of the High Court.

5   See p. 219, *post*. The wardship jurisdiction of the Chancery Division was assigned to the Family Division by the Administration of Justice Act 1970, s. 1; Sch. 1.

6   Supreme Court Act 1981, s. 6.

instance and on appeal from the Comptroller-General of Patents, Designs and Trade Marks, procedure being governed by R.S.C. Order 104.

Probate jurisdiction and procedure—Probate procedure differs according to whether the deceased died testate, i.e. leaving a valid will, or intestate, i.e. leaving no will or leaving a will which is invalid, generally through failure to comply with the due formalities which are principally contained in the Wills Act 1837.

If a person dies testate his will should appoint one or more executors. These executors must first apply to the Principal Registry of the Family Division or to a District Probate Registry for a grant of probate. This application must be accompanied by the will itself, the executors' affidavit of undertaking to administer the estate, a statement of all the deceased's property for tax purposes and various other documents. In the overwhelming majority of cases no-one will dispute the validity of the will and the grant of probate will be made as a formality. However any person who disputes the validity of a will in respect of which a grant is sought may enter a *caveat* at the Registry in question. In that event the proceedings become contentious and there will have to be a trial as to the validity of the will.[7] This trial may take place in the county court for the district where the testator resided before his death if the net value of the estate is less than £30,000.[8]

If a person dies intestate a person will have to apply to be appointed an administrator of the estate. There will then be a grant of letters of administration rather than a grant of probate. The effect is similar in that it vests the deceased's property in the administrators who must then distribute it in accordance with the intestacy provisions.

Appellate jurisdiction—Although the jurisdiction of the Chancery Division is predominately original, there is some appellate jurisdiction. A single judge of the Division has jurisdiction by statute to hear certain appeals, for example income tax appeals from the Commissioners of Inland Revenue under section 56 of the Taxes Management Act 1970. A divisional court of the Chancery Division, comprising at least two judges of the Division, has a limited jurisdiction, consisting of the hearing of appeals from county courts in bankruptcy and land registration matters. The Patents Court, as stated above, hears appeals from certain decisions of the Comptroller-General of Patents, Designs and Trade Marks.

b   Queen's Bench Division

The jurisdiction of the Queen's Bench Division is wider in scope than that of the other two divisions of the High Court. It is both civil and criminal and both original and appellate. In addition it exercises the supervisory jurisdiction formerly exercised by the Court of King's Bench. The jurisdiction of the Division is equivalent to the jurisdiction exercised by the three superior common law courts of first instance prior to 1875, as altered by subsequent statutes and rules. Procedure in this division is dealt with at length in Part IV of this book.

Original civil jurisdiction— By far the most important aspect of the business

---

[7] The procedure is governed by R.S.C. O. 76; a probate action must be commenced by writ (O. 76, r. 2).
[8] County Courts Act 1984, s. 32; the limit may be raised by Order in Council (*ibid.*, s. 145).

of the Division is its first instance jurisdiction over civil matters, principally actions in contract and tort. Jurisdiction over commercial matters is exercised in the Commercial Court, which is one of the lists in the Division, maintained in London, Liverpool and Manchester.[9] Admiralty jurisdiction, assigned to the Division by section 20 of the Supreme Court Act, is exercised by the "Admiralty Court", the judges of which are those judges nominated to be Admiralty Judges by the Lord Chancellor.[10] Admiralty business includes actions to enforce a claim for damage, loss of life or personal injury arising out of a collision between ships, claims to the possession or ownership of ships, claims for loss of or damage to goods carried in a ship, towage claims and other specified proceedings.[11] When trying admiralty actions the judge often sits with lay assessors.

Appellate civil jurisdiction—The appellate jurisdiction of the Queen's Bench Division in civil matters is fairly minor. Appeal lies from an interlocutory order of a Queen's Bench Division master to a judge in chambers[12] and a single judge also has jurisdiction to hear certain appeals from tribunals, for example from the Pensions Appeal Tribunal.[13] A judge of the Commercial Court hears appeals from arbitrations and determines questions of law arising in the course of arbitrations in accordance with the provisions of the Arbitration Act 1979.[14] A divisional court of the Queen's Bench Division consisting of two or more judges of the Division has a limited civil jurisdiction in hearing appeals by way of case stated from magistrates' courts, other than matrimonial proceedings, and the Crown Court, from the Solicitors Disciplinary Tribunal and in certain other cases.

Criminal and supervisory jurisdiction—The criminal jurisdiction of the High Court is exercised exclusively by the Queen's Bench Division.

This is entirely appellate[15] and exercised by the divisional court consisting of at least two but usually three judges of the Division. The Lord Chief Justice often sits and the hearing will then take place in his own court in the Royal Courts of Justice. The jurisdiction is exercised over appeals by way of "case stated"[16] from magistrates' courts and the Crown Court (in the exercise of that court's appellate jurisdiction).

The supervisory jurisdiction of the Division is also exercised by the divisional court. This includes jurisdiction to issue the prerogative writ of habeas corpus and to make orders of mandamus, prohibition and certiorari by which inferior courts and tribunals are compelled to exercise their powers properly and restrained from exceeding their jurisdiction. This jurisdiction,

---

[9] For details of procedure in the Commercial Court see p. 369, *post*.

[10] Supreme Court Act 1981, s. 6. Procedure in the Admiralty Court is governed by R.S.C., O. 75; see p. 371, *post*.

[11] The full jurisdiction is listed in s. 20 of the Supreme Court Act.

[12] See p. 426, *post*.

[13] Pensions Appeal Tribunals Act 1943; Tribunals and Inquiries Act 1971, s. 13.

[14] See p. 227, *post*.

[15] Prior to 1972 the Division exercised a limited original criminal jurisdiction in the form of a trial "at bar", a procedure adopted in the notorious case of *R. v. Casement*, [1917] 1 K.B. 98; the jurisdiction was, however, virtually obsolete and was abolished by the Courts Act 1971, s. 6 (now s. 46(1) of the Supreme Court Act, which provides that all proceedings on indictment must be brought before the Crown Court).

[16] For details of the procedure see p. 552, *post*.

as has been seen,[17] is invoked by application for "judicial review", the procedure being governed by R.S.C. Order 53.

Judges of the Division exercise other functions. Thus, as has been seen, they discharge the bulk of the business of the criminal division of the Court of Appeal. They also sit in the Courts-Martial Appeal Court. Disputed Parliamentary elections are determined by an election court which consists of two judges of the Queen's Bench Division.[18]

It should be noted finally that the "first-tier" jurisdiction of the Crown Court is exercised principally by the judges of the Queen's Bench Division.[19] Judges of the Queen's Bench Division on average spend approximately half their time in the Royal Courts of Justice and half "on circuit".

c Family Division

This Division (formerly named the Probate, Divorce and Admiralty Division[20]) consists of the President and such of the puisne judges as the Lord Chancellor may nominate.[1] The jurisdiction of the Division is set out in the first Schedule to the Administration of Justice Act 1970 and is both original and appellate.

Schedule 1 of the Supreme Court Act assigns to the Family Division:

"(*a*) all matrimonial causes and matters (whether at first instance or on appeal);
(*b*) all causes and matters (whether at first instance or on appeal) relating to—
    (i) legitimacy;
    (ii) the wardship, guardianship, custody or maintenance of minors (including proceedings about access), except proceedings solely for the appointment of a guardian of a minor's estate;
    (iii) affiliation or adoption;
    (iv) non-contentious or common form probate business;
(*c*) applications for consent to the marriage of a minor;
(*d*) proceedings on appeal under section 13 of the Administration of Justice Act 1960 from an order or decision made under section 63(3) of the Magistrates' Courts Act 1980 to enforce an order of a magistrates' court made in matrimonial proceedings or with respect to the guardianship of a minor."

The general effect of these provisions is that the Division has exclusive jurisdiction over matrimonial disputes and children. Prior to the 1970 Act the Chancery Division dealt with wardship and embarrassing conflicts sometimes arose between the Divisions involving issues such as whether the Divorce judge in, say, custody proceedings could disregard the order of a Chancery judge made in wardship proceedings.[2]

The appellate business of the Division comprises principally appeals from

---

[17] See pp. 174–178, *supra.*
[18] Representation of the People Act 1983, ss. 120 *et seq.* However, this is not part of the Queen's Bench Division and, indeed, is an inferior court and therefore subject to judicial review: *R. v. Cripps, Ex parte Muldoon*, [1984] Q.B. 68; [1984] 3 All E.R. 72.
[19] See p. 203, *post.*
[20] The Division was re-named by the Administration of Justice Act 1970, s. 1. The late Sir Alan Herbert described the jurisdiction as "wills, wives and wrecks"; of these, "wills" have gone to the Chancery Division and "wrecks" (other than the wrecks of marriages) to the Queen's Bench Division (*supra*).
[1] Supreme Court Act 1981, s. 5; there are at present sixteen.
[2] This occurred, for example, in *Hall v. Hall*, [1963] P. 378; [1963] 2 All E.R. 140.

magistrates' courts and county courts under the Guardianship of Minors Act 1971, from magistrates' courts and the Crown Court in affiliation proceedings and from various proceedings concerning matrimonial causes and children in magistrates' courts, notably from the making or refusal of adoption orders and maintenance orders.

F   THE CROWN COURT

1   Creation of the Crown Court

The Crown Court was created by the Courts Act 1971. In order to appreciate the jurisdiction of this court and its place in the hierarchy, it is necessary to examine briefly the system of courts that the Crown Court replaced.

Prior to the 1st January 1972, the date upon which the Courts Act came into operation, trials on indictment took place either at quarter sessions or at assizes.[3] The essential characteristics of both quarter sessions and assizes was that their jurisdiction was local. This meant not only that the courts (as a rule) tried only offences committed within the locality of their jurisdiction but also that the administration of the courts was organised on a local basis, so that the methods of administration and organisation varied from area to area.

The most serious offences were tried at assizes before a court presided over by a judge sitting, not by virtue of his normal judicial office, but under Royal commissions of *oyer and terminer* and *gaol delivery*; the persons named in the commissions usually included at least two High Court judges, almost invariably judges of the Queen's Bench Division, who would sit at the assize town for the duration of the assize. The jurisdiction of assizes was equivalent to that of the High Court since a commissioner when engaged in the exercise of his jurisdiction constituted a court of the High Court of Justice.[4]

All save the most serious offences tried on indictment were tried at quarter sessions of which there were almost 150 separate courts. Quarter sessions were of two kinds—county quarter sessions and borough quarter sessions. These courts, which as their name would indicate were held at least four times a year, were composed, in the case of county quarter sessions, by the justices of the peace of the county, almost invariably presided over by a legally qualified chairman, and in the case of borough quarter sessions, by a Recorder who sat alone and was a practising barrister of at least five years' standing. The jurisdiction of quarter sessions was both civil and criminal and original and appellate. The criminal jurisdiction comprised the trial of all indictable offences, save those which had, by statute, to be tried at assizes, jurisdiction to sentence persons committed for sentence following summary conviction and the hearing of appeals from the decisions of magistrates'

---

3   Although trial "at bar" in the High Court was still theoretically, possible; see p. 196, fn. 15, *ante.*
4   In addition to the High Court judges, county court judges and Queen's Counsel were often included in the commissions; furthermore the Master of the Rolls, Lords Justices of Appeal and former Lords Justices and High Court judges might be included in the commissions but in practice were not. The Commissioners of Assize also tried civil cases as a court of the High Court.

courts. The whole of this jurisdiction has been transferred to the Crown Court together with the civil jurisdiction of quarter sessions which comprised principally matters concerned with various forms of licensing.[5]

Before leaving the pre-1972 system, mention must also be made of the Central Criminal Court and of the Crown Courts of Liverpool and Manchester. The Central Criminal Court, established by the Central Criminal Court Act 1834 and popularly known as the "Old Bailey" after the name of the street in London in which the court is situated, was the assize court exercising criminal jurisdiction in the Greater London area. The court was a court of the High Court and its jurisdiction extended over indictable offences committed in Greater London or on the high seas; the judges of the court sat under the commissions of *oyer and terminer* and *gaol delivery* and consisted of the Lord Chancellor, the Lord Mayor of the City of London, the Lord Chief Justice and the judges of the Queen's Bench Division, the Aldermen of the City of London, the Recorder and the Common Serjeant and a number of additional judges who had to be judges of at least ten years' standing; of these only the Queen's Bench Division judges, the Recorder, the Common Serjeant and the additional judges sat in practice.

The Criminal Justice Administration Act 1956 established, as something of an experimental innovation, Crown Courts in Liverpool and Manchester presided over by the Recorders of Liverpool and Manchester who were the full time judges of the courts. The jurisdiction of these courts was solely criminal but was both original and appellate since the courts exercised the criminal jurisdiction of both assizes and quarter sessions within the area of their respective jurisdictions. These courts, which were abolished by the Courts Act 1971, must not be confused with the present Crown Court. Apart from the difference in the judiciary of the courts, the jurisdiction of the Crown Courts of Liverpool and Manchester was, as in the case of all quarter sessions and assize, local.

Of the system of courts described above one commentator has observed:[6]

"Not only have the courts been tied to geographical areas but their judges have been tied to them. This is true both of courts of quarter sessions in boroughs and counties and also of courts of assize where the judges of the High Court have been obliged to follow rigid itineraries which, since the beginning of the last century, have borne little relation to the volume of business to be dealt with or the populations which the assize towns were intended to serve. When populations are small, business is light and travelling slow, such a system has its obvious advantages and represents perhaps no more than a marginal waste of resources which is more than adequately offset by the benefit of having justice readily available on a local basis. The urbanisation of England from the late eighteenth century, together with the vast increase in population and the introduction of a rapid and efficient system of transport, have rendered a rigid system of locally organised justice no longer adequate to absorb the consequent increases in the volume of work."

In the result a Royal Commission was established under the chairmanship of Lord Beeching and the so-called Beeching Report[7] that followed

---

[5] Although certain administrative functions were transferred to local authorities (Courts Act 1971, ss. 53, 56; Sch. 8).

[6] M.D. Huebner, *An Outline of the New System*, 121 New Law Journal, p. 1136.

[7] *Report of the Royal Commission on Assizes and Quarter Sessions*: Cmnd. 4153 of 1969.

contained recommendations which formed the basis for the system introduced by the Courts Act 1971.

The Courts Act 1971 abolished all courts of assize and quarter sessions and established in their place a single court to be known as the Crown Court. The constitution and jurisdiction of the Crown Court is now contained in the Supreme Court Act 1981. It is part of the Supreme Court and a superior court of record.[8] The Courts Act further abolished the Crown Courts of Liverpool and Manchester and the Central Criminal Court, though the latter has been retained in name since it is expressly provided that when the Crown Court sits in the City of London it shall be known as the Central Criminal Court.[9]

As already indicated the essential feature of the Crown Court is that its jurisdiction is in no sense local. Section 78 of the Supreme Court Act provides that:

> "(1) any Crown Court business may be conducted at any place in England or Wales, and the sittings of the Crown Court at any place may be continuous or intermittent or occasional.
> (2) Judges of the Crown Court may sit simultaneously to take any number of different cases in the same or different places, and may adjourn cases from place to place at any time."

Thus it is important to remember that there are not various Crown Courts throughout the country, in the way that there were various quarter sessions; there is one Crown Court,[10] sittings of which may be held anywhere at any time as indicated above.

---

[8] Supreme Court Act 1981, ss. 1, 45(1). This, however, appears to be largely a matter of terminology since, in the exercise of its appellate jurisdiction, the Crown Court (as were Quarter Sessions) is amenable to the supervisory jurisdiction of the High Court as if it were an inferior court (*ibid.*, s. 29(3); see p. 177, *ante*), although it is not amenable to this jurisdiction in matters relating to trial on indictment; cf. *Smalley* v. *Crown Court at Warwick*, [1985] 1 All E.R. 769; *sub nom. In re Smalley*, [1985] 2 W.L.R. 538. In addition s. 151 of the Act, the interpretation section, provides that except where the context otherwise requires a reference in the Act, or in any other Act, to a judge of the Supreme Court shall not include a reference to a judge of the Crown Court; cf. *Sirros* v. *Moore*, [1975] Q.B. 118; [1974] 3 All E.R. 776; see p. 231, *post*.

[9] Supreme Court Act, s. 8(3); the Lord Mayor of the City and any Alderman of the City are entitled to sit as judges of the Central Criminal Court with any High Court judge, Circuit judge or Recorder. The reasons behind the preservation of this obsolete tradition are not clear. There used to be a rule to the effect that an Alderman of the City had to be present in the court; although this rule has disappeared, the central seat in the No. 1 court at the Old Bailey is still traditionally left vacant for the Lord Mayor. As a further concession to the City of London the 1971 Act provides that the holders of the offices of Recorder of London and Common Serjeant, although Circuit judges *ex officio*, continue to be appointed and remunerated in accordance with the provisions of the City of London (Courts) Act 1964 rather than in accordance with the provisions of the 1971 Act, which govern the appointment and remuneration of all other Circuit judges (s. 16; Sch. 2); finally judges sitting in the Central Criminal Court continue to be addressed as "my Lord" as opposed to "your Honour", which is the appropriate form of address for Circuit judges, deputy Circuit judges, Recorders and Assistant Recorders (see *Practice Direction (judge: mode of address)*, [1982] 1 All E.R. 320; [1982] 1 W.L.R. 101).

[10] For an example of the relevance of this fundamental principle, see *R.* v. *Slatter* [1975] 3 All E.R. 215; [1975] 1 W.L.R. 1084.

2 Constitution

The judges of the Crown Court are all the judges of the High Court, the Circuit judges and Recorders; judges of the Court sit alone as a rule, though there is provision for justices of the peace to sit, but only with one of the judges of the Court.[11] This is in contrast to the former county quarter sessions which were composed entirely of justices of the peace, albeit almost always sitting with a legally qualified chairman. In addition to the regular judges of the Court any judge of the Court of Appeal and any former Court of Appeal or puisne judge may, on the request of the Lord Chancellor, sit and act as a judge and when so sitting and acting is regarded as a judge of the High Court.[12] There is also provision for the temporary appointment of deputy High Court and Circuit judges and Assistant-Recorders.[13]

There are thus basically three tiers of judiciary. At the highest level are the High Court judges who, in practice, are almost invariably judges of the Queen's Bench Division and try principally those cases formerly heard at assizes.[14]

Below the High Court judges are the Circuit judges. The office of Circuit judge was created by the 1971 Act. Circuit judges are appointed by Her Majesty on the recommendation of the Lord Chancellor and must have been barristers of at least ten years' standing or have held the office of Recorder for at least three years.[15] In addition, before recommending any person for appointment the Lord Chancellor must take steps to satisfy himself that the proposed appointee's health is satisfactory.[16] Circuit judges retire at the age of 72 though the Lord Chancellor may authorise continuance in office from time to time up to the age of 75. The Lord Chancellor may remove a Circuit judge from office on the ground of incapacity or misbehaviour.

Whereas Circuit judges are full time appointments, Recorders are part time judges of the Crown Court. They are appointed by Her Majesty on the recommendation of the Lord Chancellor and must be barristers or solicitors of at least ten years' standing.[17] Recorders must be under the age of 72 and, like Circuit judges, are removable by the Lord Chancellor on the ground of incapacity or misbehaviour. Unlike Circuit judges, however, Recorders are appointed on a temporary basis and their appointment specifies the term for

---

[11] Supreme Court Act 1981, s. 8. A further unimportant exception to the rule that the judges of the Court sit alone is the right of the Lord Mayor and Aldermen of the City of London to sit in the Central Criminal Court (*supra*). Where justices do sit they are themselves judges of the Crown Court and must play a full part in all decisions of the court, whether on interlocutory matters or on sentence, so that in the event of disagreement the decision of the majority of the court prevails, even if the judge alone is in the minority. The summing-up and charge to the jury must, however, be given by the judge and where there is any ruling of law to be given that ruling must be determined by the judge alone; these principles were stated by the Court of Appeal in *R*. v. *Orpin*, [1975] Q.B. 283; [1974] 2 All E.R. 1121.

[12] *Ibid.*, s. 9.

[13] Courts Act 1971, s. 24.

[14] As to the distribution of business, see p. 203, *post*.

[15] Courts Act 1971, s. 16 (as amended by Administration of Justice Act 1977, s. 12). Since solicitors are eligible for appointment as Recorders it follows that the office of Circuit judge is open to members of that branch of the profession (and indeed several solicitors have been appointed as Recorders and, subsequently, Circuit judges).

[16] *Ibid.*, s. 16(4); this means that proposed appointees may be required to submit to medical examination.

[17] *Ibid.*, s. 21.

which they are appointed and the frequency and duration of the occasions during that term on which they will be required to be available to undertake the duties of Recorders; failure to comply with the requirements specified in the terms of appointment is a ground for removal from office.[18]

Finally there are the provisions for justices of the peace to sit in the Court. Their attendance is mandatory on the hearing by the Crown Court of any appeal or of proceedings on committal to the Court for sentence, on the hearing of which proceedings the judge of the Court sits with not less than two nor more than four justices of the peace.[19] In addition any jurisdiction or power of the Court may be exercised by a regular judge of the Court sitting with not more than four justices.[20] Where justices sit the decision of the Court is by majority and if the members of the Court are equally divided the regular judge has a second and casting vote.[21] As a final illustration of the departure from the principle of localised jurisdiction, section 8(2) of the 1981 Act provides that a justice of the peace shall not be disqualified from acting as a judge of the Crown Court for the reason that the proceedings are not at a place within the area for which he was appointed as a justice, or because the proceedings are not related to that area in any way.

It will be noted that the judges of the Crown Court are not, as it were, full time criminal judges (as were the Recorders of the former Crown Courts of Liverpool and Manchester). The High Court judges sit, of course, in civil cases in the High Court; the Circuit judges, as well as exercising the very limited civil jurisdiction which the Crown Court inherited from quarter sessions, discharge the functions of county court judges;[1] Recorders sit almost exclusively to try criminal cases though, as well as having the civil jurisdiction of the Crown Court, there is provision for Recorders to sit as county court judges.

The immediate effect of the Courts Act was a large number of new judicial appointments, which is thought to have placed some strain on the resources of the bar. In fact the majority of Circuit judges were simply translated from judicial offices held before the Courts Act came into force. Thus, on the 1st January 1972, the date upon which most of the provisions of the Courts Act came into force, the Vice-Chancellor of the County Palatine of Lancaster, the Recorder of London, the Common Serjeant, the Official Referees of the Supreme Court,[2] the Recorders of Liverpool and Manchester, the additional judges of the Central Criminal Court, the assistant judge of the Mayor's and City of London Court,[3] all county court judges and all whole-time chairmen

---

18 *Ibid.*, s. 21.
19 Supreme Court Act 1981, s. 74(1), although under s. 74(4) the Lord Chancellor may give directions dispensing with the requirements for justices to sit in such cases. In addition no objection can subsequently be taken to a decision on the ground that the court was not properly constituted as required by section 74 unless objection was taken at the time.
20 *Ibid.*, s. 8(1)(c).
21 *Ibid.*, s. 73(3).
1 Courts Act 1971, s. 20; see p. 210, *post.*
2 The office of Official Referee was abolished by section 25 of the Act, but the functions conferred on official referees by statute are discharged by such of the Circuit judges as the Lord Chancellor may from time to time determine, these functions being described as "official referees' business"; see p. 371, *post*).
3 This court was abolished by section 42 of the Act, though the name survives, rather in the same way as the Central Criminal Court, since the county court for the City of London is known as the Mayor's and City of London Court and the Circuit judge assigned to that

and deputy chairmen of courts of quarter sessions for Greater London, Cheshire, Durham, Kent and Lancashire automatically became Circuit judges.[4]

3 Jurisdiction and procedure

The Crown Court has exclusive jurisdiction over all trials on indictment for offences wherever committed, including proceedings on indictment for offences within the jurisdiction of the Admiralty in England.[5] In addition all jurisdiction formerly exercised by any court of quarter sessions was vested in the Crown Court.[6] This, as indicated above, includes the hearing of appeals by persons convicted summarily in magistrates' courts,[7] the sentencing of persons committed for sentence following summary conviction[8] and a limited civil jurisdiction, principally concerned with licensing appeals.

Procedure in the Court is governed by Crown Court rules[9] and follows closely procedure in quarter sessions prior to 1972. Details of criminal procedure are to be found in Part V of this work.

The Lord Chief Justice has power under section 75 of the Supreme Court Act, with the concurrence of the Lord Chancellor, to give directions relating to the distribution of Crown Court business and, on 14th October 1971, LORD WIDGERY, C.J. gave such directions.[10] The directions classify offences, for the purposes of distribution, into four classes,[11] the first of which, being the most serious, are to be tried by a High Court judge. Class 2 offences are to be tried by a High Court judge unless a particular case is released by or on the authority of a presiding judge, that is to say, a High Court judge assigned to have special responsibility for a particular circuit. All offences triable on indictment, other than those in classes, 1, 2 and 4 form Class 3 and may be listed for trial by a High Court judge, Circuit judge or Recorder, while certain indictable offences and all offences triable either way constitute Class 4 and may be tried by a High Court judge, Circuit judge or Recorder but will normally be listed for trial by a Circuit judge or Recorder.[12]

---

district under section 20 of the Act is known as the judge of the Mayor's and City of London Court.

4 Courts Act 1971, s. 16; Sch. 2.

5 Supreme Court Act 1981, s. 46.

6 Courts Act 1971, s. 8; Sch. 1; this was subject to the provisions of Sch. 8, Part I which transferred certain administrative functions of quarter sessions to local authorities.

7 See p. 550, *post.*

8 See p. 462, *post.*

9 Section 86 of the 1981 Act confers power to make Crown Court rules upon a Crown Court rule committee consisting of the Lord Chancellor together with any four or more of the following persons, namely the Lord Chief Justice, two other judges of the Supreme Court, two Circuit judges, the registrar of criminal appeals, a justice of the peace, two practising barristers and two practising solicitors. The current rules are the Crown Court Rules 1982.

10 Reported in *Practice Note*, [1971] 3 All E.R. 829; [1971] 1 W.L.R. 1535; amended by *Practice Direction (Crown Court)*, [1978] 2 All E.R. 912; [1978] 1 W.L.R. 926. The directions were given under s. 4 of the 1971 Act, the statutory predecessor of s. 75 of the 1981 Act.

11 For further details of the classification of offences and the distribution of business, see p. 483, *post.*

12 As to when Class 4 offences will be tried by a High Court judge, see p. 484, *post.*

G   EMPLOYMENT APPEAL TRIBUNAL

1   History

The Industrial Relations Act 1971, s. 99 established the National Industrial Relations Court. The Act, together with the court itself, were extremely unpopular with certain trade unions which, in consequence, declined to recognise the court and openly defied its orders.[13] In the result the Labour Government pledged itself to repeal of the Act and this was effected by section 1 of the Trade Union and Labour Relations Act 1974. This appears to have been the first instance in English legal history of a fully operative court being abolished.

With the repeal of the 1971 Act the National Industrial Relations Court ceased to exist. However the Employment Protection Act 1975, s. 87 and Schedule 6, with effect from 30th March 1976, effectively revived the court under the name of the Employment Appeal Tribunal. The provisions of the 1975 Act which brought the Employment Appeal Tribunal into existence were repealed and re-enacted by the consolidating Employment Protection (Consolidation) Act 1978.

2   Constitution

The constitution of the court is similar to that of the former National Industrial Relations Court.

Thus it consists of such number of judges as may be nominated from time to time by the Lord Chancellor from the judges of the High Court and the Court of Appeal, one of whom is appointed President, at least one nominated judge of the Court of Session and such other members as may be appointed from time to time by Her Majesty.[14] The additional members are persons having special knowledge or experience of industrial relations, either as representatives of employers or as representatives of workers, so that, although the President is a lawyer, the Tribunal consists of laymen with specialised knowledge of industrial relations. The members of the Tribunal may resign by notice in writing and may be removed by the Lord Chancellor after consultation with the Secretary of State on specified grounds, notably incapacity or misbehaviour.[15] The Tribunal, which is a superior court of record, has a central office in London and may sit at any time and in any place in Great Britain in any number of divisions concurrently. It is duly constituted when sitting with a judge and either two or four other members (or a judge and one other member by consent of the parties).[16]

---

[13] See, for example, *Goad* v. *Amalgamated Union of Engineering Workers (No. 2)*, [1973] I.C.R. 42; *Goad* v. *Amalgamated Union of Engineering Workers (No. 3)*, [1973] I.C.R. 108; *Heatons Transport (St, Helens), Ltd.* v. *Transport and General Workers Union (Interim Proceedings)*, [1972] I.C.R. 285.

[14] Employment Protection (Consolidation) Act 1978, s. 135(2); in addition the Lord Chancellor has power to appoint temporary judges or members (*ibid.*, Sch. 11, Part I, paras 4–10).

[15] *Ibid.*, Sch. 11, Part I, paras. 1–3.

[16] *Ibid.*, Sch. 11, Part I, paras. 12–16.

3 Jurisdiction

The jurisdiction of the Tribunal is limited to that which is conferred upon it by the 1978 Act. In sharp contrast to the National Industrial Relations Court, the Tribunal does not have the original jurisdiction which that court had to deal, for example, with unfair industrial practices. Its jurisdiction is limited to hearing appeals; these lie on questions of law from industrial tribunals under the Equal Pay Act 1970, the Sex Discrimination Act 1975, the Employment Protection Act 1975, the Race Relations Act 1976 and the 1978 Act.[17] In addition the Tribunal hears appeals on questions of fact or law arising in any proceedings before, or arising from any decision of, the Certification Officer under section 8 of the Trade Union and Labour Relations Act 1974 or under section 8 of the 1975 Act (under which a trade union may be certified as independent).[18]

4 Procedure

The hallmarks of procedure in the National Industrial Relations Court were speed, informality and simplicity. The Lord Chancellor has power to make rules of procedure, subject to which the Tribunal has power to regulate its own procedure.[19] The rules of procedure[20] are, in fact, somewhat similar to those which applied in the National Industrial Relations Court.

These aimed at informality. Nevertheless any person appearing before the Tribunal may be represented by counsel or by a solicitor or, indeed, may appear in person or be represented by a representative of a trade union or employers' association or by any other person whom he desires to represent him.[1]

Procedure at hearings of the Tribunal are designed to combine informality with order. No-one appears robed, there is no bench or witness box, parties and their advisers sit at tables and may address the court seated. The informality is doubtless an innovation to be welcomed, though whether abandonment of the rules of evidence is always a profitable exercise remains open to doubt. A further departure from normal court practice is that no party is to be ordered to pay costs unless, in the opinion of the Tribunal, the proceedings were unnecessary, improper or vexatious or there has been unreasonable delay or other unreasonable conduct in bringing or conducting the proceedings.[2]

The Tribunal has powers in relation to compelling the attendance and examination of witnesses, the production and inspection of documents, the enforcement of its orders and all other matters incidental to its jurisdiction under the Act, save that no person can be punished for contempt except by, or with the consent of, a judge who is a member of the court.[3]

---

[17] *Ibid.*, s. 136(1).
[18] *Ibid.*, s. 136(3).
[19] *Ibid.*, Sch. 11, Part I, para. 17.
[20] Employment Appeal Tribunal Rules 1980; see also *Practice Direction* (*Employment Appeal Tribunal*), [1977] 1 All E.R. 478; [1977] 1 W.L.R. 145.
[1] Act of 1978, Sch. 11, Part I, para. 20.
[2] *Ibid.*, Sch. 11, Part I, para. 19.
[3] *Ibid.*, Sch. 11, Part I, paras. 18, 21, 22.

Appeals—Any decision of the Employment Appeal Tribunal on a question of fact is final (except in the case of committal for contempt) but appeal on a point of law lies to the Court of Appeal.[4] The court, being a superior court of record, is not subject to the supervisory jurisdiction of the High Court.[5]

H   MAGISTRATES' COURTS

1   Constitution

A magistrates' court is defined by the Magistrates' Court Act 1980, section 148, as any justice or justices of the peace acting under any enactment or by virtue of his or their commission or under common law. Consequently magistrates' courts are composed of justices of the peace.[6] A magistrates' court must be composed of at least two and not more than seven justices of the peace in order to try an information summarily, hear a complaint or conduct an examination into the means of a person whom it is proposed to commit to prison for non-payment of a fine. However an exception is provided by the presence of a stipendiary magistrate who has all the powers of two lay justices.[7] A single lay justice has a limited jurisdiction and cannot order a person to pay more than one pound or impose imprisonment for more than fourteen days.[8] It should be noted that a single justice may discharge the function of determining the mode of trial of an offence triable summarily or on indictment and of conducting a preliminary investigation.[9]

The jurisdiction of magistrates' courts is local. Every county, the London commission areas and the City of London has a separate commission of the peace. The jurisdiction of the justices is generally confined to matters arising in or near these commission areas.[10]

2   Jurisdiction

It is common to suppose that the jurisdiction of the magistrates' courts is entirely criminal. This is very far from being true since magistrates have a wide and varied civil jurisdiction. The feature of both the civil and the criminal matters within the jurisdiction of the magistrates' courts is that they are matters of minor importance compared with the civil matters heard in the High Court and the county courts and the criminal cases tried at the Crown Court. The compensating advantage of summary procedure is its cheapness and speed.

Before examining more closely the civil and criminal jurisdiction of justices it should be remembered that sitting as magistrates' courts is not the

---

[4] *Ibid.*, s. 136(4).
[5] See p. 177, *ante.*
[6] See p. 12, *ante.*
[7] Justices of the Peace Act 1979, s. 16.
[8] Magistrates' Courts Act 1980 s. 121(5).
[9] See pp. 463, 476, *post.*
[10] Administration of Justice Act 1973; the commission areas are stated in accordance with the provisions of the Justices of the Peace Act 1979, ss. 1, 2.

only function of justices of the peace. They also sit in the Crown Court.[11] Furthermore such important functions as the conduct of preliminary investigations, the issue of summonses and warrants and the grant of bail are exercised by justices though not sitting as magistrates' "courts". It has only in recent years been confirmed that licensing sessions are "courts".[12]

a Criminal jurisdiction

The criminal jurisdiction of the magistrates' courts exists principally over summary offences.[13] Such offences are offences triable without a jury and are all statutory offences since all summary jurisdiction derives from statute. These offences are of a minor character since the maximum penalty which can be imposed in respect of a summary offence is six months imprisonment[14] and a fine limited in amount.[15] In practice most summary offenders are convicted of motoring offences under the Road Traffic Acts and Regulations made under those Acts. Indeed so numerous are the number of convictions for minor offences such as speeding and unauthorised parking that a new procedure was introduced by the Magistrates' Courts Act 1957 enabling persons to plead guilty to minor summary offences by post.[16] There are more than 2 million persons a year found guilty of summary offences in England and Wales.

In addition to their jurisdiction over summary offences magistrates' courts also have jurisdiction to try "offences triable either way"[17] and may, on conviction, impose penalties similar to those which may be imposed following conviction of summary offences.

Juvenile courts

These courts are magistrates' courts which exercise jurisdiction over offences committed by, and other matters concerning, children and young persons. The aim of the procedure in these courts is to disassociate the juvenile offenders from the criminal atmosphere and environment of the ordinary magistrates' courts, and to avoid undue publicity. Thus a juvenile court must not sit in a room in which sittings of another court are held if a sitting of that other court has been or will be held there within an hour. Proceedings are not open to the public and the only persons admitted to the court are the court officers, the parties to the case and their representatives, witnesses, *bona fide* members of the press and other persons authorised by the court to be present. In addition, to protect the juvenile, the press must not publish or broadcast the identity of any person under seventeen unless the court or the Home Secretary so orders.

---

[11] See p. 202, *ante*.

[12] *Jeffrey* v. *Evans*, [1964] 1 All E.R. 536; [1964] 1 W.L.R. 505.

[13] The jurisdiction appears to be exclusive: *R.* v. *East Powder Magistrates' Court, Ex parte Lampshire*, [1979] Q.B. 616; [1979] 2 All E.R. 329; see p. 20 *ante*.

[14] Magistrates' Courts Act 1980, s. 31(1).

[15] The limits are determined by the "standard scale" under s. 37 of the Criminal Justice Act 1982 and may be altered by the Secretary of State in the event of change in the value of money (*ibid.*, s. 48).

[16] For details of the procedure see p. 547, *post*.

[17] See Magistrates' Courts Act 1980, s. 17, Sched. 1; for details of the procedure for determining the mode of trial of such offences, see p. 458, *post*.

A juvenile court consists of justices drawn from a special panel, the chairman of which sits permanently though the other members change by rotation. There must be three lay justices to form a juvenile court of whom one at least must be a woman.[18]

A completely new procedure for the treatment of children and young persons was laid down by the Children and Young Persons Act 1969. At the time of writing, certain fundamental parts of that Act are still not in operation, in particular sections 4 and 5 which impose an absolute prohibition on charging a child with any offence except homicide and impose severe restrictions on the prosecution of young persons. The basic concept of the Act is to replace criminal proceedings, in respect of children and young persons, with "care proceedings" under section 1 of the Act.[19] Under that section any local authority, constable or authorised person who reasonably believes that there are grounds for an order may bring the child or young person in question before a juvenile court where, if one or more of the qualifying conditions is present, the court may make such an order, which may be an order requiring his parent or guardian to enter into a recognisance to take proper care of him and exercise proper control over him, a supervision order (an order placing him under the supervision of a local authority designated by a probation officer), a care order (an order committing him to the care of a local authority), a hospital order or a guardianship order. One of the qualifying conditions for the making of one of the above orders is that the child or young person is guilty of an offence, excluding homicide. Thus the child or young person may be found guilty of an offence without a trial, as such, but that finding is in no sense a conviction and he is dealt with not as a criminal but as any other child or young person in need of help. Nevertheless the court is not to find the "offence condition" satisfied unless it would have found him guilty of that offence in ordinary criminal proceedings, so that the ordinary onus of proof applies; furthermore if the "offence condition" is satisfied, the court has power to make orders for compensation (even if it makes no order under section 1) up to a maximum of £100 which the court may, in the case of a young person, and must (subject to exceptions) in the case of a child, order to be paid by the parent or guardian.[20] The power to order detention of children and young persons is limited to special circumstances where it is necessary for the protection of the public and detention will normally be in a "community home". There appears to be no immediate prospect of these provisions being brought into operation.

b   Civil jurisdiction

This aspect of the magistrates' courts' jurisdiction is very varied. It extends over the recovery of certain civil debts such as income tax, national insurance contributions, electricity, gas and water charges, rates, the grant, revocation and renewal of licences and domestic proceedings. The latter category is probably the most important aspect of the magistrates' civil jurisdiction; it is exercised principally under the Domestic Proceedings and Magistrates' Courts Act 1978 in "domestic courts".

---

[18] *Re J.S. (an infant)*, [1959] 3 All E.R. 856; [1959] 1 W.L.R. 1218.
[19] Part V of this work deals with criminal procedure as it is at the time of writing rather than as it will be if and when the whole of the 1969 Act is fully operational.
[20] Children and Young Persons Act 1969, s. 3(6).

c Domestic courts

These courts, constituted under section 80 of the 1978 Act, are magistrates' courts sitting for the purposes of hearing domestic proceedings.[1] They consist of justices drawn from a specially appointed panel to deal with such proceedings.[2] No person may be present during the proceedings except officers of the court, the parties and their legal representatives, witnesses and other persons directly concerned in the case, newspaper representatives and any other person whom the court may permit to be present.[3] There is provision for rules of court to be made requiring the magistrates to give and record reasons for their decisions (which they do not have to, and usually do not, do in ordinary proceedings) and for making available a copy of the record to prospective appellants.[4]

The 1978 Act at last disposed of the "matrimonial offence" as the basis of complaint. Although the Divorce Reform Act 1969 substituted "irretrievable breakdown" as the only ground for divorce, the principle of relief based upon the matrimonial offence continued to apply in magistrates' courts under the Matrimonial Proceedings (Magistrates' Courts) Act 1960. Indeed adultery on the part of a wife continued to be an absolute bar to her obtaining an order for maintenance for herself in a magistrates' court under the 1960 Act, although it had long ceased to be of much, if any, significance in the assessment of a wife's maintenance in the divorce county courts or the Family Division of the High Court.

Under section 1 of the 1978 Act either party to a marriage[5] may apply for an order on the ground that the other "(*a*) has failed to provide reasonable maintenance for the applicant, or (*b*) has failed to provide, or to make a proper contribution towards, reasonable maintenance for any child of the family; or (*c*) has behaved in such a way that the applicant cannot reasonably be expected to live with the respondent; or (*d*) has deserted the applicant." If any such ground is made out the court may order periodical payments and/or a lump sum (of up to £500[6]) to or for the benefit of the applicant or any child of the family;[7] in addition the court may make orders as to custody or access,[8] orders committing children to the care of the local authority[9] and various orders, for example excluding one spouse from the matrimonial home, for the protection of spouses and children.[10]

Appeals from these orders lie to the Family Division, where they are usually heard by a divisional court, although in some cases they may be heard

[1] As defined by Magistrates' Courts Act 1980, s. 65(1); these include, for example, affiliation, adoption, guardianship and matrimonial proceedings.
[2] The formation of these panels and the composition of domestic courts is dealt with by rules of court made under s. 67 of the Magistrates Courts' Act 1980; a stipendiary magistrate who is a member of a domestic court panel may sit alone (s. 67(7)).
[3] *Ibid.*, s. 69(2).
[4] *Ibid.*, s. 74(1).
[5] It is to be noted that the provisions do not apply to unmarried cohabitees as do, for example, the provisions of the Domestic Violence and Matrimonial Proceedings Act 1976.
[6] This figure may be increased by the Secretary of State.
[7] Act of 1978, s. 2; the factors the court must take into account (s. 3) are similar to those prescribed in s. 25 of the Matrimonial Causes Act 1973.
[8] *Ibid.*, s. 8.
[9] *Ibid.*, s. 10.
[10] *Ibid.*, s. 16.

by a single judge.[11] Further appeal lies to the Court of Appeal and then to the House of Lords, in each case with leave.

I   COUNTY COURTS

The county courts are courts of exclusively civil jurisdiction dealing, in the main, with minor civil claims such as small debts. They were established by the County Courts Act 1846 to meet the need for a system of courts to deal with small claims. There are two important limitations to the extent of the county courts' jurisdiction. First, the jurisdiction is entirely statutory so that if, in any matter, statute provides no jurisdiction then none exists. Nevertheless statutes which are likely to affect a large section of the community frequently confer jurisdiction on the county courts. Modern examples are to be found in the Hire-Purchase Act 1965 and the Rent Act 1977. The general common law and equity jurisdiction of the county courts is contained in the County Courts Act 1984 and is principally limited by the value of the plaintiff's claim.[12]

The second limitation on the jurisdiction of the courts is geographical. The jurisdiction of county courts is local in nature so that there must be some connecting factor between the action and the county court district in which it is tried. There are about four hundred county court districts in England and Wales grouped into circuits, each of which has at least one Circuit judge assigned to it. The administrative business of the court is supervised by the county court registrar who is a solicitor of at least seven years' standing and frequently holds the post of district registrar of the High Court. The registrar has a limited jurisdiction to try cases in which cases appeal lies to the judge. Apart from this, county courts have no appellate jurisdiction. Appeal lies from a county court to the Court of Appeal, subject to certain conditions, except in bankruptcy matters where appeal lies to a divisional court of the Chancery Division.

Details of jurisdiction and procedure in the county courts are contained in Part IV of this book.[13]

J   CORONERS' COURTS

1   The office of coroner

This ancient office dates from the twelfth century when it principally concerned the custody of the King's revenue, particularly that revenue accruing from fines and forfeiture. In addition the coroner from time to time exercised the jurisdiction of the sheriff and enquired into such matters as deodands, treasure trove and unexplained deaths. Some of these functions, together with the administrative functions once exercised by coroners, have been removed.

---

[11] R.S.C., O. 90, r. 16.

[12] For details of the financial limits, see Chapter 21, *post*; the limits may be increased by Order in Council (Act of 1984, s. 145).

[13] See p. 40, *post*.

The modern coroner's appointment and jurisdiction are governed by statute.[14] He must be a barrister, solicitor or registered medical practitioner of not less then five years' standing. He is removable by the Lord Chancellor for misbehaviour.

2 Jurisdiction

Although the coroner has jurisdiction over such matters as treasure trove and, in London, enquiring into the outbreak of fires, his jurisdiction is principally concerned with inquests into the death of persons whose bodies are "lying within his jurisdiction"[15] where there is reasonable cause for suspecting that the person has died a violent or unnatural death, or a sudden death the cause of which is unknown, or has died in prison or that the death occurred while the deceased was in police custody, or resulted from an injury caused by a police officer in the purported execution of his duty.[16]

If the case falls within the terms of section 3 of the 1887 Act (as amended) the coroner's duty is mandatory; he must hold an inquest. Moreover jurisdiction does not depend upon the death having occurred within the coroner's area—or even in the United Kingdom. It depends upon the presence of the body. Thus, where the body of an English nurse who had died in suspicious circumstances in Saudi Arabia was brought to West Yorkshire, the coroner was compelled by the High Court to hold an inquest.[17]

To hold an inquest the coroner may, and in some cases must, summon a jury of between seven and eleven members. Witnesses attend and give evidence and the coroner may compel the attendance of a witness and fine a witness for failing to attend in answer to a summons. The procedure is entirely inquisitorial in that, although interested persons may be represented and may ask questions of the witnesses, it is the coroner who conducts the proceedings and there are no speeches made to the jury. The jury return their verdict which need not be unanimous provided there are not more than two dissentients. This verdict is recorded in a document termed an "inquisition". Prior to the passing of the Criminal Law Act 1977 the jury might return a verdict of murder, manslaughter or infanticide by a named person whereupon the coroner had power, without more, to commit that person for trial. In such a case the inquest took the place of a preliminary investigation by magistrates and the inquisition performed the function of an indictment.[18] This procedure, although rarely adopted, was an anachronism and it was abolished by section 56 of the 1977 Act. A coroner's inquisition cannot now charge a person with any offence. Where criminal proceedings are on foot in respect of a death which is the subject of an inquest or for an offence alleged to have been committed in circumstances connected with the death, there are provisions in Schedule 10 of the 1977 Act for the adjournment of the inquest pending the resolution of the criminal proceedings, the decision ultimately resting with the Director of Public Prosecutions. After the

---

[14] Coroners Acts 1887–1980 (as amended).
[15] Coroners Act 1887, s. 3(1).
[16] The extension to deaths in police custody or at the hands of police officers was effected by the Administration of Justice Act 1982, s. 62.
[17] *R. v. West Yorkshire Coroner, Ex parte Smith*, [1983] Q.B. 335; [1982] 3 All E.R. 1098.
[18] See p. 487, *post.*

conclusion of the relevant criminal proceedings the coroner will be notified of the outcome by the court concerned whereupon he may resume the inquest if in his opinion there is sufficient cause to do so. If he does, then the finding of the inquest as to the cause of death must not be inconsistent with the outcome of the relevant criminal proceedings.[19]

There is no appeal from a coroner's inquisition although the proceedings are subject to judicial review by the High Court[20] and may be quashed by order of certiorari where, for example, the verdict cannot be supported by the evidence.[1]

Proceedings before a coroner's court are absolutely privileged for the purposes of defamation.[2]

K   JUDICIAL COMMITTEE OF THE PRIVY COUNCIL

1   Constitution

Prior to the Judicial Committee Act 1833 the jurisdiction of the Privy Council was exercised principally by laymen. This Act, as amended by the Judicial Committee Act 1844, the Appellate Jurisdiction Acts 1876–1947 and other Acts, created the Judicial Committee composed of the Lord President of the Council, the Lord Chancellor, ex-Lord Presidents, the Lords of Appeal in Ordinary and those members of the Privy Council who hold or have held high judicial office within the meaning of the Appellate Jurisdiction Acts 1876 and 1887. Membership has also been extended from time to time by Order in Council to persons who have held high judicial office in Commonwealth countries. In practice the Lord Chancellor and the Lords of Appeal in Ordinary are the members of the Committee who usually sit, with the result that decisions of the Privy Council enjoy great authority although they are not strictly binding on English courts.[3]

The hearing of appeals takes place at the bar of the Privy Council before not less than three and usually five members of the Committee. The members of the Committee sit unrobed and procedure is similar to procedure in the House of Lords.

2   Jurisdiction

Although all English courts derive their jurisdiction directly or indirectly from the Sovereign, the Judicial Committee of the Privy Council is slightly different in that its jurisdiction is that of the Sovereign in Council. Consequently the Privy Council does not pass judgment. It merely tenders advice to the Sovereign in person. This is by convention followed and implemented

---

[19] Coroners (Amendment) Act 1926, s. 20(7) (substituted by Criminal Law Act 1977, s. 56; Sch. 10). Procedure is governed by the Coroners' Rules 1984.

[20] See p. 177, *ante*.

[1] See, for example, *R.* v. *Coroner for Durham County, Ex parte A.-G.* (1978), *The Times*, 29 June.

[2] *McCarey* v. *Associated Newspapers, Ltd.*, [1964] 2 All E.R. 335; [1964] 1 W.L.R. 855. Being a court of record (as to which see p. 181, *ante*) a coroner's court has power to impose a fine for contempt committed in the face of the court: *R.* v. *West Yorkshire Coroner, Ex parte Smith (No. 2)*, [1985] 1 All E.R. 100; [1985] 2 W.L.R. 332.

[3] See p. 140, *ante*.

by an Order in Council. For this reason only one opinion is usually read and dissents were until recently not recorded.[4] However it is now provided by Order in Council that dissenting opinions may be delivered in open court.[5]

The main aspects of the jurisdiction of the Privy Council are as follows.

a Appeals from courts outside the United Kingdom

Since the Sovereign is the fountain of justice for all her Dominions the Privy Council has jurisdiction to hear appeals from the Isle of Man, the Channel Islands, British Colonies and Protectorates and from the highest courts of independent Commonwealth countries. However, since the Statute of Westminster 1931 Commonwealth legislatures have been competent to pass legislation excluding appeal to the Privy Council and several have done so.[6] Thus the Privy Council held in 1947 that Canada could validly enact that the decision of its own Supreme Court be final and exclusive in civil and criminal matters.[7]

Leave to appeal in criminal matters is only given in exceptional cases. Misdirection will not suffice. There must be some "clear departure from the requirements of justice" or "something which, in the particular case, deprives the accused of the substance of fair trial and the protection of the law."[8]

b Admiralty jurisdiction

Prior to 1875 appeal lay from the High Court of Admiralty to the Privy Council. When the Judicature Acts assigned jurisdiction to hear appeals from the Probate, Divorce and Admiralty Division of the High Court to the newly formed Court of Appeal the jurisdiction of the Privy Council was virtually limited to appeals from that Division when sitting as a "prize court".[9] The jurisdiction of the High Court to sit as a prize court is now exercised, as with other Admiralty jurisdiction, by the Admiralty Court of the Queen's Bench Division.[10] A prize court is a court convened to determine issues concerning the ownership of ships and cargo and the validity of their capture by enemy warships.

c Appeals from ecclesiastical courts

Since the jurisdiction of the ecclesiastical courts was drastically curtailed in 1857[11] their jurisdiction has been confined to matters affecting members of

---

[4] Cf., judgment in the criminal division of the Court of Appeal where only one judgment is delivered as a rule but for different reasons.
[5] Judicial Committee (Dissenting Opinions) Order in Council 1966; for a particularly vigorous dissent, see *Abbot* v. *R.*, [1977] A.C. 755; [1976] 3 All E.R. 140.
[6] Including Aden, Botswana, Burma, Canada, Cyprus, Ghana, Guyana, India, Lesotha, Pakistan, Sierra Leone, Sri Lanka, Tanzania and Uganda.
[7] *A.-G. for Ontario* v. *A.-G. for Canada*, [1947] A.C. 127; [1947] 1 All E.R. 137.
[8] *Ibrahim* v. *R.*, [1914] A.C. 599, at pp. 614–615, *per* LORD SUMNER; see also *Prasad* v. *R.*, [1981] 1 All E.R. 319; [1981] 1 W.L.R. 469.
[9] Now contained in Supreme Court Act 1981, s. 16(2), although jurisdiction also exists to hear appeals from the Colonial Courts of Admiralty and from the Court of Admiralty of the Cinque Ports.
[10] Supreme Court Act 1981, s. 20; see p. 196, *ante*.
[11] Court of Probate Act 1857; Matrimonial Causes Act 1857; see p. 80, *ante*.

the clergy and church buildings. The highest ecclesiastical courts are the Canterbury Court of Arches and the Chancery Court of York. Appeal from these courts lies to the Privy Council.[12] Although archbishops and bishops are not members of the Privy Council, whenever the Council is hearing an ecclesiastical appeal summonses are sent to one archbishop or the Bishop of London and four other bishops to sit as assessors, i.e. in an advisory capacity.

d   Appeals from medical tribunals

The Privy Council hears appeals by persons who have had their names erased from the medical register by the Professional Conduct Committee of the General Medical Council under the Medical Act 1983.[13]

e   Special references

Apart from its appellate jurisdiction outlined above, the Privy Council is sometimes required to advise on matters of law at the instance of the Sovereign.[14] In the exercise of this jurisdiction the Judicial Committee has advised on such diverse matters as the powers of colonial judges,[15] legislation in Jersey[16] and the eligibility of a person to sit and vote in the House of Commons.[17] The Secretary of State may recommend Her Majesty to refer to the Judicial Committee any question of whether a provision of any Measure of the Northern Ireland Assembly or Act of Parliament of Northern Ireland is void to the extent that it discriminates against any person or class of persons on the ground of religious belief or political opinion.[18]

L   COURTS OF PARTICULAR JURISDICTION

Prior to 1977 there were many   urts of local jurisdiction which constituted exceptions to the normal hierarchy of courts in that their constitution and jurisdiction were controlled locally. However the judicial functions of the vast majority of such courts which actively exercised jurisdiction were abolished by the combined effect of the Courts Act 1971, the Local Government Act 1972 and the Administration of Justice Act 1977.[19] Certain courts are outside the ordinary hierarchy because their jurisdiction is concerned with matters wholly outside the scope of the ordinary civil and criminal law. Some of these courts, such as courts-martial, derive their jurisdiction from statute while others, notably the ecclesiastical courts, are autonomous although, of course, they are recognised by the Crown. The jurisdiction of these specialist courts is usually applicable only to certain members of society

---

[12] Ecclesiastical Jurisdiction Measure 1963, s. 8.
[13] Similar powers exist under the Dentists Act 1984, the Opticians Act 1958 and the Veterinary Surgeons Act 1966.
[14] Judicial Committee Act 1833, s. 4.
[15] *Re Wills* (1840), 3 Moo. P.C.C. 216.
[16] *Re Jersey States* (1853), 9 Moo. P.C.C. 185.
[17] *Re Macmanaway*, [1951] A.C. 161.
[18] Northern Ireland Constitution Act 1973, s. 18.
[19] See p. 6, *ante*; the few that remain are listed in para. 23 of the Law Commission report, *Jurisdiction of Certain Ancient Courts* (Law Com. No. 72).

who have impliedly agreed to submit to their jurisdiction, though in some instances it extends to all members of the community.

1 Courts-martial

Courts-martial exercise jurisdiction over members of the armed forces. Their constitution, jurisdiction and procedure are governed by various statutes, principally the Army and Air Force Acts 1955, the Naval Discipline Act 1957 and the Armed Forces Act 1981.

Air Force and military courts-martial are similar in constitution and procedure.[20] The accused may be arrested for any offence against military law by a superior officer. In many instances his offence will only be a "summary" offence against Queen's Regulations in which case he will be tried by superior officers. In other cases the accused has a choice as to whether to be tried summarily or at a court-martial. Serious offences are always tried at courts-martial, except that murder, manslaughter, treason and rape committed within the United Kingdom cannot be tried at courts-martial but must be tried in the ordinary criminal courts. In all other cases the jurisdiction of civilian and military courts is concurrent. However a person who has already been convicted or acquitted by a civilian court cannot be subsequently tried at a military or Air Force court-martial, and *vice-versa*.[1]

The trial of an offence at a court-martial is in many ways similar to a trial in the ordinary criminal courts. It is preceded by an inquiry which is similar to a preliminary investigation. The accused is sent for trial on a charge sheet which may be compared with an indictment. The trial will be before at least three (or five in the case of a general court-martial) officers who are assisted by a judge advocate from the Judge Advocate General's department[2] who is a lawyer and advises on the law. Proceedings are in open court and both counsel and solicitors have a right of audience. The prosecution case is conducted by an Army or Air Force officer either personally or through a civilian counsel. The order of proceedings and rules of evidence applicable are similar to those applicable in other criminal proceedings. The accused may appear in person or be represented by counsel, solicitor or a defending officer. There is no jury and at the conclusion of the evidence the judge advocate sums up and advises on the law, leaving the members of the court to arrive at their decision which is by majority, except that the court must be unanimous where sentence of death is to be imposed.[3] An acquittal is final whereas a finding of guilt is subject to confirmation by a superior officer. Prior to confirming the finding of guilt the confirming authority may remit the finding to the court for reconsideration and may refuse to confirm the decision if it could not be supported by the evidence, was wrong in law or there was a miscarriage of justice.

The necessity for confirmation of a finding of guilt affords a safeguard to

---

[20] Naval courts-martial differ slightly in their composition, although their jurisdiction and procedure are similar.

[1] Armed Forces Act 1966, s. 25.

[2] The corresponding department in naval courts-martial is the Judge Advocate of the Fleet's department. The Judge Advocate General and the Judge Advocate of the Fleet are appointed by the Queen on the advice of the Lord Chancellor.

[3] Army Act 1955, s. 96.

the accused against injustice. A further safeguard is provided by the power of the High Court to prevent excesses or abuses of jurisdiction by means of the prerogative orders of prohibition and certiorari and by habeas corpus.[4]

Although courts-martial cannot generally exercise jurisdiction over civilians this can be done where Her Majesty's forces are in armed occupation of hostile territory. In these circumstances a state of martial law may be declared by Her Majesty's commanders. A state of martial law may also be declared in time of insurrection although it is doubtful whether such a declaration would be valid within the United Kingdom. Furthermore civilians who are employed in the service of the forces on active service outside the United Kingdom are liable to trial in "Standing Civilian Courts" which may be established outside the United Kingdom under section 6 of the Armed Forces Act 1976.

Courts-Martial Appeal Court. Until 1951 there was no appeal from conviction by a court-martial, the only remedy being a petition to the reviewing authority or, where an excess of jurisdiction was alleged, an application for prohibition, certiorari or habeas corpus.

The Courts-Martial (Appeals) Act 1951[5] created the Courts-Martial Appeal Court which is now composed of the *ex-officio* and ordinary members of the Court of Appeal, judges of the Queen's Bench Division nominated by the Lord Chief Justice, certain Scottish and Irish judges and other persons of legal experience appointed by the Lord Chancellor. In practice the composition of the court resembles closely that of the criminal division of the Court of Appeal.[6] As in the latter court, there must be at least three judges. Only one judgment is delivered and procedure is similar to that in the criminal division of the Court of Appeal. The grounds of appeal to the Courts-Martial Appeal Court and the powers of that court on determining appeals are substantially similar to those of the Court of Appeal except that there is no right of appeal against sentence.

Appeal lies from the Courts-Martial Appeal Court to the House of Lords at the instance of the prosecutor or the defence subject to the conditions under which an appeal lies from the criminal division of the Court of Appeal to the House of Lords.[7]

2   Ecclesiastical courts

These courts have a history which is as old as the common law itself. Although they have been subject to control by the Sovereign since the reign of Henry VIII and although their jurisdiction over laymen has by stages been abolished there remains a hierarchy of courts within the Church of England. In addition the General Synod of the Church of England has statutory power[8] to pass Measures concerning any matter affecting the Church of England and even concerning Acts of Parliament. These measures have

---

[4] *R. v. Governor of Wormwood Scrubs Prison, Ex parte Boydell*, [1948] 2 K.B. 193; [1948] 1 All E.R. 438.
[5] Now the Courts-Martial (Appeals) Act 1968.
[6] See p. 191, *ante.*
[7] See p. 540, *post*; Courts-Martial (Appeals) Act 1968, s. 39.
[8] Under the Church of England Assembly (Powers) Act 1919 as amended by the Synodical Government Measure 1969, s. 2.

statutory force upon receiving the Royal Assent. The most significant recent measure has been the Ecclesiastical Jurisdiction Measure 1963 which altered the hierarchy of ecclesiastical courts and abolished a large number of obsolete courts and their jurisdiction.

The ecclesiastical judicial system may now be summarised as follows. In each diocese there is a consistory court the judge of which is a chancellor appointed by the bishop. He must be at least 30 years old and either be a barrister of seven years' standing or have held high judicial office. The consistory courts' jurisdiction[9] is principally concerned with investigating allegations of conduct unbecoming a clerk in Holy Orders and persistent neglect of duty. Appeal lies from the consistory courts to the Arches Court of Canterbury, presided over by the Dean of the Arches, or the Chancery Court of York, presided over by the Auditor, both officers being barristers of ten years' standing or persons who have held high judicial office. Appeal from these two courts lies to the Privy Council.[10]

Jurisdiction equivalent to that of the consistory courts is exercised over bishops and archbishops by Commissions of Convocation. Jurisdiction over all members of the clergy in matters involving "doctrine, ritual or ceremonial" is exercised by the Court of Ecclesiastical Causes Reserved composed of five judges appointed by Her Majesty including two persons who have held high judicial office and three diocesan bishops. Finally petition lies from both the Commissions of Convocation and the Court of Ecclesiastical Causes Reserved to a Commission of Review composed of three Lords of Appeal in Ordinary and two Lords Spiritual.

The penalties which ecclesiastical courts may impose range from rebuke to deprivation of Orders and disqualification from subsequent preferment. In addition such deprivation and disqualification are automatic where a priest or deacon is sentenced to imprisonment, has an affiliation order made against him, has a decree of divorce or judicial separation pronounced against him on certain specified grounds, is found to have committed adultery in matrimonial proceedings or has had a magistrates' court order made against him in similar circumstances.[11]

Excesses of jurisdiction by the ecclesiastical courts may be controlled by the High Court by means of the prerogative orders of mandamus and prohibition. Certiorari does not, however, lie since these courts exercise and administer a different system of law.

3 Naval courts

A naval court may be summoned by an officer in command of one of Her Majesty's ships on any foreign station on a complaint to him by any member of the crew which appears to require immediate investigation, or where any British ship is wrecked, abandoned or lost in the area, or where the interests of the owner of any British ship or its cargo so require.[12] Such a court,

---

[9] For a recent reported instance of the jurisdiction of consistory courts, see *Re St. George's Church, Oakdale*, [1976] Fam. 210; [1975] 2 All E.R. 870.

[10] See p. 214, *ante*.

[11] Ecclesiastical Jurisdiction Measure 1963, s. 55 (substituted by Ecclesiastical Jurisdiction (Amendment) Measure 1974).

[12] Merchant Shipping Act 1894, s. 480.

consisting of naval officers, must investigate the matter judicially and may impose imprisonment or fine or forfeiture of wages, suspend or cancel officers' certificates, send an offender home for trial and order a ship to undergo a survey for unseaworthiness. Appeal lies from its decision to the divisional court of the Queen's Bench Division and thence, with leave, to the Court of Appeal.

4   Court of Chivalry

The jurisdiction of an English court can only be removed by statute. Nevertheless the jurisdiction of most local courts and feudal courts has fallen into obsolescence. However a modern sitting was held of the Court of Chivalry, an ancient feudal court, to decide the entitlement of a theatre to display the coat of arms of the City of Manchester.[13] Prior to this case the court had not been convened since 1737. The court determines disputes over the right to use armorial bearings and ensigns. It is presided over by the Earl Marshal, although he appointed the Lord Chief Justice to sit as his deputy in the modern case in question. The court appears to have no power to enforce its decisions.[14]

5   Restrictive Practices Court

This court of record was created by the Restrictive Trade Practices Act 1956, now repealed and replaced by the consolidating Restrictive Practices Court Act 1976 and Restrictive Trade Practices Act 1976. The function of the court is to consider "restrictive agreements" and "information agreements" relating to the supply of goods or services.[15] Cases are referred to the court by the Director General of Fair Trading or by parties to such an agreement who have been ordered to furnish particulars to the court. The scope of the court's business was temporarily increased by the Resale Prices Act 1964 which restricted minimum resale price maintenance. Any supplier or trade association was able to apply to the Restrictive Practices Court for exemption for a class of goods on the grounds that this would be in the public interest.[16] The jurisdiction of the court was extended by the Fair Trading Act 1973 in that the Director General of Fair Trading may bring proceedings in the court against any person who either does not give or does not observe a written assurance that he will refrain from a course of conduct in the course of his business which appears to the Director to be detrimental to the interests of consumers in the United Kingdom and, in accordance with statutory criteria, unfair to consumers.[17]

---

[13] *Manchester Corporation* v. *Manchester Palace of Varieties, Ltd.*, [1955] P. 133; [1955] 1 All E.R. 387.

[14] *Ibid*. Notwithstanding, the Law Commission report of 1976 (see p. 214, fn. 19, *ante*) did not recommend the abolition of the court and it was one of the few courts of local and ancient jurisdiction which did not have its jurisdiction removed by the Administration of Justice Act 1977.

[15] Restrictive Trade Practices Act 1976, s. 1; the extension to agreements relating to services was made by the Fair Trading Act 1973; for the definitions of "restrictive agreements" and "information agreements", see ss. 6, 7, 11 and 12 of the 1976 Act.

[16] Resale Prices Act 1964, s. 5. All applications have now been determined.

[17] Fair Trading Act 1973, ss. 34–35.

The court consists of three judges of the High Court appointed by the Lord Chancellor, a judge of the Court of Session of Scotland, a judge of the Supreme Court of Northern Ireland and not more than ten lay members appointed by the Queen on the recommendation of the Lord Chancellor. The court is duly constituted with a presiding judge and two lay members except that in the case of proceedings involving only issues of law the court may consist of a single judge.[18] Appeal lies from the court on a question of law, and in proceedings under Part III of the Fair Trading Act 1973 (consumer protection) on a question of fact or law, to the Court of Appeal, the Court of Session or the Court of Appeal of Northern Ireland, as the case may be.[19]

6 Court of Protection

At common law the Sovereign has always assumed care and custody of persons of unsound mind and their property. As keeper of the Queen's conscience the Lord Chancellor was detailed to exercise this authority. At the present day the Lord Chancellor and the judges of the Chancery Division administer the property of persons of unsound mind within the meaning of the Mental Health Act 1983. When exercising this function the Chancery judge sits as the Court of Protection, the constitution and jurisdiction of which is now governed by the 1983 Act.[20]

The jurisdiction of the Court of Protection should not be confused with the jurisdiction of courts under various statutes to make orders for admission of persons to approved hospitals.[1]

M TRIBUNALS AND INQUIRIES

1 Nature of tribunals and inquiries

a Statutory tribunals

The second characteristic of Dicey's Rule of Law is that all categories of people are subject to the control of the courts. There are some who regard the modern concept of administrative justice as a denial of this principle. Nonetheless administrative justice is an increasingly important aspect of the English legal system. Because of the comparative speed, cheapness and informality of tribunals as compared with the ordinary courts Parliament has during the last hundred or so years tended more and more to confer jurisdiction upon bodies which are outside the normal hierarchy of the courts. These tribunals exercise differing functions which may be administrative or judicial. They differ from ordinary courts of law in several respects but particularly in their composition. The members of the tribunals are often lawyers and sometimes even judges but equally frequently they are laymen

---

[18] Restrictive Practices Court Act 1976, s. 7.
[19] *Ibid.*, s. 10.
[20] Though the power is exercisable in the High Court if the sum involved is a small one: *Re K.*, [1969] 2 Ch. 1; [1969] 1 All E.R. 194.
[1] E.g., Mental Health Act 1983, s. 37.

with specialised knowledge of the sphere of activity with which the tribunal is dealing but with little or no knowledge of the law.

In recent years the control exercised by outside forces, notably the ordinary courts, over administrative tribunals has increased. A committee was set up in 1955 under the chairmanship of Sir Oliver Franks to consider administrative tribunals and inquiries. The committee reported in 1957[2] and its recommendations were substantially implemented by the Tribunals and Inquiries Act 1958 (now the Tribunals and Inquiries Act 1971). The 1971 Act provides that in the case of certain specified tribunals the chairman is to be selected from a panel appointed by the Lord Chancellor.[3] In addition there is a Council on Tribunals consisting of not more than fifteen nor less than ten members appointed by the Lord Chancellor and the Secretary of State.[4] The members are disqualified from membership of the House of Commons. The Council keeps under review the working of tribunals and reports on them from time to time. The tribunals subject to the scrutiny of the Council on Tribunals are listed in the First Schedule to the Act (as amended) and include Agricultural Land Tribunals, the Aircraft and Ship-building Industries Arbitration Tribunal, the Lands Tribunal, Mental Health Review Tribunals, National Insurance Tribunals, Rent Tribunals and the General and Special Commissioners of Income Tax. In this way the Lord Chancellor is able to exercise direct extrajudicial control over some of the more important tribunals.

b   Domestic tribunals

There are a number of private or professional associations which have set up their own tribunals for resolving disputes between their own members or exercising control or discipline over them. The jurisdiction of these tribunals is based primarily on contract in that, by becoming a member of the association or professional body, a person contracts to accept the jurisdiction of the governing tribunal. Nevertheless in many cases these tribunals exist on a statutory basis with a right of appeal to the courts. Examples of domestic tribunals constituted under statute are the Solicitors' Disciplinary Tribunal, under the Solicitors' Act 1974,[5] and the Professional Conduct Committee of the General Medical Council, under the Medical Act 1983. Where the tribunal is not constituted under a statute then there is no appeal to the ordinary courts. However, the High Court exercises a supervisory jurisdiction over tribunals, even where their jurisdiction is not based on statute and will intervene to prevent an abuse of natural justice.[6]

---

2   Cmnd. 218.
3   Tribunals and Inquiries Act 1971, s. 7.
4   *Ibid.*, s. 2(1); the Parliamentary Commissioner for Administration is also a member of the Council (s. 2(3)).
5   See p. 254, *post.*
6   See, for example, *Lee* v. *Showmen's Guild of Great Britain*, [1952] 2 Q.B. 329; [1952] 1 All E.R. 1175; *Byrne* v. *Kinematograph Renters Society, Ltd.*, [1958] 2 All E.R. 579; [1958] 1 W.L.R. 762; *Nagle* v. *Feilden*, [1966] 2 Q.B. 633; [1966] 1 All E.R. 689.

c Industrial Tribunals

These tribunals were first established under section 12 of the Industrial Training Act 1964 with a very limited jurisdiction under that Act. Since that date, however, the jurisdiction of the tribunals has been greatly enlarged by statutes, notably the Contracts of Employment Act 1972, the Redundancy Payments Act 1965, the Docks and Harbours Act 1966, the Equal Pay Act 1970, the Trade Union and Labour Relations Act 1974, the Health and Safety at Work Act 1974, the Sex Discrimination Act 1975 and the Employment Protection Act 1975. Many of these provisions, notably those relating to complaints of unfair dismissal (which constitute about two-thirds of the business of the tribunals these days) and claims for redundancy payment, are now consolidated in the Employment Protection (Consolidation) Act 1978.[7] The establishment of industrial tribunals is now governed by section 128 of the 1978 Act and regulations made thereunder. They have become an extremely important organ of the administration of justice; thus, although there is no fixed number of tribunals, since each may be convened as required, on average 75 tribunals currently sit in Great Britain every working day. Tribunals ordinarily consist of three members, one of whom is a legally qualified chairman, the decision being by majority. Members of tribunals are appointed because of their special knowledge and experience and they are entitled to draw on this in support of their decisions, although if evidence is given which is contrary to their knowledge and experience, the Employment Appeal Tribunal has stated that, while the tribunals are entitled to reject such evidence and to act on their own knowledge, they should first make this known to the parties and give witnesses the opportunity of dealing with it.[8]

Proceedings are relatively informal. The strict rules of evidence do not apply. Any person may appear before a tribunal in person or be represented by counsel or solicitor, or by a representative of a trade union or any employers' association or, indeed, "by any other person whom he desires to represent him".[9] Awards of costs are not usually made, unless a party has acted frivolously or vexatiously.[10]

The jurisdiction of industrial tribunals extends over a wide range of aspects of industrial law, in addition to unfair dismissal and redundancy.

Thus, for example, an employee may present a complaint to an industrial tribunal on the ground of the employer's failure to pay a "guarantee payment"[11] or maternity pay,[12] or on the ground that his employer has taken action for the purpose of preventing or deterring him from joining an "independent trade union"[13] or has failed to permit him to take time off as permitted by the Act.[14]

---

[7] Under s. 131 of the 1978 Act, the appropriate Minister has power to confer upon tribunals jurisdiction over claims for damages for breach of a contract of employment, and related claims, and to modify other enactments for this purpose.

[8] *Dugdale* v. *Kraft Foods, Ltd.*, [1977] 1 All E.R. 454; [1976] 1 W.L.R. 1288.

[9] Employment Protection (Consolidation) Act 1978, s. 128; Sch. 9, para. 6.

[10] Industrial Tribunals (Labour Relations) Regulations 1974, r. 10; however a party who by his conduct necessitates an adjournment of proceedings may be ordered to pay the costs occasioned thereby: *Ladbroke Racing, Ltd.* v. *Hickey*, [1979] I.C.R. 525.

[11] Employment Protection (Consolidation) Act 1978, s. 22.

[12] *Ibid.*, s. 36.

[13] *Ibid.*, s. 24.

[14] *Ibid.*, ss. 27–29.

Following the abolition of the National Industrial Relations Court, appeal from industrial tribunals lay in all cases to the Queen's Bench Division. However appeal now lies to the Employment Appeal Tribunal in most cases.[15]

d   Tribunals of Inquiry

When a matter of urgent public importance arises Parliament may resolve to set up a tribunal to inquire into it. The tribunal is then set up by Her Majesty or a Secretary of State and upon the tribunal may be conferred many of the procedural powers of the High Court, such as summoning witnesses, compelling the production of documents and taking evidence on oath. If a witness refuses to answer a question put to him he may be reported to the High Court and punished for contempt of court.[16] A tribunal of inquiry must generally sit in public unless the public interest requires otherwise. The tribunal has discretion whether or not to allow representation by counsel or solicitor before it.

e   Local statutory inquiries

There are a number of statutes which confer jurisdiction upon Ministers to hold local inquiries. In practice these inquiries are conducted by local inspectors but ultimately it is the Minister who assumes responsibility in Parliament. Inquiries of this nature often arise when objections are lodged against orders submitted by a local or public authority to a Minister for confirmation, or, sometimes, submitted by the Minister himself but subject to confirmation. The usual circumstance is the making of an order for the compulsory acquisition of land, or planning schemes affecting land development.

Procedure at these inquiries is governed by the statute under which they are held and often there is no right of appeal. Nevertheless the rules of natural justice must be observed and, since the Tribunals and Inquiries Act 1958, the Minister has been required to give reasons for his decision on request unless national security justifies not giving a reason.

f   Criminal Injuries Compensation Board

Tribunals are sometimes established for the purpose of determining individuals' rights to compensation from public funds. The right to compensation arises where a person has suffered loss or damage, often by reason of an act of the legislature or the executive; compulsory acquisition of land is an obvious example.

A most important addition to compensation tribunals was the Criminal Injuries Compensation Board. The scheme was established as an experimental measure in 1964 and provides *ex gratia* compensation to victims of crimes of violence (or if the victim dies, his dependants). Compensation is assessed on the same basis as common law damages (where the application is

---

[15] For details of the cases in which appeal lies to the Tribunal, see p. 205, *ante*.

[16] Tribunals of Inquiry (Evidence) Act 1921, s. 1; Contempt of Court Act 1981, s. 20; cf. *A.-G.* v. *Clough*, [1963] 1 Q.B. 773; [1963] 1 All E.R. 420; *A.-G.* v. *Mulholland*, [1963] 2 Q.B. 477; [1963] 1 All E.R. 767.

by a dependant the principles of the Fatal Accidents Act apply) and takes the form of a lump sum payment. Although there is no right to compensation claims are determined by the Board consisting of a chairman and a number of qualified members.

Applications are in the first instance dealt with by a single member, the applicant having the right, if dissatisfied with the single member's decision, to a hearing before three other members of the Board. At the hearing the applicant must prove his case on a balance of probabilities; he may (as may the Board) call, examine and cross-examine witnesses. The procedure is informal and hearings are in private. Compensation will not be awarded unless the Board is satisfied (*a*) that the injury is one for which compensation of not less than £400 would be awarded; and (*b*) that the circumstances of the injury have been the subject of criminal proceedings, or were reported to the police without delay; and (*c*) that the applicant has given the Board all reasonable assistance, particularly in relation to any medical reports that they may require. The Board may reduce the amount of compensation or reject the application altogether if, having regard to the conduct of the victim and to his character and way of life it is inappropriate that he should be granted a full award or any award at all.

The Scheme extends, subject to restrictions, to victims of violence within the family.

The Board may re-open cases to take account of a serious change in a victim's medical condition within three years of the date of a final award.

An interesting feature of the Board is the method of its creation. Whereas tribunals are usually established by statute, the Board was set up by prerogative act. The Government set out in a White Paper[17] the draft scheme, it was debated in both Houses of Parliament and, in an amended form, was announced by both Houses on June 24, 1964.[18]

The scheme is financed by a grant-in-aid, approved annually by the Appropriation Act.[19]

It seems likely that in the near future the Board will be given a statutory foundation, in view of the increasing importance (and expense) of its functions. When that is done a right of appeal to the courts, on points of law at least, will certainly be created. There is, at present, no right of appeal from the Board, although its decisions are subject to judicial review by the High Court[20] and will be quashed if the Board misconstrues its mandate or if it must, on *Wednesbury* principles,[1] be deemed to have done so.[2]

---

[17] Cmnd. 2323 of 1964.

[18] Further amendments to the scheme were announced by the Home Secretary in 1965, 1969 and 1979.

[19] The amount of compensation paid out in England and Wales in the financial year 1983–84 totalled £27,161,359 to a total of 17,930 applicants, 1,017 of whom were police officers injured on duty (Criminal Injuries Compensation Board, Twentieth Report (Cmnd. 9399 of 1984)).

[20] *R.* v. *Criminal Injuries Compensation Board, Ex parte Lain*, [1967] 2 Q.B. 864; [1967] 2 All E.R. 770.

[1] Cf. *Associated Provincial Picture Houses, Ltd.* v. *Wednesbury Corporation.*, [1948] 1 K.B. 223; [1947] 2 All E.R. 680; see p. 177, *ante*.

[2] *R.* v. *Criminal Injuries Compensation Board, Ex parte Thompstone*, [1984] 3 All E.R. 572; [1984] 1 W.L.R. 1234.

2   Control by the courts of administrative tribunals and inquiries

It is well recognised that administrative justice is a dangerous institution unless it is subject to effective safeguards and control. The Donoughmore Committee on Ministers' Powers, a predecessor of the Franks Committee, in its report in 1932 recommended four types of safeguard: first, that the supervisory jurisdiction of the High Court over tribunals be maintained in respect of excesses of jurisdiction; secondly, that the tribunals be compelled by the High Court to observe natural justice; thirdly, that reports of statutory inquiries be published; and finally, that there should be an appeal to the High Court on a question of law. The third of these safeguards is not judicial and was, in fact, implemented by the Tribunals and Inquiries Act 1958, section 12. The same Act introduced the additional safeguard of control by the Council on Tribunals. The first, second and last of the four safeguards specified by the Donoughmore Committee depend upon control by the courts through the exercise of supervisory and appellate jurisdiction.

a   Supervisory control

The supervisory jurisdiction of the High Court, exercised in practice by the Queen's Bench Division, is a common law jurisdiction and does not depend upon statute. Any provision in an Act passed before August, 1958 which excludes any of the powers of the High Court does not have effect so as to prevent the High Court from making orders of mandamus or certiorari.[3]

There are two ways in which the High Court may purport to exercise its supervisory control over tribunals. The usual method is by the issue of prerogative orders in judicial review proceedings; however these orders lie only against tribunals which are statutory, or at least of a public character[4] and do not extend to tribunals exercising a purely voluntary jurisdiction. A person aggrieved by the decision of a voluntary tribunal may, however, invoke the High Court's supervisory jurisdiction by bringing an action against the officers of the tribunal, claiming an injunction or a declaration as to his rights.[5]

In recent years the High Court has shown an increased willingness to intervene in the affairs of trade and professional bodies which have the power to deprive individuals of their livelihood.[6]

b   Appeals from tribunals

An application for judicial review is not an appeal. There is no common law right of appeal from a tribunal so that an appeal only lies where statute so provides. The Tribunals and Inquiries Act 1971, section 13, provides for any party to appeal or to require the tribunal to state a case on a point of law from certain administrative tribunals to the High Court. These appeals are heard by the divisional court of the Queen's Bench Division. Other statutes provide

---

3   Tribunals and Inquiries Act 1971, s. 14.
4   See pp. 174–178, *ante.*
5   Under R.S.C. O.15, r. 16; see p. 344, *post.*
6   *Bonsor* v. *Musicians' Union,* [1956] A.C. 104; [1955] 3 All E.R. 518; *Byrne* v. *Kinematograph Renters Society, Ltd.,* [1958] 2 All E.R. 579; [1958] 1 W.L.R. 762; *Nagle* v. *Feilden,* [1966] 2 Q.B. 633; [1966] 1 All E.R. 689.

rights of appeal to various branches of the Supreme Court and, in the case of doctors, dentists and opticians, to the Judicial Committee of the Privy Council.[7]

N ARBITRATION

1 Provisions for reference to arbitration

As an alternative to proceedings in the ordinary courts, parties, particularly in the sphere of commerce, often prefer to refer their disputes to arbitration. The jurisdiction of arbitrators usually arises out of contract, though there are numerous statutory provisions which provide for the reference of disputes to arbitration.

An agreement to refer disputes to arbitration is a contract and, as such, is subject to the ordinary law of contract. Any provision purporting to oust the jurisdiction of the courts is void, as being contrary to public policy, though there is no objection to a clause which makes reference to arbitration a condition precedent to a right of action. The effect of such a clause, known as a *Scott* v. *Avery*[8] clause, is that if a party does institute proceedings without referring the dispute to arbitration the clause may be pleaded as a defence in those proceedings and the other party may, after acknowledging service of the writ but before taking any other step in the proceedings, apply to the court for an order staying the proceedings.[9] The order is discretionary but, in the absence of some good reason, the court will stay the proceedings. Since legal aid is not available in arbitrations an impecunious plaintiff is at a severe disadvantage if proceedings (in which he would be eligible for legal aid) are stayed. The poverty or insolvency of a plaintiff is, as a rule, not a ground for refusing a stay; however, where there is a triable issue as to whether that poverty or insolvency has been brought about by the defendant's breach of contract, a stay may be refused so as to avoid a denial of justice by reason of the plaintiff being of insufficient means to pursue his cause of action effectively.[10]

2 Procedure

Procedure on arbitrations is governed (except, in relation to statutory references, where the statute in question otherwise provides) by the Arbitration Acts 1950 and 1979. The issues arising must (in the absence of contrary agreement) be decided according to the ordinary rules of English law and the normal judicial procedure will apply, including the rules of evidence (though these are often dispensed with by agreement). The arbitrator has implied

---

[7] See p. 214, *ante*.
[8] (1856), 5 H.L. Cas. 183.
[9] Arbitration Act 1950, s. 4(1). The Arbitration Act 1975, s. 1(1) makes similar provision in relation to agreements which are not "domestic arbitration agreements" as defined by s. 1(4). The Act provides for the enforcement of awards made in the territory of any State (other than the United Kingdom) which is a party to the New York Convention on the Recognition of Foreign Arbitral Awards.
[10] *Fakes* v. *Taylor Woodrow Construction, Ltd.*, [1973] Q.B. 436; [1973] 1 All E.R. 670.

power to examine witnesses, order the discovery and inspection of documents, pleadings, interrogatories and the like. If a party fails to comply with an order made by an arbitrator in the course of a reference, the High Court may extend the powers of the arbitrator so as to confer upon him power to treat the default in the same way as a High Court judge would in civil proceedings.[11] This presumably would permit the arbitrator to strike out pleadings and allow judgment in default. Apart from this provision, it has been held[12] that an arbitrator has no power to dismiss an action for want of prosecution. Nor may a court, by injunction, restrain continuance of an arbitration where the circumstances are such as would, in the context of litigation in the courts, justify dismissal for want of prosecution, although it seems that the arbitrator, faced with such delay, could fix a hearing date and make an award *ex parte* if one party failed to appear, or could debar a claimant from raising a claim of which he has failed to give adequate notice to the respondent in breach of the arbitrator's directions.[12]

3   Appointment and powers of arbitrators and umpires

In the absence of specific provision reference to arbitration connotes reference to a single arbitrator.[13] Where specific provision is made for the appointment of two arbitrators there is an implied term that, immediately after they are appointed, they shall appoint an umpire who, if the arbitrators cannot agree, may enter on the reference in their stead.[14] Under section 10 of the 1950 Act the High Court has various powers to appoint arbitrators and umpires in default of appointment by the parties. The High Court also has power to revoke the authority of an arbitrator or umpire on the ground of delay, bias or improper conduct[15] and has inherent jurisdiction to stay arbitration proceedings by injunction.

There used to be provision whereby an arbitrator might, and, if directed by the court, had to state in the form of a "special case" for the opinion of the High Court, either his award or any question of law arising in the reference.[16] The power to apply for a special case was sometimes exercised by a party to delay unduly the resolution of the dispute and to add needlessly to costs. It was thus particularly unfortunate that the power could not be restricted by the terms of the agreement, i.e. the parties could not "contract out" of the special case procedure.[17] The 1979 Act altered this situation by providing[18] that the parties may enter into an "exclusion agreement", but only if they do so after the arbitration has commenced. There will then be no power in the High Court to consider a question of law arising in the course of the arbitration; nor will there be any right of appeal (*infra*). Therefore

---

[11] Arbitration Act 1979, s. 5.

[12] *Bremer Vulkan Schiffbau und Maschinenfabrik* v. *South India Shipping Corporation* [1981] A.C. 909; [1981] 1 All E.R. 289. The decision has been much criticised but the House of Lords declined to depart from it in *Paal Wilson & Co. A/S* v. *Partenreederi Hannah Blumenthal*, [1983] 1 A.C. 854; [1983] 1 All E.R. 34.

[13] Arbitration Act 1950, s. 6.

[14] *Ibid.*, s. 8.

[15] *Ibid.*, s. 23.

[16] *Ibid.*, s. 21.

[17] *Czarnikow* v. *Roth, Schmidt & Co.*, [1922] 2 K.B. 478.

[18] Arbitration Act 1979, ss. 3, 4.

(subject to the limited power of the High Court to set aside or remit an award for misconduct (*infra*)) the arbitrator's decision will be final. Exclusion agreements entered into before the arbitration is commenced are effective only in a limited class of cases and, in particular, are invalid in the case of a "domestic arbitration agreement", that is, basically, an agreement which does not provide for arbitration outside the United Kingdom and is not one to which no United Kingdom national or resident is a party.[19]

The decision of the arbitrator is in the form of an "award", dealing with all the issues on which reference was made. The award may contain provision for the payment of money, costs or an order of specific performance (except of a contract relating to land).[20] As between the parties the award gives rise to an estoppel *in personam*[1] in relation to the issues decided, thus extinguishing any cause of action in relation thereto.

4 Intervention by the court

An arbitration award may, with leave of the High Court, be enforced in the same way as a judgment or order of that court and, where leave is granted, judgment may be entered in the terms of the award. In addition action may be brought on the award as a contractual debt.

The court's powers over arbitration proceedings were altered and extended by the 1979 Act. There is now, for the first time, a right of appeal on any question of law arising out of an award made on an arbitration agreement[2] (unless excluded by a valid "exclusion agreement" (*supra*)) but only by consent of all parties or with leave of the court; the court may not grant leave unless it considers that the determination of the question of law could affect substantially the rights of the parties and it may attach conditions to the grant of leave (for example the provision of security for the amount claimed).

In addition to the right of appeal, there is jurisdiction in the High Court (save where there is a valid exclusion agreement) to determine any question of law arising in the course of the reference,[3] but only with the consent of the arbitrator or of all the parties. This replaces the old special case procedure under section 21 of the 1950 Act.

There is an appeal from the High Court to the Court of Appeal, from decisions under sections 1 and 2 of the 1979 Act, but only (*a*) with leave of the High Court; and (*b*) if the High Court certifies that the question of law is one of general public importance or one which for some other special reason should be considered by the Court of Appeal.[4]

---

[19] *Ibid.*, s. 3(6).
[20] Arbitration Act 1950, s. 15.
[1] See p. 591, *post*.
[2] Arbitration Act 1979, s. 1(2); the appeal is by originating motion, must be brought within 21 days and is to a judge of the Commercial Court: O. 73, rr. 2(2), 5(2), 6.
[3] Arbitration Act 1979, s. 2(1); the application must be made within 14 days and is to a judge of the Commercial Court: O. 73, rr. 5(3), 6.
[4] *Ibid.*, s. 1(7); compare the conditions for leave to appeal to the House of Lords in criminal cases (p. 540, *post*). For a summary of the principles which a judge ought to apply when considering whether to grant leave to appeal (1) to the High Court; and (2) to the Court of Appeal, see *Antaios Cia Naviera S.A.* v. *Salen Rederierna A.B.*, [1984] 3 All E.R. 229; [1984] 3 W.L.R. 592. In practice appeals to the courts in arbitration cases are discouraged.

Where an arbitrator has misconducted himself or the proceedings the court may remove him and may set aside the award, or may remit it for reconsideration.

The parties may nominate any person they wish to act as arbitrator. Members of the bar are not infrequently appointed. In addition, by section 4 of the Administration of Justice Act 1970 a judge of the Commercial Court may, if in all the circumstances he thinks fit, accept appointment as sole arbitrator or as umpire where the dispute appears to him to be of a commercial character and provided the Lord Chief Justice has informed him that, having regard to the state of business in the High Court, he can be made available to do so. Where a judge has acted as arbitrator or umpire under this section appeal lies by case stated to the Court of Appeal.[5]

The arbitration procedure described above operates, as will be appreciated, as an alternative to proceedings before the ordinary courts. With this should be contrasted the procedure in county courts whereby the registrar has power to refer disputes to arbitration.[6] The essential feature of such an arbitration is that it takes place within the context of county court proceedings rather than as an alternative to such proceedings, so that the award is entered as a judgment in the proceedings and is binding as such.

---

[5]   R.S.C., O. 61, r. 2(6).
[6]   For details of the procedure, see p. 408, *post*.

CHAPTER 10

The Judiciary

A APPOINTMENT AND CONDITIONS OF TENURE OF OFFICE

The Lord Chancellor, the Lord Chief Justice, the Master of the Rolls, the President of the Family Division of the High Court, the Vice-Chancellor, the Lords of Appeal in Ordinary and the Lords Justices of Appeal are appointed by the Queen on the advice of the Prime Minister. Of these only the Lord Chancellor's appointment is made on a political basis. The puisne judges of the High Court, Circuit judges and Recorders are appointed by the Queen on the advice of the Lord Chancellor. Justices of the peace are appointed by the Lord Chancellor directiy.

Until Stuart times judges held office only during the King's pleasure and could be, and were, removed at the will of the King. Their position was altered in consequence of the Revolution settlement by the Act of Settlement 1700 which provided that:

> "Judges' commissions be made *quamdiu se bene gesserint*, and their salaries ascertained and established, but upon the address of both Houses of Parliament it may be lawful to remove them."

Thus, as long as they conducted themselves properly (*quamdiu se bene gesserint*) judges of the superior courts[1] could be removed only on an address by both Houses of Parliament. Presumably a judge who was guilty of serious neglect or misconduct could be removed by the Crown without the need for an address by Parliament.[2] This prohibition still applies to judges of the Supreme Court of Judicature,[3] except, however, for Circuit judges and Recorders who are removable by the Lord Chancellor on the ground of incapacity or misbehaviour or, in the case of a Recorder, failing to comply with the conditions of his appointment.[4]

---

[1] Except the Lord Chancellor who, because he is a Minister of the Crown, holds office at the Queen's pleasure.
[2] See *Earl of Shrewsbury's Case* (1611), 9 Co. Rep 42a, at p. 50. No English judge has been removed under the Act of Settlement procedure, though an Irish judge was so removed in 1830.
[3] It is now contained in s. 11(3) of the Supreme Court Act 1981.
[4] Courts Act 1971, ss. 17(4), 21(6); see p. 201, *ante*.

Judges of the Supreme Court (excluding Circuit judges and Recorders) and Lords of Appeal in Ordinary must, unless appointed before 1959, retire at the age of 75.[5] Their salaries are determined by the Lord Chancellor, with the consent of the Minister for the Civil Service, and charged on the Consolidated Fund.

Justices of the peace may be removed from the commission by the Lord Chancellor without showing cause. Several justices have been so removed, generally for refusing to administer a law with which they were not in sympathy. Although there is no retiring age for justices of the peace they are put on the supplemental list at the age of 70,[6] which is *de facto* retirement in that they cease to be entitled to exercise judicial functions. Justices may be put on the supplemental list before they have reached this age, either at their own request or on the ground of "age or infirmity or other like cause" or on the ground that the justice declines or neglects to take a proper part in the exercise of his judicial functions.[6]

A peculiar feature of the English system of judicial appointment has been its almost Salic preference for males over females. This tradition was only broken when, in 1965, Mrs. Justice Lane, having already been the first female county court judge, was accorded the distinction of being the first woman to be made a judge of a superior court in England, being appointed a puisne judge of the Probate, Divorce and Admiralty Division.

B   CONSTITUTIONAL POSITION

Much has been written on the question of whether judges are "servants" of the Crown. The better view seems to be that they are servants for they are appointed and, in certain circumstances, removable by the Queen and are paid out of the Consolidated Fund, although they cannot be controlled in the exercise of their office by the Queen or her Ministers. Generally the question of whether judges are properly describable as servants is unimportant though the question did arise in an acute form in 1931 when the National Economy Act of that year conferred power upon the Commissioners of Inland Revenue to reduce the remuneration of "persons in His Majesty's Service". The Commissioners purported to reduce judicial salaries. The validity of this measure, though strenuously disputed, was not decided since the Inland Revenue soon abolished these reductions under pressure of public opinion.

Whether judges are or are not Crown servants there is no doubt that the judicial function is not under the control of the legislature or the Executive. Judicial independence is a fundamental of English constitutional law. An offshoot of this principle of judicial independence is the doctrine of judicial immunity. Historically the degree of immunity has varied with the status of the judge. The old cases distinguish between judges of superior courts, who were held immune from action even if acting maliciously, and judges of

---

5   Supreme Court Act 1981, s. 11(2), (10); Judicial Pensions Act 1959, ss. 2(1), 3, Sch. 1. Circuit judges retire at the age of 72 (though the Lord Chancellor may authorise continuance in office until 75); Courts Act 1971, s. 17(1), (2).

6   Justices of the Peace Act 1979, s. 8. Stipendiary magistrates retire at 70 but may be retained in office up to the age of 72 (*ibid.*, s. 14).

inferior courts who enjoyed immunity only while acting within their jurisdiction. These principles operated somewhat capriciously; thus a Recorder of London who unlawfully imprisoned the jurors at the trial of Penn and Meade for ignoring his direction to convict was held immune from suit[7] while an unfortunate county court judge in Lancashire was held liable in damages for a mistake of law as to his jurisdiction, made quite innocently and in good faith.[8]

Such rationale as there may have been behind this dichotomy may be thought to have little relevance to modern conditions and the Court of Appeal in *Sirros* v. *Moore*,[9] rejected the principle whereby the degree of immunity depends upon the status of the court. LORD DENNING, M.R. stated the position in characteristically straightforward terms:[10]

> "Every judge of the courts of this land—from the highest to the lowest—should be protected to the same degree, and liable to the same degree. If the reason underlying this immunity is to ensure 'that they may be free in thought and independent in judgment', it applies to every judge, whatever his rank. Each should be protected from liability to damages when he is acting judicially. Each should be able to do his work in complete independence and free from fear. He should not have to turn the pages of his books with trembling fingers, asking himself: 'If I do this, shall I be liable in damages?' So long as he does his work in the honest belief that it is within his jurisdiction, then he is not liable to an action. He may be mistaken in fact. He may be ignorant in law. What he does may be outside his jurisdiction—in fact or in law—but so long as he honestly believes it to be within his jurisdiction, he should not be liable. . . Nothing will make him liable except it be shown that he was not acting judicially, knowing that he had no jurisdiction to do it."

The result in the instant case was to render immune from liability a Circuit judge, exercising the appellate jurisdiction of the Crown Court, who, without authority (but in good faith), ordered the arrest and detention of the plaintiff as the latter was lawfully leaving the court.

LORD DENNING, immediately after the passage quoted above, added:

> "This principle should cover the justices of the peace also. They should no longer be subject to 'strokes of the rodde or spur'. Aided by their clerks, they do their work with the highest degree of responsibility and competence—to the satisfaction of the entire community. They should have the same protection as the other judges."

However this *dictum* was rejected by the House of Lords in *McC.* v. *Mullan*[11] in which it was held that justices could be sued if they acted without

---

[7] *Hamond* v. *Howell* (1677), 2 Mod. Rep. 218.

[8] *Houlden* v. *Smith* (1850), 14 Q.B. 841.

[9] [1975] Q.B. 118, at p. 136; [1974] 3 All E.R. 776, at p. 785. The position of justices of the peace is now set out in Part V of the Justices of the Peace Act 1979. They cannot be held liable in respect of acts done within their jurisdiction unless the plaintiff pleads and proves that the act was done "maliciously and without reasonable cause" (s. 44). However in *McC.* v. *Mullan* the majority of the House of Lords regarded this old common law cause of action as obsolete and stated, albeit *obiter*, that it would no longer lie. There is no similar protection as regards acts done in excess of jurisdiction (s. 45) but the justice is entitled to indemnity out of local funds, in respect of both damages and costs, if he acted "reasonably and in good faith" (s. 53).

[10] [1975] Q.B., at p. 136; [1974] 3 All E.R., at p. 785.

[11] [1984] 3 All E.R. 908; [1984] 3 W.L.R. 1227.

or in excess of jurisdiction. The latter phrase, however, requires some elaboration. If justices have jurisdiction to entertain the proceedings then the mere fact that they impose a sentence or take some other course which is subsequently held to be wrong does not mean that they acted in excess of jurisdiction. They will only act without their jurisdiction if they impose a sentence or take a course which they have no power to do. In such a case they may be held liable for whatever form of trespass to the person, land or goods follows.

The House of Lords also doubted the correctness of the statements in *Sirros* v. *Moore* (including that quoted above) to the effect that the distinction between superior and inferior courts, for this purpose, no longer exists although it regarded the decision itself as defensible on narrower grounds.

The immunity which attaches to judicial proceedings is not personal to the judge. Thus no civil action lies in respect of words spoken in the course of proceedings by parties,[12] witnesses,[13] advocates[14] or in respect of the verdict of a jury.[15] Fair and accurate contemporaneous newspaper and broadcast reports of judicial proceedings in the United Kingdom are also absolutely privileged in the law of defamation.[16]

C THE JUDICIAL FUNCTION

Most of the work of the judges is judicial in the sense that they have to adjudicate upon disputes. To do this they are required, dispassionately, to find the facts upon the evidence presented to the court, to apply the law to the facts as found and then to give the "right decision". Appellate courts have repeatedly pointed out that the judicial function in the conduct of litigation goes no further than that. Thus, in relation to finding the facts, the court must act on the evidence before it; it has no duty to seek out some "independent truth" as LORD WILBERFORCE called it in the following interesting passage from his speech in a case concerning discovery of documents:[17]

> "In a contest purely between one litigant and another, such as the present, the task of the court is to do, and be seen to be doing, justice between the parties, a duty reflected by the word 'fairly' in the rule. There is no higher or additional duty to ascertain some independent truth. It often happens, from the imperfection of evidence, or the withholding of it, sometimes by the party in whose favour it would tell if presented, that an adjudication has to be made which is not, and is known not to be, the whole truth of the matter; yet, if the decision has been in accordance with the available evidence and with the law, justice will have been fairly done."

Likewise, having found the facts, judges must apply the existing rules of law to those facts. There are two aspects of this function—the interpretation of statutes and the application of the doctrine of precedent. It is the duty of

---

[12] *Astley* v. *Younge* (1759), 2 Burr. 807.
[13] *Hargreaves* v. *Bretherton*, [1959] 1 Q.B. 45; [1958] 3 All E.R. 122.
[14] *Munster* v. *Lamb* (1883), 11 Q.B.D. 588.
[15] *Bushell's Case* (1670), Vaugh. 135.
[16] Defamation Act 1952, s. 8.
[17] *Air Canada* v. *Secretary of State for Trade* (*No. 2*), [1983] 2 A.C. 394, at p. 438; [1983] 1 All E.R. 910, at p. 919; see p. 354, *post*.

judges to ascertain the intention of the legislature, if the rule of law in question is statutory, or to apply the existing law where the rule of law in question is a rule of common law or equity. The traditional view is that judges are not competent to interpret a statute other than in accordance with the literal meaning of the words used, or to alter any existing rule of common law or equity. LORD DIPLOCK explained the rationale of this view, in relation to the interpretation of statutes, in a case concerning a trade dispute in the steel industry, in the following words:[18]

> "My Lords, at a time when more and more cases involve the application of legislation which gives effect to policies that are the subject of bitter public and parliamentary controversy, it cannot be too strongly emphasised that the British Constitution, though largely unwritten, is firmly based on the separation of powers: Parliament makes the laws, the judiciary interpret them. When Parliament legislates to remedy what the majority of its members at the time perceive to be a defect or a lacuna in the existing law (whether it be the written law enacted by existing statutes or the unwritten common law as it has been expounded by the judges in decided cases), the role of the judiciary is confined to ascertaining from the words that Parliament has approved as expressing its intention what that intention was, and to giving effect to it. Where the meaning of the statutory words is plain and unambiguous it is not for the judges to invent fancied ambiguities as an excuse for failing to give effect to its plain meaning because they themselves consider that the consequences of doing so would be inexpedient, or even unjust or immoral. In controversial matters such as are involved in industrial relations there is room for differences of opinion as to what is expedient, what is just and what is morally justifiable. Under our Constitution it is Parliament's opinion on these matters that is paramount."

To similar effect, but in relation to construction of a contract, are the words of LORD BRIDGE in a shipping case:[19]

> "The ideal at which the courts should aim, in construing such clauses, is to produce a result such that in any given situation both parties seeking legal advice as to their rights and obligations can expect the same clear and confident answer from their advisers and neither will be tempted to embark on long and expensive litigation in the belief that victory depends on winning the sympathy of the court. This ideal may never be fully attainable, but we shall certainly never even approximate to it unless we strive to follow clear and consistent principles and steadfastly refuse to be blown off course by the supposed merits of individual cases."

Nevertheless strict adherence to this rule is not always possible since there is often uncertainty or ambiguity in the area of law being considered.[20] Indeed the rule cannot be applied in interpreting an Act of Parliament which makes no provision for the case in question or in deciding a case of "first impression", i.e., a case for which there is no precedent. In such a case the judge must create new law. This traditional view of the judicial function is, it

---

[18] *Duport Steels, Ltd.* v. *Sirs* [1980] 1 All E.R. 529, at p. 541; [1980] 1 W.L.R. 142, at p. 157.

[19] *A/S Awilco* v. *Fulvia SpA di Navigazione, The ChiKuma*, [1981] 1 All E.R. 652, at p. 659; [1981] 1 W.L.R. 314, at p. 322. This decision was an appeal to the House of Lords from the Court of Appeal presided over by LORD DENNING, M.R. as were both cases cited in the preceding two footnotes.

[20] For a detailed discussion of the judicial approach to statutory interpretation and to the doctrine of judicial precedent, see pp. 104, 135 *et seq., ante.*

must be said, changing. As LORD SIMON frankly stated in the case of *Jones* v. *Secretary of State for Social Services*:[1]

> "In this country it was long considered that judges were not makers of law but merely its discoverers and expounders. The theory was that every case was governed by a relevant rule of law, existing somewhere and discoverable somehow, provided sufficient learning and intellectual rigour were brought to bear. But once such a rule had been discovered, frequently the pretence was tacitly dropped that the rule was pre-existing, for example, cases like *Shelley's Case*,[2] *Merryweather* v. *Nixan*[3] or *Priestley* v. *Fowler*[4] were (rightly) regarded as new departures in the law. Nevertheless the theory, however unreal, had its value—in limiting the sphere of law-making by the judiciary (inevitably at some disadvantage in assessing the potential repercussions of any decision, and increasingly so in a complex modern industrial society), and thus also in emphasising that central feature of our constitution, the sovereignty of Parliament. But the true, even if limited, nature of judicial law-making has been more widely acknowledged of recent years."

There are other circumstances in which the judicial function goes far beyond the strict application of existing legal rules. Thus, in many cases, a judge has a discretion. This discretion is usually fettered by precedent and is always subject to principles of natural justice but it is, nonetheless, a discretion. It is sometimes possible for a judge to evolve a new rule of equity even at the present day. Indeed DENNING, J. (as he then was) virtually did this in *Central London Property Trust, Ltd.* v. *High Trees House, Ltd.*[5] However the existing framework of the law of property makes it very difficult for a new equitable right to be recognised.[6]

The self-assumed power of the House of Lords to depart from its own previous decisions[7] has had the effect of bringing into sharp relief the scope of the judicial function, for the members of the House are now free, in effect, to create new law. It is fair to say that certain judges deem it to be within their function to create new principles of law while others believe that any far-reaching change should be left to Parliament, which has greater facilities for testing the possible repercussions of law reform. The latter approach is exemplified by the following passage from the vigorous dissenting speech of LORD SIMON in the leading case of *Miliangos* v. *George Frank (Textiles), Ltd.*[8]

> "I am sure that an expert committee, including or taking evidence from departmental officials, would apprehend a great number of not immediately apparent repercussions of the decision which my noble and learned friends propose to take. Such a committee might conclude that the repercussions make the decision unacceptable. Or they might suggest some means of mitigating any adverse effect. Or they might advise that the repercussions were on balance acceptable. But at least the crucial decision would be taken in the light of all the consequences involved.

---

[1] [1972] A.C. 944, at p. 1026; [1972] 1 All E.R. 145, at p. 198; see p. 146, *ante*.
[2] (1581), Moore K.B. 136.
[3] (1799), 8 Term Rep. 186.
[4] (1837), 3 M. & W. 1.
[5] [1947] K.B. 130; [1956] 1 All E.R. 256n.
[6] See, for example, *National Provincial Bank, Ltd.* v. *Ainsworth*, [1965] A.C. 1175; [1965] 2 All E.R. 472.
[7] See p. 146, *ante*.
[8] [1976] A.C. 443, at pp. 481–482; [1975] 3 All E.R. 801, at pp. 824–825.

By contrast, the training and qualification of a judge is to elucidate the problem immediately before him, so that its features stand out in stereoscopic clarity. But the beam of light which so illuminates the immediate scene seems to throw surrounding areas into greater obscurity; the whole landscape is distorted to the view. A penumbra can be apprehended, but not much beyond; so that when the searchlight shifts a quite unexpected scene may be disclosed. The very qualifications for the judicial process thus impose limitations on its use. This is why judicial advance should be gradual. 'I am not trained to see the distant scene: one step enough for me' should be the motto on the wall opposite the judge's desk. It is, I concede, a less spectacular method of progression than somersaults and cartwheels; but it is the one best suited to the capacity and resources of a judge. We are likely to perform better the duties society imposes on us if we recognise our limitations. Within the proper limits there is more than enough to be done which is of value to society.''

Nevertheless, LORD SIMON was a lone dissenting voice in that case and the House of Lords did effect a radical reform of English law in holding that English courts have power to give judgments expressed in foreign currency.

An important example of judicial law-making by the House of Lords is afforded by the recent cases of *Ramsey (W.T.), Ltd.* v. *Inland Revenue Commissioners*[9] and *Furniss* v. *Dawson*[10] in which the House formulated and developed the principle whereby a series of prearranged steps or transactions, some of which have no commercial purpose other than the avoidance or deferment of tax, fall to be looked at together so that liability to tax is determined according to the substance of the scheme as a whole and its end result. These cases amounted to a bombshell to the tax-avoidance industry.

In the realm of criminal law judges have occasionally regarded it as within their function to enforce public morality by creating new criminal offences. The earliest criminal offences were, of course, judge-made and even until the eighteenth century the scope of the criminal law was being extended judicially.[11]

However, by the middle of the nineteenth century "times had changed and the pretensions of the judges to extend the criminal law had changed with them".[12] Accordingly it is universally accepted that judges have no power to create new criminal offences.[13] This principle must be seen in relation to the very wide criminal offences which have, in this century, been held to exist. In *R.* v. *Manley*[14] the defendant had alleged falsely that she had been attacked and robbed. The police were put to considerable trouble and expense in investigating her story and members of the public were put in suspicion. She was convicted of public mischief and her appeal against conviction, on the

---

[9] [1982] A.C. 300; [1981] 1 All E.R. 865.

[10] [1984] A.C. 474; [1984] 1 All E.R. 530.

[11] The historical alteration in the function of the judiciary in relation to the development of criminal law is illuminatingly described in the speech of LORD DIPLOCK in *Knuller (Publishing, Printing and Promotions), Ltd.* v. *Director of Public Prosecutions*, [1973] A.C. 435; [1972] 2 All E.R. 898.

[12] *Knuller (Publishing, Printing and Promotions), Ltd.* v. *Director of Public Prosecutions (supra)*, [1973] A.C. 435, at p. 474; [1972] 2 All E.R. 898, at p. 918, *per* LORD DIPLOCK.

[13] This was virtually the only point upon which all five members of the House of Lords were agreed in *Knuller (supra)*; see also *Abbott* v. *R.*, [1977] A.C. 755; [1976] 3 All E.R. 140.

[14] [1973] 1 K.B. 529; her conduct would now amount to a summary offence under the Criminal Law Act 1967, s. 5(2).

ground that no such offence was known to the law, was dismissed. Equally striking is the decision of the House of Lords in *Shaw* v. *Director of Public Prosecutions*,[15] to the effect that an agreement to publish the "Ladies Directory", containing names, addresses and photographs of persons willing to engage in prostitution and perversion, constituted a "conspiracy to corrupt public morals" which was a criminal offence. The following observation from the speech of VISCOUNT SIMONDS in that case has been widely quoted.[16]

> "In the sphere of criminal law I entertain no doubt that there remains in the courts of law a residual power to enforce the supreme and fundamental purpose of the law, to conserve not only the safety and order but also the moral welfare of the State . . . The law must be related to the changing standards of life, not yielding to every shifting impulse of the popular will but having regard to fundamental assessments of human values and the purpose of society".

In *Knuller* (*Publishing, Printing and Promotions*), *Ltd.* v. *Director of Public Prosecutions*[17] a publication of a somewhat similar kind (although this time aimed at a homosexual market) was held to give rise to the same offence. Not only was *Shaw*'s case followed but a majority of the House (*obiter*) expressed the view that there were known to the criminal law further offences of outraging public decency and conspiring so to do.

In the light of these authorities such comfort as may be drawn from the principle that judges have no power to create new criminal offences would appear to be more illusory than real. However, in the recent case of *Director of Public Prosecutions* v. *Withers*[18] the House of Lords to some extent redressed the balance by holding that conspiracy to effect a public mischief, in the sense of an agreement to do an act which, although not unlawful in itself, is injurious to the public, is not as such an offence known to the law; *a fortiori* there is no offence of public mischief as such. Conduct which has already been held to be criminal, such as that of the defendant in *R*. v. *Manley* (*supra*), remains criminal but not simply because it falls within the general rubric of "public mischief" but rather because it is a specific form of conduct which, on the authorities, constitutes an established criminal offence.

Other areas in which the judicial function goes beyond the resolution of the dispute which the judge in question is determining are "guideline" authorities in which appellate courts lay down guidelines for the guidance of judges in approaching the exercise of discretionary powers. Thus the rates of interest to be awarded on damages in personal injury actions,[19] the principles to be applied in determining applications for interlocutory injunctions[20] and the circumstances in which judges should grant leave to appeal from arbitration awards[1] are all the subject of guidelines laid down by the House of Lords. Similarly in criminal cases the modern practice of the criminal division of the Court of Appeal is, on the hearing of one or more appeals against

---

[15] [1962] A.C. 220; [1961] 2 All E.R. 446.
[16] [1962] A.C., at pp. 267–268; [1961] 2 All E.R., at p. 452.
[17] [1973] A.C. 435; [1972] 2 All E.R. 898.
[18] [1975] A.C. 842; [1974] 3 All E.R. 984.
[19] See p. 379, *post*.
[20] See p. 333, *post*.
[1] See p. 227, *ante*.

sentence relating to a particular type of offence, to give sentencing guidelines for the assistance of Crown Court judges in dealing with offences of the type.[2]

Professional judges (but not lay magistrates) must give reasons for their decisions and an appellate court will look askance at a refusal to do so and may have power to order the judge to do so.[3]

In addition to the power to apply, and to a lesser extent create, rules of law, judges exercise certain administrative functions. This is particularly true of justices of the peace who exercise many functions which are not properly termed judicial, such as licensing and the issue of summonses and warrants. Judges of the Chancery Division sitting as a Court of Protection supervise the affairs and administer the property of persons of unsound mind. The Lord Chancellor and all High Court judges are "visitors" of the Inns of Court and, as such, hear appeals from orders of the Senate of the Inns of Court and the Bar.[4] In addition much litigation in the courts is non-contentious and concerns such matters as the administration of trusts, the winding-up of companies, adoption and legitimacy. Finally sections 85 and 86 of the Supreme Court Act 1981 empower, respectively, the Supreme Court Rule Committee and the Crown Court Rule Committee to make rules of court for the purpose of regulating and prescribing the practice and procedure to be followed in the Supreme Court while in county courts the rule committee derives jurisdiction from section 75 of the County Courts Act 1984. All of these committees include judges. In addition the judiciary controls practice and procedure in the courts by the issue of Practice Directions.

D CONTEMPT OF COURT

1 General nature of contempt

Her Majesty's judges control the due administration of justice and have an inherent jurisdiction to punish conduct which is calculated to prejudice or interfere with the process of the law. Such conduct is termed a contempt of court. Contempt may be of a criminal nature or of a procedural nature, the latter being generally termed civil contempt.

Criminal contempt is a common law misdemeanour punishable by fine and imprisonment. It consists of conduct, in or out of court, which amounts to a contemptuous interference with the administration of justice. Perhaps the best known perpetrator of a criminal contempt was the prisoner who, at the Salisbury summer assizes, 1631, before Chief Justice RICHARDSON:

---

[2] This practice seems to have originated in *R*. v. *Turner* (1975), 61 Cr. App. Rep. 67 in relation to sentences for robbery and has since been followed in relation to many other sentencing areas; see, for example, *R*. v. *Clarke* (*Linda*), [1982] 3 All E.R. 232; [1982] 1 W.L.R. 1090 (partially suspended sentences); *R*. v. *Aramah* (1982), 76 Cr. App. Rep. 190 (drugs offences); *R*. v. *Boswell*, [1984] 3 All E.R. 353; [1984] 1 W.L.R. 1047 (causing death by reckless driving).

[3] *R*. v. *Knightsbridge Crown Court, Ex parte International Sporting Club* (*London*), *Ltd.*, [1982] Q.B. 304; [1981] 3 All E.R. 417, per GRIFFITHS, L.J.

[4] See p. 267, *post*.

"Ject un Brickbat a le dit Justice que narrowly mist, & pur ceo immediately fuit Indictment drawn per Noy envers le prisoner, & son dexter manus ampute & fix al Gibbet sur que mesme immediatement hange in presence de Court."

Marginally more subtle was the solicitor's clerk who decided to enliven proceedings at St. Albans Crown Court by releasing nitrous oxide ("laughing gas") down a ventilation duct into the trial court.[5]

There are many more common forms of criminal contempt such as: interference with jurors or witnesses, failure of a witness to attend court in pursuance of a subpoena, witness order or witness summons,[6] refusal to give evidence,[7] use of a tape recorder in court without the leave of the court,[8] removal of a ward of court from the jurisdiction, publication of the identity of a child in juvenile court proceedings without the express consent of the court, or the identity of a witness contrary to a clear direction prohibiting such publication,[9] scandalous abuse of a judge with reference to his office or the publication during a pending case of matter which is calculated to prejudice a fair trial.[10] It was on this ground that an injunction was granted restraining the publication in the *Sunday Times* newspaper of an article intending to show that defendants in a negligence action had not exercised due care.[11] The House of Lords held that it was a contempt of court to publish an article expressing an opinion on the merits of a specific issue which was before the court for decision in circumstances such that the article gave rise of a "real risk" that the fair trial of the action would be prejudiced. Moreover it is a contempt of court to use improper pressure to induce a litigant to settle a case on terms to which he did not wish to agree.

Contempt of Court Act 1981

This Act amended the law relating to contempt of court in certain substantive and procedural respects. In particular the "strict liability rule" (whereby conduct may be treated as a contempt of court as tending to interfere with the course of justice in legal proceedings regardless of intent to do so) is: (1) limited to "publications" (as opposed to conduct); (2) applicable only to publications which create "a substantial risk that the course of

---

[5] Although he did not get far enough in carrying out his plan for his conduct to amount to contempt: *Balogh* v. *St. Albans Crown Court*, [1975] Q.B. 73; [1974] 3 All E.R. 283.

[6] Criminal Procedure (Attendance of Witnesses) Act 1965; see p. 486, *post.*

[7] *R.* v. *Phillips* (1984), 78 Cr. App. Rep. 88.

[8] Contempt of Court Act 1981, s. 9; as to considerations relevant to the grant of leave, see *Practice Direction*, [1981] 3 All E.R. 848; [1981] 1 W.L.R. 1526.

[9] *R.* v. *Socialist Worker Printers and Publishers, Ltd., Ex parte A.-G.*, [1975] Q.B. 637; [1975] 1 All E.R. 142; but there must be a clear direction and not merely a request: *A.-G.* v. *Leveller Magazine, Ltd.*, [1979] A.C. 440; [1979] 1 All E.R. 745.

[10] E.g., *R.* v. *Bolam, Ex parte Haigh* (1949), 93 Sol. Jo 220 in which the editor of the *Daily Mirror* was gaoled for three months and the proprietors fined £10,000 for comments made pending a murder trial. On the other hand, criticism of the decision of a court does not amount to contempt, even if it contains error, provided that it was made in good faith and is reasonable. Thus in *R.* v. *Metropolitan Police Commissioner, Ex parte Blackburn (No. 2)*, [1968] 2 Q.B. 150; [1968] 2 All E.R. 319 a description of a Court of Appeal decision (by none other than LORD HAILSHAM, before his appointment as Lord Chancellor) as "a strange example of the blindness which sometimes descends on the best of judges" was held not to amount to contempt.

[11] *A.-G.* v. *Times Newspapers, Ltd.*, [1974] A.C. 273; [1973] 3 All E.R. 54, one of a number of actions resulting from the thalidomide tragedy.

justice in the proceedings in question will be seriously impeded or prejudiced"; and (3) applicable only if the proceedings in question are "active" (as determined by reference to Schedule 1 of the Act).[12] In addition the Act creates three statutory defences to the strict liability rule, *viz.* innocent publication or distribution,[13] fair and accurate reports of legal proceedings held in public, published contemporaneously and in good faith[14] and discussion of public affairs or other matters of general public interest if the risk of impediment or prejudice to particular legal proceedings is merely incidental to the discussion.[15] Quite apart from these provisions, it appears that *mens rea* is an element in contempt of court, not in the sense that the defendant must be demonstrated to have intended to be in contempt but in the sense that his conduct must have been deliberate and he must have known of the circumstances by reason of which that conduct was a contempt of court.[16]

Whereas criminal contempt consists of a positive act of interference with the administration of justice, civil (or procedural) contempt is generally committed by inaction. It is a failure to comply with an order of the court or an undertaking given to the court. Examples of civil contempt are: failure of a solicitor to comply with an undertaking,[17] failure to swear an account, refusal to comply with an order for discovery of documents or to answer interrogatories[18] and failure to comply with an injunction. Similarly mere failure to pay a judgment debt is not contempt, although wilful refusal to do so is.[19] However, if there is a reasonable alternative method available of securing compliance with a court order, the Court of Appeal has stated that that method should be adopted rather than committing the contemner to prison.[20]

2 Jurisdiction to punish contempt

Civil contempt was formerly punishable by writ of attachment but the Rules of the Supreme Court (Revision) 1965 abolished attachment so that civil contempt is now punishable by committal in the same way as criminal contempt.

The jurisdiction to punish for contempt, whether committed in or out of court, is inherent in superior courts of record. Such courts may commit for contempt and also punish contempt committed in the face of the court by immediate fine and imprisonment. Imprisonment must be for a fixed term not exceeding two years.[1]

---

12 Contempt of Court Act 1981, s. 2.
13 *Ibid.*, s. 3.
14 *Ibid.*, s. 4; but under s. 4(2) the court may order publication to be postponed for the purpose of avoiding a substantial risk of prejudice to the administration of justice in those proceedings or in other proceedings pending or imminent; see *Practice Direction*, [1981] 1 All E.R. 64; [1982] 1 W.L.R. 64; *semble* breach of such order could be a contempt of court: *R. v. Horsham Justices, Ex parte Farquharson*, [1982] Q.B. 762; [1982] 2 All E.R. 269.
15 *Ibid.*, s. 5.
16 Cf. *Re. F. (a minor) (publication of information)*, [1977] Fam. 58; [1977] 1 All E.R. 114.
17 *Re Kirby*, [1901] 1 Ch. 467.
18 See pp. 357, 360, *post.*
19 Debtors Act 1869, as amended by Administration of Justice Act 1970, s. 11.
20 *Danchevsky* v. *Danchevsky*, [1975] Fam. 17; [1974] 3 All E.R. 934.
1 Contempt of Court Act 1981, s. 14(1); previously committal could be for an indefinite term. Where the contemnor is under 21 (but not less than 17) the committal is to detention: Criminal Justice Act 1982, s. 9.

Inferior courts of record have more limited powers. They can imprison for up to one month and impose a fine not exceeding £500.[2] Although a county court is for all other purposes an inferior court it is treated as a superior court for this purpose.[3]

The powers of magistrates' courts to commit are contained in section 12 of the 1981 Act. Any person who (*a*) wilfully insults a justice, any witness before or officer of the court or any solicitor or counsel having business in the court, during his or their sitting or attendance in court or in going to or returning from the court; or (*b*) wilfully interrupts the proceedings or otherwise misbehaves in court is liable to be detained until the rising of the court and then to be committed for up to one month and fined up to £500. Appeal lies to the Crown Court.

The Queen's Bench Division, as the successor of the Court of King's Bench, protects inferior courts against contempt by punishing contempts committed in inferior courts.[4]

Until 1960 there was no appeal against punishment for criminal contempt. The law was altered by the Administration of Justice Act 1960, section 13, which provides that the defendant shall have a right of appeal from any order or decision of a court or tribunal in the exercise of jurisdiction to punish for contempt, including criminal contempt. Appeal lies to the Court of Appeal, divisional court or House of Lords as the case may be.

Contempt is punishable, and is often punished, summarily; that is to say by a procedure which is far removed from the ordinary processes of the law. No precise charges are put, often the accused is given no opportunity of consulting lawyers or of an adjournment to prepare his defence. There is no jury and the decision is made by a judge who may himself have been the person insulted. Therefore the Court of Appeal has indicated that the summary jurisdiction should not be used where a more orthodox procedure could be adopted. In the words of LAWTON, L.J.:[5]

> "In my judgment this summary and draconian jurisdiction should only be used for the purpose of ensuring that a trial in progress or about to start can be brought to a proper and dignified end without disturbance and with a fair chance of a just verdict or judgment. Contempts which are not likely to disturb the trial or affect the verdict or judgment can be dealt with by a motion to commit under R.S.C. Ord. 52, or even by indictment."

It should be noted, in conclusion, that punishment for contempt of court is by no means the only legal sanction for abuse of legal process. Many forms

---

2 Contempt of Court Act, s. 14(1), (2).
3 *Ibid.*, s. 14(4A) (added by County Courts (Penalties for Contempt) Act 1983).
4 *R. v. Davies*, [1906] 1 K.B. 32; *R. v. Daily Herald, Ex Parte Bishop of Norwich*, [1932] 2 K.B. 402. The High Court also has statutory power under the Parliamentary Commissioner Act 1967 to deal with a person whom the Commissioner certifies as having been guilty of conduct in the nature of contempt in relation to an investigation held by the Commissioner under the Act. But this jurisdiction only extends to "courts" properly so called, and not to tribunals which are not courts; it may therefore be important to ascertain whether a particular tribunal is or is not a "court": *A.-G. v. British Broadcasting Corporation*, [1981] A.C. 303; [1980] 3 All E.R. 161; see p. 180, *ante*. Note, however, that s. 20 of the 1981 Act extends the jurisdiction to tribunals to which the Tribunals of Inquiry (Evidence) Act 1921 applies.
5 *Balogh v. St Albans Crown Court*, [1975] Q.B. 73, at pp. 92–93; [1974] 3 All E.R. 283, at p. 295.

of conduct which appear to have the characteristics of criminal contempt are not punishable as contempts because they are separate criminal offences. Where they cause damage to another person they may also be torts, although contempt of court is not in itself tortious. Thus a person who intimidates a witness commits a contempt of court but may not be sued by that witness in tort.[6]

---

6 *Chapman* v. *Honig*, [1963] 2 Q.B. 502; [1963] 2 All E.R. 513.

CHAPTER 11

Juries

A HISTORICAL GROWTH OF THE JURY SYSTEM

There is ample evidence that some forms of jury trial existed in England prior to the Norman Conquest. However, although the jury system was not the creation of the common law, it was certainly one of the cornerstones of common law procedure both in civil and criminal trials.

In criminal cases there were, until 1948, two juries. The first of these was the grand jury. The grand jury was not principally a trial jury in the modern sense. It originated in the jury of presentment of the hundred and its function was to present persons for trial before the royal judges at assizes or the justices in quarter sessions.[1] This function was later assumed by justices of the peace in the form of the modern system of preliminary investigation. For this reason the grand jury (of up to 23 members) ceased to be functional and its duties had been reduced virtually to formality long before its abolition. It was virtually abolished by the Administration of Justice (Miscellaneous Provisions) Act 1933, save for a few purposes, and entirely abolished by the Criminal Justice Act 1948.

The second jury in criminal cases was the petty jury (of 12 members). This was the equivalent of the modern trial jury. The trial of criminals by jury evolved in the thirteenth century to replace trial by ordeal, which the Church condemned in 1215.[2] Originally the grand jury of presentment also exercised the function of the trial jury but by the middle of the fourteenth century the petty jury had become distinct from its predecessor. The petty jury was originally summoned for its local knowledge and the members were really witnesses rather than judges of fact. Their function changed gradually as the practice grew of examining independent witnesses and by the fifteenth century the trial jury had assumed its modern function as judges of fact. Nevertheless not until *Bushell's Case* in 1670[3] was it established that jurors could not be punished for returning a verdict contrary to the evidence or the direction of the trial judge.

In civil cases there was only ever one type of jury—the trial jury of 12

---

[1] See p. 16, *ante*.
[2] See p. 17, *ante*.
[3] Vaugh. 135.

members, which had its origins in the Assize of Clarendon 1166.[4] By 1304 it was the rule of the common law courts that all trespass actions had to be tried with a jury. The result was that, with the decline of the real actions and the personal actions of debt and detinue,[5] virtually all actions in the common law courts came to be tried with a jury and this was the position until 1854 when the steady decline of the jury in civil cases began. The function of civil juries was, originally, that of witnesses but, as with criminal juries, a similar transition from witnesses to judges of fact took place.

B JURY TRIAL AT THE PRESENT DAY

Before the present century the jury system was widely pronounced to be one of the chief safeguards of the individual against the abuse of prerogative and judicial power. The vast majority of cases, both civil and criminal, were tried by a jury and this right was thought to be essential and inviolable. Blackstone, writing of the jury in criminal cases, saw the jury as a barrier between the liberties of the people and the prerogative of the Crown.[6] LORD CAMDEN, reflecting the mood of the age, observed:

> "Trial by jury is indeed the foundation of our free constitution; take that away, and the whole fabric will soon moulder into dust."[7]

By the middle of the nineteenth century this concept of the sanctity of jury trial was disappearing. Consequently the jury began to decline as a factor in the administration of justice in both civil and criminal cases. The principal reasons for this decline were the eclipse of the royal prerogative in the administration of justice, the rapid growth in the volume of litigation in civil cases, the even more rapid growth of summary jurisdiction in criminal cases and a general appreciation that juries were both unpredictable and fallible.

1 Criminal cases

In criminal cases the loss of faith in the jury system has been far less marked than in civil cases. The situation is still that a person aged seventeen or over[8] who has a common law right to jury trial cannot, subject to minor exceptions[9] be deprived of that right without his consent. Since all common

---

[4] See p. 30, *ante.*

[5] See pp. 23, 27, *ante.*

[6] 3 Comm. 379.

[7] See Jackson, *The Machinery of Justice in England* (7th Edn.), pp. 481 *et seq.*

[8] There are special provisions for children and young persons: see p. 207, *ante.*

[9] The exceptions are incitement to commit a summary offence (Magistrates' Courts Act 1980, s. 45(1)) and offences of criminal damage, and associated offences, where the value involved does not exceed £200 (*ibid.*, s. 22(2)). The James Committee, which was established in 1973 and reported in 1975 (*The Distribution of Criminal Business between the Crown Court and Magistrates' Courts*: Cmnd. 6323) recommended (*inter alia*) that theft and other related offences where the value of the property concerned was less than £20 should become summary offences; in the face of considerable public opposition provisions to this effect in the original Bill were removed during the passage of the Bill through Parliament; see p. 455, *post.* A committee under the chairmanship of LORD ROSKILL is currently considering whether any modification of the right to jury trial in fraud cases is appropriate.

law offences were triable by jury an accused person still has a right to claim trial by jury for any common law offence, subject to those exceptions. However many offences which were formerly indictable are now triable "either way"[10] and most trials of such offences are, in fact, summary trials. Indeed the number of trials on indictment is very small compared with the number of summary trials. Modern legislation, especially that concerned with road traffic, has created a vast number of summary offences.

2 Civil proceedings

It is in civil actions that the decline of the jury has been most marked. Until 1854 most civil actions in the common law courts had to be tried before a jury. The Common Law Procedure Act 1854 provided for trial by a judge alone but only with the consent of both parties. This trend was continued by the Judicature Acts and by 1933 only about one half of civil actions in the Queen's Bench Division were tried with a jury. The Administration of Justice (Miscellaneous Provisions) Act 1933 was a landmark in the decline of the civil jury. By section 6 of that Act the right to claim a jury in a civil action was limited to cases of libel, slander, malicious prosecution, false imprisonment, seduction or breach of promise of marriage on the application of either party or on the application of a party against whom fraud was alleged.[11] The right to claim jury trial in the Queen's Bench Division in these cases is now contained in section 69 of the Supreme Court Act 1981.[12] Even in these cases a jury may be refused if the court considers that the trial will involve a prolonged examination of documents or accounts or a scientific or local investigation. In all other cases the grant of a jury is at the discretion of the court. It was once the case that this discretion was absolute or "completely untrammelled".[13] However in the leading case of *Ward* v. *James*[14] the full Court of Appeal established that this was not so and that the discretion had, in the same way as any other discretion, to be exercised judicially. Furthermore, the Court of Appeal stated that in actions for damages for personal injuries trial should be by a judge alone in the absence of special circumstances, such as a substantial dispute on the facts. The basic reason for this opposition to jury trial in personal injury cases is the unpredictability of jury awards of damages. Juries, no doubt swayed by the knowledge that the substantive defendant in a "running-down" case is almost always an insurance company[15] with apparently bottomless resources, have sometimes made disproportionate awards to successful plaintiffs in this type of action. It was following two awards of £50,000 to victims in personal injury actions in 1963[16] that the courts became acutely aware of the unsuitability of juries in

---

[10] Criminal Law Act 1977, s. 16; see p. 457, *post*.

[11] Of these, actions for seduction and breach of promise of marriage were abolished by the Law Reform (Miscellaneous Provisions) Act 1970.

[12] See p. 369, *post*. The right is confined to cases in the Queen's Bench Division.

[13] *Hope* v. *Great Western Rail. Co.*, [1937] 2 K.B. 130; [1937] 1 All E.R. 625, *per* LORD WRIGHT, M.R.

[14] [1966] 1 Q.B. 273; [1965] 1 All E.R. 563.

[15] Although the court should not be informed that the defendant in a personal injuries action is insured.

[16] *Warren* v. *King*, [1963] 3 All E.R. 521; [1964] 1 W.L.R. 1; *Morey* v. *Woodfield*, (*No. 2*), [1964] 1 Q.B. 1; [1963] 3 All E.R. 584.

this type of case. Since the majority of actions in the Queen's Bench Division are actions for damages for personal injuries,[17] *Ward* v. *James* is a further landmark in the decline of the civil jury. Immediately before this decision approximately 2 *per cent* of trials in the Queen's Bench Division took place before a jury. The figure is now minimal.

Consequently, in little more than a century, jury trial in civil cases has virtually been superseded by trial by a judge alone. Outside the Queen's Bench Division of the High Court juries are hardly ever encountered in civil actions. The Chancery Amendment Act 1858 provided power to summon a jury in the Court of Chancery. This power was transferred to the Chancery Division by the Judicature Acts but has been totally ignored. There may be a jury in defended divorce petitions and contentious probate proceedings though there seldom is in either type of case. A jury of eight may be summoned in the county court in the same circumstances as in the Queen's Bench Division but this is extremely unusual mainly because of the disproportionately high costs which it would entail. Juries may also be summoned in some of the courts of local jurisdiction. Finally coroners may, in certain cases, and in few cases must,[18] summon a jury of between seven and eleven persons.

Majority verdicts were permitted in criminal cases by the Criminal Justice Act 1967.[19] In civil cases majority verdicts (save by consent of the parties) were not receivable until the Courts Act 1971[19] in effect extended the Criminal Justice Act provisions to civil cases.

C CRITICISMS OF THE JURY SYSTEM

There are several criticisms which are commonly levelled at the present-day jury system, many of which have no doubt been instrumental in its current decline. The most frequent criticism was formerly directed at the composition of juries and, in particular, the existence of a property qualification. Thus, no less eminent an authority than LORD DEVLIN described the jury as "predominantly male, middle-aged, middle-minded and middle-class".[20] These criticisms were, to some extent, met by the Criminal Justice Act 1972 which both abolished the property qualification and extended the age limits for jurors. The relevant provisions are now contained in the Juries Act 1974, a consolidating statute. Under section 1 of this Act the basic provision is that every person is qualified to serve as a juror and liable, when summoned, to attend for jury service, if:

(a) he is registered as a parliamentary or local government elector and is not less than eighteen nor more than sixty-five years of age; and
(b) he has been ordinarily resident in the United Kingdom, the Channel

---

[17] In 1977, of 2,497 actions tried in the Queen's Bench Division 1,836 were personal injuries and Fatal Accidents Act claims.
[18] See Coroners (Amendment) Act 1926, s. 13(2) (as amended by Criminal Law Act 1977, s. 56(2)).
[19] The operative provisions are now contained in the Juries Act 1974, s. 17; see p. 513, *post* as to the procedure.
[20] Devlin, *Trial By Jury*, p. 20.

Islands or the Isle of Man for any period of at least five years since attaining the age of thirteen.

There are, however, provisions relating to ineligibility, disqualification and excusal.[1]

Thus the judiciary, members of the legal profession, court officers, police officers, ministers of religion and the mentally ill are ineligible[2] while persons who have in the last ten years served any part of a sentence of imprisonment, youth custody or detention, being a sentence of three months or more or have been to borstal or have received a suspended sentence or had imposed on them a community service order or who have at any time been sentenced to custody for life or to a term of imprisonment or youth custody for a term of five years or more are disqualified from jury service.[3]

In addition to those who are ineligible or disqualified certain persons, notably members of Parliament, serving members of the armed forces and medical practitioners, may be excused from jury service if they so wish.[4]

Thus the compositions of juries has radically changed; there are, for example, far more women sitting on juries nowadays as a result of the removal of the property qualification. Nevertheless there remain certain common prejudices which are alleged to exist in juries. The tendency to high awards of damages to victims of motor accidents has already been noted. There is also alleged to be a bias against newspapers in libel actions and against the police in malicious prosecution and false imprisonment suits. On the other hand juries are commonly supposed to sympathise with the motorist in criminal prosecutions under the Road Traffic Acts. Other commonly encountered criticisms of juries are their susceptibility to rhetoric and their lack of experience in weighing evidence. These are the factors which have led to the establishment of the Roskill Committee to consider whether any modification of the right to jury trial in fraud cases is appropriate.

A further criticism, particularly in relation to juries in criminal trials in London and other cities, is that, despite the disqualification provisions, jurors with criminal tendencies and indeed criminal records may still serve on juries and may contribute to perverse acquittals, or at any rate disagreements. The introduction of majority verdicts in criminal cases went some way to meeting this criticism. Jury "nobbling", where it is discovered, is severely punished (as the common law offence of embracery or, more commonly, perverting the course of public justice). Finally reference may be made to the controversial practice of "jury vetting" and the Attorney-General's guidelines relating thereto.[5]

Nor is the system popular with most jurors themselves. The compulsory element of jury service is undoubtedly unpopular with many because of the

---

1　The verdict of a jury is not void only because a juror was disqualified from jury service and no verdict can be challenged on the ground that a juror was not included in the relevant list of jurors or was misnamed or misdescribed or (unless objection was taken at the time) that the provisions of the Act as to the impanelling or selection of jurors has not been complied with (Juries Act 1974, s. 18).
2　The full list is contained in Sch. 1, Part 1 of the 1974 Act.
3　Act of 1974, Sch. 1, Part II (as amended).
4　For full details of the excusal provisions see Act of 1974, ss. 8–9 and Sch. 1, Part III.
5　See p. 508, *post*.

loss of time and money it may involve, although jurors are paid travelling and subsistence allowances and compensation for loss of earnings.[6]

Nevertheless, despite these criticisms, the jury remains a fundamental of the English legal system. LORD DENNING, M.R. in *Ward* v. *James* explained the place of the modern jury as follows.[7]

> "Let it not be supposed that this court is in any way opposed to trial by jury. It has been the bulwark of our liberties too long for any of us to seek to alter it. Whenever a man is on trial for serious crime, or when in a civil case a man's honour or integrity is at stake, or when one or other party must be deliberately lying, then trial by jury has no equal."

---

[6] See Juries Act 1974, s. 19. "Special juries" whose members were paid and specially qualified were finally abolished by the Courts Act 1971, s. 40(1).

[7] [1966] 1 Q.B. 273, at p. 295; [1965] 1 All E.R. 563, at p. 571.

CHAPTER 12

The Legal Profession

A · THE DIVISION OF THE LEGAL PROFESSION

A distinctive feature of the English legal system is the division of the legal profession into two separate branches—solicitors and barristers. This precise division is unknown outside Britain and the Commonwealth. Elsewhere all practitioners are described as "lawyers", a word which has no particular application in England. The division of the legal profession dates back to about 1340, the time at which professional advocacy evolved.[1] The advocates with audience in the common law courts were the serjeants[2] and barristers while the preparatory stages of an action were carried through by officers of the court in question known as attorneys. There thus developed two classes of legal practitioner; serjeants and barristers on the one hand and attorneys who were, as solicitors still are, officers of the court. Solicitors, as distinct from attorneys, first appeared in the fifteenth century and practised in the Court of Chancery. They were, at first, inferior to attorneys and could not bind their clients as attorneys could. By the eighteenth century the offices of attorney and solicitor were frequently held by the same person and the distinction between them was finally abolished by the Judicature Act 1873.

The separation of barristers and solicitors was preserved by the Inns of Court. Barristers had to be members of one of the Inns of Court and these Inns, after the sixteenth century, refused to admit attorneys or solicitors to membership. As a result the latter banded together and by 1739 had formed their own professional organisation in London. This was styled "The Society of Gentlemen Practisers in the Courts of Law and Equity" and was the forerunner of The Law Society.

Thus the separation of the legal profession has an historical foundation as has the nature of the respective functions which barristers and solicitors perform. Barristers are still primarily advocates, although many barristers in fact spend most of their time engaged in "paper-work" such as the drafting of pleadings, divorce petitions, complex settlements and opinions on special-

---

[1] For details of the history of the emergence of both branches of the profession, see Baker, *An Introduction to English Legal History* (2nd Edn.), pp. 133–143.

[2] Serjeants (*servientes regis ad legem*) were the senior advocates and had exclusive audience in the Court of Common Pleas. The rank of serjeant was abolished by the Judicature Act 1873.

ised matters such as taxation and company law. Solicitors deal with the preparatory stages of litigation such as the preparation of evidence, interviewing witnesses, issuing writs and, usually, conducting interlocutory proceedings. Solicitors have a right of audience in most courts and tribunals; this does not, however, extend to the Court of Appeal or to most proceedings in open court (as opposed to chambers) in the High Court, and rights of audience in the Crown Court are limited to such proceedings as the Lord Chancellor may direct.[3] In addition solicitors deal with a large number of non-litigious matters such as the drafting of wills, the supervision of trusts and settlements, the administration of estates and, above all, conveyancing.

There are other important distinctions between the two branches of the profession. Solicitors may enter into partnership; barristers may not. Solicitors, since they stand in a contractual relationship to their clients, may sue for their fees; barristers, whose fees are regarded as honorary rather than contractual payments, may not. Barristers appear in court (other than magistrates' courts) in wig and gown; solicitors appear in gown in certain courts, notably the county court, but are never bewigged. Solicitors are instructed by their clients directly; barristers may be instructed only by a solicitor and not by a lay client direct.[4]

Royal Commission on Legal Services

In 1976 a Royal Commission was set up to inquire into the law and practice relating to the provision of legal services in England, Wales and Northern Ireland to consider whether, and if so what, changes were desirable in the public interest in the structure, organisation, training, regulation of and entry to the legal profession.

The Commission produced its final report in October 1979.[5] Its conclusions and recommendations were (surprisingly, to some) basically favourable to the status quo, although it found that the distribution of legal services was uneven and the quality not uniform. Its recommendations have had little impact to date.

The Commission summarised its observations on the quality of service in the following words:[6]

> "The evidence before us shows that year by year most legal work is transacted well and efficiently. Most clients are satisfied with the service they receive. The judiciary is in general able to rely on the quality of work performed in the courts. City institutions, including The Stock Exchange, the British Bankers' Association and the Committee on Invisible Exports told us that the legal services available in London are of a high standard; this attracts legal and other business from abroad which contributes to our invisible exports."

---

[3] Supreme Court Act 1981, s. 83; see *Practice Direction* (*Crown Court: Right of Audience*), [1972] 1 All E.R. 608; [1972] 1 W.L.R. 307. Full details of the courts and tribunals in which solicitors have a right of audience may be found in 44 *Halsbury's Laws of England* (4th Edn.), paras. 68–70.

[4] This is a custom rather than a rule of law but is, nevertheless, strictly observed. It is a custom of fairly recent origin for, until the eighteenth century, it was customary for counsel to be instructed directly by lay clients.

[5] Report of the Royal Commission on Legal Services (Cmnd. 7648). For a summary of the principal recommendations, see 129 New Law Journal 964, 988.

[6] Report, para. 22.16.

Having said that, the Commission went on to point to certain shortcomings in the service and to suggest some remedies.[7] In particular it pointed to unacceptable delays in contentious business and noted that in the Queen's Bench Division the average lapse of time between cause of action and trial was four years. It decried "repetitious cross-examination, labouring points good and bad and general prolixity" and suggested that the remedy lay in good education and training, self-discipline, adequate research and careful preparation. It recommended *inter alia* that both solicitor and barrister should advise specifically on whether a conference before the day of trial was necessary for the proper presentation of a case (it being an occasional complaint of litigants, especially defendants in criminal cases, that they do not meet their counsel until shortly before the hearing on the day of trial), that measures should be taken to prevent parties being taken by surprise by offers of settlement at the door of the court, that The Law Society should issue guidelines on methods of office administration, that practising solicitors should plan ahead to meet the increasing need for specialisation and that written Professional Standards should be issued by both branches of the profession, failure to observe which would involve disciplinary proceedings.

On the controversial issue of fusion, the Commission recommended against it on the grounds that there would be an unacceptable reduction in the number and spread of smaller firms of solicitors and an increase in the proportion of large city firms, that while there might be some saving in small cases, in large ones the expense might be greater and, with regard to the administration of justice that:

> "a two-branch profession is more likely than a fused one to ensure the high quality of advocacy which is indispensable, so long as our system remains in its present form, to secure the proper quality of justice."[8]

As to solicitors' practising arrangements, the Commission recommended that partnership between solicitors and members of other professions should not be permitted, that incorporation of a solicitor's business with limited liability should not be permitted but that incorporation with unlimited liability should, subject to certain safeguards,[9] that legal executives should continue to perform their functions as the employees of solicitors, but not as independent practitioners,[10] that The Law Society should introduce duty solicitor schemes in all magistrates' courts,[11] that a system of citizens' law centres should be established to provide legal services, particularly in relation to social welfare law (but not to undertake community work and campaigns),[12] that the so-called "conveyancing monopoly" should be retained but with a reversion to scale charges[13] and that there should be no general extension of solicitors' rights of audience.[14] Finally the Commission made detailed recommendations on the subject of disciplinary procedures,[15] in

---

[7] Report, paras. 22.17–22.75.
[8] *Ibid.*, paras. 17.45–17.46.
[9] *Ibid.*, paras. 30.15–30.28.
[10] *Ibid.*, para. 31.26.
[11] *Ibid.*, para. 9.9.
[12] *Ibid.*, paras. 8.15–8.38.
[13] *Ibid.*, paras. 21.28–21.101.
[14] *Ibid.*, para. 18.60.
[15] *Ibid.*, paras. 25.8–25.45.

particular that The Law Society should take action when cases of bad professional work are brought to its notice, that The Law Society should ensure that independent legal advice is available for those who allege negligence against solicitors, that within The Law Society the processes of investigation and adjudication of complaints should be separated and that laymen should be involved in these processes; there were also recommendations on the subject of charges.[16]

Nor were the recommendations affecting barristers any more radical. Here again the Commission recommended that, in relation to disciplinary procedure, the processes of investigation and adjudication of complaints should be separated and that the Senate should have the responsibility of taking action when cases of bad professional work are brought to its notice.[17] It recommended that all barristers should be required to have professional indemnity insurance against negligence claims,[18] should not be compelled to have a clerk,[19] that the organisation and functions of the circuits should be reviewed[20] and that the existing restriction against partnership at the bar should be retained, as should the two-tier system of silks and juniors.[1]

Reference may also be made to the impact of European community law, since there is now provision whereby, under certain conditions, lawyers qualified in other E.E.C. member states may provide services in the United Kingdom which could otherwise be provided only by barristers and solicitors.[2]

B SOLICITORS

1 The Law Society

The controlling body in the case of solicitors is The Law Society, constituted under a Royal Charter of 1845 as amended by supplemental charters,[3] and being given the name "The Law Society" by the Supplemental Charter of 1903. Membership of the Society is voluntary although more than 85 per cent of the solicitors currently in practice are, in fact, members of the Society. The Society is governed by the President, Vice-President and a Council of not more than 70 members, the latter being elected for a period of five years; at present there are 70 members, of whom 56 are elected to represent constituencies and 14 are elected by the Council itself as specialists.

The objects of the Society remain, as defined in the Charter of 1845, as "promoting professional improvement and facilitating the acquisition of

---

[16] *Ibid.*, paras. 37.14–37.68.
[17] *Ibid.*, paras. 26.13, 26.18.
[18] *Ibid.*, para. 24.11. The Bar gave effect to this in 1983, since when failure to be properly insured has constituted professional misconduct; the cover must be for not less than £250,000 for each and every claim.
[19] *Ibid.*, para. 34.7.
[20] *Ibid.*, para. 32.54.
[1] *Ibid.*, paras. 33.66, 33.84.
[2] European Communities (Services of Lawyers) Order 1978 (S.I. 1978 No. 1910), giving effect to Council Directive 77/249, with effect from 1 March 1979. A client wishing to retain an E.E.C. lawyer to act for him, either in the capacity of barrister or solicitor, must also retain a home barrister or solicitor, as the case may be, to act with the E.E.C. lawyer. The E.E.C. lawyer cannot act as both barrister and solicitor in the same or related proceedings.
[3] In 1872, 1903, 1909 and 1954.

legal knowledge". Notwithstanding its voluntary composition The Law Society has statutory powers in respect of all solicitors and in certain matters affecting the public generally. These powers derive mainly from the Solicitors Act 1974, a consolidating statute.

By section 2 of the 1974 Act the Society may, with the concurrence of the Lord Chancellor, the Lord Chief Justice and the Master of the Rolls, make "training regulations" about education and training for persons seeking to be admitted or to practise as solicitors. Training regulations may relate to education and training, whether by service under articles or otherwise, to be undergone by persons seeking admission as solicitors or by persons who have already been admitted. A person wishing to enter into articles must satisfy the Society as to his character and suitability[4] and no person may be admitted as a solicitor until he has obtained a certificate that the Society is satisfied that he has complied with training regulations (which will involve satisfactory completion of articles, legal education and examinations) and is satisfied as to his character and his suitability to be a solicitor of the Supreme Court. The Society maintains the Roll of Solicitors and, in order to practise as a solicitor, a person must have his name on the Roll and hold a current practising certificate.

Section 32 of the Act requires the Council of The Law Society to make rules[5] governing the handling by solicitors of clients' and certain trust moneys and the right to interest thereon. Section 34 requires the Council to make rules governing the annual submission by solicitors of an accountant's report.[6] Section 31 empowers the Council to make rules regulating professional practice, conduct and discipline.[7]

As well as exercising these powers and duties The Law Society also looks after the welfare of solicitors generally and attempts to maintain good relations with other bodies and with the public. To this end the Council examines the activities of unqualified persons doing the work of solicitors and, in appropriate cases, institutes proceedings. It also organises refresher lectures on changes in the law, annual study courses, study groups and pamphlets on certain matters of general importance to solicitors, such as new legislation.

The only matters concerning solicitors which are not within the province of The Law Society are scales of remuneration, which are fixed by statute, and disciplinary proceedings, which are dealt with by the Solicitors Disciplinary Tribunal, an independent statutory body.

In addition to its control over its own members and other solicitors the Society in at least two spheres protects the interests of the public generally. First it administers the Legal Aid and Advice Scheme[8] and secondly it maintains a Compensation Fund[9] out of which it may make a hardship grant to

---

4   For this purpose there is an interviewing panel nominated by the Society.
5   The present rules are the Solicitors' Accounts Rules 1975, the Solicitors' Trust Accounts Rules 1975 and the Solicitors' Accounts (Deposit Interest) Rules 1975.
6   The present rules are the Accountant's Report Rules 1975.
7   See Solicitors Practice Rules 1936–1975.
8   The Royal Commission on Legal Services recommended that this should continue (Report, para. 6(9)).
9   Solicitors Act 1974, s. 36 and Sch. 2. The fund is made up of special annual contributions payable by solicitors on application for practising certificates. The Royal Commission found the present compensation arrangements satisfactory (Report, para. 23.15).

any person who suffers hardship through the failure of a solicitor to account for money due in connection with his practice as a solicitor or with any trust of which he is a trustee. The result is that members of the public are indemnified against loss which might be suffered as a result of any solicitor's default in the handling of their moneys. The Law Society is subrogated to the rights and remedies of the person to whom the grant was made to the extent of the grant.

By way of further protection of the public, the Society has power to take over and reorganise the practice of any solicitor who cannot safely be relied upon to continue the handling of his clients' affairs,[10] while the Council may, with the concurrence of the Master of the Rolls, make "indemnity rules" providing for the indemnity of solicitors against professional liability by the establishment of a mutual fund, by commercial insurance effected by the Society, by requiring solicitors themselves to insure or by any combination of these methods.[11]

The combined effect of the provisions above referred to is to afford to members of the public comprehensive protection against the possibility of financial loss resulting from the default or neglect of any solicitor.

2 Liabilities of a solicitor

a Liability to disciplinary proceedings

Solicitors are, of course, subject to the general criminal law. However, conduct on the part of a solicitor which falls short of a criminal offence may still result in sanctions. These are usually enforced by the Solicitors Disciplinary Tribunal although, since solicitors are officers of the Supreme Court, the High Court and Court of Appeal have inherent jurisdiction to strike the name of a solicitor from the roll or suspend him for misconduct.[12] In addition to this inherent jurisdiction the High Court has a limited statutory jurisdiction in disciplinary matters. The High Court must strike off the Roll the name of a solicitor who wilfully and knowingly assists an unqualified person to practise or act as a solicitor;[13] it must strike off the Roll or suspend from practice a person who, without the written permission of The Law Society, knowingly employs a person who has been struck off the Roll

---

[10] Solicitors Act 1974, s. 35 and Sch. 1; this important power was introduced by the Solicitors (Amendment) Act 1974. The circumstances in which the Society can intervene are detailed in Part I of Sch. 1 but can briefly be summarised as dishonesty, undue delay on the part of the personal representatives of a deceased solicitor, failure to comply with the rules referred to on p. 252, fn. 5 (*supra*), bankruptcy, imprisonment, removal from or striking off the roll or suspension from practice.

[11] *Ibid.*, s. 37; this was a further important innovation effected by the Solicitors (Amendment) Act 1974. The current rules are the Solicitors Indemnity Rules 1984 under which The Law Society maintains a "master policy" of indemnity insurance on behalf of all solicitors required to be insured, practising solicitors being required to make a fixed contribution annually by way of premium. The limit of indemnity for the basic premium under the 1984 policy was £100,000 each claim for a sole practitioner and £50,000 each claim per partner in a partnership. The scheme is by no means universally popular among practising solicitors and an unsuccessful attempt to have it declared *ultra vires* was made in *Swain* v. *The Law Society*, [1983] 1 A.C. 598; [1982] 2 All E.R. 827.

[12] This jurisdiction is preserved by the Solicitors Act 1974, s. 50(2).

[13] Solicitors Act 1974, s. 39(2).

involuntarily or suspended from practice.[14] However the Tribunal has, in all these cases, corresponding jurisdiction and, since it also has a wider jurisdiction than the High Court, proceedings are generally instituted before the Tribunal.

The Solicitors Disciplinary Tribunal is constituted by the Master of the Rolls from "solicitor members" who must be practising solicitors of not less than ten years' standing and "lay members" who must be neither solicitors nor barristers.[15] It is, nonetheless, independent of The Law Society. The Tribunal is a judicial tribunal and proceedings before it are absolutely privileged for the purposes of the law of defamation.[16] There is a quorum of three members of whom at least one must be a lay member, although the number of solicitor members present must exceed the number of lay members present; the Tribunal may receive evidence on oath and compel the attendance of witnesses by subpoena. It may also, with the concurrence of the Master of the Rolls, make rules regulating its own procedure.

Its jurisdiction is threefold. First, it hears applications to strike the name of a solicitor off the Roll, or to require him to answer allegations contained in an affidavit, or by a former solicitor whose name has been struck off the Roll to have his name restored to the Roll.[17] Secondly, it hears complaints by another party against a solicitor based either upon common law disciplinary offences of professional misconduct or upon specific offences under the 1974 Act, such as failure to comply with the Solicitors' Accounts Rules or the Solicitors' Trust Accounts Rules[18] or making a false statement in a declaration for obtaining a practising certificate.[19]

Finally, the Tribunal hears applications by The Law Society under section 43 of the Act to restrain the employment by solicitors, without the written permission of The Law Society, of clerks who have been convicted of criminal offences of dishonesty rendering their employment in a solicitor's practice undesirable or have been parties to disciplinary offences by solicitors.

The major part of the Tribunal's business is concerned with the second type of matter—complaints against solicitors in respect of professional misconduct or offences under the Solicitors Act 1974. In dealing with these applications the Tribunal may make such order as it thinks fit. In particular it may strike the solicitor's name off the Roll, suspend him from practice, order him to pay a penalty not exceeding £3,000, to be forfeit to Her Majesty, and order him to pay a reasonable contribution towards the costs of the proceedings.[20] In two cases the punishment imposable by the Tribunal is

---

[14] *Ibid.*, s. 41(4).

[15] *Ibid.*, s. 46; the Tribunal is successor of the Solicitors Disciplinary Committee which existed until 1974. The provision for "lay members" was to allay public criticism of the system whereby complaints against solicitors were investigated exclusively by solicitors; with the same object, section 45 of the Act permits the Lord Chancellor to appoint "lay observers" to examine written allegations made by members of the public concerning the Society's treatment of complaints made about solicitors or their employees.

[16] *Addis* v. *Crocker*, [1961] 1 Q.B. 11; [1960] 2 All E.R. 629.

[17] Solicitors Act 1974, s. 47(1).

[18] *Ibid.*, s. 32(3).

[19] *Ibid.*, s. 9(5).

[20] *Ibid.*, s. 47(2). The Lord Chancellor may vary the sum of £3,000 by statutory instrument, having regard to any change in the value of money (*ibid.*, s. 47(4), (5), added by Administration of Justice Act 1982, s. 56).

mandatory. It must strike off the Roll a solicitor who has committed an offence under s. 39 of the Act (assisting an unqualified person to practise) and it must either strike off or suspend from practice a solicitor who has committed an offence under s. 41 (employment of a person involuntarily disqualified from practice).

Any party may appeal from the decision of the Solicitors Disciplinary Tribunal to a divisional court of the Queen's Bench Division[1] and thence, with leave of either that court or the Court of Appeal, to the Court of Appeal.[2] Where the application is to restrain the employment of a clerk under s. 43, appeal lies only at the instance of the clerk and the decision of the High Court is final.

b Liability as an officer of the court

As stated above, the Supreme Court has both an inherent and a limited statutory jurisdiction over solicitors since they are officers of the Supreme Court. This jurisdiction is merged in the wider jurisdiction of the Disciplinary Tribunal. In addition to this jurisdiction, the sanction for which is striking off the Roll, the High Court has further powers to impose liability upon solicitors as court officers. Thus solicitors may be, and sometimes are, ordered to pay personally costs thrown away by their neglect or improperly incurred. These costs may be made payable either to the solicitor's own client or to a third party. This provision is both punitive and compensatory so that a solicitor may be ordered to pay costs even where the defaulting party is his partner or a clerk.[3] Examples of the type of default which may render a solicitor personally liable for costs are: failing to warn the court that an action has been settled or postponed, entering into a champertous agreement, acting for both sides in an action and instituting proceedings without his client's authority.

A solicitor may also be liable, as an officer of the court, for loss occasioned by his negligence or breach of duty.[4] This liability may be summarily enforced by any party who has suffered loss. This may be compared with the general civil liability of a solicitor to his client, discussed below, which is enforceable by civil proceedings.

A further way in which a solicitor may incur liability as an officer of the court is by giving an undertaking to the court or in his capacity as a solicitor. The court often makes an order, or refrains from making an order, on the faith of a personal undertaking by a solicitor appearing; for example, an undertaking to stamp a document or an unconditional undertaking not to issue execution if payment of a judgment debt is expedited. The court will enforce a solicitor's undertaking summarily, not as a contractual obligation but in order to secure the proper conduct of its officers. An undertaking to

---

[1] *Ibid.*, s. 49(1), save that appeal is to the Master of the Rolls against an order restoring or refusing to restore to the Roll the name of a solicitor who has been struck off or an order revoking or refusing to revoke an order made under s. 43.

[2] Supreme Court Act 1981, s. 18(1)(e).

[3] *Myers* v. *Elman*, [1940] A.C. 282; [1939] 4 All E.R. 484 where it was made clear that the jurisdiction ought only to be exercised in cases of "serious dereliction of duty" by a solicitor or his employee; cf. *Thew (R. & T.) Ltd.* v. *Reeves (No. 2)*, [1982] Q.B. 1283; [1982] 3 All E.R. 1086.

[4] *Marsh* v. *Joseph*, [1897] 1 Ch. 213.

pay money is an obligation *sui generis* enforceable summarily by the court and is neither a contractual obligation nor a judgment debt.[5]

Finally a solicitor is liable to be committed for contempt of court. A solicitor's liability for contempt of court is basically no different from the liability of laymen. Nevertheless solicitors, because of their close association with the court, may be guilty of contempt in a wider variety of ways. Furthermore there are various statutes and rules which impose special liability to committal upon a solicitor, for example for neglecting to inform his client of a judgment against the latter or for defaulting on an order to pay costs personally for misconduct.[6] Failure to comply with an undertaking is a contempt of court as well as rendering the solicitor liable to perform his undertaking.

c   Civil liability

The solicitor, by his position, may render himself liable to civil proceedings either at the suit of his client or of some third party, in a variety of ways. The duty which the solicitor owes to his own client is an incident of the solicitor-client relationship and is dealt with in the following section.

There are, in addition, several ways in which a solicitor may incur civil liability to persons other than his own client. In contract the solicitor's liability to third parties is governed usually by the ordinary law of agency. Thus if the solicitor contracts on behalf of an undisclosed client, the other party may elect to sue either the solicitor or the client.[7] If the solicitor acts without authority on behalf of a client he may, in accordance with general principles, be sued for breach of warranty of authority.[8] An exception to the general law of agency is that the solicitor is personally responsible for certain items of expenditure even though incurred as agent for his client, such as experts' fees and the costs of a shorthand writer. A solicitor's liability in tort is governed by the general law of torts. Thus, for example, a solicitor who fraudulently induces a third party to buy an estate with a defective title commits the tort of deceit. The position of solicitors in the tort of negligence is uncertain. The question is the extent of a solicitor's liability for negligence in accordance with the principles stated by the House of Lords in *Hedley Byrne & Co., Ltd.* v. *Heller & Partners, Ltd.*[9] It has been held, at first instance, that there is liability in negligence where the plaintiff is the client of the defendant solicitor[10] and it has been held at first

---

[5] *Re Hudson*, [1966] Ch. 209; [1966] 1 All E.R. 110. However the obligation will only be enforced summarily in clear cases; in cases where there is a triable issue the plaintiff must bring an action in the normal way: *Silver and Drake* v. *Baines*, [1971] 1 Q.B. 396; [1971] 1 All E.R. 473.

[6] Debtors Act 1869, s. 4(4).

[7] *Foster* v. *Cranfield* (1911), 46 L.Jo. 314. A solicitor has ostensible authority to bind his client to compromise of an action (whether or not he has actual authority so to do). Consequently, if an action is compromised on terms the client is bound by those terms and the other party may enforce them: cf. *Waugh* v. *H.B. Clifford & Sons, Ltd.*, [1982] Ch. 374; [1982] 1 All E.R. 1095.

[8] *Yonge* v. *Toynbee*, [1910] 1 K.B. 215.

[9] [1964] A.C. 465; [1963] 2 All E.R. 575.

[10] *Midland Bank Trust Co., Ltd.* v. *Hett, Stubbs and Kemp*, [1979] Ch. 384; [1978] 3 All E.R. 571, applying *Hedley Byrne* (*supra*) and *Arenson* v. *Casson Beckman Rutley & Co.*, [1977] A.C. 405; [1975] 3 All E.R. 901 and not following *Groom* v. *Crocker*, [1939] 1 K.B. 194; [1938] 2 All E.R. 394 and *Clark* v. *Kirby-Smith*, [1964] Ch. 506; [1964] 2 All E.R. 835.

instance[11] that there may be liability in tort in respect of negligent advice or conduct where there is no contractual relationship between the solicitor and the plaintiff.

3 Incidents of the solicitor-client relationship

a *Solicitor's duty of care to his client*

A solicitor's authority derives from the retainer given to him by his client. The effect of this retainer is to create a contractual relationship between the solicitor and the client. In most respects this relationship is, therefore, subject to the ordinary law of contract and in particular to that part of contract law concerning agency since the relationship created is, for purposes within the scope of the retainer, a principal and agent relationship. Consequently the solicitor has a right to be indemnified by his client for acts done within the scope of his authority. The solicitor's duty subsists throughout the period of his retainer. The general rule is that when retained the solicitor undertakes to complete the transaction for which he is retained. Thus a specific retainer is an entire contract with the result that, unless there is some express agreement to the contrary, the solicitor is not entitled to his remuneration until the transaction is completed (although he is entitled to be put in funds for disbursements) and if he wrongfully withdraws from the retainer he will not be entitled to a *quantum meruit* for the work he has done. However, it is now provided[12] that a solicitor engaged to conduct contentious business may require payment of a reasonable amount on account of costs and if the client refuses or fails to make that payment the solicitor may, upon giving reasonable notice to the client, withdraw from the retainer. The solicitor must then have his name withdrawn from the court record since until he does so he remains in the position of the party's solicitor *quoad* the court and the other parties to the action, with all the duties and potential liabilities that that position entails.[13]

If the solicitor is negligent the client may have an action against him for damages. Indeed, as one writer observed;[14]

> "The pursuit of actions for negligence, once rare occurrences, has now become the pastime of the disgruntled client whose affairs have gone wrong whether through ill luck, his own fault or otherwise, and no professional man or indeed technician is safe from them."

The action lies in contract and, almost certainly, in tort as well.[10] In *Rondel* v. *Worsley*[15] the majority opinion of the House of Lords was that a

---

[11] *Ross* v. *Caunters*, [1980] Ch. 297; [1979] 3 All E.R. 580 (solicitor who drew up will liable to beneficiary in respect of loss of benefit due to defects in attestation).

[12] By Solicitors Act 1974, s. 65(2).

[13] Where, the retainer having ended, the client retains a new solicitor he must file a notice of change of solicitor; where he intends to act in person he must file a notice of intention to act in person. If he files neither of these notices, then the outgoing solicitor must apply to the court for an order declaring that he has ceased to be the solicitor acting for that party; for the procedure in the High Court see R.S.C. O. 67, r. 6.

[14] *Cordery on Solicitors* (6th Edn.), p. 148.

[15] [1969] 1 A.C. 191; [1967] 3 All E.R. 993.

solicitor should not be liable for negligence in carrying out work in litigation which would have been carried out by counsel, had counsel been engaged in the case. This was confirmed by the majority of the House of Lords in *Saif Ali* v. *Sydney Mitchell & Co.*[16]

b   Fiduciary obligations

The solicitor-client relationship is regarded in equity as a fiduciary one. Several consequences flow from this. In general the solicitor must act in good faith in all dealings with his client. This involves making a full and honest disclosure of facts within the solicitor's knowledge in any financial transaction with his client. This principle derives from the equitable doctrine of fraud and has differing consequences which depend upon the nature of the transaction.

The principle is at its strongest in the case of gifts to the solicitor by his client. There is a presumption of undue influence in the case of such a gift, the effect of which is to make the gift voidable at the instance of the client. The solicitor can retain the gift only by showing that it was made after the fiduciary relationship had ceased, or that it was ratified by the client after the relationship had ceased or that the client had independent legal advice.[17]

This presumption of undue influence, which applies to gifts *inter vivos*, does not apply to gifts by will although any person may allege and prove actual undue influence by the solicitor. Nevertheless, where a solicitor prepares a will under which he receives a large benefit the court requires affirmative proof that the testator knew and fully approved of the contents of the will.[18] Where a client intends to give a large benefit to a solicitor in his will the latter should insist on the will being prepared by another solicitor.[19]

A purchase by a solicitor from his client, or a sale to his client, is not necessarily bad but the solicitor must show that the bargain is as good as the client could have obtained with due diligence elsewhere in order to rebut the presumption of undue influence. This means that the price must be fair and that the solicitor must make a full disclosure. In practice the solicitor should see that the client has independent advice. Similar conditions apply to loans between solicitor and client.[20]

c   Obligations to preserve confidence

One particular aspect of the fiduciary relationship between solicitor and client is the confidential nature of communications between them. This gives rise to two types of privilege; privilege in the tort of defamation and privilege from disclosure in evidence.

For the purposes of the law of defamation professional communications between solicitor and client are undoubtedly privileged though it is not

---

16 [1980] A.C. 198; [1978] 3 All E.R. 1033.

17 *Gibson* v. *Jeyes* (1801), 6 Ves. 266; *Lancashire Loans, Ltd.* v. *Black*, [1934] 1 K.B. 380.

18 *Wintle* v. *Nye*, [1959] 1 All E.R. 552; [1959] 1 W.L.R. 284.

19 Failure to comply with these fiduciary obligations will invariably be regarded as serious professional misconduct and the offending solicitor is liable to be struck off the Roll; see, for example, *Re A Solicitor*, [1975] Q.B. 475; [1974] 3 All E.R. 853.

20 See, generally, *Cordery on Solicitors* (7th Edn.), pp. 9–29; cf. *Spector* v. *Ageda*, [1973] Ch. 30; [1971] 3 All E.R. 417.

finally decided whether this privilege is absolute or only qualified, i.e., rebuttable by proof of malice. The Court of Appeal in *More* v. *Weaver*[1] held the privilege to be absolute, but the House of Lords in *Minter* v. *Priest*[2] expressly left the point open and the better view probably is that the privilege is only qualified.[3] In this event it is rebuttable by malice but the malice of a client is not attributable to his solicitor.[4]

The second category of privilege is privilege from disclosure in evidence of communications, oral or written, which are made between the client and his solicitor in a professional capacity. This privilege is for the protection of the client rather than the solicitor and exists so that the client may make the fullest disclosure to his solicitor. The client (but not the solicitor) may waive the privilege and, in addition, it is lost if the communication is made in furtherance of a criminal purpose, for example criminal conspiracy or an unlawful threat by the client to his solicitor. The privilege does not extend to collateral matters not disclosed confidentially such as the client's name and address. However where the privilege does exist it does not end with the termination of any proceedings to which it relates, nor with the termination of the retainer, nor with the death of the client.[5]

With these privileges, which exist for the better operation of the solicitor and client relationship, may be compared the wider privilege which attaches to all statements made in the course of judicial proceedings, such as statements made by a solicitor or witness to the court. This privilege exists for the better operation of the judicial system and its effect is to confer absolute immunity from proceedings in defamation and other torts.[6] It does not, however, create evidential privilege, except in relation to those proceedings to which the statement relates.

So stringent is the solicitor's professional duty to maintain his client's confidences that he should not disclose a communication by his client to the effect that the latter has committed a criminal offence. His duty to his client in such a case overrides his public duty and he would not be guilty of any criminal offence by reason of his non-disclosure.[7]

---

[1] [1928] 2 K.B. 520.

[2] [1930] A.C. 558.

[3] But see observations of DEVLIN, L.J., (as he then was) in *Lincoln* v. *Daniels*, [1962] 1 Q.B. 237, at p. 260; [1961] 3 All E.R. 740, at p. 751.

[4] *Egger* v. *Viscount Chelmsford*, [1965] 1 Q.B. 248; [1964] 3 All E.R. 406.

[5] *Bullivant* v. *A.-G. for Victoria*, [1901] A.C. 196.

[6] *Lincoln* v. *Daniels*, [1962] 1 Q.B. 237; [1961] 3 All E.R. 740; *Marrinan* v. *Vibart*, [1963] 1 Q.B. 528; [1962] 3 All E.R. 380; *Roy* v. *Prior*, [1971] A.C. 470; [1969] 3 All E.R. 1153.

[7] *Sykes* v. *Director of Public Prosecutions*, [1962] A.C. 528, at p. 564; [1961] 3 All E.R. 533, at p. 564, *per* LORD DENNING. However the duty yields to a contrary statutory provision; thus a solicitor's duty to produce his books of account to The Law Society for inspection overrides his contractual duty not to disclose his client's affairs: *Parry-Jones* v. *Law Society*, [1968] Ch. 195; [1968] 1 All E.R. 177; similarly, the fact that documents are, or may be, privileged does not prevent the police from seizing them if they are documents which the police have power to seize in the course of a search; *Frank Truman Export, Ltd.* v. *Metropolitan Police Commissioner*, [1977] Q.B. 952; [1977] 3 All E.R. 431; since the privilege is that of the client, the solicitor cannot claim any privilege which would not have availed the client himself: *R.* v. *Justice of the Peace for Peterborough, Ex parte Hicks*, [1978] 1 All E.R. 225; [1977] 1 W.L.R. 1371. As to the extent to which E.E.C. law recognises legal professional privilege, see *A.M. & S. Europe, Ltd.* v. *Commission of the European Communities*, [1983] Q.B. 878; [1983] 1 All E.R. 705 in which the European Court held that a general power to require

4 Remuneration

Solicitors are entitled to remuneration for their services. However the way in which this remuneration is assessed and recovered is not primarily governed by the ordinary law of contract even though the right to remuneration arises out of a contractual relationship. It is governed by various statutes and rules, passed generally for the benefit of clients, and is subject to the supervision of the courts. Even where solicitor and client make an agreement as to costs, the court may still examine its reasonableness. It should be noted that English law has always regarded "contingency fees" (that is to say fees the amount or payment of which are contingent upon the result of litigation) as unlawful on the ground that they are contrary to public policy. This principle was affirmed by the Court of Appeal in *Wallersteiner* v. *Moir* (*No. 2*)[8] in which the majority of the court refused to recognise an exception to the rule in the case of minority shareholders' actions, an exception which LORD DENNING, M.R. (dissenting on this point) was in favour of creating.

The way in which a solicitor's remuneration is assessed depends upon whether the business done on behalf of the client is contentious or non-contentious. "Contentious business" is defined by the Act[9] as:

> "Business done, whether as solicitor or advocate, in or for the purpose of proceedings begun before a court or before an arbitrator appointed under the Arbitration Act 1950, not being business which falls within the definition of non-contentious or common form probate business in the Supreme Court Act 1981, s. 128;"

The test is thus whether or not proceedings are begun. If they are, all business relating to these proceedings is contentious. If proceedings are not begun, as for example where a dispute is settled before a writ is issued, the proceedings are treated as non-contentious. Non-contentious business is any business which is not contentious within the above statutory definition and comprises a very wide range of matters including conveyancing, drafting wills and settlements, advice and many other matters. The basic difference between contentious and non-contentious business in relation to the assessment of remuneration is that in the former the amount is usually fixed by the court by taxation while in the latter it is not, being fixed in accordance with statutory orders.

a   Assessment of remuneration in contentious business

The Solicitors Act 1974, section 59 expressly authorises a solicitor to enter into a written agreement with his client regulating remuneration in content-

---

production of documents conferred upon the Commission by E.E.C. legislation was subject to legal professional privilege in relation to communications between the applicant and its independent lawyers, but only in relation to communications for the purpose of the applicant's "right of defence", that is to say in the context of litigation pending or anticipated. The basis of the decision was the fact that, while there is no express provision for legal confidentiality in the E.E.C. Treaty or Community legislation, there was recognition of such a principle in the laws of all the member states.

8   [1975] Q.B. 373; [1975] 1 All E.R. 849. The Royal Commission on Legal Services came down firmly against a contingency fee system on the ground that it "would give rise to serious dissatisfaction" and "would benefit only a limited class of litigants and would reward some lawyers disproportionately". (Report, para. 16(6).)

9   Solicitors Act 1974, s. 87(1) (as amended).

ious business.[10] In the absence of such an agreement the solicitor may submit either a bill containing detailed items or one charging a gross sum.[11]

The client has a right to have this bill taxed, in which case the appropriate basis of taxation is (unless the bill is to be paid out of the Legal Aid Fund) the "solicitor and own client" basis.[12] On this basis:

> "All costs shall be allowed except in so far as they are of an unreasonable amount or have been unreasonably incurred".[13]

All costs incurred with the express or implied approval of the client are conclusively presumed to have been reasonably incurred and, where the amount has been so approved, are presumed to have been reasonable in amount.[14] However the solicitor must expressly inform his client of any costs which are of an unusual nature and might not be allowed on a "party and party" taxation; otherwise such costs are deemed to be unreasonably incurred.[15] Many items of costs are charged on a fixed scale[16] while in respect of other items a maximum and a minimum charge are prescribed by scale.[17] Nevertheless items may be allowed on a solicitor and own client taxation which do not appear in the scale and even where a maximum amount is prescribed in the scale the taxing master may, in his discretion, allow an amount higher than that prescribed by the scale.[18]

An exception to the above basis of taxation applies where the client is legally aided. In such a case in the High Court the solicitor receives from the Legal Aid Fund only his disbursements and 90 per cent of his costs taxed on a "common fund" basis. On this basis, which is less liberal than the "solicitor and own client" basis of taxation, there is allowed "a reasonable amount in respect of all costs reasonably incurred".[19]

b   Assessment of remuneration in non-contentious business

Whereas remuneration in contentious business is usually fixed by the court, remuneration in non-contentious business is controlled differently. Save in certain exceptional cases under specific enactments,[20] the mode and amount of remuneration are regulated by orders made under section 56 of the 1974 Act.[1]

As to the mode of remuneration, orders made under section 56 may provide for remuneration—

(*a*)   according to a scale of rates of commission or a scale of percentages; or

---

[10] See p. 263, *post*.
[11] Section 64.
[12] See p. 390, *post*.
[13] R.S.C. (Revision) 1965, O. 62, r. 29 (1).
[14] O. 62, r. 29(2).
[15] O. 62, r. 29(3).
[16] O. 62, Appendix 3.
[17] O. 62, Appendix 2.
[18] O. 62, r. 32(2).
[19] O. 62, r. 28(4).
[20] Preserved by s. 75 of the 1974 Act.
[1] These orders are made by a committee consisting of the Lord Chancellor, the Lord Chief Justice, the Master of the Rolls, the President of The Law Society, a nominated solicitor who is president of a local law society and (for the purpose only of business under the Land Registration Act 1925) the Chief Land Registrar (s. 56(1)).

(*b*) by a gross sum; or

(*c*) by a fixed sum for each document prepared or perused; or

(*d*) in any other mode; or

(*e*) partly in one mode and partly in another.

The amount of remuneration may be regulated by order with reference to the following, among other, considerations—

(*a*) the position of the party for whom the solicitor is concerned, that is, whether he is vendor or purchaser, lessor or lessee, mortgagor or mortgagee or the like;

(*b*) the place where, and the circumstances in which, the business was transacted;

(*c*) the amount involved;

(*d*) the skill, labour and responsibility involved on the part of the solicitor;

(*e*) the number and importance of the documents prepared or perused.

These provisions reproduce those formerly contained in the 1957 Act and the order currently in force, the Solicitors' Remuneration Order 1972 was, in fact, made under that Act.

The basis of remuneration under this Order is a lump sum which is fair and reasonable having regard to all the circumstances of the case and in particular to:

(1) the complexity of the matter or the difficulty or novelty of the questions raised;

(2) the skill, labour, specialised knowledge and responsibility involved on the part of the solicitor;

(3) the number and importance of the documents prepared or perused, without regard to length;

(4) the place where and the circumstances in which the business or any part thereof is transacted;

(5) the time expended by the solicitor;

(6) where money or property is involved, its amount or value;

(7) whether any land involved is registered land;

(8) the importance of the matter to the client.

In *Property and Reversionary Investment Corporation, Ltd.* v. *Secretary of State for the Environment*[2] (one of the very few reported cases on taxation of costs) DONALDSON, J. (as he then was), in fixing remuneration at £5,500 for the vendors' solicitors in relation to the sale of property for the sum of £2¼ million gave some guidance as to the mode of assessing remuneration in commercial conveyancing transaction; by far the most important factor, in such cases, is the value of the property involved.

The client has no right to have a lump sum bill itemised. He has, nevertheless, two safeguards against an excessive charge. First, he has a right to have the bill taxed and secondly, without prejudice to this right, he has a right to require the solicitor to obtain a certificate from The Law Society that the sum

---

2   [1975] 2 All E.R. 436; [1975] 1 W.L.R. 1504; see also *Maltby* v. *D.J. Freeman & Co.* [1978] 2 All E.R. 913; [1978] 1 W.L.R. 431; *Treasury Solicitor* v. *Regester*, [1978] 2 All E.R. 920; [1978] 1 W.L.R. 446.

charged is fair and reasonable, or, if it is not, what is a fair and reasonable sum. It is for the solicitor to show that the charge is fair and reasonable. A solicitor can bring no proceedings on a lump sum bill until he has drawn his client's attention to the latter's rights which are set out above. The right to require the solicitor to obtain a certificate may be exercised within one month of his being informed by the solicitor of his rights as above, provided the bill has been neither taxed nor paid. If the taxing master allows less than one half the amount charged he must bring the facts of the case to the attention of The Law Society.[3]

c Special agreements as to remuneration

Solicitor and client may, in both contentious and non-contentious business, agree the amount of the solicitor's remuneration. Such agreements are, however, not freely enforceable in the same way as commercial contracts since their enforceability is regulated by statute.

In contentious business solicitor and client may make an agreement in writing, providing for remuneration by a gross sum, or by a salary, or otherwise and whether at a higher or lower rate than that at which the solicitor would otherwise have been entitled to be remunerated.[4] There is no prescribed form for the agreement and it may, for example, be contained in letters passing between solicitor and client provided that the terms of the agreement can be ascertained with certainty. However there are certain other restrictions attaching to such an agreement. Any provision exempting the solicitor from liability for negligence or any other responsibility is void.[5] The agreement itself is void if it involves any purchase by a solicitor of any part of the interest of his client in the proceedings or if it makes payment contingent upon the outcome of the proceedings.[6] The agreement cannot prejudice the rights of third parties although it may indirectly benefit them since the client cannot recover more costs from a third party than he has agreed to pay his solicitor.[7]

A provision relating to remuneration in contentious business cannot be enforced by action,[8] even though the agreement as a whole can be so enforced. It may, however, be enforced summarily by the High Court or a county court on application.[9] The court may, if it considers the agreement unfair or unreasonable, declare it void and order the costs covered thereby to be taxed as if the agreement had never been made.[10]

An agreement for remuneration in non-contentious business must likewise

---

[3] Solicitors' Remuneration Order 1972, arts. 3, 4.
[4] Act of 1974, s. 59(1).
[5] *Ibid.*, s. 60(5).
[6] *Ibid.*, s. 59(2). A solicitor is, however, justified in acting for an impoverished client on terms that he shall receive no costs or reduced costs unless the action succeeds.
[7] *Ibid.*, s. 60(3).
[8] *Ibid.*, s. 61(1).
[9] The appropriate court is the one in which the business to which the agreement relates was done if this is the High Court or a county court, or, if not, the High Court in respect of agreements to pay more than £50 or the county court for sums of less than £50 (1974 Act, s. 61(6)). Application to the High Court is usually by originating summons; application to a county court is by originating application.
[10] *Ibid.*, s. 61(2), (4).

be in writing.[11] It must also be signed by the party to be bound or his agent, a provision which is not mandatory, though desirable, in the case of agreements relating to contentious business. Such an agreement is subject to the ordinary law of contract and may be sued on in the ordinary way. Nevertheless the court has an inherent jurisdiction to order taxation in order to determine whether the sum agreed is fair and reasonable, and may cancel the agreement or reduce the amount payable if the taxing officer certifies that it is unfair or unreasonable.[12]

d   Recovery of costs

By section 69 of the Solicitors Act 1974 no action shall be brought to recover any costs due to a solicitor until one month after delivery of a bill signed by the solicitor, or by a partner in the firm if the costs are due to a firm, or accompanied by a letter so signed and referring to the bill. However, the High Court may by order dispense with this requirement if there is probable cause for believing that the party chargeable is about to quit England and Wales, to become bankrupt or compound with his creditors or do any other act which would tend to prevent or delay the solicitor obtaining payment.

Within one month of the delivery of a bill the client has a right to have it taxed and no action may be commenced on the bill until the taxation is completed.[13] After one month has elapsed the court may, upon such terms as it thinks fit, order taxation on the application of solicitor or client and may stay proceedings on the bill, or order that no action shall be taken, until taxation is completed.[14] However, except in special circumstances, the client will not obtain an order for taxation more than twelve months after the delivery of the bill or after payment, and in no event will he obtain an order more than twelve months after payment. Unless the client does not appear on the solicitor's application to have the bill taxed or the order for taxation otherwise provides the costs of the taxation depend upon its outcome. If one-fifth of the amount of the bill is taxed off the solicitor pays the costs; otherwise the client pays the costs.[15]

Subject to the above restrictions the solicitor may proceed to recover his costs as a contractual debt. He may do so by action or by proving in the client's bankruptcy or in the liquidation of a client company. As an alternative to action the solicitor may exercise his common law lien.[16] He has a general lien over all of the client's personal property in the solicitor's possession except his will. This entitles the solicitor to retain the property until payment of the full amount due. The lien is often exercised in relation to case papers. However a solicitor's lien is subordinate to the public interest that justice be achieved in the suit. Consequently a lien over a client's papers is qualified in that the solicitor is bound to hand over the client's papers to his new solicitor on the latter's undertaking to preserve the lien.[17] In addition the

---

[11] *Ibid.*, s. 57.
[12] *Ibid.*, s. 57(5).
[13] *Ibid.*, s. 70(1).
[14] *Ibid.*, s. 70(2).
[15] *Ibid.*, s. 70.
[16] See, generally, *Cordery on Solicitors* (7th Edn.), pp. 273–291.
[17] *Gamlen Chemical Co. (U.K.), Ltd.* v. *Rochem, Ltd.*, [1980] 1 All E.R. 1049; [1980] 1 W.L.R. 614.

solicitor has a particular lien over property, other than real property,[18] recovered or preserved or the proceeds of any judgment obtained in an action, for his costs in relation to that action.

It will be appreciated that in a long and expensive piece of litigation the solicitor may be in the position of having to wait a very long time in order to recover his remuneration. To remedy this section 65 of the Act enables the solicitor, in contentious business, to request payment of a reasonable sum of money on account of costs; if the client refuses or fails within a reasonable time to make that payment the solicitor may, upon giving reasonable notice, withdraw from the retainer. The solicitor will then have to apply to the court for removal of his name from the record.

5 Offences by unqualified persons

An "unqualified person" means, in the Solicitors Act 1974, a person who is not qualified under section 1 of that Act. No person shall be qualified to act as a solicitor unless:

(*a*) he has been admitted as a solicitor; and
(*b*) his name is for the time being on the Roll; and
(*c*) he has in force a practising certificate.

Thus a solicitor who has been disqualified or does not have a current practising certificate is in no better position than any layman.[19] If such a solicitor is a partner in a firm, the effect of his practising certificate lapsing will be that the partnership is automatically dissolved and reconstituted, for so long as the situation obtains, as a partnership between the remaining partners.[20]

It is an offence for an unqualified person or a body corporate to act as a solicitor or as such to take a step in any court proceeding. This is a contempt of the court in which the action or matter is proceeding. In addition it renders the offender liable on summary conviction to a fine not exceeding level 3 on the standard scale.[1]

Any unqualified person, not being a barrister, notary public or public officer acting in the course of his duty, who prepares for reward any instrument relating to real or personal estate is similarly liable on summary conviction. There are savings for wills, agreements under hand only, powers of attorney and simple stock transfers.[2]

---

[18] But note s. 73 of the 1974 Act which enables the court to make a charging order in favour of the solicitor over any property including real property.

[19] He is still, however, a solicitor for the purpose of disciplinary proceedings: *Re A Solicitor* (1963), 107 Sol. Jo. 216.

[20] *Hudgell Yeates & Co.* v. *Watson*, [1978] Q.B. 451; [1978] 2 All E.R. 363.

[1] Act of 1974, s. 21; Criminal Justice Act 1982, s. 38; as to the "standard scale", see p. 549, *post*. There is, however, no objection to any person, whether he be a professional man or not, attending a trial as a friend of any party, taking notes and quietly making suggestions and giving advice to that party: *McKenzie* v. *McKenzie*, [1971] P. 33; [1970] 3 All E.R. 1034. Note also the position of E.E.C. lawyers under the European Communities (Services of Lawyers) Order 1978; see p. 251, fn. 2, *ante*.

[2] Act of 1974, s. 22(3). No offence is committed if the unqualified person proves that the instrument was not prepared in expectation of any fee or reward. He need not, however, have a legal right to remuneration. It is sufficient that he has an expectation of gain: *Pacey* v.

None of the above provisions affects the right of any person to act for himself in any matter, contentious or non-contentious. Thus a litigant may appear in person without the need for representation by solicitor or counsel. However there are exceptional cases in which the litigant cannot appear in person. Thus in the High Court neither a corporate body nor the next friend or guardian *ad litem* of a person under disability (infant or patient) may appear in person. A solicitor must be retained.[3]

C   BARRISTERS

1   General organisation of the Bar

a   The Inns of Court

Persons may only practise as counsel in England if they have been "called to the Bar" of one of the four Inns of Court; Lincoln's Inn, the Inner Temple, the Middle Temple and Gray's Inn. These Inns are as old as professional advocacy itself in England and appear to have originated as living quarters for those legal practitioners who were not serjeants.[4] The Inns' jurisdiction is in no way statutory. It is derived from the judges (and thus indirectly from the Crown) and is subject to control by the judges.[5] One member of the Court of Appeal has explained the Inns' functions as follows:[6]

> "I would regard the Inns of Court in their disciplinary power in relation to the practising member of the Bar as equivalently established over the centuries by its practice and acceptance as if the power had been derived from statute and as unassailable. If the Inns of Court had not controlled the professional conduct of the Bar the judges themselves would have had to do so. The judges themselves, deriving their authority from the Crown, were minded in the distant past to delegate, and the undisputed view in Lord Mansfield's time was that the judges had delegated their disciplinary power over the Bar to the Inns of Court."

In the Inns of Court there are three classes of members; benchers, who are the governors of the Inn, barristers, who are called by the benchers, and students who are admitted to membership by the benchers. The benchers of an Inn, who are judges or senior members of the Bar, have absolute control over the admission of students and the call of barristers. There is an appeal from their decisions to the Lord Chancellor and the judges of the High Court

---

Atkinson, [1950] 1 K.B. 539; [1950] 1 All E.R. 320. The Royal Commission recommended maintaining the existing restrictions on conveyancing for fee or reward, and increasing the maximum penalties (Report, paras. 21.61, 21.63). Legislation to remove the present "conveyancing monopoly" is anticipated in the near future.

3   R.S.C. (Revision) 1965, O. 5, r. 6. The Administration of Justice Act 1977, s. 16 confers power upon the Lord Chancellor to confer a right of audience in county courts upon "persons in relevant legal employment" (the intention apparently being to limit the right to Fellows of the Institute of Legal Executives and then only in a narrow range of cases). The County Courts (Rights of Audience) Direction 1978 in fact grants legal executives limited rights of audience.

4   Serjeants had their own Inns ("Serjeants' Inns"). There were also several Chancery Inns (e.g. New Inn, Clifford's Inn). All these have ceased to exist.

5   *R.* v. *Gray's Inn* (1780), 1 Doug, K.B. 353, *per* LORD MANSFIELD.

6   SELLERS, L.J. in *Lincoln* v. *Daniels*, [1963] 1 Q.B. 237, at p. 250; [1961] 3 All E.R. 740, at p. 745; cf. *Re S.* (*a barrister*), [1970] 1 Q.B. 160; [1969] 1 All E.R. 949.

sitting as "visitors", a domestic tribunal. They cannot, however, be sued in respect of any act done in their official capacity nor can they be compelled by mandamus to admit a person as a student or call a student to the Bar.[7] The principal conditions which a student must satisfy before applying for call to the Bar are payment of the requisite fees, passing the Bar Final Examination and keeping eight terms.[8] No person under the age of 21 can be called to the Bar. Before a barrister can practise he must serve a pupillage under a senior member of the Bar (not a Queen's Counsel) for not less than twelve months.[9]

b The Senate of the Inns of Court and the Bar

In 1966 the four Inns, by a resolution passed by each Inn (and confirmed by a resolution of the judges of the High Court) established a new joint body known as the Senate of the Inns of Court. In 1974 this body was replaced by the Senate of the Inns of Court and the Bar constituted by agreement between the existing Senate, the Inns and the Bar. The new organisation is, broadly speaking, the governing body of the Bar. The Inns themselves have undertaken to abide by the general policy as laid down from time to time by the Senate while the judges have resolved and confirmed that disciplinary powers over barristers shall be exercised in accordance with the regulations of the Senate.[10] The Senate consists of up to ninety members, comprising the Attorney-General, the Solicitor-General and the Chairman of the Council of Legal Education, twenty four Bench Representatives (six from each Inn), twelve Hall Representatives (three from each Inn), thirty-nine Bar Representatives elected by the Bar (of whom six must be non-practising barristers) and not more than twelve additional members. The Senate has authority, within limits, to make decisions on behalf of the whole Bar. Its functions include the regulation of the admission of students and of call to the Bar, legal education and the exercise of certain disciplinary power over members of the Bar. The Inns of Court are bound by decisions of the Senate, which also acts in an advisory capacity to the Inns. The Senate also controls the policy of the Council of Legal Education, though the Bar Council retains its autonomy for the purposes of its separate powers and functions, referred to below. The Senate, through a special disciplinary committee composed of practising barristers and no more than one judge, hears and determines disciplinary charges against barristers, though the penalty to be imposed upon a barrister found guilty of professional misconduct is still imposed upon him by his own Inn, which therefore acts simply as a "rubber stamp" for the decisions of the Senate.

In one case[11] a barrister, who had been disbarred by his Inn following a hearing before the disciplinary Committee of the Senate, appealed to five judges of the Queen's Bench Division sitting as visitors to the Inn; his contention was that the benchers of the Inn, having derived their disciplinary

---

[7] *R. v. Lincoln's Inn Benchers* (1825), 4 B. & C. 855.

[8] The latter obligation is not imposed upon solicitors wishing to become barristers. There are four dining terms a year in the Inns of Court: Michaelmas, Hilary, Easter and Trinity. A term is kept by dining in Hall on a number of occasions (usually three) during the term.

[9] The number of practising barristers rose from 2,714 in 1971 to 5,032 in 1983, of whom 526 were Q.C.s.

[10] Regulations of the Senate of the Inns of Court and the Bar, reg. 2.

[11] *Re S. (a barrister)*, [1970] 1 Q.B. 160; [1969] 1 All E.R. 949.

powers by delegation from the judges could not, because of the principle *delegatus non potest delegare*, delegate those powers to the Senate. The visitors rejected this contention on the ground that the judges had a duty to determine who should have right of audience in the courts and that, although they had for three centuries acquiesced in that duty being performed by the benchers, they had never divested themselves of the duty. Consequently the transfer of jurisdiction to the Senate was not a delegation but simply a change in the manner in which the judges chose to discharge their primary duty.

> "The judges remain under the same duty unimpaired; the machinery by which they exercise their judicial duty has been changed."[12]

c   The Bar Council

The Bar Council, like the Inns of Court, has no statutory foundation. However its jurisdiction does not derive from the judges but from the consent of the Bar. In addition it is not a judicial body and has no disciplinary powers. It is of far more recent creation than the Inns, being created by consent of the whole Bar in 1894. Prior to 1974 it was independent of the Senate but, under the new Regulations, its assets together with many of its functions have been transferred to the Senate.

However the Bar Council retains certain separate powers and functions, in the performance of which it is not subject to the directions of the Senate. Its express functions are to maintain the standards, honour and independence of the Bar, to promote, preserve and improve the services and functions of the Bar and to represent and act for the Bar generally. It must call an Annual General Meeting of the Bar and has power to make its own bye-laws and regulations provided they are not inconsistent with the main Regulations.[13]

However, such functions as the regulation of standards of professional conduct, the investigation of complaints against barristers and the organisation of the Bar's finances, which were formerly the province of the Bar Council, are now dealt with by various committees of the Senate.

2   Rights and duties of barristers

The barrister's function is primarily advocacy although he deals also with such matters as drafting conveyances, pleadings and other legal documents

---

12 [1970] 1 Q.B., at p. 175; [1969] 1 All E.R., at p. 959, *per* PAULL, J. In the instant case the visitors allowed the appeal in respect of 2 out of 6 charges and substituted for the order of disbarment an order of suspension for 12 months. A further attempt to challenge the authority of the Senate in disciplinary matters was made in *Re S. (a barrister)*, [1981] Q.B. 683; [1981] 2 All E.R. 952, this time on the basis that since the Bar Council (which is part of the Senate) had investigated the complaint and preferred charges against the barrister concerned, the Senate was acting as judge in its own cause, thereby infringing the rule of natural justice *nemo judex in causa sua*, alternatively on the wider basis that a tribunal, the majority of the members of which were practising barristers, was incapable of considering fairly a charge of misconduct brought against a fellow barrister. The first of these submissions was rejected by the visitors on the ground that the Bar Council was autonomous for the purposes of the functions in question, and therefore not subject to the control of the Senate; the alternative submission was dismissed as "wholly misconceived".

13 Regulations of the Senate of the Inns of Court and the Bar, reg. 29.

and advising on the law. He has a right of audience in virtually all judicial proceedings and in the House of Lords, the Judicial Committee of the Privy Council, the Court of Appeal and the High Court of Justice this right is exclusive, except in interlocutory proceedings and bankruptcy proceedings where solicitors have a concurrent right. This exclusive right of audience does not usually prejudice the right of a litigant to appear in person.[14] However, in certain exceptional cases counsel must be retained. In criminal proceedings in the Crown Court, prosecutions must be conducted by barristers[15] and prosecutors cannot appear in person. All petitions of appeal to the House of Lords from the Court of Appeal must be signed by two counsel.

Barristers have, in most cases, exclusive eligibility by statute for judicial offices and the offices of Lord Chancellor, Attorney-General and Solicitor-General are always filled by barristers.

In addition to these rights and privileges barristers have various duties both to the court and to their clients. Their duties to the court are all based on professional etiquette. Barristers are not, in the way that solicitors are, officers of the court so that they are not strictly subject to control by the courts. It is doubtful whether the courts would exercise jurisdiction to suspend a barrister from practising, since this power is left by the judges to the Inns of Court. Nevertheless a barrister may clearly be fined or imprisoned for contempt of court to the same extent as a solicitor or, indeed, any other person. Counsel cannot, in general, be heard in court unless they are "robed", a term which includes the wearing of wig, gown and bands. A barrister may, however, appear unrobed in magistrates' courts and also when appearing as litigant in person.[16] Although counsel are not officers of the court they are officers of justice. This is particularly true in criminal proceedings so that prosecuting counsel's function is to assist the court, not to press for a conviction. Even in civil cases barristers are under a duty to draw to the attention of the court authorities which do not support their client's case. Furthermore, counsel must not mislead the court by actively concealing facts[17] from the court which are material to the case, nor must he set up any affirmative case or defence inconsistent with any admission or confession made to him by his client, nor should he take a point of law which he knows to be bad.

3 Relationship between counsel and client

The relationship between a barrister and his client is *sui generis*. It is not a contractual relationship. The payment which a barrister receives by way of a

---

[14] In addition courts have an inherent power to control their own procedure and may, therefore, hear persons who strictly have no right of audience; see *Engineers' and Managers' Association* v. *Advisory, Conciliation and Arbitration Service*, [1979] 3 All E.R. 223; [1979] 1 W.L.R. 113, where an official of a small trade union with limited resources was permitted a right of audience for the purpose of putting forward a simple point on the union's behalf.

[15] Under s. 83 of the Supreme Court Act 1981 the Lord Chancellor may confer unlimited rights of audience upon solicitors in proceedings in the Crown Court; upon the establishment of the Crown Prosecution Service under the Prosecution of Offences Act, it is anticipated that solicitors who are officers of the Service will eventually be authorised to prosecute in the Crown Court.

[16] *Practice Note*, [1961] 1 All E.R. 319.

[17] *Meek* v. *Fleming*, [1961] 2 Q.B. 366; [1961] 3 All E.R. 148.

brief fee is not a contractual payment but an *honorarium*. The result is that a barrister cannot sue for his fees.[18] Nor can he sue upon a promise to pay fees, nor prove for fees in bankruptcy. Fees due to counsel which have been paid to a firm of solicitors but have not been paid over to counsel cannot be attached or garnished.[19] Counsel's fees are, however, chargeable to income tax and are allowable as costs on taxation.

The principal safeguard that counsel has in connection with his fee is that he may refuse to accept a brief if the fee is not paid when the brief is delivered. However, as a matter of etiquette, the Council of The Law Society has stated that solicitors are personally liable to see that counsel's fees are paid whether or not the solicitor has been put in funds by the client. If the solicitor has been paid counsel's fee by the client, it is professional misconduct on the part of the solicitor not to pay it over and the matter may be referred to the Disciplinary Tribunal.[20] In exceptional cases The Law Society may authorise payment of counsel's fees out of the Compensation Fund.[1] Also, as a matter of etiquette, counsel's "right" to his fees derives from delivery of the brief not from his retainer. Thus a brief must not be marked after the termination of the proceedings to which it relates, with certain exceptions, notably in legal aid cases.

The corollary of barristers' inability to sue for their fees is their immunity from being sued in contract for professional negligence. Historically barristers have always been immune from actions in negligence because such actions could only be based on contract and were thus not possible against a barrister, with whom the client could not enter into a contractual relationship. There is a long line of authorities going back to the Year Books for the reign of Henry VI which support this immunity.[2] However, when all these old cases were decided there was no thought of the existence of the modern action for negligence in respect of professional advice. Following statements of the House of Lords in *Hedley Byrne & Co., Ltd.* v. *Heller & Partners, Ltd.*[3] that a person giving professional advice may owe a duty of care in negligence:

> "Many at the Bar have been watching carefully for signs of the cold wind of change blowing across the Strand into the Temple; some are said to have protected themselves with the comforting embraces of Lloyd's and others who provide like services."[4]

However, in the leading case of *Rondel* v. *Worsley*[5] the House of Lords, faced with this very question whether a barrister might now be held liable in

---

[18] *Wells* v. *Wells*, [1914] P. 157.

[19] *Re Le Brasseur and Oakley*, [1896] 2 Ch. 487. See *Rondel* v. *Worsley*, [1969] 1 A.C. 191; [1967] 3 All E.R. 993, in which the position of a barrister is examined and the authorities reviewed.

[20] Annual Statement of the Bar Council 1930, p. 10.

[1] Annual Statement of the Bar Council 1954, p. 26.

[2] The leading case is *Swinfen* v. *Lord Chelmsford* (1860), 5 H & N. 890. The authorities are reviewed in *Rondel* v. *Worsley*, [1969] 1 A.C. 191; [1967] 3 All E.R. 993.

[3] [1964] A.C. 465; [1963] 2 All E.R. 575.

[4] LAWTON, J. (as he then was) as first instance in *Rondel* v. *Worsley*, [1967] 1 Q.B. 443, at p. 455; [1966] 1 All E.R. 467, at p. 470. In 1983 the Bar gave effect to a resolution that failure to have proper professional indemnity insurance (for an amount of not less than £250,000 for each and every claim) constituted professional misconduct.

[5] [1969] 1 A.C. 191; [1967] 3 All E.R. 993.

negligence, decided not and dismissed the plaintiff's appeal from an order
that his statement of claim be struck out as disclosing no cause of action.
LORD DENNING, M.R., in the Court of Appeal, reviewed the authorities at
length before distinguishing *Hedley Byrne & Co., Ltd.* v. *Heller & Partners,
Ltd.*[6] The Master of the Rolls conceded that, since *Hedley Byrne*, a barrister's immunity could not be justified on the ground of his inability to sue for
his fees. Consequently LORD DENNING based counsel's immunity upon
various grounds of public policy and upon long usage from which the public
interest did not require a departure. The grounds of public policy to which
LORD DENNING adverted may be summarised as follows:[7]

(1) *Independence*—"that he may do his duty fearlessly and independently as
he ought and to prevent him being harassed by vexatious actions."
"If a barrister is to be able to do his duty fearlessly and independently he
must not be subject to the threat of an action for negligence."
(2) *Professional obligation to act*—"A barrister cannot pick or choose his
clients. He is bound to accept a brief for any man who comes before the
courts. No matter how great a rascal the man may be. No matter how given
to complaining. No matter how undeserving or unpopular his cause. The
barrister must defend him to the end;"
(3) *Duty to the court*—"He has a duty to the court which is paramount. It is
a mistake to suppose that he is the mouthpiece of his client to say what he
wants; or his tool to do what he directs. he is none of these things. He owes
allegiance to a higher cause. It is the cause of truth and justice. . . . He must
disregard the most specific instructions of his client, if they conflict with his
duty to the court;"
(4) *Protraction of litigation*—"If a barrister could be sued for negligence, it
would mean a retrial of the original case. . . . If this action were to be
permitted, it would open the door to every disgruntled client. . . . If this
action is to go for trial, it will lead to dozens of like cases."

Although the appellant's claim was "clearly as devoid of merit as it was of
any prospect of success"[8] the House of Lords gave leave to appeal in view
of the importance of the question of law involved. In the event the House of
Lords affirmed the decision of the Court of Appeal. While their lordships
differed slightly as to the emphasis to be placed upon individual heads of
public policy they concurred, in the result, in each of the above four heads
adverted to by LORD DENNING in the Court of Appeal.

The House of Lords also considered, as the Court of Appeal had done, the
question of whether barristers' immunity extended to work done in chambers in advising, settling documents and other matters which might never
come before a court. Although the majority view of the Court of Appeal had
been that the immunity did so extend the House of Lords, with the exception
of LORD PEARCE who favoured the wider immunity, expressed the opinion
that, while the immunity from action extended to pleadings and other work
done while litigation was pending, it did not extend to advisory work or work

6 [1964] A.C. 465; [1963] 2 All E.R. 575.
7 [1967] 1 Q.B., at pp. 501–504; [1966] 3 All E.R., at pp. 665–666.
8 [1967] 1 Q.B., at 516; [1966] 3 All E.R., at p. 674, *per* SALMON, L.J. (as he then was); [1969] 1
A.C., at p. 226; [1967] 3 All E.R., at p. 998, *per* LORD REID.

done on documents outside the context of litigation. These opinions were, of course, no more than *obiter dicta* although of great weight. However, in *Saif Ali* v. *Sydney Mitchell & Co.*[9] the House of Lords were once again called upon to consider the scope of barristers' immunity, but this time in relation to work done in chambers in the course of litigation. The same procedure was adopted to bring the issue before the court as had been used in *Rondel* v. *Worsley*, namely an application to strike out a pleading alleging negligence against a barrister on the ground that it disclosed no reasonable cause of action.[10] The facts were commonplace. The plaintiff was a passenger in a van being driven by M. when the same was in collision with a car owned by S. and being driven by Mrs. S., whereby the plaintiff was injured. Counsel advised suing S. on the basis that Mrs. S. (who was convicted of careless driving) had been driving as her husband's agent; thereafter, although S.'s insurers indicated in the course of negotiations that they might dispute the allegation of agency and might also "blame" M., the barrister, who was told of these facts, did not advise joining either Mrs. S. or M. to the proceedings. The limitation period of three years passed and the plaintiff upon being advised, by new advisers, that his action against S. was untenable, discontinued his action and sued his former solicitors; that firm issued a third party notice claiming to be indemnified in respect of any damages payable to the plaintiff on the ground that he, the barrister, had been negligent in his advice as to who should be joined in the plaintiff's action and in settling pleadings in accordance with that erroneous advice. The barrister applied for the third party notice and statement of claim to be struck out and the district registrar granted this application, but his order was reversed on appeal to the judge; the judge's order was in turn reversed by the Court of Appeal[11] whereupon the solicitors appealed to the House of Lords. The Court of Appeal was, as the House of Lords had been in *Rondel* v. *Worsley*, disposed to extend barristers' immunity to all matters connected with litigation which was pending or contemplated, including advice. In the House of Lords the dissenting minority (LORD RUSSELL and LORD KEITH) supported this view but the majority (LORD WILBERFORCE, LORD DIPLOCK and LORD SALMON), in allowing the solicitors' appeal, limited the immunity to those matters of pre-trial work which were so intimately connected with the conduct of the cause in court that they could fairly be said to be preliminary decisions affecting the way that the cause was conducted when it came to a hearing. Since the barrister's advice and pleadings in the instant case had in fact prevented the plaintiff's cause from coming to court at all, it could not be said to be "intimately connected" with the conduct of the plaintiff's cause in court and was therefore not within the sphere of a barrister's immunity from actions for negligence.

The test approved was taken from a New Zealand Court of Appeal case[12] and is narrower than that which had been favoured *obiter* in *Rondel* v. *Worsley*. The test may not, in practice, be easy to apply in subsequent cases. Thus if, for example, the negligent conduct was failure to plead a cause of

---

[9] [1980] A.C. 198; [1978] 3 All E.R. 1033.
[10] For this procedure, see p. 344, *post*.
[11] [1978] Q.B. 95; [1977] 3 All E.R. 744.
[12] *Rees* v. *Sinclair*, [1974] 1 N.Z.L.R. 180.

action (rather than failure to join a party) the immunity would appear to apply, although it is difficult to see why the barrister should be liable in the one case and not in the other.

Other incidents of the barrister's relationship with his client which may be noted briefly are the former's obligation to preserve the latter's confidences and counsel's authority to conduct proceedings on behalf of the client. The scope of this authority is determinable in accordance with ordinary principles of the law of agency and includes the authority to compromise proceedings on behalf of the client and the authority to make admissions on the latter's behalf in civil proceedings, though not to plead guilty in a criminal prosecution.

4 Professional conduct

The duties of solicitors towards their clients is governed both by statute and by their code of professional conduct. In the case of barristers the obligations are governed solely by the dictates of professional etiquette.[13] The rules of conduct may change from time to time and may be altered by the Inns of Court on behalf of their members or by the Senate of the Inns of Court and the Bar. In no case are the rules enforceable in any way other than by complaint to the Senate or the individual barrister's Inn followed by disciplinary proceedings before the Senate of the Inns of Court and the Bar which may result in the barrister being disbarred or suspended from practising.

Conduct and etiquette at the Bar is a complex study[14] but certain important rules of conduct should be carefully noted. Perhaps the most important rule is that, subject to a few exceptional cases, counsel may accept instructions only from a solicitor and not from a client direct.[15] Touting for business among solicitors and advertisement[16] are clearly contrary to etiquette. So too is any form of partnership or profit sharing. Counsel should not normally interview witnesses before or during a trial, nor should he consult with a client except in the presence of the solicitor. Until recently, Queen's Counsel were subject to particular rules whereby they were not permitted to appear without a junior (the "two counsel" rule), nor to do drafting work nor give written opinions on evidence. As a consequence of a recommendation of the Monopolies and Mergers Commission in 1976, the Bar Council, by a resolution dated 31 May 1977, abolished the two counsel rule, although Queen's Counsel should decline to appear without a junior if he would be unable properly to conduct that case, or other cases, or to fulfil his professional commitments unless a junior were also instructed. In practice, it is still comparatively rare to find Queen's Counsel appearing without a junior.

---

[13] *Re Harrison*, [1908] 1 Ch. 282.

[14] Details are contained in *Code of Conduct for The Bar of England and Wales*, published by the Senate.

[15] *Doe d. Bennett* v. *Hale* (1850), 15 Q.B. 171. For an unsuccessful attempt to challenge this rule, see *Re T (a barrister)*, [1982] Q.B. 430; [1981] 2 All E.R. 1105. In criminal cases the rule was, until 1980, subject to the exception of the "dock brief" whereby the defendant, on a trial on indictment, could instruct from the dock any barrister who was robed and sitting in court for the sum of £2.10. The dock brief became obsolete by reason of the extension of legal aid in criminal proceedings, but it may be noted that the litigation in *Rondel* v. *Worsley* (*supra*) arose out of a dock brief, the plaintiff having been refused legal aid.

[16] Though it is not improper for a Queen's Counsel (Q.C.) to describe himself by this title.

Furthermore, Queen's Counsel may now engage in non-contentious drafting work and may, if he has agreed to appear without a junior in a case, settle pleadings or draft other documents in that case.

D   LAW OFFICERS

1   Attorney-General and Solicitor-General

The "Law Officers", legal advisers to the Crown, are the Attorney-General and the Solicitor-General. The Attorney-General is the head of the English Bar, though neither he nor the Solicitor-General may engage in private practice while they hold office. They are assisted by Junior Counsel to the Treasury who, holding no political office, are practising barristers.

Apart from his political duties, which include advising Government Departments and answering questions in the House of Commons, the Attorney-General represents the Crown in certain civil proceedings and, as a matter of practice, in trials for treason and other important offences with a political or constitutional element. In addition he exercises the prerogative power of staying prosecutions on indictment by the entry of a *nolle prosequi* and, by statute, leave of the Attorney-General is required for the commencement of certain criminal proceedings. Mention may also be made of "relator" proceedings in which the Attorney-General appears on behalf of a section of the public, for example to restrain a public nuisance.

Thus where there is a case of public nuisance, or some other interference with the public weal (not being a criminal offence) the rule is that an ordinary member of the public cannot sue; this rule is necessary in order to avoid multiplicity of actions. In such cases the Attorney-General has power to bring proceedings. His role has in one case been defined as follows:[17]

> "It is settled in our constitutional law that in matters which concern the public at large the Attorney-General is the guardian of the public interest. Although he is a member of the government of the day, it is his duty to represent the public interest with complete objectivity and detachment. He must act independently of any external pressure from whatever quarter it may come. As the guardian of the public interest, the Attorney-General has a special duty in regard to the enforcement of the law".

However, the Court of Appeal in that case suggested that there was an exception to the general rule so that, in the last resort, if the Attorney-General refused improperly or unreasonably to exercise his power to initiate proceedings, or if there was not sufficient time, a member of the public, aggrieved by non-observance of the law, could himself come to the courts and seek a declaration and, in a proper case, an injunction, joining the Attorney-General, if need be, as a defendant. This suggestion was, however, rejected firmly by the House of Lords in the important case of *Gouriet v. Union of Post Office Workers*.[18] The defendant trade union had resolved to

---

[17] *Per* Lord Denning, M.R. in *A.-G. (ex rel. McWhirter)* v. *Independent Broadcasting Authority*, [1973] Q.B. 629, at pp. 646–647; [1973] 1 All E.R. 689, at p. 697; the case involved an unsuccessful attempt by the late Mr. Ross McWhirter to prevent the showing of a television film about the American artist Andy Warhol.

[18] [1978] A.C. 435; [1977] 3 All E.R. 70.

call on its members not to handle mail from this country to South Africa, in support of a political protest against apartheid policy. This action would have amounted to a criminal offence under section 58 of the Post Office Act 1953. The plaintiff applied to the Attorney-General (Samuel Silkin, Q.C.) for his consent to act as plaintiff in a relator action against the union for an injunction to restrain the union from acting as it threatened to do, and thereby breaking the law. The Attorney-General refused his consent. The plaintiff thereupon issued a writ in his own name claiming an injunction and the question at issue was whether he was entitled so to do. The Court of Appeal held that he was[19] but the House of Lords, after hearing ten days of argument, reversed the Court of Appeal's decision. The House held that it was a fundamental principle of English law that public rights could only be asserted in a civil action by the Attorney-General as an officer of the Crown representing the public and that, except where statute otherwise provided, a private person could only bring an action to restrain a threatened breach of the law if such breach would infringe his private rights or would inflict special damage on him. Moreover the refusal of the Attorney-General to give his consent to a relator action is not subject to review by the courts, any more than is the exercise by the Attorney-General of any other of the powers and duties vested in him.

Accordingly the plaintiff's action was struck out. It may be noted, however, that had the defendant union actually committed a criminal offence, the plaintiff (or any other private person) could have instituted and pursued a private prosecution—although the Attorney-General could have brought this to a halt by entering a *nolle prosequi*.

The Solicitor-General's position is basically that of the Attorney-General's deputy and he may exercise any power vested by statute in the Attorney-General (unless the statute in question otherwise provides) if the office of Attorney-General is vacant, the Attorney-General is unable to act through illness or the Attorney-General authorises the Solicitor-General to act.[20]

2   Director of Public Prosecutions

The term "Law Officers" does not strictly include the Director of Public Prosecutions but mention may be made at this stage of this official who is a barrister or solicitor of not less than ten years standing appointed by the Home Secretary but working under the supervision of the Attorney-General.[1] It is the duty of the Director to institute, undertake or carry on such criminal proceedings, and to give such advice and assistance to chief officers of police, justices' clerks and other persons concerned in any criminal proceedings respecting those proceedings, as the Attorney-General may direct.[2] In practice the Director investigates and prosecutes in cases of great gravity

---

[19] [1977] Q.B. 729; [1977] 1 All E.R. 696.
[20] Law Officers Act 1944, s. 1.
[1] Prosecution of Offences Act 1979, s. 1; there are also Assistant Directors, who must be barristers or solicitors of not less than seven years standing (s. 1(2)). When the new Prosecution of Offences Act is implemented the Director will be appointed by the Attorney-General and will head the Crown Prosecution Service created by that Act.
[2] *Ibid.*, s. 2.

and complexity, notably murder and crimes of interference with the judicial process such as perjury and there are provisions requiring the police to inform the Director with respect to certain offences where there appears to be a *prima facie* case for proceedings.[3] There are, in addition, certain offences which, by statute, must be prosecuted by the Director.[4] Apart from these cases, there is nothing to stop any individual instituting criminal proceedings and, indeed, most prosecutions in England are instituted and carried on by private persons (usually police officers). However if the Director wishes to stop these proceedings, he has only to take them over and offer no evidence. In this way where (as has sometimes happened in recent years) the Director has granted immunity from prosecution to a criminal informer, in return for the latter giving evidence in other cases, he can (and will) give effect to this by intervening in any private prosecution which an individual may institute against the informer.[5] Finally certain statutes prescribe the consent of the Director of Public Prosecutions as a condition precedent to the institution of criminal proceedings.[6]

---

[3]   Prosecution of Offences Regulations 1978.

[4]   E.g. election offences under the Representation of the People Act 1983.

[5]   The courts have no power to interfere with the exercise of the Director's discretion unless, perhaps, it can be shown that his decision is one that could not honestly and reasonably have been arrived at: *Turner* v. *Director of Public Prosecutions*, (1978) 68 Cr. App. Rep. 70; *Raymond* v. *A.-G.*, [1982] Q.B. 839; [1982] 2 All E.R. 487.

[6]   E.g. Sexual Offences Act 1967, s. 8. If consent is not first obtained the subsequent trial is a nullity: *R.* v. *Angel*, [1968] 2 All E.R. 607n.; [1968] 1 W.L.R. 669.

CHAPTER 13

Legal Aid and Advice

A GENERAL ADMINISTRATION OF THE LEGAL AID SCHEME

Prior to 1949 there were various provisions to enable persons to sue or be sued *in forma pauperis* and to prosecute and defend both civil and criminal proceedings with the financial assistance of various societies and authorities. These provisions have now been almost totally replaced by statute. The grant of legal aid in both civil and criminal matters is governed by the Legal Aid Acts 1974 and 1982, together with numerous regulations passed under these Acts. The Legal Aid Acts created a national scheme for providing legal aid and advice to persons within the means limits, the expense being met out of a public fund known as the Legal Aid Fund financed by the State.

The general administration of Part I of the 1974 Act, which concerns legal aid in civil litigation, legal aid in matters not involving litigation and legal advice, is in the hands of The Law Society which acts in consultation with the Bar Council and under the general guidance of the Lord Chancellor.[1] For the purposes of the scheme England and Wales is divided into 15 areas. Each area has an area secretary who may grant (but not refuse) legal aid and three committees; first, the general committee which deals with applications for legal aid and the control of certificates and green forms; secondly, the area committee which deals with appeals against refusal of legal aid and financial matters such as the assessment of bills; finally, the criminal legal aid committee deals with reviews of magistrates' court decisions to refuse legal aid together with some aspects of the conduct of criminal proceedings. Area committees also deal with complaints against solicitors and barristers on these panels which may result in their names being removed.[2]

---

[1] Legal Aid Act 1974, s. 15. An explanation of the various form of legal aid is available in the *Legal Aid Guide*, obtainable from the Law Society or any legal aid office. In addition there is an annual *Legal Aid Handbook* available from H.M.S.O. and containing the statutory provisions currently in force.

[2] A barrister or solicitor aggrieved by a decision excluding him has a right of appeal to the High Court: Legal Aid Act 1974, s. 12(4) (substituted by Administration of Justice Act 1977, s. 1; Sch. 1).

B   LEGAL ADVICE AND ASSISTANCE

1   Nature of advice and assistance (Green form scheme)

The Legal Advice and Assistance Act 1972 introduced a completely new scheme for the giving of legal advice and assistance in relation to both civil and criminal matters. The aim of the scheme was to introduce a simple and effective method of providing legal advice and assistance so as to make these services more readily accessible to the public. The scheme, which is generally known as the "green form scheme", is now contained in sections 1 to 5 of the Act[3] (as amended by sections 1 to 3 of the 1979 Act) and in regulations.[4]

Under the scheme a solicitor, and so far as may be necessary counsel, may give oral or written advice on any question of English law and as to any steps which the applicant might appropriately take (whether by way of settling any claim, bringing or defending any proceedings, making an agreement, will or other instrument or transaction, obtaining further legal or other advice or otherwise) having regard to the application of English law to his problem. In addition, the 1979 Act added to the scheme "assistance by way of representation"[5] which means taking on a person's behalf any step in the institution or conduct of any proceedings, whether before a court or tribunal or in connection with a statutory enquiry, whether by representing him in those proceedings or otherwise. This provision is potentially of very far reaching effect because it extends the scope of legal aid to tribunals (which were, in general, outside the scope of the scheme prior to the 1979 Act). The scheme does not apply to advice or assistance given in connection with any proceedings in which there is already in existence a legal aid certificate or (in criminal proceedings) a legal aid order.[6] Regulations specify the proceedings to which the scheme applies. Under the Regulations currently in operation[7] it extends to domestic proceedings in magistrates' courts, proceedings before a Mental Health Review Tribunal and to representation of a parent or guardian in certain child care proceedings. It has recently been extended to proceedings before boards of visitors of custodial institutions[8] in consequence of public disquiet as to the safeguards available to prisoners appearing before such bodies.

The normal services which are provided under the scheme comprise such matters as general advice, writing letters, negotiating settlements and the like. It does not, save in those cases to which "assistance by way of representation" applies, extend to taking any step in proceedings (other than negotiating settlement) since this is a matter for legal aid proper rather than for legal advice or assistance.

---

3   References in this chapter to "the Act" are to the Legal Aid Act 1974, unless a contrary intention appears.
4   Currently the Legal Advice and Assistance (No. 2) Regulations 1980 (as amended).
5   Legal Aid Act 1974, s. 2A (added by Legal Aid Act 1979, s. 1).
6   Legal Aid Act 1974, s. 2(1), (2).
7   Legal Advice and Assistance Regulations (No. 2) 1980 (as amended).
8   Legal Advice and Assistance (Amendment) Regulations 1984.

2 Financial provisions

Legal advice and assistance under the scheme is available to applicants whose resources are within the limits specified in section 1 of the Act as amended by Regulations made thereunder. Under the present limits[9] an applicant is eligible if his "disposable income"[10] does not exceed £108 per week or he is in receipt of supplementary benefit or family income supplement and his "disposable capital"[10] does not exceed £765, but these limits have been the subject of frequent review in the past few years, and are likely to continue to be so.

The applicant must complete a form (the "green form") which contains requirements as to details of his income and capital so that the solicitor can decide his eligibility for legal advice and assistance.[11] If he is within the financial limits the solicitor must assess the contribution (if any) to be paid by the applicant. No contribution is payable by an applicant who is in receipt of supplementary benefit or family income supplement or has a disposable income not exceeding £49 per week. Above this a contribution calculated by reference to income, but not capital, is payable. If the solicitor is properly entitled to any further charge or fee, he has a first charge upon money or property recovered (subject to exceptions) and, in relation to any further deficiency, he is entitled to be paid out of the legal aid fund.

An important limitation upon the scope of the scheme is contained in section 3 of the Act whereby advice or assistance is only immediately available to the extent that the solicitor considers that the cost of giving it will not exceed £50 (or £90 in cases leading to the preparation of an undefended divorce or judicial separation petition).[12] If this limit is to be exceeded the solicitor must obtain the approval of the appropriate legal aid office. There will then, of necessity, be some delay. Therefore the scheme is limited in that an immediate service can only be provided to a somewhat elementary extent; nevertheless, in practice, much can be done for a client even within such limits and the scheme appears to have been a considerable success.

Finally, mention should be made of section 16 of the act whereby The Law Society is empowered (*inter alia*) to establish local law centres, such centres to be staffed by solicitors employed by The Law Society. The section has not yet been brought into operation,[13] although similar provision was contained in the 1972 Act. There are, of course, legal advice centres and neighbourhood law centres in existence but these operate autonomously and quite outside the scheme described above.

The fact that the services of counsel or solicitor are given under the Act

---

9 Legal Advice and Assistance (Financial Conditions) Regulations 1984 and Legal Advice and Assistance (Financial Conditions) (No. 2) Regulations 1984.

10 As to which, see p. 281, *post*.

11 It will be noted that the solicitor makes the calculation rather than the legal aid assessment officer (as in the case of legal aid). This is essential in order to enable the service to be provided without delay and effects a considerable saving of time and administrative expenses in proceedings where "assistance by way of representation" (as opposed to legal aid proper) is available.

12 Regulations may prescribe a larger sum (Legal Aid Act 1974, s. 3(2)).

13 The Report of the Royal Commission on Legal Services, paras. 8.15–8.38 recommended the establishment of a system of citizens' law centres, to provide legal advice, assistance and representation to those in the locality; these recommendations have not, as yet, been adopted.

rather than under private instructions does not, of course, affect the professional relationship and duties which spring from the relationship. The solicitor must exercise the same degree of care and skill in giving advice as he would normally and he must preserve the applicant's confidence[14] (except that he must complete and forward to the legal aid office the appropriate forms and must give to the legal aid authority any additional information that it may require).

C   LEGAL AID IN CIVIL PROCEEDINGS

1   Courts and proceedings in which legal aid is authorised by the Act

Legal aid is now available in connection with proceedings (unless specifically excepted) in the House of Lords, the Court of Appeal, the High Court, the Employment Appeal Tribunal, any county court, coroners' courts, proceedings in the Restrictive Practices Court under Part III of the Fair Trading Act 1973 and proceedings in the Lands Tribunal. It is also available in certain proceedings in magistrates' courts, notably proceedings under the Affiliation Proceedings Act 1957, the Domestic Proceedings and Magistrates' Courts Act 1978, the Guardianship of Minors Acts 1971 and 1973 and in certain proceedings under the Children and Young Persons Act 1963, the Children Act 1975, the Child Care Act 1980, the Maintenance Orders Act 1958 and the Maintenance Orders (Reciprocal Enforcement) Act 1972.[15]

There are, however, excepted proceedings in respect of which aid is not, at present, authorised under the Act. Of these the more important are proceedings wholly or partly in respect of defamation,[16] and undefended matrimonial proceedings (that is to say proceedings for divorce or judicial separation).[17] Where a legal aid order is made for the purpose of proceedings, that order extends to the costs of a reference to the European Court[18] since the reference to that court is simply a step in the proceedings in which it is made.[19]

Legal aid is not available in proceedings before judicial and administrative

---

[14] Act of 1974, s. 2(5); cf. *Kitchen* v. *Royal Air Force Association*, [1958] 2 All E.R. 241; [1958] 1 W.L.R. 563.

[15] Legal Aid Act 1974, s. 7; Sch. 1 (as amended). It is also available in contempt proceedings under s. 12 of the Contempt of Court Act 1981, in which proceedings the court may order that a person liable to be committed for contempt be given legal aid (*ibid.*, s. 13).

[16] Though the making of a counterclaim in respect of defamation in proceedings in which legal aid is available does not prevent the grant of legal aid to a defendant to the counterclaim; Legal Aid Act 1974, Sch. 1, Part II, para. 1.

[17] Legal Aid (Matrimonial Proceedings) Regulations 1977; there are limited exceptional cases in which legal aid is still available in such proceedings and legal aid continues to be available in proceedings for ancillary relief and for proceedings relating to children. The taking of undefended divorce out of the legal aid scheme was an important reform since a high proportion of the cost of the legal aid scheme in civil proceedings was attributable to undefended divorces. The saving was estimated to be of the order of £6 million a year.

[18] As to which, see p. 185, *ante*.

[19] *R*. v. *Marlborough Street Stipendiary Magistrate, Ex parte Bouchereau*, [1977] 3 All E.R. 365; [1977] 1 W.L.R. 414.

tribunals, which most people[20] consider a notable omission in view of the increasing volume of business dealt with therein, particularly in industrial tribunals. It is for this reason that the provisions introduced by the 1979 Act for bringing "assistance by way of representation" within the advice and assistance scheme (*supra*) are potentially so important.

Nor, of course, is legal aid available in arbitrations. This may seem to confer a considerable benefit upon defendants (especially where they have insurers behind them) who can invoke an arbitration clause thereby preventing an impecunious plaintiff from pursuing his rights with proper legal representation. The mere fact that the plaintiff is insolvent does not prevent the defendant from obtaining a stay,[1] although if it appears that his insolvency was caused by the defendant's breaches of contract a stay may be refused[2] (with the result that the action will proceed and the plaintiff may apply for legal aid).

2 Conditions under which aid may be granted

Any person, not being a body corporate or an unincorporated body,[3] may apply for legal aid irrespective of nationality or residence. He must, however, be within the prescribed financial limits, this being the first condition precedent to the grant of legal aid. His "disposable income" must not exceed £5,155 a year[4] and, if required, the applicant must show that his "disposable capital" does not exceed £4,710[5] or, if it does, that he could not afford to proceed without legal aid. Disposable income and disposable capital are assessed by the assessment officer of the Department of Health and Social Security in accordance with section 11 of the Act and the Legal Aid (Assessment of Resources) Regulations 1980 as amended. These Regulations are complex. It is important to note that disposable income[6] is far less than gross income. Deductions are prescribed in respect of the maintenance of dependants, income tax, interest on loans, rates, rent and other matters so that a disposable income of £5000 may well represent, in some cases, a gross income of £16,000 or more. A spouse's resources are, as a rule, treated as the applicant's resources for these purposes. A common criticism of the disposable capital limit is that it tends to penalise those who have been prudent enough to accumulate modest savings. The Royal Commission on Legal Services, among several recommendations concerning legal aid, advice and assistance, stated that the underlying principle should be that an assisted

---

[20] Including the Lord Chancellor's Advisory Committee on Legal Aid who have recommended to the Lord Chancellor and to the Royal Commission on Legal Services the extension of the scheme to all statutory tribunals under the supervision of the Council on Tribunals: 28th Legal Aid Annual Reports (1977–78), p. 91.

[1] *Smith* v. *Pearl Assurance Co., Ltd.*, [1939] 1 All E.R. 95.

[2] *Fakes* v. *Taylor Woodrow Construction, Ltd.*, [1973] Q.B. 436; [1973] 1 All E.R. 670.

[3] Act of 1974, s. 25.

[4] The current figure is prescribed by the Legal Aid (Financial Conditions) Regulations 1984, made under section 6(2) of the Act. The figure may be further increased by Regulations under this section.

[5] This figure, currently prescribed by the 1984 Regulations, may be varied by Regulations under section 6(2).

[6] Receipts are "income" only if they have an element of recurrence so that *ad hoc* gifts are not income; *R* v. *Supplementary Benefits Commission, Ex parte Singer*, [1973] 2 All E.R. 931; [1973] 1 W.L.R. 713.

person "should not suffer an undue financial burden in pursuing his legal rights",[7] that the eligibility limits be abolished, that the free limit of disposable income should be increased to £3,000, the free limit of disposable capital to £10,000 and the contribution proportion above the free limits be reduced to one-fifth.[8]

The second condition precedent to a grant of legal aid is that the applicant must show that he has reasonable grounds for taking, defending or being a party to the proceedings.[9] In particular a certificate will not be granted in respect of proceedings at first instance where it appears to the Local Committee that the proceedings are too trivial or simple to warrant the assistance of a solicitor.

If a certificate is granted it may be marked with a contribution payable by the assisted litigant. The maximum contribution in proceedings is all the assisted person's disposable capital above a prescribed figure and one-quarter of the amount by which his annual disposable income exceeds a prescribed figure.[10]

3 Application for a certificate

An application for a legal aid certificate must be made on one of three forms approved by The Law Society (according to the nature of the proceedings). There is a fourth form on which to apply for an "emergency certificate", which may be granted where delay would cause a risk of miscarriage of justice or an unreasonable degree of hardship or other problems in the handling of the case; emergency certificates will usually authorise only the taking of immediate steps in order to protect the interests of the applicant. In most cases it takes about six weeks for an application to be granted or refused, this time being mainly attributable to the financial assessment, usually based on interview, which is undertaken by the legal aid assessment officers of the Department of Health and Social Security. The legal aid office may grant a certificate, although only the general committee can refuse an application.[11]

Assuming that the applicant's means qualify him for legal aid, he must still satisfy other criteria before a certificate will be granted.[12] In particular he must be regarded as having a reasonable case on its merits (for which purpose the opinion of counsel is often required); legal aid will not be granted where it appears that only a trivial advantage would be derived from the proceedings nor where the applicant has available rights or facilities making it unnecessary for him to obtain legal aid (for example, where he is entitled to legal representation through his insurance company or trade union). Where legal

---

[7] Report, para. 12.28.

[8] *Ibid.*, paras. 12.32, 12.40, 12.43, 12.48 and 12.52; of these recommendations, only the second has been adopted.

[9] Legal Aid Act 1974, s. 7(5).

[10] *Ibid.*, s. 9(1) (as substituted by Legal Aid Act 1979, s. 4). The figures are regularly varied by Regulations under section 9. At the time of writing the income figure is £2,145 and the capital figure is £3,000 (Legal Aid (Financial Conditions) Regulations 1984).

[11] In contempt of court proceedings an order in favour of a person liable to be committed may be made by the court in question: Contempt of Court Act 1981, s. 13.

[12] See Legal Aid (General) Regulations 1980, regs. 29–34.

aid is refused by a general committee there is a right of appeal to the appropriate area committee.

The certificate may be, and often is, limited to the taking of certain steps in the action. Thus, in the first instance it is frequently limited to the taking of counsel's opinion, on the basis of which the legal aid authority will consider whether to amend the certificate so as to extend it to enable further steps to be taken in the action or, on the contrary, to discharge it. By these powers of amendment and discharge it is possible for the legal aid authority to supervise the conduct of the litigation to some extent, or at least to see, as far as possible, that large amounts of costs are not expended in pursuing hopelessly lost causes. There is, of course, a duty on both solicitors and counsel not to advise the pursuit of cases which do not justify the support of the legal aid fund.

4 The effects on the proceedings of a party being aided

a Relationship between the assisted litigant and his solicitor and counsel

The professional relationship of solicitor and client is not prejudiced by the fact of the client being in receipt of legal aid. The solicitor's general duties are still owed to the client and he has authority to act for the client, unless the act performed is not within the scope of the certificate. Thus it has been held[13] that a solicitor is under a duty not to instruct leading counsel, even though authorised by the legal aid authority so to do, without first obtaining the client's specific agreement and authority after informing him of the probable cost and the potential effect upon the client's assets having regard to the legal aid fund's charge on property recovered or preserved in the action (as to which see *infra*). The solicitor must preserve his client's confidences though he is in some cases obliged to furnish information to the legal aid committees which would normally be privileged.

The chief effect of legal aid on the solicitor-client relationship is upon costs. The solicitor has no right to any costs from the client and he must not charge or take any sum in respect of costs. It follows that any item of costs incurred by a solicitor which is not allowed by the area committee or by the court on taxation is irrecoverable so that a disbursement of this nature will have to be met by the solicitor personally. In certain cases costs are assessed by the area committee.[14] Otherwise in High Court proceedings the court must order the assisted person's costs to be taxed pursuant to the second schedule of the 1974 Act. These costs are taxed on a "common fund" basis.[15] After taxation the solicitor may recover from the Fund the full amount allowed on taxation for disbursements and 90 *per cent*[16] of the amount allowed in respect of profit costs. Counsel receives 90 *per cent*[16] of the fee allowed on taxation (his brief is not marked with a fee before the proceedings as it must be in other cases). However taxation is not necessary where an

---

13 *Re Solicitors*, [1982] 2 All E.R. 683; [1982] 1 W.L.R. 745.
14 See Legal Aid (General) Regulations 1980, reg. 100.
15 Legal Aid Act 1974, Sch. 2, para. 4(1); see Rules of the Supreme Court (Revision) 1965, O. 62, r. 28(4), p. 389, *post*.
16 The full amount is recoverable in respect of proceedings in county courts.

assisted litigant is successful and the costs payable by the other party are agreed with the assisted party's solicitor and counsel (if any).[17]

b   Assisted litigant's liability for costs

An assisted person has, as stated above, no liability for costs towards his own solicitor and counsel. His primary liability to the Legal Aid Fund is limited to the amount of his contribution. However, if he loses his action he may be ordered to pay the costs of the other side. This does not mean that he must pay the full taxed costs of his opponent. His liabilities are limited to such amount (if any) which is a reasonable one for him to pay, having regard to the means of all the parties and their conduct in connection with the dispute.[18] In determining this amount, the assisted person's dwellinghouse, household furniture and tools and implements of his trade are not to be taken into account.[19] In addition the order may direct payment by instalments or may suspend payment *sine die*. The order may, however, be varied within six years if circumstances change.

An assisted person cannot be required by the court to pay the costs of an unsuccessful interlocutory application forthwith. Also, an assisted person is not usually ordered to give security for costs although such an order can be, and has been, made.[20]

If the assisted litigant is awarded costs, these are payable by his opponent in the ordinary way. These costs are paid directly into the Legal Aid Fund. If the sums paid out by the Fund[1] to the assisted person's solicitor and counsel exceed the amount paid in, comprising the assisted person's contribution and costs recovered from the other side, the Fund has a first charge for the balance on any property recovered or preserved in the proceedings, with certain exemptions, notably maintenance in matrimonial proceedings.[2] Thus if an assisted person is successful the public will not generally be the loser, which is the reason for the public cost of the Legal Aid scheme being relatively so low.

---

[17] The costs are then assessed by the area committee; the provision was introduced in 1983 and has been successful in reducing the number of taxations required in legal aid cases: Legal Aid (General) Regulations 1980, regs. 29–34.

[18] Legal Aid Act 1974, s. 8(1) (*e*); see *Peeling* v. *Guidice* (1963), 186 Estates Gazette 133.

[19] *Ibid.*, s. 8(4). On the other hand the court, in considering what is a reasonable amount for the assisted litigant to pay, may take into account the fact that he has been awarded damages: *Nolan* v. *C. and C. Marshall, Ltd.*, [1954] 2 Q.B. 42; [1954] 1 All E.R. 328.

[20] *Wyld* v. *Silver* (*No. 2*), [1962] 2 All E.R. 809; [1962] 1 W.L.R. 863.

[1] Including sums paid by way of advice or assistance in connection with those proceedings: Legal Aid Act 1974, s. 9(9) (as substituted by Legal Aid Act 1979, s. 5).

[2] Legal Aid Act 1974, s. 9(6). The Law Society is bound to enforce this charge, for the benefit of taxpayers generally although it will postpone enforcement in appropriate cases (but not where the charge is on money); nor is a dwelling house apparently exempt from the charge. A defendant who successfully resists a claim to a beneficial interest in his dwelling-house (for example in proceedings under section 17 of the Married Women's Property Act 1882) may find that, since the property has been "preserved" in the action, his house is charged with payment of his costs: *Till* v. *Till*, [1974] Q.B. 558; [1974] 1 All E.R. 1096. Moreover the charge extends to property received pursuant to a compromise of an action notwithstanding that the property concerned was not in issue in that action: *Van Hoorn* v. *The Law Society*, [1984] 3 All E.R. 136; see also *Hanlon* v. *The Law Society*, [1981] A.C. 124; [1980] 2 All E.R. 199; *Simmons* v. *Simmons*, [1984] Fam. 17; [1984] 1 All E.R. 83.

c Unassisted person's rights to costs

It follows from the preceding paragraph that the unassisted litigant appearing against an assisted litigant is at a substantial disadvantage in the matter of costs. If he loses he pays full costs; if he wins he recovers only limited costs, or, as often as not, no costs at all. It was to remedy this serious abuse that the Legal Aid Act 1964 was passed. This Act (the relevant provisions of which are now contained in sections 13 and 14 of the 1974 Act) was at first interpreted and applied by the courts in a very restrictive manner,[3] so much so that over the period of three years after the passing of the Act, Parliament provided no less than £120,000 for the purposes of the Act, of which only £1,155 was used. However, in *Hanning* v. *Maitland* (*No. 2*)[4] the Court of Appeal laid down broader principles for the application of the Act, stating that if the legally aided party lost the action it was usually just and equitable that the unassisted party should recover his costs from public funds, unless, for example, he has done something to bring the action on himself or has been guilty of misconduct.

Section 13 of the 1974 Act provides that an unassisted party appearing against an assisted party may be awarded the whole or any part of his costs out of the Legal Aid Fund, provided that the proceedings are finally decided in favour of the unassisted party,[5] that those proceedings were instituted by the assisted party in the court of first instance and provided "the court is satisfied that the unassisted party will suffer severe financial hardship unless the order is made".[6] "Severe financial hardship" is not, however, strictly interpreted so that in *Hanning* v. *Maitland* (*No. 2*), LORD DENNING, M.R. stated that the condition should not be construed as to exclude people of modest income or modest capital who would find it hard to bear their own costs. A company may suffer "severe financial hardship".[7] Furthermore no

---

3 See *Nowotnik* v. *Nowotnik*, [1967] P. 83; [1965] 3 All E.R. 167; *Re Spurling's Will Trusts*, [1966] 1 All E.R. 745; [1966] 1 W.L.R. 920; *Re Sl.* (*infants*), [1967] 3 All E.R. 538; [1967] 1 W.L.R. 1379.

4 [1970] 1 Q.B. 580; [1970] 1 All E.R. 812. Nevertheless the total amounts paid out of the Fund under these provisions have continued to be modest.

5 In *Kelly* v. *London Transport Executive*, [1982] 2 All E.R. 842; [1982] 1 W.L.R. 1055, it was held that where the plaintiff had failed to beat the payment into court and had been ordered to pay costs, which meant that he recovered nothing at all, the proceedings had been "finally decided in favour of the unassisted party".

6 The need to show "severe financial hardship" exists only in relation to proceedings at first instance (s. 13(3)) and not to proceedings on appeal where the applicant need only show that it is "just and equitable" that an order be made (s. 13(2)): *Parker* (*infants*) v. *Thompson*, [1966] 3 All E.R. 766; [1967] 1 W.L.R. 28; *Gallie* v. *Lee* (*No. 2*), [1971] A.C. 1039; [1971] 1 All E.R. 243 (in which case a Building Society was awarded its costs out of the Legal Aid Fund); *Lewis* v. *Averay* (*No. 2*), [1973] 2 All E.R. 229; [1973] 1 W.L.R. 510. Indeed the fact that the unassisted party has been successful in the appeal may in itself be sufficient to justify an order in his favour: *Davies* v. *Taylor* (*No. 2*), [1974] A.C. 225; [1973] 1 All E.R. 959. The practice in the Court of Appeal is for the Court to state its intention whether the Legal Aid Fund should bear all or part of the unassisted party's costs and to give The Law Society ten weeks notice to enable them to appear and object to the proposed order; then, if no objection is made within that time, an order will be made: *Maynard* v. *Osmond* (*No. 2*), [1979] 1 All E.R. 483; [1979] 1 W.L.R. 31. Proceedings on appeal, for this purpose, include interlocutory appeals: *Megarity* v. *The Law Society*, [1982] A.C. 81; [1981] 1 All E.R. 641.

7 *Thew* (*R. & T.*), *Ltd.* v. *Reeves*, [1982] Q.B. 172; [1981] 2 All E.R. 964; in *Kelly* v. *London Transport Executive* (*supra*) the Court of Appeal, with apparent reluctance, felt unable to accede to the defendants' bold contention that the loss of £8,000 in costs would amount to severe financial hardship.

order is to be made unless an order in favour of the unassisted party would be made apart from this Act; thus, in divorce suits a wife is not usually ordered to pay her husband's costs, unless she has sufficient separate estate. If an assisted wife would not be required to pay her unassisted husband's costs, the latter has no recourse to the Fund.[8]

Apart from the above provisions, which affect costs, proceedings are not generally affected by one or more of the parties being legally aided. Indeed proceedings may be lengthened since litigants are naturally not anxious to compromise proceedings which they are fighting at the public expense. This is one of the principal criticisms of the scheme to which may be added the fact that legal aid is not available before most tribunals and the inequitable position of the unassisted litigant, particularly where he is a plaintiff (and therefore at any rate at first instance, outside the scope of the provisions for payment of his costs out of the Fund). For this reason insurance companies in industrial injuries actions often make payments in settlement of unmeritorious claims by legally aided plaintiffs, simply because, in the long run, this will prove a less expensive expedient than contesting the case successfully. There is a further anomaly in that a successful assisted litigant appearing against another assisted litigant may well find himself in a worse position than if he were unassisted since an assisted party cannot obtain an order under section 13 (*supra*) against the Fund, whereas the property he recovers will be subject to The Law Society's statutory charge.

It is generally agreed that some reform of the legal aid scheme in civil cases is overdue in order to deal with the above, and other, points.

D LEGAL AID IN CRIMINAL PROCEEDINGS

Criminal proceedings, formerly outside the scope of the legal aid scheme, are now provided for in Part II of the Legal Aid Act 1974. However, in contrast to civil proceedings, the order is made by the court.

There are two basic differences between legal aid in criminal proceedings and legal aid in civil proceedings. The first is that, due to the importance of expedition in criminal proceedings, there is not time for the elaborate formalities relating to applications for certificates and assessment of resources which take place in civil cases. The result is that application is usually to the magistrates or the court of trial and any assessment of resources or contribution by the accused may take place after an order has been made. However a court, before it makes a legal aid order, must require the applicant to furnish a written statement of means and, if it appears from this statement that he will be required to make a contribution and has the means to make an immediate payment, may refuse an order unless the applicant first makes a

---

[8] Legal Aid Act 1974, s. 13(4); *Nowotnik* v. *Nowotnik* (*supra*); *Povey* v. *Povey*, [1972] Fam. 40; [1970] 3 All E.R. 612; cf. *Stewart* v. *Stewart*, [1974] 2 All E.R. 795; [1974] 1 W.L.R. 877. However, if a husband had made a *Calderbank* offer (cf. *Calderbank* v. *Calderbank*, [1976] Fam. 93; [1975] 3 All E.R. 333; p. 387, *post*) which the wife rejects, and it is subsequently held that she ought to have accepted it, then it would ordinarily follow that the husband be awarded his costs against the wife and, in such cases, the husband is likely to be awarded his costs out of the Legal Aid Fund: *McDonnell* v. *McDonnell*, [1977] 1 All E.R. 766; [1977] 1 W.L.R. 34.

payment on account.[9] In magistrates' courts the application is initially dealt with by the clerk to the justices. If he refuses legal aid, appeal is to a criminal legal aid committee of The Law Society if the offence is triable on indictment or "either way"[10] or to the justices themselves in the case of summary offences. The legal aid order will be a "through" order which covers the Crown Court as well as the committal proceedings.[11] As well as hearing appeals from refusals of legal aid by a magistrates' court, criminal legal aid committees deal with two other matters: first, where there is an application to a magistrates' court for the assignment of counsel in proceedings in that court under a legal aid order the court, if it does not grant the application, must refer it to the committee; secondly, applications by solicitors for prior authority to incur expenditure on obtaining an expert's or other report, bespeaking transcripts of shorthand notes or tape recordings of any proceedings or "performing an act which is either unusual in its nature or involves unusually large expenditure" must be made direct to the committee.[12]

The second essential difference between civil and criminal legal aid is that, while in civil proceedings there is a wide discretion in the matter of granting certificates, legal aid must be granted where it is desirable in the interests of justice,[13] and an accused will rarely be refused legal aid, on grounds other than financial ones, where he is charged with a serious crime, even if he intends to plead guilty.[14] Moreover on committal for trial on a charge of murder or on the prosecution appealing, or applying for leave to appeal, from the criminal division of the Court of Appeal or the Courts-Martial Appeal Court to the House of Lords, the court must make a legal aid order.[15]

The House of Lords does not grant legal aid although aid may be granted by the court below in respect of an appeal to the House. Where the appeal is from or the proceedings are before a divisional court of the Queen's Bench Division application is, anomalously, to the appropriate Area Committee of The Law Society since these are treated as civil proceedings for the purpose of legal aid.

In relation to all other criminal proceedings the power to grant legal aid is now contained in section 28 of the 1974 Act.[16]

---

[9] Legal Aid Act 1974, s. 39(3), (4).

[10] As to which see p. 457, *post.*

[11] Legal Aid Act 1982, s. 2. For full details of the procedure, see Legal Aid in Criminal Proceedings (General) Regulations 1968 (as amended).

[12] 1968 Regulations (as amended), regs. 14A, 14D.

[13] Legal Aid Act 1974, s. 29(1). The criteria to be followed by the court are the Widgery Criteria, *viz.* (*a*) the charge is a grave one, in the sense that the accused is in real jeopardy of losing his liberty or livelihood or suffering serious damage to his reputation; or (*b*) the charge raises a substantial question of law; or (*c*) the accused is unable to follow the proceedings or state his case; or (*d*) the nature of the defence involves tracing or interviewing witnesses or expert cross-examination; or (*e*) legal representation is desirable in the interests of someone other than the accused, for example in the case of sexual offences against young children.

[14] See *R.* v. *Howes,* [1964] 2 Q.B. 459; [1964] 2 All E.R. 172.

[15] Legal Aid Act 1974, s. 29(1).

[16] Section 28 extends to certain proceedings under the Children and Young Persons Act 1969 which are not, strictly, criminal proceedings, namely "care proceedings" brought under section 1 of the Act (see p. 208, *ante*), proceedings under sections 15 and 21 of the Act (variation and discharge of supervision and care orders) and under section 31 (removal to borstal institutions of persons committed to the care of local authorities). An order may be made at any stage of the proceedings and, apparently, may extend even to that part of the proceedings which has taken place before the order is made: *R.* v. *Tullett,* [1976] 2 All E.R. 1032; [1976] 1 W.L.R. 241.

Where a person appears before the Crown Court, whether for trial or sentence, a legal aid order may be made either by the court by which or by the court to which he is committed. Similarly on appeal from a magistrates' court to the Crown Court either of these courts may make an order.

In relation to appeals to the criminal division of the Court of Appeal, that court may grant legal aid for the purposes of the appeal and any proceedings preliminary or incidental thereto.

As a rule legal aid consists of representation by a solicitor and counsel and includes advice on the preparation of the accused's case. However in magistrates' courts legal aid does not extend to representation by counsel except in the case of an unusually grave or difficult indictable offence,[17] while in certain cases there is power to order legal aid to consist of representation by counsel only.[18]

An assisted person may be ordered by the court to pay such contribution as appears reasonable, having regard to his commitments and resources.[19] A contribution may be ordered to be paid by instalments. If the assisted person fails to pay any contribution, or any instalment thereof, this may be recovered in a magistrates' court as a civil debt or enforced as a judgment debt in the High Court or a county court.[20]

Duty Solicitor Scheme—The Legal Aid Act 1982, s. 1 authorised the creation of a scheme for the provision of advice and representation by solicitors in attendance at magistrates' courts. In consequence, with effect from October 1983, the Legal Aid (Duty Solicitor) Scheme 1983 was implemented.

The more important provisions of the scheme are as follows. Under this Scheme regional duty solicitor committees have been set up within which are local duty solicitor committees, each including at least three solicitors with "considerable current experience of advocacy in criminal cases in magistrates' courts",[1] together with others who may be justices or justices' clerks or other persons (not being practising barristers).

Each local duty solicitor committee must make arrangements for advice and representation to be provided on a rota basis by duty solicitors at courts within the scheme. It must also ensure that arrangements exist to inform all defendants who are eligible for advice or representation of the availability of the duty solicitor.[2]

The duty solicitor must inform every defendant to whom he offers advice or representation that the defendant is entitled to instruct any solicitor and

---

[17] Legal Aid Act 1974, s. 30(2). This includes an offence which is triable either way (as to which see p. 457, *post*): Interpretation Act 1978, s. 5; Sch. 1; *R. v. Guildhall Justices, Ex parte Marshall*, [1976] 1 All E.R. 767; [1976] 1 W.L.R. 335.

[18] *Ibid.*, s. 30(3), (4). Magistrates cannot order legal aid providing for more than one counsel, except in murder cases: Legal Aid in Criminal Proceedings (General) Regulations 1978. Consequently an application for the services of two counsel in other cases must be directed to the Crown Court.

[19] Legal Aid Act 1982, s. 7. Where the assisted person is under the age of 16, the order for payment of contributions may be made against anyone who is an "appropriate contributor" in relation to the assisted person (s. 7(3)), which expression includes the assisted person's father, any person who has been adjudged to be his putative father or his mother.

[20] Legal Aid Act 1974, s. 35(1), (2) and Sch. 3.

[1] Legal Aid (Duty Solicitor) Scheme 1983, reg. 8(2).

[2] *Ibid.*, reg. 10.

must not act for him if he has his own solicitor who is available to act, unless the duty solicitor is specifically asked in writing by the defendant to act for him.[3]

Provided that he has not previously received advice or representation on the same charge or charges, the defendant is entitled to have the following assistance from the duty solicitor: (*a*) advice if he is in custody; (*b*) the making of a bail application.[4] In addition, unless the duty solicitor considers that in the interests of justice or of the defendant the case should be adjourned, he must represent the defendant if he is pleading guilty and wishes the case to be concluded at that appearance in court or help him to make an application for a legal aid order in respect of any subsequent appearance of the defendant before the court.[5]

---

[3] *Ibid.*, reg. 13(1), (2).
[4] *Ibid.*, reg. 14(1).
[5] *Ibid.*, reg. 14(2). Remuneration to the solicitor is provided in accordance with the Legal Advice and Representation (Remuneration) Regulations 1983.

PART IV

Civil Procedure

The jurisdiction of the various English courts has been considered. The chapters in this section deal with civil proceedings in the Queen's Bench Division of the High Court, county court proceedings and appeals in civil cases. Procedure in the Chancery Division is basically similar to procedure in the Queen's Bench Division though there are, of course, certain differences due to the specialised nature of many Chancery matters. Procedure in the Family Division, to which brief reference has been made in Chapter 9, differs substantially from Queen's Bench Division procedure and will not be considered further in this work.

CHAPTER 14

Preliminary Considerations in an Action in the Queen's Bench Division

A RULES OF THE SUPREME COURT

Procedure in the Queen's Bench Division is governed by the Rules of the Supreme Court. These Rules are delegated legislation, being made by a Rule Committee under powers conferred formerly by the Judicature Acts and currently contained in section 84 of the Supreme Court Act 1981.

The Rules were recently revised; the current Rules[1] are the Rules of the Supreme Court (Revision) 1965 (as amended). The Rules themselves together with guides to their interpretation are to be found in the current edition of the Supreme Court Practice (the "White Book") which, formerly published annually, is now produced in a new edition every three years with periodical supplements. It must be stressed that the Rules are purely procedural and cannot affect substantive rules of law. In the words of a Master of the Rolls:

"... The relation of the rules of practice to the work of justice is intended to be that of handmaiden rather than mistress ..."[2]

Thus the Court of Appeal has in two modern cases declared certain of the Rules to be *ultra vires*, as being substantive rather than procedural.[3]

It should also be appreciated that the Rules are not an exhaustive code either of the jurisdiction of the Supreme Court or of the procedure whereby

---

[1] The Rules of the Supreme Court have their source in the Common Law Procedure Acts 1852 and 1854 and the Court of Chancery Procedure Act 1852 (15 & 16 Vict., c. 86). These were substantially reproduced in a Schedule to the Judicature Acts 1873–1875 and later embodied in the Rules of the Supreme Court 1883, a statutory instrument drawn up by the Rule Committee. The current Rules were made under s. 99 of the Judicature Act 1925, the statutory predecessor of s. 84 of the Supreme Court Act 1981.

[2] Sir RICHARD HENN-COLLINS, M.R. in *Re Coles and Ravenshear*, [1907] 1 K.B. 1, at p. 4.

[3] *Re Grosvenor Hotel, London (No. 2)*, [1965] Ch. 1233; [1964] 3 All E.R. 354; *Ward* v. *James*, [1966] 1 Q.B. 273; [1965] 1 All E.R. 563; the Rules in question have since been amended.

that jurisdiction may be invoked. The Supreme Court has, as have all courts whose jurisdiction does not derive entirely from statute, inherent powers and jurisdiction which do not derive from statute and are not necessarily formulated in statutory enactments. Thus, by way of example, the Supreme Court has inherent power to prevent abuse of the process of the court by staying proceedings or striking out claims.[4] The power of a judge to refuse to hear persons who have no right of audience before the court, or counsel who are improperly dressed, or to sit in camera, or to abort a trial and start a new one where a procedural irregularity has occurred, or to adjourn the proceedings are all inherent powers. In recent years the important developments of *Mareva*[5] injunctions and *Anton Piller*[6] orders have derived from the inherent jurisdiction of the court and the judges have formulated their own procedural requirements ancillary to the exercise of their jurisdiction in these areas.

B   DISCOVERY, INSPECTION AND RELATED PROCEDURES BEFORE COMMENCEMENT OF PROCEEDINGS

Questions concerning discovery and inspection of documents and the inspection, preservation and the like of property are dealt with during the course of proceedings, usually after the close of pleadings, and these matters are dealt with below in that context. However statutory provisions enable parties to obtain orders of this type prior to the commencement of proceedings. There are two distinct procedures.

1   Discovery and inspection of documents

By section 33(2) of the Supreme Court Act 1981[7] a person who appears to the High Court to be likely to be a party to subsequent proceedings in that court in which a claim in respect of personal injuries to a person or in respect of a person's death is likely to be made, may apply to the court[8] whereupon a party who appears to be likely to be a party to the proceedings and to be likely to have or have had in his possession, custody or power any relevant documents may be ordered to disclose whether those documents are in his custody, possession and power and, if so, to produce them to the applicant, save that if they would be privileged from production he may claim privilege from

---

4   See p. 321, *post*.
5   See p. 297, *post*.
6   See p. 296, *post*.
7   Replacing Administration of Justice Act 1970, s. 31.
8   The application is by originating summons supported by an affidavit which must (*a*) state the grounds upon which it is alleged that the applicant and the person against whom the order is sought are likely to be parties to subsequent proceedings of the type specified in section 33(2); and (*b*) specify or describe the documents concerned and showing, if practicable by reference to a draft pleading, their relevance.

    The summons and copy affidavit are served on the other party and require him to make an affidavit stating whether any documents specified or described are or have been in his custody, possession or power and, if not then in his custody, possession or power what has become of them; O. 24, r. 7A (1), (3)–(5).

production in the normal way.[9] It is immaterial that the likelihood of the claim being made is dependent upon the outcome of the discovery; the words "likely to be made" in the section are to be construed as meaning "may or may well be made" if, on discovery, the documents in question indicate that the applicant has a good cause of action.[10]

It will be noted that the above procedure is limited to personal injuries litigation. It may be utilised, for example, by a plaintiff to enable him to see his employer's accident reports or documents relating to the maintenance of a vehicle or machine which has proved defective.[11] The object of this provision is to enable personal injuries litigation to be conducted openly and with a view to early settlement if possible.

2 Inspection etc. of property

Section 33(1) of the Supreme Court Act 1981[12] empowers the High Court, in such circumstances as may be specified in rules of court, to make an order providing for the inspection, photographing, preservation, custody or detention of property (including land or chattels) which appears to the court to be property which may become the subject-matter of subsequent proceedings in the court or as to which any question may arise in such proceedings, or for the taking of samples of any such property and the carrying out of any experiment on or with any such property.

The rule made under the section[13] is not now (although it originally was) limited to personal injuries actions although the objects of the section are clearly similar to the objects of section 33(2). Unlike that provision, however, section 33(1) is not limited to personal injuries actions nor is it limited to prospective parties.

---

[9] O. 24, r. 7A (6); see p. 357, *post.*

[10] *Dunning* v. *United Liverpool Hospitals Board of Governors*, [1973] 2 All E.R. 454; [1973] 1 W.L.R. 586. This case concerned the disclosure of medical records. Applications under the rule are frequently made in this type of case, namely actions against doctors and hospitals for damages for professional negligence because, in the nature of things, a party (and his own expert witnesses) can hardly formulate his claim properly, nor can counsel advise upon merits, without knowing what took place while the plaintiff was being treated by the defendant, and this will almost always necessitate inspecting the medical records relating to the diagnosis and treatment of the plaintiff's medical condition. The standard form of order used to limit disclosure, in the first instance, to the applicant's medical adviser, but the rules do not provide for orders in this form and the House of Lords has held that they cannot properly be made: *McIvor* v. *Southern Health and Social Services Board*, [1978] 2 All E.R. 625; [1978] 1 W.L.R. 757.

[11] Cf. *Shaw* v. *Vauxhall Motors, Ltd.*, [1974] 2 All E.R. 1185; [1974] 1 W.L.R. 1035 in which an order was made for the discovery of documents relating to the inspection, maintenance and repair of a fork lift truck which was alleged to have caused an accident due to a braking defect (this being the applicant's only cause of complaint against his employers). The Court of Appeal, in the case, expressly took into account the fact that the proposed plaintiff was legally aided so that there was the public interest in saving costs to be considered.

[12] Replacing Administration of Justice Act 1969, s. 21.

[13] O. 29, r. 7A. The application is by originating summons and the procedure is similar to that under O. 24, r. 7A (*supra*). An order may be made conditional on the applicant giving security for the costs of the person against whom the order is sought (r. 7A (5)); no order will be made if it appears to the court that this would result in the disclosure of information relating to a secret process, discovery or invention not in issue in the proceedings (r. 7A (6)).

3   Anton Piller orders

In addition to the statutory powers referred to above, the High Court has an inherent jurisdiction to order a defendant to permit a plaintiff to enter the defendant's premises in order to inspect, remove or make copies of documents belonging to the plaintiff or relating to the plaintiff's property. Such an order is known as an *Anton Piller* order, after the case in which the Court of Appeal first sanctioned this type of order.[14] An order may be obtained *ex parte* but will only be made where the plaintiff shows that there is a grave danger of property being smuggled away or vital evidence destroyed; it is usually applicable to infringement of copyright cases or cases of that sort.[15] An *Anton Piller* order may, at first sight, appear to be in the nature of a search warrant issued to a private individual, but in fact it is not; it confers upon the plaintiff no right to enter the defendant's premises, but rather creates a duty to the court on the part of the defendant to permit the plaintiff to enter his premises. Failure on the part of the defendant to comply will, however, be a contempt of court.

The *Anton Piller* application has become extremely popular with plaintiffs and their advisers. By its very nature it may enable a plaintiff to strike gold in relation to wrongful acts, such as misuse of confidential information or infringement of copyright, which but for the order the plaintiff might possibly never have been in a position to prove (defendants in these matters frequently being less than frank as to voluntary discovery); all that the plaintiff risks is having to pay his opponent's costs of the application and damages if any are caused.[16] In order to minimise speculative and oppressive applications the courts have formulated several procedural safeguards. Thus the plaintiff's solicitor should attend when the order is executed; if permission to enter premises is refused no force should be used; the defendant should have the opportunity to contact his solicitor and should be advised of his right to obtain legal advice.[17] The applicant must make full disclosure to the court of all matters relevant to his application and if material facts are omitted the order will be discharged.[18]

The defendant against whom an *ex parte* order has been made may apply to have the order set aside (as can any litigant against whom an *ex parte* order is made[19]); he may even refuse compliance with the order and apply urgently to have it set aside but he does so at his peril since if his application fails he will be in contempt of court and liable to severe penalties if he has in the interim breached the order, for example by destroying records.[20]

It was held by the House of Lords in *Rank Film Distributors, Ltd.* v. *Video Information Centre*[1] that defendants could resist the making of an order on the ground of privilege against self-incrimination.[2] This was a serious inroad

---

[14] *Anton Piller K.G.* v. *Manufacturing Processes, Ltd.*, [1976] Ch. 55; [1976] 1 All E.R. 779.

[15] See, for example, *Ex parte Island Records, Ltd.*, [1978] Ch. 122; [1978] 3 All E.R. 824.

[16] The plaintiff applying for any form of interlocutory injunction has to give an undertaking as to damages and this undertaking is always written into the court order.

[17] *International Electronics, Ltd.* v. *Weigh Data, Ltd.*, [1980] F.S.R. 423.

[18] *Thermax, Ltd.* v. *Schott Industrial Glass, Ltd.*, [1981] F.S.R. 289.

[19] O. 8, r. 2.

[20] *WEA Records, Ltd.* v. *Visions Channel 4, Ltd.*, [1983] 2 All E.R. 589; [1983] 1 W.L.R. 721.

[1] [1982] A.C. 380; [1981] 2 All E.R. 76.

[2] See p. 637, *post* for details of this privilege.

into the scope of *Anton Piller* orders since, in the nature of things, persons against whom such orders are made are frequently engaged in fraudulent activity. To remedy this, section 72 of the Supreme Court Act 1981 withdrew the privilege in relation to High Court proceedings for infringement of rights pertaining to any intellectual property or for passing-off, including proceedings brought to prevent any apprehended such infringement or passing-off and proceedings brought to obtain disclosure of information relating thereto.

C MAREVA INJUNCTIONS

1 Jurisdiction

It will be appreciated that the prospective plaintiff in an action for debt or damages faces two distinct obstacles. The first is to obtain a judgment (or settlement) in his favour; the second is to enforce that judgment. It is of little consolation to most litigants to succeed in the action and yet be unable to enforce the judgment. Regrettably, where a defendant is uninsured against his liability this is a situation which often arises. Where the defendant is simply insovent this is a misfortune that the plaintiff must bear. However the courts can and will intervene to prevent a defendant from avoiding his liability to the plaintiff by disposing of his assets, and in particular removing them outside the jurisdiction of the English courts. An injunction to restrain a defendant from so doing is called a *Mareva* injunction, taking its name from the 1975 case in which the jurisdiction was first acknowledged by the Court of Appeal.[3] Since 1975 the development of this area of law and practice, particularly in the Commercial Court,[4] has been rapid. The injunction was originally confined to foreign defendants and to prohibiting removal of assets from the jurisdiction but was soon extended to United Kingdom residents and to the prohibition of dispositions of assets within the jurisdiction. The precise scope of the jurisdiction as evolved by the courts no longer calls for scrutiny because it is now given statutory embodiment in section 37(3) of the Supreme Court Act 1981 which provides:

> "The power of the High Court . . . to grant an interlocutory injunction restraining a party to any proceedings from removing from the jurisdiction of the High Court, or otherwise dealing with, assets located within that jurisdiction shall be exercisable in cases where that party is, as well as cases where he is not, domiciled, resident or present within that jurisdiction."

The words "dealing with" encompass disposing of, selling or charging assets.[5]

The most important restriction on the court's power to grant a *Mareva* injunction lies in the fact, which must never be overlooked, that the injunction is *ancillary* to a cause of action; it is not a cause of action in itself. Consequently if the plaintiff's claim is not justiciable in the English courts he

---

[3] *Mareva Compania Naviera S.A.* v. *International Bulkcarriers S.A.*, [1980] 1 All E.R. 213; [1975] 2 Lloyd's Rep. 509.
[4] As to which see p. 369, *post*.
[5] *CBS (U.K.), Ltd.* v. *Lambert*, [1983] Ch. 37; [1982] 3 All E.R. 237.

cannot obtain an injunction. Thus in a case where a plaintiff cannot obtain leave to serve a writ out of the jurisdiction under Order 11[6] he cannot found jurisdiction upon an application for an injunction to restrain the defendant from doing something within the jurisdiction.[7] However this principle will be subject to exceptions when section 25 of the Civil Jurisdiction and Judgments Act 1982 is implemented, since sub-section (1) of that section provides:

> "The High Court in England and Wales or Northern Ireland shall have power to grant interim relief where—
>
> (a) proceedings have been or are to be commenced in a Contracting State[8] other than the United Kingdom or in a part of the United Kingdom other than that in which the High Court in question exercises jurisdiction; and
>
> (b) they are or will be proceedings whose subject-matter is within the scope of the 1968 Convention. . . ."

The injunction cannot extend to assets outside the jurisdiction.[9]

2   Procedure

An applicant for a *Mareva* injunction is well advised to act quickly. To this end the customary practice is to apply *ex parte* in the first instance, sometimes even before issuing a writ (in which case the plaintiff will be required to undertake to issue a writ within a specified period or "forthwith") whereupon an order will be made to take effect until the return date on the summons which the plaintiff will have issued or undertaken to issue. The plaintiff must swear an affidavit in support of his application In *Third Chandris Shipping Corporation* v. *Unimarine S.A.*[10] the Court of Appeal stated guidelines that judges should follow on such applications: *viz.* (i) the plaintiff should make full and frank disclosure of all matters in his knowledge which are material for the judge to know; (ii) the plaintiff should give particulars of his claim and the amount thereof and of the defendant's case against it; (iii) the plaintiff should give some grounds for believing that the defendant has assets within the jurisdiction; (iv) the plaintiff should give some grounds (not merely that the defendant is abroad) for believing that there is a risk of the assets of the defendant being removed before the judgment is satisfied; (v) the plaintiff should give an undertaking in damages, in a suitable case to be supported by a bond or security. In the light of the fact that the injunction is no longer limited to restraining removal of assets from the jurisdiction, (iv) above is clearly modified.

The court has power to order discovery of documents or to administer interrogatories as to the amount, whereabouts or other details of the defendant's assets, with a view to securing the efficacy of the injunction.[11]

It is common for the plaintiff to serve copies of the injunction upon the

---

6 As to which see p. 315, *post*.

7 *The Siskina*, [1979] A.C. 210; [1977] 3 All E.R. 803.

8 "Contracting State" is defined by s. 1(3) of the Act to mean a party to the 1968 Convention on jurisdiction and the enforcement of judgments in civil and commercial matters (*viz.* Belgium, West Germany, France, Italy, Luxembourg, the Netherlands, Denmark, the Republic of Ireland and the United Kingdom).

9 *Intraco, Ltd.* v. *Notis Shipping Corporation of Liberia* [1981] 2 Lloyd's Rep. 256.

10 [1979] Q.B. 645; [1979] 2 All E.R. 972.

11 *A*. v. *C.*, [1981] Q.B. 956; [1980] 2 All E.R. 347.

defendant's bank or other body having custody of his assets, so as to fix such body with knowledge of the injunction (since such body would itself be guilty of contempt of court if it assisted the defendant to act in breach of the injunction). The receipt by a bank of such notice overrides its customer's instructions, e.g. to honour cheques.

3   Principles upon which the court acts

By section 37(1) of the Supreme Court Act the High Court may grant an injunction "in all cases in which it appears to the court to be just and convenient to do so". However, although not subject to statutory fetters, the courts have developed principles on the basis of which to grant injunctions. The general principles affecting the discretion whether to grant or refuse an interlocutory injunction are those laid down by the House of Lords in *American Cyanamid Co.* v. *Ethicon, Ltd.*[12] and will be considered in due course.[13] However there are additional principles of particular application to *Mareva* applications. As a first step the plaintiff must satisfy the court (i) that he has at least a good arguable case; and (ii) that the refusal of an injunction would involve a real risk that a judgment or award in the plaintiff's favour would remain unsatisfied because of the defendant's removal of assets from the jurisdiction or dissipation of assets within the jurisdiction.[14] An injunction will not be granted merely for the purpose of providing a plaintiff with security for a claim, even where it appears likely to succeed and even where the granting of the injunction will not cause hardship to the defendant.

An injunction will not be granted so as to give the plaintiff priority over other creditors, nor to prevent the defendant from paying his debts as they fall due or carrying on his legitimate business. So it is common for the injunction to be expressed so as to exclude periodical payments of reasonable amounts to provide for the living or other expenses of the defendant,[15] including amounts to be paid to his legal advisers to contest the litigation.

4   Position of third parties

It has been noted that service of a copy of the injunction upon a third party, such as a bank, operates in effect to freeze the account. This has led to problems and the courts are vigilant to ensure that banks and other third parties do not suffer in consequence of the grant of a *Mareva* injunction.

Thus, a bank is entitled to a variation of the injunction to enable it to set-off against any funds which it holds any right that it has in respect of facilities granted to the client, for example bank charges, interest or the balance on another account.

Similarly an injunction will not be granted, or will be discharged, where the effect would be to interfere substantially with the business of a third party.[16]

---

[12] [1975] A.C. 396; [1975] 1 All E.R. 504.

[13] See p. 333, *post*.

[14] *Ninemia Maritime Corporation* v. *Trave Schiffahrtsgesellschaft mbH & Co. K.G.*, [1984] 1 All E.R. 398; [1983] 1 W.L.R. 1412.

[15] See, for examples, *PCW (Underwriting Agencies), Ltd.* v. *Dixon*, [1983] 2 All E.R. 158.

[16] *Galaxia Maritime S.A.* v. *Mineralimportexport*, [1982] 1 All E.R. 796; [1982] 1 W.L.R. 539.

Where a bank or third party is compelled to enter the proceedings in order to obtain an order, or discharge of an order, the plaintiff will ordinarily be required to pay its cost on a solicitor and own client (indemnity) basis.[17]

D ALTERNATIVE METHODS OF COMMENCING A CIVIL ACTION

An action in the Queen's Bench Division[18] is in most cases commenced by writ of summons, generally referred to as a writ. However there are alternative methods of proceeding of which the most important is by originating summons.[19] The latter method is appropriate where the parties' dispute is such that it can be peremptorily determined. As the name indicates it is a summons which actually originates the action as opposed to the issue of an ordinary summons which is an interlocutory step in an action commenced by writ. The method which the plaintiff chooses is not in all cases optional. Thus the following proceedings in the Queen's Bench Division must be begun by writ:

(1) in which a claim is made by the plaintiff for any relief or remedy for any tort, other than trespass to land;

(2) in which a claim made by the plaintiff is based on an allegation of fraud;

(3) in which a claim is made by the plaintiff for damages for breach of duty where the damages claimed consist of or include damages in respect of the death of any person or in respect of personal injuries to any person or in respect of damage to any property:[20]

One type of action must be commenced by originating summons; where any Act requires an application to be made to the High Court other than an application in pending proceedings and no other method is prescribed.[1] A common example is an application, made before commencing an action, for discovery of documents under section 33(2) of the Supreme Court Act 1981.[2] All other actions may be commenced by writ or originating summons but the following proceedings are appropriate to be commenced by originating summons:

---

[17] *Z, Ltd.* v. *A-Z*, [1982] Q.B. 558; [1982] 1 All E.R. 556.

[18] By R.S.C., O. 1, r. 4A (*a*) "any reference to proceedings in the Queen's Bench Division shall be construed as including a reference to proceedings in the Commercial Court but not to proceedings in the Admiralty Court." The Admiralty Court is part of the Queen's Bench Division (Supreme Court Act 1981, s. 62(2)) but procedure differs in many respects from procedure in the remainder of the Division and a code of procedure is prescribed by Order 75; see p. 371, *post.*

[19] The extension of originating summons procedure in the Queen's Bench Division was an important innovation of the 1962 Rules. Prior to 1964 originating summonses were far more common in the Chancery Division and, in the Queen's Bench Division, were confined mainly to applications under s. 17 of the Married Women's Property Act 1882 (which are now assigned to the Family Division).

[20] O. 5, r. 2.

[1] O. 5, r. 3.

[2] See p. 294, *ante.*

(1) in which the sole or principal question at issue is, or is likely to be, one of the construction of an Act, or of any instrument made under an Act, or of any deed, will, contract or other document, or some other question of law, or

(2) in which there is unlikely to be any substantial dispute of fact[3]

Since these actions are not concerned with disputes as to fact it would be pedantic for the parties to have to exchange pleadings. The originating summons procedure is not, therefore, appropriate where there is a significant dispute upon the facts. Nor is it appropriate where the plaintiff intends to apply for summary judgment under Order 14, since this important Order applies only to actions commenced by writ. The tort of trespass to land is excepted from those proceedings which must be begun by writ because this action frequently involves a dispute as to title which can be resolved by reference to a single deed or contract—the very type of case with which originating summons procedure is appropriate to deal.

The only other methods of commencing proceedings in the High Court are by originating motion or petition, but these methods are applicable if, and only if, expressly authorised by the rules or by any Act.[4] Proceedings by petition occur in both the Chancery Division (for example for the winding-up of companies) and the Family Division (for example judicial separation proceedings), but not in the Queen's Bench Division, with the exception of election petitions under the Representation of the People Act 1983.

The following chapters are almost exclusively concerned with the course of an action commenced by writ. However in a later chapter we shall return to consider the uses of originating summonses, originating motions and petitions.[5]

Having considered which is the appropriate method of proceeding the plaintiff must, before issuing his writ, consider two further preliminary matters. First he must ensure that his cause of action has accrued since, in order to succeed in his action, the plaintiff must prove a cause of action which was complete at the date of the issue of the writ. So, for example, an action for the recovery of a debt would be bound to fail if the debt had not fallen due before the issue of the writ even though, when the action came to trial, the debt was clearly overdue. It is axiomatic that English courts will not adjudicate upon hypothetical, as opposed to actual, disputes.[6]

The second matter which he must consider concerns the proper parties to the action.

---

[3] O. 5, r. 4.
[4] O. 5, r. 5.
[5] See Chapter 19, *post*.
[6] *Re Barnato*, [1949] Ch. 258; cf. *Ealing London Borough Council* v. *Race Relations Board*, [1972] A.C. 342; [1972] 1 All E.R. 105 and authorities referred to therein. The power of the High Court to make a declaratory judgment or order (O. 15, r. 16; see p. 344, *post*) can be exercised in relation to future rights but is only so exercised in exceptional cases, for example where future rights affect the present situation. A declaration which relates to a purely hypothetical issue or which would serve no useful purpose will not be made; cf. *Mellstrom* v. *Garner*, [1970] 2 All E.R. 9; [1970] 1 W.L.R. 603. If a writ is issued prematurely the defect is incurable by amendment since amendment dates back to the issue of the writ (*Eshelby* v. *Federated European Bank*, [1932] 1 K.B. 254); the plaintiff's only course is to apply to discontinue the action (see p. 323, *post*).

E PARTIES

1 Joinder of parties

The names of all intended parties must appear at the head of the writ. There may be any number of plaintiffs or defendants, or both, to the action. At common law the effect of misjoinder or non-joinder of proper parties was to defeat the plaintiff's claim but nowadays "no cause or matter shall be defeated by reason of the misjoinder or nonjoinder of any party".[7] However the plaintiff must still weigh carefully his choice of parties. On the one hand he may fail to join a party from whom he is entitled to relief in which case his whole action may fail. Alternatively he may add parties whose presence is unnecessary in which event he will usually have to pay the costs occasioned by his error.

Subject to the court's power to order separate trials or add or strike out parties,[8] two or more persons may be joined as plaintiffs or defendants in the following circumstances:

(1) where (*a*) if separate actions were brought by or against each of them, as the case may be, some common question of law or fact would arise in all the actions; and (*b*) all rights to relief claimed in the action (whether they are joint, several or alternative) are in respect or arise out of the same transaction or series of transactions; and

(2) in any other case with leave of the court.[9]

The plaintiff should join all potential defendants whether relief is alleged to exist against them jointly, severally or in the alternative, for even in the latter circumstance the plaintiff, although he obviously must fail against one or more defendant, may not suffer by it. The reason is that if the court is satisfied that it was a proper course for the plaintiff to join the defendants, it may order the costs of the successful defendant to be added to the costs payable by the unsuccessful defendant.[10] Thus if a plaintiff is injured in a "running down" case he should join the drivers of all the vehicles (unless the liability of one driver, to the exclusion of the others, is *prima facie* obvious, in which event a wise course is to sue only one driver and then to join, by amendment, such other persons as the defendant "blames" in his defence);[11] where he seeks an injunction to abate a nuisance he should join both the landlord and the tenant of the premises from which the alleged nuisance comes; where he is uncertain whether a woman has contracted with him as agent of her husband or as a principal he should join both the husband and wife.[12]

In addition, under O. 15, r. 6(2), at any stage of the proceedings the court

---

[7] O. 15, r. 6(1).

[8] O. 15, rr. 5(1), 6(2).

[9] O. 15, r. 4.

[10] See p. 386, *post.*

[11] Counsel who fails to bear these precepts in mind may be liable in negligence: *Saif Ali* v. *Sydney Mitchell & Co.*, [1980] A.C. 198; [1978] 3 All E.R. 1033; see p. 272, *ante.*

[12] *Morel Brothers* v. *Earl of Westmorland*, [1904] A.C. 11; unless, of course, prior correspondence or negotiation has disclosed that there is no issue on the point.

may, of its own motion or on application (*a*) strike out any party who is not a necessary or proper party; or (*b*) add as a party any person whose presence is necessary to ensure that all matters in dispute may be effectively and completely determined or any person between whom and any party there may exist a question or issue connected with the action which in the opinion of the court it would be just and convenient to determine.[13] Thus in *Gurtner* v. *Circuit*[14] the Motor Insurers Bureau was added as a defendant to an action for damages by a pedestrian against a motor cyclist, on the basis that, since neither the original defendant nor his insurers could be traced, the Bureau might, by reason of its agreement with the Minister of Transport to satisfy all unpaid damages awarded against an uninsured motorist, have to pay any damages awarded. This gave the Bureau a legal and pecuniary interest in the proceedings sufficient to justify its joinder, notwithstanding that the plaintiff had no cause of action against the Bureau.

As in all branches of the law there are special rules which apply only to certain classes of person, usually by reason of a status. The prospective plaintiff must in particular determine whether a prospective defendant is the subject of any of these special rules.

2   Special parties

a   The Crown[15]

Until 1948, as an offshoot of the principle of sovereign immunity, the Crown could not be made a party to an action in the courts, the only redress being against Crown servants in their personal capacity. However, by the Crown Proceedings Act 1947 the Crown may now be sued in contract or tort with minor exceptions. The immunity now extends only to the reigning monarch, although there is still a rule of statutory interpretation that the Crown is not bound by a statute unless expressly named in it. An action is commenced by or against the Crown through its appropriate government department as named in a list issued by the Treasury and service is on the solicitor for that department. If there is no appropriate department proceedings are carried on in the name of the Attorney-General. Although the Crown now has few relics of substantive immunity it enjoys certain procedural advantages; for example that judgment in default cannot be entered against the Crown without leave, that judgment under Order 14 cannot be entered against the Crown and that the Crown is not liable to have any judgment enforced against it.

Action against the Crown pursuant to the provisions of the 1947 Act lies only in respect of liability arising in the United Kingdom.[16] In *Franklin* v. *A.-G.*[17] LAWSON, J. was faced with the difficult task of deciding what was

---

[13] The latter part of (*b*) was added by R.S.C. (Amendment No. 4) 1971 and appears to negative the decision of the House of Lords in *Vandervell Trustees, Ltd.* v. *White*, [1971] A.C. 912; [1970] 3 All E.R. 16.

[14] [1968] 2 Q.B. 587; [1968] 1 All E.R. 328; cf. *Sanders Lead Co. Inc.* v. *Entores Metal Brokers, Ltd.*, [1984] 1 All E.R. 857; [1984] 1 W.L.R. 452.

[15] The special rules of procedure applicable in proceedings to which the Crown is a party are contained in O. 77.

[16] Crown Proceedings Act 1947, s. 40(2).

[17] [1974] Q.B. 185; [1973] 1 All E.R. 879.

the appropriate form of proceedings to enforce a right existing against the Bank of England in relation to the plaintiff's entitlement to interest on Southern Rhodesia stock. The method of enforcement prescribed by the Colonial Stock Act 1877, s. 20 was petition of right, under the then Petitions of Right Act 1860. However, that 1860 Act had been repealed by the Crown Proceedings Act 1947 and, as noted above, no action lay under the 1947 Act since the liability of the Crown did not arise within the United Kingdom. It was held, by LAWSON, J., that the procedure was by petition of right but in the old form used prior to the Act of 1860. This would seem to be the only surviving instance of the ancient procedure of petition of right whereby the Sovereign is petitioned to "order that right be done in this matter".[18] The Sovereign then refers the petition to the Queen's Bench Division for consideration and the High Court then makes an order which appears to have the effect of a judgment against the Crown.

b　Foreign states

Foreign states, their sovereigns or other heads of state (in their public capacity),[19] their governments and departments of government are immune from the jurisdiction of the courts of the United Kingdom, subject to the exceptions provided by the State Immunity Act 1978.[20] However, that does not mean that a foreign state cannot, or should not, be made a party to an action. It may submit to the jurisdiction by taking a step in the proceedings, for example acknowledging service, and a state is not immune if it intervenes or submits to the jurisdiction (unless it does so only for the purpose of claiming immunity or asserting an interest in property in circumstances in which it could have claimed immunity had it been sued, or it takes a step in ignorance of its entitlement to immunity, provided it claims immunity as soon as reasonably practicable).[1]

Moreover the immunity does not extend to proceedings in respect of commercial transactions,[2] contracts requiring performance in the United Kingdom, certain contracts of employment, death, personal injury or damage to property caused in the United Kingdom and certain other proceedings described in the Act.[3] The effect of the Act has therefore been to restrict considerably the immunity from suit which foreign states formerly enjoyed at common law. Quite apart from the Act, the House of Lords has held that the immunity does not extend to activities, trading, commercial or otherwise, of a private law character in which the state in question has chosen to engage, but is limited to sovereign or public acts.[4]

---

[18] For the full form of the petition, see *Franklin* v. *R.*, [1974] Q.B. 202; [1973] 3 All E.R. 861.

[19] A sovereign acting in his private capacity is immune from process and he, members of his family forming part of his household and his private servants enjoy the privileges set out in the Diplomatic Privileges Act 1964: State Immunity Act 1978, s. 20. The question of whether any country is a state for the purposes of the Act is resolved by certificate of the Secretary of State, which is conclusive (*ibid.*, s. 21).

[20] Act of 1978, ss. 1, 14.

[1] *Ibid.*, s. 2.

[2] *Ibid.*, s. 3(1) (*a*) affirming *Trendtex Trading Corporation, Ltd.* v. *Central Bank of Nigeria*, [1977] Q.B. 529; [1977] 1 All E.R. 881; see p. 135, *ante*.

[3] *Ibid.*, ss. 2–11.

[4] *I Congreso del Partido*, [1983] 1 A.C. 244; [1981] 2 All E.R. 1064.

Writs and documents are served through the Foreign and Commonwealth Office to the Ministry of Foreign Affairs of the state. Foreign states enjoy certain procedural privileges under section 13 of the Act. Thus they are not liable to committal or fine for failure to disclose or produce documents and (subject to certain exceptions arising out of international conventions) the following remedies are not available against foreign states: injunctions, orders for specific performance, orders for the recovery of land or other property, all process against property of the state for the enforcement of judgments,[5] orders for the arrest, detention and sale of the property of the state in actions *in rem*.

c   Incorporated associations

An association may be incorporated either by Royal charter or under a statute, usually one of the Companies Acts. In either case the creation is a legal *persona* with an existence, for the purposes of the law, completely independent of its members.[6] It is this factor which distinguishes a corporation or company from an unincorporated association, which is merely a group of individuals referred to by a collective name. An incorporated association may enter into contracts and may commit torts and even crimes. As a legal personality it may sue and be sued in its corporate title or registered name. However, since it has no physical existence, it can only appear through a solicitor.[7] Service on a company is effected by delivering or posting the document to be served to the company's registered office.[8] In one respect a plaintiff company is at a disadvantage; if it has insufficient assets it may be required to give security for costs.[9]

d   Unincorporated associations

An association which is not incorporated, under Royal charter or statute, has no legal existence independent of the members of the association. There are for procedural purposes three classes of unincorporated association; partnerships, registered associations and unregistered associations.

Partnerships—Partners may sue and be sued in the firm name.[10] However if suing in the firm name they must on request disclose the name and address of every member of the firm.[11] If they are sued in the firm name, the partners must acknowledge service in their own names individually although proceedings continue in the name of the firm. Any person who denies that he is or

---

[5] See *Alcom, Ltd.* v. *Republic of Colombia*, [1984] 2 All E.R. 6; [1984] 2 W.L.R. 750 although the House of Lords in that case stated that the property in question (the credit balance in a bank account) would not be immune if the plaintiff could prove that funds in the account were used solely to meet liabilities incurred in commercial transactions; since the ambassador's certificate to the contrary was conclusive by virtue of section 13(5) of the Act, the plaintiff was unable to surmount this obstacle.

[6] *Salomon* v. *Salomon & Co., Ltd.*, [1897] A.C. 22.

[7] So that the litigant's right to appear in person (O. 5, r. 6) does not extend to corporations or companies. They may, however, acknowledge service (and give notice of intention to defend) by a duly authorised person instead of a solicitor (O. 12, r. 1(2)).

[8] Companies Act 1948, s. 437(1). Service on the company solicitor is also usual. Corporations are served by serving the appropriate officer, e.g. mayor, town clerk (O. 65, r. 3.)

[9] Companies Act 1948, s. 447.

[10] O. 81, r. 1.

[11] O. 81, r. 2.

was a partner when the cause of action arose should so state in his acknowledgment of service.[12] A judgment against a partnership may be executed against partnership property or against any person who has acknowledged service of the writ as a partner or failed to acknowledge service having been served as a partner, has admitted in his pleading that he is a partner or has been adjudged to be a partner.[13]

Registered associations—Certain associations are by statute registrable. This does not affect the position of the members but it does enable the association to appear in its registered name. The most common examples of such associations are Trade Unions[14] and Friendly Societies.[15]

Other unincorporated associations—Where an association is unregistered and not a partnership it cannot appear in its group name, since that name is no more than a convenient label for the members collectively.[16] Frequently the proper parties to the action will be members of the association in their private capacity. Where, however, the right or liability is common to all the members it is inconvenient, although possible, to join them all as parties. The appropriate procedure is a "representative action".

In a representative action, where numerous persons have the same interest in any proceedings, whether as plaintiffs or defendants, one or more persons may be authorised to appear on behalf of all persons so interested.[17] However a representative action is only appropriate where all the persons to be represented have a common grievance and will all benefit from the relief claimed if plaintiffs,[18] or are jointly liable if defendants.[19] Thus where the liability of defendants is several, for example in conspiracy[20] or defamation,[19] they cannot be represented and must be sued in their own names. Nevertheless an action for negligence has been allowed to proceed against representatives of the members of a club on the ground that they were joint occupiers of the club premises.[1] A judgment against representative defendants is binding on them all. However it can be executed against the actual parties but not against the persons represented without leave. An order for costs cannot be made against a person represented. The writ must define clearly the parties and the names of persons represented. Thus an order to represent "all the persons who were members of the City Livery Club on June 29, 1949" was made in one case, being a sufficient identification of the persons represented as defendants.[1]

---

[12] O. 81, r. 4; he may then apply to the court to set aside service.

[13] O. 81, r. 5; such a judgment may also be executed against the private property of any other partner, but only with leave.

[14] Trade Union and Labour Relations Act 1974, s. 2(1) (*h*) (replacing earlier legislation); an "employers' association" (as defined in s. 28(2) of the Act of 1974) may likewise sue and be sued in its own name. In *Engineers' and Managers' Association* v. *Advisory, Conciliation and Arbitration Service (No. 1)*, [1979] 3 All E.R. 223; [1979] 1 W.L.R. 1113 the Court of Appeal held that, in certain circumstances, a union might be permitted representation by one of its officers, so obviating the need for counsel to appear for it.

[15] Friendly Societies Act 1974 (consolidating earlier legislation).

[16] But see *London Association for Protection of Trade* v. *Greenlands, Ltd.*, [1916] 2 A.C. 16, where the rules of procedure appear to have been flouted.

[17] O. 15, r. 12.

[18] *Smith* v. *Cardiff Corporation*, [1954] 1 Q.B. 210; [1953] 2 All E.R. 1373; distinguished in *John* v. *Rees*, [1970] Ch. 345; [1969] 2 All E.R. 274.

[19] *Mercantile Marine Service Association* v. *Toms*, [1916] 2 K.B. 243.

[20] *Hardie and Lane, Ltd.* v. *Chiltern*, [1928] 1 K.B. 663.

[1] *Campbell* v. *Thompson*, [1953] 1 Q.B. 445; [1953] 1 All E.R. 831; see also *Wallersteiner* v.

It is important to distinguish a representative action from a "test case". The latter is popular terminology for an action the function of which is to determine the legal position of numerous individuals who are not parties to the action; for example an action based on the interpretation of a Finance Act upon which depend the tax obligations of a large section of the populace. The expression "test case" has, however, no legal meaning and only the parties to a test case are bound by the judgment. However, rights are determined conclusively through the operation of the doctrine of precedent.

e   Persons under disability: infants and patients

A married woman has, since 1935, ceased to be a person under a disability[2] and that phrase now applies only to infants and patients. An infant is a person under the age of 18.[3] A patient is a person who, by reason of mental disorder within the meaning of the Mental Health Act 1983, is incapable of managing and administering his property and affairs.[4] Infants and patients cannot appear personally.

They sue by their "next friend".[5] In the case of an infant this is usually the father or person *in loco parentis*; in the case of a patient, his receiver. In any case where there is no person competent or willing to appear as next friend, the Official Solicitor will do so. The next friend is not a party to the action (though he may, of course, be a co-plaintiff in his own right). Nevertheless his name must appear on the writ, *viz.* "AB an infant, by CD his (father and) next friend", and he is personally liable for costs with a right of indemnity from the infant or patient for costs properly incurred. Since he is not a party he cannot counterclaim in his personal capacity; nor can he be required to give security for costs.[6] The next friend cannot act in person and so must be represented by a solicitor[7] who must file two documents: (1) the next friend's written consent to act, and (2) a certificate that the next friend has no interest in the proceedings adverse to that of the infant or patient.[8]

Moir (No. 2) [1975] Q.B. 373; [1975] 1 All E.R. 849 where a minority shareholder's action was likened to a representative action on behalf of the company and it was stated by the Court of Appeal that the shareholder, after issuing proceedings, should in effect apply to the court for an order sanctioning the proceedings, the effect of which would be to give the shareholder a right to have the company pay his costs.

2   Law Reform (Married Women and Tortfeasors) Act 1935, s. 1; and see Law Reform (Husband and Wife) Act 1962.

3   Family Law Reform Act 1969, s. 1(1); the terms "infant" and "minor" are synonymous (*ibid.*, s. 1(2)).

4   This definition of a "patient" in O. 80, r. 1 is narrower than the definition in s. 145(1) of the Mental Health Act 1983, i.e. a person suffering or appearing to be suffering from mental disorder, but corresponds with the criteria under s. 94 of that Act (which applies for the purpose of deciding whether a person is within the jurisdiction of the Court of Protection); where there are proceedings in the Court of Protection application for the appointment of a next friend should be made to that court: *Re S. (F. G.) (Mental Health Patient)*, [1973] 1 All E.R. 273; [1973] 1 W.L.R. 178.

5   O. 80, r. 2(1).

6   Since he is not a "nominal plaintiff" within O. 23, r. 1(1) (*b*); *Fellows v. Barrett* (1836), 1 Keen 119; see p. 362, *post*. Nor can he give a receipt for money recovered in settlement of an action, *Leather v. Kirby*, [1965] 3 All E.R. 927n.; [1965] 1 W.L.R. 1489.

7   O. 80, r. 2(3).

8   O. 80, r. 3.

They defend by a "guardian *ad litem*" who will be the same person as the next friend would have been, or the Official Solicitor. The solicitor must file the same two documents as above. However the guardian *ad litem* is not personally liable for costs except where he has been guilty of gross misconduct, and in this respect his position differs from that of the next friend.

The next friend or guardian *ad litem* must, of course, act in the best interests of the person he represents. If he does not the court has inherent power to remove him but this power will not be exercised simply because the course which a next friend is taking is opposed by a number of other litigants.[9]

(1) Judgment on failure to give notice of intention to defend cannot be entered against an infant or patient. The proper course is to apply to the court to appoint a guardian *ad litem*.[10]

(2) No settlement of an action on behalf of an infant or patient is valid unless approved by the court.[11]

(3) Any money recovered by or on behalf of an infant or patient must be dealt with in accordance with the court's direction.[12]

(4) Allegations in a statement of claim or counterclaim are not deemed to be admitted by an infant or patient by reason only of his failure to traverse them.[13]

f   Estates of deceased persons

Prior to 1971, if at the commencement of proceedings a person named as a party was dead the action by or against that person was a nullity and could not be cured by amendment to substitute executors as parties.[14] The action had to be brought by or against the executors or administrators. However the Proceedings Against Estates Act 1970 and Order 15, rule 6A enable an action to be brought against the estate of a deceased person[15] even though no grant of probate or administration has been made; the defendant should be named in the proceedings "the personal representative of A.B. deceased." The plaintiff must then, during the period of validity for service of the writ or originating summons, apply to the court for an order appointing a person to represent the deceased's estate or, if a grant of probate of administration has been made since the commencement of proceedings, an order that the per-

---

[9] *Re Taylor's Application*, [1972] 2 Q.B. 369; [1972] 2 All E.R. 873—one of the many actions arising out of the "thalidomide" tragedy.

[10] O. 80, r. 6.

[11] O. 80, rr. 10, 11. If a settlement or compromise is reached before a writ is issued, the court's approval to it can be sought by originating summons in the expedited form (see p. 381, *post*) (O. 80, r. 11). If a settlement is reached after proceedings have begun, the application for the approval of the court is by ordinary summons, or to the trial judge if the settlement is reached during the trial. It seems arguable that O. 80, r. 10 is *ultra vires* in that, insofar as it purports to declare certain contracts void, it is more than a rule of procedure, but such an argument was rejected by the House of Lords in *Dietz* v. *Lennig Chemicals, Ltd.*, [1969] A.C. 170; [1967] 2 All E.R. 282.

[12] O. 80, r. 12. In *Leather* v. *Kirby*, [1965] 3 All E.R. 927n; [1965] 1 W.L.R. 1489, the House of Lords stated that the money should usually be paid into court or, in the case of a patient, to the Court of Protection.

[13] O. 80, r. 8; see O. 18, r. 13(1); also p. 345, *post*.

[14] *Dawson (Bradford), Ltd.* v. *Dove*, [1971] 1 Q.B. 330; [1971] 1 All E.R. 554.

[15] Proceedings commenced in the name of a deceased person as plaintiff are still a nullity.

sonal representative be made a party.[16] Before making such order the court may require notice to be given to any insurer of the deceased who has an interest in the proceedings as well as to any other person having an interest in the estate. Judgment cannot be signed until personal representatives have been appointed and any judgment signed before that time will be a nullity.[17]

---

[16] O. 15, r. 6A (4). Where no grant of probate or administration has been made any judgment or order binds the estate as if a personal representative of the deceased had been a party to the proceedings (O. 15, r. 6A (7)).
[17] *Re Amirteymour (decd.)*, [1978] 3 All E.R. 637; [1979] 1 W.L.R. 63.

CHAPTER 15

Commencing an Action by Writ

A THE WRIT AND ITS CONTENTS

A writ of summons (1) notifies the defendant of the issue of the writ, (2) informs him that he must either satisfy the claim set out on the back of the writ or return to the Court Office the accompanying acknowledgment of service stating therein whether he intends to contest the proceedings, and (3) informs him that if he fails to satisfy the claim or return the acknowledgment within the time stated or without stating therein an intention to contest the proceedings, judgment may be entered against him.[1] The writ must state the names of all the intended parties to the action, whether plaintiffs or defendants, the persons on whose behalf they are appearing, if they are appearing in a representative capacity, and the division of the High Court in which the plaintiff is suing.[2] In addition the writ must bear certain indorsements. These are of two kinds; indorsements of the plaintiff's claims and formal indorsements.

1 Indorsements of claim

The writ must be indorsed either:
(1) with a statement of claim.[3] In this event, the statement of claim on the

---

[1] R.S.C., App. A, Form No. 1 (substituted by the Rules of the Supreme Court (Writ and Appearance) 1979, with effect from 3 June 1980); the old form of writ was in the form of a royal command to the defendant to enter an appearance.

[2] In commercial actions in London, Liverpool and Manchester the writ may be marked in the top lefthand corner with the words "Commercial Court" whereupon the action will be automatically entered in the commercial list (O. 72, r. 4(1)); see p. 369, *post*. Finally a writ or originating summons by which "official referees" business is to be begun may be marked in the top lefthand corner with those words whereupon the cause will thereafter be treated as official referees' business (as to which, see p. 371, *post*).

[3] This is usually termed a "special indorsement", though this expression does not appear in the current Rules. The plaintiff may in one action claim relief against the same defendant in respect of more than one cause of action. However admiralty actions *in rem* and *in personam*

writ will be the statement of claim in the action and the plaintiff may not serve another, except by way of amendment. The advantage is a saving of time for the plaintiff may proceed to apply for summary judgment under Order 14 as soon as the defendant has given notice of intention to defend. Also where the plaintiff's claim is for an equitable remedy or a declaration, he cannot obtain judgment in default until he has served a statement of claim; or

(2) with a concise statement of the nature of the claim made or the relief or remedy required in the action.[4] In this case the plaintiff will have to serve his statement of claim, setting out his claim in detail, at the same time as service of the writ, or subsequently. However he must still indorse his writ with particulars which are sufficient to enable the defendant to identify the cause of action against him.[5] Thus "the plaintiff claims damages for breach of contract", or "the plaintiff claims damages for slander" are insufficient. The plaintiff must identify the contract which he alleges has been broken, or the publication which he alleges to defame him. In addition; in actions for libel the actual publication complained of must be identified;[6] in actions for wrongful interference with goods brought by a plaintiff who is one of two or more persons claiming any interest in the goods, unless he has the written authority of all of them to sue, the writ must be indorsed with (i) particulars of the plaintiff's title; and (ii) identification of every other person who, to his knowledge, has or claims any·interest in the goods.[7] Where the claim is for possession of land the writ must be indorsed with a statement showing whether the claim relates to a dwelling house and, if it does, whether the rateable value of the premises on every day specified by section 4 of the Rent Act 1977 in relation to the premises exceeds the sum so specified.[8] Where the action is brought to enforce a right to recover possession of goods the writ must be indorsed with a statement showing the value of the goods.[9] Where the plaintiff seeks to obtain judgment in a foreign currency, he should state this in his writ and, unless the facts themselves clearly show this (*semble* the facts set out in the general indorsement) he should plead the facts relied on to support such a claim in his statement of claim.[10]

---

cannot now be joined in one writ: *Practice Direction (Admiralty: writs)*, [1979] 2 All E.R. 155; [1979] 1 W.L.R. 426.

[4] Usually described as a "general indorsement".

[5] Although failure so to do does not render the writ a nullity. The defect may be cured by amendment, by service of a statement of claim, or even by the defendant's delay in applying to have the writ set aside; *Pontin* v. *Wood*, [1962] 1 Q.B. 594; [1962] 1 All E.R. 294.

[6] O. 82, r. 2.

[7] O. 15, r. 10A.

[8] O. 6, r. 2(1) (*c*). For the rateable value limits, see Rent Act 1977, s. 4 and for suggested forms of indorsement, see *Practice Direction (Possession Claims: Dwelling House)*, [1973] 2 All E.R. 336; [1973] 1 W.L.R. 577. Where the tenant is within the protection of the Rent Act the landlord ought to issue his proceedings in a county court since, in the High Court, he can no longer sign judgment in default without leave and, furthermore, cannot recover any costs.

[9] O. 6, r. 2(1) (*d*).

[10] *Practice Direction (Judgment: foreign currency) (No. 2)*, [1977] 1 All E.R. 544; [1977] 1 W.L.R. 197.

2 Formal indorsements

a *"Fourteen-day" costs*

Where a plaintiff's claim is for a debt or liquidated demand[11] *only*, the writ must be indorsed with a claim for fixed costs,[12] the amount being determined by the amount of the claim, and a statement that further proceedings will be stayed if, within the time limited for acknowledging service, the defendant pays the amount claimed and costs. This indorsement is only made where the claim is for a debt or liquidated demand, i.e. a specific sum of money either ascertained or readily ascertainable by arithmetic. Thus such a claim cannot be made where the action is founded on tort since damages in tort are always unliquidated. Where the plaintiff claims interest, whether pursuant to contract or under section 35A of the Supreme Court Act 1981, he must include the amount of the claim for interest calculated to the date of issue of the writ and if the defendant pays this amount (together with the amount of the claim and fixed costs) within 14 days the action is stayed and no further interest is payable.[13]

b *Solicitor and address*

The writ must be indorsed with the plaintiff's address within the jurisdiction and his solicitor's name and address if the plaintiff has a solicitor.[14] The latter is essential if the plaintiff is a body corporate, an infant or patient or a person who has no address within the jurisdiction, since these plaintiffs, contrary to the general rule, cannot appear in person.

c *District registry actions*

Where the writ is issued out of a district registry and the cause of action arose wholly or in part in the district of that registry, the writ may be indorsed with a statement to that effect.[15] The effect is that the defendant cannot apply to have the action transferred to another registry or to the Royal Courts of Justice.[16]

---

[11] Where the claim is for a debt or liquidated demand in foreign currency, the sterling equivalent of the amount claimed (immediately preceding the issue of the writ) should be certified on the writ by the plaintiff or his solicitor: *Practice Direction (Judgment: foreign currency)*, [1976] 1 All E.R. 669; [1976] 1 W.L.R. 83.

[12] O. 6, r. 2(1) (*b*). Where the claim is for less than £600 no claim for costs should be indorsed since no costs are recoverable (unless the action is one which could not be brought in a county court or is brought by the Crown): County Courts Act 1984, ss. 19, 20 (see p. 387, *post*). The scale of fixed costs is set out in Order 62, App. 3.

[13] *Practice Direction*, [1983] 1 All E.R. 934; [1983] 1 W.L.R. 377.

[14] O. 6, r. 5.

[15] O. 6, r. 4. There are in most large towns district registries which may be regarded as branch offices of the Central Office of the Supreme Court. The district registrar exercises in his registry the same powers as the masters exercise in the Central Office (O. 32, r. 23). However, whereas a master must be a barrister of ten years' standing, a district registrar must be a solicitor of seven years' standing.

[16] As to which see p. 317, *post*.

d Capacity

Where the plaintiff sues in a representative capacity, or the defendant is sued in such a capacity, the writ must be indorsed with a statement of the capacity in which he sues or is sued.[17]

Where a writ does not bear the proper formal indorsement it will not be issued until the defects have been corrected. Where, however, an indorsement of claim lacks particularity the writ will be issued and will be valid. The defect must then be cured by amendment unless the defendant acquiesces in the fault.

B ISSUE AND SERVICE OF THE WRIT

1 Issue

The writ must be issued using the prescribed form, but that form is not a writ until it has been issued. To issue his writ the plaintiff takes or sends two copies of his form to the Central Office or a district registry where one copy is stamped with the court fee[18] and filed, and the other is sealed and returned to the plaintiff. The action has now been commenced for the purpose of any statute of limitation. Leave is not generally required to issue a writ but to this rule there are five exceptions of which the two more important are: (1) where the defendant is outside the jurisdiction;[19] and (2) where the plaintiff has been declared a vexatious litigant.[20]

2 Service

Once issued the writ is valid for twelve months beginning with the date of issue.[1] However it may on application be renewed for periods of up to twelve months if the court is satisfied that it has not been possible to serve it during that period. Such an application is made *ex parte* (without giving notice to

---

[17] O. 6, r. 3(1).

[18] Currently £50: Supreme Court Fees Order 1980.

[19] O. 6, r. 7(1); see p. 315, *post.*

[20] Supreme Court Act 1981, s. 42. The other three cases in which leave is required are under the Mental Health Act 1983, s. 139(2), under the Leasehold Property (Repairs) Act 1938, s. 1, and under the Crown Proceedings Act 1947, s. 9(3). Note also the position under the Limitation Act 1980; s. 11 of the Act provides that, in personal injuries actions, "an action . . . shall not be brought" after the expiry of the appropriate period of limitation, subject to s. 33 under which the court may in certain circumstances direct that the normal limitation period shall not apply "if it appears to the court that it would be equitable to allow an action to proceed". A literal interpretation of these provisions would indicate that the plaintiff needed leave (in the form of a direction under s. 33) before he could bring an action at all, but they have not been interpreted in this way and, although the Rules do not prescribe a procedure, the appropriate procedure seems to be for the plaintiff to issue and serve his writ and then apply to the court under s. 33; if he does not do so the defendant may issue a summons to stay or dismiss the action (see p. 321, *post*) or the parties may simply get on with the action, leaving all limitation points, including the s. 33 direction to be dealt with at the trial: *Walkley* v. *Precision Forgings, Ltd.*, [1979] 2 All E.R. 548; [1979] 1 W.L.R. 606. O. 32, r. 9A empowers masters and registrars to give a direction under s. 33.

[1] O. 6, r. 8(1). Thus a writ issued on the 10th September 1965 can validly be served on the 9th September 1966 but not on the following day; see *Trow* v. *Ind Coope (West Midlands), Ltd.*, [1967] 2 Q.B. 899; [1967] 2 All E.R. 900.

the other party) on affidavit. An extension will only be granted in exceptional circumstances, generally where the defendant is untraceable; it is not an exceptional circumstance that the plaintiff failed to serve the writ through accident, mistake or a delay in obtaining a legal aid certificate[2] nor that settlement negotiations were in progress.[3] While in force the writ may be served at any time of the day or night although not on Sunday expect, in case of urgency, with the leave of the court.[4] The following are permitted methods of service.

a   Personal service or service by post

Personal service involves the plaintiff or his agent tendering the defendant a sealed copy of the writ accompanied by the appropriate form of acknowledgment of service.[5] Personal service has not been obligatory since 1979. A writ for service within the jurisdiction may, instead of being served personally on him, be served:

(*a*) by sending a copy of the writ by ordinary first class post to the defendant at his usual or last known address; or

(*b*) if there is a letter box for that address, by inserting through the letter box a copy of the writ in a sealed envelope addressed to the defendant.[6]

Where the writ is served in accordance with the provisions set out above, it is deemed, unless the contrary is shown, to be served on the seventh day after the date on which the copy was sent to or inserted through the letter box for the address in question.[7]

b   Service on the defendant's solicitor

This is an alternative to personal service. The defendant's solicitor must indorse on the writ a statement that he accepts service on behalf of the defendant.[8]

c   Acknowledgment of service

Where the defendant acknowledges service of the writ, it is deemed, unless the contrary is shown, to have been duly served on him and to have been so served on the date on which he acknowledges service.[9]

---

[2] *Baker* v. *Bowkett's Cakes, Ltd.*, [1966] 2 All E.R. 290; [1966] 1 W.L.R. 861; *Stevens* v. *Services Window and General Cleaning Co., Ltd.*, [1967] 1 Q.B. 359; [1967] 1 All E.R. 984.

[3] *Easy* v. *Universal Anchorage Co., Ltd.*, [1974] 2 All E.R. 1105; [1974] 1 W.L.R. 899.

[4] O. 65, r. 10; formerly the Sunday Observance Act 1677 (repealed by the Statute Law (Repeals) Act 1969) contained an absolute prohibition against service of process on a Sunday.

[5] O. 65, r. 2. If the person served will not accept the copy, it is sufficient to tell him of its content and leave it as nearly as possible in his possession.

[6] O. 10, r. 1(2). The copy must be a sealed copy and must be accompanied by the appropriate form of acknowledgment of service (r. 1(5)).

[7] O. 10, r. 1(3).

[8] O. 10, r. 1(4).

[9] O. 10, r. 1(5); see *The Gniezno*, [1968] P. 418; [1967] 2 All E.R. 738.

d   Substituted service

Where the plaintiff is unable to effect service as above, he may apply *ex parte* on affidavit to a master for an order for substituted service.[10] The master, if he makes such an order, will specify the form which substituted service must take, for example, service by registered or recorded delivery post to the defendant's last known address, service on the defendant's solicitor or agent or service by advertisement in the press.[11]

e   Service in pursuance of contract

The parties may by contract agree upon a method of service, in which case service in accordance with this method is sufficient.[12]

f   Actions for the recovery of land

Where no person appears to be in possession of land, the plaintiff in an action for the recovery of that land may, with leave, serve the writ by affixing it to some conspicuous part of the land, such as the door. In summary proceedings for possession of land commenced by originating summons the summons may be served by leaving a copy at the premises and where the occupants are not identified, by affixing a copy of the summons to the main door or other conspicuous part of the premises.[13]

There is only one case in which leave is needed to serve, as well as to issue, a writ. That is where it is proposed to serve it outside the jurisdiction.[14] Leave is also needed to issue the writ in such a case and one application both to issue and serve is usually made. The jurisdiction of the English courts comprises England, Wales, Berwick-on-Tweed and such part of the sea as the Crown may from time to time claim as territorial waters.[15] Leave in any case is discretionary but can only be given in those cases specified in Order 11, rr. 1 and 2. This important Order lists some sixteen cases in which leave may be granted, for example: where the subject matter of the action is land situate within the jurisdiction, where the defendant is domiciled or ordinarily resident within the jurisdiction, where the action is founded on a tort committed within the jurisdiction or concerns a contract made or broken within the jurisdiction. Since the grant of leave is discretionary, leave may be refused if

---

[10] O. 65, r. 4. An action in the Queen's Bench Division is assigned to one of the masters when the first summons in the action is issued. Masters have, with a few exceptions (set out in O. 32, r. 11), all the powers of a judge in chambers in relation to interlocutory matters. In addition masters have jurisdiction to try cases, with the consent of the parties, to assess damages and to make final orders in interpleader and garnishee disputes.

[11] *Porter* v. *Freudenberg*, [1915] 1 K.B. 857. Where the defendant is insured against his potential liability, service may be ordered on his insurers: *Gurtner* v. *Circuit*, [1968] 2 Q.B. 587; [1968] 1 All E.R. 328.

[12] O. 10, r. 3; see *British Controlled Oilfields, Ltd.* v. *Stagg* (1921), 127 L.T. 209.

[13] O. 113, r. 4.

[14] These rules will be substantially modified when section 16 of the Civil Jurisdiction and Judgments Act 1982 is implemented. This section creates a new uniform code of jurisdiction for the courts of England and Wales, Scotland and Northern Ireland in proceedings within that section, *viz.* proceedings within the scope of the 1968 Convention on jurisdiction and the enforcement of judgments in civil and commercial matters.

[15] *R.* v. *Kent Justices, Ex parte Lye*, [1967] 2 Q.B. 153; [1967] 1 All E.R. 560.

the court considers that another forum could more properly and conveniently try the case. This particularly applies where it is proposed to serve the writ in Scotland or Northern Ireland.[16] Unless service is to be effected in Scotland, Northern Ireland, the Isle of Man or the Channel Islands, notice of the writ is served and not the writ itself.[17] The effect is similar in that the plaintiff may obtain judgment on failure to give notice of intention to defend following service of notice of the writ.

If the defendant is in Scotland, Ireland, the Isle of Man, the Channel Islands or the Commonwealth the writ or notice of the writ may be served in accordance with the English methods of service. Elsewhere it must be served through the British consul, or the foreign government (where it is willing), or the foreign judicial authority in any country with which there is a Civil Procedure Convention.[18]

It may be noted that if a foreigner enters the jurisdiction he may be served, and the action proceed, irrespective of the fact that leave to serve him could not have been obtained had he remained outside the jurisdiction. Thus service of a writ upon an international art dealer at Ascot racecourse, although it may have been socially unpleasant, was held in one case[19] to have been effective to confer jurisdiction upon the English courts. However a defendant may obtain a stay of proceedings if he can show that there is another forum in which justice could be done between the parties and that to refuse a stay would produce injustice. Moreover where England is not the natural forum and the plaintiff does not offer any reasonable justification for his choice of forum the defendant may be granted a stay if the defendant establishes merely that he would be involved in substantial inconvenience and unnecessary expense if the proceedings were allowed to continue in England.[20] Where there are already proceedings pending between the parties in a foreign court which is a natural and appropriate forum for the resolution of the dispute between the parties, the court will stay a subsequent action unless the plaintiff can establish objectively by cogent evidence that even-handed justice might not be accorded to him in the foreign jurisdiction or that there was some personal or juridical advantage only available to him in the English action and of such importance that it would be unjust to deprive him of that advantage.[1]

---

16 Leave cannot be granted under O. 11, r. 1(1) (*f*) (contract (*inter alia*) made within the jurisdiction) if the defendant is domiciled or ordinarily resident in Scotland, nor under O. 11, r. 1(1) (*g*) (breach within the jurisdiction) if the defendant is domiciled or ordinarily resident in Scotland or Northern Ireland.

17 O. 11, r. 3.

18 O. 11, rr. 5, 6.

19 *Maharanee of Baroda* v. *Wildenstein*, [1972] 2 Q.B. 283; [1972] 2 All E.R. 689.

20 *MacShannon* v. *Rockware Glass, Ltd.*, [1978] A.C. 795; [1978] 1 All E.R. 625.

1 *The Abidin Daver*, [1984] A.C. 398; [1984] 1 All E.R. 470.

C ACKNOWLEDGMENT OF SERVICE[2]

1 Mode of acknowledging service

The defendant must acknowledge service within 14 days of service (including the day of service) to avoid being in default.[3] This is done by delivering or posting[4] to the Central Office or district registry the prescribed form of acknowledgment, duly completed. This is not a defence but a formal document the function of which is to avoid the plaintiff obtaining judgment in default or, if liability is admitted, to obtain a stay of execution.

2 Contents of acknowledgment of service

The form which the defendant is required to complete (on the back of which are printed notes for guidance) contains four sections. In (1) he is required to state his name; in (2) he states (by ticking the appropriate box) whether he intends to contest the proceedings; in (3) he indicates (again by ticking a box) whether, if the claim is for a debt or liquidated demand and he does not intend to contest the proceedings, he intends to apply for a stay of execution; in (4) he states (by ticking boxes) whether, if the writ was issued out of a district registry, he applies for the transfer of the action to the Royal Courts of Justice or to some other district registry.[5] Finally he (or his solicitor) must sign the form.

3 Dispute as to jurisdiction

Acknowledgment of service of a writ does not constitute waiver of any irregularity in the writ or notice or service thereof or in any order giving leave to serve the writ or notice out of the jurisdiction or extending the validity of the writ for the purpose of service.[6] A defendant who wishes to dispute the jurisdiction of the court on the ground of any such irregularity, or on any other ground, must give notice of intention to defend (in his

---

[2] Prior to 3 June 1980 the defendant was required, by the writ, to "enter an appearance" and, if he did not do so, the plaintiff could enter judgment in default of appearance. The Rules of the Supreme Court (Writ and Appearance) 1979 abolished this procedure and prescribed a procedure analogous to that previously applicable under the Matrimonial Causes Rules, namely that whereby the defendant is sent a form of acknowledgment of service on which he is invited to state whether he intends to contest the proceedings.

[3] Where service is out of the jurisdiction extra time is allowed. In proceedings within the State Immunity Act 1978 the period is two months (*ibid.*, s. 12(2)).

[4] The use of registered or recorded delivery post is not required. Ordinary pre-paid post is sufficient but it must be remembered that service is acknowledged when the document actually arrives at the court office, not when it is posted. In addition there are very detailed directions as to the precise procedure to be adopted for transacting this, and other classes of, business which may now be transacted by post; these are set out in *Practice Direction* (*Use of postal facilities: Queen's Bench Division*), [1976] 2 All E.R. 446; [1976] 1 W.L.R. 516.

[5] Such application can only be made where (*a*) the defendant does not reside or carry on business within the district of the registry out of which the writ was issued; and (*b*) there is no indorsement on the writ that the plaintiff's cause of action arose wholly or in part within that district (O. 4, r. 5(3)).

[6] O. 12, rr. 7, 8 (replacing the former procedure of entering "conditional appearance"); see, generally on this topic, *Carmel Exporters* (*Sales*), *Ltd.* v. *Sea-Land Services Inc.*, [1981] 1 All E.R. 984; [1981] 1 W.L.R. 1068.

acknowledgment of service) and must then within 14 days apply by summons to have the writ or an order for service set aside. The master may on this application try the issue of jurisdiction as a preliminary point. An acknowledgment of service may be withdrawn with leave of the court and may be amended, so as to change the defendant's statement that he does or does not intend to contest the proceedings, without leave before judgment is obtained.

4   Judgment on failure to give notice of intention to defend

If any defendant fails to give "notice of intention to defend" within the time limited the plaintiff is entitled to enter judgment in default. He must either file an affidavit of service proving due service of the writ, or notice of the writ on the defendant (which, if service was effected by post (*supra*) must contain a statement to the effect that in the deponent's opinion the copy of the writ will have come to the knowledge of the defendant within seven days thereafter and that the copy writ has not been returned through the post undelivered) or produce the writ indorsed with a statement by the defendant's solicitor that he accepts service on the defendant's behalf. In some cases leave must also be obtained: examples are cases where the defendant is the Crown[7] or has served notice to reopen a credit agreement under the Consumer Credit Act 1974,[8] or the action is a mortgage action[9] or an action in tort between spouses.[10] In addition judgment in default cannot be entered against an infant or patient.[11]

Where there are several defendants some of whom do not give notice, the plaintiff may enter judgment against those who do not appear without prejudice to his right to proceed against the others, if their liability is joint or several. However, where the liability of defendants is alternative, a judgment against one, albeit a default judgment, is a bar to a claim against any other.[12]

The type of default judgment which the plaintiff obtains depends upon the indorsements on the writ.

(1)   Where the writ was indorsed with a claim for a debt or liquidated demand or for the recovery of land the plaintiff is entitled to *final* judgment in default for the amount claimed or the recovery of land and costs on a fixed scale.[13] Thus a final judgment is final both as to liability and as to *quantum*.

(2)   Where the writ was indorsed with a claim for unliquidated damages or a claim relating to the detention of goods the plaintiff is entitled to apply by summons for judgment for delivery of the goods without giving him the alternative of paying their assessed value, or enter *interlocutory* judgment in default.[14] This is final as to liability but leaves the amount of damages and costs to be assessed. Notice of the assessment, which will take place before a

---

[7] O. 77, r. 9.
[8] O. 83, r. 3.
[9] O. 88, r. 6.
[10] O. 89, r. 2.
[11] The plaintiff must first apply to have a guardian *ad litem* appointed: O. 80, r. 6.
[12] *Morel Brothers* v. *Earl of Westmorland*, [1903] 1 K.B. 64, (affirmed [1904] A.C. 11).
[13] O. 13, rr. 1, 4. Leave is required where the action is for possession of premises to which the Rent Act 1977 applies (O. 13, r. 4(2)) or a mortgage action (O. 88, r. 6).
[14] O. 13, rr. 2, 3.

master or referee, is served upon the defendant who may attend the hearing and give evidence affecting the amount of liability, although he can no longer dispute his liability.

(3) Where the writ was indorsed with any other claim, for example for an injunction, a declaration, a decree of specific performance, an account or the appointment of a receiver, the plaintiff cannot obtain judgment in default.[15] He must first serve a statement of claim, unless this was indorsed on the writ, and the action proceeds as if notice of intention to defend had been given. Then if the defendant does not serve a defence within the time limited, the plaintiff may apply for judgment in default of defence, for such relief as he appears entitled to on his statement of claim.[16]

5 Setting aside a default judgment[17]

If the default judgment was irregularly or fraudulently obtained or is for an amount larger than is due the defendant has a right to have it set aside. In any other case, he may apply to have it set aside but he will have to show why he has failed to give notice of intention to defend, and also that he has a triable defence, which he will normally have to disclose by affidavit. In addition a third party who is affected by the judgment may apply to have it set aside even though not a party to the action. Thus an insurance company may apply to have a judgment against the insured set aside,[18] so also may a person in possession of land which the plaintiff has recovered by default.

Where a judgment regularly obtained is set aside it will almost invariably be on condition that the defendant pay the extra costs incurred.

Where, after judgment has been entered against a defendant purporting to have been served by post, a copy of the writ is returned to the plaintiff through the post undelivered, the plaintiff, before taking any further step must either—

(*a*) request judgment to be set aside on the ground that the writ has not been duly served; or

(*b*) apply to the court for directions.[19]

If he takes course (*a*) the court must set aside the judgment, whereas if he elects for course (*b*) the court may set the judgment aside or direct that the writ be treated as having been duly served or make such other order and give such other direction as the circumstances may require.[20] Accordingly, course (*b*) is preferable since, if there seems to be no reasonable prospect of

---

15 However the fact that there is a claim for a *Mareva* injunction in addition to a liquidated demand will not prevent the plaintiff from signing judgment in default for the sum claimed and then applying for his injunction; although this course is not envisaged by the Rules the court has inherent jurisdiction to control its own process and were it not to sanction this procedure a recalcitrant debtor could avoid a *Mareva* injunction against himself by simply failing to acknowledge service: *Stewart Chartering, Ltd.* v. *C. & O. Managements S.A.*, [1980] 1 All E.R. 718; [1980] 1 W.L.R. 460.

16 O. 19, r. 7(1). The application may be by motion, but is usually by summons unless an injunction is sought (which is generally outside the master's jurisdiction: O. 32, r. 11).

17 O. 13, r. 9.

18 *Windsor* v. *Chalcraft*, [1939] 1 K.B. 279; [1938] 2 All E.R. 751.

19 O. 13, r. 7(3).

20 O. 13, r. 7(4), (5).

ascertaining the defendant's whereabouts the court may order the judgment to stand or, perhaps, order some form of substituted service.

6   Application for stay of execution

It will be appreciated that, in order to avoid a default judgment, the defendant must return the form of acknowledgment of service containing a statement to the effect that he intends to contest the proceedings (by ticking the appropriate box). The acknowledgment of service then constitutes "notice of intention to defend".[1] If he does not intend to contest the proceedings, one might legitimately wonder why he should trouble to return the acknowledgment of service at all. The answer is that if the claim is for a debt or liquidated demand, he may state that he intends to apply for a stay of execution of the judgment and, if he does so state, execution is automatically stayed for 14 days from the acknowledgment of service and if within that time the defendant issues and serves a summons for such a stay, supported by an affidavit in accordance with Order 47, rule 1,[2] the stay continues until that summons is heard, unless the court otherwise directs.

Accordingly this procedure enables a debtor who has no defence to the claim to obtain a breathing space by means of stay of execution; his alternative (but more expensive) way of achieving delay is to give notice of intention to defend, thereby compelling the plaintiff to issue an Order 14 summons to obtain a judgment.[3]

---

[1]   O. 1, r. 4(1).
[2]   See p. 391, *post*.
[3]   For details of Order 14 procedure, see p. 326, *post*.

CHAPTER 16

Proceedings After Acknowledgment of Service

After the defendant has acknowledged service (assuming he gives notice of intention to defend), the action will normally proceed to the stage where the parties disclose their respective cases by the exchange of pleadings; however there are several courses which the action may take before that stage is reached and the procedure applicable to each of these must be considered. The principal possibilities are as follows:

A The proceedings may be stayed, discontinued or dismissed.
B The proceedings may be settled.
C There may be an application for summary judgment under Order 14.
D There may be a summons for an account to be taken under Order 43, rule 1.
E There may be an application for judgment on admissions of fact.
F The defendant may make a payment into court.
G There may be an application for a trial without pleadings under Order 18, rule 21.
H There may be an application for interim relief.
I The defendant may issue third party proceedings or may interplead.

Each of these courses merits individual consideration.

A STAY, DISCONTINUANCE AND DISMISSAL

1 Stay

The power of the court to stay proceedings may exist: (*a*) by statute; (*b*) under the Rules of the Supreme Court; or (*c*) under the inherent jurisdiction. Certain Acts of Parliament contain specific provisions empowering or requiring the court to stay proceedings. Of these, the most commonly encountered, in practice, are the Arbitration Act 1950, s. 4 (power to stay an action brought contrary to an arbitration agreement),[1] Bankruptcy Act 1914, s. 9 (stay of proceedings against a debtor after presentation of a bankruptcy petition) and Companies Act 1948, ss. 226, 307 (stay of proceedings against a company after the presentation of a winding up petition or in a voluntary winding up).[2] The Rules contain some provisions empowering or requiring the court to stay proceedings, generally until a party complies with an order.[3]

The power to stay under the inherent jurisdiction is expressly acknowledged and preserved by section 49(3) of the Supreme Court Act 1981 and is exercisable in a wide range of circumstances. Thus the court may stay proceedings which are obviously frivolous, vexatious, groundless or an abuse of the process of the court. It is necessary for the applicant for a stay to show that the action could not possibly succeed. Commencing a second action while there is in being an action based on the same facts is *prima facie* an abuse of the process of the court.[4] Other circumstances in which the court may stay proceedings in the exercise of its inherent jurisdiction include the existence of concurrent proceedings in the courts of another country,[5] the fact that the case ought properly to be litigated in another country[6] (in particular where the dispute arises out of a contract containing a foreign jurisdiction clause[7]) or the fact that the subject matter of the action is *res judicata*.[8] In addition it appears that there is inherent jurisdiction to order a stay whenever it is just and reasonable to do so, even though no party has failed to comply with any specific obligation. This was done in *Edmeades* v. *Thames Board Mills, Ltd.*[9] The plaintiff, in an action for damages for personal injuries, refused to submit to a medical examination by the defendant's doctor for the purpose of enabling the defendant to check on the injuries which the plaintiff claimed to have sustained. The Court of Appeal ordered a stay of the action until the plaintiff submitted to such examination. The decision is a remarkable one, since there is no power in any court to order a person to submit to medical examination.[10] It is odd that a person should be denied the use of the legal process to enforce his rights simply because he refuses to do that which he is in no way obliged to do.[11]

---

[1] See p. 225, *ante*.

[2] See also the Law Reform (Husband and Wife) Act 1962, s. 1(2) which enables actions in tort to be stayed if the court considers that no substantial benefit would accrue to either party from the continuation of the proceedings or that the dispute could more conveniently be disposed of under s. 17 of the Married Women's Property Act 1882.

[3] See, for example, O. 18, r. 19 (p. 344, *post*); O. 6, r. 5; O. 21, r. 5; O. 81, r. 2. Note also O. 114, r. 4, whereby, on an order being made referring a question to the European Court for a preliminary ruling under Article 177 of the E.E.C. Treaty, proceedings are (unless the court otherwise orders) stayed until the European Court has given a preliminary ruling on the question before it; see p. 379, *post*.

[4] *Slough Estates, Ltd.* v. *Slough Borough Council*, [1968] Ch. 299; [1967] 2 All E.R. 270.

[5] *The Abidin Daver*, [1984] A.C. 398; [1984] 1 All E.R. 470; see p. 316, *ante*.

[6] *MacShannon* v. *Rockware Glass, Ltd.*, [1978] A.C. 795; [1978] 1 All E.R. 625; see p. 316, *ante*. This ground is known as *forum non conveniens* and is expressly preserved by s. 49 of the Civil Jurisdiction and Judgments Act 1982.

[7] *The Eleftheria*, [1970] P. 94; [1969] 2 All E.R. 641.

[8] See p. 589, *post*.

[9] [1969] 2 Q.B. 67; [1969] 2 All E.R. 127.

[10] Although the creation of such a power has been recommended: *Report of the Committee on Personal Injuries Litigation* (Cmnd. 3691 of 1968), para. 312.

[11] This view was apparently shared by LAWSON, J. who, in holding in *Baugh* v. *Delta Water*

2 Discontinuance

The parties and their solicitors will, at every stage of the proceedings, be attempting to resolve their dispute without the expense of a trial. In fact very few actions come to trial. If the plaintiff is satisfied that his cause of action was misconceived or has ceased to exist he may at any time consent to judgment being entered against him with costs. The result will be to determine finally the issues he has raised on his writ and pleadings. However the plaintiff is better advised simply to discontinue his action since this course will not prevent him from suing again at a more convenient time. If he acts before a defence is served or within 14 days of service of a defence, the plaintiff may without leave serve a written notice on the defendant to the effect that he is discontinuing the whole or any part of his action.[12] He may serve a notice of discontinuance at a later stage of the action but only with leave (unless the defendant agrees in writing), and a condition of the grant of leave may be that the plaintiff shall take no further proceeding in the matter. Alternatively leave may be refused and judgment entered for the defendant. If a defendant has served a defence, he may withdraw it in whole or in part by giving written notice to the plaintiff.[13] The plaintiff may then enter judgment in default of defence. If a subsequent action is brought in respect of a cause of action previously discontinued, the master may order the proceedings to be stayed until the costs of the discontinued action have been paid.[14]

3 Dismissal

In a case in which the court has inherent power to stay proceedings, it will sometimes make an order dismissing the action, and the courts do not usually in such cases simply stay the proceedings if, for example, they are an abuse of the process of the court or are groundless. On the other hand if, of course, the ground upon which they are stayed is one that can be removed

---

Fittings, Ltd., [1971] 3 All E.R. 258; [1971] 1 W.L.R. 1295 that there was no power to require a widow to submit to medical examination by staying the action if she refused, (at any rate in the absence of any reason for supposing that her medical condition was out of the ordinary), expressed the opinion that *Edmeades* was wrongly decided, an opinion which soon brought a sharp rebuke by the Court of Appeal in *Lane* v. *Willis*, [1972] 1 All E.R. 430; [1972] 1 W.L.R. 326, in which case *Edmeades* was approved. Cf. *Norman* v. *Hardy*, [1974] 1 All E.R. 1170; [1974] 1 W.L.R. 1048 in which GOULDING, J. declined to stay a pending action, which was registered as such under the Land Charges Act 1972, on the ground that it was not right to stay an action in circumstances not covered by the Rules of the Supreme Court for the purpose of bringing about a vacation of the register which the judge had no power to effect by direct order.

[12] O. 21, r. 2(1). However a party in whose favour an interim payment has been ordered (as to which see p. 335, *post*) may not discontinue except with the leave of the court or the consent of all other parties (O. 21, r. 2(2A)). This Rule was introduced to remedy the omission which was disclosed in *Castanho* v. *Brown & Root (U.K.), Ltd.*, [1981] A.C. 557; [1981] 1 All E.R. 143 in which case the plaintiff, having obtained interim payments totalling £27,250 in his personal injuries action, together with an admission of liability, then served notice of discontinuance with a view to commencing another action in the United States based on the same accident. This was held to be an abuse of the process of the Court so that the court had jurisdiction to strike out the notice.

[13] O. 21, r. 2(2) (*a*).

[14] O. 21, r. 5.

(for example by a party complying with a court order), then it will be appropriate for the court to stay the proceedings rather than to dismiss them.

Dismissal for want of prosecution—One particular occasion of the exercise of the court's power to dismiss actions under its inherent jurisdiction is encountered in cases where the plaintiff has been guilty of "want of prosecution". It is of great practical importance and covers two distinct circumstances: (*a*) cases where the plaintiff has failed to comply with a peremptory (or "unless") order of the court; in such cases the action is liable to be dismissed on account of the contumelious conduct of the party in failing to comply with the court's peremptory order; (*b*) cases in which the plaintiff has simply delayed getting on with the action; these are more common.

If the time limits prescribed by the Rules were strictly observed most actions would be disposed of in a matter of months. In practice the time limits are, for one reason or another, not observed and even the simplest actions often take an unconscionable time to come to trial. The blame for delay must, as a rule, rest with the plaintiff and the ultimate sanction is that the action may be dismissed for want of prosecution. A dismissal, not being an adjudication on the merits, does not estop the plaintiff from issuing a fresh writ founded on the same cause of action.[15] However in *Birkett* v. *James*[16] the House of Lords held that in cases in which the limitation period had not expired (so that if the action were dismissed the plaintiff could simply issue a fresh writ), the court would not, save in rare and exceptional cases, dismiss an action for want of prosecution. The rare and exceptional cases contemplated are those in which the plaintiff's default has been contumelious or cases, such as *Spring Grove Services, Ltd.* v. *Deane*[15] where some factors other than mere delay have prejudiced the defendant. In such cases, on the basis that the court would stay a second action as being an abuse of the process of the court, it may dismiss the first action notwithstanding the fact that the limitation period has not expired. As stated above, such cases are likely to be very rare.

There have in recent years been numerous reported cases on this topic, starting with *Allen* v. *Sir Alfred McAlpine & Sons, Ltd.*[17] in which the Court of Appeal set out the principles on which the court would approach applications to dismiss. These are: (1) that the delay must be inordinate, (2) that it must be inexcusable, and (3) that the defendant must have been prejudiced by the delay. In considering whether delay has been inordinate, the whole history of the action is considered including delay prior to the issue of the writ and delay for which the defendant has been responsible. An inordinate delay will be inexcusable unless the plaintiff has some reason for it. Even if the delay is inordinate and inexcusable the action may not be struck out if the defendant has not been prejudiced, for example where liability is admitted.[18]

---

[15] *Pople* v. *Evans*, [1969] 2 Ch. 255; [1968] 2 All E.R. 743. However the court has power to strike out such an action as being an abuse of the process of the court. This has been done in only one reported case, *Spring Grove Services, Ltd.* v. *Deane* (1972), 116 Sol. Jo. 844, which case was exceptional in that the defence depended essentially on the evidence of two witnesses who were no longer available to the defendant when the second action was brought; cf. *Department of Health and Social Security* v. *Ereira*, [1973] 3 All E.R. 421.

[16] [1978] A.C. 297; [1977] 2 All E.R. 801.

[17] [1968] 2 Q.B. 299; [1968] 1 All E.R. 543; approved in *Birkett* v. *James* (*supra*).

[18] *Marlton* (*an infant*) v. *Lee-Leviten*, [1968] 2 All E.R. 874; [1968] 1 W.L.R. 1214.

Moreover, in *Birkett* v. *James* the House of Lords held that prejudice occurring prior to the issue of the writ was not sufficient, since delay during this period is permitted by the Limitation Acts. Thus the plaintiff has to demonstrate new prejudice over and above that which has occurred due to permissible delay in instituting proceedings. It need not be great but it must be "more than minimal". Nevertheless actions may be, and have been, struck out even where liability has been admitted by the defendant (thus providing an unexpected windfall for the defendant or, more often, his insurers). Thus in *Paxton* v. *Allsopp*[19] an action for damages for personal injuries arising out of a car accident was struck out even though liability had been admitted, and, indeed, an offer of £2,050 had been made by the defendant's solicitors and rejected some years earlier. The reason for striking out was that, not only was the delay inordinate and inexcusable, but the defendant was prejudiced in that oral examination of the medical witnesses would be impossible after such a length of time. The case was, it should be pointed out, an extreme one since the application to strike out was made more than 13 years after the accident.[20]

Without prejudice to the above, O. 3, r. 6 provides that where a year or more has elapsed since the last proceeding in an action, the party who desires to proceed must give to every other party not less than one month's notice of intention to proceed (whereupon the other party may, of course, apply to have the action dismissed for want of prosecution).

B. SETTLEMENT

The parties (or their insurance companies) are likely to be in constant communication to effect a settlement of the action. This they may do with complete candour since letters which pass between them are privileged from production and any offer or admission of liability made therein is said to be made "without prejudice".[1] The nature of a settlement is that it is a contract whereby the parties abandon their previous rights and obligations in return for the creation of new rights and obligations. Since the new obligations are contractual, they must, in accordance with general principles, either be under seal or made for consideration. These releases are termed, therefore, a "release under seal" and a "release by way of accord and satisfaction"; the latter is more common and has been defined as:[2]

> "The purchase of a release from an obligation, whether arising under contract or tort, by means of any valuable consideration, not being the actual performance of the obligation itself. The accord is the agreement by which the obligation is discharged. The satisfaction is the consideration which makes the agreement operative."

---

[19] [1971] 3 All E.R. 370; [1971] 1 W.L.R. 1310; see also *Gloria* v. *Sokoloff*, [1969] 1 All E.R. 204; *Sweeney* v. *Sir Robert McAlpine & Sons, Ltd.*, [1974] 1 All E.R. 474; [1974] 1 W.L.R. 200; *Bremer Vulkan Schiffbau und Maschinenfabrik* v. *South India Shipping Corporation*, [1981] A.C. 909; [1981] 1 All E.R. 289.

[20] See also *Biss* v. *Lambeth, Southwark and Lewisham Health Authority*, [1978] 2 All E.R. 125; [1978] 1 W.L.R. 382.

[1] See p. 668, *post.*

[2] *British Russian Gazette, Ltd.* v. *Associated Newspapers, Ltd.*, [1933] 2 K.B. 616, at pp. 643 644.

The parties may effect a settlement without the consent of the court by giving notice of withdrawal before trial. Where an order of the court is required, which will usually be the case when the action is settled during the trial, the required terms will be drawn up and indorsed on counsels' briefs, or, more usually, the parties will submit to judgment on agreed terms. The settlement of any action on behalf of an infant or patient must be approved by the court.[3]

C SUMMARY JUDGMENT UNDER ORDER 14

This procedure was introduced by the Judicature Acts 1873-1875, and involves the only Order which is universally recognised by number. It will be appreciated that the defendant's purpose in giving notice of intention to defend is frequently to gain time. Order 14 procedure enables the plaintiff to bring the matter to an early determination where the defendant has no triable defence to liability.[4]

The rule applies to every action in the Queen's Bench Division (or Chancery Division) begun by writ other than one which includes:

(*a*) a claim by the plaintiff for libel, slander, malicious prosecution, false imprisonment; or,

(*b*) a claim by the plaintiff based on an allegation of fraud;[5] or is

(*c*) an Admiralty action *in rem*.

Provided the defendant has given notice of intention to defend and the plaintiff has served a statement of claim, the plaintiff may issue the appropriate summons. To do so he or a person duly authorised by him must first swear an affidavit setting out his cause of action, the amount claimed, if liquidated, and his belief that there is no defence to his claim except as to the amount of damages. The plaintiff should not swear to this lightly, for if he issues an Order 14 summons where the case is not a proper one, or where he must have known that the defendant had a triable defence, the master may order him forthwith to pay the whole costs of the application.[6]

The plaintiff, having filed his affidavit, then takes out a summons which must be served on the defendant, together with a copy of his affidavit, not less than 10 clear days before the return day (i.e. the day appointed for the hearing of the summons).[7] The defendant, if he contests the summons, must attend on the return day and show that he has a triable defence. This is usually done by an affidavit, but it can be done "otherwise",[8] for example by oral testimony.

---

3 O. 80, rr. 11, 12; see p. 308, *ante*.
4 O. 86 provides a procedure, similar to O. 14, in actions commenced by writ in the Chancery Division for specific performance or rescission of agreements relating to land or for the forfeiture or return of any deposit made under such an agreement.
5 O. 14, r. 1(2). "Fraud" appears to be confined to common law deceit: *Barclays Bank, Ltd.* v. *Cole*, [1967] 2 Q.B. 738; [1966] 3 All E.R. 948.
6 O. 14, r. 7(1); except where the plaintiff is an assisted person. See the remarks of LORD GODDARD, C.J. in *M. Pocock* v. *A.D.A.C., Ltd.*, [1952] 1 T.L.R. 29 (*infra*).
7 O. 14, r. 2. As to the meaning of "clear days" in the Rules, see O. 3, r. 2(4).
8 O. 14, r. 4(1). The defendant must show that he has a triable defence, although he need not set out every element of that defence. A general denial of liability is not sufficient. There is no

At the hearing of the summons the master[9] may make the following orders.

(1) He may give judgment for the plaintiff, final or interlocutory.[10] This must be done unless the defendant satisfies the court "that there is an issue or question in dispute which ought to be tried or that there ought for some other reason to be a trial."[11] If he has any defence on a question of law or fact then he must be given leave to defend the action, even if the master strongly doubts that the defence will succeed.

(2) He may give the defendant unconditional leave to defend the action. In this case the action will proceed to trial in the usual way.

(3) He may give the defendant conditional leave to defend. This may be done where the master is almost, but not quite, sure that there is no triable defence.[12] The effect is that the defendant may present his defence provided he makes a payment into court of the whole or part of the sum claimed. The court must not impose a condition with which it is impossible for the defendant to comply. If the defendant wishes to avoid or limit a financial condition on the ground of his own impecuniosity the onus is on him to make a full and frank disclosure of his means. Moreover he cannot complain because a financial condition is difficult for him to fulfil; he must prove that it will be impossible for him to fulfil.[13] The defendant may appeal to a judge in chambers against any condition imposed.

(4) He may give judgment for the plaintiff as to part and to the defendant leave to defend as to part of the claim.

(5) He may give judgment for the plaintiff with a stay of execution pending the trial of a counterclaim.

(6) If the application was not made in good faith or the case was not within the order, a libel action for example, the master may order the plaintiff to pay the costs of the application forthwith.[14] This is an extreme sanction which will rarely be invoked although LORD GODDARD, C.J. suggested otherwise:[15]

"I wish it to be known as a practice rule that the proper course for a Master to take, if he considers that in a summons under O. 14 it is clear that the plaintiff

---

express requirement for the defendant to serve his affidavit on the plaintiff. However the summons contains a notice requiring the defendant to send a copy of his affidavit to the plaintiff to reach him not less than three days before the return day (so that the plaintiff may swear an affidavit in answer if he wishes). If the defendant sends his affidavit late or not at all, thereby necessitating an adjournment of the summons, he will usually have to pay the costs thrown away in any event; see *Practice Direction (Order 14: Return Date)*, [1970] 1 All E.R. 343; [1970] 1 W.L.R. 258.

9 The summons is almost always returnable before a master. However if an injunction is sought (which a master has no power to grant) the summons should be made returnable before a judge: *Shell-Mex and B.P. Ltd.* v. *Manchester Garages, Ltd.*, [1971] 1 All E.R. 841; [1971] 1 W.L.R. 612.

10 If the judgment is a money judgment, he may also award interest: *Gardner Steel, Ltd.* v. *Sheffield Brothers (Profiles), Ltd.*, [1978] 3 All E.R. 399; [1978] 1 W.L.R. 916.

11 O. 14, r. 3(1); the latter part of this sub-rule is wide enough to enable leave to defend to be given where, even though the defendant cannot point to a specific defence, it is just that the plaintiff be put to strict proof of his case: *Miles* v. *Bull*, [1969] 1 Q.B. 258; [1968] 3 All E.R. 632.

12 *Fieldrank, Ltd.* v. *E. Stein*, [1961] 3 All E.R. 681 n.; [1961] 1 W.L.R. 1287.

13 *M. V. Yorke Motors (a firm)* v. *Edwards*, [1982] 1 All E.R. 1024; [1982] 1 W.L.R. 444.

14 O. 14, r. 7(1).

15 *M. Pocock* v. *A.D.A.C., Ltd.*, [1952] 1 T.L.R. 29, at p. 34.

knew that there was an arguable defence to the claim, is to dismiss the summons with costs. Masters should use their powers under O. 14 much more freely.''

(7) If the master gives leave to defend or orders a stay of execution pending the trial of a counterclaim, he must give all directions as to the further conduct of the action as if the summons were a summons for directions; in particular he may, with the consent of all parties, order the action to be tried by himself or another master[16] or may transfer the action to a county court where it is transferable under the County Courts Act 1984.[17]

A defendant may apply for summary judgment on a counterclaim, provided it is not a claim which is outside the scope of the Order.[18] In addition any judgment under Order 14 may be set aside by the court on such terms as it thinks just.[19] This rather likens a judgment under Order 14 to a judgment on failure to give notice of intention to defend.

Order 14 proceedings constitute an invaluable means of combating delaying tactics on the part of a defendant who owes money but simply wishes to postpone the evil day of payment. However, in order to obtain a judgment for part of the sum claimed, the plaintiff has to identify a part of the claim which is separately quantifiable (for example, individual invoices in a claim for the balance of an account). If the plaintiff cannot do this, then there is no power under Order 14 to give judgment for any sum at all, even though there may be no doubt whatsoever but that a substantial sum is due. Thus in a claim for the balance of an account[20] or for unliquidated damages,[1] the defendant can keep the plaintiff out of his money pending a trial (or arbitration) simply by denying that the account is accurate (if he can raise a triable issue as to its accuracy) or by putting the plaintiff to proof of his damages. However the plaintiff may in such cases obtain an interim payment[2] and it is common for the plaintiff to apply for an interim payment as an alternative to summary judgment.

D   ACCOUNT SUMMONS

The plaintiff may indorse his writ with a claim for an account to be taken. This procedure dates back to the early days of the common law where it was available to the feudal lord against his bailiff or steward. It was extended in equity to any principal and agent relationship, such as landlord and rent-collector.[3] It is appropriate where the defendant is an accounting party that is to say a person who has received money on the plaintiff's behalf. The plaintiff is not in possession of sufficient details to frame an action for a debt. His remedy is to ask the court to compel his agent to account for monies received and to pay them to the plaintiff.

---

[16] O. 14, r. 6.
[17] See p. 422, *post*.
[18] O. 14, r. 5.
[19] O. 14, r. 11.
[20] *Contract Discount Corporation, Ltd.* v. *Furlong*, [1948] 1 All E.R. 274.
[1] *The Fuohsan Maru*, [1978] 2 All E.R. 254.
[2] See p. 335, *post*.
[3] See *London, Chatham and Dover Rail. Co.* v. *South Eastern Rail. Co.*, [1892] 1 Ch. 120.

To do so he may, at any time after the time limited for acknowledging service of the writ, or after the defendant has acknowledged service, take out a summons. The application is usually supported by an affidavit setting out the grounds on which the plaintiff relies. Unless the defendant can show that there is some preliminary issue to be tried or that he has already accounted, the master will order an account to be taken and the amount found due to be paid to the plaintiff within a specified time. The plaintiff's rights thus become crystallised into a judgment debt in the normal way. Simple accounts may be taken by a master in the Queen's Bench Division, but the proceedings are usually transferred to the Chancery Division or to an official referee.[4]

E JUDGMENT ON ADMISSIONS OF FACT

Where admissions of fact are made by a party "either by his pleadings or otherwise" any other party may apply to the court for such judgment or order as upon those admissions he may be entitled to, without waiting for the determination of any other question between the parties, and the court may on the hearing of the application give such judgment or make such order as it thinks just.[5]

The admissions may be made in the pleadings in which event, of course, the application will not be made at the early stages of the proceedings presently being considered. On the other hand, they may be made "otherwise", as the wording of the rule indicates; so admissions might be made in an affidavit sworn in opposition to Order 14 proceedings; or in the course of correspondence prior to the issue of proceedings, provided this was not "without prejudice".[6] However, the power to give judgment on admissions will only be exercised in the clearest cases. So, for example, the fact that a defendant has pleaded guilty to manslaughter does not enable the widow of the deceased to obtain judgment in a Fatal Accidents Act claim, because the defendant might wish to raise, for example, a plea of contributory negligence or *volenti non fit injuria*.[7] So also where, in a personal injuries action, the defendants' solicitors wrote to the plaintiff a letter informing him that they were authorised to inform him that "the defendants now admit that the incident alleged in . . . the statement of claim resulted from negligence for which they were responsible" the Court of Appeal, perhaps surprisingly, refused the plaintiff judgment on this admission since, although it amounted to an admission of negligence, it did not admit damage, which is an essential element of the tort of negligence.[8]

---

[4] See p. 371, *post.*

[5] O. 27, r. 3; the application may be made by summons or motion, but in the Queen's Bench Division is in practice made by summons.

[6] See p. 668, *post.*

[7] *Murphy* v. *Culhane*, [1977] Q.B. 94; [1976] 3 All E.R. 533.

[8] *Rankine* v. *Garton Sons & Co., Ltd.*, [1979] 2 All E.R. 1185. The decision seems highly technical since if the plaintiff had gone under Order 14 it is difficult to see on what basis judgment could have been withheld.

F PAYMENT INTO COURT

1 Method of payment

In any action for debt or damages the defendant may, at any time[9] pay money into court in satisfaction of any or all of the plaintiff's claims.[10] To do so he deposits his payment at the Bank of England, Law Courts Branch, and serves a written notice to this effect on the plaintiff and on every co-defendant.[11] Where the plaintiff has included in his writ two or more claims the defendant may either: (1) make a separate payment in respect of each, or (2) make one payment in respect of any or all of those claims.[12] The latter course is usually disadvantageous to the plaintiff, since he must either continue with all of his claims or accept the payment and abandon them all. Accordingly where the payment in of a lump sum in respect of several causes of action embarrasses the plaintiff, he may apply to the court by summons for an order that the defendant apportion his payment in respect of the several causes of action.[13] However, the defendant will not be required to sever his payment in unless the causes of action are substantially different, i.e. where a jury might be directed to make separate awards of damages. Where the causes of action are technically different but substantially the same, for example several meanings of the same words in a defamation action, the defendant, if he makes one payment in respect of them all, will not be required to sever it.[14]

Where the defendant has a counterclaim for damages he may expressly take this into account when paying money into court;[15] thus if he values the plaintiff's claim at £1,000 and his counterclaim at £200, he will pay into court £800. It will be appreciated that where he values his counterclaim in excess of the plaintiff's claim, he should not take it into account when paying in since, as we shall see, the effect of the plaintiff accepting the payment will be that the defendant cannot proceed with his counterclaim.

If the claim is for a debt or liquidated demand in foreign currency the defendant may pay into court in that currency, whereupon the currency will be held in a special account.[16]

The plaintiff's cause of action is deemed to include such interest as might be awarded in the judgment.[17] Consequently it is incumbent upon the defendant to make a payment which takes account of the interest which

---

9 Even before service of the writ.

10 O. 22, r. 1(1). This may be done after the trial of an action has begun.

11 Money standing in court carries no interest unless the court orders it to be placed in a deposit or short-term investment account. Consequently, if the sum is of any size, the defendant should apply to a master for the money to be transferred to the Short-Term Investment Account established under section 6(1) of the Administration of Justice Act 1965; for the procedure applicable, see *Practice Direction* (*Short-Term Investment Account*), [1973] 2 All E.R. 64; [1973] 1 W.L.R. 500.

12 O. 22, r. 1(4). Until 1965 this was not possible in defamation actions.

13 O. 22, r. 1(5). This order cannot be made in relation to money paid into court after the trial or hearing of the action has begun (O. 22, r. 3(3)).

14 *Pedley* v. *Cambridge Newspapers, Ltd.*, [1964] 2 All E.R. 794; [1964] 1 W.L.R. 988; decided under O. 82, r. 4, before that rule was amended; see fn. 13, *supra*.

15 O. 22, r. 2.

16 *The Halcyon the Great*, [1975] 1 All E.R. 882; [1975] 1 W.L.R. 515; see *Practice Direction* (*Foreign Currency*), [1976] 1 All E.R. 669; [1976] 1 W.L.R. 83.

17 O. 22, r. 1(8).

will have notionally accrued on the debt or damages up to the date of payment in.

2 Effects of a payment into court

The plaintiff must, within 3 days of receiving the defendant's notice of payment in, acknowledge receipt. He may then within 21 days, or later with leave, take the money out of court in respect of any cause of action for which a payment in was made.[18] If the defendant made a general payment in the plaintiff must take "all or nothing". The effect is that all the causes of action in respect of which the plaintiff accepted a payment in are stayed, as is any counterclaim which the defendant took into account under O. 22, r. 2. The plaintiff may then:

(1) tax and sign judgment for his costs to the date of payment in (but only if his whole claim is satisfied);[19] and

(2) in actions for defamation, apply to a judge in chambers by summons for leave to make in open court a statement in terms approved by the judge.[20] This is so that he may vindicate his reputation publicly.

Alternatively the plaintiff may leave the money in court and continue with his action. In this event the court must not be told of the existence of a payment into court until all questions of liability and damages have been determined.[1] This is especially so in jury actions, notably defamation, for if the jury knew of a substantial payment into court they would obviously be likely to look upon it as an admission of liability by the defendant, rather than a genuine attempt to effect a settlement. To this rule there are two exceptions—the defences of tender before action and apology under section 2 of the Libel Act 1843. In both these cases payment into court is an element in a defence and will therefore appear on the pleadings and be disclosed to the court.

As long as the plaintiff recovers more than the amount paid in the payment in will have been of no avail to the defendant. However, if he recovers less or no more than the amount paid in then, although costs are discretionary, the plaintiff will usually have to pay the whole costs of the action in respect of which payment was made, from the date of payment in.[2] The modern

---

[18] O. 22, r. 3. He requires, under O. 22, r. 4, an order of the court in some cases; *viz.* (*a*) where the payment is made by some, but not all, defendants sued jointly or in the alternative by him, (*b*) where the payment in was made as part of a plea of tender before action, (*c*) in actions by an infant or patient (O. 80, r. 12), (*d*) in actions under the Fatal Accidents Act and the Law Reform (Miscellaneous Provisions) Act 1934, or under the Fatal Accidents Act alone where more than one person is entitled to the money. Where the payment in was made or increased after the trial has begun the plaintiff may accept the money within two days of receiving notice but before the judge begins to deliver judgment or sum up to the jury. Save by consent, an application for leave to take out of court a sum paid in after the time for acceptance has expired should not be made to the trial judge since this would necessitate disclosing to the judge the fact (and probably the amount) of a payment in, which is specifically prohibited by O. 22, r. 7 (*infra*); *Gaskins* v. *British Aluminium Co., Ltd.*, [1976] Q.B. 524; [1976] 1 All E.R. 208.

[19] O. 62, r. 10(2).

[20] O. 82, r. 5(1).

[1] O. 22, r. 7; *Monk* v. *Redwing Aircraft Co.*, [1942] 1 K.B. 182; [1942] 1 All E.R. 133; *Millensted* v. *Grosvenor House (Park Lane), Ltd.*, [1937] 1 K.B. 717; [1937] 1 All E.R. 736.

[2] O. 62, r. 5. *Findlay* v. *Railway Executive*, [1950] 2 All E.R. 969.

tendency of the courts is to look at the action as a whole and not as several causes of action tried together. Thus if the plaintiff does not recover in the aggregate more than the total payment in by the defendant he may have to pay the costs of the whole action from the date of payment in.[3] To put it simply, the plaintiff is gambling to "beat the payment in".[4]

Where the plaintiff beats the payment in only by reason of interest that has accrued since the date of payment in it is to be anticipated that he would not be regarded as having beaten the payment in at all and that the trial judge would therefore order him to pay the defendant's costs from the date of payment in. In such a case it will be necessary for the judge to make a calculation of what the interest would have been at the date of payment in.

Where a defendant claims an indemnity or contribution from a third party or tortfeasor liable in respect of the same damage, that third party or tortfeasor cannot make a payment into court. He can, however, obtain a similar advantage by making a written offer to the defendant to pay a specified contribution to any debt or damages recovered against the defendant. If the defendant refuses this offer it may be drawn to the attention of the trial judge, who may take it into account when making an order as to costs, as if the offer were a payment into court.[5]

Finally it should be noted that the plaintiff may make a payment into court in respect of a counterclaim against him[6] and that a party may, with leave, withdraw a payment in.[7]

G   TRIAL WITHOUT PLEADINGS

This procedure enables either the plaintiff or the defendant to obtain a trial without pleadings or without further pleadings as the case may be. The application may be made in any action commenced by writ other than one which includes:

(*a*) a claim by the plaintiff for libel, slander, malicious prosecution or false imprisonment; or

(*b*) a claim by the plaintiff based on an allegation of fraud,

provided that any defendant has given notice of intention to defend.[8] The object of this procedure is to enable the parties to determine their dispute

---

3   *Hultquist* v. *Universal Pattern and Precision Engineering Co., Ltd.*, [1960] 2 Q.B. 467; [1960] 2 All E.R. 266.
4   LORD DENNING, M.R. in *Mason* v. *Mason*, [1965] 3 All E.R. 492; [1966] 1 W.L.R. 757 pointed out the desirability of a new rule which would have the effect of concealing the existence and amount of a payment in from the Court of Appeal so that the court would not be embarrassed by its knowledge of a payment in. With effect from the 1 April, 1976 such a rule was introduced (O. 59, r. 12A).
5   O. 16, r. 10; O. 62, r. 5; *Bragg* v. *Crosville Motor Services, Ltd.*, [1959] 1 All E.R. 613; [1959] 1 W.L.R. 324. A similar course may be taken in proceedings such as matrimonial property disputes, where the Rules make no provision for payment into court: *Calderbank* v. *Calderbank*, [1976] Fam. 93; [1975] 3 All E.R. 333 or in arbitrations where a "sealed offer" may be made.
6   O. 22, r. 6.
7   O. 22, r. 1(3); cf. *Sherratt (W.A.), Ltd.* v. *John Bromley (Church Stretton), Ltd.*, [1985] 1 All E.R. 216.
8   O. 18, r. 21.

without the delay and expense of pleadings or other interlocutory applications. However it is only appropriate where there is no substantial dispute as to fact, as, for example, where the action turns on the construction of a document. In this respect, and also in the conduct of the proceedings, the procedure is very similar to originating summons procedure, except that it applies to a wider range of proceedings in the Queen's Bench Division, such as a negligence action where the sole issue is the assessment of damages. Since there are no pleadings the parties must agree on a statement of the issues in dispute. This may be done by letter.[9] In a commercial case application for a trial without pleadings is frequently made in conjunction with an application for transfer to the Commercial Court.[10]

If the master makes an order for a trial without pleadings he must, and if he dismisses the application he may, give directions as to the further conduct of the action as if the summons were a summons for directions.

H INTERIM RELIEF

1 Interlocutory injunction

The power of the High Court to grant injunctions is, of course, inherited from equity. In addition to the court's inherent power to grant an injunction by way of final remedy, section 37(1) of the Supreme Court Act 1981 empowers the court to grant an injunction by an interlocutory order "in all cases in which it appears to the court to be just or convenient so to do." It may be noted that the injunction need not be directed at achieving the same relief as that which is sought by way of final relief in the proceedings. The most obvious example of this is the *Mareva* injunction, which has already been considered in detail.[11]

There has, recently, been a restatement of the principles to be considered by the court when faced with an application for an interlocutory injunction. It was formerly thought that the most important consideration was the relative strength of the parties' cases so that, in order to obtain an interlocutory injunction, the plaintiff had first to establish that he had a strong *prima facie* case.[12] The disadvantage of this approach was that it necessitated a close examination of the merits as disclosed in the affidavits sworn on behalf of each side, sometimes amounting almost to a trial of the action.[13]

In *American Cyanamid Co.* v. *Ethicon, Ltd.*[14] LORD DIPLOCK stated that the approach referred to above was incorrect and, in a speech with which the remainder of their Lordships agreed, laid down the following principles:[15]

---

9 *Hill* v. *Scott*, [1895] 2 Q.B. 371.
10 See p. 370, *post*.
11 See p. 297, *ante*.
12 See *J. T. Stratford & Son, Ltd.* v. *Lindley*, [1965] A.C. 269; [1964] 3 All E.R. 102.
13 Although there was the correlative advantage that, very often, the parties would either agree to treat the hearing of the motion as the trial of the action or, in fact, compromise the action on the basis of the decision of the motion. Many "leading cases" were decided in this way; cf. *Fellowes & Son* v. *Fisher*, [1976] Q.B. 122, at p. 133; [1975] 2 All E.R. 829, at p. 837.
14 [1975] A.C. 396; [1975] 1 All E.R. 504.
15 [1975] A.C., at pp. 408–409; [1975] 1 All E.R., at pp. 510–511.

(1) The plaintiff must first satisfy the court "that the claim is not frivolous or vexatious; in other words that there is a serious question to be tried".

(2) The court should then go on to consider the "balance of convenience".

(3) As to that, the court should first consider whether, if the plaintiff were to succeed at the trial in establishing his right to a permanent injunction, he would be adequately compensated by an award of damages for the loss he would have sustained by refusal of an interlocutory injunction.[16]

(4) If damages would not provide an adequate remedy (for example because the defendant may be impecunious) the court should consider whether the defendant would be adequately compensated by the plaintiff's undertaking as to damages (*infra*) in the event of an interlocutory injunction being granted but a permanent injunction being refused at the trial.

(5) Where other matters are equal, it is a "council of prudence to take such measures as are calculated to preserve the status quo".

(6) Finally, "if the extent of the uncompensatable disadvantage to each party would not differ widely, it may not be improper to take into account in tipping the balance the relative strength of each party's case as revealed by the affidavit evidence."

LORD DIPLOCK made it clear that there may be special factors which operate in "individual cases" in addition to the principles enumerated above. Nevertheless it is clear that the courts should not embark on anything resembling a trial of the action.

The Court of Appeal has, in subsequent cases, shown little enthusiasm for these new principles and LORD DENNING, M.R., in particular, treated these cases as "individual cases" taking them outside the *American Cyanamid* case.[17] In *Cayne* v. *Global Natural Resources plc*[18] the Court of Appeal pointed out that where the grant or refusal of an interlocutory injunction will have the practical effect of putting an end to the action the task of the court is to do its best to avoid injustice, and to balance the risk of doing an injustice to either party. In such cases the *American Cyanamid* guidelines cannot apply and unless the plaintiff can show an overwhelming case he will not be granted an injunction the effect of which would be tantamount to shutting the defendant out from contesting the action. MAY, L.J. justified this departure by observing:[19]

> "I think that one must be very careful to apply the relevant passages from Lord Diplock's familiar speech in the *Cyanamid* case not as rules but only as guidelines, which is what I am certain Lord Diplock intended them to be."

A master having no power to grant injunctions, application must be made to a judge. In cases of extreme urgency application can be made *ex parte* on affidavit, in which event an injunction will be granted for a very short period until an application by summons or motion can be brought before the court. Otherwise application is by summons to a judge in chambers in the Queen's

---

[16] *Donmar Productions, Ltd.* v. *Bart*, [1967] 2 All E.R. 338n; [1967] 1 W.L.R. 740; cf. *Hampstead and Suburban Properties, Ltd.* v. *Diomedous*, [1969] 1 Ch. 248; [1968] 3 All E.R. 545.

[17] *Fellowes & Son* v. *Fisher* (*supra*); *Hubbard* v. *Pitt*, [1976] Q.B. 142; [1975] 3 All E.R. 1.

[18] [1984] 1 All E.R. 225.

[19] [1984] 1 All E.R., at p. 237.

Bench Division or by motion in open court in the Chancery Division.[20]

As an alternative to injunction the court will usually accept an undertaking from the defendant (which has precisely the same effect). In addition, as a condition of being granted an interlocutory injunction the plaintiff is always required to give his undertaking as to damages, that is an undertaking to indemnify the defendant in respect of any damages which the latter sustains by reason of the injunction in the event of the action failing.[1] For this reason it is generally improvident for a plaintiff to apply for an interlocutory injunction unless he has a strong case in circumstances in which the injunction will cause the defendant heavy expense, for example by delaying building works.

2 Interim payment of damages

One long-standing criticism of civil procedure in the English courts was that wholly innocent parties, such as injured passengers in road accidents, had to wait for long periods for their damages while disputes between other parties, such as the car drivers (in fact, their insurers) were being resolved. The Report of the Committee on Personal Injuries Litigation[2] recommended that in such litigation, courts should have power to make interim payments and effect was given to this recommendation by the Administration of Justice Act 1969. This was replaced by section 32(1) of the Supreme Court Act 1981 which authorises rules of court enabling the High Court.

> "in such circumstances as may be prescribed to make an order requiring a party to the proceedings to make an interim payment of such amount as may be specified in the order, with provision for the payment to be made to such other party to the proceedings as may be so specified or, if the order so provides, by paying it into court."

The power was first exercised in personal injuries actions in 1970 and was extended in 1980 to all actions in which there is a money claim, whether by way of debt, damages, account, *quantum meruit* or whatever. The application for an interim payment may be made at any time after expiry of the time limited for acknowledgment of service and is by summons supported by an affidavit which must:

(*a*) verify the amount of the damages, debt or other sum to which the application relates and the grounds of the application;

(*b*) exhibit any documentary evidence relied on by the plaintiff in support of the application; and

(*c*) if the plaintiff's claim is made under the Fatal Accidents Act 1976, contain the particulars mentioned in section 2(4) of that Act.[3]

---

[20] O. 29, r. 1.

[1] Where the Crown engages in litigation for the purpose of asserting a proprietary or contractual right, the ordinary rule applies; however where the Crown has commenced proceedings for an injunction for the purpose of enforcing the law in the manner prescribed by statute, no undertaking as to damages will be required: *Hoffman-La Roche (F.) & Co. A.G.* v. *Secretary of State for Trade and Industry*, [1975] A.C. 295, at p. 329; [1974] 2 All E.R. 1128.

[2] Cmnd. 3691 of 1968.

[3] O. 29, r. 10.

By O. 29, r. 11 an interim payment in an action for damages may be ordered only in three circumstances:

(*a*) where the defendant has admitted liability;

(*b*) where the plaintiff has obtained judgment against the respondent to the application for damages to be assessed; or

(*c*) where if the action proceeded to trial the plaintiff would obtain judgment for substantial damages. Thus the power to order a payment on account of damages is limited to clear cases.[4]

The fact of the interim payment being made must not be pleaded nor disclosed to the court at the trial until all questions of liability and damages have been decided.[5] On giving final judgment the court may make an order so as to adjust the position between the parties in relation to sums already paid by way of interim payment; such an adjustment may involve repayment by the plaintiff or compensating payments between two or more defendants.[6] Where, after making an interim payment, a defendant pays money into court under Order 22, rule 1,[7] the notice of payment must state that the defendant has taken into account the interim payment.

Power to order interim payments extends to actions for possession of land; where it appears to the court that in the event of final judgment the defendant would be held liable to pay to the plaintiff a sum in respect of the defendant's use and occupation of the land during the pendency of the action, the court may order an interim payment on account of that sum.[8] The order may be for a lump sum or for periodical payments during the pendency of the action, or both.[9]

Those provisions enable, for example, a landlord to be awarded sums equivalent to rent against a tenant who is holding over at the end of his lease.

I   THIRD PARTY AND INTERPLEADER PROCEEDINGS

1   Third party proceedings

Irrespective of his liability to the plaintiff, the defendant may have a right to relief from a third party which relates to the original subject matter of the action or which is substantially the same as the relief or remedy claimed by the plaintiff.[10] Thus if the plaintiff is a lessor and sues the defendant lessee for breach of covenant, the defendant may be able to claim relief from a

---

[4] It is further limited in that no order can be made unless the defendant is insured against his liability, a public authority or a person whose means and resources are such as to enable him to make the interim payment; O. 29, r. 11(2).

[5] O. 29, r. 15; cf. the rules relating to payments into court, p. 331, *ante.*

[6] O. 29, r. 17.

[7] See p. 330, *ante.*

[8] O. 29, r. 12.

[9] O. 29, r. 13.

[10] O. 16, r. 1. Until Rules made in 1929, a third party notice could only be issued for a contribution or indemnity. It now applies to a much wider range of proceedings by virtue of the wide provisions of the present rule. Cf. *Myers* v. *N. and J. Sherick, Ltd.*, [1974] 1 All E.R. 81; [1974] 1 W.L.R. 31.

sub-lessee.[11] Usually the right claimed by the defendant is to an indemnity or a contribution. A right to indemnity may exist by contract, by statute[12] or by a rule of common law or equity. A common example is the right of an agent to be indemnified by his principal in respect of acts performed within the scope of his authority.[13] A contribution is, in effect, a partial indemnity. It arises where a person is sued and there are other persons liable in respect of the same damage. The others, who may be joint trustees, joint debtors or joint tortfeasors, for example, have a duty to contribute.[14]

In any of the above cases the defendant may bring a separate action for the remedy sought against the third party. However he will save time and costs by issuing a third party notice. He may do this without leave before serving his defence and with leave thereafter.[15] The notice must contain particulars of the nature of the claim and the relief sought and must be served on the third party together with a copy of the statement of claim and all pleadings thus far served in the action.[16]

The effect of this procedure is to make the third party a defendant in relation to the original defendant. The action then proceeds between them as if the defendant had issued a writ against the third party in the ordinary way. Thus if the third party does not give notice of intention to defend, the defendant is entitled to sign judgment in default. If his claim was for an indemnity the extent of this judgment will be the amount that the plaintiff recovers from the defendant.[17]

The third party may counterclaim against the defendant, but not against the plaintiff.[18] He can, however, interrogate the plaintiff. Alternatively the third party may join a fourth party and so on.[19] Although the third party does not, strictly speaking, stand in any relationship to the plaintiff the court is enabled by Order 16, rules 8 and 9 to determine any issue arising between the third party and the plaintiff. Third party proceedings are independent of the main action to the extent that they may continue to trial even after the issue between the plaintiff and defendant has been disposed of by final order.[20]

---

[11] *Pontifex* v. *Foord* (1884), 12 Q.B.D. 152.

[12] Examples are: ss. 76, 77 of the Law of Property Act 1925, and Sch. 2 (implied covenants); Civil Aviation Act 1982, s. 76(3).

[13] *Read* v. *Anderson* (1882), 10 Q.B.D. 108; *Johnson* v. *Kearley*, [1908] 2 K.B. 514.

[14] See Civil Liability (Contribution) Act 1978, s. 1 (repealing and replacing Law Reform (Married Women and Tortfeasors) Act 1935, s. 6).

[15] O. 16, rr. 1, 2.

[16] O. 16, r. 3. Note also O. 15, r. 10A(2) whereby a defendant to an action for wrongful interference with goods (under the Torts (Interference with Goods) Act 1977) who wishes to set up the title of a third party against the plaintiff's claim (*jus tertii*) may at any time after giving notice of intention to defend apply for directions as to whether any such person should be joined in the action; the application is by summons which must be served on the third party in question and if the latter does not appear on the hearing of the summons the court may by order deprive him of any right of action he might otherwise have against the defendant: O. 15, r. 10A(4).

[17] O. 16, r. 5. But it cannot, without leave, be enforced until the defendant has satisfied the judgment against himself: O. 16, r. 7(2).

[18] *Barclays Bank, Ltd.* v. *Tom*, [1923] 1 K.B. 221.

[19] O. 16, r. 9. The procedure between a third party and a fourth party is similar to the procedure as between the defendant and the third party.

[20] *Stott* v. *West Yorkshire Road Car Co., Ltd.*, [1971] 2 Q.B. 651; [1971] 3 All E.R. 534.

2   Stakeholder's interpleader

This is a procedure which is appropriate where a person is under a liability in respect of a debt or in respect of any money, goods or chattels and he is, or expects to be, sued by two or more rival claimants.[1] For example, an estate agent who is holding a purchaser's deposit or a repairer in possession of goods may find that there is a claim by a third party other than the depositor, such as the vendor or a hire purchase finance company. If he delivers the money or goods to the claimant who turns out not to have been entitled, he is liable to the rightful owner in the tort of conversion. If he wrongly withholds possession he is liable for wrongful interference with goods. In this situation he should interplead.

To do this he takes out an ordinary summons, if an action is pending, or an originating summons, if not, which he serves on all the rival claimants calling upon them to appear before a master or district registrar and specify their claims. The stakeholder, when he takes out the summons, must swear an affidavit stating that he claims no interest in the subject matter in dispute other than for charges or costs, that he does not collude with any of the claimants and that he is willing to pay or transfer the subject matter into court.[2] On the return day the court will, if the claimants appear, make an order in one of the following forms:[3]

(1) that any claimant be made a defendant in a pending action in addition to, or in substitution for, the stakeholder;

(2) that an issue between the claimants be stated and tried, directing which shall be plaintiff and which defendant;

(3) that the issue be determined by the master if both parties consent, or one requests, or the question is solely one of law.[4]

(4) that the proceedings be transferred to a county court if the subject matter or its value does not exceed the county court limit.[5]

In addition the master may order the money or goods in issue to be paid or deposited in court pending the determination of the issue.[6] If the subject matter is money the stakeholder may deduct his charges and his taxed costs. Otherwise these will be paid after the determination of the issue.

---

[1] O. 17, r. 1.

[2] O. 17, r. 3.

[3] O. 17, r. 5.

[4] The Court of Appeal has stated that the issue should not, however, be determined summarily if there is a serious claim to chattels of considerable value or there is a prospect of difficult questions of law arising; in such a case a proper trial of the claim should be ordered; *Fredericks and Pelhams Timber Buildings* v. *Wilkins (Read, Claimant)*, [1971] 3 All E.R. 545; [1971] 1 W.L.R. 1197.

[5] County Courts Act 1984, s. 44.

[6] Under O. 29, r. 4 the court has power on the application of any party to order a sale of perishable property which is the subject-matter of proceedings or as to which any question arises.

CHAPTER 17

Pleadings

A THE NATURE AND FUNCTION OF PLEADINGS

If the action has not been brought to an end in one of the ways referred to in the preceding Chapter the parties must proceed to the exchange of pleadings. Before embarking upon consideration of this important topic it is important to bear in mind the distinction between modern pleadings and the pleadings which formed the basis of the common law writ system at common law. Pleadings at common law had to state a conclusion of law in one of the prescribed forms. Pleadings in Chancery went to the other extreme and simply set out *en masse* all the relevant facts leaving the judge to decide where equity lay. The modern system of pleading strikes a happy balance between the common law and Chancery systems. The modern system has its origins in the Common Law Procedure Acts 1852 and 1854 and the first set of Rules of the Supreme Court in 1875.[1]

Pleadings are written statements served by each party on his opponent, containing the allegations of fact on which the party pleadings relies. They serve various purposes. Principally they enable each party to determine exactly which facts are alleged against him. This may save a party from preparing evidence to meet allegations which are not being made against him. Also it enables parties to establish their "common ground", that is to say facts on which they are in agreement, thus saving the expense of proving these matters at the trial.

Secondly, the action is decided upon the pleadings. Thus the parties and their successors may, by reference to the pleadings, determine in the future exactly what the case decided, so that they may not have to, and indeed may not be allowed to, fight the same issues again. Similarly reference to the pleadings in an action may disclose the *ratio decidendi* of the case for the purpose of the doctrine of precedent, since any fact not pleaded will not usually be regarded as a fact upon which a judgment is based.

The classic definition of what pleadings must contain is now to be found in O. 18, r. 7(1):

---

[1] See p. 83, *ante.*

"... , every pleading must contain, and contain only, a statement in a summary form of the material facts on which the party pleading relies for his claim or defence, as the case may be, but not the evidence by which those facts are to be proved, and the statement must be as brief as the nature of the case admits ..."

Thus pleadings must contain facts not law.[2] However, this only means that conclusions of law (such as the existence of a duty of care in negligence) need not be pleaded, not that a point of law cannot be raised on the pleadings.[3] Only material facts should be pleaded. Thus immaterial facts, such as character or motive, must not be pleaded since they form no part of a cause of action or defence.[4] Evidence should not be pleaded. However, the line between facts and evidence is by no means clearly defined. It is suggested that evidence be confined to its narrow meaning, *viz.* the means of proof.[5] By way of exception to the rule that evidence need not be pleaded, Order 18, rule 7A provides that a party intending to adduce evidence of another party's conviction, pursuant to section 11 of the Civil Evidence Act 1968[6] must include in his pleading a statement of his intention with particulars of the conviction and the date thereof, the court which made the conviction and the issue in the proceedings to which the conviction is relevant. If the person convicted intends to deny the conviction, allege that it was erroneous or deny its relevance he must make the denial or allegation in his pleading.

Finally, pleadings must contain all the material facts. The reason is that at the trial a party will be confined to his pleadings and will not be allowed to raise any matter not pleaded since this would take his opponent by surprise— the very contingency which pleadings are designed to avoid.[7] Thus where, in an action based on negligence, the plaintiffs relied in their pleaded case upon vicarious liability, they were not allowed in the House of Lords to allege that the defendants were negligent personally, since this was an allegation which they had not pleaded.[8] On the other hand a variation from the pleaded case, as opposed to a complete departure, is permissible; thus where, in one case, the plaintiff in his statement of claim alleged that a large stone had struck him on the head, he was not prevented from showing at the trial that his injuries had in fact been caused by several stones.[9]

Without prejudice to the generality of the above principles the Rules prescribe certain criteria as to the contents of pleadings generally. The most important of these are as follows.

---

[2] *North Western Salt Co., Ltd.* v. *Electrolytic Alkali Co., Ltd.*, [1914] A.C. 461; *Gautret* v. *Egerton* (1867), L.R. 2 C.P. 371.

[3] O. 18, r. 11.

[4] *Rassam* v. *Budge*, [1893] 1 Q.B. 571; *Plato Films, Ltd.* v. *Speidel*, [1961] A.C. 1090; [1961] 1 All E.R. 876; but see *Goody* v. *Odhams Press, Ltd.*, [1967] 1 Q.B. 333; [1966] 3 All E.R. 369.

[5] *Davy* v. *Garrett* (1878), 7 Ch.D. 473; *North Western Salt Co., Ltd.* v. *Electrolytic Alkali Co., Ltd.*, [1914] A.C. 461; see p. 559, *post.*

[6] As to the admissibility and effect of such evidence, see p. 581, *post*. The rule also applies to findings of adultery and paternity as evidence in civil proceedings under section 12 of the Civil Evidence Act 1968.

[7] Although where a party has pleaded conclusions of law he is not precluded, at the trial, from seeking to draw different conclusions of law from the facts pleaded: *Re Vandervell's Trusts (No. 2)*, [1974] Ch. 269; [1974] 3 All E.R. 205.

[8] *Esso Petroleum Co., Ltd.* v. *Southport Corporation*, [1956] A.C. 218; [1955] 3 All E.R. 864.

[9] *McCarron* v. *Cementation Co., Ltd.* (1964), *The Times*, 26 October; see also *Waghorn* v. *George Wimpey & Co., Ltd.*, [1970] 1 All E.R. 474; [1969] 1 W.L.R. 1764; *Farrell* v. *Secretary of State for Defence*, [1980] 1 All E.R. 166; [1980] 1 W.L.R. 172.

(1) Every pleading must contain the necessary particulars of any claim, defence or other matter pleaded, including particulars of any misrepresentation, fraud, breach of trust, wilful default or undue influence on which the party pleading relies.[10]

(2) A party must give particulars of any alleged condition of mind of any person other than knowledge (for example, fraudulent intention or malice).[11]

(3) A party must in any pleading *subsequent* to a statement of claim plead any matter, for example any relevant statute of limitation, fraud or other fact showing illegality which he alleges makes any claim or defence of the other party not maintainable or which if not specifically pleaded might take the other party by surprise or which raises issues of fact not arising out of the preceding pleading.[12]

Thus, for example, if in a "running down" action the defendant driver's case is that his vehicle had a latent mechanical defect which caused it to go out of control, he cannot simply deny negligence in his defence and then raise the specific suggestion of latent defect at the trial since this would take the other party by surprise. He must plead the defence of latent mechanical defect specifically so that the plaintiff can inspect the vehicle, or have it inspected by his own expert, and join the manufacturer or person who last repaired or serviced the vehicle as a second defendant.

It will be observed that the above rules are of two kinds: (3) relates to matters which must be pleaded, whereas (1) and (2) relate to particulars which must be given of matters which are pleaded.

B THE EXCHANGE OF PLEADINGS

1 Statement of claim[13]

The plaintiff may have indorsed his writ with a statement of claim. This is a pleading and the plaintiff may not serve another statement of claim except by way of amendment. If the writ was only generally indorsed the plaintiff may serve his statement of claim at any time before the defendant gives notice of intention to defend or within 14 days thereof. If he does not the defendant may (although he is not obliged so to do) apply to have the action dismissed for want of prosecution.

---

[10] O. 18, r. 12(1) (*a*). If these matters are not pleaded, in view of their gravity, judges are very slow to allow a party to rely upon them, directly or indirectly; see, for example, *Belmont Finance Corporation, Ltd.* v. *Williams Furniture, Ltd.*, [1979] Ch. 250; [1979] 1 All E.R. 118.

[11] O. 18, r. 12(1) (*b*); *Fowler* v. *Lanning*, [1959] 1 Q.B. 426; [1959] 1 All E.R. 290. "Condition of mind" includes the condition of mind of the party pleading, if he relies upon it: *Feeney* v. *Rix*, [1969] Ch. 693; [1968] 3 All E.R. 22. Although the rule excludes "knowledge" it is necessary to give particulars of the facts alleged to give rise to knowledge; O. 18, r. 12(4); cf. *Astrovlanis Compania Naviera S.A.* v. *Linard*, [1972] 2 Q.B. 611; [1972] 2 All E.R. 647 in which the former practice of the Commercial Court not to order particulars of an allegation of "scuttling" (i.e. conniving at the loss of a vessel in order to make an insurance claim in respect thereof) was held to be wrong and inconsistent with O. 18, r. 12(1) (*a*).

[12] O. 18, r. 8(1).

[13] Before 1875 this was called a "declaration"; the modern defence was called a "plea" and the reply, a "replication".

The statement of claim is a statement of all the facts which are alleged to constitute the plaintiff's cause of action, and a statement of the relief or remedy required. Thus if the action is for breach of contract, the statement of claim must set out the date, time and place at which the contract was made, the parties to the contract, the term alleged to have been broken and details of the breach. It is bad pleading to allege a breach of contract without alleging the existence of a contract, since that may be just what the defendant wishes to deny. Similarly in a tort action the plaintiff must allege all the elements of the tort in question, although he need not name the tort. Otherwise, his statement of claim discloses no cause of action. Thus a statement of claim that alleged, "laconically", that at a stated time and place "the defendant shot the plaintiff" was held to disclose no cause of action, since it did not allege a mental element which is an element in the tort of trespass to the person.[14] The one limitation on the contents of the statement of claim is that it must contain only allegations in respect of causes of action mentioned in the indorsement on the writ or arising from facts mentioned on the writ.[15]

In addition to the general criteria for the contents of pleadings, referred to above, there are certain other matters which the plaintiff must have in mind when preparing the statement of claim. The more important of these are as follows:

(1) In libel and slander the plaintiff must give particulars of facts to support any sense of the words other than their ordinary meaning (innuendo).[16]

(2) In actions under the Fatal Accidents Act 1976, the plaintiff must serve:

> "full particulars of the dependants for whom and on whose behalf such action shall be brought, and of the nature of the claim in respect of which damages are sought to be recovered".[17]

(3) The plaintiff should set out in his statement of claim all reliefs and remedies to which he claims to be entitled, though he need not specifically claim costs.[18] The reliefs and remedies which the plaintiff may claim merit some attention.

a   Debt or damages

For procedural purposes there are only two kinds of damages—general and special.

General damages—These are such damages as the law will presume to have resulted from the defendant's act. These damages (which include damages for pain, suffering, loss of amenities and inconvenience) need not be specifically pleaded and the plaintiff cannot as a rule be required to give particulars of them. However, where a plaintiff has suffered damage of an unusual

---

[14] *Fowler* v. *Lanning*, [1959] 1 Q.B. 426; [1959] 1 All E.R. 290.

[15] O. 18, r. 15(2). The rule is, however, of no great practical importance since the plaintiff can raise a new cause of action by amending the writ; see *Brickfield Properties, Ltd.* v. *Newton*, [1971] 3 All E.R. 382; [1971] 1 W.L.R. 862.

[16] O. 82, r. 3; *Grubb* v. *Bristol United Press*, [1963] 1 Q.B. 309; 2 All E.R. 380; *Lewis* v. *Daily Telegraph, Ltd.*, [1964] A.C. 234; [1963] 2 All E.R. 151. The precise words of the publications relied upon should be set out *verbatim; Collins* v. *Jones*, [1955] 1 Q.B. 564; [1955] 2 All E.R. 145.

[17] Fatal Accidents Act 1976, s. 2(4).

[18] O. 18, r. 15(1).

character he must in his pleadings warn the defendant of the fact that damages will be claimed in respect of such damage, thus showing the defendant the case he has to meet and assisting him in computing a payment into court.[19] Once again the general rule is that the plaintiff must not take the defendant by surprise. So, for example, future loss of earnings in a personal injuries action are general damages; nevertheless a plaintiff who alleges a continuing or future loss of earnings must make this clear. A claim for exemplary damages must be specifically pleaded together with the facts on which the party pleading relies.[20] General damages are claimed generally by the words "and the plaintiff claims damages".

Special damages—These are such damages as the law will not presume in the plaintiff's favour, such as loss of earnings, loss of business profits, and medical expenses. These damages must be specifically pleaded and proved at the trial. Where special damage is an element in the plaintiff's cause of action, he must plead it or his statement of claim will disclose no cause of action. It is important to note that any special damage not pleaded cannot be recovered at the trial, unless leave to amend is given.

If the claim is for a debt or damages in a foreign currency the statement of claim should make this clear and should set out the facts relied upon to support such a claim.[1]

b Interest

The High Court has power under section 35A of the Supreme Court Act 1981[2] to award simple interest on debts and damages. Apart from this provision the plaintiff may have a right to interest arising out of contract or under the Bills of Exchange Act 1882. In any of these cases the claim for interest must be specifically pleaded.[3] The statement of claim must plead (i) the cause of action, with particulars, the sum claimed and the date when payment was due; (ii) the rate of interest claimed and the amount claimed from the date when payment was due to the date of issue of the writ, (iii) a claim for further interest from the issue of the writ, showing the daily rate.[4]

c Other relief

There are various other forms of relief available. Of these an order for the possession of land or delivery of a chattel, being common law remedies, are available as of right, whereas the equitable remedies of injunction, specific performance, rectification rescission, account and discovery are discretionary. Where an order, such as an injunction, is sought it is usual to plead the precise terms of the order sought.

---

[19] *Perestrello e Companhia Limitada* v. *United Paint Co., Ltd.*, [1969] 3 All E.R. 479; [1969] 1 W.L.R. 570. This requirement cuts across the traditional distinction between general and special damages.

[20] O. 18, r. 8(3), negativing *Cassell & Co., Ltd.* v. *Broome*, [1972] A.C. 1027; [1972] 1 All E.R. 801.

[1] *Practice Direction (Judgment: Foreign Currency)*, [1977] 1 All E.R. 544; [1977] 1 W.L.R. 197.

[2] Added by Administration of Justice Act 1982, s. 15(1), Sch. 1.

[3] O. 18, r. 8(4).

[4] *Practice Direction (interest: pleading)*, [1983] 1 All E.R. 934; [1983] 1 W.L.R. 377.

d Declaration

Where the plaintiff claims no relief, legal or equitable, but seeks an adjudication upon his rights he may simply claim a declaration. The power of the High Court to make declarations of right or title is an inherent one deriving from the practice of the Court of Chancery; it is now codified in O. 15, r. 16 and provides a useful means whereby a party may ascertain his legal position before embarking upon a course of action. However, it is axiomatic that the courts will not adjudicate upon hypothetical questions so that no declaration will be granted where the defendant has neither committed nor threatened any wrongful act.[5] The procedure of applying for a declaration is particularly appropriate where a party seeks the court's decision as to status; thus declarations are frequently sought and made on such issues as whether a person is legitimate or whether a foreign divorce decree has effectively dissolved an English marriage. However, if the proceedings are directed at challenging the decision of a public body the applicant must proceed for judicial review[6] and the courts will not allow him to proceed by way of action for a declaration, thereby avoiding the procedural restrictions of judicial review proceedings, in particular the three months time limit.[7]

2 Defence (and counterclaim)

The defendant must serve a defence on the plaintiff within 14 days of the expiration of the time limited for acknowledging service of the writ or of receiving the statement of claim, whichever is the later.[8] If he does not, the plaintiff may enter judgment, final or interlocutory, in default of defence.[9] The procedure is similar to judgment on failure to give notice of intention to defend and the same limitations apply. This time limit may, as may all time limits under the Rules, be extended by agreement or by order of the master. Before drafting his defence, there are preliminary matters which the defendant must consider. For example, the statement of claim served on him may disclose no cause of action, or may introduce a new cause of action not indorsed on the writ. In such a case the defendant may apply by summons to a master to strike out the statement of claim.[10] A less radical course is to

---

[5] *Ealing London Borough* v. *Race Relations Board*, [1971] 1 Q.B. 309; [1971] 1 All E.R. 424; *Mellstrom* v. *Garner*, [1970] 2 All E.R. 9; [1970] 1 W.L.R. 603.

[6] See p. 174, *ante.*

[7] *O'Reilly* v. *Mackman*, [1983] 2 A.C. 237; [1983] 3 All E.R. 1124.

[8] The effect of this is that where the statement of claim is indorsed on the writ, the defendant has 28 days in which to serve a defence. Unless the court otherwise directs the time for serving pleadings does not run during the month of August (O. 3, r. 3). This Rule, introduced in 1982, effectively reduces the "long vacation" from two months to one and indeed there are now sittings of the High Court in London and elsewhere (albeit to a very limited extent) in September.

[9] The plaintiff or his solicitor must certify that the defendant is in default on the back of the court copy of the judgment which he tenders for entry: *Practice Direction (Judgment by Default)*, [1979] 2 All E.R. 1062; [1979] 1 W.L.R. 851.

[10] O. 18, r. 19. This is a most important rule. It enables the court to stay or dismiss an action, or strike out any pleading "on the ground that—(a) it discloses no reasonable cause of action or defence, as the case may be; or (b) it is scandalous, frivolous or vexatious; or (c) it may prejudice, embarrass or delay the fair trial of the action; or (d) it is otherwise an abuse of the process of the court". Apart from this rule the court has an inherent jurisdiction under which it can deal with any case within this rule. This wide power is only exercised in the clearest

apply for particulars.[11] There may be a third party from whom the defendant has a right to relief in respect of the subject matter of the action, the other driver in a running-down action for example. In this case the defendant should institute third party proceedings to join that party to the action.[12] Alternatively the defendant may have found himself in the midst of a dispute in which he has no interest; for example a garage owner may be in possession of a car which is claimed by a hire purchase finance company and by the hirer or an estate agent in possession of a deposit when a sale of property has fallen through. In such a case he should interplead.[13] However if the defendant wishes to serve a defence to the statement of claim, he may frame it in the following ways.

a Defence generally

The defendant must deal individually with each allegation in the statement of claim. A general denial of liability is insufficient and will result in the defendant having to give lengthy particulars, incurring extra costs. In particular it is expressly provided[14] that:

"A party must in any pleading subsequent to a statement of claim plead specifically any matter, for example, performance, release, any relevant statute of limitation, fraud or any fact showing illegality—

(*a*) which he alleges makes any claim or defence of the opposite party not maintainable; or

(*b*) which, if not specifically pleaded, might take the opposite party by surprise; or

(*c*) which raises issues of fact not arising out of the preceding pleadings."

In respect of each allegation in the statement of claim the defendant may:

(i) Admit; or,
(ii) Traverse; and/or,
(iii) Confess and avoid; and/or,
(iv) Object in point of law.

Admissions—An admission on the pleadings may be express or implied. An admission is implied from a failure to traverse, since the Rules expressly provide that every allegation of fact in a statement of claim or counterclaim that is not traversed is deemed to be admitted, except against an infant or patient, and excepting also allegations as to damages.[15] Admission should not be regarded as a sign of weakness on the part of the defendant. Indeed there is no point in denying facts which your opponent can easily prove against you, or which are purely formal.

Thus, if the defendant's case is that his conduct does not amount to a breach of contract, there is no point in denying the existence of the contract.

---

cases; cf. *Hubbuck & Sons* v. *Wilkinson*, [1899] 1 Q.B. 86; *Remmington* v. *Scoles*, [1897] 2 Ch. 1; *Drummond-Jackson* v. *British Medical Association*, [1970] 1 All E.R. 1094; [1970] 1 W.L.R. 688.

[11] See p. 352, *post*.
[12] See p. 336, *ante*.
[13] See p. 338, *ante*.
[14] O. 18, r. 8(1).
[15] O. 18, r. 13(1), (4); O. 80, r. 8.

Similarly, in an action for malicious prosecution, where the dispute is invariably as to whether the defendant was malicious and whether he had a reasonable and probable cause for instigating a prosecution, it is pedantic to deny that there was a prosecution which terminated in favour of the plaintiff, since this can easily be proved. Indeed, a party who denies facts that he should properly admit may be penalised in the matter of costs.[16]

Traverses—A traverse is simply a denial. It is unnecessary to traverse allegations of law. On the other hand it is essential that the defendant traverse positively and unambiguously every allegation of fact in the statement of claim that he disputes.[17] A paragraph in the statement of claim may contain two allegations of fact; for example "the plaintiff paid the defendant £5,000." This incorporates two allegations; first, that the plaintiff paid the defendant a sum of money; secondly, that the sum was £5,000. Accordingly a traverse that "the plaintiff did not pay the defendant £5,000" is insufficient if the defendant contends that the plaintiff paid him nothing at all. A proper traverse would be; "the plaintiff did not pay the defendant £5,000 *or any other sum*".

Pleas in confession and avoidance—This form of defence involves admitting the literal truth of an allegation (confession), but at the same time setting up other facts which alter or nullify its effect (avoidance). Thus where the statement of claim alleges the existence of a contract, the defendant may wish to allege that that contract has been discharged or frustrated or that he has been released, or that the action is statute-barred. All these pleas are pleas in avoidance. Similarly, the defendant may be prepared to admit a battery on the plaintiff, but may allege that it was performed in self-defence or under a right conferred by law. It is perhaps unfortunate that the Rules allow a party to plead inconsistent defences. Thus the defendant may both traverse and confess and avoid the same facts. For example, he may deny that he struck the plaintiff at all and yet plead that he did so in self-defence.

Objections in point of law—As a rule no party is obliged to take a point of law in his pleadings. Thus even where the statement of claim contains an apparent defect in law or discloses no cause of action, the defendant may elect to remain silent until the trial.[18] Indeed there are occasions where it is politic to do so, since by that time it may be too late for the plaintiff to set his pleadings in order by amendment. However, where the point of law could effectively dispose of the whole question, the Rules provide the means for the defendant to raise this point at an early stage in the proceedings, thus forestalling a trial. The defendant may apply by summons to have the point set down for trial as a preliminary point.[19] In an extreme case, as already noted, the defendant may apply to have the plaintiff's statement of claim

---

[16] O. 62, r. 3(5).

[17] The defendant need not and should not traverse allegations which the plaintiff has not pleaded; although a general traverse is insufficient, it is common form for the defence to conclude with a general traverse in addition to the specific traverses, *viz.* "save as hereinbefore specifically admitted, the defendant denies each and every allegation contained in the statement of claim as though the same were herein set out and traversed *seriatim*". See *Warner* v. *Sampson*, [1959] 1 Q.B. 297; [1959] 1 All E.R. 120.

[18] *MacDougall* v. *Knight* (1890), 25 Q.B.D. 1; *Independent Automatic Sales, Ltd.* v. *Knowles and Foster*, [1962] 3 All E.R. 27; [1962] 1 W.L.R. 974.

[19] O. 33, rr. 2, 4.

struck out on the ground that it is frivolous, vexatious or discloses no cause of action or is otherwise an abuse of the process of the court.

b   Special defences: set-off and counterclaim

In addition to pleading to the statement of claim in any or all of the above ways, in certain cases the defendant may raise a defence which is peculiar to one type of action. Thus the defences of fair comment, justification and offer of amends are peculiar to actions for defamation. These defences must always be specifically pleaded. In particular, the defences of tender before action[20] and apology under the Libel Acts 1843–45[1] are interesting from a procedural standpoint in that both require payment into court as an element in the defence. The payment in differs from a payment under the Rules of the Supreme Court, O. 22 in that the latter can only affect costs[2] while the former is an element in a defence to liability.

At this stage it is appropriate to consider the defence of set-off and, more important still, counterclaim.

Set-off[3]—A defence may contain a set-off which may be pleaded to the whole or to any part of the plaintiff's claim. Thus it may be pleaded in conjunction with a plea of tender before action, whereby the defendant has tendered a sum less than the sum claimed by the plaintiff because he pleads a set-off in respect of the balance.

The common law courts prior to 1875 recognised the set-off although it was limited in its scope to cases where both the plaintiff's claim and the amount to be set off were liquidated. The defence was also recognised in equity, where its scope was, however, greater and extended to unliquidated claims. With the fusion of the administration of law and equity in 1875 the equitable set-off became available throughout the Supreme Court. This is still the case, as evidenced by the wide phrasing of the present Order 18, r. 17:

> "Where a claim by a defendant to a sum of money (whether of an ascertained amount or not) is relied on as a defence to the whole or part of a claim made by the plaintiff, it may be included in the defence and set-off against the plaintiff's claim, whether or not it is also added as a counterclaim."

Thus, for example, in an action for the price of goods, it is well established that the defendant can plead by way of set-off a claim for damages in respect of the defective state of the goods;[4] similarly in a landlord's action for rent the defendant tenant can raise a set-off in respect of defects in the premises

---

[20] O. 18, r. 16. This old common law defence can only be pleaded to an action for a debt or liquidated demand; it is that the defendant tendered the whole sum due before issue of the writ.

[1] This defence, which is obsolete, is available to a newspaper or other periodical which publishes a libel without actual malice or gross negligence. The defence is never used because it cannot be pleaded in conjunction with any other defence and, in any event, the defence of unintentional defamation under the Defamation Act 1952, s. 4 is more favourable to the defendant.

[2] See p. 330, *ante.*

[3] O. 18, r. 17.

[4] In this particular instance the common law in fact permitted an "abatement of price" (*Mondel* v. *Steel* (1841), 8 M. & W. 858) but now that there can be a set-off in any event the historical source of the defendant's remedy is unimportant.

which affect the tenant's enjoyment of them.[5] On the other hand the equitable set-off historically developed from the power of the Court of Chancery to restrain a litigant at common law from enforcing his rights in the common law courts (where, of course, the only set-off permitted was a legal set-off). Therefore it was not, and is not, available unless the defendant's claim by way of set-off is such that it would be inequitable for the plaintiff to obtain judgment without taking it into account. This will not be the case, in general, where the transactions giving rise to the plaintiff's claim and the defendant's purported set-off are wholly unconnected. Thus the House of Lords in two recent cases has refused to permit a set-off for unliquidated damages against a claim on a bill of exchange[6] or for damages for short delivery of cargo against a claim for freight charges.[7]

In such cases the defendant's proper course is to counterclaim, and then to apply for a stay of execution[8] on the claim pending trial of the counterclaim.

It must also be noted that both the claim and the set-off must be monetary. Thus if the plaintiff seeks an injunction or a declaration of title, for example, there can be no set-off to these claims. There are other limitations to pleading a set-off; *viz.*

(1) Both claim and set-off must exist between the same parties in the same capacity. Thus, if the plaintiff sues as trustee or executor of an estate, the defendant cannot set-off a debt owed to him by the plaintiff in the latter's personal capacity.[9]

(2) If the set-off overtops the plaintiff's claim the defendant cannot recover the excess except by way of counterclaim. Since a set-off is only a defence, it can only operate to extinguish or reduce *pro tanto* the plaintiff's claim.[10]

(3) If the original claim is settled or discontinued the set-off is *ipso facto* terminated, since it depends for its existence on the original claim.

(4) The amount to be set-off must have been due when the writ was issued.[11]

Counterclaim[12]—A counterclaim is not a defence but, since it is pleaded at this stage, it is conveniently considered here. A counterclaim is a cross action and may best be regarded as the defendant's statement of claim. Thus the subject matter of a counterclaim can be anything which could be the subject matter of an action commenced by writ. It need not relate to the plaintiff's claim, nor indeed need it claim the same remedy as that sought by the plaintiff.[13] If the claim and counterclaim are of a totally different nature and cannot conveniently be tried together, the court may order the counterclaim to be tried separately, or even transferred to a county court. The counter-

[5] *British Anzani (Felixstowe), Ltd.* v. *International Marine Management* U. K.), *Ltd.*, [1980] Q. B. 137; [1979] 2 All E.R. 1063.
[6] *Nova (Jersey) Knit, Ltd.* v. *Kammgarn Spinnerei GmbH*, [1977] 2 All E.R. 463; [1977] 1 W.L.R. 713.
[7] *Aries Tanker Corporation* v. *Total Transport, Ltd.*, [1977] 1 All E.R. 398; [1977] 1 W.L.R. 185.
[8] As to which, see p. 391, *post.*
[9] *Rees* v. *Watts* (1855), 11 Exch. 410; *Phillips* v. *Howell*, [1901] 2 Ch. 773.
[10] The balance should be claimed by counterclaim: *Stooke* v. *Taylor* (1880), 5 Q.B.D. 569.
[11] *Richards* v. *James* (1848), 2 Exch. 471.
[12] O. 18, r. 18.
[13] O. 15, r. 2(1); *Beddall* v. *Maitland* (1881), 17 Ch.D. 181.

claim must exist against the plaintiff but not necessarily in the capacity in which he sues (provided that he is a party to the action and not, for example, an infant's next friend). Thus if the plaintiff sues as trustee or executor, the defendant may counterclaim either against the plaintiff personally or against the estate that the plaintiff is representing.[14] In addition the defendant by his counterclaim may join new parties to the action, who are in the position of defendants *quoad* the original defendant (though not *quoad* the plaintiff).[15] If both claim and counterclaim succeed the court will usually make one order as to damages.[16] There is a discretion as to costs and the court may either make one order as to costs (in which case the counterclaim is in effect treated as if it were a set-off) or two orders as to costs. In the latter case the defendant would be entitled to the costs of his successful counterclaim but would be liable for the costs of the plaintiff's claim, since a counterclaim is not a defence. In practice, where the claim and counterclaim arise out of the same transaction or series of transactions, for example, trading debts between the parties, the court will make just one order as to costs—in favour of the party who recovers the balance between the claim and counterclaim.[17]

For almost all purposes the counterclaiming defendant is in the same position as a plaintiff. He may obtain judgment in default of defence to his counterclaim[18] (though not on failure to give notice of intention to defend except by third parties,[19] since acknowledgment by the plaintiff is not required); he may also obtain judgment under Order 14 on his counterclaim.[20] In certain situations the counterclaiming defendant is in a better position than he would be as plaintiff. Of these the most important, in practice, arises where the defendant's cause of action has become statute-barred. Provided the plaintiff has issued his writ within the limitation period the defendant may counterclaim notwithstanding that his cause of action would, if he were the plaintiff, be statute-barred.[1] The defendant cannot, however, counterclaim until he has been served with a statement of claim.[2]

3 Defence to counterclaim and reply

If the defendant has raised a counterclaim, the plaintiff must serve a defence to it, or the defendant will be entitled to judgment in default on his counterclaim. This pleading must be drafted in the same way as a defence, although

---

[14] *Re Richardson*, [1933] W.N. 90; *Stumore* v. *Campbell & Co.*, [1892] 1 Q.B. 314.

[15] O. 15, r. 3(1). There must, however, be a claim against the plaintiff as well; *Furness* v. *Booth* (1876), 4 Ch.D. 587. It is permissible that the liability of the plaintiff and of the third party be alternative: *Smith* v. *Buskell*, [1919] 2 K.B. 362.

[16] O. 15, r. 2(4).

[17] *Provincial Bill Posting Co.* v. *Low Moor Iron Co.*, [1909] 2 K.B. 344; *Chell Engineering, Ltd.* v. *Unit Tool and Engineering Co., Ltd.*, [1950] 1 All E.R. 378; *Childs* v. *Gibson*, [1954] 2 All E.R. 243; [1954] 1 W.L.R. 809.

[18] O. 19, r. 8.

[19] O. 15, r. 3(5).

[20] O. 14, r. 5.

[1] Limitation Act 1980, s. 35; cf. *Henriksens Rederi A/S* v. *Rolimpex*, [1974] Q.B. 233; [1973] 3 All E.R. 589 for an enlightening analysis of the nature of set-off and counter-claim, legal and equitable.

[2] See *The Gniezno*, [1968] P. 418; [1967] 2 All E.R. 738.

the plaintiff cannot himself counterclaim since he is confined to the causes of action raised in his statement of claim.

The plaintiff need not serve a reply to reaffirm the allegations in his statement of claim that the defendant has traversed. These are already in issue.[3] However he must serve a reply if he wishes to make admissions, rebut positive allegations in the defence or raise an objection in point of law in answer to a plea of confession and avoidance.

> "The reply is the proper place for meeting the defence by confession and avoidance."[4]

Thus where the defendant has pleaded fair comment or qualified privilege in an action for defamation, the plaintiff may rebut the defence by proving malice. This will be alleged in his reply.[5] If the defence of a statute of limitation is raised, the plaintiff, in his reply, may plead fraud or a written acknowledgment, which prevent time from running. The plaintiff cannot, however, raise a new cause of action in his reply since this constitutes a "departure" which is expressly forbidden by O. 18, r. 10.

A reply or a defence to counterclaim must be served within 14 days. If both are pleaded they must be incorporated in the same document.[6]

4   Subsequent pleadings

No pleading subsequent to a reply or a defence to counterclaim shall be served except with the leave of the court.[7] A rejoinder (by the defendant) may be necessary to rebut affirmative allegations in a defence to counterclaim. Surrejoinder (by the plaintiff), rebutter (by the defendant) and surrebutter (by the plaintiff) are virtually obsolete because of the rule prohibiting departures in pleading.

C   AMENDMENT OF WRIT AND PLEADINGS

1   Writ

Where there is some defect in the writ or in any pleading it can almost always be cured by amendment. Nevertheless the party at fault should act quickly so as to avoid increasing the extra costs which he will have to pay. The plaintiff may amend the writ[8] *once* without leave before the close of pleadings. An amended writ must be served on the defendant. The writ does not include any statement of claim indorsed upon it, since this is a pleading and not part of the writ. Amendments to the writ can be of a technical nature, for example, correction of a misspelling or an incorrect date; moreover the writ can with leave be amended under Order 20 to correct the name of a party, even if this has the effect of substituting a new party, if the court is satisfied that the mistake was a genuine one and not misleading as to the true identity of the

---

3   O. 18, r. 14(1).
4   JAMES, L.J. in *Hall* v. *Eve* (1876), 4 Ch.D. 341, at p. 345.
5   O. 82, r. 3(3).
6   O. 18, r. 3.
7   O. 18, r. 4.
8   O. 20, r. 1(1).

party intended;[9] similarly an amendment may be allowed which adds or substitutes a new cause of action provided it arises out of substantially the same facts as the original cause of action. Amendments to alter the parties to the action to add or substitute a new cause of action can be made without leave only before the writ has been served.[10] Leave may be granted to make these amendments even after the period of limitation current at the date of issue of the writ has expired, if the courts think it just. In this way a new statute-barred cause of action may be raised, or a party may be "brought in" by amendment at a time when he could no longer be sued in a fresh action.[11] Apart from the provisions of O. 20, new parties may be added by order of the court following an application by summons[12] but a new cause of action arising since the issue of the writ, against a defendant, can never be added. The proper procedure in this case is to issue a second writ and apply to have the actions consolidated. It will be appreciated, however, that in this case the Limitation Act comes into play since time will be deemed to have run up to the time of issue of the new writ.

2 Pleadings

Any party may amend his pleadings once without leave before the close of pleadings.[13] As long as the proposed amendment does not amount to pleading a completely new cause of action and causes no injustice to an opponent it is permissible. Thus a party will be allowed to withdraw an admission mistakenly made.[14] A plaintiff may be allowed to amend his statement of claim even where the original disclosed no cause of action. To adopt any other approach would be a regression to the formalism of pleading at common law. The court's attitude is well illustrated in the judgment of BOWEN, L.J. in *Cropper* v. *Smith*:[15]

> "I know of no kind of error or mistake which, if not fraudulent or intended to overreach, the Court ought not to correct, if it can be done without injustice to the other party. Courts do not exist for the sake of discipline, but for the sake of deciding matters in controversy, and I do not regard such amendment as a matter of favour or grace. . . . It seems to me that as soon as it appears that the way in which a party has framed his case will not lead to a decision of the real matter in controversy it is as much a matter of right on his part to have it corrected if it can be done without injustice, as anything else in the case is a matter of right."

[9] See *Evans Construction Co., Ltd.* v. *Charrington & Co., Ltd.*, [1983] Q.B. 810; [1983] 1 All E.R. 310.

[10] O. 20, r. 1(3).

[11] See *Rodriguez* v. *Parker*, [1976] 1 Q.B. 116; [1966] 2 All E.R. 349; *Mitchell* v. *Harris Engineering Co., Ltd.*, [1967] 2 Q.B. 703; [1967] 2 All E.R. 682; *Chatsworth Investments, Ltd.* v. *Cussins (Contractors), Ltd.*, [1969] 1 All E.R. 143; [1969] 1 W.L.R. 1; *Sterman* v. *E.W. and W.J. Moore*, [1970] 1 Q.B. 596; [1970] 1 All E.R. 581; cf. *Braniff* v. *Holland and Hannen and Cubitts (Southern), Ltd.*, [1969] 3 All E.R. 959; [1969] 1 W.L.R. 1533; *Brickfield Properties, Ltd.* v. *Newton*, [1971] 3 All E.R. 328; [1971] 1 W.L.R. 863.

[12] Under O. 15, rr. 6, 7. The court will not, however, grant an application so as to deprive the proposed defendant of a defence of limitation; therein lies the great advantage of adding a party under O. 20 rather than under O. 15 (where possible). By s. 35 of the Limitation Act 1980 a new claim (including a new cause of action and a claim against an added or substituted party) is deemed to have been commenced on the same date as the original action.

[13] O. 20, r. 1(3).

[14] *Hollis* v. *Burton*, [1892] 3 Ch. 226.

[15] (1884), 26 Ch.D. 700, at pp. 710–711.

The amended pleading must be served on the opponent who may himself serve an amended pleading to it within 14 days.[16] Alternatively he may allow his original pleading to stand, or he may apply to the master to disallow the amendment on the ground that it causes injustice.[17]

The writ and pleadings may be amended after the close of pleadings but only with leave.[18] The application is by summons, usually the summons for directions. Amendment may even be allowed at the trial if the judge is satisfied that no injustice is thereby caused.[19] If amendment is allowed it is almost always on terms that the party amending pays the costs thrown away in any event and if the amendment necessitates an adjournment of the trial he will usually be ordered to pay the costs thrown away by the adjournment.

D PARTICULARS

If a pleading is vague or too general the party on whom it is served may apply for particulars. The application should first be by letter, and the court will not usually make an order until there has been an application to the other side by letter. If particulars are not forthcoming application may be made by summons for an order for further and better particulars.[20] The functions of particulars are broadly twofold. First they prevent the party giving them from framing his case too widely, since at the trial he will be confined to his particulars as if they had been incorporated in his pleading. Thus if he relies in his particulars on conduct which he alleges amounts to negligence, he cannot at the trial give evidence as to other conduct (unless he obtains leave to amend his particulars). Secondly the party who is served with particulars is thereby better acquainted with the case against him so that he will not be taken by surprise at the trial. Any particulars which ought to have been included in the pleadings may be ordered,[1] for example particulars of special damages. However particulars cannot be ordered of matters which have not been specifically pleaded, nor can particulars be required of a simply traverse.[2] Particulars are most often sought in respect of the statement of claim.

Particulars cannot be required of any matter not pleaded. In this respect they differ from interrogatories which may, as we shall see, relate to any relevant matter whether pleaded or not.

E THE CLOSE OF PLEADINGS

The pleadings are deemed to be closed:

---

[16] O. 20, r. 3.

[17] O. 20, r. 4. The application is by summons and is usually made on the summons for directions.

[18] O. 20, r. 5. The court may even amend a pleading on its own motion; see *Nottage* v. *Jackson* (1883), 11 Q.B.D. 627.

[19] *Ives* v. *Brown*, [1919] 2 Ch. 314; but see *Esso Petroleum Co., Ltd.* v. *Southport Corporation*, [1956] A.C. 218; [1955] 3 All E.R. 864.

[20] O. 18, r. 12(3), (6): *Milbank* v. *Milbank*, [1900] 1 Ch. 376.

[1] See p. 340, *ante*.

[2] *Weinberger* v. *Inglis*, [1918] 1 Ch. 133; see also *Chapple* v. *Electrical Trades Union*, [1961] 3 All E.R. 612; [1961] 1 W.L.R. 1290.

(*a*) at the expiration of 14 days after service of the reply or defence to counter-claim, or

(*b*) if neither a reply nor a defence to counterclaim is served, at the expiration of 14 days after service of the defence.[3]

Where the time for serving any of these pleadings is extended with leave, the close of pleadings is postponed until the expiry of such further time. The close of pleadings is important for three purposes:

(1) subsequent amendment of the writ and pleadings may only be made with leave;

(2) there is an implied joinder of issue on the pleading last served (unless the last pleading was a counterclaim); and

(3) the time is fixed within which discovery of documents must be made and the summons for directions taken out. These are the next stages in the action.

---

[3] O. 18, r. 20.

CHAPTER 18

Procedure from the Close of
Pleadings to the Trial

A DISCOVERY AND INSPECTION OF DOCUMENTS

Discovery of documents is the procedure whereby a party discloses, to the court or to any other party, the relevant documents in the action that he has, or has had, in his possession, custody or power.

Documentary evidence plays an important part in nearly all civil cases. In an action for breach of contract, for example, the transactions between the parties may be contained entirely in letters which have passed between them. One party's letters may not be intelligible unless read in conjunction with letters in the possession of the other party. Similarly, in an industrial injuries action, the employers are likely to have internal accident reports, machine maintenance records, records of complaints and the like which it is very much in the plaintiff's interests to see, while, on the other hand, the plaintiff may have documents relating to his medical condition, or to his earnings since the accident or state benefits which he has received, all of which may be highly relevant to the quantification of his claim by the defendants. Accordingly a party will want to have his opponent disclose which documents the latter has, or has had, in his possession (discovery), and, secondly, to inspect and take copies of those documents in his opponent's possession (inspection).[1] Sometimes a party may have documents which are relevant to the litigation, and therefore disclosable, but which he wishes to safeguard against circulation either to third parties, or occasionally to the plaintiff himself for extraneous reasons. As to this point, the position is that on discovery each party impliedly undertakes not to use the documents which are disclosed for any ulterior or improper purpose. Thus where the plaintiff, in proceedings against his employers, obtained discovery of an internal

---

[1] "Inspection" is not limited to ocular inspection but includes examination by any of the senses. Thus, a tape-recording is a document, inspection of which would be effected by playing the same upon a tape recorder to the inspecting party; *Grant* v. *Southwestern and County Properties, Ltd.*, [1975] Ch. 185; [1974] 2 All E.R. 465; similar considerations apply to untransmitted television film: *Senior* v. *Holdsworth*, [1976] Q.B. 23; [1975] 2 All E.R. 1009 (the so-called "Windsor pop festival" action).

memorandum about him which contained an alleged libel, it was held that he could not found a libel action upon that publication, since this would be an abuse of the process of the court.[2] Nor will a third party be permitted to use, and indeed he will by injunction be restrained from using, for an ulterior purpose (for example, the sale of confidential information to a newspaper) documents which he has obtained from a party who has himself obtained them in the course of discovery in an action.[3]

If there is a real risk of the plaintiff using documents for an improper collateral purpose, the court may restrict inspection, for example to a party's legal advisers.[4]

Discovery may take place in two ways, under the Rules.

1 Discovery without order

Until 1964 discovery of documents was dependent upon the order of a master, which was made in most cases on the summons for directions. While discovery by order still exists, one of the major alterations in procedure effected by the 1962 Rules was the introduction of "automatic" discovery. Parties must now in any action commenced by writ, with certain exceptions, make discovery by exchanging lists within 14 days of the close of pleadings.[5] The lists are in a prescribed form[6] and annexed are two schedules, as follows:

SCHEDULE 1

Part 1

Relevant documents, listed numerically, which the party has in his possession, custody or power[7] and which he does not object to produce.

Part 2

Relevant documents as above which he objects to produce.[8]

---

2 *Riddick* v. *Thames Board Mills, Ltd.*, [1977] Q.B. 881; [1977] 3 All E.R. 677.
3 *Distillers Co. (Biochemicals), Ltd.* v. *Times Newspapers, Ltd.*, [1975] Q.B. 613; [1975] 1 All E.R. 41. Misuse of documents in this way is a contempt of court; see *Home Office* v. *Harman*, [1983] A.C. 280; [1982] 1 All E.R. 532.
4 For a discussion of this power, and some illustrations of the difficulties involved in its exercise, see *Church of Scientology of California* v. *Department of Health and Social Security*, [1979] 3 All E.R. 97; [1979] 1 W.L.R. 723.
5 O. 24, r. 2. If any party does not comply he may be ordered to do so and may also be ordered to file an affidavit verifying his list: O. 24, r. 3(2).
6 O. 24, r. 5(1).
7 This comprises documents of which a party has an enforceable right to obtain possession; for example a director of a company of which he is, in effect, the alter ego, would have the right to obtain possession of that company's documents (which he would, therefore, have to disclose) whereas a company director *simpliciter*, though he has a right to inspect the company's documents, has no right to possess them (so that he could not, in those circumstances, be required to disclose them): *B.* v. *B. (Matrimonial Proceedings: Discovery)*, [1978] Fam. 181; [1979] 1 All E.R. 801.
8 The list must contain a sufficient statement of the grounds of the privilege claimed: O. 24, r. 5(2).

SCHEDULE 2

Relevant documents, listed as above, which have been, but at the date of service of the list are not, in the possession, custody or power of the party in question.[9]

Notice to inspect

A party serving a list of documents must also serve on his opponent a notice to inspect the documents in the list (other than those which he objects to produce) setting out a time within 7 days and place where the documents in Part 1 of the first schedule may be inspected.[10]

The right to inspect includes the right to take copies of the documents in question, although these will, as a matter of courtesy, be supplied on payment by the solicitors for the party in question.[11]

The foregoing provisions for automatic discovery do not apply to actions commenced by originating summons. There are certain other proceedings to which the procedure is not applicable; notably actions to which the Crown is a party, and actions arising out of an accident on land involving a vehicle, where the defendant must not make discovery unless ordered to do so.[12] In addition, the court may, on the application of any party, made by summons, waive discovery by all or any of the parties or restrict discovery to certain classes of documents for disposing fairly of the action or for saving costs.[13]

2 Discovery by order

There are two important circumstances in which an order for discovery will be required. The first is where the action is one of those to which the above rule relating to automatic discovery is not applicable or where any party has failed to comply with that rule. In such a case there must be an application for an order for discovery of all relevant documents, if discovery is required. The second case arises where a party is dissatisfied with his opponent's list. He may then apply for discovery of particular documents.

A party who is served with a list of documents may believe that relevant documents which the maker of the list has, or has had, in his possession, custody or power are not included in his list. This may be due to a *bona fide* belief on the maker's part that the document in question is not relevant to the action, or to an omission, accidental or deliberate. In either case application may be made by summons to the master for an order for discovery of the documents in question. This application must be accompanied by an affidavit setting out the grounds for the deponent's belief and identifying the documents of which discovery is required. If the other party admits the existence of the documents in question but denies their relevance, the master may inspect them in order to decide whether they are in fact relevant. In

---

[9] He must state what has become of them and who is presently in possession of them.

[10] O. 24, r. 9. As to the court's power to restrict inspection, see *Church of Scientology of California* v. *Department of Health and Social Security* (p. 355, fn. 4, *supra*); there is, however, no apparent power to withhold inspection entirely (*ibid.*).

[11] *Ormerod, Grierson & Co.* v. *St. George's Ironworks*, [1905] 1 Ch. 505.

[12] O. 77, r. 12(1); O. 24, r. 2(2).

[13] O. 24, r. 2(5).

addition that party may be required to make an affidavit stating whether or not any particular document is, or has at any time been, in his possession, custody or power and, if it no longer is, what has become of it.[14]

Finally, independent of the above provisions, any party may at any time require inspection of any document referred to in any other party's pleadings or affidavits.[15]

If any party fails to comply with an order for discovery the master may order his statement of claim to be struck out, if he is a plaintiff, or his defence to be struck out and judgment entered against him, if a defendant. In a case of extreme and wilful disobedience the offender may be committed for contempt of court.[16]

There is another issue which may be raised in connection with discovery. This arises where a party refuses to produce a document in his possession, custody or power.

3 Documents privileged from production

The only circumstance in which a party may refuse to produce a document is where that document is one of a class which the law recognises as privileged. The privilege which attaches to documents must be carefully distinguished from privilege in the law of defamation. Thus a document which attracts qualified privilege for the purposes of defamation, the minutes of a company meeting for example, is not necessarily privileged from discovery. The former rule is a rule of law, the latter a rule of evidence or procedure.

A party who wishes to claim privilege for a document cannot merely omit to include it in his list. He must include it in the second part of the first schedule to his list, together with a statement in the body of the list of the ground upon which he claims privilege for it. The principal classes of documents which the law recognises as being privileged from production are: documents which relate solely to the deponent's own case, incriminating documents, documents attracting legal professional privilege and documents whose production would be injurious to the public interest. These classes of evidential privilege are considered fully elsewhere in this work.[17]

4 Discovery and inspection against other persons

We have already examined the procedure introduced by the Administration of Justice Act 1970, whereby orders for discovery and inspection of documents against proposed parties may be made before the commencement of proceedings.[18]

---

[14] O. 14, r. 7; *Astra-National Productions, Ltd.* v. *Neo-Art Productions, Ltd.*, [1928] W.N. 218.

[15] O. 24, r. 10.

[16] O. 24, r. 16. The object of this rule is to secure compliance with the rules and orders of the court, relating to discovery, and not to punish a party for non-compliance; thus where a summons is taken out for a punitive order under rule 16 and the defaulting party complies before the hearing of that summons, it is wrong to make an order requiring payment into court of the balance of the claim: *Husband's of Marchwood, Ltd.* v. *Drummond Walker Developments, Ltd.*, [1975] 2 All E.R. 30; [1975] 1 W.L.R. 603.

[17] See pp. 598, 636, *post.*

[18] See p. 294, *ante.*

Under section 34 of the Supreme Court Act 1981 there is, in addition, power, in actions for damages for death or personal injuries, to order a person who is not a party to the proceedings and who appears to be likely to have or have had in his possession, custody or power any documents which are relevant to an issue arising out of the action to disclose whether these documents are in his possession, custody or power and to produce those which he has to the applicant.

This power is exercisable only after the commencement of proceedings, the application being by summons (which must be served on the person against whom the order is sought and on all parties to the action) supported by affidavit.[19] As stated above, the procedure is limited in its application to personal injuries litigation where it may be used, for example, by defendants to obtain a sight of the plaintiff's hospital notes or by plaintiffs to obtain copies of manufacturers' instructions for using and maintaining machines, reports by employers to the Health and Safety at Work Executive and documents of that type.

5 Action for discovery

Save for the limited exception, in personal injuries actions, discussed above there is, as a rule, no procedure for obtaining discovery against persons who are not parties to an action. They can, of course, be compelled to attend the trial and to produce, at that stage, documents in their possession (by means of *subpoena duces tecum*) but there is a rule, sometimes known as the "mere witness" rule, whereby discovery cannot be obtained against a person against whom no relief is sought but who might be a witness in an action. It follows that if a party wishes to inspect documents in the possession of a person against whom he has no cause of action, he cannot sue that person simply for the purpose of obtaining evidence, by way of discovery of documents, for use against the party against whom there is a cause of action. This rule appears to have little in the way of logic to commend it but it is, nevertheless, too firmly entrenched to be altered save by way of legislation.

However, a limited exception to the rule was formulated by the House of Lords in the case of *Norwich Pharmacal Co.* v. *Customs and Excise Commissioners*.[20] The facts of the case were unusual. The appellants, who were the owners of a patent covering a chemical compound, learned from information published by the respondents that a number of consignments of the compound had been imported between 1960 and 1970, none of which had been licensed by the appellants. The appellants therefore knew that others were infringing their patent but did not know their identity. The respondents refused to disclose the identity of the importers whereupon the appellants brought an action against the respondents seeking an order for discovery of documents relating to the importations. The House of Lords granted such an order; the reasoning behind the decision was expressed by LORD REID, as follows:[1]

---

[19] O. 24, r. 7A.

[20] [1974] A.C. 133; [1973] 2 All E.R. 943, applied in *Loose* v. *Williamson*, [1978] 3 All E.R. 89; [1978] 1 W.L.R. 639.

[1] [1974] A.C., at p. 175; [1973] 2 All E.R., at p. 948.

". . . if through no fault of his own a person gets mixed up in the tortious acts of others so as to facilitate their wrong doing he may incur no personal liability but he comes under a duty to assist the person who has been wronged by giving him full information and disclosing the identity of the wrongdoers."

Discovery, being historically an equitable remedy, is the method by which the duty referred to is capable of enforcement. The procedure has been used in several subsequent cases, notably *British Steel Corporation* v. *Granada Television, Ltd.*[2] and *Harrington* v. *North London Polytechnic.*[3] These cases demonstrate that the remedy extends not only to disclosure of documents but also to requiring the defendant to provide information by answering questions on oath or otherwise.

B INSPECTION OF PROPERTY

1 Inspection of property inter partes

The court has power, on the application of any party, to make an order for the detention, custody or preservation of any property which is the subject matter of the action or as to which any question may arise therein or for the inspection of any such property in the possession of a party to the action and, for the purpose of enabling such an order to be carried out, may authorise any person to enter a party's land or building.[4] The application is often made on the summons for directions but may, if need be, be made by summons at any stage of the proceedings. The procedure is widely used in personal injuries actions, usually to enable an expert engineer on behalf of the plaintiff to inspect the defendant's factory premises, but is not confined to such actions.

As has already been noted,[5] section 33(1) of the Supreme Court Act 1981 enables an order to be made before the commencement of proceedings.

2 Orders against third persons

Analogous to the power of the court to order discovery and inspection of documents against strangers to the proceedings is the power, now contained in section 34(3) of the Supreme Court Act 1981, to make orders for the inspection, photographing, preservation, custody or detention of property[6] which is not the property of, or in the possession of, any party to the proceedings but which is the subject matter of the proceedings or as to which any question arises in the proceedings; orders may also be made for the taking of samples of any such property and the carrying out of any experiment in relation thereto.

Application for such an order is by summons supported by affidavit. No

---

2 [1981] A.C. 1096; [1981] 1 All E.R. 417.
3 [1984] 3 All E.R. 666; [1984] 1 W.L.R. 1293.
4 O. 29, r. 2. There is no express power to order photographing but this is obviously an oversight since inspection will often be worthless without a right to take photographs.
5 See p. 295, *ante.*
6 "Property" includes any land, chattel or other corporeal property of any description: Supreme Court Act 1981, s. 35(5).

order will be made if it appears that compliance would result in the disclosure of information relating to a secret process, discovery or invention not in issue in the proceedings.[7]

C   INTERROGATORIES

Interrogatories are questions answerable on oath which any party may, with leave of the master, administer to his opponent.[8] The purpose of interrogatories is twofold; first to obtain admissions, and secondly to limit the scope of one's opponent's case. It may thus seem that answers to interrogatories are similar to particulars. In fact, they differ in several important respects.

(1) The scope of particulars is limited to matters raised in the pleadings. Thus particulars cannot be required of matters not pleaded. Interrogatories, on the other hand, may relate to any matter relevant to the action.[9] For example, in an action for defamation, a defendant cannot ask the plaintiff to give particulars of why the words complained of are untrue since it is no part of the plaintiff's case to allege or prove the falsity of the words in question. However, if the defendant pleads justification, he may administer interrogatories to the plaintiff the function of which is to elicit from the plaintiff how far the latter is prepared to admit that the words, or any part of them, are true.[10] Broadly speaking, any question which could be asked of a witness at the trial may be asked in the form of an interrogatory, with the notable exception of questions as to the witness's credit or credibility.[11]

(2) Particulars cannot relate to evidence. Interrogatories are usually aimed at evidential matters, although they cannot extend to asking a party to disclose his means of proof or to name his witnesses.[12]

(3) An application for particulars may be made as soon as the pleading in question has been served. Interrogatories, however, will never be ordered before delivery of the defence (since that may contain admissions rendering them unnecessary) and will hardly ever be ordered before discovery of documents takes place (since an opponent's documents may contain the answers sought). In practice an application for leave to administer interrogatories should not be made before the hearing of the summons for directions.

(4) Particulars are not given on oath. Interrogatories must always be answered on affidavit (though parties often agree to accept answers by open letter, which answers can be put in at the trial in the same way as sworn answers).

(5) A party may apply for particulars by letter on his own initiative. Indeed he should do so. Interrogatories may only be administered by order of a master. The proper course is to apply to the master for leave to administer the proposed interrogatories. The master will only allow those which he

---

[7] O. 29, r. 7A(6).
[8] O. 26, r. 1.
[9] O. 26, r. 1(1) (*a*); *Nash* v. *Leyton*, [1911] 2 Ch. 71.
[10] *Marriott* v. *Chamberlain* (1886), 17 Q.B.D. 154; *Peter Walker & Son, Ltd.* v. *Hodgson*, [1909] 1 K.B. 239.
[11] *Kennedy* v. *Dodson*, [1895] 1 Ch. 334.
[12] *Marriott* v. *Chamberlain* (*supra*); *Knapp* v. *Harvey*, [1911] 2 K.B. 725.

"considers necessary either for disposing fairly of the cause or matter or for saving costs".[13] He will not allow relevant questions to be put, such as questions relating to the character of a party or witness; nor will the master allow interrogatories as to the contents of a document. Finally, the master will not allow "fishing" interrogatories; these are questions which are not asked in furtherance of a genuine inquiry, but in the hope that the answers which are given may lend support to a case which is insufficient as it stands.[14]

The interrogatories ordered must be answered on oath within the time prescribed by the master. The only ground upon which a party may refuse to answer is that of privilege. The privilege must be claimed on oath[15] and the grounds are the same as those for the privilege from production of documents. Other objections must be taken at the hearing of the summons at which the order for interrogatories is made or not at all. Answers to interrogatories are binding and the party administering them is in a position of advantage since he may put in evidence at the trial all *or any* of the answers. He cannot be compelled to put in any answer which does not favour his case.[16]

If a party's answers are evasive or ambiguous he may be ordered to make a further answer either on affidavit or by oral examination.[17] The final sanctions for failing to comply with an order for interrogatories are the same as for disobedience to any other interlocutory order. Thus the defaulter's statement of claim may be struck out if he is a plaintiff or his defence if a defendant. In an extreme case of wilful disobedience the offender may be committed for contempt of court.[18]

D SECURITY FOR COSTS

As a rule no party can be required to deposit money or a bond as security for the costs of a pending action. This rule applies even if the party concerned is insolvent or even bankrupt.[19] However there are exceptions to this rule, as there are to most rules. In these exceptional cases the defendant may apply by summons, usually on the summons for directions, for an order that the plaintiff provide security for costs:

---

[13] O. 26, r. 1(3). Although interrogatories directed to ascertaining the identity of other wrongdoers against whom the plaintiff may have a cause of action may be allowed under the principles stated in *Norwich Pharmacal Co.* v. *Customs and Excise Commissioners* (p. 358, *ante*); *Loose* v. *Williamson*, [1978] 3 All E.R. 89; [1978] 1 W.L.R. 639, in which GOULDING, J. ordered the defendants, who were the owners of vessels seen fishing within the territory of the plaintiff's shellfish fishery, to disclose the names and addresses of the persons who had been on those vessels on the occasion in question. The objection that the interrogatories were "fishing" interrogatories (in the sense referred to in the text) was overruled; see also *Harrington* v. *North London Polytechnic*, [1984] 3 All E.R. 666; [1984] 1 W.L.R. 1293.

[14] See *Hooton* v. *Dalby*, [1907] 2 K.B. 18; *Pankhurst* v. *Hamilton* (1886), 2 T.L.R. 682.

[15] O. 26, r. 4; *Dalgleish* v. *Lowther*, [1899] 2 Q.B. 590.

[16] O. 26, r. 7. The court may, however, order an answer to be put in where it is so closely connected with another answer which has been put in evidence that the court considers that one ought not to be used without the other.

[17] O. 26, r. 5. The test is whether the answer is sufficient, not whether it is true; *Lyell* v. *Kennedy* (*No. 3*) (1884), 27 Ch.D. 1.

[18] O. 26. r. 6.

[19] *Cowell* v. *Taylor* (1885), 31 Ch.D. 34; *Cook* v. *Whellock* (1890), 24 Q.B.D. 658; *Rhodes* v. *Dawson* (1886), 16 Q.B.D. 548.

(*a*) where the plaintiff is ordinarily resident out of the jurisdiction.[20] However security will not be ordered on this ground if the plaintiff has substantial property within the jurisdiction out of which costs may be defrayed, since the basis of the exception is that the defendant, if successful, would not be able to enforce an order for his costs;[1]

(*b*) where the plaintiff is a nominal plaintiff suing for the benefit of a third party and there is reason to believe that he would be unable to pay the defendant's costs if ordered to do so;[2] a person suing in a representative capacity is not a nominal plaintiff;

(*c*) where the plaintiff has deliberately misstated his address on the writ, or has changed his address since the issue of the writ in order to evade the consequences of litigation;[3]

(*d*) where a plaintiff company may not be able to pay costs awarded against it.[4]

In addition, orders for the disclosure of documents or the inspection of property before the commencement of proceedings, or for the disclosure of documents or the inspection of property in relation to persons who are not parties to the proceedings[5] may be made conditional upon the applicant's giving security for costs.[6] However, in these cases, unlike the above cases, no application for security is made.

These are the only cases in which security for costs, as such, may be ordered. However it is as well to bear in mind that under Order 14 a defendant may be ordered to pay a sum into court as a condition of being granted leave to defend the action[7] and that an applicant for a *Mareva* injunction may sometimes be required to support his cross-undertaking as to damages by a bond or security.[8]

A counterclaiming defendant may sometimes be ordered to give security for costs[9] but, otherwise, security cannot be ordered to be given by a defendant or someone compelled to litigate.

---

[20] O. 23, r. 1(1) (*a*). As to the meaning of the words "ordinarily resident", see *Levene* v. *Inland Revenue Commissioners*, [1928] A.C. 217 and *Lysaght* v. *Inland Revenue Commissioners*, [1928] A.C. 234. This rule does not conflict with the Treaty of Rome, but the court may take into account the fact that the plaintiff is an E.E.C. resident and refuse to order security: *Landi Den Hartog B.V.* v. *Stopps*, [1976] F.S.R. 497. The High Court may by issue of the prerogative writ *ne exeat regno* restrain a defendant from leaving the jurisdiction, subject to the conditions contained in the Debtors Act 1869, s. 6, of which the most important is that the defendant's absence will materially prejudice the plaintiff in prosecuting his action; see, generally, the judgment of MEGARRY, J. in *Felton* v. *Callis*, [1969] 1 Q.B. 200; [1968] 3 All E.R. 673. Note also the power to grant *Mareva* injunctions (see p. 297, *ante*).

[1] See *Kevorkian* v. *Burney*, [1937] 4 All E.R. 468.

[2] O. 23, r. 1(1) (*b*). The next friend of a person under a disability is not a nominal plaintiff; *Fellows* v. *Barrett* (1830), 1 Keen. 119. An example of a nominal plaintiff is one who, before action, assigns to a third party any damages he may recover; see *Semler* v. *Murphy*, [1968] Ch. 183; [1967] 2 All E.R. 185.

[3] O. 23, r. 1(1) (*c*), (*d*); O. 23, r. 1(2); *Knight* v. *Ponsonby*, [1925] 1 K.B. 545.

[4] Companies Act 1948, s. 447.

[5] Supreme Court Act 1981, ss. 33–35; see pp. 294, 358, *ante*.

[6] O. 24, r. 7A(5); O. 29, r. 7A(6).

[7] See p. 327, *ante*.

[8] *Third Chandris Shipping Corporation* v. *Unimarine S.A.*, [1979] Q.B. 645; [1979] 2 All E.R. 972; see p. 298, *ante*.

[9] When his counterclaim is in the nature of a cross-action rather than simply by way of a defence; cf. *Visco* v. *Minter*, [1969] P. 82; [1969] 2 All E.R. 714.

Application for security should first be made by letter and then, if this fails by summons. In order to assist the court as to the appropriate amount of security, it is helpful for solicitors to prepare a skeleton bill of costs to date. The court will order such security as appears just in all the circumstances of the case. Normally a discount from the defendant's assessment will be made to take account of the court's expectation of any reduction by the taxing officer of the fees particularised, but there is not (as used to be thought) any justification for a "conventional approach" of fixing security at two-thirds of the estimated party and party costs.[10] A party who has obtained security may apply for further security as the action proceeds and the costs increase.

E DIRECTIONS

1 Automatic directions

The majority of actions in the Queen's Bench Division are personal injury actions. Prior to 1980 a summons for directions had to be issued in all such actions even though the directions sought and obtained were in most cases standard. Following recommendations of the Cantley Working Party on Personal Injuries Litigation,[11] a system of automatic directions in personal injury actions was introduced as Order 25, rule 8. This rule applies to any action for personal injuries except (*a*) any Admiralty action; and (*b*) any action where the pleadings contain an allegation of negligent medical treatment. The effect of the rule is that when the pleadings are closed the following directions take effect automatically:

(*a*) save where liability is admitted or where the action arises out of a road accident (in which cases discovery is limited to disclosure by the plaintiff of documents relating to special damages) there must be discovery of documents within 14 days and inspection within seven days thereafter;

(*b*) where any party intends to rely on expert evidence he must within 10 weeks disclose the substance of that evidence to the other parties in the form of a written report, which shall be agreed if possible;[12]

(*c*) unless such reports are agreed, the parties shall be at liberty to call as expert witnesses those witnesses whose reports have been disclosed, limited to two medical experts and one expert of any other kind;

(*d*) photographs, a sketch plan and the contents of any police accident report book shall be receivable in evidence at the trial, and shall be agreed if possible;

(*e*) the action shall be tried at the trial centre of the place where the action is proceeding or at such other trial centre as the parties may in writing agree;[13]

(*f*) the action shall be tried by Judge alone, as a case of substance or difficulty (Category B) and shall be set down within six months;

(*g*) the court shall be notified, on setting down, of the estimated length of the trial.

---

[10] *Procon (G.B.), Ltd.* v. *Provincial Building Co., Ltd.*, [1984] 2 All E.R. 368; [1984] 1 W.L.R. 557, in which the principles are stated by the Court of Appeal.

[11] Cmnd. 1476 of 1979.

[12] Where more than one party intends to rely on expert evidence, disclosure is by mutual exchange of reports (r. 8(2)).

[13] Except where the Crown is a party, since the Crown has a right to trial in London (O. 77, r. 13).

It should be noted that there is nothing to prevent any party from applying by summons for further or different directions or orders. In addition the court may elect to transfer the action to a county court in accordance with the powers contained in section 40 of the County Courts Act 1984[14] and, in particular, where it considers "that the proceedings are not likely to raise any important question of law or fact and are suitable for determination by a county court" irrespective of the amount of damages likely to be involved. In London every action set down under automatic directions is forthwith examined by a master and if it appears to him that the question of transfer ought to be considered, the parties are directed to attend the master at a given date and time for this purpose.[15]

2   Summons for directions

In cases outside the automatic directions procedure, directions are given by the master or district registrar on the hearing of a summons for directions.

The plaintiff must, within one month of the close of pleadings, take out a summons for directions returnable in not less than 14 days.[16] To do so he issues the summons, using the appropriate form, at the Central Office or a district registry, and serves it on all defendants to the action. If he does not do so the defendant has two courses open to him. He may apply to have the plaintiff's action dismissed for want of prosecution, or he may issue the summons himself and serve it on the plaintiff.[17] The plaintiff must issue a summons for directions in every action commenced by writ with a few exceptions, the chief of which are: automatic directions cases, cases where directions have already been given following an application for summary judgment under Order 14 or for a trial without pleadings under Order 18, r. 21, actions for an account and actions which have been referred to an official referee or transferred to the Commercial Court.[18]

The general functions of the summons for directions are summarised in Order 25, r. 1(1), so that:

(*a*) all matters which must or can be dealt with on interlocutory applications and have not already been dealt with may so far as possible be dealt with, and

(*b*) such directions may be given as to the future course of the action as appear best adapted to secure the just, expeditious and economical disposal thereof.

The summons for directions has been described as a "stocktaking" of all the interlocutory matters in the action. It is possible for a party to issue a separate summons for each interlocutory application which he wishes to make, but to save time and expense it is generally prudent to await the

---

[14] See p. 422, *post*.

[15] *Practice Direction*, [1984] 2 All E.R. 672; [1984] 1 W.L.R. 1023.

[16] O. 25, r. 1(1). In Admiralty actions the period is seven weeks and the summons will be returnable before a judge of the Admiralty Court; O. 75, r. 25; see p. 371, *post*. There is a *lacuna* in the Rules of the Supreme Court in that if no defence is served the close of pleadings never occurs and there is no provision for applying for directions; fortunately the High Court has an inherent power to give directions on application; *Austin* v. *Wildig*, [1969] 1 All E.R. 99; [1969] 1 W.L.R. 67.

[17] O. 25, r. 1(4).

[18] The full list of exceptions is embodied in O. 25, r. 1(2).

summons for directions to apply for all the orders required.[19] The form on which the summons is issued sets out in outline matters on which directions may be given, leaving the parties to fill in their detailed requirements and also to add any other application for which the form does not provide (such as an order for the admission of a certified copy of notes of evidence taken in other proceedings). The applicant must delete the number[20] of any paragraph on the form which contains a matter on which he does not require directions. On the return day, and on adjourned hearings, the master will give directions for which the parties have applied and will also give directions of his own motion on certain matters, such as the mode and place of trial, whether or not the parties have applied for them.[1]

3 Matters dealt with on the summons

The standard form lists 30 matters upon which the parties may apply for directions, and leaves space for any others not listed. Certain matters which are, in fact, dealt with on the summons for directions, such as particulars of pleading, amendment of writ and pleadings, discovery and inspection of documents, security for costs and interrogatories have already been encountered.[2] It remains to consider the other principal matters which are dealt with at this important stage of the proceedings.

a Consolidation of actions[3]

This is a procedure which enables a party to have separate issues tried together, whether or not they could have been joined on one writ.[4] It arises frequently in defamation actions where one plaintiff wishes to sue several defendants for separate publications of substantially the same defamatory matter.[5] The application to consolidate should be made as early as possible and will often be made before the summons for directions in which case a separate summons will be required. The plaintiffs in a consolidated action must generally be represented by one firm of solicitors, so that, where more than one firm has been instructed, consolidation will be impossible unless the plaintiffs agree to be represented by one of the firms alone.[6]

---

[19] There is a general rule that particulars will not be ordered before the summons for directions; nevertheless in exceptional cases, for example cases where the pleading is so vague that the other party cannot properly ascertain the case against him, particulars may be ordered; *Cyril Leonard & Co.* v. *Simo Securities Trust. Ltd.*, [1971] 3 All E.R. 1313; [1971] 1 W.L.R. 80.

[20] He must not, however, delete the text.

[1] *Nagy* v. *Co-operative Press*, [1949] 2 K.B. 198; [1949] 1 All E.R. 1019. If the directions sought are uncontested or agreed (when it is still necessary to obtain directions as to the mode and place of trial, before the action can be set down for trial) the plaintiff can apply by post for the directions he requires and the order may be drawn in the High Court office, personal attendance being dispensed with: *Practice Direction (use of postal facilities: Queen's Bench Division)*, [1976] 2 All E.R. 312; [1976] 1 W.L.R. 489.

[2] See pp. 350–363, *ante*.

[3] O. 4, r. 10.

[4] In fact cases are normally consolidated only where the parties could have been joined on one writ under O. 15, r. 4.

[5] See Defamation Act 1952, s. 13; *Stone* v. *Press Association*, [1897] 2 Q.B. 159; *Daws* v. *Daily Sketch*, [1960] 1 All E.R. 397; [1960] 1 W.L.R. 126.

[6] *Lewis* v. *Daily Telegraph (No. 2)*, [1964] 2 Q.B. 601; [1964] 1 All E.R. 705. This case indicates that there is a power to "deconsolidate" consolidated actions.

A simple alternative to consolidation is for the master to order separate actions to be set down for trial consecutively in the same list, so that they will come before the same judge on the same day. The effect is to avoid the duplication of such expenses as witness fees.

b   Evidence

Order 38, r. 1, provides that:

> "subject to the provisions of these rules and of the Civil Evidence Act 1968 and the Civil Evidence Act 1972, and any other enactment relating to evidence, any fact required to be proved at the trial of any action begun by writ by the evidence of witnesses shall be proved by the examination of the witnesses orally and in open court".

Nevertheless the rules provide for enabling and even compelling parties to reduce costs, particularly witness fees, by adopting alternative methods of proof. The most common method of reducing costs is by the use of admissions. A party need produce no proof of any matter admitted in his favour. Admissions on the pleadings may be express or implied from a failure to traverse.[7] Admissions may also be made in answer to interrogatories. A useful means of compelling an opponent to admit a fact is to serve him with a "notice to admit facts", calling upon him to admit the facts listed in the notice.[8] If he will not admit these facts and they are proved at the trial, unless the court otherwise orders, he will bear the costs of proof.[9] This is, of course, a powerful weapon but it must not be abused. A party should not be asked to admit the facts in issue or any inference of fact, such as negligence. He should only, in practice, be asked to admit facts of a formal nature or facts which can easily be proved against him if he does not admit them. If admissions are made which clearly establish one party's liability the other party may, without waiting for a trial, apply for judgment based on those admissions.[10] Similar to such a notice is a "notice to admit documents", calling upon the party served to admit the authenticity of the documents listed, though not the truth of their contents. The effect of failure to admit is, again, that the party who was served with the notice has to pay the costs of proving the documents at the trial, unless the court otherwise orders, which may involve an extra witness, such as a handwriting expert.[11]

Wide powers are conferred on the master by Order 38 as to the means of proof. Thus he may order evidence to be given at the trial by affidavit or in any other specified manner.[12] For example, he may order the date on which an important event occurred to be proved by production of a newspaper containing a report of the event. In addition he may restrict the number of medical or other expert witnesses who may be called at the trial.[13]

---

[7] O. 18, r. 13; see p. 345, *ante*.

[8] O. 27, r. 2.

[9] O. 62, r. 3.

[10] O. 27, r. 3; see p. 329, *ante*.

[11] O. 27, r. 5.

[12] O. 38, rr. 1, 2.

[13] O. 38, r. 4. Note the restrictions embodied in the automatic direction (*c*) (*supra*).

c   Disclosure of experts' reports

Many actions involve the giving of expert evidence. Thus, for example, in actions for damages for personal injuries there is invariably medical evidence concerning the extent of the plaintiff's injuries. In practice the plaintiff's advisers will obtain a medical report (upon which the pleaded case will be based); thereafter the defendants will have the plaintiff medically examined and will in consequence obtain their own medical report. These reports, coming into existence as they do in contemplation of litigation, are privileged from disclosure[14] so that neither party can be directly compelled to disclose his expert evidence to the other side.[15] This has, for some time, been widely thought to be an unsatisfactory state of affairs, particularly in personal injuries actions where, not only might a party be taken by surprise at the trial, but also the ignorance of the strength or weakness of the other party's case may act as a factor inhibiting settlement of the claim or the making of a realistic payment into court. In the result, following recommendations made by committees which had considered this and associated problems,[16] the Civil Evidence Act 1972 authorised the making of rules of court designed to compel parties to disclose medical or other expert reports upon which they propose to rely.

To this end it is now provided that, except with leave of the court or where all parties agree, no expert evidence may be adduced at the trial unless the party seeking to adduce the evidence has applied for a direction in relation thereto and has complied with any directions given on such application.[17] In relation to medical reports in personal injuries actions the court will direct disclosure unless it considers that there is sufficient reason for not doing so.[18] In relation to other classes of expert evidence the court may direct disclosure of experts' reports; in considering whether to do so the court must have regard to all the circumstances but circumstances which may justify not ordering disclosure are that the evidence is or will be based upon a version of the facts which is in dispute between the parties or that it is or will be based upon facts which are neither ascertainable by the expert by the exercise of his own powers of observation, nor within his general professional knowledge or expertise.[19]

Although these rules were introduced in order to assist the progress of personal injuries litigation, it is fair to say that they are regarded with scant enthusiasm in some quarters. This may be due to difficulty in adjusting to their novelty, since they do involve a radical departure from pre-existing practice. On the other hand, especially in relation to engineers' reports in personal injuries actions, there is a natural reluctance to make available to

---

[14] See p. 639, *post*.

[15] *Causton* v. *Mann Egerton (Johnsons), Ltd.*, [1974] 1 All E.R. 453; [1974] 1 W.L.R. 162.

[16] *Report of Committee on Personal Injuries Litigation* (Cmnd. 3691 of 1969); *Seventeenth Report of the Law Reform Committee on Evidence of Opinion and Expert Evidence* (Cmnd. 4489 of 1970).

[17] O. 38, r. 36(1); see *Practice Direction*, [1974] 2 All E.R. 966; [1974] 1 W.L.R. 904.

[18] "Sufficient reason" may be that the pleadings contain an allegation of negligent medical treatment or that the medical report may contain an expression of opinion as to the manner in which the injuries were sustained or as the genuineness of the plaintiff's symptoms: O. 38, r. 37(2).

[19] O. 38, r. 38.

the other side lines of attack flowing from adverse comments in a party's own expert's report. Accordingly a practice seems rapidly to have grown up whereby engineers prepare their reports in two parts, one for disclosure to the other side (often containing non-contentious matters such as measurements and details of the workings of machinery), the other not being for disclosure and containing opinions as to negligence, contributory negligence and the like. This practice appears not to conform to the spirit of the rules, nor to their letter since O. 38, rr. 37–38 refer to the "substance" of the evidence to be relied upon at the trial.[20]

d   Place of trial

The master sometimes exercises his power to transfer the action to another division of the High Court or to a county court.[1] In other cases he must direct where and in what manner the action is to be tried.[2] This must be the last matter upon which the master gives directions. The place of trial will be either London or a centre at which the Lord Chancellor has directed sittings of the High Court to be held, pursuant to section 71 of the Supreme Court Act 1981. No party, other than the Crown,[3] has a right to trial in London, and the place of trial will be fixed where it is most convenient for all parties having regard to such matters as the availablity of witnesses. This will generally be London, if service was acknowledged in London, or the centre for the district in the registry of which service was acknowledged though the place of acknowledgment of service is not conclusive since the jurisdiction of the High Court, unlike that of county courts, is in no way local.

e   Mode of trial

The master or district registrar will determine the mode of trial. Order 33, rule 2 sets out the possible modes of trial, *viz.* trial before—

(*a*) a judge alone;
(*b*) a judge with a jury;
(*c*) a judge with the assistance of assessors;
(*d*) an official referee with or without the assistance of assessors;
(*e*) a master;
(*f*) a special referee.

If the master orders trial in London, he must fix the list in which the case is to be set down for trial. There are six such lists in the Queen's Bench Division, *viz.* Crown Office List, Jury List, Non-Jury List, Short Cause List, Commercial List, Arbitration Case List and Admiralty List.[4] Cases which are to be tried without a jury and which are not likely to last more than four hours are set down in the Short-Cause List. Most actions are tried in the Non-Jury

---

[20] As ACKNER, J. (as he then was) pointed out in deprecating this practice in *Ollett* v. *Bristol Aerojet, Ltd.*, [1979] 3 All E.R. 544; [1979] 1 W.L.R. 1197.
[1] See p. 422, *post.*
[2] O. 33, r. 4.
[3] O. 77, r. 13(1).
[4] See *Practice Direction*, [1981] 3 All E.R. 61; [1981] 1 W.L.R. 1296. For directions outside London see *Practice Direction*, [1972] 1 All E.R. 287; [1972] 1 W.L.R. 5.

List by a judge sitting alone. Provisions relating to jury trial are now contained in section 69 of the Supreme Court Act 1981 which provides that the only cases in which either party has a right[5] to a jury are actions to be tried in the Queen's Bench Division where

(*a*) a charge of fraud against the party; or

(*b*) a claim for libel, slander, malicious prosecution or false imprisonment is in issue unless in either case the trial requires any prolonged examination of documents or accounts or any scientific or local investigation which cannot conveniently be made with a jury.[6] In any other case the master has a discretion whether or not to order a jury. In *Ward* v. *James*,[7] the Court of Appeal formulated the principle that, in the absence of special circumstances, it is a wrong exercise of the master's discretion to order a jury in an action based on a claim for damages for personal injuries.

Thus the law is that the discretion as to the mode of trial is a judicial rather than an absolute one, and that, in the absence of special circumstances, it is a wrong exercise of that discretion to order a jury in a personal injuries action. In the result jury trial has virtually disappeared in personal injuries actions. Indeed it is extremely rare in any case other than those in which the right to jury trial has been preserved by statute. Thus in *Williams* v. *Beesley*,[8] an action alleging professional negligence against a solicitor, the House of Lords refused to order trial by jury, LORD DIPLOCK stating that:[9]

> "The fact that a case involves issues of credibility is not a ground for departing from the usual rule that cases, other than those in which a prima facie right to trial by jury is conferred by statute, should be tried by judge alone."

The Commercial Court

A separate list is kept in London, Liverpool and Manchester to hear "commercial actions", which are defined by Order 72, r. 1(2) to include—

> "any cause arising out of the ordinary transactions of merchants and traders and, without prejudice to the generality of the foregoing words, any cause relating to the construction of a mercantile document, the export or import of merchandise, affreightment, insurance, banking, mercantile agency and mercantile usage."

---

5 The right must be claimed before the master first fixes the place and mode of trial (O. 33, r. 5). "Fraud", in this context, is limited to deceit: *Barclays Bank, Ltd.* v. *Cole*, [1967] 2 Q.B. 738; [1966] 3 All E.R. 948.

6 Even though a case does, *prima facie*, fall within this exception, jury trial may be ordered where a party's honour or reputation is at stake: *Rothermere* v. *Times Newspapers, Ltd.*, [1973] 1 All E.R. 1013; [1973] 1 W.L.R. 448. Rules may provide for additional cases (Supreme Court Act 1981, s. 69(1) (*c*)). It will be noted that the right to jury trial is limited to the Queen's Bench Division. If an action involving a charge of fraud is started in the Chancery Division, therefore, it will be tried by a judge alone; however an application could be made under O. 4, r. 3 to have the action transferred to the Queen's Bench Division and a transfer would be ordered if the Chancery master or judge considered the case suitable for jury trial: see *Stafford Winfield Cook & Partners, Ltd.* v. *Winfield*, [1980] 3 All E.R. 759; [1981] 1 W.L.R. 458.

7 [1966] 1 Q.B. 273; [1965] 1 All E.R. 563.

8 [1973] 3 All E.R. 144; [1973] 1 W.L.R. 1295, an exceptional instance of leave being granted to appeal to the House of Lords on an interlocutory appeal.

9 [1973] 3 All E.R., at p. 146; [1973] 1 W.L.R., at p. 1298.

The judges of the Commercial Court are such of the puisne judges of the High Court as the Lord Chancellor may from time to time nominate[10] and are usually judges of the Queen's Bench Division with special experience in commercial matters. Except by consent their powers are no greater than those of any other judge. However, procedure in the court is more flexible than the normal procedure. Thus the pleadings must be in the form of points of claim, defence, counterclaim, defence to counterclaim or reply and must be as brief as possible. Applications for particulars are not allowed unless essential. By consent the strict rules of evidence are relaxed. Thus evidence is admitted which would generally be excluded, and witness fees may be saved by deciding the case on documentary evidence alone. Moreover the judges regard it as their duty to be available at short notice at any stage of the action on the initiative of either party, so that disputes being dealt with in the Commercial Court are dealt with as quickly as possible. However, such is the popularity of the Commercial Court that a date for a trial of any substance is currently liable to be fixed at between one and two years from the date of the application to fix. A summons for directions may be taken out before the pleadings are closed. Summonses are heard by the judges and in London the current practice is for all five judges of the Court to sit on Fridays for the sole purpose of dealing with summonses. In a recent case the Master of the Rolls, SIR JOHN DONALDSON (himself a sometime member of the Court) paid it the following tribute:[11]

> "It may be situated in London, but, unlike the courts of Kuwait, those of Scotland or other English courts (other perhaps than the Admiralty Court), it is far more than a national or domestic court; it is an international commercial court the overwhelming majority of whose judgments are concerned with the rights and obligations of foreign nationals. It is a court which has an unrivalled expertise in marine insurance where that insurance is governed by English law. This is the result of the sheer volume of work of this nature which comes to the court and to the practitioners from whom the judges of the court are appointed."

A writ or originating summons issued out of London, Liverpool or Manchester may be marked in the top left hand corner, with the words "Commercial Court" and on the issue of the writ or summons so marked, the action will be entered immediately in the commerical list.[12] Actions may be transferred to the Commercial Court apart from this rule and, indeed, actions commenced in the Commercial Court under the rule may be removed from the list. Any party who seeks the removal of an action from the Commercial Court, when it has been set down in that list, must apply within 7 days of giving notice of intention to defend.[13]

Any party to an action in the Commercial Court may take out a summons for directions in the action before the close of pleadings, and should do so as early as possible in the action. This is principally because the directions required may, in fact, relate to the framing of the pleadings. The summons is heard by a Commercial judge rather than a master.

---

[10] Supreme Court Act 1981, s. 6. There are at present five at any one time.
[11] *Amin Rasheed Shipping Corporation* v. *Kuwait Insurance Co.*, [1983] 1 All E.R. 873, at p. 882; [1983] 1 W.L.R. 228, at p. 240 (affirmed [1984] A.C. 50; [1983] 2 All E.R. 884).
[12] O. 72, r. 4.
[13] O. 72, r. 6.

The Admiralty Court

The Admiralty jurisdiction of the High Court, assigned to the Queen's Bench Division by the Administration of Justice Act 1970, is administered by the Admiralty Court, created by that Act as part of the Queen's Bench Division and consisting of such of the puisne judges of the High Court as the Lord Chancellor may from time to time nominate to be Admiralty Judges.[14] Procedure is governed by R.S.C. Order 75. There are special forms of writ for the commencement of proceedings and special rules of procedure, depending upon the type of Admiralty proceeding. To take but one example, in actions to enforce a claim for damage, loss of life or personal injury arising out of a collision between ships, each party must lodge a document known as a "preliminary act" which contains a statement of the material facts relating to the collision including such matters as the state of the weather, the course steered and speed of the ships, the lights on the ships, alterations in course, the angle of the ships at the moment of contact and what sound signals were given and heard. The preliminary acts are sealed and are not opened before the close of pleadings.[15]

Official referees

The office and title of "official referee" was created by the Judicature Act 1873 and abolished by the Courts Act 1971. However the title survives and is used to describe those Circuit judges who are nominated by the Lord Chancellor[16] to deal with "official referees' business" which is defined by Order 36, rule 1(2) to include a cause or matter—

> "(a) which involves a prolonged examination of documents or accounts, or a technical scientific or local investigation such as could more conveniently be conducted by an official referee; or
> (b) for which trial by an official referee is desirable in the interests of one or more of the parties on grounds of expedition, economy or convenience or otherwise."

In practice the bulk of the work of the official referees concerns building disputes, civil or mechanical engineering matters, actions against architects, engineers, surveyors and other professionals, for breach of duty, claims by and against local authorities relating to their statutory duties concerning building regulations and claims involving adjudication over lists of complaints or defects. In the latter type of case the pleadings often consist of or include a "Scott Schedule" (so named after a former official referee) which is a document containing a list of numbered items and divided across the page into a number of columns in which there are completed by the parties in turn, their respective contentions in respect of those items, the final column being left blank for the purpose of the judge completing his adjudication on that item.

As in the Commercial Court, actions may be allocated to an official referee at the time that the writ is issued (by marking it "official referees' business") or may subsequently be transferred to an official referee. Thereafter all

---

[14] Supreme Court Act 1981, s. 6.
[15] O. 75, r. 18.
[16] Under s. 68(1) of the Supreme Court Act 1981 (as amended); the Lord Chancellor may also nominate deputy Circuit judges or Recorders (*ibid.*).

summonses are heard by the official referee (rather than a master or registrar) to whom the case is allocated.

An application for directions (including an application to fix a date for trial) must be made by the plaintiff within 14 days of the giving of notice of intention to defend or the date of the order transferring the cause or matter, whichever is the later.[17] Unfortunately, as in the Commercial Court, the current state of the lists is such that the interval between the application and the fixed date is usually measured in years rather than months.

It should be noted that the court has power to order any issue to be tried before, at or after the trial of the action and may order different issues to be tried separately.[18] Thus the master can order the assessment of damages, for example, to be postponed until after the trial on the issues of liability.[19] Under these provisions a preliminary point of law is often tried before the facts where this may effectively dispose of the action.[20] However, in *Tilling* v. *Whiteman*[1] the House of Lords stated that this course should only be adopted where the facts are complicated and the legal issues short and easily decided, for otherwise (as happened in that case) very considerable costs may be incurred in litigating through the appellate courts a point of law based on hypothetical facts which might never have required determination if the facts of the case had first been found.

Having dealt with all the interlocutory matters raised on the summons for directions including, finally, the mode and place of trial, the master will give an estimate of the length of trial, together with a provisional assessment of the substance, difficulty or public importance of the case.[2] He will then fix a period within which the plaintiff must set the action down for trial. When the plaintiff has done so he must, within 24 hours, inform all the other parties.[3] The parties must then proceed to prepare their cases for trial.

---

[17] O. 36, r. 6.

[18] O. 33, rr. 3, 4(2).

[19] This power has been sparingly exercised; see observations of WINN, L.J. in *Stevens* v. *William Nash, Ltd.*, [1966] 3 All E.R. 156; [1966] 1 W.L.R. 1550, and in *Hawkins* v. *New Mendip Engineering, Ltd.*, [1966] 3 All E.R. 228; [1966] 1 W.L.R. 1341. Cf. *Coenen* v. *Payne*, [1974] 2 All E.R. 1109; [1974] 1 W.L.R. 984. One advantage of trying the issue of liability before damages is that a judgment on liability for damages to be assessed enables the plaintiff to apply for an interim payment; see p. 335, *ante*.

[20] See, for example: *Everett* v. *Ribbands*, [1952] 2 Q.B. 198; [1952] 1 All E.R. 832; *Carl-Zeiss-Stiftung* v. *Herbert Smith & Co.*, [1969] 1 Ch. 93; [1968] 2 All E.R. 1002.

[1] [1980] A.C. 1; [1979] 1 All E.R. 737.

[2] The assessment is as follows: "A"—cases of great substance or great difficulty or of public importance; "B"—cases of substance or difficulty; "C"—other cases: *Practice Direction* (*Summons for Directions*), [1972] 1 All E.R. 288; [1972] 1 W.L.R. 3.

[3] O. 34, r. 8. In addition, where the trial is set down for trial outside London, the plaintiff must, after giving to the defendant 7 days' notice of his intention so to do, lodge with the district registrar a certificate of readiness for trial containing certain particulars, notably whether the order made on the summons for directions has been complied with, and in particular whether medical or experts' reports have been submitted for agreement and, if so, whether they have been agreed (or if not how many medical or expert witnesses are to be called), whether plans and photographs have been agreed, an up-to-date estimate of the length of the trial and a statement that the plaintiff is ready and wishes the action to be brought on for trial: *Practice Direction* (*Trial out of London*), [1972] 1 All E.R. 287; [1972] 1 W.L.R. 5.

F TRIAL

1 Preparation of evidence

At an early stage of the action the papers will have been sent to counsel. Counsel will normally settle the pleadings but, in any event, he will usually be instructed before the summons for directions so as to obtain his advice on interlocutory matters. Cases are won and lost in their preparation. Counsel will therefore wish to consider which applications should be made, whether the pleadings require amendment and similar matters.

The first consideration upon preparing an action for trial is on whom the burden of proof rests. The general rule is *quis affirmat debet probare*; thus where any allegation of fact is in issue the party who alleges that fact must prove it. The pleadings will disclose where the general burden lies. If an allegation in the statement of claim is admitted (expressly or impliedly) it need not be proved at all. If it is traversed then the burden rests on the plaintiff. If it is the subject of a plea in confession and avoidance, then the burden is on the defendant to prove the matters in avoidance. However, the burden may shift during the action by the effect of presumptions. If a presumption is raised in favour of a party, the effect is to shift the burden of disproving the matter presumed to his opponent.[4]

Having decided which matters he must prove, counsel will decide how he proposes to prove them. The two principal methods of proof are by witnesses and by documents.

a Witnesses

Counsel will name the witnesses whom he requires. There is no property in a witness, so that there is no objection to interviewing or calling any witness even if he has been served with a subpoena by an opponent.[5] It is, of course, wrong to call a witness whose testimony is unlikely to support one's case, since a party cannot cross-examine a witness he has called, unless the court gives leave to treat the witness as hostile.[6] Also, to intimidate or otherwise tamper with a witness amounts to a contempt of court.[7]

Usually a witness wil be prepared to attend voluntarily if he is tendered a reasonable fee. Where he will not, his attendance may be compelled by *subpoena ad testificandum*.[8] A witness who fails to comply may be committed for contempt of court. Where a witness will not, or may not, be able to attend the trial his testimony may, by order of the court, be taken before a special examiner.[9]

---

4 See p. 606, *post*.
5 See observations of LORD DENNING, M.R. in *Fullam* v. *Newcastle Chronicle and Journal, Ltd.*, [1977] 3 All E.R. 32; [1977] 1 W.L.R. 651; see also *Harmony Shipping Co. S.A.* v. *Davis*, [1979] 3 All E.R. 177; [1979] 1 W.L.R. 1380; see p. 627, fn. 1, *post*.
6 See p. 634, *post*.
7 *Chapman* v. *Honig*, [1963] 2 Q.B. 502; [1963] 2 All E.R. 513.
8 O. 38, r. 14. Where the witness is a prisoner an order may be obtained for his attendance by an application *ex parte* to a judge in chambers under the Criminal Procedure Act 1853, s. 9. Where he is in custody on civil process, his attendance is secured by writ of *habeas corpus ad testificandum* upon application *ex parte* on affidavit to a judge in chambers.
9 O. 39. Where the witness is in another country a "letter of request" is issued to the judicial authorities of that country. A deposition taken under this Order may be put in evidence at the

b   Documents

Documentary evidence, especially in contract cases, frequently forms the basis of a party's case. Where he is in possession of the documents himself, he is in no difficulty. However the documents which are needed by a party may be in the possession of an opponent or of a third party. If they are in the possession of a third party, the proper course is to serve him with a *subpoena duces tecum*, i.e. "attend and bring the document with you". If the documents are in the possession of an opponent he should be served with a "notice to produce" the documents required. This does not have the effect of a subpoena, but if he does not produce the document, he cannot use the document himself and the party who served the notice may give secondary evidence of its contents.[10] In addition, if he has served a list of documents under Order 24 he is deemed to have been served with a notice to produce all the documents in his list.[11]

Formal proof of a document may be dispensed with if one's opponent is prepared to admit the authenticity of the documents in question. Accordingly, he should be served with a "notice to admit" these documents.[12] However, a party who has been served with a list of documents is deemed to admit the authenticity of every document in his list[13] unless he serves express notice of non-admission within 21 days after inspection.

Since automatic discovery now takes place in nearly all actions commenced by writ, it follows that express notices to produce and notices to admit documents will rarely be necessary.

c   Special damage calculation

The obligation to plead special damages fully has already been noted.[14] However, by the time the action comes on for trial the special damage claim, particularly in personal injury actions, will usually be out of date in consequence of time off work since the Statement of Claim, increase in wage rates, further statutory benefits and so on. Much court time is taken up in investigating these matters and to avoid waste of time, it is now the practice[15] that in any personal injury action in which there is a claim for loss of earnings, loss of future earning capacity, medical or other expenses or loss of pension rights, particulars (where appropriate in the form of a schedule) must be served by the claimant on all other parties not later than seven days after the case appears in the Warned List in London. Within seven days thereafter every party seved with particulars must indicate whether and to what extent each item claimed is agreed and, if not agreed, the reason why not and any counter-proposals. Where there is a fixed date for hearing, the plaintiff's particulars must be served not less than 28 days before that date and the answer not later than 14 days thereafter. In cases for hearing outside London

---

trial either by consent of the other side or on proof that the deponent is dead, outside the jurisdiction or unable from sickness or other infirmity to attend the trial (O. 38, r. 9).

[10] O. 27, r. 5(4); *Sharpe* v. *Lamb* (1840), 11 Ad. & El. 805.

[11] O. 27, r. 4(3).

[12] O. 27, r. 5(1).

[13] O. 27, r. 4(1).

[14] See p. 343, *ante*.

[15] *Practice Direction*, [1984] 3 All E.R. 165; [1984] 1 W.L.R. 1127.

the particulars must be served not later than the lodging of the certificate of readiness and the answer not later than 14 days thereafter.

Failure to comply with these directions may result in penalising the defaulting party in costs.

d   Notices under the Civil Evidence Act 1968

Where it is desired to put in evidence at the trial statements admissible under the provisions of the Civil Evidence Act 1968,[16] the party desiring to do so must within 21 days after setting down serve on every other party a notice containing prescribed particulars of (if the statement is oral) the time, place and circumstances in which the statement was made, the persons by whom and to whom it was made and the substance of the statement or, if material, the words used.[17] In the case of written statements admissible by virtue of the Act, the notice must annex a copy of the document in question as well as containing certain prescribed particulars relating to the circumstances of its compilation.[18]

If the party giving the notice alleges that the maker cannot be called as a witness at the trial because he is dead, beyond the seas, unfit by reason of his bodily or mental condition to attend as a witness, cannot be found or cannot reasonably be expected to have any recollection of matters relevant to the accuracy of his statement, the notice must contain a statement to this effect;[19] otherwise a party served with a notice may within 21 days serve a counter-notice requiring the maker of any statement to be called as a witness by the party who served the original notice, in which event if that person is not called as a witness, his statement is not admissible under the 1968 Act.[20]

When the evidence for each side has been prepared the parties must await trial. Neither party need serve any notice of the date of trial on his opponent. Accordingly (unless the case has been given a fixed date) all parties must watch carefully the lists. The Week's List is published on Mondays and contains the cases expected to be tried in that week. Each day there is published a Daily Cause List containing the actions to be heard that day and a Warned List consisting of actions likely to be tried in the near future. Thus neither side has any excuse if his case is not ready when the action comes on for trial. If one party fails to appear the trial may proceed in his absence.[1] However, if application is made within 7 days, a judgment obtained in the

---

16 See pp. 664–665, *post*.

17 O. 38, r. 22(1).

18 O. 38, rr. 22(2), 23(1), 24.

19 O. 38. rr. 22(3), 23(2), 24(3), 25. Any issue as to whether these conditions are satisfied in relation to the maker of a statement may be determined conclusively before the trial on an application by summons (O. 38, r. 27). The conditions appear to be disjunctive so that if, for example, it is established that the witness is abroad, his statement is admissible and it is not necessary to prove, in addition, that he cannot be found: *Piermay Shipping Co. S.A.* v. *Chester*, [1978] 1 All E.R. 1233; [1978] 1 W.L.R. 411.

20 O. 38, r. 26. The court has, however, discretion to admit statements under the Civil Evidence Act 1968 in cases where the proper notice was not served but it will not exercise this discretion in favour of a party who, for example, has deliberately not served a notice in order to retain the possibility of surprising an opponent; cf. *Ford* v. *Lewis*, [1971] 2 All E.R. 983; [1971] 1 W.L.R. 623.

1 O. 35, r. 1.

absence of a party may be set aside, generally on condition that he pay the costs thrown away.[2] Although adjournment is possible, last minute postponements are looked upon with disfavour by the judge in charge of the list and may result in the offending firm of solicitors being penalised personally with the extra costs incurred.[3]

2   Procedure at the trial

If the action is to be tried with a jury, a jury of 12 is sworn. The trial then begins.

a   Right to begin

If damages are unliquidated or the burden of proving any single issue on the pleadings rests on the plaintiff, then the plaintiff begins. Thus the only case where the defendant has the right to begin is a case in which the plaintiff claims only liquidated damages and the defendant has not traversed any allegation in the statement of claim. The right to begin and the right to the last word are advantages which are probably exaggerated, especially in the absence of a jury.

b   Case for the plaintiff

Counsel for the plaintiff opens his case stating the facts on which the plaintiff relies in the order in which they appear on the pleadings, which should be chronological order. He should not rely upon any fact which he is not permitted to prove, which means, of course, that he cannot allege any fact not pleaded, although he may, even at this late stage, be allowed to amend the pleadings. Neither counsel must disclose the existence of any interim payment, nor of any payment into court, unless the defendant has raised one of the two defences in which the payment is an essential element.[4] The plaintiff's witnesses are then called and sworn. They are examined and may be cross-examined and re-examined.[5] In the course of cross-examining the plaintiff's witnesses, counsel for the defendant must "put his case" which includes making clear which part of the plaintiff's case is challenged and what positive allegations are being made in relation to the evidence of the plaintiff's witnesses, so that they may have the opportunity of dealing with those allegations. This is important to the efficient conduct of trials because if counsel for·the plaintiff calls a witness whose evidence is not challenged on a particular point, then he is entitled to assume that the point is not in issue and he will not call any other witnesses to deal with it. If the defence lead evidence as to matters which should have been put but were not put to the plaintiff's witnesses, judicial rebuke is virtually inevitable and, unless counsel was responsible for the oversight (in which event he will, in the interests of

---

2   O. 35, r. 2. There can be an appeal against such a judgment, though this is rarely appropriate: *Armour* v. *Bate*, [1891] 2 Q.B. 233.

3   O. 62, r. 8.

4   O. 22, r. 7; see p. 347, *ante*.

5   See p. 633, *post*. It is a matter for the judge's discretion as to whether he allows other witnesses to remain in court while evidence is being given: *Moore* v. *Lambeth County Court Registrar*, [1969] 1 All E.R. 782; [1969] 1 W.L.R. 141.

his client, immediately accept responsibility for it), the judge is likely to infer, and find, that the evidence in question is a recent invention. His documents, including answers to interrogatories which he wishes to put in, are then put in evidence. Finally counsel argues the propositions of law upon which he relies, citing to the court all relevant authorities on the point whether they support his own case or that of his opponent. If they tend to support his opponent's case, he must attempt to distinguish them from the present case on their facts. He cannot, however, ignore them, since this would infringe his duty to the court.

c Case for the defence

At the close of the plaintiff's case the defendant has the following courses open to him:

(1) he may submit "no case to answer". This is a submission that the plaintiff has failed to make out a *prima facie* case, or to establish the elements of a recognised cause of action. The submission is rare in a civil action since the objection will usually have been taken long before the trial. If it is made, the judge, before deciding, may require the defendant to "stand on his submission", which means that he can call no evidence if his submission fails, although this is not usual in jury actions.[6] Counsel for the plaintiff has a right to reply to the submission. If it succeeds, judgment is entered for the defendant. If it fails and the defendant has been put to his election, judgment is entered for the plaintiff.

(2) He may state that he intends to call no evidence, oral or documentary. Counsel for the plaintiff will then address the court followed by defence counsel who thus obtains the right to the last word.[7]

(3) In most cases the defence will be a mixture of law and fact and the defendant will want to put in some evidence. In this event defence counsel may make an opening speech outlining his defence. His witnesses give their evidence in the same way as those of the plaintiff followed by the defendant's documents and legal submissions. The plaintiff may be permitted to adduce evidence in rebuttal where the defence case has raised matters which could not reasonably have been foreseen. Defence counsel then makes a closing speech, following which counsel for the plaintiff has a right to make a closing speech in reply. Where a party in his closing speech raises any fresh point of law, the other party is entitled to reply but only in relation to that point.

d Verdict and judgment

At the conclusion of all the evidence and the legal argument for both sides the judge sums up (if there is a jury) or either gives judgment or reserves his judgment if there is not. He must direct the jury (if there is one) as to the issues in the case, stating on whom the burden of proving the individual issues rests, and outlining the evidence in support of those issues. He must

---

6 *Laurie* v. *Raglan Building Co., Ltd.*, [1942] 1 K.B. 152; [1941] 3 All E.R. 332; *Young* v. *Rank*, [1950] 2 K.B. 510; [1950] 2 All E.R. 166; *Storey* v. *Storey*, [1961] P. 63; [1960] 3 All E.R. 279.

7 O. 35, r. 7. This rule applies expressly to jury actions, but, in the Queen's Bench Division, applies in practice to non-jury actions as well; see *Weller* v. *O'Brien*, [1962] 3 All E.R. 65; [1962] 1 W.L.R. 885.

also direct upon the standard of proof required from the party on whom the burden rests. He will direct on the law applicable to the issues of fact, for example, whether the words are capable of bearing the defamatory meaning alleged or whether the defendant owes the plaintiff a duty of care in negligence. He must leave the actual issues of fact and the assessment of damages to the jury. While he can suggest a conclusion of fact to the jury, the judge should not tell the jury of the limits within which an award of damages should fall, since this would amount to an attempt by the judge to assess damages. A modern tendency is for the judge to pose a series of questions to the jury calling for their decision on the facts and, if they find for the plaintiff on any issue, the amount of damages.[8]

Where the plaintiff has sought an equitable remedy as an alternative or in addition to damages, the grant of this remedy is in the discretion of the judge.

It remains for judgment to be entered in accordance with the verdict. A judgment crystallises the rights of the parties in respect of the subject matter of the action. Thus they are estopped from litigating the same issues of fact again.[9] Even if fresh damage becomes apparent the plaintiff cannot sue because his right is extinguished.[10] Counsel for the unsuccessful party may apply for a stay of execution pending an appeal. This may be granted on terms. After judgment on the issues of liability and damages the judge may make orders as to interest and costs.

Damages—Historically damages have always been expressed in English currency. This has caused hardship in cases in which sterling has been devalued so that a party who bargained for payment in foreign currency has been awarded damages in sterling, the rate of exchange being calculated at the date upon which his entitlement to payment arose (the "breach-date" rule). Accordingly in 1975 the House of Lords changed this rule.[11] Since 1975 the English courts have shown an increasing willingness to give judgment in foreign currency. At first limited to contract actions where the sum was due under the contract in a foreign currency and the proper law of the contract was the law of that country in whose currency the obligation was expressed,[11] the power is now exercised in cases where the plaintiff's loss would be most truly expressed in a foreign currency, in which case judgment will be given in that currency,[12] and in tort actions, where damages may be awarded in a

---

[8] However where a jury delivers a general verdict, the judge is not then entitled to ask questions to ascertain the grounds for the verdict: *Arnold* v. *Jeffreys*, [1914] 1 K.B. 512; *Barnes* v. *Hill*, [1967] 1 Q.B. 579; [1967] 1 All E.R. 347.

[9] Clerical mistakes in judgments or orders, or errors arising therein from any accidental slip or omission, may at any time be corrected by the court on motion or summons without an appeal (O. 20, r. 11—the "slip rule").

[10] There is an exception to this rule; if special damage is an element in a cause of action, fresh special damage arising out of the same cause of action may be the basis of a second action: *Darley Main Colliery Co.* v. *Mitchell* (1886), 11 App. Cas. 127; *West Leigh Colliery Co.* v. *Tunnicliffe*, [1908] A.C. 27.

[11] *Miliangos* v. *George Frank* (*Textiles*), *Ltd.*, [1976] A.C. 443; [1975] 3 All E.R. 801 not following *Re United Railways of the Havana and Regla Warehouses, Ltd.*, [1961] A.C. 1007; [1960] 2 All E.R. 332; for the significance of this decision in relation to the doctrine of judicial precedent, see p. 147, *ante*.

[12] *The Folias*, [1979] A.C. 685; [1979] 1 All E.R. 421.

currency which the plaintiff has used to make good the loss which he has suffered.[13]

Nevertheless a judgment can only be enforced in terms of sterling. Accordingly if enforcement becomes necessary the judgment will be converted into its sterling equivalent at the date when leave is given to enforce the judgment.

Finally, there is at present no procedure for successive awards of damages in the same action. Damages have to be assessed once and for all at the trial. This may cause hardship to either side, since subsequent events may demonstrate the hypotheses upon which the award of damages were based to be false with the result that the damages were too high or too low. This is particularly so in personal injury actions where, for example, an award of damages for loss of future earning capacity must necessarily be highly speculative. To remedy this situation section 32A of the Supreme Court Act contains provision for "provisional damages" in personal injury actions. Rules of court are required to implement the terms of this section and to date no such Rules have been made.

Interest—Section 35A of the Supreme Court Act 1981[14] empowers the court to award simple (but not compound) interest on debts or damages "at such rate as the court thinks fit or as rules of court may provide". In commercial cases the usual rate is 1 *per cent* above United Kingdom clearing banks' base rates over the relevant period.[15]

In personal injury actions the position is more complicated. Section 35A provides that in the absence of special reasons, the court must grant interest on awards exceeding £200. The principles applicable are as follows:[16]

(1) that the plaintiff is awarded interest on general damages for pain, suffering and loss of amenities from the date of service of the writ to the date of trial at a conventional rate of 2 *per cent per annum*;

(2) that the plaintiff is awarded interest on special damages from the date of the accident to the date of trial at half the rates which during that period were payable on money in court placed on short-term investment account;[17]

(3) that no interest is awarded on future loss of earnings or other prospective financial losses.

e References to the European Court

As has been noted[18] Article 177 of the E.E.C. Treaty (to which English courts are bound to give effect[19]) confers power upon English judges to request the Court of Justice of the European Communities (the European Court) to give a preliminary ruling concerning: (*a*) the interpretation of the E.E.C. treaty; (*b*) the validity and interpretation of acts of the institutions of the

---

13 *The Despina R*, [1979] A.C. 685; [1979] 1 All E.R. 421.
14 Added by Administration of Justice Act 1982, s. 15, Sch. 1 and replacing s. 3 of the Law Reform (Miscellaneous Provisions) Act 1934.
15 See *Polish Steam Ship Co.* v. *Atlantic Maritime Co.*, [1984] 3 All E.R. 59; [1984] 3 W.L.R. 300.
16 As laid down by the Court of Appeal in *Jefford* v. *Gee*, [1970] 2 Q.B. 130; [1970] 1 All E.R. 202 and restated with modification by the House of Lords in *Wright* v. *British Railways Board*, [1983] 2 A.C. 773; [1983] 2 All E.R. 698.
17 See *Dexter* v. *Courtaulds, Ltd.*, [1984] 1 All E.R. 70; [1984] 1 W.L.R. 372.
18 See p. 185, *ante*.
19 European Communities Act 1972, s. 2(1).

Community; (c) the interpretation of the statutes of bodies established by an act of the Council where those statutes so provide.[20]

The decision whether to refer a question for a preliminary ruling is within the discretion of the judge and the procedure on a reference is governed by Order 114. A master has no power to make such an order but a judge may do so either following application or of his own motion. If an order is made it should set out in a schedule the request for the preliminary ruling and the proceedings will, unless otherwise ordered, be stayed until the European Court has given its ruling. The following principles should be noted:

(1) As will be apparent from the terms of Article 177 it is only questions of Community law which can be referred to the European Court, and not questions of internal domestic law.

(2) Furthermore an English court will not refer a question if the decision of that question is not necessary to enable the English court to give judgment.

(3) For this purpose a decision on the question is necessary only if it would be conclusive of the very case before the court so that, following the decision of the European Court nothing would remain for the English court to do but to give judgment in accordance with that decision.

(4) If the same, or substantially the same, point has already been decided by the European Court in a previous case, an English court can follow that decision without troubling the European Court.

(5) If the point is reasonably clear and free from doubt there is no need for the point to be referred.

(6) Even if the English court considers the decision of a question to be necessary so that a reference would be justified, it must still, in exercising its discretion whether or not to refer the question, take into account all the circumstances of the case, including such matters as the length of time which may elapse if the question is referred, the importance of not overloading the European Court with references, the difficulty and importance of the point, the expense involved and the wishes of the parties.

The principles set out above are a summary of those stated by LORD DENNING, M.R. in the leading case of *H.P. Bulmer, Ltd.* v. *Bollinger S.A.*[1] and appear to have been extracted by LORD DENNING from authorities of the legal systems of the Common Market countries. They may be taken, at least for the time being, as being an authoritative statement of the principles to be applied by English courts when considering whether or not to refer a question to the European Court. As will be apparent from (3) above the decision whether or not to refer the question will not usually be taken until the conclusion of the evidence and presumably also of the argument, in the trial, that is to say the issue of whether or not to refer will be the last issue to be determined before judgment is delivered. Nevertheless the rules themselves make express provision for the making of an application for an order before the trial.[2]

---

[20] Similar provisions are contained in Article 150 of the Euratom Treaty and in Article 41 of the E.C.S.C. Treaty.

[1] [1974] Ch. 401; [1974] 2 All E.R. 1226; see also *Customs & Excise Commissioners* v. *ApS Samex*, [1983] 1 All E.R. 1042; *Henn and Darby* v. *Director of Public Prosecutions.* [1981] A.C. 850; [1980] 2 All E.R. 166 (with particular reference to criminal cases).

[2] O. 114, r. 2(2); the application is by motion.

CHAPTER 19

Originating Summonses, Motions and Petitions

A USES OF THE ORIGINATING SUMMONS

Although most actions in the Queen's Bench Division are commenced by writ, and many must be commenced in this way, the plaintiff may in some cases proceed by originating summons.[1] An originating summons is defined as "every summons other than a summons in a pending cause or matter".[2] The procedure is aptly named since it actually raises the point at issue in the first instance, thus dispensing with the need for pleadings. It is the proper method for making applications under certain statutes; for example, applications to approve the compromise of an action by an infant or patient, interpleader applications where an action is not pending and summary proceedings for possession of land occupied by trespassers.[3] In addition it is a streamlined method of obtaining the court's decision on a point of law or on the construction of a document or statute.

B ORIGINATING SUMMONS PROCEDURE

There are now three forms of originating summons;[4] (1) originating summons between parties, general form; (2) originating summons between parties, expedited form; (3) *ex parte* originating summons (this form is used mainly in the Chancery Division). The first form is the usual one in the Queen's Bench Division. The second form differs in that it makes provision

---

[1] See pp. 300–301, *ante*.
[2] O. 1, r. 4.
[3] O. 113. This Order was introduced to combat difficulties posed by "squatters" in cases in which it was not possible to identify by name the trespassers against whom an order was sought. The Order provides a swift and summary procedure whereby the plaintiff may proceed by originating summons, to which no acknowledgment of service is required, supported by affidavit; an order for possession may then be made by a judge without the necessity for a trial and a writ of possession issued without leave.
[4] O. 7, r. 2 (as amended by Rules of the Supreme Court (Writ and Appearance) 1979).

for a date of hearing to be inserted (rather like an ordinary summons in a pending action) but it can only be used in a small number of cases, specified in the Rules. The summons is issued in the same way as a writ, out of the Central Office or a district registry. It remains in force and is renewable in the same way as a writ and must be served on the defendant as if it were a writ, leave being required to serve it outside the jurisdiction.

> "Every originating summons must include a statement of the questions on which the plaintiff seeks the determination or direction of the High Court or, as the case may be, a concise statement of the relief or remedy claimed in the proceedings begun by the originating summons with sufficient particulars to identify the cause or causes of action in respect of which the plaintiff claims that relief or remedy."[5]

Although an originating summons is not a pleading[6] it is in many ways similar to a statement of claim and it seems that the inherent jurisdiction of the court and under Order 18, r. 19 to strike out any pleading extends to an originating summons.[7]

The plaintiff must, within 14 days after any defendant has acknowledged service, file with the court the affidavit evidence on which he intends to rely (in the case of an *ex parte* summons he must file this not less than four clear days before the date fixed for the hearing) and must serve copies thereof on all defendants. A defendant who has acknowledged service must then within 28 days file and serve any affidavit evidence upon which he intends to rely and the plaintiff may within 14 days thereafter file and serve further affidavit evidence in reply.[8]

The plaintiff will then obtain an appointment for the attendance of the parties before the court for the hearing of the summons.[9] Any defendant who has acknowledged service may raise a counterclaim whether or not that counterclaim could have been commenced by originating summons had he been the plaintiff; if the court cannot conveniently hear the counterclaim with the originating summons, it may order that it be struck out or tried separately.[10]

C DIRECTIONS OF THE COURT

The first hearing of the summons will usually be before a master who may adopt the following courses:

(1) If the liability of the defendant in respect of the claim is established, the

---

[5] O. 7, r. 3(1).

[6] *Lewis* v. *Packer*, [1960] 1 All E.R. 720; [1960] 1 W.L.R. 452.

[7] O. 18, r. 19(3); *Punton* v. *Ministry of Pensions*, [1963] 1 All E.R. 275; [1963] 1 W.L.R. 186. Moreover, although O. 18, r. 19(2) provides that no evidence is admissible on an application to strike out a pleading as disclosing no reasonable cause of action, it appears that an affidavit sworn in support of an originating summons can be referred to on an application on this ground made in relation to an originating summons: *Re Caines*, [1978] 2 All E.R. 1; [1978] 1 W.L.R. 540.

[8] O. 28, r. 1A. These time limits are abridged where the summons is in the expedited form or is an *ex parte* originating summons (O. 28, r. 2(2)).

[9] O. 28, r. 2.

[10] O. 28, r. 7.

master may make such order against him as the case may require. The issues raised are thus determined. However, if such an order is made against a defendant who does not appear at the hearing, it may subsequently be varied or revoked by the court on such terms as the court thinks just.[11]

(2) The master may order the proceedings to continue as if the action had been begun by writ (whether or not it could have been begun by writ), and may order that any affidavit shall stand as a pleading. In this event the master will treat the summons as if it were a summons for directions and will, accordingly, give directions on such matters as discovery of documents and the mode and place of trial.[12]

(3) The master may order the action to be transferred to the appropriate county court.

(4) Unless one of the above orders is made, the court will "give such directions as to the further conduct of the proceedings as it thinks best adapted to secure the just, expeditious and economical disposal thereof".[13] This includes most directions which would be given on the hearing of the summons for directions in an action commenced by writ. In particular the court must determine the mode and place of trial. This will usually be before a judge in open court, the evidence being given in most cases by affidavit. In addition the court is bound to consider at as early a stage as practicable whether there is or may be a dispute as to fact and whether the summons should be heard on oral evidence. The court may, if it thinks fit, order that no further evidence shall be filed and that the summons shall be heard on oral evidence or partly on oral evidence and partly on affidavit evidence, with or without cross examination of the deponents as it may direct.[14]

D ORIGINATING MOTIONS

After writs and originating summonses, the third possible method of commencing proceedings in the Queen's Bench Division (and, indeed, in the High Court generally) is by originating application. Relatively few classes of case are appropriately commenced in this way in the Queen's Bench Division. An application under any enactment for an order directing a Minister, tribunal or other person to state a case for determination by the High Court is by originating motion. So also is an appeal from an arbitration to a Commercial judge under the Arbitration Act 1979[15] and an application for committal for contempt of court where there are no pending proceedings.[16] Perhaps the most important type of case dealt with under this procedure in this Division is an application for "judicial review".[17] The application for

---

[11] O. 28, r. 4(1).

[12] O. 28, r. 8. However an action based on an allegation of fraud (which must be commenced by writ; see p. 300, *ante*) cannot be continued as if commenced by writ; *Re 462 Green Lane, Ilford, Gooding* v. *Booland*, [1971] 1 All E.R. 315; [1971] 1 W.L.R. 138; cf. *Re Deadman, Smith* v. *Garland*, [1971] 2 All E.R. 101; [1971] 1 W.L.R. 426.

[13] O. 28, r. 4(3).

[14] O. 28, r. 4(4).

[15] O. 73, r. 2(2); see p. 227, *ante*.

[16] O. 52, r. 3.

[17] See p. 175, *ante*. The procedure is governed by O. 53 (substituted by R.S.C. (Amendment No. 3) 1977).

leave is made to a judge in chambers (in most cases) *ex parte* and, if leave is granted, the originating motion may be issued. On the hearing the court (usually the divisional court) may make any one of the prerogative orders and may, in addition, award damages,[18] or grant an injunction or a declaration (the applicant being permitted to join claims for such relief if they arise out of or are connected with the subject-matter of his application[19]). Parties may make interlocutory applications, for example for discovery and interrogatories, in the course of proceedings for judicial review, and these may be made to a judge or master.[20]

In the case of originating motions, other than for judicial review, the motion must include a concise statement of the nature of the claim made or the relief or remedy required,[1] and must be issued out of the Central Office in proceedings in the Queen's Bench Division. It will be served on the respondents to the motion, who will attend before the court on the day fixed for the hearing of the motion, whereupon on that hearing, or future adjourned hearings of the motion, the issue in question will be tried, either on affidavit or on oral evidence as the parties may agree or the judge may direct.

E PETITIONS

The final method of commencing proceedings in the High Court is by petition. Many forms of proceedings in the other two Divisions are commenced in this way, and there are generally specific rules, for example in bankruptcy, winding-up of companies and matrimonial causes, relating to these proceedings.[2]

In the Queen's Bench Division the only proceedings commenced by petition appear to be election petitions under the Representation of the People Act 1983, concerning disputes arising out of the conduct of local government or Parliamentary elections. Such proceedings are, happily, rare.

---

[18] The order does not create any substantive rights (it would be *ultra vires* if it did) so that the applicant must have a claim for damages which he could have pursued by writ.

[19] O. 53, r. 2.

[20] O. 53, r. 8.

[1] O. 8, r. 3; procedure on originating and other motions is dealt with in O. 8.

[2] Although O. 9 contains a few general rules.

CHAPTER 20

Costs and the Enforcement of Judgments

A COSTS

1 Who must pay costs

There are two sets of costs. First there are the costs which each party will have to pay to his own solicitor. These must be paid irrespective of the outcome of the action and, subject to the Rules, depend upon the contract between solicitor and client. Secondly there are the costs which one side may be ordered to pay to his opponent. These must be assessed or "taxed" by the court and will very rarely cover the full amount that a party has to pay to his own solicitor. It follows that even a litigant who is completely successful will often have to pay some costs himself. These represent the difference between the amount he pays his solicitor and the amount he recovers from his opponent, and are sometimes described as "irrecoverable costs". If the judge makes no order as to costs each party pays his own costs. In most cases, however, the judge will order one side to pay all or a proportion of the costs of his opponent. At common law a successful litigant had a right to costs but this right has been virtually removed by legislation so that at the present day the award of costs is discretionary. It is not, of course, an absolute discretion and it is a wrong exercise of the discretion to deprive a party of his costs if he has been completely successful and guilty of no misconduct.[1] In addition there are statutory fetters on the exercise of this discretion, of which the following should be specially noted.[2]

a Costs should follow the event

Unless there are special factors present, a successful party may expect his costs from an unsuccessful opponent. Nevertheless there is clearly a power to

---

[1] *Donald Campbell & Co., Ltd*, v. *Pollak*, [1927] A.C. 732. See remarks of VISCOUNT CAVE, L.C., at pp. 811–812.
[2] Though mention may also be made of the Slander of Women Act 1891, s. 1 and the Rent Act 1977, s. 141(4).

deprive a successful party of his costs on the ground that he has conducted the litigation dishonestly or recovered only a small part of his claim.[3] In an extreme case a successful plaintiff may have to pay the costs of the defendant.[4] There is jurisdiction to order a successful defendant to pay costs but this jurisdiction is only exercisable in the most exceptional circumstances.[5]

There has been a considerable volume of litigation as to what is "the event" in an action.[6] In a simple action involving one plaintiff, one defendant and a single issue, no difficulty arises; the event is judgment on that issue. However, where there are several parties or several issues the situation is more complex.

Several parties—Where a plaintiff properly joins several defendants and succeeds against some but fails against others, the court may, in its discretion, order the costs of a successful defendant to be paid directly or indirectly by an unsuccessful defendant.[7] Conversely, where one defendant is sued by several plaintiffs, some of whom succeed and some of whom fail, the defendant should make a special application for the extra costs he has incurred through the presence of an unsuccessful plaintiff.[8]

Several causes of action—Where several causes of action are tried together the court will, if the issues are severable, order the costs of them to be taxed separately.[9] The effect is that the plaintiff will recover the costs of the causes of action upon which he succeeds, and the defendant will be awarded the costs of the others. However this method of taxation is not possible where the several causes of action arise out of the same transaction. In such cases the judge may order that the whole of the successful plaintiff's costs be taxed, but that he shall recover only a fixed proportion of the taxed costs from the defendant.[10]

Costs of interlocutory proceedings—There will be various interlocutory applications made by each party throughout the action. There are two possibilities with respect to the costs of these applications. The court may make a special order as to the costs of the individual application upon making or refusing an interlocutory order.[11] Alternatively the court may order that the costs of the application be "costs in the cause" which means that the party who is eventually successful will recover the costs of the application. A modification of the latter order is "plaintiff's costs in cause"

---

[3] *Barnes* v. *Maltby* (1889), 5 T.L.R. 207; *O'Connor* v. *Star Newspaper Co., Ltd.* (1893), 68 L.T. 146.

[4] See *Alltrans Express, Ltd.* v. *CVA Holdings, Ltd.*, [1984] 1 All E.R. 685; [1984] 1 W.L.R. 394.

[5] *Knight* v. *Clifton*, [1971] Ch. 700; [1971] 2 All E.R. 378. There was no such power prior to the Judicature Act 1890 (now Supreme Court Act 1981, s. 51(1)). An order against a successful defendant was made in *Ottway* v. *Jones*, [1955] 2 All E.R. 585; [1955] 1 W.L.R. 706.

[6] See *Reid, Hewitt & Co.* v. *Joseph*, [1918] A.C. 717.

[7] *Bullock* v. *L.G.O. Co.*, [1907] 1 K.B. 264; *Sanderson* v. *Blyth Theatre Co.*, [1903] 2 K.B. 533.

[8] *Keen* v. *Towler* (1924), 41 T.L.R. 86.

[9] As to what is an "issue", see *Howell* v. *Dering*, [1915] 1 K.B. 54, at p. 63; *Reid, Hewitt & Co.* v. *Joseph*, [1918] A.C. 717. Any item of costs attributable to more than one issue will be divided between the issues.

[10] O. 62, r. 9(4); *Cinema Press, Ltd.* v. *Pictures and Pleasures, Ltd.*, [1945] K.B. 356; [1945] 1 All E.R. 440; cf. *Cassell & Co., Ltd.* v. *Broome (No. 2)*, [1972] A.C. 1027; [1972] 1 All E.R. 801.

[11] O. 62, r. 4; *viz.* costs to be the plaintiff's (or defendant's) "in any event". In this case the court is treating an interlocutory order as an "event" within r. 3.

or "defendant's costs in cause", the effect of which is that if the plaintiff, in the former case, or the defendant, in the latter, is eventually successful, he will be awarded his costs of the interlocutory application in question, whereas if he is ultimately unsuccessful, each party pays his own costs of the interlocutory application. This type of order is the usual one on, for example, an application for an interlocutory injunction; if an interlocutory injunction is granted, the usual order is "plaintiff's costs in cause", and if it is refused, the usual order is "defendant's costs in cause". On a summons for directions the normal order is "costs in cause", on the basis that there has to be a summons, irrespective of what orders are made on the summons.

b   Payment into court

It has been noted that a payment into court (unless it is an element in a substantive defence) can affect only costs and not liability or damages. The effect is that if the successful plaintiff recovers no more than the amount paid in, in respect of one or more causes of action, he will be ordered to pay the defendant's costs of those causes of action from the date of payment in. He will still be entitled to his costs to the date of payment in, though these are often small consolation by comparison.[12]

c   County Courts Act 1984, ss. 19, 20

This is the most important of the statutory fetters on the judge's discretion as to costs. The purpose of the sections is to encourage parties to conduct their litigation in the county court rather than the High Court wherever possible. The sections provide that where an action founded on contract or tort is commenced in the High Court which is within the jurisdiction of the county court:[13]

(1) if the plaintiff recovers less than the lower limit (currently £600[14]) he will be entitled to no costs whatever;

(2) if the plaintiff recovers less than the higher limit (currently £3,000[14]) he will be entitled to costs on the appropriate county court scale only,

unless in either case the judge is satisfied that there was reasonable ground for supposing the amount recoverable in respect of the plaintiff's claim to be in excess of the county court maximum, or the defendant objected to the transfer of the action to the county court.

Because of this provision a party must hesitate before commencing a High Court action where the sum in dispute is within the county court limits. If in doubt a safer course is to commence proceedings in the county court and then apply to have them transferred to the High Court.

This provision does not operate if the plaintiff recovers any relief other than damages, such as an injunction.[15] Nor does it apply to counterclaims,

---

[12] O. 62, r. 5(6); *Hultquist* v. *Universal Pattern and Precision Engineering Co., Ltd.*, [1960] 2 Q.B. 467; [1960] 2 All E.R. 266. In cases in which the rules make no provision for payment into court, a similar objective may be attained by making an open offer (or in Lands Tribunal cases or arbitrations a "sealed offer"); see observations of CAIRNS, L.J. in *Calderbank* v. *Calderbank*, [1976] Fam. 93, at p. 105; [1975] 3 All E.R. 333, at p. 342.

[13] As to which see pp. 401–403, *post*.

[14] The figures may be increased by Order in Council under s. 145 of the Act.

[15] *Keates* v. *Woodward*, [1902] 1 K.B. 532. Nor does it apply where an award in excess of the limits is reduced by reason of the plaintiff's contributory negligence.

since a defendant has no control over the court in which an action is commenced. Where the sections do apply, however, they should be carefully borne in mind when advising a plaintiff whether to proceed in the High Court or in a county court, since the wrong choice may well cost the plaintiff the fruits of his action.

Having considered the question of which side must pay costs, the judge must decide what is to be the basis of taxation, for this will determine how much of an opponent's costs the loser will have to pay.

2   The taxation of costs

a   Bases of taxation

It was stated at the beginning of this chapter that there are two sets of costs; costs as between a solicitor and his own client, and costs as between the parties. The bases upon which these bills are taxed differ.

Regarding costs between a solicitor and his own client, each party must pay his own solicitor's costs as a contractual debt.[16] Very often the client will simply pay the bill presented to him without knowing or wishing to know of his right to have it taxed. He has, however, a right to have the bill taxed. In this case the bill will be taxed on a "solicitor and own client" basis. This means that "all costs are to be allowed except in so far as they are unreasonable in amount or have been unreasonably incurred."[17] All costs incurred with the express or implied approval of the client are deemed to be reasonable.[18] The result is that the client must pay his solicitor all costs unless they are both unauthorised and certified by the taxing master to be unreasonable, in which case the solicitor will have to pay them personally.

There is one exception to this principle. Where a litigant is legally aided, his solicitor recovers from the Fund his disbursements and 90 *per cent* of his profit costs taxed on a "common fund" basis.[19] This is far less than the complete indemnity which a "solicitor and own client" taxation provides. There is allowed, on this basis, a reasonable sum in respect of all costs reasonably incurred or incurred with the prior approval of the Area Committee. Reasonableness, both as to items and as to amount, depends upon all the circumstances of the case, such as its length, the sum involved and the complexity and novelty of the issues raised.

As to the costs between the parties, the court has jurisdiction to award a

---

[16] A lay litigant appearing in person used not to be entitled to remuneration for the time and labour expended in preparation of his case, though a solicitor acting in person was so entitled: *Buckland* v. *Watts*, [1970] 1 Q.B. 27; [1969] 2 All E.R. 985. This rule was, however, abrogated by the Litigants in Person (Costs and Expenses) Act 1975 which came into operation on 1 April 1976. The lay litigant is, however, restricted in that the maximum amount recoverable by him is two-thirds of the sum which would have been allowed to him if he had been represented by a solicitor and the maximum rate of remuneration for work done in leisure time is £6 an hour in respect of time reasonably spent: O. 62, r. 28A. A party employing a salaried solicitor is, generally, entitled to have his bill of costs taxed as though it were the bill of an independent solicitor: *Re Eastwood, Lloyds Bank, Ltd.* v. *Eastwood*, [1975] Ch. 112; [1974] 3 All E.R. 603.

[17] O. 62, r. 29(1); see p. 261, *ante*.

[18] O. 62, r. 29(2).

[19] Legal Aid Act 1974, Sched. 2; counsel is awarded 90 *per cent* of his fees.

fixed sum by way of costs to be paid by a party to his opponent.[20] In any other case the costs must be taxed. There are now three possible bases of taxation which may be ordered:

(1) party and party;
(2) common fund;
(3) solicitor and own client.

(1) "Party and party" is the usual basis of taxation between the parties and it is also the least generous to the party in whose favour the order is made. On this basis are allowed "all such costs as were necessary or proper for the attainment of justice or for enforcing or defending the rights of the party whose costs are being taxed".[1] The taxing master must decide not only which items are reasonable, but also what is a reasonable amount in respect of each item. As to items allowable the master will not allow costs which may be termed luxuries, or costs thrown away by neglect or excessive caution.[2] As to scale the taxing master will have regard to Order 62, Appendix 2, in which certain items carry fixed costs while others are discretionary as to amount. Where an item is discretionary Part X of Appendix 2 lists factors to which the master must have regard. These include the complexity and novelty of the questions involved, the skill, specialised knowledge and responsibility required by the solicitor or counsel, the amount involved and similar considerations.

(2) Where a party has conducted his litigation in a manner which incurs the disapproval of the court, for example where he has been dilatory and unco-operative[3] he may, as a penalty, be ordered to pay costs on a "common fund" basis. Where this is so a reasonable amount will be allowed to his opponent for all costs reasonably incurred.[4] This is more generous than a party and party taxation both as to amount and as to items allowable,[5] although it does not amount to a complete indemnity. In settlements of actions on behalf of infants, for example under the Fatal Accidents Act 1976, it is usual for costs to be paid on a common fund basis, the solicitors waiving any further entitlement to costs; this is so that the court, when deciding whether to approve the settlement, will know precisely how much

---

[20] O. 62, r. 9(4) (b). This must not exceed the amount a party would have to pay if the costs were taxed: *Wilmott* v. *Barker* (1881), 17 Ch.D. 772.

[1] O. 62, r. 28(2). However, where a country solicitor attended appeal proceedings in London personally, rather than instructing London agents, in a case of which he had been in charge for a number of years, it was held that his costs were, in the circumstances, reasonably incurred: *Garthwaite* v. *Sherwood*, [1976] 2 All E.R. 1015; [1976] 1 W.L.R. 705.

[2] *Smith* v. *Buller* (1875), L.R. 19 Eq. 473, at p. 475; the costs of taking a shorthand note and supplying transcripts thereof are not usually allowed on a party and party taxation (*Re Blyth* (1882), 10 Q.B.D. 207). The Royal Commission on Legal Services recommended abolition of this basis of taxation and the substitution of common fund as the normal basis of taxation (Report (Cmnd. 7648 of 1979) para. 37.32).

[3] See, for example, *Preston* v. *Preston*, [1982] Fam. 17; [1982] 1 All E.R. 41.

[4] O. 62, r. 28(3), (4). *Gibbs* v. *Gibbs*, [1952] P. 332; [1952] 1 All E.R. 942; *Reed* v. *Gray*, [1952] Ch. 337; [1952] 1 All E.R. 241. However where the taxing master believes the full value of the work done to have been allowed on a party and party taxation, he cannot allow any further costs on a common fund taxation (*Lyon* v. *Lyon*, [1953] P. 1; [1952] 2 All E.R. 831).

[5] E.g., the cost of taking a shorthand note may be allowed on a common fund taxation where it would not be allowed on a party and party taxation (*Re De Nicols*, [1906] W.N. 192).

the plaintiff will receive. However costs of such actions, if contested, will normally be on the party and party basis.[6]

It must be noted that this basis of taxation does not apply by reason only of one of the parties being legally aided. Where a party is awarded his costs out of the Legal Aid Fund under the Legal Aid Act 1974, s. 13 the basis of taxation will usually be party and party,[7] although the Fund pays the assisted litigant's costs on a common fund basis.

(3) The "solicitor and own client" basis of taxation applies between each party and his own solicitor. However, the court rarely orders a party to pay his opponent's costs on this basis except by consent, as a term of a settlement of the action. Orders have been made in cases of contempt of court[8] and are customarily made in favour of innocent third parties affected by *Mareva* injunctions, who have to go to court to obtain variations of the order.[9] In such cases, however, the party in whose favour the order is made has to prove that the costs were reasonable in amount and reasonably incurred and the fact that they were incurred with his approval is not conclusive[9] (as it is between a litigant and his own solicitor (*supra*)). Accordingly a party who is awarded costs must still pay the difference between a solicitor and own client taxation, which is the basis of his personal liability, and a party and party taxation, which he receives from his opponent. The extent of this liability for extra costs will depend upon the degree of extravagance which he has authorised in the conduct of his case.

b   Review of taxation

Any party who is dissatisfied with a taxation of a bill of costs may apply in writing to the same taxing master for a review of his decision. The application must be made within 14 days and must set out the disputed items and a summary of the grounds of objection.[10] The taxing master will then review his taxation of those items and certify his grounds and reasons for allowing, disallowing or altering the amount of disputed items.[11] If still dissatisfied either party may apply within 14 days by summons to a judge in chambers for an order for a further review. The judge may review the taxation himself or refer it to another taxing master.[12]

B   ENFORCEMENT OF JUDGMENTS

1   Judgments for the payment of money

a   Enforcement in the High Court

The judgment creditor's rights in respect of which he brought the action are

---

[6] Although in *K.* v. *J. M. P. Co., Ltd.*, [1976] Q.B. 85; [1975] 1 All E.R. 1030 the trial judge awarded costs on a common fund basis and the Court of Appeal dismissed an appeal against this order.

[7] Legal Aid Act 1974, s. 13(6); see p. 285, *ante.*

[8] *E.M.I. Records, Ltd.* v. *Ian Cameron Wallace, Ltd.*, [1983] Ch. 59; [1982] 2 All E.R. 980.

[9] *Project Development Co., Ltd. S.A.* v. *K.M.K. Securities, Ltd.* (*Syndicate Bank intervening*), [1983] 1 All E.R. 465; [1982] 1 W.L.R. 1470.

[10] O. 62, r. 33.

[11] O. 62, r. 34; see *Re Fraser, Leach* v. *Public Trustee*, [1958] 1 All E.R. 26; [1958] 1 W.L.R.

[12] O. 62, r. 35.

extinguished by the judgment. In their place he has a judgment debt. He will wish to enforce this debt which may consist of an award of damages and taxed costs, in addition to which may be included interest at a statutory rate from the date of judgment.[13] The judgment creditor may proceed to enforce the judgment[14] by any of the following five methods prescribed by Order 45, rule I:

    (i) writ of *fieri facias*;
    (ii) garnishee proceedings;
    (iii) a charging order;
    (iv) the appointment of a receiver;
    (v) writ of sequestration.

Writ of fieri facias (fi.-fa.)—This is directed to the sheriff of the county in which is situated the property which it is proposed to seize. Where the debtor has property in more than one county concurrent writs may be issued.[15] The writ commands the sheriff to cause to be made (*fieri facias*) in the name of Her Majesty out of the debtor's chattels a sum sufficient to satisfy the judgment debt and interest together with the costs of execution, unless the judgment is for less than £600 and does not include an order for costs. The sheriff may enter the judgment debtor's land (although he may not effect a forcible entry)[16] or the land of a third party if the debtor's goods are to be found thereon. He may seize and sell chattels, choses in action such as banknotes or cheques, promissory notes and a lease belonging to the judgment debtor, which he may assign. He cannot, however, seize property which is exempt from execution. This comprises freehold interests in land, equitable interests in land or chattels, fixtures attached to land, wearing apparel, bedding and tools and implements of trade to a specified value[17] and goods belonging to a third party. The latter provision operates to exempt property which is subject to a hire purchase agreement.

A writ of execution may be issued within the six years following the judgment or order, or later with leave.[18] It may be executed within 12 months of issue on any day not excepting Sunday.[19] There are several other cases in which leave is required, notably where the writ is to be executed against the

---

[13] The rate is currently 14 *per cent per annum*: Judgments Act 1838, ss. 17, 18 as amended by Judgments Act 1838 (Judgments Debts (Rate of Interest)) Order 1985, made under Administration of Justice Act 1970, s. 44. This means the date upon which judgment is pronounced, not the date when it is perfected by entry in the appropriate record book: *Parsons* v. *Mather and Platt, Ltd.*, [1977] 2 All E.R. 715; [1977] 1 W.L.R. 855.

[14] A stay of execution, for example pending trial of a counterclaim or appeal, is often ordered by the court. However, although this operates to stay execution by *fi.-fa.* (*infra*) it does not prevent the judgment creditor proceeding by one or more of the other methods of enforcement since these do not constitute "execution"; they are alternatives to execution: *Berliner Industriebank Aktiengesellschaft* v. *Jost*, [1971] 2 Q.B. 463; [1971] 2 All E.R. 1513. The Court of Appeal pointed out the need for some modification of the normal form of order.

[15] O. 47, r. 2.

[16] *Semayne's Case* (1604), 5 Co. Rep. 91.

[17] Small Debts Act 1845, s. 8 (as amended). The current exemptions are £100 for wearing apparel and bedding and £150 for tools of a trade: Protection from Execution (Prescribed Value) Order 1980, made under Administration of Justice Act 1956, s. 37(2); the Lord Chancellor has power to prescribe higher figures (*ibid.*).

[18] O. 46, r. 2(1) (*a*).

[19] The Sunday Observance Act 1677 having been repealed by the Statute Law (Repeals) Act 1969.

property of a partner in a firm where the judgment is against the firm,[20] against any person not a party to the original proceedings'such as an assignee and against persons represented in a representative action.[1]

It is not unusual for a sheriff to find that goods which he has seized or is about to seize in execution are claimed by a third party such as a hire purchase finance company. His proper course of action in such a situation is to interplead. To do this he issues an interpleader summons serving it on the execution creditor and the claimant.[2] All three parties attend before the master on the return day. The master may try the issue himself, direct an issue to be stated and tried or otherwise deal with the summons as he might deal with a stakeholder's interpleader summons.[3]

The sheriff must make arrangements for the sale of the property seized in execution. Such sale should normally be by public auction and should not take place on the judgment debtor's premises.[4] In practice the sheriff himself takes no part in enforcement and a local auctioneer, acting as a sheriff's officer, usually takes possession of the goods and arranges the auction, or they are left in the possession of the judgment debtor subject to periodic inspection by the sheriff's officers. This arrangement is termed "walking possession" of the goods. In practice the judgment debtor will invariably pay the debt if he can to avoid a sale of his property. Comparatively few sales take place because the court may stay execution on application if the applicant is unable from any cause to pay the money.[5]

Garnishee proceedings—The purpose of these proceedings is to enable the judgment creditor to have assigned to him the benefit of any debt owed by a third party (the garnishee) to the judgment debtor. A garnishee order will only issue in respect of a legal debt presently owing to the judgment debtor. A common object of garnishee proceedings is a credit balance at the judgment debtor's bank.[6] Earnings may be garnished but only where the right to them has accrued, so that future earnings cannot be garnished. There is, in

---

[20] O. 81, r. 5(4).

[1] O. 15, r. 12(3); p. 306, *ante*.

[2] O. 17, r. 1(1) (*b*).

[3] See p. 338, *ante*.

[4] O. 47, r. 6; *Watson* v. *Murray & Co.*, [1955] 2 Q.B. 1; [1955] 1 All E.R. 350.

[5] O. 47, r. 1(1) (*b*). It may also do so if there are special circumstances which render it inexpedient to enforce the judgment or order (O. 47, r. 1(*a*)); under this rule execution may be suspended where a debtor company has entered into an informal scheme of arrangement with the majority of its creditors and where not to stay execution would bring down the company and compel it into a winding-up or, at least, a statutory scheme of arrangement: *Prestige Publications, Ltd.* v. *Chelsea Football and Athletic Co., Ltd.* (1978), 122 Sol. Jo. 436. The case is a good illustration of the modern tendency of the courts not to permit one creditor to steal a march over other creditors of an insolvent debtor; see also *Rainbow* v. *Moorgate Properties, Ltd*, [1975] 2 All E.R. 821; [1975] 1 W.L.R. 788 (see p. 395, *post*); *Wilson* (*Birmingham*), *Ltd.* v. *Metropolitan Property Developments, Ltd.*, [1975] 2 All E.R. 821; *Roberts Petroleum, Ltd.* v. *Bernard Kenny, Ltd.*, [1983] 2 A.C. 192; [1983] 1 All E.R. 564. In these cases similar principles were applied to prevent creditors obtaining and enforcing garnishee orders and charging orders (as to which see *infra*) so as to obtain preference over other creditors.

[6] *Rogers* v. *Whitely*, [1892] A.C. 118. The Supreme Court Act 1981, s. 40 brought within the scope of garnishee orders "any deposit account with a bank or other deposit-taking institution"; this includes, for example, the National Savings Bank and the Post Office. A debt which is not assignable, such as state pension, maintenance or the pay of a member of the armed forces, cannot be attached.

fact, no way of seizing or intercepting the judgment debtor's future earnings in the Queen's Bench Division.[7]

The judgment debtor may be required to attend before a master to submit to an oral examination as to what debts are owing to him and as to what property or means, if any, he has of satisfying the judgment.[8] When these matters have been ascertained, by examination or otherwise, the judgment creditor may apply *ex parte* on affidavit for an order *nisi* which is served on the garnishee personally and, unless the court otherwise directs, on the judgment debtor.[9] This order calls upon the garnishee either to pay the debt, or so much of it as may be sufficient to satisfy the balance of the judgment debt, to the judgment creditor or show cause for not so doing. If the garnishee fails to comply or show cause the order is made absolute and execution may issue against the garnishee to the extent of his obligation, which is, in effect, assigned to the execution creditor.[10] If the garnishee disputes liability to pay the debt claimed to be due from him[11] the master may determine the question at issue summarily or determine the manner in which it shall be tried, no consent being required to trial before a master.[12]

Where money is standing to the credit of the judgment debtor in court, garnishee proceedings cannot be taken in respect of that money but the judgment creditor can apply by summons for an order for the payment out of all or any part of such money. This summons must be served on the judgment debtor at least 7 days before the return day.[13]

Charging order—The judgment creditor may apply *ex parte* on affidavit for an order imposing a charge on property of the kind specified in section 2 of the Charging Orders Act 1979. This comprises any interest held by the debtor beneficially in (1) land; (2) securities of various kinds; (3) funds in court; and (4) any interest under a trust. In addition where the debtor is a trustee of property his interest may be the subject of a charging order if the judgment or order was made against him in his capacity as trustee or the whole beneficial interest under the trust is his alone or shared with others who are all jointly liable to the creditor for the same debt. Thus, for example, if the property in question is a house in the joint names of husband and wife, the legal estate may be charged if both the husband and wife are liable to the judgment creditor, whereas if only one is liable, then all that can be charged is the beneficial interest of that one.

An order may also be made charging a partnership interest.

(1) If he discovers that the judgment debtor has land or an interest in land within the jurisdiction, the judgment creditor may apply for an order

---

[7] *Mapelson* v. *Sears* (1911), 105 L.T. 639. Future earnings may be attached in respect of a maintenance order under the Attachment of Earnings Act 1971, s. 1. Attachment of earnings orders may be obtained in respect of judgment debts only by transferring the judgment to a county court; see p. 413, *post*.

[8] O. 48, r. 1.

[9] O. 49, r. 3(1). The immediate effect of the order is to bind the debt specified in the order from the moment of service of the order.

[10] O. 49, r. 4. The order absolute may be enforced in the same manner as any other order for the payment of money.

[11] He may, for example, allege a counterclaim against the judgment debtor: *Hale* v. *Victoria Plumbing Co., Ltd., and En-Tout-Cas Co., Ltd.*, [1966] 2 Q.B. 746; [1966] 2 All E.R. 672.

[12] O. 49, r. 5.

[13] O. 49, r. 9.

creating a charge over the land or over the interest in the land.[14] An order *nisi* is made in the first instance specifying the time and place for further consideration of the matter and imposing the charge until that time. Unless the judgment debtor pays the debt or shows cause at that time the order will be made absolute. The charge so created is a general equitable charge and the judgment creditor should register it in the Land Charges Registry under the provisions of the Land Charges Act 1925. There are two important advantages of registration; a purchaser takes the land subject to the charge (registration amounting to notice) and priority is obtained over subsequent chargees. A land charge may be enforced by an order for sale in the Chancery Division.[15]

(2) If the judgment debtor has government stock or stock or shares in any registered company these cannot be seized in execution of a writ of *fi.-fa.* because a share certificate is not a negotiable instrument. It is simply evidence of obligations owed by the company which has issued it to the person named in the certificate. The judgment creditor's proper course is to apply for an order *nisi* creating a charge over the shares.[16] The effect of such an order is that no subsequent disposition by the judgment debtor is valid as against the judgment creditor. Unless the judgment debtor shows cause the charging order is made absolute. There is no provision for registering a charge on securities corresponding to the registration of land charges. The judgment creditor, to prevent a disposition of the securities by the judgment debtor, must serve on the company in which the shares are held a "stop notice". The effect is that the company on whom the notice is served must not register a transfer of the shares without serving notice on the judgment creditor, who may apply to the Chancery Division for an order prohibiting the transfer.[17] After the expiration of six months from the charging order *nisi* the judgment creditor may proceed to realise his charge by an order for sale obtainable in the Chancery Division.

(3) The judgment debtor may have an interest in funds or securities in court. This might occur, for example, where the judgment debtor has made a payment into court as security for costs. The court may make a "stop order" prohibiting any dealing with the whole or any part of the funds in question. Application for such an order is by summons in the cause or matter relating to the funds in court or, if there is no such cause or matter, by originating summons.[18] The summons must be served on every person whose interest may be affected by the order and on the Accountant General. The judgment creditor may enforce his charge by applying by summons for an order for payment out of the money or so much of it as is sufficient to satisfy his charge.[19]

(4) In relation to partnership property the sheriff cannot levy execution upon property belonging to a partnership in which the debtor is a partner

---

[14] O. 50, r. 1. This was introduced by the Administration of Justice Act 1956, s. 35(1) to replace the old writ of *elegit*.

[15] O. 31, r. 1.

[16] Charging Orders Act 1979, s. 2(2) (*b*); the order may extend to any dividend or interest payable (*ibid.*, s. 2(3)).

[17] O. 50, r. 15.

[18] O. 50, r. 10.

[19] O. 49, r. 9. If the judgment debtor is insolvent the judgment creditor is in the position of a secured creditor to the extent of the sum in court: *Sherratt (W.A.), Ltd.* v. *John Bromley (Church Stretton), Ltd.*, [1985] 1 All E.R. 216.

(unless the judgment is against the firm). Nonetheless the judgment creditor may apply by summons to the master for an order charging the partner's interest in the partnership property.[20] The jurisdiction to create such a charge derives from section 23 of the Partnership Act 1890. The creation of a charge on a partnership interest gives the other partners the option of purchasing the interest charged.[1] Failing this the judgment creditor may apply by summons for the appointment of a receiver who will receive on behalf of the judgment creditor money accruing from the debtor's interest in the partnership.[2]

The power of the court to make charging orders, and indeed garnishee orders, is a discretionary one. It will be appreciated that the effect of such orders is to give the plaintiff priority over unsecured creditors of the defendant. Accordingly such orders should not be made against an insolvent defendant so as to place the plaintiff at an advantage over other creditors if it would be inequitable so to do.[3]

Appointment of a receiver by way of equitable execution.[4]—This is a method of enforcement directed at the interception of certain classes of income and profits before they reach the debtor so that he does not have the opportunity of disposing of them to the detriment of the judgment creditor. The judgment creditor may apply by summons or motion to the court to appoint some person as a receiver to receive income such as rents or profits in respect of any interest in land, legal or equitable, or of any interest in chattels which could not be reached by a writ of *fi.-fa.*[5] It should be stressed, however, that a receiver cannot be appointed to receive the judgment debtor's future earnings of employment for, as stated earlier, there is no direct means of attaching earnings in the Queen's Bench Division.

Before appointing a receiver the court will consider whether the probable costs of the appointment are justified by the amount claimed and the amount likely to be recovered by the receiver, and may direct an enquiry on these matters before making an appointment.[6] The general powers and duties of receivers appointed by the court are contained in Order 30. The receiver is usually required to provide a guarantee as security for what he receives as receiver.[7] The receiver is allowed a proper remuneration which is fixed by court. His obligation is to submit accounts to the court for approval as and when ordered to do so and to pay into court the amounts shown by his accounts to be due.[8]

Prior to 1971, committal for contempt of court was an indirect means of enforcing a judgment debt. However section 11 of the Administration of

---

[20] O. 81, r. 10.
[1] Partnership Act 1890, s. 23(3).
[2] O. 51, r. 3; O. 30; *infra.*
[3] *Rainbow* v. *Moorgate Properties, Ltd.*, [1975] 2 All E.R. 821; [1975] 1 W.L.R. 788; *Roberts Petroleum, Ltd.* v. *Bernard Kenny, Ltd.*, [1983] 2 A.C. 192; [1983] 1 All E.R. 564 (p. 392, fn. 5, *supra*); see also, to similar effect, Charging Orders Act 1979, s. 1(5).
[4] O. 51, r. 3. The expression "equitable execution" is explained by the fact that this method of enforcement originated in the Court of Chancery. It is, however, misleading since it is not confined to equitable interests, nor is it a method of execution. It is a method of enforcement alternative to execution: see *Re Shepherd* (1889), 43 Ch.D. 131, at p. 137.
[5] The power is now contained in Supreme Court Act 1981, s. 37.
[6] O. 51, r. 1.
[7] O. 30, r. 2.
[8] O. 30, rr. 3–6.

Justice Act 1970 limited the jurisdiction of the High Court to commit to prison in respect of non-payment of a debt due under a judgment or order to cases of default in respect of maintenance orders. Since these orders are invariably made in the Family Division, committal in the Queen's Bench Division for non-payment of a debt is effectively abolished (though, as will be seen, it remains a sanction for failure to comply with orders other than orders for the payment of money).

There remains, however, one process of contempt in respect of failure to pay judgment debts—the procedure by writ of sequestration.

Writ of sequestration[9]—In cases of contempt of court a committal order is sometimes accompanied by a writ of sequestration. The two have much in common in that they are both indirect methods of enforcement being in the nature of punitive measures. As indicated above, although committal to prison in respect of a judgment debt (other than a maintenance order) has been abolished, a writ of sequestration may still issue in respect of continuous failure to comply with an order for the payment of money, although the procedure is very rarely used in such cases, save occasionally against corporate bodies. A writ of sequestration may issue in any case in which a person refuses or neglects to do an act within a specified time or disobeys an order requiring him to abstain from doing some act.[9] The writ commissions not less than four persons[10] to enter upon and take possession of all the real and personal estate of the judgment debtor and to keep the same under sequestration until the debtor complies with the judgment. If a fine has been imposed for contempt of court and remains unpaid, a writ of sequestration may issue to enforce payment of the fine. The procedure on application is by notice of motion for leave to issue the writ stating the grounds of the application and accompanied by an affidavit in support.[11] The application must be heard in open court.[12]

A writ of sequestration is a practical alternative to committal where the judgment debtor is a corporation and the writ may issue, with leave, against the property of any director or other officer of the body.

In relation to a writ of sequestration, the position of third parties is similar to that of third parties in relation to injunctions; although they are not directly bound by the order, they must not knowingly take any step which would obstruct enforcement of the order. Thus, for example, a bank is under a duty to disclose to sequestrators balances which are held to the credit of the contemner and to pay over such sums on demand (unless a third party, such as the bank itself, has a prior charge on the balance).[13]

---

9 O. 45, r. 5.
10 As to the position of sequestrators and their potential liability for negligence, see *Inland Revenue Commissioners* v. *Hoogstraten*, [1984] 3 All E.R. 25; [1984] 3 W.L.R. 933.
11 O. 46, r. 5.
12 Except in the special cases set out in O. 52, r. 6 where the application may be heard in private, notably where the case involves the wardship, adoption, guardianship, custody or maintenance of infants, proceedings relating to mental patients, cases where a secret process, discovery or invention is involved or where it appears to the court that in the interests of the administration of justice or for reasons of national security the application should be heard in private.
13 *Eckman* v. *Midland Bank, Ltd.*, [1973] Q.B. 519; [1973] 1 All E.R. 609, a decision of the now defunct National Industrial Relations Court, arising out of the refusal of the Amalgamated Union of Engineering Workers to recognise or comply with orders of that court.

b Other methods of enforcing judgments for the payment of money

County court enforcement—A judgment of the High Court for the payment
of money may be enforced in a county court as if it were a judgment of the
county court.[14] This is done by registering the judgment in the county court
for the district where the debtor resides. There are two methods of enforcement available in county courts which are not available in the Queen's Bench
Division—judgment summonses and attachment of earnings orders. The
primary advantage of the judgment summons, as opposed to the power of
the High Court to require a debtor to attend an examination as to his means
under Order 48, rule 1, is that the county court has power to make an order
for payment by instalments in the first instance. Secondly, an attachment of
earnings order may now be obtained, under the provisions of the Attachment of Earnings Act 1971, in a county court in respect of a High Court
judgment debt. Both of these methods of enforcement are extremely practical in relation to debtors who have insufficient assets to satisfy the judgment
but who have earnings out of which the debt, or at least part of it, might be
recoverable.[15]

Bankruptcy—Where the debtor's total debts amount to at least £200 the
judgment creditor may serve upon him a bankruptcy notice calling upon him
to pay the judgment debt within ten days. Failure to comply by the judgment
debtor constitutes an "act of bankruptcy" and the judgment creditor may
proceed to institute bankruptcy proceedings.[16] Bankruptcy proceedings are,
in general, an unsatisfactory method of enforcement though the mere threat
of bankruptcy proceedings may be a sufficient sanction where the judgment
debtor is a person, such as a solicitor, whose livelihood cannot survive
bankruptcy.

2 Judgments and orders other than for the payment of money

a Judgments for possession of land[17]

A judgment or order for the giving of possession of land may be enforced by
any one or more of the following three methods:

(1) *Writ of possession*—This is the direct method of enforcement. It directs
the sheriff to enter the land and cause the plaintiff to have possession of it.
The writ cannot be issued without leave,[18] application for which is *ex parte*
on affidavit, and leave cannot be granted unless it is shown that every person
in actual possession of the whole or any part of the land has received sufficient notice of the proceedings to enable him to apply to the court for any
relief to which he may be entitled, such as relief against forfeiture.[19] In

---

[14] County Courts Act 1984, s. 105.
[15] For details of procedure see pp. 416–418, *post*.
[16] Bankruptcy Act 1914, ss. 1(1), 4, as amended by the Insolvency Act 1976 which increased the
    figure from £50 (which had stood since 1914); the figure may be increased or reduced by
    regulations (Act of 1976, s. 1(2)).
[17] O. 45, r. 3.
[18] Except where the judgment or order was given or made in a mortgage action (O. 45, r. 3. (2))
    or where the order was made in summary proceedings for possession of land against trespas-
    sers following the issue of an originating summons under Order 113 (O. 113, r. 7); as to this
    procedure, see p. 381, *ante*.
[19] O. 45, r. 3(3).

practice judgments or orders for the possession of land are always enforced in this way.

(2) *Order of committal*; and (3) *writ of sequestration* are, in theory at least, indirect methods of enforcement but are almost never employed in this context. The procedure on application for leave to issue a writ of sequestration has already been noted; committal procedure is considered below.

b   Judgments for delivery of goods[20]

The appropriate writ of execution for a judgment for the delivery of goods depends upon whether or not the judgment contains an alternative provision for payment of the assessed value of the goods.

Writ of specific delivery—This is the appropriate writ where the judgment orders the delivery of specific goods without an alternative provision for the payment of their assessed value. It directs the sheriff to seize the goods described in the writ and deliver them to the plaintiff.

Writ of delivery—This is appropriate where the judgment orders the delivery of goods with an alternative provision for payment of their assessed value. The writ directs the sheriff to seize the goods described and deliver them to the plaintiff and, if he cannot obtain the goods, to levy execution upon the goods and chattels of the defendant to an extent sufficient to realise the assessed value of the goods. If the alternative course is adopted the writ has the same effect as a writ of *fi.-fa.*

Whether a writ of delivery or a writ of specific delivery is issued the sheriff is authorised to enforce by execution the payment of any money ordered to be paid by way of damages or costs by the judgment or order which is to be enforced by the writ together with the costs of execution and interest. *Order of committal* and *writ of sequestration* are theoretically available as indirect methods of enforcement but, as in the case of orders for the possession of land, their use is generally inappropriate in this context.

c   Judgments to do or abstain from doing any act

Where the judgment or order requires the defendant to perform any act other than the payment of money or the delivery of goods or land or requires him to abstain from doing any act, it is enforceable only by: (1) *order of committal*; and (2) *writ of sequestration*.

The order to which these rules apply may have been, for example, an injunction[1] (mandatory or prohibitory), an order to deliver an account, an order to produce a document or an order to answer an interrogatory.

Procedure by writ of sequestration has already been noted. In cases of contempt a writ of sequestration is an appropriate method of enforcement against a corporate body and is often joined with a committal order in respect of the officers of the corporate body.[2]

---

[20] O. 45, r. 4.

[1] An undertaking given to the court is equivalent to an injunction against the person giving the undertaking so that breach of the undertaking is contempt of court: cf. *Biba, Ltd.* v. *Stratford Investments, Ltd.*, [1973] Ch. 281; [1972] 3 All E.R. 1041.

[2] See, for example, *Worthington* v. *Ad Lib Club, Ltd.*, [1965] Ch. 236; [1964] 3 All E.R. 674.

Committal orders—A committal order is an order committing a person to prison for contempt of court. An order may be made where a person required by a judgment or order to do an act within a time specified in the judgment or order refuses or neglects to do it within that time,[3] or a person disobeys a judgment or order requiring him to abstain from doing an act. A master or registrar has no power to make a committal order. The order is made by a judge following a motion in open court.[4] Notice of motion must have been served on the person sought to be committed together with a copy of the affidavit which must support the application. Personal service is generally required.[5] Committal must be either for a fixed period although earlier discharge may be ordered if the court deems that the contemner has "purged his contempt" and releases him, generally on his undertaking to perform (or abstain from repeating, as the case may be) the act in respect of which he was committed. As an alternative to imprisonment there is jurisdiction to impose a fine for contempt.

It was formerly held that a person might not be committed for a mere neglect as opposed to a "wilful and contumacious disobedience of a court order".[6] However in *Knight* v. *Clifton*[7] the Court of Appeal rejected this principle and asserted that in proceedings for committal for breach of an order of the court there is no need to prove that the conduct in question was wilful or contumacious; when an injunction prohibits an act, the performance of that act is a contempt irrespective of questions of intention unless otherwise stated on the face of the order. This authority was cited with apparent approval by the House of Lords in *Heaton's Transport (St. Helens), Ltd.* v. *Transport and General Workers Union*,[8] inasmuch as the House of Lords accepted that wilfulness was not an element in contempt of court; however it appeared also to accept that conduct which was "casual or accidental and unintentional" would not amount to contempt. To this extent the assertion in *Knight* v. *Clifton* that questions of intention are irrelevant is probably too wide.

---

3 Save where the act is the payment of money, in which case (except in the case of maintenance orders) there is no power of committal (Administration of Justice Act 1970, s. 11); see p. 396, *ante*.
4 Except in the cases set out in O. 52, r. 6 in which the court may sit in private; see p. 396 (n), *ante*.
5 O. 52, r. 4.
6 See for example, *Worthington* v. *Ad Lib Club, Ltd.*, [1965] Ch. 236; [1964] 3 All E.R. 674.
7 [1971] Ch. 700; [1971] 2 All E.R. 378, disapproving *Worthington* v. *Ad Lib Club, Ltd.* (*supra*); see also *Re Mileage Conference of Tyre Manufacturers' Agreement*, [1966] 2 All E.R. 849; [1966] 1 W.L.R. 1137 in which breach of an undertaking was held to be contempt where the persons concerned had taken all reasonable care to avoid a breach.
8 [1973] A.C. 15; [1972] 3 All E.R. 101.

CHAPTER 21

Procedure in County Courts

A CONSTITUTION AND JURISDICTION OF COUNTY COURTS

1 Origins and constitution

It will be recalled that one of the principal deficiencies of the English legal system, until the reforms of the nineteenth century, was the lack of a system of courts to deal with civil actions involving only a small amount of money.[1] As a result, the modern county courts were established by the County Courts Act 1846. The upper limit of the new courts' jurisdiction was originally fixed at £20 but this figure has been progressively increased and presently stands at £5,000 in most cases. The jurisdiction of the county courts is now principally contained in the County Courts Act 1984, a consolidating statute. Procedure in the county courts is regulated by the County Court Rules made by a Rule Committee under powers conferred by the Act.[2] The rules presently in force are the County Court Rules 1981 (as amended). These and other rules relating to county court practice and procedure are to be found in the County Court Practice (the "Green Book") which, although not an official publication, is accepted as authoritative in the same way as the White Book is accepted in the Supreme Court.

England and Wales is divided into districts each having one or more county courts.[3] These courts are, for administrative convenience, grouped into circuits with one or more judges presiding over each circuit. Each court has a sitting at least once a month.

a Judges of county courts

The office of county court judge, as such, was abolished by the Courts Act 1971 and on the date on which that Act came into operation, January 1st,

---

[1] See p. 77, *ante.*

[2] Section 75. In any case not expressly provided for in the Act or Rules, the principles of High Court procedure apply (s. 76); see *Williamson* v. *Rider*, [1963] 1 Q.B. 89; [1962] 2 All E.R. 268.

[3] *Ibid.*, ss. 1, 2; the places at which county courts are to be held and the names of those courts are specified in the Civil Courts Order 1983; they are set out in Appendix 1 of the Green Book.

1972, all existing county court judges automatically became Circuit judges.[4] Although every Circuit judge is, by virtue of his office, enabled to sit in any county court the Lord Chancellor is bound to assign one or more Circuit judges to each county court district.[5]

b   Registrars

These are appointed by the Lord Chancellor and must be solicitors of at least 7 years' standing.[6] The county court registrar exercises both an administrative and a judicial function. In his administrative capacity he maintains the court records, arranges for the issue and service of summonses, accounts for money paid into court and exercises a large number of similar functions. In practice he delegates much of this work to subordinate court officers, notably the clerks and bailiffs. The scope of his judicial function is narrower than that of the judge. He has power to hear and determine (*a*) any action or matter in which the defendant fails to appear at the hearing or admits the claim; (*b*) any action or matter in which the sum claimed or the amount involved does not exceed £500; (*c*) actions in which mortgagees of land claim possession; and (*d*) by leave of the judge and with the consent of the parties, any other action or matter.[7] He also deals with interlocutory matters and the taxation of costs.

2   Jurisdiction

Because county courts are the creation of statute, their jurisdiction derives entirely from statute. The general jurisdiction of the county court is to be found in the County Courts Act 1984. Nevertheless extensive jurisdiction is conferred upon the county court by other statutes. This latter jurisdiction is usually concurrent with the High Court or magistrates' courts although in a few cases it is exclusive to the county court.[8]

a   Jurisdiction under the County Courts Act 1984

The jurisdiction of the county court under the 1984 Act may be classified as follows:

(1) *Actions founded on contract or tort* where the debt, demand or damage claimed does not exceed "the county court limit" (currently £5,000) except actions for defamation.[9] The plaintiff may not divide his cause of action so as to bring separate actions on the same facts claiming less than the limit in

---

4   Courts Act 1971, s. 16; Sch. 2; as to the position of Circuit judges, see p. 201, *ante*.
5   County Courts Act 1984, s. 5. In addition every judge of the Court of Appeal, every judge of the High Court and every Recorder is capable of sitting as a county court judge if he consents so to do and may be required, under s. 5(3), so to act on such occasions as the Lord Chancellor considers desirable. It is difficult to envisage any judge of the Court of Appeal or High Court sitting as a county court judge.
6   *Ibid.*, s. 9; the Lord Chancellor may appoint assistant registrars (s. 7) and deputy registrars (s. 8), who must be similarly qualified.
7   C.C.R., O. 21, r. 5.
8   For example, under the Rent Act 1977, the Race Relations act 1976 and the Domestic Violence and Matrimonial Proceedings Act 1976, s. 1.
9   County Courts Act 1984, s. 15; under s. 145 the limit may be raised by Order in Council.

each. He can, however, abandon his right to recover any damages in excess of the limit.[10] In an action for the return of specific goods the county court has jurisdiction if the value of the goods claimed does not exceed the limit. Where the plaintiff claims an injunction or a declaration the court has jurisdiction to grant these remedies but only ancillary to a claim for relief (usually debt or damages) which is otherwise within the substantive jurisdiction. Accordingly if the plaintiff seeks, for example, an injunction to compel the defendant to abate a nuisance, he must claim damages, even if only nominal, to give the county court jurisdiction. This is obviously artificial[11] and, in actions relating to land (which are within the rateable value limits applicable under s. 21 (*infra*)) it is provided[12] that a county court may grant an injunction or declaration other than by way of ancillary relief.

Section 18 of the Act enables the parties to confer jurisdiction on a particular county court in any action which, if commenced in the High Court, would have been assigned to the Queen's Bench Division. This section operates to extend the jurisdiction of a particular county court to any action in contract or tort, including such actions as libel and slander, up to any amount. The parties must agree to this increased jurisdiction by memorandum signed by the parties or their solicitors.

(2) *Actions for the recovery of land* or where the title to any hereditament or right over land is in question, where the net annual value for rating does not exceed the county court limit (currently £1,000).[13]

(3) *Equity proceedings* where the sum involved does not exceed the county court limit (currently £30,000) or more by written memorandum signed by the parties or their solicitors, and then only where the proceedings fall within certain specified categories. These categories are set out in section 23 of the Act and include: the administration of estates of deceased persons, the declaration and execution of trusts, the foreclosure and redemption of mortgages,[14] the rectification or cancellation of deeds, the maintenance and advancement out of trust funds of infants and proceedings for relief against fraud or mistake. These categories cannot be extended even if both parties are willing to extend them.

(4) *Admiralty proceedings*, but only in certain specified proceedings and only in county courts which have been appointed by the Lord Chancellor to exercise jurisdiction in admiralty matters.[15] All these courts, with the excep-

---

10 County Courts Act 1984, s. 17.

11 See, for example, *Hatt & Co. (Bath), Ltd.* v. *Pearce*, [1978] 2 All E.R. 474; [1978] 1 W.L.R. 885 in which the plaintiffs, in order to pave the way for an application for an interlocutory injunction to restrain the defendant from continuing employment in breach of covenant, issued proceedings claiming £1 damages for breach of contract, a course which the Court of Appeal held to be valid.

12 County Courts Act 1984, s. 22.

13 *Ibid.*, s. 21. The title to land may come in question in an action which is not for the recovery of the land but only for damages, for example in trespass, where the defendant sets up his title as a defence. The value for rating is determined by reference to the valuation list in force at the time that the proceedings are commenced (s. 147(2)).

14 Mortgage proceedings outside the financial limit may nevertheless be within the county court jurisdiction if there is a claim for the recovery of land having a net annual value for rating not exceeding £1000; see *West Penwith Rural District Council* v. *Gunnell*, [1968] 2 All E.R. 1005; [1968] 1 W.L.R. 1153.

15 County Courts Act 1984, ss. 26, 27.

tion of the Mayor's and City of London Court, are on or near the coast. The admiralty proceedings in question are set out in section 27 of the Act. They include claims for damage to a ship or for damage to or loss of goods carried by sea, towage and pilotage disputes. The limit of jurisdiction is in each case £5,000 (or £15,000 in salvage claims), but this limit can be increased by memorandum of agreement, although the extent of the proceedings over which the county court has jurisdiction cannot be so increased.

(5) *Contentious probate proceedings* where there is an application for a grant or revocation of probate or letters of administration, where the net value of the estate at the time of death was less than the county court limit (currently £30,000). The applicant must swear an affidavit containing the value of the estate and also the place of abode of the deceased, since only the county court for that district has jurisdiction.[16]

(6) *Set-off and counterclaim*. Where there is a counterclaim, or set-off and counterclaim, which involves a claim outside the jurisdiction of the county court, such as a claim in respect of libel or a claim in tort for more than £5,000, the Act expressly provides that the county court shall have jurisdiction to hear and determine the whole proceedings, notwithstanding.[17] However, in such a case, any party may apply to the High Court for an order that the proceedings be transferred in whole or in part to the High Court.[18] The master may then order the whole proceedings to be determined in the High Court, or in a county court, or that the counterclaim, or set-off and counterclaim, be transferred to the High Court leaving the plaintiff's claim to be determined in the county court.

(7) *Proceedings transferred from High Court*. Section 40 of the Act specifies circumstances in which proceedings may be transferred from the High Court to a county court. These will be considered below[19] but at this stage it should be noted that one circumstance is that in which the High Court considers that the proceedings "are not likely to raise any important question of law or fact and are suitable for determination by a county court". Where an action is transferred, the jurisdiction of the county court is unlimited.

b   Jurisdiction under other statutes

Apart from the County Courts Act 1984, there are more than 150 statutes which confer jurisdiction in certain matters either on the county courts generally, or upon particular county courts. Of these mention may be made of the Rent Act 1977 and the Hire-Purchase Act 1965 both of which are fertile sources of county court litigation. Special attention should be drawn to the Matrimonial Causes Act 1967 which conferred jurisdiction upon those county courts nominated by the Lord Chancellor as "divorce county courts" to hear undefended matrimonial causes,[20] and to the Domestic Violence and Matrimonial Proceedings Act 1976 under which a county court judge may, by injunction, exercise powers which include restraining a party from molesting the other party or a child living with the applicant, excluding one

---

[16] *Ibid.*, s. 32.
[17] *Ibid.*, s. 43; *Hardwicke* v. *Gilroy*, [1944] K.B. 460; [1944] 1 All E.R. 521.
[18] *Ibid.*, s. 42(1) (c).
[19] See p. 422, *post*.
[20] See p. 419, *post*, for a brief outline of procedure under the Matrimonial Causes Rules 1977.

party from the "matrimonial home" or requiring him (or her) to permit the other to enter and remain in the home.[1]

B   PROCEDURE IN THE COUNTY COURT

1   Actions

a   Choice of county court

Unlike that of the High Court, the jurisdiction of county courts is local. This means that the plaintiff must usually commence proceedings:

(1) in the court for the district in which the defendant or one of the defendants resides or carries on business; or

(2) in the court for the district where the cause of action arose wholly or in part.[2]

If the plaintiff commences proceedings in any other county court the judge of that court may transfer the proceedings to a court which does have jurisdiction, order them to be struck out, or allow them to continue in his court.[3]

b   Parties

The County Court Rules regulating the choice and joinder of parties are parallel to the provisions of the Rules of the Supreme Court. Thus two or more persons may be joined as plaintiffs or defendants if their rights or liabilities arise out of the same transaction or series of transactions and, if separate actions were brought, any common question of law or fact would arise.[4]

Parties to whom special rules of procedure apply in the High Court, such as partners, companies and persons under disability, are in a similar position in the county court. An infant must generally, as in the High Court, sue by his "next friend" who must file an undertaking to be responsible for costs.[5] However, an infant may sue in his own name for any sum not exceeding the county court limit which may be due to him for wages or piece work or for work as a servant.[6]

---

[1] Act of 1976, s. 1. The Act extends to men and women living together but not married to one another and "matrimonial home" is construed accordingly. Under s. 2 the judge may attach to the injunction a "power of arrest" which gives to police officers a power to arrest without warrant persons whom they reasonably suspect of being in breach of such an injunction. Nor can the police grant bail in such a case, but the person arrested must be brought before a judge within 24 hours of his arrest.

[2] O. 4, r. 2(1). Oddly enough the matrimonial jurisdiction of divorce county courts is not local; a petition may be filed in any divorce county court (Matrimonial Causes Rules, 1977, r. 12(1)).

[3] O. 16, r. 2.

[4] O. 5, r. 2.

[5] O. 10, r. 2.

[6] County Courts Act 1984, s. 47.

c Commencement of proceedings

All proceedings, the object of which is to obtain relief against any other person, must (subject to any express provision to the contrary) be brought by *action* and commenced by *plaint*.[7] An action in which a claim is made for any relief other than the payment of money is termed a "fixed date action"; every other action is a "default action".[8] The plaintiff or his solicitor commences a default or fixed date action by filing in the court office a request for the summons (formerly called a *praecipe*) setting out the names, addresses and descriptions of all parties and the nature and amount of the claim. He must also file particulars of claim and the sum claimed with a copy for each defendant. Upon filing these documents the registrar issues to the plaintiff a plaint note containing the title of the action, the reference number of the plaint and a date and time for the return day. He also prepares, from the plaintiff's request, and issues a summons to which are annexed the particulars of claim. The summons and particulars are then served on every defendant at least 21 clear days before the return day.[9] The defendant is also served with forms of admission, defence and counterclaim.

A county court summons may be served by the plaintiff or his agent, in which case he must file an affidavit of service,[10] but it is usually served by the county court bailiff. The summons may be served by an officer of the court sending it by first-class post to the defendant at the address stated in the request for the summons or, if the plaintiff so requests, by the plaintiff delivering the summons to the defendant personally.[11] The defendant's solicitor may accept service on the defendant's behalf, in which case he must indorse on the bailiff's copy summons a statement to this effect. Substituted service may be ordered by the registrar following application by the plaintiff on affidavit. A summons may not be served out of the jurisdiction without leave of the judge. The circumstances in which leave may be granted are similar (though not identical) to those contained in Order 11, rule 1 of the Rules of the Supreme Court.[12]

d Defence

A defendant who is served with a summons has open to him the following courses of action.[13]

---

[7] O. 3, r. 1.

[8] O. 3, r. 2.

[9] O. 7, r. 10(5).

[10] O. 7, r. 6.

[11] O. 7, r. 10. Service by post is deemed to be effected on the seventh day after the date on which the summons was sent (O. 10, r. 7(3)). Consequently service may be deemed to be validly effected even though the defendant never actually receives the summons. The defendant's remedy is to apply to set aside judgment, though this is a matter of discretion rather than of right; see *Cooper* v. *Scott-Farnell*, [1969] 1 All E.R. 178; [1969] 1 W.L.R. 120. However where a summons sent by post has been returned undelivered, notice of non-service is sent to the plaintiff who is informed that he may request bailiff service; if he so requests the court bailiff then effects service by (*a*) inserting the summons through the letterbox at the address stated in the request for the summons; or (*b*) delivering the summons to some person, apparently not less than 16 years old, at that address; or (*c*) delivering the summons to the defendant personally (O. 10, r. 7(4)).

[12] O. 8, r. 2; see p. 315, *ante*. Service on a Sunday, Christmas Day or Good Friday is prohibited except, in case of urgency, with leave of the court: O. 7, r. 3.

[13] O. 9.

(1) In any action for debt or damages he may within 14 days of service pay into court the whole amount of the claim; the action is then stayed and if the defendant also pays in the costs stated on the summons he will not be liable for any further costs unless the court otherwise orders.[14] Alternatively he may pay into court some lesser amount, either in satisfaction of the plaintiff's claims or on account of a sum admitted by him to be due to the plaintiff. In the former case the payment in operates in the same way as a payment into court in the High Court under R.S.C. Order 22.[15] Thus if the payment in is accepted, the proceedings are stayed in respect of the causes of action to which the payment in relates while if the plaintiff goes on but then, at the trial, fails to "beat the payment in" he will normally be held liable for all costs subsequent to the date of payment in.

(2) Where the defendant admits the whole or any part of the claim but desires time to pay he may, within 14 days, file the form of admission attached to the summons and state how he proposes to pay the admitted sum, for example by fixed instalments. The registrar sends notice of this admission to the plaintiff who must, within 14 days, inform the court office whether or not he accepts the offer. If he does accept, the registrar will enter judgment accordingly. If he does not accept, the registrar must inform the defendant whereupon the action proceeds.[16] If the defendant admits the whole or any part of the plaintiff's claim, the plaintiff may apply to the court for such judgment as he may be entitled to on the admission; an alternative course for the plaintiff is to apply for an interim payment.[17]

(3) If the defendant denies liability or wishes to plead a set-off or counterclaim he must, within 14 days, file the forms of defence and counterclaim if appropriate. The registrar will serve copies of these upon the plaintiff.

(4) In a default action if the defendant takes none of the above courses, the plaintiff may obtain judgment for the amount of the claim (if the claim is liquidated[18]) or interlocutory judgment for damages to be assessed (if the claim is for unliquidated damages) together with costs. In a fixed date action (*viz.* an action in which there is a claim for some relief other than the payment of money) the defendant may appear on the return day without having filed a defence and dispute the plaintiff's claim. However he will be ordered to pay any extra costs incurred by his failure to file a defence.

e   Pre-trial review and other interlocutory proceedings

In the case of a fixed date action (other than an action for recovery of land) the return day on the summons will be, unless the court otherwise directs, a day fixed for the preliminary consideration of the action by the registrar, known as a "pre-trial review". In the case of default action, where a defence or counterclaim is delivered the court will fix either a day for the hearing of

---

[14] O. 11, rr. 1, 2.
[15] See p. 330, *ante.*
[16] O. 9, r. 3.
[17] O. 13, r. 12; this rule applies R.S.C. O. 29 (subject to minor exceptions) to county court proceedings where the sum claimed or the amount involved exceeds £500; for details of the High Court procedure, see p. 335, *ante.*
[18] In county courts a claim for the cost of repairs executed to a motor vehicle is treated as a liquidated claim unless the court otherwise orders (O. 1, r. 10).

the action or a day for a pre-trial review.[19] The pre-trial review is analogous to the summons for directions in High Court actions[20] and the registrar is enjoined to "consider the course of the proceedings and give all such directions as appear to him necessary or desirable for securing the just, expeditious and economical disposal of the action".[1] In particular the registrar must endeavour to secure that the parties make all such admissions and agreements as ought reasonably to be made by them and may record in the order any admission or agreement so made or any refusal to make any admission or agreement. Evidence on the pre-trial review may be given by affidavit. If the defendant does not appear on the pre-trial review and has not delivered an admission or defence, the registrar may, if he thinks fit, enter judgment for the plaintiff; if the defendant does not appear on the pre-trial review and has delivered a defence, the plaintiff may proceed to prove his case (generally by affidavit) and may ask for judgment in the same way as if the defendant had not appeared at the trial.

Every party must apply on the pre-trial review for any interlocutory order which he seeks and if he does not and makes a subsequent interlocutory application, he will usually have to pay the extra costs incurred. Interlocutory orders are, in practice, required rather less frequently than in High Court actions.

The interlocutory orders which the county court has power to make are similar to the orders which may be made in the High Court, the following being frequently encountered—third party proceedings,[2] further and better particulars of claim,[3] discovery and inspection of documents,[4] interrogatories[5], amendment of pleadings[6] security for costs,[7] interim payments.[8] After giving all necessary directions the registrar must, if the action remains to be tried, fix a day for the trial and give notice thereof to every party.[9]

The pre-trial review operates, therefore, both as a summons for directions in actions which are destined to proceed to trial and as a means of the plaintiff obtaining judgment (either by default or by proving his case, as above) in other cases, without the need of a proper trial in open court.

f Premature determination of proceedings

A high proportion of actions never come to trial, being prematurely determined by agreement, by the defendant admitting liability, by the plaintiff discontinuing his claim, or by a judgment or order given or made on a pre-trial review. In addition Order 9, rule 14 now, in effect, applies High Court

---

[19] O. 3, r. 3 (fixed date); O. 9, r. 5 (default).
[20] See p. 364, *ante*.
[1] O. 17, r. 1.
[2] O. 12.
[3] O. 6, r. 7.
[4] O. 14, rr. 1–10; the automatic discovery provisions in the High Court (p. 355, *ante*) do not apply in county courts.
[5] O. 14, r. 11.
[6] O. 15.
[7] O. 13, r. 8.
[8] O. 13, r. 12.
[9] O. 17, r. 9.

Order 14 procedure to default actions in which the plaintiff's claim exceeds £500 and the defendant has delivered a "document purporting to be a defence."[10]

If the parties arrive at a settlement, the plaintiff must give notice of this to the registrar who notes it in the minute book. The action is thus determined. However the consent of the court is required to a settlement of an action by or on behalf of a person under disability.[11] Some actions are brought solely for obtaining the court's sanction for a settlement which has already been reached. The particulars of claim in such an action contain only an outline of the claim, the terms of the proposed settlement and a request for the court's approval, which will be given in chambers by the judge or registrar. The judge or registrar will direct how the money is to be dealt with; in the case of an infant the money is usually paid into court and invested or applied for his benefit until he attains his majority, when he can demand payment of the capital.

As has already been noted the defendant may pay money into court at any time before judgment. If the plaintiff takes the money out of court proceedings are stayed and the plaintiff may tax and sign judgment for his costs.

The plaintiff may, at any time before trial, discontinue his action by giving notice in the prescribed form to the registrar and to the defendant, who will be entitled to his costs incurred before receiving notice of discontinuance.[12]

g   References to arbitration or for inquiry and report or to the European Court

(1) *Arbitration*—Before 1973 the power of county courts to refer cases to arbitration was limited to those cases in which the parties consented. Accordingly it was excercised only rarely. However, the Administration of Justice Act 1973 created wide powers to refer proceedings to arbitration and the relevant provisions are now to be found in section 64 of the Act and Order 19 of the Rules. The position is that either party may apply by notice for the case to be referred to arbitration, which may be ordered to take place before the judge, registrar or an outside arbitrator. In addition any proceedings in which the sum claimed or the amount involved does not exceed £500 automatically stand referred for arbitration by the registrar[13] upon receipt by the court of a defence to the claim. However in such cases the registrar may on the application of any party rescind the reference if he is satisfied

(*a*) that a difficult question of law or a question of fact of exceptional complexity is involved; or

(*b*) that a charge of fraud is in issue; or

(*c*) that the parties are agreed that the dispute should be tried in court; or

(*d*) that it would be unreasonable for the claim to proceed to arbitration having regard to its subject matter, the circumstances of the parties or the interests of any other person likely to be affected by the award.[14]

---

[10] For details of O. 14 procedure in the High Court, see p. 326, *ante*; the procedure was not extended to county courts until 1982.

[11] O. 10, r. 10.

[12] O. 18, rr. 1, 2.

[13] But the registrar may, on the application of any party, refer the proceedings for arbitration by the judge or an outside arbitrator (O. 19, r. 2(3)).

[14] O. 19, r. 2(4).

The advantage of arbitration is that it provides a procedure for small claims which is not only expeditious but inexpensive and informal. Thus the hearing is informal and the strict rules of evidence do not apply, the arbitrator may adopt any procedure he wishes so as to afford each party a fair and equal opportunity to present his case and may, with the consent of the parties, consult any expert or call for an expert report on any matter in dispute or invite an expert to attend the hearing as assessor.[15] Furthermore since in cases automatically referrred no solicitors' charges are usually allowed as between party and party litigants in, for example, consumer disputes can freely take their case to the county court in the knowledge that they are not at risk for substantial costs. In this way the county court is able to exercise its original function as a "small-claims" court, readily accessible to litigants in person.

The order for reference will usually be made at the pre-trial review.

(2) *Inquiry and report*—Section 65 of the Act empowers the court to refer "to the registrar or a referee for inquiry and report" proceedings which require any prolonged examination of documents or any scientific or local investigation, proceedings concerning matters of account, other proceedings with the consent of the parties and any question arising in any proceedings.

Such an order may be made either on application or by the court of its own motion and, as will be apparent from the terms of the section, is usually appropriate in complex cases, such as building disputes, where there is a great deal of detailed or expert evidence to be heard; the reference may be to the registrar or to an independent referee who will conduct the inquiry and make a report to the court. The procedure differs from arbitration in that it does not, as arbitration does, involve the adjudication being made by the person to whom the reference is made—judgment will still be given by the judge (or registrar) trying the case.

(3) *Reference to European Court*—County courts, like the High Court and the Court of Appeal, have power to refer questions for a preliminary ruling under Article 177 of the E.E.C. Treaty. The circumstances in which such a reference may be made and the principles which govern the court's discretion whether or not to refer have been considered elsewhere in this work; the rules applicable in county courts are substantially similar to those which apply in the High Court.[16] In view of the costs involved it seems unlikely that there will be many references to the European Court from county courts, although the terms of Article 177 have compelled the enactment of rules to deal with such a contingency.

h Trial

Unless it is settled or discontinued or disposed of at the pre-trial review the action comes on for trial on the day fixed. If the plaintiff does not appear when the case is called his action will be struck out and he will have to apply to have it reinstated at another time. If the defendant does not appear the trial may proceed in his absence and judgment may be entered against him. The trial will be before the registrar, the judge or, very rarely, the judge and a

---

[15] O. 19, r. 5 (which sets out the term of reference for arbitrations which are to apply unless the court otherwise directs).

[16] See p. 379, *ante*; the reference cannot be made by the registrar (O. 19, r. 11).

jury. In busy county courts there is a judge's court and a registrar's court. It is then usually the practice to set down actions where the claim is less than £500 and actions where the defendant is not expected to appear in the registrar's list, other actions being set down in the judge's list. The county court jury is obsolescent. No party has a right to claim trial with a jury unless there is in issue a charge of fraud against him or claim in respect of libel, slander, malicious prosecution or false imprisonment unless the trial requires any prolonged examination of documents or accounts or any scientific or local investigation which cannot conveniently be made with a jury.[17] In any other case he may be granted a jury, 8 in number. In fact actions which would be heard by a jury are usually heard in the High Court. The conduct of the trial is similar to that in the High Court. Solicitors, however, have a right of audience in the county court and frequently appear.[18] Also, if the action is not determined in one day, the registrar must fix another date to continue the hearing which will not necessarily be the next day.

If the defendant admits the plaintiff's claim or does not appear judgment will be entered for the plaintiff. Where this judgment is for the payment of money the court may order the sum to be paid forthwith or within a specified time, or may order payment by fixed instalments.[19]

If the plaintiff does not succeed in proving his case the court may either give judgment for the defendant or non-suit the plaintiff. The non-suit has long been abolished in the High Court but still exists in the county court. It differs from a judgment for the defendant in that it does not decide the case affirmatively against the plaintiff, so that he is not estopped from bringing a subsequent action on the same facts. However a second action may be stayed until the plaintiff has complied with an order for costs made against him in the former action.[20]

2   Rent actions

Much of the time of the average county court is taken up by landlords' actions for the recovery of premises and arrears of rent from tenants. Indeed the jurisdiction of county courts in actions for the recovery of possession of dwellings which are within the rateable value limits of the Rent Act 1977 is virtually exclusive.

A new summary procedure for the recovery of arrears of rent from a tenant or former tenant who is still in occupation of the demised premises was introduced in 1972 and is now embodied in Order 24, rules 8–11. The action, known as a "rent action" is commenced by the filing of a special form of request for a summons in the court for the district in which the land

---

[17] County Courts Act 1984, s. 66. The application for an order for trial by jury must be made not less than 10 clear days before the return day: O. 13, r. 10.

[18] Moreover the Lord Chancellor has power under s. 61 of the Act to confer rights of audience in county courts upon persons in "relevant legal employment", and this power has been exercised to enable Fellows of the Institute of Legal Executives to be heard on (*a*) unopposed applications for an adjournment; and (*b*) applications for judgment by consent: County Courts (Right of Audience) Direction 1978.

[19] County Courts Act 1984, s. 71.

[20] O. 21, r. 2. At any time before the facts are found the plaintiff has an absolute right to elect to be non-suited; thereafter the court has a discretion: *Clack* v. *Arthurs Engineering, Ltd.*, [1959] 2 Q.B. 211; [1959] 2 All E.R. 503.

is situated. The summons fixes a return day for the hearing, there being no pre-trial review, and must be served on the defendant not less than 7 clear days before the return day. There is no provision for the defendant to serve a defence or counterclaim and the usual forms of admission, defence and counterclaim are not sent to the defendant; nor is there any provision for his making an admission and a written request for time to pay. The form of summons simply requires the defendant to pay into court the whole of the claim (or such part as he admits) or to attend court on the return day, failing which judgment may be given in his absence.

3   Proceedings other than actions

Where, subject to any Act or Rule, the object of proceedings is to obtain relief against any person or to compel any person to do or abstain from doing any act, the proper method of proceeding is by action, the procedure for which has been described above. Proceedings in the county court which do not fall into this category are commenced by originating application unless any Act or Rule requires that they be commenced otherwise.[1]

An originating application may be likened to an originating summons in the High Court. It is appropriate where the applicant seeks an order of the court which does not amount to a claim for relief from another person. Thus the person who seeks an adoption order, a declaration of legitimacy, or an order under the Landlord and Tenant Acts will commence proceedings by originating application. Notice of the application must be served on the proper respondent; for example, an application for a declaration of legitimacy must be served on the Attorney-General and all persons whose interests might be affected by the declaration. If the respondent wishes to resist the application he must file an answer, following which there will be a hearing before the judge or registrar. Since there is no plaint, but only an application, the parties are described not as "plaintiff" and "defendant" but as "applicant" and "respondent".

4   Costs in the county court

The position as to costs between a party and his own solicitor has already been considered in connection with High Court litigation. As between the parties, the court has a judicial discretion over costs,[2] but as a rule the successful party will recover his costs from his opponent, as in the High Court.

a   Scales of costs

The essential distinction between High Court and county court costs is that the latter are fixed in amount by reference to scales[3] according to the sum

---

[1] O. 3, r. 4. Proceedings may also be commenced by petition where any Act or Rule so provides.

[2] O. 38, r. 1.

[3] These scales do not apply to bankruptcy, divorce or Companies Act proceedings (where special scales apply).

claimed or recovered in the action or, where the claim is not only a money claim, according to the discretion of the court.

For the regulation of solicitors' charges and disbursements, other than court fees, there are four scales of costs:

Exceeding £   25   but not exceeding £   100   Lower Scale
Exceeding £   100 but not exceeding £   500   Scale 1
Exceeding £   500 but not exceeding £3,000   Scale 2
Exceeding £3,000   Scale 3[4]

If the plaintiff succeeds the scale is determined by the amount for which he recovers judgment. If the plaintiff fails the scale is determined by the amount of the plaintiff's claim. The court has a discretion to award costs on a higher or lower scale than the one applicable in certain cases, notably if the judge certifies that a difficult question of law or fact is involved.[4] Where the claim is less than £25 the court cannot allow any solicitors' charges unless the judge certifies that a "difficult question of law or a question of fact of exceptional complexity" is involved.[5] No fee for counsel can be awarded where the defendant, in an action for money alone, delivers no defence and does not appear at the hearing, unless the judge or registrar at the hearing otherwise orders.[6] The judge has no power to award a fixed sum by way of costs (except on the lower scale or by consent), although he may direct the registrar to allow or disallow any specific item on taxation.[7]

b   Assessment of costs

Certain items are fixed in amount. For example, when a summons is issued in an action where the only relief claimed is a sum of money liquidated or unliquidated, the court fee and the charges of the plaintiff's solicitor for the issue of the summons are fixed and are entered on the summons. Accordingly, if the defendant within 14 days of service pays the sum claimed and costs into court, or pays in a lesser sum with an admission of liability which the plaintiff accepts in satisfaction, the defendant is generally liable for no further costs beyond those stated on the summons. This may, of course, cause hardship to a plaintiff who has already incurred expense, for example by obtaining a medical report or by having particulars of claim settled by counsel. Where costs are on the Lower Scale they must be assessed at a lump sum.[8] In other cases the costs will be taxed according to the appropriate scale; the basis of taxation within the scale is similar to that applicable in the High Court so that taxation will almost always be on a "party and party" basis.[9] The registrar may fix and allow costs without taxation if the successful party so requests. Otherwise they must be taxed unless the parties agree an amount of costs in lieu of taxation.[10]

---

[4] O. 38, r. 3. The figures may be varied by Order in Council.
[5] O. 38, r. 4(6).
[6] O. 38, r. 8.
[7] O. 38, r. 6.
[8] O. 38, r. 19.
[9] O. 38, r. 23; see p. 389, *ante.*
[10] O. 38, r. 19.

c Taxation of costs

The registrar is the taxing officer of the court. The successful party must, within 3 months of the order for costs, lodge a bill of costs with the registrar and obtain an appointment for taxation. He must serve a copy of this bill on his opponent and give him not less than 14 days' notice of the appointment.[11] On taxation the registrar will allow, in accordance with the scale, a reasonable amount for each item incurred. The judge may, at the trial, expressly authorise the registrar to allow an amount in respect of certain items, such as counsel's fee, in excess of the scale maximum. In this event the registrar may allow such sum as he considers reasonable in respect of these items. Where an item is not provided for in the scales the registrar may or may not in his discretion make an allowance in respect of it. The registrar certifies the total amount due on taxation in his *allocatur* which is endorsed on the bill.

d Review of taxation[12]

Any party not satisfied with a taxation may apply to the registrar to review his taxation; the application must set out the disputed items and the grounds of objection. The registrar will then certify in writing his reasons for allowing or disallowing the disputed items. If dissatisfied with this review, any party may apply to the judge for a review. The judge then has the equivalent powers of the registrar in his review. He cannot upset the discretion of the registrar unless the exercise of this discretion was based upon a wrong principle of law.[13] There is a further appeal to the Court of Appeal, with leave of the judge, if a question of legal principle is involved.[14]

5 Execution and enforcement of judgments

a Judgments for the payment of money

Where the judgment or order directs the payment of money, the methods of enforcing the judgment are similar to those available in the High Court, i.e. execution against the debtor's personal property, garnishee proceedings, appointment of a receiver, creation of a charge over the debtor's land, or partnership interest or other assets,[15] and bankruptcy proceedings. County court judgments used not to carry interest. This was an anomalous and unjust, state of affairs since High Court judgments have carried interest since the Judgments Act 1838. It has now been remedied by order made under section 74 of the Act.[15] Furthermore the important jurisdiction to make attachment of earnings orders under the Attachment of Earnings Act 1971, which in the High Court is limited to the enforcement of maintenance orders, is, in county courts, exercisable in respect of maintenance orders, judgment debts of £15 or more and administration orders.[16]

---

11 O. 38, r. 20.
12 O. 38, r. 24.
13 *White* v. *Altrincham Urban District Council*, [1936] 2 K.B. 138; [1936] 1 All E.R. 923.
14 *Goodman* v. *Blake* (1887), 19 Q.B.D. 77; Supreme Court Act 1981, s. 18(1) (*f*).
15 See p. 393, *ante* for details of assets which may be the subject of a charging order.
16 Attachment of Earnings Act 1971, s. 1(2); see p. 417, *post*. Under the same section, magistrates' courts have power to make attachment of earnings orders in respect of maintenance

Finally mention may be made of the judgment summons. This was, until recently, a widely used procedure to enforce both county court and High Court judgments. However, as noted below, the drastic curtailment of the power to commit to prison for default in paying civil debts in favour of the power to make attachment of earnings orders has rendered judgment summonses inappropriate in all but a very few cases.

Execution—Execution is effected by warrant of execution issued to the county court bailiff which is in the nature of a writ of *fieri facias*.[17] The warrant directs the bailiff to execute upon the debtor's personal property for the judgment debt, costs and interest. The rules relating to property which is exempt from execution, method of execution and interpleader proceedings are similar to those in the High Court. A judgment creditor seeking the issue of a warrant of execution must file the appropriate request in the court office. A notice is usually sent to the defendant telling him that a warrant has been issued and that if he pays the debt there will be no need to execute the warrant. This often results in the warrant being paid out. As an alternative the plaintiff may agree to suspend the warrant on condition that the debt and costs are paid within a specified time or by instalments.[18] In fact most warrants are paid out or suspended in this way and only in a small proportion of cases does the warrant have to be executed. The warrant, once issued, remains in force for one year from the date of issue unless renewed. The bailiff seizes sufficient goods to satisfy the warrant and either deposits them in a proper place, such as a warehouse or auction room, or takes "walking possession" of them. There will then be a sale of such goods as are sufficient to satisfy the judgment debt including costs. In order that the bailiff does not sell too much, he will have the goods "appraised", usually by a local auctioneer who also deals with the storage and sale of the goods. The sale is usually by public auction following advertisement and, where the execution is for a sum exceeding £20, must be by public auction unless the court directs otherwise.[19]

The jurisdiction of the county courts is local. This rule applies to the county courts' jurisdiction over the execution of warrants. Thus where the debtor has property outside the jurisdiction of the county court from which the warrant against him was issued (called the "home court"), the warrant must be sent to the registrar of the county court for that district for execution.[20]

A judgment obtained in the High Court for the payment of money, whatever the sum, may be executed in the county court.[1] The execution creditor must file in the court for the district where execution is to be levied a request for a warrant of execution.

---

orders, fines and analogous impositions and legal aid contributions; accordingly the use of attachment of earnings orders to enforce ordinary judgment debts is confined to county courts.

17 County Courts Act 1984, s. 85.
18 If a suspended warrant has taken effect, there is no power to suspend it further: *Moore* v. *Lambeth County Court Registrar*, [1969] 1 All E.R. 782; [1969] 1 W.L.R. 141; cf., however, *R.* v. *Bloomsbury and Marylebone County Court, Ex parte Villerwest, Ltd.*, [1976] 1 All E.R. 897; [1976] 1 W.L.R. 362.
19 County Courts Act 1984, s. 97.
20 *Ibid.*, s. 103.
1 *Ibid.*, s. 105.

Attachment of earnings—Prior to 1970, attachment of earnings orders could only be made in matrimonial causes under the provisions of the Maintenance Orders Act 1958. Following recommendations of the Payne Committee[2] the procedure was extended by the Administration of Justice Act 1970 to judgment debts generally in virtual substitution for the powers of committal to prison under the Debtors Act 1869, though, as noted below, the power of committal was retained in a few cases. The relevant provisions of the 1970 Act were repealed and consolidated by the Attachment of Earnings Act 1971.

An application for an attachment of earnings order may be made by the person entitled to the benefit of the judgment or order, where the relevant order is an administration order[3] by any of the creditors scheduled to the order or (where the application is for an order to secure maintenance payments) by the judgment debtor himself.[4] The application is generally to the court for the district in which the debtor resides and must be served, in the same manner as a fixed date summons, not less than 21 clear days before the return day. The debtor must then, within 8 days of service, complete and return a form containing full details of his employment, pay and income, financial liabilities and proposals for payment of the debt,[5] which proposals are notified to the applicant. The registrar may by notice require any person appearing to have the debtor in his employment to supply particulars of the debtor's earnings.

The application is heard by the registrar who may hear it in chambers, evidence being given by affidavit. If the debtor does not attend, the registrar may adjourn the hearing and notify the debtor of the date of the adjourned hearing; if the debtor then fails to attend or attends but refuses to give evidence, he may be imprisoned by the judge for up to 14 days.

An attachment of earnings order may be made in respect of any sums payable by way of wages or salary or by way of pension.[6] The order requires the debtor's employer to make periodical deductions from the debtor's earnings and to pay them to the collecting officer of the court; the order specifies the "normal deduction rate" and the "protected earnings rate", the latter being the amount which the court decides the debtor must retain out of his earnings in any event.[7] It is the duty of both debtor and employer to notify the court of changes in the debtor's employment. As long as an attachment of earnings order is in force, no execution for the recovery of the judgment debt may issue without the leave of the court.[8]

There was for some time a general opposition to the concept of attachment of earnings orders on the ground that a debtor might be prejudiced in his employment by his employer's knowledge that he was a debtor. This

---

2   Cmnd. 3909 of 1969.
3   *Infra.*
4   Attachment of Earnings Act 1971, s. 3(1).
5   *Ibid.*, s. 14; O. 25, r. 81: Form N56. Failure to comply with this or other requirements under the Act is an offence punishable as a contempt of court with imprisonment for not more than 14 days (*ibid.*, s. 23).
6   Attachment of Earnings Act 1971, s. 24. Certain classes of payment are excluded, notably the pay of members of the forces, social security payments, disablement or disability pensions and seamen's wages.
7   *Ibid.*, s. 6. There is provision for variation and discharge of orders in sections 9–11 of the Act.
8   *Ibid.*, s. 8.

opposition has been overcome, no doubt as a result of acknowledgment of the fact that debt is not the social disgrace which it was in Victorian times and as a result of the expense and futility of keeping debtors in prison, though the power to imprison certain classes of recalcitrant debtors, notably husbands who will not maintain their wives and families, has been retained and is enforceable by judgment summons.

Judgment summons—This is a method of enforcing a judgment for the payment of money in that it enables the court to ascertain the debtor's means, to order payment of the debt by instalments (where the debt is a High Court debt it is not likely that the debtor will have had an opportunity to pay by instalments) and, as a final sanction, to imprison the debtor.

Imprisonment for civil debt as such was abolished by the Debtors Act 1869, section 4. However there remained a few cases under that Act in which a defaulting judgment debtor might be committed to prison. These are contained in section 5 of the Act which empowers any court to commit to prison for a term not exceeding six weeks or until payment of the sum due any person who defaults in paying a debt, or instalment of a debt, due from him under any order of that or any other competent court. This power can only be exercised by a judge who must be satisfied that the defaulter has, or has had, since the date of the judgment against him, the means to pay. It does not, therefore, render a defaulter liable to imprisonment where he simply has not the means to pay. His conduct must be in the nature of a contempt.[9] However the power to commit under section 5 of the Debtors Act was severely curtailed by the Administration of Justice Act 1970, and the power is now exercisable by county courts only in respect of High Court or county court maintenance orders and orders for the payment of certain debts of a public nature such as income tax and national insurance contributions.[10]

Imprisonment does not extinguish the debt, although the debtor cannot be committed twice in respect of the same debt (though he can be committed separately in respect of separate instalments of the same debt). Since the 1970 Act, imprisonment in respect of civil debt is extremely rare and the judgment summons is of far less practical importance than formerly. Furthermore on a judgment summons the court has power, instead of making a committal order, to make an attachment of earnings order.[11]

The plaintiff must file the appropriate request in the office of the county court for the district where the debtor resides or carries on business. Where the judgment in question is not a county court judgment he must also produce an office copy of the judgment or order, an affidavit verifying the amount due and a copy of the sheriff's return to any writ of execution issued in the High Court.[12] The county court will then issue a judgment summons which is served on the defendant not less than 14 days before the day fixed for the hearing.[13]

At the hearing there will be an enquiry into the debtor's means. The judgment creditor may give evidence, orally or by affidavit, as to the debtor's means and the debtor will also be required to undergo a sworn examination

---

9 *Re Edgcome*, [1902] 2 K.B. 403.
10 Administration of Justice Act 1970, s. 11, Sch. 4.
11 Attachment of Earnings Act 1971, s. 3(4), (6).
12 O. 25, r. 11.
13 O. 28, r. 3.

as to his means. If he does not appear at the hearing the judge may adjourn the hearing and order the defendant to attend the adjourned hearing. This order must be served personally on the defendant not less than 5 clear days before the date fixed for the adjourned hearing.[14] If he does not attend then the judge may commit him to prison for not more than 14 days.[15]

If the judge is satisfied that the debtor has had the means to pay the debt but has not done so he may commit the defendant to prison for a term not exceeding six weeks. In fact the judge usually makes an order for payment by instalments if this has not already been done. If the judgment summons was issued in respect of a default on an instalment the judge will more readily make a committal order but even then it will usually be suspended provided the debt is paid within a specified time.

Administration orders—The great advantage of attachment of earnings orders is that they provide a means of intercepting the earnings of judgment debtors and thereby ensuring, so far as possible, that the debtor with insufficient assets to justify execution process pays his debts, albeit slowly. By the nature of things it is often the case that a judgment debtor has outstanding against him not one but several judgment debts. In such a case there is provision in the Attachment of Earnings Act 1971[16] for the making of a "consolidated attachment order" which is an attachment of earnings order for the payment of two or more judgment debts.

An alternative procedure in the case of insolvent debtors lies in the power of county courts to make administration orders. An administration order is an order providing for the administration of the debtor's estate by the court. The court may make such an order, under section 112 of the County Courts Act 1984 on the application of a debtor whose total debts do not exceed the county court limit and who is unable to pay forthwith the amount of a judgment obtained against him in a county court. The court also has an independent power under section 4 of the Attachment of Earnings Act 1971 to make an administration order on an application for an attachment of earnings order to secure payment of a judgment debt if of the opinion that the case is one in which all the debtor's liabilities should be dealt with together; if of opinion that it may be such a case the court may order the debtor to furnish to the court a list of all his creditors and the amounts which he owes to them and if it appears that his total indebtedness does not exceed the county court limit the court may make an administration order.

Where an administration order has been made, any creditor, on proof of his debt before the registrar, is entitled to be scheduled as a creditor of the debtor for the amount of his proof.[17] Where the debtor applies for an order, he must file a request, verified on oath.[18] Any person who becomes a creditor after the date of the order may be scheduled as a creditor but payment to him

---

[14] O. 27, r. 8; O. 28, r. 4.
[15] County Courts Act 1984, s. 110.
[16] S. 17. Application for a consolidated attachment order may be made by the debtor or by any person who has obtained or is entitled to apply for an attachment of earnings order or, in certain circumstances, the court may make such an order of its own motion. Payments made under the order are divided *pro rata* among the creditors (O. 25, r. 90).
[17] County Courts Act 1984, s. 113.
[18] O. 39, rr. 1, 3.

is deferred until those who were creditors before the making of the order have been paid.

The effect of an administration order is that no creditor has any remedy against the person or property of the debtor in respect of any debt which the debtor has notified to the court or which has been scheduled to the order except with leave of the court.[19] Furthermore no creditor whose name is included in the schedule may, without the leave of the county court, present or join in a bankruptcy petition unless his name was notified to the county court by the debtor, he is a creditor for a sum exceeding £400 and the petition is presented within 28 days of the creditor receiving notice that his name has been notified to the court.[20]

The court will, under the order, administer the debtor's estate and distribute his assets and instalments paid by him *pro rata* among his creditors. As has been noted, an administration order may itself be enforced by an attachment of earnings order. Further, if the debtor fails to make any payment which he is required to make by an administration order, the court may, if it thinks fit, revoke the administration order and make a receiving order against that person.[1]

b   Other judgments

Warrants of delivery and possession—A judgment for the recovery of land or for the delivery of possession of land may be enforced by warrant of possession which corresponds to the writ of possession available in the High Court.[2]

Similarly, a judgment for the delivery of specific goods is enforced by warrant of delivery. There are different forms of warrant of delivery which enable the bailiff either to execute upon the defendant's goods to the value of the chattel, as if the warrant were a warrant of execution, or to seize the specific chattel which is the subject matter of the warrant.[3]

Committal—The power of county courts to commit a person for contempt of court may be compared with the power of committal in the High Court. Thus where a person has failed to comply with any order of the court, he may be committed. A copy of the order in question must be served on the defendant personally, warning him of the consequences of his disobedience. If the defendant still fails to comply with the order he will be required to attend the court and show cause why he should not be committed to prison. If he does not show cause, the judge may order a warrant of committal to issue for his arrest and imprisonment.[4]

There are various other penal sanctions available to the county court.

---

[19] County Courts Act 1984, s. 114(1).

[20] *Ibid.*, s. 112(4).

[1] Insolvency Act 1976, s. 11(1).

[2] O. 26, r. 17. There is power to suspend warrants (and this is often exercised in landlord and tenant cases). If a suspended warrant has taken effect there is no power to suspend it further (*Moore* v. *Lambeth County Court Registrar*, [1969] 1 All E.R. 782; [1969] 1 W.L.R. 141) except in Rent Act cases, where the power to suspend possession is indefinite (*Yates* v. *Morris*, [1951] 1 K.B. 77; [1950] 2 All E.R. 577).

[3] O. 26, r. 16.

[4] O. 29, r. 1.

Thus a person who assaults an officer of the court in the execution of his duty is liable to imprisonment for up to 3 months or to a fine not exceeding level 5 on the standard scale,[5] while a person who wilfully insults the judge, any juror or witness or any officer of the court or wilfully interrupts the proceedings or otherwise misbehaves in court may by order of the judge be taken into custody and detained until the rising of the court and thereafter is liable to be committed to prison for up to one month and to a fine not exceeding level 4 on the standard scale.[6] These provisions are additional to the general provisions of the Contempt of Court Act 1981.[7]

C MATRIMONIAL CAUSES PROCEDURE

A matrimonial cause is commenced by filing a petition in any divorce county court. The form of petition is prescribed by the Matrimonial Causes Rules 1977; in addition to various formal matters the petition must contain the names of the parties, details of the marriage, the names of all children of the family, particulars of previous proceedings between the parties and details of grounds upon which relief is sought. In a divorce suit the petition must state that "the said marriage has broken down irretrievably" and must then allege which of the five facts set out in section 1(2) of the Matrimonial Causes Act 1973 the petitioner relies upon as proof of breakdown. The petition concludes with a prayer for the relief sought, which, in the case of divorce, is "that the said marriage may be dissolved", including any claim for a financial provision, costs or custody of children of the family.

The petitioner must file copies of the petition for each person to be served and their names and addresses are annexed to the petition. With the petition the petitioner must file a written statement containing details of the present and proposed arrangements for the residence, education, financial provision and access of all children of the family under 16.[8] In addition, where a solicitor is acting for a petitioner for divorce or judicial separation a certificate as to whether or not he has discussed with the petitioner the possibility of a reconciliation must be filed with the petition. Unless the petitioner otherwise requests the petition, together with forms of Notice of Proceedings and Acknowledgment of Service, is served by post through the court. There is no entry of appearance although a party may, within 8 days of service, give "notice of intention to defend." Within 21 days of the time limited for giving notice of intention to defend the respondent may file an answer. If an answer to the petition is filed the proceedings become defended and *must* then be transferred to the High Court (Family Division).[9] The answer contains the

---

5 County Courts Act 1984, s. 14; as to the "standard scale" see p. 549, *post*.

6 *Ibid.*, s. 118.

7 As to which, see p. 238, *ante*.

8 And those minor children over 16 who are receiving instruction at an educational establishment or undergoing training for a trade, profession or vocation: Matrimonial Causes Rules 1977, r. 8(2); Form 4.

9 This will change when Part V of the Matrimonial and Family Proceedings Act 1984 is implemented. Under s. 33 of that Act the Lord Chancellor may designate any county court as a divorce county court and any court so designated will have jurisdiction to hear and determine any matrimonial cause and to try such a cause if designated as a court of trial. By s. 37 the President of the Family Division may, with the concurrence of the Lord Chancellor, give

respondent's defence to the allegations in the petition, together with any claim for relief which the respondent wishes to make. If an answer is filed the petitioner has 14 days in which to file a reply. The following interlocutory proceedings are similar to those in the Queen's Bench Division and may include such matters as particulars of pleading, discovery of documents and interrogatories. These are closed by the registrar giving "directions for trial"[10] whereupon the case is set down in the High Court (if defended) or a divorce county court (if undefended). The trial is similar to the trial of any other civil action and takes place before a judge who deals with the relief sought and ancillary matters such as custody and costs. Financial matters are usually dealt with by registrars, with a right of appeal to a judge, the appeal taking the form of a complete rehearing.[11]

Special procedure list

On December 1, 1973 a new procedure was introduced[12] for the granting of decrees nisi of divorce or decrees of judicial separation, virtually without a hearing. Originally limited to cases of two years' separation and consent, it now extends to undefended petitions for divorce or judicial separation on any ground.

In cases to which these rules apply there is a special form of application for directions for trial which must be lodged together with an affidavit of evidence by the petitioner (and by any corroborative witness) in the prescribed form. If the registrar is satisfied that the petitioner has sufficiently proved the contents of the petition and is entitled to a decree he files a certificate to this effect whereupon a day will be fixed for the pronouncement of a decree by a judge in open court, notification of the day and place fixed being given to the parties. Where there are children of the family to whom section 41 of the 1973 Act applies (in relation to whose welfare the court has certain duties of enquiry under that section) and the respondent has neither applied for custody of or access to the children, nor returned an acknowledgment of service stating that he objects to the petitioner's claim for custody or wishes to apply on his own account, nor filed a statement as to arrangements for children proposing arrangements which differ materially from the petitioner's proposals, the registrar will fix an appointment for a judge in chambers to consider the arrangements for the children and notify the parties of that appointment.

On the day fixed it is unnecessary for the petitioner to appear at court or be represented, the cases are called on in a group, and, if no cause is shown to the contrary, decrees are automatically pronounced.[13]

---

directions with respect to the distribution and transfer between the High Court and county court of "family business" (*viz.* business of any description which in the High Court is assigned exclusively to the Family Division (s. 32)). It is therefore to be anticipated that, when appropriate family proceedings rules have been formulated and implemented, a high proportion of contested family business will be heard in county courts.

10 M.C.R., r. 33; cf. the summons for directions in the Queen's Bench Division; see p. 364, *ante*.
11 G. (*formerly P.*) v. *P.* (*ancillary relief: appeal*), [1978] 1 All E.R. 1099; [1978] 1 W.L.R. 1376; cf. appeals from masters (and district registrars) to judges in the Queen's Bench Division (p. 426, *post*).
12 Matrimonial Causes (Amendment No. 2) Rules 1973.
13 See *Practice Direction* (*Matrimonial Causes: Special Procedure*), [1977] 1 All E.R. 845; [1977] 1 W.L.R. 320.

D TRANSFER OF PROCEEDINGS

1 From one county court to another

It must be remembered that the jurisdiction of the county courts is local, so that the plaintiff is restricted in his choice of venue. This must generally be in the court for the district in which the defendant or one of the defendants resides or carries on business, or where the cause of action wholly or in part arose. Where proceedings are commenced in the wrong county court, the judge of that court may transfer them to the court in which they ought to have been commenced.[14]

Where an action is commenced in the proper court it may still be transferred to another county court. The judge or registrar may transfer the proceedings to another court if he is satisfied that they can more conveniently or fairly be tried in that court. Secondly, where an action has been commenced in a county court against a defendant who does not reside or carry on business within the district of that court, the latter may after delivering a defence apply *ex parte* in writing for an order transferring the proceedings to the county court for the district in which he does reside or carry on business.[15]

Finally, a judgment summons can only be issued in the county court for the district in which the defendant resides or carries on business and certain other proceedings for enforcement are confined to the debtor's local court. Thus where the action in which the judgment was obtained took place in some other court, proceedings must be transferred to the court having jurisdiction over the enforcement proceedings. The action is then transferred for all purposes to the latter court, so that money paid by the defendant must be paid to the court to which the proceedings are tranferred.[16]

2 From a county court to the High Court

Proceedings may be transferred from the county court in which they were commenced to the High Court in the following circumstances (*inter alia*):[17]

(1) the High Court may at any stage order a transfer if it "thinks it desirable that the proceedings, or any part of them, should be heard and determined in the High Court";[18]

(2) a county court may, either of its own motion or on the application of any party, transfer the whole or any part of the proceedings if:

---

[14] See p. 404, *ante*.

[15] O. 16, rr. 1, 4. There is power, under the Matrimonial Causes Rules 1977, r. 32(2) to transfer a matrimonial cause from one divorce county court to another.

[16] O. 25, r. 2. The proceedings in question are judgment summonses, applications for charging orders under s. 1 of the Charging Orders Act 1979, for attachment of earnings orders and for orders for the oral examination of a debtor under O. 25, r. 3.

[17] The Matrimonial Causes Rules 1977 contain various provisions for transfer of matrimonial causes to the High Court, the most important being r. 18(5) under which a matrimonial cause which becomes defended must be so transferred. This rule will be abrogated when Part V of the Matrimonial and Family Proceedings Act 1984 is brought into force and rules thereunder made; but s. 39 of that Act confers an unrestricted power on county courts to transfer family proceedings to the High Court, either of the court's own motion or on the application of any party to the proceedings.

[18] County Courts Act 1984, s. 41.

(*a*) the court considers that some important question of law or fact is likely to arise; or

(*b*) the court considers that the amount recoverable on a claim or counterclaim is likely to exceed the county court limit; or

(*c*) any counterclaim or set-off and counterclaim involves matters beyond the jurisdiction of the county court.[19]

The procedure in the High Court on transferred actions is governed by R.S.C. Order 78. The master must give all directions as to the future conduct of the proceedings as he would on a summons for directions.

3   From the High Court to a county court

The following are the circumstances in which actions may be transferred from the High Court to a county court:

(1) if the parties consent to the transfer;

(2) if the High Court is satisfied that the amount remaining in dispute is within the county court limit; or that the amount recoverable in respect of the claim or counterclaim is likely to be within the limit;

(3) if the High Court is satisfied in the case of proceedings not involving an unliquidated claim, that the subject matter of the proceedings is likely to be within the county court jurisdiction;

(4) if "the High Court considers that the proceedings are not likely to raise any important question of law or fact and are suitable for determination by a county court".[20]

Proceedings transferred under the above provisions, contained in section 40 of the Act, will be transferred to such county court as is considered convenient to the parties. Where proceedings are transferred the county court has jurisdiction to award any relief, including any amount of damages, which could have been awarded by the High Court.

In addition the following proceedings may be transferred:

(5) interpleader proceedings in which it appears that the amount or value of the matter in dispute does not exceed the county court limit;[1]

(6) a matrimonial cause which, having been transferred to the High Court, subsequently becomes undefended.[2]

In addition, as has been noted, county court proceedings may be transferred to the High Court, and *vice versa*, for the purpose of the enforcement of judgments.[3]

---

[19] *Ibid.*, s. 42.

[20] *Ibid.*, s. 40.

[1] *Ibid.*, s. 44.

[2] Matrimonial Causes Rules 1977, r. 27. When s. 38 of the Matrimonial and Family Proceedings Act 1984 is implemented the following "family proceedings" will be transferable to county courts by the High Court, either of its own motion or on the application of any party to the proceedings: (*a*) all family proceedings which are within the county court jurisdiction; (*b*) wardship proceedings, except applications for an order that a minor be made, or cease to be, a ward of court; (*c*) all family proceedings transferred from a county court to the High Court.

[3] The provisions are contained in ss. 105–106 of the County Courts Act 1984.

CHAPTER 22

Civil Appeals

A RIGHTS OF APPEAL

There is no common law right of appeal from a superior court. It was established in *Darlow* v. *Shuttleworth*[1] that the common law jurisdiction of the Court of King's Bench to hear proceedings in error from the inferior courts of local jurisdiction was transferred by the Judicature Acts to the divisional court of the Queen's Bench Division. However since this right of appeal is confined to situations in which proceedings in error might have been brought at common law and since the local courts have ceased to function[2] common law rights of appeal are virtually obsolete. Apart from this all rights of appeal are statutory. The basic rights of appeal in the Supreme Court are now contained in the Supreme Court Act 1981 although numerous statutes create particular rights of appeal in special cases.

1 Appeal to the Court of Appeal: Civil Division

The fulcrum of the system of civil appeals is the civil division of the Court of Appeal. In a number of cases the Court of Appeal hears appeals directly from the decision of the court below. In other cases the appeal lies to the High Court in the first instance and then to the Court of Appeal.

Section 16(1) of the Supreme Court Act 1981 provides—

> "Subject as otherwise provided by this or any other Act . . . the Court of Appeal shall have jurisdiction to hear and determine appeals from any judgment or order of the High Court."[3]

Appeals from county courts lie, subject to the conditions set out in section 77 of the County Courts Act 1984, to the Court of Appeal with the single exception of appeals from orders in bankruptcy matters which lie in the first instance to a divisional court of the Chancery Division and thence with special leave to the Court of Appeal.

---

[1] [1902] 1 K.B. 721.
[2] See p. 6, *ante.*
[3] Where the House of Lords grants leave to appeal direct from the High Court to the House, appeal to the Court of Appeal is excluded (Administration of Justice Act 1969, s. 13(2)).

The Court of Appeal also has jurisdiction to hear appeals from the Employment Appeal Tribunal,[4] the Restrictive Practices Court,[5] the Lands Tribunal[6] and certain other statutory tribunals[7] and from Commercial judges sitting as arbitrators or umpires under section 4 of the Administration of Justice Act 1970.

Leave to appeal

As a general rule appeal lies to the Court of Appeal as of right but in certain cases leave is required. The more important cases in which leave is required are:

(1) from the determination of an appeal by a divisional court of the High Court;[8] leave may be given either by the divisional court or by the Court of Appeal;

(2) from a consent order or an order which is solely an order as to costs which by law are left to the discretion of the court; leave can only be granted by the court below;[9]

(3) from an interlocutory order or judgment made or given by a judge (with certain exceptions, notably where the liberty of the subject or the custody of infants is involved or where an injunction or the appointment of a receiver has been granted or refused);[10]

---

[4] Employment Protection (Consolidation) Act 1978, s. 136(4); appeal lies only on a point of law.

[5] Restrictive Practices Court Act 1976, s. 10; save in relation to proceedings under Part III of the Fair Trading Act 1973 (consumer protection) appeal lies only on a point of law.

[6] Lands Tribunal Act 1949, s. 3(4). Appeal from tribunals is by case stated on a point of law. The procedure is governed by O. 61.

[7] Transport Tribunal, Electricity Arbitration Tribunal, Gas Arbitration Tribunal, Foreign Compensation Commission and Iron and Steel Arbitration Tribunal.

[8] Supreme Court Act 1981, s. 18(1) (*e*). Leave may be granted by the House of Lords for an appeal direct to the House from the divisional court (Administration of Justice Act 1969, s. 12(2) (*c*)). See also Tribunals and Inquiries Act 1971, s. 13(4) as to appeals under that Act.

[9] Supreme Court Act 1981, s. 18(1) (*f*). Although the Court of Appeal will, despite this statutory restriction, entertain on appeal where it adjudges that the court below has in effect failed to exercise its discretion at all; see *Alltrans Express, Ltd.* v. *CVA Holdings, Ltd.*, [1984] 1 All E.R. 685; [1984] 1 W.L.R. 394 and the cases cited therein. Where there are genuine grounds of appeal in addition to an appeal against an order as to costs the appeal is not as to costs only even if all the other grounds of appeal are unsuccessful: *Wheeler* v. *Somerfield*, [1966] 2 Q.B. 94; [1966] 2 All E.R. 305.

[10] Supreme Court Act 1981, s. 18(1)(*h*). Whether an order is final or interlocutory depends on the nature of the application to the court rather than the nature of the order made. Thus, for example, the refusal of a county court judge to order a new trial is an interlocutory order as is an order dismissing an action for want of prosecution (see p. 323, *ante*), even though the practical effect may be final in that the action is at an end; the test stated above was laid down by the Court of Appeal in *Salter Rex & Co.* v. *Ghosh*, [1971] 2 Q.B. 597; [1971] 2 All E.R. 865 and applied in *Moran* v. *Lloyd's*, [1983] Q.B. 542; [1983] 2 All E.R. 200 and *White* v. *Brunton*, [1984] Q.B. 570; [1984] 2 All E.R. 606. Section 60 of the Supreme Court Act 1981 enables rules of court to be made providing for orders or judgments to be treated as final or interlocutory for the purposes of appeal to the Court of Appeal. Note, finally, that an order refusing unconditional leave to defend (in Order 14 proceedings, see p. 327, *ante*) is not treated as an interlocutory order for this purpose (Supreme Court Act 1981, s. 18(2)). An order referring a question to the European Court for a preliminary ruling is deemed to be a final order (O. 114) so that no leave to appeal against it is required, although an order refusing to refer a question is an interlocutory order.

(4) from the decision of a county court judge, where the claim (or counter-claim if larger) is for an amount not exceeding one half of the limit of county court jurisdiction, in most cases,[11] or where the determination was by the judge in his appellate capacity; leave is not, however, required where the determination sought to be appealed from includes or preserves an injunction or relates to the custody of or access to a child;

(5) from the decision of a Commercial judge on an arbitration appeal.[12]

Right of appeal excluded

Although section 16 of the Supreme Court Act 1981 confers a general right of appeal from the High Court to the Court of Appeal there are certain cases specified in the Act and in the Rules in which the right of appeal is excluded. Of these the most important are:

(1) from any judgment of the High Court in any criminal cause or matter.[13] In fact it is not true to say that these appeals do not lie to the Court of Appeal; they do not lie to the civil division of the Court of Appeal but they generally do lie to the criminal division with the notable exception of appeals from the divisional court of the Queen's Bench Division which lie, under the Administration of Justice Act 1960, direct to the House of Lords;[14]

(2) from a decision which is provided by any statute to be final;[15]

(3) from a decree absolute for dissolution or nullity of marriage provided that the party wishing to appeal had time and opportunity to appeal from the decree nisi;[16]

(4) from any judgment order or decision of a Circuit judge in the course of official referees' business except as provided in Order 58, rule 4.[17]

Appeals from the registrar and the single judge

An application for leave to appeal to the Court of Appeal is determined by a single judge and there is no appeal from his decision.[18] Other applications are, according to their nature, heard either by the full court, or by a single

---

[11] For the complete list, see County Court Appeals Order 1981.

[12] Arbitration Act 1979, s. 1(7); in this case a second prerequisite is that the judge certify that the question of law to which his decision relates either is of general public importance or is one which for some other special reason should be considered by the Court of Appeal. Note also O. 58, r. 7 under which appeal from the summary determination by a judge of a stakeholder's interpleader lies only with leave.

[13] Supreme Court Act 1981, s. 18(1) (a).

[14] See p. 555, *post*.

[15] Supreme Court Act 1981, s. 18(1) (c); *Lane* v. *Esdaile*, [1891] A.C. 210. Statutes under which an appeal to the High Court is final are listed in O. 94, r. 6.

[16] *Ibid.*, s. 18(1) (d).

[17] Under O. 58, r. 4 (1) an appeal lies (a) from a decision of an official referee on a point of law or as to costs only; and (b) from a decision of an official referee on a question of fact relevant to a charge of fraud or breach of professional duty. There is, in addition, a right to appeal against a committal order made by an official referee under the Administration of Justice Act 1960, s. 13. Apart from these cases the decision of an official referee cannot be called in question "by appeal or otherwise" (O. 58, r. 4(3)). For this reason cases involving important questions, such as the commercial reputation of a party, should be ordered to be tried by a judge and not before an official referee: *Simplicity Products Co.* v. *Domestic Installations Co., Ltd.*, [1973] 2 All E.R. 619; [1973] 1 W.L.R. 837.

[18] Supreme Court Act 1981, s. 54(6).

judge or by the registrar of civil appeals. An appeal lies from the registrar to a single judge.[19] Appeal from decisions of a single judge (other than the determination of an application for leave to appeal) lies to the full court.[20]

2   Appeals from masters and registrars

The general rule is that an appeal lies as of right from any order of a Queen's Bench Division master to a judge in chambers.[1] In certain exceptional cases, set out in Order 58, rule 2, appeal lies from a master direct to the Court of Appeal. These are appeals from any judgment, order or decision (other than an interlocutory judgment, order or decision) given or made:

(*a*) on the hearing or determination of any cause, matter, question or issue tried before or referred to him under Order 36, rule 11 (power to order trial by or reference of issues of fact to a master);
(*b*) on an assessment of damages;[2]

Appeals from masters and registrars take the form of a complete rehearing; that is to say the issue which was argued below is argued out again *de novo* before the judge. Since it is a complete rehearing, the parties are not confined to the points which were taken before the master. Nor are they confined to the evidence which was before the master and it is quite common for further evidence, in the form of affidavits, to be put in before the judge.

3   Appeal to the House of Lords

In civil matters appeal lies from the civil division of the Court of Appeal to the House of Lords only with leave of the Court of Appeal or of the House of Lords.[3] There is no requirement that the appeal be based on a point of law, though almost always appeal to the House of Lords is based upon a point of law rather than on an issue of fact or an award of damages. Although leave is the only prerequisite for appealing, no appeal lies from the decision of the Court of Appeal where any statute expresses the decision of the Court of Appeal to be final. Thus, for example, the decision of the Court is final on any appeal from a county court in probate proceedings[4] and from the determination by a divisional court of the Chancery Division of a bankruptcy appeal from a county court.[5]

---

19 O. 59, r. 14(11); the appeal is by way of fresh application made within 10 days of the registrar's determination (*ibid*.) and the single judge approaches the matter *de novo* unfettered by the registrar's decision: *Van Stillevoldt (C.M.) B.V.* v. *El Carriers Inc.*, [1983] 1 All E.R. 699; [1983] 1 W.L.R. 207.

20 O. 59, r. 14(12); the appeal is by way of fresh application made within 10 days of the single judge's determination.

1 O. 58, r. 1. Likewise, appeal from any order of a district registrar (O. 58, r. 3).

2 This rule was amended in 1978 (by R.S.C. (Amendment No. 2) 1978) following criticisms of its drafting by the Court of Appeal in *Rainbow* v. *Moorgate Properties, Ltd.*, [1975] 2 All E.R. 821; [1975] 1 W.L.R. 788. In addition, before the amendment, interpleader and garnishee issues used to go direct to the Court of Appeal, but these now go to a judge in chambers in the usual way.

3 Administration of Justice (Appeals) Act 1934, s. 1.

4 County Courts Act 1984, s. 82.

5 Bankruptcy Act 1914, s. 108(2) (*a*).

The Administration of Justice Act 1969, Part II provides for a "leap-frog" appeal direct from the High Court to the House of Lords subject to the grant of a certificate by the trial judge and of leave by the House of Lords in any case in which appeal lies to the Court of Appeal (with or without leave).[6]

For the purpose of European Community law the House of Lords is clearly "a Court or tribunal of a Member State, against whose decisions there is no judicial remedy under national law" within the meaning of Article 177(3) of the E.E.C. Treaty, so that where a question arises concerning (*a*) the interpretation of the Treaty; (*b*) the validity and interpretation of acts of the institutions of the Community; or (*c*) the interpretation of the statutes of bodies established by an act of the Council, where those statutes so provide, the House of Lords is bound to refer that question to the European Court for a preliminary ruling (unless, of course, the High Court or Court of Appeal has already referred the question in the same case) and, having obtained the ruling, is bound to follow it.[7]

B PROCEDURE IN THE COURT OF APPEAL

Substantial amendments to procedure in the Court of Appeal were made by the Supreme Court Act 1981 and, more particularly, by a revision of Order 59 in 1982. These changes, and the reasons for them, were fully explained by the Master of the Rolls, SIR JOHN DONALDSON in a statement made at the beginning of the 1982 Michaelmas sittings.[8] The most important changes were: the creation of a new office of registrar of civil appeals,[9] much wider use of two-judge courts, allocation of interlocutory applications to the registrar or to a single judge, standardisation of the time for appealing, alteration of the listing arrangements and the introduction of a practice of handing down written judgments.

An appeal is initiated by serving notice of motion in respect of the whole or any part of the judgment or order in respect of which the appeal is brought. This notice must set out the grounds of appeal shortly but with sufficient particularity to enable the respondent to ascertain exactly what issues are being raised against him. Thus, merely to complain that the trial judge

---

[6] See p. 423, *ante*; the principal conditions precedent to the grant of a certificate are (1) the consent of all parties, and (2) that the case involves a point of law of general public importance either relating to the construction of an enactment or being a point on which the judge was bound by precedent: *American Cyanamid Co.* v. *Upjohn Co.*, [1970] 3 All E.R. 785; [1970] 1 W.L.R. 1507, a case concerning a petition for revocation of a patent, was the first "leap-frog" appeal heard by the House of Lords.

[7] See, generally, *Bulmer (H. P.), Ltd.* v. *J. Bollinger, S. A.*, [1974] Ch. 401; [1974] 2 All E.R. 1226.

[8] The statement is reported as *Practice Note*, [1982] 3 All E.R. 376; [1982] 1 W.L.R. 1312 and repays study in that it contains a readable, concise but virtually comprehensive guide to current procedure in the Civil Division of the Court of Appeal.

[9] Supreme Court Act 1981, s. 89(1), Sch. 2. He must be a barrister or solicitor of not less than 10 years' standing (*ibid.*). His functions include supervising the listing of appeals, giving directions as to the conduct of pending appeals (under O. 59, r. 9(3), (4)) and hearing interlocutory applications such as applications for extension of time, leave to amend a notice of appeal, security for costs, leave to adduce further evidence, expedition and vacating a hearing date.

misdirected the jury would be inadequate; the particular nature of the mis-direction must be specified. The notice must also contain a statement of the order for which the apellant is applying to the court, and the list in which he proposes to set down the appeal. The notice must be served on all parties interested in the appeal and upon such other persons as the Court of Appeal may direct.[10] Notice of appeal must be served within 4 weeks[11] of the date upon which judgment in the court below was signed or entered, though this time may be extended either by the Court of Appeal or, if application is made before the time expires, by the court below. Having served the notice of appeal, the appellant must within 7 days apply to set down the appeal. To do so he produces an office copy of the judgment or order appealed from, together with two copies of his notice of appeal, one of which must bear the appropriate judicature fee stamp and an office copy of any list of exhibits made at the hearing.[12] The appeal is then set down in the appropriate list to await hearing. The next stage in the procedure is that the appeal will appear in the List of Forthcoming Appeals. Then, within 14 days, the appellant must lodge with the registrar bundles of the copy documents which are going to be required for the use of the court on the hearing; these include the notice of appeal, any respondent's notice, the judgment or order of the court below, the pleadings, a transcript of the official shorthand note of the judge's reasons (or a note of them if there is no official shorthand note), such part of the transcript of the official shorthand note of the evidence (or the judge's note if there is no official shorthand note) as is relevant to the appeal and such affidavits and exhibits used below as are relevant to the appeal.[13]

After the documents have been lodged the registrar may give such directions "as appear best adapted to secure the just, expeditious and economical disposal of the appeal" and may summon the parties to appear before him for this purpose.[14]

Thereafter the appeal will appear in the Warned List and will be listed for hearing. In order to save the time of the court in recording counsel's arguments, and in order to enable the court to examine those arguments in advance of the hearing, it is currently the practice in most cases for counsel to submit in advance of the hearing "skeleton arguments" containing a numbered list of the points which each counsel proposes to argue and the references to the material to which counsel will refer in support of these points.[15]

Appeals may be heard by two or three judges of the Court.[16]

---

[10] O. 59, r. 3. Appeals from tribunals to the Court of Appeal are by case stated, the procedure being governed by O. 61.

[11] O. 59, r. 4. The only exceptions to the standard 4-week period are: (1) 6 weeks in the case of appeals under s. 14 of the Social Security Act 1980 (O. 59, r. 21); and (2); 14 days in the case of appeal from an order referring a question to the European Court (O. 114, r. 6).

[12] O. 59, r. 5.

[13] O. 59, r. 9; see also *Practice Note*, [1983] 2 All E.R. 416 for further directions as to the manner in which the bundles should be prepared, bound and paginated.

[14] O. 59, r. 9(3), (4).

[15] *Practice Note*, [1983] 2 All E.R. 34; [1983] 1 W.L.R. 1055.

[16] Supreme Court Act 1981, s. 54; if they are equally divided the case must, on the application of any party, be re-argued before another court containing an uneven number of judges (*ibid.*, s. 54(5)). The Court of Appeal has indicated that in complex cases, where a difference of judicial opinion may be anticipated, counsel should apply for a hearing before an uneven number: *Wandsworth London Borough Council* v. *Winder*, [1984] 3 All E.R. 83; [1984] 3 W.L.R. 563.

Except in the case of applications for a new trial or to set aside a verdict, appeal is "by way of rehearing". That is to say the Court hears full legal argument from both sides and may substitute its own judgment for that of the court below. However it is not a complete rehearing, as it is before the judge in chambers or in the Crown Court in criminal cases, since the Court does not, in practice, hear again the testimony of the trial witnesses, but merely sees transcripts of their evidence.[17]

In addition the appellant is normally confined to the points of law which he raised in the court below. He may in certain circumstances, discussed below, be allowed to take new points on appeal but he cannot, except with leave of the Court of Appeal, rely on any grounds of appeal or apply for any relief not specified in his notice of appeal.[18]

Cross-appeal

A respondent who, not having appealed from the decision of the court below, seeks to have the judgment or order of the court below either varied or affirmed on other grounds need not enter a separate notice of appeal. His proper course is to serve on the appellant, and on any other party directly affected, a "respondent's notice" specifying the grounds of his contention and any alteration in the judgment or order which he requests. Thus, for example, if the appellant is appealing against a finding as to his liability the respondent may, by his notice, appeal against his award of damages. A respondent's notice must be served within 21 days of service of the notice of appeal, and the respondent must, within 2 days after service of the notice, file two copies of the notice.[19]

C POWERS OF THE COURT OF APPEAL

The Court of Appeal has all the powers, authority and jurisdiction of the court or tribunal from which the appeal was brought in any matter before it.[20] The Court has power to examine trial witnesses though it rarely does so, being content in most cases to rely upon the judge's note or a transcript of the official shorthand note. It has power to receive further evidence orally, by affidavit or by deposition taken before an examiner but, where there was a trial or hearing on the merits, the Court of Appeal will not admit further evidence (other than evidence as to matters which have occurred since the trial) except on special grounds.[1] In *Ladd* v. *Marshall*[2] DENNING, L.J. (as he then was), prescribed the following three conditions for the reception of fresh evidence in the Court of Appeal:[3]

---

[17] O. 59, r. 12.

[18] O. 59, r. 3(3).

[19] O. 59, r. 6.

[20] Supreme Court Act 1981, s. 15. These powers are both statutory and inherent. Thus the Court of Appeal may strike out a notice of appeal in the same way as the High Court may strike out a statement of claim either under O. 18, r. 19 or in exercise of its inherent power: *Aviagents, Ltd* v. *Balstravest Investments, Ltd.*, [1966] 1 All E.R. 450; [1966] 1 W.L.R. 150.

[1] O. 59, r. 10(2). A hearing under O. 14 (as to which see p. 326, *ante*) is a "hearing on the merits" for this purpose: *Langdale* v. *Danby*, [1982] 3 All E.R. 129; [1982] 1 W.L.R. 1123.

[2] [1954] 3 All E.R. 745; [1954] 1 W.L.R. 1489; applied in *Roe* v. *Robert McGregor & Sons, Ltd.*, [1968] 2 All E.R. 636; [1968] 1 W.L.R. 925.

[3] [1954] 3 All E.R. 745, at p. 748; [1954] 1 W.L.R. 1489, at p. 1491.

"First, it must be shown that the evidence could not have been obtained with reasonable diligence for use at the trial; secondly, the evidence must be such that, if given, it would probably have an important influence on the result of the case, though it need not be decisive; thirdly, the evidence must be such as is presumably to be believed, or, in other words, it must be apparently credible though it need not be incontrovertible."[4]

This statement was approved by the House of Lords in *Skone* v. *Skone*[5] where the evidence consisted of a bundle of love letters written by the co-respondent in a divorce suit to the wife which tended to prove adultery between them. The trial judge had dismissed the husband's petition and accepted the co-respondent's evidence to the effect that adultery had not taken place. It was argued that these letters (which were in the possession of the wife) could have been obtained by seeking discovery of documents from the wife. The House of Lords rejected this argument on the basis that the husband had no reason to suspect the existence of such letters, that the letters, if genuine, falsified the judge's finding to such an extent that it would be unjust to leave matters where they were and, furthermore, that there was a strong *prima facie* case of deception of the court.

It must be emphasised that these rigorous conditions need not be satisfied in respect of evidence of matters occurring after the trial. Evidence will be admitted of matters occurring after the trial where the basis on which the trial judge gave his decision has been clearly falsified by subsequent events.[6]

Since appeal to the Court of Appeal is "by way of rehearing" the Court of Appeal has full power to make any order which should have been made in the court below[7] and to substitute its own order as to liability, quantum or costs for that of the court below. In addition the Court of Appeal is not confined to the points raised in the notice of appeal or respondent's notice. It may, though it rarely does, take any point of law or fact so far as is necessary to ensure the determination on the merits of the real question in issue between the parties. Should the Court of Appeal wish to decide an issue of fact which has not been pleaded, an extremely infrequent contingency, it may allow the pleading to be amended.[8]

The Court has power to order an appellant to give security for the costs of an appeal in any case in which he could be required to give security for costs under Order 23[9] and, in addition, in "special circumstances"[10] generally where the appellant would be unable to pay the costs of the appeal if

---

[4] Compare the somewhat wider provisions for the reception of fresh evidence in the criminal division of the Court of Appeal; see p. 536, *post*.
[5] [1971] 2 All E.R. 582; [1971] 1 W.L.R. 812.
[6] *Mulholland* v. *Mitchell*, [1971] A.C. 666; [1971] 1 All E.R. 307 (in which the plaintiff's condition had unexpectedly deteriorated between the trial and the hearing of the appeal) and *McCann* v. *Sheppard*, [1973] 2 All E.R. 881; [1973] 1 W.L.R. 540 (in which the plaintiff had died while his appeal was pending). Where the fresh evidence becomes available to a party during the trial he must adduce it then and there, even though this may necessitate an adjournment. He must not disregard it and thereafter found an application for a new trial upon the fresh evidence: *Cowling* v. *Matbro, Ltd.*, [1969] 2 All E.R. 664; [1969] 1 W.L.R. 598.
[7] O. 59, r. 10(3).
[8] See *Bell* v. *Lever Brothers, Ltd.*, [1932] A.C. 161, at p. 216.
[9] See p. 361, *ante*.
[10] O. 59, r. 10(5).

unsuccessful. Although an appeal does not operate as a stay of execution the Court of Appeal has power to order a stay of execution though it will only do so if there is some good reason, since it inclines against depriving a person of the fruits of his litigation. If a stay of execution is ordered on an appeal from the High Court, interest is allowed on the judgment debt unless there is an express order to the contrary.[11]

Special note should be taken of the power, which the High Court also possesses, to refer a question to the European Court for a preliminary ruling. The procedure is governed by Order 114 and the principles upon which the Court of Appeal should act are those set out in the judgment of LORD DENNING, M.R. in *Bulmer (H.P.), Ltd* v. *J. Bollinger, S.A.*[12]

In addition to the powers of the Court of Appeal listed above there is an extremely important power which the High Court does not possess.[13] This is the power to order a new trial, the exercise of which is considered in detail below.

D THE APPROACH OF THE COURT OF APPEAL TO THE DETERMINATION OF APPEALS

1 Appeal on a point of law

Most appeals to the Court of Appeal are based on a point of law. It has already been stated that, notwithstanding the general power of the Court of Appeal to take a point not raised therein, the Court usually confines itself to the points raised in the notice of appeal or respondent's notice. Furthermore there is a general rule that a party cannot take on appeal a point which he did not take in the court below.[14] To this rule there are two important exceptions. The first occurs where the point of law was expressly reserved in the court below. This might occur where the court below was not free to consider the point because it was bound by precedent on that point, whereas the Court of Appeal might be free to reconsider the precedent in question. Secondly, the Court of Appeal will allow a point to be taken, and indeed will take the point itself, where not to do so would result in an abuse of the court's process.

---

[11] O. 59, r. 13.
[12] [1974] Ch. 401; [1974] 2 All E.R. 1226; see p. 380, *ante* for a summary of these principles. *Quaere* whether, in a case in which there is no appeal from the Court of Appeal to the House of Lords, the former is bound to refer the point to the European Court or simply empowered to do so; this depends upon whether the Court of Appeal in such a case is "a Court or tribunal of a Member State, against whose decisions there is no judicial remedy under national law" (Article 177(3) of the E.E.C. Treaty). It is submitted that the use of the plural "decisions" confines Article 177(3) to the House of Lords and does not extend to the Court of Appeal in an individual case in which the decision is final.
[13] Although s. 17(2) of the Supreme Court Act 1981 enables rules of court to provide for an application for a new trial to be determined by the High Court where the trial was by a judge alone and no error of the court at the trial is alleged.
[14] The rule is not, however, invariable so that where all the findings of fact upon which the application of the point of law depends were made by the trial judge, the Court of Appeal may allow the point to be taken: *Donaghey* v. *P. O'Brien & Co.*, [1966] 2 All E.R. 822; [1966] 1 W.L.R. 1170 (affirmed on this point, though reversed on another ground, *sub. nom. Donaghey* v. *Boulton and Paul, Ltd.*, [1968] A.C. 1; [1967] 2 All E.R. 1014); cf. *Wilson* v. *Liverpool City Council*, [1971] 1 All E.R. 628; [1971] 1 W.L.R. 302.

Thus the illegality of a contract may be raised on appeal even though the point was overlooked in the court below.[15]

2 Appeal against a finding of fact

Since the appeal is by way of rehearing the Court of Appeal has power to substitute its own finding of fact, direct or inferential, for that of the trial judge or jury. There are, however, three restrictions upon this general power to upset findings of fact made at the trial. First, the Court of Appeal in practice confines itself to issues of fact raised in the notice of appeal or respondent's notice. Secondly, the Court of Appeal cannot make a finding in relation to a fact not pleaded, although it can give leave to amend the pleadings.[16] Finally, the Court does not as a rule upset direct findings of fact, whether they were made by a judge or by a jury. The reason for this is that, as stated earlier, the Court of Appeal does not have the advantage, which the judge and jury had, of seeing the trial witnesses and observing their demeanour.[17] Consequently the jurisdiction exercised by the Court of Appeal in relation to findings of fact is confined to inferential findings of fact. The Court has power to substitute its own inference from the facts as found for that of the trial judge or jury and will not hesitate to do so. Thus, for example, in one case the Court of Appeal reduced a plaintiff's award of damages by half on the basis of his contributory negligence even though there had been no finding of contributory negligence at the trial.[18] Contributory negligence, like negligence, is an inference of fact to be drawn from the facts as found. In a recent medical negligence action, where the crucial issue of fact was whether a hospital registrar had pulled "too long and too hard" on the head of the infant plaintiff in the course of his birth, LORD BRIDGE explained his willingness to uphold an appeal from the trial judge's finding in the plaintiff's favour in the following words.[19]

> "My Lords, I recognise that this is a question of pure fact and that in the realm of fact, as the authorities repeatedly emphasise, the advantages which the judge derives from seeing and hearing the witnesses must always be respected by an appellate court. At the same time the importance of the part played by those advantages in assisting the judge to any particular conclusion of fact varies through a wide spectrum from, at one end, a straight conflict of primary fact between witnesses, where credibility is crucial and the appellate court can hardly ever interfere, to, at the other end, an inference from undisputed primary facts, where the appellate court is in just as good a position as the trial judge to make the decision."

---

[15] See *Snell* v. *Unity Finance, Ltd.*, [1964] 2 Q.B. 203; [1963] 3 All E.R. 50; cf. *Oscroft* v. *Benabo*, [1967] 2 All E.R. 548; [1967] 1 W.L.R. 1087.

[16] See *Bell* v. *Lever Brothers, Ltd.*, [1932] A.C. 161.

[17] The Court of Appeal feels no such inhibition when the evidence at the trial was given by written statement or deposition; see *Gallie* v. *Lee*, [1969] 1 All E.R. 1062, at p. 1079; [1969] 2 W.L.R. 901, at p. 921 (affirmed [1971] A.C. 1004; [1970] 3 All E.R. 961).

[18] *Hicks* v. *British Transport Commission*, [1958] 2 All E.R. 39; [1958] 1 W.L.R. 493; see also *Benmax* v. *Austin Motor Co., Ltd.*, [1955] A.C. 370; [1955] 1 All E.R. 326; *Qualcast (Wolverhampton), Ltd.* v. *Haynes*, [1959] A.C. 743; [1959] 2 All E.R. 38.

[19] *Whitehouse* v. *Jordan*, [1981] 1 All E.R. 267, at p. 286; [1981] 1 W.L.R. 246, at p. 269.

Where a jury has returned a general verdict it is impossible to distinguish direct findings of fact from inferential findings and, indeed, the jury cannot be asked, after they have returned a general verdict, to state what their direct findings of fact were.[20] The Court of Appeal, therefore, can only upset the general verdict of a jury if it cannot be supported by the evidence or is a verdict which no reasonable men could have reached.[1]

3 Appeal against the exercise of a discretion

In many circumstances the judge has a discretion as to whether, and in what manner, to exercise his powers. Commonly encountered instances of judicial discretion are the discretion as to costs, the discretion whether to grant or refuse an injunction and the discretion as to the mode of trial, in particular in relation to the question of whether or not to order jury trial. However, no discretion is absolute[2] and there may be a successful appeal to the Court of Appeal in relation to the exercise of a judicial discretion if the appellant can show that the judge exercised his discretion under a mistake of law,[3] or under a misapprehension as to the facts, or that he took into account irrelevant matters or gave insufficient weight, or too much weight, to certain factors[4] or that he failed to exercise his discretion at all.[5] If the judge gives no reasons, or insufficient reasons for the exercise of his discretion, the court may infer that he has gone wrong in one respect or another.[6] The burden of proof is on the party who alleges that the discretion was wrongly exercised and, in any event, the Court of Appeal will only allow the appeal if satisfied that the judge's conclusion is one which involves injustice or was clearly wrong.[7] In *Hadmor Productions, Ltd.* v. *Hamilton* LORD DIPLOCK explained the extent of the appellate court's powers as follows.[8]

> "Before adverting to the evidence that was before the judge and the additional evidence that was before the Court of Appeal, it is I think appropriate to remind your Lordships of the limited function of an appellate court in an appeal of this

[20] *Barnes* v. *Hill*, [1967] 1 Q.B. 579; [1967] 1 All E.R. 347.

[1] *Mechanical and General Inventions Co., Ltd.* v. *Austin*, [1935] A.C. 347.

[2] R.S.C. (Revision) 1962, O. 36, r. 1 described the discretion as to the mode of trial as an "absolute one" but the Court of Appeal in *Ward* v. *James*, [1966] 1 Q.B. 273, at p. 293; [1965] 1 All E.R. 563, at p. 568 stated that the word "absolute" either added nothing or, if it did, was *ultra vires*. R.S.C. (Revision) 1965, O. 33 omits the reference to an "absolute" discretion.

[3] *Evans* v. *Bartlam*, [1937] A.C. 473; [1937] 2 All E.R. 646.

[4] *Re F.* (*a minor*) (*wardship: appeal*), [1976] Fam. 238; [1976] 1 All E.R. 417; *Birkett* v. *James*, [1978] A.C. 297; [1977] 2 All E.R. 801.

[5] *Evans* v. *Bartlam*, *supra*.

[6] *Ward* v. *James*, [1966] 1 Q.B. 273; [1965] 1 All E.R. 563; In *Re a Debtor* (*No. 12 of 1970*), [1971] 1 All E.R. 504; [1971] 1 W.L.R. 261 (affirmed [1971] 2 All E.R. 1494; [1971] 1 W.L.R. 1212).

[7] *Beck* v. *Value Capital, Ltd.* (*No. 2*), [1976] 2 All E.R. 102; [1976] 1 W.L.R. 572.

[8] [1983] 1 A.C. 191, at p. 220; [1982] 1 All E.R. 1042, at p. 1046. The appeal was from a decision of the Court of Appeal, presided over by the then Master of the Rolls, LORD DENNING, who was thought by some to be inclined to substitute his own discretion for that of the judge below rather more freely than precedent would allow. LORD DIPLOCK had occasion to repeat, almost *verbatim*, the passage quoted above, in *Garden Cottage Foods, Ltd.* v. *Milk Marketing Board*, [1984] A.C. 130; [1983] 2 All E.R. 770, once again in reversing the decision of the Court of Appeal presided over by LORD DENNING.

kind. An interlocutory injunction is a discretionary relief and the discretion whether or not to grant it is vested in the High Court judge by whom the application for it is heard. On an appeal from the judge's grant or refusal of an interlocutory injunction the function of an appellate court, whether it be the Court of Appeal or your Lordships' House, is not to exercise an independent discretion of its own. It must defer to the judge's exercise of his discretion and must not interfere with it merely on the ground that the members of the appellate court would have exercised the discretion differently. The function of the appellate court is initially one of review only. It may set aside the judge's exercise of his discretion on the ground that it was based on a misunderstanding of the law or of the evidence before him or on an inference that particular facts existed or did not exist, which, although it was one that might legitimately have been drawn on the evidence that was before the judge, can be demonstrated to be wrong by further evidence that has become available by the time of the appeal, or on the ground that there has been a change of circumstances after the judge made his order that would have justified his acceding to an application to vary it. Since reasons given by judges for granting or refusing interlocutory injunctions may sometimes be sketchy, there may also be occasional cases where even though no erroneous assumption of law of fact can be identified the judge's decision to grant or refuse the injunction is so aberrant that it must be set aside on the ground that no reasonable judge regardful of his duty to act judicially could have reached it. It is only if and after the appellate court has reached the conclusion that the judge's exercise of his discretion must be set aside for one or other of these reasons that it becomes entitled to exercise an original discretion of its own.''

4   Appeal against an award of damages

The approach adopted by the Court of Appeal when determining an appeal against an award of damages differs according to whether the award was made by a jury or by a judge sitting alone. Where unliquidated damages are claimed, the Court will not interfere with the award of a jury unless the damages awarded are so large or, more rarely, so small that no jury could reasonably have given them.[9] The reason for this is that the assessment of damages is historically the province of the jury in any case. Thus juries know of no fixed scale of damages comparable to that applied by judges, and the law does not consider it desirable that they should be made aware of any such scale.[10] In the matter of damages; "the views of juries may form a valuable corrective to the views of judges".[11] However a new trial may be ordered if it appears to the court either that the jury took into account irrelevant factors or failed to consider matters which it ought to have considered and in consequence awarded damages which were excessive or inadequate. The case of *Lewis* v. *Daily Telegraph, Ltd.*[12] provides a good example. In that case two national newspapers published on the same day paragraphs alleged to be defamatory of the plaintiffs. The jury in the first action awarded the plain-

---

[9] *Johnston* v. *Great Western Rail. Co.*, [1904] 2 K.B. 250. The award must be an "entirely erroneous" estimate: *Banbury* v. *Bank of Montreal*, [1918] A.C. 626, at p. 694. The principle was reaffirmed by the House of Lords in *Cassell & Co., Ltd.* v. *Broome*, [1972] A.C. 1027; [1972] 1 All E.R. 801 where the House, by a bare majority, upheld an award of £40,000 for libel although unanimous in regarding the sum as excessive.

[10] The desirability of not informing juries of awards of damages in comparable cases was reiterated by LORD DENNING, M.R. in *Ward* v. *James* (*supra*).

[11] *Per* MORRIS, L.J. in *Scott* v. *Musial*, [1959] 2 Q.B. 429; [1959] 3 All E.R. 193.

[12] [1964] A.C. 234; [1963] 2 All E.R. 151.

tiffs a total of £100,000; in the second action two days later in which there were factors which a jury might be entitled to take into account as aggravating damages, a different jury awarded the plaintiffs a further £117,000. New trials of both actions were ordered on the ground (*inter alia*) that the damages in each case were excessive. The House of Lords, affirming the decision of the Court of Appeal, stated that in such a case, pursuant to section 12 of the Defamation Act 1952, each jury should be directed to consider how far the damage suffered can reasonably be attributed solely to the libel with which they are concerned, and how far it ought to be regarded as the joint result of the two libels, bearing in mind that the plaintiff ought not to be compensated twice for the same loss.

Where the award of damages appealed against was made by a judge sitting alone the Court of Appeal will not hesitate to interfere with the assessment, not only on the ground that the judge applied a wrong principle of law in making the assessment, but also on the ground that the award is out of scale with awards in similar cases. There is, of course, no prescribed scale of damages in any type of action but, nevertheless, there is a certain degree of parity in awards in respect of similar types of damage particularly in actions for damages for personal injuries.[13] In such cases the Court of Appeal will not make small adjustments to the sum awarded though it will make a substantial adjustment if that is found necessary. In practice the Court will rarely interfere unless an adjustment of at least 20 or 25 *per cent* is envisaged. It is this diversity of approach to awards of damages made by judges and juries respectively that has led to the virtual disappearance of jury trial in personal injuries actions.[14]

5 Exercise of the power to order a new trial

The Court of Appeal has power under section 17 of the Supreme Court Act 1981 and Order 59, rule 11 to order a new trial. It may exercise this power on an appeal from a judge and jury or from a judge alone just as it can on a motion for a new trial following a trial with a jury.[15] A new trial may be ordered on any one issue without disturbing the finding of the court below on any other issue. Thus the Court of Appeal may order a new trial on the issue of damages while affirming the decision on the question of liability. Indeed if the only ground of application is the amount of damages the Court should limit the new trial to that issue and leave the findings as to liability undisturbed.[16] If there is a new trial that trial is completely independent of the first trial. The mode of trial need not be the same, no estoppels arise as a result of the first trial and the parties may raise new points and may contest issues left uncontested at the first trial. The costs of the first trial are

---

13 See observations of LORD DENNING, M.R. on scales of damages in personal injuries actions in *Ward* v. *James*, [1966] 1 Q.B. 273, at pp. 296 *et seq.*; [1965] 1 All E.R. 563, at pp. 572 *et seq.* For an illustration of the tendency to standardise damages see *Bastow* v. *Bagley & Co., Ltd.*, [1961] 3 All E.R. 1101; [1961] 1 W.L.R. 1494. See also *Brown* v. *Thompson*, [1968] 2 All E.R. 708; [1968] 1 W.L.R. 1003.

14 See p. 244, *ante*.

15 Compare the very limited power of the criminal division of the Court of Appeal to order a new trial; see p. 537, *post*.

16 *Tolley* v. *Fry & Sons, Ltd.*, [1931] A.C. 333, at p. 341.

sometimes ordered to await the outcome of the new trial though, as a rule, the successful applicant ought to be allowed the costs of his application.[17]

There are several grounds upon which a new trial may be ordered of which the more important are set out below.

a   Misdirection

The judge has a duty to provide the jury with an adequate direction as to what are the issues to be decided, what is the law applicable to those issues and what is the effect in law of the evidence received. If this is not done there is a misdirection. The expression "misdirection" includes a failure to direct at all.[18]

b   Improper admission or rejection of evidence

c   Wrongful withdrawal of a question from the jury

It is expressly provided by Order 59, rule 11(2) that the Court is not bound to order a new trial on any of the above three grounds "unless in the opinion of the Court of Appeal some substantial wrong or miscarriage has been thereby occasioned".[19] There will not have been an operative miscarriage of justice unless the appellant has lost a chance of success which was fairly open to him. The burden is on the party supporting the verdict to show that, on the evidence, there has been no miscarriage of justice.

d   Perverse jury verdict

The Court of Appeal is slow to order a new trial on this ground and there is a heavy burden on the applicant. He must show not merely that the verdict is one which reasonable men *ought* not to have reached but that it is one which no jury of reasonable men, properly directed, *could* have found upon the evidence. This may occur either because there was no evidence at all in support of a material fact or because such evidence as there was could not reasonably be believed.

e   Jury verdict as to damages

The limited circumstances in which the Court of Appeal is prepared to upset a jury verdict as to damages have already been noted.[20] Where the Court of Appeal does decide that damages awarded by a jury are excessive or inadequate it has no power to substitute its own award without the consent of all parties concerned although it may increase or reduce an award in respect of any distinct head of damages erroneously included in or excluded from the sum awarded, with consent of the party who will be adversely affected by the increase or reduction.[1]

---

[17] *Hamilton* v. *Seal*, [1904] 2 K.B. 262; cf. *Bray* v. *Ford*, [1896] A.C. 44.

[18] *Hobbs* v. *Tinling & Co. Ltd.*, [1929] 2 K.B. 1.

[19] Compare the wording of the proviso to s. 2(1) of the Criminal Appeal Act 1968; see p. 533, *post*.

[20] See p. 434, *ante*.

[1] O. 59, r. 11(4).

f Discovery of fresh evidence

The principles upon which the Court of Appeal acts when considering applications for a new trial on the ground of the discovery of fresh evidence are similar to those applicable where the Court is asked to receive fresh evidence on the hearing of an appeal.[2]

A common example of fresh evidence which will justify a new trial is the discovery that one of the trial witnesses gave false evidence.[3]

g Misconduct or other irregularity at the trial

A new trial may be ordered on the ground of misconduct on the part of the judge, the jury, counsel, court officers or other persons, provided that the misconduct in question prevented either party from having a fair trial. It is not sufficient that either judge or jury expressed a strong opinion in favour of one party during the trial. However new trials have been ordered where the verdict of the jury was reached by drawing lots,[4] where the jury expressed a strong opinion in favour of the plaintiff before hearing the defendant's evidence,[5] where the court was misled by counsel[6] and where the judge's constant interruptions prevented one side from conducting an effective cross-examination.[7]

h Surprise

The applicant for a new trial on the ground of surprise must swear an affidavit setting out the facts on which he relies. He may allege, for example, that the action came on for trial unexpectedly when his witnesses were not available or that his opponent was allowed to present his case in a way for which the applicant was not prepared. Thus where, in a personal injuries action, the plaintiff at the end of the trial confronted the defendants with, and succeeded on, a case based on allegations which had not been pleaded and which the defendants had not come to the trial prepared to meet, a new trial was ordered.[8] The application will only succeed if the surprise has occasioned a substantial miscarriage of justice.

i Judgment obtained by fraud

There are alternative methods of challenging a judgment obtained by fraud. The first is by a motion for a new trial. Alternatively the party affected may bring an action to have the judgment set aside. In either case the party has the burden of particularising and proving the fraud alleged.[9]

---

2 See p. 430, *ante.*
3 *Piotrowska* v. *Piotrowski*, [1958] 2 All E.R. 729 n.; [1958] 1 W.L.R. 797. A new trial was ordered in *Skone* v. *Skone*, [1971] 2 All E.R. 582; [1971] 1 W.L.R. 812; see p. 430, *ante.*
4 *Harvey* v. *Hewitt* (1840), 8 Dowl. 598.
5 *Allum* v. *Boultbee* (1854), 9 Exch. 738.
6 *Meek* v. *Fleming*, [1961] 2 Q.B. 366; [1961] 3 All E.R. 148.
7 *Jones* v. *National Coal Board*, [1957] 2 Q.B. 55; [1957] 2 All E.R. 155.
8 *Lloyde* v. *West Midlands Gas Board*, [1971] 2 All E.R. 1240; [1971] 1 W.L.R. 749.
9 *Hip Foong Hong* v. *H. Neotia & Co.*, [1918] A.C. 888.

PART V

Criminal Procedure

SUMMARY

CHAPTER 23

Compelling Appearance and Determining Mode of Trial

A COMPELLING THE APPEARANCE OF THE DEFENDANT

A person accused or suspected of having committed an offence may be brought before the court in one of three ways:

(i) by summons; this is a document, sent to or served on the defendant, ordering him to appear in court;

(ii) by warrant for his arrest; this is an order to the police, or in certain circumstances to private persons, to arrest the defendant and bring him before the court;

(a summons and a warrant are generally known as "process")

(iii) by arrest without warrant, where permitted by law.

Each of these will be considered in turn.

1 Information

Both a summons and a warrant are obtained by the laying of information before a magistrate.

> "An information is nothing more than what the word imports, namely the statement by which the magistrate is informed of the offence for which the summons or warrant is required. . . ."[1]

---

[1] HUDDLESTON, B., in *R*. v. *Hughes* (1879), 4 Q.B.D. 614, at p. 633; cited with approval by the House of Lords in *R*. v. *Manchester Stipendiary Magistrate, Ex parte Hill*, [1983] 1 A.C. 328; *sub nom. Hill* v. *Anderton*, [1982] 2 All E.R. 963, in which it was held that the information was "laid" when received at the office of the clerk to the justices for the relevant area, and that it was not necessary for it to be personally received by the clerk or any justice; it was sufficient that it was received by a member of staff expressly or impliedly authorised to receive it for onward transmission to a justice or the justices' clerk.

It is not necessary for the person requiring the issue of process to attend to lay the information personally; it may be laid by his counsel or solicitor or other person authorised for the purpose.[2]

It is, of course, fundamental that any person[3] may lay information—not only a police officer—unless there is a specific rule to the contrary in the case of the particular offence alleged. To take two examples, proceedings under section 70 of the Race Relations Act 1976, prohibiting incitement to racial hatred, can only be instituted by or with the consent of the Attorney-General,[4] and proceedings under section 4 of the Criminal Law Act 1967, which provides penalties for assisting offenders, can only be instituted by or with the consent of the Director of Public Prosecutions.[4] Where consent or authority is required for the issue of process, the magistrate before whom information is laid should see that the consent or authority is produced before issuing process.[5]

In general there is no time limit on the prosecution of an indictable offence. *Kenny* records four cases in which convictions of murder were obtained 35, 30, 23 and 19 years after the actual murders.[6] In some cases Parliament has for reasons of policy imposed a time limit; thus a prosecution for unlawful sexual intercourse with a girl under sixteen may not be commenced more than twelve months after the commission of the offence.[7] It seems that a prosecution is commenced when information is laid,[8] or (presumably) at the moment of arrest, where the defendant is arrested without warrant. Furthermore every court has a right to decline to hear proceedings on the ground that they are oppressive and an abuse of the process of the court,[9] and delay may itself render proceedings both vexatious and an abuse of process if sufficiently prolonged. However, in the absence of some improper use of the court's procedure, the court should not refuse to hear proceedings.[10]

An information is sufficient in form if it describes the specific offence alleged in ordinary language. Technical terms should be avoided as far as possible. It is not necessary to set out in the information all the elements of the offence, and in particular it is not necessary to "specify or negative" any exemption or general defence;[11] however the information should give such

---

[2] Magistrates' Courts Rules 1981, r. 4(1).

[3] On the subject of prosecutions by private persons, see Jackson, *Machinery of Justice in England* (7th Edn.), pp. 213–215, and Edwards, *Law Officers of the Crown*, especially chapter 16. The Prosecution of Offences Bill, when implemented, will establish a Crown Prosecution Service for England and Wales, headed by the Director of Public Prosecutions, who will have a general duty to take over the conduct of criminal proceedings instituted by the police and to institute and have the conduct of criminal proceedings in certain other cases.

[4] Failure to obtain consent appears to make proceedings a nullity: *R.* v. *Angel*, [1968] 2 All E.R. 607n; [1968] 1 W.L.R. 669.

[5] *Price* v. *Humphries*, [1958] 2 Q.B. 353, at p. 357; [1958] 2 All E.R. 725, at p. 727. Considerable limitations on the power to issue process in the case of young offenders are contained in section 5 of the Children and Young Persons Act 1969. Only a "qualified informant" i.e. a police officer, a children's officer or the N.S.P.C.C. may obtain process. These provisions are not yet in force.

[6] *Kenny's Outlines of Criminal Law* (19th Edn. 1966), p. 547. See also the singular case of *Collins*, convicted of manslaughter 21 years after the event: *The Times*, October 8, 1971.

[7] Sexual Offences Act 1956, s. 37, and Sched. II(10) (*b*).

[8] *R.* v. *Wakely*, [1920] 1 K.B. 688.

[9] *Mills* v. *Cooper*, [1967] 2 Q.B. 459; [1967] 2 All E.R. 100.

[10] *R.* v. *Grays Justices, Ex parte Graham*, [1982] Q.B. 1239; [1982] 3 All E.R. 653.

[11] Magistrates' Courts Rules 1981, r. 4(3).

particulars as may be necessary for explaining the nature of the charge and where the offence charged is statutory there should be a reference to the relevant section of the Act.[12] Further, a magistrates' court must not proceed to the trial of an information which charges more than one offence; such an information must be amended, so as to charge one offence only, before the commencement of the trial.[13] However, a single document may contain two or more informations in which event there is no reason why they cannot be tried together.[14]

An information may normally be in any form; if, however, a warrant is sought in the first instance the information should be in writing and substantiated on oath.[15]

Failure to conform to these rules will not necessarily mean that the issue of process is invalid (with possible liability in false imprisonment) since section 123(1) of the Magistrates' Courts Act provides that:

> "No objection shall be allowed to any information . . . or to any summons or warrant . . . for any defect in it in substance or in form, or for any variance between it and the evidence adduced on behalf of the prosecutor."[16]

The section indicates that:

> "technical objections to informations are not to prevail, even though they touch the substance of the charge. There have been, however, many decisions under that section which show that the section does not operate to prevent an objection being effective where the error alleged is fundamental. . . ."[17]

It is a question of fact and degree in each case whether the error is indeed fundamental. Thus it was held in *Meek* v. *Powell*[18] that where an information charges an offence under a statute which has been repealed this is a fundamental defect which cannot be cured by the section, but only by amendment or dismissal of the summons. Equally, the section cannot "save" an information that is bad because it does not charge any offence at all,[19] or, presumably, one that is bad for duplicity.[20] Again, in *Wright* v. *Nicholson*[1] the appellant had been convicted on an information alleging that the offence charged had been committed on August 17. On appeal to Quarter Sessions the victim simply said "in August". It was held that at that stage there ought to have been an amendment of the information, and then, to avoid injustice, an adjournment of the hearing, since the appellant indicated that he could establish an alibi for the whole of August. Even apart from

---

[12] *Ibid.*, r. 100.

[13] *Ibid.*, r. 12(1). See p. 544, *post.*

[14] *Ibid.*, r. 12(2); see *Shah* v. *Swallow*, [1984] 2 All E.R. 528; *sub. nom. Director of Public Prosecutions* v. *Shah*, [1984] 1 W.L.R. 886.

[15] Magistrates' Courts Act 1980, s. 1(1), (3).

[16] If, however, the variance between a summons or a warrant and the evidence adduced is such that the defendant has been misled, the court must, on the application of the defendant, adjourn the hearing.

[17] HUMPHREYS, J. in *Atterton* v. *Browne*, [1945] K.B. 122, at p. 127, dealing with a section of the Summary Jurisdiction Act 1848 in similar terms to s. 123(1).

[18] [1952] 1 K.B. 164; [1952] 1 All E.R. 347. *Quaere* whether the defendant could waive the irregularity. See also *Hunter* v. *Coombs*, [1962] 1 All E.R. 904; [1962] 1 W.L.R. 573.

[19] *Garman* v. *Plaice*, [1969] 1 All E.R. 62, at p. 64; [1969] 1 W.L.R. 19, at p. 23.

[20] For the meaning of this, see p. 544, *post.*

[1] [1970] 1 All E.R. 12; [1970] 1 W.L.R. 142.

section 123, it is well settled at common law that: "where a person is before justices who have jurisdiction to try the case they need not inquire how he came there, but may try it."[2] Thus in *R*. v. *Hughes*[3] the defendant made a wilfully false statement on oath at the trial of a person who had been brought before the court by·illegal process. It was held that this latter fact did not affect the defendant's liability for perjury.

If and when the defendant is committed for trial he is entitled to a sight of the information, if it is sworn; before committal, and seemingly in any case where the information is not sworn, the defendant's only right is to apply for particulars of the charge to be given. This may be done at any time, application being in the first instance to the prosecutor, although application may be made to the magistrates' court for an order if particulars are refused or those given are thought to be insufficient.[4]

2   Conditions for issue of process

Before issuing process a magistrate must be satisfied of two matters: (1) that as a matter of law he has jurisdiction to issue process; and (2) that in the particular case there is sufficient evidence against the person named in the information to justify the issue of process. As to jurisdiction, section 1(2) of the Magistrates' Courts Act provides that a justice of the peace.[5] for any area[6] may, on information being laid before him, issue a summons or a warrant in the following cases.

(*a*) If the offence[7] was committed or is suspected to have been committed within the area.

(*b*) If it appears to the magistrate issuing process necessary or expedient, with a view to the better administration of justice, that the person charged should be tried jointly with, or in the same place as, some other person who is charged with an offence, and who is in custody, or is being or is to be proceeded against, within the area.[8]

The effect of this provision is shown by the decision of the Court of Criminal Appeal in *R*. v. *Blandford, R*. v. *Freestone*.[9] In that case property had been stolen, and received in Montgomeryshire. The two defendants had received other property, stolen in the same incident from the same prosecutors; however they had received their share in the county borough of Southampton and the county of Stafford respectively. The court held that they had

---

2   LORD COLERIDGE, C.J. in *Dixon* v. *Wells* (1890), 25 Q.B.D. 249, at p. 255.
3   (1879), 4 Q.B.D. 614; see also *R*. v. *Brentford Justices, Ex parte Catlin*, [1975] Q.B. 455; [1975] 2 All E.R. 201.
4   *R*. v. *Aylesbury Justices, Ex parte Wisbey*, [1965] 1 All E.R. 602; [1965] 1 W.L.R. 339 (a case arising out of the great train robbery trial). It was held that the defendant was entitled to particulars of an information charging perjury on a particular day in the trial, since it did not state what piece of evidence was alleged to be false.
5   Section 1 and certain other sections of the Magistrates' Courts Act use the term "justice of the peace", which is synonymous with "magistrate".
6   "Area" means any county, any London commission area and the City of London (*ibid.*, s. 1(8)).
7   By Magistrates' Courts Act 1980, s. 150(5), except where the context otherwise requires references in the Act to an offence include references to an alleged offence.
8   *Ibid.*, s. 1(2) (*b*).
9   [1955] 1 All E.R. 681; [1955] 1 W.L.R. 331.

been validly summoned to appear in Montgomeryshire to answer the charge of receiving.

> "[the provision] operates although the persons are not to be tried jointly. It is enough if some other person is charged with an offence . . . connected with the offence in which the summons has been issued against the other defendant. . . . The fact that persons resident within that jurisdiction are being charged with offences so similar or closely connected that the witnesses for the prosecution or some of them will be the same in both cases may . . . be a good reason for the justice exercising the discretion [to issue process] vested in him by the section. Further . . . where there are offences which are so similar or closely connected, uniformity in the treatment of the accused persons may be desirable."[10]

However the court went on to point out that a magistrate must bear in mind the interests of the defendant before issuing process under this subsection, since the defendant might be caused great difficulty and expense in preparing his defence and procuring the attendance of witnesses.[10]

(*c*) If the person charged resides or is believed to reside in the area.[11]

(*d*) If under any enactment a magistrates' court for the area has jurisdiction to try the offence.[12] Jurisdiction to try is dealt with below.[13], but here it may be noted that summary offences may be tried at the same magistrates' court provided that the court has jurisdiction to try one of them. Thus, if the court has jurisdiction to try offence A, it may also try offences B and C, committed by the same defendant which otherwise it would not have jurisdiction to try. It follows that it may issue process in respect of B and C.

It will be seen that a magistrate is concerned generally with offences committed in, or persons resident in, that area for which he is a magistrate.[14] However section 3 of the 1980 Act lays down certain rules which enable a commonsense view to be taken of whether an offence is committed "within" the area. Thus an offence committed on or within 500 yards of the boundary between two local jurisdictions may be regarded as having been committed in either jurisdiction, as may an offence begun in one jurisdiction and completed in another. Again where an offence has been committed on a vehicle engaged on a journey through two or more local jurisdictions, the offence may be treated for the purpose of section 1 as having been committed in any of them.

As to the point of sufficiency of evidence, namely (2) above, it is in the magistrates' judicial discretion whether he issues process; there is however some authority for saying that if he refused to hear an application for process at all or if he refused to issue process, in spite of being satisfied both as to jurisdiction and as to the evidence in the case, because of "extraneous and extra-judicial" matters, then in either case mandamus would lie to order him to issue process.[15] Assuming, however, that he has decided to issue process,

---

[10] *R. v. Blandford, R. v. Freestone*, [1955] 1 All E.R. 681, at pp. 683–684; [1955] 1 W.L.R. 331, at pp. 334–335.

[11] Magistrates' Courts Act 1980, s. 1(2) (*c*).

[12] *Ibid.*, s. 1(2) (*d*).

[13] See p. 543, *post*.

[14] This "local" jurisdiction contrasts sharply with the jurisdiction of the Crown Court.

[15] *R. v. Adamson* (1875), 1 Q.B.D. 201. The persons against whom process was sought had broken up a meeting addressed by Dr. Kenealy, the defender of the Tichborne claimant, and the extraneous and extra-judicial matter was the magistrate's own opinion of the Tichborne

he must then consider whether to issue a summons or a warrant. Subject to certain exceptions,[16] this too is a matter for his discretion. The discretion must, it should be emphasised, be exercised by the justice or the clerk to the justices[17] personally since the function is a judicial one which cannot be delegated. Thus in *R. v. Gateshead Justices, Ex parte Tesco Stores, Ltd.*[18] it was held that process was invalid where the summons had been "rubber-stamped" with a facsimile of the clerk's signature by a member of his staff. The resulting conviction was quashed. This decision caused considerable consternation since the practice which it had held to be invalid was widely adopted throughout the country at that time. However the House of Lords in *R. v. Manchester Stipendiary Magistrate, Ex parte Hill,* [19] while affirming the principle that the function of issuing summonses could not be delegated as it had been in the *Gateshead* case, pointed out that the decision in the case was in fact incorrect since the information itself, and therefore the trial of that information, was valid, even though the summons was not. Thus no defect in the summons (or warrant) will invalidate the trial of a valid information.

3 Summons

"A summons is a citation proceeding upon an information . . . laid before the magistrate who issues the summons, and conveying to the person cited the fact that the magistrate is satisfied that there is a *prima facie* case against him."

A summons must state shortly the matter of the information and then set out the time and place at which the defendant is required by the summons to appear. A single summons may be issued in respect of several informations, but must state the matter of each information separately and has effect as several summonses, one for each information.[20] In all cases the summons must either be signed by the magistrate issuing it or must state his name, with the signature of the clerk of the court to authenticate it in either event.

A variation of the *Gateshead* point arose in *R. v. Fairford Justices, Ex parte Brewster.*[1] In that case informations were laid just under six months after the commission of the alleged offences to which they related;[2] on the basis of those informations two defective summonses were issued approximately a year later and, subsequently, two effective summonses were issued some nineteen months after the alleged offences. The applicant, perhaps not surprisingly, applied for an order of prohibition to restrain the justices from hearing the informations. His application was refused. Accordingly, while

---

case, then recent and highly controversial. See also *R. v. Metropolitan Police Commissioner, Ex parte Blackburn*, [1968] 2 Q.B. 118; [1968] 1 All E.R. 763, an attempt to secure more sustained enforcement of the then gaming laws.

[16] See p. 448, *post.*

[17] The clerk is authorised to perform this (among other) functions by Rules made under s. 28 of the Justices of Peace Act 1979 (or its statutory predecessor).

[18] [1981] Q.B. 470; [1981] 1 All E.R. 1027.

[19] [1983] 1 A.C. 328; *sub. nom. Hill* v. *Anderton*, [1982] 2 All E.R. 963.

[20] MATHEW, J. in *Dixon* v. *Wells* (1890), 25 Q.B.D. 249, at p. 257.

[1] [1976] Q.B. 600; [1975] 2 All E.R. 757.

[2] Six months being the "limitation period" during which information must be laid for a summary offence if magistrates are to have jurisdiction to try it: Magistrates' Courts Act 1980, s. 127.

the information must be laid within six months, it appears to be immaterial that a summons based on that information is either defective, issued without consideration of the information or issued a very long time after the laying of the information, although it should, perhaps, be pointed out that in the latter case LORD WIDGERY, C.J. stated (*obiter*) that the divisional court would have power to provide a remedy in cases of excessive delay—presumably by issue of the prerogative order of prohibition.[3]

The summons must then be served on the defendant; this may be effected by: (1) delivering it to him; (2) leaving it for him with some person at his last known or usual place of abode; or (3) sending it by post in a letter addressed to him at his last known or usual place of abode.[4] If a person summoned for an indictable offence fails to appear at the trial, service of the summons by methods (2) or (3) above must not be treated as proved unless it is first shown that the summons came to the defendant's knowledge; for this purpose, however, a letter or other communication purporting to be written by or on behalf of the defendant and giving rise to the reasonable inference that the summons came to his knowledge shall be admissible as evidence of that fact.[5] This limitation does not apply to a summary offence, but it is now provided[6] that where a summons has been issued under section 1 of the Act of 1980, and the court has begun to try the information to which the summons relates, the defendant may at any time during or after the hearing make a statutory declaration[7] that he did not know of the summons until a date specified by him. Thereafter the information remains valid (with the result that subsequent proceedings will not be barred by lapse of time),[8] but all subsequent proceedings are void. There may be a fresh trial but not before any of the same magistrates.[9] A summons remains in force even though the magistrate who issued it ceases for any reason to be a magistrate[10] and with certain exceptions (for example under the Road Traffic Act 1972) it may be served at any time after issue.

4   Warrant[11]

A warrant, unlike a summons, is an order for the arrest of the defendant. It is addressed to the officers of the police area in which the warrant is issued and such other persons as are named in the warrant, and directs them to arrest a particular person. That person must be mentioned by name or otherwise described;[12] general warrants, i.e. warrants which do not name the person to

---

[3] As to which, see *R.* v. *Grays Justices, Ex parte Graham*, [1982] Q.B. 1239; [1982] 3 All E.R. 653; p. 442, *ante*.
[4] Magistrates' Courts Rules 1981, r. 99.
[5] *Ibid.*, r. 99(2).
[6] Under s. 14 of the Magistrates' Courts Act.
[7] With liability for perjury if it is false.
[8] Under s. 127 of the Magistrates' Courts Act (*supra*).
[9] *Ibid.*, s. 14(4).
[10] *Ibid.*, s. 124: *quaere* as to the death of the person laying information.
[11] Strictly called "a warrant of arrest" there being various other types of warrant, such as a search warrant.
[12] Magistrates' Courts Rules 1981, r. 96(2).

be arrested, have been held to be illegal at common law ever since a series of famous cases[13] in the eighteenth century.

A warrant must contain a statement of the offence charged in the information and, like a summons, must be signed by the magistrate or clerk issuing it.[14]

A warrant may be executed (i.e. the arrest effected) anywhere in the United Kingdom, at any time,[15] by any person to whom the warrant is directed or by any police officer acting within his police area;[16] an officer making the arrest need not have the warrant in his possession at the time but must show it to the defendant as soon as is practicable, if the defendant demands to see it.[17] This duty is equivalent to the duty imposed on a person making an arrest without warrant to inform the defendant of the reason for his arrest. In the unlikely event of a warrant being addressed to a private person he could of course make the arrest, but by the terms of section 125 would actually have to have the warrant in his possession as well as having to show it on demand.

When a magistrate issues a warrant he may at the same time endorse it with a direction that the person named in the warrant shall, on arrest, be released on bail, on such terms as may be specified in the endorsement. The warrant is then said to be "backed for bail", and the officer in charge of the police station to which the defendant is taken after arrest must release him (subject to approving any surety tendered in compliance with the endorsement).[18] Special provisions apply in relation to the execution of warrants in Eire.[19]

As stated above,[20] the magistrate's discretion as to whether to issue a summons or a warrant is now limited, by section 1(4) of the 1980 Act. No warrant may be issued against a person who is seventeen or over, unless the offence is indictable or punishable with imprisonment, or unless the defendant's address in not "sufficiently established" for a summons to be served on him. Even before the Act a magistrate would not normally issue a warrant unless he was satisfied that a summons would be ineffectual to secure the defendant's presence.

5   Arrest without warrant

Finally, the defendant may be arrested without warrant. Until recent years the law placed police officers and private persons in equal difficulties. A police constable might have had to "decide at a moment's notice a point that has puzzled the appellate courts several times"[1] while a private person's

---

13 Notably *Money* v. *Leach* (1765), 3 Burr. 1742.
14 Magistrates' Courts Rules 1981, rr. 96(2), 95; Magistrates' Courts Act 1980, ss. 123, 124 and Rules, r. 100 (*ante*, pp. 442 and 443 and *supra*) apply to a warrant.
15 Until withdrawn: Magistrates' Courts Act 1980, s. 125(1).
16 *Ibid.*, s. 125(2).
17 *Ibid.*, s. 125(3). This is reasonable from the point of view of the police (since there may be many police seeking to make the arrest, but only one warrant) and also for the purpose of protecting the liberty of the subject.
18 *Ibid.*, s. 117.
19 For Eire, see the Backing of Warrants (Republic of Ireland) Act 1965 which resolved the difficulties revealed by the decision of the House of Lords in *Metropolitan Police Commissioner* v. *Hammond*, [1965] A.C. 810; [1964] 2 All E.R. 722.
20 See p. 446, *ante*.
1 Winfield and Jolowicz on *Tort* (10th Edn. 1971), p. 40.

powers were "so limited and illogical that he is well advised not to try arresting anyone".[2] However the law was greatly simplified[3] by the Criminal Law Act 1967. The Act created a new category of offence (called an "arrestable offence") for which arrest without warrant[4] is permissible. An arrestable offence is any offence for which a person not previously convicted may by statute be sentenced to five years' imprisonment or more, any offence for which the penalty is fixed by law, and attempt to commit any of the offences in these two categories.[5]

These provisions will be repealed and replaced when Part III of the Police and Criminal Evidence Act 1984 is brought into operation. These provisions extend the powers of summary arrest to certain specific statutory offences.[6] Further where a constable has reasonable grounds for suspecting that any offence which is not an arrestable offence has been committed or attempted, or is being committed or attempted, he may arrest the relevant person if it appears to him that service of a summons is impracticable or inappropriate because any of the "general arrest conditions" is satisfied.[7]

Where an offence is arrestable (1) any person may arrest without warrant anyone who is, or is reasonably suspected by the person arresting to be, in the act of committing the offence; (2) any person may arrest without warrant any person whom he reasonably believes to have committed such an offence, or who is in fact guilty of it (reasonably suspected or not). If it is later discovered that no offence was committed by anyone (if for example a taking apparently amounting to theft is discovered to be innocent[8]) a police officer can escape liability for false imprisonment by proving reasonable cause to believe that an arrestable offence had been committed. A private person will however be liable.[9] This rule previously governed the lawfulness of arrest in the case of felonies; it has been criticised,[10] but is preserved by s. 24(5) of the Police and Criminal Evidence Act. If the rule discourages arrest by private persons it may perhaps be justified; (3) a police officer may arrest without warrant anyone who is, or whom he reasonably suspects to be, about to commit an arrestable offence.[11]

---

2 Jackson, *op. cit.* (6th Edn.), p. 165.
3 As one of the surprisingly large number of consequences flowing from the abolition of the distinction between felonies and misdemeanours.
4 Called by the Act "summary arrest". The concept of an "arrestable offence" is used in sections 4 and 5 of the Act, which replace the old law as to accessories after the fact to felony and misprision of felony.
5 Section 2(1). Therefore, theft and many offences under the Theft Act are arrestable.
6 Police and Criminal Evidence Act 1984, s. 24(2).
7 *Ibid.*, s. 25; the "general arrest conditions" are defined in s. 25(3) and include giving a false name or address, arrest necessary to prevent physical injury, damage to property, an offence against public decency or unlawful obstruction of the highway or to protect a child or other vulnerable person.
8 Thus a person shopping in a store may be arrested by a store detective for alleged shoplifting. At the trial the defendant may raise some defence going to show that although he or she took the articles, that taking was (legally) innocent; thus he may suggest that he picked the goods up and later forgot to pay for them. If the defendant is acquitted the store detective and, vicariously, the store will have no defence to an action for false imprisonment.
9 *Walters* v. *W.H. Smith & Son, Ltd.*, [1914] 1 K.B. 595.
10 As one respect "in which the common law has become fossilized": DIPLOCK, L.J. (as he then was) in *Dallison* v. *Caffery*, [1965] 1 Q.B. 348, at p. 370; [1964] 2 All E.R. 610, at p. 619.
11 Criminal Law Act 1967, s. 2(2)–(5). These provisions are repeated in s. 24(4)–(7) of the 1984 Act.

For the purpose of exercising a right of arrest conferred by section 2, a police officer may enter any place (by force if need be) and search it.[12] More generally section 3 provides that a person may use such force as is reasonable in the circumstances in the prevention of crime, or in effecting or assisting in the lawful arrest of offenders or suspected offenders or persons unlawfully at large. The section replaces the common law rules on the subject.

Additionally, a large number of statutes now authorise arrest without warrant in the case of individual offences.[13] For example, it is permissible to arrest a person found committing any indictable offence by night.[14] Where a statute authorises arrest, it is a question of construction of the particular statute as to whether the defendant in an action for false imprisonment, arising out of an arrest purportedly made under the Act, must show that the offence was actually committed by the plaintiff, or whether there is a wider right to arrest if the person arrested was apparently committing the offence in question. There is no general rule, one way or the other, which can be applied to all such statutes.[15] In *Wiltshire* v. *Barrett*[16] the Court of Appeal had to consider section 6(4) of the Road Traffic Act 1960 (now Road Traffic Act 1972, s. 5(5)), which permits a police officer to arrest without warrant "a person committing" an offence under section 6 (driving while under the influence of drink or drugs). The Court held that the power of arrest extended to a person apparently committing the offence.

> ". . . This statute is concerned with the safety of all of Her Majesty's subjects who use the roads in this country. It is of the first importance that any person who is unfit to drive through drink should not be allowed to drive on the road, and that the police should have power to stop him from driving any further. The most effective way to do it is by arresting him then and there. The police have to act at once, on the facts as they appear on the spot: and they should be justified by the facts as they appear to them at the time and not on any *ex post facto* analysis of the situation."[17]

Finally, quite apart from statute, any person may arrest in cases where a breach of the peace has been committed or is reasonably apprehended.[18]

It will be observed that the right to arrest is discretionary; no-one is bound to arrest a person liable to be arrested. The relevance of this fact, in relation to police officers, was considered by the House of Lords in *Holgate-Mohammed* v. *Duke*.[19] The plaintiff sued for damages for wrongful arrest and succeeded in the county court on the basis that, although the conditions

---

[12] *Ibid.*, s. 2(6). This power is preserved by s. 17 of the 1984 Act, which codifies the powers of entry and search of premises by police officers; cf. *Swales* v. *Cox*, [1981] Q.B. 849; [1981] 1 All E.R. 1115.

[13] The Criminal Law Act does not affect the power to arrest in these cases (s. 2(7)), and the offences are not strictly "arrestable". The 1984 Act also preserves the power to arrest in those cases (which are listed in Sch. 2 of the Act).

[14] Prevention of Offences Act 1851, s. 11. This section is repealed by the 1984 Act.

[15] See *Barnard* v. *Gorman*, [1941] A.C. 378; [1941] 3 All E.R. 45. The authorities are reviewed in *Wills* v. *Bowley*, [1983] 1 A.C. 57; [1982] 2 All E.R. 654.

[16] [1966] 1 Q.B. 312; [1965] 2 All E.R. 271.

[17] [1966] 1 Q.B. 312, at p. 321; [1965] 2 All E.R. 271, at p. 274, *per* LORD DENNING, M.R.

[18] *R.* v. *Howell*, [1982] Q.B. 416; [1981] 3 All E.R. 383; *Albert* v. *Lavin*, [1982] A.C. 546; [1981] 3 All E.R. 878. But not simply because the person arrested is obstructing the officer in the execution of his duty: *Wershof* v. *Metropolitan Police Commissioner*, [1978] 3 All E.R. 540.

[19] [1984] A.C. 437; [1984] 1 All E.R. 1054.

for arrest were present, the arresting police officer had exercised his power of arrest in order to bring pressure on the plaintiff to induce a confession and that this was a wrongful exercise of the power of arrest. The decision was reversed on appeal on the narrow ground that, being a public officer charged with a statutory power, the policeman's exercise of discretion could only be attacked on *Wednesbury* principles[20] and that since inducement of a confession was a matter which the officer was entitled to take into account in the exercise of his discretion whether to arrest or not, that exercise would be upheld. Presumably similar considerations would apply to the exercise of the discretion by a private individual although, not being a public officer, *Wednesbury* principles would not, strictly, apply to him.

The courts, and in particular the House of Lords,[1] have laid down certain rules governing the procedure in all cases of arrest without warrant. Every person arresting another without a warrant must inform that other of the reason for his arrest, or at least the facts said to constitute a crime on his part; he need not tell him the exact charge, which may in any event be difficult or impossible to determine until after full examination of the facts. Neither need he even give the information as to the facts of the case

> "if the arrested man is caught red-handed, and the crime is patent to high Heaven. Nor, obviously, is explanation a necessary prelude to arrest when it is important to secure a possibly violent criminal."[2]

Further, the utmost duty resting on the person making the arrest is to do what is reasonable in the circumstances, in discharge of his obligations; thus an arrest was held to be lawful where the defendant was unaware, because of total deafness and inability to lip-read, that he was being arrested but the police officer was likewise unaware of his disability and went through the motions of arrest as for a person not under disability.[3] It seems also that an initially unlawful arrest may be "cured" by the supply of further information at a later stage.[4]

Subject to these limitations, failure to give the defendant the reason for his arrest, or giving him a false reason (even if in fact there is a lawful ground for his arrest, of which the police do not inform him[5]) makes the arrest unlawful.

> "Is citizen A bound to submit unresistingly to arrest by citizen B in ignorance of the charge made against him? I think, my Lords, that cannot be the law of England. Blind, unquestioning obedience is the law of tyrants and of slaves: it does not yet flourish on English soil."[6]

On the other hand LORD SIMONDS expressly sanctioned[7] "holding

---

[20] As to which see p. 178, *ante*.
[1] In *Christie* v. *Leachinsky*, [1947] A.C. 573; [1947] 1 All E.R. 567.
[2] LORD SIMONDS in *Christie* v. *Leachinsky*, [1947] A.C. 573, at p. 593; [1947] 1 All E.R. 567, at p. 575.
[3] *Wheatley* v. *Lodge*, [1971] 1 All E.R. 173; [1971] 1 W.L.R. 29; see also *R.* v. *Inwood*, [1973] 2 All E.R. 645; [1973] 1 W.L.R. 647.
[4] *R.* v. *Kulynycz*, [1971] 1 Q.B. 367; [1970] 3 All E.R. 881.
[5] As in *Christie*'s case itself.
[6] *Christie* v. *Leachinsky*, [1947] A.C. 573, at p. 591; [1947] 1 All E.R. 567, at p. 575, *per* LORD SIMONDS. It is perhaps instructive to compare the same judge's speech in *Shaw* v. *Director of Public Prosecutions*, [1962] A.C. 220; [1961] 2 All E.R. 446; see p. 236, *ante*.
[7] *Christie* v. *Leachinsky*, [1947] A.C. 573, at p. 593; [1947] 1 All E.R. 567, at p. 575, and see the speech of LORD DU PARCQ, at pp. 604 and 577 of the respective reports.

charges", i.e. minor charges made pending investigation of a major one, provided, of course, that there is reasonable belief in the minor charge.

The Police and Criminal Evidence Act 1984, s. 28 in effect codifies the above provisions, save that the obligation to inform the person arrested both that he is under arrest and of the ground for the arrest apply regardless of whether such fact or ground is obvious.[8] There is, of course, no power to detain a person other than pursuant to a lawful arrest (any attempt to do so will justify issue of the prerogative writ of *habeas corpus*). This was confirmed (if it required confirmation) by LAWTON, L.J. in the following terms:[9]

> "it must be clearly understood that neither customs officers nor police officers have any right to detain somebody for the purposes of getting them to help with their inquiries. Police officers either arrest for an offence or they do not arrest at all. Customs either detain for an offence or they do not detain at all. The law is clear. Neither arrest nor detention can properly be carried out without the accused person being told the offence for which he is being arrested. There is no such offence as 'helping police with their inquiries'. This is a phrase which has crept into use, largely because of the need for the press to be careful about how they report what has happened when somebody has been arrested but not charged. If the idea is getting around amongst either Customs and Excise Officers or police officers that they can arrest or detain people, as the case may be, for this particular purpose, the sooner they disabuse themselves of that idea, the better."

The question of whether or not there has been a lawful arrest usually arises in a subsequent civil action for damages for assault or false imprisonment, or in prosecutions for assaulting police officers in the execution of their duty (since it is no part of a constable's duty to detain unlawfully).[10]

For these reasons the question of the validity of an arrest is infinitely more important than the question of the validity of a summons.

A private person arresting without a warrant must hand the person arrested to the police or to a magistrate as soon as reasonably practicable; he will not, however, be liable in false imprisonment if he holds the person arrested for a reasonable time in order to consider the position.[11] A police officer has greater latitude:

> "He can do what is reasonable to investigate the matter, and to see whether the suspicions are supported or not by further evidence. He can . . . take the person suspected to his own house to see whether any of the stolen property is there; . . . he can take the person suspected to the place where he says that he was working, for there he may find persons to confirm or refute his alibi. . . ."[12]

---

8 S. 28(2), (4).
9 *R.* v. *Lemsatef*, [1977] 2 All E.R. 835, at p. 839; [1977] 1 W.L.R. 812, at p. 816.
10 *Ludlow* v. *Burgess*, [1971] Crim. L.R. 238. The question used to arise in proceedings for driving with excess alcohol (since lawful arrest was a condition precedent to the requiring of specimens of blood or urine) and considerable ingenuity was displayed in challenging the legality of the arrest on behalf of drunken drivers who had no other defence. However the amendment of ss. 6–12 of the Road Traffic Act 1972 effected by the Transport Act 1981 put an end to this point since the lawfulness of the arrest is no longer relevant to these offences.
11 *John Lewis & Co., Ltd.* v. *Tims*, [1952] A.C. 676; [1952] 1 All E.R. 1203.
12 LORD DENNING, M.R. in *Dallison* v. *Caffery*, [1965] 1 Q.B. 348, at p. 367; [1964] 2 All E.R. 610, at p. 617 (where the defendant police officer had done both these things).

When a person is taken into custody without a warrant a police officer not below the rank of inspector, or the police officer in charge of the station, whatever his rank, may grant bail; further, if it will not be practicable to bring the defendant before a magistrates' court within 24 hours the officer must enquire into the case and is obliged to grant bail in accordance with the Bail Act 1976 unless the offence appears to him to be a serious one.[13] The defendant may also be bailed to appear at the police station for further enquiry.[14] If detained in custody, he must be brought before a magistrates' court as soon as practicable and, in any event, within 48 hours.[15] At the other end of the scale it may become apparent that the defendant has not in fact committed any offence; in this case he may be released without formality, and there is no obligation to take him before any court.[16] Where any person has been arrested and is being held in custody in a police station or other premises, he is entitled to have intimation of his arrest and of the place where he is being held sent to one person reasonably named by him, without delay or with no more delay than is necessary if some delay is necessary in the interest of the investigation or prevention of crime or the apprehension of offenders.[17]

In this way, it will be seen that English law attempts to give substantial protection to a person arrested without warrant, both in requiring him to be brought before a court within a reasonable time or released on bail, and in requiring that he be given particulars of what is alleged against him.

Nevertheless the protection which English law attempts to provide against wrongful detention is, of necessity, insufficient to prevent all abuses. Thus it sometimes happens that suspects are arrested and taken into police custody, for questioning. If they are detained without being charged or brought before a magistrate, the remedy is to apply for a writ of *habeas corpus* but the procedure for obtaining such a writ[18] necessarily takes a few days even if someone is able to instruct a solicitor to take immediate steps on behalf of a person who is being detained in the manner described. If the police then charge the person concerned just before the application for *habeas corpus* is to be heard the detention will cease to be unlawful. By these means the police are able, in practice, to hold and interrogate a suspect for at least a few days before charging him.

Police and Criminal Evidence Act 1984—The law, as set out above, relating to detention after arrest will be substantially modified when Parts IV and V of the 1984 Act are brought into operation. These Parts of the Act provide a comprehensive statutory code to replace the existing common law and statutory provisions. Under the new provisions the detention of a suspect is subject to periodic review by the station custody officer (if the suspect has been charged) or by an officer of at least the rank of inspector who has

---

[13] Magistrates' Courts Act 1980, s. 43.

[14] *Ibid.*, s. 43(2).

[15] *Ibid.*, s. 43(4); the 48-hour maximum was laid down (by reference to the 48-hour period referred to in the Prevention of Terrorism (Temporary Provisions) Act 1976) in *R. v. Holmes, Ex parte Sherman*, [1981] 2 All E.R 612.

[16] *Wiltshire* v. *Barrett*, [1966] 1 Q.B. 312; [1965] 2 All E.R. 271; p. 450, *ante.*

[17] Criminal Law Act 1977, s. 62 (to be replaced by s. 56 of the Police and Criminal Evidence Act 1984).

[18] The procedure is set out in R.S.C., Order 54.

not been directly involved in the investigation (if the suspect has not been charged). The first review must take place not later than six hours after detention was first authorised and there must thereafter be review at intervals of not more than nine hours.[19] At each review, which is carried out for the purpose of considering whether to authorise continued detention, the suspect (unless he has a solicitor present) must be given the opportunity to make representations to the review officer.

The basic maximum period for which a person may be kept in police detention without being charged is 24 hours,[20] although in certain circumstances an officer of the rank of superintendent or above who is responsible for the police station at which the suspect is being detained may authorise extension of this period to 36 hours[1] and further extensions may be authorised by a "warrant of further detention" issued by a magistrates' court which may be for up to a further 36 hours in the first instance and thereafter for further periods, with a maximum total period of detention without charge of 96 hours.[2]

After charge the person charged must be brought before the local magistrates' court "as soon as is practicable and in any event not later than the first sitting after he is charged with the offence".[3]

Part V of the Act contains detailed provisions relating to the questioning and treatment of persons in police custody, including provisions relating to searches,[4] the right to have someone informed following arrest,[5] access to legal advice[6] and fingerprinting.[7] In addition section 60 requires the Secretary of State to make provision for the tape-recording of interviews of suspects.

It is currently thought that the changes indicated above may be brought into operation some time in 1986.

B   CLASSIFICATION OF OFFENCES

Prior to the implementation of Part III of the Criminal Law Act the law relating to the classification of criminal offences and the determination of the appropriate mode of trial, summary or on indictment, was complex.[8] Thus there were provisions for summary offences to be tried on indictment and for indictable offences to be tried summarily, while there was a third class of offences, colloquially (though not by statute) called "hybrid" offences which might take on the character of either summary offences or indictable offences according to the election of the parties. With a view to simplifying the procedure and to considering methods of reducing the ever

---

[19] Police and Criminal Evidence Act 1984, s. 40.
[20] *Ibid.*, s. 41.
[1] *Ibid.*, s. 42.
[2] *Ibid.*, ss. 43–44.
[3] *Ibid.*, s. 46(2).
[4] *Ibid.*, ss. 54–55.
[5] *Ibid.*, s. 56.
[6] *Ibid.*, s. 58.
[7] *Ibid.*, s. 61.
[8] Details of the former rules may be found in Chapter 23 of the fourth edition of this work.

increasing case load of the Crown Court a committee was set up under the late Lord Justice James to "consider within the framework of the existing court structure what should be the distribution of criminal business between the Crown Court and magistrates' courts; and what changes in law and practice are desirable to that end". The committee, the Interdepartmental Committee on the Distribution of Criminal Business Between the Crown Court and Magistrates' Courts, reported in November 1975.[9]

The committee's recommendations were largely (but not entirely) adopted and it was upon them that Part III of the Criminal Law Act 1977 was based.

As regards mode of trial there are now three classes of offence, namely—

> "(a) offences triable only on indictment;
> (b) offences triable only summarily; and
> (c) offences triable either way."[10]

However, while the above classification is the only important one for the purposes of criminal procedure, it is important to note that "offences triable only on indictment" is not a phrase synonymous with "indictable offences"; the latter phrase means offences which, if committed by an adult, are triable on indictment, whether exclusively so triable or triable either way.[11] Thus an indictable offence may, in the case of an adult, be triable either way by reason of provisions to that effect in the Criminal Law Act while, as we shall see, such offences may be tried summarily in the case of children and young persons. The classification of an offence as an "indictable offence" may be important when construing an Act of Parliament or a private or public document. Thus in *Hastings and Folkestone Glassworks, Ltd.* v. *Kalson*[12] articles of association of a company provided that a director could be disqualified on being convicted of "an indictable offence".[13] The Court of Appeal held that he could be disqualified on being convicted of a hybrid offence, even one which in the particular case had been tried summarily.

> "An 'indictable offence' without any qualifying context can mean nothing else but an offence in respect of which an indictment would lie . . . It is none the less 'indictable' because, if the prosecution chose, it could proceed in respect of it summarily. . . . The measure of gravity is to be sought in my opinion, in what can happen to persons guilty of that class of offence, not what does happen."[14]

At common law all offences are indictable offences; an offence can only be a summary offence if the statute creating it so provides, since all summary jurisdiction derives from statute. Likewise an offence triable either way (while, as has been noted, it may be an indictable offence) is only so triable if statute so provides. Bearing these factors in mind, the classification of offences as regards mode of trial may be looked at more closely.

---

[9] *The Distribution of Criminal Business between the Crown Court and Magistrates' Courts* (Cmnd, 6323).

[10] Criminal Law Act 1977, s. 14.

[11] Interpretation Act 1978, s. 5; Sch. 1; a "summary offence" means an offence which, if committed by an adult, is triable only summarily; an "offence triable either way" means an offence which, if committed by an adult, is triable either on indictment or summarily (*ibid.*).

[12] [1949] 1 K.B. 214; [1948] 2 All E.R. 1013; see also *R.* v. *Guildhall Justices, Ex parte Marshall*, [1976] 1 All E.R. 767; [1976] 1 W.L.R. 335 (see p. 288, *ante*).

[13] With the exception of an offence "under the Road Traffic Act 1930, or any statutory provision in lieu or modification thereof".

[14] ASQUITH, L.J., [1949] 1 K.B., at pp. 220–221; [1948] 2 All E.R., at pp. 1016–1017.

1   Offences triable only on indictment

Since offences can only fall within one of the other two categories if statute so provides, it follows that where there is no express statutory provision an offence is triable only on indictment. This involves a trial by judge and jury in the Crown Court, usually preceded by a hearing in the magistrates' court; this is not a trial, but merely an enquiry, known as a "preliminary enquiry" or, more generally, "committal proceedings."[15]

In practice only the gravest indictable offences are triable only on indictment; these include any offences for which a person may be sentenced to death, murder, genocide, manslaughter, infanticide, child destruction, abortion, rape, sexual intercourse with a girl under 13, sedition, mutiny, piracy, offences under section 1 of the Official Secrets Act 1911, robbery, wounding or causing grievous bodily harm "with intent", blackmail, assault with intent to rob, aggravated burglary and burglary comprising the commission of, or an intention to commit, an offence triable only on indictment.

It will, however, be recalled that these are triable only on indictment if committed by an adult; as we shall see, in the case of children and young persons, all indictable offences (other than homicide) may, and in most cases must, be tried summarily.

2   Offences triable only summarily

The expressions "summary offence" and "offence triable only summarily" may be taken as synonymous. A statute creating a summary offence will first define the offence and then state that it is punishable "on summary conviction" with a particular penalty, thereby indicating that the offence is a summary one. In addition a number of offences which, prior to the Criminal Law Act 1977, were not summary offences according to the statute creating them, became summary offences by reason of section 15 of the 1977 Act. These comprise the offences mentioned in Schedule 1 of the Act (which were formerly hybrid offences); of these the most important in practice are offences of drunken driving, driving with excess alcohol, being in charge of a motor vehicle when unfit to drive through drink or drugs or with excess alcohol and failing to provide a specimen of blood or urine for a laboratory test.[16] These offences accounted for a large number of cases annually in the Crown Court since drivers generally believed that juries were more likely to be sympathetic than magistrates so that acquittal was on the cards provided some, albeit highly technical, defence could be put forward. In addition to the offences in the first Schedule to the 1977 Act, incitement to commit a summary offence and offences under the Night Poaching Act 1828 (which were formerly triable only on indictment) became summary offences. Finally, offences under section 1 of the Criminal Damage Act 1971 (excluding arson) are triable only summarily if the "value involved" does not exceed £200.[17]

---

[15] See p. 476, *post*.

[16] Road Traffic Act 1972, ss. 5(1), 5(2), 6(1), 8(7) (as amended by Transport Act 1981).

[17] Magistrates' Courts Act 1980, s. 22 (replacing Criminal Law Act 1977, s. 23); the "value involved" is, where the property is destroyed, its open market value and where it is damaged, the market price of repair (Sch. 2); the figure of £200 may be increased by the Secretary of State by stautory instrument (*ibid.*, s 143(1)).

Section 22 prescribes a procedure for determining whether offences under section 1 of the Criminal Damage Act 1971 are to be regarded as summary or as triable either way (if the value involved exceeds £200). The court begins by hearing any representations made by the prosecutor or the accused as to the value involved; if it appears to the court clear that the value involved does not exceed the prescribed sum, it will proceed to summary trial. If it is clear that it does exceed that sum, then it will treat the offence as triable either way (which, of course, it then is).[18] If it is not clear whether or not the value involved does exceed the prescribed sum, then the accused is given the choice and told that if he consents to summary trial, his liability to imprisonment or a fine will be limited to the maximum that magistrates have power to impose;[19] the nature of the offence will then be determined in accordance with the accused's decision. If a person is convicted, either by a magistrates' court or by the Crown Court, he cannot appeal on the ground that the magistrates were mistaken as to the value involved.[20]

Following summary trial of an offence triable only summarily, the maximum sentence which magistrates can impose is imprisonment for not more than six months for any one offence (or a total of twelve months in the case of consecutive sentences for two or more offences)[1] and a fine not exceeding £2000.[2]

3 Offences triable either way

The third class of offence is offences triable either way. Those made so triable under the 1977 Act are now listed in Schedule 1 of the Magistrates' Courts Act 1980, which consists of 35 paragraphs incorporating some 66 separate offences; these include inflicting bodily injury, with or without a weapon, assault occasioning actual bodily harm, common assault, bigamy, certain forms of perjury and forgery, unlawful sexual intercourse with a girl under 16, all indictable offences under the Theft Act 1968 (except robbery, blackmail, assault with intent to rob and certain burglaries), arson, offences under section 1 of the Criminal Damage Act 1971 where the value involved exceeds £200 (*supra*) and indecent assault. In addition many other statutes expressly provide for an offence to be triable either summarily or on indictment (the former "hybrid" offences) and these are now triable either way.[3]

---

[18] The court must hear "representations", meaning submissions, assertions of fact and sometimes production of documents; however the court is not bound to hear evidence of the value involved: *R. v. Canterbury and St. Augustine Justices, Ex parte Klisiak*, [1982] Q.B. 398; [1981] 2 All E.R. 129; moreover it is permissible for the prosecution to limit the charge to certain items below the prescribed value, even though in fact other damaged items would take the value above the prescribed value (so as to ensure summary trial) (*ibid.*).

[19] In this case imprisonment for not more than three months or a fine of not more than £1000 (Magistrates' Courts Act, s. 33(1) (as amended)); the figure of £1000 may be increased by statutory instrument (*ibid.*, s. 43(1)).

[20] *Ibid.*, s. 22(8).

[1] *Ibid.*, ss. 31(1), 133.

[2] *Ibid.*, s. 32. (This figure also may be increased by statutory instrument (s. 143(4)(5).)

[3] *Ibid.*, s. 17(2).

C   PROCEDURE FOR DETERMINING MODE OF TRIAL

The procedure for determining the mode of trial differs according to whether or not the accused is an adult. If he is, then, as has been noted, he will always be tried on indictment for an offence triable only on indictment and will always be tried summarily for a summary offence; only in the case of an "either way" offence are there alternative possibilities. In the case of children and young persons the position is quite different. Before considering these procedures it should be noted that if magistrates mistakenly adopt a procedure which is not permitted, for example by "trying" a case which is triable only on indictment or by committing for trial in the case of an offence triable only summarily, then their "trial" or "committal" will be a complete nullity. Even if the defendant has been "sentenced" he may later be committed for trial and properly tried, if the offence was triable only on indictment.[4]

1   Adults charged with "either way" offences

Before any evidence is called, a magistrates' court[5] before whom a person aged 17 or over appears charged with an offence triable either way must adopt the following procedure:

(1) If the prosecution is being carried on by the Attorney-General, the Solicitor-General or the Director of Public Prosecutions and he applies for the offence to be tried on indictment, then it must be tried in that way and the court must proceed as examining justices.[6] In any other case the following steps apply.

(2) The court must first cause the charge to be written down, if this has not already been done, and read to the accused.

(3) First the prosecutor and then the accused are given an opportunity to make representations as to which mode of trial would be more suitable.

(4) The court then considers whether the offence appears more suitable for summary trial or for trial on indictment, having regard to the representations referred to in (3) above, to the nature of the case, whether the circumstances make the offence one of serious character, whether the punishment which a magistrates' court would have power to inflict for it would be adequate and "any other circumstances which appear to the court to make it more suitable for the offence to be tried in one way rather than the other."[7]

Although the Act is silent on the point, it is clear on principle that the "circumstances" to be taken into account by the justices in reaching their decision cannot include the accused's past record, unless, presumably, the accused himself relies upon this. It would be invidious to permit the prosecution to make representations concerning the accused's past record because

---

4   *R. v. West*, [1964] 1 Q.B. 15; [1962] 2 All E.R. 624 is a modern example of a case in which this occurred.
5   A single justice may discharge this function, but could not (unless a stipendiary) go on to conduct a summary trial: Magistrates' Courts Act 1980, s. 18(5).
6   *Ibid.*, s. 19(4).
7   *Ibid.*, s. 19(3).

the justices would then (improperly) know of it when conducting the ensuing trial or committal proceedings as the case may be.

(5) If, following consideration as above, it appears to the court that the offence is more suitable for trial on indictment, then it must tell the accused that it has so decided and will then proceed as examining justices, the accused having no power to prevent this course even if neither he nor the prosecution has requested it.[8]

(6) If, on the other hand, "it appears to the court that the offence is more suitable for summary trial", then the court must explain to the accused in ordinary language that he can either consent to summary trial or, if he wishes, be tried by a jury and that if he is tried summarily and convicted he may be committed for sentence to the Crown Court under section 38 of the Magistrates' Courts Act 1980 if the court, on obtaining information about his character and antecedents, is of opinion that they are such that greater punishment should be inflicted than the magistrates have power to inflict.[9]

This power to commit for sentence is considered below[10] but it should at once be appreciated that the accused cannot limit his potential sentence to the maximum that magistrates can impose by opting for summary trial where the offence is triable either way.

The procedure for explaining to the accused his options is similar to that which used to apply to indictable offences triable summarily (when that was still possible) and there was adequate authority for the proposition that failure to give the accused the warning of his liability to committal for sentence renders both the committal and the conviction bad;[11] the defendant will not have been in peril from the moment that the warning should have been given but was not, and a fresh charge may be brought against him. This position will still obtain under section 20 of the 1980 Act.

Although the magistrates have a discretion to proceed (subject to the accused's consent) to summary trial of an either way offence "if it appears to the court that the offence is more suitable for summary trial" it is not intended that they should do so in grave cases. LORD GODDARD, C.J. repeatedly emphasised during the period that he was Lord Chief Justice that:

> ". . . the fact that justices have power to try cases is no reason why they should necessarily do so. When a case is of a serious character . . . it ought to go to trial on indictment. It is not merely a question of sentence; it may be that when the case does go for trial the court of trial will think it necessary only to impose a nominal sentence or even bind over. That is not the point; serious cases ought to be dealt with by superior courts."[12]

Severer condemnation still was reserved for magistrates who, at the express request of both the prosecution and the defence, reduced a charge of wounding with intent (which is not triable summarily) to one of unlawful wounding (which is), presumably with the object of holding the summary trial which was in fact held.

---

[8] *Ibid.*, s. 21.
[9] *Ibid.*, s. 20(2).
[10] See p. 463, *post.*
[11] *R.* v. *Kent Justices, Ex parte Machin*, [1952] 2 Q.B. 355; [1952] 1 All E.R. 1123.
[12] *R.* v. *Norfolk Justices, Ex parte Director of Public Prosecutions*, [1950] 2 K.B. 558, at p. 567; [1950] 2 All E.R. 42, at pp. 44–45.

"Here is a case in which a man's life has been seriously imperilled and if he had died . . . the accused would have been charged with murder. It was never intended that . . . justices should deal with such a case. . . . For justices to exercise jurisdiction under that section by treating a case of this sort as nothing much more than common assault is a most extraordinary state of affairs. Justices should remember that they have to deal with matters of this sort judicially, and, although they must take into account what the prosecution and the defence say with regard to whether or not it is a proper case for the charge to be reduced, they are not bound to assent to dealing with the case summarily because the prosecution want to get the matter dealt with there and then." [13]

Again, in a case [14] where a number of serious charges against two defendants had been summarily dealt with at the express request of the prosecution, LORD PARKER, C.J., said: [15]

"This court is quite unable to understand how . . . the prosecution invited the magistrates' court . . . to deal summarily with the indictable offences. . . . No doubt it is convenient in the interests of expedition, and possibly in order to obtain a plea of guilty, [16] for the prosecution to invite the magistrates' court to deal with indictable offences summarily. But there is something more involved than convenience and expedition. Above all there is the proper administration of criminal justice to be considered, questions such as the protection of society and the stamping out of this sort of criminal enterprise if it is possible. . . . The court would like to observe that while in their view the prosecution was at fault . . . that is no excuse for the magistrates' court. Their duty in the case of indictable offences is to begin to enquire into the matter as examining justices, and only to deal with the case summarily if the matter can be brought fairly and squarely within section 19(2) of the Magistrates' Courts Act 1952."

(7) After explaining to the accused, as provided under (6) above, his options, the court asks him whether he consents to be tried summarily or wishes to be tried by a jury. If he consents to summary trial, the magistrates proceed to try him; if he does not consent, they proceed as examining justices. [17]

(8) There are provisions in section 25 of the Act whereby the magistrates may change from summary trial to committal proceedings and *vice versa*. Where the court has begun to try an either way offence summarily it may, at any time before the conclusion of the evidence for the prosecution, discontinue the summary trial and proceed as examining justices. [18] This will neces-

---

13 *R.* v. *Bodmin Justices, Ex parte McEwen*, [1947] K.B. 321, at pp. 324–325; [1947] 1 All E.R. 109, at p. 111.

14 *R.* v. *Coe*, [1969] 1 All E.R. 65; [1968] 1 W.L.R. 1950, C.A. One only of the defendants was committed for sentence, and the Court of Appeal was considering his application for leave to appeal against sentence.

15 [1969] 1 All E.R., at p. 67; [1968] 1 W.L.R., at p. 1953. See also the remarks of the Divisional Court in *R.* v. *King's Lynn Justices, Ex parte Carter*, [1969] 1 Q.B. 488, at p. 494; [1968] 3 All E.R. 858, at pp. 859–860. The court consisted of the same judges as in *R.* v. *Coe*; for a further point arising from the case see p. 463, *post*. Although both of the Lords Chief Justice were considering summary trial of indictable offences, all of the old indictable offences which could be tried summarily are now either way offences, so that the principles enunciated hold good.

16 This is an interesting reference to "plea-bargaining", i.e. the defendant pleading guilty in exchange for the prosecution dropping another charge or agreeing to summary trial; see p. 502, *post*.

17 Magistrates' Courts Act 1980, s. 20(3).

18 *Ibid.*, s. 25(2); but this cannot be done following a plea of guilty; *R.* v. *Dudley Justices, Ex*

sitate starting all over again and the court may adjourn the hearing without remanding the accused.

Conversely, if the court has already begun proceedings as a preliminary enquiry it may at any time, if it appears to the court having regard to any representations made by prosecutor or accused with consent of the accused (and with the consent of the Attorney-General, the Solicitor-General or the Director of Public Prosecutions if any of them is the prosecutor) proceed to try the information summarily.[19] As indicated, this can only be done with the accused's consent and, before asking him whether he consents, the court must in ordinary language explain to him what is proposed, that it can only be done with his consent and (unless it has already done so) must explain the court's power to commit to the Crown Court for sentence.[20] If the magistrates do change from a preliminary enquiry to a summary trial evidence already given is deemed to have been given in and for the purposes of the summary trial.[1] Where, however, the defendant pleads not guilty the court must recall for cross-examination any witness who has already given evidence, unless not required by either side for that purpose.[2] The reason for this is that at a preliminary enquiry the defence will usually be reserved completely, or at any rate hardly pressed, and cross-examination of the same witness may vary very much according to whether proceedings are to be regarded as the preliminary enquiry or the trial proper.

The accused must usually be present in court in person during the proceedings at which the mode of trial is determined.[3] However, the court may proceed in the absence of the accused if they consider that by reason of his disorderly conduct before them it is not practicable for the proceedings to be conducted in his presence. In addition, where the accused is represented by counsel or a solicitor who in his absence signifies to the court the accused's consent to the proceedings for determining how he is to be tried for the offence being conducted in his absence, and the court is satisfied that there is good reason for proceeding in the absence of the accused, then the court may proceed in the accused's absence.[4] In either case the consents required either to summary trial under (6) above (in this case there is no need for the court to explain its power to commit for sentence) or to summary trial of an offence under section 1 of the Criminal Damage Act 1971 (where it is not clear whether the value involved exceeds the prescribed limit)[5] may be given by the accused's counsel or solicitor.[6]

2   Children and young persons

Section 4 of the Children and Young Persons Act 1969 imposes a complete prohibition on prosecution of a child for any offence except "homicide"

---

parte Gillard, [1985] 1 All E.R. 8; [1984] 1 W.L.R. 1318 (an appeal to the House of Lords is pending).

[19] *Ibid.*, s. 25(3).
[20] *Ibid.*, s. 25(4).
[1] *Ibid.*, s. 28.
[2] Magistrates' Courts Rules 1981, r. 21.
[3] Magistrates' Courts Act 1980, s. 18(2).
[4] *Ibid.*, ss. 18(3), 23(1).
[5] See p. 457, *ante*.
[6] Magistrates' Courts Act 1980, ss. 23(3), (4).

(that is to say all offences of unlawful homicide) and section 5 of the same Act imposes considerable restrictions upon the prosecution of a young person, subject to the same exception. Criminal proceedings will, in such cases, be replaced by "care proceedings" under section 1 and succeeding sections of the Act. However these important provisions have still not been brought into force and in the meantime the law remains as follows.

Whenever a child or young person appears before a magistrates' court charged with any indictable offence except "homicide" he must, subject to certain exceptions, be tried summarily.[7]

As indicated this will not apply to any offence of unlawful homicide. Nor will it apply (*a*) in the case of a young person (14 or over) charged with an offence for which the penalty is in the case of an adult 14 years' imprisonment or more, not being an offence for which the sentence is fixed by law, and the court considers that if he is found guilty it ought to be possible to sentence him to detention under section 53(2) of the Children and Young Persons Act 1933[8]; or (*b*) in the case of a child or young person charged jointly with an adult (17 or over) if the court considers it necessary in the interests of justice to commit them both for trial.[9] In this case the court may also commit the child or young person for any other indictable offence with which he is charged at the same time (whether jointly with an adult or not) if that other offence arises out of circumstances which are the same as or connected with those giving rise to the first offence.[10]

A child or young person not accused jointly with an adult will be tried in a juvenile court.[11] However, if charged jointly with an adult he will be tried in an ordinary magistrates' court unless the adult pleads guilty or is not tried summarily (so that they are no longer jointly charged) in which events the court may before any evidence is called in the case of the child or young person remit him to a juvenile court for trial.[12]

If tried summarily the child or young person is, basically, liable to sentence in the same way as an adult, save that he cannot be sentenced to imprisonment (although he may be liable to detention or youth custody) and he can only be fined £400 (if a young person) or £100 (if a child).[13]

D COMMITTAL FOR SENTENCE

In nine cases a defendant may be tried in, or in one case brought before, a magistrates' court but committed to the Crown Court to be sentenced or otherwise dealt with. The case then becomes:

---

[7] *Ibid.*, s. 24(1); "appears" means appears or is brought before the court when the court makes its decision as to the mode of trial so that an accused who attains the age of 17 before this occasion is treated as an adult notwithstanding that he was a young person when he appeared at an earlier remand hearing: *R.* v. *Islington North Juvenile Court, Ex parte Daley*, [1983] 1 A.C. 347; *sub nom. Re Daley*, [1982] 2 All E.R. 974.

[8] See p. 522, *post.*

[9] These two exceptions are set out in s. 24(1) of the 1980 Act.

[10] *Ibid.*, s. 24(2).

[11] See p. 207, *ante.*

[12] Magistrates' Courts Act 1980, s. 29.

[13] *Ibid.*, s. 24(3), (4) (as amended); the figures may be increased by Order in Council (and were increased in 1984).

". . . a sort of composite case in which power is given to one court to convict and to another to give judgment; and until the judgment is given the hearing of the case is not complete"[14]

Although the nine cases vary in detail, there are basically three objects of committal for sentence, namely to ensure that (*a*) a defendant receives greater punishment than a magistrates' court has power to inflict, if thought to deserve it, (*b*) the same court which made an order should deal with its breach and (*c*) generally, there should be uniformity in sentencing. It may be noted at this stage that where the magistrates exercise their power under section 1(1) of the Powers of Criminal Courts Act 1973[15] to defer sentence, it is usually wrong when the defendant comes before them again to be dealt with to commit him for sentence.[16] Furthermore, if the justices do decide to commit the defendant for sentence they must be scrupulously careful to leave all questions associated with sentence to the Crown Court. They cannot therefore impose any order such as a compensation order and all matters relating to sentence are out of the justices' hands.[17]

1 Summary trial of an adult for an "either way" offence

It has already been noted that if a magistrates' court tries an adult for an either way offence and convicts him, but considers that, having regard to the defendant's character and antecedents, greater punishment should be inflicted than the justices have power to impose, they may commit the defendant to the Crown Court for sentence.

This power is contained in section 38 of the Magistrates' Courts Act 1980. The magistrates' court is not limited to considering the actual past record of the defendant, but may also take into account the general circumstances of the offender and also of the offence, since:

" 'character' in my opinion relates to something more than the fact that a person has been previously convicted, and the word 'antecedents' is as wide as can be conceived."[18]

Neither need there be any offences to be taken into consideration. In *R.* v. *King's Lynn Justices, Ex parte Carter*,[19] the defendants, all of previous good character, pleaded guilty in the magistrates' court to larceny as servants of goods to the value of nearly £3,500. The prosecution alleged an organised conspiracy to steal over a long period, although the defendants denied this. All three defendants were committed for sentence, and the Queen's Bench Divisional Court held that the committals were lawful, in spite of the absence of previous convictions or offences to be taken into consideration, assuming the magistrates to have accepted the prosecution allegation of a conspiracy.

---

[14] LORD GODDARD, C.J. in *R.* v. *Norfolk Justices, Ex parte Director of Public Prosecutions*, [1950] 2 K.B. 558, at p. 568; [1950] 2 All E.R. 42, at p. 46.

[15] See p. 518, *post*.

[16] *R.* v. *Gilby*, [1975] 2 All E.R. 743; [1975] 1 W.L.R. 924; cf. *R.* v. *Harling* (1977), 65 Cr. App. Rep. 320.

[17] *R.* v. *Brogan*, [1975] 1 All E.R. 879; [1975] 1 W.L.R. 383.

[18] LORD GODDARD, C.J. in *R.* v. *Vallett*, [1951] 1 All E.R. 231, at pp. 231–232.

[19] [1969] 1 K.B. 488; [1968] 3 All E.R. 858.

"As I see it . . . the expression 'character and antecedents' being as wide as it possibly can be, justices are entitled to take into consideration in deciding whether or not to commit . . . matters revealed in the course of the case connected with the offence charged which reflect in any way on the defendant's character."[20]

The court also pointed out that where the court did make proper enquiry into the circumstances of the offence, and then decided to try summarily, they could not rely on those circumstances again to justify committal for sentence, on their own, but had to find fresh circumstances (e.g. offences to be taken into consideration).[1]

Although the power to commit extends to all either way offences tried summarily, it does not apply to cases under the Criminal Damage Act 1971 where the magistrates proceed to summary trial on the basis that the value involved does not exceed the relevant sum.[2]

Committal will normally be to the most convenient location of the Crown Court. In selecting this the justices must have regard to directions given by the presiding judge or judges of the Circuit.[3] Committal may be in custody or on bail, but the Court of Appeal has indicated that:

". . . the cases must be rare when magistrates' courts can properly commit for [sentence] on bail because the whole purpose of the committal is to have the man sent to prison, and have him sent to prison for a longer period than the magistrates' court could impose."[4]

However, the defendant may give notice of appeal against conviction and may then, *qua* appellant, be released on bail, although, where a possibly severe sentence awaits him, bail will only be granted "with extreme care, and only in really exceptional cases".[5] There is no appeal against the order of committal as such;[6] if the defendant thinks that the committal was bad in law, for example because he was not warned that he might be committed, he should apply to a divisional court of the Queen's Bench Division for an order of certiorari or prohibition; the Crown Court will not, of course, sentence him until the result of his application is known, since the order of committal may be held to be a nullity. On such an application the divisional court can only hear argument as to the legality of the committal and cannot entertain any suggestion that the committal was too harsh a step to take having regard to the facts; this is an argument to be addressed (although not in so many words) to the Crown Court when the defendant appears there for sentence.

---

[20] LORD PARKER, C.J., [1969] 1 K.B., at p. 497; [1968] 3 All E.R., at p. 862.

[1] See, for example, *R. v. Tower Bridge Magistrate, Ex parte Osman*, [1971] 2 All E.R. 1018; [1971] 1 W.L.R. 1109. The cases cited dealt, of course, with the trial of indictable offences summarily under the pre-Criminal Law Act provisions. However, since all those offences which were formerly indictable offences triable summarily are now "either way" offences, the cases are still relevant.

[2] Magistrates' Courts Act 1980, s. 33(1) (*b*); see p. 457, *ante*.

[3] *Practice Note*, reported at [1971] 3 All E.R. 829; [1971] 1 W.L.R. 1535, paras. 6–9. The Note contains Directions given by the Lord Chief Justice as to distribution of Crown Court business, see p. 203, *ante*. There may be transfer from one location of the Crown Court to another: Directions, paragraph 14. See also 483, *post*.

[4] *R. v. Coe*, [1969] 1 All E.R. 65, at p. 68; [1968] 1 W.L.R. 1950, at p. 1954; see p. 460, *ante*.

[5] *Re Whitehouse*, [1951] 1 K.B. 673, at p. 675; [1951] 1 All E.R. 353, at p. 354.

[6] *R. v. London Sessions, Ex parte Rogers*, [1951] 2 K.B. 74; [1951] 1 All E.R. 343.

On such appearance, procedure is as if the defendant had been committed for trial to the Crown Court and had pleaded guilty to the charge. No actual plea will be taken, since that stage of the trial is concluded, but otherwise the position is as if the defendant had pleaded guilty at the Crown Court itself. Thus notices required to be served three days before the "trial" may be served three days before the hearing at the Crown Court,[7] and, if the defendant has been granted bail, but fails to surrender, the Crown Court may issue a bench warrant.[8] It might then be thought that the Crown Court could allow the defendant to withdraw his plea of guilty (if such was tendered) in the magistrates' court, before he was sentenced, and it is now clear from *R. v. Mutford and Lothingland Justices, Ex parte Harber*,[9] following the decision of the House of Lords in *S. (An Infant)* v. *Manchester City Recorder*,[10] that this is permissible. The Crown Court certainly has such a power when trying a case on indictment.[11]

At the hearing there should be formal identification by the police of the defendant as the person who appeared at the magistrates' court and was committed; if there is no police officer present who can give this information, the defendant may, it seems, be asked whether he was the person who appeared and was committed. The Crown Court will enquire into the circumstances of the case as it would following a plea of guilty before itself; prosecuting counsel will give the court an outline of the facts, and the defendant's antecedents, and defending counsel (or solicitor) will address the court in mitigation. The Crown Court can then pass any sentence up to the maximum which the particular indictable offence carries and can deal with the defendant in any manner in which it could deal with him if he had just been convicted of the offence on indictment before the court.[12] The position as to appeal itself against this sentence is considered below.[13]

If the defendant appeals against conviction, as well as being committed for sentence, the Crown Court will of course hear his appeal first, since, if this succeeds, there will be no cause to sentence him. This is logical but leads to the undesirable result that the court may hear his appeal against conviction with knowledge that he has been committed for sentence on the basis of his "character and antecedents". This phrase is now widely interpreted, but may include previous convictions.[14]

2 Young persons: Magistrates' Courts Act 1980, s. 37[15]

The maximum period of youth custody that a magistrates' court has power

---

[7] *R. v. Grant*, [1951] 1 K.B. 500; [1951] 1 All E.R. 28.

[8] Bail Act 1976, s. 7.

[9] [1971] 2 Q.B. 291; [1971] 1 All E.R. 81. The Crown Court can only take into consideration what took place in the magistrates' court: *R. v. Marylebone Justices, Ex parte Westminster City Council*, [1971] 1 All E.R. 1025; [1971] 1 W.L.R. 567.

[10] [1971] A.C. 481; [1969] 3 All E.R. 1230.

[11] See p. 502, *post.*

[12] Powers of Criminal Courts Act 1973, s. 42.

[13] See p. 529, *post.*

[14] See p. 463, *ante*, and *R. v. Dorset Quarter Sessions, Ex parte O'Brien*, [1956] 1 Q.B. 452n; [1956] 1 All E.R. 449.

[15] In its original form this section (which was the successor to s. 28 of the 1952 Act) provided for committal with a recommendation for Borstal training. Borstal training was abolished by

to impose corresponds with its maximum power of imprisonment, *viz.* 6 months or 12 months for consecutive sentences[16]

Section 37(1) of the 1980 Act provides:

> "Where a person who is not less than 15 nor more than 16 years old is convicted by a magistrates' court of an offence punishable on conviction on indictment with a term of imprisonment exceeding six months, then, if the court is of opinion that he should be sentenced to a greater term of youth custody than it has power to impose, the court may commit him in custody or on bail to the Crown Court for sentence."

The power exists only in relation to male offenders. Since an offender aged less than 17 cannot be sentenced to a term of youth custody exceeding 12 months in any event,[17] the power of committal under s. 37 is of limited application.

3   Offences under the Bail Act 1976

The Bail Act 1976 created three new summary offences: the first two consist of failure of a person released on bail in criminal proceedings, without reasonable cause, to surrender to custody, or, having reasonable cause, to surrender at the appointed place as soon after the appointed time as reasonably practicable;[18] the third offence is that of agreeing to indemnify sureties in criminal proceedings.[19] Each of these offences is a summary offence (and therefore triable only summarily[20]); in each case the magistrates have power to impose imprisonment for up to three months or a fine of up to level 5 or both. However, exceptionally, the Act provides that in each case if the court thinks—

(*a*)   that the circumstances of the offence are such that greater punishments should be inflicted for that offence than the court has power to inflict, or

(*b*)   in a case where it commits that person for trial to the Crown Court for another offence, that it would be appropriate for him to be dealt with by that court for the bail offence,

it may commit him in custody or on bail to the Crown Court for sentence.[1] In the Crown Court the convicted person is liable to imprisonment for up to 12 months or a fine or both.[2]

This form of statutory provision, namely one that provides for committal for sentence in the case of a purely summary offence, is wholly exceptional.

---

s. 1(3) of the Criminal Justice Act 1982 and the present s. 37(1) was substituted by the 1982 Act (s. 77, Sch. 14).

[16] Magistrates' Courts Act 1980, s. 133 (as amended).

[17] Criminal Justice Act 1982, s. 7(8).

[18] Bail Act 1976, s. 6(1); the marginal note refers to the offence as "absconding" although that word does not appear in the body of the section.

[19] *Ibid.*, s. 9(1).

[20] Although the offences under s. 6 may alternatively be punished as contempts of court (s. 6(5)).

[1] Bail Act 1976, ss. 6(6), 9(3).

[2] *Ibid.*, ss. 6(7), 9(4).

4 Committal under the Powers of Criminal Courts Act 1973:[3] probation and conditional discharge

If a defendant has been put on probation, or given a conditional discharge, by the Crown Court, and is subsequently convicted by a magistrates' court of an offence committed during the period of probation or of conditional discharge, the magistrates' court may commit him in custody or on bail, until he can be brought before the court by which the order was made.[4] The process is analogous to those already discussed, although the defendant is not committed directly to the Crown Court and is committed to be dealt with for the original offence only.

5 Committal under the Powers of Criminal Courts Act 1973[5] and the Criminal Law Act 1977:[6] suspended sentences

Where the defendant has been convicted by the magistrates' court of an offence (i) punishable with imprisonment, and (ii) committed during the operational period of a suspended sentence passed by the Crown Court, the magistrates' court may commit him, in custody or on bail, to the Crown Court. If it does not commit him, it must at least notify the conviction to the court which originally imposed the sentence.

6 Committal under the Powers of Criminal Courts Act 1973:[7] community service orders

Where a community service order has been made in respect of an offender[8] by the Crown Court and it appears on information to a justice that the offender has failed to comply with the requirements of the order, he may be brought before a magistrates' court and committed in custody or on bail to the Crown Court where the order may be revoked and the offender dealt with as if the order had not been made. Similar powers of committal for sentence and sentence exist where the offender appears before a magistrates' court on an application, which may be made by the relevant officer or by the offender himself, to extend the duration of an existing community service order.

7 Committal under the Criminal Justice Act 1967:[9] prisoners on licence

Where a person released on licence from the Parole Board is convicted by a magistrates' court of an offence punishable on indictment with

---

[3] Section 8(6).
[4] Committal must normally be to the Crown Court where the order was made or sentence passed: *Practice Note*, [1971] 3 All E.R. 829; [1971] 1 W.L.R. 1535, para. 6 This is in accordance with the terms of the sections, as originally passed.
[5] Section 24(2).
[6] Section 47; Sch. 9, para. 2. This extends the powers to commit to cases where the original sentence was partly suspended under the 1977 Act; see p. 521, *post*.
[7] Sections 16(3), 17(2).
[8] Under s. 14 of the Powers of Criminal Courts Act 1973; see p. 524, *post*.
[9] Section 62(6), (7).

imprisonment, the court may commit him for sentence to the Crown Court, in custody or on bail. That court may revoke the licence.

8 Committal under the Mental Health Act 1983[10]

A magistrates' court may make an order under the Mental Health Act 1983 committing the defendant, if he is fourteen or over, to a hospital, but it cannot at the same time make an order restricting the defendant's discharge for a fixed number of years. If, therefore, the court considers that a hospital order is appropriate but that it must in the particular case be accompanied by restrictions on release, the magistrates' court may, instead of making a hospital or any other order, commit the defendant to the Crown Court to be dealt with. Committal must be in custody; if, however, the magistrates' court is satisfied that arrangements have been made by a hospital to receive the defendant in the event of the Crown Court making a hospital order, the court may itself direct the defendant to be admitted to that hospital and to be detained there, pending determination of the case by the Crown Court. The Crown Court may make a hospital order, with or without restrictions, or it may deal with the defendant in any way in which the magistrates' court could have done.

9 Incorrigible rogues

A person deemed to be an "incorrigible rogue", within the meaning of section 5 of the Vagrancy Act 1824, for one of the various causes there specified, may be committed to the "house of correction"—that is, in custody or on bail to the Crown Court for sentence. The Crown Court may impose up to a year's imprisonment. A person is deemed to be a rogue within section 5 if, *inter alia*, he breaks or escapes out of a place of legal confinement before the expiry of his sentence or if he is apprehended as a rogue and vagabond and violently resists the constable "or other peace officer" so arresting him.

It is not of course for every offence that the defendant can be committed for sentence. Thus the defendant may be convicted of two or more offences, and *prima facie* liable to be committed in respect of only one. Now, however, for the sake of uniformity, where a defendant is committed for sentence under any of the above cases, except section 43 of the Mental Health Act 1983, in respect of an offence, he may also be committed in respect of other offences.[11] If the offence in respect of which the committal is being made (the "relevant offence") is an offence triable either way, then the other offences may be any other offences whatsoever in respect of which the committing court has power to deal with him (being an offence of which he has been

---

[10] Section 43.
[11] Criminal Justice Act 1967, s. 56(1) (as substituted by Criminal Law Act 1977, s. 46). This has, of course, no application to a committal of someone in respect of a community service order since such a committal does not arise out of a subsequent conviction but simply out of failure to comply with the terms of the original order (*supra*).

convicted by that or any other court[12]). If, on the other hand, the relevant offence is a summary offence, then the other offences are limited to offences of which the committing court has convicted the defendant, being offences punishable with imprisonment or disqualification from driving, or in respect of which there is in existence a suspended sentence which the committing court has power to implement.[13] Where there is a committal in respect of the "second offence", the Crown Court can only deal with the defendant as the magistrates could have done; subject to this, they have all duties and powers of sentence transferred to them, except that the magistrates' court may impose an order of interim disqualification from driving, pending the defendant's appearance at the higher court.

E BAIL

1 Nature of bail

A person is "granted bail" when he is released from the custody of the law subject to a duty to surrender to custody at some future time. The "custody" is the custody of a court unless bail was granted by a police officer, in which event it is the custody of the officer. Considerable changes in the law were effected by the Bail Act 1976. Previously bail involved entering into a "recognisance" which is an acknowledgement of a debt to the Queen payable on default of compliance with the conditions of the recognisance. The 1976 Act abolished personal recognisances[14] from the accused but preserved them for sureties (where these are required). Bail may be granted to an accused person conditionally or unconditionally. If granted bail the accused is under a duty to surrender to custody when required; if he fails without reasonable cause to do so he commits an offence under section 6(1) of the 1976 Act, punishable either on summary conviction or as a contempt of court.[15]

If bail is granted conditionally, the conditions may consist of the provision of a surety or sureties to secure the person's surrender to custody,[16] the provision of security (if it appears that he is unlikely to remain in Great Britain until the time appointed for him to surrender to custody),[17] requirements to secure that he surrenders to custody, does not commit any offence while on bail, does not interfere with witnesses or otherwise obstruct the course of justice or makes himself available for the purpose of enabling inquiries or a report to be made to assist the court in dealing with him for the offence.[18] Conditions commonly imposed include surrender of passport,

---

[12] This could arise where the offender (if an adult) had been convicted of offences by other magistrates' courts and those courts had remitted him to the committing court to be dealt with for those offences under s. 39 of the Magistrates' Courts Act; see p. 549, *post*.

[13] Under s. 24(1) of the Powers of Criminal Courts Act 1973.

[14] Bail Act 1976, s. 3(2).

[15] *Ibid.*, s. 6(1); if he has reasonable cause, it is an offence under s. 6(2) to fail to surrender at the appointed place as soon after the appointed time as is reasonably practicable; as to penalties and committal to the Crown Court for sentence for these offences, see p. 466, *ante*.

[16] *Ibid.*, s. 3(4).

[17] *Ibid.*, s. 3(5). This security may be forfeited, in whole or in part, if the defendant fails to surrender (*ibid.*, s. 5(7)).

[18] Bail Act 1976, s. 3(6); these conditions may be imposed only by a court (not by a police officer). In murder cases, unless satisfactory reports on the accused's mental condition have

reporting to a police station at prescribed times, not visiting specified premises and not approaching specified persons. Conditions imposed by a court may be varied by that court on the application of the person bailed, the prosecutor or a constable.[19]

2   Occasions for the grant of bail

The question of when bail may be granted to a person may arise at various stages of his case, from the moment that he is arrested to the final determination of any appeal arising out of his conviction. Bail in cases of treason can only be granted by order of a High Court judge or the Home Secretary.[20]

In other cases, bail may be granted as follows:

a   By the police

We have seen that a warrant of arrest may be "backed for bail" in which event the officer in charge of the station to which the defendant is taken after his arrest must release him, subject to approving any surety tendered in compliance with the endorsement on the warrant[1] and, also, that where the arrest is without a warrant the police have certain powers and duties under section 43 of the Magistrates' Courts Act 1980 in relation to the grant of bail.[2]

b   By magistrates

Magistrates have power to grant bail at various stages of proceedings. When an accused person is first brought before a magistrates' court charged with an offence it quite often happens that the prosecution is not ready to proceed in which event the proceedings are adjourned and the accused is remanded, either in custody or on bail. This may arise in the course of summary proceedings or where the offence is triable only on indictment (in which event the magistrates will eventually conduct a preliminary enquiry) or where it is triable "either way".[3]

Secondly, if, after holding a preliminary enquiry, magistrates decide to commit the accused to the Crown Court for trial, that committal may be in custody or on bail.[4]

Thirdly, following summary conviction, the magistrates have power if they commit the defendant to the Crown Court for sentence (where this is open to them)[5] to commit in custody or on bail.[6]

---

already been obtained, the court must impose as conditions of bail (*a*) a requirement that the accused shall undergo examination by two medical practitioners for the purpose of enabling such reports to be prepared; and (*b*) a requirement that he shall for that purpose attend such an institution or place as the court directs (*ibid.*, s. 3(6A)).

[19] *Ibid.*, s. 3(8).
[20] Magistrates' Courts Act 1980, s. 41.
[1] *Ibid.*, s. 117; see p. 448, *ante*.
[2] See p. 453, *ante*.
[3] *Ibid.*, s. 18(4); see p. 458, *ante*.
[4] *Ibid.*, s. 6(3).
[5] See pp. 462–469, *ante* for the cases in which they may do this.
[6] Magistrates' Courts Act 1980, s. 38 and the other provisions permitting committal, except Mental Health Act 1983, s. 43.

Finally, following conviction, if the magistrates adjourn for the purpose of considering sentence they may remand the defendant on bail or in custody[7] and, having imposed a custodial sentence, they may, if a person has given notice of appeal or applied to the magistrates to state a case,[8] grant bail.[9]

If bail is refused on a remand, the maximum period of remand is eight clear days[10] unless he is already serving a custodial sentence, in which event it is 28 clear days.[11] There may, of course, be further remands thereafter.[12]

Where magistrates adjourn a summary trial, committal proceedings or the determination of the method of trial of an either way offence and remand the accused in custody, they may, if the accused is an adult, order that he be brought up for any subsequent remands before an alternate magistrates' court nearer to the prison where he is to be confined on remand.[13]

Although successive applications for bail may be made to a magistrates' court (and for that matter to any court having power to grant bail), if bail has been refused a court will not entertain a further application unless there has been a change of circumstances.[14]

c By the Crown Court

The Crown Court may grant bail to any person—[15]

(a) who has been committed in custody for appearance (trial or sentence) before the Crown Court; or

(b) who is in custody pursuant to a sentence imposed by a magistrates' court and has appealed against conviction or sentence; or

(c) who is in the custody of the Crown Court pending the disposal of his case by the Crown Court; or

(d) who, after the decision of the Crown Court in his case, has applied to the Crown Court to state a case for the High Court;[16] or

(e) who has applied to the High Court for an order of certiorari, or for leave to apply, in respect of proceedings in the Crown Court;[17] or

---

[7] Magistrates' Courts Act 1980, s. 128(1); if the remand is for medical examination and report, it must not be for more than three weeks, if in custody, or four weeks, if on bail and, if on bail, conditions as to undergoing medical examination must be imposed (*ibid.*, s. 30).

[8] As to this procedure, see p. 552, *post.*

[9] Magistrates' Courts Act 1980, s. 113.

[10] *Ibid.*, s. 128(6); "clear days" means omitting the day of the remand and the day fixed for appearance.

[11] *Ibid.*, s. 131(1).

[12] *Ibid.*, s. 129(1).

[13] *Ibid.*, s. 130; this is a security measure introduced by the Criminal Law Act 1977 to minimise the risks inherent in transporting dangerous prisoners over long distances; in particular it was prompted by the escape of William Hughes while being transported from Leicester Prison to Chesterfield magistrates' court on January 12, 1977, and the tragic consequences of that escape. There are provisions for remands to be made in the absence of the accused (ss. 128, 129).

[14] *R.* v. *Nottingham Justices, Ex parte Davies*, [1981] Q.B. 38; [1980] 2 All E.R. 775 (see also Bail Act 1976, s. 5(6A)); however, even though refused bail on remand the accused is entitled to have his right to bail fully reviewed at the stage of committal for trial: *R.* v. *Reading Crown Court, Ex parte Malik*, [1981] Q.B. 451; [1981] 1 All E.R. 249.

[15] Supreme Court Act 1981, s. 81 (as amended).

[16] See p. 555, *post.*

[17] This only applies to appellate proceedings in the Crown Court, because while it is sitting as a court of trial it is not amenable to prerogative order; see p. 177, *ante.*

(*f*) to whom the Crown Court has granted a certificate under the Criminal Appeal Act 1968 (case fit for appeal).

(*g*) who has been remanded in custody by a magistrates' court, where he has been refused bail by that court after hearing full argument.[18]

d   By the High Court

Whenever a magistrates' court withholds bail in criminal proceedings or imposes conditions in granting bail, the High Court may grant bail or vary the conditions.[19]

The High Court may also grant bail pending any application for certiorari or for the statement of a case by the Crown Court or a magistrates' court, or pending appeal from the Queen's Bench divisional court to the House of Lords.[20]

The application for bail in the High Court is by summons to the prosecutor before a judge in chambers in the Queen's Bench Division to show cause why bail should not be granted, or why the variation in conditions of bail proposed by the applicant should not be made; the procedural requirements may be dispensed with if the judge assigns the official solicitor to act for the applicant (which he may do if the applicant gives notice to the judge stating his desire to apply for bail and requesting that the official solicitor should act for him).[1]

If an applicant for bail in the High Court is refused bail by a judge in chambers, he cannot make fresh applications to any other judge or to the divisional court[2] and there is no appeal against the judge's decision.

e   By the Court of Appeal

The Court of Appeal has power to grant bail pending appeal to that court or pending a retrial ordered by that court following such an appeal[3] or pending appeal from that court to the House of Lords.[4] It is rare for the Court of Appeal to grant bail, but it occasionally does so, for example where the sentence appealed against is a short one so that it might be served by the time the appeal comes on for hearing, or where there is a strong *prima facie* likelihood of success.[5]

---

[18] Cases (*f*) and (*g*) were added by the Criminal Justice Act 1982. Previously the Crown Court had no power to grant bail pending appeal to the Court of Appeal, nor prior to committal for trial (in the former case application had to be made to the Court of Appeal, in the latter to a High Court judge in chambers).

[19] Criminal Justice Act 1967, s. 22 (as amended by Bail Act 1976, Sch. 2).

[20] Administration of Justice Act 1960, s. 4.

[1] R.S.C. (Revision) 1965, O. 79, r. 9(4).

[2] *Ibid.*, O. 79, r. 9(11); cf. *Re Kray*, [1965] Ch. 736; [1965] 1 All E.R. 710.

[3] Criminal Appeal Act 1968, ss. 8(2), 19; the power may be exercised by the single judge (*ibid.*, ss. 31, 45(2)).

[4] *Ibid.*, s. 36. By s. 37, if the prosecutor is appealing to the House of Lords and, but for the decision of the Court of Appeal, the appellant would be liable to be detained, the Court of Appeal may make an order providing for his detention or directing that he shall not be released except on bail; there is similar provision on prosecution appeals from the Queen's Bench divisional court (Administration of Justice Act, 1960, s. 5).

[5] *R. v. Watton* (1978), 68 Cr. App. Rep. 293.

3 The right to bail

The marginal note to section 4 of the Bail Act 1976 is "General right to bail of accused persons and others" (the "others" being persons who are brought up for breach of the requirements of probation or community service orders,[6] or persons who have been remanded following conviction for reports[7]). The section created a new statutory presumption in favour of granting bail and provides that, except as provided in Schedule 1 to the Act, bail shall be granted to a person who appears before a magistrates' court or the Crown Court in the course of or in connection with proceedings or applies for bail in connection with proceedings. It does not apply (save in the case of remand for reports (*supra*)) after conviction.

Schedule 1 contains detailed provisions relating to circumstances in which bail may justifiably be withheld. These vary according to whether the accused is charged with an "imprisonable offence" or a "non-imprisonable offence", that is to say whether or not the offence is punishable with imprisonment (even if the accused himself, for example by reason of his age, would not be liable to be imprisoned for it).

If the offence is non-imprisonable the only circumstances in which bail may be withheld are:

(1) if the defendant having previously been granted bail, has failed to comply with his obligation to surrender to custody and the court believes that he would so fail again;

(2) if the court is satisfied that the defendant should be kept in custody for his own protection or, if he is a child or young person, for his own welfare;

(3) if he is already in custody pursuant to a court sentence;[8]

(4) if, having been granted bail in the instant proceedings, he has been arrested for absconding or breaking the conditions of his bail.[9]

If the offence is imprisonable, there is a much wider range of circumstances in which bail may be justifiably withheld, in addition to those listed above. These are as follows:

(5) if the court is satisfied that there are substantial grounds for believing that the defendant, if released on bail (whether subject to conditions or not) would—
  (*a*) fail to surrender to custody; or
  (*b*) commit an offence while on bail; or
  (*c*) interfere with witnesses or otherwise obstruct the course of justice;

(6) where it has not been practicable for want of time to obtain sufficient information to enable the court to make its decision;

(7) where a case is adjourned for inquiries or report and it appears that it would be impracticable to complete the inquiries or make the report without keeping the defendant in custody.[10]

---

6 Powers of Criminal Courts Act 1973, ss. 6, 16.
7 Bail Act 1976, s. 4(4).
8 Or a sentence of an authority acting under the Army, Air Force or Naval Discipline Acts.
9 Bail Act 1976, Sch. 1, Part II.
10 *Ibid.*, Sch. 1, Part I.

In considering the grounds referred to under (5) above the court must have regard to the nature and seriousness of the offence or default, the character, antecedents, associations and community ties of the defendant, the defendant's record in relation to fulfilling his obligations under previous grants of bail in criminal proceedings, the strength of the evidence against him and any other considerations which appear to be relevant.[11]

The Act[12] contains detailed provisions for recording the decisions of both courts and police officers in relation to bail and entitling defendants to copies of records of such decisions.

Where a court withholds bail or imposes or varies conditions of bail in the case of a person who has a "right to bail" in criminal proceedings, it must give reasons and these are recorded with the record of the decision.[13]

Where a magistrates' court withholds bail from a person who is not represented by counsel or solicitor, the court must inform him of his right to apply to the High Court (and, on committal for trial, to the Crown Court) for bail.[14]

4   Sureties

As already noted, the 1976 Act abolished personal recognisances from defendants (although persons unlikely to remain in Great Britain may be required to provide security). Recognisances still exist, however, in relation to sureties; these are persons who are sometimes colloquially said to "stand bail" for the accused. If a person is granted bail subject to the provision of sureties, the court must fix the amounts of the sureties and must also be satisfied that the proposed sureties are suitable having regard to their financial resources, character and any previous convictions and proximity (whether in point of kinship, place of residence or otherwise) to the defendant.[15] In practice courts are usually guided by the police in matters relating to the suitability of proposed sureties.

Before sureties are taken it is the practice to explain the nature of the obligations being undertaken so as to ensure that the proposed surety understands them and to warn of the consequences of the defendant failing to answer to his bail. These are, *prima facie*, forfeiture of the amount of the recognisance and possible imprisonment in default. The court has power to order the surety, in the event of default by the defendant, to forfeit the whole of the amount of the recognisance or part thereof.[16] Before exercising its discretion the court must give the surety the opportunity to be heard and must take into account circumstances relating either to means or to the surety's culpability for the non-appearance of the defendant which might make it fair and just for the surety not to be ordered to forfeit the whole

---

[11] *Ibid.*, Sch. 1, Part I, para. 9.
[12] Section 5.
[13] *Ibid.*, s. 5(3), (4).
[14] *Ibid.*, s. 5(6).
[15] *Ibid.*, s. 8(2).
[16] Magistrates' Courts Act 1980, s. 120(3); Powers of Criminal Courts Act 1973, s. 31.

amount of the recognisance.[17] Imprisonment may be ordered in default of payment, of up to 12 months.[18]

It is an offence, punishable on summary conviction or as a contempt of court, to agree to indemnify a surety in criminal proceedings (or, in the case of the surety himself, to be indemnified).[19]

An order of the Crown Court estreating the recognisance of a surety for a defendant who has failed to surrender to his bail to stand trial is not a "matter relating to trial on indictment" (within s. 29(3) of the Supreme Court Act 1981) so that the order is subject to judicial review.[20]

---

[17] *R.* v. *Southampton Justices, Ex parte Green*, [1976] Q.B. 11; [1975] 2 All E.R. 1073.
[18] Powers of Criminal Courts Act 1973, s. 31(3).
[19] Bail Act 1976, s. 9; for powers of committal to the Crown Court for sentence, see p. 466, *ante.*
[20] *Smalley* v. *Crown Court at Warwick*, [1985] 1 All E.R. 769; *sub nom. In re Smalley*, [1985] 2 W.L.R. 538.

CHAPTER 24

Trial of an Indictable Offence

A   PRELIMINARY ENQUIRY : COMMITTAL

1   Introduction

The first stage of the trial of an indictable offence will be the preliminary enquiry before justices. The prosecution is rarely, if ever, ready to proceed on the defendant's first appearance before the magistrates' court; usually the defendant will be remanded in custody or on bail.[1] As regards jurisdiction, the magistrates' court at the preliminary enquiry has jurisdiction over any offence committed by a person who appears or is brought before the court, whether or not the offence alleged was committed in the county for which the magistrates' court acts.[2] It will be seen that these words are wide enough to cover all the cases set out above[3] in which a magistrate may issue process in the case of an indictable offence; thus the jurisdiction of the single magistrate issuing process and the magistrates' court sitting for the purpose of the preliminary enquiry are made co-extensive. It has been noted that magistrates also possess this very wide jurisdiction in a number of other cases (although not for the trial of a summary offence). A single lay magistrate may sit for the purpose of committal proceedings.[4]

Great changes in the form of committal proceedings were made by the Criminal Justice Act 1967. In all committal proceedings prior to the Act prosecution witnesses had to give evidence orally, and the magistrates had to go through the motions of satisfying themselves that there was sufficient evidence to put the defendant on trial by jury, although no-one, least of all the defendant, questioned this.[5] The result was a great waste of time in many

---

[1]   See p. 470, *ante*.
[2]   Magistrates' Courts Act 1980, s. 2(3). The rules as to offences committed on boundaries or on journeys apply: see p. 445, *ante*. There is power to remand to an alternate court nearer to the prison where the accused, if remanded in custody, is confined: *ibid*., s. 130(1); see p. 471, *ante*.
[3]   See p. 444, *ante*.
[4]   Magistrates' Courts Act 1980, s. 4(1).
[5]   It is outside the scope of this work to consider the merits of having committal proceedings at all. For a full discussion, see Napley, *Law and Practice under the Criminal Justice Act*, pp. 14–19.

cases, especially long ones. Further, it was expressly provided that magistrates were not bound to sit in open court at the preliminary enquiry. Whether they should do so was the subject of much controversy. There are certain obvious arguments both in favour of publicity and against it; thus it may be argued that the general public (including the twelve jurors who will try the accused if there is a committal for trial) may be improperly prejudiced by evidence given at proceedings which are not the trial of the accused and at which the defence side of the case is very rarely heard. On the other hand there are undoubted arguments in favour of courts generally being open to the public; thus there are a number of examples[6] of persons, having read of the preliminary enquiry, coming forward with evidence for the defence. The matter received considerable attention at the trial of Dr. Adams for murder in 1957; the trial judge, DEVLIN, J. (as he then was), stating that he was speaking with the authority of the then Lord Chief Justice (LORD GODDARD), said that it would have been far better if the preliminary proceedings in that case had been held in private. Dr. Adams's case was a somewhat extreme one since the preliminary proceedings and the trial itself received a quite exceptional amount of publicity and at the preliminary enquiry there was a reference to the deaths of certain other of Dr. Adams's patients, besides the patient of whose murder he was eventually charged at the trial; no further mention was made of these patients and no evidence in respect of them was led at the trial, but there was obviously a grave risk of prejudice. The remarks of DEVLIN, J. were not apparently intended to be of general application; nevertheless, following the case, a committee was set up, under the chairmanship of LORD TUCKER, to consider the matter. In 1958 the committee reported[7] that in their opinion no details of the preliminary enquiry should be made public beyond the name of the accused and the charge, until the accused had been committed for trial or discharged by the magistrates.

2 Procedure

a Committal without consideration of the evidence

This change, desirable or not, could hardly be put into effect until there was a complete reform of committal proceedings, designed to save time in the type of case mentioned above, but to preserve the existing advantages of committal proceedings, namely to give the defendant fair notice of the evidence against him and a chance to defeat a weak case at an early stage. This reform was brought about by the 1967 Act. It is now open to the court to commit for trial "without consideration of the evidence" if *all* the evidence before it consists of written statements in the form required by the Act. Provided that all conditions are satisfied, the statements are admissible in committal proceedings to the same extent that oral evidence to the same effect, by the makers of statements, would be. Such statements will normally be of the prosecution witnesses, the defence not revealing its case at this early stage. The statements must be signed with a declaration that the statement is true to

---

6 Set out in the Tucker Report, *infra*, paragraphs 45–49. The committee was sceptical about the value of committal proceedings for this purpose.
7 Cmnd. 479 of 1958.

the best of the maker's knowledge or belief; before it is tendered to the court a copy must be given to all other parties (i.e., normally by the prosecution to the defence), none of whom must object to the statement being tendered to the court.[8] Normally, the prosecution will have ascertained in advance that there will be no objection, and would not use the procedure otherwise. They will also inform the court that all their evidence is in the form of written statements, copies of which have been given to the defence.

Thus far, statements having been tendered to the defence without objection, the court must cause the charge to be written down and read to the defendant if not already done, and then may itself receive the statements and commit for trial, at once, on the statements, without any consideration of the strength of the prosecution evidence contained in them, or even reading them.[9] The court will however consider the statements and will therefore depart from this procedure if counsel or a solicitor for the defendant or any of the defendants submits that they contain insufficient evidence to put his client on trial by jury,[10] and, not unnaturally, does not and cannot commit under this procedure if the defendant wishes to give evidence himself or call witnesses.[9] In any event, every statement must be authenticated by a signature from one of the magistrates, but signature of a single certificate now suffices. By this certificate he is treated as signing each statement individually.

This shortened procedure is commonly called a "section 6(2) committal" or "short committal" or "committal for trial without consideration of the evidence".[11] It does however seem necessary to consider it for certain questions other than testing its strength—such as determining whether the defendant should be released on bail, and to what court he should be committed. The procedure may not be used if the defendant, or any of the defendants (if there are more than one), has no solicitor acting for him in the case (whether present in court or not).[12]

The magistrates do not have to use the procedure; it is optional, and either the court or any party may require any witness to attend and give evidence in person.[13]

A common criticism of the procedure is that persons are sometimes committed for trial where the evidence against them does not justify a committal. This may arise if the defendant's legal representative does not give adequate consideration to the contents of the witness statements.[14]

---

[8] Magistrates' Courts Act 1980, s. 102(2). Service on the solicitor for the defendant suffices, but where there is more than one defendant, there must be one copy of the statements for each defendant: *R. v. Bott: R. v. Baker*, [1968] 1 All E.R. 1119; [1968] 1 W.L.R. 583.

[9] Magistrates' Courts Rules 1981, r. 6(1)–(3).

[10] Magistrates' Courts Act 1980, s. 6(2)(*b*).

[11] This form of committal used to be known as a "section 1 committal" (having been introduced by s. 1 of the Criminal Justice Act 1967) prior to the consolidation of the 1967 Act provisions in the Magistrates' Courts Act 1980.

[12] Magistrates' Courts Act 1980, s. 6(2)(*a*) (as amended).

[13] *Ibid.*, s. 102(4).

[14] In order to meet this criticism, the James Committee (*The Distribution of Criminal Business between the Crown Court and Magistrates' Courts*: Cmnd. 6323 of 1975) recommended that both the prosecution and the defence advocate should be required to sign a certificate to the effect that they have examined the witness's statements and satisfied themselves that the case is suitable for committal for trial without consideration of the evidence.

It was formerly held[15] that where the defendant, although under seventeen, was liable to be committed for trial under section 6(1) of the Children and Young Persons Act 1969,[16] it was not possible to use the section 6(2) procedure. The reason was that section 6(1) used the phrase ". . . if [the court] is of opinion that there is sufficient evidence to put the accused on trial" and this was construed to exclude section 6(2). However, section 24(1) of the 1980 Act expressly permits use of the procedure on committal for trial of persons under the age of seventeen.

b   *"Old-style" committal*

If it is not possible to use the section 6(2) procedure the court can only proceed with what is now called an "old-style committal". On appearing, the defendant is not of course asked to plead, since this is not the trial of the charge against him; indeed it may well not be until a later stage in the enquiry (as will be seen) that any specific charge is recorded in writing. In accordance with the general provisions of section 122 of the Magistrates' Courts Act either party may be represented by counsel or solicitor; if represented, the defendant would normally be deemed to be present if in fact physically absent, but in the particular case of the preliminary enquiry section 4(3) of the Act provides that evidence before examining justices must be given in the presence of the accused. To this rule the only exceptions are those contained in section 4(4) of the Act, *viz.* committal proceedings may proceed in the absence of the accused in two circumstances: (*a*) if the examining justices consider that by reason of his disorderly conduct before them, it is not practicable for the evidence to be given in the accused's presence; or (*b*) he cannot be present for reasons of health but is represented by counsel or solicitor and has consented to the evidence being given in his absence.

The prosecutor may make an opening speech, outlining for the benefit of the justices the facts against the accused; it is a matter for his discretion whether he does so. He will then call his evidence, which may consist of witnesses giving evidence orally or of written statements. If witnesses give evidence orally their evidence must be given on oath, subject to any enactment or rule of law permitting or authorising the reception of unsworn evidence.[17] They will first be examined in chief by the prosecution; they will then be subject to cross-examination on behalf of the defence and, if cross-examined, to re-examination on behalf of the prosecution.[18] As each witness for the prosecution gives his or her evidence it will be recorded either by the

---

[15] *R.* v. *Coleshill Justices, Ex parte Davies,* [1971] 3 All E.R. 929; [1971] 1 W.L.R. 1684; and see *R.* v. *L.* and *W.,* [1971] Crim. L.R. 481. In the latter case the judge held that, though not expressly prohibited, it was contrary to the spirit of the Children and Young Persons Act 1969 to use the voluntary bill procedure (for which see p. 488, *post*).

[16] See p. 462, *ante.*

[17] Magistrates' Courts Act 1980, s. 98.

[18] The divisional court will not, while committal proceedings are being heard, exercise jurisdiction to issue a prerogative order to control the manner in which they are conducted. Accordingly where a magistrate refused to allow a particular line of cross-examination by defence counsel, the divisional court refused to consider issuing an order of mandamus directing the magistrate to allow the cross-examination: *R.* v. *Wells Street Stipendiary Magistrate, Ex parte Seillon,* [1978] 3 All E.R. 257; [1978] 1 W.L.R. 1002; compare *R.* v. *Horseferry Road Stipendiary Magistrate, Ex parte Adams,* [1978] 1 All E.R. 373; [1977] 1 W.L.R. 1197 (*infra*).

clerk to the justices or by one of the clerk's assistants; then, as soon as possible after the examination of the witness is concluded, the whole record of that witness's evidence must be read over to him in the presence and hearing of the defendant (save in cases in which the evidence was given in his absence under section 4(4) of the Act, in which event the deposition must record this fact).[19] After making any corrections that are necessary the witness must sign the document.[19] The record of the witness's evidence is called a "deposition"; as will be seen,[20] depositions are documents of considerable importance in the general process of the trial of an indictable offence. A deposition must be authenticated in the same way as a written statement, by signature of a magistrate, but again signature of a single certificate suffices.[1]

It is also open to the prosecution to tender written statements, in exactly the same form as those used under the section 6(2) procedure. Again, copies must be given to each of the defendants before they are tendered to the court and none of the defendants must object to their use. The court or any party has power to require the attendance of the maker. This procedure is very useful in the case of a witness, such as the owner of the property in many cases of theft or handling, whose evidence is not disputed by anyone but is necessary for the prosecution to prove their case. The statement must be read aloud unless the court otherwise directs, and the court may direct that an "account" be given of any part not read aloud.[2] The function of committal proceedings is simply to ensure that no-one shall stand trial unless there is a *prima facie* case against him. Accordingly there is no greater obligation upon the prosecution than to adduce sufficient evidence to establish a *prima facie* case. The prosecution is not obliged to call all of the witnesses who will be called at the trial and cannot be compelled to call any particular witness even if that witness be the principal witness against the accused.[3]

After the whole of the evidence of the prosecution has been given the defence may submit that there is no case to answer, either on the charge brought against the accused (assuming that a specific charge has been formulated at this stage; as noted above,[4] this is not necessarily so) or generally. In other words it may be submitted either that the charge brought should be reduced to a lesser charge (murder to manslaughter for example) or that the accused should be discharged altogether as being completely innocent of any crime. Such a submission is only likely to succeed in the clearest of cases, since, it will be recalled, the magistrates are not concerned at this stage to assess the actual guilt or innocence of the defendant; their only duty is to decide whether there is sufficient evidence against the accused to put him on trial for any indictable offence. In rare cases the magistrates themselves (no doubt advised by their clerk; this being a case in which he could take the

---

[19] Magistrates' Courts Rules 1981, r. 7(2).
[20] See p. 486, *post*.
[1] Magistrates' Courts Rules, r. 7(3).
[2] Magistrates' Courts Act 1980, s. 102(5).
[3] *R.* v. *Epping and Harlow Justices, Ex parte Massaro*, [1973] Q.B. 433; [1973] 1 All E.R. 1011. The witness in this case was a little girl who was the victim of an alleged sexual assault by the accused. Although the defence were anxious to cross-examine her at the committal proceedings the prosecution decided not to call her and the accused was committed for trial on other evidence. The divisional court refused an application for an order of certiorari and upheld the validity of the committal. See, also, Magistrates' Courts Act 1980, s. 103.
[4] See p. 479, *ante*.

initiative in advising them) may take the same point on behalf of a defendant. If no submission of "no case" is made, or if it is rejected, the magistrates must cause the charge to be written down, if this has not already been
done, and then, if he is not represented by counsel or a solicitor, read out to
the defendant and its nature explained to him in ordinary language.[5] Then,
before the defendant is allowed to say anything in answer to the charge the
court must administer to him the statutory caution,[6] which is as follows:

> "You will have an opportunity to give evidence on oath before us and to call
> witnesses. But first I am going to ask you whether you wish to say anything in
> answer to the charge. You need not say anything unless you wish to do so; and
> you have nothing to hope from any promise, and nothing to fear from any
> threat, that may have been held out to induce you to make any admission or
> confession of guilt. Anything you say will be taken down and may be given in
> evidence at your trial. Do you wish to say anything in answer to the charge?"

Although the rule says that "words to that effect" may be used in place of
the actual words of the caution, it is customary for these exact words to be
used. It is one example of the English tradition of fair treatment of the
defendant that, although he may be willing and anxious to admit his guilt
once the charge has been read over to him and its nature explained, he will
not be allowed to do so until the statutory caution has been put to him. It will
be noted that although the defendant is told that anything he says may be
given in evidence at his trial it will not necessarily be given in evidence against
him.[7]

Whatever the defendant says in answer to the charge, once the statutory
caution is complete, must be taken down in writing, read over to him and
signed by one of the examining justices and also by the defendant if he so
wishes.[8] This statement may then be given in evidence at the trial of the
defendant (assuming that he is committed for trial) without the need for
further proof. The only limitation on this procedure is that laid down by the
Court of Criminal Appeal in *R. v. Morry*.[9] In that case the defendant was
given the statutory caution in the form stated above; he then made a speech
of some three hours' duration, "defending himself as an advocate". Only
part of what he said was in fact transmitted to the court of trial. It was held
by the Court of Criminal Appeal that: (1) the magistrates'. signature was
conclusive as to the contents of the statement and that no evidence could be
called at the trial to prove that the whole statement was not transmitted; and
(2) (in effect the reason for (1)):

> "The procedure under s. 12 was never intended to apply to a man making an
> oration as an advocate on his own behalf. That is not the time at which all the
> arguments should be put."[10]

The defendant was not handicapped for he could make the same statement
to the judge and jury at his trial; in the particular case the defendant had

---

[5] Magistrates' Courts Rules 1981, r. 7(6).

[6] *Ibid.*, r. 7(7).

[7] Cf. the position under the Judges' Rules; see p. 670, *post.*

[8] Magistrates' Courts Rules 1981, r. 7(8).

[9] [1946] K.B. 153; [1945] 2 All E.R. 632. The court was concerned with section 12(2) and (4) of
the Criminal Justice Act 1925 which is in similar terms to rule 7(7) and (8).

[10] HILBERY, J., in *R. v. Morry*, [1946] K.B. 153, at pp. 155–156; [1945] 2 All E.R. 632, at p. 634.

signed not merely the end of his statement but each individual sheet of it "so that a more unmeritorious objection can scarcely be conceived".[10]

Once the defendant has made such answer as he wishes to the statutory caution, the court must further give him an opportunity to give evidence himself, and to call witnesses.[11] If he wishes to take this course, he must be permitted to do so, even if he has already made an unsuccessful submission of no case to answer.[12] He can, therefore, have "two bites at the cherry" since he may again try to persuade the magistrates, at the conclusion of all the evidence, that there is no *prima facie* case to justify committal.[12]

However, in practice, if a submission of no case fails, it is overwhelmingly likely that the magistrates will ultimately commit and, therefore, it may do the defendant no good, and indeed positive harm, tactically, to give evidence and thereby reveal his case at this stage, especially if there is no question of being committed on a lesser charge. There have been many comments from judges on the desirability of evidence being called for the defence as early as possible, but in spite of this the defendant frequently "reserves his defence".[13] If defence evidence is called at this stage, the procedure is as follows. It is unusual for the defendant's solicitor or counsel to make an opening speech, but he may do so, in his discretion; except in one case, set out below, he has only one chance to address the court and as a matter of tactics he will usually take it after his evidence and not before. Defence evidence will then be called. Any evidence, whether that of the defendant himself or any of his witnesses, will be reproduced in the form of depositions, or may be by written statement, in exactly the same way as the evidence of prosecution witnesses. The only exception is that a witness "merely"[14] as to the accused's character will not have his evidence taken in the form of a deposition, in the rather unlikely event of such a witness being called at the preliminary enquiry. It has been said that "Good character may tend to prove the innocence of the accused, and, if so, his deposition must be taken . . ."[15] However it may be difficult in a particular case to decide whether evidence as to character does in fact exculpate the defendant until the evidence has already been given, by which time it will be too late to take a deposition if such is found to be necessary.

As to speeches, defending counsel or solicitor may, as a rule, make one speech on behalf of his client (as already noted). If however (1) the defendant himself gives evidence, (2) witnesses are called on his behalf, and (3) the court gives leave, he may address the court both before and after the defence evidence; but in this case the prosecutor will have the right to reply. His reply will be heard immediately after the evidence for the defence is concluded; then will come the second speech for the defence.[16]

---

11 Magistrates' Courts Rules 1981, r. 7(10).
12 *R. v. Horseferry Road Stipendiary Magistrate, Ex parte Adams*, [1978] 1 All E.R. 373; [1977] 1 W.L.R. 1197, where the divisional court issued an order of certiorari quashing committal proceedings in which the magistrate had refused to permit the accused, following an unsuccessful submission of no case, to give evidence on his own behalf.
13 It is commonly (but strictly inaccurately) also stated that he "pleads not guilty".
14 Magistrates' Courts Rules 1981, r. 7(2).
15 *Stone's Justices Manual* (114th Edn.) p. 6060.
16 Magistrates' Courts Rules 1981, r. 7(11).

3 Committal for trial

On committal for trial, four questions arise: (1) what should the charge be; (2) to which location of the Crown Court should the defendant be committed; (3) should the defendant be committed in custody or on bail and (4) should there be an "alibi warning"? Each of these questions will be considered in turn.

a Charges

In an old-style committal it is for the justices to consider, on all the evidence, what charge is appropriate, the only limitation being that it must be properly founded on evidence appearing in the depositions. As seen, their power to dismiss the charge completely only arises at the end of the prosecution evidence.

There is no power to reduce the charge on a section 6(2) committal; therefore, if such a committal is to be used, the prosecution may be wise to bring charges in the alternative. As already seen, so long as the section 6(2) procedure is used, no question of dismissing the charge arises.

b Court of trial

The Crown Court is a single court but sits in a number of different locations. These are described as first-tier, second-tier and third-tier centres. First-tier centres deal with both civil and criminal cases and are visited by High Court and Circuit judges; second-tier centres deal with criminal cases only but are visited by both High Court and Circuit judges, while third-tier centres deal with criminal cases only and are visited only by Circuit judges. Each circuit contains a number of each type of centre. Thus, for example, on the Midland and Oxford Circuit, Birmingham and Stafford are first-tier centres, Leicester and Worcester are second-tier centres and Coventry and Wolverhampton are third tier centres. Offences in turn are divided into four classes,[17] each containing a number of offences. Offences in Class 1 must be tried by a High Court judge; examples are murder and any offence for which a person may be sentenced to death. Offences in Class 2 must be tried by a High Court judge unless a presiding judge of the Circuit releases any particular case for trial by a Circuit judge or Recorder; examples are manslaughter, abortion and rape. Offences in Class 3 are normally to be tried by a High Court judge, but may be tried by a Circuit judge or Recorder; these are all offences triable only on indictment not falling within any other Class. Offences in Class 4 will normally be tried by a Circuit judge or Recorder,[18] although they may also be tried by a High Court judge; examples are wounding or causing grievous bodily harm with intent, forgery, conspiracy and all offences triable either way.[19]

Therefore, when a magistrates' court commits for trial a person charged

---

[17] By the Directions set out in *Practice Note*, [1971] 3 All E.R. 829; [1971] 1 W.L.R. 1535, para. 1 (as amended); see p. 203, *ante*.

[18] By paragraph 13 of the Directions, proceedings listed for hearing by a Circuit judge or Recorder are suitable for allocation to a court comprising Justices of the Peace.

[19] See p. 203, *ante*.

with any offence within Classes 1-3,[20] it must specify, as the place of trial, the location of the Crown Court where a High Court judge regularly sits. In the case of an offence in Class 4 the magistrates' court must simply specify the most convenient location of the Crown Court. If, however, the magistrates think that an offence[1] although within Class 4 should be tried by a High Court judge, they should commit as for an offence in Classes 1-3, giving their reasons in a notice included with the papers sent to the Crown Court. The Directions specify a number of reasons which "should influence the justices in favour of trial by a High Court judge", for example that widespread public concern is involved, the case involves violence of a serious nature, the accused holds a public position or is a professional or other person owing a duty to the public, or a novel or difficult issue of law is likely to be involved. In selecting the most convenient location of the Crown Court, the magistrates should have regard to (i) the convenience of the defence, the prosecution and the witnesses, (ii) the expediting of the trial and (iii) the location or locations designated by a presiding judge of the Circuit in question as being the "normal" location or locations for committal.[2]

The Crown Court has jurisdiction to alter the location of any trial on indictment, whether previously fixed by itself or the magistrates.[3] A corresponding power, vested in the High Court by the Administration of Justice (Miscellaneous Provisions) Act 1938, was sometimes used where there was such strong bias against the defendant that there was little chance of finding an impartial jury to try him.[4]

c   Bail

The magistrates must consider whether to release the defendant on bail, or to commit in custody. Factors which must be considered, including the imposition of conditions, have already been explained.[5]

d   Alibi warning

Finally, there will be the question of what is commonly called "the alibi warning". At his trial the defendant will not be allowed to adduce evidence in support of an alibi—except with leave of the court—unless he has given to the prosecutor particulars of the alibi within seven days from the end of the committal proceedings. Therefore, if there is any question at the trial as to the time or place of an alleged offence, this must be resolved on the material available to the defendant, namely the charges and the depositions.[6] Notice may of course be given before the committal proceedings, or during them; if

---

[20] Even if there is one or more further offences within Class 4 and not of a type suitable to be tried by a High Court judge.

[1] Even if there is one or more other offences within Class 4, and not of a type suitable to be tried by a High Court judge.

[2] Directions, paras. 2-5 and Magistrates' Courts Act 1980, s. 7.

[3] Supreme Court Act 1981, s. 76.

[4] Since jurors at that time had to come from the locality.

[5] See p. 470, *ante*.

[6] *R.* v. *Lewis*, [1969] 2 Q.B. 1; [1969] 1 All E.R. 79. The court stated this "with confidence", but said, "It will no doubt be proved in future that there are many difficulties in section 11"; for some of these, see p. 512, *post*. The prosecutor should send a copy of any notice received by him to the court of trial, to assist in estimating the length of the trial: *Practice Direction*, [1969] 1 All E.R. 1042; [1969] 1 W.L.R. 603.

it has not been given up to then, the warning must contain the name and address of the prosecutor, on whom notice may be served.

If the court of trial is satisfied that the warning was not given, evidence in support of an alibi may be called without leave.[7] In practice the warning may be inappropriate, because there is obviously no question of a defence of alibi; the clerk to the justices may confirm this by reference to the defendant's counsel or solicitor, and then not give the warning.[8]

4 Publicity

It would have been inappropriate to reform committal proceedings without solving the vexed question of publicity. By section 8 of the 1980 Act, it is generally unlawful to publish any report of committal proceedings, apart from various formal matters such as the court, the names of the justices, defendants and advocates, a summary of the charges and the decision as to whether or not to commit. The evidence, called by either side, may not be published until the end of the trial,[9] if the defendant is committed, or the end of committal proceedings, if he is not. It is open to the defendants or any one of them to apply, and the court must then order that the restriction is not to apply if all defendants so require; if one or more objects to such an order the court will make an order only if it is in the interests of justice to do so.[10] The restrictions on publicity apply equally to proceedings in the magistrates' court before the court proceeds to inquire into the information as examining justices.[11] This might arise in the case of an either way offence where the court began a summary trial but then changed to committal proceedings.[12]

In addition to the general restrictions imposed by the Act, there are specific restrictions in rape cases imposed by the Sexual Offences (Amendment) Act 1976. Under that Act it is an offence to publish matter likely to lead members of the public to identify a woman as the complainant[13] or the defendant as the person accused.[14] In relation to committal proceedings the accused can apply to the court to remove the restriction relating to publicising his identity (but not that of the complainant).[15]

All the above applies to publicity in the press, and on radio and television. As regards admission of the public to committal proceedings, the Act

---

[7] Criminal Justice Act 1967, s. 11(3).

[8] Magistrates' Courts Rules 1981, r. 7(9).

[9] By which time it will have been superseded by evidence given at the trial and will be of no general interest. See also the court's powers under s. 4 of the Contempt of Court Act 1981 (p. 239, *ante*).

[10] Magistrates' Courts Act 1980, s. 8 (as amended).

[11] *Ibid.*, s. 8(8); but this does not render unlawful any report published before the court decides to proceed as examining justices (*ibid.*).

[12] Under s. 25 of the Act; see p. 460, *ante*.

[13] Sexual Offences (Amendment) Act 1976, s. 4. The Act applies to "rape offences", and not to cases of indecent assault or other sexual offences. The restrictions on publicity apply equally to the trial and subsequent proceedings.

[14] *Ibid.*, s. 6(1).

[15] *Ibid.*, s. 6(2). In addition he can apply to the Crown Court for a direction removing the restriction in relation to his own or the complainant's identity, but such a direction may only be given if required for the purpose of inducing likely witnesses to come forward and if the conduct of the applicant's defence at the trial is likely to be substantially prejudiced if the direction is not given (*ibid.*, ss. 4(2), 6(2)).

expressly states that examining justices must sit in public unless (*a*) statute directs to the contrary or (*b*) the magistrates consider that the ends of justice would not be served by them sitting in open court, as regards the whole or any part of the committal proceedings.[16] Thus publicity is encouraged as regards the attendance of members of the public in court, but not as regards reports to a wider public in the press and on television. Further, where the defendant is committed, or discharged after decision not to commit, there must be published on that day or the next, in a part of the magistrates' court to which the public have access, certain details such as the defendant's name and address, the charge or charges and (if there is a committal) the court of trial.[17]

5   Securing the attendance of witnesses

Formerly, on committal for trial, most, if not all, witnesses giving evidence at the preliminary enquiry would have been bound over in a certain sum to appear at the court of trial and give evidence. A new scheme was created by the Criminal Procedure (Attendance of Witnesses) Act 1965; it applies to all witnesses giving evidence before the magistrates except the defendant and any witness of his merely as to character. As soon as possible after the witness has signed his deposition[18] he must be handed a document called a witness order, commanding him to appear at the court of trial. No sum of money is liable to be forfeited if the witness fails to appear, but disobedience to a witness order is contempt of the trial court and as such is punishable summarily by imprisonment for a period not exceeding three months or by other penalty imposed by the court of trial, unless the witness can satisfy the court that he had "just excuse" for failure to attend.[19]

If, however, the magistrates consider that the evidence of a particular witness at the trial is unlikely to be disputed or even required they may make in the case of that witness a conditional witness order, which requires him to attend at the court of trial only if notice is given to him to do so. On committing the defendant for trial the court must inform him of his right to require the attendance at the trial of a witness in respect of whom a conditional witness order has been made, and the necessary steps which he must take.[20]

The depositions and a number of other documents will be forwarded to the trial court by the clerk to the justices.[1] The defendant's right to see the information has already been noted. The general importance of the depositions is that, subject to a notice of additional evidence being served, what is in the depositions will be the evidence called against the defendant at the

---

[16] Magistrates' Courts Act 1980, s. 4(2).
[17] *Ibid.*, s. 6(5). It is not stated how long the notice must be displayed. But this has effect subject to the restrictions imposed by the Sexual Offences (Amendment) Act 1976 (*supra*) so that the name of the defendant will not be included, nor will any matter likely to lead members of the public to identify him or the complainant.
[18] A term which includes in this context statements tendered for the purpose of section 6(2) committal proceedings.
[19] Act of 1965, s. 3.
[20] *Ibid.*, s. 1(3).
[1] See generally, Magistrates' Courts Rules 1981, r. 11.

trial; the indictment can only be drawn from material appearing in the depositions, prosecuting counsel at the trial must confine himself in his opening speech to what appears in them and any departure from a deposition is regarded as an appropriate subject for cross-examination of a witness.

The names of the witnesses to be called by the prosecution are listed on the back of the indictment.[2] The defendant is entitled to assume that all of those witnesses will be present at court so that he need take no step to secure the attendance of any of them at his trial. However, although it is the obligation of the prosecution to have at court all witnesses whose names are on the back of the indictment, the prosecution may in certain circumstances refrain from calling such a witness. These circumstances will, in due course, be considered.[3]

B PREFERMENT OF BILL

1 Introduction

"A bill of indictment is a written or printed accusation of crime made at the suit of the Crown against one or more persons."[4] There is an important difference between a bill of indictment and an indictment proper. A bill of indictment may be preferred by any person[5] against any other person before the Crown Court; however a bill of indictment is of no legal validity in itself. It only becomes a legal document when it is turned into an indictment proper by being signed by the appropriate officer of the court, who in turn can only sign the draft bill if he is satisfied that one of four things has happened: either (1) the person charged has been committed for trial by examining justices; this is naturally the most common; (2) the "voluntary bill" procedure has been followed; (3) the bill is preferred pursuant to an order made under section 9 of the Perjury Act 1911; or (4) the bill is preferred by direction of the Court of Appeal.[5] The three latter contingencies are considered below. If one of these four is satisfied, the judge of the court may direct the appropriate officer to sign the bill, either on his own motion or on the application of the prosecution. After it has been signed, the proper officer must on request supply to the defendant a copy free of charge.[6]

Where the bill is preferred on the authority of a committal for trial it may charge any offence which appears on the depositions, or statements, in addition to or in place of the offence or offences for which he was committed, subject to the normal rules as to joinder of offences.[7] It is immaterial that the "added" offences involve a higher penalty than the original charge or

---

[2] In fact the practice varies from court to court and there is no statutory requirement to this effect; if their names are not so listed the defendant is entitled to assume that those witnesses who were tendered at the committal stage will be called.

[3] See p. 510, *post.*

[4] Archbold, *Pleading, Evidence and Practice in Criminal Cases* (41st Edn.), para. 1.

[5] Except in those cases where a private person has no right to institute proceedings: see p. 442, *ante.*

[6] Indictment Rules 1971, r. 10(1).

[7] Administration of Justice (Miscellaneous Provisions) Act 1933, s. 2(2)(i). For the rules as to joinder, see p. 491, *post.* The bill must be preferred within 28 days of committal, although the Crown Court has power to extend this period (Indictments (Procedure) Rules 1971, r. 5 (as amended)).

charges. This rule does not in any way destroy what has already been described as one of the main purposes or advantages of the preliminary enquiry, namely to give the defendant fair notice of the case against him, since he will necessarily have knowledge of the facts alleged to constitute the offence, if not of the precise charge based on those facts. However, there are obvious possibilities of injustice, and the Court of Appeal has said[8] that whenever it is decided to bring such "fresh" charges, the police ought to see the defendant and warn him of the charges under caution, so that he may make a statement in answer if he wishes.

The whole of the indictment may consist of such "substitute" charge or charges. If the defendant considers that one or more of such charges does not fairly arise out of the facts in the depositions he may move to quash the indictment. It is then for the trial judge to rule on the sufficiency of the indictment. "The question in its nature is one of legal objection to the indictment, and is appropriate matter for a motion to quash it."[9]

Where however the defendant was committed for trial in respect of two offences which had been repealed by statute, it was held that he was never lawfully committed at all, and it was immaterial that the third count of the indictment was in respect of an offence which both existed and was disclosed by the depositions.[10]

It cannot be denied that there is a certain risk of hardship to the defendant in this procedure, since he may go to trouble and expense to defeat a particular charge at the stage of committal proceedings, only to find (on the assumption that he is committed for trial in respect of other matters) that the same charge appears in the indictment.

> ". . . We think it right to say that . . . it is an undesirable practice and can easily in some cases work hardship on defendants, and the right to prefer in the indictment charges which the magistrate has rejected is one which ought to be very carefully regarded."[11]

2   Voluntary bills

The voluntary bill procedure must now be considered. The essence of the procedure is that the prosecution apply to a High Court[12] judge for leave to prefer a bill of indictment against the accused; the judge in his discretion grants or refuses[13] leave, with the result that if leave is granted the bill is preferred forthwith and there is no need for any committal proceedings. At the same time the defendant loses the advantage of knowing in advance the substance of the case against him; indeed the applicant himself cannot attend unless permitted by the judge to do so, and even if there is a hearing it is not in

---

8 In *R. v. Dickson*, [1969] 1 All E.R. 729; [1969] 1 W.L.R. 405, where the defendant's solicitors had six days' notice of "fresh" charges.

9 HILBERY, J. in *R. v. Morry*, [1946] K.B. 153, at p. 157; [1945] 2 All E.R. 632, at p. 636.

10 *R. v. Lamb*, [1969] 1 All E.R. 45; [1968] 1 W.L.R. 1946.

11 FINNEMORE, J. in *R. v. Dawson*; *R. v. Wenlock*, [1960] 1 All E.R. 558, at p. 562; [1960] 1 W.L.R. 163, at p. 168.

12 A Circuit judge has no power to give leave to prefer a bill of indictment: *R. v. Thompson*, [1975] 2 All E.R. 1028; [1975] 1 W.L.R. 1425.

13 See, for example, *Re Roberts*, [1967] 1 W.L.R. 47. The exercise of the judge's discretion is not open to review: *R. v. Rothfield*, [1937] 4 All E.R. 320.

open court.[14] Regular use of the voluntary bill procedure could therefore lead to hardship, and there are indications in the rules that the procedure[15] is to be regarded as a somewhat exceptional one.

All applications must be accompanied by the proposed bill of indictment and, unless the application is being made by or on behalf of the Director of Public Prosecutions, an affidavit by the applicant that the statements contained in this application are true to the best of his knowledge, information and belief. It has been held[16] to be sufficient compliance with these rules if the proposed indictment is actually before the judge at the time when he deals with the application. There must also be the depositions, where appropriate, and the statements of witnesses proposed to be called for the prosecution, in so far as their evidence does not appear from the depositions. The application must also state whether there has been any previous application for a voluntary bill, whether there have been any committal proceedings and the result in each case. Most applications for a voluntary bill are made after the magistrates have refused to commit.[17] Where there have been no committal proceedings, the application must state why the present procedure is being used; again, if the defendant has been committed for trial the application must contain a statement as to the reason why it is being made. There might, of course, be perfectly good reasons; thus the voluntary bill procedure is obviously much quicker than proceedings by way of preliminary enquiry, and it might be thought desirable to use it if certain co-defendants had already been committed for trial and were awaiting trial. By the voluntary bill procedure, considerable delay and hardship to them might be avoided. Nevertheless the requirement that the bill must state specifically why the present procedure is being used instead of committal proceedings (if such is the case) shows that indiscriminate use of the procedure is to be avoided.

3 Perjury Act 1911

Section 9 of the Perjury Act provides that where a judge (including a justice of the peace) is of opinion that any person has committed perjury in proceedings before him he may order the prosecution of that person for perjury and may commit him in custody or on bail to take his trial. This procedure, which is a combination of the voluntary bill procedure and committal for trial by examining justices, has fallen into disuse; even in the clearest cases the judge will normally send the papers to the Director of Public Prosecutions for him to consider the matter and take proceedings if thought fit, rather than take the initiative himself.

---

[14] See, generally, *R. v. Raymond*, [1981] Q.B. 910; [1981] 2 All E.R. 246 where an attempt to challenge the validity of the voluntary bill procedure (on the ground that it was inconsistent with the *audi alteram partem* principle) was rejected by the Court of Appeal.

[15] Now contained in the Indictments (Procedure) Rules 1971.

[16] In *R. v. Rothfield*, [1937] 4 All E.R. 320.

[17] Although, since committal proceedings are not a trial, the prosecution may validly institute fresh committal proceedings based on the same charge: *R. v. Manchester City Stipendiary Magistrate, Ex parte Snelson*, [1978] 2 All E.R. 62; [1977] 1 W.L.R. 911; LORD WIDGERY, C.J. in that case indicated that the safeguard against repeated committal proceedings lay in the inherent power of the court (exercisable by the prerogative order of prohibition) to stop proceedings which had become vexatious or an abuse of the process of the court.

4   Criminal Appeal Act 1968

Section 8 of this Act provides that, where the Court of Appeal orders a new trial under the Act, that trial is to be on a fresh indictment preferred by the direction of the Court of Appeal.

C   INDICTMENT

1   Form and contents

The rules as to the form of indictments are now contained in the Indictments Act 1915 and the Indictment Rules 1971. The Act in particular effected a much needed simplification in the law, the previous rules being technical to the point of absurdity. At present, drafting of the indictment is primarily the responsibility of the appropriate officer of the court, but in cases where more than ordinary care may be requisite in framing the indictment, it is often drawn by counsel. In *R.* v. *Martin*[18] the Court of Criminal Appeal said that counsel should be instructed "in all cases of difficulty".

An indictment is in three parts: introductory matters, statement of offence and particulars of offence. The introductory matters are twofold, first the court of trial and secondly the name of the defendant, appearing in the form:

THE QUEEN v. [Defendant] . . . charged as follows:—

As regards the statement of offence and particulars of offence, the Rules now provide[19] that every indictment must contain, and need not contain more than, a statement of the specific offence with which the defendant is charged, describing the offence shortly, together with such particulars as are necessary to give reasonable information as to the nature of the charge. Where, however, the offence is created by statute, there must be a reference to the statute and to the relevant section, and all the essential elements of the offence must be disclosed in the particulars, unless the defendant is not prejudiced or embarrassed by failure to describe any such element.[20] The fact that an indictment is defective does not render the trial a nullity. Thus in *R.* v. *Nelson*[1] the indictment was defective in that the statement of offence did not refer to the statute which the defendant was alleged to have contravened. Although this was a ground of appeal on a point of law, the Court of Appeal held that it did not render the trial a nullity so that the court had jurisdiction to hear the appeal (which it dismissed by the application of the proviso to section 2(1) of the Criminal Appeal Act 1968).

If the error had been noticed prior to conviction, it could have been cured

---

[18] [1962] 1 Q.B. 221; [1961] 2 All E.R. 747.
[19] Indictment Rules, r. 5(1). Cf. the rules for the contents of an information; see p. 443, *ante*. Rule 5 further provides for a form of indictment for individual offences to be approved by the Lord Chief Justice.
[20] *Ibid.*, r. 6. It is not necessary for the indictment to specify or negative any exception, exemption, excuse, proviso or qualification. There is again an analogy with the rules for the contents of an information.
[1] (1977), 65 Cr. App. Rep. 119; see also *R.* v. *Ayres*, [1984] A.C. 447; [1984] 1 All E.R. 619 where the House of Lords applied the proviso in a case where the wrong offence had been charged (common law conspiracy as opposed to conspiracy under s. 1 of the Criminal Law Act 1977).

by amendment of the indictment, but an indictment cannot be amended after conviction.[2]

2 Joinder: separate trials

Hitherto the indictment has been considered as charging one offence only. However, within certain limits, a single indictment may charge more than one offence, or be drawn in respect of more than one defendant, or both. The rules relating to joinder (the technical term used) of offenders or offences must therefore now be considered. So far as joinder of offenders is concerned, the basic rule is that where two or more persons join in the commission of an offence, all or any number of them may be jointly indicted for that offence, or each may be indicted separately. In the latter case there would be no power in any court to order "consolidation" of the indictments, however desirable this might seem from the point of view of saving time and expense.[3] However, joinder is now very common. None of the Indictment Rules deals specifically with joinder of offenders (as distinct from offences) and the matter depends upon decisions of the courts, particularly of the Court of Criminal Appeal. The latest formulation of the rule on this subject is as follows:[4]

> "As a general rule it is, of course, no more proper to have tried by the same jury offenders on charges of committing individual offences that have nothing to do with each other than it is to try before the same jury offences committed by the same person that have nothing to do with each other. Where, however, the matters which constitute the individual offences of the several offenders are upon the available evidence so related, whether in time or by other factors, that the interests of justice are best served by their being tried together, then they can properly be the subject of counts in one indictment and can . . . be tried together. Such a rule, of course, includes cases where there is evidence that several offenders acted in concert but is not limited to such cases.

The court stressed that:

> ". . . It is the interests of justice as a whole that must be the governing factor and . . . amongst those interests are those of the accused."

This formulation will no doubt govern the practice of the courts for a considerable time to come.[5]

Conspiracy counts—In cases involving several offences of a similar character committed by two or more persons, there was until recently a tendency among prosecutors to formulate the charges as conspiracies instead of (or, in some cases, in addition to) counts charging specific offences. Although this practice was deprecated by the House of Lords[6] it persisted with the result

---

[2] Save, perhaps, as to immaterial matters: *R*. v. *Dossi* (1918), 87 L.J.K.B. 1024; as to amendment generally, see p. 496, *post*.

[3] *Crane* v. *Director of Public Prosecutions*, [1921] 2 A.C. 299.

[4] *R*. v. *Assim*, [1966] 2 Q.B. 249, at pp. 261–262; [1966] 2 All E.R. 881, at pp. 887–888.

[5] There is no objection to joining in one indictment counts founded on separate committals so that offenders separately committed may be tried together: *R*. v. *Groom*, [1977] Q.B. 6; [1976] 2 All E.R. 321.

[6] In *Verrier* v. *Director of Public Prosecutions*, [1967] 2 A.C. 195; [1966] 3 All E.R. 568.

that in 1977 LORD WIDGERY, C.J. after consultation with the judges of the Queen's Bench Division, announced a *Practice Direction*[7] as follows:

> "1. In any case where an indictment contains substantive counts and a related conspiracy count, the judge should require the prosecution to justify the joinder, or, failing justification, to elect whether to proceed on the substantive or on the conspiracy counts.
> "2. A joinder is justified for this purpose if the judge considers that the interests of justice demand it."

Justification might exist where the substantive offences which the prosecution is in a position to prove do not adequately reflect the extent and persistence of the defendants' criminality. Thus, for example, there might be evidence to show that a person had been engaged for some time in the importation of drugs of various kinds, although the prosecution might only be able to prove one specific importation.[8]

The question of joinder of offenders used to require careful consideration since there was formerly a rule that where persons were jointly charged they had to be acquitted if it was shown that each of them had committed an offence independently.[9] The rule was much criticised and the authority embodying it was eventually overruled by the House of Lords in *Director of Public Prosecutions* v. *Merriman*.[10] The law, as stated in that case, is that where two or more defendants are jointly charged with an offence, each may be convicted of that offence either if he acted in concert with another defendant in committing that offence or if he independently committed the offence; thus persons jointly charged can, in effect, be found guilty either as principals or as accessories of one another (or, indeed, of persons not before the court).

If these rules are broken, the indictment is bad and may properly be made the subject of a motion to quash. Even if the indictment is good on the face of it, it is essentially a matter for the discretion of the court whether several offenders can properly be tried together at the same time.

> "The discretion, no doubt, must be exercised judicially, that is, not capriciously. The judge must consider the interests of justice as well as the interests of the prisoners."[11]

Further there is no rule that where the defence of one co-accused is to blame the other for the crime a separate trial must be ordered, although that is obviously a matter which the trial judge will take into consideration.[12] Separate trials might also be ordered where prejudice would result from a joint trial; thus evidence might be admissible against one co-defendant but not against another, or one of the co-defendants might already have been convicted in respect of substantially similar offences.

---

[7] Reported at [1977] 2 All E.R. 540; [1977] 1 W.L.R. 537.
[8] Although conspiracy has ceased, subject to certain exceptions, to be a common law offence and has become a statutory offence (Criminal Law Act 1977, ss. 1–5) the principles of the Practice Direction remain unaffected.
[9] *R.* v. *Scaramanga*, [1963] 2 Q.B. 807; [1963] 2 All E.R. 852.
[10] [1973] A.C. 584; [1972] 3 All E.R. 42.
[11] LORD GODDARD, C.J. in *R.* v. *Grondkowski*; *R.* v. *Malinowski*, [1946] K.B. 369, at p. 372.
[12] See, among many cases, *R.* v. *Bywaters* (1922), 17 Cr. App. Rep. 660.

"The real test after all, which must be applied by a court of criminal appeal on a matter which is essentially one of discretion is, has the exercise of the discretion resulted in a miscarriage of justice?"[13]

So far as joinder of offences is concerned, the basic rule is to be found in Rule 9 of the 1971 Rules:

"Charges for any offences may be joined in the same indictment if those charges are founded on the same facts or form or are a part of a series of offences of the same or a similar character."

It is a matter of fact and degree in each case as to whether this rule is satisfied. Thus it has been held[14] that there should not be included in the same indictment one count charging rape and another count charging indecent assault on another woman at another time; wholly disconnected and dissimilar offences ought not be joined in the same indictment even against the same person. On the other hand it may be proper to join counts alleging rape upon one person and indecent assault upon another where the two cases are of such similarity that evidence of each incident would be admissible in relation to the other as relevant "similar fact" evidence.[15] The modern tendency of some judges is to assimilate the rules regarding joinder of offences with those governing the admissibility of similar fact evidence. Thus if a person is charged with sexual offences against two boys, the question of whether the offences could be joined in one indictment would depend upon whether the evidence in relation to the offences against one boy would be admissible evidence in relation to the alleged offences against the other boy (and *vice versa*). This approach was advocated by LORD CROSS in *Boardman* v. *Director of Public Prosecutions* in the following terms:[16]

"When in a case of this sort the prosecution wishes to adduce 'similar fact' evidence which the defence says is inadmissible, the question whether it is admissible ought, if possible, to be decided in the absence of the jury at the outset of the trial and if it is decided that the evidence is inadmissible and the accused is being charged in the same indictment with offences against the other men the charges relating to the different persons ought to be tried separately. If they are tried together the judge will, of course, have to tell the jury that in considering whether the accused is guilty of the offence alleged against him by A they must put out of mind the fact—which they know—that B and C are making similar allegations against him. But, as the Court of Criminal Appeal said in *R.* v. *Sims*,[17] it is asking too much of any jury to tell them to perform mental gymnastics of this sort."

This passage is much canvassed by defence counsel seeking an order for separate trials of counts joined in a single indictment. However it is fair to state that the statement of LORD CROSS is not only contrary to the plain words of Rule 9 of the 1971 Rules but also inconsistent with the practice which undoubtedly obtains in the criminal courts. Moreover the decision in

---

[13] LORD GODDARD, C.J. in *R.* v. *Grondkowski*, [1946] K.B. 369, at p. 374.

[14] *R.* v. *Muir* (1938), 26 Cr. App. Rep. 164.

[15] *R.* v. *Wilson* (*S.C.*) (1973), 58 Cr. App. Rep. 169; as to the rules governing the admissibility of "similar fact" evidence, see p. 571, *post*.

[16] [1975] A.C. 421, at p. 459; [1974] 3 All E.R. 887, at p. 910.

[17] [1946] K.B. 531; [1946] 1 All E.R. 697.

R. v. Sims[18] affords no support for LORD CROSS's somewhat radical view.

Thus where, for example, a defendant is charged with a number of bank robberies, they are almost always tried together although, in the ordinary way, the evidence on one robbery count will be wholly inadmissible on the other counts, the jury simply having to perform the "mental gymnastics" required in order to give separate consideration to each count. The trial judge in every case has a discretion and so long as he does not err in law, takes into account all relevant matters and excludes consideration of irrelevant matters, the Court of Appeal will not interfere.[19] Thus, in one case,[20] the House of Lords held that two charges were properly joined in the same indictment where the defendant was charged first with attempted larceny from a public house and secondly with robbery, following a fracas, in another public house in the same area 15 days later. Although the offences were not founded on the same facts, two could make a series, and the offences had the same essential ingredient of theft or attempted theft in a public house. It used to be the rule[1] that no other offence should be charged in any indictment alleging murder or manslaughter, the charge of murder being regarded as too serious a matter to be complicated by having alternative counts inserted in the indictment. This rule was progressively abrogated by the Homicide Act 1957 which allowed two murders to be joined in one indictment and, later, by the decision of the House of Lords in *Connelly* v. *Director of Public Prosecutions*[2] and a *Practice Direction*[3] consequent thereon. There is now no special rule as regards murder or manslaughter.

If the rules as to joinder of offences are infringed the indictment again is bad and is liable to be quashed. Even on the assumption that joinder is legally permissible, the judge may in his discretion order one or more counts to be tried separately from the rest of the indictment, on the ground that the defendant would be prejudiced or embarrassed by the joinder. Thus in a case in which the defendant had been tried on an indictment containing no less than forty counts of obtaining or attempting to obtain by false pretences HAWKINS, J. observed:[4]

> "Though not illegal, it is hardly fair to put a man upon his trial on such an indictment for it is almost impossible that he should not be grievously prejudiced as regards each one of the charges by the evidence which is given on the others. In such a case it would not be unreasonable for the defendant to make an application that each count or set of counts should be taken separately."

The sentiment was echoed by a Lord Chief Justice:

> "The risk, the danger, the logical fallacy is indeed quite manifest. . . . It is so easy to derive from a series of unsatisfactory accusations, if there are enough of them, an accusation which at least appears satisfactory. It is so easy to collect

---

[18] [1946] K.B. 531; [1946] 1 All E.R. 697.
[19] *R. v. Scarrott*, [1978] Q.B. 1016; [1978] 1 All E.R. 672.
[20] *Ludlow* v. *Metropolitan Police Commissioner*, [1971] A.C. 29; [1970] 1 All E.R. 567. The House was considering the appropriate provision of the 1915 Rules, which was materially the same as Rule 9. See also *R. v. Kray*, [1970] 1 Q.B. 125; [1969] 3 All E.R. 941.
[1] Laid down in *R. v. Jones*, [1918] 1 K.B. 416. There was also the possibility of a compromise verdict in a murder case.
[2] [1964] A.C. 1254; [1964] 2 All E.R. 401; see p. 503, *post*.
[3] [1964] 3 All E.R. 509; [1964] 1 W.L.R. 1244.
[4] *R. v. King*, [1897] 1 Q.B. 214, at p. 216.

from a mass of ingredients, not one of which is sufficient, a totality which appear to contain what is missing."[5]

Alternatively, the offences may be numerous and complicated, or difficult to disentangle, so that a joint trial would cause confusion, and embarrassment to the defence.[6] Conversely, it may be very material (though not conclusive) in favour of a joint trial that evidence given in support of one count is admissible, to prove system, on other counts.[7] The test is essentially one of prejudice to the defendant, and the Court of Appeal will not interfere with the judge's discretion unless it can see that justice has not been done or unless compelled to do so by some overwhelming fact. Even if the judge gives a bad reason, the Court of Appeal will not interfere if satisfied that there was a good reason.[8]

Where two or more offences are joined in one indictment each one must be alleged in a separate count or paragraph of the indictment.[9] Well before the passing of the Indictments Act this rule was uniform and well established. Where an indictment contravenes this rule it is said to be bad for duplicity. Thus in *R. v. Molloy*[10] the defendant was charged in an indictment, the particulars of which stated that in a certain place and at a certain time he "stole, or with intent to steal, ripped and severed or broke" certain articles. The indictment was clearly bad for duplicity since, under the relevant Act, the Larceny Act 1916, stealing and ripping with intent to steal were distinct offences; they should therefore have been put in separate counts of the indictment and separate pleas taken in respect of each. Similarly in *R. v. Nicholls*[11] the defendant was charged on an indictment of which the statement of offence and particulars of offence were as follows:

> *Statement of offence*: warehousebreaking contrary to sections 16(1) and 27(2) of the Larceny Act 1916. *Particulars of offence*: the defendant on a particular named day "broke and entered a warehouse with intent to steal therein and stole therein . . .".

This indictment again was bad for duplicity, since both the statement of offence and the particulars of offence contained two separate offences, warehousebreaking with intent to steal and warehousebreaking and stealing. The matter was not a mere technicality, since the first offence carried a maximum of seven years' imprisonment and the second a maximum of fourteen.

There are exceptions or apparent exceptions to this rule. Where an offence created by statute is defined as doing or not doing different acts in the alternative, or in any one of different capacities or with any one of different intentions, or where some part of the offence is stated in the alternative, the

---

[5] LORD HEWART, C.J. in *R. v. Bailey*, [1924] 2 K.B. 300, at p. 305.
[6] Cf. *Ludlow*'s case (*supra*), [1971] A.C. 29, at p. 41; [1970] 1 All E.R. 567, at p. 576. See also *R. v. Fitzpatrick*, [1962] 3 All E.R. 840; [1963] 1 W.L.R. 7.
[7] *R. v. Flack*, [1969] 2 All E.R. 784; [1969] 1 W.L.R. 937; and see *R. v. Sims* (*supra*); cf. *Boardman* v. *Director of Public Prosecutions* (*supra*).
[8] *R. v. Flack* (*supra*).
[9] Indictment Rules 1971, r. 4(2). Each count is equivalent to a separate indictment (for one consequence of this, see p. 498, *post*). Counts must be numbered consecutively: r. 4(3).
[10] [1921] 2 K.B. 364.
[11] [1960] 2 All E.R. 449; [1960] 1 W.L.R. 658.

indictment may follow the statute and charge the offence in a single count.[12] Thus it was held under the old law that a single count in an indictment might charge driving while under the influence of a drink or a drug; the words of the relevant section in the Road Traffic Act charge a single offence, namely driving while incapable of having proper control, whether that incapacity is caused by drink or drugs.[13]

Again, s. 1(1) of the Children and Young Persons Act 1933 makes it an offence wilfully to assault, ill-treat, neglect, abandon or expose a child. It has been held that the section describes in detail various forms of cruelty to a child, and that if the indictment selects one out of the five verbs it is immaterial that the conduct proved might be more aptly described by one of the others. Therefore a count in the indictment may properly charge more than one or even presumably all five forms of cruelty.[14]

Where the sentence for an offence varies according to the factual ingredients of it, for example the age of the victim of a sexual offence, the proper course is for the prosecution to charge the variations in separate counts, so that the jury can decide on whether or not the ingredients of the more serious or less serious form of the offence are present.[15]

Finally, section 22(1) of the Theft Act 1968 contains a single offence of handling stolen goods, but specifies various alternative methods of committing that offence. Consequently an indictment which charged handling stolen goods *simpliciter*, without particularising the species of handling would not be defective.[16] However, in fairness to the defendant it is the practice to particularise the precise form of handling relied upon by the prosecution, and, in cases of doubt, to include two counts, one for receiving and the other for dishonestly undertaking or assisting in the "retention, removal, disposal or realisation by or for the benefit of another person" of the stolen goods.[17] If the prosecution rely upon one species of handling, it is not open to the jury to convict on the basis of some other form·of handling;[16] it is for this reason that the prosecution is wise to include alternative counts.

3   Objecting to the indictment: amendment

If the defendant desires to object to the validity of the indictment he should do so before he is arraigned. The Court of Appeal does not readily hear objections to the validity of an indictment where the objection was not taken at the trial, although failure to take it is not insuperable. When objection is taken the court may (unless it rules against the objection altogether) either quash the indictment or amend it. Quashing the indictment may arise from causes other than formal defects in it and will be considered below.[18] As to amendment section 5(1) of the 1915 Act provides:

---

[12] Indictment Rules 1971, r. 7.
[13] *Thomson* v. *Knights*, [1947] K.B. 336; [1947] 1 All E.R. 112. See also *R.* v. *Inman*, [1967] 1 Q.B. 140; [1966] 3 All E.R. 414, and see p. 544, *post*.
[14] *R.* v. *Hayles*, [1969] 1 Q.B. 364; [1969] 1 All E.R. 34.
[15] *R.* v. *Courtie*, [1984] A.C. 463; [1984] 1 All E.R. 740.
[16] *R.* v. *Nicklin*, [1977] 2 All E.R. 444; [1977] 1 W.L.R. 403.
[17] *Griffiths* v. *Freeman*, [1970] 1 All E.R. 1117; [1970] 1 W.L.R. 659.
[18] See p. 506, *post*.

"Where before trial, or at any stage of a trial, it appears to the court that the indictment is defective, the court shall make such order for the amendment of the indictment as the court thinks necessary to meet the circumstances of the case, unless, having regard to the merits of the case, the required amendments cannot be made without injustice. . . ."

Since amendment of the indictment includes the addition of a new count, the court's powers would appear to be very wide;

"In our opinion, any alteration in matters of description, and probably in many other respects, may be made in order to meet the evidence in the case so long as the amendment causes no injustice to the accused person."[19]

Thus in *R. v. Pople*[20] the defendants were charged with obtaining certain quantities of cash by false pretences (under the Larceny Act 1916). At the close of the prosecution case, and because of the state of the prosecution evidence, the prosecution were permitted to amend the indictment by the substitution of cheques for the amounts in question instead of cash as originally alleged. It was held that in substance the charge was unaltered and that the amendment was properly made. Again in *R. v. Hall*[1] a charge of stealing 3 pictures was amended to stealing 8, there being evidence of stealing 8 on the depositions. The court applied what had been said in *R. v. Martin*, that

"An indictment which charges offences which are not disclosed in the depositions and fails to charge an offence which is, lacks the most essential quality of an indictment."[2]

A new count may be added before the defendant is arraigned, and even after arraignment a count can be added charging a completely new offence;[3] the question is one of degree depending on the facts of the particular case.[4]

Application for amendment may be made by either side and at any time. Since counsel for the prosecution has general responsibility for the correctness of the indictment he should not open his case without being satisfied on the point and should make any necessary application for amendment before the defendant is arraigned, having inspected the indictment for the purpose. Defending counsel should also inspect, in his own client's interests. Amendment may be made by the judge of his own motion, but before doing so he should give both sides the opportunity of commenting on the proposed amendment.[5]

---

[19] HUMPHREYS, J. in *R. v. Pople*, [1951] 1 K.B. 53, at p. 57; [1950] 2 All E.R. 679, at p. 681.
[20] *Supra.*
[1] [1968] 2 Q.B. 788; [1968] 2 All E.R. 1009.
[2] *Per curiam* in *R. v. Martin*, [1962] 1 Q.B. 221; [1961] 2 All E.R. 747.
[3] *R. v. Radley* (1973), 58 Cr. App. Rep. 394 where the amendment was made at the conclusion of the prosecution opening; cf. *R. v. Tirado* (1974), 59 Cr. App. Rep. 80.
[4] It seems that an amendment on an immaterial matter can be made at or after verdict: *R. v. Dossi* (1918), 87 L.J.K.B. 1024. Compare the position which arose in *Wright* v. *Nicholson* (p. 443, *ante*).
[5] *R. v. West*, [1948] 1 K.B. 709, at p. 717; [1948] 1 All E.R. 718, at p. 721.

D   ARRAIGNMENT AND PLEAS

1   Attendance of the accused

The general course of the trial of an indictable offence will now be considered. On the day fixed for the trial to begin the defendant, if he has been
detained in custody, will be brought from the prison or remand centre where
he has been detained and lodged in the cells beneath the dock. If he has been
on bail he must surrender to his bail and will then be placed in the cells to
await his trial. It may be that the defendant has been on bail and does not
appear, in which case by a long established procedure, now codified in
section 7 of the Bail Act 1976, the court of trial may issue a warrant, called a
"bench warrant," for the arrest of the defendant; this is a summary procedure and will not normally be used unless the arrest of the defendant is a
matter of urgency.

Still further powers are provided by section 7(3) of the 1976 Act by which a
constable may arrest without warrant any person who has been released on
bail in criminal proceedings if (*inter alia*) he has reasonable grounds for
believing that the person is unlikely to appear at the time and place required.

2   Arraignment

Assuming that the defendant has appeared at, or has been brought to, the
court, the first formal step in his trial will be the arraignment.

> "Arraignment is the process of calling an accused forward to answer an indict-
> ment. It is only after arraignment, which concludes with the plea of the accused
> to the indictment, that it is known whether there will be a trial and, if so, what
> manner of trial."[6]

Nevertheless, where a plea of not guilty is "vicariously offered or tacitly
conveyed" and a trial ensues, that trial will not be a nullity despite the
absence of a formal arraignment.[7]

The defendant will be brought from the cells into the dock and the proper
officer will first ask him his name. Assuming that he is the person named in
the indictment he will then be asked to plead. The indictment will be read to
him (omitting only the introductory matters) and he will be asked to plead to
it; further, where the indictment contains more than one count, each should
be put to the defendant separately and he should be asked to plead separately.[8] The reason is that

> ". . . Every count in an indictment is equivalent to a separate indictment; the
> prisoner can be tried on one or all of the counts. The verdicts have to be taken
> separately, and the right practice is that he should be asked to plead to each count
> as each count is read to him."[9]

---

[6] *R.* v. *Vickers*, [1975] 2 All E.R. 945, at p. 948; [1975] 1 W.L.R. 811, at p. 814, *per* SCARMAN,
L.J.
[7] *R.* v. *Williams (Roy)*, [1978] Q.B. 373; [1977] 1 All E.R. 874.
[8] *R.* v. *Boyle*, [1954] 2 Q.B. 292; [1954] 2 All E.R. 721; see p. 495, *ante*.
[9] LORD GODDARD, C.J. in *R.* v. *Boyle*, [1954] 2 Q.B. 292, at p. 296; [1954] 2 All E.R. 721, at
p. 722.

Unfitness to plead

On arraignment the defendant may, of course, simply say nothing. If this occurs, the first question is whether the defendant is mute of malice, that is to say, able to speak but refusing to do so, or whether he is mute by visitation of God, that is to say, temporarily or permanently unable to speak. If there is any doubt a jury must be sworn to try the issue.[10] Witnesses may be called on either side and counsel may address the jury; the judge will then sum up the case to the jury, who will retire if necessary and then give a verdict.[11] If the finding is that the defendant is mute of malice the court may then order the proper officer of the court to enter a plea of not guilty on behalf of the defendant (assuming that he still declines to speak);[12] the trial will then proceed as if the defendant had himself pleaded not guilty. If, however, the finding is that the defendant is mute by visitation of God, the defendant may yet be perfectly well able to defend himself, and a plea of not guilty should be entered by the court and the trial should proceed in the ordinary way. However there may well be some question of whether the defendant is fit to plead, the test for which is whether he is fit to challenge jurors, instruct counsel, understand the evidence and give evidence himself.[13] The procedure to be followed is now contained in section 4 of the Criminal Procedure (Insanity) Act 1964. A jury must be sworn to try the issue. It may be the same jury which has just found the defendant mute by visitation of God, although it seems that evidence given on the first trial within a trial, as to the defendant's muteness, must be led in full again on the question of unfitness. Again, evidence may be called by either side and speeches will be made; the judge will direct the jury, who will return a verdict.[14] If the finding is that the defendant is unfit to plead the trial does not proceed, but the defendant is not free to go; he is liable to be detained in hospital. If the finding is one of fitness to plead, the defendant will then be called upon to plead to the indictment; if he still declines to answer, a plea of not guilty may be entered on his behalf, as in the case of a person mute of malice.[12]

It is important to note the precise relationship between the issue of whether the defendant is mute of malice or mute by visitation of God, and the issue of unfitness to plead. If a defendant refuses or cannot answer on the indictment being put to him, the criminal court must necessarily enquire as to the cause for his not replying. It by no means follows that there will be a further enquiry as to unfitness; for instance the defendant may be found mute of malice, which of itself does not raise any question of unfitness. Even if he is found mute by visitation of God this may be for some reason which involves no question of unfitness to plead. Conversely, the question of unfitness may arise even though there is no doubt whatever about the defendant's ability and willingness to speak, as in the case of *R. v. Podola.*[15] The question of

---

[10] There is no right to challenge jurors empanelled to try this issue: *R. v. Paling* (1978), 67 Cr. App. Rep. 299.

[11] Not necessarily unanimous: see pp. 513–514, *post.*

[12] Criminal Law Act 1967, s. 6(1) (c).

[13] *R. v. Berry* (1977) 66 Cr. App. Rep. 156; not whether he is able to defend himself properly and well: *R. v. Robertson*, [1968] 3 All E.R. 557; [1968] 1 W.L.R. 1767.

[14] Again not necessarily unanimous, see pp. 513–514, *post.*

[15] [1960] 1 Q.B. 325; [1959] 3 All E.R. 418.

unfitness may be raised by either side, or the judge himself may raise it;[16] it must normally be determined as soon as it is raised,[17] but the court may postpone the issue until any time up to the opening of the case for the defence if it considers it expedient to do so and in the interests of the defendant. If, before the question falls to be determined, the jury return a verdict of acquittal on the count or each of the counts on which the accused is being tried, the question is not determined.[18] This change in procedure, effected[19] by the 1964 Act, gives the defendant the opportunity of submitting "no case to answer" at the close of the prosecution case and obtaining an acquittal without putting in issue his state of mind.

The court should have regard to the facts of the case; if there are reasonable chances of the prosecution case being successfully challenged, so that the defence is not called on, it is clearly in the defendant's interest to have the issue postponed. The court should also consider the supposed disability and whether the defendant would have to be confined, in the public interest, whatever the result of the trial.[20] Thus in *R. v. Burles*[1] the defendant had been charged with manslaughter of a fellow inmate in a hospital. He was severely subnormal and unable to communicate except with those who knew him well. The Crown admitted that there was insufficient evidence to convict. The Court of Appeal held that this was a clear case where the issue of unfitness should have been postponed.

3 Pleas

Assuming that all questions of fitness to plead have been disposed of adversely to the defendant, in the sense that the trial on the substantive issues must go on, the possible pleas open to the defendant are as follows:

a Plea of guilty

On the assumption that the plea covers the whole indictment counsel briefed for the prosecution will give a brief outline of the facts and then call the police officer in charge of the case to give the antecedent history of the defendant, in the form of a sheet setting out the defendant's home and educational background, previous jobs, criminal record and anything else thought to be relevant. He may be cross-examined by defending counsel. There is then a plea in mitigation made by counsel for the defence, sometimes supported by witnesses (very rarely the defendant). The defendant will then usually be given the opportunity of saying something himself to the court, after which sentence will be passed. If there are two defendants, one of whom is pleading guilty and the other not guilty, the one pleading guilty will not normally be sentenced until the trial of the other defendant, is con-

---

[16] *R. v. Dashwood*, [1943] K.B. 1; [1942] 2 All E.R. 586; and see *R. v. McCarthy*, [1967] 1 Q.B. 68; [1966] 1 All E.R. 447.

[17] Criminal Procedure (Insanity) Act 1964, s. 4(3).

[18] *Ibid.*, s. 4(2).

[19] Following the procedure devised for the occasion by DEVLIN, J. (as he then was), in *R. v. Roberts*, [1954] 2 Q.B. 329, [1953] 2 All E.R. 340—a notable example of "judicial valour".

[20] *R. v. Webb*, [1969] 2 Q.B. 278; [1969] 2 All E.R. 626.

[1] [1970] 2 Q.B. 191; [1970] 1 All E.R. 642.

cluded.[2] It is customary for the normal rules of evidence to be relaxed at proceedings following a plea of guilty. Thus in a case where normal "antecedent evidence" had been given LORD GODDARD, C.J. said:[3]

> "That evidence would be quite properly admissible . . . after verdict. What happens after verdict is very different from what happens before verdict. After verdict, there is no longer an issue between the Crown and the prisoner. The issue has been determined by the verdict of the jury and there is no more room for evidence except to inform the mind of the court as to what the prisoner's previous history has been for the purpose of enabling the court . . . to assess the proper sentence."

The rules of evidence do not apply to "antecedent evidence", which is invariably given by a single police officer on the basis of files concerning the defendant which the officer has in court. Nevertheless the officer should not make allegations against the defendant which he has reason to think that the latter would deny and which he cannot properly prove.[4]

If the defendant pleads guilty to some, but not all, counts or pleads guilty to a lesser offence, the prosecution must decide whether to proceed on the remaining counts or "accept" the defendant's pleas, in which event the counts to which he has not pleaded guilty will be left "on the file". Although the defendant will never have been in peril of conviction on those counts, so that he could theoretically be tried on them, in practice this would not be permitted without leave of the court and, indeed, the counts on the file are sometimes ordered to be marked with words such as "not to be proceeded with without the leave of this court or of the Court of Appeal". However, even if the prosecution is content to adopt this course, the judge must consent to it and, if he does not, he may order the trial to proceed.[5]

b Plea of not guilty

It should be noted that this is not necessarily a positive assertion that the defendant is innocent but merely a request or a challenge to the prosecution to prove the case against him. The trial will then proceed in the manner to be described.

As to pleas of guilty and not guilty generally, certain observations may be made. First, the defendant may plead guilty to one count in the indictment but not guilty to another, or even admit part of an offence contained in a single count but not the rest of the offence.[6] He may also plead not guilty to the offence charged but guilty to some other offence of which he may lawfully be convicted by way of alternative verdict;[7] thus he may plead not guilty

---

2 Contrary to the former practice, the modern tendency of judges is to adhere to this principle (*viz.* sentencing all defendants at the same time) even where the defendant who has pleaded guilty is to give evidence either for the Crown ("Queen's evidence") or a co-defendant; cf. *R.* v. *Weeker* (1982), 74 Cr. App. Rep. 161.

3 *R.* v. *Butterwasser*, [1948] 1 K.B. 4, at p. 8; [1947] 2 All E.R. 415, at pp. 416–417.

4 *R.* v. *Robinson* (1969), 53 Cr. App. Rep. 314, where the officer described the defendant as the principal drug "pusher" in the Midlands, "evidence" the reception of which the Court of Appeal described as "a clear and obvious injustice"; see also *R.* v. *Wilkins* (1977), 66 Cr. App. Rep. 49.

5 *R.* v. *Broad* (1978), 68 Cr. App. Rep. 281.

6 See *Machent* v. *Quinn*, [1970] 2 All E.R. 255, p. 516, *post.*

7 Criminal Law Act 1967, s. 6(1) (*b*).

to murder but guilty to manslaughter. The whole question of alternative verdicts is now regulated by section 6(3) of the Criminal Law Act 1967. This enables the jury to acquit of the offence charged, but to convict of another offence which the court has jurisdiction to try and which is expressly or by implication alleged in the indictment. The section only applies to a trial on indictment, and not to treason, or murder (which is dealt with by s. 6(2)). Where another offence is expressly alleged there is no difficulty, but the question of what offences are included "by implication" presents difficulties. For many years courts applied the so-called "red pencil test" whereby all the averments in the indictment which had not been proved were struck out and the defendant could only be convicted of an alternative offence if the remaining averments were sufficient to constitute that offence; put another way, the test was whether the lesser offence was an essential ingredient of the greater one.[8] However in *R.* v. *Wilson (Clarence)*[9] the House of Lords rejected this test, overruled the authority for it[8] and substituted a wider test, *viz.* whether the allegations in the indictment are capable of including the elements of the alternative offence. Thus assault occasioning actual bodily harm was an alternative verdict on a count charging inflicting grievous bodily harm since, although the count charged did not *necessarily* include an allegation of assault (grievous bodily harm can be inflicted without an assault) it was *capable* of including such an allegation. The point arises, of course, when the judge comes to sum up the case to the jury. Where nothing appears on the depositions which can be said to reduce the crime charged to the lesser offence of which the defendant wishes to plead guilty it is the duty of counsel for the Crown to present the offence charged in the indictment, leaving it to the jury "in the exercise of their undoubted prerogative" to return a verdict of guilty of the lesser offence.[10] Secondly, the defendant may change his plea once the trial has started but in this case the appropriate verdict must be returned by the jury which will have been sworn to try the case;[11] it may seem a formality that if the defendant changes his plea, for example, from not guilty to guilty the foreman of the jury should be required to stand up and say that the defendant is guilty but ". . . once a prisoner is in charge of a jury he can only be either convicted or discharged by the verdict of the jury".[12] Thirdly, whether the plea is guilty or not guilty it must always come from the defendant himself.[13] This is important since pressure of various sorts may have been brought to bear on the defendant to plead guilty;[14] the requirement that he must personally plead is a safeguard at least against the grosser type of intimidation. Finally, in certain circumstances a plea of guilty may be withdrawn and a plea of not guilty entered.

---

[8] *R.* v. *Springfield* (1969), 53 Cr. App. Rep. 608.

[9] [1984] A.C. 242; [1983] 3 All E.R. 448.

[10] *R.* v. *Soanes*, [1948] 1 All E.R. 289.

[11] *R.* v. *Heyes*, [1951] 1 K.B. 29; [1950] 2 All E.R. 587.

[12] LORD GODDARD, C.J. in *R.* v. *Heyes*, [1951] 1 K.B. 29, at p. 30; [1950] 2 All E.R. 587, at p. 588.

[13] Otherwise, if a plea of guilty is entered, all subsequent proceedings will be ineffective: *R.* v. *Ellis* (1973), 57 Cr. App. Rep. 571.

[14] See *R.* v. *Turner (No. 1)*, [1970] 2 Q.B. 321; [1970] 2 All E.R. 281; see p. 460, *ante.*

"The question . . . is entirely a matter for the trial judge. If the court came to the conclusion that there was a question of mistake or misunderstanding, or that it would be desirable on any ground that the prisoner should be allowed to join issue, no doubt the court would allow him to do it. For example, it has been known for a prisoner charged with receiving stolen goods to acknowledge that he received them, and to plead guilty, adding 'but I did not know that they were stolen'. In such a case, the trial judge might well allow the prisoner to change his plea. . . ."[15]

However a plea of guilty cannot in any circumstances be withdrawn after the defendant has been sentenced.[16]

Where on being arraigned the defendant pleads not guilty and the prosecution propose to offer no evidence against him, the presiding judge may order a verdict of not guilty to be recorded without the defendant being given in charge to a jury.[17]

c   Autrefois acquit and autrefois convict

These are by far the most important of a number of so-called "special pleas in bar" which can be raised by the defendant when the indictment is put to him. The substance of the pleas in bar is that there is some reason why the court should not proceed to try the defendant, which should be made the subject of immediate enquiry, so that if the reason is found to be a valid one the defendant should be released and further proceedings stayed.[18] The general principle of the two pleas of *autrefois acquit* and *autrefois convict* is that the same person should not be put in jeopardy twice for the same offence founded on the same facts—not, it may be noted at once, merely for the same facts. The two pleas were extensively considered by the House of Lords in *Connelly* v. *Director of Public Prosecutions*.[19]

"Principle and authority establish: (1) that a man cannot be tried for a crime in respect of which he has previously been convicted or acquitted; (2) that a man cannot be tried for a crime in respect of which he could on some previous indictment have been convicted; (3) that the same rule applies if the crime in respect of which he is being charged is in effect the same, or is substantially the same as either the principal or a different crime in respect of which he has been acquitted or could have been convicted or has been convicted; (4) that one test as to whether the rule applies is whether the evidence which is necessary to support the second indictment, or whether the facts which constitute the second offence, would have been sufficient to procure a legal conviction upon the first indictment either as to the offence charged or as to an offence of which, on the indictment, the accused could have been found guilty; (5) that this test must be subject to the proviso that the offence charged in the second indictment had in fact been committed at the time of the first charge; thus if there is an assault and

---

[15] *R.* v. *McNally*, [1954] 2 All E.R. 372; [1954] 1 W.L.R. 933, at p. 934; see *R.* v. *Ingleson*, p. 528, *post*; *S. (An Infant)* v. *Manchester City Recorder*, [1971] A.C. 481; [1969] 3 All E.R. 1230, and p. 465, *ante*.

[16] *R.* v. *McNally (supra)* disapproving *R.* v. *Blakemore* (1948), 33 Cr. App. Rep. 49. There may, however, be an appeal against conviction; see p. 528, *post*.

[17] Criminal Justice Act 1967, s. 17. This is in contrast with the situation in *R.* v. *Heyes (supra)* where the trial had already proceeded some way.

[18] See the remarks of LORD GODDARD, C.J. in *R.* v. *Chairman, County of London Quarter Sessions, Ex parte Downes*, [1954] 1 Q.B. 1, at pp. 5–6; [1953] 2 All E.R. 750, at p. 751.

[19] [1964] A.C. 1254; [1964] 2 All E.R. 401.

a prosecution and a conviction in respect of it there is no bar to a charge of murder if the assaulted person later dies; (6) that on a plea of *autrefois acquit* or *autrefois convict* a man is not restricted to a comparison between the later indictment and some previous indictment or to the records of the court, but that he may prove by evidence all such questions as to the identity of persons, dates and facts as are necessary to enable him to show that he is being charged with an offence which is either the same, or is substantially the same, as one in respect of which he has been acquitted or convicted or as one in respect of which he could have been convicted; (7) that what has to be considered is whether the crime or offence charged in the later indictment is the same or is in effect or is substantially the same as the crime charged (or in respect of which there could have been a conviction) in a former indictment and that it is immaterial that the facts under examination or the witnesses being called in the later proceedings are the same as those in some earlier proceedings; (8) that apart from circumstances under which there may be a plea of *autrefois acquit*, a man may be able to show that a matter has been decided by a court competent to decide it, so that the principle of *res judicata* applies; (9) that, apart from cases where indictments are preferred and where pleas in bar may therefore be entered, the fundamental principle applies that a man is not to be prosecuted twice for the same crime.''[20]

The eighth of these propositions was directed at the possibility of "issue estoppel" applying in a criminal case. However the House of Lords in *R*. v. *Humphrys*[1] stated that this doctrine had no application in criminal proceedings. With this exception, the above propositions must be regarded as settling for some considerable time to come the law as to both *autrefois acquit* and *autrefois convict*. Some comment may now be offered on them. It is very well settled that neither plea applies unless the previous conviction or acquittal was before a court with jurisdiction to try both the offence and the defendant. Thus in *R*. v. *Hogan*; *R*. v. *Tompkins*[2] the two appellants, who had escaped from prison, had been recaptured and sentenced by a "court" of visiting justices to certain loss of privileges. They were subsequently charged on indictment with a number of offences, among them prison breach and escape from prison. It was held that the court was in no way concerned with the proceedings before the visiting justices, which were a mere matter of the internal running of the prison. In fact the trial judge struck out the count charging prison breach on hearing that the appellants had been dealt with under prison rules, but the court of Criminal Appeal held that this was unnecessary as a matter of law, although sensible from the point of view of the sentence ultimately to be passed on the defendants.

Again in *Lewis* v. *Mogan*[3] the respondent, a seaman, had neglected his duties and had been punished summarily by the master of his ship to the extent of forfeiting a day's pay. He was subsequently charged before a magistrates' court with being absent from duty without leave, contrary to the then existing Defence (General) Regulations 1939. The justices upheld a plea of *autrefois convict*, but the divisional court of the King's Bench Division held that this was incorrect:

---

[20] [1964] A.C., at pp. 1305, *et seq.*; [1964] 2 All E.R., at p. 412, *per* LORD MORRIS.
[1] [1977] A.C. 1; [1976] 2 All E.R. 497; see p. 593, *post*, for a discussion of this case and of the nature of issue estoppel.
[2] [1960] 2 Q.B. 513; [1960] 3 All E.R. 149.
[3] [1943] K.B. 376; [1943] 2 All E.R. 272.

"the master of the ship in dealing with the respondent was not in any way acting as a court of competent jurisdiction. . . . He was acting in a domestic way. . . ."[4]

In addition the previous proceedings must actually have resulted in a verdict of guilty or not guilty; mere disagreement or discharge of the jury is not enough. Thus if a judge, for whatever reason, does not ask for the jury's verdict (even though they have reached a verdict) but discharges them without taking a verdict there is no bar to the accused being tried again.[5] When the criminal division of the Court of Appeal quashes a conviction it is required by statute to direct that a verdict of acquittal be entered;[6] this therefore is sufficient (indeed it was the case in *Connelly*'s case itself).

Apart from these two preliminary points the court, in assessing a plea of *autrefois convict* or *autrefois acquit*, must now address itself closely to the principles laid down in *Connelly*'s case, with reference to the facts before the court. Vital to the operation of the doctrine is the whole rule as to alternative verdict offences.[7] As has already been noted a defendant on being charged with certain crimes may plead, or be found, guilty of certain other crimes and not guilty of the crime charged, without the need for any fresh indictment. Thus for example a defendant charged with murder may be found guilty of manslaughter, and a person charged with any indictable offence may be found not guilty of the "full" offence but guilty of an attempt to commit that offence. The House of Lords made it clear that the doctrine of *autrefois acquit* and *autrefois convict* applies to any offence which was an alternative verdict offence to the original offence of which the defendant was convicted or acquitted; thus if the defendant is acquitted of murder the defence of *autrefois acquit* will be open to him if he is charged with manslaughter or attempted murder arising out of the death of the same person. (The same would of course be true if the charge were actually murder arising out of the same facts.)

Uncertainty arises out of the rule that the doctrine also applies if the second offence is substantially the same as the first one; this must be a matter for the common sense of the court, it being quite immaterial that the second charge is founded on the same facts as the first. Thus in *R. v. Thomas*[8] the defendant had been found guilty of wounding his wife with intent to murder her and had been sentenced. The wife later died as a result of the injuries and the defendant was charged with murder. It was held that the plea of *autrefois convict* was not open to him.

The operation of the rule may now be illustrated generally from the facts of *Connelly v. Director of Public Prosecutions* itself. Connelly and three other men were charged in an indictment with murder. In a separate indictment Connelly was charged with robbery with aggravation; the separate

---

4 CHARLES, J., in *Lewis* v. *Mogan*, [1943] K.B., at p. 379; [1943] 2 All E.R., at p. 274.
5 *R.* v. *Robinson*, [1975] Q.B. 508; [1975] 1 All E.R. 360. It follows that where a judge adopts such a course the accused is completely without remedy.
6 Criminal Appeal Act 1968, s. 2(2): unless it orders a new trial; see p. 537, *post*. Moreover if proceedings in an inferior court are quashed by *certiorari* (as to which see p. 175, *ante*) the defendant will not have been in peril: cf. *Weight* v. *Mackay*, [1984] 2 All E.R. 673; *sub. nom. R.* v. *Bournemouth Crown Court, Ex parte Weight*, [1984] 1 W.L.R. 980.
7 See p. 502, *ante*.
8 [1950] 1 K.B. 26; [1949] 2 All E.R. 662.

indictment was necessary because of the then existing rule[9] that it was incorrect to charge other offences along with murder in a single indictment. Connelly was convicted of murder and sentenced; the trial judge ordered that the indictment for robbery should not be proceeded with without leave of the trial court or the Court of Criminal Appeal. Connelly appealed against his conviction of murder and the appeal was allowed[10] on the ground that the trial judge had not dealt fully and fairly with certain evidence for the defence and had exceeded the proper limits of comment in his summing-up when dealing with the defence raised to the murder charge. The court then ordered that the robbery trial should be held. When charged with robbery the defendant pleaded *autrefois acquit* (the effect of the quashing of the murder conviction being, as stated above, that the defendant was acquitted on the charge of murder). The House of Lords held that the plea failed. Clearly the second charge was not exactly the same as the first; neither was it even substantially the same; nor was robbery an alternative verdict offence to murder.[11]

Two further comments may be made on *Connelly*'s case. First, much of the difficulty arose from the old rule that other offences could not be joined in the same indictment as murder; as already noted[12] the House of Lords demolished this rule and a subsequent *Practice Direction* completed the process. Secondly the observations made in the case concerning the doctrine of issue estoppel in English criminal law have not been adopted subsequently.[13]

d   Demurrer, plea to the jurisdiction and pardon

All these three are extremely rare and may be mentioned briefly. By a demurrer the defendant alleges that even if all the facts alleged against him are true they do not constitute the offence charged. It is in essence an objection to the form or substance of the indictment, and is not therefore to be resolved by examination of the depositions.[14] Pleas that the court has no jurisdiction to try the offence or the defendant, or that the defendant has already received a pardon in respect of the offence in question may be raised as such, but they may also be raised on a motion to quash the indictment, or even under the cloak of a general plea of not guilty.

If any of the special pleas is raised but fails the defendant will then be arraigned in the manner described and will be called on to plead to the general issue. The trial will proceed.

4   Motion to quash the indictment

Instead of entering any plea, general or special, the defendant may move to quash the indictment. This may be done on several grounds. If any of the rules, already described[15] as to the framing of the indictment have not been

---

9 As to the present position, see p. 494, *ante*.

10 (1963), *The Times*, 5th April.

11 The position presumably remains the same under the Criminal Law Act 1967.

12 See p. 494, *ante*.

13 See p. 593, *post*.

14 *R. v. Inner London Quarter Sessions, Ex parte Metropolitan Police Commissioner*, [1970] 2 Q.B. 80; [1969] 3 All E.R. 1537. ". . . I hope that now demurrer in criminal cases will be allowed to die naturally."—LORD PARKER, C.J., at pp. 85 and 1541 of the respective reports.

15 See pp. 490–496, *ante*.

followed this may be made the ground for a motion to quash; however it has already been seen that the court possesses ample power to amend the indictment and it will only be rarely that a motion to quash on this ground will succeed. It could only do so on the ground of some grave defect of substance, such as the insufficiency of the particulars of offence, or duplicity. An indictment may also be quashed on the ground that the offence charged in it is not one known to the law. Yet another ground is that the appropriate officer did not have jurisdiction to sign it; as has already been seen he can sign it only if certain conditions are satisfied. The most usual of these conditions is that the defendant has been committed for trial by examining justices; yet "committed" means properly committed, so that if there was some defect in the proceedings before examining justices the indictment is liable to be quashed. Thus in *R. v. Bibby*,[16] the witnesses before examining justices were examined by the chief constable from a prepared type-written statement, analogous to a proof of evidence, copies of which were handed to the magistrates and their clerk. Nothing was taken down by the magistrates in writing but the statement was checked by the clerk as the witnesses gave evidence and was ultimately signed by the witnesses. The defendants were not furnished with copies of the statements. It was held that, since there was a grave irregularity in the proceedings before examining justices, there was no lawful committal for trial and both the indictment itself and the "trial" were complete nullities.

It has been said that if the indictment is clearly bad the court not only can but must quash it and that in other cases the court may quash it if the indictment is such as to cause embarrassment to the defendants in their defence and to prejudice the fair trial of the case. The latter proposition is perhaps doubtful since the passing of the Indictments Act, with the wide and generous powers of amendment which it confers, and it is unlikely that there will now be any extension of the cases in which an indictment is liable to be quashed. Quashing does not amount to an acquittal, and the Crown is at liberty to bring a fresh indictment on the same facts.

5 Preliminary points of law

It sometimes happens that there is a point of law involved in a case the decision of which may effectively dispose of the whole case. Thus, for example, the basic facts alleged by the prosecution may be admitted by the defence, the sole issue being whether those admitted facts amount to the offence charged. In cases of this sort it is obviously a sterile exercise to go through the motions of trial by jury when the outcome of the case will depend entirely upon the judge's decision as to the law. Accordingly there is an informal but well recognized procedure whereby, following a plea of not guilty, the judge hears argument upon the law (before empanelling a jury); if a ruling is given which, in the view of the accused and his advisers, is fatal to the defence, the accused can then change his plea.[17]

---

[16] [1936] 2 K.B. 442; [1936] 2 All E.R. 89. It will be noted that the chief constable was anticipating the procedure now allowed by the Criminal Justice Act 1967.

[17] See, for example, *Director of Public Prosecutions v. Doot*, [1973] A.C. 807; [1973] 1 All E.R. 940. An accused who has pleaded guilty in such circumstances can, of course, appeal against his conviction on the ground that the preliminary point of law was wrongly decided against; see p. 528, *post*.

However it is necessary for a plea of not guilty to be taken before the point of law is argued and the Court of Appeal has discouraged the practice of hearing argument on agreed facts before the accused has even pleaded.[18]

6   Empanelling the jury: challenges

Assuming that there is a plea of not guilty to some part of the indictment the next stage of the trial will be the swearing of the jury. The Juries Act confers on the Lord Chancellor general responsibility for the summoning of jurors.[19] From all the jurors summoned, twelve will be chosen by ballot[20] and will take their place in the jury box. They must be sworn; but before they are sworn the clerk of the court will address the defendant as follows:

> "Prisoner at the bar, the names that you are about to hear called are the names of the jurors who are to try you. If therefore you object to them or to any of them you must do so as they come to the book to be sworn and before they are sworn, and your objection shall be heard."

This is to give the defendant a right to challenge members of the jury if he so wishes. Challenges may be peremptory or for cause. A person arraigned may challenge up to three jurors without disclosing, or even having, any cause;[1] he will do so, as the form of the clerk's statement implies, as the juror is about to be sworn. Such a challenge is called a "peremptory" challenge. Neither the prosecution nor the court has any discretion in the matter and if the defendant is denied his right of peremptory challenge the trial is a nullity.[2] Mere failure to inform him of the right will not have the same or (apparently) any effect, certainly if the defendant is represented.[3] The defendant is not, however, permitted to question jurors, for example, as to their occupations or political views. The Crown has no right of peremptory challenge as such, although, as will be seen, the Crown has a right to "stand by" jurors which in many cases will lead to the same result. In addition to the defendant's right of peremptory challenge he has an unlimited number of challenges for cause, either to the whole panel summoned or to an individual juror. There are certain specified causes in each case and the burden is on the party making the challenge to show such a cause. The issue is tried by the presiding judge himself and if he rules in favour of the objection being

---

[18] *R. v. Vickers*, [1975] 2 All E.R. 945; [1975] 1 W.L.R. 811.

[19] Juries Act 1974, s. 2.

[20] *Ibid.*, s. 11. The police may "vet" potential jurors by search of criminal records. In addition in 1980, following expressions of public concern at the practice of "jury vetting", the Attorney-General published guidelines on this topic (reported at [1980] 3 All E.R. 785) indicating the circumstances in which further vetting might take place. These guidelines indicate that in exceptional cases (cases in which national security is involved and terrorist cases) the Attorney-General may authorise a check on records of police special branches; the results of any such check will be sent to the Director of Public Prosecutions who may then advise prosecuting counsel accordingly. Prosecuting counsel may then make use of this information by asking jurors to stand by for the Crown as they come to be called (*infra*).

[1] Juries Act 1974, s. 12(1), as amended by Criminal Law Act 1977, s. 43 (which reduced the number of peremptory challenges from seven to three).

[2] *R. v. Williams* (1925), 19 Cr. App. Rep. 67. The appellant had challenged a woman juror "because she was a woman".

[3] *R. v. Berkeley*, [1969] 2 Q.B. 446; [1969] 3 All E.R. 6.

upheld that juror will stand down. The swearing of the other jurors, if there are any others to be sworn, will then continue.

As noted above the Crown has a right to make a provisional challenge in the form of "standing by" a juror. By this procedure, the juror is asked to stand down, but consideration of the cause of challenge (since a challenge made by the Crown must be for cause) is postponed. It will usually then happen that there are enough "spare" jurors for a whole jury to be assembled, however many more challenges are made, so that the trial can proceed and the cause of the Crown's challenge is never made the subject of enquiry. In effect the practice of standing by a juror gives the Crown a far wider right of peremptory challenge than that accorded by statute to the defendant. The Crown will usually act on the basis of knowledge of a potential juror's criminal record[4] or, in exceptional cases, of other matter's disclosed on an authorised check of the records of police special branches.[5] The defendant has no such right; but in an exceptional case the judge might allow a defendant to do so or even do so himself.[6]

Each member of the jury must be sworn individually;[7] there is then an opportunity given to the parties to challenge each separately. The form of the juror's oath is as follows:

"I swear by Almighty God that I will faithfully try the defendant and give a true verdict according to the evidence."[8]

The appropriate officer of the court then tells the jury of the substance of the offence to which the defendant has pleaded not guilty and informs them that it is their duty, having heard the evidence, to say whether he is guilty or not.

E COURSE OF THE TRIAL

1 Hearing

Prosecuting counsel starts by making an opening speech. This will be an outline of the allegations against the defendant and of the evidence which it is proposed to call in support of the allegations. No reference should be made to any item of evidence if counsel has been informed that there is going to be an objection to the admissibility of that evidence. Such objection will be tried by the judge, in the absence of the jury, at the time in the trial when the evidence would otherwise have been called. The institution of the opening speech has been criticised[9] on the ground that counsel may make allegations which are not borne out by the evidence of his witnesses (even before they are the subject of cross-examination) yet the jury may recollect only the statements of counsel, since they came first. Only in limited circumstances has defending counsel the right to make an opening speech.[10] It is a strict rule that

---

[4] Cf. *R.* v. *Mason*, [1981] Q.B. 881; [1980] 3 All E.R. 777.

[5] See p. 508, fn. 2, *ante*.

[6] See, generally, *R.* v. *Chandler*, [1964] 2 Q.B. 322; [1964] 1 All E.R. 761.

[7] Juries Act 1974, s. 11(3).

[8] *Practice Note*, [1984] 3 All E.R. 528; [1984] 1 W.L.R. 1217.

[9] For such criticism see Blom Cooper, *The A6 Murder; R.* v. *James Hanratty: The Semblance of Truth*, pp. 92–98.

[10] See p. 512, *post*.

prosecuting counsel should limit his observations to what appears in the depositions, or witness statements. The only exception arises in the case of those witnesses in respect of whom a notice of additional evidence has been served. Even this practice is not strictly required by law, but the court has an inherent discretion to prevent oppressive conduct towards the defendant[11] and it is most unlikely that a judge would allow additional evidence to be called unless a notice of additional evidence, setting out a summary of that witness's evidence, had been served on the defendant.

Prosecution witnesses will then be called[12] and will be subject to examination-in-chief by prosecuting counsel, cross-examination by defending counsel and re-examination by prosecuting counsel. In certain circumstances, however, the witness may not appear in person, but the deposition or statement taken or served before the committing justices may simply be read in the place of actual appearance. The most common example of this occurs where a conditional witness order has been made under the Criminal Procedure (Attendance of Witnesses) Act 1965, and neither side has requested the personal appearance of the witness in question. A deposition may also be read where it is proved by the oath of a credible witness that the deponent is dead, so ill as not to be able to travel, or kept out of the way by procurement of the defendant or on his behalf.[13] It must also be proved that the deposition was taken in the presence of the defendant and that he, or his counsel or solicitor, had full opportunity of cross-examining the witnesses.[13] The charge at the trial need not be the same as the charge before the justices (even assuming that a definite charge had been formulated at the time that the witness gave his evidence) although there is some authority to the effect that

---

11 See the remarks of LORD DEVLIN, in *Connelly* v. *Director of Public Prosecutions*, [1964] A.C. 1254, at pp. 1346 *et seq.*; [1964] 2 All E.R. 401, at pp. 438 *et seq.*

12 It is the duty of the prosecution to take all reasonable steps to secure the attendance at the trial of all witnesses (other then those subject to a conditional witness order) named on the back of the indictment (*R.* v. *Cavanagh*, [1974] 2 All E.R. 704; [1972] 1 W.L.R. 676). However the prosecution has a discretion whether to call a particular witness and, having called him, whether to adduce his evidence in chief or merely to tender him for cross-examination. Where the witness's evidence is capable of belief the prosecution should call him even though his evidence is unfavourable to the prosecution case and if they do not do so, the judge may intervene and direct that he be called; on the other hand if the witness's evidence does not appear to be capable of belief the prosecution need not call him and it will then be for the defence to call him if they wish to do so; *R.* v. *Oliva*, [1965] 3 All E.R. 116; [1965] 1 W.L.R. 1028. Furthermore, if the prosecution knows of the identity of witnesses whose evidence might be materially favourable to the defence, and decides not to call those witnesses, it should notify the defence of the existence of those witnesses and failure to do so may result in a conviction being quashed: *R.* v. *Leyland Magistrates, Ex parte Hawthorn*, [1979] Q.B. 283; [1979] 1 All E.R. 209. The Attorney-General has issued guidelines (reported at [1982] 1 All E.R. 734) on the disclosure of "unused material" to the defence. In general the prosecution must disclose all such material to the defence although there is a discretion not to make disclosure in certain specified cases, including (i) where disclosure might lead to attempts to persuade the witness to change his story or to intimidate him; (ii) the statement is believed to be untrue and might be of use in cross-examination of the witness if called by the defence; (iii) the statement is "sensitive" and it is not in the public interest to disclose it; for full details reference should be made to the text of the guidelines.

13 Criminal Justice Act 1925, s. 13(1). This is a statutory clarification of a common law exception to the hearsay rule (as to which see p. 675, *post*) and, although the statute does not expressly so provide, a transcript of a witness's evidence at a previous trial may be given on a retrial, by virtue of the common law rule, where, for example, the witness is too ill to travel: *R.* v. *Thompson*, [1982] Q.B. 647; [1982] 1 All E.R. 907.

it must be substantially the same.[14] Even if the case falls within the statute, so that the depositions can properly be read, it is still within the discretion of the trial judge as to whether he will allow the prosecution to read them; thus leave might be refused in the case of a witness who was so ill that he might never be able to attend the trial, yet whose evidence constituted the whole, or almost the whole, case for the prosecution.[15] In such a case the defendant would in effect have no right to challenge the case against him. Again, if the defendant states at the preliminary enquiry that he will plead guilty, and conditional witness orders are made in the case of all witnesses in consequence, but at the trial the defendant changes his mind and pleads not guilty, the depositions should not be read, even though the statute strictly allows this course.[16]

> "In our view it was never contemplated by this Act, which was passed simply with the object of saving time and expense in cases where no possible injustice could be done to anybody, that it should be used to abolish in such a case as this the ordinary methods of trial by jury."[17]

Facts may also be proved by written statements, which are admissible in precisely the same circumstances as have already been discussed in connection with committal proceedings.[18] Alternatively either side may now make admissions.[19]

When all the witnesses for the prosecution have been examined, prosecuting counsel will close his case by saying "that is the case for the prosecution" or words to that effect. There may then be a submission by defending counsel that there is no case to answer as regards the whole or some part of the indictment. This may be put in two ways; first that there is no evidence that the crime alleged against the accused was committed by him; secondly that the evidence, taken at its highest, is so tenuous that a jury could not properly convict on it.[20] This is a matter for the judge to determine and, although there is no set rule, it is usually regarded as desirable that the argument on the submission should take place in the absence of the jury. Prosecuting counsel has, of course, a right to reply to defending counsel's submission. If the submission is upheld the trial will end as regards that part of the indictment at least, although the jury should be instructed to return a formal verdict of not guilty; this is analogous to the case where the defendant changes his plea to guilty in the course of the trial.[1] Even if no formal verdict is taken, the case, once withdrawn from the jury, is completely "dead" and

---

[14] In *R. v. Abbatto and Healy*, [1955] Crim. L.R. 645 the defendants were committed for trial on a charge of assault with intent to rob. Their victim then died and they were charged with murder and further committed for trial on this charge. It was held that the victim's deposition was admissible at the trial.

[15] As in *R. v. Linley*, [1959] Crim. L.R. 123. The test is whether it would be unfair to the accused to admit the statement: *R. v. Blithing*, [1984] R.T.R. 18.

[16] *R. v. Collins*, [1938] 3 All E.R. 130.

[17] *Ibid.*, at p. 132, *per* HUMPHREYS, J.

[18] Criminal Justice Act 1967, s. 9; see p. 480, *ante*.

[19] *Ibid.*, s. 10. In *R. v. Lewis* (1971), 55 Cr. App. Rep. 386 defending counsel admitted every allegation in the opening speech for the prosecution, whereupon the prosecution called no evidence. The Court of Appeal approved of the procedure in the particular case, but said that the procedure should only be adopted "rarely and with extreme caution".

[20] *R. v. Galbraith*, [1981] 2 All E.R. 1060; [1981] 1 W.L.R. 1039.

[1] See p. 502, *ante*.

cannot be revived by the defendant's own evidence or evidence given by a prosecution witness who is allowed to be recalled.[2] Similarly where two men are jointly charged, and a successful submission is made on behalf of one of them, he is to be regarded as no longer charged during what remains of the trial.[3]

If the submission is simply rejected the trial will proceed. Even if no submission is made the judge may at any time after the close of the prosecution's case ask the jury whether they think that the prosecution case has been proved and invite them to return a verdict of not guilty if they think that it has not; the Court of Criminal Appeal has indicated that the more desirable practice may be for the judge to take the initiative and direct the jury to return a verdict of not guilty.[4]

The defence case will then open, assuming that the trial is proceeding as to part or all of the indictment. Defence counsel has no right to make an opening speech to the jury unless he is calling witnesses as to fact other than the defendant (whether or not he is also calling the defendant); even then the matter is in his discretion. Witnesses for the defence are then called. If the defendant is giving evidence it is the general rule that he should give evidence before other witnesses; he must be in court, and if he heard the evidence of other witnesses before him, he might be tempted to "trim" his own evidence.[5] A witness about whose evidence there could be no controversy may of course be taken before the defendant. What evidence is called for the defence depends on the nature of the case, but it has already been seen that "evidence in support of an alibi" cannot be called, without leave, unless prior notice has been given.[6] It has however been held that the statutory definition of "evidence in support of an alibi" postulates an offence committed in a particular place at a particular time; where therefore the indictment alleged no place, for the commission of the crime, more precise than "the city of Cardiff", section 11 did not apply.[7] All defence witnesses are subject to examination-in-chief, cross-examination and re-examination in the normal way. Where there is more than one defendant cross-examination of prosecution witnesses and speeches will normally be taken in the order in which the defendants' names appear on the indictment, although there is no fixed rule on the matter. Once the case for the defence has been closed the prosecution may be allowed to call rebutting evidence, in the discretion of the judge. This is a necessary right, since apart from the "alibi defence", there is no obligation on the defendant to reveal his case until the actual presentation of it in court. However, the general rule has been established that rebutting evidence should be allowed only where evidence has been

---

[2] *R. v. Plain*, [1967] 1 All E.R. 614; [1967] 1 W.L.R. 565. The corollary of this is that if the submission is wrongly rejected the accused is entitled to have his subsequent conviction quashed by the Court of Appeal, even though evidence subsequently given would support that conviction: *R. v. Cockley*, [1984] Crim. L.R. 429.

[3] *R. v. Meek* (1966), 110 Sol. Jo. 867.

[4] *R. v. Young*, [1964] 2 All E.R. 480; [1964] 1 W.L.R. 717.

[5] *R. v. Smith*, [1968] 2 All E.R. 115; [1968] 1 W.L.R. 636. This rule is given statutory force by Police and Criminal Evidence Act 1984, s. 79.

[6] Criminal Justice Act 1967, s. 11, and see p. 484, *ante*.

[7] *R. v. Hassan*, [1970] 1 Q.B. 423; [1970] 1 All E.R. 745. *Quaere* how far the section can apply at all to an offence of a continuing nature; as to the court's discretion see *R. v. Sullivan*, [1971] 1 Q.B. 253; [1970] 2 All E.R. 681.

called on behalf of the defendant which could not fairly have been foreseen by the prosecution; it has even been said that such evidence should only be allowed where the defence has called evidence "which no human ingenuity can foresee".[8] This may go too far, and in one case evidence was allowed, for example, in rebuttal of a claim made by the defendant in evidence that the charge against him was false and concocted.[9] Rebutting evidence may be called at any time up to the conclusion of the summing-up and retirement of the jury and defending counsel has a right to cross-examine the witnesses called in rebuttal. Further, if evidence is called after the conclusion of the speeches, counsel may deliver supplemental speeches dealing with the new evidence.

The judge has a right to recall witnesses himself or even call witnesses whom neither side has called; he may also question witnesses to clarify matters of doubt or to probe further into matters which he thinks have not been sufficiently investigated. If the evidence called by the judge falls into the category of rebutting evidence the rules stated above apply to it and breach of them would be a matter for consideration on appeal.[10] Equally, the judge may not himself introduce evidence after the jury have retired to consider their verdict.

Closing speeches then follow. Each side may address the jury, except that where a defendant is unrepresented and either gives no evidence at all or only gives evidence himself the prosecution have no right to sum up their case.[11] In all cases the rule is that prosecuting counsel speaks first and is then followed by counsel for the defendant.[12] The judge will then sum up[13] and invite the jury to consider their verdict. Towards or at the end of his summing up he will direct them as to majority verdicts, saying that while the law in certain circumstances permits majority verdict the circumstances have not yet arisen and the jury should endeavour to reach a unanimous verdict.[14]

2 Verdict

The Criminal Justice Act 1967[15] introduced into English law the majority verdict. A verdict need not be unanimous if where there are not less than

---

[8] *R. v. Day,* [1940] 1 All E.R. 402, at p. 405.
[9] *R. v. Milliken* (1969), 53 Cr. App. Rep. 330.
[10] As in *R. v. Cleghorn,* [1967] 2 Q.B. 584; [1967] 1 All E.R. 996. Contrast *R. v. Tregear,* [1967] 2 Q.B. 574; 1 All E.R. 989.
[11] *R. v. Harrison* (1923), 17 Cr. App. Rep. 156. Where the defendant is represented but calls no evidence, counsel for the prosecution has a right to make a closing speech but the Court of Appeal has stated that it is a right which it should rarely be necessary to exercise save in long and complex cases: *R. v. Bryant* [1979] Q.B. 108; [1978] 2 All E.R. 689; an instructive case on the history of the procedure relating to speeches in criminal trials.
[12] Criminal Procedure (Right of Reply) Act 1964.
[13] If the issue of referring a question to the European Court for a preliminary ruling arises (as to which, see p. 185, *ante*) the judge may, on application or otherwise, order the question to be referred and the proceedings will then be adjourned until the European Court has given its preliminary ruling: cf. the Crown Court (References to the European Court) Rules 1972 and *R. v. Landy,* [1981] 1 All E.R. 1172; [1981] 1 W.L.R. 355.
[14] *Practice Direction,* [1967] 3 All E.R. 137; [1967] 1 W.L.R. 1198. Errors in the summing-up should be corrected by counsel before the jury retire: *R. v. Southgate,* [1963] 2 All E.R. 833; [1963] 1 W.L.R. 809.
[15] Section 13 (now Juries Act 1974, s. 17).

eleven jurors, ten agree on the verdict, and where there are ten, if nine agree.[16] The court cannot accept any majority verdict unless the jury have had not less than two hours of deliberation, or such longer period as the court thinks reasonable having regard to the nature and complexity of the case,[17] nor can the court accept a majority verdict of guilty unless the foreman of the jury states in open court the number of jurors who agreed on, and dissented from the verdict.[18] The *Practice Direction*[19] contains procedure whereby it is hoped to conceal the fact that an acquittal was by a majority. Majority verdicts are novel in English law,[20] and there are various precautions. When the jury first retire, it is on the basis that they are to reach a unanimous verdict. After two hours (or the further time allowed) they will be told that they should still try to be unanimous, but that a majority verdict will be accepted. The procedure may have to be modified according to the circumstances, if there is more than one count in the indictment.

The two hours include time spent back in court, when the jury were receiving further guidance.[1] To avoid difficulties arising from "travelling time" between the court and the jury-room, an ample margin (say 10 minutes) over two hours should be allowed.[2] In any event the judge is entitled to discharge the jury from giving a verdict, if they are disagreed, and need not accept a majority verdict.[3]

Section 17 applies to any verdict of a jury on any issue.

In very clear cases the jury will return a verdict without leaving the jury box, but normally they will retire to a room provided for the purpose. They are put in charge of officers of the court called jury bailiffs who must take an oath not, without leave of the court, to allow any person to speak to the jury or to speak to them themselves without such leave, except only to ask them if they are agreed on their verdict. Once they have retired to consider their verdict the jury can separate only with leave of the court, which in turn can be given only in case of "evident necessity",[4] such as a juror being taken ill in the course of the jury's deliberations. They do not have to stay in the same jury room until they have reached a conclusion, but they must not separate, subject to the very limited exception noted above, and it is desirable if not

---

[16] Majority verdicts are not considered desirable in retrials: cf. *R.* v. *Mansfield*, [1978] 1 All E.R. 134; [1977] 1 W.L.R. 1102.

[17] Juries Act 1974, s. 17(4).

[18] *Ibid.*, s. 17(3). The requirement of this sub-section is mandatory so that if, for whatever reason, the foreman does not so state the conviction will inevitably be quashed: *R.* v. *Barry*, [1975] 2 All E.R. 760; [1975] 1 W.L.R. 1190.

[19] *Supra.*

[20] Verdicts by a bare majority have been permissible in Scotland for many years. The number of jurors is fifteen.

[1] *R.* v. *Adams*, [1968] 3 All E.R. 437; [1969] 1 W.L.R. 106.

[2] *R.* v. *Bateson*, [1969] 3 All E.R. 1372; *Practice Note*, [1970] 2 All E.R. 215; [1970] 1 W.L.R. 916.

[3] *R.* v. *Elia*, [1968] 2 All E.R. 587.

[4] *R.* v. *Neal*, [1949] 2 K.B. 590; [1949] 2 All E.R. 438. Breach of this rule will almost invariably amount to a material irregularity resulting in a subsequent conviction being quashed: *R.* v. *Goodson*, [1975] 1 All E.R. 760; [1975] 1 W.L.R. 549 (where a juror, after retirement, was permitted by the jury bailiff to leave the jury room, following which he was seen making a telephone call); but compare *R.* v. *Alexander*, [1974] 1 All E.R. 539; [1974] 1 W.L.R. 422 in which the irregularity was a trifling one (juror returned to court simply to collect one or more of the exhibits and was observed throughout) and was held to be of insufficient gravity to justify quashing the conviction.

essential for them always to be in the custody of one of the court bailiffs while, for example, staying at a hotel overnight. The jury may, of course, ask for further guidance from the judge upon any point of law or evidence arising in the case, but both the request for information and the answer to it must be given in open court; if the jury have asked for guidance in the form of a note sent to the judge, this note should be read out *verbatim* and then the answer given.[5]

Breach of this rule (however worthy the motives for the breach, as, for example, to save a child embarrassment) will almost certainly lead to the quashing of the conviction. Thus in *R. v. Davis*[6] a jury retired and after some deliberation sent a request for certain guidance to the presiding judge. He did not return to court, neither did he inform either counsel of the contents of the request, but merely sent an answer back through the medium of the clerk of the peace. This was then repeated. The Court of Criminal Appeal held that this was wholly irregular.

> "It is at the very basis of the whole of the administration of justice in this country that everything in the course of doing justice shall be done in open court, so that everybody concerned may know precisely what has taken place and what has led either to the conviction or the acquittal. . . ."[7]

The matter was made worse by the fact that certain parts of the clerk's statements to the jury amounted to the introduction of fresh evidence, and, as has already been noted, no fresh evidence whatever can be introduced after the jury have retired.[8]

On appeal, the court will not permit any enquiry into what happened in the jury room, or how the jury reached their verdict.[9]

When the jury have concluded their deliberations they will return to court and one of their number, whom they have appointed foreman, will stand up and, subject to the possibility of a majority verdict, in answer to questions put by the appropriate officer of the court, deliver the verdict of the jury.[10] It has already been noted that there may be a verdict that the defendant is not guilty of the crime charged but guilty of some other, alternative, offence.[11] Theoretically it is still possible for a jury to return a "special verdict", which is in form a statement of the facts as found, leaving it to the court to decide of what offences, if any, the defendant is guilty upon those facts. However, special verdicts are now rare if not obsolete, and the Court of Criminal Appeal has said that they ought only to be found in the most exceptional

---

[5] *R. v. Green*, [1950] 1 All E.R. 38.

[6] (1960), 44 Cr. App. Rep. 235.

[7] *R. v. Davis (supra)*, at p. 240, *per* HILBERY, J. See also *R. v. Townsend*, [1982] 1 All E.R. 509.

[8] The fresh evidence was also inaccurate.

[9] See, among many cases, *R. v. Thompson*, [1962] 1 All E.R. 65. Cf. Contempt of Court Act 1981, s. 8(1) whereby it is a contempt of court "to obtain, disclose or solicit any particulars of statements made, opinions expressed, arguments advanced or votes cast by members of a jury in the course of their deliberations in any legal proceedings".

[10] Once a verdict is given in the presence and hearing of all the jury, their assent to it is conclusively presumed: *R. v. Roads*, [1967] 2 Q.B. 108; [1967] 2 All E.R. 84.

[11] See p. 502, *ante*. Or the defendant may be found not guilty in relation to certain items or articles named in the indictment but guilty in relation to others: *Machent* v. *Quinn*, [1970] 2 All E.R. 255.

circumstances.[12] Reference may, however, be made to the "special verdict" of "not guilty by reason of insanity" which may be returned under section 1 of the Criminal Procedure (Insanity) Act 1964. This is described as a "special verdict" but is, of course, of a completely different character from the special verdict discussed above. It is, in fact, a special form of acquittal.

No verdict is complete until the jury have dealt with all verdicts which may possibly be returned on the indictment, and if a defendant is discharged by the judge before the jury have completed their verdict, that is to say before giving a verdict not only in relation to the crime charged but also as to all alternatives which are relevant in the particular case, that discharge is a complete nullity.[13]

This is important, since as has been seen[14] s. 6(3) of the Criminal Law Act 1967 now enables a jury to find the defendant not guilty of the offence charged in the indictment, but guilty of another expressly or impliedly alleged. The judge is not bound to record the first verdict which the jury return but may ask them to reconsider it.[15] He may also do this if the verdict is ambiguous, or is one which cannot properly be returned on the indictment. However, subject to these exceptional cases, the judge is bound to accept the jury's verdict whether he agrees with it or not.[16] He is not, on the other hand, bound to take a verdict even though the jury has agreed upon it but can simply discharge the jury.[16]

The provisions as to majority verdicts have already been discussed. If the majority verdict is guilty the foreman must state in open court the number of jurors who respectively agreed to and dissented from the verdict.[17] In *R. v. Pigg*[18] the House of Lords held that the words "ten agreed" (in answer to the question how many agreed and how many dissented) was sufficient compliance with the statute. If after such discussion as is practicable in the circumstances the jury still cannot reach the necessary measure of agreement the judge has no option but to discharge them. The defendant will then be remanded in custody or on bail to be tried afresh. Theoretically this could happen several times, but if successive juries disagree the practice is for the prosecution to offer no evidence at a third trial. On a retrial, the fact that there has been a previous trial is usually irrelevant and inadmissible, but it may become necessary to refer to it, for example for the purpose of proving that the defendant or a witness made some particular statement or admission. Thus in *R. v. McGregor*[19] the defendant was charged with receiving. At an earlier, abortive, trial he had admitted possession. A police officer was allowed to give evidence of this admission.

Other circumstances in which the jury may be discharged are: (1) illness. If during the course of a criminal trial a juror falls ill he may be discharged by

---

12 *R. v. Bourne* (1952), 36 Cr. App. Rep. 125. A special verdict was found in the celebrated case of *R. v. Dudley and Stephens* (1884), 14 Q.B.D. 273; for what was incorrectly called a "special verdict" see *R. v. Parker*, [1969] 2 All E.R. 15; [1969] 2 Q.B. 248.
13 *R. v. Carter; R. v. Canavan*, [1964] 2 Q.B. 1; [1964] 1 All E.R. 187.
14 See p. 502, *ante.*
15 See, for example, *R. v. Philpott* (1912), 7 Cr. App. Rep. 140.
16 See *R. v. Robinson*, [1975] Q.B. 508; [1975] 1 All E.R. 360 in which the authorities are reviewed.
17 Juries Act 1974, s. 17(3).
18 [1983] 1 All E.R. 56; [1983] 1 W.L.R. 6.
19 [1968] 1 Q.B. 371; [1967] 2 All E.R. 267.

the judge from further service, and depending on the facts, normally will be so discharged. The judge may then discharge the whole jury, but does not have to do so; neither is discharge of the single juror fatal to the continuance of the trial, since statute now provides[20] that when, in the course of a trial, any member of the jury dies or is discharged the trial may nevertheless continue provided that the number of jurors does not fall below nine. If, however, the charge is murder or any offence punishable by death the prosecution and every accused must consent in writing to the trial continuing, even if only one juror is discharged or dies;[20] (2) misconduct of a juror, such as holding improper conversations with a member of the public about the case or absenting himself from his colleagues at the time when the jury were in the course of retiring to consider their verdict; and (3) improper revelation to the jury of the defendant's past criminal record. In such a case the jury is frequently discharged in the defendant's own interest, although every case depends on its own facts. It is material to consider which side brought out the record and what the degree of prejudice could have been.[1]

3 Passing sentence

If the defendant has been found guilty on any part of the indictment the court will then proceed to sentence. There is first such an enquiry into the defendant's antecedents as normally follows a plea of guilty, as has already been described.[2] The defendant is then customarily given an opportunity of making such observations as he wishes, in addition to his counsel's speech in mitigation. It should always be made clear whether separate sentences are intended to be consecutive or concurrent.[3] In the course of this part of the trial it not infrequently happens that the defendant asks for other offences to be taken into consideration. This practice is based on convention and has no statutory foundation; yet at the same time it is extremely convenient both from the point of view of the police and of the defendant. If there are other offences which the defendant has committed but which are still untried (or unknown), then the defendant may admit them to the court of trial and ask the judge to take them into consideration when sentencing him for the offence of which he has just been convicted. In practice he will probably tell the police well before the hearing that he wishes certain offences to be taken into consideration or the police may suggest the matter to him and he will then be supplied with an appropriate form of admission; however there seems to be nothing to prevent a court taking an offence into consideration even if the defendant does not either admit it or ask for it to be taken into consideration until the actual trial. However:

---

[20] Juries Act 1974, s. 16. The judge may discharge a juror "whether as being through illness incapable of continuing to act or for any other reason" (s. 16(1)). This is a matter left to the discretion of the trial judge, although the Court of Appeal will interfere if injustice has resulted. In *R.* v. *Hambery*, [1977] Q.B. 924; [1977] 3 All E.R. 561 the trial judge discharged a lady juror in order to permit her to go away on holiday, a course which the Court of Appeal saw no reason to criticise.

[1] *R.* v. *Weaver and Weaver*, [1968] 1 Q.B. 353; [1967] 1 All E.R. 277; see also *R.* v. *Palin*, [1969] 3 All E.R. 689; [1969] 1 W.L.R. 1544.

[2] See pp. 500–501, *ante*.

[3] *Practice Direction*, [1962] 1 All E.R. 417; [1962] 1 W.L.R 191; for difficulties which arose when this was not made clear, see the litigation in the name of *Re Hastings*, for example, that reported at [1958] 1 All E.R. 707; [1958] 1 W.L.R. 372.

"If justice is to be done it is essential that the practice should not be followed except with the express and unequivocal assent of the offender himself. Accordingly, he should be informed explicitly of each offence which the judge proposes to take into consideration; and should explicitly admit that he committed them and should state his desire that they should be taken into consideration in determining the sentence to be passed on him."[4]

Once the defendant has served his sentence he will not, by long established custom, be prosecuted in respect of any of the offences which have been taken into consideration, although if he were prosecuted the defence of *autrefois convict* would not be open to him, there having been no trial, let alone conviction, in respect of those offences.[5] If, however, his conviction were quashed, a prosecution might be brought.

The mere fact that the defendant asks for the offence to be taken into consideration does not, of course, compel the court to do so. Certain limitations have been laid down in the cases. Broadly, the offence to be taken into consideration should be of the same character as the offence of which the defendant has been convicted; if the defendant has already been separately committed for trial in respect of the offence to be taken into consideration the judge should obtain the consent of the prosecution before doing so.[6] Even if the prosecution does consent the judge ought to consider whether the public interest requires a separate enquiry. Neither ought the court to take into consideration: (1) an offence carrying disqualification.[7] The reason is that in very many cases it will be desirable if not obligatory to disqualify the defendant, yet there can only be a disqualification on conviction, and taking other offences into consideration does not amount to a conviction in respect of them; (2) a breach of probation. This should be separately considered and a separate sentence passed in respect of it, for otherwise the original offence in respect of which the defendant was put on probation will not rank as a conviction in the future and the defendant will appear to have a better record than is in fact the case.

A sentence takes effect from the beginning of the day on which it is imposed, unless the court otherwise directs. Any sentence imposed, or other order made, by the Crown Court may be varied or rescinded by the Crown Court within the period of 28 days from the date of such sentence or order.[8]

4   Deferment of sentence

As an alternative to passing sentence immediately upon an offender, the judge has power to defer sentence "for the purpose of enabling the court or any other court to which it falls to deal with him to have regard, in dealing with him to his conduct after conviction (including, where appropriate, the making by him of reparation for his offence) or to any change in his circum-

---

4   *R*. v. *Anderson*, [1978] A.C. 964, at p. 977; [1978] 2 All E.R. 512, at pp. 515–516, *per* LORD DIPLOCK.
5   *R*. v. *Nicholson*, [1947] 2 All E.R. 535.
6   *R*. v. *McLean*, [1911] 1 K.B. 332.
7   *R* v. *Williams*, [1962] 3 All E.R. 639; [1962] 1 W.L.R. 1268.
8   Supreme Court Act 1981, s. 47(2); cf. *R*. v. *Menocal*, [1980] A.C. 598; [1979] 2 All E.R. 510.

stances".[9] The deferment can only be made if the offender consents and the court is satisfied, having regard to the nature of the offence and the character and circumstances of the offender, that it would be in the interests of justice so to do.[10]

The power to defer sentence is intended for cases such as those in which a persistent offender has at last shown an inclination to settle down and work or those in which persons have, under domestic or financial pressure, stolen from their employers sums which they say they propose to repay. Accordingly it will not be appropriate to defer sentence where the offence is so minor that it would not merit a sentence of imprisonment in any event, nor, at the other end of the scale, where the offence is so serious that it must inevitably result in a substantial custodial sentence since, as a matter of principle, a substantial custodial sentence is not appropriate in a case where, when the offender returns to the court to be dealt with following deferment, the information before the court relating to his conduct during the period of deferment is not unfavourable to him.[11]

The period of deferment may be anything up to six months and there must not be a further deferment on the specified date.[12] Furthermore, where sentence is deferred, all aspects of the sentence should be deferred; the sentence must not be "split" by, for example, imposing an immediate disqualification from driving, but deferring the remainder of the sentence.[13]

F SENTENCES AND ORDERS

1 Death

The death penalty was abolished for nearly all murders in 1957,[14] and finally abolished in 1965,[15] for the other murders. The provisions of the 1965 Act were expressed to be temporary and experimental, but Parliament in 1969 decided that abolition was to be permanent. Death continues to be the penalty for treason and piracy with violence.[16]

---

9 Powers of Criminal Courts Act 1973, s. 1 (as amended). Although this specific procedure was introduced by the Criminal Justice Act 1972 there has always been power at common law to postpone passing the whole, or any part of a sentence and there is statutory power to adjourn after conviction for social enquiry report upon the convicted person (Act of 1973, s. 45). These powers are expressly preserved by section 1(7) of the 1973 Act; cf. *R.* v. *Annesley*, [1976] 1 All E.R. 589; [1976] 1 W.L.R. 106.

10 *Ibid.*, s. 1(3); cf. *R.* v. *McQuaide*, [1975] Crim. L.R. 246.

11 *R.* v. *Gilby*, [1975] 2 All E.R. 743; [1975] 1 W.L.R. 924; see, generally, *R.* v. *George*, [1984] 3 All E.R. 13; [1984] 1 W.L.R. 1082.

12 Act of 1973, s. 1(2).

13 *R.* v. *Fairhead*, [1975] 2 All E.R. 737; but cf. *R.* v. *Annesley* (*supra*). However, a restitution order may be made under the Theft Act 1968, even if the passing of sentence is in other respects deferred: Theft Act 1968, s. 28(1) (as amended by Criminal Law Act 1977, Sch. 12).

14 Homicide Act 1957, ss. 5–9.

15 Murder (Abolition of Death Penalty) Act 1965.

16 The death penalty for arson of Her Majesty's ships and dockyards was abolished by s. 11(2) of the Criminal Damage Act 1971.

2   Imprisonment and fine

Life imprisonment is the fixed penalty for murder[17] and the maximum penalty for manslaughter[18] and a large number of other offences. It is of course rarely imposed.

In the case of a life sentence for murder, the court may declare the minimum period which in its view should elapse before the defendant is released on licence.[19] Such a recommendation is not binding on the Home Secretary who must however consult the trial judge if available and the Lord Chief Justice before permitting release on licence. It was formerly doubted whether a judge had power to recommend that a prisoner convicted of murder should never be released, but such an order was made in *R.* v. *Skingle and Sparrow*.[20]

Imprisonment for a specified period of years or months is also the maximum penalty for a great number of offences in English law; very often statute prescribes a fine as an additional or alternative penalty, but in any event any court may now fine for any offence except where the penalty is fixed by law.[1] Where the defendant is convicted of several offences in respect of which terms of imprisonment are imposed, those terms may be ordered to be consecutive or concurrent; similarly a term may be ordered to run consecutively or concurrently to a term which the defendant is already serving.[2]

A sentence of imprisonment may be imposed but suspended, i.e. ordered not to take effect immediately.[3] The sentence must not be for more than two years and the period of suspension must be between one and two years.[4] The effect of a suspended sentence is that so far as that sentence is concerned, the defendant is not liable to be imprisoned unless (i) during the period of suspension he commits another offence punishable with imprisonment, and thereafter (ii) a court orders that the sentence shall take effect.[5] When suspended sentences were first introduced there was a tendency for courts to impose a suspended sentence upon persons who, but for the existence of the power to impose suspended sentences, would not have received a sentence of imprisonment at all. The effect was to increase the prison population signifi-

---

[17] Murder (Abolition of Death Penalty) Act 1965, s. 1(1). For the position as to appeal, see p. 529, *post*.

[18] Offences against the Person Act 1861, s. 5.

[19] The power is limited to murder cases and does not apply to life sentences for other offences: *R.* v. *Flemming*, [1973] 2 All E.R. 401; as to an appeal, see p. 529, *post*.

[20] (1971), *The Times*, 16th October (reported, but not on this point, *sub nom. R.* v. *Sparrow*, [1973] 2 All E.R. 129; [1973] 1 W.L.R. 488).

[1] Powers of Criminal Courts Act 1973, s. 30. Where the offender is a child or young person, the court should normally order the fine to be paid by his parent or guardian (Children and Young Persons Act 1933, s. 55). The Crown Court must fix a period of imprisonment (or detention if the offender is under 21) in default (1973 Act, s. 31(2)). The period varies according to the amount of the fine and there is a Table for this purpose contained in s. 69 of the Criminal Justice Act 1982, the maximum period being 12 months.

[2] A term of imprisonment cannot be consecutive to a sentence of life imprisonment: *R.* v. *Foy*, [1962] 2 All E.R. 246; [1962] 1 W.L.R. 609.

[3] Powers of Criminal Courts Act 1973, ss. 22–25. Where the court passes a suspended sentence for a term of more than six months, it has power under section 26 to make a "suspended sentence supervision order" which places the offender under the supervision of a probation officer during the period of the suspended sentence. There is no power to make such an order when only a part of the sentence is suspended under the Criminal Law Act 1977, s. 47 (*infra*).

[4] Powers of Criminal Courts Act 1973, s. 22(1).

[5] *Ibid.*, s. 23.

cantly since, when the offender committed another offence, he would usually be imprisoned. Accordingly it is now expressly provided[6] that a court shall not impose a suspended sentence unless the case appears to be one in which a sentence of imprisonment would have been appropriate in the absence of any power to suspend such a sentence. Further, where a court passes a sentence of imprisonment of not less than three months and not more than two years, it may suspend part of the sentence, the defendant thereby serving part of the sentence immediately, the remainder being held in suspense; the part to be served in prison must be at least 28 days and the part to be held in suspense must be not less than one quarter of the whole term.[7] The court which deals with a suspended sentence after re-conviction is not bound to order it to take effect, if it thinks that it would be unjust to do so in view of all the circumstances. These include the facts of the subsequent offence.

No person under 21 years of age may be sentenced to imprisonment by any court.[8] If an offender under that age requires custodial treatment it must be detention or youth custody. Further, no person who has not previously been sentenced to imprisonment should be so sentenced unless the court is of opinion, having obtained and considered information about the circumstances and after taking into account any information relevant to his character and his physical and mental condition, that no other method of dealing with him is appropriate and unless the court considers it unnecessary, a social inquiry report should be obtained for this purpose.[9] Finally, an unrepresented defendant who has not previously been sentenced to imprisonment cannot be sentenced to a term of imprisonment (unless he was refused legal aid on the ground that his means were such that he did not require assistance or, having been informed of his right to apply for legal aid, he did not do so).[10] The effect of this provision is that a court which is minded to imprison an unrepresented defendant has to adjourn the hearing and inform the defendant of his right to apply for legal aid.

3 Youth custody, detention centre and attendance centre orders

The Criminal Justice Act 1982 abolished Borstal training. Apart from the powers of detention for grave offences under the Children and Young

---

[6] *Ibid.*, s. 22(2).

[7] Criminal Law Act 1977, s. 47 (as amended). These periods may be varied by Order of the Secretary of State (s. 47(9)); guidelines as to circumstances in which partially suspended sentences are appropriate were laid down by the Court of Appeal in *R. v. Clarke*, [1982] 3 All E.R. 232; [1982] 1 W.L.R. 1090.

[8] Criminal Justice Act 1982, s. 1. However, if convicted of an offence punishable with more than 14 years' imprisonment and the court is of the opinion that no other method of dealing with him is appropriate, he may be ordered to be detained for such period not exceeding the maximum term of imprisonment which the offence carries in such place as the Secretary of State may direct: Children and Young Persons Act 1933, s. 53(2) (as amended); by section 53(1) a person convicted of murder or any offence punishable by death who was under the age of 18 at the time the offence was committed must be ordered to be so detained during Her Majesty's pleasure.

[9] Powers of Criminal Courts Act 1973, ss. 20, 20A (as amended).

[10] *Ibid.*, s. 21(1) (as amended).

Persons Act 1933[11] the custodial sentences which may be imposed on offenders under 21 are as follows.[12]

a Custody for life—By section 8(1) of the 1982 Act custody for life is the appropriate sentence for a person under the age of 21 who is convicted of an offence for which the sentence is fixed by law as imprisonment for life (unless he is liable to be detained under section 53(1) of the Children and Young Persons Act 1933). Under section 8(2) the sentence may be imposed upon a person who is at least 17 but under 21 and who would, if over 21, be liable to imprisonment for life.

b Youth custody—A person who is at least 15 but under 21 and convicted of an offence punishable with imprisonment in the case of a person aged over 21 may be sentenced to youth custody. The total period of custody (there may be consecutive sentences as in the case of imprisonment) must exceed 4 months in the case of a male offender or be at least 21 days if the offender is female.[13] The sentence may only be imposed if the court considers, for reasons which must be stated in open court, that the only appropriate method of dealing with the offender is to pass a custodial sentence.[14] If the offender is under 17 the maximum sentence is 12 months.[15]

c Detention centre order—This form of order may be imposed on a male offender who is at least 14 but under 21 and convicted of an offence punishable with imprisonment in the case of a person aged over 21. The order may not be for less than 21 days nor for more than 4 months.[16]

The restrictions on imposing sentences of youth custody apply, *mutatis mutandis*, to detention centre orders.[17]

Section 15 of the Act contains provisions whereby a person under 22 who is released from a term of detention under a detention centre order or a term of youth custody is under the supervision of a probation officer or local authority social worker for not less than 3 months (or until he attains the age of 22).

A major criticism of these provisions is the absence of any provision for a suspended sentence or order and it is to be anticipated that such provision will be introduced in the not too distant future.

d Attendance centre order—Prior to the 1982 Act the power to make these

---

[11] See p. 521, fn. 8, *ante*.

[12] The restrictions on imprisoning unrepresented defendants imposed by s. 21 of the 1973 Act (*supra*) apply *mutatis mutandis* to the making of detention centre orders, sentences of youth custody or custody for life and orders under s. 53(2) of the Children and Young Persons Act 1933 (Criminal Justice Act 1982, s. 3(1)).

[13] Criminal Justice Act 1982, s. 7. The Act contains detailed provisions relating to the accommodation of young offenders (ss. 11, 12), computation of sentences (s. 10) and conversion of youth custody to imprisonment (s. 13).

[14] *Ibid.*, s. 6(1)(*b*); by s. 1(4) this must be because the accused is unable or unwilling to respond to non-custodial penalties, or because a custodial sentence is necessary for the protection of the public, or because the offence was so serious that a non-custodial sentence cannot be justified; a social inquiry report should usually be obtained (s. 2).

[15] *Ibid.*, s. 7(8).

[16] *Ibid.*, s. 4. Consequently, if this period is regarded as inadequate it will be necessary to impose a sentence of youth custody.

[17] *Viz.* (1) the court must consider that the only appropriate method of dealing with the offender is to pass a custodial sentence (s. 4(1)(*b*)); (2) this must be because he is unable or unwilling to respond to non-custodial penalties, or because a custodial sentence is necessary for the protection of the public, or because the offence was so serious that a non-custodial sentence cannot be justified (s. 1(4)); (3) a social inquiry report should usually be obtained (s. 2).

orders was confined to magistrates' courts. It now extends to the Crown Court and an order may be made requiring an offender who is under 21 and has not previously been the subject of a custodial sentence or order to attend an attendance centre for a total period of not less than 12 (unless the offender is under 14) or more than 24 (if he is under 17) or 36 (if he is at least 17) hours.[18] The Home Office regards the aims of the attendance centre as being (*a*) to vindicate the law by imposing loss of leisure, a punishment that is generally understood by children; (*b*) to bring the offender for a period under the influence of representatives of authority of the state; and (*c*) to teach him something of the constructive use of leisure. In practice, courts often use this power when dealing with football hooligans, specifying attendance on Saturday afternoons.

4 Probation

Except where the sentence is fixed by law, a court may make a probation order in respect of an offender aged 17 or over where it thinks it right to do so provided that the offender himself is willing to be bound by the order.[19] This will require the offender to be under the supervision of a probation officer for between six months and three years, and conditions, e.g. as to residence, may also be imposed.[20] Additionally, there is power to include in the order a requirement that the offender shall attend a "day training centre" (if there is a place for him).[1] However, these centres are intended for offenders of a particular type, for example the "socially inadequate pest" so that a requirement of attendance should not be imposed in ordinary cases.[2] The object of the order is to re-establish the offender in the community with the assistance of a probation officer. Probation being instead of punishment, a fine cannot be imposed, along with probation, for the same offence.[3] An offender who fails to comply with the terms of his probation, whether by committing another offence or otherwise, is liable to be sentenced for the original offence.

5 Absolute and conditional discharge

Where a court thinks it inappropriate to pass any sentence, or make a probation order, it may discharge the offender either absolutely, without any condition, or subject to the condition that he does not commit any further

---

[18] Criminal Justice Act 1982, s. 17.
[19] Powers of Criminal Courts Act 1973, s. 2; *R.* v. *Marquis*, [1974] 2 All E.R. 1216; [1974] 1 W.L.R. 1087.
[20] Where the court is satisfied on the evidence of a medical practitioner approved for the purposes of the Mental Health Act 1983 that the medical condition of the offender is such that he requires and may be susceptible to treatment, the order may include a requirement to submit to treatment, either as a resident patient in a hospital or mental nursing home or as a non-resident patient at a specified institution or place (Act of 1973, s. 3). Subject to this, however, probation orders should not contain conditions which impose a custodial element amounting in substance to the imposition of a sentence: *Cullen* v. *Rogers*, [1982] 2 All E.R. 570; *sub nom. Rogers* v. *Cullen*, [1982] 1 W.L.R. 729.
[1] Powers of Criminal Courts Act 1973, s. 4.
[2] *R.* v. *Cardwell* (1974), 58 Cr. App. Rep. 241.
[3] *R.* v. *Parry*, [1951] 2 K.B. 590; [1950] 2 All E.R. 1179.

offence for a period fixed by the court, not exceeding three years.[4] If he commits another offence in that period he is liable to be sentenced for his original offence.

If, following conviction, the offender is put on probation or discharged, absolutely or conditionally, that order is not a sentence against which the offender can appeal.[5]

6   Community service orders

With the aim of reducing the prison population the Criminal Justice Act 1972 introduced community service orders, whereby convicted persons of or over seventeen years of age are required to perform unpaid work in the interests of the community.[6] The scheme is an experimental one and orders may only be made in respect of an offender who lives in an area where community service arrangements exist.

The relevant provisions are now set out in sections 14 to 17 of the Powers of Criminal Courts Act 1973. The aggregate of the hours to be worked (not less than 40, not more than 240) must be specified in the order and, as with probation orders, the consent of the offender to the order is required.[7] An offender who does not comply with the order is liable, as in the case of non-compliance with probation orders, to be fined up to £50 and sentenced anew for the offence in respect of which the order was made.

7   Compensation, restitution and criminal bankruptcy

Compensation—A court by or before which a person is convicted of an offence may, instead of or in addition to dealing with him in any other way, make an order requiring him to pay compensation for any personal injury, loss or damage resulting from that offence (or any other offence which is taken into consideration). However, no compensation order may be made in favour of the dependants of a deceased person in consequence of his death, nor in respect of injury, loss or damage due to a road accident.[8]

In determining whether to make an order and the amount of such order the court must have regard to the offender's means. In practice the power to make compensation orders has been exercised somewhat sparingly. In particular, the Court of Appeal has repeatedly stated that no order should be

---

4   Powers of Criminal Courts Act 1973, s. 7.
5   *R*. v. *Tucker*, [1974] 2 All E.R. 639; [1974] 1 W.L.R. 615. The reason is that there is deemed to have been no conviction (Act of 1973, s. 13(1)) although the offender can appeal against the conviction in respect of which the order was made (*ibid.*, s. 13(4)); see Samuels, *Probation Neither a Conviction Nor a Sentence*, 125 New Law Journal, p. 912. However, if the proper procedure is not followed, for example, because the effects of the order are not explained to the defendant, the order may be a nullity, in which case the Court of Appeal will have jurisdiction to entertain an appeal, at least to the extent of declaring the order a nullity: *R*. v. *Wehner*, [1977] 3 All E.R. 553; [1977] 1 W.L.R. 1143.
6   See, generally, Griffiths, *Community Service by Offenders*, 126 New Law Journal, p. 169.
7   As to the power of magistrates to commit to the Crown Court offenders who do not comply with such orders, see p. 467, *ante*.
8   Powers of Criminal Courts Act 1973, s. 35(1) (as amended), (2); except, where the vehicle was the subject of an offence under the Theft Act 1968, in respect of damage to *that* vehicle: *Quigley* v. *Stokes*, [1977] 2 All E.R. 317; [1977] 1 W.L.R. 434.

made where it might result in the accused committing further offences in order to discharge his obligations; for this reason a substantial compensation order will not usually be appropriate where the offender is imprisoned since the need to discharge the order may hinder his rehabilitation on his release.[9]

If there are subsequent civil proceedings, the damages are assessed without reference to the order, but the order is taken into account when enforcing the judgment.[10] Compensation is of such amount as the court considers appropriate, having regard to any evidence and to any representations made by or on behalf of the accused or the prosecutor.[11]

Restitution—Where goods have been stolen and either a person is convicted of any offence with reference to the theft or such offence is taken into consideration on conviction of any other offence, the court may order anyone in possession of the goods to restore them to any person entitled to recover them from him, or may order the restoration of any goods directly or indirectly representing the stolen goods (e.g. the proceeds of sale), or may order a sum not exceeding the value of the goods to be paid out of any money of the person convicted which was taken out of his possession on his apprehension.[12] However, it should be borne in mind that this provision does not give the police power to seize money or other property when apprehending someone, in anticipation of a compensation or restitution order being made in due course.[13] The police may, however, justifiably take possession of money or other property which they reasonably believe to be material evidence in relation to crime.[14]

A restitution order, under the above provisions, should only be made in clear and obvious cases. If there is any serious dispute concerning the ownership of the goods in question, this should be left to be determined by a civil court in the normal way and no order should be made.[15]

Criminal bankruptcy—Where a person is convicted before the Crown Court and it appears that loss or damage has been suffered as a result of that offence (or that offence taken together with any other relevant offence) amounting to a sum in excess of £15,000, the court may, in addition to dealing with the offender in any other way (but not if it makes a compensation order against him), make a criminal bankruptcy order.[16] The making of the order is deemed to be an act of bankruptcy with the result that the Director of Public Prosecutions (acting as the Official Petitioner) may institute bankruptcy proceedings.[17]

---

[9] See *R.* v. *Oddy*, [1974] 2 All E.R. 666 and cases cited therein.

[10] For the detail of this, see s. 38 of the 1973 Act. Where the offender is a child or young person, the court should normally order payment by his parent or guardian (Children and Young Persons Act 1969, s. 3(6)).

[11] Act of 1973, s. 35(1A) (added by Criminal Justice Act 1982).

[12] Theft Act 1968, s. 28 (as amended by Criminal Justice Act 1972).

[13] *Malone* v. *Commissioner of Police of the Metropolis (No. 2)*, [1980] Q.B. 49; [1979] 1 All E.R. 256; cf. *Chief Constable of Kent* v. *V.*, [1983] Q.B. 34; [1982] 3 All E.R. 36; see p. 52, *ante*.

[14] *Ghani* v. *Jones*, [1970] 1 Q.B. 693; [1969] 3 All E.R. 1700.

[15] *R.* v. *Ferguson*, [1970] 2 All E.R. 820.

[16] Powers of Criminal Courts Act 1973, s. 39(1); "relevant offence" means any other offence of which the defendant is convicted in the same proceedings or which the court takes into consideration (as to which see p. 517, *ante*) (s. 39(2)).

[17] The procedure is set out in Schedule 2 of the 1973 Act.

8   Miscellaneous orders

The principal sentences and orders the court has power to make have been considered above. There are, in addition, various other forms of order which may be made, detailed consideration of which is beyond the scope of his work. However, it may be noted that the Crown Court has, in addition to the powers detailed above, power to make orders for costs either out of central funds or *inter partes*,[18] orders depriving offenders of property used, or intended for use, for the purposes of crime,[19] orders disqualifying an offender from holding or obtaining a licence to drive a motor vehicle,[20] orders authorising the admission to and detention in specified hospitals of offenders suffering from mental illness, psychopathic disorder, subnormality or severe subnormality[1] and recommendations for deportation of non-"patrials".[2]

Where the Crown Court imposes a fine, forfeits a recognisance or makes an order for costs, it may order the person concerned to be searched and any money found on him to be applied towards payment of the fine or other sum.[3]

---

[18] Costs in Criminal Cases Act 1973, ss. 3, 4.

[19] Powers of Criminal Courts Act 1973, s. 43. The power is limited to personal property and so cannot extend to the defendant's house: *R. v. Khan*, [1982] 3 All E.R. 969; [1982] 1 W.L.R. 1405, one of several unsuccessful attempts by the courts to relieve drugs dealers of their ill-gotten gains; see also *R. v. Cuthbertson*, [1981] A.C. 470; [1980] 2 All E.R. 401.

[20] Road Traffic Act 1972, s. 93; Transport Act 1981, s. 19; Powers of Criminal Courts Act 1973, s. 44.

[1] Mental Health Act 1983, s. 37.

[2] Immigration Act 1971, s. 6.

[3] Powers of Criminal Courts Act 1973, s. 34A. This section was added by the Criminal Law Act 1977, s. 49; curiously the Crown Court did not previously have this power, although magistrates' courts did.

CHAPTER 25

Appeal Following Trial on Indictment

A RIGHTS OF APPEAL

It is now necessary to consider the rights of appeal available to a person convicted on indictment and, exceptionally, to the prosecution following acquittal. It must be borne in mind, as a fundamental principle, that it is the mode of trial which determines the rights of appeal, not the nature of the offence. Thus if the defendant is convicted at the Crown Court his appeal lies, if at all, to the criminal division of the Court of Appeal. It does not matter whether he was convicted of an indictable or "either way" offence. Equally, appeal following summary conviction lies to those courts having jurisdiction over summary appeals—the Crown Court and the divisional court of the Queen's Bench Division—irrespective of the fact that the defendant was convicted of an "either way" offence.

The whole law as to appeals following conviction on indictment is now to be found in the Criminal Appeal Act 1968, which consolidated the Criminal Appeal Acts of 1907, 1964 and 1966. There is no right of appeal except such as is conferred by the Act. Recent cases have demonstrated deficiencies in the system of appeals, consequent upon this rule. Thus there is no appeal against the refusal of an order for costs, nor as to the taxation of costs,[1] nor against an order that solicitors pay costs personally,[2] nor against an order refusing particulars of an indictment,[3] nor against an order that a defendant pay a contribution towards the legal aid costs of his defence.[4] These are serious *lacunae*; in particular they operate to give Crown Court judges an unfettered discretion as to costs following acquittal since if a judge decides to refuse to award an acquitted defendant his costs out of central funds there is nothing whatsoever that he can do about it.[5] However, where the Crown Court

---

[1] *Re Central Funds Costs Order*, [1975] 3 All E.R. 238; [1975] 1 W.L.R. 1227.
[2] *R.* v. *Smith*, [1975] Q.B. 531; [1974] 1 All E.R. 651.
[3] *R.* v. *Collins*, [1970] 1 Q.B. 710; [1969] 3 All E.R. 1562.
[4] *R.* v. *Hayden*, [1975] 2 All E.R. 558; [1975] 1 W.L.R. 852.
[5] Bearing in mind that the Crown Court is not subject to the prerogative orders in matters relating to trial on indictment (*Ex parte Meredith*, [1973] 2 All E.R. 234; [1973] 1 W.L.R. 435).

makes an order which is defective in law (as opposed to one that it is within the discretion of the court to make) it seems that the Court of Appeal will assume jurisdiction to entertain an appeal.[6]

1   Appeal against conviction

By section 1 of the Criminal Appeal Act 1968 a person convicted on indictment may appeal to the Court of Appeal:

(*a*) against his conviction on any ground which involves a question of law alone; and

(*b*) with the leave of the Court of Appeal, against his conviction on any ground which involves a question of fact alone, or a question of mixed law and fact, or any other ground which appears to the court to be a sufficient ground of appeal.

The trial judge may also grant a certificate that the case is fit for appeal, on a question of fact or mixed law and fact; he should not give the certificate merely for the asking, but only if he is satisfied that there is a substantial point and one worthy of consideration by the Court of Appeal.[7] Where leave to appeal is required, it may be granted, in the first instance by a single judge of the court; if he refuses, the applicant may have his case considered by the Court itself.[8]

There is nothing in the Act to prevent an appeal against conviction even though the defendant pleaded guilty at his trial. However an appeal in these circumstances will as a rule only be entertained if either (1) the defendant did not appreciate the nature of the charge, or (2) he did not intend to admit that he was guilty of it, or, (3) on the admitted facts, he could not in point of law have been guilty of the offence to which he pleaded guilty.[9] With the more generous provision of legal aid, cases of the first and second type are increasingly rare.[10]

One such case was *R. v. Ingleson*.[11] The defendant in that case pleaded guilty to receiving and subsequently handed to the judge a written statement which, if believed, was a complete exculpation, and concluded with the words "I am guilty of [receiving] not knowing them to have been stolen." It

---

[6] See *R. v. Wehner*, [1977] 3 All E.R. 553; [1977] 1 W.L.R. 1143; *R. v. Reilly*, [1982] Q.B. 1208; [1982] 3 All E.R. 27; *R. v. Cain*, [1984] 2 All E.R. 737; [1984] 3 W.L.R. 393.

[7] *R. v. Eyles* (1963), 47 Cr. App. Rep. 260; cf. *R. v. Smith*, [1974] Q.B. 354; [1974] 1 All E.R. 632.

[8] Criminal Appeal Act 1968, s. 31. See also p. 539, *post*.

[9] *R. v. Forde*, [1923] 2 K.B. 400, at p. 403; *R. v. Gould*, [1968] 2 Q.B. 65; [1968] 1 All E.R. 849; cf. *R. v. Vickers*, [1975] 1 W.L.R. 811; see p. 507, *ante*.

[10] But see *R. v. Phillips*, [1982] 1 All E.R. 245 where the appellant, who had been (although represented by counsel) in "a hopeless muddle and very confused" was permitted to appeal. In this case the convictions in question were quashed since the prosecution, on pleas of not guilty, would not have proceeded on the counts in question. But for this concession, *semble* the proceedings would have to be treated as a nullity.

[11] [1915] 1 K.B. 512; cf. p. 503, *ante* and, for a further example, *R. v. Clarke*, [1972] 1 All E.R. 219 in which case the appellant had changed her plea to guilty after the trial judge had construed the defence of absence of intention as one of insanity thereby exposing the appellant, if her defence succeeded, to a finding that she was insane. The resulting conviction was quashed.

was held on appeal that the plea of guilty was wrongly received and that the proceedings were a nullity.

Furthermore, even where the defendant was fit to plead, knew what he was doing, intended to make the plea he did and pleaded without equivocation after receiving expert advice, the court may nevertheless entertain and allow the appeal if satisfied that the conviction is unsafe or unsatisfactory.[12]

2 Appeal against sentence

The defendant may appeal against the sentence passed on his conviction, unless the sentence is one fixed by law, but only with the leave of the Court of Appeal.[13] An application for leave may be determined by a single judge of the Court of Appeal but, if he refuses leave, the appellant has a right to have his application determined by the full court.

"Sentence" includes certain sentences passed by the Crown Court on defendants committed to that court for sentence, as well as sentences passed in the normal way on defendants convicted at the Crown Court.[14] There is no appeal against a sentence fixed by law (such as death for treason or life imprisonment for murder) or against a recommendation made by a trial judge that a defendant convicted of murder shall not be released before a certain number of years.[15] There may also be an appeal against an order for disqualification from driving, an order that the accused pay the whole or any part of the costs of the prosecution,[16] a compensation order,[17] a binding-over order,[18] an order revoking a parole licence[19] or against a recommendation for deportation whether or not in any case there is an appeal against the sentence otherwise imposed on the defendant (since a recommendation for deportation cannot be imposed on its own).[20]

The prosecution has no right of appeal against sentence (indeed it is a principle of our system that the prosecution does not address the court upon, or otherwise concern itself with, sentence) but it may be noted that a clause in the Prosecution of Offences Bill currently before Parliament (if not removed during the passage of the Bill would have empowered the Attorney-General to refer to the Court of Appeal sentences imposed by the Crown Court for the "opinion" of the Court of Appeal.

---

[12] *R.* v. *Lee*, [1984] 1 All E.R. 1080; [1984] 1 W.L.R. 578; see p. 531, *post.*

[13] Criminal Appeal Act 1968, s. 9.

[14] *Ibid.*, s. 10. For cases in which persons may be committed to the Crown Court for sentence see pp. 462–469, *ante.* It is not open to the Court of Appeal to review the validity of the committal; if it is sought to attack the validity of a committal for sentence, this must be done by application for prerogative order (*R.* v. *Birtles*, [1975] 3 All E.R. 395; [1975] 1 W.L.R. 1623).

[15] *R.* v. *Aitken*, [1966] 2 All E.R. 453; [1966] 1 W.L.R. 1076.

[16] *R.* v. *Hayden*, [1975] 2 All E.R. 558; [1975] 1 W.L.R. 852.

[17] Powers of Criminal Courts Act 1973, s. 36(3) (*b*).

[18] *R.* v. *Williams*, [1982] 3 All E.R. 1092; [1982] 1 W.L.R. 1398.

[19] *R.* v. *Welch*, [1982] 2 All E.R. 824; [1982] 1 W.L.R. 976.

[20] See Criminal Appeal Act 1968, s. 50(1), defining sentence to include "any order make by a court when dealing with an offender". No appeal lies against a "criminal bankruptcy order" (for which see p. 525, *ante*), but where a conviction is quashed the order will normally be rescinded. Further, despite the statutory prohibition, an appeal will be entertained where the decision of the Crown Court was defective in law: *R.* v. *Cain* (*supra*).

3   Application to the Home Secretary

By section 17(1) (*a*) of the 1968 Act any person convicted on indictment may apply to the Home Secretary and the Home Secretary may, even in the absence of such application, refer the whole case to the Court of Appeal, in which event the case is treated for all purposes as an appeal by the person convicted. It follows that there may be an appeal to the House of Lords. Alternatively the Home Secretary may refer any point arising in the case to the Court of Appeal for consideration and the opinion of the Court on that point.[1] This may, in effect, give the defendant "two bites at the cherry" since the Home Secretary may refer a case even though there has already been an unsuccessful appeal.[2]

4   Appeal against a verdict of "not guilty by reason of insanity" or against findings of fitness and unfitness to plead

Although the verdict of "not guilty by reason of insanity" is, in form, an acquittal, the defendant may appeal against the verdict, in effect, as if it were a conviction. The defendant may appeal, in the same way, against the finding of a jury that he is unfit to plead.[3] It had already been held[4] that the defendant has the right to appeal against a finding, on a preliminary issue, that he is fit to plead.

The powers of the Court of Appeal in dealing with appeals of this nature are dealt with below.[5]

5   Appeal following acquittal

The Criminal Justice Act 1972[6] for the first time gave the prosecution a limited right of appeal on a point of law' following an acquittal on indictment. It is important to note that the procedure is in the nature of a reference rather than an appeal properly so called, so that the outcome of the reference has no effect upon the acquittal in that case.[7] "The Attorney-General may, if he desires the opinion of the Court of Appeal on a point of law which has arisen in the case, refer that point to the court, and the court shall, in accordance with this section, consider the point and give their opinion on it."[6]

The Act and the rules made under it[8] go to great lengths to protect the acquitted person. Not only is his acquittal unaffected, he may appear to present argument in the Court of Appeal, is entitled to be represented by

---

1   Act of 1968, s. 17(1) (*b*).
2   See, for example, *R*. v. *Chard*, [1984] A.C. 279; [1983] 3 All E.R. 637; this case affirms that where the reference is under s. 17(1) (*a*) the appellant is entitled to re-open the whole case and argue grounds unconnected with the reasons for the Home Secretary's reference.
3   Criminal Appeal Act 1968, ss. 12, 15.
4   *R*. v. *Podola*, [1960] 1 Q.B. 325; [1959] 3 All E.R. 418.
5   See p. 538, *post*.
6   Section 36(1); this provision came into operation on October 1, 1973 and the first reference under it was *Re Attorney-General's Reference (No. 1 of 1974)*, [1974] Q.B. 744; [1974] 2 All E.R. 899.
7   Act of 1972, s. 36(7).
8   Criminal Appeal (Reference of Points of Law) Rules 1973.

counsel and have his costs paid out of central funds and his identity must not be disclosed during the proceedings in the Court of Appeal except by his consent.

The power to refer is, in fact, sparingly exercised, although LORD WIDGERY, while he was Lord Chief Justice stated that:[9]

> "It would be a mistake to think, and we hope people will not think, that references by the Attorney-General are confined to cases where very heavy questions of law arise and that they should not be used in other cases. On the contrary, we hope to see this procedure used extensively for short but important points which require a quick ruling of this court before a potentially false decision of law has too wide a circulation in the courts."

The Court of Appeal, following a reference under section 36, may of their own motion or on application, refer the point to the House of Lords if it appears that the point ought to be considered by that House.[10]

B POWERS OF THE COURT OF APPEAL

1 Power to quash conviction

The Court may allow an appeal against conviction if they think that either:

(*a*) *Under all the circumstances of the case the conviction*[11] *is unsafe or unsatisfactory*—This formula was substituted by the Criminal Appeal Act 1966 for the formula contained in the Criminal Appeal Act 1907: "the verdict is unreasonable or cannot be supported having regard to the evidence". Two criticisms were made of the old formula and the courts' interpretation of it. First, the two parts of the formula were always treated as synonymous, in spite of it being the apparent intention of the draftsmen of the 1907 Act by the use of the word "or", that they should mean something different. Secondly, the Court adopted what was widely considered to be a very narrow view of its powers, refusing to interfere except in cases (usually of joint trials) where there was literally no evidence against the defendant yet the jury had convicted. The attitude of the Court has been stated as follows:[12]

> "[The Court] is not here to consider whether the jury was right or wrong . . . [but] to review the proceedings below with the assistance of counsel to see if the proceedings were properly conducted and, if not, to see whether any irregularities which arose in the course of the proceedings were sufficient to render the

---

[9] *Re Attorney-General's Reference (No. 1 of 1975)*, [1975] Q.B. 773, at p. 778; [1975] 2 All E.R. 684, at p. 685.
[10] Criminal Justice Act 1972, s. 36(3).
[11] "Conviction" was substituted for "verdict of the jury" by the Criminal Law Act 1977, s. 44. The previous wording appeared to preclude an appeal if the accused pleaded guilty, unless the count to which the accused pleaded guilty disclosed no offence known to the law or (perhaps) on the admitted facts he could not in point of law have been guilty of the offence; this, presumably erroneous, drafting in the 1968 Act went judicially unnoticed until *Director of Public Prosecutions* v. *Shannon*, [1975] A.C. 717; [1974] 2 All E.R. 1009, in which case LORD SALMON drew attention to the need for some amendment to s. 2(1) of the 1968 Act.
[12] LORD WIDGERY, C.J., giving the judgment of the Court of Appeal in *R.* v. *Anderson*, [1972] 1 Q.B. 304 at p. 309, [1971] 3 All E.R. 1152, at p. 1156; for another point arising from the case see p. 655, *post*.

finding of the jury unsafe or unsatisfactory. . . . If we come to the conclusion that there were such irregularities, then we quash the convictions and since there is no machinery in English law for a re-trial in such circumstances, the matter rests in that somewhat inconclusive state.''

It was suggested in the first edition of this work that, in future, where, in cases of disputed identity, there was only one witness identifying the defendant, the court would say that a verdict of guilty based on such evidence was unsafe or unsatisfactory. This suggestion appeared to be supported by *R.* v. *Cooper*, where it was said that:

"until the passing of the Criminal Appeal Act 1966 . . . it was almost unheard of for this court to interfere in such a case. However, now our powers are somewhat different in cases of this kind the court must in the end ask itself a subjective question, whether we are content to let the matter stand as it is, or whether there is not some lurking doubt in our minds which makes us wonder whether an injustice has been done.''[13]

Nevertheless persons may validly be convicted on the evidence of a single identifying witness. Occasional, but well-publicised, miscarriages of justice have occurred in such circumstances and in 1976 these led the full Court of Appeal to lay down certain guidelines to be followed by trial judges in cases of disputed identification.[14] These include the need to warn the jury of the special need for caution before convicting in reliance on the correctness of the identification, to direct the jury to examine closely the circumstances of the purported identification and to remind the jury of any specific weaknesses which have appeared in the identification evidence. Where in the opinion of the judge the quality of the identifying evidence is poor he should withdraw the case from the jury and direct acquittal unless there is other evidence which supports the correctness of the identification. Failure to follow the guidelines is likely to result in a conviction being quashed. However:

"Having regard to public disquiet about the possibility of miscarriages of justice in this class of case, some explanation of the jurisdiction of this court may be opportune. That jurisdiction is statutory: we can do no more than the Criminal Appeal Act 1968 authorises us to do. It does not authorise us to retry cases. It is for the jury in each case to decide which witnesses should be believed. On matters of credibility this court will only interfere in three circumstances: first, if the jury has been misdirected as to how to assess the evidence; secondly, if there has been no direction at all when there should have been one; and, thirdly, if on the whole of the evidence the jury must have taken a perverse view of a witness, but this is rare.

The limitations, such as they are, on our jurisidiction do not mean that we cannot interfere to prevent miscarriages of justice. In 1966 Parliament released appellate jurisdiction in criminal cases tried on indictment from the limitations which the Criminal Appeal Act 1907 and the case law based on it had put on the old Court of Criminal Appeal. The jurisdiction of this court is wider. We do not hesitate to use our extended jurisdiction whenever the evidence in a case justifies our doing so. In assessing a case, however, it is our duty to use our experience of

---

[13] [1969] 1 Q.B. 267, at p. 271; [1969] 1 All E.R. 32, at p. 34, *per* WIDGERY, L.J. (as he then was). The phrase "lurking doubt" is now much canvassed in the Court; see, e.g. *R.* v. *Milliken* (1969), 53 Cr. App. Rep. 330. For another point arising from the case, see p. 513, *ante*.

[14] *R.* v. *Turnbull*, [1977] Q.B. 224; [1976] 3 All E.R. 549.

the administration of justice. In every division of this court that experience is likely to be extensive and helps us to detect the specious, the irrelevant and what is intended to deceive."[15]

(*b*) *The judgment of the court should be set aside on the ground of a wrong decision of any question of law*—This formula appeared in the 1907 Act and is unchanged. It covers misdirection in the summing-up either as to the law applicable or as to the facts (including failure to put the defence to the jury), wrongful rejection of a submission that there is no case to answer, wrongful admission or exclusion of evidence and defects in the indictment. Thus if the judge fails to give the jury an appropriate warning as to corroboration in those cases where such direction is required this omission will normally lead to the quashing of the conviction;[16] or

(*c*) *There was a material irregularity in the course of the trial*—This formula was introduced by the 1966 Act; it replaced the words in the 1907 Act: "on any ground there was a miscarriage of justice". These latter words have been held to cover a variety of errors in the course of the trial, such as unfair conduct or undue interruption by the judge, improper disclosure to the jury of the defendant's previous record, tampering with a juror, misconduct of a juror and failure to inform an undefended person of his right to call witnesses. The altered formula appears to cover residual cases in the same way.[17] It is not perhaps easy to see the significance of the word "material" since if the irregularity is not material the Court has another way of reflecting that fact in its order. This must now be considered.

2 Applying the proviso

On an appeal against conviction the Court may dismiss the appeal, even though of the opinion that the point raised might be decided in favour of the appellant, if it is considered that no miscarriage of justice has actually occurred.[18] In section 4(1) of the 1907 Act the word "substantial" appeared before "miscarriage"; this seemed "devoid of practical significance"[19] and was deleted by section 4(1) of the 1966 Act. Where the Court exercises this power it is said to "apply the proviso".[20] It appears that the proviso was intended in substitution of a general power to order a new trial; yet it is now clear that, whether or not it is regarded as desirable that the Court should have power to order a new trial, the proviso is not an adequate substitute for that power. A mass of case law has grown up around the original artless

---

[15] [1977] Q.B., at p. 231; [1976] 3 All E.R., at p. 554, *per* LORD WIDGERY, C.J.
[16] *R.* v. *Trigg*, [1963] 1 All E.R. 490; [1963] 1 W.L.R. 305; see p. 619, *post*. The "question of law" may have been decided before the trial or even before plea so that a defendant who has pleaded guilty following a decision of a preliminary point against him may appeal against his conviction (*R.* v. *Vickers*, [1975] 2 All E.R. 945; [1975] 1 W.L.R. 811; see p. 507, *ante*).
[17] See *R.* v. *Hood*, [1968] 2 All E.R. 56; [1968] 1 W.L.R. 773, where one of the jurors knew or suspected that the defendant might have previous convictions. The Court of Appeal deprecated this but dismissed the appeal by application of the proviso (*infra*). See also the cases arising out of defective indictments (p. 490, *ante*).
[18] Criminal Appeal Act 1968, s. 2(1).
[19] *Report of the Interdepartmental Committee on the Court of Criminal Appeal* (Donovan Report) (Cmnd. 2755), para. 164.
[20] Because the paragraph in question of the 1968 Act (and of the 1907 Act) begins "Provided that . . ."

words of the 1907 Act and LORD GODDARD publicly stated that the Court finds great difficulty in applying the proviso. The test is whether a reasonable jury, after a proper summing-up, could have failed to convict the defendant;[1] the Court assumes a reasonable jury, puts itself in the place of that jury and asks itself whether the only reasonable verdict was one of guilty. If so, it applies the proviso. It can only proceed on evidence that could lawfully have come before the jury.[2]

The Court has, on occasion, applied the proviso despite a substantial misdirection in law. The test is by no means one of the degree of error. Research[3] has shown that in 96 cases where the Court of Criminal Appeal or the House of Lords applied the proviso 44 were cases involving substantial misdirection of the jury. The proviso has even been applied where the trial judge omitted to tell the jury that the burden of proof was on the prosecution.[4] If, however, wrongfully admitted evidence may have had a substantial effect on the jury's verdict the Court will not apply the proviso. It almost certainly will not do so where a defence was wrongly withdrawn from the jury[5] or where alibi evidence was wrongly excluded,[6] or generally, however obvious the guilt of a defendant may seem, if the Court's desire for fair treatment of defendants outweighs this consideration. It has been said that:[7]

> "We are not aware of any precedent for applying the proviso in a case where cross-examination as to character has been deliberately [and wrongly] admitted by the trial judge."

There were in fact a number of precedents and the House of Lords did apply the proviso very shortly afterwards in the same circumstances in *Stirland* v. *Director of Public Prosecutions*.[8] The fact that on a previous trial the jury disagreed is no automatic bar to application of the proviso, although no doubt a relevant factor.[9]

If the proviso is applied the appeal is dismissed. The court has no power to substitute an alternative verdict. Accordingly where evidence was wrongly admitted on a charge of murder with the result that the Court of Appeal felt

---

1   *Stirland* v. *Director of Public Prosecutions*, [1944] A.C. 315; [1944] 2 All E.R. 13; see also (among many cases) *R.* v. *Haddy*, [1944] K.B. 442; [1944] 1 All E.R. 319. For the proper attitude to application of the proviso in a murder case, see *Anderson* v. *R.*, [1972] A.C. 100; [1971] 3 All E.R. 768.

2   *R.* v. *Sowden*, [1964] 3 All E.R. 770; [1964] 1 W.L.R. 1454, where the defendant wrote out, for the purpose of mitigation, a statement substantially admitting the prosecution case. The court felt unable to take this into account.

3   Cf. Knight: *Convicting the Guilty*, [1966] Crim. L.R. 24.

4   *R.* v. *Sparrow* (1962), 46 Cr. App. Rep. 288, and see *R.* v. *Cashmore*, [1971] 2 Q.B. 572n; [1971] 2 All E.R. 970, where the Courts-Martial Appeal Court applied the proviso despite a summing-up described as being "in many respects defective".

5   *R.* v. *Badjan* (1966), 50 Cr. App. Rep. 141.

6   *R.* v. *Lewis*, [1969] 2 Q.B. 1; [1969] 1 All E.R. 79; see p. 603, *post*.

7   *R.* v. *Turner*, [1944] K.B. 463, at p. 471; [1944] 1 All E.R. 599, at p. 602.

8   [1944] A.C. 315; [1944] 2 All E.R. 13; cf. *R.* v. *Bruce*, [1975] 3 All E.R. 277; [1975] 1 W.L.R. 1252.

9   See *Customs and Excise Commissioners* v. *Harz*, [1967] 1 A.C. 760; [1967] 1 All E.R. 177, *per* LORD MORRIS OF BORTH-Y-GEST (a decision given before the introduction of majority verdicts). When the leading case of *Woolmington* v. *Director of Public Prosecutions* was before the Court of Criminal Appeal that Court applied the proviso even though the jury had disagreed at the first trial. The appellant succeeded in the House of Lords on the same point which was raised in the Court of Criminal Appeal; see p. 614, *post*.

compelled to quash the conviction, it had no power to substitute a verdict of manslaughter even though defence counsel had, at the trial, conceded that the verdict must at least be manslaughter.[10]

3 Power to substitute an alternative verdict

Where the defendant has been convicted of an offence and (1) the jury could on the same indictment have found him guilty of some other offence; and (2) it appears to the Court of Appeal that the jury must have been satisfied of the facts proving him guilty of that other offence, the Court may, instead of allowing or dismissing the appeal against conviction, substitute a verdict of guilty of that other offence and pass sentence on the defendant for it.[11] The sentence must not be greater than that passed on the defendant at the trial, and must not, of course, exceed the maximum permitted by law for the substituted offence.[12] The Court exercises this power with care, particularly in the light of (2) above, which involves some consideration of a verdict for which necessarily no reasons were given; further, it is a material, though not decisive, point against exercising the power if the jury were not given any direction as to the alternative offence.[13] Where the indictment contains counts for two offences (such as theft and handling) which are in the circumstances alternative to each other, and the jury convict of one but acquit of the other, the Court cannot substitute a verdict of guilty of the latter, even if that seems the correct verdict, since the jury expressly acquitted. The proper course, if there is a conviction on one is for the jury to be discharged from giving a verdict on the other whereupon the Court of Appeal may substitute a verdict of guilty.[14] This may also be important from the point of view of a retrial.[15]

4 Appeal against sentence

On an appeal against sentence the Court may reduce the sentence or it may vary it, by substituting one form of detention or treatment for another. The facts of each case differ so much that it is difficult to lay down any general principle on which the Court acts but it is commonly said that the Court will only interfere where the sentence is "wrong in principle" and not merely on the ground that the members of the Court themselves would have passed a different sentence. Where the appeal is against conviction only there is no power to interfere with the sentence in any way. Formerly the court had power to increase sentence, but this power was taken away by section 4(2) of the 1966 Act.[16] It had some effect as a deterrent against frivolous appeals,

---

[10] *R. v. Deacon*, [1973] 2 All E.R. 1145; [1973] 1 W.L.R. 696; for details of the case see p. 631, *post*.

[11] Criminal Appeal Act 1968, s. 3(1).

[12] *Ibid.*, s. 3(2).

[13] See, generally, *R. v. Caslin*, [1961] 1 All E.R. 246; [1961] 1 W.L.R. 59. This case was decided under the corresponding provisions of the Criminal Appeal Act 1907, but appears still to be good law.

[14] *R. v. Melvin and Eden*, [1953] 1 Q.B. 481; [1953] 1 All E.R. 294.

[15] See p. 537, *post*.

[16] Although it may do so on one count, if the conviction on another is quashed subject to the proviso that the sentence on the indictment as a whole must not be of greater severity than the

but was largely ineffective since in cases where the Court was thinking of increasing sentence it felt obliged to give the defendant legal aid; counsel would then realise what the Court had in mind and advise the defendant to discontinue his appeal. Further, the power undoubtedly acted as a deterrent to some meritorious appeals, since counsel might think that the sentence was on the high side, yet not so high that the Court was bound to interfere; in that case he did not dare to advise an appeal against sentence in case the Court disagreed with his estimate and in fact increased the sentence. The power was of some use in avoiding disparity of sentence between co-defendants, but only in a very few cases.[17] In fact the Court exercised the power to increase only very rarely, and abolition of the power has probably made little difference. It may be noted that a variation of sentence can result in the defendant being detained for longer than would otherwise have been the case. Thus a hospital order under the Mental Health Act cannot be regarded as more severe than a sentence of imprisonment.[18]

5   Power to receive fresh evidence and to order a new trial

a   Power to receive fresh evidence

Section 23 is complementary to sections 7 and 8 of the Act insofar as it deals with fresh evidence. It does not deal at all with the powers of the Court on the reception of fresh evidence but materially affects the conditions subject to which it can be received. The Court cannot now refuse to hear fresh evidence merely on the ground that it was available at the trial, provided that a reasonable explanation is given for failure to adduce it. The evidence must of course be admissible, and "likely to be credible"; equally the Court is under no duty to receive the evidence if it would not in any event be any ground for allowing the appeal or if it bears only upon an issue which was not raised at the trial.[19] Subject however to these conditions, the Court *must* receive the evidence. Fresh evidence is typically received in cases where, for example, some eye-witness or alibi witness not previously available has later been discovered. In *R. v. Lomas*[20] however the Court allowed fresh evidence of expert opinion, stating that the case depended on exceptional facts and was to be no encouragement to similar applications in the future.

Where the court entertains an appeal against conviction following and notwithstanding a plea of guilty[1] it will almost always require evidence to justify this exceptional course and the evidence will, in the nature of things,

---

sentence passed at the trial: Criminal Appeal Act 1968, s. 4; for difficulties which arose under the 1966 Act, see *R. v. Craig*, [1967] 1 All E.R. 1052; [1967] 1 W.L.R. 645.

[17] Thus in *R. v. Ryall*; *R. v. Gardiner*, [1962] Crim. L.R. 853, the appellants had been convicted at different Assizes of "wage-snatches" committed in remarkably similar circumstances and had been sentenced to 5 and 10 years' imprisonment respectively. Their appeals were heard on the same day, and the court increased Ryall's sentence, and reduced Gardiner's sentence, to 7 years.

[18] *R. v. Bennett*, [1968] 2 All E.R. 753; [1968] 1 W.L.R. 998.

[19] Thus in *R. v. Melville*, [1976] 1 All E.R. 395; [1976] 1 W.L.R. 181 the Court refused to admit fresh medical evidence relating to the appellant's state of mind (tendered with a view to canvassing a defence of diminished responsibility) when that issue had not been raised at his trial.

[20] [1969] 1 All E.R. 920; [1969] 1 W.L.R. 306.

[1] As to which see p. 528, *ante*.

be fresh evidence. This occurred in *R.* v. *Lee.*[2] The appellant had pleaded guilty to various counts of arson and manslaughter on 11 indictments. Following articles in the *Sunday Times* which suggested that he could not have committed some of the offences as well as making allegations as to how his confessions had been obtained and how it had been sought to corroborate them, the Court of Appeal, stating the case to be "wholly exceptional, if not unique", permitted evidence to be called by both the appellant and the Crown.

b Power to order a new trial

The power to order a new trial, first introduced by the Criminal Appeal Act 1964, is now contained in sections 7 and 8 of the 1968 Act. Assuming that the Court receives the fresh evidence in the first place, and is then satisfied that if given at the trial it would have created a reasonable doubt in the mind of the jury it must still allow the appeal and quash the conviction but may now order a new trial if it considers that the interests of justice so require. One circumstance in which a new trial might not be ordered is where a considerable length of time has elapsed since the relevant events took place.[3] The new trial may be for the offence charged at the first trial, for any offence which is an alternative verdict offence to that offence or for any offence which was charged in the indictment at the first trial but in respect of which the jury were discharged from giving a verdict, in consequence of convicting the defendant of the first-mentioned offence.

6 Venire de novo

The appeal court has always had the power to order a *venire de novo* where proceedings in the court of trial were so defective as to amount to a nullity. To the defendant this no doubt seems very like ordering a new trial, but strictly the court is ordering not a new trial but a proper one. It has not, unfortunately, been established what degree of irregularity suffices to render proceedings a nullity; there are only particular examples in the cases of proceedings which have been held to be a nullity. This has been held to be so where the judge at the trial was not properly qualified,[4] where the defendant specifically asked for but was denied his right of peremptory challenges,[5] or where a plea of not guilty was misheard and dealt with as a plea of guilty.[6] "To constitute a mistrial the proceedings must have been abortive from beginning to end. . . .";[7] thus there was held not to be a mistrial where the

---

2 [1984] 1 All E.R. 1080; [1984] 1 W.L.R. 578.
3 *R.* v. *Pedrini*, [1964] Crim. L.R. 719; see generally for the proper approach to fresh evidence *R.* v. *Flower*, [1966] 1 Q.B. 146; [1965] 3 All E.R. 669 and *R.* v. *Stafford and Luvaglio* (1969), 53 Cr. App. Rep. 1 where the Court of Appeal indicated reluctance to hear fresh evidence which involved raising a line of defence wholly different from that raised at the trial. Fresh evidence may be found in additional evidence from a witness who appeared at the trial (as in *R.* v. *Flower*).
4 *R.* v. *Cronin*, [1940] 1 All E.R. 618.
5 *R.* v. *Williams* (1925), 19 Cr. App. Rep. 67. *Aliter* if he made no request; *ibid.*
6 *R.* v. *Scothern*, [1961] Crim. L.R. 326.
7 *R.* v. *Middlesex Justices, Ex parte Director of Public Prosecutions*, [1952] 2 Q.B. 758, at p. 769; [1952] 2 All E.R. 312, at p. 314, *per* LORD GODDARD, C.J.

defendant was arraigned and technically put in peril on the charge, although by reason of the misconduct of the judge in procuring an acquittal against the weight of evidence he soon ceased to be in peril.[7]

However, a *venire de novo* was ordered where the defendant, having been told that if he pleaded guilty a non-custodial sentence would be imposed, did plead guilty and was sentenced to immediate imprisonment.[8]

The House of Lords considered the scope of *venire de novo* in *R. v. Rose.*[9] In that case there had been a material irregularity in the course of the trial (the judge having sent messages to the jury imposing time limits on their deliberations). The Court of Appeal had quashed the convictions, feeling unable to apply the proviso. The House of Lords affirmed the decision, holding that there was no power to issue a writ of *venire de novo* where the trial had been validly commenced and had proceeded to an unequivocal verdict from the jury.

7 Orders for admission to hospital; Criminal Procedure (Insanity) Act 1964 and Criminal Appeal Act 1968, ss. 12–16

It has been noted that the Criminal Procedure (Insanity) Act 1964 created a right of appeal against a finding of "not guilty by reason of insanity" (called in the Act a "special verdict"), and against a finding of unfitness to plead. On appeal against a hospital order the Court will consider whether the order was right at the time when it was made, and will not review the applicant's subsequent progress.[10] If an appeal against the special verdict is allowed, the Court may at the same time conclude that the defendant was guilty of an offence; in that case the Court may substitute a verdict of guilty of that offence, provided it is the offence charged at the trial or an offence of which the defendant could have been found guilty by way of alternative verdict.[11] In any other case, the Court must simply substitute a verdict of acquittal, but may make an order that the defendant be admitted to hospital for observation.[12] Where the Court allows an appeal against a finding of unfitness to plead, the appellant may be tried for the offence originally charged.[13] Conversely, the defendant may have been convicted of an offence at the trial (whether or not insanity or unfitness to plead were alleged) but the Court of Appeal may be of opinion that the special verdict should have been returned or a finding of unfitness made. In this case the Court of Appeal may quash the conviction, enter a special verdict or a finding of unfitness and order the defendant to be admitted to hospital.[14]

---

[8] *R. v. Ryan* (1978), 67 Cr. App. Rep. 177—one of a number of cases of the so-called "plea-bargaining" type.

[9] [1982] A.C. 822; [1982] 2 All E.R. 731.

[10] *R. v. McNaney*, [1969] 2 All E.R. 35; [1969] 1 W.L.R. 623.

[11] Criminal Appeal Act 1968, s. 13(4).

[12] *Ibid.*, s. 14.

[13] *Ibid.*, s. 16.

[14] *Ibid.*, s. 6.

8 Procedural powers of the court[15]

As noted above, some appeals to the Court may be brought without leave, but in most cases there must be an application to the Court itself for leave. The time limit for giving notice of appeal, or application for leave to appeal, is 28 days from the date of conviction or sentence. This time may be extended by the Court, except in a case involving sentence of death. Such application is made in the first instance to a single judge of the Court, who considers it in private.[16] A single judge has most of the powers of a court of three judges (besides, of course, the power to grant leave); exceptionally he does not have any of the powers relating to fresh evidence. An application may of course be abandoned, and notice of abandonment cannot be withdrawn although it may be treated as a nullity if the abandonment was not the result of a deliberate and informed decision in the sense that "the mind of the appellant did not go with his act of abandonment."[17] For example, where an application for leave to appeal was granted but, because of a postal strike, was not communicated to the applicant before he gave notice of abandonment, he was permitted to withdraw his notice.[18] If the single judge refuses leave to appeal (or to exercise any other of his powers) the application may be considered by a court of two judges.[19] Both the single judge and the court may grant legal aid and bail. Bail, for obvious reasons, is very rarely granted;[20] indeed almost the only cases where it will be granted are where the defendant has obtained (or does not need) leave to appeal and has a very good chance of succeeding on appeal, or where the defendant has been given a comparatively short sentence after a long and complex trial.[1] In the latter case he might otherwise have served much of his sentence before the appeal was heard. Time spent on bail does not, of course, count as part of the sentence.[2] Conversely, time spent in custody pending the determination of the appeal now counts as part of the defendant's sentence, subject to any direction to the contrary (for which reasons must be given). No such direction may be given where the defendant obtained leave to appeal, from the Court of Appeal or the trial court, or where the case has been referred to the Court by the Home Secretary.[2]

---

15 If the issue of referring a question to the European Court for a preliminary ruling arises (as to which, see p. 185, *ante*) the Court may, on application or otherwise, order the question to be referred. Such order may be made at any time before determination of the appeal or application and there will be no determination by the Court until the European Court has given its preliminary ruling: cf. the Criminal Appeal (References to the European Court) Rules 1972.

16 This practice is not invariable, and some applications for leave to appeal against conviction may go direct to a court of three judges. See the Donovan Report, paras. 229–241.

17 *R. v. Medway*, [1976] Q.B. 779; [1976] 1 All E.R. 527.

18 *R. v. Noble*, [1971] 3 All E.R. 361; [1971] 1 W.L.R. 1772.

19 Criminal Appeal Act 1968, s. 31(2); Supreme Court Act 1981, s. 55(4). The application must normally be made to the Court within 14 days of communication of the notice of refusal by the single judge, but the Court has jurisdiction to extend the time even though the further application is not made until after the 14 days have expired: *R. v. Ward*, [1971] 3 All E.R. 619; [1971] 1 W.L.R. 1450; *R. v. Doherty*, [1971] 3 All E.R. 622; [1971] 1 W.L.R. 1454.

20 If the appeal is dismissed, it may embarrass the court to order the defendant's return to prison. "The court is always anxious in such a case, because although a man may have been on bail he will have had the appeal hanging over him for all this time": LORD PARKER, C.J. in *R. v. Cavendish*, [1961] 2 All E.R. 856, at p. 858; [1961] 1 W.L.R. 1083, at p. 1085.

1 *R. v. Watton* (1978), 68 Cr. App. Rep. 293; see p. 472, *ante*.

2 Criminal Appeal Act 1968, s. 29.

Once an appeal has been heard and dismissed, or a notice of appeal abandoned, it cannot be re-opened and the applicant's only recourse is to petition the Home Secretary (who, as seen, may refer the case to the Court). A case may only be re-listed for further argument if there was "some procedural defect" in the hearing, such as papers being lost.[3]

C   APPEAL TO THE HOUSE OF LORDS

A further appeal lies by either prosecution or defence from the Court of Appeal (criminal division) to the House of Lords if (1) the Court of Appeal certifies that a point of law of general public importance is involved in the decision; and (2) either the Court of Appeal or the House of Lords gives leave to appeal on the ground that the point is one which ought to be considered by the House.[4] The certificate is a necessary condition to avoid the House of Lords being inundated with hopeless applications. If the Court of Appeal is satisfied that there is a point of law of general public importance involved it will give the certificate, as it were, automatically. There will always, nevertheless, be an element of discretion as to whether an appeal is allowed to proceed, since even if the point were of general public importance it might still not be worthy of consideration by the House of Lords in the particular case; for example it might already be the subject of clear and satisfactory decisions of lower courts. This element of discretion is preserved by the requirement that there must be leave to appeal. It will be observed that only the Court of Appeal can give the certificate, and if that court refuses the certificate there can be no further proceedings.[5] On the other hand, the Court of Appeal may give a certificate and yet refuse leave, in which case a petition may be made to the House of Lords for leave to appeal, the petition being heard by the Appeals Committee of the House.

It is proper and convenient that the certificate should state what the point of law of general public importance is;[6] however, it seems that other points may be raised by either side once the case is before the House of Lords on the point certified.[7] However, the grant of a certificate on some point affecting the validity of the conviction does not enable the appellant to argue that the sentence is invalid.[6] The House of Lords may exercise similar powers to those of the court below. As to applying the proviso,[8] however, VISCOUNT SIMONDS said in *Jones* v. *Director of Public Prosecutions* that the House of Lords:

> "may feel some difficulty about exercising a jurisdiction which demands an examination not only of the particular question of law that is raised but of all the circumstances of the case."[9]

---

[3] *R.* v. *Grantham*, [1969] 2 Q.B. 574; [1969] 2 All E.R. 545; a decision of the Courts-Martial Appeal Court, but stated to apply to the Court of Appeal.

[4] Criminal Appeal Act 1968, s. 33. Application for leave must be made within 14 days of the Court of Appeal decision, if made to that court, or within 14 days of the Court of Appeal's refusal to grant leave if made to the House of Lords (s. 34).

[5] *Gelberg* v. *Miller*, [1961] 1 All E.R. 618n.; [1961] 1 W.L.R. 459.

[6] *Jones* v. *Director of Public Prosecutions*, [1962] A.C. 635; [1962] 1 All E.R. 569.

[7] *A.-G. for Northern Ireland* v. *Gallagher*, [1963] A.C. 349; [1961] 3 All E.R. 299.

[8] To s. 2(1) of the 1968 Act, see pp. 533–535, *ante*.

[9] [1962] A.C. 635, at p. 660; [1962] 1 All E.R. 569, at p. 573.

Notwithstanding, the House of Lords did apply the proviso in the case of *Myers* v. *Director of Public Prosecutions.*[10]

The procedure described above does not apply following the hearing of an Attorney-General's reference after acquittal.[11] In these cases the court may of its own motion or in pursuance of an application refer the point of law in the case to the House of Lords "if it appears to the court that the point ought to be considered by that House"[12] and there is, accordingly, no need for a certificate that a point of law of general public importance is involved. Indeed the point of law need not be a point of general public importance, although no doubt the Court of Appeal would only refer such a point to the House, as a matter of practice.

Finally, in the event of a question being raised, in an appeal, requiring a reference to the European Court for a preliminary ruling, the determination of the appeal will be postponed to await the ruling of the European Court.[13]

---

[10] [1965] A.C. 1001; [1964] 2 All E.R. 881; see p. 662, *post.*
[11] Under the Criminal Justice Act 1972, s. 36; see p. 530, *ante.*
[12] *Ibid.*, s. 36(3).
[13] See p. 185, *ante.*

CHAPTER 26

Summary Procedure

A PROCESS

The rules as to process are the same as in the case of an indictable offence, except that a summons cannot be issued merely on the ground that the defendant resides or is, or is believed to reside or be, in the area in question and a warrant cannot be issued in any case where a summons has already been issued. In any event, as has already been noted,[1] a warrant cannot be issued for the arrest of an adult in the case of a summary offence, unless the offence is punishable with imprisonment or the defendant's address is "not sufficiently established" for a summons to be served on him. Even where a warrant may lawfully be issued, it is rarely thought necessary in the case of any summary offence. The position therefore is that a summons or a warrant may be issued if:

(*a*) the summary offence was committed or is suspected to have been committed within the area; or

(*b*) it appears to the magistrate issuing process necessary or expedient, with a view to the better administration of justice, that the person charged should be tried jointly with or in the same place as some other person who is charged with an offence and who is in custody or is to be proceeded against within the area; or

(*c*) the person charged resides or is, or is believed to reside or be within the area; or

(*d*) under any enactment the magistrates' court has jurisdiction to try the offence. In this context, there should be noted section 2(6) of the Magistrates' Courts Act 1980, permitting a magistrates' court to try a number of offences provided that it has jurisdiction to try any one of them; or[2]

(*e*) the offence was committed outside England and Wales and, where it is an offence exclusively punishable on summary conviction, if a magistrates' court for the area would have jurisdiction to try the offence if the offender were before it.[3]

---

[1] See p. 448, *ante*.
[2] See p. 445, *ante*.
[3] Magistrates' Courts Act 1980, s. 1(2); see the rules as to offences committed on boundaries etc. which also apply here, p. 445, *ante*.

B JURISDICTION

A magistrates' court for an area[4] has jurisdiction to try summary offences committed within that area. It also has jurisdiction as a court of trial in the following circumstances: (1) where a person is brought before the court on a summons or warrant issued under section 1(2) (*b*) of the Act (to be tried jointly with another person over whom the court has jurisdiction);[5] (2) in relation to "either way" offences, in any case where it has jurisdiction as examining justices;[6] (3) in relation to the trial of juveniles for indictable offences, in any case where it has jurisdiction as examining justices; (4) where it has jurisdiction to try an offender for a summary offence, it can also try him for any other summary offence.

C THE COURSE OF THE TRIAL

1 Time-limit

Unless expressly provided to the contrary a magistrates' court cannot try an information charging a summary offence unless the information was laid within six months from the time when the offence was committed.[7] However, it may try summarily an "either-way" offence outside the period, since this statutory time limit is confined to summary offences.[8] Time runs from the time of commission of the offence, not from the time of its discovery; however, it is sufficient if the information is laid within the six months, even if the trial takes place outside that time. It is in each case a question of construction of the statute whether the offence in question is a continuing offence, that is, committed each day that the act or state of affairs in question continues, or whether it is a "once and for all" offence in that it is committed on one day and one day only. Thus in *R. v. Wimbledon Justices, Ex parte Derwent*[9] a statute made it an offence to let or offer to let a house in excess of a certain rent. The divisional court held that a person lets a house once and for all when he demises it by means of a lease and that an information laid six months after the date of the demise was out of time. Proceedings could therefore be restrained by prohibition since:

> ". . . If in a case brought before justices it can be seen on the face of the proceedings that the offence is alleged to have been committed more than six months before the information was laid, justices have no power to enter upon the case at all, because they have no jurisdiction to sit as a court of summary jurisdiction in the case of an offence alleged to have been committed more than six months before the proceedings were instituted."[10]

---

[4] *Viz.* a county, a London commission area or the City of London (Magistrates' Courts Act 1980, s. 2(1)). The provisions as to offences committed on boundaries, etc. (p. 445, *ante*) also apply here.
[5] See p. 444, *ante*.
[6] See p. 476, *ante*.
[7] Magistrates' Courts Act 1980, s. 127(1).
[8] *Ibid.*, s. 127(2).
[9] [1953] 1 Q.B. 380; [1953] 1 All E.R. 390.
[10] [1953] 1 Q.B. 380, at p. 385; [1953] 1 All E.R. 390, at p. 391, *per* LORD GODDARD, C.J.

Even where the offence is continuing it seems that the time limit runs from each day, so that the magistrates cannot hear any information that charges the offence as occurring more than six months before the date of the information;[11] in other words the matter is to be regarded as if the defendant committed the offence once every day. Where an information is laid in time it may be amended to charge a different offence, after the expiry of six months from the commission of that offence, provided that this does not cause injustice.[12]

2   Number of offences

A magistrates' court must not proceed to the trial of an information which charges more than one offence.[13] This is a natural rule, since the information fulfils the same function in summary trial as the indictment in the case of trial at the Crown Court; the same considerations of, *inter alia*, fairness to the defendant, which prohibit duplicity in an indictment, also prohibit an information charging more than one offence. Thus in *Ware* v. *Fox*[14] an information charged the defendant with being concerned in the management of premises which were used for the purpose of smoking cannabis or cannabis resin or dealing in cannabis or cannabis resin. The Queen's Bench divisional court held that on the proper construction of the relevant statute[15] the information alleged two offences, namely managing premises used for smoking and managing premises used for dealing and was bad for duplicity. By contrast, section 5 of the Public Order Act 1936 creates the offence of using "threatening, abusive or insulting words or behaviour . . . with intent to provoke a breach of the peace or whereby a breach of the peace is likely to be occasioned". It was held in *Vernon* v. *Paddon*[16] that the section creates one offence, the essential feature of which is conduct intended to provoke a breach of the peace or whereby such a breach was likely to be occasioned. Where an information is found to charge more than one offence the prosecutor should be called on to elect before the trial begins on which offence to proceed; if he declines to make his election the information should be dismissed.[17] It is essential that the matter should be put right at the outset, since, as will be noted below, the magistrates must state the substance of the information to the defendant and ask him to plead to it; therefore the information must be in order for a proper plea to be received, and the defendant cannot be required to plead to an information that is bad for duplicity. It is very doubtful whether this irregularity is one which can be cured by the operation of section 123 of the Magistrates' Courts Act.[18] In any event if the information is not amended:

---

[11] *R.* v. *Chertsey Justices, Ex parte Franks*, [1961] 2 Q.B. 152; [1961] 1 All E.R. 825.

[12] *R.* v. *Newcastle-upon-Tyne Justices, Ex parte John Bryce (Contractors), Ltd.*, [1976] 2 All E.R. 611; [1976] 1 W.L.R. 517.

[13] Magistrates' Courts Rules 1981, r. 12(1). However, two or more informations may be set out in a single document (*ibid.*, r. 12(2)); see *Shah* v. *Swallow*, [1984] 2 All E.R. 528; *sub nom. Director of Public Prosecutions* v. *Shah*, [1984] 1 W.L.R. 886.

[14] [1967] 1 All E.R. 100; [1967] 1 W.L.R. 379.

[15] Dangerous Drugs Act 1965, s. 5.

[16] [1973] 3 All E.R. 302; [1973] 1 W.L.R. 663.

[17] *Edwards* v. *Jones*, [1947] K.B. 659; [1947] 1 All E.R. 385.

[18] See p. 443, *ante*.

"If a conviction is to be drawn up, how is it to be done? The information has to be dealt with as a whole. . . . To split it into halves and say that one bit is proved and another bit is disproved involves, to my mind, an operation as impossible as a few years ago splitting the atom was thought to be."[19]

To avoid the difficulty the information itself should always be in court from the beginning of proceedings.[20]

It is however quite permissible, and indeed common, for two informations against the same defendant, or (where the cases are related) against different defendants, to be tried together. It was formerly thought that this could only be done by consent but the House of Lords in *Clayton* v. *Chief Constable of Norfolk*[1] held that, although magistrates should first seek consent to such a course, they could nevertheless in the exercise of their discretion order a joint trial even without the consent of the parties, although they should not do so where it would not be fair and just to a defendant.

Where there are informations charging an offence and an attempt to commit that offence, these may be ordered to be tried together without the consent of the defendant[2] and this will usually be done.

3 Hearing

If the defendant appears at the hearing the court must state to him the substance of the information and ask him whether he pleads guilty or not guilty. In spite of these words, the same pleas as are open to a defendant charged with an indictable offence may be raised by a defendant charged with a summary offence. If the plea is one of not guilty the prosecutor may make an opening speech, and will then call his evidence. Where the prosecutor is unrepresented, it is open to the magistrates, in their discretion, to permit their clerk to examine prosecution witnesses.[3] Section 98 of the Magistrates' Courts Act, already cited,[4] will apply, and the witnesses will be subject to cross-examination and re-examination according to the circumstances of the case. At the conclusion of the evidence for the prosecution the defendant may address the court, whether or not he calls evidence; if he is calling evidence it will follow at once. The defendant may then address the court a second time but only if he himself has given evidence, another witness has been called on his behalf, and the court gives leave.[5] If the defendant addresses the court twice the prosecutor has a right to address the court a second time immediately before the defendant's second speech.[5] The court will then retire if necessary and convict the defendant or dismiss the charge.

If on the other hand the defendant pleads guilty the court may convict him

---

[19] [1947] K.B. 659, at p. 667; [1947] 1 All E.R. 830, at p. 834, *per* OLIVER, J.

[20] *Per* LORD PARKER, C.J. and SALMON, J. (as he then was) in *Hargreaves* v. *Alderson*, [1964] 2 Q.B. 159; [1962] 3 All E.R. 1019; see also *Garman* v. *Plaice*, [1969] 3 All E.R. 342; [1969] 1 W.L.R. 19.

[1] [1983] 2 A.C. 473; [1983] 1 All E.R. 984. This does not, however, enable a summons and cross-summons to be tried together; this cannot be done *semble* even by consent: *R.* v. *Epsom Justices, Ex parte Gibbons*, [1983] 3 All E.R. 523; [1983] 3 W.L.R. 873.

[2] Criminal Attempts Act 1981, s. 4(2).

[3] *Simms* v. *Moore*, [1970] 2 Q.B. 327; [1970] 3 All E.R. 1.

[4] See p. 479, *ante*.

[5] Magistrates' Courts Rules 1981, r. 14.

without hearing evidence.[6] The wording of the subsection shows that it is often desirable to hear some evidence, particularly where it is part of the prosecution's case that the offence was committed in circumstances of aggravation, or perhaps if a committal for sentence to the Crown Court is contemplated or if the plea of guilty tendered may be "equivocal".[7] In any event the court retains full power over the case until sentence is passed and has discretion to allow a change of plea until that time if justice so requires.[8]

Whether there is a plea of guilty or finding of guilt, there will normally be such an enquiry into the past record of the defendant as follows conviction of an indictable offence; the court may then adjourn, for not more than four weeks at a time, for enquiries to be made or for the purpose of determining the best way to deal with the case.[9] When the court resumes it need not be composed of the same magistrates; if, however, there are any newcomers the court which sentences or deals with the offender must make such enquiry into the facts and circumstances of the case as are necessary to acquaint the newcomers fully with those facts and circumstances.[10] This must be done even though the court will *ex hypothesi* have held some such enquiry before; the use of the words "the court" seems to prohibit the newcomers being given information privately before the court sits.[11]

Finally, note should be taken of the power which magistrates have under the Justices of the Peace Act 1361 to bind over to keep the peace or be of good behaviour a defendant even where he is acquitted.[12]

D   ABSENCES

1   General effects of absence[13]

It sometimes happens that one or both of the parties fails to appear at the trial or adjourned trial of the information. If the defendant does not appear the court may hear the case in his absence provided that, where a summons was issued, either, the court is satisfied that the summons was served on the defendant within what appears to be a reasonable time before the hearing, or the defendant appeared on a previous occasion to answer the information.[14]

---

6 Magistrates' Courts Act 1980, s. 9(3).

7 See p. 550, *post*.

8 *S. (An Infant)* v. *Manchester City Recorder*, [1971] A.C. 481; [1969] 3 All E.R. 1230.

9 Magistrates' Courts Act 1980, s. 10(3); the period is three weeks if the defendant is in custody.

10 *Ibid.*, s. 98(7). This is perhaps the nearest that English law comes to allowing special "sentencing tribunals".

11 In the event of a question arising which might require reference to the European Court for a preliminary ruling (as to which, see p. 185, *ante*) the justices may, on application or otherwise, order the question to be referred and the hearing will then be adjourned pending receipt of the European Court's ruling; for a case in which this was done, and observations as to the approach which magistrates should adopt to this problem, see *R.* v. *Plymouth Justices, Ex parte Rogers*, [1982] Q.B. 863; [1982] 2 All E.R. 175.

12 See *Veater* v. *G.*, [1981] 2 All E.R. 304; [1981] 1 W.L.R. 567.

13 Magistrates' Courts Act 1980, ss. 11–16. As to absence during the initial procedure on information for an offence triable either way, see p. 461, *ante*.

14 The mode of service is prescribed by Magistrates' Courts Rules 1981, r. 99. If the court proceeds in the absence of the defendant in a case where he has not been duly served in accordance with this rule, the "hearing" is a complete nullity: *R.* v. *Seisdon Justices, Ex parte Dougan*, [1983] 1 All E.R. 6; [1982] 1 W.L.R. 1476.

Alternatively the court may adjourn the hearing, with or without issuing a warrant for the arrest of the defendant; but a warrant can only be issued if the court is satisfied as to the matters stated above, and if the information is substantiated on oath. There is a further restriction on the issue of a warrant: if the court adjourns the trial after hearing evidence, or convicting the defendant without hearing evidence on a plea of guilty, the court must not issue a warrant unless it thinks it undesirable, by reason of the gravity of the offence, to continue the hearing in his absence. In any event, a warrant cannot be issued unless the offence is punishable by imprisonment or unless the court, having convicted the defendant, proposes to disqualify him.

If the prosecutor fails to appear the court may dismiss the information or, if evidence has been received on a previous occasion, continue the hearing.[15] This is one example of the importance of the stage of the trial at which the justices begin to hear evidence. Alternatively the court may adjourn the trial. If neither side appears, the court may again dismiss the information or, if evidence has been received on a previous occasion, continue the hearing;[16] alternatively the hearing may simply be adjourned.

2 Pleading guilty by post

The Magistrates' Courts Act 1957 provided a new and convenient procedure whereby the defendant can plead guilty in cases where his appearance at court would be no more than a formality, if not a serious waste of time and money. It is now governed by section 12 of the 1980 Act. The procedure laid down by the Act is generally acknowledged to have worked well and is extensively used, particularly in motoring cases; however, it has no application at all to (1) juvenile court proceedings; (2) offences triable either way; or (3) offences for which the accused is liable to be sentenced to imprisonment for a term exceeding three months. Where the Act does apply, procedure is as follows. The prosecutor will serve with the summons a notice in prescribed terms as to the effect of section 12 of the Act and a concise statement of such facts as he will place before the court if the defendant does decide to plead guilty by post. Although the Act is silent on the point it seems that it is entirely within the discretion of the prosecutor as to whether he will make use of the Act and serve the above documents with the summons, even on the assumption that the Act applies to the offence charged. Where, however, the prosecutor does elect to use the procedure, he must serve the documents and then inform the clerk to the justices that he has done so. It is then for the defendant or his solicitor to inform the clerk that he desires to plead guilty without appearing, if that is so, by sending, appropriately completed, the part of the notice described above. He does not, of course, have to use the procedure, and even if he does at first give notification that he is not going to appear he may change his mind and appear.

If, however, he does not appear the court may proceed to hear the case in his absence (whether or not the prosecutor is also absent) provided that it is satisfied that the notice and statement of facts were served on the defendant with the summons. Before accepting the plea of guilty and convicting the

---

15 Magistrates' Courts Act 1980, s. 15.
16 *Ibid.*, s. 16.

defendant in his absence the court must cause to be read out aloud the defendant's notification that he is going to plead guilty, the statement of facts served on the defendant and any statement by way of mitigation which the defendant himself may have submitted. The statement of facts read out must be precisely the same as that served upon the defendant. These rules must be meticulously observed, and breach of them may be a ground for quashing the conviction by means of certiorari.

> "We all know that these matters have to be dealt with expeditiously. . . . It seems to me, however, to be quite clear that, before the magistrates can exercise jurisdiction in a case of this sort, they must strictly observe the conditions of the statute. Mere knowledge of the contents of the accused's submission, the mere reading of it to themselves, is not sufficient; the submission must be read in open court."[17]

The rule that the precise statement of facts must be read out is also important, because after hearing it the magistrates may decide that the case is too grave to be dealt with in the way contemplated by the parties and may adjourn the case for the defendant to be present.

Assuming that, after hearing the notification of intention to plead guilty, the statement of facts and the submissions in mitigation, the magistrates accept the plea, they will record a conviction and (in the majority of cases to which the Act applies) impose a fine. Where they think it desirable to imprison the defendant or to impose any disqualification on him they must adjourn the hearing[18] without imposing any penalty whatever. There must then be sent to the defendant a notice stating the time and place of the adjourned hearing and the reason for the present adjournment (that is that the court is considering imprisonment or disqualification). If he chooses not to appear after receiving notice of what the court has in mind the court can proceed to disqualify him in his absence;[19] they cannot however sentence him to imprisonment or detention in a detention centre in his absence.[20] In such a case the proper course is to issue a warrant for the defendant's arrest.[1]

Thus a person can never be sentenced to imprisonment in his absence and can only be disqualified in his absence following an adjournment for the purpose of giving him an opportunity to appear. However, a person may be committed to prison, for default in payment of a fine, in his absence.[2]

---

17 *R*. v. *Oldham Justices, Ex parte Morrissey*, [1958] 3 All E.R. 559n, at p. 560; [1959] 1 W.L.R. 58, at p. 59, *per* LORD PARKER, C.J.
18 Under Magistrates' Courts Act 1980, s. 10(3); see p. 546, *ante*. This applies even if disqualification is mandatory under the "totting-up" provisions; further there may even in this case be grounds for mitigating the normal consequences of conviction, which the defendant should have the chance to state: *R*. v. *Llandrindod Wells Justices, Ex parte Gibson*, [1968] 2 All E.R. 20; [1968] 1 W.L.R. 598.
19 *Ibid*., s. 11(4).
20 *Ibid*., s. 11(3).
1 *Ibid*., s. 13(3).
2 *Ibid*., s. 82(5); *R*. v. *Dudley Magistrates' Court, Ex parte Payne*, [1979] 2 All E.R. 1089; [1979] 1 W.L.R. 891.

E SENTENCE

The types of sentence imposable by magistrates are basically similar to those available to the Crown Court, although the extent of magistrates' powers in relation to severity of sentence is more limited. They can only sentence to imprisonment for up to six months in respect of any one offence[3] (or 12 months in the case of consecutive sentences).[4]

Their powers relating to the imposition of fines and the making of compensation orders are restricted. Since all summary jurisdiction derives from statute the amount of the maximum fine for any offence is prescribed by statute. However where a statute provides for imprisonment or other detention but makes no express provision for a fine, there is a general power to fine instead of imposing a custodial sentence.[5]

As a result of inflation statutory fines may quickly become too low and, to combat this phenomenon, the Criminal Justice Act 1982, section 37 introduced "the standard scale" of fines for summary offences. This scale consists of 5 levels and the ensuing sections of the 1982 Act provide for the substitution of a level on the standard scale for the figures prescribed by existing statutory provisions. Thus, for example, a summary offence formerly punishable with a fine of £100 became punishable with a fine up to level 3. To keep pace with inflation these levels may be increased by order of the Secretary of State.[6]

The maximum compensation that magistrates can order under a compensation order is similarly limited.[7]

Finally, reference should be made to the provisions, now contained in section 39 of the 1980 Act, whereby a person over 17 who has been convicted before different magistrates' courts of two or more offences punishable with imprisonment or disqualification from driving, may be remitted to be dealt with by one of the courts concerned.

---

[3] Magistrates' Courts Act 1980, s. 31(1); they can, of course, commit to the Crown Court for sentence in the circumstances noted at pp. 462–469, *ante.*

[4] *Ibid.*, s. 133.

[5] *Ibid.*, s. 34(3); the maximum fine is £400 for a summary offence or "the prescribed sum" for an either way offence (currently £2,000). These figures may be varied by order of the Secretary for State under s. 143 of the Act, and were altered to the above figures in 1984.

[6] *Ibid.*, s. 143 (as amended by Criminal Justice Act 1982, s. 48). They were increased by the Criminal Penalties Etc. (Increase) Order 1984, under which the maximum fine (level 5) became £2,000.

[7] *Ibid.*, s. 40(1); s. 143 applies to s. 40(1) and the maximum was increased to £2,000 in 1984 by the Order above referred to.

CHAPTER 27

Appeal Following Summary Trial

A defendant convicted by a magistrates' court may appeal either (1) to the Crown Court; or (2) by case stated to the Queen's Bench Division of the High Court and subsequently (3) to the House of Lords, in certain circumstances. In addition to those rights of appeal there is the possibility of applying for judicial review. Each of these will be considered in turn.

A APPEAL TO THE CROWN COURT

Where the defendant has been convicted in the magistrates' court of either a summary offence or an "either-way" offence tried summarily he may appeal to the Crown Court, if he pleaded guilty against his sentence only, or if he pleaded not guilty against both conviction and sentence.[1] It will be seen that there is an express statutory prohibition against an appeal against conviction if the defendant pleaded guilty. This may be contrasted with the position following trial on indictment, where, as already noted,[2] there is nothing in the Criminal Appeal Act to prevent an appeal against conviction to the Court of Appeal even if the defendant pleaded guilty. It has been observed[2] that the judges have laid down that appeals against conviction following a plea of guilty will only be entertained by the Court of Appeal in certain exceptional circumstances; so in the case of appeals to the Crown Court also, the judges have given a construction to the statute which evades the effect of the exact words used by Parliament, but on this occasion in favour of the defendant. It has been held that to make a plea of guilty binding and effective it must be unambiguous;[3] if therefore the defendant says the actual word "guilty" but adds to it a statement which, if true, amounts to a defence to the charge, or if from the circumstances it is clear that he is denying the charge but has

---

[1] Magistrates' Courts Act 1980, s. 108(1).
[2] See p. 528, ante.
[3] R. v. Durham Quarter Sessions, Ex parte Virgo, [1952] 2 Q.B. 1; [1952] 1 All E.R. 446; cf. R. v. Ingleson, cited at p. 528, ante.

pleaded guilty through ignorance of the law, a plea of guilty accepted in these circumstances is a nullity.[4] The Crown Court can, therefore, hear an appeal against the "conviction" which is equally a nullity, and under powers presently to be considered can remit the case to the magistrates with an expression of opinion that a plea of not guilty ought to be entered. Where on the other hand there has been a deliberate and unequivocal plea of guilty no appeal against conviction can be entertained.[5]

The expression "sentence" includes any order made on conviction by a magistrates' court, with certain exceptions, namely: (1) a probation order or an order for absolute or conditional discharge, although if on a later date sentence is passed in respect of the offence for which the probation order or order for conditional discharge was made, that is following "breach" of the order, there may be an appeal against that later sentence; (2) an order for the payment of costs; (3) an order for the destruction of an animal, made under the Protection of Animals Act 1911; and (4) any order, if the court has no discretion as to the making of the order or its terms, for example if the court is bound to order endorsement of a driving licence.[6] It has already been noted[7] that there is no appeal against a committal for sentence, in the cases already discussed in which there may be such a committal, although there may be an appeal against the conviction on which the committal is based. There is a right of appeal against an order to enter into recognisances to keep the peace or be of good behaviour,[8] and this right exists where such an order has been made following acquittal.[9]

With limited exceptions only the defendant may appeal. Procedure is that an appeal must be commenced by giving notice of appeal, to the clerk of the magistrates' court, and to the other party, within 21 days after the day on which the decision of the magistrates' court was given (meaning the day on which sentence is passed if there is an adjournment of the case after conviction). The Crown Court may extend the time, either in relation to a notice not yet given or to a notice already given but out of time.

Proceedings before the Crown Court take the form of a complete rehearing of the case;[10] the prosecution must open the case and call its witnesses afresh and either side may introduce fresh evidence without any leave. This is of course in sharp contrast to proceedings in the Court of Appeal. The Crown Court may confirm, reverse or vary the decision of the magistrates' court,[11] or remit the case with an expression of their opinion;[12] as already seen this latter procedure will be appropriate where an "equivocal" plea of guilty has been entered, which in all the circumstances the Crown Court considers should have been treated as a plea of not guilty.

As regards appeals against sentence, the Crown Court may impose any

---

[4] *R.* v. *Blandford Justices, Ex parte G.*, [1967] 1 Q.B. 82; [1966] 1 All E.R. 1921; see p. 546, *ante.*

[5] *P. Foster Haulage, Ltd.* v. *Roberts*, [1978] 2 All E.R. 751.

[6] Magistrates' Courts Act 1980, s. 108(3).

[7] See p. 464, *ante.*

[8] Magistrates' Courts (Appeals from Binding Over Orders) Act 1956.

[9] *Shaw* v. *Hamilton*, [1982] 2 All E.R. 718; [1982] 1 W.L.R. 1308.

[10] Supreme Court Act 1981, s. 48. Although the prosecution cannot alter the case by amending the information (*Garfield* v. *Maddocks*, [1974] Q.B. 7; [1973] 2 All E.R. 303).

[11] *Ibid.*, s. 48(2) (*a*).

[12] *Ibid.*, s. 48(2) (*b*).

sentence which the magistrates' court could have passed, whether more or less severe than that which they actually passed. The court may also do this if the appeal is against conviction only.[13] Again, there is a sharp contrast between appeals to the Crown Court and appeals to the Court of Appeal following trial on indictment, since the Court of Appeal never has had the power to interfere with the sentence in any way if the appeal is against conviction only and, in addition, cannot now increase sentence;[14] the Crown Court can do both. Finally, the Crown Court may:

> "make such other order in the matter as the court thinks just, and by such order exercise any power which the said authority might have exercised."[15]

The wording is liberal, but it was held;[16] on an almost identical provision in the previous legislation, that Quarter Sessions had no power to vary the sentence by quashing the sentence passed at the magistrates' court and committing to itself for sentence. The reason lies in the point already noted[17] that committal for sentence is not itself a sentence; if therefore magistrates elect to sit as a sentencing court instead of as a committing court Quarter Sessions could not go behind that election. Their power was to interfere with a sentence, not a decision as to whether the defendant should be committed or sentenced. This is presumably still true for the Crown Court.

If the appeal is against sentence only it may proceed on the basis of the facts relevant to sentence produced before the magistrates, if counsel for the appellant agrees to that course; there will then be no need for any evidence whatever to be called before the Crown Court. The same strictness of proof is not demanded in matters relevant to sentence as in matters relevant to conviction. In fact proceedings on an appeal against sentence normally take the same course as if the defendant had just been convicted, or had pleaded guilty, before the court.

From the Crown Court a further appeal lies by way of case stated to the Queen's Bench Division of the High Court; this will be considered below.

B APPEAL BY CASE STATED TO THE QUEEN'S BENCH DIVISION FROM MAGISTRATES' COURTS AND THE CROWN COURT

1 Magistrates' Courts

Any person who was a party to proceedings before a magistrates' court or (although not a party) is aggrieved by the conviction, order, determination

---

[13] Supreme Court Act 1981, s. 9(4). However the Crown Court cannot impose a sentence which the magistrates could not have imposed. Thus an unrepresented defendant who has not previously been sentenced to imprisonment cannot (subject to minor exceptions, as to which see p. 521, *ante*) be sentenced to imprisonment (Powers of Criminal Courts Act 1973, s. 21(1)). Accordingly, on appeal in such a case, the Crown Court cannot impose a sentence of imprisonment even though the accused is legally represented on his appeal: *R. v. Birmingham Justices, Ex parte Wyatt*, [1975] 3 All E.R. 847; [1976] 1 W.L.R. 260.

[14] See p. 535, *ante*.

[15] Supreme Court Act 1981, s. 48(2) (*c*). Note, in addition, the provisions as to ordering questions to be referred to the European Court for preliminary ruling (Crown Court (References to the European Court) Rules 1972); see pp. 185, 513, *ante*.

[16] In *R. v. Bullock*, [1964] 1 Q.B. 481; [1963] 3 All E.R. 506.

[17] See p. 463, *ante*.

or other proceeding may appeal against the proceeding on the ground that it is wrong in law or in excess of jurisdiction by applying to the magistrates' court to state a case for the opinion of a divisional court of the Queen's Bench Division of the High Court.[18] Thus, either the defendant or the prosecutor in a criminal case may make application for a case to be stated. Application may also be made by a person aggrieved, but:

> "the words 'person aggrieved' do not really mean a man who is disappointed of a benefit which he might have received if some other order had been made (still less does it mean someone having a merely sympathetic interest in the proceedings). A 'person aggrieved' must be a man who has suffered a legal grievance, a man against whom a decision has been pronounced which has wrongfully deprived him of something, or wrongfully refused him something, or wrongfully affected his title to something."[19]

A party to proceedings who has succeeded in part only may appeal against the incompleteness of his success. Executors of a person who has died since the hearing of the case in the magistrates' court are "interested", at any rate if a fine has been imposed, since the money to pay this would come out of the estate of the deceased; they may accordingly bring an appeal by way of case stated.[20] If the deceased had been sentenced to imprisonment the executors appear not to be "interested".[1]

Application must be made in writing, within 21 days after the day on which the decision of the magistrates' court was given;[2] again, if the magistrates adjourn after conviction, the day on which sentence is actually passed is the first day on which time begins to run.[2] The application should be delivered to the clerk of the magistrates' court whose decision is being questioned or sent to him by post; the names of the magistrates constituting the court do not have to be given and it is therefore immaterial that there is an error in their names.[3]

The application must identify the point of law on which the opinion of the High Court is sought.[4]

The magistrates may refuse to state a case only on the ground that the application is in their opinion frivolous, and may not refuse to state a case if the application is made by or under the direction of the Attorney-General, even in the unlikely event of such an application being considered frivolous.[5] On refusal the magistrates must give the applicant a certificate of refusal if he so requires; he may then apply to the High Court for an order of mandamus directing the justices to state a case.[6] On the making of the application,

---

[18] Magistrates' Courts Act 1980, s. 111(1).

[19] *Ex parte Sidebotham* (1880), 14 Ch.D. 458, at p. 465, *per* JAMES, L.J., described as "the best definition of the expression 'aggrieved' " in *R. v. London Sessions, Ex parte Westminster Corporation*, [1951] 2 K.B. 508, at p. 511; [1951] 1 All E.R. 1032, at p. 1033, *per* LORD GODDARD, C.J.

[20] *Hodgson v. Lakeman*, [1943] K.B. 15. *Aliter* in an appeal following trial on indictment: *R. v. Jefferies*, [1969] 1 Q.B. 120; [1968] 3 All E.R. 238.

[1] *R. v. Rowe*, [1955] 1 Q.B. 573; [1955] 2 All E.R. 234.

[2] Magistrates' Courts Act 1980, s. 111(2), (3).

[3] *R. v. Oxford (Bullingdon) Justices, Ex parte Bird*, [1948] 1 K.B. 100.

[4] Magistrates' Courts Rules 1981, r. 76(1).

[5] Magistrates' Courts Act 1980, s. 111(5).

[6] *Ibid.*, s. 111(6).

whether granted or refused, the applicant loses his right to appeal to the Crown Court.[7]

A "case" will normally contain a statement of the information as laid, the facts found, the contentions of the parties, the cases cited, the decision and the question or questions for the decision of the High Court. If one or other of the parties is contending that there was no evidence on which the magistrates could come to their decision, a statement of the evidence should be included. This form, originally settled by LORD GODDARD, C.J., should always be used. The case may be stated by all the justices whose decision is questioned or by any two of them[8] and may be stated in relation to a number of different prosecutions, even against different defendants on different days, provided that they raise precisely the same point. Under no circumstances should the case state that the decision was that of a majority, if that was the position.[9] The case should in any event be submitted to both parties for their consideration and in the event of any difficulty it should be left to the parties themselves to produce a draft and submit it to the magistrates for their consideration.[10] If, in spite of this, a party to an appeal considers that the facts have been improperly stated in the case he may apply to the Queen's Bench Division for the case to be remitted to the justices for restatement of the facts, the application being accompanied by an affidavit setting out the facts which it is alleged should go in the case.[11]

Periods of 21 days are allowed for delivering the draft case to the parties, for the parties to make representations and for the justices to prepare the final case.[12] These time-limits are not inflexible and may be extended, but in such event a written statement of the reasons for the delay must accompany the final case.[13]

On the hearing the court will hear and determine the questions of law arising, after argument by counsel for the parties. The court may allow argument on a point not raised in the court below or even take such a point itself,[14] provided that in each case the point is one of pure law, not requiring any evidence. The magistrates themselves may file an affidavit, setting out the grounds of the decision and any facts which they may consider to have a bearing on the issues;[15] in view of the existence of the case this procedure will rarely be appropriate. Unless misconduct is alleged there is no need for the justices to be represented by counsel. The court may reverse, affirm or amend the decision in respect of which the case has been stated, or may remit the matter to the magistrates with its opinion, or make such other order as it sees fit.[16]

---

[7] *Ibid.*, s. 111(4).

[8] Magistrates' Courts Rules 1981, r. 78(2).

[9] *More O'Ferrall, Ltd.* v. *Harrow U.D.C.*, [1947] K.B. 66, at p. 70; [1946] 2 All E.R. 489, at p. 491.

[10] *Cowlishaw* v. *Chalkley*, [1955] 1 All E.R. 367 n., [1955] 1 W.L.R. 101.

[11] *Spicer* v. *Warbley*, [1953] 1 All E.R. 284; [1953] 1 W.L.R. 334.

[12] Magistrates' Courts Rules 1981, rr. 77, 78.

[13] *Ibid.*, r. 79.

[14] *Whitehead* v. *Haines*, [1965] 1 Q.B. 200; [1964] 2 All E.R. 530.

[15] Review of Justices' Decisions Act 1872.

[16] Summary Jurisdiction Act 1857, s. 6. If a question arises which is appropriate to be referred to the European Court for a preliminary ruling (as to which, see p. 185, *ante*) the court may, of its own motion or on application, make an order whereupon proceedings will be stayed pending receipt of the ruling, unless the divisional court otherwise orders; R.S.C., O. 114.

2 The Crown Court

The Crown Court may also state a case for the opinion of the High Court. Either party to any order, judgment or other decision of the Crown Court, other than one relating solely to trial on indictment, may apply for a case to be stated on the ground that the decision is wrong in law or in excess of jurisdiction.[17] Thus, either party to an appeal from the magistrates' court, against conviction or sentence may apply, as (apparently) may a person sentenced at the Crown Court after committal for sentence from a magistrates' court. These provisions are in several respects an extension of the old law; however, a person aggrieved by the Crown Court's decision, but not a party, still has no right of appeal. Application should be made in writing to the appropriate officer of the Crown Court within 21 days after the decision; again, the Crown Court may only refuse to state a case if the application is considered frivolous.[18] The powers of the Queen's Bench Division appear to be the same as those exercisable on an appeal from the magistrates.[19]

C APPEAL TO THE HOUSE OF LORDS

Finally it should be noted that an appeal to the House of Lords may be made from the divisional court of the Queen's Bench Division, subject to the same conditions as those governing appeals from the Court of Appeal in the case of trial on indictment.[20] Thus there must be a certificate from the divisional court that a point of law of general public importance is involved in its decision and either the divisional court or the House of Lords must give leave to appeal on the ground that the point is one which ought to be considered by the House of Lords. In this way a summary offence may be considered by four courts; the magistrates' court, the Crown Court, the divisional court of the Queen's Bench Division and the House of Lords.[1]

D JUDICIAL REVIEW

Magistrates' courts and the Crown Court, in the exercise of their jurisdiction over summary offences, are inferior courts and therefore their proceedings

---

[17] Supreme Court Act 1981, s. 28. Certain decisions of the Crown Court are made final: see s. 28(2) (*b*).
[18] Crown Court Rules 1982, r. 26.
[19] The case of *Harris, Simon & Co., Ltd.* v. *Manchester City Council*, [1975] 1 All E.R. 412; [1975] 1 W.L.R. 100 has demonstrated a little known legal oddity whereby under the Manchester General Improvement Act 1851 an objection to the Manchester City Council's resolution to stop up two streets is made by way of appeal to the Crown Court (as successor to the jurisdiction of Quarter Sessions) where the objection is heard as an appeal by judge and jury. Since juries do not make detailed findings of fact, the divisional court on an appeal by way of case stated approached the case on the basis that the appeal could succeed only if the judge had misdirected the jury or if their conclusion was perverse, in the sense of being a conclusion which no reasonable jury could have reached. This instance of an appeal by way of case stated from the verdict of a jury appears to be unique.
[20] Administration of Justice Act 1960, s. 1; see p. 540, *ante.*
[1] *Spicer* v. *Holt*, [1977] A.C. 987; [1976] 3 All E.R. 71 is a case in which this happened. It might, in addition, be considered by the European Court, to the extent that a question arising in the proceedings was referred to that Court for a preliminary ruling; see p. 185, *ante.*

are amenable to judicial review by the High Court.[2] This procedure may be appropriate where there is no right of appeal. Thus, for example, it has been noted[3] that there is no right of appeal from an order for the payment of costs; nevertheless the High Court has on *Wednesbury* principles[4] been prepared to quash an order for costs which was so far outside the normal sum imposed as to involve an error of law.[5] Similarly, following an appeal against sentence from a magistrates' court to the Crown Court, there is no further appeal (except by way of case stated if a point of law is involved); nevertheless in *R. v. St. Albans Crown Court, Ex parte Cinnamond*[6] a disqualification of 18 months for careless driving, although within the jurisdiction of the court, was quashed as being so far outside the normal sentence imposed by courts for this offence as to enable the divisional court to hold that it must have involved an error of law.

---

2 See pp. 174–178, *ante* for details of this jurisdiction and procedure.
3 See p. 551, *ante*.
4 As to which see p. 178, *ante*.
5 *R. v. Tottenham Justices, Ex parte Joshi*, [1982] 2 All E.R. 507; [1982] 1 W.L.R. 631.
6 [1981] Q.B. 480; [1981] 1 All E.R. 802.

Outline of the Law of Evidence

CHAPTER 28

What is Evidence?

A NATURE OF JUDICIAL EVIDENCE

All litigation involves the court making findings of fact and applying the law to those facts. It is sometimes stated, erroneously, that one case turned solely on its facts while another was decided on a point of law. In fact there can be no litigation, civil or criminal, which does not involve a mixture of law and fact. It is a fundamental principle of English law that the courts do not adjudicate upon hypothetical legal problems, so that a factual situation must form the basis of every case. The law of evidence is concerned with the means by which facts are presented to the court. The facts which are presented to the court as the basis of the dispute which is the subject of the litigation are termed the "facts in issue". The law of evidence does not determine which facts are facts in issue in any particular case. This question is determined by reference to the substantive law, and, in civil cases, to the pleadings. Thus in a prosecution for murder, if the accused pleads not guilty it is for the prosecution to prove the elements of that crime according to the common law definition of murder. This involves proving that the accused unlawfully killed the deceased and that he did so with malice aforethought. These facts are thus facts in issue. If the defence of insanity is raised the accused's sanity becomes a fact in issue. These are matters of substantive law. The province of the law of evidence is the means by which these facts in issue may validly be proved. Thus Blackstone defined judicial evidence as:

> "That which demonstrates, makes clear, or ascertains the truth of the very fact or point in issue, either on the one side or on the other."[1]

It ought to be noted that the word "evidence" is variously used in two distinct senses. In its narrower, and more usual, meaning "evidence" connotes the means by which the facts in issue are proved. This is the meaning inherent in Taylor's classic definition of judicial evidence as:

> "All the legal means, exclusive of mere argument, which tend to prove or disprove any matter of fact, the truth of which is submitted to judicial investigation."[2]

---

[1] Comm. 367.
[2] *A Treatise on the Law of Evidence* (12th Edn.), 1, 1.

The second, and wider, sense in which the word "evidence" is used is to describe those facts which may be proved, rather than the means by which they are proved. Facts may often be proved as evidence of the existence of other facts. This type of evidence is known as "circumstantial evidence".[3] For example, in a prosecution for murder a witness may testify to the fact that he sold the murder weapon to the accused. This fact is not in itself a fact in issue but it is relevant as tending to show that the accused killed the deceased, which is, of course, a fact in issue. In the above example, therefore, the word "evidence" may be used to describe both the testimony of the witness and the fact to which he testifies. Phipson's definition of judicial evidence embodies both these meanings of the word "evidence":

> "First, the means, apart from argument and inference, whereby the court is informed as to the issues of fact as ascertained by the pleadings; secondly, the subject-matter of such means."[4]

This definition applies rather to civil than to criminal proceedings since only in the former are the facts in issue ascertained by reference to the pleadings, there being, of course, no pleadings in criminal cases where facts in issue are ascertained by reference to substantive law.

Thus the law of evidence deals, to a limited extent, with what facts may be proved as well as with how those facts may be proved.[5] Where the question arises as to what facts may or must be proved in any case, this question may depend upon a consideration of the law of evidence, of substantive law or of rules of procedure. For this reason there is an overlap between evidence and substantive law and between evidence and procedure. Just as substantive law may sometimes be seen to be "secreted in the interstices of procedure", so may it be secreted in the law of evidence.

1   Relationship between evidence and substantive law

As stated above the question of whether or not a fact may be proved to the court is sometimes dependent upon rules of evidence and sometimes upon rules of law. It is sometimes asserted that rules which determine what facts may be proved are not rules of evidence at all. Thus the thirteenth report of the Law Reform Committee in 1966 dealing with hearsay evidence in civil proceedings[6] stated that:

> "Questions as to *what* facts must be proved to give rise to a cause of action or to a defence thereto, or as to *what* facts may not be proved, are questions of substantive law . . . even though the answer to such a question may sometimes be disguised as a rule of evidence."

Nevertheless although such rules sometimes have the effect of rules of law they are generally treated as rules of evidence. Usually it will be of purely academic interest whether a rule is treated as a rule of evidence or as a rule of law. However, the classification is important in at least two circumstances.

---

3   See p. 562, *post.*
4   *Law of Evidence* (13th Edn.), p. 2.
5   In fact the word "evidence" is sometimes used in a third sense as meaning "admissible evidence"; for example in the words "that's not evidence".
6   Cmnd. 2964.

First, in conflict of laws cases any rule which the English courts classify as a rule of evidence is applied in a case irrespective of which system of substantive law is appropriate to decide the case. For example in *Leroux* v. *Brown*,[7] a contract, valid according to the law by which it was to be construed, was held unenforceable in the English courts because of the absence of writing required under the Statute of Frauds, the requirement being treated as a matter of evidence.

The second circumstance in which the classification of a rule as a rule of evidence or a rule of law is critical occurs in the interpretation of statutes. Since courts are bound to adopt the procedure (including rules of evidence since these are procedural) obtaining at the hearing, there is a presumption that statutes concerned with procedural matters are retrospective in the sense that the statutory rule in question applies irrespective of the date of the events to which the evidence is directed. This is contrary to the general presumption against retrospective operation which applies to statutes which affect substantive law.[8]

Having illustrated that it is sometimes important to distinguish a rule of evidence from a rule of law it must, unfortunately, be stated that there is no acid test by which evidence may be distinguished from law. Estoppel, for example, is a rule of evidence which sometimes has the effect of a rule of law in that it, in effect, creates a right by preventing the other party from denying that right. The doctrine of *Central London Property Trust, Ltd.* v. *High Trees House, Ltd.*[9] is a form of estoppel and therefore a rule of evidence though it has the effect of a rule of law by creating a contractual obligation which would not otherwise exist. Presumptions are rules of evidence but they may also sometimes have the effect of a rule of law. For example there was, until 1963,[10] a rule that a husband who had sexual intercourse with his wife knowing that she had committed a matrimonial offence was thereby irrebuttably presumed to have condoned that offence. It has been established that this was a rule of evidence[11] though it had the effect of removing a right completely. In truth every presumption which is irrebuttable has the effect of a rule of law since it creates or extinguishes some right or obligation.

2· Relationship between evidence and procedure

Evidence is often regarded as a branch of procedure. The term "adjective law" is used to describe evidence and procedure and is distinct from "substantive law" which determines rights and liabilities. Since evidence is a branch of procedure it might appear that any statutory power to make rules of procedure would include a power to make rules of evidence. For this reason "evidence" as a branch of procedure is limited to its narrower meaning as governing the way in which facts may be proved rather than what facts may be proved. Thus a rule of court which provided for the admission of

---

[7] (1852), 12 C.B. 801.
[8] See p. 100, *ante*: for a modern illustration of the importance of classification in the interpretation of statutes, see *Blyth* v. *Blyth*, [1966] A.C. 643; [1966] 1 All E.R. 524.
[9] [1947] K.B. 130; [1956] 1 All E.R. 256n.
[10] Matrimonial Causes Act 1963, s. 1.
[11] *Blyth* v. *Blyth* (*supra*). The Divorce Reform Act 1969 removed the point of the case since condonation is no longer a bar to divorce.

facts otherwise irrelevant would be *ultra vires* as being a rule of law rather than a rule of procedure. The power to make rules governing the means of proof in the Supreme Court is now contained in section 84 of the Supreme Court Act 1981 and rules are made[12] under this section.

B CLASSIFICATIONS OF JUDICIAL EVIDENCE

While it is important to characterise rules of evidence so as to distinguish them from rules of law it is less important to arrive at a subsidiary classification of the rules themselves. Nevertheless, though certain classifications are of little practical importance, certain major subdivisions of evidence cannot be ignored since the courts and even, occasionally, the legislature refer specifically to certain types of evidence; for example, hearsay. For this reason the major subdivisions of judicial evidence are set out briefly below.

1   Direct and circumstantial

Direct evidence is evidence of the facts in issue themselves; the testimony of an eye-witness or a written confession, for example. Circumstantial evidence is evidence of other facts from which a fact in issue may be inferred. For example, in a prosecution for murder the testimony of a witness who claims to have seen the killing is direct evidence since the killing of the deceased by the accused is a fact in issue. On the other hand evidence that the accused purchased a gun, that his fingerprints were found on the gun, that the bullet which caused death was fired from the same gun and that the accused had previously threatened the deceased are all items of circumstantial evidence. None of the above facts are themselves facts in issue but each supports the existence of a fact in issue; that the accused shot the deceased. It will be appreciated from the above example that circumstantial evidence is certainly no less cogent than direct evidence. Direct evidence may more easily be fabricated or inaccurate than a strong chain of circumstantial evidence. Incidentally it may be noted that the phrase "circumstantial evidence" may be used to describe either the fact which is proved or the means of its proof. Thus where a witness testifies that the accused's fingerprints were found on the murder weapon, both his testimony and the fact to which he testifies are described as circumstantial evidence.

2   Original and hearsay

This classification relates to the means of proof. Original evidence[13] is proof of a fact by "first-hand" proof. This is usually the testimony of a witness who perceived the fact with his own senses, though either a document or an object (real evidence) may constitute original evidence. For example a letter

---

[12] The Rules of the Supreme Court (Revision) 1965 (as amended), the principal rules currently in operation, were made under s. 99 of the Judicature Act 1925, the precursor of s. 84 of the 1981 Act; see p. 293, *ante*.

[13] It is fair to warn the student that this terminology is not universal. "Original evidence" is described by some commentators as "direct evidence". See, for example, Nokes, *An Introduction to Evidence* (4th Edn.), p. 10.

containing a threat is original evidence of the words of the threat; the production of a knife in court is original evidence of the length of the blade. Hearsay evidence is "second-hand" evidence. It consists of evidence of what someone else said or wrote as proof of the truth of what was said or written. Hearsay evidence may be oral or written. For example a policeman's notebook containing the statement of a witness to an accident is hearsay evidence of the accident. It should be noted that evidence of what another person said or wrote is not necessarily hearsay. If it is submitted to prove not the truth of what was said or written, but merely the fact that it was said or written, it is original, not hearsay, evidence. For example the testimony of a witness that he heard X threaten Y is original evidence, since its purpose is to prove that a statement was made. On the other hand, the testimony of a witness to the effect that he heard X, immediately before being shot, shout out Y's name is hearsay, since its purpose is to prove the truth of what X stated, i.e., that Y was his murderer. The distinction between original and hearsay evidence is of great importance because hearsay evidence is generally excluded as a means of proof.[14]

3 Best and secondary

The "best evidence" rule is one of the oldest common law rules of evidence. It is self-explanatory; the best (or most direct) evidence of a fact must be adduced. Thus the best evidence of the contents or existence of a document is the production of the original; a copy is secondary evidence. The best evidence of the condition of a physical object is the production of that object to the court. The rule also operated to exclude circumstantial evidence where direct evidence was available.[15] The best evidence rule is of declining importance. It is no longer a bar to the reception of circumstantial evidence and it does not now apply to real evidence.[16] It does, however, still apply to proof of the contents of private documents although, even here, it is subject to several exceptions.[17]

4 Oral, documentary and real

This is the modern classification of means of proof. Oral evidence is the testimony of witnesses, documentary evidence the production of documents and real evidence the production of physical objects for the inspection of the court. The distinction between documentary and real evidence is important since the best evidence rule applies to the former but not to the latter. Although the distinction is generally self-evident, difficulty may arise where a physical object bears an inscription; for example a tombstone, a car number plate or a banner. The test of whether these objects are to be treated as real or documentary evidence is the purpose for which they are produced. If they are tendered as proof of their physical existence they are real evidence while if they are submitted as evidence of the matter inscribed they are documents.

---

[14] See p. 657, *post.*
[15] *Williams* v. *East India Co.* (1802), 3 East 192.
[16] *Hocking* v. *Ahlquist Brothers, Ltd.,* [1944] K.B. 120; [1943] 2 All E.R. 722; see p. 650, *post.*
[17] See p. 641, *post.*

As an alternative to the production of an object in court, the judge and jury may leave the court to inspect an object or a site. Such an inspection is termed a "view" and may be classified as real evidence.[18] It is less easy to characterise the demeanour of witnesses. The court is undoubtedly entitled to have regard to the physical characteristics and demeanour of witnesses, particularly in assessing their cogency. This is usually described as real evidence though demeanour is sometimes regarded as an ancillary of oral evidence. Where the physical characteristic of a witness is a fact in issue, such as facial disfigurement, it is undoubtedly a form of real evidence.[19]

C   FUNCTIONS OF JUDGE AND JURY

The respective functions of judge and jury differ irrespective of whether they are trying a civil or a criminal case. This demarcation between the function of the judge and that of the jury obtains even where there is no jury, as is the case in most civil actions at the present day. In these cases the judge discharges the functions of both judge and jury but the functions themselves remain distinct, so that different considerations must be observed by the judge according to whether he is acting *qua* judge or *qua* jury.

The general rule is that the judge decides questions of law while the jury decides questions of fact and assesses damages. Where the question is one of mixed law and fact it is for the judge to determine the point of law and for the jury to decide the facts, assuming that the judge's decision on the law does not effectively dispose of the question in issue in which event the facts must not be left to the jury. For example, where an innuendo is pleaded in the tort of defamation it is for the judge to decide whether the words are capable of bearing the defamatory meaning alleged. If he decides this question, which is a question of law, in the affirmative it is then for the jury to decide whether the words are, in fact, defamatory.[20] However this question must be left to the jury only if the judge decides that the words are capable of bearing the alleged meaning. If he decides to the contrary he must withdraw the question from the jury and failure to do so is a ground of appeal on a point of law.[1] Since every case, civil or criminal, involves mixed law and fact it follows that the issues of fact must be withdrawn from the jury where the judge's decision on any question of law conclusively determines the case. Such a finding is sometimes made following a submission of "no case to answer" by the defence. A finding of no case to answer may be based on a point of law or on the point that there is no evidence, or insufficient evidence, of an essential fact in the case of the plaintiff or prosecution. Thus where, in a prosecution for dangerous driving, the prosecution failed to call any evidence to identify

---

[18] *L.G.O. Co., Ltd.* v. *Lavell*, [1901] 1 Ch. 135; *Buckingham* v. *Daily News, Ltd.*, [1956] 2 Q.B. 535; [1956] 2 All E.R. 904; see p. 650, *post*.

[19] See *Cole* v. *United Dairies (London), Ltd.*, [1941] 1 K.B. 100; [1940] 4 All E.R. 318.

[20] This practice constitutes an exception to the general rule that the construction of documents and the determination of the ordinary meaning of words are matters of law for the judge; the exception does not appear to be confined to defamation cases (*R.* v. *Sunair Holidays, Ltd.*, [1973] 2 All E.R. 1233; [1973] 1 W.L.R. 1105).

[1] *Nevill* v. *Fine Arts and General Insurance Co.*, [1897] A.C. 68.

the accused as the driver of the car it was held that there was no case to answer.[2]

As well as determining questions of law and deciding whether there is evidence in support of material allegations of fact, the judge also decides all questions concerning the admissibility of evidence, even where the question of admissibility depends upon a preliminary finding of fact, such as whether an original documents has been destroyed or whether a confession is voluntary.[3] Although most questions regarding the admissibility of evidence are determined by the judge in the presence of the jury, the jury in a criminal case is invariably required to retire while the judge decides on the admissibility of evidence whose admission would be highly prejudicial to the accused, such as a confession or evidence of the accused's previous convictions.

Finally the judge, even when sitting with a jury, decides certain questions of fact by way of exception to the general rule that issues of fact are for the jury. It has already been noted that the judge decides questions of fact upon which the admissibility of evidence depends. In addition the judge decides other isolated issues of fact such as questions of foreign law, which must be proved as a question of fact[4] or whether a convenant in restraint of trade is reasonable.[5] Other questions of reasonableness are nowadays treated as questions of fact for the jury, such as whether the defendant in an action for negligence acted as a reasonable man.

Having dealt with these introductory matters the law of evidence may be divided into three parts: (1) what facts may be proved (relevance and admissibility); (2) on whom is the burden of proving these facts and what standard of proof is required of that party, and (3) how may these facts be proved (and how may they not be proved). The ensuing chapters deal with these questions.

---

2 *Middleton* v. *Rowlett*, [1954] 2 All E.R. 277; [1954] 1 W.L.R. 831.
3 *Chan Wai-Keung* v. *R.*, [1967] 2 A.C. 160; [1967] 1 All E.R. 948.
4 See p. 657, *post.*
5 *Mason* v. *Provident Clothing and Supply Co., Ltd.*, [1913] A.C. 724, at p. 732.

CHAPTER 29

Relevance and Admissibility

A GENERAL CONDITIONS OF RELEVANCE AND ADMISSIBILITY

When discussing the relevance and admissibility of evidence, the word "evidence" is used as meaning facts, rather than the means by which facts may be proved (except in so far as facts may be proved by other facts). Thus it is very confusing to speak of hearsay evidence as being relevant or irrelevant since hearsay evidence is a means of proof. Similarly opinion evidence is neither relevant nor irrelevant, it is a means of proving facts which may in themselves either be relevant or not. Confusion arises particularly since hearsay and opinion evidence are almost always described as "inadmissible". It would be more logical to speak of hearsay and opinion as "unpermitted" means of proof, leaving admissibility to relate solely to the issue of *what* facts may be proved irrespective of *how* they may be proved.

In order to be receivable by the court evidence must be both relevant and admissible. Relevant facts form a wider category than admissible facts. All admissible facts are relevant[1] though not all relevant facts are admissible. Two classes of facts are relevant; the facts in issue and other facts from which the facts in issue may be inferred (circumstantial evidence). There is rarely any difficulty in determining whether or not a fact is or is not a fact in issue. This question is determined by reference to the substantive law and, in civil cases, to the pleadings if there are any. Difficulty is encountered, however, in determining whether a fact, not in itself in issue, is relevant as circumstantial evidence. Basically the question of whether or not one fact may be inferred from proof of another is a question of logic. Stephen defined the word "relevant" as meaning that.

> "Any two facts to which it is applied are so related to each other that according to the common course of events one either taken by itself or in connection with other facts proves or renders probable the past, present or future existence or non-existence of the other."[2]

---

[1] It is arguable that facts upon which the admissibility of evidence depends, such as whether a document has been lost or whether a prospective witness has died, are admissible but not relevant within the general definition. It is probably better to regard such facts as indirectly relevant; see Cross, *Evidence* (5th Edn.), p. 25, text and footnotes.

[2] *Digest of the Law of Evidence* (12th Edn.), art. 1.

Obviously there are endless combinations and permutations of facts and in each case it will be for the judge to decide whether or not one fact is logically probative of a fact in issue and therefore relevant as circumstantial evidence. Circumstantial evidence may exist prior to a fact in issue, contemporaneously with it or subsequent to it. Thus, if the speed of a vehicle at a given moment is a fact in issue, evidence may be received of the speed of the vehicle a few moments earlier.[3] Evidence is also admissible of facts which supply a motive for conduct the existence of which is in issue. Thus familiarity between a husband and another woman may be evidence in support of subsequent alleged adultery. The purchase of poison by an accused murderer[4] and the financial standing of a person accused of arson with intent to defraud an insurance company[5] have been held to be relevant evidence. These are examples of circumstantial evidence existing prior to the facts in issue. Circumstantial evidence may exist subsequent to the facts in issue. Thus a promise to marry the mother of an illegitimate child was admitted in *Lloyd* v. *Powell Duffryn Steam Coal Co., Ltd.*[6] as evidence of the paternity of the child. Similarly an illegitimate child's physical appearance or blood-group would be evidence of paternity. Evidence that a person was alive on a given day obviously proves that he was alive on an earlier day and is therefore relevant.[7] Attempts by parties to suborn witnesses to commit perjury,[8] to tamper with evidence[4] or to give a false alibi to the police[9] have all been held to be relevant to issues of guilt or liability. The third class of circumstantial evidence consists of facts contemporaneous with the facts in issue. It is on this basis that the whereabouts of an accused person at the time of the alleged crime is relevant. Similarly the fact that a man and a woman spent a night together in a hotel bedroom is evidence of adultery. Those facts which are relevant to the facts in issue on account of their proximity or contemporaneity are often denoted by the expression *res gestae*. So much evidence is received under this head that it merits separate consideration.

Res gestae

This expression has been described as:

> "A phrase adopted to provide a respectable legal cloak for a variety of cases to which no formula of precision can be applied."[10]

and as an expression which:

> "like many Latin phrases, is often used to cover situations insufficiently analysed in clear English terms."[11]

---

[3] *Beresford* v. *St. Albans Justices* (1905), 22 T.L.R. 1.
[4] *R.* v. *Palmer* (1856), unreported. See Stephen, *History of the Criminal Law,* III, p. 389.
[5] *R.* v. *Grant* (1865), 4 F. & F. 322.
[6] [1914] A.C. 733.
[7] *Re Watkins,* [1953] 2 All E.R. 1113; [1953] 1 W.L.R. 1323.
[8] *Moriarty* v. *London, Chatham and Dover Rail. Co.* (1870), L.R. 5 Q.B. 314.
[9] *R.* v. *Knight,* [1966] 1 All E.R. 647; [1966] 1 W.L.R. 230.
[10] *Homes* v. *Newman,* [1931] 2 Ch. 112, at p. 120 *per* LORD TOMLIN.
[11] *Ratten* v. *R.,* [1972] A.C. 378, at p. 388; [1971] All E.R. 801, at p. 806, *per* LORD WILBERFORCE.

Nevertheless the expression is commonly used to describe facts or statements which either form part of or accompany the facts in issue. Thus the facts in issue are themselves strictly part of the *res gestae* but, since the relevance of a fact in issue is never in dispute, the question before the court is usually whether other evidence is part of the *res gestae*. The evidence alleged to form part of the *res gestae* may be either an act or a statement. In either event its admissibility depends upon its proximity, in time or in place, to a fact in issue.

The criteria for admissibility were restated by the Privy Council in *Ratten* v. *R.*[12] and the speech of LORD WILBERFORCE may be taken to have settled the law for the time being:

> "The possibility of concoction, or fabrication, where it exists, is . . . probably the real test which judges in fact apply. In their Lordships' opinion this should be recognised and applied directly as the relevant test: the test should not be the uncertain one whether the making of the statement was in some sense part of the event or transaction. This may often be difficult to establish: such external matters as the time which elapses between the events and the speaking of the words (or vice versa), and differences in location being relevant factors but not, taken by themselves, decisive criteria. As regards statements made after the event, it must be for the judge, by preliminary ruling, to satisfy himself that the statement was so clearly made in circumstances of spontaneity or involvement in the event that the possibility of concoction can be disregarded. Conversely, if he considers that the statement was made by way of narrative of a detached prior event so that the speaker was so disengaged from it as to be able to construct or adapt his account, he should exclude it. And the same must in principle be true of statements made before the event. The test should not be the uncertain one, whether the making of the statement should be regarded as part of the event or transaction. This may often be difficult to show. But if the drama, leading up to the climax, has commenced and assumed such intensity and pressure that the utterance can safely be regarded as a true reflection of what was unrolling or actually happening, it ought to be received. The expression *res gestae* may conveniently sum up these criteria, but the reality of them must always be kept in mind: it is this that lies behind the best reasoned of the judges' rulings."

In the instant case the evidence in question was that of a telephone operator who stated that, at about the time the deceased was shot by her husband, a woman telephoned from the deceased's premises in a hysterical state and said "Get me the police please". The defendant's version of events was that the gun had discharged by accident while he was cleaning it. Evidence of the telephone conversation was held admissible on the basis that it was a fact which showed that a telephone call was made and the mental state of the caller. However the Privy Council went on to state that even if it was hearsay evidence it was admissible as part of the *res gestae* on the basis of the principles stated above.

It is indeed where the evidence alleged to be relevant as part of the *res gestae* is a statement rather than a fact that difficulty arises. This is because a statement may be treated either as a fact in itself or as proof of another fact. In the latter case the statement is *prima facie* inadmissible hearsay. For example, the exclamation "Stop it Harry, you're frightening me" made by a

---

[12] [1972] A.C. 378, at p. 389; [1971] 3 All E.R. 801, at p. 807; followed in *R.* v. *Nye and Loan* (1978), 66 Cr. App. Rep. 252 and in *R.* v. *Turnbull* (*infra*).

victim of rape is in itself a relevant fact since the making of the statement tends to prove absence of consent which is a fact in issue. However it is also hearsay evidence of the identity of the assailant if the statement is reported by a third party who overheard it. Were a statement identifying the assailant made subsequently it would be inadmissible as proof of identity[13] It is admissible in the first place only because it forms part of the *res gestae*. It is in this context that it becomes important to determine the scope of the *res gestae*, for a statement which is hearsay evidence of another fact, such as identity or the state of mind of the maker, is only admissible as proof of that fact if it forms part of the *res gestae*. This is a genuine exception to the rule against hearsay.[14]

Thus the test as to admissibility now appears to be whether the statement is "made in circumstances of spontaneity or involvement" as opposed to being made "by way of narrative of a detached prior event". The old requirement of contemporaneity having been abolished many old cases must now be regarded as incorrectly decided on their facts. In the well-known case of *R.* v. *Bedingfield*[13] the deceased emerged from a room with her throat cut and was heard to utter the words "See what Bedingfield has done to me"[15] following which she died. COCKBURN, C.J. held this statement inadmissible as hearsay and not forming part of the *res gestae* since "it was something stated by her after it was all over, whatever it was, and after the act was completed". Applying the criteria laid down in *Ratten* v. *R.* the evidence would clearly be admissible.[16] On the same reasoning the House of Lords in *R.* v. *Christie*[17] refused to regard as part of the *res gestae* a statement made by a small boy which identified the accused, the statement being made some minutes after the alleged incident; the Privy Council in *Teper* v. *R*,[18] rejected a similar statement made some twenty-five minutes after the start of a fire in respect of which the accused, who was identified by the statement, was charged with arson. However, both of these cases would appear to be clear examples of "narrative of a detached prior event" and would appear therefore to be correctly decided on their facts.

In addition to the above criteria, the statement must explain a fact in issue. Clearly a statement cannot be relevant to a fact in issue if it concerns facts other than the facts in issue. Thus in *Agassiz* v. *London Tramway Co., Ltd.*[19] a statement made shortly after an accident by the conductor of a tramcar to

---

13 See *R.* v. *Bedingfield* (1897), 14 Cox C.C. 341.

14 See p. 666, *post.*

15 The precise words used were not proved at the trial and slightly different words such as "See what Harry's done!" are sometimes attributed to the deceased.

16 In *R.* v. *Turnbull*, [1984] Crim. L.R. 620 the Court of Appeal expressed no doubt that if the events in *Bedingfield* had occurred in the present day the statement would be admitted; in that case the court upheld the trial judge's admission of statements of the deceased, identifying the defendant as his assailant, made in a public house into which the deceased had staggered having been stabbed in a car park about 100 yards away and, subsequently, in an ambulance on his way to hospital, where he died about half an hour after admission.

17 [1914] A.C. 545.

18 [1952] A.C. 480; [1952] 2 All E.R. 447; compare *Davies* v. *Fortior, Ltd.*, [1952] 1 All E.R. 1359 where a statement made within two minutes of an accident was admitted in a civil case. In *Tickle* v. *Tickle*, [1968] 2 All E.R. 154; [1968] 1 W.L.R. 937, evidence was received of a statement made by a doctor concerning a patient's health, where the patient's belief in the state of his health was something "savouring of a *res*".

19 (1873), 21 W.R. 199.

the effect that the driver had been off the line five or six times earlier in the day was held inadmissible as referring not to a fact in issue but to earlier conduct.

Evidence, in order to be receivable, must be admissible as well as relevant. Admissible evidence comprises all relevant evidence which is not subject to a rule of exclusion. Thus relevance depends upon logic whereas admissibility is a question of law. It follows that there are two separate bases upon which evidence is excluded; it may be irrelevant or, alternatively, relevant but subject to a rule of exclusion and therefore inadmissible. In practice it is common to refer to the evidence as inadmissible in either case.

B   IRRELEVANT EVIDENCE

Any fact which is not in issue and which does not tend to prove a fact in issue is irrelevant. Having stated this fact it might be supposed that any classification of irrelevant evidence would be superfluous. However the law regards as irrelevant various classes of facts which the layman might suppose to be relevant. For example, the fact that a person has behaved in a certain way on a number of previous occasions is generally irrelevant to the issue of whether he has behaved in that way on the occasion in question though many would doubtless consider such evidence to be valuable. Similarly the character and previous convictions of a person accused of crime might seem to many indicative of guilt, but the law excludes such facts as irrelevant. Consequently, in this section certain classes of facts are examined which, although they may appear to have probative value, are as a rule regarded as irrelevant and therefore inadmissible.

1   Res inter alios acta

One of the oldest rules of evidence is that *res inter alios acta alteri nocere non debet* (no one should be harmed by things done between strangers). The rule is no longer one of fundamental importance since it has been superseded by the wider rules relating to relevance, though certain aspects of the rule still exist. For example an admission or confession is binding only upon the maker and not upon third parties who are implicated, although there are exceptions to this principle.[20] Similarly conduct on the part of third persons having no interest in the litigation is generally irrelevant. Thus in *Wright* v. *Doe* d. *Tatham*[1] the fact that letters were written to a testator on the assumption that he was sane was held not to be evidence of his sanity.

Nevertheless there are a number of circumstances in which the conduct or statements of strangers to the procedings are admitted as relevant. For example, on a charge of handling stolen goods, the fact of the goods being stolen must be proved; in order to prove his legitimacy a person may show that his parents lived together as man and wife;[2] an admission by a predecessor in title binds his successors in title;[3] an admission by an agent may bind his

---

[20] See pp. 666, 669, *post*.
[1] (1838), 4 Bing. N.C. 489.
[2] *Doe* d. *Fleming* v. *Fleming* (1827), 4 Bing. 266.
[3] *Woolway* v. *Rowe* (1834), 1 Ad. & El. 114.

principal;[4] the conduct of a managing director may be relevant on a charge against a limited company of conspiracy to defraud.[5] In all these circumstances, and in many others, facts are admitted which would fall within the description *res inter alios acta*. For this reason it is better to regard the operation of the rule as being confined to the few special examples given above.

2 Similar facts

As a rule evidence that a person has behaved in a certain way on other occasions is not relevant to prove that he behaved in a similar way on the occasion in question merely because of the similarity of the conduct. Such evidence is described as "similar fact" evidence and is excluded as irrelevant. The existence of this rule is recognised and illustrated in a number of leading cases. Perhaps the best-known statement of the rule is to be found in the advice of the Privy Council delivered by LORD HERSCHELL, L.C. in *Makin v. A-G. for New South Wales:*[6]

> "It is undoubtedly not competent for the prosecution to adduce evidence tending to show that the accused has been guilty of criminal acts other than those covered by the indictment, for the purpose of leading to the conclusion that the accused is a person likely from his criminal conduct or character to have committed the offence for which he is being tried. On the other hand, the mere fact that the evidence adduced tends to show the commission of other crimes does not render it inadmissible if it be relevant to an issue before the jury, and it may be so relevant if it bears upon the question whether the acts alleged to constitute the crime charged in the indictment were designed or accidental, or to rebut a defence which would otherwise be open to the accused."

The rule generally operates to exclude evidence of other conduct by the accused in criminal cases, though it is not confined to such evidence. Thus in *Harris v. Director of Public Prosecutions*[7] a policeman was indicted on eight counts of larceny from an office in a Bradford market. The counts were tried together and the eight offences were committed in a somewhat similar manner at times when the accused might have been on duty in the vicinity. Harris was acquitted on seven counts but convicted on the eighth count. His conviction was quashed on the eighth count since the summing-up had not warned the jury that what had occurred on the earlier occasions was irrelevant to the accused's guilt on the eighth count. Similarly in *R. v. Rodley*[8] a conviction of burglary (with intent to ravish) was quashed by the Court of Criminal Appeal because of the wrongful admission of evidence that the accused had entered another house by the chimney later the same night and had consensual sexual intercourse with the occupant.[9] The rule also applies in civil cases. The fact that a brewer had supplied good beer to other publicans

---

4 *Re Devala Provident Gold Mining Co.* (1883), 22 Ch.D. 593.
5 *R. v. I.C.R. Haulage, Ltd.*, [1944] K.B. 551; [1944] 1 All E.R. 691.
6 [1894] A.C. 57, at p. 65; This statement was expressly approved by the House of Lords in *Director of Public Prosecutions* v. *Boardman* (*infra*).
7 [1952] A.C. 694; [1952] 1 All E.R. 1044.
8 [1913] 3 K.B. 468.
9 See also *Noor Mohamed* v. *R.*, [1949] A.C. 182; [1949] 1 All E.R. 365; *R.* v. *Holmes* (1871), L.R. 10 C.C.R. 334.

was not evidence that he had not supplied bad beer to the defendant publican in *Holcombe* v. *Hewson*.[10] On the issue of whether a person has been negligent on a particular occasion it is not relevant either that he has or has not been negligent on other occasions, even though performing similar conduct on all the occasions in question.

However, as appears from the celebrated statement of the rule quoted above, not all similar fact evidence is irrelevant. It is not relevant merely because of its similarity to a fact in issue but, if it is otherwise logically relevant, conduct on other occasions is admissible. Thus on a charge of rape the fact that the prosecutrix has had consensual sexual intercourse with the accused on other occasions is relevant to the issue of consent and therefore admissible evidence notwithstanding that it is similar fact evidence.[11]

In *Director of Public Prosecutions* v. *Boardman*[12] the House of Lords once again[13] had occasion to examine this difficult branch of the law of evidence. The appellant, the headmaster of a boarding school for boys, was charged with sexual offences in relation to two pupils. There were certain similarities between the alleged offences, notably that the appellant's request and desire was that he should play the passive part and the boy the active part and that, on each occasion, an approach by the appellant was made during a nocturnal visit to a dormitory. The House of Lords, not without hesitation for it was clearly (and was stated by certain of their Lordships to be) a borderline case, dismissed the appeal, holding that the evidence on each count was admissible in relation to the other.

The statements of law embodied in their Lordships' speeches are basically little more than a reaffirmation of the principles set out in *Makin*'s case. As LORD HAILSHAM observed:[14]

> "Attempts to codify the rules of common sense are to be resisted."

The basic test, in determining whether a case falls on one side of the line or the other, is whether, as a matter of logic and common sense, the "striking resemblances" or "unusual features" which the facts have in common are such that to ignore them would affront common sense. Thus, to adopt an example given by LORD HAILSHAM:[14]

> "In a sex case . . . whilst a repeated homosexual act by itself might be insufficient to admit the evidence as confirmatory of identity or design, the fact that it was alleged to have been performed wearing the ceremonial headdress of a Red Indian chief or other eccentric garb might well in appropriate circumstances suffice."

---

[10] (1810), 2 Camp. 391.

[11] *R.* v. *Riley* (1887), 18 Q.B.D. 481.

[12] [1975] A.C. 421, [1974] 3 All E.R. 887.

[13] In *Director of Public Prosecutions* v. *Kilbourne*, [1973] A.C. 729; [1973] 1 All E.R. 440 the question of the admissibility of similar fact evidence arose but, eventually, was not dealt with by the House of Lords by reason of counsel for the respondent's agreement that there were striking features of resemblance between the acts alleged to have been committed in one count and those alleged to have been committed in the others. Accordingly the *ratio* of the case is concerned with corroboration (as to which, see p. 623, *post*).

[14] [1975] A.C., at p. 454; [1974] 3 All E.R., at p. 906.

LORD SALMON used the phrase[15] "Uniquely or strikingly similar" while LORD CROSS suggested[16] that the test was:

> "whether the similar fact evidence taken together with the other evidence . . . would point so strongly to his guilt that only an ultra-cautious jury, if they accepted it as true, would acquit in face of it."

Nevertheless, while counsel on behalf of defendants frequently cite these passages in an attempt to exclude similar fact evidence, it is clear that the courts will admit such evidence in circumstances in which the similarities are far less striking than those in LORD HAILSHAM's example. Thus in *R*. v. *Rance*, LORD WIDGERY C.J. said:[17]

> "It seems to us that one must be careful not to attach too much importance to Lord Salmon's vivid phrase 'uniquely or strikingly similar'. The gist of what is being said both by Lord Cross and by Lord Salmon is that evidence is admissible as similar fact evidence if, but only if, it goes beyond showing a tendency to commit crimes of this kind and is positively probative in regard to the crime now charged. That, we think is the test which we have to apply on the question of the correctness or otherwise of the admission of the similar fact evidence in this case."

Various attempts have been made to classify the types of case in which similar fact evidence will be admitted. These cases are generally treated as exceptions to the rule excluding similar fact evidence and the most important of them are set out below. Nevertheless, in *Boardman* the House of Lords demonstrated little, if any, enthusiasm for this approach. The categories are clearly not closed and are best regarded as specific instances of the application of the second proposition of LORD HERSCHELL in the passage from *Makin*'s case quoted above.

a System

Conduct on other occasions is treated as relevant to conduct which is in issue where, taken together, they may be said to form part of a systematic course of conduct. This principle is construed very narrowly. The mere fact that conduct is repeated on several occasions does not constitute a system. The question is one of degree. In *Harris* v. *Director of Public Prosecutions*,[18] eight offences of larceny from the same office in the same market did not constitute a system. However in *Makin* v. *A-G. for New South Wales*[19] a system was established by the prosecution. The accused man and woman were charged with the murder of a child whose body was found in their garden. They had adopted the child on receipt of a small sum from its mother for its support. Evidence was held admissible that other children had been adopted by the accused in the same way and that their bodies had been found buried in the gardens of houses occupied by the accused. The purpose of

---

[15] [1975] A.C., at p. 462; [1974] 3 All E.R., at p. 913.
[16] [1975] A.C., at p. 451; [1974] 3 All E.R., at p. 909.
[17] (1975), 62 Cr. App. Rep. 118, at p. 121; applied by the Court of Appeal in *R*. v. *Mansfield*, [1978] 1 All E.R. 134; [1977] 1 W.L.R. 1102 and in *R*. v. *Scarrott*, [1978] Q.B. 1016; [1978] 1 All E.R. 672.
[18] [1952] A.C. 694; [1952] 1 All E.R. 1044.
[19] [1894] A.C. 57.

proving a system, and thereby rendering admissible conduct on other occasions, may be to prove either the *actus reus* or the *mens rea* of a crime. Thus in *Makin*'s case the similar fact evidence tended to show the unlikelihood of the death being due to natural causes and was thus evidence of an *actus reus*. A similar case is *R. v. Smith*,[20] the famous "brides in the bath" murder. The deceased, who had gone through a ceremony of marriage with the accused, was drowned in her bath having insured her life in favour of the accused. The death was claimed by the accused to have been caused by an attack of epilepsy. Evidence was admitted that two other women with whom Smith had gone through ceremonies of marriage had also drowned in their baths in circumstances in which the accused would gain financially by their death.

Evidence of system may also serve to prove the *mens rea* of an offence, in which case it may be doubly relevant as it also serves to rebut a defence of accident or mistake. For example in *R. v. Mortimer*,[1] on a charge of murdering a lady cyclist by running her down, evidence was admitted that the accused had intentionally driven his car at other lady cyclists thus proving that his conduct was intentional and not merely negligent.

b Rebutting defences

The purpose of establishing a system is to prove either *mens rea* or *actus reus*. This incidentally involves rebutting such defences as accident or mistake. Nevertheless similar fact evidence which operates to rebut a defence may be regarded as a separate category. The evidence need not amount to a systematic course of conduct. Thus in *R. v. Armstrong*[2] the accused, a solicitor, charged with murdering his wife by arsenic poisoning, raised the defence that she had committed suicide. Evidence was admitted of a subsequent attempt by the accused to poison a rival solicitor with arsenic. Similarly in *R. v. Bond*[3] evidence that the accused, a doctor, had used instruments upon a woman to perform an abortion on an earlier occasion was admitted in order to rebut the defence that his use of similar instruments on the occasion in question was to carry out a *bona fide* examination.

In *R. v. Barrington*[4] the accused was charged with indecently assaulting three young girls, the prosecution case being that he had lured them to premises on the pretext that they were required as baby-sitters and, once there, had shown them pornographic pictures, asked them to pose for photographs in the nude and indecently assaulted them. When the girls gave evidence to this effect they were cross-examined along the lines that their evidence was false and they had put their heads together to concoct a case against the accused. In those circumstances the prosecution successfully applied to call three other girls whose evidence was that they too had been lured to the premises on the pretext of baby-sitting and then shown pornographic pictures and asked to pose for nude photographs. The Court of Appeal upheld the admission of this evidence both on the ground advanced by the prosecu-

---

[20] (1915), 11 Cr. App. Rep. 229.
[1] (1936), 25 Cr. App. Rep. 150; for a recent illustration of the principle in a civil case, see *Mood Music Publishing Co., Ltd. v. De Wolfe, Ltd.,* [1976] Ch. 119; [1976] 1 All E.R. 763.
[2] [1922] 2 K.B. 555.
[3] [1906] 2 K.B. 389.
[4] [1981] 1 All E.R. 1132; [1981] 1 W.L.R. 419

tion, namely as tending to rebut the defence, and on the wider ground of "striking similarity" between the surrounding circumstances of the alleged offences and those of the visits of the three other girls. The case is of particular interest because the similar fact evidence did not, as will have been observed, include evidence of the actual commission of offences similar to those with which the accused was charged.

c Identity

There are various way of proving identity by circumstantial evidence. A comparison of fingerprints or handwriting is circumstantial evidence of identity. So also is the physical resemblance or blood group of an illegitimate child evidence of the identity of the father. In exceptional circumstances the conduct of a person on other occasions may identify him as the perpetrator of conduct which is a fact in issue, provided that the conduct is sufficiently idiosyncratic. In *R. v. Straffen*[5] the accused was charged with the murder of a small girl. Evidence was admitted that the accused had previously murdered two other small girls.[6] The evidence served to identify Straffen because of the peculiar similarity shared by the three murders; all three victims were young girls, all were strangled, there was no sexual assault or other apparent motive and no attempt to conceal the bodies.

d Knowledge

Similar fact evidence may support *mens rea* in a criminal case or a relevant mental element in a civil case. If a person acts in a certain way on more than one occasion this may tend to show that he knew what he was doing and was not ignorant or mistaken. For example in *R. v. Francis*[7] the accused was charged with obtaining an advance from a pawnbroker by the false pretence that a worthless ring was valuable. In order to prove knowledge of the falsity of this pretence evidence was admitted that the accused had made similar pretences to other pawnbrokers in order to obtain advances.

Certain statutes provide for the admission of evidence of conduct on the part of an accused person on other occasions. Thus section 27(3) of the Theft Act 1968[8] provides:

> "Where a person is being proceeded against for handling stolen goods (but not for any offence other than handling stolen goods), then at any stage of the proceedings, if evidence has been given of his having or arranging to have in his possession the goods the subject of the charge, or of his undertaking or assisting in, or arranging to undertake or assist in, their retention, removal, disposal, or realisation, the following evidence shall be admissible for the purpose of proving that he knew or believed the goods to be stolen goods:—
>
> (*a*) evidence that he has had in his possession, or has undertaken or assisted in the retention, removal, disposal or realisation of, stolen goods from any theft taking place not earlier than twelve months before the offence charged; and
>
> (*b*) (provided that seven days' notice in writing has been given to him of the

---

5 [1952] 2 Q.B. 911; [1952] 2 All E.R. 657.
6 In respect of these murders Straffen had been found unfit to plead and had been ordered to be detained in a Broadmoor institution, from which he had escaped.
7 (1874), L.R. 2 C.C.R. 128.
8 Replacing *s.* 43(1) of the Larceny Act 1916.

intention to prove the conviction) evidence that he has within the five years preceding the date of the offence charged been convicted of theft or of handling stolen goods.''

Most of the cases concerning the relevance of similar fact evidence are criminal cases but the principles apply equally in civil cases. Thus similar fact evidence frequently tends to prove knowledge in cases where liability depends upon knowledge. For example the tendency of a servant to play dangerous practical jokes is admissible to show that his master was negligent in employing him.[9]

3   Character

Character is usually regarded as *res inter alios acta*. The fact that a person is of good or bad character is generally irrelevant to the issue of whether or not he has performed a certain act on the occasion in question. Consequently evidence of character is, as a rule, irrelevant and inadmissible. Nonetheless there are numerous exceptions to this rule. For example reputation, which is one facet of character, is a fact in issue in defamation; admissible similar fact evidence may demonstrate character, in the sense of disposition, directly or by implication. Thus evidence that a person has strangled two small girls is, incidentally, evidence of bad character. Before examining the exceptional circumstances in which evidence of character may be adduced it will be convenient to consider what the word "character" comprises. For the purposes of the law of evidence there are three aspects of character:—reputation, disposition and convictions. The question of which of these three aspects of character are admissible in any particular circumstance differs according to the circumstances in which a person's character is admitted in evidence.

The strange case of *Lowery* v. *R*.[10] is most instructive in its demonstration of the various aspects of character. L. and K. were charged with the murder of a young girl who had been killed at a time and in a place when L. and K. were present and when no one else was present. The defence of each defendant was that the other alone was the killer and that he took no part whatsoever. L. gave evidence of his own good character, of his happy domestic circumstances and financial prospects and of the fact that he had neither interest nor motive to commit the offence. Furthermore he stated that he was in fear of K. K., in turn was permitted to adduce evidence from a psychologist who had interviewed both of the accused and had submitted them to tests commonly employed by psychologists in making assessments of personality. The psychologist concluded that K. was an immature, emotionally shallow youth, who seemed likely to be led and dominated by more aggressive and dominant men. In relation to the personality of L. the finding was that he showed a strong aggressive drive with weak control of his aggressive impulses, callousness and impulsiveness; furthermore, one test indicated some sadistic pleasure in observing the sufferings of others. Both L.

---

9 *Hudson* v. *Ridge Manufacturing Co., Ltd.*, [1957] 2 Q.B. 348; [1957] 2 All E.R. 229; see also *Bebee* v. *Sales* (1916), 32 T.L.R. 413.
10 [1974] A.C. 85; [1973] 3 All E.R. 662; cf. *R.* v. *Turner* (*Tarence*), [1975] Q.B. 834; [1975] 1 All E.R. 70 in which the Court of Appeal adjudged *Lowery* to have been decided on its special facts; see also *R.* v. *Rimmer and Beech*, [1983] Crim. L.R. 250.

and K. were convicted; L. (perhaps not surprisingly) appealed, contending that the evidence of the psychologist had been wrongly admitted. His appeal was dismissed. The *ratio* of the Privy Council's decision is obscure but the speech of LORD MORRIS makes it clear that the evidence was admissible not because it related to criminal tendency but on the basis that it was scientific evidence as to the respective personalities of the two accused. This reasoning, without more, could clearly have far-reaching consequences if it were to be applied in other cases for it seems logical to suggest that it would enable the prosecution in almost any criminal case to lead evidence (if available) as to the personality of a defendant so as to show that it was such as to dispose him to commit the criminal act in question. Nevertheless this has not happened and there is no indication of any attempt by prosecutors to invoke generally what would be a fundamental change in criminal procedure and evidence. Indeed, in *Lowery* LORD MORRIS indicated that there was no suggestion that the contested evidence either could or would have been adduced by the prosecution. Accordingly the *ratio* of the case must be taken to be much narrower than the general proposition that scientific evidence of the characteristics of a defendant's personality is admissible in criminal proceedings. If *Lowery* does lay down any general principle it is probably no broader than that where two defendants are charged with the same offence and one seeks to blame the other, that other is entitled to adduce scientific evidence both as to his own personality and as to that of his co-accused with a view to showing that the one is more likely to have committed the offence than the other. It is clear on the authorities, however, that this principle is limited to scientific evidence of disposition and would not enable one defendant to lead evidence as to the reputation or criminal convictions of the other.[11]

a Character of the parties in civil cases

Character is relevant in civil cases only in very limited circumstances. The character of the parties *qua* parties (as opposed to *qua* witnesses, where different considerations apply) is generally irrelevant. Character witnesses, as such, are hardly ever encountered at civil trials, even where issues bearing upon character are involved. Thus in *A-G.* v. *Bowman*[12] the defendant to an information for keeping false weights was not permitted to call a witness as to character because the proceedings were civil, notwithstanding that the information necessarily involved an imputation on his character.

There are, however, exceptions. In certain civil cases the character of a party is a fact in issue. In defamation, for example, the plaintiff's reputation is in issue and the plaintiff may seek to establish his good character while the defendant attempts to prove the plaintiff's bad character.[13] The plaintiff's reputation is also relevant, in defamation, to the issue of the amount of damages recoverable by him, but evidence of the defendant in mitigation of damages is confined to evidence of general reputation and he cannot prove specific facts which demonstrate the plaintiff's bad character.[14]

---

[11] Though he might well be entitled to *cross-examine* that other upon these matters; see p. 587, *post*.

[12] (1791), 2 Bos. & P. 532.

[13] However, in prosecutions for criminal libel, evidence of the general bad character of the prosecutor is not admissible: *Gleaves* v. *Deakin*, [1980] A.C. 477; [1979] 2 All E.R. 497.

[14] *Plato Films, Ltd.,* v. *Speidel*, [1961] A.C. 1090; [1961] 1 All E.R. 876. However the fact that

b   Character of the accused in criminal cases

The character of the accused in a criminal case is, by the nature of criminal proceedings, an important matter and, if admitted, likely to have a significant effect upon the deliberations of the average jury. Although the general rule excluding evidence of character still applies, there are several exceptions to this rule where the character of which it is sought to admit evidence is that of the accused. It must be stressed once again that, notwithstanding the rule excluding evidence of character, facts which are otherwise relevant may bear upon the character of the accused. Thus relevant similar fact evidence very often indicates the accused's disposition, which is one aspect of his character. Similarly evidence of the accused's previous convictions, which is admissible under several statutes, is evidence of another aspect of his character. However, apart from these instances and the limited circumstances in which a defendant may adduce evidence of the disposition of a co-defendant (as demonstrated by *Lowery* v. *R.*), the accused's character may only be introduced in evidence by the accused himself or by the prosecution in certain well-defined circumstances.

The accused may always attempt to prove his good character. He may do this by his own testimony, by calling character witnesses or by cross-examination of prosecution witnesses. The significance of this is two-fold. First, it goes to support the accused's credibility and, secondly, it is evidence which the jury should consider so as to ask themselves "whether they think it likely that a person with such a character would have committed the offence",[15] and the judge should direct the jury in these terms. There is scant logic in the latter aspect of relevance since it is well established that the accused's bad character (when admissible) goes only to credibility and is not relevant to the issue of whether the jury "think it likely that a person with such a character would have committed the offence". Whether most juries follow, let alone apply, this distinction is open to doubt. Moreover the accused is limited to giving or calling evidence of general reputation, including disposition. Thus in *R.* v. *Redgrave*[16] the accused, charged with an offence of importuning, was not permitted to lead detailed evidence of his heterosexual relationships in order to show that he was not disposed to make homosexual approaches. If the accused does try to prove his good character by any of these methods he is said to "put his character in issue". The effect is that the prosecution may then give evidence of his bad character in rebuttal.[17] Such

---

the plaintiff has previous convictions is admissible in defamation for the purpose of mitigating damages: *Goody* v. *Odhams Press, Ltd.,* [1967] 1 Q.B. 333; [1966] 3 All E.R. 369. The Rehabilitation of Offenders Act 1974 has some, albeit slight, effect in such cases since section 4(1)(*a*) of that Act provides that no evidence shall be admissible to prove that a "rehabilitated person" has been convicted for any offence which was the subject of a "spent conviction" while section 4(1)(*b*) provides a shield against answering any questions relating to the witness's spent convictions. The length of the period which must elapse before a conviction is spent varies according to the sentence imposed but convictions in respect of which a sentence in excess of thirty months' imprisonment was imposed are excluded from rehabilitation (s. 5).

15 *R.* v. *Stannard* (1837), 7 C.C.P. 673, at p. 675, *per* WILLIAMS, J., cited with approval by the Court of Appeal in *R.* v. *Bryant*, [1979] Q.B. 108; [1978] 2 All E.R. 689.

16 (1981), 74 Cr. App. Rep. 10.

17 The accused does not put his character in issue by attacking the character of the prosecution witnesses; *R.* v. *Butterwasser*, [1948] 1 K.B. 4; [1947] 2 All E.R. 415; cf. Criminal Evidence Act 1898, s. 1 (*f*) (ii); see p. 585, *post*. Nor does he do so by eliciting evidence as to the bad

evidence may relate to the accused's general reputation though not to any individual witness's opinion as to the accused's character.[18] It may also relate to the accused's previous convictions. Consequently if the accused has a number of previous convictions he must beware of seeking to establish his good character for in so doing he may let in evidence of his convictions. There is authority for saying that the accused's character is indivisible. The effect is that if evidence is admitted of his character this evidence may relate to any aspect of his character, not merely to that segment of it which seems relevant to the offence with which he is charged. In *R.* v. *Winfield*[19] the accused was charged with indecent assault upon a woman. He called a witness to testify as to his good behaviour with women, whereupon the prosecution was allowed to cross-examine that witness as to a previous conviction of the accused involving dishonesty.

Apart from this common law provision there are certain statutes which enable evidence to be given of the accused's bad character (as opposed to previous convictions).[20] The most important of these statutes, the Criminal Evidence Act 1898, is discussed below.

Finally, after conviction and before sentence it is common for the court to receive evidence of the accused's character and antecedents in order to decide upon the most appropriate sentence. This procedure is informal and the strict rules of evidence relating to means of proof are not usually observed.[1]

c Character of third parties

Evidence of the character of persons other than the parties in civil actions and the accused in criminal cases, where those persons are not called as witnesses, is only receivable in a few special circumstances. Historically such evidence was most often led in prosecutions for rape and similar offences where defendants, running the defence of consent, frequently sought to impugn the character of the victim by cross-examining, and leading evidence, as to her reputation for sexual conduct. This was widely regarded as an invasion of privacy and, more important, as a factor which discouraged victims of sexual offences from reporting them to the police. The law was changed by the Sexual Offences (Amendment) Act 1976, section 2 of which provides that in prosecutions for rape and allied offences, except with leave of the judge, no evidence and no question in cross-examination shall be adduced or asked by or on behalf of the defendant about any sexual experience of a complainant with a person other than the defendant. The section only protects women (so that it does not extend to, for example, male homosexuals); nor does it apply in prosecutions for sexual offences which are not rape offences, such as indecent assult or unlawful sexual intercourse.

---

character of other persons who, for example, had the opportunity to commit the offence of which the accused stands charged: *R.* v. *Lee*, [1976] 1 All E.R. 570; [1976] 1 W.L.R. 71.

[18] *R.* v. *Rowton* (1865), Le. & Ca. 501.

[19] (1939), 27 Cr. App. Rep. 139; see p. 588, *post.*

[20] See, for example, Official Secrets Act 1911, s. 1(2).

[1] The statement of the defendant's record will contain all previous convictions, but those which are "spent" in accordance with the provisions of the Rehabilitation of Offenders Act 1974 should be marked as such and should not be referred to in open court without the authority of the judge (*Practice Note (rehabilitation of offenders)*, [1975] 2 All E.R. 1072; [1975] 1 W.L.R. 1065).

Evidence of bad reputation, where admissible, is confined to general reputation and proof of specific instances is not allowed.[2]

d Character of witnesses (other than the accused in a criminal case)

Witnesses may be cross-examined as to credit in order to show that they are persons who ought not to be believed on account of their bad character. This applies notwithstanding that the witness is also a party to a civil action[3] or is the prosecutor in a criminal case.[4] Moreover a witness may be called to testify that he would not believe another witness on oath. The former may testify as to his opinion of the impugned witness's credibility or as to the latter's reputation for untruthfulness, though he may not (unless asked in cross-examination) give evidence as to particular facts or incidents upon which his opinion is based.[5] This rule does not apply, however, where the witness is the accused in a criminal case since the accused may only be cross-examined as to credit under the Criminal Evidence Act 1898.[6] While being cross-examined as to credit an opposing witness may be asked any questions, even if totally irrelevant to any fact in issue, concerning his bad reputation, disposition or previous convictions.[7] However the cross-examining party must accept the answer of the witness as final. He cannot adduce evidence to rebut it. This is a practical rule which exists in order to avoid multiplication of collateral issues. Thus in *A-G.* v. *Hitchcock*[8] the defendant was not permitted to adduce evidence to rebut a prosecution witness's denial that the latter had been offered a bribe. Similarly the prosecutrix on a charge of a sexual offence may, if she is a witness, be asked whether she has had sexual intercourse with other men (subject to the restrictions contained in the Sexual Offences (Amendment) Act 1976 (*supra*)) but if she denies this fact evidence cannot be given to rebut her denial.[9]

There are, however, four exceptions to this general rule against rebuttal. Thus if a witness denies a previous conviction or his own previous inconsistent statement evidence may be given, under the Criminal Procedure Act 1865, of this conviction or statement. To these statutory exceptions may be added the common law rules permitting evidence to prove bias in a witness or

---

2 *R.* v. *Holmes* (1871), L.R. 1 C.C.R. 334. In civil cases the bad character of a wife in actions for damages for adultery and of a daughter in seduction actions were relevant on this basis. The actions in question have now been abolished.

3 *Hobbs* v. *Tinling & Co., Ltd.,* [1929] 2 K.B. 1.

4 *R.* v. *Holmes* (*supra*).

5 *R.* v. *Richardson, R.* v. *Longman*, [1969] 1 Q.B. 299; [1968] 2 All E.R. 761.

6 See p. 583, *post*.

7 Save (in most civil proceedings) in relation to convictions "spent" under the provisions of the Rehabilitation of Offenders Act 1974 (Act of 1974, s. 4(1)(*b*)).

8 (1847), 1 Ex. 91; but compare *R.* v. *Busby* (1982), 75 Cr. App. Rep. 79 where the Court of Appeal held that evidence from a potential defence witness, to the effect that police officers in the case had threatened him in order to stop him giving evidence, ought to have been admitted as being relevant to an issue in the case, namely whether the police officers were prepared to go to any lengths to secure the defendant's conviction. The officers had denied the suggestion and the trial judge had excluded the evidence to rebut this denial as going simply to credit. The trial judge's ruling is difficult to understand because, at the very least, the evidence would have been admissible to prove bias.

9 *R.* v. *Holmes* (*supra*). Evidence can, of course, be given of previous acts of sexual intercourse with the accused since this is a fact relevant to the issue of consent: *R.* v. *Riley* (1887), 18 Q.B.D. 481.

to prove a general reputation for untruthfulness. However, in *R. v. Thorne*[10] the trial judge refused to allow defence counsel to cross-examine a police officer about verdicts of acquittal which had been returned in other cases in which a witness in the instant case, an informer giving "Queen's evidence", had testified. The Court of Appeal upheld this decision since those acquittals were no evidence of bias, against the defendants in the instant case, nor did they establish a general reputation for untruthfulness, or indeed prove that the witness had lied in the earlier cases (since acquittal shows no more than that a jury is not satisfied beyond reasonable doubt).

4 Convictions

As a general rule evidence of a person's previous convictions is excluded as irrelevant in the same way as evidence of similar facts and of character are excluded. All are illustrations of the older general rule excluding *res inter alios acta*. Before considering in detail the exceptional circumstances in which previous convictions may be put in evidence it is necessary to consider the evidential nature of convictions and the relationship between bad character and previous convictions.

In criminal proceedings, at common law, a conviction is only evidence of the fact that a person has been convicted. It is not evidence that he performed the conduct upon which his conviction is based. To quote BLACKBURN, J. (as he then was):[11]

> ". . . A judgment of conviction on an indictment for forging a bill of exchange, though conclusive as to the prisoner being a convicted felon, is not only not conclusive, but is not even admissible evidence of the forgery in an action on the bill. . . ."

This much-criticised rule may have strange effects. For example, if evidence were admissible, as relevant similar fact evidence, that a person had murdered two little girls these murders could not be proved by evidence of convictions for these murders, though they could be proved by evidence of confessions or pleas of guilty made in the course of those proceedings.[12] The fact that the person had murdered the girls would be relevant; the fact that he had been convicted of those murders would not. The rule will be altered, and criminal proceedings brought into line with civil proceedings in this respect, when section 74 of the Police and Criminal Evidence Act 1984 is brought into operation.

In relation to civil proceedings, this rule[13] has been abrogated by the Civil Evidence Act 1968. That Act provides that in any civil proceedings the fact that a person has been convicted of an offence by any court in the United Kingdom, or by a court-martial there or elsewhere, shall be admissible to prove that he committed that offence, whether or not he pleaded guilty and

---

[10] (1978), 66 Cr. App. Rep. 6.
[11] *Castrique v. Imrie* (1870), L.R. 4 H.L. 414, at p. 434.
[12] *R. v. Straffen*, [1952] 2 Q.B. 911; [1952] 2 All E.R. 657.
[13] The rule was known as the Rule in *Hollington v. Hewthorn & Co., Ltd.*, [1943] K.B. 587; [1943] 2 All E.R. 35. However, in *Hunter v. Chief Constable of West Midlands*, [1982] A.C 529; [1981] 3 All E.R. 727 the House of Lords expressed the view that this case had been wrongly decided.

whether or not he is a party to the civil proceedings.[14] The effect is to raise a presumption that he committed the offence, unless the contrary is proved.[15] Thus the conviction is admissible but not conclusive evidence, save in defamation actions, where proof of the conviction is expressed by the Act[16] to be conclusive. The position will be the same, in relation to criminal proceedings, under the 1984 Act (*supra*).

There is an interrelationship between character and convictions. That is not to say that whenever evidence of character is admissible evidence of convictions is admissible, or *vice versa*. If the whole of a person's character is admissible this includes evidence of his previous convictions. However, if only his reputation is relevant, as in defamation for example, evidence of previous convictions is inadmissible. Conversely, convictions are not only relevant as evidence of character. A previous conviction may be an element in a criminal offence or a fact in issue in a civil case in which case it will be relevant where general bad character is irrelevant.

The circumstances in which previous convictions are receivable in evidence are now examined in relation to the persons whose convictions it is sought to prove.

a   Witnesses (other than the accused in a criminal case)

In the course, of cross-examination of an opposing witness as to credit, the witness may be cross-examined as to his previous convictions.[17] This is to show that he ought not to be believed. Consequently the conviction need not be relevant to a fact in issue. The admission of such evidence may appear to contradict the general rule that only relevant evidence is admissible. In fact it is true to say that such evidence is indirectly relevant. It is indirectly relevant to a fact in issue in that it tends to show the falsity of other relevant evidence.

If the witness denies a previous conviction, this conviction may be proved by the cross-examining party under the Criminal Procedure Act 1865, section 6. This Act, despite its misleading short title, applies to both civil and criminal proceedings, though in the latter special rules apply where the witness is the accused himself.

b   Parties in civil cases

The previous convictions of a party in a civil case can only be proved where the fact of conviction is a relevant fact[18] or where the conviction is admissible under the Civil Evidence Act 1968 as proof of a relevant fact or to discredit

---

14 Civil Evidence Act 1968, s. 11(1); unless the conviction is "spent" under the provisions of the Rehabilitation of Offenders Act 1974, in which event evidence of it will not be admissible (s. 4(1)(*a*)) unless the court is satisfied that justice cannot be done except by admitting such evidence (s. 7(3)). Section 12 of the 1968 Act introduced a similar rule in respect of (*a*) the fact that a person has been found guilty of adultery in any matrimonial proceedings; and (*b*) the fact that a person has been adjudged to be the father of a child in affiliation proceedings.

15 *Ibid.*, s. 11(2)(*a*).

16 Section 13(1). This section must be read subject to section 8 of the Rehabilitation of Offenders Act 1974 whereby, while a defendant may justify a defamatory statement by proving a spent conviction he is precluded from relying upon justification (and therefore upon the conviction) if the publication is proved to have been made with malice (s. 8(5)).

17 Save (in most civil proceedings) in relation to convictions spent under the provisions of the Rehabilitation of Offenders Act 1974 (Act of 1974, s. 4(1)(*b*)).

18 *Ingram* v. *Ingram*, [1956] P. 390; [1956] 1 All E.R. 785.

the testimony of the party as a witness. Thus the fact of conviction would be a fact in issue in a defamation action where the defendant alleged that the plaintiff had been convicted and sought to justify the allegation, or in an action for malicious prosecution where the defendant alleged that the plaintiff had been convicted. Similarly, where the fact of a spouse having been convicted is alleged to amount to, or be part of, a course of intolerable conduct in a divorce suit, that conviction may be proved.[19]

Similarly, where the defendants in a libel action imputed dishonesty to a company which was the proprietor of a computer school, they were permitted in support of justification, to plead details of the convictions and sentences of the founder of the school.[20]

c Accused persons

The extent to which an accused person, as a witness, may be cross-examined as to his previous convictions is dealt with below. However the accused's previous convictions may sometimes be proved irrespective of whether he is a witness. For example, where the accused raises a plea of *autrefois convict* the conviction in question is relevant as a fact in issue.[1] Also, there are several statutory provisions enabling the prosecution to give evidence of the accused's previous convictions. For example the Theft Act 1968, s. 27(3),[2] allows proof of convictions as a means of proving facts in issue.

Finally, where the accused puts his character in issue by seeking to establish his good character, the prosecution may be allowed to prove his previous convictions as part of his bad character.

Cross-examination of the accused as to his character and previous convictions is governed by the Criminal Evidence Act 1898, section 1 (as amended). That Act made the accused a competent though not a compellable witness for the defence. Consequently, the accused has a choice as to whether or not to give evidence. If he does elect to give evidence the accused's position differs from that of other witnesses in that he cannot be freely cross-examined as to credit. The extent to which he can be cross-examined is governed by section 1 proviso (f) of the 1898 Act (as amended)[3] and the judicial interpretation of this important provision.

---

[19] For convictions as evidence of bad character see *Goody* v. *Odhams Press, Ltd.,* [1967] 1 Q.B. 333; [1966] 3 All E.R. 369 in which the Court of Appeal held that previous convictions in the relevant sector of the plaintiff's life, and within such a period of time as to affect his current reputation, were admissible in mitigation of damages.

[20] *London Computer Operators Training, Ltd.* v. *British Broadcasting Corporation,* [1973] 2 All E.R. 170; [1973] 1 W.L.R. 424; the decision is interesting in that the convicted person was not a party to the action and is explicable only on the basis of the wide meaning of the words complained of, which were capable of meaning that the company was being run by persons of questionable honesty.

[1] See p. 503, *ante.* See also *R.* v. *B.,* [1979] 3 All E.R. 460; [1979] 1 W.L.R. 1185, where the previous convictions of a boy under 14 were admitted to rebut the presumption (which exists in favour of children between 10 and 14) that he did not know the difference between right and wrong.

[2] See p. 575, *ante*; see also Official Secrets Act 1911, s. 1(2).

[3] The amendment, effected by s. 1 of the Criminal Evidence Act 1979, was to substitute the words "in the same proceedings" for the words "with the same offence" in (*f*) (iii); this was to nullify the decision of the House of Lords in *Metropolitan Police Commissioner* v. *Hills,* [1980] A.C. 26; [1978] 2 All E.R. 1105. In that case two cars collided causing one of them to leave the road and kill a pedestrian. The two drivers were prosecuted in the same indictment

Section 1(f) is negative in expression. It provides that:

"A person charged and called as a witness in pursuance of this Act shall not be asked, and if asked shall not be required to answer, any question tending to show that he has committed or been convicted of or has been charged with any offence other than that wherewith he is then charged, or is of bad character, unless—

(i) the proof that he has committed or been convicted of such other offence is admissible evidence to show that he is guilty of the offence wherewith he is then charged; or

(ii) he has personally or by his advocate asked questions of the witnesses for the prosecution with a view to establish his own good character, or has given evidence of his good character, or the nature or conduct of the defence is such as to involve imputations on the character of the prosecutor or the witnesses for the prosecution; or

(iii) he has given evidence against any other person charged in the same proceedings."

Section 1(f) may thus be regarded as a shield against cross-examination as to character and convictions which is lost in certain circumstances. The effect of the shield of section 1(f) being lost is that the accused may be cross-examined upon his character and previous convictions.[4] A strict interpretation of the section would suggest that the accused, if he loses the shield, may be asked questions to show that he has been charged with other offences. Were this interpretation adopted the section would operate to admit evidence of previous acquittals as well as of previous convictions. It is not presumed, however, that the framers of the 1898 Act intended to affect the general rule that all evidence must be relevant in order to be admissible. Consequently evidence that the accused has been "charged" with an offence is not generally admissible in spite of the wording of section 1(f). This was the basis of the decision of the House of Lords in *Maxwell* v. *Director of Public Prosecutions*[5] which held that, although a doctor on a charge of manslaughter had put his character in issue, he ought not to have been cross-

---

for separate offences of causing death by dangerous driving. In the nature of things each driver's defence was that it was the other man's fault. One of the defendants had a bad driving record but the House of Lords held that the trial judge had been wrong to allow the other defendant to cross-examine him as to this record since the defendants were charged with separate offences and not "the same offence". The House of Lords pointed out the need for reform of the law, and expressed the hope that the Home Secretary would refer the matter to the Criminal Law Revision Committee for consideration without delay. This was duly done and that Committee's consequent recommendation was embodied in the 1979 Act.

4　He may not, however, if he is twenty-one or over be cross-examined as to offences of which he was found guilty while under the age of fourteen: Children and Young Persons Act 1963, s. 16(2). The restriction upon adducing evidence of spent convictions does not apply in any criminal proceedings (Rehabilitation of Offenders Act 1974, s. 7(2)(*a*); however, as a matter of practice, it is recommended by the Lord Chief Justice that both court and counsel should give effect to the general intention of Parliament by never referring to a spent conviction when such reference can be reasonably avoided (*Practice Note (rehabilitation of offenders)*, [1975] 2 All E.R. 1072; [1975] 1 W.L.R. 1065).

5　[1935] A.C. 309. LORD SANKEY, L.C. in that case recognised that questions relating to a previous charge would be admissible under s. 1(f) if the fact of the charge being made were otherwise relevant, for example where the fact of a previous charge is a fact in issue (see *R. v. Waldman* (1934), 24 Cr. App. Rep. 204). A previous charge is a fact in issue where a defence is raised under s. 6(3) of the Sexual Offences Act 1956.

examined as to a similar charge upon which he had been acquitted. Further-more "charged" is interpreted as meaning "charged in court" so that section 1(f) cannot operate to admit evidence that an accused person has been questioned about or suspected of a criminal offence of which he has never been formally charged unless he can be proved to have committed the offence.[6]

It should be noted that the shield afforded by section 1(f) only protects the accused from questions "tending to show" his previous convictions or bad character. The words "tending to show" were interpreted narrowly by the House of Lords in *Jones* v. *Director of Public Prosecutions*[7] as meaning "tending to reveal" or "tending to make known", with the effect that questions relating to matters which have already been revealed to the court are not excluded by section 1(f). The facts of this somewhat unusual case were as follows. Jones was charged with murdering a young girl, a Girl Guide. He first advanced an admittedly false alibi and later asserted an uncorroborated alibi. His explanation as to why he had not raised this alibi earlier was that he had been in trouble with the police before and was afraid that the police would not believe his uncorroborated alibi. In fact Jones had been previously convicted of raping another Girl Guide at which trial he had raised an alibi, similar to the one now raised, that he had been with an unnamed prostitute. He was cross-examined concerning the remarkable similarity between the two alibis. Although the fact of his previous convic-tion was not brought out, the cross-examination did tend to show that he was of bad character in that he had been in trouble with the police. His appeal against conviction was dismissed, the House of Lords holding that the cross-examination did not "tend to show", in the sense of "tend to reveal", that Jones had been in trouble with the police, since he had already revealed this himself.[8] Consequently the shield of section 1(f) did not exist.

Where the shield does exist it is lost only in the circumstances specified in section 1(f). There are four circumstances in which the shield is lost. These are as follows:

(1) *where the fact of commission or conviction of the earlier offence is relevant similar fact evidence.* (This adds nothing to the common law since relevant similar fact evidence would be admissible apart from the provisions of the 1898 Act);

(2) *where the accused tries to establish his own good character.* (This also adds nothing to the common law since the effect of the accused putting his character in issue is, as noted above, to let in evidence of his bad character including his previous convictions);

(3) *where the conduct of the defence involves imputations on the charac-ter of the prosecutor or the prosecution witnesses.* A mere denial that the testimony of the prosecution witnesses is true does not amount to an imputation upon their character,[9] though a statement that the prosecutor is

---

6   *Stirland* v. *Director of Public Prosecutions*, [1944] A.C. 315; [1944] 2 All E.R. 13.
7   [1962] A.C. 635; [1962] 1 All E.R. 569.
8   This was the *ratio* of the case since it was the basis of the speeches of the majority; LORDS SIMONDS, REID and MORRIS. LORDS DENNING and DEVLIN arrived at the same decision but dissented from the reasoning of the majority.
9   *R.* v. *Rouse*, [1904] 1 K.B. 184.

such a horrible liar that even his own brother would not speak to him has been held to amount to an imputation within section 1(f) (ii).[10]

The cases are not entirely consistent. Thus an allegation that the prosecutor was an habitual drunkard was held in one case not to be an imputation[11] though a statement that the prosecutor was drunk, driving disgracefully and shouting abuse at other drivers was, in another case, held to be an imputation.[12] Similarly, criticism of the method of holding an identification parade has been held not to be objectionable[13] though a suggestion that the accused's confession was dictated by one policeman to another was held to amount to an imputation.[14] In practice the question often arises out of the manner in which a defendant challenges police evidence concerning oral interviews (colloquially known as "verbals") or the obtaining of written confessions. If the defendant simply challenges the accuracy of the record, this will not amount to an imputation whereas if he goes so far as to allege that police officers have invented admissions so as to facilitate his conviction, this will let in his character. Consequently defence counsel representing a defendant who has a bad criminal record will usually strive to go no further than he need for the purpose of "putting his case" and will suggest that the officer's evidence is "mistaken" or, simply, "challenged". However, while this is perfectly feasible when only one or two answers are disputed, it is not possible when the defendant's challenge is so fundamental that there is no room for mistake and the conflict between the officer's version and the defendant's can, as a matter of common sense, only be explained on the basis that one or other is deliberately lying.[15]

The situation referred to above is but one example of the difficulty which arises when the proper conduct of the defence necessitates imputations upon the prosecution. In such a case the accused appears to be faced with the invidious choice of being hindered in the conduct of his defence or rendering himself liable to cross-examination upon his character and convictions. It must be borne in mind that, even where the shield of section 1(f)(ii) is lost, the trial judge has a discretion to refuse the prosecution leave to cross-examine as to character.

In *R. v. Britzman*[16] LAWTON, L.J. in the Court of Appeal set out some guidelines for the exercise of this discretion.

> "First, it should be used if there is nothing more than a denial, however emphatic or offensively made, of an act or even a short series of acts amounting to one incident or in what was said to have been a short interview. Examples are

---

[10] *R. v. Rappolt* (1911), 6 Cr. App. Rep. 156.
[11] *R. v. Westfall* (1912), 7 Cr. App. Rep. 176.
[12] *R. v. Brown (No. 2)* (1960), 124 J.P. 391. An allegation by a defendant that he had a homosexual relationship with a prosecution witness (a variation of the so-called "Portsmouth" defence) was held to involve an imputation on the character of that witness in *R. v. Bishop*, [1975] Q.B. 274; [1974] 2 All E.R. 1206, on the basis that such an allegation still carried with it a certain stigma.
[13] *R. v. Preston*, [1909] 1 K.B. 568.
[14] *R. v. Clark*, [1955] 2 Q.B. 469; [1955] 3 All E.R. 29; see also *R. v. Dunkley*, [1927] 1 K.B. 323.
[15] See, for example, *R. v. Tanner* (1977), 66 Cr. App. Rep. 56. There is no rule that the discretion must be exercised in favour of the accused where the proper conduct of his defence necessitates imputations on the prosecution: *Selvey* v. *Director of Public Prosecutions*, [1970] A.C. 304; [1968] 2 All E.R. 497.
[16] [1983] 1 All E.R. 369, at pp. 373–374; [1983] 1 W.L.R. 350, at p. 355.

provided by the kind of evidence given in pickpocket cases and where the defendant is alleged to have said: 'Who grassed on me this time?' The position would be different however if there were a denial of evidence of a long period of detailed observation extending over hours and just as in this case and in *R.* v. *Tanner*, where there were denials of long conversations.

Second, cross-examination should only be allowed if the judge is sure that there is no possibility of mistake, misunderstanding or confusion and that the jury will inevitably have to decide whether the prosecution witnesses have fabricated evidence. Defendants sometimes make wild allegations when giving evidence. Allowance should be made for the strain of being in the witness box and the exaggerated use of language which sometimes results from such strain or lack of education or mental instability. Particular care should be used when a defendant is led into making allegations during cross-examination. The defendant who, during cross-examination, is driven to explaining away the evidence by saying it has been made up or planted on him usually convicts himself without having his previous convictions brought out. Finally, there is no need for the prosecution to rely on section 1(*f*)(ii) if the evidence against a defendant is overwhelming."

Where cross-examination as to previous convictions is admitted, it is important to remember that evidence of the accused's convictions (or, indeed, bad character generally) is not relevant to prove the commission of the offence charged. It is only relevant to the credibility of the defendant's evidence and the jury must be directed to this effect. Nevertheless judges are well aware of the difficulty experienced by the average juror in performing the mental gymnastics necessary to give effect to this principle and, in practice, common sense indicates that disclosure that a defendant has previous convictions for offences of a similar character to the offence charged is likely to be highly prejudicial to a fair trial. Consequently where a defendant has previous convictions for similar offences, the discretion to exclude cross-examination (or at any rate to limit it so as not to disclose the precise nature of his previous conviction) will normally be exercised in the defendant's favour.[17]

(4) *where the accused has given evidence against a co-accused*. The question of whether evidence is given "against" a co-accused must be answered objectively. The test is whether it supports the prosecution case in a material respect or undermines the defence of the co-accused.[18] Thus there need be no intention on the part of the accused to give evidence adverse to his co-accused so long as the evidence has that effect. Evidence cannot be said to have been given against a co-accused where, although it is inconsistent with that co-accused's own testimony, its effect, if believed, would be to result, not in the co-accused's conviction, but in his acquittal.[19] On the other hand where the

---

[17] For example, in *R.* v. *John and Braithwaite* (1983) (unreported) convictions for purse-snatching were quashed by the Court of Appeal, presided over by LORD LANE, C.J. despite a "perfectly adequate direction" by the trial judge on the ground that, although the defendants had attacked the character of police witnesses and thereby "let in" character, the trial judge had wrongly exercised his discretion by permitting cross-examination concerning previous convictions of both defendants for precisely similar offences. See also, to similar effect, *R.* v. *Watts*, [1983] 3 All E.R. 101 (where LORD LANE, C.J. described this branch of the law as being in "an unhappy state").

[18] *R.* v. *Varley*, [1982] 2 All E.R. 519, where the authorities are reviewed and summarised; *R.* v. *Stannard*, [1965] 2 Q.B. 1; [1964] 1 All E.R. 34; *Murdoch* v. *Taylor*, [1965] A.C. 574; [1965] 1 All E.R. 406.

[19] *R.* v. *Bruce*, [1975] 3 All E.R. 277; [1975] 1 W.L.R. 1252; *sed contra* where the evidence is

circumstances are such that one or other of two defendants must have committed the offence charged, it seems that evidence on the part of one defendant which goes no further than a denial of the offence is evidence "against" the other.[20] Where the evidence is given against a co-accused the accused who gives the evidence renders himself liable to cross-examination under section 1(f) (iii) by both the prosecution and his co-accused. The discretion which exists to exclude cross-examination by the prosecution does not exist to exclude cross-examination by a co-accused. There is no discretion to exclude such cross-examination.[1] The combined effect of the above rules may impede an accused in the proper conduct of his defence. If the conduct of his defence involves imputations "against" a co-accused there is no discretion to exclude cross-examination by that co-accused upon the first accused's character and convictions. The only safeguard is the power to order separate trials where the defence of one accused is likely to involve evidence against another but, in practice, this is never done.[2]

Where cross-examination of the accused upon his character and convictions is allowed under the 1898 Act the whole of the accused's character and convictions is admissible, not merely that part of the accused's character which appears relevant to the offence charged. The accused's character appears to be indivisible.[3] The prosecution may prove any conviction which the accused denies in cross-examination.[4]

C   RULES OF EXCLUSION APPLICABLE TO RELEVANT FACTS

When considering rules of exclusion it is necessary to remember that the word "evidence" comprises both facts and means of proof. Consequently a rule of exclusion may exclude either facts or a particular method of proving facts. The principal rule of exclusion, the hearsay rule, falls into the latter category and, together with the rules excluding opinion and secondary evidence of documents, is dealt with below.[5] This section is confined to rules of

---

such that it does more to undermine the co-accused's defence than the Crown's case: *R.* v. *Hatton* (1976), 64 Cr. App. Rep. 88.

[20] *R.* v. *Davis*, [1975] 1 All E.R. 233; [1975] 1 W.L.R. 345. In view of the absence of any discretion to exclude cross-examination on behalf of a co-accused in such circumstances, it will be appreciated that a defendant who has previous convictions is at a considerable disadvantage where his co-defendant has no convictions. Many would regard this as unattractive and even unfair but it is a result which flows ineluctably from the decision of the House of Lords in *Murdoch* v. *Taylor* (*infra*).

[1] *R.* v. *Ellis*, [1961] 2 All E.R. 928; [1961] 1 W.L.R. 1064; *R.* v. *Stannard* (*supra*); *Murdoch* v. *Taylor*, [1965] A.C. 574; [1965] 1 All E.R. 406.

[2] The fact that the defence of one co-accused involves imputations on the character of another co-accused (therefore giving the latter a right to avail himself of the opportunity of cross-examining the former upon his character and convictions) does not override the principle that in most cases it is in the interests of justice that all co-accused should be tried together: *R.* v. *Hoggins*, [1967] 3 All E.R. 334, [1976] 1 W.L.R. 1223.

[3] *R.* v. *Winfield*, [1939] 4 All E.R. 164. The report of this case in 27 Cr. App. Rep. 139 suggests that the cross-examination was of a defence witness rather than of the accused himself; see p. 579, *ante*.

[4] Criminal Procedure Act 1865, s. 6.

[5] See p. 652, *et seq.*, *post*.

exclusion which exclude facts. To these rules may be added the discretion of the court to exclude relevant evidence.

1 Estoppel

Estoppel is a rule of evidence whereby a party is prohibited from asserting or denying a fact. This prohibition may arise in various ways but whenever it does arise it has the effect of rendering relevant facts inadmissible. Estoppel has sometimes been described as a rule of substantive law rather than a rule of evidence.[6] Indeed it may have the effect of a rule of substantive law where it prevents a party from asserting or denying a fact in issue since it operates in such a case to create a right against the party estopped, by preventing him from denying that right. Nevertheless estoppel is a rule of evidence rather than a rule of substantive law, even though it may affect substantive rights and so have the same effect as a rule of law. Thus a party may waive an estoppel in his favour and, in any event, estoppel cannot be used as a cause of action but only as a defence.[7]

It is also occasionally stated that estoppel is a rule of procedure or pleading. The reason for this proposition is that an estoppel must be expressly pleaded. This is an exception to the general rule that evidence need not be pleaded.[8] Failure to plead an estoppel may operate as a waiver of the benefit of the estoppel. Nevertheless 'it does not follow that estoppel is a rule of pleading merely because it must be expressly pleaded. The Limitation Acts must be expressly pleaded but these cannot be said to be rules of pleading. It is best to classify estoppel as a rule of evidence to which special rules of procedure apply. Estoppels may arise in three ways, by record, by deed or by conduct. These three types of estoppel must be considered individually.

a Estoppel by record

The oldest form of estoppel is estoppel by record, alternatively known as judgment estoppel since the record in question is almost always a court record. A matter which a party is estopped by a court record from reopening is said to be *res judicata*. The doctrine of estoppel by record is based on two well-known maxims of the common law: *interest reipublicae est ut sit finis litium* (it is in the public interest that there be an end to litigation) and *nemo debet bis vexari pro eadem causa* (no one should be in jeopardy twice on the same ground). The effect of the doctrine is that a person cannot raise an allegation which has previously been decided against him by a court of competent jurisdiction.[9] A judgment may be assailed by an appeal, where a

---

6 See, for example, observations of LORD WRIGHT in *Canadian and Dominion Sugar Co., Ltd.* v. *Canadian National (West Indies) Steamships, Ltd.*, [1947] A.C. 46, at p. 56.

7 *Combe* v. *Combe*, [1951] 2 K.B. 215; [1951] 1 All E.R. 767.

8 R.S.C., O.18, r. 7 (1); see p. 340, *ante*.

9 This includes a foreign court (*Black-Clawson International, Ltd.* v. *Papierwerke Waldhof-Aschaffenburg AG*, [1975] A.C. 591; [1975] 1 All E.R. 810). Conversely, it is now provided by s. 34 of the Civil Jurisdiction and Judgments Act 1982 that no proceedings may be brought by a person in England and Wales on a cause of action in respect of which a judgment has been given in his favour in proceedings between the same parties, or their privies, in a court in another part of the United Kingdom or in a court of an overseas country, unless that judgment is not enforceable or entitled to recognition in England and Wales.

right of appeal exists, or by applying to have the judgment set aside where it was obtained fraudulently or collusively. Similarly an estoppel is not raised by the record of a court acting in excess of jurisdiction.[10] Although the estoppel is known as estoppel by "record", it is the decision of the court which, in truth, gives rise to the estoppel. Thus the court considering the question of estoppel can, and indeed must, look behind the record in the earlier case so as to see what was really decided. Thus no estoppel is raised by a decision which involves no adjudication on the merits of the case, for example a dismissal for want of prosecution.[11] Conversely an estoppel arises before the decision has been formally recorded in the court records. Thus where, following the hearing of an unfair dismissal complaint before an industrial tribunal, the chairman announced the tribunal's decision orally but died before it could be put into writing, supported by reasons and sent in that form to the parties (as required by rules of procedure), the Employment Appeal Tribunal held that the announcement of the decision orally gave rise to an estoppel preventing the parties from litigating again the issue which had been decided.[12]

Judgments in rem—For the purposes of the doctrine of estoppel by record there are two classes of judgments—judgments *in rem* and judgments *in personam*. A judgment *in rem* is a judgment which involves a determination of a person's right or status against the whole world; a judgment *in personam* is a judgment which determines one party's right against another party to the litigation. The importance of the distinction is that a judgment *in rem* raises an estoppel against the whole world, including the Crown and the House of Lords,[13] whereas a judgment *in personam* operates only against the parties to the action upon which the judgment is founded and their privies. Common examples of judgments *in rem* are orders adjudicating a person bankrupt,[14] a decree absolute of divorce or nullity,[15] a declaration of legitimacy[13] and a grant of probate.[16] Thus if a person has obtained a decree absolute of nullity neither the other spouse nor any other person can assert that the marriage is valid; if a grant of probate has been obtained no person can deny the title of the executors. Generally there is no difficulty in determining whether a judgment is a judgment *in rem*, or a judgment *in personam*, the question being determined by reference to substantive law. However difficulty may arise when an action between individuals indirectly bears upon the status of one of them. In such a case the judgment *in personam* may at first sight have the appearance of a judgment *in rem*. Thus in *B.* v *A-G.*[17] a husband, N.E.B., had admitted paternity of B. in divorce proceedings brought against him by the mother, and a custody order in respect of B. was made on the basis of that admission. Several years later in proceedings for maintenance by the mother N.E.B. was held to be estopped by the earlier finding of the court from denying that B. was his son. In the present proceedings B. sought

---

[10] *R.* v. *Hutchings* (1881), 6 Q.B.D. 300.
[11] *Pople* v. *Evans*, [1969] 2 Ch. 255; [1968] 2 All E.R. 743.
[12] *Jowett* v. *Earl of Bradford*, [1977] 2 All E.R. 33.
[13] *Ampthill Peerage Case*, [1977] A.C. 547; [1976] 2 All E.R. 411.
[14] Bankruptcy Act 1914, s. 137(2).
[15] *Salvesen* v. *Administrator of Austrian Property*, [1927] A.C. 641.
[16] *Allen* v. *Dundas* (1789), 3 Term Rep. 125.
[17] [1965] P. 278; [1965] 1 All E.R. 62.

a declaration of legitimacy and alleged that N.E.B. and other persons were estopped from denying that he, B., was the legitimate son of N.E.B. WILLMER, L.J. held that they were not so estopped since the earlier judgment was a judgment *in personam* which, although it had raised an estoppel against N.E.B. in favour of the mother, did not raise an estoppel in favour of B. who was not a party to the earlier proceedings.

Judgments in personam—A judgment *in personam* is binding only on the parties to the litigation and their privies.[18] The scope of an estoppel raised by a judgment *in personam* is narrowly defined. There must be both an identity of parties and an identity of issue between the judgment alleged to give rise to the estoppel and the issue before the court. The necessity for an identity of parties is illustrated by the case of *Townsend* v. *Bishop*.[19] The owner of a car brought an action against the owner of a lorry in respect of damage to his car caused in an accident in which the car was being driven by the owner's son. In this action the court held that the accident was caused by the negligence of the car owner's son. It was held in the instant action for personal injuries brought by the car owner's son against the owner of the lorry that the former was not estopped by the judgment in the first case from denying that he had been negligent.[20] Not only must the judgment alleged to create the estoppel have affected the same parties, it must also have affected those parties in the capacity in which they appear in the action in which the estoppel is pleaded. Thus a judgment against a person appearing in his personal capacity will not raise an estoppel against him in an action in which he subsequently appears in a representative capacity, notwithstanding that both actions arise out of the same incident.[1]

The second test to be applied in deciding whether a judgment *in personam* gives rise to an estoppel in subsequent proceedings between the same parties is whether there is an identity of issue. The same facts may give rise to several causes of action because several different rights are infringed. In order to decide whether the first case necessarily decides the issue raised in the second case, the facts upon which the judgment in the first case was based must be examined. A party cannot raise an allegation of fact which has already been determined against him even though he is pleading a different cause of action. For example, cruelty and constructive desertion were, prior to the Divorce Reform Act 1969, separate grounds for divorce but in both cases the respondent spouse's conduct had to be grave and weighty. If a cruelty

---

18 Privies are persons claiming as successors of a party. Privity may be of blood or of estate. For example an executor and an heir are both privies of a testator; an assignee of a lease is the privy of the original lessee.

19 [1939] 1 All E.R. 805.

20 See also *Gleeson* v. *J. Wippell & Co., Ltd.,* [1977] 3 All E.R. 54; [1977] 1 W.L.R. 510. The plaintiff had designed a type of shirt. W. Ltd. designed a similar shirt which they sent to D. Ltd. to copy and manufacture. The plaintiff first sued D. Ltd. alleging that they had infringed her copyright in the design drawings of her shirt, that W. Ltd. had copied her drawings and that D. Ltd., by copying W. Ltd.'s shirt, were infringing her copyright. The court dismissed her action against D. Ltd., holding that W. Ltd. had known nothing of the plaintiff's shirt and had not copied her drawings. The plaintiff then brought an action against W. Ltd. based upon the same facts. It was held that, since W. Ltd. had not been a party to the first action, and since D. Ltd. and W. Ltd. had no privity of interest, the plaintiff was not estopped from pursuing her action against W. Ltd.

1 *Marginson* v. *Blackburn Borough Council*, [1939] 2 K.B. 426; [1938] 2 All E.R. 539.

petition had been dismissed because the conduct alleged to amount to cruelty was found not to be sufficiently grave and weighty, the petitioner was estopped from founding a petition for constructive desertion on the same conduct.[2] This form of estoppel is termed "issue estoppel" and may be contrasted with "cause of action estoppel". Both are forms of estoppel by record but the first is raised by the court's determination of a single issue of fact while the second is raised by the court's determination of a cause of action.[3] Issue estoppel is illustrated by the decision of STREATFIELD, J. in *Wood* v. *Luscombe*[4]. A collision occurred between two motor cycles driven by W. and L. In an action by L. against W. they were found equally to blame. A pillion passenger in the accident subsequently brought an action against L. and L. brought in W. as a third party, claiming a contribution under the Law Reform (Married Women and Tortfeasors) Act 1935.[5] It was held that W. was estopped from denying that he and L. were equally to blame in the accident, since this issue, the issue of blame, was determined by the judgment in the first action.

An estoppel is binding only on the parties to the litigation. An estoppel cannot bind the court. This principle is demonstrated clearly in matrimonial proceedings, in which the court is concerned to preserve the sanctity of marriage as well as to do justice between the parties. The mere fact that one spouse is estopped from denying conduct such as adultery or desertion does not prevent the court from enquiring into the facts since the court must be satisfied that the marriage has broken down irretrievably before granting a decree.[6] Similarly, a custody order made in favour of a wife in undefended divorce proceedings (which imports a finding that the children to whom the order relates are children of the family) does not estop the husband from denying in maintenance proceedings that they are children of the family.[7]

There is a rule that findings in criminal cases do not give rise to estoppels in civil cases, and *vice-versa*. To this rule section 13 (1) of the Civil Evidence Act 1968 affords an isolated exception;[8] this sub-section provides, in effect, that

---

[2] *Hill* v. *Hill*, [1954] P. 291; [1954] 1 All E.R 491; *Thoday* v. *Thoday*, [1964] P. 181; [1964] 1 All E.R. 341. The Divorce Reform Act 1969 abolished cruelty and constructive desertion as grounds of divorce *per se*.

[3] See *Thoday* v. *Thoday*, [1964] P. 181, at p. 196; [1964] 1 All E.R. 341, at p. 352, *per* DIPLOCK, L.J. (as he then was), where "issue estoppel" and "cause of action estoppel" are distinguished and explained.

[4] [1966] 1 Q.B. 169; [1964] 3 All E.R. 972; not following *Randolph* v. *Tuck*, [1962] 1 Q.B. 175; [1961] 1 All E.R. 814.

[5] Now the Civil Liability (Contribution) Act 1978, s. 1 (1).

[6] *Harriman* v. *Harriman*, [1909] P. 123; *Winnan* v. *Winnan*, [1949] P. 174; [1948] 2 All E.R. 862.

[7] *Rowe* v. *Rowe*, [1980] Fam. 47; [1979] 2 All E.R. 1123.

[8] See p. 58, *ante*; the sub-section was passed to overrule cases in which persons convicted of crimes have brought successful defamation actions against persons who published statements to the effect that the convicted persons were guilty of the crimes of which they had been convicted (*Hinds* v. *Sparks*, [1964] Crim. L.R. 717; *Goody* v. *Odhams Press, Ltd.*, [1967] 1 Q.B. 333; [1966] 3 All E.R. 369). The rule was considered by the House of Lords in *Hunter* v. *Chief Constable of West Midlands*, [1982] A.C. 529; [1981] 2 All E.R. 727. In that case the plaintiff was one of six I.R.A. men convicted of 21 murders arising out of the Birmingham public house bombings in 1974. At his trial he had objected to the admissibility of his alleged confession on the ground that it had been induced by violence on the part of the police. His objection was overruled, the confession admitted and he was duly convicted. He now brought a civil action based upon the same allegations of violence as had been rejected by the trial

a plaintiff in a defamation action is estopped from denying the truth of an allegation that he is guilty of an offence of which he has been convicted by a criminal court.

Criminal cases—Estoppel in criminal cases is limited to "cause of action estoppel" in the form of the plea of *autrefois acquit*.[9] This plea can be raised where the accused has previously been acquitted of the offence with which he is now charged or of an offence so similar that acquittal necessarily involves acquittal of the present charge, or where the accused was at the first trial in peril of conviction of the offence now charged. In any of these circumstances the accused cannot be tried again. The doctrine of "issue estoppel" is not recognised in English criminal law.[10] The reason for this is that it is, by the nature of criminal verdicts, usually impossible to isolate any one issue from the others. Thus a general verdict of "not guilty" does not make it clear which of the issues have been determined in favour of the accused. It is clear that a verdict of not guilty cannot be regarded as determining every issue of fact in favour of the accused. Nevertheless in *Connelly v. Director of Public Prosecutions*[11] certain members of the House of Lords suggested that issue estoppel could exist in criminal cases. LORD DEVLIN explained the distinction between issue estoppel and *autrefois acquit* as follows:[12]

> "The difference between issue estoppel and the autrefois principle is that, while the latter prevents the prosecution from impugning the validity of the verdict as a whole, the former prevents it from raising again any of the separate issues of fact which the jury have decided or are presumed to have decided, in reaching their verdict in the accused's favour."

In *Connelly's* case it was held that neither the principle of *autrefois acquit* nor issue estoppel was applicable. Connelly was charged with murder. At his trial he raised the two defences of alibi and no intent to kill but the jury returned a general verdict of guilty. This conviction was quashed on appeal on the ground of misdirection by the trial judge. Connelly was subsequently indicted for robbery in respect of the same incident. It was held by the House of Lords that, since he had never been in peril of conviction for robbery, the plea of *autrefois acquit* failed and that, since no single issue could be determined in Connelly's favour from the judgment in the first trial, issue estoppel could not arise.

In *R. v. Humphrys*[13] the interesting point arose as to whether, following an acquittal, the Crown were estopped from seeking to prove that the defendant had, in fact, committed the offence of which he had been acquitted in a subsequent prosecution of the defendant for perjury in relation to his evidence given at his trial. Prosecution of a defendant for perjury in relation to evidence given at his trial is, in practice, rare (whether the trial resulted in conviction or acquittal); no doubt the reason for this is the prospect of an

---

judge. The Court of Appeal had ordered the action to be struck out both on the ground of issue estoppel and on the ground that it was an abuse of the process of the court (see p. 322, *ante*). The House of Lords upheld this decision, but on the second ground alone.

[9] See p. 503, *ante*.

[10] Although it is in Australia: *R. v. Wilkes* (1948), 77 C.L.R. 511; *Mraz v. R. (No 2)* (1956), 96 C.L.R. 62.

[11] [1964] A.C. 1254; [1964] 2 All E.R. 401; see p. 503, *ante*.

[12] [1964] A.C. 1254, at p. 1343; [1964] 2 All E.R. 401, at p. 436.

[13] [1977] A.C. 1; [1976] 2 All E.R. 497.

unsatisfactory situation in the event of conflict between the verdicts of the two juries concerned. Nevertheless it is surprising that the point in *R*. v. *Humphrys* had not been the subject of reported decision before. The Court of Appeal held that issue estoppel did apply[14] and declined the invitation of the Crown to carve out an exception for charges of perjury from the general principles of issue estoppel, stating that such a course, if appropriate, was for the House of Lords or Parliament to take. The Court of Appeal accordingly allowed the appeal but granted leave to appeal to the House of Lords, certifying that a point of law of general public importance was involved. The House of Lords reversed the Court of Appeal's decision, holding that the doctrine of issue estoppel had no application to criminal proceedings. The rationale of this rule appears to be largely pragmatic and it may lead to what many would regard as capricious results. Thus if, for example, a defendant was prosecuted for causing grievous bodily harm and acquitted and, subsequent to that acquittal, the victim died, he could then be prosecuted for murder. No doubt the Attorney-General would enter a *nolle prosequi* or the Director of Public Prosecutions take over the case and offer no evidence[15] in such cases, but this would make the individual's freedom dependent upon the exercise of executive discretion. Conversely if a defendant were convicted of causing grievous bodily harm and the victim subsequently died the defendant, in a prosecution for murder, would be free to raise again all the defences which had been disbelieved and rejected at his first trial.[16]

Judicial review proceedings—In *R*. v. *Secretary of State for the Environment, Ex parte Hackney London Borough Council*[17] the Queen's Bench divisional court held that issue estoppel did not apply in proceedings for judicial review.[18] The grounds for this decison were: (1) the absence of formal pleadings in such proceedings, so that it is frequently difficult if not impossible to identify a particular "issue" decided by the "first" application; (2) the absence of any *lis* between either the Crown and the respondent or the *ex parte* applicant and the respondent; and (3) the fact that a decision

---

[14] [1976] Q.B. 191; [1975] 2 All E.R. 1023. This decision, if upheld, would have led logically to the surprising conclusion that if a person was convicted of any criminal offence, however minor, following a trial in which he gave evidence denying the criminal act involved, his conviction would be virtually automatic if he were prosecuted for perjury in relation to the evidence which he gave at his trial.

[15] See p. 276, *ante*.

[16] In *R*. v. *Hogan*, [1974] Q.B. 398; [1974] 2 All E.R. 142 this very situation arose and LAWSON, J., after a careful analysis of the English, Australian and United States authorities, held that the defendant was estopped at his trial for murder from denying those issues which had necessarily been decided against him by the verdict of the jury at his first trial for causing grievous bodily harm; in *R*. v. *Humphrys* (*supra*) the House of Lords overruled this case. It is very difficult to reconcile the recent decision of the Court of Appeal in *R*. v. *Hay* (1983), 77 Cr. App. Rep. 70 with the *Humphrys* principle. In this case the accused signed a confession to both arson and burglary. He was first tried for arson, at which trial he alleged that the confession had been fabricated by the police and he was acquitted. He was then tried for the burglary at which trial the judge excluded evidence of his acquittal. He was convicted but the Court of Appeal quashed the conviction holding that the jury should have been told of the acquittal and directed that it was conclusive evidence that his confession (so far as it related to the arson) was untrue and that in deciding the issue between the accused and the police in relation to the burglary they should bear in mind that the admissions relating to the arson had to be treated as untrue.

[17] [1983] 3 All E.R. 358, [1983] 1 W.L.R. 524.

[18] For details of this procedure, see p. 174, *ante*.

in judicial review proceedings is not "final" in the sense necessary for issue estoppel to operate; the nature of the relief, in many cases, leaves open reconsideration by the statutory or other tribunal of the matter in dispute. The court also "ventured a reservation" as to whether issue estoppel could ever operate against the Crown.

b Estoppel by deed

The doctrine of estoppel by deed is a reminder of the peculiar sanctity accorded by the common law to deeds. However, equity has made such substantial inroads into the common law rules concerning the enforcement of obligations under seal[19] that the common law doctrine of estoppel by deed is now scarcely any wider than the doctrine of estoppel by agreement discussed below.

At common law a party to a deed is estopped from denying the truth of statements in the deed. A recital in a deed will raise an estoppel against the party making it. It may also raise an estoppel against other parties to the deed[20] provided that the statement is one which the parties have mutually agreed to admit as true. However, if the recital is intended to be the statement of one party only, the estoppel operates only against that party and not again other parties to the deed.[1] Apart from this limitation, a deed only raises an estoppel in an action upon the deed between the parties to the deed and their privies. In addition the doctrine of estoppel does not prevent a party from setting up any plea such as fraud, undue influence, mistake or illegality which would give him a right to rescind the deed in equity.

c Estoppel by conduct

> "Where one by his words or conduct wilfully causes another to believe in the existence of a certain state of things, and induces him to act on that belief, or to alter his own previous position the former is concluded from averring against the latter a different state of things as existing at that time."[2]

This classic statement illustrates the common law doctrine of estoppel by conduct. The conduct which gives rise to the estoppel may exist in an agreement, a representation or in negligence. Consequently it is usual to subdivide the doctrine of estoppel by conduct in this way.

Estoppel by agreement—If two persons enter into an agreement on the basis that a certain state of affairs exists, each of them is estopped from denying that this state of affairs does exist. Perhaps the commonest illustration of estoppel by agreement is the principle that neither a landlord nor a tenant may deny the title of the landlord since the lease is entered into on the basis that the landlord has a good title. The practical result is that the landlord

---

[19] A document does not, however, have to bear a physical seal in order to be classified as a deed; it is sufficient that it has been executed by a party as if it were his deed—it is common these days for the letters "L.S." (*locus sigilli*), in a circle, to appear instead of a seal: *First National Securities, Ltd.* v. *Jones*, [1978] Ch. 109; [1978] 2 All E.R. 221.

[20] *Bowman* v. *Taylor* (1834), 2 Ad. & El. 278.

[1] *Greer* v. *Kettle*, [1938] A.C. 156; [1937] 4 All E.R. 396. Intention is ascertained by construing the deed (*ibid*).

[2] *Pickard* v. *Sears* (1837), 6 Ad. & El. 469.

cannot refuse to perform his covenants such as repairing covenants; nor can the tenant refuse to pay rent or carry out repairs by denying the landlord's title.[3] Estoppel by agreement only lasts, however, during the existence of the agreement so that after the tenancy has expired, the tenant is no longer estopped from denying the landlord's title.[4] Other relationships to which the doctrine of estoppel by agreement applies are those between licensor and licensee, bailor and bailee and principal and agent.

Estoppel by representation—Anyone who makes a representation of existing fact with intention that the person to whom it is made should act upon it is estopped from denying the truth of that fact, in an action by someone who has acted to his detriment upon the faith of the representation. There are many varieties of the doctrine of estoppel by representation. A typical example is agency by estoppel. A person who represents another as being his agent is estopped from denying that that person acted with his authority. Thus a husband who pays for goods ordered from tradesmen by his wife is estopped from denying that his wife has authority to pledge his credit.[5] The husband, if he wishes to terminate his wife's agency by estoppel, must expressly inform the tradesmen that she no longer has authority to pledge his credit.[6] Another form of estoppel by representation occurs where a person represents himself as a partner in a firm. He is liable as a partner to anyone who has given credit to the firm on the faith of his representation.[7]

There are, however, restrictions on the doctrine of estoppel by representation at common law. The representation must be a representation of existing fact. A representation as to the law will not raise an estoppel; nor will a representation as to future intention.[8] However, a representation as to future intention may give rise to an estoppel in equity, sometimes described as a quasi-estoppel or promissory estoppel. The doctrine of equitable or quasi-estoppel is enshrined in the judgment of DENNING, J. (as he then was) in *Central London Property Trust, Ltd.* v. *High Trees House, Ltd.*[9] where it was suggested that a representation as to future intention which is acted upon may estop the person making the representation from resiling from his representation.[10] There is, however, a basic difference between common law estoppel by representation and equitable estoppel by representation. The difference is that a person can take the benefit of an equitable estoppel only if it is just and equitable for him to do so whereas there is no such limitation on the common law doctrine of estoppel. Thus if a person agrees to accept a lesser sum in satisfaction of a contractual debt he may be estopped from suing for the balance, but only if it would be inequitable, and contrary to the justice of the case, to allow him to do so.[11] Where there is a duty to disclose facts, failure to do so amounts to a representation for the purposes of

---

[3] *Cooke* v. *Loxley* (1792), 5 Term Rep. 4.
[4] *Harrison* v. *Wells*, [1967] 1 Q.B. 263; [1966] 3 All E.R. 524.
[5] *Drew* v. *Nunn* (1879), 4 Q.B.D. 661; cf. *Spiro* v. *Lintern*, [1973] 3 All E.R. 319; [1973] 1 W.L.R. 1002.
[6] *Debenham* v. *Mellon* (1880), 6 App. Cas. 24.
[7] Partnership Act 1890, s. 14 (1).
[8] *Jorden* v. *Money* (1854), 5 H.L. Cas. 185.
[9] [1947] K.B. 130; [1956] 1 All E.R. 256n.
[10] See *Tool Metal Manufacturing Co., Ltd.* v. *Tungsten Electric Co., Ltd.,* [1955] 2 All E.R. 657; [1955] 1 W.L.R. 761; *Inwards* v. *Baker,* [1965] 2 Q.B. 29; [1965] 1 All E.R. 446.
[11] *D. and C. Builders, Ltd.* v. *Rees*, [1966] 2 Q.B. 617; [1965] 3 All E.R. 837.

estoppel. This point is illustrated by the decision of the House of Lords in *Greenwood* v. *Martins Bank, Ltd.*[12] In that case a husband's failure to inform the bank that his wife was forging his signature on cheques was held to estop him from setting up the forgeries in an action by the bank to recover the sums paid to his wife and debited to his account.

There are two further restrictions on the doctrine of estoppel by representation which should be noted. First, estoppel is a defence and cannot, as a rule, be used to found a cause of action. Thus a person who makes a promise, not under seal and unsupported by consideration, to pay money to another cannot be sued by that other upon his promise on the basis that he is estopped from denying his promise. This extension of the *High Trees* principle was firmly rejected by the Court of Appeal in *Combe* v. *Combe.*[13] However where the effect of the estoppel is to create a proprietary interest (sometimes called a "proprietary estoppel") the estoppel can give rise to a cause of action in that proceedings can be taken to enforce the interest so created.[14] In such cases estoppel is clearly to be regarded rather as a rule of substantive law than as a rule of evidence. The second restriction is that an estoppel cannot be pleaded where to do so would give effect to something illegal, immoral or contrary to public policy. This is an extension of the general principle that an estoppel cannot bind the court. Thus an infant who represents himself as being of full age in order to obtain a loan of money is not estopped from pleading his infancy as a defence to an action on the loan.[15] Similarly a wife who agrees not to apply to the court for maintenance is not estopped from making such an application.[16]

Estoppel by negligence—Where a person by his negligence causes another, to whom he owes a duty of care, to believe in the existence of a fact, and that other acts to his detriment upon that belief, the negligent party is estopped from denying that fact. This situation usually arises where the negligent party facilitates the commission of a fraud upon the other party. Thus in *Coventry, Sheppard & Co.* v. *Great Eastern Rail. Co.,*[17] a servant of the defendant company negligently issued two delivery orders in respect of one consignment of wheat enabling a fraudulent third party to obtain two advances of money on the security of the goods. The company was held to be estopped from denying that there were two consignments. Similarly a person who carelessly draws a cheque so as to enable a fraudulent holder to fill in additional figures is liable to have his account debited with the amount paid to the rogue.[18] The scope of estoppel by negligence is not wider than the tort of negligence in that negligence can only give rise to an estoppel where a duty of care is owed by the negligent party to the person who acts to his detriment.

---

[12] [1933] A.C. 51.

[13] [1951] 2 K.B. 215; [1951] 1 All E.R. 767.

[14] See *Crabb* v. *Arun District Council*, [1976] Ch. 179; [1975] 3 All E.R. 865 and cases cited therein.

[15] *R. Leslie, Ltd.* v. *Sheill*, [1914] 3 K.B. 607; see also *Kok Hoong* v. *Leong Cheong Kweng Mines, Ltd.*, [1964] A.C. 993; [1964] 1 All E.R. 300.

[16] *Hyman* v. *Hyman*, [1929] A.C. 601; Matrimonial Causes Act 1973, s. 34.

[17] (1883), 11 Q.B.D. 776.

[18] *London Joint Stock Bank* v. *Macmillan*, [1918] A.C. 777; the decision in this case was not based primarily upon estoppel, though the principle is similar.

2   Public policy

a   Public interest privilege

Relevant evidence must be excluded if its disclosure would be prejudicial to the public interest. The evidence in question is, in fact, usually documentary. Where the Crown (usually through a department of State) is involved the privilege is sometimes described as "Crown privilege" but "public interest privilege" is much wider than Crown privilege.[19] In cases of Crown privilege the objection to production is usually taken at the stage of discovery of documents[20] although it may be taken at the trial. In actions between private persons the privilege exists and cannot be waived by any person (other than the Crown) and the objection to production is usually taken at the trial. Privilege can be claimed on behalf of the Crown for a document regardless of who has possession of the document and is not confined to documents emanating from or in the possession of a department of State. Indeed, even if neither party takes the objection, the judge must exclude evidence if it appears that its reception would be injurious to the public interest. The scope of Crown privilege is properly a matter of constitutional law rather than of evidence or procedure. Basically there are two problems: the scope of the "public interest" and the question of who is to decide whether or not the reception of evidence would be contrary to that interest. Until recent years, in cases involving the Crown (or departments of State) these two problems merged into one since it was accepted as being the law that the executive rather than the judiciary was the final arbiter of a claim of Crown privilege. The result was that the scope of the State interest was determined by the Crown. It is this fact which accounts for the wide variety of matters which the State interest has been held to comprise. Thus evidence has been excluded of such diverse matters as communications between the Commander-in-Chief in India and the Indian Government,[1] a company's balance sheets in the possession of the Inland Revenue authorities,[2] medical and police reports on the condition of a prisoner alleged to have assaulted a fellow prisoner,[3] and communications between the Secretary of State for War and the Soldiers', Sailors' and Airmen's Families' Association concerning the latter's attempts to effect a reconciliation between a soldier and his wife.[4] In the two most recent of these cases, *Ellis* v. *Home Office* and *Broome* v. *Broome*, the claim of the appropriate Minister of the Crown was regarded as conclusive. This principle had been established by VISCOUNT SIMON, L.C. in the leading case of *Duncan* v. *Cammell, Laird & Co., Ltd.*[5] In that case the House of Lords upheld the refusal of the First Lord of the Admiralty to allow discovery of documents relating to the details of construction of submarines in time of war. The Lord Chancellor, however, went further and stated, in effect, that the decision as to whether or not to exclude evidence as contrary to the public interest rested with the Minister and that the judge could not go

---

[19] See *Neilson* v. *Laugharne*, [1981] Q.B. 736; [1981] 1 All E.R. 829.
[20] Crown Proceedings Act 1947, s. 28.
[1] *Chatterton* v. *Secretary of State for India*, [1895] 2 Q.B. 189.
[2] *Re Joseph Hargreaves, Ltd.*, [1900] 1 Ch. 347.
[3] *Ellis* v. *Home Office*, [1953] 2 Q.B. 135; [1953] 2 All E.R. 149.
[4] *Broome* v. *Broome*, [1955] P. 190; [1953] 1 All E.R. 201.
[5] [1942] A.C. 624; [1942] 1 All E.R. 587.

behind the Minister's decision. There followed a line of cases in which the affidavit of the appropriate Minister, generally expressed in a common form, was accepted by the judiciary with varying degrees of reluctance as conclusive. In some of these cases the Minister's refusal to allow evidence to be adduced appeared to cause considerable hardship to litigants. In addition it was widely felt that the judiciary ought to have the power to examine the evidence in question in order to satisfy itself that its reception would, indeed, be contrary to the public interest rather than having to rely upon the Minister's assertion. The result was, in 1968, a restatement of the law by the House of Lords in *Conway* v. *Rimmer*.[6]

The speeches of the House of Lords in *Conway* v. *Rimmer* vary considerably in their respective statements of the law. However, certain basic principles emerge. First, there are documents which, because either of their contents or of the class to which they belong, are conclusively privileged from disclosure. This category would include, for example, documents containing official secrets (privileged on account of their contents) and cabinet minutes (privileged on account of the class to which they belong). In respect of such documents their lordships anticipated that no difficulty would arise and that the courts would never need to go behind the certificate of a Minister claiming privilege (though it seems implicit that a court would have power to call for such a document for examination if it chose to do so). Since *Duncan* v. *Cammell, Laird & Co., Ltd.* concerned documents in this category, the House of Lords in *Conway* v. *Rimmer* expressed the view that the case was correctly decided on its facts but distinguishable.

In relation to documents outside the limited category referred to above the court will, even in the face of a Minister's certificate claiming privilege, look at the documents and attempt to strike a balance between the public interest in maintaining confidence and the principle that the administration of justice should not be impeded by the withholding of evidence.[7] When a Minister's certificate asserts that certain documents are of a class which ought in the public interest to be withheld from disclosure then, unless his reasons are of a kind which judicial experience is not competent to weigh, the final decision rests with the court.

In the event the House of Lords in *Conway* v. *Rimmer* did order disclosure of the documents in issue, which comprised reports concerning a probationary police constable made by a police superintendent, including a report to the Chief Constable. Subsequently, in *Rogers* v. *Secretary of State for Home Department*[8] a claim for privilege was upheld, by the House of Lords, in respect of letters passing between the Gaming Board and the Chief Constable

---

6 [1968] A.C. 910; [1968] 1 All E.R. 874. See also *Re Grosvenor Hotel, London (No. 2)*, [1965] Ch. 1210; [1964] 3 All E.R. 354; *Wednesbury Corporation* v. *Ministry of Housing and Local Government*, [1965] 1 All E.R. 186; [1965] 1 W.L.R. 261.

7 *Burmah Oil Co., Ltd* v. *Bank of England (A-G intervening)*, [1980] A.C. 1090; [1979] 3 All E.R. 700. However before ordering discovery, or even inspecting the document in question, the court must be satisfied that the documents are likely to assist the applicant's case or damage the other side's case and that the applicant is not just undertaking a "fishing expedition": *Air Canada* v. *Secretary of State for Trade (No.2)*, [1983] 2 A.C. 394; [1983] 1 All E.R. 910.

8 [1973] A.C. 388; [1972] 2 All E.R. 1057; see also *Crompton (Alfred) Amusement Machines, Ltd.* v. *Customs and Excise Commissioner (No. 2)*. [1974] A.C. 405; [1973] 2 All E.R. 1169; *Neilson* v. *Laugharne*, [1981] Q.B. 736; [1981] 1 All E.R. 829.

of Sussex concerning the character and reputation of an applicant for bingo club licences on the basis that the public interest required that protection be given to persons supplying information to the Gaming Board for otherwise they might refuse to give the information requested thus hindering the Gaming Board in the proper exercise of its public duties.

The public interest is not, however, confined to evidence in the possession of the Crown or departments of State or to proceedings to which the Crown is a party. Occasionally the public interest may justify a claim for privilege in proceedings between parties. The origin of the modern "public interest privilege" (as opposed to the narrower "Crown privilege") is the decision of the House of Lords in *Crompton (Alfred) Amusement Machines, Ltd. v. Customs and Excise Commissioners (No. 2)*[9] where LORD CROSS, speaking on behalf of all members of the House, observed:[10]

> " 'Confidentiality' is not a separate head of privilege, but it may be a very material consideration to bear in mind when privilege is claimed on the ground of public interest. What the court has to do is to weigh on the one hand the considerations which suggest that it is in the public interest that the documents in question should be disclosed and on the other hand those which suggest that it is in the public interest that they should not be disclosed and to balance one against the other."

A good illustration of this balancing exercise is the leading case of *D. v. National Society for the Prevention of Cruelty to Children.*[11] The defendant society, which is an "authorised person" under the Children and Young Persons Act 1969, for the purpose of bringing care proceedings under the Act, invites information from members of the public concerning children who might need protection from abuse; it promises that such information will be treated as confidential and, without an effective promise of confidentiality, it may be appreciated that members of the public might be deterred from bringing cases to the attention of the society. In the instant case somebody told the society that the plaintiff's daughter had been ill-treated; the society sent one of its inspectors to the plaintiff's home whereupon the information supplied proved to be untrue. The plaintiff, not unnaturally, wished to know the source of the complaint against her and to this end she brought an action against the society claiming damages for negligence in the manner of investigating the complaint and seeking an order that the society disclose to her all documents relating to the complaint and the identity of the informant. The House of Lords, reversing the decision of the Court of Appeal, held that the society was entitled to withhold discovery of these documents, in the public interest. The public interest to be protected was the effective functioning of an organisation authorised by Act of Parliament to bring proceedings for the welfare of children. The House added, however, that the fact that a communication was made in confidence would not in itself be a sufficient ground to justify non-disclosure of either the informa-

---

9 [1974] A.C. 405; [1973] 2 All E.R. 1169.
10 [1974] A.C., at p. 433, [1973] 2 All E.R., at p. 1184.
11 [1978] A.C. 171; [1977] 1 All E.R. 589. Furthermore, the court always has a discretion to refuse to order discovery, by which it may permit confidential documents to be withheld: *Science Research Council* v. *Nassé*, [1980] A.C. 1028; 3 All E.R. 673.

tion communicated or the identity of the informant, if these would be relevant in a court of law.

One final aspect of the public interest may be quoted here. The sources of information leading to the detection of crime are privileged from disclosure. Thus in *Marks* v. *Beyfus*,[12] a civil action based on conspiracy to prosecute the plaintiff maliciously, the Director of Public Prosecutions declined to answer questions concerning the information leading to the plaintiff's prosecution. His refusal was upheld by the Court of Appeal. Indeed the Court of Appeal went further and stated that the judge ought not to have allowed the Director to answer had he wished to do so. For this reason the exclusion must be regarded as being based on public policy rather than private privilege.

b Judicial proceedings

Judges of superior courts cannot be compelled to give evidence of what took place in the course of proceedings before them. The rationale of this rule is the need for preserving the dignity of the judiciary. The privilege does not extend to arbitrators who may be required to give evidence as to what occurred during the arbitrations.

The general immunity which attaches to judicial proceedings extends to prevent jurors from giving evidence which would tend to cast doubts upon their verdict. Thus jurors cannot give evidence of discussions in the jury room. Nor can a juror testify that he did not understand the evidence; nor that he intended to give a verdict contrary to that returned;[13] nor that the verdict was arrived at by drawing lots.[14]

c Illegally obtained evidence

An involuntary or induced confession of guilt by an accused person is inadmissible. The admissibility of confessions is dealt with in a later chapter.[15] Oddly enough there is no rule of public policy which excludes facts discovered as a result of an inadmissible confession. For example evidence may be given that stolen goods were discovered at the accused's lodgings even though the confession leading to this discovery was induced and therefore inadmissible.[16] Similarly there is no rule excluding evidence of facts discovered in consequence of illegal searches. Indeed the authorities favour the admissibility of such evidence.[17] In *R*. v. *Sang*[18] the House of Lords held that the fact that evidence might have been obtained against an accused improperly by the use of an *agent provocateur* or by a policeman and an informer inciting the accused to commit a crime was not a ground upon which a judge could exclude the evidence. Courts are concerned with how evidence is used at the trial, not with how it was obtained in the first place and, except in the

---

[12] (1890), 25 Q.B.D. 494.

[13] *Jackson* v. *Williamson* (1788), 2 Term Rep. 281; *Boston* v. *W.S. Bagshaw & Sons,* [1966] 2 All E.R. 906; [1966] 1 W.L.R. 1135.

[14] *Owen* v. *Warburton* (1805), 1 B. & P.N.R. 326.

[15] See p. 669, *post.*

[16] *R.* v. *Gould* (1840), 9 C & P. 364. This position will be preserved by the Police and Criminal Evidence Act 1984, s. 76(4).

[17] *Elias* v. *Pasmore,* [1934] 2 K.B. 164; *Kuruma Son of Kaniu* v. *R.,* [1955] A.C. 197; [1955] 1 All E.R. 236; *Rumping* v. *Director of Public Prosecutions,* [1964] A.C. 814; [1962] 3 All E.R. 256.

[18] [1980] A.C. 402; [1979] 2 All E.R. 1222.

case of admissions, confessions and evidence obtained from the accused after the commission of the offence (as to which see *infra*), a judge had no discretion to exclude relevant evidence merely because it had been obtained by improper or unfair means. Thus an attempt, in effect, to introduce a defence of "entrapment" into the English criminal law via the law of evidence, failed.

LORD DIPLOCK expressed the position as follows:[19]

> "A fair trial according to law involves, in the case of a trial on indictment, that it should take place before a judge and a jury; that the case against the accused should be proved to the satisfaction of the jury beyond all reasonable doubt on evidence that is admissible in law; and, as a corollary to this, that there should be excluded from the jury information about the accused which is likely to have an influence on their minds prejudicial to the accused which is out of proportion to the true probative value of admissible evidence conveying that information. If these conditions are fulfilled and the jury receive correct instructions from the judge as to the law applicable to the case, the requirement that the accused should have a fair trial according to law is, in my view, satisfied; for the fairness of a trial according to law is not all one-sided; it requires that those who are undoubtedly guilty should be convicted as well as that those about whose guilt there is any reasonable doubt should be acquitted. However much the judge may dislike the way in which a particular piece of evidence was obtained before proceedings were commenced, if it is admissible evidence probative of the accused's guilt it is not part of his judicial function to exclude it for this reason."

This passage cannot, however, be taken entirely at face value because LORD DIPLOCK was expressly excluding from his consideration admissions, confessions and evidence obtained from the accused after the commission of the offence. Indeed the Privy Council, including LORD DIPLOCK, had recently held[20] in favour of excluding from the prosecution case evidence given by a defendant during a "trial within a trial", although such evidence would, on general principles, be both relevant and admissible and, indeed, would be admissible in cross-examination of the accused as to inconsistency, as the Privy Council accepted.

Accordingly the principle to be deduced from *R.* v. *Sang* is that evidence, if admissible, cannot be excluded simply because it has been improperly or illegally obtained.

3   Discretion to exclude relevant evidence

Apart from the positive rules of exclusion discussed above, there is an overriding judicial discretion to exclude relevant evidence in criminal proceedings where its prejudicial effect would outweigh its probative value.[1] Thus the permissible scope of cross-examination of an accused person by the prosecution under the provisions of the Criminal Evidence Act 1898, section

[19] [1980] A.C., at pp. 436–437; [1979] 2 All E.R., at p. 1230.
[20] *Wong Kam-ming* v. *R.,* [1980] A.C. 247; [1979] 1 All E.R. 939; see p. 669, *post.*
[1] *Harris* v. *Director of Public Prosecutions*, [1952] A.C. 694; [1952] 1 All E.R. 1044; *R.* v. *Sang* (*supra*). This discretion is codified in s. 78(1) of the Police and Criminal Evidence Act 1984 "if it appears to the court that, having regard to all the circumstances, including the circumstances in which the evidence was obtained, the admission of the evidence would have such an adverse effect on the fairness of the proceedings that the court ought not to admit it."

1(f) is within the discretion of the trial judge.[2] There is a discretion to allow rebutting evidence after the close of the defence evidence in both civil and criminal proceedings. The question of whether to conduct a view of the *locus in quo* is within the discretion of the trial judge. These may, however, be regarded as instances of the court exercising control over its own procedure, rather than as rules of evidence.

Where a statute provides for the reception of evidence, the question of whether the judge has a discretion to exclude such evidence is primarily one of statutory interpretation. Thus if a statute provides that some fact *may* be given in evidence there is a discretion to exclude it. Conversely, where the statute is couched in mandatory terms there is no discretion to exclude the evidence rendered admissible by the statute. Thus the House of Lords has held that there is no discretion to exclude cross-examination of one accused by a co-accused under section 1(f) (iii) of the Criminal Evidence Act 1898 even though there is a discretion to exclude cross-examination by the prosecution under the section.[3]

Evidence of alibi

Special mention should be made of the discretionary rule of exclusion in relation to alibi defences, introduced by section 11 of the Criminal Justice Act 1967. This section provides that on a trial on indictment the defendant shall not without leave of the court adduce evidence in support of an alibi unless within 7 days of the conclusion of the committal proceedings he gives to the prosecution notice of particulars of the alibi. The notice must contain certain prescribed particulars, so as to enable the prosecution to investigate the alleged alibi. However the rule of exclusion only operates if the defendant was informed at the preliminary investigation of his obligation to give the prescribed notice. Moreover, although there is a statutory time limit, the discretion to exclude alibi evidence must be exercised judicially and the fact that the notice has been served late does not by itself, as a general rule, justify the court refusing leave to admit the evidence.[4] Furthermore, notice is only required in relation to the occasion on which an offence with which he is charged is alleged to have been committed. Accordingly evidence of the accused's whereabouts on other occasions is not subject to the restriction imposed by the section, however significant that evidence may be in relation to the issues in the case. Thus if the accused is charged with a robbery which is alleged to have been committed on a Monday, and part of the prosecution case is that the accused was seen on the following Tuesday driving a van which contained the stolen goods, he may tender alibi evidence concerning his whereabouts on the Tuesday without giving the statutory notice.[5]

---

2 *Maxwell* v. *Director of Public Prosecutions*, [1935] A.C. 309, at pp. 319, 321; see p. 586, *ante*.
3 *Murdoch* v. *Taylor*, [1965] A.C. 574; [1965] 1 All E.R. 406; see p. 588, *ante*.
4 *R.* v. *Sullivan*, [1971] 1 Q.B. 253; [1970] 2 All E.R. 681.
5 *R.* v. *Lewis*, [1969] 2 Q.B. 1; [1969] All E.R. 79, per WIDGERY, L.J. (as he then was). See also p. 512, *ante*.

CHAPTER 30

The Onus of Proof

A FACTS WHICH MAY BE ESTABLISHED BY MEANS OTHER THAN PROOF

The general rule is that a party seeking to rely upon a fact must prove its existence to the tribunal. There are, however, certain matters which do not require affirmative proof. Thus facts which are admitted in civil or criminal cases need not be proved. Similarly English courts take judicial notice of a number of matters with the result that neither party need adduce proof of these matters. Finally a fact which is presumed in favour of a party need not be proved by that party, although the presumption sometimes arises only on proof of a prior basic fact; whether or not his opponent may disprove the fact depends upon the classification of the presumption as rebuttable or irrebuttable.

1 Formal admissions

Formal admissions must be distinguished from informal admissions and confessions. An informal admission and a confession are means of proving the fact admitted or confessed. For example, if a car driver, following an accident, admits that he was driving on the wrong side of the road and that he failed to give a proper signal, this statement may be put in evidence at the trial as a means of proving the facts stated by the driver. The driver may, however, attempt to explain away his statement at the trial and may produce evidence to contradict its truth. If, on the other hand, the driver in a civil action to which he is a party formally admits in the course of the proceedings that he was driving on the wrong side of the road his opponent need not prove that fact at all; it is admitted in his favour. Thus an informal admission is a means of proving the fact admitted whereas a formal admission dispenses with the need for proving that fact.

   At common law formal admissions were not receivable in criminal cases (except, of course, for pleas of guilty, which dispense with the need for a trial). Provision for formal admissions in criminal cases, by or on behalf of either prosecution or defence, was introduced by section 10 of the Criminal Justice Act 1967. An admission may, by virtue of that section, be made either at or before the trial, but if made other than in court, must be in writing. An admission made for the purpose of proceedings relating to any matter is treated as an admission for the purpose of any subsequent criminal proceedings relating to that matter, including any appeal or retrial, but may, at any stage, be withdrawn with leave of the court.

In civil cases rules of court provide for the means by which formal admissions may be made. In the High Court the Rules of the Supreme Court provide for formal admissions at various stages of the proceedings. Thus admissions may be made on the pleadings. An admission on the pleadings may be express or implied, in some circumstances, by a failure to traverse (deny) an allegation. Alternatively an admission may be made in answer to interrogatories or to a notice to admit facts or documents or on the hearing of the summons for directions.[1] Finally admissions may be made during the course of the trial. Counsel or solicitors acting as advocates have a general authority to make admissions binding upon their clients.[2]

2 Judicial notice

There are certain facts of which the court recognises the existence, in civil and criminal cases alike, without the need for proof. Such facts are said to be judicially noticed. The rationale of the principle of judicial notice is that there are matters which are so notorious that it would be pedantic to require proof of them. Certain matters must, by statute, be judicially noticed. These include the authenticity of signatures on certain public or official documents[3] and the contents of every Act of Parliament passed after 1850 unless the contrary is provided by the Act.[4] Apart from these statutory provisions it is impossible to classify satisfactorily the innumerable facts of which the courts take judicial notice. The issue depends to a certain extent upon the degree of notoriety of the fact in question. Thus judicial notice has been taken of the fact that a fortnight is an impossibly short period of human gestation[5] though not that 360 days is an impossibly long period.[6] Judicial notice has been taken of such widely divergent matters as the fact that camels are domestic animals,[7] that the value of money has declined since 1189,[8] that the streets of London are full of traffic,[9] that Great Britain is at war[10] and that many motorists prefer not to mix lubricating oils in the engines of their cars.[11]

---

[1] See pp. 345, 360, 364, 374, *ante.*

[2] *Swinfen* v. *Lord Chelmsford* (1860), 5 H. & N. 890.

[3] Evidence Act 1845, s. 2; Bankruptcy Act 1914, s. 142.

[4] Interpretation Act 1978, ss. 3, 22 (1) and Sch. 12. By section 3(2) of the European Communities Act 1972: "Judicial notice shall be taken of the Treaties, of the Official Journal of the Communities and of any decision of, or expression of opinion by, the European Court on any such questions as aforesaid; and the Official Journal shall be admissible as evidence of any instrument or other act thereby communicated of any of the Communities or of any Community institution.'

[5] *R.* v. *Luffe* (1807), 8 East 193.

[6] *Preston-Jones* v. *Preston-Jones,* [1951] A.C. 391; [1951] 1 All E.R. 124.

[7] *McQuaker* v. *Goddard,* [1940] 1 K.B. 687; [1940] 1 All E.R. 471.

[8] *Bryant* v. *Foot* (1868), L.R. 3 Q.B. 497.

[9] *Dennis* v. *White & Co.,* [1916] 2 K.B. 1.

[10] *Re a Petition of Right,* [1915] 3 K.B. 643.

[11] *Petrofina (Gt. Britain), Ltd* v. *Martin,* [1966] Ch. 146, at p. 190; [1966] 1 All E.R. 126, at p. 144, per Diplock, L.J. (as he then was).

In many cases the court will take judicial notice of a fact without inquiry. Nevertheless in some cases the judge will consult sources to which it is proper for him to refer before deciding whether to take judicial notice of a particular fact. These sources are examined for reference rather than as evidence and it is for this reason that the fact ascertained is regarded as judicially noticed rather than proved. For example, the court takes judicial notice of the meaning of ordinary English words but the judge may still wish to consult a dictionary for reference. In *McQuaker* v. *Goddard*[12] the trial judge took judicial notice of the fact that a camel is a domestic animal only after consulting reference books and hearing witnesses. Similarly, although the courts take judicial notice of the sovereignty of a foreign State, the certificate of the appropriate Secretary of State is conclusive in cases of uncertainty.[13] In such cases the dividing line between judicial notice and proof is sometimes a very thin one.

It is sometimes said that the courts take judicial notice of the law of England. This is merely an alternative method of saying that law need not be proved. Actually certain rules of law must be proved. Private Acts of Parliament, certain Statutory Instruments and any custom not settled by judicial decision must be proved. Apart from these exceptions law need not be proved. However this principle only extends to English law and, in the House of Lords, to the law of Scotland and Northern Ireland.[14] Foreign law is, paradoxically, a question of fact and must be proved as such although it is a question of fact to be decided by the judge not by the jury.[15]

3 Presumptions

In certain circumstances the court presumes a fact in favour of a party who is thereby relieved of the burden of proving it. In a few of these cases the law provides that the party against whom the fact is presumed cannot deny its existence. The presumption is then said to be irrebuttable. However, in most cases the presumption is rebuttable. Consequently the effect of a presumption is usually to shift a burden of proof from the party in whose favour the presumption is raised to his opponent. It would be possible to consider presumptions as one aspect of the burden of proof but, since the burden of proof is a wider topic much of which is unconnected with presumptions and since not all presumptions shift the burden of proof, it is more convenient to deal with presumptions separately.

Presumptions may take two forms: direct and inferential, the latter being of greater practical importance. A direct presumption is a presumption which arises without proof of a basic fact. Direct presumptions are really rules of law which determine where the general burden of proof shall lie.

---

12 [1940] 1 K.B. 687; [1940] 1 All E.R. 471.
13 *Duff Development Co.* v. *Government of Kelantan*, [1924] A.C. 797.
14 *MacShannon* v. *Rockware Glass, Ltd.,* [1978] A.C. 795; [1978] 1 All E.R. 625.
15 Administration of Justice Act 1920, s. 15; Supreme Court Act 1981, s. 69(5). By s. 3(1) of the European Communities Act 1972: "For the purposes of all legal proceedings any question as to the meaning or effect of any of the Treaties, or as to the validity, meaning or effect of any Community instrument, shall be treated as a question of law and, if not referred to the European Court, be for determination as such in accordance with the principles laid down by and any relevant decision of the European Court.

The best known direct presumptions are the presumption of innocence and the presumption of sanity. An accused person is presumed innocent until the prosecution has proved his guilt beyond reasonable doubt. Similarly, every person is presumed sane until the contrary is proven. It will be appreciated that since these two presumptions arise without the need for proving any preliminary basic fact they do not shift a burden of proof; they merely determine where the burden shall lie in the first place. Inferential presumptions, on the other hand, have the effect of shifting a burden of proof from the party who proves the basic fact upon which the presumption depends to the party against whom the presumption is raised. A typical example is the presumption of legitimacy. It is for the person who alleges that he is legitimate to prove his legitimacy. There is, however, a presumption of legitimacy in favour of a person who was born or conceived in lawful wedlock unless his conception must have occurred while his parents were separated by court order. The result is that if the party seeking to prove his legitimacy can prove the basic fact of birth or conception in lawful wedlock the presumption arises in his favour and a burden of proof is cast upon his opponent to prove illegitimacy. However, while almost all inferential presumptions merely have the effect of shifting a burden of proof, certain inferential presumptions are irrebuttable[16] with the effect that proof of the basic fact amounts to proof of the fact presumed. In such a case the presumption does not merely affect the burden of proof; it dispenses with the need for proof completely. There is sometimes said to be a presumption that every person knows the law, but this is not so. There is, however, a rule that ignorance of law is no defence. Thus a recent attempt to persuade the Court of Appeal that the draftsman of a settlement, being presumed to be aware of the fiscal consequences of what he was doing, must have intended the settlement to produce consequences least favourable to the Inland Revenue, was conspicuously unsuccessful.[17]

Various classifications of presumptions have been attempted.[18] Although none of them is wholly satisfactory, the orthodox classification into irrebuttable presumptions of law, rebuttable presumptions of law and rebuttable presumptions of fact is the classification most widely adopted.

a Irrebuttable presumptions of law

Irrebuttable presumptions of law, sometimes described as conclusive presumptions, are not really presumptions but are rather rules of substantive law couched in presumptive terms. For example section 50 of the Children and Young Persons Act 1933[19] provides that "it shall be conclusively presumed that no child under the age of ten years can be guilty of any offence". Since the presumption is irrebuttable it is really a rule of law to the effect that a child under the age of ten cannot commit a crime. This is not a rule of evidence at all and the allusion to "presumption" in the section is

---

[16] For example, the presumption of death in order of seniority contained in s. 184 of the Law of Property Act 1925 (*infra*).

[17] *Inland Revenue Commissioners* v. *Cookson*, [1977] 2 All E.R. 331; [1977] 1 W.L.R. 962.

[18] The best known unorthodox classification is that suggested by LORD DENNING in (1945), 61 L.Q.R. 379. It has not been generally adopted.

[19] As amended by the Children and Young Persons Act 1963.

misleading. There are several rules of law customarily expressed in the form of presumptions. For example, a boy under the age of fourteen years is presumed to be incapable of committing an offence involving sexual potency as principal offender. Similarly, where two or more persons have died in circumstances rendering it uncertain which of them survived the other, such deaths shall (subject to any order of the court), for all purposes affecting the title to property, be presumed to have occurred in order of seniority, and accordingly the younger shall be deemed to have survived the elder.[20] This latter "presumption" differs from the other examples in that it depends upon proof of the basic fact of uncertainty in the order of deaths. It is, nonetheless, rather a rule of substantive law than a rule of evidence.

b   Rebuttable presumptions of law

A rebuttable presumption of law is a rule of law compelling the court to infer the existence of the fact presumed. The direct presumptions of innocence and sanity mentioned above are rebuttable presumptions of law. Most rebuttable presumptions of law, however, depend upon proof of a basic fact. The presumption of legitimacy is an example. There are virtually innumerable other examples, some of the best known of which are the presumption of death from seven years' absence unheard of,[1] the presumption that a document proved or purporting to be not less than twenty years old and produced from proper custody has been duly executed,[2] the presumption that alterations to a deed have been made before execution and that alterations to a will have been made after execution,[3] the presumption that official acts have been duly performed[4] (*omnia praesumuntur rite esse acta*) and the equitable presumption that property purchased by a parent in his child's name constitutes a gift rather than the creation of a trust.[5] In all of these cases the court is bound, on proof of the basic fact, to give effect to the presumption and infer the existence of the fact presumed. The effect of this is to cast the burden of disproving the existence of the fact presumed upon the party against whom the presumption is raised.

c   Rebuttable presumptions of fact

Presumptions of fact are merely specific and frequently recurring instances of the operation of circumstantial evidence. The nature of circumstantial

---

[20] Law of Property Act 1925, s. 184.

[1] This presumption, though basically a common law presumption, has been codified with variations in several statutes, notably the Matrimonial Causes Act 1973, s. 19(3); see also Offences Against the Person Act 1861, s. 57. Moreover, the presumption cannot be raised in order to fix the precise date of death for succession purposes: *Re Phenés Trusts* (1870), L.R. 5 Ch. 139. Consequently there is very little of the original common law presumption left in operation.

[2] Evidence Act 1938, s. 4.

[3] *Doe* d. *Tatum* v. *Catamore* (1851), 16 Q.B. 745.

[4] There are innumerable variations of this presumption, examples are: that a marriage has been duly celebrated; that a licence has been duly granted; that a public officer has been duly appointed and that a public seal is authentic.

[5] This is termed the "presumption of advancement": *Shephard* v. *Cartwright*, [1955] A.C. 431 [1954] 3 All E.R. 649. It applies also to purchases made by a husband in his wife's name though it is nowadays easily rebutted.

evidence is that it consists of facts from which other facts may be presumed to exist. The basic difference between a presumption of fact and a presumption of law is that in the case of the former there is no rule of law which compels the court to apply the presumption whereas in the latter case the court not only may, but must, apply the presumption.

The variety of presumptions of fact is infinite but certain examples are noteworthy on account of frequency of their recurrence. The presumption of continuance, for example, may arise in various forms. Thus if a car is being driven by a certain person immediately after an incident it may be inferred that the same person was driving at the time of the incident.[6] Similarly the fact of a person being alive may be presumed from the fact of his being alive and healthy at an earlier date.[7] It must be stressed, however, that continuance is a presumption of fact not a presumption of law so that the court is not bound to presume a person to be alive from the fact of his being known to be alive at an antecedent date.[8] Other examples of presumptions of fact are the presumption of guilty knowledge raised by the fact of possession of recently stolen goods,[9] the presumption that, where a person conceals evidence, that evidence would be to his disadvantage if produced (*omnia praesumuntur contra spoliatorem*)[10] and the presumption that a person intends the natural consequences of his acts.[11] The latter presumption has often been treated as a presumption of law and, occasionally, as an irrebuttable presumption of law.[12] That it is, in criminal proceedings, a rebuttable presumption of fact is now laid down by section 8 of the Criminal Justice Act 1967.

It must once again be stressed that the operation of a presumption (other than an irrebuttable presumption of law) is not conclusive of liability; the person against whom the presumption is invoked may well be able to rebut it by his evidence. An interesting illustration of this is the case of *Moore v Maxwells of Emsworth, Ltd.*[13] In that case the driver of a lorry towing a trailer discovered that the tail light of the trailer had failed. Accordingly he stopped and, while he was attempting to repair the fuse, another vehicle ran into the unlit trailer. The court found as a fact that the lorry driver had taken all reasonable steps to avoid creating or prolonging the danger presented by the stationary unlit vehicle so that, although the presence of an unlit vehicle on the road gave rise to a presumption of negligence, that presumption had been rebutted by the evidence, with the result that the action by the owner of the other vehicle failed. A difficult academic question is whether rebuttable presumptions affect only the onus of proof or whether they are of some evidential weight in themselves. It will be appreciated that a presumption which is of no weight in itself, but which merely determines the onus of

---

[6] *Beresford* v. *St Albans Justices* (1905), 22 T.L.R. 1.

[7] *Chard* v. *Chard*, [1956] P. 259; [1955] 3 All E.R. 721.

[8] *R.* v. *Lumley* (1869), L.R. 1 C.C.R. 196.

[9] *R.* v. *Langmead* (1864), 9 Cox 464. *R.* v. *Smythe* (1980), 72 Cr. App. Rep. 8.

[10] *Armory* v. *Delamirie* (1721), 1 Swa. 505; *Moriarty* v. *London, Chatham and Dover Rail Co.* (1870), L.R. 5 Q.B. 314.

[11] *Hosegood* v. *Hosegood* (1950), 66 T.L.R. (pt. 1) 735; *R.* v. *Steane*, [1947] K.B. 997; [1947] 1 All E.R. 813.

[12] See the notorious case of *Director of Public Prosecutions* v. *Smith*, [1961] A.C. 290; [1960] 3 All E.R. 161.

[13] [1968] 2 All E.R. 779; [1968] 1 W.L.R. 1077.

proof, ceases to have any effect when evidence one way or the other has been adduced because the court will then decide upon the evidence (unless it finds the evidence so finely balanced that it is not satisfied either way, in which event the party on whom the burden of proof lies will fail). This point was clearly made by LORD REID when explaining the effect of the presumption of legitimacy:[14]

> ". . . the presumption of legitimacy now merely determines the onus of proof. Once evidence has been led it must be weighed without using the presumption as a make-weight in the scale for legitimacy. So even weak evidence against legitimacy must prevail if there is not other evidence to counterbalance it. The presumption will only come in at that stage in the very rare case of the evidence being so evenly balanced that the court is unable to reach a decision on it. I cannot recollect ever having seen or heard a case of any kind where the court could not reach a decision on the evidence before it."

Despite this, REES, J. in *T (H).* v. *T (H.),*[15] while expressly applying LORD REID's dictum, founded his decision on the presumption, being unable to accept the evidence of either the husband or the wife as constituting proof even on a balance of probabilities; accordingly the presumption of legitimacy prevailed.

In *Stupple* v. *Royal Insurance Co., Ltd.*[16] the Court of Appeal was called upon to consider the effect in a civil case of a conviction admissible by virtue of section 11 of the Civil Evidence Act 1968;[17] unfortunately the Court failed to lay down any principle as to whether the conviction merely operated to shift the onus of proof on to the party denying the correctness of the conviction or whether the conviction was of weight in itself. LORD DENNING, M.R. regarded the conviction as entitled to great weight; however BUCKLEY, L.J. regarded it as being of no weight and WINN, L.J. expressed no opinion. In *Hunter* v. *Chief Constable of West Midlands*[18] (the Birmingham public house bombings case), LORD DENNING went further and expressed the view that a party to civil proceedings could only rebut the presumption raised by the conviction by proving that the conviction was obtained by fraud or collusion or by obtaining fresh evidence, but the House of Lords[19] expressly disagreed with this statement, although LORD DIPLOCK (with whom all the other law lords agreed) evidently accepted that the conviction was in itself of evidential weight, since he explained[20]

> "Section 11 makes the conviction *prima facie* evidence that the person convicted did commit the offence of which he was found guilty, but does not make it conclusive evidence: the defendant is permitted by the Act to prove the contrary if he can . . . The burden of proof of 'the contrary' that lies on a defendant under s. 11 is the ordinary burden in a civil action, i.e. proof on a balance of probabilities, although in the face of a conviction after a full hearing this is likely to be an uphill task."

---

[14] *S.* v. *McC; W.* v. *W.,* [1972] A.C. 24, at p. 41; [1970] 3 All E.R. 107, at p. 109.
[15] [1971] 1 All E.R. 590; [1971] 1 W.L.R. 429.
[16] [1971] 1 Q.B. 50; [1970] 3 All E.R. 230.
[17] See p. 581, *ante.*
[18] [1980] Q.B. 283; [1980] 2 All E.R. 227; see p. 592, fn. 8, *ante.*
[19] [1982] A.C. 529; [1981] 3 All E.R. 727.
[20] [1982] A.C., at p. 544; [1981] 3 All E.R., at pp. 735–736.

B THE BURDEN OF PROOF

1 Nature and incidence of the burden of proof

Basically the expression "burden of proof" is simple to define. It means the obligation of proving a fact or facts. Nonetheless much recondite learning has been expended in tracing the different senses in which the expression has been used.[1] The expression has been used in at least three different senses; first to connote a party's general obligation to prove his case ("general burden"), secondly to connote a party's specific obligation to prove any individual issue or fact relevant to that issue ("specific burden") and thirdly to connote the obligation of adducing evidence in support of a disputed fact ("evidential burden"). The difference between the general, specific and evidential burdens may be ilustrated by a hypothetical action for negligence. The general burden of proving negligence on the part of the defendant rests on the plaintiff. In addition the burden is on the plaintiff of proving specific acts on the part of the defendant which are alleged to amount to negligence, such as driving too fast, failing to observe traffic signals or failing to keep his vehicle properly maintained. Finally the plaintiff has the burden of adducing evidence in support of each of these facts. If the defendant in the same action alleges contributory negligence on the part of the plaintiff it is for the defendant to discharge the specific burden of proving fault on the part of the plaintiff and also to adduce evidence in support of his allegation. Similarly, in a prosecution for murder the general burden of proving guilt is upon the prosecution, the specific burden of proving the elements of the crime, that the defendant's unlawful act done with malice aforethought caused the death of the victim, death occurring within a year and a day,[2] is on the prosecution but the specific burden of proving insanity, for example, rests on the accused. It will be apparent from these illustrations that the general burden is composed of a number of specific burdens and that the question of which specific burdens go to make up the general burden is to be determined by reference to substantive law. For this reason the general burden and specific burdens are collectively referred to as the "legal burden of proof". It will be equally apparent that not every specific burden is imposed upon the party having the general burden. Thus the specific burden of proving insanity in a criminal case is on the accused the general burden of proving guilt is on the prosecution.

It might be supposed that the evidential burden would always follow the legal burden. This is usually, though not invariably, the case. For example, in a prosecution for murder the burden of negativing provocation is on the prosecution but the jury need not be directed to consider provocation unless there is some evidence of provocation. This evidence may be found in the testimony of the prosecution witnesses but if it is not the accused must adduce some evidence in support of a plea of provocation. In other

---

[1] See, for example, Cross, *Evidence* (5th Edn.) pp. 85–93.
[2] If death occurs after this time it is conclusively presumed that the death was caused by something other than the infliction of the original injury by the defendant cf. *R* v. *Dyson*, [1908] 2 K.B. 454. This may the regarded as an example of an irrebuttable presumption; see p. 607, *ante*.

words the accused has the evidential burden.[3] Similar considerations arise where the accused pleads self-defence[4] or non-insane automatism[5] in a criminal case.

It is frequently asserted that a specific burden of proof or an evidential burden may shift during the course of proceedings. Thus the orthodox view of the effect of raising a presumption of law is that it shifts the burden of proof on to the party against whom the presumption operates. For example if a person claiming an interest in property under a settlement asserts that he is legitimate, he has the specific burden of proving his legitimacy. If he can prove that he was born or conceived in lawful wedlock the presumption of legitimacy applies and the court must then infer that he is legitimate unless an opponent can rebut the presumption by proving that the claimant is not the child of both spouses and, therefore, illegitimate. In such a case it is usually stated that the presumption operates to shift the burden of proof. In fact, if the case is inspected closely, it appears that although the party denying the claimant's legitimacy has *a* specific burden of proof it is not the *same* specific burden as the claimant had. The true position is that because one party has discharged his specific burden of proof a different burden has been cast on his opponent. The late Professor Nokes explained this extremely clearly in the following words:[6]

> "The prosecutor or plaintiff has one burden, that is, the obligation to prove one set of facts; while the accused or the defendant may have another burden, that is, an obligation to adduce evidence of different facts, such as payment of a debt, or other matters in disproof of the opposing evidence. The shifting of the burden means that A. lays down his load and B. picks up another load. But A. never tosses his load to B., and B. never tosses it back to A. What shifts is the obligation; but it is an obligation to prove different facts."

Thus it appears that while a party cannot shift his burden of proof, if he discharges his burden of proof, for example by proving facts which give rise to a presumption in his favour, the effect may be to impose upon his opponent a different burden—the burden of proving facts to negative the legal effect of the facts proved by the first party. A good illustration of the operation of this principle is the effect of the maxim *res ipsa loquitur* (the thing speaks for itself). *Prima facie* a person alleging negligence must prove the acts alleged to constitute negligence on the part of the defendant. However if he can prove that something under the management or control of the defendant has caused damaged, but there is no explanation as to how the accident occurred[7] and that the accident is such as would not in the ordinary course of things have occurred without negligence the court must presume negligence. The maxim, which is in effect a presumption of law, has been applied to a variety of situations. The effect of the plaintiff invoking the maxim is to place upon the defendant a burden which he may discharge by

---

3 *Mancini* v. *Director of Public Prosecutions*, [1942] A.C. 1; [1941] 3 All E.R. 272.
4 *R.* v. *Lobell*, [1957] 1 Q.B. 547; [1957] 1 All E.R. 734.
5 *Hill* v. *Baxter*, [1958] 1 Q.B. 277; [1958] 1 All E.R. 193; see also *Bratty* v. *A-G. for Northern Ireland*, [1963] A.C. 386; [1961] 3 All E.R. 523.
6 *An Introduction to Evidence* (4th Edn.), p. 480.
7 The doctrine depends upon the absence of explanation: *Barkway* v. *South Wales Transport Co., Ltd.*, [1950] A.C. 185; [1950] 1 All E.R. 392.

proving either that he used all reasonable care or that the accident occurred in a manner which does not connote negligence on his part.[8]

2 The burden of proof in civil cases

In civil cases the general burden of proof is upon the party who would fail if no evidence at all were adduced. This party also has the right to begin. The effect of this rule is that the general burden, and also the right to begin, are upon the plaintiff if the burden of proving any single issue of fact is upon him or if damages are unliquidated. *Prima facie* the burden of proving every fact which he alleges is upon the plaintiff but in practice many of these facts will be admitted by the defendant in which case they need not be proved.

The incidence of particular burdens of proof in civil cases depends upon substantive law and upon the pleadings in a case tried with pleadings. Thus the plaintiff must prove every fact which is an essential element in his cause of action. In addition the plaintiff must prove any positive allegation to rebut a defence or to show an exception to the defence pleaded. In terms of the pleadings the plaintiff must prove every fact in his statement of claim (unless, of course, the fact in question is judicially noticed, admitted or presumed in the plaintiff's favour) and every positive allegation in a reply served by him. Thus in a libel action the plaintiff must prove publication and, if the defendant pleads qualified privilege, malice. Similarly in an action for breach of contract where the defence of frustration is pleaded the plaintiff must prove a breach of contract and also negligence if he alleges that to negative the defence of frustration.[9] The defendant has the burden of proving any particular defence which he raises. If his defence to an allegation made by the plaintiff is a mere traverse or denial the effect is simply to put that fact in issue leaving the burden of proving that fact upon the plaintiff. If, however, the defendant raises positive allegations in his defence or confesses and avoids one of the plaintiff's allegations, then the burden is upon the defendant to prove the fact alleged or matter in avoidance. Thus if the defendant in a libel action merely denies publication he assumes no particular burden of proof. However, if he alleges qualified privilege, justification, fair comment or unintentional defamation the burden of proving these positive allegations is upon him. It follows that in civil cases the particular burdens may be distributed between the parties although the general burden almost always rests upon the plaintiff.

A particular burden is no less upon a party because his allegation is negative rather than positive in character. Thus in an action for malicious prosecution it is for the plaintiff to allege and prove that the defendant had no reasonable and probable cause for the prosecution.[10] Similarly, where the statutory defence of unintentional defamation is raised it is for the defendant to show absence of malice.[11] It follows that a party gains no advantage by

---

[8] *Barkway* v. *South Wales Transport Co., Ltd.* (*supra*); *Moore* v. *R. Fox & Sons,* [1956] 1 Q.B. 596; [1956] 1 All E.R. 182; cf. *Lloyde* v. *West Midlands Gas Board,* [1971] 2 All E.R. 1240; [1971] 1 W.L.R. 749.

[9] *Joseph Constantine Steamship Line, Ltd.* v. *Imperial Smelting Corporation, Ltd.,* [1942] A.C. 154; [1941] 2 All E.R. 165.

[10] *Abrath* v. *North Eastern Rail. Co.* (1883), 11 Q.B.D. 440.

[11] Defamation Act 1952, s. 4.

couching a positive allegation in negative terms. Thus whether a landlord alleges that the tenant "did not repair" the premises in question or whether he alleges that the tenant "let the house become dilapidated" the burden of proving this fact is upon the landlord.[12]

Finally it may be observed that where the admissibility of evidence is in issue the party who alleges that an item of evidence is admissible bears the burden of proving this fact. For example, a party who wishes to put in secondary evidence of a private document must account for the absence of the original; a party seeking to prove a dying declaration must prove that the declarant is dead together with the other conditions of admissibility of such declarations.[13]

3   The burden of proof in criminal cases

In criminal proceedings the effect of the presumption of innocence is that the general burden of proving guilt is upon the prosecution. Consequently the prosecution always has the right to begin except where the accused raises a special plea in bar such as *autrefois acquit.*

In addition to the general burden of proving guilt the prosecution must also discharge the particular burden of proving every element in the crime charged; this includes (subject to the exceptions noted below) the burden of disproving all defences of which there is some evidence. The number of specific burdens which combine to make up the general burden in criminal proceedings is ascertained by reference to the substantive criminal law. The leading case on the subject of the burden of proof in criminal proceedings is *Woolmington* v. *Director of Public Prosecutions.*[14] The accused, charged with murdering his wife, claimed that the killing was an accident. The trial judge in his summing-up directed the jury that if the Crown proved that the accused killed the deceased the burden rested on the accused to prove provocation or accident. The conviction was quashed in the House of Lords on the ground of this misdirection. In the hallowed words of LORD SANKEY, L.C.:[15]

> "Throughout the web of the English criminal law one golden thread is always to be seen, that it is the duty of the prosecution to prove the prisoner's guilt, subject to . . . the defence of insanity and subject also to any statutory exception."

Nevertheless a legal burden is sometimes cast on the defence in criminal cases. Basically there are few situations in which a legal (as opposed to an evidential) burden of proof is on the defence.

(1) The burden of proving insanity is on the defence where this issue is raised at the instance of the defence. This may be seen as the effect of the direct presumption of sanity.[16] Similarly the burden of proving unfitness to

---

[12] *Seward* v. *Leggatt* (1836), 7 C & P. 613.

[13] See p. 672, *post.*

[14] [1935] A.C. 462; cf. *R.* v. *Bone,* [1968] 2 All E.R. 644; [1968] 1 W.L.R. 583 in which the defendant's conviction was quashed because of the trial judge's failure to direct that, in relation to the defence of duress, it was for the prosecution to disprove that defence rather than for the defendant to prove it.

[15] [1935] A.C. 462, at p. 481.

[16] *M'Naughton's Case* (1843), 10 Cl. & Fin. 200.

plead[17] or diminished responsibility[18] is upon the accused where either of these issues is raised at the instance of the defence.[19]

(2) Several statutory provisions impose a specific burden upon the defence. The statutory defence of diminished responsibility has already been mentioned. To this may be added certain statutes which impose a burden on the accused only after the prosecution has proved particular facts.[20] For example, section 6(2) of the Road Traffic Act 1972[1] provides that, on a prosecution for being in charge of a motor vehicle on a road or other public place having consumed alcohol in such a quantity that the proportion thereof in his breath, blood or urine exceeds the prescribed limit, a person shall not be convicted if he proves that there was no likelihood of his driving it whilst the proportion of alcohol in his breath, blood or urine remained likely to exceed the prescribed limit.

(3) As stated above, the burden of proving a special plea in bar is upon the accused.

(4) Finally, where an enactment makes the commission of a particular act an offence subject to a proviso, exception, excuse or qualification, the burden of proving that the case falls within such proviso, exception, excuse or qualification is upon the defendant. So far as proceedings in magistrates' courts are concerned, there is an express provision to this effect in section 102 of the Magistrates' Courts Act 1980. In relation to proceedings on indictment it was for some time thought that the rule applied only to "facts peculiarly within the accused's own knowledge"[2] so that if the prosecution was in a position to ascertain whether or not the defendant was within some proviso, exception, excuse or qualification, then no burden rested upon the defendant to prove that he was, the burden rather being upon the prosecution to prove that he was not, in accordance with fundamental principle.

However in *R. v. Edwards*[3] the Court of Appeal dispelled any such notion by holding that the Magistrates' Courts Act provision did no more than set out the common law rule in statutory form. Accordingly it may now be taken as settled law that the burden of proof is upon the defendant in the circumstances specified above. Most of the cases are connected with licensing; thus it has been held that the burden is upon the defendant of proving that he has a licence to sell by retail intoxicating liquor,[4] a driving licence[5] or legal authority to be in possession of hares.[6]

---

[17] *R. v. Podola*, [1960] 1 Q.B. 325; [1959] 3 All E.R. 418.
[18] Homicide Act 1957, s. 2(2); *R. v. Dunbar*, [1958] 1 Q.B. 1; [1957] 2 All E.R. 737.
[19] Where insanity, diminished responsibility or unfitness to plead is raised at the instance of the prosecution the burden of proof is presumably on the prosecution. Section 6 of the Criminal Procedure (Insanity) Act 1964 permits the prosecution to allege insanity where the accused raises the issue of diminished responsibility and *vice versa*.
[20] Other statutes which impose a specific burden on the accused are: Libel Act 1843, s. 6; Prevention of Corruption Act 1916, s. 2; Companies Act 1948, s. 283(3); Customs and Excise Management Act 1979, s. 154.
[1] As substituted by Transport Act 1981, s. 25 and Sch. 8.
[2] An expression taken from the judgment of BAYLEY, J. in *R. v. Turner* (1816), 5 M. & S. 206; cf. *John v. Humphreys*, [1955] 1 All E.R. 793; [1955] 1 W.L.R. 325.
[3] [1975] Q.B. 27; [1974] 2 All E.R. 1085.
[4] *R. v. Edwards* (*supra*).
[5] *John v. Humphreys* (*supra*).
[6] *R. v. Turner* (*supra*).

In addition to the exceptional circumstances listed above in which a legal burden of proof is imposed upon the defence there are many cases, not capable of classification, in which an evidential burden is cast upon the defence. These arise principally where the burden is upon the prosecution of proving a negative averment or disproving a possible defence. Thus in a case such as *Woolmington*, although the legal burden of disproving provocation or accident is upon the prosecution, there is a burden upon the defence to adduce some evidence in support of these defences if such evidence has not been given during the course of the prosecution case. This is a commonsense rule for otherwise the prosecution would be faced with the intolerable burden of disproving every conceivable defence no matter how fanciful. LORD SIMON has explained the relationship between legal and evidential burdens of proof in criminal cases as follows:[7]

> "In the criminal law the probative burden of every issue lies on the prosecution (except for the single common law exception of insanity and some statutory exceptions). But the prosecution may adduce evidence sufficient, at a certain stage in the trial, to discharge provisionally the probative burden and thus call for some explanation on behalf of the accused (generally by evidence; though forensic analysis discounting the prosecution's case sometimes suffices): the evidential burden has shifted, though the probative burden remains on the prosecution. Again, the accused may raise a case fit for the consideration of the jury on a fresh issue. For example, although the prosecution may have provisionally discharged the onus of proving an assault, the accused may raise an issue of self-defence in a form fit for the consideration of the jury: if so, the evidential burden of disproving it will shift to the prosecution, which has, of course, also (once the defence is raised in a form fit for the consideration of the jury) the probative burden of disproving it. In this way the evidential burden of proof will often shift backwards and forwards during a trial, the probative burden remaining throughout on the prosecution."

A good example of the impact of the evidential burden of proof is afforded by the recent decision of the Queen's Bench divisional court in *R. v. Newcastle-upon-Tyne Justices, Ex parte Hindle*.[8] The defendant was charged with driving with excess alcohol in his blood contrary to section 6(1) of the Road Traffic Act 1972. When seen by the police he said that he had had a drink since the accident.[9] Since, in accordance with ordinary principles, the burden would be on the prosecution to negative this line of defence the magistrates dismissed the information on a submission of no case to answer at the close of the prosecution case. The divisional court held that this was wrong since the defendant's statement to the police was entirely self-serving and was not evidence in his favour[10] with the result that he had failed to discharge the evidential burden necessary to raise the legal burden of disproving his defence. The decision could also be regarded as an application of a presumption of fact (namely that the alcohol in his blood when he was seen by the police was there at the time of his earlier accident) which it was for

---

[7] *Director of Public Prosecutions* v. *Morgan*, [1976] A.C. 182, at p. 217 [1975] 2 All E.R. 347, at p. 364.

[8] [1984] 1 All E.R. 770.

[9] The well-known "hip-flask" defence, which the Transport Act 1981, s. 25 and Sch. 8 was passed to counter by substituting a new s. 10(2) of the Road Traffic Act 1972.

[10] As to which, see p. 661, *post*.

the defendant to rebut, by proving consumption of alcohol in the intervening period.

C THE STANDARD OF PROOF

1 The two standards of proof

Once it is determined on whom the burden of proof rests the question arises as to what standard of proof that party must satisfy in order to discharge his burden. If the burden in question is merely an evidential burden the question of standard of proof does not really arise since the burden is, by definition, discharged merely by adducing an item of credible evidence. Where the burden is a legal burden the traditional view of English law is that there are two alternative standards of proof; proof beyond reasonable doubt, which is the appropriate standard in criminal cases, and proof on a balance of probabilities, which is the standard in civil cases. In fact the modern view is that these two standards are not perhaps as radically different as they are often stated to be. Thus, it has been stated, whether the case is civil or criminal, the judge or juror is primarily concerned with deciding whether or not he is satisfied that the case is made out. Where the allegation in question is of a grave or serious nature it will naturally require a higher degree of proof to satisfy him. Nevertheless, although it is certainly true that the degree of proof required varies with the gravity of the allegation in both civil and criminal proceedings, it can probably not be maintained that there is no practical difference between proof on a balance of probabilities and proof beyond reasonable doubt. Many cases must arise where the reasonable juror would feel that an allegation of fact was more likely than not to be true but would not be prepared to say that he felt sure that it was true.

Consequently the traditional view that there are two standards of proof still obtains. There are, however, within these two standards varying degrees of proof which differ according to the gravity of the allegation of fact which is to be proved. This principle was very clearly explained in the judgment of DENNING, L.J. (as he then was) in *Bater* v. *Bater*:[11]

> "The difference of opinion which has been evoked about the standard of proof in recent years may well turn out to be more a matter of words than anything else. It is of course true that by our law a higher standard of proof is required in criminal cases than in civil cases. But this is subject to the qualification that there is no absolute standard in either case. In criminal cases the charge must be proved beyond reasonable doubt, but there may be degrees of proof within that standard. . . . A civil court, when considering a charge of fraud, will naturally require for itself a higher degree of probability than that which it would require when asking if negligence is established. It does not adopt so high a degree as a criminal court, even when it is considering a charge of a criminal nature; but still it does require a degree of probability which is commensurate with the occasion."

---

[11] [1951] P. 35, at p. 37; [1950] 2 All E.R. 458, at p. 459; approved in *Hornal* v. *Neuberger Products, Ltd.,* [1957] 1 Q.B. 247; [1956] 3 All E.R. 970, and in *Blyth* v. *Blyth,* [1966] A.C. 643; [1966] 1 All E.R. 524.

2 The standard of proof in civil cases

The standard of proof applicable in civil cases is proof on a balance of probabilities. This standard applies, as a general rule, whether the burden of proof to be discharged is the general burden or a particular burden. It also applies where the allegation to be proved is of a criminal charge. There are old authorities to the effect that an allegation of crime, even if made in a civil case, had to be proved beyond reasonable doubt. These authorities have now been discredited and the present law is that an allegation of a criminal offence made in the course of civil proceedings need only be proved on a preponderance of probability, although, of course, the degree of probability will be higher in the case of such an allegation. The leading modern authority is *Hornal* v. *Neuberger Products, Ltd*[12] in which case the Court of Appeal upheld an award of damages for fraud made by a county court judge who had expressly stated that he was satisfied on a balance of probabilities that the false statement had been made as alleged but that he was not satisfied beyond reasonable doubt. The reasoning of the Court of Appeal has been applied to an allegation of unlawful killing.[13] On the same basis it used to be thought that an allegation of a matrimonial offence made in matrimonial proceedings had to be proved beyond reasonable doubt. This view of the law was based on the quasi-criminal nature of matrimonial offences, notably adultery.[14] However, since it is now established that criminal allegations made in civil proceedings need only be proved on a balance of probabilities, it is understandable, as laid down by the House of Lords in *Blyth* v. *Blyth*[15] that the same civil standard applies in matrimonial proceedings which are, after all, civil not criminal proceedings.

There remain, after *Hornal* v. *Neuberger Products, Ltd.* and *Blyth* v. *Blyth*, very few instances in which an allegation of fact made in civil proceedings must be proved beyond reasonable doubt. It is now enacted that the presumption of legitimacy can be rebutted by proof on a balance of probabilities that the child is in fact illegitimate. The standard of proof of contempt of court is beyond reasonable doubt[16], since contempt is quasi-criminal in nature.[17] The case of *Judd* v. *Minister of Pensions and National Insurance*[18] furnishes another illustration. These cases are, however, exceptional.

---

[12] [1957] 1 Q.B. 247; [1956] 3 All E.R. 970.
[13] *Re Dellow's Will Trusts*, [1964] 1 All E.R. 771; [1964] 1 W.L.R. 451. Proof of breach of a recognisance, in proceedings to forfeit or estreat that recognisance, is on a balance of probabilities since such proceedings are civil in character. *R.* v. *Marlow Justices, Ex parte O'Sullivan*, [1984] Q.B. 381; [1983] 3 All E.R. 578.
[14] The leading authorities in support of the old view are: *Ginesi* v. *Ginesi*, [1948] P. 179; [1948] 1 All E.R. 373; *Preston-Jones* v. *Preston-Jones*, [1951] A.C. 391; [1951] 1 All E.R. 124.
[15] [1966] A.C. 643; [1966] 1 All E.R. 524.
[16] Family Law Reform Act 1969, s. 26; at common law proof beyond reasonable doubt was required: *Preston-Jones* v *Preston-Jones* (*supra*).
[17] *Re Bramblevale, Ltd.,* [1970] Ch. 128; [1969] 3 All E.R. 1062.
[18] [1966] 2 Q.B. 580; [1965] 3 All E.R. 642. The case turned on the construction of article 4 of the Royal Warrant 1949, which expressly provides that the Minister cannot disallow a claim by a member of the armed forces to a disablement award unless satisfied beyond reasonable doubt that the claimant's injury was not due to, or aggravated by, war service; see also *M.E.P.C., Ltd.* v. *Christian-Edwards*, [1981] A.C. 205; [1979] 3 All E.R. 752.

3 The standard of proof in criminal cases

Proof beyond reasonable doubt is generally described as the criminal standard of proof. However it is the standard appropriate in criminal proceedings only where the burden of proof is upon the prosecution.[19] It is trite law that the prosecution must prove the guilt of the accused beyond reasonable doubt. The words "beyond reasonable doubt" in this context have been subjected to considerable judicial analysis. In *Miller* v. *Minister of Pensions*,[20] DENNING, J. (as he then was) observed that

> "Proof beyond a reasonable doubt does not mean proof beyond the shadow of a doubt. . . . If the evidence is so strong against a man as to leave only a remote possibility in his favour, which can be dismissed with the sentence 'of course it is possible but not in the least probable' the case is proved beyond reasonable doubt, but nothing short of that will suffice."

Several attempts have been made to change the hallowed formula "beyond reasonable doubt". LORD GODDARD, C.J. in *R.* v. *Summers*[1] deprecated these words and suggested that an appropriate direction to the jury be that they should "feel sure" that the accused is guilty, an alternative which LORD GODDARD reiterated in *R.* v. *Hepworth and Fearnley*[2] in which case he suggested, as a further alternative, "completely satisfied". These days the most common direction to the jury is in the following (or very similar) terms: "Before you can convict the defendant you must be satisfied so that you are sure of his guilt."

In the few cases in which the burden of proving a fact is upon the defence in a criminal case the appropriate standard of proof is proof on a balance of probabilities—the civil standard.[3]

D CORROBORATION

As a general rule English law does not require corroboration or confirmative evidence. No doubt a jury may in practice be impressed with the cogency of several items of evidence tendered in support of the same fact but, as a matter of law, any party may discharge his burden of proof by adducing one item of evidence. Nevertheless there are exceptional circumstances in which corroboration is required either as a matter of practice or, by statute, as a matter of law. The distinction is important because where corroboration is required

---

[19] Where the admissibility of evidence is in issue, the judge decides all issues of fact upon which admissibility depends (for example, whether a confession is voluntary). In these cases the judge must be satisfied beyond reasonable doubt before admitting evidence against a defendant: cf. *R.* v. *Ewing*, [1983] Q.B. 1039; [1983] 2 All E.R. 645.

[20] [1947] 2 All E.R. 372.

[1] [1952] 1 All E.R. 1059.

[2] [1955] 2 Q.B. 600; [1955] 2 All E.R. 918. Whichever of these formulations is adopted, an appellate court will not interfere (*Walters* v. *R.*, [1960] 2 A.C. 26) although expressions such as "reasonably sure" and "pretty sure" have been disapproved by the Court of Appeal; cf. *R.* v. *Head and Warrener* (1961), 45 Cr. App. Rep. 225.

[3] *R.* v. *Carr-Briant*, [1943] K.B. 607 (Prevention of Corruption Act 1916, s. 2); *Sodeman* v. *R.*, [1936] 2 All E.R. 1138 (insanity); *R.* v. *Dunbar*, [1958] 1 Q.B. 1; [1957] 2 All E.R. 737 (diminished responsibility); *R.* v. *Podola*, [1960] 1 Q.B. 325; [1959] 3 All E.R. 418 (unfitness to plead).

by statute the court cannot act on uncorroborated evidence whereas where corroboration is required only as a matter of practice the court can act on uncorroborated evidence, though it will do so only with hesitation and only after warning the jury, if there is one, of the danger of so doing. The principal circumstances in which corroboration is required, either as a matter of practice, or by statute, are discussed below.[4]

1   Cases in which corroboration is required by statute

a   Perjury

Section 13 of the Perjury Act 1911 provides that a person cannot be convicted of perjury solely upon the evidence of one witness as to the falsity of any statement alleged to be false. The origin of this rule[5] is somewhat obscure but is usually attributed to the undesirability of matching "oath against oath". The explanation for its incorporation in the common law is that perjury was a crime which was originally punished in the Court of Star Chamber,[6] whose procedure was influenced by civil law systems, which systems generally adopted the rule that corroboration was required in criminal cases. There is no limitation on the form which the corroborative evidence may take. A second witness is sufficient but not essential and the court may act on documentary evidence or on the fact that the accused has frequently repeated statements contradicting the impugned statement. The mere fact that the accused has made inconsistent statements is not, however, sufficient.

b   Affiliation

The Affiliation Proceedings Act 1957, section 4 (as amended) provides that justices may make an affiliation order against the putative father but shall not do so, in a case where evidence is given by the mother, unless her evidence is corroborated in some material particular to the satisfaction of the justices.[7] The usual form which the corroborative evidence takes is evidence of acts of sexual intercourse between the parties during the time when the child must have been conceived. Likewise evidence of acts of familiarity has been held to amount to corroboration even where these acts took place at a time prior to conception.[8] Mere evidence of opportunity, unsupported by evidence of affection, is, however, insufficient.[9] Where the corroborative evidence consists of letters written by the father to the mother the handwriting may be proved by the mother, notwithstanding that it is her testimony which the letters corroborate.[10]

---

4   The list is not exhaustive; see *Gallie* v. *Lee*, [1969] 2 Ch. 17, at p. 38; [1969] 1 All E.R. 1062, at p. 1079, *per* RUSSELL, L.J. (as he then was).

5   The statutory provision merely codifies the common law: *R.* v. *Muscot* (1813), 10 Mod. Rep. 192.

6   See p. 13, *ante*.

7   Under the 1957 Act the mother had to give evidence in all cases; however the effect of the amendment to section 4 by the Affiliation Proceedings (Amendment) Act 1972 is that she does not, although, if she does (i.e. in almost all contested cases), corroboration of her evidence is essential.

8   *Moore* v. *Hewitt*, [1947] K.B. 831; [1947] 2 All E.R. 270.

9   *Burbury* v. *Jackson*, [1917] 1 K.B. 16.

10   *Jeffery* v. *Johnson*, [1952] 2 Q.B. 8; [1952] 1 All E.R. 450; overruling *Moore* v. *Hewitt* (*supra*) on this point.

c Procuration of women

Several sections of the Sexual Offences Act 1956,[11] which punish various forms of procuration of women, provide that a person shall not be convicted on the evidence of one witness only, unless the witness is corroborated in some material particular by evidence implicating the accused. Since the witness in question is usually the victim herself it will be appreciated that the need for corroboration stems from the fact that the witness whose evidence requires corroboration has a motive to misrepresent. The same principle underlies the need for corroboration in affiliation proceedings and (formerly) breach of promise actions.[12] In addition the allegation in question in such cases is easy to make but generally, by its nature, difficult to refute. Once again no particular form of corroboration is prescribed but there is an express provision that the corroborative evidence must implicate the accused. This is a principle which applies generally to corroborative evidence in criminal proceedings.

d Unsworn evidence of children

A child of tender years who can understand the duty of telling the truth but who does not understand the nature of an oath may give unsworn evidence in a criminal case. This provision is contained in section 38 of the Children and Young Persons Act 1933. However, because of the inherent possibility of such evidence being unreliable, the same section also provides that the accused cannot be convicted unless the child's evidence is corroborated by some other material evidence implicating the accused. Once again the corroborative evidence must implicate the accused. The unsworn evidence of another child cannot amount to corroboration although the sworn evidence of one child can be mutually corroborative with the unsworn evidence of another. Thus if A. gives sworn evidence and B. gives unsworn evidence, the former corroborates the latter and *vice versa*.[13] If the prosecution calls as one of its witnesses a child who gives unsworn evidence which is not corroborated, a literal interpretation of the words of section 38 ("the accused shall not be liable to be convicted of the offence") might be thought to lead to the conclusion that acquittal was inevitable, irrespective of the remainder of the evidence before the jury. This is not, however, so. The jury must disregard the unsworn evidence but may nonetheless convict if there is sufficient other evidence.[13]

e Speed limits

A person charged with driving a motor vehicle at a speed greater than the maximum allowed shall not be convicted solely on the evidence of one witness to the effect that in his opinion the person charged was driving the vehicle at such greater speed. This provision is now contained in section

---

[11] Section 2 (procuring a woman by threats or intimidation to have unlawful sexual intercourse); s. 3 (procuring a woman by false pretences); s. 4 (administering drugs to obtain or facilitate intercourse); s. 22 (causing the prostitution of a woman) and s. 23 (procuration of a female infant).

[12] These actions were abolished by the Law Reform (Miscellaneous Provisions) Act 1970.

[13] *Director of Public Prosecutions* v. *Hester*, [1973] A.C. 296; [1972] 3 All E.R. 1056.

78A(2) of the Road Traffic Regulation Act 1967. Section 77(7) contains a similar provision applicable to offences of not attaining minimum speed limits. It should be noted that it is only the opinion of a witness which requires corroboration. Evidence other than an opinion does not require corroboration under the section. Consequently, the recording of a mechanical device such as a speedometer, being a statement of fact rather than an opinion, does not require corroboration.[14]

In all the above cases corroboration is essential.[15] The effect is that the absence of corroborative evidence is fatal to the claim or prosecution. In addition to these statutory cases there are several cases in which corroboration is desirable though not, as a matter of law, essential. In these cases, which are discussed below, the lack of corroboration is not necessarily fatal though the judge must warn the jury, if there is one, of the absence of corroboration and of the danger of acting on uncorroborated evidence. In addition the judge must explain what evidence is capable of amounting to corroboration and also the general nature of corroborative evidence.[16] The categories set out below are not exhaustive. Thus in *R. v. Bagshaw*,[17] a case concerning alleged ill-treatment of patients at Rampton Hospital, the Court of Appeal quashed convictions because the trial judge had failed to give full corroboration "warnings" in respect of the evidence of the three complainants (although he had directed the jury to approach their evidence with "the very greatest caution"). The Court of Appeal held that although mental patients were not *per se* a category of witnesses whose evidence called for corroboration, the complainants in the instant case were witnesses in respect of whom the "full warning" was essential.

Nevertheless, corroboration is not required, nor need the warning be given, simply because a witness may have a motive to give false evidence, although in such cases the judge should direct the jury to approach the witness's evidence with caution.[18]

2   Cases in which corroboration is required as a matter of practice

a   Accomplices

It is now settled that the trial judge must warn the jury of the danger of convicting the accused on the uncorroborated testimony of an accomplice.

---

[14] *Nicholas v. Penny* [1950] 2 K.B. 466; [1950] 2 All E.R. 89.

[15] Other statutory provisions requiring corroboration are the Treason Act 1795, s. 1 (compassing the death of the Sovereign etc.) and the Representation of the People Act 1983, s. 168(5) (personation at elections).

[16] *R. v. Goddard*, [1962] 3 All E.R. 582; [1962] 1 W.L.R. 1282.

[17] [1984] 1 All E.R. 971; [1984] 1 W.L.R. 477; cf. *R. v. Spencer*, [1985] 1 All E.R. 673; [1985] 2 W.L.R. 197, in which a differently constituted Court of Appeal held, in further appeals arising out of the Rampton Hospital trials, that full corroboration warnings were not necessary and that *R. v. Bagshaw* was either decided *perineuriam* (as to which see p. 149, *ante*) or on its special facts; an appeal to the House of Lords is pending, on the hearing of which this branch of the law will doubtless be clarified.

[18] *R. v. Beck*, [1982] 1 All E.R. 807; [1982] 1 W.L.R. 461.

This was finally established by the House of Lords in the leading case of *Davies* v. *Director of Public Prosecutions*[19] in which case it was established that this, although a rule of practice, now has the force of a rule of law. The effect is that where the judge fails to warn the jury the accused's conviction will be quashed, even if in fact there is ample corroborative evidence, unless the appellate court can apply the proviso to section 2 (1) of the Criminal Appeal Act 1968.[20] The rationale of the rule is presumably the likely tendency of accomplices to try to shift the blame on to one another.

Davies's case is also a leading authority on the question of who is an accomplice. LORD SIMONDS, L.C. classified accomplices as (1) participants in the crime alleged, whatever the degree of participation, (2) receivers of stolen goods in relation to those who are alleged to have stolen those goods; and (3) parties to another crime alleged to have been committed by the accused of which "similar fact" evidence would be admissible. The facts of *Davies*'s case were that the accused was charged with murder by stabbing the deceased, a member of a rival gang. The witness whose testimony was in question was a member of the same gang as the accused and had joined in an assault on the deceased but had not been party to the stabbing and was not aware that the accused had a knife. It was held that the witness was not an accomplice so that the rule requiring corroboration did not apply. The speech of LORD SIMONDS in *Davies*'s case clearly indicated that a person indicted jointly with the accused and giving evidence against him is not to be regarded as an accomplice. Nevertheless it has been held that there is a rule of practice (though not of law) that the trial judge should give the jury a similar warning in respect of the evidence of a co-accused.

Where persons are accomplices within either of the first two categories of LORD SIMONDS, L.C.'s classification, one accomplice's testimony cannot be corroborated by the testimony of the other[1] for obvious reasons. Apart from this there is no particular restriction on the form which the corroborative evidence may take. It must, however, implicate the accused.[2]

Until recently it was thought that accomplices within the third category according to that classification could not corroborate one another's testimony. This led to enormous difficulties because, of course, the whole point of admitting similar fact evidence is to support the evidence to which it bears a similarity. A direction was given to juries to the effect that the evidence of similar incidents "may help the jury to determine the truth of the matter" although it could not amount to corroboration.[3] This was a distinction without a difference and it was at last laid to rest by the House of Lords in *Director of Public Prosecutions* v. *Kilbourne*.[4] The accused was

---

[19] [1954] A.C. 378; [1954] 1 All E.R. 507.
[20] See p. 533, *ante*.
[1] *R.* v. *Prater*, [1960] 2 Q.B. 464; [1960] 1 All E.R. 298. However, the testimony of one co-accused against another co-accused may be corroborated by the former's wife: *R.* v. *Allen; R.* v. *Evans*, [1965] 2 Q.B. 295; [1964] 3 All E.R. 401.
[2] *R.* v. *Baskerville*, [1916] 2 K.B. 658; as to the position where the accomplice's evidence is partly favourable to the accused and partly unfavourable, see *R.* v. *Royce-Bentley*, [1974] 2 All E.R. 347; [1974] 1 W.L.R. 535.
[3] *R.* v. *Campbell*, [1956] 2 Q.B. 432, at pp. 438–439; [1956] 2 All E.R. 272, at p. 276, *per* LORD GODDARD, C.J.
[4] [1973] A.C. 729; [1973] 1 All E.R. 440.

charged on an indictment containing seven counts; counts 1 to 4 alleged sexual offences against four boys, while counts 5 to 7 alleged sexual offences involving two other boys a year later. All the boys gave sworn evidence. Since the evidence of one group of boys was admissible in relation to the charges concerning the other group[5] the House of Lords held that it was immaterial that each boy was technically an accomplice in relation to the offence committed against him, so that the evidence of each was capable of corroborating the other.

b   Sexual offences

It has already been noted that in the case of certain offences under the Sexual Offences Act 1956 corroboration is essential. In other cases involving prosecution for sexual offences corroboration is required as a matter of practice although it is not essential. The obvious underlying reasons are the inherent likelihood of the victim's testimony being exaggerated or fanciful coupled with the difficulty of refuting the victim's allegations.

The corroborative evidence must support the allegations of the complainant in some material particular and must implicate the accused. It follows that the distressed condition of the victim shortly after the alleged offence is not sufficient corroboration because it does not implicate the accused. However, evidence of the complainant's distressed condition coupled with evidence that the accused was seen with the complainant shortly before or after the incident is sufficient.[6] Evidence of a complaint made by the victim of a sexual offence cannot amount to corroboration (because it is not independent evidence) but it may be admissible to show consistency.[7]

c   Matrimonial causes

It used to be a rule of practice, though not a rule of law, that testimony alleging a matrimonial offence should be corroborated. The rule applied whether the testimony was that of the petitioner, of the respondent or of an accomplice to the matrimonial offence.[8] The court would, however, act on uncorroborated evidence if satisfied that it was reliable, especially in undefended suits. In divorce county courts and in the Family Division of the High Court the rule has little, if any, practical application now that the concept of the matrimonial offence has given way to that of irretrievable breakdown of marriage as the basis for divorce.

d   Sworn evidence of children

It will be recalled that the unsworn testimony of a child in criminal proceedings must, by statute, be corroborated. Where a child gives sworn evidence,

---

5   As to which, see p. 572, *ante*.
6   *R.* v. *Redpath* (1962), 46 Cr. App. Rep. 319; *R.* v. *Knight*, [1966] 1 All E.R. 647; [1966] 1 W.L.R. 230.
7   *R.* v. *Whitehead*, [1929] 1 K.B. 99; *R.* v. *Christie,* [1914] A.C. 545. Complaints are admissible only for the purpose of showing consistency (unless forming part of the *res gestae*) and only if made by the victim of a sexual assault, male or female, as soon after the incidents as may be reasonably expected. In addition the complaint must have been made voluntarily and not in answer to a leading question: *R.* v. *Whitehead* (*supra*).
8   *Statham* v. *Statham*, [1929] P. 131; *Galler* v. *Galler*, [1954] P. 252; [1954] 1 All E.R. 536; *Alli* v. *Alli*, [1965] 3 All E.R. 480.

as he can do in any case provided he can comprehend the nature of an oath, the jury should be warned of the risk of acting on the uncorroborated evidence of the child. This does not, however, apply in every case in which the witness is under 18. Whether he is to be regarded as a "child" for this purpose, so that a warning is given to the jury, is essentially a matter for the trial judge.[9] Virtually all of the authorities are criminal cases though the same rule presumably applies in a civil case. Nevertheless a jury can act on the uncorroborated evidence of a child if satisfied that it is true. The sworn evidence of one child can be corroborated by the sworn evidence of another child and by the unsworn evidence of another child.[10]

3 The nature of corroboration

The first requirement of corroboration is that it must consist of admissible evidence. Irrelevant or otherwise inadmissible evidence, such as conduct on other occasions showing criminal disposition, does not become admissible merely because it appears to be corroborative.

Generally there is no prescribed form which corroborative evidence must take. Certain minor statutory provisions expressly require two or more credible witnesses[11] but, in the absence of such express stipulation, corroboration need not involve a second witness.

There are, however, two conditions which corroborative evidence must satisfy. First it must be independent of the evidence to be corroborated; secondly it must, in a criminal case, implicate the accused. The rule against self-corroboration is of fairly recent origin, not being finally established until the case of *R.* v. *Lillyman*[12] in 1896. However it is now well settled that corroborative evidence "must be extraneous to the witness who is to be corroborated".[13] It is for this reason that the complaint of a victim of a sexual offence made soon after the offence, although admissible to show consistency, is not capable of amounting to corroboration of the victim's testimony. The relevance of such evidence is simply that it adds weight or cogency to the evidence which requires corroboration for, as will be appreciated, the question of corroboration can only arise at all if the witness requiring corroboration is credible. If his evidence is not credible it should be rejected and the accused acquitted, even if there could be found evidence capable of amounting to corroboration, since:

> "Corroboration can only be afforded to or by a witness who is otherwise to be believed. If a witness's testimony falls of its own inanition the question of his needing, or being capable of giving, corroboration does not arise."[14]

---

[9] *R.* v. *Morgan*, [1978] 3 All E.R. 13; [1978] 1 W.L.R. 735.

[10] *Director of Public Prosecutions* v. *Hester*, [1973] A.C. 296; [1972] 3 All E.R. 1056.

[11] Examples are Treason Act 1795, s. 1; Places of Religious Worship Act 1812; Representation of the People Act 1983, s. 168 (5).

[12] [1896] 2 Q.B. 167.

[13] *R.* v. *Whitehead*, [1929] 1 K.B. 99, at p. 102, *per* LORD HEWART, C.J. See also s. 6 (4) of the Civil Evidence Act 1968, which provides that the previous statement of a witness admitted under the provisions of that Act shall not amount to corroboration of the evidence of that witness.

[14] *Director of Public Prosecutions* v. *Kilbourne*, [1973] A.C. 729, at p. 746; [1973] 1 All E.R. 440, at p. 452, *per* LORD HAILSHAM, L.C.

A document may amount to corroboration even though its authenticity is proved by the witness whose testimony it corroborates.[15] This does not, of course, amount to self-corroboration since the corroborative evidence exists in the contents of the document not in the witness's testimony as to its authenticity.

The second condition for the sufficiency of corroborative evidence is that in a criminal case it must implicate the accused. For this reason the distressed condition of the victim of an assault shortly after the assault, although relevant, is not corroboration of testimony identifying the accused as the assailant. However, evidence of distressed condition shortly after the accused was seen with the victim may amount to corroboration.[16]

Corroboration frequently exists in the conduct of the person against whom it will operate. This is generally the accused in a criminal case but may be, for example, the putative father in affiliation proceedings. The fact that the accused ran away,[16] gave a false alibi[17] or behaved on previous occasions in the manner now alleged[18] may corroborate the testimony against him. Lies told by a defendant, either before the trial or in the course of his evidence during the trial (assuming the jury is satisfied that he has lied and that the statement is proved to be a lie by evidence other than that of the witness whose evidence has to be corroborated) are capable of constituting corroboration.[19] However it is important to bear in mind that irrelevant evidence does not become relevant merely because of its value as corroboration. Consequently irrelevant "similar fact" evidence cannot amount to corroboration. For the same reason the silence of an accused person or his failure to give evidence at his trial cannot amount to corroboration of testimony against him.[20]

---

[15] *Jeffrey* v. *Johnson*, [1952] 2 Q.B. 8; [1952] 1 All E.R. 450.

[16] *R.* v. *Knight*, [1966] 1 All E.R. 647; [1966] 1 W.L.R. 230.

[17] *Credland* v. *Knowler* (1951), 35 Cr. App. Rep. 48.

[18] *R.* v. *Hartley*, [1941] 1 K.B. 5; *R.* v. *Sims*, [1946] K.B. 531; [1946] 1 All E.R. 697.

[19] *R.* v. *Lucas*, [1981] Q.B. 720; [1981] 2 All E.R. 1008; however a careful direction to the jury is required in such cases and, in particular, they should in appropriate cases be reminded that people sometimes lie in an attempt to bolster up a just cause, or out of shame or out of a wish to conceal disgraceful behaviour from their family (*ibid.*).

[20] *R.* v. *Whitehead*, [1929] 1 K.B. 99; *R.* v. *Jackson*, [1953] 1 All E.R. 872; [1953] 1 W.L.R. 591. In *R.* v. *Chapman*, [1973] Q.B. 774; [1973] 2 All E.R. 624 a Circuit judge directed the jury that if they rejected the defendant's evidence, that fact could corroborate the evidence of an accomplice against him. The Court of Appeal (none of the members of which had ever before heard of a direction in similar terms) held that the direction was wrong but, despite the absence of corroboration of an accomplice's evidence, applied the proviso and dismissed the appeal.

CHAPTER 31

The Means of Proof

Having decided what facts may be proved, upon whom the onus of proving those facts lies and the nature of this burden the question arises as to how these facts are to be proved. Assuming that the fact in question is not admitted, judicially noticed or presumed in favour of the party who would otherwise have to prove it there are three ways in which a fact may be proved: (1) by the testimony of witnesses; (2) by documentary evidence; (3) by "real" evidence. Each of these means of proof is considered in detail below.

A WITNESSES

1 Competence and compellability

The general rule is that all persons are both competent and compellable as witnesses in judicial proceedings. This is so even if the witness has been proofed or, in the case of an expert witness, retained by the other side. There is no property in a witness.[1] The attendance of witnesses in magistrates' courts is compelled by summons or warrant. In criminal trials at the Crown Court attendance is compelled by witness order or witness summons, failure to comply with either of which is punishable as a contempt of the trial court.[2] Attendance in the High Court is compelled by subpoena failure to comply with which is a contempt of court.

In civil cases the court can neither compel a party to call any witness nor call a witness itself. In criminal proceedings and in proceedings for contempt

---

[1] *Harmony Shipping Co. S. A. v. Davis*, [1979] 3 All E.R. 177; [1979] 1 W.L.R. 1380; in that case a handwriting expert retained by the plaintiffs inadvertently gave advice to the defendants concerning the same documents. It was held that the defendants could compel him to give evidence. The principle applies equally in criminal cases. Thus in *R. v. King*, [1983] 1 All E.R. 929; [1983] 1 W.L.R. 411 the Crown enterprisingly subpoenaed a handwriting expert retained by the defendant and obtained from him documents sent by the defendant which included, as luck would have it, a document which was highly prejudicial to the defence case.

[2] Criminal Procedure (Attendance of Witnesses) Act 1965; see p. 486, *ante*.

of court,[3] however, the court may, of its own volition, call any witness without the consent of the parties.

There are several exceptions to the general rule, stated above, that all persons are both competent and compellable as witnesses. The most important of these exceptions are set out below. Before considering these exceptions, however, it is important to note that the compellability of a witness is a separate matter from any privilege which that witness may validly claim in respect of any fact as to which it is sought to elicit his testimony. Thus a witness does not cease to be compellable merely because he may claim privilege from answering any specific question or for the contents of a document.

a Children

Infancy, in the legal sense, is not a disability for the purposes of competence as a witness. On the other hand young children may be incompetent to give evidence simply because of immaturity. The rule is that a child may only give sworn evidence if he appears, on examination by the court, to be able to appreciate the nature and consequences of an oath or "to entertain of the danger and impiety of falsehood" as was said in an early case.[4] It is not necessary for the child to be aware of the existence of God; it is sufficient if the judge is satisfied that the child appreciates the solemnity of the occasion and the duty when on oath to tell the truth.[5]

At common law a child's inability to appreciate the nature and consequences of an oath would prevent him from giving evidence in either civil or criminal proceedings. There is a statutory exception to this rule applicable only to criminal cases. This is now contained in section 38 of the Children and Young Persons Act 1933 which provides that a child who does not understand the nature of an oath may give unsworn testimony in criminal proceedings if "in the opinion of the court, he is possessed of sufficient intelligence to justify the reception of the evidence, and understands the duty of speaking the truth". As a safeguard the section goes on to provide that the unsworn evidence of a child given on behalf of the prosecution must be corroborated. The trial judge may determine the competence of a child to give sworn or unsworn evidence by a preliminary examination of the child known as *voire dire*.

If a child is competent in accordance with the above rules he is also compellable. To this rule, however, there is an exception created by the Children and Young Persons Act 1963 and now contained in s. 103 of the Magistrates' Courts Act 1980. This section provides that, subject to certain exceptions, a child should not be called as a witness for the prosecution in proceedings before examining justices enquiring into a sexual offence but, instead, a written statement of the child's evidence shall be admissible in evidence of any matter of which the child's oral testimony would be admissible. The purpose of the section is to spare children the strain and

---

3 *Yianni* v. *Yianni*, [1966] 1 All E.R. 230; [1966] 1 W.L.R. 120.
4 *R.* v. *Brasier* (1799), 1 Leach 199.
5 *R.* v. *Hayes*, [1977] 2 All E.R. 288; [1977] 1 W.L.R. 234.

embarrassment of repeating at the preliminary investigation and again at the trial details of sexual offences.[6]

b Mentally defective persons

The mere fact of mental illness does not render a person incompetent as a witness. However, as in the case of children, the disability will render him incompetent if he is intellectually incapable of understanding the nature of an oath. The derangement may be intermittent in which case the witness is competent during lucid intervals.[7] Even if a person is found by the judge to be competent as a witness it is open to the opposing side to cross-examine the witness as to his credibility and, indeed, to call a separate witness as to his credibility.[8]

c Accused persons in criminal cases

The general rule is that accused persons are not competent witnesses for the prosecution in criminal cases.[9] This rule is of practical importance where there are two or more persons tried together. The effect is that neither co-accused may give evidence for the prosecution against the other, although each may, of course, give evidence on his own behalf which may support the prosecution case incidentally. If the prosecution wishes to make use of the evidence of one participant in a crime against any other participant in the same crime the solution is not to indict them together for there is no rule that an accomplice is not competent for the prosecution. Alternatively if one co-accused decides to turn "Queen's evidence" the prosecution may decide to offer no evidence against him in which event he will be formally acquitted and thereby become a competent witness against the other co-accused. The same effect may be achieved by the filing of a *nolle prosequi* in respect of one accused person or by one accused pleading guilty.[10]

It is only since the Criminal Evidence Act 1898 that an accused person has been a competent defence witness at his own trial. Where there are co-accused each is competent but not compellable on behalf of the other. Although neither is competent for the prosecution against the other, either

---

[6] However the defence may object to this procedure being followed (but cannot insist on the child being called; see p. 180, *ante*) and the prosecution may require the attendance of the child for the purpose of establishing the identity of any person: Magistrates' Courts Act 1980, s. 103(2)(*a*), (*b*).

[7] *R.* v. *Hill* (1851), 2 Den 254.

[8] *Toohey* v. *Metropolitan Police Commissioner*, [1965] A.C. 595; [1965] 1 All E.R. 506.

[9] There used to be an odd exception to this rule in prosecutions for public nuisance under the Evidence Act 1877 but this disappeared when that Act was repealed by the Statute Law (Repeals) Act 1981.

[10] Whether the judge sentences the defendant, who has pleaded guilty and is to give evidence, before or after he gives evidence is a matter for the judge's discretion. It was formerly the practice to sentence him before he gave evidence (so that his evidence was not tainted by the hope that the nature or quality of it might affect his sentence) but the modern tendency is to defer sentence until the completion of the trial (when the judge will have a clearer picture of the extent of the relative culpability of the various defendants): cf. *R.* v. *Weekes* (1982), 74 Cr. App. Rep. 161; *R.* v. *Coffey* (1982), 74 Cr. App. Rep. 168. It is not proper for the prosecution to call as a witness an accomplice against whom separate proceedings are pending or anticipated: *R.* v. *Pipe* (1967), 51 Cr. App. Rep. 17.

may give evidence against the other on his own behalf.[11] The prosecution may not comment upon the failure of an accused person to give evidence, or to give sworn evidence, although the judge may do so.[12]

It should be noted finally that none of the above rules apply to the parties in civil cases, so that one party may be compelled to give evidence on behalf of his opponent.

d Spouses

At common law spouses were incompetent to give evidence either for or against one another in both civil and criminal cases. In civil cases the Evidence (Amendment) Act 1853 rendered the husbands and wives of parties both competent and compellable so that there are now no special rules applying to spouses in civil cases. In criminal cases, however, the situation is more complicated. The general rule in criminal cases is that the spouse of the accused is competent, but not compellable, for the defence and is incompetent for the prosecution.[13] There are several important exceptions to this rule. Most of these exceptions have the effect of making the accused's spouse a competent witness for the prosecution though a very few render the accused's spouse compellable for the prosecution or the defence.

The accused's spouse is a competent witness for the prosecution in those cases listed in the schedule to the Criminal Evidence Act 1898 as amended.[14] This schedule has been much amended and the main offences now comprised are bigamy, child destruction, various offences against children under the Children and Young Persons Act 1933, and the Indecency with Children Act 1960, and offences against the property of a spouse. In addition section 39 of the Sexual Offences Act 1956, renders the accused's spouse competent, though not compellable, for the prosecution in cases involving charges of almost every offence contained in that Act, section 2 of the Protection of Children Act 1978 contains similar provision while section 30 of the Theft Act 1968 renders a spouse conpetent as a witness against the other spouse in proceedings brought by the former and in proceedings brought by a third person for an offence with reference to the person or property of the accused's spouse.

Both section 39 of the Sexual Offences Act and section 2 of the Protection of Children Act expressly provide that nothing in that section shall make a spouse compellable to give evidence and that the prosecution must not comment upon the failure of any spouse to do so. The Criminal Evidence Act 1898, which made spouses competent witnesses in criminal proceedings,

---

[11] The right of a defendant to make an unsworn statement from the dock (which had been preserved by the Criminal Evidence Act 1898) was abolished by s. 72 of the Criminal Justice Act 1982. It had become much abused.

[12] *R.* v. *Rhodes*, [1899] 1 Q.B. 77; as to the permissible scope of such comment, see *R.* v. *Sparrow*, [1973] 2 All E.R. 129; [1973] 1 W.L.R. 488, in which the authorities are reviewed.

[13] When s. 80 of the Police and Criminal Evidence Act 1984 is brought into force these rules will be changed. The general rule will be that spouses will be competent for the prosecution but not compellable (except in relation to assaults on the spouse and assaults or sexual offences against persons under 16) and will be both competent and compellable on behalf of the defence. After they have ceased to be married, spouses will be competent and compellable as if they had never been married (reversing *R.* v. *Algar*, [1954] 1 Q.B. 279; [1953] 2 All E.R. 1381).

[14] Criminal Evidence Act 1898, s. 4(1).

contains no such express provisions but in *Leach* v. *R.*[15] the House of Lords held that the 1898 Act did not make a spouse compellable as a witness.

It may be that a spouse is compellable as a witness against the other in treason cases and possibly in prosecutions for abduction of females although in each case the position is open to doubt and, indeed, in the present climate of judicial opinion it seems unlikely, particularly in the case of abduction, that a spouse would be held compellable. It was formerly thought that a spouse was compellable on a prosecution arising out of a charge of personal violence committed against that spouse by the other, but the House of Lords has held that this is not so.[16]

An interesting application of the rules set out above arose in *R.* v. *Deacon.*[17] An argument took place between the appellant, his wife and the wife's brother in the course of which the appellant shot and killed the brother and wounded the wife. The appellant was charged with murder of the brother and attempted murder of the wife, the two charges being tried together. The wife, who was the sole eye-witness, gave evidence and the appellant was convicted of the murder. On appeal his conviction was quashed since the wife had not been a competent witness for the Crown on that count.[18]

It should be noted that where a spouse who is competent but not compellable does elect to give evidence, he or she then becomes an ordinary witness and they are compellable to answer all permissible questions that could be put to any witness.[19]

e Miscellaneous

The Sovereign is not a compellable witness; nor are foreign Sovereigns, ambassadors, High Commissioners and various grades of diplomatic staff. In any legal proceedings to which a bank is not a party a banker or bank officer cannot be compelled either to produce any banker's book the contents of which can be proved by secondary evidence, or to prove any matter therein recorded.[20] Finally, there appears to be a residual power in courts to set aside a *subpoena* (which, of course, means that the witness is, in effect, not compellable) if the court considers that it would be oppressive to compel a person to give evidence.[1] It is doubtful whether this power would be held to exist in criminal proceedings, and virtually certain that it would not be exercised to deprive a defendant of the means of compelling the attendance of a witness whose presence he required.

---

[15] [1912] A.C. 1305.

[16] *Hoskyn* v. *Metropolitan Police Commissioner*, [1979] A.C. 474; [1978] 2 All E.R. 136. Prior to the repeal of the Evidence Act 1877 (see p. 629, fn. 9, *ante*) a spouse was compellable for the prosecution in cases under that Act.

[17] [1973] 2 All E.R. 1145; [1973] 1 W.L.R. 696.

[18] The appellant was extremely fortunate in that, although the appellant's own evidence was consistent with a manslaughter verdict, the Court of Appeal refused to substitute such a verdict. Furthermore (for reasons which the Court of Appeal did not understand) no verdict was taken on the second count and a few days later the Crown was refused leave to proceed on that charge.

[19] *R.* v. *Pitt*, [1983] Q.B. 25; [1982] 3 All E.R. 63.

[20] Bankers' Books Evidence Act 1879, s. 6.

[1] *Morgan* v. *Morgan*, [1977] Fam. 122; [1977] 2 All E.R. 515.

2   Oaths, affirmations and unsworn evidence

a   Oaths

The general rule is that all witnesses must give evidence on oath. Any person having authority to hear evidence has power to administer an oath[2] but the oath is generally administered by the clerk of the court or other court official. The usual form of oath differs slightly between criminal and civil proceedings. In civil proceedings it runs thus:

> "I swear by Almighty God that the evidence which I shall give shall be the truth, the whole truth, and nothing but the truth."

The witness holds the New Testament, or in the case of Jews the Old Testament, in his uplifted hand.[3] This form of oath is appropriate only to members of the Christian and Jewish faiths. Any person who objects to take the usual oath may take any form of oath, according to his religious belief, which he declares to be binding on his conscience.

The form of oath for use in juvenile courts and by children and young persons in other courts begins with the words "I promise before Almighty God" instead of "I swear by Almighty God that".[4]

b   Affirmations

As an alternative to an oath any person who objects to being sworn is permitted to "make his solemn affirmation" instead of taking an oath.[5] This substitutes the words "I (*name*) do solemnly, sincerely and truly declare and affirm" for "I swear by Almighty God that".[6] A witness is also permitted to affirm if it is not reasonably practicable without inconvenience or delay to administer the form of oath appropriate to the witness's religious belief (for example, because the book on which the witness wishes to swear is not available).[7]

It would be wholly incorrect to classify evidence given on affirmation as unsworn evidence since an affirmation is equivalent to an oath and a false statement on affirmation amounts to perjury.[8]

c   Unsworn evidence

In a few clearly-defined circumstances a witness may give unsworn evidence. Thus young children in criminal cases who cannot understand the nature and consequences of an oath but who can appreciate the duty of telling the truth may give unsworn evidence.[9] In addition, persons called simply to produce a document and advocates may be permitted to give unsworn evidence in any proceedings.

---

2   Evidence Act 1851, s. 16.
3   Oaths Act 1978.
4   Children and Young Persons Act 1963, s. 28.
5   Oaths Act 1978, s. 5(1); until 1869 persons without religious belief were incompetent as witnesses.
6   Oaths Act 1978, s. 6.
7   *Ibid.*, s. 5(2).
8   *Ibid.*, s. 5(4); Perjury Act 1911, s. 15(2) (as amended).
9   Children and Young Persons Act 1933, s. 38; see p. 621, *ante*.

3 The examination of witnesses

Two basic rules exist in relation to the giving of testimony by a witness. The first is that the testimony should be given orally and in open court. There are, however, on the grounds of expedience, numerous exceptions to this rule. Thus there are many provisions enabling evidence to be taken before trial. Rules of court frequently provide for evidence to be given by affidavit.[10] The evidence of witnesses who are ill or abroad and will thus be unable to attend at the trial may be taken before a special examiner or by a foreign court or judge by letters of request. Depositions taken in the presence of the accused at a preliminary investigation may be read in evidence at the accused's trial if the witness's attendance has not been required or he is proved by the oath of a credible witness to be dead, insane, too ill to travel or kept out of the way by or on behalf of the accused.[11] To these should be added the important provisions of section 9 of the Criminal Justice Act 1967 and section 102 of the Magistrates' Courts Act 1980 providing, subject to conditions, for proof by written statement in criminal proceedings[12] and of section 2 of the Civil Evidence Act 1968 and section 1 of the Civil Evidence Act 1972 relating to proof by out-of-court statement in civil proceedings.[13] In addition there are certain circumstances in which legal proceedings need not take place in open court.[14]

The second basic rule relating to the testimony of witnesses is that it must be confined to facts which the witness personally perceived. This rule operates to exclude opinions and hearsay as means of proof. The numerous exceptions to this rule are discussed below.[15]

Where a witness does give evidence at the trial, there are three stages to his examination; examination-in-chief, cross-examination and re-examination. The two latter stages need not always take place and re-examination is, by definition, only possible where there has been cross-examination.

a Examination-in-chief

This is the first stage in the examination of a witness and is carried out by the party calling the witness, generally through solicitor or counsel. There are a number of rigid rules which must be observed in examination-in-chief. Leading questions may not be asked. A leading question is a question framed in such a way as to suggest the answer desired. "Did you then see the accused attack the deceased?" is an extreme example. It is sometimes said that any question which can be answered with a simple "yes" or "no" is a leading question. This is often, though not invariably, true. There are certain instances in which leading questions may be asked. Thus a witness is frequently led upon the introductory part of his testimony. "Are you John Smith?" is a leading question of a type which is very commonly put.

It follows from the prohibition against leading questions that a party cannot cross-examine his own witness. No doubt counsel is frequently

---

[10] Answers to interrogatories, for example; see p. 360, *ante*. See also the Evidence (Proceedings in Other Jurisdictions) Act 1975.
[11] Criminal Justice Act 1925, s. 13(3).
[12] See pp. 478, 511, *ante*.
[13] See p. 664, *post*.
[14] See p. 181, *ante* for a discussion of this topic.
[15] See Chapter 32, *post*.

annoyed by the failure of a witness to give the answer desired, paricularly if the witness has previously given the desired answer in a deposition or proof. Nevertheless a witness cannot be questioned by the party calling him upon a previous inconsistent statement. There is, however, one important exception to this rule: where the judge gives leave to treat a witness as "hostile" the party calling the witness may cross-examine him upon his previous inconsistent statement. Cross-examination of a hostile witness is limited to putting to him a previous inconsistent statement. His credit may not be impeached by general questions about his character or convictions.[16] If the witness denies his previous statement, this statement may be put in evidence. In criminal cases the statement is only evidence of the inconsistency of the witness; it is not evidence of the truth of the earlier statement.[17] However in civil proceedings the statement, and any statement put in evidence to rebut it, is admissible as evidence of any fact stated therein of which direct oral evidence by the maker would be admissible.[18] In the light of these rules it might logically be supposed that in a criminal case if a witness manifested his hostility by simply refusing to give any evidence at all, it would not be permissible to put his previous statement to him since, first, it cannot be evidence of the truth of its contents and, secondly, it cannot contradict evidence where none has been given. Nonetheless in *R. v. Thompson*[19] the Court of Appeal permitted this very course. The defendant was charged with incest with his daughter. She, when called by the prosecution, answered some preliminary questions but then indicated that she would not give evidence against her father. Thereupon prosecuting counsel successfully applied to put to her the statement she had previously made to the police. It will be appreciated that if (as happened in *Thompson*) the witness admits authorship of the statement and confirms the truth of its contents, then the contents become part of the witness's evidence and the effect of the hostile witness's recalcitrance is nullified. This may justify the course taken in *Thompson* as a matter of expedience, but it remains logically suspect. Above all it must be remembered that an unfavourable witness is not necesarily a hostile witness. In order to be classified as hostile the witness must do more than fail to match up to his deposition or proof. He must exhibit, some hostility or animosity to the party calling him. It would seem to follow that there is no way in which a party may discredit the testimony of a witness called by him who is unfavourable but not hostile. In fact this may be done by calling another witness whose testimony contradicts that of the first witness. A written statement of a witness, admissible by virtue of section 2 of the Civil Evidence Act 1968, cannot, subject to minor exceptions, be put in before the conclusion of that witness's evidence-in-chief. It cannot therefore be used as an indirect means of discrediting one's own witness.[20]

---

16 Criminal Procedure Act 1865, s. 3.
17 The jury must be directed to this effect: *R. v. Golder*, [1960] 3 All E.R. 457; [1960] 1 W.L.R. 1169.
18 Civil Evidence Act 1968, s. 3(1).
19 (1976), 64 Cr. App. Rep. 96.
20 Civil Evidence Act 1968, s. 2(2).

b Cross-examination

Following examination-in-chief the witness may be cross-examined by or on behalf of the opposing party or parties. Cross-examination may comprise a far wider range of questions than examination-in-chief. In addition leading questions may be put to the witness. There are three possible lines of cross-examination. First a witness may be cross-examined as to the facts in issue. The object of this line of questioning is to establish information concerning the facts in issue that is favourable to the cross-examining party. The object of the two remaining lines of questioning is to discredit the witness. This is achieved by cross-examination as to credit or credibility.

A witness (other than the accused in a criminal case) may be asked questions whose purpose is to discredit him by showing that he is a person who ought not to be believed. Almost any question may be put[1] extending to such matters as the witness's character, convictions, general reputation or unchastity, save (in the latter case) where the witness is a woman in a rape case, in which circumstances she is shielded from such cross-examination, without the leave of the judge, by section 2 of the Sexual Offences (Amendment) Act 1976.[2] However, insofar as the question relates solely to the witness's credit and not to a relevant fact, the witness's answer is final and evidence cannot be called to rebut it. This is a rule of commonsense to avoid evidence being given upon a multiplicity of collateral issues in the light of which the facts in issue might become obscured. It has been noted in an earlier chapter, however, that there are four types of answer which may be rebutted; denials of a previous inconsistent statement, a previous conviction, bias or a general reputation for untruthfulness.[3] Since a witness's answer upon a collateral issue is generally final it is important to distinguish a collateral issue from a fact in issue. Thus in *R. v. Holmes*[4] the prosecutrix in a prosecution for a sexual offence denied consensual intercourse with men other than the accused. It was held that her denial was final and could not be rebutted. Conversely in *R. v. Riley*[5] evidence was admitted to rebut the denial of the prosecutrix of past acts of intercourse with the accused since these acts were relevant to the issue of consent.

It is important to note that, whereas cross-examination as to credit is aimed at the character of the witness, cross-examination as to credibility is directed at some physical or mental attribute on the part of the witness which is likely to affect the credibility of his testimony. Thus questions to impeach credibility may relate to such matters as the witness's hearing, memory or eyesight. Whereas the answer to a question going to the witness's credit is generally final, evidence may be called to impeach the credibility of a

---

[1] But neither prosecution (*R. v. Stubbs*, [1982] 1 All E.R. 424; [1982] 1 W.L.R. 509) nor judge (*R. v. Winter* (1980), 74 Cr. App. Rep. 16) is permitted to question a defendant about the contents of his legal aid application.

[2] See p. 579, *ante*. The Court of Appeal in *R. v. Viola*, [1982] 2 All E.R. 73; [1982] 1 W.L.R. 1138 gave some guidance as to when a judge should give leave under the Act. Broadly speaking he should not do so where the questions go only to credit but should do so where the cross-examination is relevant to an issue in the case, such as consent, although the Lord Chief Justice recognised that there would inevitably be a "grey area" between these two situations.

[3] See p. 580, *ante*.

[4] (1871), L.R. 1 C.C.R. 334.

[5] (1887), 18 Q.B.D. 481.

witness. Consequently a witness who denies deafness or short-sightedness is liable to have his denial rebutted by affirmative evidence. This principle emerges from the decision of the House of Lords in *Toohey* v. *Metropolitan Police Commissioner*.[6] In that case the chief prosecution witness, who was the victim of an alleged assault by the appellant, was examined shortly after the alleged assault by a police surgeon. The police surgeon was permitted to give evidence as to the witness's appearance and condition but the trial judge did not allow him to advance his medical opinion, based on examination, to the effect that the witness was prone to hysteria. This hysteria would certainly have an effect upon the credibility of the witness and for this reason the House of Lords, allowing the appeal, stated that evidence of it ought to have been admitted.

c   Re-examination

Following cross-examination a witness may be re-examined by the party calling him. The object of re-examination is to reinstate any part of the witness's testimony which has been shaken in cross-examination. As in examination-in-chief leading questions may not be asked. Furthermore a party cannot use re-examination as an opportunity for raising matters which he omitted to raise in examination-in-chief unless the form of the cross-examination necessitates this.

4   Privilege

Privilege is a rule of evidence whereby a witness may be justified in refusing to answer a question or produce a document or a party may refuse to produce a document or answer an interrogatory. There are only a limited number of occasions of private privilege and the courts are slow to recognise any new occasion of privilege. Privilege as a rule of evidence must be carefully distinguished from privilege in the law of defamation. The mere fact that words are spoken on an occasion of qualified privilege in the law of defamation does not mean that a witness may refuse to disclose in evidence what was said. Privilege is sometimes said to be public or private. In this section, however, only the occasions of privilege are examined. Public, including Crown, privilege is one aspect of the principle whereby evidence may be excluded on the basis of public policy and has been considered in the context of rules of exclusion of facts. In addition there are certain basic differences between private privilege and public privilege which render it somewhat confusing to classify them as separate aspects of the same principle. In the first place private privilege attaches to the person claiming the privilege rather than to the evidence in respect of which it is claimed. Thus a third party may always give evidence of a fact notwithstanding that a party to the action could claim privilege from disclosing that fact. In *Calcraft* v. *Guest*,[7] for example, the Court of Appeal allowed copies of witnesses' proofs and notes on evidence to be proved notwithstanding that the plaintiff could claim

---

[6]   [1965] A.C. 595; [1965] 1 All E.R. 506.
[7]   [1898] 1 Q.B. 759.

privilege from producing the originals. In *Rumping* v. *Director of Public Prosecutions*[8] a third party was able to disclose a confidential letter written by the defendant to his wife, notwithstanding that his wife could have claimed privilege from disclosure if she has been in possession of the letter. However the public interest in the ascertainment of truth in litigation which underlies the above principle, is outweighed by the public interest in the proper administration of justice. So where a litigant either steals or obtains by stealth or a trick his opponent's documents, he will not be permitted to make use of them in evidence.[9]

It follows from the above statement that secondary evidence may be given of a fact where private privilege could be claimed in respect of primary evidence of that fact. This is not so in the case of Crown privilege where secondary evidence as well as primary evidence is excluded. Finally a person may always waive his private privilege[10] whereas only the Crown may waive a claim to Crown privilege. Indeed the court may refuse to admit evidence whose disclosure would be prejudicial to the public interest though no formal claim to privilege has been made.[11]

The following are the existing occasions of private privilege.

a Incrimination

No person may be compelled to answer any question the answer to which would tend to incriminate himself or, in civil proceedings only, his spouse.[12] An answer is regarded as incriminating if it would expose the deponent to any criminal charge or statutory penalty. The fact that a person swears that his answer would be incriminating is not conclusive. If the privilege is claimed for a document the court may inspect the document in order to determine whether its contents are incriminating. Where privilege is claimed for an oral answer the judge must decide from the surrounding circumstances whether there is a real danger of incrimination. If there is no real and appreciable danger the claim to privilege will not be upheld even if there is a remote possibility of criminal sanctions. Thus in *R.* v. *Boyes*[13] a witness who had been handed a royal pardon was obliged to answer a question although there remained a possibility of his being impeached, because a pardon cannot be pleaded as a defence to an impeachment. Nevertheless a claim to privilege is not defeated merely because prosecution for the offence in question is very rare.[14]

In criminal proceedings the privilege extends to answers which would tend

---

8 [1964] A.C. 814; [1962] 3 All E.R. 256.
9 *I.T.C. Film Distributors, Ltd.* v. *Video Exchange, Ltd.*, [1982] Ch. 431; [1982] 2 All E.R. 241.
10 Waiver may be inadvertent, for example by mistakenly sending a document to one's opponent. Similarly disclosure of part of a document may result in a waiver of privilege in respect of the remainder of the document: *Great Atlantic Insurance Co.* v. *Home Insurance Co.*, [1981] 2 All E.R. 485; [1981] 1 W.L.R. 529.
11 *Duncan* v. *Cammell Laird & Co., Ltd.*, [1942] A.C. 624; [1942] 1 All E.R. 587; see p. 598, *ante.*
12 Civil Evidence Act 1968, s. 14(1)(*b*).
13 (1861), 1 B. & S. 311; see also *Khan* v. *Khan*, [1982] 2 All E.R. 60; [1982] 1 W.L.R. 513.
14 *Triplex Safety Glass Co., Ltd.* v. *Lancegaye Safety Glass (1934), Ltd.*, [1939] 2 K.B. 395; [1939] 2 All E.R. 613.

to expose the deponent to forfeiture, including forfeiture of a lease.[15] It does not, however, extend to answers which would expose the deponent to other civil liability such as an action for debt or to ill-fame generally.[16]

There are a number of statutory exceptions to the rule that a person cannot be required to incriminate himself. The most important exceptions occur in the case of the accused at a criminal trial. Section 1(*e*) of the Criminal Evidence Act 1898 provides that the accused may be asked any question in cross-examination notwithstanding that it would tend to incriminate him as to the offence charged. The considerations which apply where the answer would tend to incriminate the accused as to other offences are contained in section 1(f) of the 1898 Act and have already been considered.[17] Several other statutes,[18] concerned chiefly with the examination of debtors, create exceptions to the general rule, but the statute concerned generally provides that the answer may not be used in subsequent criminal proceedings.

b   Marital privilege

There are two heads of privilege which have their origin in the confidential relationship between spouses. By virtue of section 16 of the Civil Evidence Act 1968, they apply only in criminal proceedings. These are (1) communications between spouses (Criminal Evidence Act 1898, section 1(*d*); and (2) evidence as to marital intercourse (Matrimonial Causes Act 1965, section 43(1)). Both will be abolished when section 80(9) of the Police and Criminal Evidence Act 1984 is brought into operation. Accordingly it is not proposed to consider them further.[19]

c   Legal professional privilege

The legal profession is unique in at least one respect. This is that legal professional communications attract evidential privilege. This privilege does not exist in respect of communications made in pursuance of other relationships of an apparently equally confidential nature. Thus there is no privilege for communications between doctor and patient,[20] priest and penitent[1] or banker and customer[2]. It should be noted, however, that the law does respect

---

[15] *Earl of Mexborough* v. *Whitwood Urban District Council*, [1897] 2 Q.B. 111. The Civil Evidence Act 1968, s. 14(1)(*a*), abolished this rule in relation to civil proceedings. However, in civil proceedings, the privilege does extend to answers or documents which would tend to expose a person to a statutory penalty. In *Rio Tinto Zinc Corporation* v. *Westinghouse Electric Corporation*, [1978] A.C. 547; [1978] 1 All E.R. 434, a corporation was held to be entitled to claim privilege for documents tending to show that it was party to an international cartel of uranium producers on the ground that this would constitute a breach of Article 85 of the E.E.C. Treaty in respect of which the European Commission had power to impose fines upon the corporation. Section 16(5) of the 1968 Act abolished the rule whereby a witness in proceedings instituted in consequence of adultery could decline to answer any question tending to show that he or she had been guilty of adultery.

[16] *Nast* v. *Nast*, [1972] Fam. 142; [1972] 1 All E.R. 1171.

[17] See p. 578, *ante*.

[18] Examples are: Bankruptcy Act 1914, s. 15; Companies Act 1948, s. 270; Theft Act 1968, s. 31(1); Criminal Damage Act 1971, s. 9; Supreme Court Act 1981, s. 72 (as to which see p. 297, *ante*).

[19] Details may be obtained from consideration of previous editions of this work.

[20] *R.* v. *Kingston* (1776), 20 State Tr. 355; *Hunter* v. *Mann*, [1974] Q.B. 767; [1974] 2 All E.R. 414.

[1] *Wheeler* v. *Le Marchant* (1881), 17 Ch.D. 675, at p. 681; see 123 New Law Journal, p. 815.

[2] Bankers' Books Evidence Act 1879, s. 7.

the confidential nature of these relationships in that it may, in appropriate circumstances, restrain a party from making public that which was divulged in confidence.[3] This is a principle of public policy and it may be displaced by the stronger principle of public policy that requires full disclosure in judicial proceedings. The result is that the courts might compel a person to disclose in evidence in judicial proceedings that which they would restrain him from disclosing anywhere else.[4]

There are two separate heads of legal professional privilege.

Communications between solicitor and client—Oral and written communications between solicitor and client are privileged provided they were made in confidence and for the purpose of obtaining or giving legal advice. The rationale of this privilege is that the client may be able to make a full and frank disclosure of his affairs to his solicitor. Provided the communication is a professional and not a merely social or business one there is no requirement that any litigation be pending or anticipated. The privilege does not depend upon a retainer and exists even if there is no retainer or if the retainer has terminated.[5] The privilege is that of the client, not of the solicitor, so that only the client can waive it. Apart from this the privilege is lost in respect of a confidential professional communication only if it was made in furtherance of a fraudulent or criminal purpose, for example seeking advice upon the commission of a crime or fraud.[6]

Communications made in pursuance of litigation—Communications, generally written, made in pursuance of litigation that is pending or anticipated are privileged from disclosure in that or any other litigation. This head of privilege is wider than the first head in that it is not confined to the solicitor-client relationship. It extends to communications between, for example, counsel and solicitor, an insured person and his insurance company, solicitor and prospective witness and, in proceedings under the Patents Act 1977, to communications between a party and his patent agent.[7] In one case[8] the privilege was held to justify the defendants' refusal to disclose a statement made by the plaintiff to the defendants' insurers; the statement had been made shortly after the accident in respect of which the plaintiff's action was brought. However, where a document is brought into existence for more than one purpose privilege will only be held to exist if the dominant purpose is that of submitting it to a legal adviser for advice and use in litigation. So where the British Railways Board, following a fatal accident to one of its employees, held an enquiry, the results of which were recorded in an

---

[3] See *R.* v. *Statutory Visitors to St. Lawrence's Hospital,* [1953] 2 All E.R. 766; [1953] 1 W.L.R. 1158; *Duchess of Argyll* v. *Duke of Argyll,* [1967] Ch. 302; [1965] 1 All E.R. 611; *D.* v. *National Society for the Prevention of Cruelty to Children,* [1978] A.C. 171; [1977] 1 All E.R. 589 (see p. 600, *ante*).

[4] See, for example, *Jones* v. *G. D. Searle & Co. Ltd.,* [1978] 3 All E.R. 654; [1979] 1 W.L.R. 101.

[5] *Calcraft* v. *Guest,* [1898] 1 Q.B. 759, at p. 761; *Minter* v. *Priest,* [1930] A.C. 558. The privilege extends to communications with a foreign legal adviser: *Re Duncan, Garfield* v. *Fay,* [1968] P. 306; [1968] 2 All E.R. 395.

[6] *R.* v. *Cox and Railton* (1884), 14 Q.B.D. 153. See *Butler* v. *Board of Trade,* [1971] Ch. 680; [1970] 3 All E.R. 593 and *Crescent Farm (Sidcup) Sports, Ltd.* v. *Sterling Offices, Ltd.,* [1972] Ch. 553; [1971] 2 All E.R. 1192, where the authorities are reviewed.

[7] Patents Act 1977, s. 104.

[8] *Britten* v. *F. H. Pilcher & Sons,* [1969] 1 All E.R. 491.

internal enquiry report headed "For the information of the Board's solicitor", the report was held nevertheless not to be privileged in an action brought by the deceased's widow against the Board since the report was prepared for another purpose as well, namely to establish the cause of the accident so that appropriate safety measures could be taken, and the purpose for advice and use in anticipated litigation was merely one of the purposes and not the dominant purpose.[9]

The privilege is also limited in that the communication must be referable to litigation pending or anticipated. Thus in *Wheeler* v. *Le Marchant*[10] certain reports from a surveyor to the defendant's solicitor were held not to attract privilege since, although they were prepared in respect of property which was the subject matter of the litigation, no litigation was pending or anticipated when the reports were made.

It should be noted, finally, that legal professional privilege can only be claimed by a party or a witness. Thus if the other party to litigation has secondary evidence of a confidential professional communication there is no way to prevent him from giving this evidence,[11] unless he has obtained the information by stealth or a trick.[12]

d   Sources of information

Aside from cases of public interest privilege,[13] there is no common law privilege from disclosing sources of information. Attempts to establish such a privilege on behalf of journalists and newspaper proprietors had conspicuously failed[14] before Parliament intervened to create a limited privilege by the Contempt of Court Act 1981, section 10 of which provides

> "No court may require a person to disclose, nor is any person guilty of contempt of court for refusing to disclose, the source of information contained in a publication for which he is responsible, unless it be established to the satisfaction of the court that disclosure is necessary in the interests of justice or national security or for the prevention of disorder or crime."

The restricted scope of the privilege will be obvious. First, there must be a "publication" within the meaning of the Act.[15] Secondly, the three exceptions are very wide in scope so that the practical impact of the section is likely to be slight.[16]

---

9 *Waugh* v. *British Railways Board*, [1980] A.C. 521; [1979] 2 All E.R. 1169.
10 (1881), 17 Ch.D. 675.
11 *Calcraft* v. *Guest*, [1898] 1 Q.B. 759.
12 *I.T.C. Film Distributors, Ltd.* v. *Video Exchange, Ltd.*, [1982] Ch. 431; [1982] 2 All E.R. 241.
13 As to which see p. 598, *ante*.
14 See *A.-G.* v. *Clough*, [1963] 1 Q.B. 773; [1963] 1 All E.R. 420; *A-G.* v. *Foster, A-G.* v. *Mulholland*, [1963] 2 Q.B. 477; [1963] 1 All E.R. 767; *British Steel Corporation* v. *Granada Television, Ltd.*, [1981] A.C. 1096; [1981] 1 All E.R. 417.
15 Defined by s. 2(1) of the Act to include "any speech, writing, broadcast or other communication in whatever form, which is addressed to the public at large or any section of the public."
16 For a consideration of the scope and construction of s. 10, see *Secretary of State for Defence* v. *Guardian Newspapers, Ltd.*, [1984] Ch. 156; [1984] 3 All E.R. 601.

e   Title deeds

An ancient instance of private privilege is the privilege whereby a witness may refuse to produce deeds or documents of title. The common law basis of the rule is the sanctity of an Englishman's property in land, although the privilege is not confined to documents of title to land. If it would also tend to prove the title of his opponent, where that title is in issue, the privilege is lost.[17] By virtue of the Civil Evidence Act 1968, s. 16(1)(*b*) the privilege now extends only to criminal proceedings.

B   DOCUMENTARY EVIDENCE

A party who wishes to rely upon the contents of a document[18] as a means of proving a fact has to prove two separate matters. First he must prove what the document in question contains. This must usually be done by producing the document itself. His second obligation is to prove that the document upon which he relies is authentic or has been duly executed. These matters must be dealt with separately.

1   Proof of the contents of a document

a   Application of the "best evidence" rule

One of the fundamental rules of evidence at common law was the best evidence rule. The rule is self-explanatory, its effect being that a fact could only be proved by the best, or most cogent, evidence available. The rule has long ceased to be a basic rule of evidence and its operation is now primarily confined to documentary evidence. In this sphere the basic rule is still that the contents of a document may be proved only by production of the original, although there are now many exceptions to this rule. The rule is well illustrated by the case of *Macdonnell* v. *Evans*.[19] One of the plaintiff's witnesses was asked in cross-examination whether a letter of his, which defendant's counsel produced, was written in answer to another letter charging the witness with forgery. The question was disallowed by the Court of Common Pleas since it purported to prove the contents of that letter without producing the original. The best evidence rule was recently applied in respect of tape recordings. In *R.* v. *Stevenson*[20] the trial judge rejected tape recordings on

---

[17] *Morris* v. *Edwards* (1890), L.R. 15 A.C. 309.
[18] The word "document" probably comprises any form of permanent record of a fact and includes, for example, tape recordings; see *R.* v. *Maqsud Ali*, [1966] 1 Q.B. 688; [1965] 2 All E.R. 464; *Grant* v. *Southwestern and County Properties, Ltd.,* [1975] Ch. 185; [1974] 2 All E.R. 465. The Civil Evidence Act 1968, s. 10(1) defines a document, for the purposes of Part 1 of that Act, as including, in addition to a document in writing "(*a*) any map, plan, graph or drawing; (*b*) any photograph; (*c*) any disc, tape, sound track or other device in which sounds or other data (not being visual images) are embodied so as to be capable (with or without the aid of some other equipment) of being reproduced therefrom; and (*d*) any film, negative, tape or other device in which one or more visual images are embodied so as to be capable (as aforesaid) of being reproduced therefrom".
[19] (1852) 11 C.B. 930.
[20] [1971] 1 All E.R. 678; [1971] 1 W.L.R. 1.

the ground that there was clear evidence that some interference with the tapes might have taken place with the result that it was likely that the proffered evidence was not the original or best evidence.

There may be a number of originals of one document. Thus where an agreement is drawn up in two identical documents, each of which is executed by both parties, both documents are duplicate originals.[1] On the other hand a deed and a counterpart, each of which is executed by only one party to the transaction, are not duplicate originals; each is a separate original and neither is regarded as a duplicate of the other.

b   Exceptions

Having stated the general rule that the original of a document must be put in evidence, it is necessary to examine the existing exceptions to the rule. These exceptions are very wide in scope and largely nullify the effect of the rule. Where one of these exceptions can be shown to apply, secondary evidence of the contents of the document may be given. Where secondary evidence of a document is admissible in this way there is no prescribed form which this secondary evidence must take. There are no degrees of secondary evidence. Consequently a photographic copy, strange as it may seem, is not, in theory at least, preferable to oral testimony as to the contents of the document in question[2] though a photographic copy is undoubtedly more cogent than oral testimony. The principal circumstances in which secondary evidence of a document may be given are as follows.

(1) Where a party has, in civil proceedings, failed to comply with a notice to produce a document, the party serving the notice may put a copy in evidence. In addition the party failing to comply with the notice cannot himself rely upon the original. Express notices to produce are now comparatively rare in civil proceedings in the High Court because the present Rules of the Supreme Court[3] provide that a party serving a list of documents in his custody, possession or power on another party is deemed to have been served by that other party with a notice to produce at the trial the documents specified in the list. Notwithstanding the fact that the party served with the notice may claim privilege from production of the original, his opponent may make use of a copy thus nullifying the privilege.[4]

A notice to produce is not required where the document in question is itself a notice, such as a notice to quit, a notice of intended prosecution or, indeed, a notice to produce.[5]

(2) Where the original is in the possession of a third party who may justifiably decline to produce it, a copy is admissible. This situation may arise where the third party is out of the jurisdiction and cannot be served with a *subpoena duces tecum*.[6] This principle does not apply, however, where the

---

[1] *Forbes* v. *Samuel,* [1913] 3 K.B. 706.
[2] *Brown* v. *Woodman* (1834), 6 C. & P. 206.
[3] See p. 374, *ante.*
[4] See p. 374, *ante.*
[5] *R.* v. *Turner,* [1910] 1. K.B. 346.
[6] The principle applies in criminal, as well as civil, proceedings: *R.* v. *Nowaz,* [1976] 3 All E.R. 5; [1976] 1 W.L.R. 830.

third party has not been served with a *subpoena* or has unlawfully failed to obey a *subpoena*.[7] In such a case the remedy is to institute proceedings to have the witness committed for contempt of court.

(3) Where the original has been lost or destroyed, its production is excused. This principle is based, as is the one above, on expedience since it would be pedantic to require a party to do the impossible. Adequate proof must be tendered that the document has, in fact, been lost or destroyed.

(4) A copy may be admitted where production of the original would be physically impossible or, at least, highly inconvenient. Thus inscriptions on walls or tombstones are commonly proved by oral testimony though a tombstone has been produced in the House of Lords.[8] On the same basis the copy of a notice was admitted where the original was required by statute to remain affixed to a factory wall in *Owner* v. *Bee Hive Spinning Co., Ltd.*[9]

(5) Where the document is a public document, special rules apply. A public document has been defined as "a document that is made for the purpose of the public making use of it, and being able to refer to it".[10] The distinguishing feature of a public document is often its authentication by a public officer. Public registers, court records and Parliamentary records are typical classes of public documents. The best evidence rule does not apply to public documents. Consequently the contents of a public document may always be proved by secondary evidence. However, in the case of public documents the appropriate form of secondary evidence required to constitute proof is usually prescribed by statute. Thus the statement that there are no degrees of secondary evidence is not accurate in relation to public documents.

Judicial notice is taken of the contents of certain public documents such as Public Acts of Parliament. Old Private Acts, Statutory Instruments and other Parliamentary documents are proved by production of the Queen's Printer's copy. The contents of public registers are proved by certified or office copies. Thus a birth, death or marriage is proved by a certificate of entry in the appropriate register.[11] The method of proving judgments and convictions varies according to the court in question. House of Lords judgments are proved by production of an officially printed copy of the Journal of the House. Judgments of the Supreme Court may be proved by production of an office copy[12] and those of the county court by certified copy of the registrar's book.[13] There are numerous statutory provisions governing the methods by which a conviction may be proved, proof generally being by a certified copy of the court record signed by the clerk or other officer having custody of the record.[14]

(6) Bankers' books do not come within the definition of public documents. Nevertheless, for the purpose of saving the time of banks and their staff, the Bankers' Books Evidence Act 1879, sections 3 to 5, provide that an examined

---

[7] *R.* v. *Llanfaethly (Inhabitants)* (1853), 2 E. & B. 940.
[8] *Boosey* v. *Davidson* (1849), 13 Q.B. 257, at p. 265.
[9] [1914] 1 K.B. 108.
[10] *Sturla* v. *Freccia* (1880), 5 App. Cas. 623, at p. 643, *per* LORD BLACKBURN.
[11] Births and Deaths Registration Act 1953, s. 34; Marriage Act 1949, s. 65.
[12] R.S.C. (Revision) 1965, O. 38, r. 10.
[13] County Courts Act 1984, s. 73.
[14] Evidence Act 1851, s. 13 (to be replaced by Police and Criminal Evidence Act 1984, s. 73); see also Civil Evidence Act 1968, s. 11(4).

copy of any entry in a bankers' book[15] kept in the ordinary course of business shall be received in all legal proceedings as *prima facie* evidence of such entry.

(7) Any document admissible by virtue of section 2, 4 or 5 of the Civil Evidence Act 1968 may be proved by the production of a copy of that document authenticated in such manner as the court may approve.[16]

2   Proof of execution of private documents

This section is concerned with the methods by which a party may prove the validity or due execution of a private document. No question of proof of execution arises in connection with public documents since the statutes which enable the contents of public documents to be proved by means of copies also provide that the mere production of the appropriately sealed or certified copy shall be sufficient proof of execution.[17] This is an illustration of the presumption of regularity, *omnia praesumuntur rite esse acta*.[18] Nevertheless the presumption is always rebuttable and the validity or due execution of a public document may be impeached.

In civil cases it is often not necessary for a party to prove the execution of documents in his possession since, unless authenticity is in issue, they will usually be formally admitted by his opponent. Indeed it is usual in civil cases to have an "agreed bundle" of documents for use in the course of the trial. Admission is made in answer to a notice to admit the documents in question, express or implied.[19] If a private document is not admitted in civil or criminal proceedings it must be formally proved. There are three methods of proving documents: by proof of handwriting, by proof of attestation and by presumption.

a   *Proof of handwriting*

Probably the commonest method of proving the validity or execution of a private document is by identification of the handwriting. Handwriting is a matter which may be proved by ordinary or by expert witnesses. The usual method of proving handwriting is by calling the writer as a witness or, if he is already a witness, putting the document to him in the witness box. Alternatively a witness who saw the document written or is familiar with the handwriting of the writer by reason of their family or business connection may identify the handwriting in the document in question. The least common, and probably least cogent, method of proving handwriting is by comparison of the document in question with an authenticated specimen of the handwriting of the person who is alleged to be the author of that document. The

---

15 Bankers' books include ledgers, day books, cash books, account books and other records used in the ordinary business of the bank, whether in writing or kept on microfilm, magnetic tape or any other form of mechanical or electronic data retrieval mechanism: Bankers' Books Evidence Act 1897, s. 9 (as substituted by Banking Act 1979, Sch. 6).
16 Civil Evidence Act 1968, s. 6(1); see pp. 664–665, *post*.
17 Evidence Act 1845, s. 1; Evidence Act 1851, s. 14; Supreme Court Act 1981, s. 132.
18 See p. 608, *ante*.
19 R.S.C. (Revision) 1965, O. 27, rr. 4, 5; see p. 374, *ante*

comparison may be made by the judge or jury[20] or by an ordinary witness but is usually made by an expert witness—a graphologist.[1]

b Proof of attestation

Attestation is the signature of a document by a person who is not a party to the document as a witness to signature of one of the parties. The principal classes of documents which require attestation under the modern law are wills and codicils.[2] If it is necessary to prove the execution of a will one of the attesting witnesses must be called to prove attestation. Only if none of the attesting witnesses can be called may attestation be proved by proof of the handwriting of one of them. Certain other documents by law require attestation[3] while many others are, as a matter of practice, needlessly attested. In the case of these other documents the attesting witness may be called though this is not essential, as it is in the case of wills, and the handwriting of such a witness may be proved.[4]

c Proof by presumption

In any proceedings, civil or criminal, there is a presumption, now contained in section 4 of the Evidence Act 1938, that a document which is not less than twenty years old is validly executed. The document must appear to be duly executed and must be produced from proper custody. This means that the document must have been produced from a place in which it might properly be expected to be kept, such as a deed box, bank or solicitor's office. For the purpose of determining the age of a document there is a presumption, which is rebuttable, that the document was executed on the date it bears.

There are certain other presumptions which apply in relation both to the contents and to the due execution of documents. Thus parties to a conveyance are presumed to be of full age.[5] Alterations in a deed are presumed to have been made before execution; alterations in a will are presumed to have been made after execution.

Before leaving the subject of the execution of documents it is necessary to refer briefly to the Stamp Act 1891. This Act, as amended, creates obligations to stamp certain classes of documents either with a fixed stamp or, in some cases, with an *ad valorem* stamp. One of the methods of enforcing the obligation to pay stamp duty is to prohibit the use in evidence of unstamped documents which ought to be stamped. Stamp objections are taken by the court,[6] not by counsel, in civil proceedings and are not taken at all in criminal proceedings. Stamping must generally take place on or before execution, though many documents may be stamped late on payment of the unpaid duty and prescribed penalties.[7]

---

[20] Criminal Procedure Act 1865, s. 8. This is, in practice, almost never done.
[1] *R.* v. *Silverlock*, [1894] 2 Q.B. 766.
[2] Wills Act 1837, s. 9.
[3] Examples are: chattel mortgages (Bills of Sale (1878) Amendment Act 1882, s. 10), deeds under the seal of a corporation (Law of Property Act 1925, s. 74).
[4] Evidence Act 1938, s. 15.
[5] Law of Property Act 1925, s. 15.
[6] Stamp Act 1891, s. 14.
[7] *Ibid.*, ss. 14(1), 15.

3   Extrinsic evidence in relation to documents: the parol evidence rule

Where a transaction is recorded in a document extrinsic evidence is inadmissible as a substitute for that document, to vary or contradict the terms of the document or to interpret the document. This rule is often described as the "parol evidence" rule. The rule is a rule of exclusion, though it is difficult to classify it with other exclusionary rules of evidence. The reason for this difficulty is that the first aspect of the rule primarily excludes extrinsic evidence as a means of proof whereas the second and third parts of the rule exclude facts. In addition the second and third parts of the rule, which together exclude evidence adduced to vary, contradict or interpret a document, are best regarded as rules of substantive law rather than rules of evidence. This, coupled with the highly technical and complex rules of construction which are involved, render it undesirable to examine the parol evidence rule in any detail in a general work of this nature. Consequently only the barest outline of the three aspects of the parol evidence rule appears below.[8]

a   *Extrinsic evidence in substitution for documents*

The first aspect of the parol evidence rule excludes parol evidence as a means of proving the contents of a document or as a substitute for a document. Parol evidence is any evidence, oral or written, which is extrinsic to the document the contents of which it is sought to prove. It will be readily appreciated that this aspect of the parol evidence rule is largely co-extensive with the best evidence rule in relation to documents. The latter rule has already been discussed and the several exceptions which have been noted may also be classified as exceptions to the parol evidence rule.[9] However, the parol evidence rule is somewhat wider than the best evidence rule in this respect. Thus certain rules of substantive or procedural law require some transactions either to be recorded[10] in or evidenced[11] by writing. In these cases the transactions are either void or unenforceable by action at common law in the absence of writing. There are certain exceptional cases, even where the need for writing arises by statute, in which parol evidence is admissible. Thus in actions for specific performance of contracts for the sale of interests in land, parol evidence may be admitted to prove the contract in question[12] or to prove a sufficient act of part performance. Similarly extrinsic evidence may be admitted to connect two or more documents in order to show that the transaction in question was contained in more than one document.[13] These are further exceptions to the parol evidence rule.

Even where there is no substantive rule of law or procedure requiring a memorandum in writing to prove a transaction, the parol evidence rule applies to cases where the parties have chosen to record their transactions in a document.

---

[8] For a more detailed discussion of the rule reference should be made to Cross, *Evidence* (5th Edn.), p. 608; Nokes, *An Introduction to Evidence* (4th Edn.), p. 239.

[9] See p. 641, *ante*.

[10] For example, Wills Act 1837; Law of Property Act 1925, s. 52.

[11] For example: Statute of Frauds (1677), s. 4; Law of Property Act 1925, s. 40.

[12] *Chaproniere* v. *Lambert*, [1917] 2 Ch. 356.

[13] *Pearce* v. *Gardner*, [1897], 1 Q.B. 688; compare *Boydell* v. *Drummond* (1809), 11 East 142.

b   Extrinsic evidence to vary or contradict the contents of a document

This aspect of the parol evidence rule is entirely different from the best evidence rule in relation to documents. This aspect of the rule applies where a party wishes to adduce extrinsic evidence, not as an alternative means of proving the contents of a document, but in order to contradict or vary the express terms of the document. The general rule, which is probably based simply on commercial expedience, prohibits such evidence and applies to any written transaction whether or not it is required by law to be in writing. In *Angell* v. *Duke*[14] the defendant agreed in writing to let a house to the plaintiff together with the furniture in the house. The plaintiff sought to adduce evidence that the defendant had orally agreed to supply additional furniture but this evidence was excluded since it would contradict the written agreement which referred only to furniture already in the house. Similarly in *Henderson* v. *Arthur*[15] evidence was excluded of the prior agreement of the lessor to accept rent in arrears where the lease itself provided for the payment of rent in advance.

There are, however, a number of important exceptions to this principle. First, it is permissible to adduce evidence to prove the nature of a written transaction. Thus an apparent sale may be shown, in fact, to be a mortgage;[16] an apparent gift may be shown, in fact, to amount to the creation of a trust. Similarly evidence may be adduced to supplement the terms of a written transaction. For example, in *Re Huxtable*[17] a testator bequeathed £4,000 to a beneficiary "for charitable purposes agreed between us". Extrinsic evidence was admitted to show what these purposes were. It may be noted, however, that supplementary terms cannot contradict the terms they are admitted to supplement. Thus in *Re Huxtable,* while evidence was admitted to identify the charitable purposes referred to in the will, evidence was not admitted of a prior agreement that only the income of the bequest, and not the capital, was to be devoted to these purposes since this would have contradicted the terms of the bequest. The supplemental term may take the form of a collateral warranty which may be defined as a separate promise which is understood to form part of the consideration for entering into the main contract. Thus in *De Lassalle* v. *Guildford*[18] the plaintiff refused to execute a lease unless the defendant landlord warranted that the drains were in good order. A verbal warranty was given and the lease consequently executed. Although the lease contained no provision as to the drains it was held by the Court of Appeal that the plaintiff could sue for breach of warranty.

Evidence may also be admissible of a subsequent variation or discharge of a written agreement. This variation or discharge may be oral notwithstanding that the original agreement was in writing or even under seal.[19] Where the original agreement is required by law to be evidenced in writing evidence of a

---

[14] (1875), 32 L.T. 320.
[15] [1907] 1 K.B. 10.
[16] *Re Duke of Marlborough*, [1894] 2 Ch. 133.
[17] [1902] 2 Ch. 793.
[18] [1901] 2 K.B. 215.
[19] This is a rule of equity: *Berry* v. *Berry*, [1929] 2 K.B. 316.

verbal discharge of this agreement is admissible[20] though evidence of a verbal variation is not.[1]

Finally, in relation to wills, note must be taken of the Administration of Justice Act 1982. Section 20 of that Act permits rectification of a will which is so expressed that it fails to carry out the testator's intentions in consequence (*a*) of a clerical error; or (*b*) of a failure to understand his instructions, while section 21 provides for the admission of extrinsic evidence, including evidence of the testator's intention, to interpret a will:

> "(*a*) in so far as any part of it is meaningless;
> (*b*) in so far as the language used in any part of it is ambiguous on the face of it;
> (*c*) in so far as evidence, other than evidence of the testator's intention, shows that the language used in any part of it is ambiguous in the light of surrounding circumstances."

c Extrinsic evidence as an aid to interpretation

The construction of documents is far too wide a topic to be considered even in outline in a general work of this nature. Many of the rules concerning the interpretation of statutes discussed elsewhere in this book[2] apply equally to the construction of deeds and documents. The basic rule, common to the interpretation of both statutes and documents, is that the intention of the draftsman is to be ascertained from the words used, not from extrinsic evidence. This rule excluding extrinsic facts as an aid to interpretation is in character a rule of evidence, though the topic of construction of documents has become so specialised as to become in effect a branch of substantive law. Stated simply, the rule, which is generally classified as the third aspect of the parol evidence rule, is that extrinsic facts may not be proved in order to ascertain the intention of the writer of a document in construing that document. There are several exceptions to this rule of exclusion. The exceptions fall into two classes. The first category of cases in which extrinsic evidence is admitted comprises those cases where extrinsic evidence is admitted to show the meaning of the words used. The second category of exceptions comprises those cases where, having ascertained the meaning of the words used, equivocation results and it is necessary to resort to extrinsic evidence in order to determine which of alternative results the writer intended. The process of ascertaining the meaning of words used in a document is properly called "interpretation"; the process of determining the legal effect of the words is properly called "construction", though the two words are frequently used in the alternative to describe the same process.

In most of the cases in which extrinsic evidence has been admitted, it has been admitted as an aid to interpretation rather than as an aid to construction. The reason for this is that parties to an agreement frequently use words which bear a meaning to them, or to persons in their trade or locality, which is not a meaning in common usage. In these cases it is clearly essential to have regard to extrinsic facts to ascertain the meaning of the words used. These facts may consist of the parties' previous agreements or dealings or a

---

[20] *Morris* v. *Baron & Co.,* [1918] A.C. 1.
[1] *Goss* v. *Nugent* (1833), 5 B. & Ad. 58.
[2] See p. 102, *et seq, ante.*

customary trade or local usage. Thus in *Kell* v. *Charmer*[3] evidence was admitted of the marking practice of jewellers in order to ascertain that a legacy of "the sum of i.x.x." meant £100 and that "the sum of o.x.x." was £200. Similarly in *Smith* v. *Wilson*[4] the Court of King's Bench was prepared to admit evidence of a local custom to the effect that, in counting rabbits, a hundred consisted of six score so that the figure 10,000 in fact meant 12,000 in the lease in question.

There have been comparatively few cases in which extrinsic evidence has been admitted as an aid to construction, as opposed to interpretation. Most of these cases have turned on the construction of wills which is an extremely specialised subject. Where a document, having been interpreted, discloses an ambiguity, extrinsic evidence of the intention of the writer may be admitted in order to resolve the ambiguity. The ambiguity may be patent, such as would arise if the same property were made the subject of bequests to different persons in a will, but is generally latent. Thus in *Doe* d. *Gord* v. *Needs*[5] a testator devised property to "George Gord the son of Gord". There were in existence two George Gords, one the son of G. Gord, the other the son of J. Gord. Evidence was admitted of the testator's statements of intention to show that the bequest was intended for the son of G. Gord. An odd illustration of this principle is contained in *Re Jackson*.[6] In that case a testatrix left property to her "nephew" Arthur Murphy. Since she had two legitimate nephews of that name extrinsic evidence was admitted to show that the intended beneficiary was, in fact, an illegitimate nephew also named Arthur Murphy. The striking feature of *Re Jackson* is that had there been but one legitimate Arthur Murphy he would have benefited to the exclusion of the intended beneficiary since there was a rule of construction that words of relationship exclude illegitimates. This occurred in *Re Fish*[7] where a bequest to a "niece" E.W. was construed as a bequest to a legitimate niece of that description even though there was adequate extrinsic evidence to show that an illegitimate "niece" E.W. was, in fact, intended.[8]

C REAL EVIDENCE

The principal methods of proof—the testimony of witnesses and documentary evidence—have been considered. The third and final means of proof is real evidence. Real evidence has been defined as "material objects, other than documents, produced for the inspection of the court".[9] This definition is open to criticism on more than one ground. The physical appearance of a party is not commonly described as a "material object" and yet is classifiable as real evidence. A "view" is not "produced" and yet most commentators regard a view as one type of real evidence. Finally a document may be

---

3 (1856), 23 Beav. 195.
4 (1832), 3 B. & Ad. 728.
5 (1836), 2 M. & W. 129.
6 [1933] Ch. 237.
7 [1894] 2 Ch. 83. The rule of construction was abrogated by Family Law Reform Act 1969, s. 15.
8 But see now Administration of Justice Act 1982, ss. 20, 21 (*supra*).
9 Phipson, "Real Evidence" (1920), 29 Yale L.J. 705, at p. 717.

classified as real evidence if it is tendered as proof of something other than its contents.

The basic difference between real evidence and the more common methods of proof is that where the evidence is real evidence the fact which it is sought to prove is actually perceived by the court. There are at least three types of real evidence. The first, and most common, type of real evidence consists of material objects produced for the inspection of the court. In the course of proceedings they are referred to as "exhibits". Commonly encountered exhibits are weapons, clothing, goods alleged to have been stolen and samples. In *Line* v. *Taylor*[10] a dog was produced in court at Hertford Assizes and the jury, from the expression of the dog's eyes and other indications, concluded that it was not of a vicious disposition.

The second type of real evidence consists of the physical appearance of persons. A person's wounds or disfigurement are frequently inspected by the court particularly where such evidence is relevant to the assessment of damages in a personal injuries action.[11] The appearance of a person may also be relevant to the issue of identity. Thus a child's physical resemblance to his putative father may be evidence in affiliation proceedings though it is very weak evidence of paternity.[12] The demeanour of a witness in the witness-box is classified by some commentators as real evidence on the basis that it is a fact of indirect relevance in that it affects testimony. The alternative view is that the demeanour of a witness merely affects cogency and is not evidence at all.

Finally, it is usual to classify a view as real evidence since the fact which it is sought to prove is actually perceived by the court. A view is an inspection outside the court of a place or object where the physical characteristics of that place or object are relevant facts. Thus in *Buckingham* v. *Daily News, Ltd.*[13] the Court of Appeal held that an inspection by the trial judge of the working of a machine did form part of the evidence. It is within the judge's discretion whether or not to hold a view; neither side can either compel or prevent the judge from holding a view.[14] On the other hand, since a view is evidence, it is not permissible in a jury trial for some of the jurors to view the *locus in quo* without the others. So where a judge invited one member of a jury to visit an area at night to examine the effectiveness of the street lighting and "report back" to the other jurors, the resulting conviction was quashed on appeal.[15]

It should be noted that the best evidence rule has no application to real evidence. Even if an object could very easily be brought into court there is no obligation to do so and the fact of its physical characteristics may be proved by testimony or documentary evidence such as a photograph.[16] Since, it will

---

[10] (1862), 3 F. & F. 731.

[11] *Cole* v. *United Dairies (London), Ltd.*, [1941] 1 K.B. 100;[1940] 4 All E.R. 318.

[12] *Slingsby* v. *A.-G.* (1916), 33 T.L.R. 120.

[13] [1956] 2 Q.B. 534; [1956] 2 All E.R. 904. There is nothing improper in a judge going to examine the *locus in quo* for himself, unaccompanied by the parties though this is not, strictly, a "view": *Salisbury* v. *Woodland*, [1970] 1 Q.B. 324; [1969] 3 All E.R. 863.

[14] R.S.C., O. 35, r. 8(1); cf. *Tito* v. *Waddell*, [1975] 3 All E.R. 997; [1975] 1 W.L.R. 1303 in which MEGARRY, J. visited two islands in the Western Pacific, in order to view them, in the course of a long Chancery action.

[15] *R.* v. *Gurney,* [1977] R.T.R. 211.

[16] *Hocking* v. *Ahlquist Brothers, Ltd.,* [1944] K.B. 120; [1943] All E.R. 722.

be recalled, the best evidence rule does apply to documentary evidence it is important to distinguish documentary evidence from real evidence. A document is regarded as documentary evidence if it is tendered as a means of proving a fact to which the contents of the document relate. On the other hand a document is real evidence if it is adduced simply to prove its physical characteristics. Thus a tombstone is real evidence if tendered as proof of its height, weight or other physical characteristic. It is a document, however, if its inscription is adduced as evidence of, for example, the date of a person's death. On the same basis a coffin plate[17] and a ring[18] have been treated as documents whereas a banner[19] and a driving-licence[20] have been regarded as objects. In *Castle* v. *Cross*[1] the Queen's Bench divisional court held that the test record print-out of an automatic breath-testing device was real evidence admissible to prove that the machine did not have a sufficient sample of breath which it required to enable it to perform an analysis.

---

[17] *R.* v. *Hinley* (1843), 1 Cox C.C. 12.
[18] *R.* v. *Farr* (1864), 4 F. & F. 336.
[19] *R.* v. *Hunt* (1820), 3 B. & Ald. 566. The basis of this decision is questionable since the inscriptions on the banners in question seem to have been relevant.
[20] *Martin* v. *White*, [1910] 1 K.B. 665.
[1] [1985] 1 All E.R. 87; [1984] 1 W.L.R. 1372.

CHAPTER 32

Means of Proof which are Generally Inadmissible

It has already been noted that the word "evidence" is used alternatively to describe facts and the means of proving facts. Consequently evidentiary rules of exclusion may exclude facts altogether or, alternatively, may exclude a particular method of proof. The principal rules of exclusion of facts were considered in Chapter 30. This chapter is concerned with the rules excluding certain methods of proving facts. In the preceding chapter it was noted that secondary evidence of the contents of a private document is, subject to several exceptions, inadmissible. There are two other inadmissible methods of proving facts; by opinion and by hearsay evidence. A witness's testimony must relate to a fact which he has directly perceived. It cannot relate to his opinion as to the existence of a fact which it is required to prove nor can it relate to a third person's assertion of the existence of that fact. These two rules of exclusion, together with the various exceptions to them, must be examined in detail.

A OPINIONS

The general rule is that a witness may testify only as to facts which he has directly perceived. He may not state a belief in facts which is based on anything but direct perception. This is the rule excluding proof by opinion. The rationale of this rule of exclusion is that it is the function of the tribunal, not of the witnesses, to draw conclusions from the facts proved.[1] The function of witnesses, and indeed of any method of proof, is simply to place those facts before the court.

It is essential to distinguish opinion as a means of proof from opinion as a fact in itself. Where a person's opinion is, in itself, a relevant fact there is no rule excluding proof of that opinion. Opinion, in the sense of belief in a fact, is a fact in issue in several different types of action. Thus in defamation

---

[1] See *North Cheshire and Manchester Brewery Co., Ltd.* v. *Manchester Brewery Co., Ltd.*, [1899] A.C. 43.

actions where the defence of fair comment is raised the defendant's opinion is relevant. Similarly in an action based on malicious prosecution the defendant's opinion as to whether there was a reasonable ground for the prosecution is a fact in issue. A dying declaration by a victim of homicide is only admissible if the declarant was in settled hopeless expectation of death,[2] which involves evidence of the deceased's belief or opinion. On a prosecution for having unlawful sexual intercourse with a girl under the age of sixteen the accused's opinion that the girl was over sixteen is an element in a defence to that crime.[3]

Thus evidence of an opinion is not excluded where the opinion is, in itself, a fact in issue. In addition, where opinion is tendered as a means of proving some independent fact there are a number of circumstances in which the opinion is admissible despite the general rule of exclusion. These exceptions fall into two categories according to whether the opinion tendered is that of an ordinary witness or of an "expert".

1 The opinions of ordinary witnesses

The general rule excluding the opinion of an ordinary witness as a means of proof has already been noted. It is, however, often difficult to distinguish opinion from testimony based upon perception. A person's opinion is his belief in the existence of a fact. That belief may be based upon perception, impression or inference and there are many cases in which the witness himself would not be able to identify the basis of his belief. No difficulty arises where the fact to which the witness is testifying is clearly inferential and incapable of perception, such as negligence or cruelty. In these cases the witness's evidence is clearly based upon opinion. Difficulty does arise, however, where the witness testifies as to a fact which he has perceived. Thus if a witness testified that a vehicle was, at a given moment, mobile rather than stationary no one would doubt that the witness was testifying as to his direct perception of a fact. On the other hand if a witness testified as to the speed at which the vehicle was moving it is generally accepted that the witness would be giving an opinion. Yet there is no theoretical distinction between the fact of whether a vehicle was moving at a given moment and the fact of the speed at which it was moving at that moment. Speed is not an inference of fact; it is a direct fact capable of precise measurement and perception. Nevertheless it is not capable of precise perception by an ordinary witness. Thus a witness who testifies as to the speed of a vehicle is testifying as to his impression of that fact rather than his precise perception of it. Herein lies the distinction between fact and opinion. A belief based on inference or impression is an opinion; a belief based on direct perception of a fact capable of precise perception is not an opinion and the statement of a witness as to that belief is testimony relating to facts. This distinction is acknowledged in the terms of section 3(2) of the Civil Evidence Act 1972. By that subsection:

> "It is hereby declared that where a person is called as a witness in any civil proceedings, a statement of opinion by him on any relevant matter on which he is

---

[2] See p. 672, *post*.
[3] Sexual Offences Act 1956, s. 6(3).

not qualified to give expert evidence, if made as a way of conveying relevant facts personally perceived by him, is admissible as evidence of what he perceived.''

The object of this provision is to make it easier for a witness to communicate to the court as accurate an impression as possible of what he perceived with his own physical senses. It would, for example, enable a witness to give evidence to the effect that a vehicle was travelling at a very high speed or that it appeared to be out of control; it would not, on the other hand, permit a witness to give his opinion as to blameworthiness or negligence, since these are inferential facts incapable of perception.

Opinion evidence is admissible where the fact to which the witness's testimony relates is incapable of precise perception by an ordinary witness. In these cases a witness may relate his belief based on impression, which is an opinion. Thus opinion evidence is admissible on matters such as the speed of vehicles,[4] the value of common objects,[5] the identification of handwriting, the identification of a person or an object[6] or a person's age. Age is not usually proved by opinion because direct evidence such as a birth certificate is generally available. Indeed where precise age is a fact in issue, as for example where infancy is raised as a defence to an action based on contract, age cannot be proved by opinion.[7]

Although an opinion based upon impression is sometimes admissible the opinion of an ordinary witness based upon inference is not. For this reason a witness would never be allowed to give his opinion as to whether a car driver was negligent, whether a husband was cruel towards his wife or whether the use of a trade name was calculated to deceive.[8] For the same reason sanity and insanity are not matters upon which an ordinary (as opposed to an expert) witness may testify.[9] Sanity is a question of mixed law and fact and, insofar as it is a question of fact, it depends upon inferences of fact rather than upon direct perception or impression. Drunkenness, on the other hand, is solely a question of fact. It is uncertain whether it is an inference of fact or a fact in itself capable of perfection. If drunkenness is an inference of fact, logic would suggest that an ordinary witness should not be permitted to testify that a person appeared to be drunk so that his testimony should be confined to his perception of direct facts such as unsteady gait, incoherent speech or alcoholic breath leaving the court to draw the inference of drunkenness from these facts. Nevertheless, in practice, there is no doubt that an ordinary witness is sometimes permitted to give his opinion to the effect that a person was drunk. Furthermore, the words of section 3(2) of the Civil Evidence Act would seem to be wide enough to permit a witness to express such an opinion in civil proceedings.

---

4   Though, as a safeguard, a person cannot be convicted of speeding on the uncorroborated opinion of one witness as to his speed: Road Traffic Regulation Act 1967, s. 78A (2). See *Nicholas* v. *Penny*, [1950] 2 K.B. 466; [1950] 2 All E.R. 89; see p. 621, *ante*.
5   *R.* v. *Beckett* (1913), 8 Cr. App. Rep. 204.
6   *Fryer* v. *Gathercole* (1849), 4 Exch. 262.
7   *Haines* v. *Guthrie* (1884), 13 Q.B.D. 818.
8   *North Cheshire and Manchester Brewery Co., Ltd.* v. *Manchester Brewery Co., Ltd.*, [1899] A.C. 83.
9   *Wright* v. *Doe d. Tatham* (1838), 4 Bing N.C. 489.

2 The opinions of expert witnesses

The rule excluding proof by opinion is subject to an important exception in favour of the opinions of persons whom the court accepts as expert witnesses.[10] The circumstances in which the opinions of experts are admissible are wider in scope than the circumstances, mentioned above, in which the opinions of ordinary witnesses are admissible. The basic distinction is that, whereas an ordinary witness can only give an opinion based upon impression, an expert witness's opinion may be based either upon impression or upon inference. Thus the expert witness is permitted to draw an inference from facts whereas the ordinary witness is not, though the court is in no way bound to accept that inference.

It is for the judge to decide both the question of whether a witness is qualified to give an expert opinion and the question of whether the fact to which his opinion relates is a matter which permits of expertise. There is no particular standard which an expert witness must satisfy. Usually he will be professionally qualifed or experienced but in *R.* v. *Silverlock*[11] a solicitor was permitted to give expert evidence on the subject of handwriting comparison although his expertise was only acquired through his own private study over a period of some ten years. However the qualifications and expertise of an expert witness may always be challenged by cross-examination.

The second point upon which the judge must satisfy himself is that the fact which the witness's opinion is tendered to prove is something which may be the subject of expertise. Thus expert evidence will not, at common law, be admitted to the effect that a party was negligent[12] or that a publication tends to deprave or corrupt,[13] although in *Director of Public Prosecutions* v. *A. and B. C. Chewing Gum, Ltd.*[14] the Queen's Bench divisional court stated that on a prosecution under section 1 of the 1959 Act the evidence of child psychiatrists should be admitted on the question of the possible effects that a particular publication might have upon a child. This case was, however, in *R.* v. *Anderson*[15] regarded as exceptional, the principle being confirmed that expert evidence is not admissible on the issue of whether or not a publication is obscene, the question of obscenity being entirely one for the jury, though expert evidence is admissible on the issue whether, if the article is found to be obscene, its publication is justified as being for the public good "on the ground that it is in the interests of science, literature, art or learning, or of other objects of general concern."[16] "Other objects of general concern", however, must fall within the same field or dimension as "science, literature,

---

[10] The admissibility of expert evidence is restricted by rules of court (R.S.C. O. 38, rr. 34–44; see p. 367, *ante*).

[11] [1894] 2 Q.B. 766.

[12] *R.* v. *Davies*, [1962] 3 All E.R. 97; [1962] 1 W.L.R. 1111.

[13] Obscene Publications Act 1959, s. 1; *R.* v. *Penguin Books, Ltd.*, [1961] Crim. L.R. 176.

[14] [1968] 1 Q.B. 159; [1967] 2 All E.R. 504.

[15] [1972] 1 Q.B. 304; [1971] 3 All E.R. 1152—the notorious "*Oz*" prosecution.

[16] Obscene Publications Act 1959, s. 4(1); s. 4(2) expressly provides for the opinions of experts to be admitted either to establish or negative the defence under s. 4(1); see also *R.* v. *Turner*, [1975] Q.B. 834; [1975] 1 All E.R. 70; in which the Court of Appeal upheld the trial judge's decision to exclude the evidence of a psychiatrist on how an ordinary person who was not suffering from mental illness was likely to react to the stresses and strains of life, and (*b*) what reliance they could place upon the evidence of someone who was not mentally disordered, both matters being within the experience and knowledge of the judge and jury.

art or learning" so that evidence cannot be directed to the psychotherapeutic value of pornography for certain categories of persons, such as sexual deviants, with a view to demonstrating that the material published relieved their sexual tensions, thereby diverting them from anti-social and possibly criminal activities directed against others.[17] Similarly "learning" means a product of scholarship and does not include sex education.[18]

At this stage it is necessary to consider section 3(1) of the Civil Evidence Act 1972. By that subsection, subject to rules of court governing procedure:

> "Where a person is called as a witness in any civil proceedings, his opinion on any relevant matter on which he is qualified to give expert evidence should be admissible in evidence."

The first point to note is that the provision is only applicable to civil proceedings so that the authorities referred to above are unaffected. However in civil proceedings the scope of the subsection is by no means self evident. It appears to contemplate the giving of expert evidence on matters which permit of expertise but the use of the words "any relevant matter" (which are defined by s. 3(3) to include "an issue in the proceedings") suggest that expert opinion will be admitted on such matters as whether a person has been negligent. Thus, in cases of industrial injury (which are the cases in which expert evidence is most frequently called) an expert in industrial safety could arguably be permitted to express an opinion as to whether or not a system of work adopted by employers was or was not safe; in practice, most High Court judges would decline to admit such opinion although the witness could (and often does) say that the precautions adopted by the defendants are lower than those commonly adopted by other employers in the relevant industry.

Expert opinion is limited to matters involving specialist knowledge. In some of these matters the opinion of an ordinary witness is also admissible, though possibly less cogent. Handwriting, intoxication and value are examples of subjects upon which either expert or ordinary opinion is admissible. Subjects such as sanity, banking practice, fingerprints, ballistics, shipping, trade customs and foreign law are a few of those upon which expert opinion has been received. Many of the cases on this topic have turned upon proof of foreign law. There is a presumption that foreign law is the same as English law, the effect of which is that any party who alleges that a rule of foreign law is different from the corresponding rule of English law has the specific burden of proving that fact. Proof is almost always by the opinion of an expert witness. In *Bristow* v. *Sequeville*[19] it was suggested that only a practi-

---

[17] *R.* v. *Jordan*, [1977] A.C. 699; [1976] 3 All E.R. 775. This had become a standard line of defence in obscene publications cases. When the provisions of the 1959 Act were extended to cinematograph exhibitions (by the Criminal Law Act 1977, s. 53) the defence under s. 4, in relation to cinematograph exhibitions, was formulated rather differently, no doubt with this line of defence in mind, *viz.*, "if it is proved that publication of the film or soundtrack is justified as being for the public good on the ground that it is in the interests of drama, opera, ballet or any other art, or of literature or learning" (1959 Act, s. 4(1A)).

[18] *A.-G.'s Reference (No. 3 of 1977)*, [1978] 3 All E.R. 1166; [1978] 1 W.L.R. 1123; an unsuccessful attempt to justify evidence of the type that was excluded by the decision in *Jordan (supra)*.

[19] (1850), 5 Exch. 275.

tioner could be an expert upon foreign law and the evidence of a jurisconsult was rejected on the basis that he was not a competent expert. This principle was almost certainly too narrow, for non-practising lawyers,[20] teachers of law[1] and even persons without legal qualification[2] have been permitted to voice an opinion upon the subject of foreign law. Any doubt which existed is now removed in relation to civil proceedings by section 4(1) of the Civil Evidence Act 1972 which declares that expert evidence as to foreign law may be given by "a person who is suitably qualified to do so on account of his knowledge or experience . . . irrespective of whether he has acted or is entitled to act as a legal practitioner". This provision is, it is submitted, no more than declaratory of the common law, so that a similar approach is appropriate in criminal proceedings.

If there has been a finding as to foreign law in any proceedings, civil or criminal, that finding is receivable in evidence in subsequent civil proceedings, if reported or recorded in citable form,[3] for the purpose of proving the law of the territory in question.[4]

An expert witness is entitled to draw on and refer to the works of others (including unpublished work) in his field of expertise as part of the process of arriving at his conclusion. Reliance on the work of others and reference to it in evidence does not infringe the hearsay rule. The Court of Appeal so held in *R. v. Abadom*,[5] upholding the admissibility of evidence from a Home Office forensic scientist as to the incidence of a particular type of glass in all controlled glass samples analysed and statistically collated in the Home Office Central Research Establishment; this evidence was given in support of his opinion as to the likelihood of certain fragments of glass (found in the accused's clothing) having come from a particular window. The decision is likely to be of great practical importance.

B HEARSAY

1 The rule against hearsay

a Nature of hearsay evidence

The rule against hearsay is probably the best known and certainly the most important evidentiary rule of exclusion. Expressed simply, hearsay is that which another person was heard to say. This would be a totally inadequate and misleading statement of the hearsay rule, however, for two basic reasons.

---

[20] *Barford* v. *Barford*, [1918] P. 140.
[1] *Brailey* v. *Rhodesia Consolidated, Ltd.*, [1910] 2 Ch. 95.
[2] *De Beeche* v. *South American Stores etc., Ltd.*, [1935] A.C. 148. The witness, a banker, was an expert on foreign banking law.
[3] As to authorities in citable form, see p. 132, *ante*.
[4] Civil Evidence Act 1972, s. 4(2); this method of proof is subject to rules of court (s. 4(3)). It will be appreciated that these provisions do not have the effect of elevating findings as to foreign law to the status of findings of law; they remain findings of fact and it will, accordingly, always be open to the other party to call expert evidence to prove that foreign law is not as found in the previously decided case.
[5] [1983] 1 All E.R. 364; [1983] 1 W.L.R. 126.

First, the rule against hearsay is not confined to oral statements. A document may be inadmissible by reason of the hearsay rule. Thus a birth certificate is hearsay evidence of a date of birth, although it is in fact admissible as an exception to the hearsay rule. There is, in addition, authority for the proposition that conduct may be hearsay. For example, if in answer to a question, a person shook his head, evidence of this conduct would be inadmissible since it is equivalent to the person uttering the word "no". Similarly the fact that a person pointed at another is hearsay evidence of identification of that other person.[6] These are, however, exceptional circumstances and it is probably accurate to regard conduct as hearsay only when the conduct can be described as a means of expressing a fact as an alternative to expressing it in words. This is illustrated by the well-known case of *Wright* v. *Doe* d. *Tatham*[7] in which three letters written to a testator on the assumption that he was sane were held by the House of Lords to be inadmissible evidence of his sanity since they infringed both the rule excluding proof by opinion and the rule excluding proof by hearsay. Thus the conduct of the writers of the letters in treating the testator as sane was treated as hearsay on the basis that it amounted to an assertion of sanity.

The paragraph above illustrates that hearsay evidence is not confined to oral or even to oral and written statements. On the other hand not every oral or written statement made by a person other than the witness testifying is hearsay evidence. It must be remembered that the rule against hearsay is only a rule excluding a means of proof; it is not a rule excluding facts. Consequently evidence of an oral or written statement only infringes the hearsay rule if that statement is tendered as a means of proving the truth of the matter stated. Where the statement is tendered as a fact rather than as a means of proving a fact it is not hearsay. Some authors describe statements which are facts as "admissible hearsay" as opposed to "inadmissible hearsay" which, they say, consists of statements tendered as a means of proving other facts. There is no objection to this terminology except that statements which were admitted pursuant to one of the many exceptions to the hearsay rule would be difficult to classify. Consequently it is probably safest to treat statements which are not tendered as a means of proof not as being hearsay at all.

The distinction between statements as facts and statements as proof was clearly defined in the advice of the Judicial Committee of the Privy Council in *Subramaniam* v. *Public Prosecutor*.[8]

> "Evidence of a statement made to a witness by a person who is not himself called as a witness may or may not be hearsay. It is hearsay and inadmissible when the object of the evidence is to establish the truth of what is contained in the statement. It is not hearsay and is admissible when it is proposed to establish by the evidence, not the truth of the statement, but the fact that it was made."

The case itself illustrates this point very clearly. The appellant, on a charge of unlawful possession of firearms, set up the defence of duress. At his trial he was not allowed to testify to threats which Malayan terrorists had allegedly made to him, the trial judge regarding these threats as hearsay. The

---

[6] See *Chandra Sekera* v. *R.*, [1937] A.C. 220 (signs made by a dying woman).
[7] (1838), 4 Bing N.C. 489.
[8] [1956] 1 W.L.R. 965, at p. 969.

Privy Council advised that this was wrong since the threats were original evidence of the fact of duress and should have been admitted. Since it is of vital importance to be able to recognise whether a statement is or is not hearsay it will be convenient to classify the situations in which a statement is original as opposed to hearsay evidence.

(1) Statements by a person as to his present health, feelings or state of mind are original evidence. Thus in *Gilbey* v. *Great Western Rail. Co.*[9] COZENS-HARDY, M.R. observed that:

> "Statements made by a workman to his wife of his sensations at the time, about the pains in his side, or head, or what not, whether the statements were made by groans, or by actions, or were verbal statements, would be admissible to prove those sensations."

Nevertheless the Master of the Rolls excluded evidence of the workman's statements as to the cause of these feelings since this was hearsay evidence of the accident in question.

(2) The making of a statement is, in certain cases, a fact in issue. Obvious examples occur in the torts of libel, slander and malicious falsehood where, in each case, the plaintiff must prove publication of a statement concerning himself or his property. Indeed if the plaintiff were prevented from adducing such evidence these causes of action could not exist. There are numerous other types of action in which the statement is in itself a fact in issue. In actions in contract an offer, acceptance, waiver, repudiation or release may all be facts in issue and will usually consist of assertions by one of the parties.

(3) In many other cases oral or written statements, though not themselves facts in issue, may constitute circumstantial evidence of facts in issue. Thus evidence would undoubtedly be admissible that a person was speaking incoherently or singing if his sobriety, or even his sanity, were a fact in issue. It is on this basis that the evidence of the threats ought to have been admitted in *Subramaniam* v. *Public Prosecutor*[10] since they amounted to facts from which duress, which was a fact in issue, might be inferred. Similarly a male person under the age of twenty-four charged with unlawful sexual intercourse with a girl under the age of sixteen[11] may testify to the fact that the girl told him she was over sixteen since this fact tends to support his belief in her age, that belief being a fact in issue.

(4) Where conduct is relevant, accompanying statements may explain or identify the nature of the conduct. Thus delivery of a chattel is equally consistent with the transaction being a bailment or a gift in which event words accompanying the delivery and explaining the nature of the transaction would be admissible.[12] Such statements often form part of the *res gestae*[13] in which event it is unnecessary to decide whether they constitute hearsay or not since, even if they do, they are admissible as an exception to the rule against hearsay.

(5) In a few cases the previous statements of a witness may be put in evidence. There is a common law rule excluding such evidence, sometimes

---

[9] (1910), 102 L.T. 202.
[10] *Supra.*
[11] Sexual Offences Act 1956, s. 6.
[12] See *Hayslep* v. *Gymer* (1834), 1 Ad. & El. 162.
[13] See p. 567, *ante.*

known as the rule against narrative. There are, however, exceptions to the rule against narrative. First, as has already been noted,[14] in criminal cases evidence is admissible of the complaint of a victim of a sexual assault. The admissibility of such complaints in no way infringes the hearsay rule because the complaint is, strictly speaking, not evidence of the truth of the content of the complaint but only of the consistency of the complainant. Nonetheless it is questionable whether the average jury is able to distinguish the fact of the complaint from its content. Secondly, any opposing witness or a party's own hostile witness may be cross-examined upon his previous inconsistent statement in both civil and criminal cases. If the witness denies the previous statement it may be put in evidence.[15] Finally, in civil proceedings a witness's previous statement is admissible under section 2 of the Civil Evidence Act 1968 and, when admitted, constitutes evidence of any fact stated therein. However, section 2(2) provides that the statement of a person whom a party has called or intends to call as a witness may not be given in evidence without the leave of the court and, generally, may not be given in evidence even then before the close of the witness's examination-in-chief. Thus the main use of such statements will be in re-examination to bolster the evidence of a witness who has been cross-examined upon, for example, a previous inconsistent statement.

(6) A witness may refer to a document in order to "refresh his memory", although he cannot read from a prepared statement. The distinction is often artificial because a witness is frequently allowed to testify to matters concerning which he could not possibly have any personal recollection, simply because he has before him a written record of the matter to which he may refer. There are limits, however, on the use of documents to refresh the witness's memory. The document must have been compiled by the witness contemporaneously with, or at least very shortly after, the matter recorded. Thus a document such as a ship's log, a diary and a policeman's notebook have been used to refresh memory though the witness's proof before trial is not a valid aid to recollection. Indeed in criminal cases the evidence of police officers is usually given by reference to notebooks, the accuracy of the notes being the subject of vigorous cross-examination on behalf of defendants. The opposite party has a right to inspect the document and to cross-examine the witness upon its contents. In addition the judge and jury may inspect the document for the purpose of assessing the witness's credibility.[16] In a criminal case the document does not constitute evidence of the facts recorded; however in civil proceedings any statement made in a document by a person who uses that document to refresh his memory is admissible as evidence of any fact stated therein of which direct oral evidence would be admissible.[17]

---

[14] See p. 624, fn. 7, *ante*.

[15] Criminal Procedure Act 1865, ss. 3–5; in civil proceedings such a statement is evidence of any fact stated therein of which direct oral evidence would be admissible (Civil Evidence Act 1968, s. 3(1)) but in criminal cases it merely shows inconsistency and is not evidence of the truth of any fact contained in the statement.

[16] *R.* v. *Bass*, [1953] 1 Q.B. 680; [1953] 1 All E.R. 1064.

[17] Civil Evidence Act 1968, s. 3(2).

b Formulation of the hearsay rule

Having illustrated that evidence of what another person said or wrote on a previous occasion is not always hearsay evidence it is possible to attempt a formulation or definition of the hearsay rule. Perhaps the most comprehensive formulation of the hearsay rule is that which has been suggested by Professor Rupert Cross:[18]

> "Express or implied assertions of persons other than the witness who is testifying and assertions in documents produced to the court when no witness is testifying are inadmissible as evidence of the truth of that which was asserted."

Numerous other formulations of the rule have been attempted but many of these are open to criticism. Phipson's exposition of the rule ran as follows:[19]

> "Oral or written statements made by persons who are not parties and are not called as witnesses are inadmissible to prove the truth of the matters stated."

This statement brings out the basic point that a statement is only hearsay when it is adduced to prove the truth of the matter stated but it is open to criticism on other grounds. First, it has been noted that conduct may amount to hearsay so that the rule is not limited to "oral or written statements". Secondly, there is no rule that a witness may testify as to what another said merely because that other is a party or is called as a witness. It is true that a witness's testimony as to what he himself said or wrote on a previous occasion is not hearsay but it is clear that, for example, a prosecution witness's testimony concerning statements made to him by the accused would be hearsay if adduced as evidence of their truth. Other commentators suggest that hearsay is limited to "out of court" assertions[20] but this ignores the fact that a statement may be excluded as hearsay even though it was made on oath at a former trial.[1]

In the context of civil proceedings the hearsay rule now has a statutory definition; section 1(1) of the Civil Evidence Act 1968 in effect defines hearsay as:

> "in any civil proceedings a statement[2] other than one made by a person while giving oral evidence in those proceedings . . . as evidence of any fact stated therein."

In fact this definition would comprise not only statements made by a person other than the witness testifying but also previous statements made by the witness himself. At common law previous statements of the witness testifying are not within the hearsay rule; in fact such statements remain admissible in civil proceedings by virtue of the provisions of the 1968 Act to

---

[18] Cross, *Evidence* (3rd Edn.), p. 387. The formulation was not preserved in later editions of the work.

[19] Phipson, *Law of Evidence* (9th Edn.), p. 221. This definition is referred to (but not adopted) in the current (13th) edition.

[20] See, for example, Nokes, *An Introduction to Evidence* (4th Edn.), p. 271.

[1] *R. v. Eriswell (Inhabitants)* (1790), 3 Term Rep. 707.

[2] " 'Statement' includes any representation of fact, whether made in words or otherwise". Civil Evidence Act 1968, s. 10(1).

at least the extent to which they were admissible prior to the Act. Thus the 1968 Act has in no way enlarged the hearsay rule; nevertheless it should be pointed out that to this extent the substance of section 1(1), set out above, does not set out (nor of course was it intended so to do) a true definition of the hearsay rule. It merely classifies the statements to which Part I of the 1968 Act applies and, as noted above, these statements include, as well as hearsay, previous statements of the witness who is testifying.

c   Arguments for the retention of the hearsay rule

The principal arguments in favour of the retention of the hearsay rule are as follows.

(1) *Unreliability*—One of the main arguments in favour of the rule excluding hearsay is that the evidence is unreliable due to the possibility of inaccurate repetition or fabrication. This argument has some force in relation to the repetition of oral statements since it is no doubt possible that the witness who testifies as to what he heard another say may have misheard or misunderstood, though the possibility of fabrication is no greater than the possibility which exists in relation to documentary evidence. Assuming that the authenticity of a document can be proved the fact that the writer is not called as a witness can scarcely be said to diminish the accuracy of the facts recorded in the document. Indeed the hearsay rule sometimes operates to exclude a document the accuracy and reliability of which are unimpeachable. Perhaps the most striking recent illustration of the capricious operation of the hearsay rule is to be found in the case of *Myers* v. *Director of Public Prosecutions*.[3] Myers was charged with various offences in relation to stolen cars. The prosecution case was that Myers would buy wrecked cars with their log books and would then disguise stolen cars so as to conform with the details contained in the log books of the wrecked cars. For this purpose he transferred small plates containing the engine and chassis numbers from the wrecked cars to the stolen cars. The trial judge allowed the admission in evidence of a car manufacturer's records which contained, in relation to each car manufactured, the engine and chassis number and also the cylinder block number which was indelibly stamped on the engine. These records showed that the cylinder block numbers of the cars in question belonged to the stolen cars. The House of Lords held that these records were hearsay evidence and should not have been admitted. None of the majority of their Lordships (LORD REID, LORD MORRIS OF BORTH-Y-GEST and LORD HODSON) doubted the accuracy or reliability of the manufacturer's records but all thought it beyond the judicial function to create a new exception to the hearsay rule merely on the ground of expedience. LORD PEARCE and LORD DONOVAN, however, dissented on this point. LORD DONOVAN expressed his reason as follows:[4]

> "The common law is moulded by the judges, and it is still their province to adapt it from time to time so as to make it serve the interests of those it binds.

---

[3]   [1965] A.C. 1001; [1964] 2 All E.R. 881.

[4]   [1965] A.C. 1001, at p. 1047; [1964] 2 All E.R. 881, at p. 902. In fact the conviction was upheld by the application of the proviso to s. 4(1) of the Criminal Appeal Act 1907 (now s. 2(1) of the Criminal Appeal Act 1968); see p. 533, *ante*.

Particularly is this so in the field of procedural law. Here the question posed is—'Shall the courts admit as evidence of a particular fact authentic and reliable records by which alone the fact may be satisfactorily proved?' I think the courts themselves are able to give an affirmative answer to that question.''

Following this decision the Criminal Evidence Act 1965 was passed to provide for the reception of trade or business records in criminal proceedings thus nullifying the effect of *Myers*'s case. Nevertheless the case illustrates that hearsay evidence is by no means necessarily unreliable.

(2) *Hearsay evidence is unsworn and not subject to cross-examination*—The second main reason advanced for the retention of the hearsay rule is that the statement in question is not made on oath and the person against whom the evidence is given has no opportunity of cross-examining the maker. The absence of an oath is not a cogent reason because some evidence may be unsworn and, in any case, the fact that the statement was made on oath would not be a ground for excepting it from the operation of the rule.[5] The lack of opportunity for cross-examination is a real objection to the reception of hearsay evidence but it is arguable that this should affect the cogency of the evidence rather than its admissibility.

(3) *Best evidence rule*—It is doubtful whether there is any historical connection between the hearsay rule and the best evidence rule though the latter is sometimes advanced as a reason for the existence of the former. In any event hearsay evidence is excluded even though original evidence is not available because, for example, the maker of the statement is dead or cannot be found.

d   *Arguments for the abolition of the hearsay rule*

The Law Reform Committee Thirteenth Report (*Hearsay Evidence in Civil Proceedings*)[6] specified five disadvantages of the rule against hearsay.

(1) Injustice is caused where a witness who could prove a fact in issue is dead or unavailable to be called.

(2) The rule adds to the cost of proving facts in issue which are not really in dispute.

(3) The rule adds greatly to the technicality of the law of evidence because of its numerous exceptions.

(4) The court is deprived of material which would be of value in ascertaining the truth.

(5) The rule often confuses witnesses and prevents them from telling their story in the witness box in the natural way. A casual visitor to the criminal courts will often hear questions put by prosecuting counsel to a police officer in the following form: "Did you make certain inquiries?" the affirmative answer being followed by "As a result of these inquiries what did you do?" By these means counsel is able to elicit that which he could not ask directly— the substance of the answers given by some third party to the witness. Such is the capricious operation of the rule against hearsay.

---

[5] *R. v. Eriswell (Inhabitants)* (1790), 3 Term Rep. 707.

[6] Cmnd. 2964 of 1966. Part I of the Civil Evidence Act 1968 was based upon recommendations contained in this Report.

2   The hearsay rule in civil proceedings

The hearsay rule, as formulated above, applies (subject to the exceptions noted below) in all criminal proceedings. In relation to civil proceedings, however, a very substantial inroad into the hearsay rule was made by the Civil Evidence Act 1968.

a   The distinction between first-hand and second-hand hearsay

As a preliminary to examining the provisions of the Civil Evidence Act 1968, it is essential to clarify the distinction between first-hand and second-hand (or "double") hearsay; at common law the distinction was of little importance but under the 1968 Act, as will appear, it is paramount. The distinction is essentially a simple one and can best be explained by reference to the definition of hearsay contained in section 1(1) of the 1968 Act:

> "a statement other than one made by a person while giving oral evidence in those proceedings . . . as evidence of any fact stated therein."

If the maker of the statement in question had personal knowledge of the facts contained in his statement, the statement is first-hand hearsay. If, on the other hand, the maker of the statement did not have personal knowledge of the facts stated, so that his evidence of those facts would be hearsay, evidence of the contents of his statement (assuming, of course, that he is not the person giving that evidence) is second-hand hearsay. This may be illustrated by the following example. A foreman makes out an accident report and sends it to his employers; the employers seek to put the report in as evidence of the circumstances of the accident. If the foreman saw the accident the report is first-hand hearsay; if, however, the foreman did not see the accident but simply took down statements made to him by other employees who did see the accident, the report is second-hand hearsay.

b   Admissibility of first-hand hearsay

Section 2(1) of the 1968 Act provides:

> "In any civil proceedings a statement made, whether orally or in a document or otherwise, by any person, whether called as a witness in those proceedings or not, shall, subject to this section and to rules of court, be admissible as evidence of any fact[7] stated therein of which direct oral evidence by him would be admissible."

This sub-section has the effect of rendering first-hand hearsay admissible in civil proceedings and is, therefore, the most far-reaching provision in the 1968 Act. Where the statement was made otherwise than in a document no evidence other than direct oral evidence by the maker or any person who heard or otherwise perceived it being made is admissible for the purpose of proving it, unless the statement was made by a person while giving oral evidence in some other legal proceedings (whether civil or criminal) in which event it may be proved in any manner authorised by the court.[8]

---

[7]   The section is extended to admissible statements of opinion by section 1(1) of the Civil Evidence Act 1972.

[8]   Act of 1968, s. 2(3); cf. R.S.C., O. 38, r. 28 as to the means by which a party may obtain directions. Where the statement is contained in a document it may, subject to any rules of

In estimating the weight to be attached to a statement admitted under this section the court must have regard to all the circumstances from which any inference can reasonably be drawn as to the accuracy or otherwise of the statement and, in particular, to the question whether or not the statement was made contemporaneously with the occurrence or existence of the facts stated, and to the question whether or not the maker of the statement had any incentive to conceal or misrepresent the facts.[9] Furthermore where the maker is not called as a witness, any evidence which would have been admissible for the purpose of destroying or supporting his credibility, including a previous inconsistent statement (which is then evidence of the facts therein stated), if he had been called as a witness, is admissible in his absence.[10]

The admissibility of statements under section 2 is expressly made subject to Rules of Court. In the Supreme Court the relevant Rules are R.S.C., O. 38, rr. 20–44. These Rules contain detailed procedural requirements with which a party must comply in order to avail himself of section 2 of the Act.[11] Nevertheless there is a discretionary power to allow a party to adduce a statement in evidence notwithstanding that he has failed either to serve the requisite notice or to comply with a counter-notice.

c Admissibility of second-hand hearsay

The Civil Evidence Act 1968 abrogated the hearsay rule in civil proceedings only in relation to first-hand hearsay. Second-hand hearsay remains, *prima facie*, inadmissible. Sections 4 and 5 of the Act do, in fact, permit second-hand hearsay evidence in certain circumstances. However, these sections are best regarded as special exceptions to the hearsay rule and are hereinafter dealt with accordingly in that context.

3 Exceptions to the rule against hearsay

Of all the arguments against the retention of the hearsay rule, however, surely the most forceful is the existence of so many exceptions formulated by the judiciary and, in more modern times, by Parliament. These exceptions, of which there are probably more than seventy, have little in common. Some are based on the fact that the maker of the statement is deposing to a fact to his own disadvantage, others on the basis that the declarant is dead (though death alone is not a ground for receiving hearsay evidence) while many appear to be based almost solely on expedience. They now apply principally in criminal proceedings, their application to civil proceedings being superseded by section 2 of the Civil Evidence Act 1968 except where the statement in question is second-hand hearsay, in which event it will be admissible only if falling within one of the prescribed exceptions.

---

court, be proved by the production of that document or (whether or not that document is still in existence) by the production of a copy, authenticated in such manner as the court may approve; *ibid.*, s. 6(3).

[9] Civil Evidence Act 1968, s. 6(1).

[10] *Ibid*, s. 7(1), (3). The admissibility of such evidence is subject to compliance with certain procedural requirements; see R.S.C., O. 38, rr. 30, 31.

[11] See p. 375, *ante* for details of the procedure.

a   Statements forming part of the res gestae

The general nature of *res gestae* has already been considered in connection with relevance.[12] The traditional view of English law is that a statement admitted as part of the *res gestae* was not hearsay evidence because it did not constitute proof of the truth of the matter stated.[13] However the modern tendency is to regard the admission of such statements as a genuine exception to the hearsay rule.[14] No doubt there are many statements admitted as part of the *res gestae* which do not infringe the hearsay rule because the statement is admitted to prove something other than the truth of the matter stated. On the other hand there are certainly many cases in which statements have been admitted when the only purpose for their admission has been to provide proof of the matter stated.[15]

b   Informal admissions

It was observed in an earlier chapter[16] that self-serving statements made by parties to litigation on a previous occasion are not usually admissible. On the other hand evidence is admissible of the earlier statement of a party where that statement is adverse to the interest of the maker. Since the earlier statement is usually proved by a person other than the maker it is hearsay, but admitted as an exception to the hearsay rule. In civil proceedings the statement will usually be admissible under section 2 of the Civil Evidence Act 1968, but, where it is not, the 1968 Act expressly provides for the retention of the common law rule that it may be received as an admission.[17] Such statements are described as informal admissions and it is important to distinguish them from formal admissions. The latter dispense with the need for proof and can only be made in the course of proceedings.[18] Informal admissions do not dispense with the need for proof; they are one means of proof. Consequently it is always open to a party to attempt to explain away or qualify his own informal admission. The informal admission of an accused person is described as a confession when made to a person in authority, such as a police officer. Confessions are dealt with separately because their reception is subject to additional conditions. The rationale of this exception to the hearsay rule is simply the intrinsic unlikelihood of a person making a statement against his own interest unless that statement were true.

An informal admission may take many forms. It may be made orally or in writing and may be express or implied. It also appears that, in certain circumstances, mere passive conduct or silence may amount to an admission. The leading authority for this proposition is the decision of the Court of Appeal in *Bessela* v. *Stern*.[19] In this action for breach of promise of marriage the

---

[12] See p. 567, *ante*.
[13] See *R.* v. *Christie*, [1914] A.C. 545, at p. 553, *per* LORD ATKINSON.
[14] See *Teper* v. *R.*, [1952] A.C. 480; [1952] 2 All E.R. 447; *Ratten* v. *R.*, [1972] A.C. 378; [1971] 3 All E.R. 801; Cross, *Evidence* (5th Edn.), p. 575.
[15] See, for examples: *R.* v. *Foster* (1834), 6 C. & P. 325; *The Schwalbe* (1861), 4 L.T. 160; *Davies* v. *Fortior, Ltd.*, [1952] 1 All E.R. 1359.
[16] See p. 624, *ante*.
[17] Civil Evidence Act 1968, s. 9(2)(*a*).
[18] See p. 604, *ante*.
[19] (1877), 2 C.P.D. 265.

plaintiff was proved to have said to the defendant—"You always promised to marry me, and you don't keep your word." The defendant did not answer and it was held that his silence corroborated the plaintiff's testimony. It was stressed in *Bessela* v. *Stern*, however, that the defendant's silence only amounted to an admission because in the circumstances he might have been expected to deny the allegation.[20] It is uncertain how far this principle applies in criminal cases. Clearly the conduct of an accused person may amount to an admission; so may silence coupled with demeanour.[1] In *Parkes* v. *R.*[2] the appellant was charged with murder of a young woman. The woman's mother found her daughter bleeding from stab wounds whereupon she went into the yard at the premises where she saw the appellant with a knife in his hands. She twice accused him of stabbing her daughter but he made no reply and, indeed, when she threatened to detain him he attempted to stab her. The trial judge in Jamaica directed the jury that the failure of the appellant to reply to the mother's accusations coupled with his conduct immediately after those accusations were made were matters from which the jury might infer that the appellant accepted the truth of the accusation. The Privy Council dismissed the appellant's appeal from his conviction of murder.

On the other hand, where an accused person is being questioned by police officers his silence will not be capable of amounting to an admission[3] unless it can properly be regarded as an acceptance by him of the truth of what the police officers are putting to him. In a case in which the defendant had, while being interrogated by the police, answered some questions but declined to answer others, LAWTON, L.J. stated the law as follows:[4]

> "Some comment on the appellant's lack of frankness before he was cautioned was justified, provided the jury's attention was directed to the right issue which was whether in the circumstances the appellant's silence amounted to an acceptance by him of what the detective sergeant had said. If he accepted what had been said, then the next question should have been whether guilt could reasonably be inferred from what he had accepted. To suggest, as the judge did, that the appellant's silence could indicate guilt was to short circuit the intellectual process which has to be followed."

The failure of an accused person to give evidence at his trial is not evidence against him.[5] Nevertheless the judge may comment upon the failure of the accused to give evidence on his own behalf.[6]

It may be noted, finally, that an admission is generally evidence only against the maker and not against a third party even though he is implicated by the admission. This is very important in criminal cases where a statement by one accused person admitting guilty conduct on the part of himself and his co-accused is not evidence against the latter. Similarly, in divorce

---

[20] Compare *Wiedemann* v. *Walpole*, [1891] 2 Q.B. 534 where the facts were similar except that the plaintiff's allegation was contained in a letter to the defendant. The Court of Appeal held that the failure of the defendant to send a letter of denial did not constitute an admission of a promise to marry.
[1] *R.* v. *Christie*, [1914] A.C. 545.
[2] [1976] 3 All E.R. 380; [1976] 1 W.L.R. 1251.
[3] *Hall* v. *R.*, [1971] 1 All E.R. 322; [1971] 1 W.L.R. 298.
[4] *R.* v. *Chandler*, [1976] 3 All E.R. 105, at pp. 110–111; [1976] 1 W.L.R. 585, at p. 590.
[5] *R.* v. *Naylor*, [1933] 1 K.B. 685.
[6] *R.* v. *Littleboy*, [1934] 2 K.B. 408; see p. 630, *ante*.

proceedings a decree may be granted against A on the ground of irretrievable breakdown, based upon his adultery with B while B may be found not to have committed adultery with A. This odd result can, and often does, occur because the admission by A is not evidence against B and there might be insufficient evidence, apart from the admission, to warrant a finding of adultery.[7] There are certain exceptional cases in which the out of court admission of one party is evidence against another. These exceptions are based either upon agency or upon privity between the parties. An admission made by an agent acting on behalf of his principal binds the latter in accordance with the general law of agency. Similarly the admission of a predecessor in title binds a party provided that the admission was made in relation to the title.[8]

"Without prejudice" communications

Where a communication is made as part of a *bona fide* attempt to effect a compromise or settlement of a civil dispute, that communication is said to be made "without prejudice". This is so that parties and their advisers may freely attempt to settle their disputes out of court without fear that any admission of liability they may make will be used against them. A solicitor making such an offer by letter will usually mark the letter with the words "without prejudice". However, it is the nature of the communication, not its description, which is the basis of the privilege. Thus a communication may be impliedly without prejudice. *Mutatis mutandis* a party cannot magically clothe his written or oral statements with immunity simply by expressing them to be without prejudice. For example a libel or a threat would be actionable notwithstanding that the letter containing it were headed "without prejudice".[9] The privilege attaches to oral or written communications provided they were made in the course of an attempt to compromise a dispute. The communication in question is often a letter between solicitors or between insurance companies but extends to communications between spouses before a probation officer or marriage guidance counsellor.[10]

The rule extends, however, only to communications made in an attempt to compromise. Where the negotiations actually result in a contractual settlement, the documents containing the terms thereof may be put in evidence notwithstanding that one or more of them was originally expressed to be "without prejudice".[11] Furthermore, where a party in a "without prejudice" letter expressly reserves the right to bring the letter to the attention of the court on the issue of costs after judgment in the action if the offer is refused, he may do so.[12]

---

[7] *Rutherford* v. *Richardson*, [1923] A.C. 1, at p. 6.

[8] *Woolway* v. *Rowe* (1834), 1 Ad. & El. 114.

[9] *Kurtz & Co.* v. *Spence & Sons* (1887), 58 L.T. 438.

[10] *Mole* v. *Mole*, [1951] P. 21; [1950] 2 All E.R. 328; *Theodoropoulas* v. *Theodoropoulas*, [1964] P. 311; [1963] 2 All E.R. 772.

[11] *Tomlin* v. *Standard Telephones and Cables, Ltd.*, [1969] 3 All E.R. 201; [1969] 1 W.L.R. 1378.

[12] *Cutts* v. *Head*, [1984] 1 All E.R. 597; [1984] 2 W.L.R. 349; the judgment of OLIVER, L.J. in that case contains a valuable review of the authorities on "without prejudice" communications.

c Confessions

The distinction between admissions in criminal cases and confessions is largely one of terminology. In this section the word "confession" is used to denote a statement made by a person charged with a crime which tends to prove any element in the prosecution case. It is customarily used to describe a statement made to a policeman or other person in authority, though its admissibility is in no way dependent on this.

The burden is on the prosecution to prove beyond reasonable doubt that a confession was voluntary. This involves proving that the confession "has not been obtained from him either by fear of prejudice or hope of advantage exercised or held out by a person in authority".[13] Where the defence wish to contest the admissibility of a confession statement this is done in the absence of the jury by means of what is usually known as a "trial within a trial" whereby the prosecution call their evidence as to the circumstances in which the alleged confession was made, the defence call any evidence they wish to call (usually that of the defendant) following which there are submissions and the trial judge decides whether or not to allow the confession to be given in evidence before the jury. The procedure to be followed in relation to a trial within a trial (or *voire dire* as it is more formally known) was considered by the Privy Council in *Wong Kam-ming* v. *R.*[14] That case has established two important principles: first, that the prosecution is not entitled to cross-examine the accused as to the truth of the disputed statement, since the sole issue is whether the statement has been made voluntarily; secondly, whether the statement is excluded or admitted, the prosecution is not entitled as part of its case to adduce evidence of the testimony of the defendant on the *voire dire*. However where the accused gives evidence and this is inconsistent with evidence which he gave on the *voire dire*, he may be cross-examined as to the latter and, if he denies that he previously gave inconsistent evidence, his testimony on the *voire dire* may be proved (generally by calling the shorthand-writer) in rebuttal under section 4 of the Criminal Procedure Act 1865.[15]

The rules governing the admissibility of confessions are based rather upon policy than upon logic, being aimed principally at preventing abusive and oppressive conduct on the part of the police. Thus as LORD HAILSHAM stated in *Director of Public Prosecutions* v. *Ping Lin*:[16]

---

[13] *Ibrahim* v. *R.*, [1914] A.C. 599, at p. 609, *per* LORD SUMNER; applied in *R.* v. *Rennie*, [1982] 1 All E.R. 385; [1982] 1 W.L.R. 64 where LORD LANE, C.J. pointed out that to LORD SUMNER's words should now be added "or by oppression". When section 76 of the Police and Criminal Evidence Act 1984 is brought into force a confession will be excluded if obtained "(*a*) by oppression of the person who made it; or (*b*) in consequence of anything said or done which was likely, in the circumstances existing at the time, to render unreliable any confession which might be made by him in consequence thereof." In addition s. 77 prescribes a requirement for the judge to give a warning to the jury concerning confessions made by mentally handicapped defendants otherwise than in the presence of an independent person.

[14] [1980] A.C. 247; [1979] 1 All E.R. 939; applied in *R.* v. *Brophy*, [1982] A.C. 476; [1981] 2 All E.R. 705.

[15] See p. 580, *ante*.

[16] [1976] A.C. 574, at p. 600; [1975] 3 All E.R. 175, at p. 182. For the reasons given by LORD HAILSHAM, and because of the existence of many recent authorities, and particularly *Ping Lin* itself, the nineteenth century cases referred to in previous editions of this book have been omitted and the old distinction between inducements of a spiritual nature and those of a temporal nature may be taken to have been laid to rest.

"It bears, it is true, all the marks of its origin at a time when the savage code of the 18th century was in full force. At that time almost every serious crime was punishable by death or transportation. The law enforcement officers formed no disciplined police force and were not subject to effective control by the Central Government Watch Committees or an inspectorate. There was no legal aid. There was no system of appeal. To crown it all the accused was unable to give evidence on his own behalf and was therefore largely at the mercy of any evidence, either perjured or oppressively obtained, that might be brought against him. The judiciary were therefore compelled to devise artificial rules designed to protect him against dangers now avoided by other and more rational means."

Nevertheless, as LORD HAILSHAM went on to point out, the rules survive and the decision of the House of Lords in that case simply reaffirms the text contained in the classical words of LORD SUMNER in *Ibrahim* v. *R.*, set out above. The issue is to be decided as one of fact and causation, that is to say whether the Crown has proved that the statement was not made as a result of something said or done by a person in authority. There has, as the House of Lords pointed out with displeasure, been a considerable number of cases turning on the various permutations of fact which arise in such cases. There ought, in future, to be fewer reported cases on the topic since the House of Lords made it clear that, where a judge has admitted a confession as voluntary, an appellate court ought only to interfere if satisfied that the judge has made a completely wrong assessment of the evidence or has failed to apply the correct principle.

It was formerly thought that an inducement was of no effect unless bearing directly upon the proceedings so that a collateral inducement, such as an offer to allow the prisoner to see his wife, was unobjectionable. However, this principle was discredited by the House of Lords in *Customs and Excise Commissioners* v. *Harz*[17] and it now seems that there is no distinction between a direct and a collateral inducement.

The inducement will only affect the admissibility of a confession if made by a person in authority or, at least, a person whom the prisoner believes to be a person in authority.[18] The person concerned is usually a policeman but may be a magistrate, prison officer, private prosecutor, employer or even the prisoner's father. The authority which he must be shown to possess, or appear to possess, is the authority to carry out the threat or fulfil the promise. The intention of the person in authority is irrelevant if, in fact, it is found to have operated as a threat or inducement.[19]

Although the judge has ruled a confession admissible, the defendant may still urge on the jury that it was made as a result of inducement or coercion and it is then for the jury to assess for itself the probative value of the confession having regard to such factors.[20]

Judges' Rules. At this stage it is necessary to note the substance and effect of the Judges' Rules. These rules have been drawn up by the judges of the Queen's Bench Division for the guidance of the police in questioning suspects and charging persons in custody. The latest set of rules are the Judges'

---

[17] [1967] 1 A.C. 760; [1967] 1 All E.R. 177; see *Sparks* v. *R.,* [1964] A.C. 964; [1964] 1 All E.R. 727.

[18] See *Deokinanan* v. *R.,* [1969] 1 A.C. 20; [1968] 2 All E.R. 346.

[19] *Director of Public Prosecutions* v. *Ping Lin* (*supra*).

[20] *R.* v. *M'Carthy* (1980), 70 Cr. App. Rep. 270.

Rules 1964.[1] These rules are only guides for the police; they do not have the force of law. The most important of the rules are those which relate to cautions. The 1964 rules provide for two cautions. A person must be given the "usual caution" when a police officer who has evidence which would afford reasonable grounds for suspecting that person wishes to question him. The usual caution runs: "You are not obliged to say anything unless you wish to do so but what you say may be put into writing and given in evidence." Whether or not the usual caution has been previously administered a person must receive the "formal caution" when he is formally charged or informed that he may be prosecuted. The formal caution is: "Do you wish to say anything? You are not obliged to say anything unless you wish to do so, but whatever you say will be taken down in writing and may be given in evidence." The words "against you" used to be added to the above version of the formal caution but were deleted by the Judges' Rules 1912. This formal caution may be compared with the statutory caution which is administered by examining justices to the accused at a preliminary investigation.[2] An accused person should not normally be questioned after he has been charged but if he is so questioned, for example in order to clarify an ambiguity, he must be cautioned a third time.

Should the accused wish to make a written statement after caution he must first be given the opportunity to writing this statement himself. If he cannot or does not wish to write it himself a police officer may offer to write it for him and the accused must certify that the statement as written is true.

Failure to comply with the Judges' Rules does not necessarily render a confession to the police inadmissible,[3] unless it is shown that the confession was not made voluntarily. Thus in *R. v. Prager*[4] a confession made as a result of prolonged interrogation was held to have been rightly admitted despite a failure to caution until a late stage of the interrogation.

Thus the test of admissibility is whether the confession was voluntary in the sense described above. In the authorities cited this test has invariably depended upon the conduct of the person provoking the confession, that is to say the nature and effect of any threat or inducement made. However there is no good reason why a confession should not be ruled involuntary without there having been any improper threat or inducement. Thus, if a defendant was so frightened or his mind so unbalanced that he was not in control of his will, a confession made in those circumstances might well be held to be involuntary and therefore inadmissible. Although there is Commonwealth authority to support this proposition, it has not yet been applied in this country, so as to exclude successfully a defendant's confession.[5]

---

[1] Home Office Circular No. 31, 1964, Appendix A, reissued with up-to-date Administrative Directions under Home Office Circular 89/1978, Appendix A; *Practice Note,* [1964] 1 All E.R. 237; [1964] 1 W.L.R. 152.

[2] Magistrates' Courts Rules 1981, r. 7(7); see p. 481, *ante.*

[3] See, for example, *R. v. Voisin,* [1918] 1 K.B. 581; *R. v. Mills and Lemon,* [1947] K.B. 297; [1946] 2 All E.R. 776.

[4] [1972] 1 All E.R. 1114; [1972] 1 W.L.R. 260.

[5] See *R. v. Isequilla,* [1975] 1 All E.R. 77; [1975] 1 W.L.R. 716 in which the Commonwealth authorities are reviewed; in that case the Court of Appeal expressed the view that the exclusion of a confession was, on principle, confined to cases of impropriety in the conduct of the person to whom the statement was made, but this statement was disapproved by the House of

A confession, in the same way as an admission, if admissible, is evidence only against the maker, not against a third person such as an accomplice or a co-accused.

d   Statements of persons since deceased

It is on the ground of expedience that certain statements are admissible in evidence when the maker can be proved to be dead. It would, nevertheless, be wrong to suppose that the hearsay rule has no application in relation to the statements of persons since deceased. The fact that the maker of a statement has died does not necessarily mean that a witness may report the statement even though there may be no other means of proving the fact contained in the statement. No statement is admissible solely on the ground that the maker is dead. Nevertheless several exceptions to the hearsay rule operate only where the maker of the statement is dead. The most important of these exceptions are set out below.

Dying declarations—On a charge of murder or manslaughter an oral or written statement made by the deceased concerning his injury is admissible provided that it can be proved that he was, at the time of making the statement, in settled hopeless expectation of death and would have been a competent witness had he lived. Such a statement is termed a "dying declaration". Dying declarations are admissible only on charges of murder or manslaughter. There is no logical reason for excluding dying declarations in other proceedings but there is clear authority against this.[6] The rationale of this exception to the hearsay rule is that dying declarations are made:

> "when every motive to falsehood is silenced, and the mind is induced by the most powerful considerations to speak the truth; a situation so solemn and so awful is considered by law as creating an obligation equal to that which is imposed by a positive oath administered in a court of justice."[7]

For this reason in *R. v. Pike*[8] the court refused to admit a statement made by a four-year-old child on the basis that the declarant would not have been capable of appreciating the awfulness of her state.

Apart from the condition that the declarant would have been competent as a witness had he lived the main condition for the admissibility of dying declarations is that the declarant must have been in "settled hopeless expectation" of death. The test is purely subjective. Thus it is not sufficient that the declarant was, in fact, certainly about to die if he was not appreciative of this fact. It was for this reason that the statement of the deceased in *R. v. Bedingfield*[9] could not be admitted under this exception since, although her

Lords in *Director of Public Prosecutions v. Ping Lin*, [1976] A.C. 574; [1975] 3 All E.R. 175 and it may now be taken to be the law that a confession may, in an appropriate case, be excluded without there having been any improper (or indeed proper) threat or inducement to the defendant although such cases are likely to be rare to the point of non-existence since a confession is not excluded simply because the accused, in making it, harboured a self-generated fear of prejudice or hope of advantage; cf. *R. v. Rennie*, [1982] 1 All E.R. 385; [1982] 1 W.L.R. 64.

6   *R. v. Mead* (1824), 2 B. & C. 605.
7   *R. v. Woodcock* (1789), 1 Leach 500, *per* EYRE, C.B.
8   (1829), 3 C. & P. 598.
9   (1879), 14 Cox C.C. 341; see p. 569, *ante*.

throat was cut from ear to ear, there was no evidence that she was conscious of her impending death. On the other hand if the declarant was in settled hopeless expectation of death a statement will be admissible even though death does not immediately occur.[10]

As a rule it is the prosecution who seek to adduce evidence of dying declarations since their value often lies in the fact that they identify the accused with the death. However in *R.* v. *Scaife*[11] a dying declaration was admitted in favour of the accused since the deceased had said "I don't think he would have struck me if I had not provoked him".

A dying declaration does not require corroboration and in *Nembhard* v. *R.*[12] the appellant's conviction for murder of a police officer was upheld by the Privy Council even though the dying declaration of the victim was the only evidence which implicated the appellant.

Declarations against interest—A statement is admissible if it is against the pecuniary or proprietary interest of the deceased. The rationale of the admission of such statements is that a person would be unlikely to make a statement against his interest unless it were true. Nevertheless such statements are only admissible if the maker can be proved to be dead. It may seem logical to suppose that a person still living would be just as unlikely to have made an untrue statement against his own interest. Such statements are not, however, admissible unless they fall within the definition of admissions or confessions or, of course, are admissible under the provisions of the Civil Evidence Act 1968.

Apart from the death of the declarant the principal condition for the admissibility of declarations against interest is that the declaration be against the pecuniary or proprietary interest of the deceased. It is generally accepted that the deceased must have known, at the time of making the statement, that it was against his interest[13] and must also have had personal knowledge of the facts stated.[14] No interest other than a pecuniary or proprietary interest will suffice. Thus in *Ward* v. *H.S. Pitt & Co.*[15] the Court of Appeal held that an admission of paternity made by a deceased putative father was not admissible as a declaration against interest merely because it might involve possible future liability for the maintenance of the child.[16] On the other hand a pecuniary interest is something less than a pecuniary obligation. In *Coward* v. *Motor Insurers' Bureau*[17] the Court of Appeal admitted proof of oral declarations by the deceased to the effect that he had gratuitously promised to pay money in return for lifts to work. Notwithstanding the fact that there was no contractual or other legal obligation to pay the money the statements were against the deceased's pecuniary interest and therefore admissible.

If a statement is admitted as being against the pecuniary or proprietary

---

[10] *R.* v. *Perry*, [1909] 2 K.B. 697.
[11] (1836), 2 Lew. C.C. 150.
[12] [1982] 1 All E.R. 183; [1981] 1 W.L.R. 1515.
[13] *Tucker* v. *Oldbury Urban Council*, [1912] 2 K.B. 317.
[14] *Lloyd* v. *Powell Duffryn Steam Coal Co.*, [1914] A.C. 733.
[15] [1913] 2 K.B. 130.
[16] But see the judgment of WILLMER, L.J. in *B.* v. *A-G.*, [1965] P. 278; [1965] 1 All E.R. 62.
[17] [1963] 1 Q.B. 259; [1962] 1 All E.R. 531.

interest of the deceased it constitutes proof of any collateral fact contained in the statement. Indeed the purpose for which it sought to adduce proof of the statement is often in order to prove some collateral fact. *Higham* v. *Ridgway*[18] affords a good illustration of this. In this leading case an entry in the books of a deceased male midwife was admitted in evidence because it acknowledged receipt of his fee, a receipt being a declaration against pecuniary interest. This entry was admitted, however, as evidence of the date of the child's birth which was the fact which it was sought to prove.

Declarations in the course of duty—Written or oral statements made by a deceased person in pursuance of a duty to record acts performed by him are admissible as an exception to the hearsay rule. However this exception is of very little importance since, in so far as it applied to civil proceedings, it was effectively abolished by section 1 of the Civil Evidence Act 1968.[19] Thus it can now only apply in criminal cases and the Criminal Evidence Act 1965[20] is framed sufficiently widely to incorporate most declarations within the common law exception. Nevertheless it is possible to envisage statements which would fall outside the provisions of the 1965 Act but which might be admissible in criminal proceedings by virtue of the common law rule as declarations made in the course of duty. The conditions for the admissibility of these declarations are extremely restrictive. Apart from the death of the declarant, which is an essential condition,[1] there must have been a duty both to act and to record, the record must have been made contemporaneously with the act and the deceased must have had no motive to misrepresent the facts recorded.[2]

Declarations concerning pedigree—A peculiar exception to the hearsay rule operates to admit declarations of deceased persons concerning the pedigree of their relatives where this is the subject of proceedings. The rationale of this exception is somewhat obscure but appears to be based principally on the personal knowledge possessed by the declarant. Oddly enough, this exception to the hearsay rule was expressly preserved by the Civil Evidence Act 1968.[3] Nevertheless the mere possession of personal knowledge is insufficient. The declarant must have been a relative, either by blood or marriage, of the person whose pedigree is the subject of the proceedings. Thus is *Johnson* v. *Lawson*[4] the Court of Common Pleas rejected the declaration of a family housekeeper though she had known the family for twenty-four years. At common law a bastard was regarded as having no relatives but in more recent times the courts have extended this exception to the hearsay rule so as to admit declarations by the mother[5] of an illegitimate

---

[18] (1808), 10 East 109.
[19] Nevertheless any statement which would have been admissible in civil proceedings by virtue of this exception will now be admissible under section 2 of the 1968 Act.
[20] See p. 679, *post.*
[1] This was established in *Price* v. *Torrington* (1703), 1 Salk. 285.
[2] *The Henry Coxon* (1878), 3 P.D. 156.
[3] Section 9(3), (4)(*b*).
[4] (1824), 2 Bing. 86.
[5] *Re Jenion,* [1952] Ch. 454; [1952] 1 All E.R. 1228.

child though it is uncertain whether the declaration of a putative father is admissible.[6]

The exception is limited to pedigree cases, that is to say cases in which the relationship by blood or marriage between two or more persons is in issue. The issue of pedigree generally arises in proceedings involving legitimacy or succession to property. One further condition for the admissibility of pedigree declarations must be mentioned. The declaration must have been made *ante litem motam* (before any dispute has arisen). The obvious reason for this restriction is that a statement made in the course of a dispute may be biased.[7]

Declarations as to public or general rights—A very old exception to the hearsay rule, the basis of which is simple expedience, admits declarations of deceased persons of competent knowledge as to the reputed existence of public or general rights. As with pedigree declarations, this exception to the hearsay rule was expressly preserved, in relation to civil proceedings, by the Civil Evidence Act 1968.[8] A public right is a right enjoyed by every member of the public, such as the right to use a highway. A general right is a right possessed by a class of persons, such as the inhabitants of a parish. Rights of common and customary manorial rights are typical general rights. Since a customary right must be proved to be of immemorial antiquity it is common for a customary right be proved by evidence of reputation which frequently involves the admission of the declaration of a deceased person.[9] Such declarations may take any form but are generally documentary.

This exception to the hearsay rule bears a certain affinity to the foregoing exception concerning pedigree declarations. As is the case with pedigree declarations a declaration as to public or general rights must have been made *ante litem motam*. If a general right is alleged the declaration must have been made by a person with competent knowledge of the reputed right. Where the alleged right is a public right any member of the public may be a competent declarant. On the other hand where a general right is alleged it seems that the declarant must have been a member of the class of persons for whose benefit the right is alleged to exist. It was for this reason that the declarations of deceased officers of the Crown were not admitted in one case[10] to prove whether the city of Chester was within the county of Cheshire.

Evidence given in previous proceedings—Where a witness who has given evidence in previous proceedings has died, a transcript of his evidence in those proceedings may be given in evidence in subsequent proceedings. This rule appears to date back at least as far as the eighteenth century[11] although, oddly enough, its application does not seem to have been considered in any

---

[6] *B. v. A.-G.,* [1965] P. 278; [1965] 1 All E.R. 62.

[7] *Butler* v. *Mountgarrett* (1859), 7 H.L. Cas. 633.

[8] Section 9(3), (4)(*c*).

[9] *Weeks* v. *Sparke* (1813), 1 M. & S. 679. The declaration must be confined to reputation. A declaration relating to a specific fact such as the siting of a boundary is not within the exception: *Mercer* v. *Denne,* [1905] 2 Ch. 538.

[10] *Rogers* v. *Wood* (1831), 2 B. & Ad. 245; cf. *Knight* v. *David,* [1971] 3 All E.R. 1066; [1971] 1 W.L.R. 1671.

[11] *R.* v. *Radbourne* (1787), 1 Leach 457.

case in this century prior to *R. v. Hall.*[12] In that case there had been a retrial of the defendant on forgery charges, the jury having failed to agree at the first trial. Between the two trials a witness, who although called for the Crown gave some evidence upon which the defendant wished to rely, died. The trial judge rejected an application by the defence to admit the transcript of the witness's evidence given at the first trial on the ground that, although there was statutory provision for the admissibility of a deposition taken before examining justices where the deponent had died,[13] there was no such provision in relation to transcripts of evidence given at a former trial. The Court of Appeal, after reviewing the authorities, affirmed the common law principle referred to above and allowed the defendant's appeal. However, the court went on to state that in such a case there would, in a criminal case, be a residual discretion to exclude such evidence where its admission would operate unfairly against a defendant.

The effect of section 1 of the Civil Evidence Act 1968 is to confine the application of this exception to the hearsay rule to criminal proceedings.

e   Statements in public documents

Mention has already been made of public documents for the purpose of noting that the best evidence rule does not apply in relation to public documents so that they may be proved by copies.[14] It will be recalled that a public document is "a document that is made for the purpose of the public making use of it, and being able to refer to it".[15] Where a public document, or a copy, is admitted in evidence as a means of proving a fact stated in the document, the admission of the document clearly constitutes an exception to the hearsay rule. The basis of this exception is the intrinsic unlikelihood of inaccuracy in a document prepared by public officers. There are many classes of public documents of which the following may be mentioned by way of illustration: public statutes,[16] registers of births, marriages and deaths, parish registers, reports of official inquiries, ordinance survey maps and the London Gazette.

Strictly speaking, a document is only a public document if made in the performance of a legal duty to record. On this basis the courts have from time to time rejected documents such as the results of private surveys, the register of attendances at a work-house and non-parochial records of births, marriages and deaths kept by nonconformist ministers. Nevertheless the modern tendency is to treat analogous documents such as these as if they were public documents. Thus certificates of various kinds such as a bishop's certificate upon an ecclesiastical matter are generally admitted as proof of

---

[12] [1973] Q.B. 496; [1973] 1 All E.R. 1.

[13] Criminal Justice Act 1925, s. 13; see p. 510, *ante.*

[14] See p. 643, *ante.*

[15] *Sturla* v. *Freccia* (1880), 5 App. Cas. 623, at p. 643, *per* Lord Blackburn. This case, as did similar old authorities, clearly contemplated as a condition of admissibility that the official making the record should either have had personal knowledge of the matters he was recording or at least should have enquired into the accuracy of the facts. However, in modern times, the complexity of public records is such that the functions formerly performed by one official may be divided between two or more; in that event the record is "double hearsay" but, nevertheless the courts are prepared to receive the record in evidence: *R. v. Halpin*, [1975] Q.B. 907; [1975] 2 All E.R. 1124.

[16] Since judicial notice is taken of public statutes the question is purely academic; see p. 606, *ante.*

the fact certified. Similarly there are now numerous statutes which provide for proof by documents which are not, in the strictest sense, public documents. For example, the registration of a company may be proved by the certificate of the Registrar of Companies;[17] a conviction may be proved by the certificate of the clerk of the court;[18] the proportion of alcohol or any drug found in a specimen of breath, blood or urine taken under the provisions of the Road Traffic Act 1972 may, subject to certain conditions, be proved by a certificate signed by an authorised analyst (in the case of blood or urine) or a statement automatically produced by an approved device (in the case of breath specimens).[19] In this connection reference may once again be made to section 3 of the Bankers' Books Evidence Act 1879, which provides that a copy of any entry in a bankers' book shall be received as *prima facie* evidence of such entry and of the matters, transactions and accounts therein recorded.[20]

f Documentary records under the Civil Evidence Act 1968, ss. 4 and 5

Section 4 of the 1968 Act provides for the admissibility of certain documentary records as evidence of any fact[1] stated therein of which direct oral evidence would be admissible. The conditions for the admissibility of such documents are as follows.

(1) The document must be, or form part of, a record compiled by a person acting under a duty.[2]

(2) It must have been compiled from information which was supplied[3] by a person (whether acting under a duty or not) who had, or may reasonably be supposed to have had, personal knowledge of the matters dealt with in that information and which, if not supplied by that person to the compiler of the record directly, was supplied by him to the compiler of the record indirectly through one or more intermediaries each acting under a duty.

It will be appreciated that if the person having personal knowledge of the information supplied is called as a witness, the document is not hearsay at all, while if the compiler is called as a witness the document is first-hand hearsay and therefore admissible in any event under section 2 of the 1968 Act. Where, however, neither the supplier nor the compiler is called, the

---

[17] Companies Act 1980, s. 3.

[18] Evidence Act 1851, s. 14; Criminal Procedure Act 1865, s. 6. These provisions are to be replaced by Police and Criminal Evidence Act 1984, s. 73.

[19] Road Traffic Act 1972, s. 10 (as amended by Transport Act 1981, s. 25 and Sch. 8); see also Road Traffic Act 1960, s. 242; Road Traffic Act 1972, ss. 181, 182.

[20] See p. 643, *ante*.

[1] Or admissible statement of opinion (Civil Evidence Act 1972, s. 1(1)).

[2] References to a person acting under a duty include a reference to a person acting in the course of any trade, business, profession or other occupation in which he is engaged or employed or for the purposes of any paid or unpaid office held by him (s. 4(3)).

[3] In *Barkway* v. *South Wales Transport Co., Ltd.*, [1949] 1 K.B. 54; [1948] 2 All E.R. 460 (a decision on the Evidence Act 1938) a shorthand writer's transcript of evidence was held inadmissible on the ground that it was not "supplied" to him. The point was not taken that such evidence was admissible at common law; it is submitted that it would have been admissible by reason of the exception to the hearsay rule in favour of evidence given in previous proceedings by persons since deceased; see p. 675, *ante*. However, since section 1 of the Civil Evidence Act 1968 has, in effect, abolished this exception in relation to civil proceedings, the principle of *Barkway*'s case has been retained by the adherence to the word "supplied" in section 4.

document is second-hand hearsay and admissible only if it satisfies the conditions of section 4, set out above.

Prior to the enactment of section 4 of the 1968 Act a similar exception to the hearsay rule in civil proceedings existed under the Evidence Act 1938 (which was repealed when section 4 came into operation). The 1938 Act contained certain restrictions on admissibility which are not reproduced in the present enactment. Thus the original document had to be in existence and it had to be authenticated by the maker; neither of these requirements exists under the 1968 Act. Furthermore, under the 1938 Act the statement was inadmissible if made by an interested person whereas under the 1968 Act the statement of an interested party is not *ipso facto* excluded. However it is provided by section 6(3) that in estimating the weight to be attached to a statement admissible under section 4 the court must have regard to all the circumstances from which any inference can reasonably be drawn as to the accuracy or otherwise of the statement and, in particular, to the question whether or not the person who originally supplied the information from which the record was compiled did so contemporaneously with the occurrence or existence of the facts dealt with in that information, and to the question whether or not that person, or any person concerned with compiling or keeping the record, had any incentive to conceal or misrepresent the facts.

Any evidence which, if the person supplying the information had been called as a witness, would be admissible for the purpose of destroying or supporting his credibility, including a previous inconsistent statement (which is then evidence of the truth of any fact stated therein) is admissible in his absence.[4]

Section 4 renders admissible a great variety of reports and records including such documents as accident reports, medical reports, police notebooks, manufacturers' records, invoices and estimates. Its extension, by section 1 of the Civil Evidence Act 1972, to opinion evidence enables unchallenged expert opinions to be given without the expense of calling the expert in question. As a sign, perhaps, of the times specific provision was made by section 5 of the 1968 Act for the admissibility of statements contained in documents produced by computers.[5] Such statements are admissible of any fact stated therein of which direct oral evidence would be admissible, subject to the conditions set out in the section. The principal conditions are: that the computer producing the record must have been used regularly to store or process information for the purpose of any activities regularly carried on, over the period during which the record was produced, by any body or individual; that over that period the computer was regularly supplied in the ordinary course of these activities with information of the kind contained in the statement or of the kind from which the information therein is derived (the information contained in the statement must either reproduce or be derived from information supplied to the computer in the ordinary course of those activities); that throughout the material time the computer was operating properly or, if it was not, that this did not affect the

---

[4] Civil Evidence Act 1968, s. 7. Admissibility is, however, subject to compliance with certain procedural requirements; see R.S.C., O. 38, rr. 30, 31.
[5] A "computer" means any device for storing and processing information: s. 5(6).

production of the document or the accuracy of its contents.[6]

As with statements admissible under section 2 of the 1968 Act, the procedure which must be followed by a party wishing to put in evidence a document under section 4 or 5 of the Act is laid down by Rules of Court made pursuant to section 8.[7]

g Trade or business records under the Criminal Evidence Act 1965

The most significant limitation of the Civil Evidence Act 1968 is that it applies only in civil proceedings. The need for a corresponding measure in the context of criminal proceedings was indicated by the decision of the House of Lords in *Myers* v. *Director of Public Prosecutions*.[8] The point at issue in this case was the admissibility of car manufacturers' records as a means of identifying disguised stolen cars. There could be no doubt as to the accuracy of the records. Notwithstanding, the House of Lords rejected these records as being hearsay and not within any recognised exception to the hearsay rule. The immediate result of *Myers* v. *Director of Public Prosecutions* was the passing of the Criminal Evidence Act 1965. This Act provides for the admission in evidence in criminal proceedings of certain trade or business records where direct oral evidence of the fact recorded would be admissible. The two basic conditions for admissibility are set out in section 1(1) of the Act: (*a*) the document must be, or form part of, a trade or business record compiled in the course of that trade or business from information supplied (directly or indirectly) by persons having personal knowledge of the matters recorded;[9] and (*b*) the person who supplied the information must be dead, beyond the seas, unfit by reason of his bodily or mental condition to attend, or cannot be identified or found or cannot be expected (having regard to the time which has elapsed and to all the circumstances) to have any recollection of the information which he supplied.

There have been several recent cases on the topic of whether a computer print-out is admissible under the provisions of the 1965 Act. In *R.* v. *Pettigrew*[10] the Court of Appeal held inadmissible a Bank of England computer print-out listing the serial numbers of a batch of £5 notes dispatched from the Bank to Newcastle (tendered by the prosecution to prove that three £5 notes in the possession of the defendant came from this batch) on the ground that there was no person who had "personal knowledge" of the numbers recorded. However in *R.* v. *Ewing*[11] the Court of Appeal upheld

---

[6] S. 5(2); see s. 6(3)(c) as to factors affecting the weight to be attached to a statement admissible under section 5. Section 5 is limited to factual statements and does not extend to statements of opinion (Civil Evidence Act 1972, s. 1(1)).

[7] See p. 375, *ante*.

[8] [1965] A.C. 1001; [1964] 2 All E.R. 881; see p. 662, *ante*.

[9] Since a national health service hospital is not a "business", a person's medical record kept by such a hospital is not admissible under the Act: *R.* v. *Crayden*, [1978] 2 All E.R. 700; [1978] 1 W.L.R. 604; cf. *R.* v. *Gwilliam*, [1968] 3 All E.R. 821; [1968] 1 W.L.R. 1839. The "record" need not be a permanent record, as long as it is a document which embodies a history of events in some form which is not evanescent; thus bills of lading and cargo manifests were held admissible under the Act in *R.* v. *Jones*, [1978] 2 All E.R. 718; [1978] 1 W.L.R. 195.

[10] (1980), 71 Cr. App. Rep. 39.

[11] [1983] Q.B. 1039; [1983] 2 All E.R. 645. See also *R.* v. *Wood* (1983), 76 Cr. App. Rep. 23 in which computer analyses of certain metals were admitted to prove the chemical composition of those metals (for the purpose of comparison with an analysis of metals found in the

the admission of a bank computer print-out of movements in a customer's account (tendered to prove a payment into that account) on the basis that the computer operator had personal knowledge of the payment in but, although not identified, could not be expected to have any recollection of it. It will be appreciated that in a civil case the print-out would have been clearly admissible under section 5 of the Civil Evidence Act 1968 (*supra*).

It will be appreciated from the above that the Criminal Evidence Act 1965 is far narrower in scope than section 4 of the Civil Evidence Act 1968. Thus the 1965 Act is restricted to trade or business records; the 1968 Act is not restricted to any particular class of documents. Furthermore, under the 1965 Act the document is admissible only in the absence of the person who supplied the information recorded (though if called as a witness he could, no doubt, refer to the document at common law in order to refresh his memory); if the supplier of the information is called as a witness in civil proceedings the document may still be put in evidence under section 4 of the 1968 Act, but only with leave of the court.[12]

The 1965 Act will be repealed when Part VII of the Police and Criminal Evidence Act 1984 is brought into operation. Section 68 of that Act provides for the admissibility of documentary records in circumstances closely analagous to those in which the 1968 Act presently applies in civil proceedings while section 69 contains certain safeguards relating to the admissibility of computer records.

---

accused's possession). The individual who programmed the computer was called as were the individuals who had run the programme. In those circumstances the print-outs were not treated as hearsay at all.
[12] Civil Evidence Act 1968, s. 4(2)(*a*).

Index

A

COURT OF APPEAL—*contd.*
criminal division—*contd.*
verdict, alternative, power to substitute, 535
cross-appeal, 429
damages, appeal against award of, 434, 435
discretion, appeal against exercise of, 433
finding of fact, appeal against, 432, 433
judges of, 427
Lords Justices, appointment and numbers, 190
master, appeal from, 426
new trial, power to order, 435, 436, 536
notice of appeal, service, 427
point of law, appeals on, 431, 432
powers of, 429–431
procedure for appealing to, 427–429
registrar, appeal from, 426
service, 427
Supreme Court, as division of, 82, 83, 189

COURT OF PROTECTION,
Chancery judges sitting as, 237

COURTS,
Admiralty, 191, 192*n*, 196
attributes of, 180
Central Criminal Court. *See* CENTRAL CRIMINAL COURT
classification, 183–228
common law. *See* COMMON LAW
consistory, 217
contempt of. *See* CONTEMPT OF COURT
county. *See* COUNTY COURTS
divisional, 196, 152
domestic, 209. *See also* DOMESTIC COURTS
evidence, restricting publicity of, 182
jurisdiction, generally, 179
open justice, principle of, 181–183
prize court, 213
record, of, 180, 181
sitting *in camera*, 182
superior and inferior, 180
valuation courts, 180

COURTS-MARTIAL,
civilians, jurisdiction over, 216
constitution and procedure, 215, 216
Courts-Martial Appeal Court—
appeal from, to House of Lords, 189, 216
creation and composition, 216
legal aid, 287
jurisdiction, 215

CRIME,
classification of offences, 454–457
criminal injuries. *See* CRIMINAL INJURIES COMPENSATION BOARD

CRIME—*contd.*
judicial functions, 235
public mischief no offence, 236

CRIMINAL INJURIES COMPENSATION BOARD,
assessment of compensation, 223
establishment and purpose of, 222, 223
membership, 223
procedure, 222, 223
quashing of decisions, 223

CRIMINAL JURISDICTION,
Court of Appeal, 190, 191
courts-martial, 189, 215, 216
Crown Courts, 202, 203
House of Lords, appeals to, 188, 189
judges not to create new offences, 235
magistrates' courts, 207
Queen's Bench Division, 196
recorders, 201, 202

CRIMINAL PROCEEDINGS,
accused, attendance of, 498
arraignment, 498–500
bail. *See* BAIL
compelling appearance of defendant—
process—
arrest, 448–452. *See also* ARREST
conditions for issue of, 444–446
generally, 441
information, 441–444
summons, 446, 447
hearing, 509–513
indictment, 487 *et seq. See also* INDICTMENT
jury; empanelling of, 508, 509. *See also* JURY
mode of trial, procedure for determining, 458–462
offences, classification of—
generally, 454–457
indictment, triable on, 456
summary offences, 456, 457
triable either way, 457
orders, 519–526
pleas—
autrefois acquit and *autrefois convict*, 503–506
demurrer, 506
guilty, 500, 501
jurisdiction, to 506
not guilty, 501–503
pardon, 506
red pencil test, overworking of authority for, 502
points of law, preliminary, 507, 508
preliminary enquiry—
committal for trial, 476, 477
generally, 476, 477
publicity, 485, 486
witnesses, securing attendance of, 486, 487

STATEMENT OF CLAIM—*contd.*
reliefs and remedies to be claimed in,
341–343
tort, in, 342
writ, indorsement on, 310, 311, 341

STATUTES,
ambiguity in, 103, 104
codification, 58, 59, 91
common law and equity contrasted, 59
construction—
aids to—
external, 121–123
internal, 116–121
judicial precedents, 124, 125
presumptions in—
alteration of law, against, 113, 114
Crown, do not bind, 116
generally, 113–116
rules of, 110–113
generally, 93, 94
history, 58, 59
interpretation—
ejusdem generis rule, 112
generally, 561
Interpretation Act 1978 . . . 113
judicial, 104–110, 232, 233
literal approach, 105–107
mischief rule, 111
need for, 102–104
penal provisions to be construed
narrowly, 112, 113
presumption in, 113
punctuation, 120
purposive approach, 107–110
rules of, 110–113
law reform, as source of, 59
must be read as whole, 110, 111
operation—
cessation, 100, 101
commencement, 98–100
extension, 98
retrospective, 99, 100
presumption against, 561
publication, 94
Royal Assent, 94
uncertainty, 104

STATUTORY INSTRUMENTS,
European law, 60
generally, 96

STAY,
execution, of, application for, 320
proceedings, of—
generally, 321, 322
inherent jurisdiction, 322
Rules, under, 322
statutory jurisdiction, 321, 322

SUMMARY TRIAL,
appeal following—
case stated, by, 552–554

SUMMARY TRIAL—*contd.*
appeal following—*contd.*
Crown Court, to, 550–552
House of Lords, to, 555
arrest, issue of warrant of, 542
child or young person, of, 462
course of—
hearing, 545, 546
number of offences, 544, 545
time limit, 543, 544
jurisdiction, 206, 207
maximum sentence and fine, 457
offences triable by, 456, 457
parties, absence of, 546–548
post, plea of guilty by, 547, 548
process, generally, 542
sentence, 549
standard scale of fines, 549
summons, issue of, 542

SUMMONS,
county court—
issue and service, 405
criminal proceedings—
defective, 446
delay in issuing, 447
form and contents, 446
meaning, 446
service, 447
signature, 446
directions, for—
consolidation of actions, 365, 366
disclosure of experts' reports, 367,
368
evidence, 366
form, 365, 366
functions of, 364, 365
generally, 364, 365
issue, 364
matters dealt with on, 365
mode of trial, 368, 369
place of trial, 368
judgment. *See* JUDGMENT SUMMONS
originating. *See* ORIGINATING SUMMONS
writ of. *See* WRIT OF SUMMONS

SUPERIOR COURTS,
generally, 180

SUPREME COURT OF JUDICATURE,
creation, 81, 82, 189
divisions of, 81–83, 189, 190
Rules. *See* RULES OF SUPREME COURT

SURPRISE,
new trial on ground of, 437

SYSTEM,
course of conduct in, 573, 574

T

TAXATION OF COSTS. *See* COSTS